8.9   The HOW and WHY of Constructing an Administrative Expense Budget, page 391

8.10 The HOW and WHY of Constructing a Budgeted Income Statement, page 392

8.11 The HOW and WHY of Constructing a Cash Receipts Budget with an Accounts Receivable Aging Schedule, page 395

8.12 The HOW and WHY of Constructing a Cash Budget, page 397

8.13 The HOW and WHY of Constructing a Flexible Budget for Varying Levels of Activity, page 404

8.14 The HOW and WHY of Constructing a Flexible Budget for the Actual Level of Activity, page 406

Examples for Chapter 9

9.1   The HOW and WHY of Computing Standard Quantities Allowed (*SQ* and *SH*), page 446

9.2   The HOW and WHY of Computing the Direct Materials Price Variance (*MPV*) and Direct Materials Usage Variance (*MUV*), page 448

9.3   The HOW and WHY of Computing the Direct Labor Rate Variance (*LRV*) and Direct Labor Efficiency Variance (*LEV*), page 453

9.4   The HOW and WHY of Using Control Limits to Determine When to Investigate a Variance, page 456

9.5   The HOW and WHY of Closing the Balances in the Variance Accounts at the End of the Year, page 459

9.6   The HOW and WHY of Calculating the Total Variable Overhead Variance, page 461

9.7   The HOW and WHY of Computing the Variable Overhead Spending Variance and the Variable Overhead Efficiency Variance, page 463

9.8   The HOW and WHY of Computing the Fixed Overhead Spending Variance and the Fixed Overhead Volume Variance, page 467

9.9   The HOW and WHY of Computing the Mix Variance, page 473

9.10 The HOW and WHY of Computing the Yield Variance, page 475

Examples for Chapter 10

10.1 The HOW and WHY of Calculating Average Operating Assets, Margin, Turnover, and Return on Investment (ROI), page 506

10.2 The HOW and WHY of Calculating Residual Income, page 510

10.3 The HOW and WHY of Calculating the Weighted Average Cost of Capital and EVA, page 514

10.4 The HOW and WHY of Calculating Market-Based and Negotiated Transfer Prices, page 526

10.5 The HOW and WHY of Calculating Cost-Based Transfer Prices, page 528

Examples for Chapter 11

11.1 The HOW and WHY of Using Net Benefit to Evaluate Risk Response Alternatives, page 566

11.2 The HOW and WHY of Exploiting Internal Linkages to Reduce Costs and Increase Value, page 569

11.3 The HOW and WHY of Activity-Based Supplier Costing, page 573

11.4 The HOW and WHY of Activity-Based Customer Costing, page 576

11.5 The HOW and WHY of Activity-Based Life-Cycle Cost Reduction, page 581

11.6 The HOW and WHY of Backflush Costing, page 593

Examples for Chapter 12

12.1 The HOW and WHY of Value- and Non-Value-Added Cost Reporting, page 635

12.2 The HOW and WHY of Non-Value-Added Cost Trend Reporting, page 636

12.3 The HOW and WHY of Kaizen Costing, page 639

12.4 The HOW and WHY of Activity-Based Flexible Budgeting, page 643

12.5 The HOW and WHY of Activity Capacity Management, page 645

Examples for Chapter 13

13.1 The HOW and WHY of Calculating Cycle Time and Velocity, page 685

13.2 The HOW and WHY of Calculating Manufacturing Cycle Efficiency (MCE), page 686

13.3 The HOW and WHY of Strategy Mapping, page 690

Examples for Chapter 14

14.1 The HOW and WHY of Preparing a Quality Cost Report, page 714

14.2 The HOW and WHY of Preparing Interim Quality Performance Reports, page 722

14.3 The HOW and WHY of Multiple-Period Quality Trend Reporting, page 724

14.4 The HOW and WHY of Long-Range Quality Performance Reporting, page 727

14.5 The HOW and WHY of an Environmental Cost Report, page 733

14.6 The HOW and WHY of Activity-Based Environmental Cost Assignments, page 737

Examples for Chapter 15

15.1 The HOW and WHY of Cellular Manufacturing, page 773

15.2 The HOW and WHY of Value-Stream Product Costing, page 779

15.3 The HOW and WHY of Profile Productivity Measurement, page 787

15.4 The HOW and WHY of Profit-Linked Productivity Measurement, page 789

Examples for Chapter 16

16.1 The HOW and WHY of Basic Cost Calculations and the Contribution-Margin-Based Income Statement, page 816

16.2 The HOW and WHY of Calculating the Units Needed to Break Even and to Achieve a Target Profit, page 819

16.3 The HOW and WHY of Calculating Revenue for Break-Even and for a Target Profit, page 822

16.4 The HOW and WHY of Calculating the Number of Units to Generate an After-Tax Target Profit, page 824

16.5 The HOW and WHY of Calculating the Break-Even Number of Units in a Multiproduct Firm, page 828

16.6 The HOW and WHY of Calculating Margin of Safety, page 837

16.7 The HOW and WHY of Calculating Degree of Operating Leverage and Percent Change in Profit, page 839

Examples for Chapter 17

17.1 The HOW and WHY of Structuring a Make-or-Buy Decision, page 877

17.2 The HOW and WHY of Structuring a Keep-or-Drop Product Line Decision, page 882

17.3 The HOW and WHY of Structuring a Special-Order Decision, page 886

17.4 The HOW and WHY of Structuring a Sell at Split-Off or Process Further Decision, page 888

Examples for Chapter 18

18.1 The HOW and WHY of Calculating a Markup on Cost, page 918

18.2 The HOW and WHY of Calculating Cost and Profit by Customer Class, page 924

18.3 The HOW and WHY of Calculating Inventory Cost and Preparing the Income Statement Using Absorption Costing, page 929

18.4 The HOW and WHY of Calculating Inventory Cost and Preparing the Income Statement Using Variable Costing, page 932

18.5 The HOW and WHY of Calculating the Sales Price Variance, the Sales Volume Variance, and the Overall Sales Variance, page 938

18.6 The HOW and WHY of Calculating the Contribution Margin Variance, page 939

18.7 The HOW and WHY of Calculating the Contribution Margin Volume Variance, page 940

18.8 The HOW and WHY of Calculating the Sales Mix Variance, page 942

18.9 The HOW and WHY of Calculating the Market Share Variance and the Market Size Variance, page 943

Examples for Chapter 19

19.1 The HOW and WHY of Calculating the Payback Period, page 976

19.2 The HOW and WHY of Calculating the Accounting Rate of Return, page 978

19.3 The HOW and WHY of Analyzing NPV, page 979

19.4 The HOW and WHY of Calculating the Internal Rate of Return, page 981

19.5 The HOW and WHY of Determining NPV and IRR for Mutually Exclusive Projects, page 984

19.6 The HOW and WHY of Calculating After-Tax Cash Flows, page 988

Examples for Chapter 20

20.1 The HOW and WHY of Calculating the EOQ, page 1023

20.2 The HOW and WHY of Reordering, page 1024

20.3 The HOW and WHY of Solving Constrained Optimization Problems with One Internal Constraint, page 1035

20.4 The HOW and WHY of Solving Linear Programming Problems with Two Variables, page 1036

20.5 The HOW and WHY of a Drum-Buffer-Rope System, page 1042

Examples for Chapter 21

21.1 The HOW and WHY of Locating in a Foreign Trade Zone, page 1062

21.2 The HOW and WHY of Exchanging One Currency for Another, page 1066

21.3 The HOW and WHY of Calculating Exchange Gains and Losses, page 1068

21.4 The HOW and WHY of Hedging Currency Exchange Rates, page 1069

21.5 The HOW and WHY of Using the Comparable Uncontrolled Price Method, the Resale Price Method, and the Cost-Plus Method in Calculating Transfer Prices, page 1078

Brief Contents

CHAPTER 1 Introduction to Cost Management 2

CHAPTER 2 Basic Cost Management Concepts 28

CHAPTER 3 Cost Behavior and Forecasting 78

CHAPTER 4 Activity-Based Costing 144

MAKING THE CONNECTION 210

CHAPTER 5 Product and Service Costing: Job-Order System 216

CHAPTER 6 Process Costing 262

CHAPTER 7 Allocating Costs of Support Departments and Joint Products 316

CHAPTER 8 Budgeting for Planning and Control 372

CHAPTER 9 Standard Costing: A Functional-Based Control Approach 440

CHAPTER 10 Decentralization: Responsibility Accounting, Performance Evaluation, and Transfer Pricing 498

MAKING THE CONNECTION 546

CHAPTER 11 Strategic Cost Management 552

CHAPTER 12 Activity-Based Management 626

CHAPTER 13 Strategic-Based Control Systems and the Balanced Scorecard 672

CHAPTER 14 Quality and Environmental Cost Management 706

CHAPTER 15 Lean Accounting and Productivity Measurement 766

MAKING THE CONNECTION 806

CHAPTER 16 Cost-Volume-Profit Analysis 812

CHAPTER 17 Activity Resource Usage Model and Tactical Decision Making 866

CHAPTER 18 Pricing and Profitability Analysis 912

CHAPTER 19 Capital Investment 972

CHAPTER 20 Inventory Management: Economic Order Quantity, JIT, and the Theory of Constraints 1018

CHAPTER 21 International Issues in Cost Management 1058

MAKING THE CONNECTION 1090

Glossary 1094

Check Figures 1106

Subject Index 1111

Company Index 1124

Examples 1126

*This book is dedicated to our students—past, present, and future—
who are at the heart of our passion for teaching.*

FIFTH EDITION

Cost Management

Don R. Hansen
Oklahoma State University

Maryanne M. Mowen
Oklahoma State University

Dan L. Heitger
Miami University

CENGAGE

Australia • Brazil • Canada • Mexico • Singapore • United Kingdom • United States

Cost Management, Fifth Edition
Don R. Hansen, Maryanne M. Mowen,
Dan L. Heitger

Senior Vice President, Higher Education & Skills
Product: Erin Joyner

Vice President, Higher Education & Skills Product:
Michael Schenk

Product Director: Jason Fremder

Associate Product Manager: Jonathan Gross

Product Assistant: Matthew Schiesl

Learning Designer: Emily Lehmann

In-house Subject Matter Expert: Eileen Byron

Senior Digital Delivery Lead: Sally Nieman

Senior Content Manager: Tim Bailey

Executive Marketing Manager: Nathan Anderson

Intellectual Property Analyst: Ashley Maynard

Manufacturing Planner: Ron Montgomery

Production Service: Lumina Datamatics, Inc.

Cover Designer: Christopher Doughman

Internal Designer: Harasymczuk Design

Cover Image: Arthimedes/ShutterStock.com

For product information and technology assistance, contact us at
Cengage **Customer & Sales Support, 1-800-354-9706**
or support.cengage.com.

For permission to use material from this text or product,
submit all requests online at **www.cengage.com/permissions.**

Microsoft Excel® is a registered trademark of Microsoft Corporation. © 2020 Microsoft.

Library of Congress Control Number: 2020950802

Student Edition ISBN: 978-0-357-14109-0

Loose-Leaf Edition ISBN: 978-0-357-14110-6

Cengage
200, Pier 4 Boulevard
Boston, MA 02210
USA

Cengage is a leading provider of customized learning solutions with employees residing in nearly 40 different countries and sales in more than 125 countries around the world. Find your local representative at **www.cengage.com.**

To learn more about Cengage platforms and services, register or access your online learning solution, or purchase materials for your course, visit **www.cengage.com.**

Printed in the United States of America
Print Number: 01   Print Year: 2021

Dear Colleague,

As experienced cost management instructors who are "in the teaching trenches"—both face-to-face and online—we have created (over the years and with this revision of the fifth edition) *the book that we would want to (and do) use* to *best excite, motivate, educate,* and *prepare* our accounting students for success in the real world! Offering cutting edge and up-to-date coverage has always been one of the distinguishing features of our text. Students *should be exposed* to ongoing developments in the real world of cost management. Furthermore, they should have the opportunity to see how real-world organizations use both the traditional and the innovative data analytic models that are so prevalent in cost management.

We are confident that the fifth edition continues to build on the cutting-edge reputation that *Cost Management* has developed. We continue to offer coverage of such innovative topics as time-driven activity-based costing (TDABC), Duration-Based Costing (DBC), the Balanced Scorecard, lean accounting, and the theory of constraints. Moreover, there are a number of new features in the fifth edition that add to the overall value proposition of the text. We are absolutely sure that both instructors and students will be excited, motivated, educated, and better prepared by the following new features:

1. *A new exciting opening chapter feature* that applies one or more of the chapter's main cost management topics to various real companies. for example, the book kicks off the first three chapters by focusing on Kroger, Amazon, and Airbnb—all of which are large, highly recognizable, and relatable companies (which includes service companies in the "gig" economy that students find so interesting). Additional chapter openers feature such companies as Marvel Studios, University of Pittsburgh Medical Center, Wells Fargo, Big Pharma, Cardinal Health, SpaceX, and Delta Air Lines. We chose these particular companies to motivate students—they **know of**, **relate to**, and perhaps even **shop at** these inherently interesting companies, all of which motivates students to study the chapter's particular cost management topics.

2. *A new data analytics framework* is introduced in Chapter 2 and applied in every chapter using four end-of-chapter exercises and text examples as appropriate. The value of our approach is that an instructor can choose to cover the role of data analytics within *Cost Management* heavily, lightly, or even not at all. This approach gives instructors maximum flexibility to apply effective data analytics coverage in whatever way best fits their particular comfort and desire. The book's new data analytics icon makes it easy to identify the data analytic content throughout the book.

3. *Updated real-world application examples within the text* relate each chapter's given topics to highly recognizable companies, such as Boeing, Royal Dutch Shell, Walmart, Pfizer, and the Mayo Clinic, thereby continuing the real-world applicability introduced by the opening chapter feature company.

4. *New chapter on the role that cost management plays in various and timely international business decisions* A full chapter on international business helps students see how global involvement requires additional approaches to cost accounting knowledge. Ways of involving the business in international trade, including importing and exporting, joint ventures, and wholly owned subsidiaries are discussed. The impact of foreign currency translation on profitability is addressed along with the new cryptocurrencies such as Bitcoin and Ethereum. A section on ethics in international business helps students understand the complexity of doing business in different cultures.

5. *New forensic accounting applications* are added for particular cost management issues. As the field of forensic accounting continues to grow in various capacities, the book highlights where appropriate (in Chapters 1, 3, 17, and 18) the role that forensic accounting plays in important cost management decisions, such as cost behavior assessments, loss valuation forecasts, differential analysis in lost profit estimations, and predatory pricing considerations.

6. ***Updated and expanded coverage of TDABC and DBC*** has been added. in particular, the relationship between TDABC and DBC is presented, and additional end-of-chapter exercises for the topics are provided. DBC is also integrated into the lean accounting framework with appropriate end-of-chapter exercises.

Our goal is both to provide up-to-date coverage of current and developing cost management topics and analytical models and to provide students with insights concerning their real-world use. We understand that cost management is learned by doing—by the practice and use of the various models and concepts. Therefore, we have developed a set of rich and challenging exercises and problems.

In conclusion, we would like to reiterate the overall value proposition that we confidently offer:

We affirm that our cost management text will excite, motivate, educate, and prepare accounting students for success in the real world.

Sincerely,

Don Hansen, Maryanne Mowen, Dan Heitger

Tools for Progressively Learning, Understanding, and Applying Cost Concepts

- *Brief Exercises* (formerly Cornerstone Exercises) are structured like the "Examples" (formerly "Cornerstone Examples") in the text. They provide students with precise guidance and detailed practice before moving on to the more complex questions. The "What If" feature challenges students to think beyond the numbers and understand the concepts behind the equations.

- *Exercises* are longer and more complex versions of the Brief Exercises. They allow students to apply what they've learned with the additional support of Show Me How videos in select Exercises.

- *Problems* are designed to cross learning objectives and bring concepts together. They challenge students to apply their knowledge in a variety of real-world scenarios.

- *Making the Connection: Integrative Exercises* are cumulative exercises, covering Chapters 1 to 4, 5 to 10, 11 to 15, and 16 to 21. Now incorporating data analytics, these comprehensive exercises allow students to demonstrate their mastery of learning objectives by bringing together important concepts across multiple chapters.

Additional Resources

Additional instructor and student resources for this product are available online. Instructor assets include a Guide to Teaching Online, Solutions Manual, Educator Guide, PowerPoint® slides, PowerPoint Guide for Instructors, Excel® template solutions, and a test bank powered by Cognero®. Student assets include Excel® template files for completing selected end-of-chapter exercises and problems. Sign up or sign in at **www.cengage.com** to search for and access this product and its online resources.

Key Changes to This Edition

There is now an Opening Scenario for each chapter that illustrates a real organization using one or more of the chapter's topics. The text introduces a data analytics framework and each chapter provides four end-of-chapter items (exercises and problems) that allow students to test their knowledge and understanding of this new framework. Moreover, the four Integrative Exercises are revised and incorporate one or more requirements that pertain to the new data analytics framework.

There are additional important changes for specific chapters. Selected chapters have updated the existing real-world application examples, continuing the objective of emphasizing the real-world applicability of the chapter's topics that began with the new Opening Scenarios. Additionally, some chapters now have new forensic accounting applications with associated end-of-chapter exercises. Two chapters also have new material on time-driven activity-based costing (TDABC) and Duration-Based Costing (DBC) with additional end-of-chapter exercises.

The growing importance and relevance of international business activities led to the creation of a completely new chapter, International Issues in Cost Management. This chapter covers such critical topics as location in foreign trade zones, currency translation, cryptocurrency, international implications of transfer pricing, and ethics.

The Discussion Questions and Review Problems and Solutions that had been included in the text are now available to instructors in Instructors' Resources and other online resources. This streamlines the text while retaining them online for students.

The changes are detailed in the chapter-by-chapter listing that follows.

Chapter 1: Introduction to Cost Management

1. Added new Opening Scenario featuring the importance of various cost management topics to the effective management of **The Kroger Co.**

2. Expanded the Factors Affecting the Use of Cost Management, including business sustainability, forensic accounting, and an introductory discussion of data analytics.

Chapter 2: Basic Cost Management Concepts

1. Added a new Opening Scenario featuring the importance of cost structure and the accounting information system to decision makers at **Amazon**.

2. Added new section on data analytics, including comprehensive yet practical framework (Exhibits 2.5 and 2.6) for understanding the role of data analytics within cost management and applying this role to improved decision making.

3. Added a new comprehensive Exhibit 2.7 regarding Understanding Difference Cost Definition.

Chapter 3: Cost Behavior and Forecasting

1. Added a new Opening Scenario featuring the importance of using cost behavior and cost terminology, such as discretionary versus nondiscretionary costs, for **Airbnb** hosts to be financially successful.

2. Added a new Real-World Example on business sustainability at **FedEx**.

3. Added a new subsection on the role of cost behavior in forensic accounting, including a new exercise on using cost behavior insights to estimate damages in a lawsuit.

4. Increased the coverage and examples of nonlinear cost behavior.

Chapter 4: Activity-Based Costing

1. Added an Opening Scenario. The scenario shows how the **University of Pittsburgh Medical Center** (UPMC) implements an activity-based costing system to improve its efficiency.

2. Added additional coverage of time equations for TDABC and a section that compares TDABC with DBC.

3. Added new exercises and problems dealing with TDABC and DBC.

Chapter 5: Product and Service Costing: Job-Order System

1. Added Opening Scenario featuring **Marvel Studios'** use of accountants on *Avengers: Endgame*.

2. Added explanation of how data analytics can be used in job-order costing.

Chapter 6: Process Costing

1. Added an Opening Scenario. **LafargeHolcim**, the largest cement producer in the world, is used to illustrate the importance of process costing.

Chapter 7: Allocating Costs of Support Departments and Joint Products

1. Added Opening Scenario featuring the way **IBM**, **Hewlett-Packard**, and **Dow Chemical** have converted support departments into shared service centers.

2. Added four exercises and problems that deal with the data analytics framework.

Chapter 8: Budgeting for Planning and Control

1. Added Opening Scenario showing how companies such as **Lufthansa AG**, **Cathay Pacific Airlines**, and **PPG** used budgeting to respond rapidly to the impact of the corona virus pandemic.

2. Added ways in which **Kimberly-Clark** used budgeting techniques to manage production of diapers and toilet paper during the pandemic lockdown.

3. Added how **Marriott** and **Delta Air Lines** reduced CEO compensation to conserve cash during budget crunch.

Chapter 9: Standard Costing: A Functional-Based Control Approach

1. Added Opening Scenario spotlighting ways in which hospitals and medical centers use standard costing and variance analysis to give them early warning of potential problems.

Chapter 10: Decentralization: Responsibility Accounting, Performance Evaluation, and Transfer Pricing

1. Added Opening Scenario showing how **Nike Vaporfly** shoes contributed to sales and ROI of the company.

Chapter 11: Strategic Cost Management

1. Added a new section on Enterprise Risk Management and its role in cost management analyses and improved decision making, including new exercises and problems.

2. Added a new Opening Scenario featuring **Cardinal Health's** use of Enterprise Risk Management to help achieve its strategy.

Chapter 12: Activity-Based Management

1. Added an Opening Scenario. **Ipsen Signes**, a French pharmaceutical company, and winner of the Shingo Prize, was used to illustrate the importance of waste reduction through activity management.

Chapter 13: Strategic-Based Control Systems and the Balanced Scorecard

1. Added a new Opening Scenario featuring the failed strategic-based control system at Wells Fargo.

2. Added two new Real-World Examples applying strategic-based control systems and business sustainability at **Royal Dutch Shell**.

3. Added a new Real-World Example that focuses on how companies, such as **Sentieo**, use sentiment analysis and other data analytic techniques to glean insights from customer social media data and investor earnings calls.

Chapter 14: Quality and Environmental Cost Management

1. Added an Opening Scenario. The scenario shows how **Baxter International**, a large medical products company, manages product and environmental quality.

2. Updated the winners of the Baldrige Award.

3. Updated the section on ISO 9000 standards.

Chapter 15: Lean Accounting and Productivity Measurement

1. Added an Opening Scenario. The scenario describes how **Nestle Waters UK** used lean manufacturing an lean accounting to reduce costs and become more efficient.

2. Updated the list of Shingo Prize recipients.

3. Updated a Real-World Example box.

4. Revised and expanded the section on value-stream costing. DBC was added as a costing method for the lean accounting setting and associated end-of chapter exercises and problems were added.

Chapter 16: Cost-Volume-Profit Analysis

1. Added Opening Scenario discussing the meaning of break-even analysis for social media giants such as Instagram, Snapchat, and Twitter.

2. Added the way in which **Mayo Clinic** used cost-volume-profit analysis to see the impact of changing product mix on its overall profit.

Chapter 17: Activity Resource Usage Model and Tactical Decision Making

1. Added new Opening Scenario showcasing the importance of special order decisions at **Delta Air Lines**.

2. Added new Opening Scenario featuring **CVS'** product drop decision to discontinue the sale of all tobacco products.

3. Added comprehensive new product keep or drop or add for restaurant service company.

4. Added new Real-World Example illustrating a special order decision at Pfizer.

5. Added new subsection on the role of differential analysis in forensic accounting, including a new exercise that uses relevant analysis to estimate damages in a lawsuit.

6. Added numerous brief Real-World examples throughout the text regarding the use of relevant analysis in various tactical decisions.

Chapter 18: Pricing and Profitability Analysis

1. Added new Opening Scenario focusing on setting prices in pharmaceutical companies such as **Pfizer**.

2. Added new Real-World Example focusing on the use of data analytics in estimating price elasticity in the medical industry.

3. Added a new sub-section on the role of costs in forensic accounting pricing cases, including a new exercise involving cost plus pricing in forensic accounting environments.

4. Added new problem on loss leader pricing (a variant of cost-based pricing).

5. Added new Ethical real company example regarding EpiPen pricing considerations.

Chapter 19: Capital Investment

1. Added an Opening Scenario. in the scenario, **SpaceX** is used to illustrate the role and importance of capital budgeting.

2. The tax rate used for calculating after-tax cash flows was revised to reflect the new corporate tax rate. Associated examples, exercises, and problems were revised to reflect this new rate.

Chapter 20: Inventory Management: Economic Order Quantity, JIT, and the Theory of Constraints

1. Added an Opening Scenario. The scenarios shows how **Dr. Reddy's Laboratories** Limited used the theory of constraints to improve product quality and inventory management.

2. Updated two Real-World Example boxes.

Chapter 21: International Issues in Cost Management

This chapter is new to this edition and includes:

1. Discussion of the role of the accountant in international business.

2. Importing, exporting, joint ventures, and wholly owned subsidiaries.

3. Foreign currency translation, including a discussion of cryptocurrencies.

4. Transfer pricing in the international arena.

5. A discussion of ethics in global business.

Technology

What is CengageNOWv2?

CengageNOWv2 is a powerful course management and online homework tool that provides robust instructor control and customization to optimize the student learning experience and meet desired outcomes.

CengageNOWv2 includes the following:

- Integrated eBook.
- End-of-chapter homework with static and algorithmic versions.
- Adaptive Study Plan with quizzing is an assignable/gradable study center that adapts to each student's unique needs and provides a remediation pathway to keep students progressing.
- Test Bank has been updated for this edition of *Cost Management* with a focus on evaluating students' knowledge of fundamental accounting concepts.
- Course management tools and flexible assignment options.
- Reporting and grade book options.
- Quick Lesson videos are short, animated clips that provide an overview of each of the new chapter-opener scenarios. Each video is followed by questions to test student comprehension.
- Show Me How demonstration videos for selected exercises.

Completing Homework

Students sometimes struggle with accounting homework. By using CengageNOWv2's powerful instructor tools, you can fine-tune the amount of help that your students receive as they work on their homework. Help your students succeed by making the right amount of assistance available at the right time!

Show Me How videos are available for the selected end-of-chapter exercises. These videos provide students with both a detailed walk-through of a similar problem and problem-solving strategies without giving away the answer.

CengageNOWv2 provides multiple layers of guidance to keep students on track and progressing.

- Check My Work Feedback provides general guidance and hints as students work through homework assignments.
- Check My Work Feedback in CNOWv2 only reports on what students have attempted, which prevents them from "guessing" their way through assignments.

- Explanations are available after the assignment has been submitted and provide a detailed description of how the student should have arrived at the solution.

To view a demo of CengageNOWv2, please visit **www.cengage .com/cnowv2/**.

CENGAGE UNLIMITED

Cengage Unlimited is a first of-its-kind digital subscription designed specifically to lower costs. Students get total access to everything Cengage has to offer on demand—in one place. That's over 20,000 eBooks, 2,300 digital learning products, and dozens of study tools across 70 disciplines and over 675 courses. Currently available in select markets.

Details at **www.cengage.com/unlimited**.

Cengage Mobile App

The *Cengage Mobile App* lets students study wherever and whenever the mood strikes. Now available with *CengageNOWv2*, it features a full interactive eBook—readable online or off—with 24/7 course access and study tools to power on-the-go learning. Plus, the app allows you to engage your students with instant in-class polling and take attendance with a tap. Find details at **www.cengage.com/mobile-app/**.

MindTap eReader

The MindTap eReader for *Cost Management*, fifth edition, is the most robust digital reading experience available. Hallmark features include the following:

- Fully optimized for the iPad
- Note-taking, highlighting, and more
- Embedded digital media

The MindTap eReader also features ReadSpeaker®, an online text-to-speech application that vocalizes, or "speech-enables," online educational content. This feature is ideally suited for both instructors and learners who would like to listen to content instead of (or in addition to) reading it.

Additional instructor and student resources for this product are available online. Instructor assets include a Solutions Manual, Solutions to Excel templates Educator's Guide, PowerPoint® slides, Guide to Online Teaching, and a test bank powered by Cognero®. Student assets include Excel templates for selected exercises and problems. Sign up or sign in at **www.cengage.com** to search for and access this product and its online resources.

Acknowledgments

We would like to thank the following reviewers for their feedback about digital assets:

Michael Bohanon, *Cleary University and Baker College*
Teresa Brown, *Central New Mexico Community College*
Shannon Charles, *University of Utah*
Jon Erickson, *Utah State University*
Ronald Fory, *University of North Texas at Dallas*
Gaurav Gupta, *Pacific Lutheran University*
Vicki Jobst, *Benedictine University*
Mehmet Kocakulah, *University of Southern Indiana*
Ping Lin, *California State U., Long Beach*
Li-Lin (Sunny) Liu, *CSUDH*
Louella Moore, *Washburn*

Misty Price, *Pasco-Hernando State College*
Kathy Rankin, *Chatham University*
Ann Reichle, *Mid-Plains Community College*
Richelle, *Finlandia University*
Anthony Ross, *Concordia University Texas*
Perry Sellers, *LSCS*
Steven Smith, *Brigham Young University*
Lateef Syed, *Robert Morris University, Illinois*
Domenic Tavella, *Pennsylvania State University, Greater Allegheny*
Cammy Wayne, *Harper College*

About The Authors

Dr. Don R. Hansen is Professor Emeritus of Oklahoma State University. He received his Ph.D. from the University of Arizona in 1977. He has an undergraduate degree in mathematics from Brigham Young University. He has published articles in both accounting and engineering journals including *The Accounting Review*, *The Journal of Management Accounting Research*, *Accounting Organizations and Society*, *Accounting Horizons*, and *IIE Transactions*. He has served on the editorial board of *The Accounting Review*. His outside interests include family, church activities, reading, movies, and watching sports.

Dr. Maryanne M. Mowen is Associate Professor Emerita of Accounting at Oklahoma State University. She received her Ph.D. from Arizona State University. She brings an interdisciplinary perspective to teaching and writing in cost and management accounting, with degrees in history and economics. She has taught classes in ethics and the impact of the Sarbanes-Oxley Act on accountants. Her scholarly research is in the areas of management accounting, behavioral decision theory, and compliance with the Sarbanes-Oxley Act. She has published articles in journals such as *Decision Science*, *The Journal of Economics and Psychology*, and *The Journal of Management Accounting Research*. Dr. Mowen has served as a consultant to mid-sized and Fortune 100 companies and works with corporate controllers on management accounting issues. She has served as a counselor to SCORE in assisting small and start-up businesses. She enjoys hiking, traveling, reading mysteries, and working crossword puzzles.

Dr. Dan L. Heitger is the Deloitte Professor of Accounting and Co-Director of the William Isaac & Michael Oxley Center for Business Leadership at Miami University. He received his Ph.D. from Michigan State University and his undergraduate degree in accounting from Indiana University. He actively works with executives and students of all levels in developing and teaching courses in management accounting, cost management, business sustainability, risk management, governance, stakeholder management, and business reporting. He has cofounded two organizations that provide executive education and consulting services for organizations ranging from large international companies to small entrepreneurial start-ups. His interactions with business professionals, through executive education, consulting, and the Center, allow him to bring a current and real-world perspective to his writing. His published research focuses on cost and management accounting, risk management issues, and business sustainability reporting and has appeared in *Harvard Business Review*, *Behavioral Research in Accounting*, *Accounting Horizons*, *Issues in Accounting Education*, *Journal of Accounting and Public Practice*, *Journal of Accountancy*, and *Strategic Finance*. His top priority is spending time with his family such as hiking with them in the National Park System.

Contents

CHAPTER 1

Introduction to Cost Management   2

Financial Accounting Versus Cost Management: A Systems Framework   4

Financial Accounting Information System   4

The Cost Management Information System   4

Different Systems for Different Purposes   5

Factors Affecting the Use of Cost Management   6

Global Competition   7

Growth in the Service Industry   7

Advances in Digital Information Technology and the Manufacturing Environment   7

Customer Orientation   9

Total Quality Management   9

Data Analytics   10

Forensic Accounting   11

Business Sustainability   12

The Role of the Management Accountant   13

Line and Staff Positions   13

Exhibit 1.1 Partial Organizational Chart: Manufacturing Company   14

Information for Planning, Controlling, Continuous Improvement, and Decision Making   14

Exhibit 1.2 Performance Report Illustrated   15

Accounting and Ethical Conduct   15

Benefits of Ethical Behavior   16

Standards of Ethical Conduct for Management Accountants   16

Exhibit 1.3 Statement of Ethical Professional Practice: Institute of Management Accountants (IMA)   17

Certification   18

The Certificate in Management Accounting   18

The Certificate in Public Accounting   18

The Certificate in Internal Auditing   18

CHAPTER 2

Basic Cost Management Concepts   28

A Systems Framework   30

Accounting Information Systems   30

Exhibit 2.1 Operational Model of the Home Theater System   31

Exhibit 2.2 Operational Model of an Accounting Information System   32

Exhibit 2.3 The Value Chain   33

Relationship to Other Operational Systems and Functions   34

Different Systems for Different Purposes   35

Exhibit 2.4 Subsystems of the Accounting Information System   36

The Growing Importance of Data Analytics within Cost Management   36

A Framework for Understanding the Role of Data Analytics in Cost Management   36

Exhibit 2.5 The Role of Data Analytics in Cost Management   37

Data Analytic Types and Cost Management Analyses   39

Exhibit 2.6 Matching Data Analytic Types to Cost Management Analyses   40

Cost Assignment: Direct Tracing, Driver Tracing, and Allocation   40

Cost Objects   40

Accuracy of Cost Assignments   41

Product and Service Costs   43

Different Costs for Different Purposes   44

Exhibit 2.7 Understanding Different Cost Definitions   45

Product Costs and External Financial Reporting   46

Example 2.1 The HOW and WHY of Calculating Prime Cost, Conversion Cost, Variable Product Cost, and Total Product Cost   48

External Financial Statements   49

Income Statement: Manufacturing Firm   50

Example 2.2 The HOW and WHY of Preparing the Statement of Cost of Goods Manufactured   50

Example 2.3 The HOW and WHY of Preparing the Statement of Cost of Goods Sold   52

Example 2.4 The HOW and WHY of Preparing the Income Statement for a Manufacturing Firm   53

Income Statement: Service Organization   54

Traditional and Activity-Based Cost Management Systems   54

Traditional Cost Management Systems: A Brief Overview   55

Activity-Based Cost Management Systems: A Brief Overview   55

Exhibit 2.8 Activity-Based Management Model   56

Choice of a Cost Management System   57

Exhibit 2.9 Comparison of Traditional and Activity-Based Cost Management Systems   57

Exhibit 2.10 Trade-Off between Measurement and Error Costs   58

Exhibit 2.11 Shifting Measurement and Error Costs   59

CHAPTER 3

Cost Behavior and Forecasting   78

Basics of Cost Behavior   80

Cost Objects   81

Measures of Output   81

Fixed Costs   82

Exhibit 3.1 Fixed Cost Behavior   83
Variable Costs   83
Cost Behavior and Its Role in Forensic Accounting   84
Exhibit 3.2 Variable Cost Behavior   84
Linearity Assumption   85
Exhibit 3.3 Nonlinearity of Variable Costs   86
Exhibit 3.4 Relevant Range for Variable Costs   86
Mixed Costs   87
Example 3.1 The HOW and WHY of Forming an Equation to Describe Mixed Cost   87
Exhibit 3.5 Mixed Cost Behavior   88
Time Horizon   88

Resources, Activities, and Cost Behavior   88
Flexible Resources   89
Committed Resources   89
Implications for Control and Decision Making   90
Step-Cost Behavior   90
Exhibit 3.6 Step-Cost Function   91
Exhibit 3.7 Step-Fixed Costs   92
Example 3.2 The HOW and WHY of Calculating Activity Availability, Capacity Used, and Unused Capacity   92
Activities and Mixed Cost Behavior   93

Methods of Determining Cost Behavior   94
Example 3.3 The HOW and WHY of Using Account Analysis to Determine Fixed and Variable Costs   94

Quantitative Methods for Separating Mixed Costs into Fixed and Variable Components   96
Example 3.4 The HOW and WHY of Using the High-Low Method to Determine Fixed Cost and Variable Rate   97
The High-Low Method   98
Scatterplot Method   99
Exhibit 3.8 Scattergraph for Anderson Company's Materials Handling Costs   100
Exhibit 3.9 Scattergraphs for Various Cost Behavior Patterns   101
The Method of Least Squares   102
Exhibit 3.10 Deviations of Data from a Line   102
Using Regression Programs   103
Exhibit 3.11 Spreadsheet Data for Anderson Company's Materials Handling Cost   104
Exhibit 3.12 Regression Results for Anderson Company's Materials Handling Cost   105
Example 3.5 The HOW and WHY of Using the Regression Results for Fixed Cost and Variable Rate to Construct and Use a Cost Formula   105

Reliability of Cost Formulas   106
Hypothesis Test of Parameters   106
Goodness of Fit Measures   107
Exhibit 3.13 Correlation Illustrated   108
Standard Errors   108

Multiple Regression   109
Exhibit 3.14 Multiple Regression Results for Anderson Company's Materials Handling Cost   111

Example 3.6 The HOW and WHY of Constructing a Cost Equation Using the Results from Multiple Regression   111

Nonlinear Cost Behavior and the Learning Curve   112
Semi-Variable Cost Behavior   112
Exhibit 3.15 Semi-Variable Cost: Increasing Rate   113
Exhibit 3.16 Semi-Variable Cost: Decreasing Rate   114
Cumulative Average-Time Learning Curve   114
Example 3.7 The HOW and WHY of Calculating the Cumulative Average-Time Learning Curve   115
Exhibit 3.17 Spreadsheet for Cumulative Average-Time Learning Model   117
Exhibit 3.18 Graph of Cumulative Total Hours Required and the Cumulative Average Time per Unit   117
Incremental Unit-Time Learning Curve   118

Managerial Judgment   118

CHAPTER 4

Activity-Based Costing   144

Unit-Level Product Costing   147
Exhibit 4.1 Unit-Based Product-Costing Model   147
Overhead Assignment: Plantwide Rates   148
Example 4.1 The HOW and WHY of Applied Overhead and Unit Overhead Cost: Plantwide Rates   148
Calculation and Disposition of Overhead Variances   149
Overhead Application: Departmental Rates   150
Example 4.2 The HOW and WHY of Overhead Variances and Their Disposal   150
Example 4.3 The HOW and WHY of Departmental Overhead Rates: Their Assignment and Rationale   152

Limitations of Plantwide and Departmental Rates   153
Non-Unit-Related Overhead Costs   153
Product Diversity   154
The Failure of Unit-Based Overhead Rates   154
Exhibit 4.2 Product-Costing Data   154
Unit Cost Computation: Plantwide and Departmental Overhead Rates   155
Exhibit 4.3 Unit Product Cost: Plantwide and Departmental Rates   155
Example 4.4 The HOW and WHY of Consumption Ratios   156
Example 4.5 The HOW and WHY of Activity-Based Costing   157
Exhibit 4.4 Comparison of Unit Costs   159

Activity-Based Costing System   160
Activity Identification, Definition, and Classification   160
Exhibit 4.5 Activity-Based Costing Model   161
Exhibit 4.6 Design Steps for an ABC System   161
Exhibit 4.7 Sample Activity Inventory   162
Assigning Costs to Activities   163
Exhibit 4.8 Activity Dictionary: Cardiology Unit   164

Example 4.6 The HOW and WHY of Assigning Resource Costs to Activities   165
Exhibit 4.9 Unbundling of General Ledger Costs   167
Cost Objects and Bills of Activities   167
Exhibit 4.10 Bill of Activities: Cardiology Unit   167
Classifying Activities   168
Exhibit 4.11 Assigning Costs: Final Cost Objects   168
Reducing the Size and Complexity of an ABC System   169
Before-the-Fact Simplification: TDABC   169
Example 4.7 The HOW and WHY of TDABC   170
Duration-Based Costing (DBC)   173
Example 4.8 The HOW and WHY of DBC   174
After-the-Fact Simplification   176
Exhibit 4.12 Data for Patterson Company   177
Example 4.9 The HOW and WHY of Approximately Relevant ABC Systems   178
Example 4.10 The HOW and WHY of Equally Accurate Reduced ABC Systems   180

MAKING THE CONNECTION: INTEGRATIVE EXERCISE PART 1 (CHAPTERS 1–4)   210

CHAPTER 5

Product and Service Costing: Job-Order System   216

Characteristics of the Production Process   217
Manufacturing Firms versus Service Firms   218
Exhibit 5.1 Continuum of Services and Manufactured Products   218
Exhibit 5.2 Features of Service Firms and Their Interface with the Cost Management System   219
Unique versus Standardized Products and Services   221
Setting Up the Cost Accounting System   222
Cost Accumulation   222
Exhibit 5.3 Relationship of Cost Accumulation, Cost Measurement, and Cost Assignment   222
Cost Measurement   223
Cost Assignment   224
Choosing the Activity Level   226
Exhibit 5.4 Measures of Activity Level   226
The Job-Order Costing System: General Description   227
Overview of the Job-Order Costing System   227
Exhibit 5.5 The Job-Order Cost Sheet   228
Materials Requisitions   228
Exhibit 5.6 Materials Requisition Form   229
Job Time Tickets   229
Exhibit 5.7 Time Ticket   229
Overhead Application   230
Unit Cost Calculation   230
Example 5.1 The HOW and WHY of Setting Up a Simplified Job-Order Cost Sheet   230

Job-Order Costing: Specific Cost Flow Description   231
Accounting for Direct Materials   232
Exhibit 5.8 Summary of Direct Materials Cost Flows   232
Accounting for Direct Labor Cost   233
Accounting for Overhead   233
Exhibit 5.9 Summary of Direct Labor Cost Flows   233
Exhibit 5.10 Summary of Overhead Cost Flows   235
Accounting for Finished Goods Inventory   235
Exhibit 5.11 Completed Job-Order Cost Sheet   236
Exhibit 5.12 Summary of Finished Goods Cost Flow   236
Exhibit 5.13 Statement of Cost of Goods Manufactured   237
Accounting for Cost of Goods Sold   237
Exhibit 5.14 Statement of Cost of Goods Sold   238
Example 5.2 The HOW and WHY of Using a Job-Order Cost Sheet to Determine the Balances of Work in Process, Finished Goods, and Cost of Goods Sold   238
Exhibit 5.15 All Signs Company Summary of Manufacturing Cost Flows   239
Accounting for Nonmanufacturing Costs   240
Data Analytics in Job-Order Costing   240
Exhibit 5.16 Income Statement   241
Job-Order Costing with Activity-Based Costing   241
Example 5.3 The HOW and WHY of Using Activity-Based Costing in Job-Order Costing   242
Accounting for Spoiled Units in a Traditional Job-Order Costing System   243
Example 5.4 The HOW and WHY of Accounting for Normal and Abnormal Spoilage in a Job-Order Environment   243

CHAPTER 6

Process Costing   262

Basic Operational and Cost Concepts   264
Cost Flows   264
Exhibit 6.1 An Operational Process System: Antihistamine Manufacturing   265
Exhibit 6.2 Comparison of Cost Accumulation Methods   265
Example 6.1 The HOW and WHY of Cost Flows: Process Costing   266
The Production Report   267
Exhibit 6.3 Process Cost Flows Illustrated Using T-Accounts: No Ending WIP   267
Exhibit 6.4 Basic Features of a Process-Costing System   268
Unit Costs   268
Process Costing with No Work-in-Process Inventories   268
Service Organizations   269
Example 6.2 The HOW and WHY of Process Costing: Services with No WIP Inventories   269
JIT Manufacturing Firms   270
The Role of Activity-Based Costing   270

Process Costing with Ending Work-In-Process Inventories   270

Physical Flow and Equivalent Units   271

Example 6.3 The HOW and WHY of Physical Flow Analysis and Equivalent Units: EWIP Only   271

Calculating Unit Costs, Assigning Costs to Inventories, and Reconciliation   273

Example 6.4 The HOW and WHY of Unit Cost, Inventory Valuation, and Cost Reconciliation: EWIP Only   273

The Five Steps of the Production Report   274

Example 6.5 The HOW and WHY of a Production Report   274

Nonuniform Application of Productive Inputs   275

Example 6.6 The HOW and WHY of Equivalent Units and Unit Costs with Nonuniform Inputs   275

Beginning Work-in-Process Inventories   277

FIFO Costing Method   277

Example 6.7 The HOW and WHY of Physical Flow Analysis and Equivalent Units: FIFO Method   278

Example 6.8 The HOW and WHY of Unit Cost and Cost Assignment: FIFO   279

Step 4 of FIFO Revisited   281

Production Report and Journal Entries   281

Exhibit 6.5 Production Report: Blending Department   282

Weighted Average Costing Method   282

Example 6.9 The HOW and WHY of Physical Flow Analysis and Equivalent Units: Weighted Average Method   283

Example 6.10 The HOW and WHY of Unit Cost and Cost Assignment: Weighted Average Method   284

Production Report   286

FIFO Compared with Weighted Average   286

Exhibit 6.6 Production Report: Blending Department   286

Treatment of Transferred-in Goods   287

Exhibit 6.7 Production and Cost Data: Encapsulating Department   289

Exhibit 6.8 Equivalent Units of Production: Weighted Average Method   289

Operation Costing   290

Exhibit 6.9 Production Report: Encapsulating Department   290

Basics of Operation Costing   291

Exhibit 6.10 Basic Features of Operation Costing   292

Operation Costing Example   293

CHAPTER 7

Allocating Costs of Support Departments and Joint Products   316

An Overview of Cost Allocation   317

Types of Departments   318

Exhibit 7.1 Examples of Departmentalization for a Manufacturing Firm and a Service Firm   319

Exhibit 7.2 Steps in Allocating Support Department Costs to Producing Departments   319

Exhibit 7.3 Examples of Possible Activity Drivers for Support Departments   320

Types of Allocation Bases   320

Objectives of Allocation   320

Allocating One Department's Costs to Other Departments   322

A Single Charging Rate   322

Example 7.1 The HOW and WHY of Calculating and Using a Single Charging Rate   323

Multiple Charging Rates   324

Example 7.2 The HOW and WHY of Calculating and Using Multiple Charging Rates   325

Budgeted versus Actual Usage   327

Exhibit 7.4 Use of Budgeted Data for Product Costing: Comparison of Single- and Dual-Rate Methods   328

Exhibit 7.5 Use of Actual Data for Performance Evaluation Purposes: Comparison of Single- and Dual-Rate Methods   328

Fixed versus Variable Bases: A Note of Caution   329

Choosing a Support Department Cost Allocation Method   329

Exhibit 7.6 Data for Support and Producing Departments   330

Direct Method of Allocation   330

Exhibit 7.7 Allocation of Support Department Costs to Producing Departments Using the Direct Method   331

Example 7.3 The HOW and WHY of Allocating Support Department Costs to Producing Departments Using the Direct Method   331

Sequential Method of Allocation   332

Exhibit 7.8 Allocation of Support Department Costs to Producing Departments Using the Sequential Method   333

Example 7.4 The HOW and WHY of Allocating Support Department Costs to Producing Departments Using the Sequential (Step) Method   334

Reciprocal Method of Allocation   336

Total Cost of Support Departments   336

Example 7.5 The HOW and WHY of Allocating Support Department Costs to Producing Departments Using the Reciprocal Method   336

Comparison of the Three Methods   338

Exhibit 7.9 Comparison of Support Department Cost Allocations Using the Direct, Sequential, and Reciprocal Methods   339

Departmental Overhead Rates and Product Costing   339

Example 7.6 The HOW and WHY of Using Allocated Support Department Costs to Calculate Departmental Overhead Rates   339

Support Department Cost Allocation Benefits   340

Accounting for Joint Production Processes   341

Exhibit 7.10 Joint Production Process   342

Cost Separability and the Need for Allocation   342

Exhibit 7.11 Independent Multiple-Product Production Using the Same Material   342

Accounting for Joint Product Costs   343

Example 7.7 The HOW and WHY of Using the Physical Units Method to Allocate Joint Product Costs   344

Example 7.8 The HOW and WHY of Using the Weighted Average Method to Allocate Joint Product Costs   345

Allocation Based on Relative Market Value   346

Sales-Value-at-Split-Off Method   347

Example 7.9 The HOW and WHY of Using the Sales-Value-at-Split-Off Method to Allocate Joint Product Costs   347

Example 7.10 The HOW and WHY of Using the Net Realizable Value Method to Allocate Joint Product Costs   349

Example 7.11 The HOW and WHY of Using the Constant Gross Margin Percentage Method to Allocate Joint Product Costs   350

Accounting for By-Products   351

Ethical Implications of Cost Allocation   353

CHAPTER 8

Budgeting for Planning and Control   372

The Role of Budgeting in Planning and Control   373

Purposes of Budgeting   374

Exhibit 8.1 The Master Budget and Its Interrelationships   374

The Budgeting Process   375

Exhibit 8.2 Components of the Master Budget   376

Gathering Information for Budgeting   377

Exhibit 8.3 Short-Term Bookings Forecast for Oil Field Equipment Company   378

Preparing the Operating Budget   379

Sales Budget   379

Production Budget   379

Example 8.1 The HOW and WHY of Constructing a Sales Budget   380

Example 8.2 The HOW and WHY of Constructing a Production Budget   381

Direct Materials Purchases Budget   382

Example 8.3 The HOW and WHY of Constructing a Direct Materials Purchases Budget   383

Direct Labor Budget   384

Example 8.4 The HOW and WHY of Constructing a Direct Labor Budget   385

Overhead Budget   386

Ending Finished Goods Inventory Budget   386

Example 8.5 The HOW and WHY of Constructing an Overhead Budget   386

Example 8.6 The HOW and WHY of Preparing the Ending Finished Goods Inventory Budget   387

Cost of Goods Sold Budget   388

Example 8.7 The HOW and WHY of Preparing the Cost of Goods Sold Budget   388

Marketing Expense Budget   389

Example 8.8 The HOW and WHY of Constructing a Marketing Expense Budget   389

Administrative Expense Budget   390

Additional Operating Budgets   390

Example 8.9 The HOW and WHY of Constructing an Administrative Expense Budget   391

Budgeted Income Statement   392

Example 8.10 The HOW and WHY of Constructing a Budgeted Income Statement   392

Operating Budgets for Merchandising and Service Firms   393

Preparing the Financial Budget   394

The Cash Budget   394

Exhibit 8.4 The Cash Budget   395

Example 8.11 The HOW and WHY of Constructing a Cash Receipts Budget with an Accounts Receivable Aging Schedule   395

Example 8.12 The HOW and WHY of Constructing a Cash Budget   397

Budgeted Balance Sheet   399

Exhibit 8.5 Balance Sheet for ABT, Inc.   399

Exhibit 8.6 Budgeted Balance Sheet for ABT, Inc.   400

Shortcomings of the Traditional Master Budget Process   400

Flexible Budgets for Planning and Control   402

Static Budgets versus Flexible Budgets   403

Exhibit 8.7 ABT Performance Report for Quarter 1: Comparison of Actual with Static (Master) Budget Amounts   403

Example 8.13 The HOW and WHY of Constructing a Flexible Budget for Varying Levels of Activity   404

Example 8.14 The HOW and WHY of Constructing a Flexible Budget for the Actual Level of Activity   406

Exhibit 8.8 Managerial Performance Report: Quarterly Production (in thousands)   407

Activity-Based Budgets   408

Exhibit 8.9 Traditional Budget for the Secure-Care Department   409

Exhibit 8.10 Flexible Budget for the Secure-Care Department   410

Exhibit 8.11 Activity-Based Budget for the Secure-Care Department   411

The Behavioral Dimension of Budgeting   412

Characteristics of a Good Budgetary System   412

CHAPTER 9

Standard Costing: A Functional-Based Control Approach   440

Developing Unit Input Standards   442

Establishing Standards   442

Kaizen Standards   443

Usage of Standard Costing Systems   443

Exhibit 9.1 Cost Assignment Approaches   444

Standard Cost Sheets   445

Exhibit 9.2 Standard Cost Sheet for Deluxe Strawberry Frozen Yogurt   445

Example 9.1 The HOW and WHY of Computing Standard Quantities Allowed (*SQ* and *SH*)   446

Variance Analysis and Accounting: Direct Materials and Direct Labor   447

Calculating the Direct Materials Price Variance and Direct Materials Usage Variance   447

Example 9.2 The HOW and WHY of Computing the Direct Materials Price Variance (*MPV*) and Direct Materials Usage Variance (*MUV*)   448

Exhibit 9.3 Standard Bill of Materials   451

Accounting for Direct Materials Price and Usage Variances   452

Example 9.3 The HOW and WHY of Computing the Direct Labor Rate Variance (*LRV*) and Direct Labor Efficiency Variance (*LEV*)   453

Investigating Direct Materials and Labor Variances   455

Example 9.4 The HOW and WHY of Using Control Limits to Determine When to Investigate a Variance   456

Disposition of Direct Materials and Direct Labor Variances   458

Example 9.5 The HOW and WHY of Closing the Balances in the Variance Accounts at the End of the Year   459

Variance Analysis: Overhead Costs   460

Four-Variance Method for Calculating Overhead Variances   461

Example 9.6 The HOW and WHY of Calculating the Total Variable Overhead Variance   461

Calculating the Variable Overhead Spending Variance and Variable Overhead Efficiency Variance   462

Example 9.7 The HOW and WHY of Computing the Variable Overhead Spending Variance and the Variable Overhead Efficiency Variance   463

Interpreting the Variable Overhead Variances   464

Exhibit 9.4 Variable Overhead Spending Variance by Item   465

Four-Variance Analysis: The Two Fixed Overhead Variances   466

Calculating the Fixed Overhead Spending Variance and Fixed Overhead Volume Variance   466

Exhibit 9.5 Variable Overhead Spending and Efficiency Variances by Item   466

Example 9.8 The HOW and WHY of Computing the Fixed Overhead Spending Variance and the Fixed Overhead Volume Variance   467

Interpreting the Fixed Overhead Variances   469

Exhibit 9.6 Fixed Overhead Spending Variance by Item   469

Accounting for Overhead Variances   470

Two- and Three-Variance Analysis Methods   471

Exhibit 9.7 Two-Variance Analysis: Helado Company   471

Exhibit 9.8 Three-Variance Analysis: Helado Company   472

Mix and Yield Variances: Materials and Labor   472

Example 9.9 The HOW and WHY of Computing the Mix Variance   473

Example 9.10 The HOW and WHY of Computing the Yield Variance   475

Direct Labor Mix and Yield Variances   476

CHAPTER 10

Decentralization: Responsibility Accounting, Performance Evaluation, and Transfer Pricing   498

Responsibility Accounting   500

Types of Responsibility Centers   500

The Role of Information and Accountability   501

Decentralization   501

Reasons for Decentralization   502

The Units of Decentralization   504

Measuring the Performance of Investment Centers   505

Return on Investment   505

Example 10.1 The HOW and WHY of Calculating Average Operating Assets, Margin, Turnover, and Return on Investment (ROI)   506

Residual Income   510

Example 10.2 The HOW and WHY of Calculating Residual Income   510

Project I   511

Project II   511

Economic Value Added   513

Example 10.3 The HOW and WHY of Calculating the Weighted Average Cost of Capital and EVA   514

Multiple Measures of Performance   516

Measuring and Rewarding the Performance of Managers   517

Incentive Pay for Managers—Encouraging Goal Congruence   517

Managerial Rewards   518

Transfer Pricing   520

The Impact of Transfer Pricing on Income   520

Setting Transfer Prices   520

Exhibit 10.1 Impact of Transfer Price on Transferring Divisions and the Company as a Whole   520

Market Price   521

Negotiated Transfer Prices   522

Exhibit 10.2 Summary of Sales and Production Data   523

Exhibit 10.3 Comparative Income Statements   523

Exhibit 10.4 Comparative Statements   525

Example 10.4 The HOW and WHY of Calculating Market-Based and Negotiated Transfer Prices   526

Cost-Based Transfer Prices   527

Example 10.5 The HOW and WHY of Calculating Cost-Based Transfer Prices   528

MAKING THE CONNECTION: INTEGRATIVE EXERCISE PART 2 (CHAPTERS 5–10)   546

CHAPTER 11

Strategic Cost Management 552

Strategic Cost Management: Basic Concepts 554

Strategic Positioning: The Key to Creating and Sustaining a Competitive Advantage 555

Value-Chain Framework, Linkages, and Activities 556

Exhibit 11.1 Value Chain for the Petroleum Industry 557

Organizational Activities and Cost Drivers 558

Exhibit 11.2 Organizational Activities and Drivers 558

Operational Activities and Drivers 559

Exhibit 11.3 Operational Activities and Drivers 559

Exhibit 11.4 Organizational and Operational Activity Relationships 560

Enterprise Risk Management 560

Determining Risk Appetite 561

Identifying Top Risks 561

Exhibit 11.5 Key Steps within the ERM Process 561

Assessing Inherent Risks 562

Exhibit 11.6 Key Elements of a Portfolio Risk Management Perspective 563

Exhibit 11.7 Enterprise Risk Management at Bayer 564

Responding to Risks 564

Net Benefit of Risk Response 565

Example 11.1 The HOW and WHY of Using Net Benefit to Evaluate Risk Response Alternatives 566

Monitoring the ERM Process 568

Value-Chain Analysis 568

Exploiting Internal Linkages 569

Exhibit 11.8 Internal Value Chain 569

Example 11.2 The HOW and WHY of Exploiting Internal Linkages to Reduce Costs and Increase Value 569

Exhibit 11.9 Step-Cost Behavior: Purchasing Activity 571

Exploiting Supplier Linkages 571

Example 11.3 The HOW and WHY of Activity-Based Supplier Costing 573

Exploiting Customer Linkages 574

Example 11.4 The HOW and WHY of Activity-Based Customer Costing 576

Life-Cycle Cost Management 577

Product Life-Cycle Viewpoints 577

Exhibit 11.10 Product Sales Revenue Life Cycle: Marketing Viewpoint 578

Exhibit 11.11 Product Cost Life Cycle: Production Viewpoint 579

Interactive Viewpoint 579

Exhibit 11.12 Typical Relationships of Product Life-Cycle Viewpoints 580

Example 11.5 The How and Why of Activity-Based Life-Cycle Cost Reduction 581

Role of Target Costing 583

Exhibit 11.13 Target-Costing Model 584

Just-In-Time (JIT) Manufacturing and Purchasing 585

Inventory Effects 586

Plant Layout 587

Grouping of Employees 587

Exhibit 11.14 Plant Layout Pattern: Traditional versus JIT 588

Employee Empowerment 588

Exhibit 11.5 Comparison of JIT Approaches with Traditional Manufacturing and Purchasing 589

Total Quality Control 589

JIT and Its Effect on the Cost Management System 589

Traceability of Overhead Costs 589

Product Costing 590

Exhibit 11.16 Product Cost Assignment: Traditional Versus JIT Manufacturing 590

JIT's Effect on Job-Order and Process-Costing Systems 591

Backflush Costing 591

Example 11.6 The HOW and WHY of Backflush Costing 593

CHAPTER 12

Activity-Based Management 626

The Relationship of Activity-Based Costing and Activity-Based Management 628

Exhibit 12.1 The Two-Dimensional Activity-Based Management Model 628

Process Value Analysis 629

Driver Analysis: Defining Root Causes 629

Activity Analysis: Identifying and Assessing Value Content 630

Assessing Activity Performance 633

Financial Measures of Activity Efficiency 633

Reporting Value- and Non-Value-Added Costs 634

Exhibit 12.2 Formulas for Value- and Non-Value-Added Costs 635

Example 12.1 The HOW and WHY of Value- and Non-Value-Added Cost Reporting 635

Trend Reporting of Non-Value-Added Costs 636

Example 12.2 The HOW and WHY of Non-Value-Added Cost Trend Reporting 636

Drivers and Behavioral Effects 637

The Role of Kaizen Standards 638

Exhibit 12.3 Kaizen Cost Reduction Process 639

Example 12.3 The HOW and WHY of Kaizen Costing 639

Benchmarking 640

Activity Flexible Budgeting 641

Exhibit 12.4 Flexible Budget: Direct Labor Hours 642

Exhibit 12.5 Activity Flexible Budget 642
Exhibit 12.6 Activity-Based Performance Report 643
**Example 12.4 The HOW and WHY of Activity-Based
Flexible Budgeting 643**
Activity Capacity Management 644
**Example 12.5 The HOW and WHY of Activity Capacity
Management 645**

Implementing Activity-Based Management 646
Discussion of the ABM Implementation Model 647
Exhibit 12.7 ABM Implementation Model 647
Why ABM Implementations Fail 648

**Financial-Based Versus Activity-Based Responsibility
Accounting 649**
Exhibit 12.8 The Responsibility Accounting Model 650
Assigning Responsibility 650
Exhibit 12.9 Responsibility Assignments Compared 651
Establishing Performance Measures 651
Exhibit 12.10 Performance Measures Compared 652
Evaluating Performance 652
Assigning Rewards 652
Exhibit 12.11 Performance Evaluation Compared 652
Exhibit 12.12 Rewards Compared 653

CHAPTER 13

Strategic-Based Control Systems and the Balanced Scorecard 672

Strategic-Based Control Systems 674
Exhibit 13.1 The Three Elements of a Strategic-Based Control
System 675
Company Strategy 676
Performance Measures 676
Exhibit 13.2 Balancing Performance Measure
Characteristics 678
Incentive Programs 678

Basic Concepts of the Balanced Scorecard 680
Strategy Translation 680
Exhibit 13.3 Strategy Translation Process 681
The Financial Perspective, Objectives, and Measures 681
Exhibit 13.4 Summary of Objectives and Measures: Financial
Perspective 682
Customer Perspective, Objectives, and Measures 682
Core Objectives and Measures 682
Customer Value 683
Exhibit 13.5 Summary of Objectives and Measures: Customer
Perspective 683
Process Perspective, Objectives, and Measures 684
Innovation Process: Objectives and Measures 684
Operations Process: Objectives and Measures 684
Cycle Time and Velocity 684
**Example 13.1 The HOW and WHY of Calculating Cycle
Time and Velocity 685**

Manufacturing Cycle Efficiency (MCE) 686
**Example 13.2 The HOW and WHY of Calculating
Manufacturing Cycle Efficiency (MCE) 686**
Post-Sales Service Process: Objectives and Measures 687
Learning and Growth Perspective 687
Exhibit 13.6 Summary of Objectives and Measures: Process
Perspective 687

Linking Measures to Strategy 688
Exhibit 13.7 Summary of Objectives and Measures: Learning
and Growth Perspective 689
The Concept of a Testable Strategy with Strategic
Feedback 689
**Example 13.3 The HOW and WHY of Strategy
Mapping 690**
Exhibit 13.8 Strategy Map for Example 13.3 691

Strategic Alignment 692
Communicating the Strategy 692
Targets and Incentives 692
Exhibit 13.9 Targets and Weighting Scheme
Illustrated 693
Resource Allocation 694

CHAPTER 14

Quality and Environmental Cost Management 706

Costs of Quality 709
Quality Defined 709
Costs of Quality Defined 710
Quality Cost Measurement 711
Exhibit 14.1 Examples of Quality Costs by Category 711
Exhibit 14.2 The Taguchi Quality Loss Function 712
Exhibit 14.3 Quality Loss Computation Illustrated 713

Reporting Quality Costs 713
**Example 14.1 The HOW and WHY of Preparing a Quality
Cost Report 714**
Optimal Distribution of Quality Costs: Zero-Defects
with Robust Quality View 715
Exhibit 14.4 Quality Cost Categories: Relative Contribution
Graphs 715
Exhibit 14.5 Robust Quality and the Zero-Defects Quality
Graph 716
The Role of Activity-Based Cost Management 717

Quality Cost Information and Decision Making 717
Decision-Making Contexts 718
Certifying Quality Through ISO 9000 720

Controlling Quality Costs 720
Choosing the Quality Standard 721
Types of Quality Performance Reports 722
**Example 14.2 The HOW and WHY of Preparing Interim
Quality Performance Reports 722**

Example 14.3 The HOW and WHY of Multiple-Period Quality Trend Reporting   724
Exhibit 14.6 Multiple-Period Trend Graph: Total Quality Costs   725
Exhibit 14.7 Multiple-Period Trend Graph: Individual Quality Cost Categories   726
Exhibit 14.8 Multiple-Period Trend Graph: Relative Quality Costs   726
Example 14.4 The HOW and WHY of Long-Range Quality Performance Reporting   727

Defining, Measuring, and Controlling Environmental Costs   729
The Ecoefficiency Paradigm   729
Exhibit 14.9 Ecoefficiency Relationships   730
Environmental Costs Defined   732
Environmental Cost Report   732
Exhibit 14.10 Classification of Environmental Costs by Activity Type   733
Example 14.5 The HOW and WHY of an Environmental Cost Report   733
Exhibit 14.11 Relative Distribution: Environmental Costs   734
Environmental Cost Reduction   735
An Environmental Financial Report   735
Exhibit 14.12 Environmental Financial Statement   735

Environmental Costing   736
Environmental Product Costs   736
Activity-Based Environmental Cost Assignments   737
Example 14.6 The HOW and WHY of Activity-Based Environmental Cost Assignments   737

CHAPTER 15

Lean Accounting and Productivity Measurement   766

Lean Manufacturing   768
Value by Product   770
Value Stream   770
Exhibit 15.1 Order Fulfillment Value Stream   770
Exhibit 15.2 Matrix Approach to Identifying Value Streams   771
Value Flow   771
Exhibit 15.3 Garn's Current Departmental Layout: Model A Aluminum Wheel Production   772
Exhibit 15.4 Garn's Proposed Manufacturing Cell (Model A)   772
Example 15.1 The HOW and WHY of Cellular Manufacturing   773
Pull Value   774
Pursue Perfection   774

Lean Accounting   775
Focused Value Streams and Traceability of Overhead Costs   776
Exhibit 15.5 Value-Stream Costs   776
Value-Stream Costing   777

Exhibit 15.6 Steel Wheel Value-Stream Costs and Production Hours   779
Example 15.2 The HOW and WHY of Value-Stream Product Costing   779
Value-Stream Reporting   780
Exhibit 15.7 Garn Autoparts Profit and Loss Statement   781
Decision Making   781
Performance Measurement   781
Exhibit 15.8 ABS Value-Stream Box Scorecard   782

Productive Efficiency   783
Partial Productivity Measurement Defined   783
Exhibit 15.9 Improving Technical Efficiency   784
Exhibit 15.10 Improving Allocative Efficiency   785
Partial Measures and Measuring Changes in Productive Efficiency   785
Advantages of Partial Measures   785
Disadvantages of Partial Measures   786

Total Productivity Measurement   786
Profile Productivity Measurement   786
Example 15.3 The HOW and WHY of Profile Productivity Measurement   787
Profit-Linked Productivity Measurement   788
Example 15.4 The HOW and WHY of Profit-Linked Productivity Measurement   789

MAKING THE CONNECTION: INTEGRATIVE EXERCISE PART 3 (CHAPTERS 11–15)   806

CHAPTER 16

Cost-Volume-Profit Analysis   812

The Break-Even Point and Target Profit in Units and Sales Revenue   815
Basic Concepts for CVP Analysis   816
Example 16.1 The HOW and WHY of Basic Cost Calculations and the Contribution-Margin-Based Income Statement   816
The Equation Method for Break-Even and Target Income   818
Example 16.2 The HOW and WHY of Calculating the Units Needed to Break Even and to Achieve a Target Profit   819
Contribution Margin Approach   820
Exhibit 16.1 Division of Revenue into Variable Cost and Contribution Margin   821
Example 16.3 The HOW and WHY of Calculating Revenue for Break-Even and for a Target Profit   822
Comparison of the Two Approaches   823

After-Tax Profit Targets   824
Example 16.4 The HOW and WHY of Calculating the Number of Units to Generate an After-Tax Target Profit   824

Multiple-Product Analysis   826
Break-Even Point in Units for the Multiple-Product Setting   826

Example 16.5 The HOW and WHY of Calculating the Break-Even Number of Units in a Multiproduct Firm   828
Sales-Revenue Approach   830
Graphical Representation of CVP Relationships   831
The Profit-Volume Graph   831
Exhibit 16.2 Profit-Volume Graph   832
The Cost-Volume-Profit Graph   832
Exhibit 16.3 Cost-Volume-Profit Graph   833
Assumptions of Cost-Volume-Profit Analysis   833
Exhibit 16.4 Cost and Revenue Relationships   834
Changes in the CVP Variables   835
Exhibit 16.5 Summary of the Effects of Alternative 1   836
Exhibit 16.6 Summary of the Effects of Alternative 2   836
Introducing Risk and Uncertainty   836
Exhibit 16.7 Summary of the Effects of Alternative 3   837
Example 16.6 The HOW and WHY of Calculating Margin of Safety   837
Example 16.7 The HOW and WHY of Calculating Degree of Operating Leverage and Percent Change in Profit   839
Sensitivity Analysis and CVP   840
Exhibit 16.8 Differences Between Manual and Automated Systems   840
CVP Analysis and Non-Unit Cost Drivers   842
Example Comparing Conventional and ABC Analysis   842
Strategic Implications: Conventional CVP Analysis Versus ABC Analysis   843
CVP Analysis and JIT   844
CVP Analysis, Multiple Drivers, and Nonprofit Entities   845
Exhibit 16.9 Summary of Important Equations   846

CHAPTER 17

Activity Resource Usage Model and Tactical Decision Making   866
Tactical Decision Making   868
The Tactical Decision-Making Process   869
Qualitative Factors   870
Exhibit 17.1 Decision Model: Tactical Decision-Making Process   871
Relevant Costs and Revenues   872
Relevant Costs Illustrated   872
Irrelevant Cost Illustrated   873
Relevancy, Cost Behavior, and the Activity Resource Usage Model   874
Flexible Resources   874
Committed Resources   874
Exhibit 17.2 Resource Demand and Supply   876
Illustrative Examples of Tactical Decision Making   876
Make-or-Buy Decisions   876
Example 17.1 The HOW and WHY of Structuring a Make-or-Buy Decision   877
Exhibit 17.3 Activity and Cost Information   879
Keep-or-Drop Decisions   881

Example 17.2 The HOW and WHY of Structuring A Keep-or-Drop Product Line Decision   882
Special-Order Decisions   885
Example 17.3 The HOW and WHY of Structuring a Special-Order Decision   886
Decisions to Sell or Process Further   887
Example 17.4 The HOW and WHY of Structuring a Sell at Split-Off or Process Further Decision   888
The Role of Differential Analysis in Forensic Accounting   889
Relevant Costing and Ethical Behavior   891
Relevant Cost Analysis in Personal Decision Making   891

CHAPTER 18

Pricing and Profitability Analysis   912
Basic Pricing Concepts   914
Demand and Supply   914
Price Elasticity of Demand   915
Market Structure and Price   916
Exhibit 18.1 Characteristics of the Four Basic Types of Market Structure   917
Cost and Pricing Policies   917
Cost-Based Pricing   917
Example 18.1 The HOW and WHY of Calculating a Markup on Cost   918
Target Costing and Pricing   919
Other Pricing Policies   921
The Legal System and Pricing   922
Predatory Pricing   922
Price Discrimination   923
Example 18.2 The HOW and WHY of Calculating Cost and Profit by Customer Class   924
The Role of Costs in Forensic Accounting Pricing Cases   926
Measuring Profit   927
Reasons for Measuring Profit   927
Absorption-Costing Approach to Measuring Profit   928
Example 18.3 The HOW and WHY of Calculating Inventory Cost and Preparing the Income Statement Using Absorption Costing   929
Variable-Costing Approach to Measuring Profit   931
Example 18.4 The HOW and WHY of Calculating Inventory Cost and Preparing the Income Statement Using Variable Costing   932
Exhibit 18.2 Changes in Inventory Under Absorption and Variable Costing   934
Profitability of Segments and Divisions   934
Exhibit 18.3 Alden Company Absorption-Costing Income Statement (In thousands of dollars)   935
Exhibit 18.4 Alden Company Variable-Costing Income Statement (In thousands of dollars)   936
Analysis of Profit-Related Variances   937
Sales Price and Sales Volume Variances   937

Example 18.5 The HOW and WHY of Calculating the Sales Price Variance, the Sales Volume Variance, and the Overall Sales Variance 938
Contribution Margin Variance 939
Example 18.6 The HOW and WHY of Calculating the Contribution Margin Variance 939
Example 18.7 The HOW and WHY of Calculating the Contribution Margin Volume Variance 940
Example 18.8 The HOW and WHY of Calculating the Sales Mix Variance 942
Market Share and Market Size Variances 942
Example 18.9 The HOW and WHY of Calculating the Market Share Variance and the Market Size Variance 943
The Product Life Cycle 944
Exhibit 18.5 Product Life Cycle and Profitability 945
Exhibit 18.6 Impact of the Product Life Cycle on Cost Management 945
Exhibit 18.7 Product Life-Cycle Costs in the ABC Categories 946
Limitations of Profit Measurement 947

CHAPTER 19

Capital Investment 972

Capital Investment Decisions 974
Payback and Accounting Rate of Return: Nondiscounting Methods 975
Payback Period 976
Example 19.1 The HOW and WHY of Calculating the Payback Period 976
Accounting Rate of Return 977
Example 19.2 The HOW and WHY of Calculating the Accounting Rate of Return 978
The Net Present Value Method 979
Example 19.3 The HOW and WHY of Analyzing NPV 979
Internal Rate of Return 981
Example 19.4 The HOW and WHY of Calculating the Internal Rate of Return 981
NPV Versus IRR: Mutually Exclusive Projects 982
NPV Compared with IRR 983
Exhibit 19.1 NPV and IRR: Conflicting Signals 983
Exhibit 19.2 Modified Comparison of Projects A and B 984
Exhibit 19.3 Modified Cash Flows with Additional Opportunity 984
Example 19.5 The HOW and WHY of Determining NPV and IRR for Mutually Exclusive Projects 984
Computing After-Tax Cash Flows 986
Conversion of Gross Cash Flows to After-Tax Cash Flows 986
Exhibit 19.4 Tax Effects of the Sale of M1 and M2 987
Example 19.6 The HOW and WHY of Calculating After-Tax Cash Flows 988

MACRS Depreciation 989
Exhibit 19.5 MACRS Depreciation Rates 990
Exhibit 19.6 Value of Accelerated Methods Illustrated 991
Capital Investment: Advanced Technology and Environmental Considerations 991
How Investment Differs 992
How Estimates of Operating Cash Flows Differ 992
An Example: Investing in Advanced Technology 993
Exhibit 19.7 Investment Data: Direct, Intangible, and Indirect Benefits 994
Salvage Value 995
Discount Rates 995
Exhibit 19A.1 Present Value of an Uneven Series of Cash Flows 999
Exhibit 19A.2 Present Value of a Uniform Series of Cash Flows 999
Appendix B: Present Value Tables 1001
Exhibit 19B.1 Present Value of $1 1001
Exhibit 19B.2 Present Value of an Annuity of $1 in Arrears 1002

CHAPTER 20

Inventory Management: Economic Order Quantity, JIT, and the Theory of Constraints 1018

Just-in-Case Inventory Management 1020
Justifying Inventory 1021
Exhibit 20.1 Traditional Reasons for Carrying Inventory 1021
Economic Order Quantity: A Model for Balancing Acquisition and Carrying Costs 1022
Example 20.1 The HOW and WHY of Calculating the EOQ 1023
Example 20.2 The HOW and WHY of Reordering 1024
Exhibit 20.2 The Reorder Point 1025
An Example Involving Setups 1025
Exhibit 20.3 EOQ and Reorder Point Illustrated 1026
EOQ and Inventory Management 1026
JIT Inventory Management 1027
A Pull System 1028
Setup and Carrying Costs: The JIT/Lean Approach 1028
Due-Date Performance: The JIT (Lean) Solution 1029
Avoidance of Shutdown and Process Reliability: The JIT/Lean Approach 1030
Exhibit 20.4 Withdrawal Kanban 1031
Exhibit 20.5 Production Kanban 1031
Exhibit 20.6 Vendor Kanban 1031
Exhibit 20.7 The Kanban Process 1032
Discounts and Price Increases: JIT Purchasing Versus Holding Inventories 1033
JIT's Limitations 1033

Basic Concepts of Constrained Optimization   1034

One Binding Internal Constraint   1034

Example 20.3 The HOW and WHY of Solving Constrained Optimization Problems with One Internal Constraint   1035

Multiple Internal Binding Constraints   1036

Exhibit 20.8 Constraint Data: Schaller Company   1036

Example 20.4 The HOW and WHY of Solving Linear Programming Problems with Two Variables   1036

Exhibit 20.9 Graphical Solution   1038

Theory of Constraints   1038

Operational Measures   1038

Five-Step Method for Improving Performance   1040

Exhibit 20.10 Drum-Buffer-Rope System: General Description   1041

Example 20.5 The HOW and WHY of a Drum-Buffer-Rope System   1042

Exhibit 20.11 Drum-Buffer-Rope: Schaller Company   1043

Exhibit 20.12 New Constraint Set: Schaller Company   1044

CHAPTER 21

International Issues in Cost Management   1058

Cost Accounting in the International Environment   1060

Levels of Involvement in International Trade   1061

Importing and Exporting   1061

Example 21.1 The HOW and WHY of Locating in a Foreign Trade Zone   1062

Wholly Owned Subsidiaries   1064

Joint Ventures   1064

Foreign Currency Exchange   1065

Managing Transaction Risk   1066

Exhibit 21.1 Spot Rates for Major Currencies September 11, 2020   1066

Example 21.2 The HOW and WHY of Exchanging One Currency for Another   1066

Example 21.3 The HOW and WHY of Calculating Exchange Gains and Losses   1068

Example 21.4 The HOW and WHY of Hedging Currency Exchange Rates   1069

Cryptocurrencies   1070

Managing Economic Risk   1071

Managing Translation Risk   1072

Decentralization and Performance Evaluation in the Multinational Firm   1074

Advantages of Decentralization in the MNC   1074

Measuring Performance in the Multinational Firm   1075

Transfer Pricing and the Multinational Firm   1077

Performance Evaluation   1078

Income Taxes and Transfer Pricing   1078

Example 21.5 The HOW and WHY of Using the Comparable Uncontrolled Price Method, the Resale Price Method, and the Cost-Plus Method in Calculating Transfer Prices   1078

Ethics in the International Environment   1080

MAKING THE CONNECTION: INTEGRATIVE EXERCISE PART 4 (CHAPTERS 16–21)   1090

Glossary   1094

Check Figures   1106

Subject Index   1111

Company Index   1124

Examples   1126

1 Introduction to Cost Management

After studying this chapter, you should be able to:

1 ▸ Describe cost management and explain how it differs from financial accounting.

2 ▸ Identify factors and trends affecting the use of cost management.

3 ▸ Describe how management accountants function within an organization.

4 ▸ Understand the importance of ethical behavior for management accountants.

5 ▸ Identify the three forms of certification available to internal accountants.

THE IMPORTANCE OF COST MANAGEMENT

at The Kroger Company

The Kroger Company represents one of the largest and most respected grocery companies in the United States with annual sales in excess of $120 billion, over 2,800 stores, more than 460,000 employees, 11 million daily customers, and consistent placement within the top 20 of the annual Fortune 500 list. Kroger supermarket stores average approximately 160,000 square feet in size and cost over $25 million to build. In addition to being a traditional brick-and-mortar grocery store, Kroger continues to expand its product and service offerings. For example, many new and renovated Kroger stores feature a wine tasting bar, full menu sit-down bistro, ready-to-eat food bar, coffee shop, and an ever-expanding pharmacy. Furthermore, Kroger continues to diversify its service offerings through online ordering and curbside pickup (i.e., where employees shop, bag, and drop off grocery items to customers outside of the store), home grocery delivery, and fuel stations. Kroger also pursues various alternative profit stream activities, such as gift cards, money services (check cashing, money transfers), and other specialty-targeted customer services based on the insights gleaned from Kroger's 10 petabytes of customer loyalty program data.

Given that it generates over $335 million in daily sales, a casual observer might assume that Kroger does not care much about understanding or controlling its costs. However, nothing could be further from the financial truth. Although Kroger does generate astonishingly large sales, it also operates in an extremely competitive industry with razor-thin profit margins. For example, its sales of $122.286 billion generate a net income of $1.64 billion, which is only a 1.34 percent return on sales.[1] In other words, almost 99 percent of Kroger's sales are consumed by its vast expenses! As a result of its thin profit margin, Kroger, like other grocers, cares deeply about cost management. Effectively understanding and managing its numerous costs can mean the difference between being a successful and respected Fortune 20 company and falling into a net loss financial position that struggles to remain in business. Kroger's heavy reliance on effective cost management is typical of most companies. For example, a recent global survey of 1,219 executives (e.g., presidents, chief executive officers, chief financial officers, and chief operational officers) directly involved in cost management within their organizations found that 71 percent of businesses plan to undertake cost reduction initiatives over the next 24 months.[2] Furthermore, these cost reduction efforts are significant as 66 percent of respondents note that they are targeting cost reductions of 10 percent or higher. Interestingly, 81 percent of respondents report that they have been unable to fully meet their past cost reduction targets, with the majority of these respondents falling 25 or more percent short of meeting their targets. Collectively, these results indicate that cost

1 See https://www.wsj.com/market-data/quotes/KR/financials/annual/income-statement, accessed August 3, 2020.
2 O. Aguilar and J. Girzadas, "Deloitte 2019 Global Cost Survey," https://www2.deloitte.com/global/en/pages/operations/articles/gx-global-cost-management-survey.html, accessed August 3, 2020.

management represents an extremely important yet challenging endeavor for most organizations, thereby demonstrating the great value of understanding cost management. Therefore, the various cost management topics discussed briefly in this chapter and examined more thoroughly throughout the book apply not only to Kroger but also to most companies.

Describe cost management and explain how it differs from financial accounting.

FINANCIAL ACCOUNTING VERSUS COST MANAGEMENT: A SYSTEMS FRAMEWORK

A systems framework helps us understand the variety of topics that appear in the field of cost management. It also facilitates our ability to understand the differences between financial accounting and cost management. An **accounting information system** consists of interrelated manual and computer parts and uses processes such as collecting, recording, summarizing, analyzing, and managing data to transform inputs into information that is provided to users.

The accounting information system within an organization has two major subsystems: (1) *the financial accounting information system* and (2) *the cost management accounting information system.* One of the major differences between the two systems is the targeted user.

Financial Accounting Information System

The **financial accounting** information system is primarily concerned with producing outputs for external users. It uses well-specified economic events as inputs, and its processes follow certain rules and conventions. For financial accounting, the nature of the inputs and the rules and conventions governing processes are defined by the Securities and Exchange Commission (SEC) and the Financial Accounting Standards Board (FASB). Among its outputs are financial statements such as the balance sheet, income statement, and statement of cash flows for external users (investors, creditors, government agencies, and other outside users). Financial accounting information is used for investment decisions, stewardship evaluation, activity monitoring, and regulatory measures.

The Cost Management Information System

The **cost management** information system is primarily concerned with producing outputs for internal users using inputs and processes needed to satisfy management objectives. The cost management information system is not bound by externally imposed criteria that define inputs and processes. Instead, the criteria that govern the inputs and processes are set by people in the company. The cost management information system has three broad objectives that provide information for:

1. Costing out services, products, and other objects of interest to management

2. Planning and control

3. Decision making

The information requirements for satisfying the first objective depend on the nature of the object being costed and the reason management wants to know the cost. For example, product costs that satisfy the FASB rules are needed to value inventories for the balance sheet and to calculate the cost of goods sold expense on the income statement. These product costs include the cost of materials, labor, and overhead. In other cases, managers may want to know all costs that are associated with a product for purposes of tactical and strategic profitability analysis. If so, then additional cost information may be needed concerning product design, development, marketing, and distribution. For example, pharmaceutical companies, such as **Merck** might want to associate research and development costs with individual drugs or drug families. The desire for management to understand such cost associations is logical given that the development of a single new drug often costs in excess of $2 billion and faces a regulator approval rate of only 12 percent.[3]

Cost information also is used for planning and control. It should help managers decide what should be done, why it should be done, how it should be done, and how well it is being done. For example, information about the expected revenues and costs for a new product could be used as an input for target costing. At this stage, the expected revenues and costs may cover the entire life of the new product. Thus, projected costs of design, development, testing, production, marketing, distribution, and servicing would be essential information.

Finally, cost information is a critical input for many managerial decisions. For example, a manager may need to decide whether to continue making a component internally or to buy it from an external supplier. In this case, the manager would need to know the cost of materials, labor, and other productive inputs associated with the manufacture of the component and which of these costs would vanish if the product is no longer produced. Also needed is information concerning the cost of purchasing the component, including any increase in cost for internal activities such as receiving and storing goods. As illustrated by this example, companies increasingly utilize a proactive cost management perspective to improve resource allocation and investment decisions across the company.

Cost management has a much broader focus than that found in traditional costing systems. It is concerned not only with how much something costs but also with the factors that drive costs, such as cycle time, quality, and process productivity. Thus, cost management requires a deep understanding of a firm's cost structure. Managers must be able to determine the long- and short-run costs of activities and processes as well as the costs of goods, services, customers, suppliers, and other objects of interest. Causes of these costs are also carefully studied.

Different Systems for Different Purposes

The financial accounting and cost management systems show us that different systems exist to satisfy different purposes. As indicated, these two systems are subsystems of the accounting information system. The cost management information system also has two major subsystems: *the cost accounting information system* and *the operational control information system*. The objectives of these two subsystems correspond to the first and second objectives mentioned earlier for the cost management information system (the costing and control objectives). The output of these two cost systems satisfies the third objective (the decision-making objective).

The **cost accounting information system** is a cost management subsystem designed to assign costs to individual products and services and other objects as specified by management. For external financial reporting, the cost accounting system must assign costs to products in order to value inventories and determine cost of sales. Furthermore, these assignments must conform to the rules and conventions set by the SEC and the FASB.

---

3 T. Sullivan, "A Tough Road: Cost to Develop One New Drug Is $2.6 Billion; Approval Rate for Drugs Entering Clinical Development Is Less Than 12%," March 21, 2019, https://www.policymed.com/2014/12/a-tough-road-cost-to-develop-one-new-drug-is-26-billion-approval-rate-for-drugs-entering-clinical-de.html, accessed August 3, 2020.

These rules and conventions do not require that all costs assigned to individual products be causally related to the demands of individual products. Thus, using financial accounting principles to define product costs may lead to under- and overstatements of individual product costs. For reporting inventory values and cost of sales, this may not matter. Inventory values and cost of sales are reported in the aggregate, and the under- and overstatements may wash out to the extent that the values reported on the financial statements are reasonably accurate.

At the individual product level, however, distorted product costs can cause managers to make significant decision errors. For example, a manager might erroneously deemphasize and overprice a product that is, in reality, highly profitable. For decision making, accurate product costs are needed. If possible, the cost accounting system should produce product costs that simultaneously are accurate and satisfy financial reporting conventions. If not, then the cost system must produce two sets of product costs: one that satisfies financial reporting criteria and one that satisfies management decision-making needs.

The **operational control information system** is a cost management subsystem designed to provide accurate and timely feedback concerning the performance of managers and others relative to their planning and control of activities. Operational control is concerned with what activities should be performed and assessing how well they are performed. It focuses on identifying opportunities for improvement and helping to find ways to improve. A good operational control information system provides information that helps managers engage in a program of continuous improvement of all aspects of their businesses.

Product cost information plays a role in this process but, by itself, is not sufficient. The information needed for planning and control is broader and encompasses the entire value chain. For example, every profit-making manufacturing and service organization exists to serve customers. Thus, one objective of an operational control system is to improve the value received by customers. Products and services should be produced that fit specific customer needs. (Observe how this affects the design and development system in the value chain.) Quality, affordable prices, and low post-purchase costs for operating and maintaining the product are also important to customers.

A second, related objective is to improve profits by providing this value. Well-designed, quality products that are affordable can be offered only if they also provide an acceptable return to the owners of the company. Cost information concerning quality, different product designs, and post-purchase customer needs is vital for managerial planning and control.

OBJECTIVE 2

Identify factors and trends affecting the use of cost management.

FACTORS AFFECTING THE USE OF COST MANAGEMENT

Worldwide competitive pressures, growth in the service industry, expansion of data analytics, and advances in digital and manufacturing technologies have changed the nature of our economy and caused many manufacturing and service industries to dramatically change the way in which they operate. Changes in these important factors, in turn, have prompted the development of innovative and relevant cost management practices. For example, activity-based accounting systems have been developed and implemented in many organizations. Additionally, the focus of cost management accounting systems has broadened to enable managers to better serve the needs of customers and manage the firm's business processes that are used to create customer value. Furthermore, cost management practices increasingly are informing decisions in important emerging areas such as forensic accounting, enterprise risk management, and business sustainability.

Global Competition

Vastly improved transportation and communication systems have led to a global market for many manufacturing and service firms. Several decades ago, firms neither knew nor cared what similar firms in Japan, Brazil, India, Germany, Africa, and China were producing. These foreign firms were not competitors because their markets were separated by geographical distance. Now, both small and large firms are affected by the opportunities and challenges offered by global competition. **Stillwater Designs**, a small firm that designs and markets Kicker speakers, has significant markets in Europe. The manufacture of the Kicker speakers is mostly outsourced to Asian producers. At the other end of the size scale, **Apple**; **Google**; **Mars, Inc.**; **Procter & Gamble**; **The Coca-Cola Company**; and **Yum! Brands** have developed sizable markets in China. For example, Apple manufactures over 500,000 iPhones every day in a Chinese factory with 350,000 employees and ships them around the world aboard massive Boeing 747 jets. For example, the 6,300-mile iPhone trek from Zhengzhou, China, to San Francisco, California, takes only three days.[4] Similarly, service providers, such as investment bankers and management consultants, can communicate with foreign offices instantly. Improved transportation and communication in conjunction with higher quality products that carry lower prices have upped the ante for all firms. This global competitive environment has increased the demand not only for more cost information but also for more accurate cost information. Cost information plays a vital role in reducing costs, improving productivity, and assessing product-line profitability.

Growth in the Service Industry

The service industry—including financial services, transportation, technology, medical, and travel—represents a significant and growing portion of the economy. For example, the global financial services market is estimated at approximately $25 trillion. Furthermore, the service industry now comprises approximately three quarters of the U.S. economy and employment. Interestingly, new products oftentimes spur the use of new services in order to function as customers desire, such as cars that utilize navigation services and smart televisions that utilize streaming services.[5] Furthermore, the gig economy, which refers to the use of short-term contracts to provide a service, represents one of the most impactful newer service sectors. For example, many well-known startup service companies, such as **Airbnb**, **Instacart**, and **Uber**, have arisen out of the gig economy. The significant growth in the service industry has made managers in the industry more conscious of the need to have accurate cost information for planning, controlling, continuous improvement, and decision making. Thus, the changes in the service sector add to the demand for innovative and relevant cost management information.

Advances in Digital Information Technology and the Manufacturing Environment

Significant advances in information technology have led to advancements in the manufacturing environment. For example, **enterprise resource planning (ERP) software** has the objective of providing an integrated system capability—a system that can run all the operations of a company and provide access to real-time data from the various functional areas of a company that span the entire value chain. Extracting and analyzing this real-time data enables managers to continuously improve the efficiency of organizational units and processes. In addition, when combined with ERP systems, automated manufacturing allows for a considerable amount of information to be collected that informs managers about what is happening within an organization. Information can be captured and analyzed regarding product movement through the factory, completed

---

4 D. Barboza, "An iPhone's Journey, from the Factory Floor to the Retail Store," *The New York Times*, https://www.nytimes.com/2016/12/29/technology/iphone-china-apple-stores.html, accessed August 3, 2020.

5 "The American Economy Is Experiencing a Paradigm Shift," *The Atlantic*, https://www.theatlantic.com/sponsored/citi-2018/the-american-economy-is-experiencing-a-paradigm-shift/2008/, accessed August 3, 2020.

production, materials used, scrap generated, and final product cost. The same real-time data usage occurs within service companies as well. For example, **UPS** utilizes its multibillion-dollar investments in information technology to provide customers with cutting-edge services, such as processing an astonishing 295 million daily package tracking requests from customers.

As a result of these technological advances in information technology, cost accountants have the flexibility to respond to the managerial need for more complex product costing methods, such as activity-based costing (ABC). Simplified and improved costing systems such as time-driven activity-based costing (TDABC) have been developed in order to deal with these issues while preserving the benefits of enhanced accuracy. ABC software is classified as online analytic software and facilitates improved decision making around areas such as cost estimation, product pricing, and planning and budgeting. This vast computing capability now makes it possible for accountants to generate individualized reports on an as-needed basis.

Furthermore, manufacturing management approaches such as the theory of constraints and just-in-time have allowed firms to increase quality, reduce inventories, eliminate waste, and reduce costs. Product costing systems, control systems, allocation, inventory management, cost structure, capital budgeting, variable costing, and many other accounting practices are being affected as well.

Theory of Constraints   The **theory of constraints** is a method used to continuously improve manufacturing and nonmanufacturing activities. It is characterized as a "thinking process" that begins by recognizing that all resources are finite. Some resources, however, are more critical than others. The most critical limiting factor, called a *constraint*, becomes the focus of attention. By managing this constraint, performance can be improved. To manage the constraint, it must be identified and exploited (i.e., performance must be maximized subject to the constraint). All other actions are subordinate to the exploitation decision. Finally, to improve performance, the constraint must be elevated. The process is repeated until the constraint is eliminated (i.e., it is no longer the critical performance-limiting factor). The process then begins anew with the resource that has now become the critical limiting factor. Using this method, lead times and, thus, inventories can be reduced.

Just-in-Time Manufacturing   A demand-pull system, **just-in-time (JIT) manufacturing**, strives to produce a product only when it is needed and only in the quantities demanded by customers. Demand, measured by customer orders, pulls products through the manufacturing process. Each operation produces only what is necessary to satisfy the demand of the succeeding operation. No production takes place until a signal from a succeeding process indicates the need to produce. Parts and materials arrive just in time to be used in production. JIT manufacturing typically reduces inventories to much lower levels than those found in conventional systems, increases the emphasis on quality control, and produces fundamental changes in the way production is organized and carried out. Basically, JIT manufacturing focuses on continual improvement by reducing inventory costs and dealing with other economic problems. Reducing inventories frees up capital that can be used for more productive investments. Increasing quality enhances the competitive ability of the firm. Finally, changing from a traditional manufacturing setup to JIT manufacturing allows the firm to focus more on quality and productivity and, at the same time, allows a more accurate assessment of what it costs to produce products.

Lean Manufacturing   JIT is a critical part of a more comprehensive approach referred to as *lean manufacturing*. **Lean manufacturing** is the persistent pursuit and elimination of waste that simultaneously embodies respect for people. Waste is anything that does not add value to the end user (customer). As a result of eliminating waste, lead time is decreased, production processes are streamlined, and costs are decreased. Depending on the nature of the value streams created in lean manufacturing, a more accurate assessment of product costs may result.

Customer Orientation

Firms concentrate on the delivery of value to the customer with the objective of establishing a competitive advantage. As such, companies increasingly utilize advances in digital information technologies, including data analytics, to estimate the profitability of their current and potential future customers. For example, during its annual investor conference, **The Kroger Company** (featured in the opening chapter scenario) Chief Financial Officer described the importance it places on customers by referring to the company's "obsession with increasing customer loyalty."[6] Interestingly, using various data analytic techniques and cost management perspectives, Kroger estimates that the value of a loyal customer is approximately eight times that of a nonloyal customer when considered over time along the value chain. Accountants and managers refer to a firm's **value chain** as the set of activities required to design, develop, produce, market, and deliver products and services to customers. As a result, a key question to be asked about any process or activity is whether it is important to the customer. The cost management system must track information relating to a wide variety of activities important to customers (e.g., product quality, environmental performance, new product development, and delivery performance). Customers now count the delivery of the product or service as part of the product. The cost management system utilizes various techniques to provide insights on these activities. For example, **activity-based management** identifies the activities produced at each stage of the development process and assesses their costs. Also, **target costing** encourages managers to assess the overall cost impact of product designs over the product's life cycle and simultaneously provides incentives to make design changes to reduce costs. Companies must compete not only in technological and manufacturing terms but also in terms of the speed of delivery and response. Firms such as **FedEx** have exploited this desire by identifying and developing a market the **U.S. Postal Service** could not serve.

Companies have internal customers as well. The staff functions of a company exist to serve the line functions. The accounting department creates cost reports for production managers. Accounting departments that are "customer driven" assess the value of the reports to be sure that they communicate significant information in a timely and readable fashion. Reports that do not measure up are dropped.

Total Quality Management

Continuous improvement and elimination of waste are the two foundation principles that govern a state of manufacturing excellence. Manufacturing excellence is the key to survival in today's world-class competitive environment. Producing products and services that actually perform according to specifications and with little waste are the twin objectives of world-class firms. A philosophy of **total quality management**, in which managers strive to create an environment that will enable organizations to produce defect-free products and services, has replaced the acceptable quality attitudes of the past. The emphasis on quality applies to services as well as products.

Advocate Good Samaritan Hospital is an acute care facility located in Downers Grove, Illinois. Good Samaritan Hospital received the Malcolm Baldrige National Quality Award in the health-care category. This award is presented to organizations that demonstrate quality and performance excellence. Furthermore, Good Samaritan Hospital improved its mortality rate (actual mortality/expected mortality) from 0.73 to 0.25. In addition, the ratio of observed to expected renal failures decreased from 3.0 to 0.86. Finally, by creating a culture of patient safety, Good Samaritan Hospital decreased its malpractice expenses by 83 percent, thereby saving $10 million.

REAL-WORLD EXAMPLE

---

6 "Kroger Co (KR) Q3 2019 Earnings Call Transcript," The Motley Fool (December 5, 2015), https://www.fool.com /earnings/call-transcripts/2019/12/05/kroger-co-kr-q3-2019-earnings-call-transcript.aspx, accessed August 3, 2020.

The message is clear. Pursuing an objective of high quality promises major benefits. Cost management supports this objective by providing crucial information concerning quality-related activities and quality costs. Savings associated with quality initiatives can be reported as well. Managers need to know which quality-related activities add value and which ones do not. They also need to know what quality costs are and how they change over time.

Data Analytics

Cost management provides significant value to organizations through its unique ability to analyze relevant financial and nonfinancial information and provide reliable insights that improve strategic and operational decision making across the organization. Organizations rely on employees from different functional areas to perform various cost management analyses. As studied throughout this book, these organizational decisions rely on numerous cost management analyses, including hospital breakeven point, new chief executive officer selection, restaurant margin of safety, existing product profit and loss, research and development cost allocation, special order offer, store operating hours, new geographic service line launch cost, risk response net benefit, grocery store product placement, and capital project return on investment.

However, conducting cost management analyses that provide value-adding decision insights increasingly requires an understanding of and comfort with the rapidly growing role of data analytics within these analyses.[7,8] Oftentimes these analyses utilize very large data sets—data sets so large that they exceed the ability of commonly used software to capture and analyze the relationships (hence, the big data label that has become popular). Analyzing these big data sets can provide significant insights that help companies to reduce costs, improve quality, decrease cycle times, detect fraudulent activity, and enhance decision making. Software for analyzing big data sets has been developed by companies such as **Oracle** and **SAP**; moreover, software such as Microsoft Power BI and Tableau provide similar analytical capabilities for individuals, small businesses, and large businesses.

Although defined formally in Chapter 2, *data analytics* generally refers to the practice of identifying and analyzing appropriate data and then communicating the resulting insights to help improve organizational decision making. For example, executives increasingly expect their accountants to utilize data analytics in forecasting the financial consequences of various decisions.[9] The Institute of Management Accountants' *Competency Framework* more specifically describes the growing importance of data analytics as accountants work to effectively "extract, transform, and analyze data to gain insights, improve predictions, and support decision making."[10] Additionally, as companies externally disclose increasing amounts of financial and nonfinancial business sustainability performance data (e.g., regarding economic, environmental, social, regulatory, and political issues), management accounting must consider data visualization challenges regarding how best to communicate data such that internal decision makers and key external stakeholders understand the "complete story" of the organization's performance. For example, as explained in the *Competency Framework*, data analytics plays an increasingly large role in a number of important traditional and emerging management accounting analyses, including the following:

- *Forecasting*—Using analytical tools and data mining techniques to discover key and relevant trends, both historical and predictive in nature
- *Budgeting*—Projecting the amount and timing of financial and operational resources required to allow the organization to achieve its long-term strategic goals

7 Brian Ballou, Dan Heitger, and Dale Stoel, "Data-Driven Decision-Making and Its Impact on Accounting Undergraduate Curriculum," *Journal of Accounting Education*, Elsevier Ltd., Vol. 44 (2018): 14–24.

8 Stathis Gould, "Building Data Science and Analytics Capabilities in Finance and Accounting," International Federation of Accountants, September 26, 2019, https://www.ifac.org/knowledge-gateway/preparing-future-ready-professionals /discussion/building-data-science-and, accessed August 3, 2020.

9 Jeff Thomson, "What Does 2020 Hold for Management Accountants?" *Forbes*, January 6, 2020, https://www.forbes .com/sites/jeffthomson/2020/01/06/what-does-2020-hold-for-management-accountants/#7bb1df5970ef, accessed August 3, 2020.

10 Institute of Management Accountants, *IMA Management Accounting Competency Framework*, 2019, https://www .imanet.org/career-resources/management-accounting-competencies?ssopc=1, accessed August 3, 2020.

- *Extraction*—Identifying, transforming, and querying the data necessary to conduct important financial analyses that often involve multiple data sets and information systems
- *Governance*—Considering the degree of accuracy, decision relevance, and security of the increasing amount and types of data used in various financial estimates, including those involving enterprise risk management issues
- *Visualization*—Determining how best to present complex analytical tools and organizational performance results in a manner that is transparent and understandable to investors and other key stakeholders

In summary, the growing presence of data analytics continues to increase significantly the responsibilities and importance of cost management. Chapter 2 discusses data analytics in more detail, including a framework that specifically applies the growing role of data analytics to cost management analyses.

Forensic Accounting

Accountants increasingly provide important inputs used in resolving organizations' various legal disputes, including civil and fraud cases. These inputs consist primarily of accounting measures of the economic consequences resulting from such disputes. For example, a business might use cost behavior concepts to measure what its cost would have been if a supplier trucking company had not violated the terms of its product delivery agreement. As another example, a business might use product profitability information to determine damages after a competitor illegally interferes with its product sales activity over some period of time. Therefore, experts define **forensic accounting** as the action of identifying, recording, settling, extracting, reporting, and verifying past financial data or other accounting activities for settling current or prospective legal disputes or using such past financial data for projecting future financial data to settle legal disputes.[11]

Although any type of accounting information potentially can be relevant to the measurement of economic consequences, management accounting—including cost management information—is particularly relevant to these measurements. However, the court (i.e., the judge, jury, and attorneys on both sides) often is not sophisticated in understanding and applying accounting information to case issues. Fortunately, forensic accounting experts are uniquely able to provide the court with relevant and reliable cost management and other accounting information to meet its needs. Therefore, it is essential that forensic accountants provide the court with knowledge and insight into the relevant accounting issues in an attempt to help it reach a fair and reasonable case decision. In so doing, forensic accountants are expected to clearly and concisely explain why they selected particular accounting information, how they arrived at their accounting measurements, and how such measures should be interpreted.

More specifically, forensic accountants provide accounting measurement services in several different but related areas: (1) fraud investigations (i.e., finding fraud and measuring the cost of resulting damages, preventing or minimizing fraud, and testifying in fraud cases); (2) litigation support (i.e., litigation consulting, preparing expert opinion reports, and testifying at trials or in other formats); and (3) performing business valuations (i.e., both adversarial and nonadversarial). Each of these dispute areas frequently relies on the estimation of certain costs, typically generated by using various data analytic techniques, to assess the nature and amount of the dispute's economic consequences. Examples of common disputes include whether the terms of a service contract have been violated by one of the contracting parties, the financial consequences resulting from an injury to an employee using an improperly serviced machine, and the amount of lost sales resulting from a company failing to provide essential parts as called for in the customer contract. In order to estimate the appropriate amount of damages within each dispute, a forensic accountant must determine what accounting information is relevant to the situation, the correct financial amount of any relevant accounting information, and how the relevant accounting information should be used or interpreted in resolving the dispute. Therefore, this book provides examples where appropriate of how cost management insights inform important forensic accounting analyses.

---

11 L. Crumbley, L. Heitger, and G. Smith, *Forensic and Investigative Accounting*, 8e (New York: CCH, 2017).

Business Sustainability

Companies operate in an increasingly complex and interconnected global business environment. As such, the decisions made by companies have increasingly wide and deep footprints for their stakeholders, including investors, customers, suppliers, regulators, employees, nongovernmental agencies, and communities. As a result, stakeholders seek more information regarding a company's various activities beyond the financial statements and other information traditionally contained with a 10-K annual report. **Business sustainability** refers to a company's ability to create value over the long term by measuring performance, managing risks, and communicating effectively to key stakeholders in a manner that consistently reflects the achievement of its strategy. Therefore, stakeholders increasingly desire information that can help them assess the company's business sustainability performance, which a growing number of investors interpret as a leading indicator of future financial performance. In response to these stakeholder requests, companies voluntarily disclose varying but significant types and amounts of qualitative and quantitative information regarding their business sustainability performance. For example, KPMG survey evidence finds that over 90 percent of the world's largest companies choose to disclose business sustainability information to some degree.[12]

American Electric Power (AEP) Ohio is an electric utility that serves nearly 1.5 million customers. The company has a long history of effectively measuring and managing its performance regarding various business sustainability issues, such as energy efficiency, and transparently reporting such performance to external stakeholders. The Environmental Protection Agency selected AEP Ohio to receive the ENERGY STAR Partner of the Year Award.[13] This award recognized AEP Ohio for its innovation and promotion to customers of energy efficiency programs, which generated an estimated 1.5 billion kilowatt hours in energy savings. AEP Ohio helped generate these energy savings in part by supporting the construction of thousands of ENERGY STAR–certified homes; providing incentives and training to over 15,000 retailers on the benefits of ENERGY STAR–certified electrical pumps, appliances, and thermostats; and implementing an annual marketing plan that generated 8.5 million media impressions involving the company's energy efficiency programs.

These business sustainability disclosures pertain to numerous issues, including the company's employee safety at overseas clothing manufacturing plants; compliance with Environmental Protection Agency rules on air, soil, and water pollution; status regarding product and service innovation efforts; carbon emissions across product and service life cycles; supplier selection processes; and employee engagement endeavors. Companies typically include these disclosures in an annual corporate sustainability report (CSR), also referred to as a *responsibility* or *citizenship report*. Ideally, the items disclosed within a CSR should link clearly to the company's strategy and reflect its most important risks and opportunities. For example, a large delivery company, such as **Amazon**, **UPS**, or **FedEx**, should focus relatively heavily on measuring, managing, and publicly disclosing its activities involving carbon emissions, whereas a public university should instead focus relatively heavily on campus safety or student job placement upon graduation. As business sustainability performance and disclosures often involve cost management expertise, this book provides examples where appropriate to demonstrate the growing importance of cost management within business sustainability.

12 J. Blasco and A. King, "The Road Ahead: The KPMG Survey of Corporate Responsibility Reporting 2017,"
    https://assets.kpmg/content/dam/kpmg/xx/pdf/2017/10/kpmg-survey-of-corporate-responsibility-reporting-2017.pdf,
    accessed August 3, 2020.

13 "AEP Ohio—An AEP Company: Partner of the Year Sustained Excellence Energy Efficiency Program Delivery,"
    https://www.energystar.gov/about/content/aep_ohio_aep_company, accessed August 3, 2020.

THE ROLE OF THE MANAGEMENT ACCOUNTANT

World-class firms are those that are at the cutting edge of customer support. They know their market and their product. They strive continually to improve product design, manufacture, and delivery. These companies can compete with the best of the best in a global environment. The titles of employees who perform important cost management analyses vary widely across organizations and include management accountants, internal auditors, finance personnel, corporate accountants, consultants, risk managers, and advisors. However, regardless of their title, accountants also can be termed world class. Those who merit this designation are intelligent and well prepared. They not only have the education and training to accumulate and provide financial information, but also stay up to date in their field and in business. In addition, world-class accountants must be familiar with the customs and financial accounting rules of the countries in which their firm operates.

Line and Staff Positions

The role of cost and management accountants in an organization is one of support and teamwork. They assist those who are responsible for carrying out an organization's basic objectives. Positions that have direct responsibility for the basic objectives of an organization are referred to as **line positions**. In general, individuals in line positions participate in activities that produce and sell their company's product or service. Positions that are supportive in nature and have only indirect responsibility for an organization's basic objectives are called **staff positions**.

In an organization whose basic mission is to produce and sell laser printers, the vice presidents of manufacturing and marketing, the factory manager, and the assemblers are all line positions. The vice presidents of finance and human resources, the cost accountant, and the purchasing manager are all staff positions.

The partial organization chart, shown in Exhibit 1.1, illustrates the organizational positions for production and finance. Because one of the basic objectives of the organization is to produce, those directly involved in production hold line positions. Although management accountants such as controllers and cost accounting managers may exercise considerable influence in the organization, they have no authority over the managers in the production area. The managers in line positions are the ones who set policy and make the decisions that impact production. By supplying and interpreting accounting information, however, accountants can have significant input into policies and decisions. Accountants also participate in project teams that are involved in decision making.

The Controller The **controller**, the chief accounting officer, supervises all accounting departments. Because of the critical role that management accounting plays in the operation of an organization, the controller is often viewed as a member of the top management team and encouraged to participate in planning, controlling, and decision-making activities. As the chief accounting officer, the controller has responsibility for both internal and external accounting requirements. This charge may include direct responsibility for internal auditing, cost accounting, financial accounting (including Securities and Exchange Commission [SEC] reports and financial statements), systems accounting (including analysis, design, and internal controls), budgeting support, economic analysis, and taxes. The duties and organization of the controller's office vary from firm to firm. In some companies, the internal audit department may report directly to the financial vice president; similarly, the systems department may report directly to the financial vice president or even to another staff vice president. A possible organization of a controller's office is also shown in Exhibit 1.1.

The Treasurer The **treasurer** is responsible for the finance function. Specifically, the treasurer raises capital and manages cash (banking and custody), investments, and investor relations. The treasurer may also be in charge of credit and collections as well as insurance. As shown in Exhibit 1.1, the treasurer reports to the financial vice president.

Exhibit 1.1   Partial Organizational Chart: Manufacturing Company

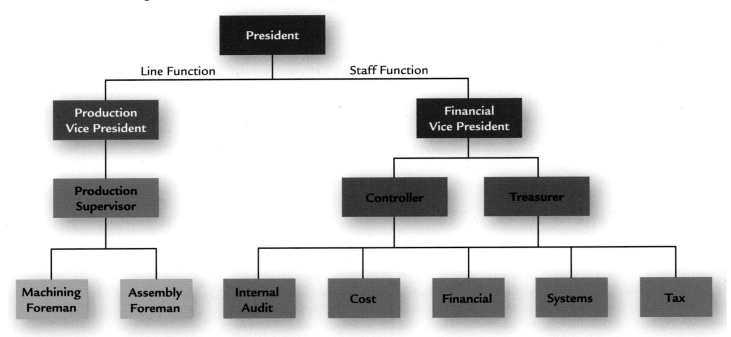

Information for Planning, Controlling, Continuous Improvement, and Decision Making

The cost and management accountant is responsible for generating financial information required by the firm for internal and external reporting. This involves responsibility for collecting, processing, and reporting information that will help managers in their planning, controlling, and other decision-making activities.

Planning   The detailed formulation of future actions to achieve a particular end is the management activity called **planning**. Planning therefore requires setting objectives and identifying methods to achieve those objectives. A firm may have the objective of increasing its short- and long-term profitability by improving the overall quality of its products. By improving product quality, the firm should be able to reduce scrap and rework, decrease the number of customer complaints and the amount of warranty work, reduce the resources currently assigned to inspection, and so on, thus increasing profitability. This is accomplished by working with suppliers to improve the quality of incoming raw materials, establishing quality control circles, and studying defects to ascertain their cause.

Controlling   The processes of monitoring a plan's implementation and taking corrective action as needed are referred to as **controlling**. Control is usually achieved with the use of **feedback**. Feedback is information that can be used to evaluate or correct the steps that are actually being taken to implement a plan. Based on the feedback, a manager may decide to let the implementation continue as is, take corrective action of some type to put the actions back in harmony with the original plan, or do some midstream replanning.

Feedback is a critical facet of the control function. It is here that accounting once again plays a vital role. Accounting reports that provide feedback by comparing planned (budgeted) data with actual data are called **performance reports**. Exhibit 1.2 shows a performance report that compares budgeted sales and cost of goods sold with the actual amounts for the month of August. Deviations from the planned amounts that increase profits are labeled "favorable,"

Golding Foods, Inc.			
Performance Report			
For the Month Ended August 31, 20×1			
Budget Item	**Actual**	**Budgeted**	**Variance**
Sales	$800,000	$900,000	$100,000 U
Cost of goods sold	600,000	650,000	50,000 F

Note: U = Unfavorable; F = Favorable.

Exhibit 1.2
Performance Report Illustrated

while those that decrease profits are called "unfavorable." These performance reports can have a dramatic impact on managerial actions—but they must be realistic and supportive of management plans. Revenue and spending targets must be based (as closely as possible) on actual operating conditions.

Continuous Improvement In a dynamic environment, firms must continually improve their performance to remain competitive or to establish a competitive advantage. A company pursuing continuous improvement has the goal of performing better than before and better than competitors. **Continuous improvement** has been defined as "the relentless pursuit of improvement in the delivery of value to customers."[14] In practical terms, continuous improvement means searching for ways to increase overall efficiency by reducing waste, improving quality, and reducing costs. Cost management supports continuous improvement by providing information that helps identify ways to improve and then reports on the progress of the methods that have been implemented. It also plays a critical role by developing a control system that locks in and maintains any improvements realized.

Decision Making The process of choosing among competing alternatives is **decision making**. Decisions can be improved if information about the alternatives is gathered and made available to managers. One of the major roles of the accounting information system is to supply information that facilitates decision making. This pervasive managerial function is an important part of both planning and control. A manager cannot plan without making decisions. Managers must choose among competing objectives and methods to carry out the chosen objectives. Only one of numerous mutually exclusive plans can be chosen. Similar comments can be made concerning the control function.

ACCOUNTING AND ETHICAL CONDUCT

OBJECTIVE ◀ 4
Understand the importance of ethical behavior for management accountants.

Business ethics is learning what is right or wrong in the work environment and choosing what is right. Well-known and staggering ethical breakdowns, such as the one that occurred at Wells Fargo involving millions of fake customer accounts and billions of dollars in corporate fines, serve as stark reminders of the constant need for organizations to behave ethically. Business ethics could also be described as the science of conduct for the work environment. Principles of personal ethical behavior include concern for the well-being of others, respect for others, trustworthiness and honesty, fairness, doing good, and preventing harm to others. For professionals such as accountants, managers, engineers, and physicians, ethical behavior principles can be expanded to include concepts such as objectivity, full disclosure, confidentiality, due diligence, and avoiding conflicts of interest.

---

14 W. Maguire and D. Heath, "Capacity Management for Continuous Improvement," *Journal of Cost Management* (January 1997): 26–31.

Benefits of Ethical Behavior

Attention to business ethics can bring significant benefits to a company. Companies with a strong code of ethics can create strong customer and employee loyalty. Observing ethical practices now can avoid later litigation costs. Companies in business for the long term find that it pays to treat all of their constituents honestly and fairly. Furthermore, a company that values people more than profit and is viewed as operating with integrity and honor is more likely to be a commercially successful and responsible business. These observations are supported by a number of studies concerning ethics and financial performance. These studies find that there is a positive correlation between ethical performance and economic performance.[15, 16] Simply put, being ethical pays.

Standards of Ethical Conduct for Management Accountants

Organizations and professional associations often establish a code of ethics or standards of conduct for their managers and employees. All firms subject to the Sarbanes-Oxley Act must disclose whether they have established a code of ethics for senior financial officers and, if not, must explain why. Although a code of ethics is not mandated by law, it certainly is encouraged strongly.

In addition to establishing a code of ethics, most companies have established ethics training programs and whistle-blower hotlines or other mechanisms for employees to report ethical behavioral breakdowns within their company. However, while important, the mere presence of such ethical codes, training programs, and reporting mechanisms certainly does not guarantee highly ethical behavior. Therefore, investors and other key stakeholders increasingly look for companies to measure and disclose evidence of highly ethical behavior. As discussed earlier in the chapter, the majority of companies voluntarily report various measures of business sustainability performance, some of which include evidence of ethical behavior. For example, Cleveland Clinic, one of the top-rated hospitals in the world, enthusiastically discloses its frequent inclusion by the Ethisphere Institute as one of the World's Most Ethical Companies.[17]

The Institute of Management Accountants (IMA) has established ethical standards for management accountants. Management accountants are subject to this professional code and have been advised that "they shall not commit acts contrary to these standards nor shall they condone the commission of such acts by others in their organizations."[18] The standards and the recommended resolution of ethical conflict are presented in Exhibit 1.3. The code has five major divisions: competence, confidentiality, integrity, credibility, and resolution of ethical conflict.

To illustrate an application of the code, suppose that the vice president of finance has informed Adrianna Nunez, a divisional controller, that the division's accounting staff will be reduced by 20 percent within the next four weeks. Furthermore, Adrianna Nunez is instructed to refrain from mentioning the layoffs because of the potential uproar that would be caused. One of the targeted layoffs is a cost accounting manager who happens to be a good friend. Adrianna Nunez also knows that her good friend is planning to buy a new sports utility vehicle within the next week. Adrianna is strongly tempted to inform her friend so that she can avoid tying up cash that she may need until a new position is found. Would it be unethical for Adrianna to share her confidential information with her friend? This situation is an example of an ethical dilemma. Informing the friend would violate II-1, the requirement that confidential information must not be disclosed unless authorized. Resolution of the conflict may be as simple as chatting with the vice president, explaining the difficulty, and obtaining permission to disclose the layoff.

---

15 Curtis C. Verschoor, "Principles Build Profits," *Management Accounting* (October 1997): 42–46; Simon Webley and Elise Moore, "Does Business Ethics Pay?" Executive Summary, Institute of Business Ethics, http://www.ibe.org.uk as of May 11, 2004; Han Donker, Deborah Poff, and Saiff Zahir, "Corporate Values, Codes of Ethics, and Firm Performance: A Look at the Canadian Context," *Journal of Business Ethics* (October 2008): 527–537.

16 S. Vollmer, "The Board's Role in Promoting an Ethical Culture," *Journal of Accountancy* (July 1, 2018), https://www.journalofaccountancy.com/issues/2018/jul/corporate-board-role-ethical-culture.html, accessed 3 August 2020.

17 See https://newsroom.clevelandclinic.org/2020/02/25/cleveland-clinic-again-named-one-of-worlds-most-ethical-companies/, accessed August 3, 2020.

18 Statement on Management Accounting No. 1C, "Standards of Ethical Conduct for Management Accountants" (Montvale, NJ: Institute of Management Accountants, 1983).

Members of IMA shall behave ethically. A commitment to ethical professional practice includes overarching principles that express our values and standards that guide our conduct.

PRINCIPLES

IMA's overarching ethical principles include: Honesty, Fairness, Objectivity, and Responsibility. Members shall act in accordance with these principles and shall encourage others within their organizations to adhere to them.

STANDARDS

IMA members have a responsibility to comply with and uphold the standards of Competence, Confidentiality, Integrity, and Credibility. Failure to comply may result in disciplinary action.

I. COMPETENCE

1. Maintain an appropriate level of professional leadership and expertise by enhancing knowledge and skills.
2. Perform professional duties in accordance with relevant laws, regulations, and technical standards.
3. Provide decision support information and recommendations that are accurate, clear, concise, and timely. Recognize and help manage risk.

II. CONFIDENTIALITY

1. Keep information confidential except when disclosure is authorized or legally required.
2. Inform all relevant parties regarding appropriate use of confidential information. Monitor to ensure compliance.
3. Refrain from using confidential information for unethical or illegal advantage.

III. INTEGRITY

1. Mitigate actual conflicts of interest. Regularly communicate with business associates to avoid apparent conflicts of interest. Advise all parties of any potential conflicts of interest.
2. Refrain from engaging in any conduct that would prejudice carrying out duties ethically.
3. Abstain from engaging in or supporting any activity that might discredit the profession.
4. Contribute to a positive ethical culture and place integrity of the profession above personal interests.

IV. CREDIBILITY

1. Communicate information fairly and objectively.
2. Provide all relevant information that could reasonably be expected to influence an intended user's understanding of the reports, analyses, or recommendations.
3. Report delays or deficiencies in information, timeliness, processing, or internal controls in conformance with organization policy and/or applicable law.
4. Communicate professional limitations or other constraints that would preclude responsible judgment or successful performance of an activity.

RESOLVING ETHICAL ISSUES

In applying the Standards of Ethical Professional Practice, the member may encounter unethical issues or behavior. In these situations, the member should not ignore them, but rather should actively seek resolution of the issue. In determining which steps to follow, the member should consider all risks involved and whether protections exist against retaliation.

When faced with unethical issues, the member should follow the established policies of his or her organization, including use of an anonymous reporting system if available.

If the organization does not have established policies, the member should consider the following courses of action:

- The resolution process could include a discussion with the member's immediate supervisor. If the supervisor appears to be involved, the issue could be presented to the next level of management.
- IMA offers an anonymous helpline that the member may call to request how key elements of the *IMA Statement of Ethical Professional Practice* could be applied to the ethical issue.
- The member should consider consulting his or her own attorney to learn of any legal obligations, rights, and risks concerning the issue.

If resolution efforts are not successful, the member may wish to consider disassociating from the organization.

Source: Institute of Management Accountants (www.imanet.org). Adapted with permission.

Exhibit 1.3

Statement of Ethical Professional Practice: Institute of Management Accountants (IMA)

OBJECTIVE 5

Identify the three forms of certification available to internal accountants.

CERTIFICATION

A variety of certifications are available to management accountants. Three of the major certifications available are a Certificate in Management Accounting, a Certificate in Public Accounting, and a Certificate in Internal Auditing. Each certification offers particular advantages to a cost or management accountant. In each case, an applicant must meet specific educational and experience requirements and pass a qualifying examination to become certified. Thus, all three certifications offer evidence that the holder has achieved a minimum level of professional competence. Furthermore, all three certifications require the holder to engage in continuing professional education in order to maintain certification. Because certification reveals a commitment to professional competency, most organizations encourage their management accountants to be certified.

The Certificate in Management Accounting

In 1974, the Institute of Management Accountants (IMA) developed the Certificate in Management Accounting to meet the specific needs of management accountants. A **Certified Management Accountant (CMA)** has passed a rigorous qualifying examination, has met an experience requirement, and participates in continuing education.

One of the key requirements for obtaining the CMA certificate or designation is passing a qualifying examination. The exam consists of two parts: (1) Technology and Analytics and (2) Strategic Financial Management. Each part has a four-hour examination and consists of 100 multiple-choice questions, as well as two essays. The exam features an increasing emphasis on data governance, technology-enabled finance transformation, data analytics, ethics, and strategic decision making.

One of the main purposes of creating the CMA program was to establish management accounting as a recognized, professional discipline, separate from the profession of public accounting. Since its inception, the CMA program has been very successful. Many firms now sponsor and pay for classes that prepare their management accountants for the qualifying examination, as well as provide other financial incentives to encourage acquisition of the CMA certificate.

The Certificate in Public Accounting

The Certificate in Public Accounting is the oldest certification in accounting. Unlike the CMA designation, the purpose of the Certificate in Public Accounting is to provide evidence of a minimal professional qualification for external auditors. The responsibility of external auditors is to provide assurance concerning the reliability of the information contained in a firm's financial statements. Only **Certified Public Accountants (CPAs)** are permitted (by law) to serve as external auditors. CPAs must pass a national examination and be licensed by the state in which they practice. Although the Certificate in Public Accounting does not focus as heavily on management accounting as the CMA, many management accountants hold it because of its widespread recognition across business.

The Certificate in Internal Auditing

Another certification available to internal accountants is the Certificate in Internal Auditing. The forces that led to the creation of this certification in 1974 are similar to those that resulted in the CMA program. As an important part of the company's control environment, internal auditors evaluate and appraise various activities within the company. While internal auditors are independent of the departments being audited, they do report to the top management of the company. Since internal auditing differs from both external auditing and management accounting, many internal auditors felt a need for a specialized certification. To attain the status of a **Certified Internal Auditor (CIA)**, an individual must pass a comprehensive examination designed to ensure technical competence and have two years' work experience.

SUMMARY OF LEARNING OBJECTIVES

LO1. Describe cost management and explain how it differs from financial accounting.
- Management accounting differs from financial accounting primarily in its targeted users. Management accounting information is intended for internal users, whereas financial accounting information is directed toward external users.
- Management accounting is not bound by the externally imposed rules of financial reporting.
- Management accounting provides more detail than financial accounting, and it tends to be broader and multidisciplinary.

LO2. Identify factors and trends affecting the use of cost management.
- These factors and trends include:
  - More intense global competition
  - Growth in the service industry
  - Advances in digital information technology and the manufacturing environment
  - Focus on customer orientation
  - Total quality management
  - Expansion of the use of data analytics
  - Emergence of forensic accounting
  - Increase in interest in business sustainability
- Many traditional management accounting practices will be altered because of the revolution taking place among many manufacturing firms.
- Deregulation and growth in the service sector of our economy are also increasing the demand for management accounting practices.

LO3. Describe how management accountants function within an organization.
- Management accountants are responsible for:
  - Identifying
  - Collecting
  - Measuring
  - Analyzing
  - Preparing
  - Interpreting
  - Communicating information used by management to achieve the basic objectives of the organization
- Management accountants need to be sensitive to the information needs of managers.
- Management accountants serve as staff members of the organization and are responsible for providing information; they are usually intimately involved in the management process as valued members of the management team.

LO4. Understand the importance of ethical behavior for management accountants.
- Management accounting aids managers in their efforts to improve the economic performance of the firm.
- Unfortunately, some managers have overemphasized the economic dimension and have engaged in unethical and illegal actions. Many of these actions have relied on the management accounting system to bring about and even support that unethical behavior.
- To emphasize the importance of the ever-present constraint of ethical behavior on profit-maximizing behavior, this text presents ethical issues in many of the problems appearing at the end of each chapter.

LO5. Identify the three forms of certification available to internal accountants.
- Three major certifications are available to internal accountants:
  - The CMA
  - The CPA
  - The CIA

- The CMA certificate is designed especially for management accountants. The prestige of the CMA certificate or designation has increased significantly over the years and is now well regarded by the industrial world.
- The CPA certificate is primarily intended for those practicing public accounting; however, this certification is also highly regarded and is held by many management accountants.
- The CIA certificate serves internal auditors and is also well respected.

KEY TERMS

Accounting information system, 4	**Financial accounting**, 4
Activity-based management, 9	**Forensic accounting**, 11
Business ethics, 15	**Just-in-time (JIT) manufacturing**, 8
Business sustainability, 12	**Lean manufacturing**, 8
Certified Internal Auditor (CIA), 18	**Line positions**, 13
Certified Management Accountant (CMA), 18	**Operational control information system**, 6
Certified Public Accountants (CPAs), 18	**Performance reports**, 14
Continuous improvement, 15	**Planning**, 14
Controller, 13	**Staff positions**, 13
Controlling, 14	**Target costing**, 9
Cost accounting information system, 5	**Theory of constraints**, 8
Cost management, 4	**Total quality management**, 9
Decision making, 15	**Treasurer**, 13
Enterprise resource planning (ERP) software, 7	**Value chain**, 9
Feedback, 14	

EXERCISES

OBJECTIVE **Exercise 1-1 Financial Accounting and Cost Management**

Classify each of the following actions as either being associated with the financial accounting information system (FS) or the cost management information system (CMS):

a. Determining the total compensation of the CEO of a public company
b. Issuing a quarterly earnings report
c. Determining the unit product cost using TDABC
d. Calculating the number of units that must be sold to break even
e. Preparing a required report for the SEC
f. Preparing a sales budget
g. Using cost and revenue information to decide whether to keep, or drop, a product line
h. Preparing an annual statement of financial position that conforms to generally accepted accounting principles (GAAP)
i. Using cost and revenue information to decide whether to invest in a new production system or not
j. Reducing costs by improving the overall quality of a product
k. Using a debt-equity ratio and liquidity ratios from a balance sheet to assess the likelihood of bankruptcy
l. Using a public company's financial statements to decide whether or not to buy its stock

Exercise 1-2 Customer Orientation, Quality, and Business Sustainability

OBJECTIVE 2

Hepworth Communications produces cell phones. One of the four major electronic components is produced internally. The other three components are purchased from external suppliers. The electronic components and other parts are assembled (by the Assembly Department) and then tested (by the Testing Department). Any units that fail the test are sent to the Rework Department where the unit is taken apart and the failed component is replaced. Data from the Testing Department reveal that the internally produced component (made by the Component Department) is the most frequent cause of product failure. One out of every 50 phones fails because of a faulty internally produced component.

Barry Norton is the manager of the Component Department. In a recent performance evaluation, the plant manager told Barry that he needed to be more sensitive to the needs of the department's customers. This charge puzzled Barry somewhat—after all, the component is not sold to anyone but is used in producing the plant's cell phones.

Required:

1. Who are Barry's customers?
2. Explain the plant manager's charge to Barry to be more sensitive to his customers. Explain also how this increased sensitivity could improve the company's business sustainability regarding its competitive ability.
3. What role would cost management play in helping Barry be more sensitive to his customers?

Exercise 1-3 Identifying Cost Management Information System Objectives

OBJECTIVE 1

Consider the following actions associated with a cost management information system:
a. Eliminating a non-value-added activity
b. Determining how much it costs to perform a heart transplant
c. Calculating the cost of inspecting components from an outside supplier
d. Developing and using a budgeted income statement for a division
e. Eliminating the need to inspect by improving the quality of products and processes
f. Determining whether selling a product at split-off is more profitable than processing it further before selling it
g. Calculating the cost of producing an e-book
h. Using a trend report on quality costs to assess the effectiveness of a quality improvement program
i. Determining the units that must be sold to break even
j. Calculating the cost to perform a tooth extraction
k. Determining the total cost of moving goods
l. Using JIT purchasing and manufacturing to significantly reduce inventories
m. Using unit product cost to help develop a bid price

Required:

Classify the above actions as being associated with one of the following objectives of a cost management information system:
1. Costing of products, services, and other objects of interest
2. Planning and control
3. Decision making

Exercise 1-4 Ethical Behavior

OBJECTIVE 3 4

Consider the following thoughts of a manager at the end of the company's third quarter:

If I can increase my reported profit by $2 million, the actual earnings per share will exceed analysts' expectations, and stock prices will increase. The stock options that I am holding will become more valuable. The extra income will also make me eligible to receive a significant bonus. With a son headed to college, it would be good if I could cash in some of these options to help pay his expenses. However, my vice president of finance indicates that such an increase is unlikely. The projected profit for the fourth quarter will just about meet the expected earnings per share. There may be ways, though, that I can achieve the desired outcome. First, I can instruct all divisional managers that their preventive maintenance budgets are reduced by 25 percent for the fourth quarter. That should reduce maintenance expenses by approximately $1 million. Second, I can increase the estimated life of the existing equipment, producing a reduction of depreciation by another $500,000. Third, I can reduce the salary increases for those being promoted by 50 percent. And that should easily put us over the needed increase of $2 million.

Required:

Comment on the ethical content of the earnings management being considered by the manager. Is there an ethical dilemma? What is the right choice for the manager to make? Is there any way to redesign the accounting reporting system to discourage the type of behavior the manager is contemplating?

OBJECTIVE ▸3▸   **Exercise 1-5 Behavioral Impact of Cost Information**

Bill Christensen, the production manager, was grumbling about the new quality cost system the plant controller wanted to put into place. "If we start trying to track every bit of spoiled material, we'll never get any work done. Everybody knows when they ruin something. Why bother to keep track? This is a waste of time. Besides, this isn't the first time scrap reduction has been emphasized. You tell my workers to reduce scrap, and I'll guarantee it will go away, but not in the way you would like."

Required:

1. Why do you suppose that the controller wants a written record of spoiled material? If "everybody knows" what the spoilage rate is, what benefits can come from keeping a written record?
2. Now consider the production manager's position. In what way(s) could she be correct? What did she mean by her remark concerning scrap reduction? Can this be avoided? Explain.

OBJECTIVE ▸3▸   **Exercise 1-6 Managerial Uses of Accounting Information**

Each of the following scenarios requires the use of accounting information to carry out one or more of the following managerial activities: (1) planning, (2) control and evaluation, (3) continuous improvement, or (4) decision making.

a. **MANAGER:** At the last board meeting, we established an objective of earning an after-tax profit equal to 20 percent of sales. I need to know the revenue that we need to earn in order to meet this objective, given that we have $250,000 to spend on the promotional campaign. Once I have estimated sales in units, we then need to outline a promotional campaign that conforms to our budget and that will take us where we want to be. However, to compute the targeted sales revenue, I need to know the unit sales price, the unit variable cost, and the associated fixed production and support costs. I also need to know the tax rate.

b. **MANAGER:** We have problems with our procurement process. Our accounts payable department is spending 80 percent of its time resolving discrepancies between the purchase order, receiving order, and supplier's invoice. Incorrect part numbers on the purchase orders, incorrect quantities ordered, and wrong parts sent (or the incorrect quantity) are just a few examples of sources of discrepancies. A complete redesign of the process has been suggested, which will allow us to eliminate virtually all of the errors and, at the same time, significantly reduce the number of clerks needed in purchasing, receiving, and accounts payable. This redesign promises to significantly reduce costs, decrease lead time, and increase customer satisfaction.

c. **MANAGER:** This overhead cost report indicates that we have spent significantly more on inspection, purchasing, and production than was budgeted. An investigation has revealed that the source of the problem is faulty components from suppliers. A supplier evaluation has revealed that by selecting five suppliers with the best quality records (out of 15 currently used), the number of defective components will be dramatically reduced, thus producing significant overhead savings by reducing the demand for inspections, reordering, and rework.

d. **MANAGER:** A large local firm has approached me and has offered to sell us one of the components used in our small engines—a component that we are currently producing internally. I need to know costs that we would avoid if this component is purchased so that I can assess the economic merits of this offer.

e. **MANAGER:** Currently, our deluxe lawn mower is losing money. We need to increase profits. I would like to know how much our profits would be if we reduce our variable costs by $50 per mower while maintaining our current sales volume. Also, marketing claims that if we increase advertising expenditures by $1,000,000 and cut prices by 15 percent, we can increase the number of mowers sold by 25 percent. I would like to know which approach offers the most profit, or if a combination of the approaches may be best.

f. **MANAGER:** We are implementing a major quality improvement program. We will be increasing the investment in prevention and detection activities with the expectation of driving down both internal and external failure costs. I expect to see trend reports for all categories of quality costs. I want to see if improving quality really does reduce costs and improve profitability.

g. **MANAGER:** Our engineering design department has proposed a new design for our product. The new design promises to reduce post-purchase costs and, as a consequence, increase market share. I need to know the cost of producing this new design because it uses some new components and requires some different manufacturing processes. I would then like to have a projected income statement based on the new market share and new production costs. The planned selling price will be the same, or maybe even 10 percent lower. Projections based on the two price scenarios would be needed.

h. **MANAGER:** My engineers have said that by redesigning our two main production processes, we can reduce move time by 90 percent and wait time by 85 percent. This would decrease cycle time and virtually eliminate the need to carry finished goods inventories. On-time deliveries would also increase dramatically. This would produce cost savings of nearly $20,000,000 per year. Market share and revenues would also increase.

Required:

1. Describe each of the four managerial responsibilities.
2. Identify the managerial activity or activities applicable for each scenario, and indicate the role of accounting information in the activity.

Exercise 1-7 Line versus Staff

OBJECTIVE ▶ 3

The job responsibilities of three employees of Ruido Speakers, Inc., are described as follows:

Kaylin Hepworth, production manager, is responsible for production of the plastic casing in which the speaker components are placed. She supervises the line workers, helps develop the production schedule, and is responsible for meeting the production budget. She also takes an active role in reducing production costs.

Joseph Nguyen, plant manager, supervises all personnel in the plant. Kaylin and other production managers report directly to Joseph. Joseph is in charge of all that takes place in the plant, including production, logistics, personnel, and accounting. He helps develop the plant's production budgets and is responsible for controlling plant costs.

Leo Tidwell, plant controller, is responsible for all of the accounting functions within the plant. He supervises three cost accounting managers and four staff accountants. He is responsible for preparing all cost of production reports. For example, he prepares periodic performance reports that compare actual costs with budgeted costs. He helps explain and interpret the reports and provides advice to the plant manager on how to control costs.

Required:

Identify Kaylin, Joseph, and Leo as line or staff, and explain your reasons.

PROBLEMS

OBJECTIVE ▶ **1**

Problem 1-8 Financial Accounting versus Cost Management

Jade Shultz is a junior majoring in hotel and restaurant management. She wants to work for a large hotel chain with the goal of eventually managing a hotel. She is considering the possibility of taking a course in either financial accounting or cost management. Before choosing, however, she has asked you to provide her with some information about the advantages that each course offers.

Required:

Prepare a letter advising Jade about the differences and similarities between financial accounting and cost management. Describe the advantages each might offer the manager of a hotel.

OBJECTIVE ▶ **4**

Problem 1-9 Ethical Issues

John Rodriguez and Patty Jorgenson are both cost accounting managers for a manufacturing division. During lunch yesterday, Patty told John that she was planning on quitting her job in three months because she had accepted a position as controller of a small company in a neighboring state. The starting date was timed to coincide with the retirement of the current controller. Patty was excited because it allowed her to live near her family. Today, the divisional controller took John to lunch and informed him that he was taking a position at headquarters and that he had recommended that Patty be promoted to his position. He indicated to John that it was a close call between him and Patty and that he wanted to let John know personally about the decision before it was announced officially.

Required:

What should John do? Describe how you would deal with his ethical dilemma (considering the IMA code of ethics in your response).

OBJECTIVE ▶ **4**

Problem 1-10 Ethical Issues

Emily Henson, controller of an oil exploration division, has just been approached by Tim Wilson, the divisional manager. Tim told Emily that the projected quarterly profits were unacceptable and that expenses need to be reduced. He suggested that a clean and easy way to reduce expenses is to assign the exploration and drilling costs of four dry holes to those of two successful holes. By doing so, the costs could be capitalized and not expensed, reducing the costs that need to be recognized for the quarter. He further argued that the treatment is reasonable because the exploration and drilling all occurred in the same field; thus, the unsuccessful efforts really were the costs of identifying the successful holes. "Besides," he argued, "even if the treatment is wrong, it can be corrected in the annual financial statements. Next quarter's revenues will be more and can absorb any reversal without causing any severe damage to that quarter's profits. It's this quarter's profits that need some help."

Emily was uncomfortable with the request because generally accepted accounting principles do not sanction the type of accounting measures proposed by Tim.

Required:

1. Using the code of ethics for management accountants, recommend the approach that Emily should take.
2. Suppose Tim insists that his suggested accounting treatment be implemented. What should Emily do?

Problem 1-11 Ethical Issues

OBJECTIVE ◀ 4

CMA

Silverado, Inc., is a closely held brokerage firm that has been very successful over the past five years, consistently providing most members of the top management group with 50 percent bonuses. In addition, both the chief financial officer and the chief executive officer have received 100 percent bonuses. Silverado expects this trend to continue.

Recently, the top management group of Silverado, which holds 40 percent of the outstanding shares of common stock, has learned that a major corporation is interested in acquiring Silver-ado. Silverado's management is concerned that this corporation may make an attractive offer to the other shareholders and that management would be unable to prevent the takeover. If the acquisition occurs, this executive group is uncertain about continued employment in the new corporate structure. As a consequence, the management group is considering changes to several accounting policies and practices that, although not in accordance with generally accepted accounting principles, would make the company a less attractive acquisition. Management has told Kala Smith, Silverado's controller, to implement some of these changes. Kala has also been informed that Silverado's management does not intend to disclose these changes at once to anyone outside the immediate top management group.

Required:

Using the code of ethics for management accountants, evaluate the changes that Silverado's management is considering, and discuss the specific steps that Kala should take to resolve the situation. *(CMA adapted*)*

Problem 1-12 Ethical Issues

OBJECTIVE ◀ 4

CMA

Emery Manufacturing Company produces component parts for the farm equipment industry and has recently undergone a major computer system conversion. Samson Achebe, the controller, has established a troubleshooting team to alleviate accounting problems that have occurred since the conversion. Samson has chosen Gus Swanson, assistant controller, to head the team that will include Linda Wheeler, cost accountant; Cindy Lopez, financial analyst; Randy Lewis, general accounting supervisor; and Max Crandall, financial accountant.

The team has been meeting weekly for the last month. Gus insists on being part of all the team conversations in order to gather information, to make the final decision on any ideas or actions that the team develops, and to prepare a weekly report for Samson. He has also used this team as a forum to discuss issues and disputes about him and other members of Emery's top management team. At last week's meeting, Gus told the team that he thought a competitor might purchase the common stock of Emery, because he had overheard Samson talking about this on the telephone. As a result, most of Emery's employees now informally discuss the sale of Emery's common stock and how it will affect their jobs.

Required:

Is Gus Swanson's discussion with the team about the prospective sale of Emery unethical? Discuss, citing specific standards from the code of ethical conduct to support your position. *(CMA adapted)*

Problem 1-13 Ethical Issues

OBJECTIVE ◀ 4

CMA

The external auditors for Heart Health Procedures (HHP) are currently performing the annual audit of HHP's financial statements. As part of the audit, the external auditors have prepared

*A number of accounting certifications require cost and managerial accounting expertise and test for it on their exams. These questions are similar in subject matter and format to certification exam questions.

a representation letter to be signed by HHP's chief executive officer (CEO) and chief financial officer (CFO). The letter provides, among other items, a representation that appropriate provisions have been made for:

Reductions of any excess or obsolete inventories to net realizable values, and Losses from any purchase commitments for inventory quantities in excess of requirements or at prices in excess of market.

HHP began operations by developing a unique balloon process to open obstructed arteries to the heart. In the last several years, HHP's market share has grown significantly because its major competitor was forced by the Food and Drug Administration (FDA) to cease its balloon operations. HHP purchases the balloon's primary and most expensive component from a sole supplier. Two years ago, HHP entered into a five-year contract with this supplier at the then current price, with inflation escalators built into each of the five years. The long-term contract was deemed necessary to ensure adequate supplies and discourage new competition. During the past year, however, HHP's major competitor developed a technically superior product, which utilizes an innovative, less costly component. This new product was recently approved by the FDA and has been introduced to the medical community, receiving high acceptance. It is expected that HHP's market share, which has already seen softness, will experience a large decline and that the primary component used in the HHP balloon will decrease in price as a result of the competitor's use of its recently developed superior, cheaper component. The new component has been licensed by the major competitor to several outside supply sources to maintain available quantity and price competitiveness. At this time, HHP is investigating the purchase of this new component.

HHP's officers are on a bonus plan that is tied to overall corporate profits. Maria Silva, vice president of manufacturing, is responsible for both manufacturing and warehousing. During the course of the audit, she advised the CEO and CFO that she was not aware of any obsolete inventory or any inventory or purchase commitments where current or expected prices were significantly below acquisition or commitment prices. Maria took this position even though you, the assistant controller, had apprised her of both the existing excess inventory attributable to the declining market share and the significant loss associated with the remaining years of the five-year purchase commitment.

You have brought this situation to the attention of your superior, the controller, who also participates in the bonus plan and reports directly to the CFO. You worked closely with the external audit staff and subsequently ascertained that the external audit manager was unaware of the inventory and purchase commitment problems. You are concerned about the situation and are not sure how to handle the matter.

Required:

1. Assuming that the controller did not apprise the CEO and CFO of the situation, explain the ethical considerations of the controller's apparent lack of action by discussing specific provisions of the Standards of Ethical Conduct for Management Accountants.
2. Assuming you believe the controller has acted unethically and not apprised the CEO and CFO of the findings, describe the steps that you should take to resolve the situation. Refer to the Standards of Ethical Conduct for Management Accountants in your answer.
3. Describe actions that HHP can take to improve the ethical situation within the company. *(CMA adapted)*

2 Basic Cost Management Concepts

After studying this chapter, you should be able to:

1 ▸ Describe a cost management information system, its objectives, and its major subsystems, and indicate how it relates to other operating and information systems.

2 ▸ Define data analytics, and describe its role in cost management.

3 ▸ Explain the cost assignment process.

4 ▸ Define tangible and intangible products, and explain why there are different product cost definitions.

5 ▸ Prepare income statements for manufacturing and service organizations.

6 ▸ Explain the differences between traditional and contemporary cost management systems.

Interim Archives/Archive Photos/Getty Images

THE IMPORTANCE OF THE ACCOUNTING INFORMATION SYSTEM

at Amazon

Have you ever wanted to buy something in a store but could not find it or perhaps had to wait longer to obtain it than you had hoped? If so, you very likely logged onto Amazon.com and easily found what you wanted and had it shipped to your doorstep in just a few days. **Amazon** generates annual net income in excess of $10 billion on astonishingly high sales that exceed $230 billion, making it one of the world's largest companies.[1] Generating such large sales numbers requires Amazon to incur an extremely large number of costs, including its $15 minimum wage for its nearly 1,000,000 employees.[2] Amazon's approximate 4 percent return on sales is impressive, especially when compared to its decade-long struggle to generate its first positive net income. However, this measure also indicates that 96 percent of the company's revenues are consumed by costs across the value chain. As one example, Amazon reaped large increases in sales revenue during the COVID-19 pandemic. However, the company also incurred approximately $4 billion in additional expenses (more than the increase in sales) for factors such as escalating labor and delivery logistics costs and customers' shift in product mix toward less-profitable categories such as grocery.[3]

As a result of its considerable costs, Amazon's cost management experts must understand thoroughly the company's complex cost structure and the accounting information system that provides critical insights into these costs. For example, Amazon's cost accounting information system must provide relatively accurate cost estimates for its numerous services, such as overnight versus two-day delivery to different locations, so that the company can set prices high enough to cover all costs and generate a positive profit. In addition, the operational control information system must provide insights useful for other important decisions, such as the value that customers likely would place on potential new service offerings and website product features.

Finally, in addition to being one of the world's largest companies, Amazon also is one of the most highly recognized companies as it engages with many different stakeholder groups. Customers represent perhaps the most important group. For example, membership in Amazon Prime, the company's paid delivery service, has grown continually since its 2005 inception to over 118 million U.S. users.[4] With such great recognition, the company also faces considerable public and regulatory scrutiny, both of which must be measured and managed carefully by Amazon as negative attention on either of these items can lead to lower revenues and/or higher costs.[5] Thus, the company's accounting information system will continue to play a critical role in Amazon's cost management decision making and future success.

1   "Fortune 500 U.S. List for 2019," *Fortune*, https://fortune.com/fortune500/2019/amazon-com/
2   "Amazon Employee Headcount Could Near 1M in 2020," *Fox Business* (February 7, 2020), https://www
    .foxbusiness.com/markets/amazon-hiring-expectations-2020
3   "Amazon Will Spend $4 Billion or More on Coronavirus Response, Potentially Wiping Out Q2 Profit,"
    MarketWatch (May 2, 2020), https://www.marketwatch.com/story/amazon-says-it-may-lose-money-while
    -spending-on-covid-19-response-stock-sinks-in-late-trading-2020-04-30
4   D. Reisinger, "Amazon Prime's Numbers (and Influence) Continue to Grow," *Fortune* (January 16, 2020),
    https://fortune.com/2020/01/16/amazon-prime-subscriptions/, accessed August 5, 2020.
5   T. Garcia, "Amazon Could Face Renewed Antitrust Scrutiny Due to Covid-19 Sales, Analyst Says," *MarketWatch*
    (May 11, 2020), https://www.marketwatch.com/story/amazon-could-face-renewed-antitrust-scrutiny-due
    -to-covid-19-sales-analyst-says-2020-05-08, accessed August 5, 2020.

The study of cost accounting and cost management requires an understanding of fundamental cost concepts, terms, and the associated information systems that produce them. We need a basic framework to help us make sense of the variety of topics that appear in the field of cost accounting and cost management. A systems perspective provides a useful framework for achieving this objective. But what is an *information system?* Are there different systems for different purposes? Similarly, what is meant by *cost?* Are there different costs for different purposes? This chapter addresses these basic questions and provides the necessary foundation for the study of the rest of the text. In providing this foundation, we make no attempt to be exhaustive in our coverage of different systems and costs. Other system and cost concepts will be discussed in later chapters. However, a thorough understanding of the concepts presented in this chapter is essential for success with later chapters.

OBJECTIVE

Describe a cost management information system, its objectives, and its major subsystems, and indicate how it relates to other operating and information systems.

A SYSTEMS FRAMEWORK

A **system** is a set of interrelated parts that performs one or more processes to accomplish specific objectives. Consider a home theater system. This system has a number of interrelated parts such as the speakers, the receiver, the amplifier, the television, and the DVD player. The most obvious process (or series of actions designed to accomplish an objective) is the playing of a movie; another is the delivery of surround sound throughout the room. The primary objective of the system is to provide a theater-quality experience while watching a movie. Notice that each part of the system is critical for achievement of the overall objective. For example, if the speakers were missing, the amplifier and receiver would not be able to provide theater-quality sound even if the other parts were present and functional.

A system works by using processes to transform inputs into outputs that satisfy the system's objectives. Consider the movie-playing process. This process requires inputs such as a movie (typically on Blu-ray or DVD), a Blu-ray or DVD player, a television set, and electricity. The inputs are transformed into the replay of the movie, an output of this process. The output of the process, delivery of surround sound, is obviously critical to achieving the overall objective of the system. The encoded sound on the DVD, the amplifier, and the speakers become inputs to the delivery process. This process transforms the inputs so that tracks of sound are delivered to each of the speakers throughout the room. In this way, the theater experience is reproduced at home (minus, of course, the people on cell phones or the sticky floors that are all too often part of the theater experience). The operational model for the home theater experience is shown in Exhibit 2.1.

Accounting Information Systems

An information system is designed to provide information to people in the company who might need it. For example, the human resource (HR) information system and materials requirements planning (MRP) system are both information systems. The HR system tracks people as they are hired. It includes data on date of hire, entry-level title and salary/wages, and any information needed for determining employee benefits. The MRP is a computerized system that keeps track of the purchase and use of raw materials used in manufacturing. These systems may also have subsystems. For example, a subsystem of the HR system is the payroll system. This is a transaction processing system. The payroll system uses information from the HR database along with information on taxes and benefits needed to pay the employees and to remit appropriate amounts to various governmental agencies, in order to process periodic payroll transactions.

An **accounting information system** is one that consists of interrelated manual and computer parts and uses processes such as collecting, classifying, summarizing, analyzing, and managing data to provide information to users. Like any system, an accounting information system has objectives, interrelated parts, processes, and outputs. The overall objective of an accounting information system is to provide information to users. The interrelated parts include database(s) and database management programs. The databases are simply collections of data or information, usually in digital form.

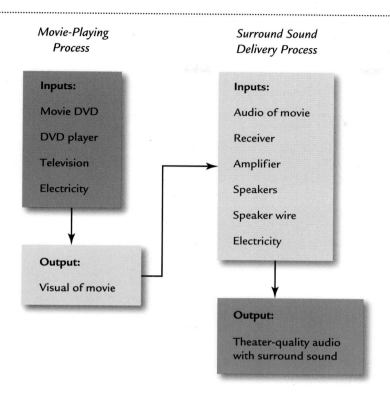

Exhibit 2.1

Operational Model of the Home Theater System

The database management system is needed to control, maintain, and use a given database. For accounting purposes, databases are formed to keep track of orders, sales, and other transactions. The database management system allows the company to handle billing, accounts receivable and cash receipts, inventory, general ledger, and cost accounting. Each of these interrelated parts is itself a system and is therefore referred to as a *subsystem* of the accounting information system. Processes of the database management system may include collecting, classifying, summarizing, and managing data. Some processes may also be formal decision models—models that use inputs and provide recommended decisions as the information output. The outputs are data and reports that provide needed information for users.

Two key features of the accounting information system distinguish it from other information systems. First, an accounting information system's inputs are usually economic events. Second, the operational model of an accounting information system is critically involved with the user of information, since the output of the information system influences users and may serve as the basis for action. This is particularly true for tactical and strategic decisions but less true for day-to-day decisions. In other cases, the output may serve to confirm that the actions taken had the intended effects.[6] Another possible output is feedback, which becomes an input for subsequent operational system performance. The operational model for an accounting information system is illustrated in Exhibit 2.2. Examples of the inputs, processes, and outputs are provided in the exhibit. (The list is not intended to be exhaustive.) Notice that personal communication is an information output. Often, users may not wish to wait for formal reports and can obtain needed information on a timelier basis by communicating directly with accountants.

The accounting information system can be divided into two major subsystems: (1) the *financial accounting information system* and (2) the *cost management information system.*

---

6 This role of information is described in William J. Bruns, Jr., and Sharon M. McKinnon, "Information and Managers: A Field Study," *Journal of Management Accounting Research* 5 (Fall 1993): 86–108. The paper reports on a field study of how managers use accounting information. The authors point out that formal information output does not seem to be used for day-to-day decisions. Managers often use interpersonal relationships to acquire information for daily use. Support for this view can be found in David Marginson, "Information Processing and Management Control: A Note Exploring the Role Played by Information Media in Reducing Role Ambiguity," *Management Accounting Research* 17 (June 2006): 187–197.

Exhibit 2.2

Operational Model of an
Accounting Information System

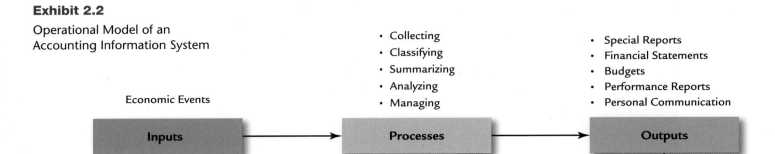

While we emphasize the second, it should be noted that the two systems need not be independent.[7] Ideally, the two systems should be integrated and have linked databases. Output of each
of the two systems can be used as input for the other system.

Financial Accounting Information System   The **financial accounting information
system** is primarily concerned with producing outputs for *external* users. It uses well-specified
economic events (e.g., payment of wages, purchases of materials) as inputs, and its processes follow
certain rules and conventions. For financial accounting, the nature of the inputs and the rules and
conventions governing processes are defined by the Securities and Exchange Commission (SEC),
the Financial Accounting Standards Board (FASB), and potentially the International Accounting
Standards Board (IASB). Among its outputs are financial statements such as the balance sheet,
income statement, and statement of cash flows for external users (investors, creditors, government
agencies, and other outside users). Financial accounting information is used for investment decisions, stewardship evaluation, activity monitoring, and regulatory measures.

The Cost Management Information System   The **cost management information
system** is primarily concerned with producing outputs for *internal* users using inputs and processes needed to satisfy management objectives. The cost management information system is
not bound by externally imposed criteria that define inputs and processes. Instead, the criteria
that govern the inputs and processes are set by people in the company. The cost management
information system provides information for three broad objectives:

1. Costing services, products, and other objects of interest to management
2. Planning and control
3. Decision making

How much does a product or service cost? That depends on the reason why management
wants to know the cost. For example, product costs calculated in accordance with GAAP (Generally Accepted Accounting Principles) are needed to value inventories for the balance sheet
and to calculate the cost of goods sold expense on the income statement. These product costs
include the cost of materials, labor, and overhead. In other cases, managers may want to know
all costs that are associated with a service for purposes of tactical and strategic profitability analysis. For example, a bank might want to know the costs and revenues associated with providing

---

7   Much of the material from this point on in this section relies on information found in the following articles: Robert
S. Kaplan, "The Four-Stage Model of Cost Systems Design," *Management Accounting* (February 1990): 22–26; Steven
C. Schnoebelen, "Integrating an Advanced Cost Management System into Operating Systems (Part 1)," *Journal of Cost
Management* (Winter 1993): 50–54; and Steven C. Schnoebelen, "Integrating an Advanced Cost Management System
into Operating Systems (Part 2)," *Journal of Cost Management* (Spring 1993): 60–67.

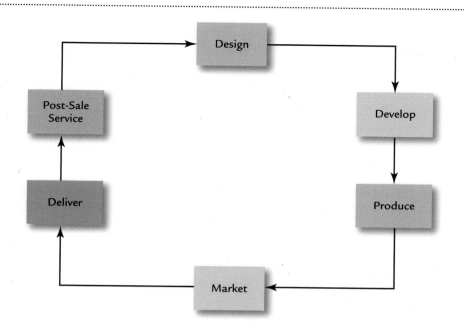

Exhibit 2.3

The Value Chain

small business loans. Then additional cost information may be needed concerning service provision, the cost of funds, collection costs, and so on.

Cost information is also needed for planning and control. It should help managers decide what should be done, why it should be done, how it should be done, and how well it is being done. For example, pharmaceutical companies may want to consider life cycle costing of individual drugs or drug families. The expected revenues and costs may cover the entire life of the new product. Thus, projected costs of research, development, testing, production, marketing, distribution, and servicing would be essential information. These costs form the basis of the value chain.

The **value chain** is the set of activities required to design, develop, produce, market, deliver, and provide post-sales service for the products and services sold to customers. Exhibit 2.3 illustrates the business processes of the value chain. Emphasizing customer value forces managers to determine which activities in the value chain are important to customers. The cost management information system should track information about the wide variety of activities that span the value chain. Consider, for example, the delivery segment. Timely delivery of a product or service is part of the total product and, thus, is of value to the customer. Customer value can be increased by increasing the speed of delivery and response. Federal Express exploited this part of the value chain and successfully developed a service that was not being offered by the U.S. Postal Service. Today, many customers believe that delivery delayed is delivery denied. This indicates that a good cost management information system ought to develop and measure indicators of customer satisfaction.

An example of a company that has streamlined the value-chain activities is Stillwater Designs, Inc., which created Kicker speakers. Originally, the company designed, manufactured, and distributed its automotive speakers. The manufacturing phase, however, was one that could be outsourced—and was. Now, Kicker concentrates on research and development, as well as sales and distribution.[8]

REAL-WORLD EXAMPLE

8 Based on conversations with Kickers' top management: http://kicker.com

Companies have internal customers as well. For example, the procurement process acquires and delivers parts and materials to producing departments. Providing high-quality parts on a timely basis to managers of producing departments is just as vital for procurement as it is for the company as a whole to provide high-quality goods to external customers. The emphasis on managing the internal value chain and servicing internal customers has revealed the importance of a cross-functional perspective. Internal and external value chains will be discussed in more detail in Chapter 11.

Finally, cost information is important for many managerial decisions. For example, a manager may need to decide whether to continue making a component in-house or to buy it from an external supplier. In this case, the manager would need to know the cost of materials, labor, and other productive resources associated with the manufacture of the component and which of these costs would disappear if the product were no longer produced. Also needed is information about the cost of purchasing the component, including any increase in cost for internal activities such as receiving and storing goods.

Relationship to Other Operational Systems and Functions

The cost information produced by the cost management information system benefits the whole organization and should have an organization-wide perspective. Managers in many different areas of a business require cost information. For example, an engineering manager must make strategic decisions concerning product design. Later costs of production, marketing, and servicing can vary widely, depending on the design. An engineer at Hewlett-Packard once told us that 70 percent of eventual product costs are "locked in" during the design process. To provide accurate cost information for the different design options, the cost management system must not only interact with the design and development system but also with the production, marketing, and customer service systems. Cost information for tactical decision making is also important. For example, a sales manager needs reliable and accurate cost information when faced with a decision concerning an order that may be sold for less than the normal selling price. Such a sale may only be feasible if the production system has idle capacity. In this case, a sound decision requires interaction among the cost management system, the marketing and distribution system, and the production system. These two examples illustrate that the cost management system should have an organization-wide perspective and that it must be properly integrated with the non-financial functions and systems within an organization. In the past, little effort was made to integrate the cost management system with other operational systems. The current competitive environment, however, dictates that companies pay much greater attention to cost management in all functional areas.

An integrated cost management system receives information from and provides information to all operational systems. To the extent possible, the cost management system should be integrated with the organization's operational systems. Integration reduces redundant storage and use of data, improves the timeliness of information, and increases the efficiency of producing reliable and accurate information. One way of accomplishing this is to implement an enterprise resource planning (ERP) system. ERP systems are integrative, cross-functional systems that coordinate information to facilitate timely and accurate reporting and decision making. Ideally, in an ERP system, data must be input only once; then it is available to people across the company for whatever purpose it may serve. In this way, information collected for one need may be used for others as well. For example, a sales order entered into an ERP system is used by marketing to update customer records, by production to schedule the manufacture of the goods ordered, and by accounting to record the sale.

Different Systems for Different Purposes

The financial accounting and cost management systems show us that different systems exist to satisfy different purposes. As indicated, these two systems are subsystems of the accounting information system. The cost management information system also has two major subsystems: the *cost accounting information system* and the *operational control information system*. The objectives of these two subsystems correspond to the first and second objectives mentioned earlier for the cost management information system (the costing, and planning and control objectives). The output of these two cost systems satisfies the third objective (the decision-making objective).

The **cost accounting information system** is a cost management subsystem designed to assign costs to individual products and services and other objects of interest to managers. For external financial reporting, the cost accounting system must assign costs to products in order to value inventories and determine cost of sales. Furthermore, these assignments must conform to the rules and conventions set by the SEC, the FASB, and (potentially) the IASB. These rules and conventions do not require that all costs assigned to individual products be causally related to the demands of individual products. Thus, using financial accounting principles to define product costs may lead to under- and overstatements of individual product costs. For reporting inventory values and cost of sales, this may not matter. Inventory values and cost of sales are reported in the aggregate, and the under- and overstatements may wash out to the extent that the values reported on the financial statements are reasonably accurate.

At the individual product level, however, distorted product costs can cause managers to make poor decisions. For example, a manager might erroneously deemphasize and overprice a product that is, in reality, highly profitable at a lower price. For decision making, accurate product costs are needed. If possible, the cost accounting system should produce product costs that simultaneously are accurate and satisfy financial reporting conventions. If not, then the cost system must produce two sets of product costs: one that satisfies financial reporting criteria and one that satisfies management decision-making needs.

The **operational control information system** is a cost management subsystem designed to provide accurate and timely feedback concerning the performance of managers and others relative to their planning and control of activities. It helps to ensure that the day-to-day activities support the long-range strategic objectives of the organization. Operational control is concerned with determining what activities should be performed and assessing how well they are performed. It identifies opportunities for improvement. A good operational control information system provides information that helps managers engage in a program of continuous improvement of all aspects of their businesses.

While product cost information is important to this process, it is not sufficient. The information needed for planning and control is broader and encompasses the entire value chain. For example, every profit-making manufacturing and service organization exists to serve customers. Thus, one objective of an operational control system is to improve the value received by customers. Products and services should be produced that fit specific customer needs. (Observe how this affects the design and development system in the value chain.) Quality, affordable prices, and low post-purchase costs for operating and maintaining the product are also important to customers.

A second, related objective is to improve profits by providing this value. Well-designed, quality, affordable products can be offered only if they also provide an acceptable return to company owners. Cost information concerning quality, different product designs, and post-purchase customer needs is vital for managerial planning and control.

Exhibit 2.4 illustrates the various subsystems of the accounting information system that we have been discussing.

Exhibit 2.4

Subsystems of the Accounting
Information System

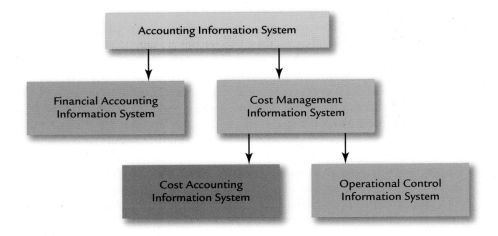

Define data analytics, and describe its
role in cost management.

THE GROWING IMPORTANCE OF DATA ANALYTICS WITHIN COST MANAGEMENT

Organizations operate in an increasingly complex and interconnected global business environment. As a result, organizational decisions impact investors and other key stakeholders, such as employees, customers, suppliers, regulators, and community residents, in increasingly broad and deep ways. The rapid expansion in the amount of data available to organizations and their stakeholders presents an important opportunity increasingly used by organizations to better understand and manage their impacts within this business environment. For example, accounting experts estimate that the size of the digital universe, including the amounts of traditional business data and rapidly growing machine-generated data, grows exponentially by doubling every two years.[9] Not surprisingly, organizations increasingly expect accountants to be able to collect, transform, and incorporate such data—also known as *big data*—into various cost management analyses to improve organizational decisions. **Data analytics** represents the process through which an organization utilizes various amounts and types of data to help connect strategy and other key goals to improved decision making throughout the organization. Developing accounting expertise with data analytics requires a concerted effort and wide-ranging practice.[10] Therefore, each chapter in this book emphasizes, where appropriate, the role played by data analytics in various cost management analyses.

A Framework for Understanding the Role of Data Analytics in Cost Management

Exhibit 2.5 presents an overview of the broad role that data analytics plays within various cost management analyses.[11] Traditionally, data analytics in cost management has been defined rather narrowly by focusing primarily on the use of analytical methods within various scenario models, such as relatively simple high-low analyses or more complex regression

---

9   "Value-Based Data Risk Management: What Data Is Worth Fighting For?" Deloitte Development LLC (2018), https://www2.deloitte.com/content/dam/Deloitte/us/Documents/risk/us-risk-value-based-data-risk-management.pdf, accessed August 5, 2020.

10 Raef Lawson and Institute of Management Accountants, "The Impact of Big Data on Finance," *Strategic Finance* (February 1, 2020), https://sfmagazine.com/post-entry/february-2020-the-impact-of-big-data-on-finance/, accessed August 5, 2020; and Institute of Management Accountants, *IMA Management Accounting Competency Framework*, 2019, https://www.imanet.org/career-resources/management-accounting-competencies, accessed August 5, 2020.

11 Author survey. 2020. This framework was developed by the textbook authors based on extensive data they collected from an online survey and face-to-face interviews with 35 accounting professionals representing a wide range of industry focus, geographic locations, and years of experience.

Step	Core Issue	Question Answered	Cost Management Application Example
1	What	What am I measuring?	The cost of innovating Apple's product and service offerings, including the cost objects (e.g., research and development) involved with such innovation efforts.
2	Why	Why am I measuring it?	Apple's strategy requires that it strives for continuous and industry-leading innovation.
3	How	How am I measuring it?	Consider the cost drivers (e.g., activities required by cutting-edge scientists and new product engineers; laboratory and testing facilities) for Apple's continuous innovation cost objects.
4	Where	Where can I find the data needed to conduct my desired statistical analysis?	Apple can collect and analyze in-house data regarding the existence and performance of its new product features as compared to external data regarding competitors' product offerings.
5	Which	Which analytical method should be employed in my analysis?	Time-series multiple regression analyses of Apple's core innovation activity drivers help management better understand the relationship between various research and development costs and innovation outcomes.
6	When	When is my analysis complete and ready to be used in decision making?	Apple's newest innovation involves a first-mover product launch, and thus, the cost analysis concludes sooner because the profit margin is wider for mature products that face more competition.
7	Who	Who in the business needs to understand my analysis, and how should I communicate its results?	An innovation cost analysis helps sales personnel better understand which new product features are more or less costly and relies on less sophisticated statistical and accounting terminology as compared to an analysis intended for product engineers.

Exhibit 2.5

The Role of Data Analytics in Cost Management

DATA ANALYTICS

analyses. Such analytical methods remain important. However, accountants must define data analytics much more broadly in order to be able to provide value-adding insights to business decision makers.

Therefore, before crunching numbers using analytical methods, accountants should begin their data analytic journey by clearly understanding *what* they are trying to measure, as well as *why* it should be measured. For example, an item should be measured when doing so is expected to provide important decision insights, such as assessing the success or failure of the company's strategy. On the contrary, an item should not be measured simply because the underlying data are available or because other companies measure it. Such unnecessary efforts often waste resources and divert attention away from potentially more valuable uses of limited data analytic resources. Finally, understanding the why of data analytics also provides useful insights into how accurate the measure must be, given the decision it ultimately intends to inform. For example, the framework likely would be employed more intensely to a decision involving the discontinuation of an entire product line rather than to the discontinuation of only a product feature.

The next two steps go hand in hand and concern *how* to measure an item and *where* to find the data for such measurements. One important consideration involves whether the measurement should be quantitative or qualitative in nature. Quantitative measurement implies the use of data expressed using numerical quantities, such as a count of the number of new model jet skis sold or a ratio of its full cost to sales. Also, data used in quantitative measurement usually are structured in nature and arise from formal sources, such as information systems. Qualitative measurement implies the use of data expressed in categories, such as customer reviews of new model jet skis. Data used in qualitative measurement usually are unstructured in nature and arise from less formal sources, including various internal business documents, texts, customer loyalty programs, or focus group transcripts. The challenge of how to measure is particularly strong when the item has never before been measured. For example, mystery or secret shopper programs were first created to help accountants assess difficult-to-measure business environments, such as customer experiences at newly redesigned **Mobil** gas station pumps or different **Victoria's Secret** store layouts.

The how and where steps often present accountants with the greatest challenge across the entire data analytic framework. For example, appropriate data must be identified (e.g., knowing which data are necessary to the measurement of interest), obtained (e.g., either internally from existing legacy and new information systems or externally through licensed access to an industry database), and transformed into a usable format (e.g., combining data from multiple sources, converting data into a single usable format, and cleansing data to improve its accuracy). These efforts—sometimes referred to as "extract, transform, and load"—are important as some experts estimate the cost of using bad data (i.e., incomplete, poorly defined, or inaccurate) to be as high as 15 to 25 percent of a company's revenue.[12] While these steps can be outsourced to third parties, accountants must be sure to understand them sufficiently so that the resulting data are used appropriately throughout the data analytic framework. Interestingly, creativity becomes particularly valuable in these steps because accountants often do not have access to the data they most prefer and, instead, must find a way to utilize the data to which they do have access in a manner that ultimately provides the needed decision insights.

Deciding *which* analytical method to employ in the analysis represents the next step. An analytical method (e.g., a quantitative or qualitative model) includes any method that converts raw data into useful information with decision insights. Examples of analytical methods in cost management include models for costing, linear programming, net present value, activity-based costing, and cost-volume-profit scenarios. The choice of analytical method should depend on other aspects of the framework, such as the strategic or operational importance of the decision it will inform, as well as the complexity of the particular business scenario being assessed. For example, a single food truck likely would require only a simple method (e.g., high-low method) for understanding its cost drivers and constructing the associated cost functions, whereas a large restaurant chain likely would benefit from a more complex method (e.g., multiple regression) given its greater product- and service-line diversity with respect to resource consumption. Additionally, sentiment analysis might use qualitative data from social media sites to interpret and classify customer reactions to the company's product or service performance or employee perception of the company's work culture.

Another challenging aspect within data analytics involves deciding *when* the analysis is complete. For example, few cost management analyses contain a set of clearly enumerated steps for their performance, obvious starting and ending points, or check figures for confirming the final result. In other words, many cost management tasks involve data analyses where it is not

---

12   Thomas Redman, "Seizing Opportunity in Data Quality," *MIT Sloan Management Review* (November 27, 2017), https://sloanreview.mit.edu/article/seizing-opportunity-in-data-quality/, accessed August 5, 2020.

clear "what to do first," "when it is finished," or "whether the answer is correct." Instead, many cost management analyses that involve data analytic measures require the use of considerable judgment to determine when the analysis has reached the point at which its results will sufficiently improve the decision for which it was conducted.

The final step in the framework focuses on *who* within the business will be using the results of cost management analysis. As such, this step revolves around the need for clear and concise communication to the eventual decision maker. Oftentimes this step involves data visualization tools, such as Tableau or Microsoft Power BI. Depending on the cost management task for which data analytics was employed, the end user could vary widely from a fellow accountant to an executive with no accounting experience and very little familiarity with the steps by which the results were created. Therefore, the perspective of the end user should be considered, and care should be taken to use communication tools (e.g., visual charts versus numeric tables versus qualitative descriptions) and approaches (e.g., face-to-face versus email versus virtual conference) that most effectively and efficiently lead to user understanding. Decision makers who do not understand analyses frequently disregard them as ineffective or incorrect. Therefore, accountants must be sure that the results of their analyses are clearly understood so that they inform decision making as intended.

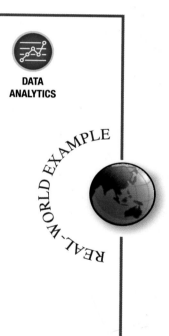

DATA ANALYTICS

The **Walt Disney Company** invested $1 billion in its MagicBand big data behavioral analytic system. The MagicBand is a waterproof wristband worn by theme park guests that, along with smartphone apps, allows Disney to track vast quantities of data regarding guest behavior while vacationing within its theme parks and resort hotels. Guest data include park entrance time, park stay duration, purchases (e.g., meals, beverages, Mickey Premium ice-cream bars, merchandise, apparel, and toys), preferred ride and attraction patterns, hotel room entry, and favorite characters for dining and photographic encounters.[13] Disney employs over 1,000 personnel to conduct various data analyses that increase profitability and improve overall guest experiences.[14] For example, such analyses enable Disney to more evenly spread out throughout the year its increasing total park attendance by charging higher prices during peak demand periods, schedule its 80,000 cast member employees and ride capacities to better match guest preferences, and stock various food and beverage options to more effectively capture guest tastes. In addition, data are transferred to Disney personnel in real time, thereby allowing the operations team to make quick decisions that improve current guest experiences, such as adding staff or rerouting guests to less busy park areas. Finally, Disney uses machine learning through a neural network to collect data regarding audience reactions to various Disney events, such as movie screenings and theme park rides, that managers analyze using sentiment analysis. Such predictive data analytic techniques help Disney Imagineers better ideate and deliver on important guest events, such as dining restaurant decisions, thereby improving the overall guest experience and increasing Disney's profitability.

Data Analytic Types and Cost Management Analyses

As discussed in the previous section, accountants increasingly are expected to be familiar with each step within the framework of Exhibit 2.5, that is, "The Role of Data Analytics in Management Accounting." However, many accountants are unlikely to be experts within each step. For instance, Step 5 (Which Analytical Method Should Be Employed in My Analysis?) represents one example where accountants are likely to seek assistance and expertise from subject matter

---

13 Austin Carr, "Disneyland Makes Surveillance Palatable—and Profitable," *Bloomberg* (July 15, 2019), https://www
.bloomberg.com/news/articles/2019-07-15/disneyland-is-tracking-guests-and-generating-big-profits-doing-it-jy49hb9t,
accessed August 5, 2020.

14 Angelica Mari, "Doing Analytics the Disney Way," *ComputerWeekly.com* (April 26, 2018), https://www.computerweekly
.com/news/252439803/Doing-analytics-the-Disney-way, accessed August 5, 2020.

Exhibit 2.6

Matching Data Analytic Types to Cost Management Analyses

DATA ANALYTICS

Data Analytic Type	Question Answered	Cost Management Analysis Example
Descriptive	What is happening?	A profit and loss analysis assesses historic trends in the company's profitability.
Diagnostic	Why is it happening?	What-if (i.e., sensitivity), root cause, and activity driver analyses decipher the significant drivers that cause changes in key revenues and costs.
Predictive	What is likely to happen?	Forecasting and budgeting analyses predict customer demand patterns to help the company more effectively synchronize its service provision and product manufacturing capabilities.
Prescriptive	What do I need to do?	Strategic cost management analysis identifies specific process reengineering actions to reduce the cost of service provision and product manufacturing activities.

experts, including statisticians, business analysts, and computer scientists, inside and outside of their organization to help run and interpret analytical methods. Therefore, Exhibit 2.6 presents a deeper dive into Steps 1 to 3 and Step 5 of Exhibit 2.5. Specifically, Exhibit 2.6 illustrates that the business question to be answered should drive the specific data analytic tool type to employ in conducting the relevant cost management analysis.

OBJECTIVE 3

Explain the cost assignment process.

COST ASSIGNMENT: DIRECT TRACING, DRIVER TRACING, AND ALLOCATION

To study cost accounting and operational control systems, we need to understand the meaning of cost and to become familiar with the cost terminology associated with the two systems. We must also understand the process used to assign costs. Cost assignment is one of the key processes of the cost accounting system. Improving the cost assignment process has been one of the major developments in the cost management field in the past 30 or so years. First, let's define cost.

Cost is the cash or cash equivalent value sacrificed for goods and services that are expected to bring a current or future benefit to the organization. We say *cash equivalent* because noncash assets can be exchanged for the desired goods or services. For example, it may be possible to trade equipment for materials used in production.

Costs are incurred to produce future benefits. In a profit-making firm, future benefits usually mean revenues. As costs are used up in the production of revenues, they are said to expire. Expired costs are called **expenses**. In each period, expenses are deducted from revenues on the income statement to determine the period's profit. A **loss** is a cost that expires without producing any revenue benefit. For example, the cost of uninsured inventory destroyed by a flood would be classified as a loss on the income statement.

Many costs do not expire in a given period. These unexpired costs are classified as **assets** and appear on the balance sheet. Computers and factory buildings are examples of assets lasting more than one period. Note that the main difference between a cost being classified as an expense or as an asset is timing. This distinction is important and will be referred to in the development of other cost concepts later in the text.

Cost Objects

Cost accounting information systems are structured to measure and assign costs to cost objects. **Cost objects** can be anything for which costs are measured and assigned; they may include products, customers, departments, projects, activities, and so on. For example, if we want to determine what it costs to produce a bicycle, then the cost object is the bicycle. If we want to determine the cost of operating a maintenance department within a factory, then the cost object is the maintenance department. If we want to determine the cost of developing a new toy, then the cost object is the new toy development project. Activities are a special kind of cost object. An **activity** is a basic unit of work performed within an organization. An activity can also be defined as an aggregation of actions within an organization useful to managers for purposes of planning, controlling, and decision making. In recent years, activities have emerged as important cost objects. Activities play a prominent role in assigning costs to other cost objects and are essential elements of an activity-based cost accounting system. Examples of activities include setting up equipment for production, moving materials and goods, purchasing parts, billing customers, paying bills, maintaining equipment, expediting orders, designing products, and inspecting products. Notice that an activity is described by an action verb (e.g., paying or designing) and an object that receives the action (e.g., bills or products).

Accuracy of Cost Assignments

Assigning costs *accurately* to cost objects is crucial. Accuracy is not evaluated based on knowledge of some underlying "true" cost. Rather, it is a relative concept and has to do with the reasonableness and logic of the cost assignment methods that are being used. The objective is to measure and assign as accurately as possible the cost of the resources used by a cost object. Some cost assignment methods are clearly more accurate than others. For example, suppose you want to determine the cost of lunch for Elaine Day, a student who frequents Hideaway, an off-campus pizza parlor. One cost assignment approach is to count the number of customers at the Hideaway between 12:00 P.M. and 1:00 P.M. and then divide that into the total sales receipts earned by Hideaway during this period. Suppose that this comes to $6.25 per lunchtime customer. Based on this approach we would conclude that Elaine spends $6.25 per day for lunch. Another approach is to go with Elaine and observe how much she spends. Suppose that she has a chef's salad and a medium drink each day, costing $4.50. It is easy to see which cost assignment is more accurate. The $6.25 cost assignment is distorted by the consumption patterns of other customers (cost objects). As it turns out, most lunchtime clients order the luncheon special for $5.95 (a mini-pizza, small salad, and medium drink).

Distorted cost assignments can produce poor decisions. For example, if a plant manager is trying to decide whether to continue producing power internally or to buy it from a local utility company, then an accurate assessment of how much it is costing to produce the power internally is fundamental to the analysis. If the cost of internal power production is overstated, the manager might decide to shut down the internal power department in favor of buying power from an outside company, whereas a more accurate cost assignment might suggest the opposite. It is easy to see that poor cost assignments can prove to be costly.

Traceability Understanding the relationship of costs to cost objects can increase the accuracy of cost assignments. Costs are directly or indirectly associated with cost objects. **Indirect costs** are costs that cannot be traced easily and accurately to a cost object. **Direct costs** are those costs that can be traced easily and accurately to a cost object.[15] For costs to be traced easily means that the costs can be assigned in an economically feasible way. For costs to be traced accurately means that the costs are assigned using a *causal relationship*. Thus, **traceability** is the ability to assign a cost directly to a cost object in an economically feasible way by means of a causal relationship. The more costs that can be traced to the object, the greater the accuracy of the cost assignments. One additional point needs to be emphasized. Cost management systems typically deal with many cost objects. Thus, it is possible for a particular cost item to be classified as both

---

15 This definition of direct costs is based on the glossary prepared by Computer Aided Manufacturing International, Inc. (CAM-I). See Norm Raffish and Peter B. B. Turney, "Glossary of Activity-Based Management," *Journal of Cost Management* (Fall 1991): 53–63. Other terms defined in this chapter and in the text also follow the CAM-I glossary.

a direct cost and an indirect cost. It all depends on *which* cost object is the point of reference. For example, if the plant is the cost object, then the cost of heating and cooling the plant is a direct cost; however, if the cost objects are products produced in the plant, then this utility cost is an indirect cost.

Methods of Tracing   Traceability means that costs can be assigned easily and accurately, using a causal relationship. Tracing costs to cost objects can occur in one of two ways: (1) *direct tracing* and (2) *driver tracing*. **Direct tracing** is the process of identifying and assigning costs to a cost object that are specifically or physically associated with the cost object. Direct tracing is most often accomplished by *physical observation*. For example, assume that the power department is the cost object. The salary of the power department's supervisor and the fuel used to produce power are examples of costs that can be specifically identified (by physical observation) with the cost object (the power department). As a second example, consider a pair of blue jeans. The materials (denim, zipper, buttons, and thread) and labor (to cut the denim according to the pattern and sew the pieces together) are physically observable; therefore, the costs of materials and labor can be directly charged to a pair of jeans. Ideally, all costs should be charged to cost objects using direct tracing.

Unfortunately, it is often impossible to physically observe the exact amount of resources being used by a cost object. The next best approach is to use cause-and-effect reasoning to identify factors—called *drivers*—that can be observed and which measure a cost object's resource consumption. **Drivers** are factors that *cause* changes in resource usage, activity usage, costs, and revenues. **Driver tracing** is the use of *drivers* to assign costs to cost objects. Although less precise than direct tracing, driver tracing can be accurate if the cause-and-effect relationship is sound. Consider the cost of electricity for the jeans manufacturing plant. The factory manager might want to know how much electricity is used to run the sewing machines. Physically observing how much electricity is used would require a meter to measure the power consumption of the sewing machines, which may not be practical. Thus, a driver such as "machine hours" could be used to assign the cost of electricity. If the electrical cost per machine hour is $0.10 and the sewing machines use 200,000 machine hours in a year, then $20,000 of the electricity cost ($0.10 × 200,000) would be assigned to the sewing activity. The use of drivers to assign costs to activities will be explained in more detail in Chapter 4.

Assigning Indirect Costs   Indirect costs cannot be traced to cost objects. Either there is no causal relationship between the cost and the cost object, or tracing is not economically feasible. Assignment of indirect costs to cost objects is called **allocation**. Since no causal relationship exists, allocating indirect costs is based on *convenience* or some *assumed* linkage. For example, consider the cost of heating and lighting a plant that manufactures five products. Suppose that this utility cost is to be assigned to the five products. Clearly, it is difficult to see any causal relationship. A convenient way to allocate this cost is simply to assign it in proportion to the direct labor hours used by each product. Arbitrarily allocating indirect costs to cost objects reduces the overall accuracy of the cost assignments. Accordingly, the best costing policy may be that of assigning only traceable direct costs to cost objects. However, it must be admitted that allocations of indirect costs may serve other purposes besides accuracy. For example, allocating indirect costs to products may be required for external reporting. Nonetheless, most managerial uses of cost assignments are better served by accuracy. At the very least, direct and indirect cost assignments should be reported separately.

Cost Assignment Summarized   There are three methods of assigning costs to cost objects: direct tracing, driver tracing, and allocation. Of the three methods, direct tracing is the most precise since it relies on physically observable causal relationships. Driver tracing relies on causal factors called drivers to assign costs to cost objects. The precision of driver tracing depends on the strength of the causal relationship described by the driver. Identifying drivers and assessing the quality of the causal relationship are more costly than either direct tracing or allocation. Allocation, while the simplest and least expensive method, is the least accurate cost assignment method; its use should be avoided where possible. In many cases, the benefits of increased accuracy by driver tracing outweigh its additional measurement cost. This cost-benefit issue is discussed more fully later in the chapter. The process really entails choosing among competing cost management systems.

PRODUCT AND SERVICE COSTS

OBJECTIVE **4**

Define tangible and intangible products, and explain why there are different product cost definitions.

One of the most important cost objects is the output of organizations. The two types of output are tangible products and services. **Tangible products** are goods produced by converting raw materials into finished products through the use of labor and capital inputs such as plant, land, and machinery. Televisions, hamburgers, automobiles, computers, clothes, and furniture are examples of tangible products. **Services** are tasks or activities performed for a customer or an activity performed by a customer using an organization's products or facilities. Services are also produced using materials, labor, and capital inputs. Insurance coverage, medical care, dental care, funeral care, and accounting are examples of service activities performed for customers. Car rental, video rental, and skiing are examples of services where the customer uses an organization's products or facilities.

Services differ from tangible products on three important dimensions: intangibility, perishability, and inseparability. **Intangibility** means that buyers of services cannot see, feel, hear, or taste a service before it is bought. Thus, services are *intangible products*. **Perishability** means that services cannot be stored (there are a few unusual cases where tangible goods cannot be stored). Finally, **inseparability** means that producers of services and buyers of services must usually be in direct contact for an exchange to take place. In effect, services are often inseparable from their producers. For example, an eye examination requires both the patient and the optometrist to be present. However, producers of tangible products need not have direct contact with the buyers of their goods. Buyers of automobiles, for instance, never need to have contact with the engineers and assembly line workers who produce automobiles.

Organizations that produce tangible products are called *manufacturing* organizations. Those that produce intangible products are called *service* organizations. Managers of organizations that produce goods or services need to know how much individual products cost for a number of reasons, including profitability analysis and strategic decisions concerning product design, pricing, and product mix.

For example, McDonald's Corporation needed to know the cost of individual products to determine whether to keep them on the Dollar Menu. The double cheeseburger, a very popular item, rose in cost to well over $1. Many franchisees refused to sell the item as part of the Dollar Menu—some charging over $2 for it.[16] Soon thereafter, McDonald's exchanged the double cheeseburger for a double hamburger with just one slice of cheese to bring down the cost. Several years later, the Dollar Menu was changed to the Extra Value Meals menu and the McPick 2 was introduced as a way to better match cost with price.

REAL-WORLD EXAMPLE

Service companies also relate cost to profit.

---

16 Richard Gibson, "Franchisees Balk at Dollar Menu," *The Wall Street Journal* (November 14, 2007): B3; and "McDonald's Hikes Price on Its McPick 2 Value Meal to $5," *FoxNews.com* (February 24, 2016), http://www.foxnews.com /leisure/2016/02/24/mcdonald-raises-prices-on-its-mcpick-value-meal-options/

A number of professional sports teams, including the **Brooklyn Nets**, go the extra mile to keep season ticket holders happy. Realizing there are numerous competing entertainment options, they hire hospitality specialists to offer season ticket holders more services, such as special tours of the locker room or meet-the-team events.[17] While the additional services are not cheap, they are an important part of maintaining consistent revenue even in the face of a disappointing win-loss record or the loss of a star player such as when the **Cleveland Cavaliers** lost LeBron James to the **Los Angeles Lakers**.

Given the importance of cost to both manufacturing and service firms, when we discuss product costs, we are referring to both intangible and tangible products.

Sustainability

Sustainable development means that companies can meet the needs of the present without compromising the ability of future generations to meet their own needs. Although it sounds simple, this takes considerable effort and requires companies to use skills not required in the past. Take energy usage, for example. The objective is to decrease energy usage to the extent possible while still maintaining productivity. How is that done? It is not just a matter of buying more energy-efficient machinery. Companies on the cutting edge may monitor every device or machine, generating considerable data. Data analytics come into play as these data are analyzed so that managers can improve overall equipment effectiveness, look for instances of energy spikes or overuse that may signal the need for maintenance, look for use of equipment during downtimes or vacations, and so on.

Many school districts and colleges and universities have used a less high-tech approach. They amass significant data on their various types of energy usage and cost. These data are then analyzed to find patterns. Is there a surcharge for usage during peak hours? If so, the company can adjust its use of electricity during those hours and deliberately use machinery more during nonpeak hours. Many school districts, for example, pay close attention to utility costs. If peak time is between 10:00 A.M. and 2:00 P.M., teachers are encouraged to do their photocopying before and after those times. They are encouraged to turn out the classroom lights during recess or lunch periods. For each hour a classroom light is turned off, $0.10 is saved. No big deal, you think? Well, if there are 40 classrooms in a school, and each teacher does this for each of the 180 school days, a total of $720 per year is saved. This is real money to a school needing funds for supplies, teacher enrichment, and so on. Over an entire school district, small savings add up. The key is to ensure that the savings do not interfere with learning. Is a child staying in the classroom during recess? Leave the lights on. Does a teacher need to photocopy some quizzes for a pop quiz in the middle of the day? Do it. But in general, teachers and school support staff are asked to think first and make the best overall decision.

Different Costs for Different Purposes

A fundamental cost management principle is "different costs for different purposes." Product cost definitions can differ according to the objective being served. Exhibit 2.7 illustrates this principle by displaying the costs that should be considered for several important yet different

---

17   Kevin Kleps, "As Basketball Side Struggles Mightily, Cavs' Business Team Is Trying to 'Overdeliver' with Fans, Partners," *Crain's Cleveland Business* (February 24, 2020).

decisions that involve particular managerial objectives. Exhibit 2.7 also provides numerous examples of costs across the value chain. (The value chain was introduced in Chapter 1 and also is discussed in detail in Chapter 11.) For example, in making decisions regarding external financial reporting (i.e., which must adhere to FASB rules and conventions), such as inventory and cost of goods sold, manufacturing organizations should consider only product costs (i.e., the production costs as shown in green). However, in making pricing decisions, all traceable costs across the entire value chain should be considered (i.e., from research and design costs shown in purple through customer service costs shown in orange) as companies need to generate enough sales revenues to exceed their full costs if they are to make a positive net income. Furthermore, in special-order tactical decisions that do not require the company to incur any additional research and design or development costs (shown in yellow), only costs to manufacture, ship (e.g., marketing and distribution costs as shown in blue), and service the special-order product should be considered when deciding whether to accept or reject the order. Decisions involving other managerial objectives, some of which are displayed in Exhibit 2.7, use other product cost definitions. For example, often costs incurred prior to production are referred to as **upstream costs**, while costs incurred after production are referred to as **downstream costs**.

Exhibit 2.7 also pertains to merchandising and service organizations. For merchandising organizations, such as American Eagle, product cost consists solely of the cost to purchase inventory and prepare it for sale. For service organizations, such as Berkshire Hathaway, Inc., there is no product cost because they do not manufacture physical products but instead provide services. However, just as for manufacturing organizations, merchandising and service organizations consider costs up and down the value chain, as appropriate, to understand the particular costs associated with the decision under consideration.

Exhibit 2.7

Understanding Different Cost Definitions

Understanding Different Cost Definitions

	← Upstream Costs →			← Downstream Costs →	
	Period	*Period*	*Product*	*Period*	*Period*
VALUE CHAIN COMPONENT	**RESEARCH AND DESIGN**	**DEVELOPMENT**	**PRODUCTION**	**MARKETING AND DISTRIBUTION**	**CUSTOMER SERVICE**
COST EXAMPLES	• Study emerging health trends • Brainstorm self-driving car capabilities • Scout movie filming locations	• Engineer aircraft to designed specifications • Write television show script • Create prototype of new product design	• Determine cost to produce products • Assess prime costs: Direct materials and direct labor • Assess conversion costs: Direct labor and overhead	• Lease warehouse for finished products • Ship sold items to customers • Demonstrate lawn and gardening services	• Investigate customer quality complaints • Perform warranty inspections and repairs • Replace faulty fiber optic cables
MANAGERIAL OBJECTIVE					
External Financial Reporting					
• Inventory, cost of goods sold, and gross margin			X		
• Operating expenses (aggregated costs)	X	X		X	X
Internal Strategic Analyses					
• New product development	X	X	X	X	X
• Pricing decisions	X	X	X	X	X
• Product mix decisions	X	X	X	X	X
• Customer profitability decisions	X	X	X	X	X
• Special-order tactical decisions			X	X	X

Product Costs and External Financial Reporting

An important objective of a cost management system is the calculation of product costs for external financial reporting. Externally imposed conventions require costs to be classified in terms of the special purposes, or functions, they serve. Costs are subdivided into two major functional categories: production and nonproduction. **Production** (or **product**) **costs** are those costs associated with manufacturing goods or providing services. **Nonproduction costs** are those costs associated with the functions of selling and administration. For tangible goods, production and nonproduction costs are often referred to as *manufacturing costs* and *nonmanufacturing costs,* respectively. Production costs can be further classified as *direct materials, direct labor,* and *overhead.* Only these three cost elements can be assigned to products for external financial reporting.

Direct Materials　**Direct materials** are those materials traceable to the good or service being produced. The cost of these materials can be directly charged to products because physical observation can be used to measure the quantity used by each product. Materials that become part of a tangible product or those materials that are used in providing a service are usually classified as direct materials. For example, steel in an automobile, wood in furniture, alcohol in cologne, denim in jeans, braces for correcting teeth, surgical gauze and anesthesia for an operation, ribbon in a corsage, and soft drinks on an airline are all direct materials.

Direct Labor　**Direct labor** is labor that is traceable to the goods or services being produced. As with direct materials, physical observation is used to measure the quantity of labor used to produce a product or service. Employees who convert raw materials into a product or who provide a service to customers are classified as direct labor. Workers on an assembly line at Dell, a chef in a restaurant, a surgical nurse for an open-heart operation, and a pilot for Southwest Airlines are examples of direct labor.

Overhead　All production costs other than direct materials and direct labor are lumped into one category called **overhead**. In a manufacturing firm, overhead is also known as *factory burden* or *manufacturing overhead.* The overhead cost category contains a wide variety of items. Many inputs other than direct labor and direct materials are needed to produce products. Examples include depreciation on buildings and equipment, maintenance, supplies, supervision, materials handling, power, property taxes, landscaping of factory grounds, and plant security. **Supplies** are generally those materials necessary for production that do not become part of the finished product or are not used in providing a service. Dishwasher detergent in a fast-food restaurant and oil for production equipment are examples of supplies.

Direct materials that form an insignificant part of the final product are usually lumped into the overhead category called **indirect materials**. This treatment is justified on the basis of cost and convenience. The cost of the tracing is greater than the benefit of increased accuracy. The glue used in making furniture or toys is an example.

The cost of overtime for direct labor is usually assigned to overhead as well. The rationale is that typically no particular production run caused the overtime. Accordingly, overtime cost is common to all production runs and is therefore an indirect manufacturing cost. Note that *only* the overtime cost itself is treated this way. If workers are paid $16 per hour regular rate and a premium of $8 per overtime hour, then only the $8 overtime premium is assigned to overhead. The $16 regular rate is still regarded as a direct labor cost. In certain cases, however, overtime is associated with a particular production run, such as a special order taken when production is at 100 percent capacity. In these special cases, it is appropriate to treat overtime premiums as a direct labor cost.

A number of materials and labor costs may go into the calculation of direct materials and direct labor. For example, a recent article broke down the manufacturing costs of designer jeans.[18] One pair of luxury denim jeans had the following materials and labor costs:

Materials:

Front pocket linings	$ 1.90
Fabric transport from North Carolina	0.70
Denim fabric	29.15
Total materials	$31.75

Trim:

Signature script labor	$ 0.15
Labels	0.18
Stitched American flag	1.61
Buttons	0.21
Rivets (6)	0.48
Hangtag	0.18
Zipper	0.37
Packaging	0.14
Total trim	$ 3.32

Labor:

Marking and grading	$ 0.40
Cutting	1.50
Sewing	9.50
American flag label	0.25
Total labor	$11.65

REAL-WORLD EXAMPLE

The cost estimates became a little fuzzier when overhead was considered. With prime costs (direct materials and direct labor) of $46.72 and a wholesale price of $140 to $160, it appears that overhead, selling, and administrative expenses fall somewhere between $94 and $113. Of course, the wholesale price is the cost of getting the jeans made. The additional costs involved in selling the jeans to the customer, the administrative costs of the designing company (e.g., 7 For All Mankind or True Religion), and the costs of the retail store that carries them account for the difference between the wholesale cost, an average of $150 per pair, and the retail cost of $300. As Binkley points out, "Someone has to pay for giant billboards and ads in fashion magazines."

Prime and Conversion Costs The manufacturing and nonmanufacturing classifications give rise to some related cost concepts. The functional distinction between manufacturing and nonmanufacturing costs is the basis for the concepts of noninventoriable costs and inventoriable costs—at least for purposes of external reporting. Combinations of different production costs also produce the concepts of prime costs and conversion costs.

Prime cost is the sum of direct materials cost and direct labor cost. **Conversion cost** is the sum of direct labor cost and overhead cost. For a manufacturing firm, conversion cost can be interpreted as the cost of converting raw materials into a final product. **Example 2.1** shows how and why to calculate prime cost, conversion cost, and product cost.

---

18 Christina Binkley, "How Can Jeans Cost $300?" *The Wall Street Journal* (July 7, 2011): D1. All cost examples in this box are taken from this article.

EXAMPLE 2.1

The HOW and WHY of Calculating Prime Cost, Conversion Cost, Variable Product Cost, and Total Product Cost

Information:

Carreker Company manufactures cell phones. For next year, Carreker predicts that 30,000 units will be produced, with the following total costs:

Direct materials	$150,000
Direct labor	90,000
Variable overhead	30,000
Fixed overhead	450,000

Why:

Product costs are basic to management control and decision making. Managers use these costs for budgeting to check the impact of an increase or a decrease in unit sales on operating income. Since fixed costs stay the same when units change, knowledge of prime cost, conversion cost, variable product cost, and overall product cost give important information, allowing analysis of costs at differing levels of production.

Required:

1. Calculate the prime cost per unit.

2. Calculate the conversion cost per unit.

3. Calculate the total variable product cost per unit.

4. Calculate the total product (manufacturing) cost per unit.

5. *What if* 32,000 cell phones could be manufactured next year? Explain in words how that would affect the unit prime cost, the unit conversion cost, the unit variable product cost, and the unit total product cost.

Solution:

1. Unit prime cost = (Direct materials + Direct labor)/Number of units
    = ($150,000 + $90,000)/30,000 = $8

2. Unit conversion cost = (Direct labor + Overhead)/Number of units
    = ($90,000 + $30,000 + $450,000)/30,000
    = $19

3. Unit variable product cost = (Direct materials + Direct labor + Variable overhead)/Number of units
    = ($150,000 + $90,000 + $30,000)/30,000
    = $9

4. Unit product cost = (Direct materials + Direct labor + Variable overhead + Fixed overhead)/Number of units
    = ($150,000 + $90,000 + $30,000 + $450,000)/30,000
    = $24

5. If the number of units produced increases, there will be no impact on any unit variable cost. Thus, unit prime cost and unit variable cost would stay the same. However, unit conversion cost and unit product cost would go down because of fixed factory overhead. Fixed overhead will remain the same in total but will decrease per unit as the number of units goes up. Conversely, if the number of units goes down, unit fixed overhead will increase.

Nonproduction Costs Nonproduction costs are divided into two categories: marketing (selling) costs and administrative costs. Marketing and administrative costs are not inventoried and are called *period* costs. **Period costs** are expensed in the period in which they are incurred. Thus, period costs are not inventoried and are not assigned to products. Period costs appear on the income statement—not the balance sheet. In a manufacturing organization, the level of these costs can be significant (often greater than 25 percent of sales revenue), and controlling them may bring greater cost savings than the same control exercised in the area of production costs.

For example, **Domino Sugar Company** offers wellness programs at its Baltimore sugar refinery. "The company is behind it because we want a healthy work force," said Mark Triche, director of finance. "We know it's going to decrease costs."[19] **Procter & Gamble (P&G)** spends enormous amounts on marketing in order to develop and dominate the market for its consumer products in China. A campaign to encourage Chinese parents to use the company's Pampers disposable diapers included advertising, mass carnivals, and in-store promotions in urban centers, as well as a viral web campaign. Couple those with the cost of free samples and salaries for the thousands of Chinese who distribute them, and we can understand why marketing expense in China is a significant portion of P&G's budget.[20]

For service organizations, the relative importance of selling and administrative costs depends on the nature of the service being produced. Physicians and dentists, for example, generally do very little marketing and thus have very low selling costs. An airline, on the other hand, may incur substantial marketing costs.

Those costs necessary to market and distribute a product or service are **marketing (selling) costs**. They are often referred to as *order-getting* and *order-filling* costs. Examples of marketing costs include the following: salaries and commissions of sales personnel, advertising, warehousing, shipping, and customer service. The first two items are examples of order-getting costs; the last three are order-filling costs.

All costs that cannot be reasonably assigned to either marketing or production are **administrative costs**. Administration is responsible for ensuring that the various activities of the organization are properly integrated in accordance with the overall mission of the firm. The president of the firm, for example, is concerned with the efficiency of *both* marketing and production as they carry out their respective roles. Proper integration of these two functions is essential for maximizing the overall profits of a firm. Examples of administrative costs are top-executive salaries, legal fees, printing and distributing the annual report, and general accounting. Research and development also is part of administrative costs and is expensed in the period incurred. Exhibit 2.7 provides numerous cost examples within each value chain component.

EXTERNAL FINANCIAL STATEMENTS

OBJECTIVE 5

Prepare income statements for manufacturing and service organizations.

The functional classification is the cost classification required for external reporting. In preparing an income statement, production and nonproduction costs are separated. The reason for the separation is that production costs are product costs—costs that are inventoried until the units are sold—and the nonproduction costs of marketing and administration are viewed

---

19 Lorraine Mirabella, "Firms Invest in Health," *baltimoresun.com* (May 27, 2009), http://articles.baltimoresun.com/2009-05-27/business/0905260059_1_wellness-programs-domino-sugar-corporate-wellness
20 Joseph Kahn, "P&G Viewed China as a National Market and Is Conquering It," *The Wall Street Journal* (September 12, 1995): A1, A6; and Joel Backaler, "How Procter & Gamble Cultivates Customers in China," *Forbes.com* (April 27, 2010), http://www.forbes.com/sites/china/2010/04/27/how-procter-and-gamble-cultivates-customers-in-china/

as period costs. Thus, production costs attached to the units sold are recognized as an expense (cost of goods sold) on the income statement. Production costs attached to units that are not sold are reported as inventory on the balance sheet. Marketing and administrative expenses are viewed as costs of the period and must be deducted each and every period as expenses on the income statement. Nonproduction costs never appear on the balance sheet.

Income Statement: Manufacturing Firm

The income statement prepared for external parties follows the standard format taught in an introductory financial accounting course. This income statement is frequently referred to as **absorption-costing income** or **full-costing income** because *all* manufacturing costs (direct materials, direct labor, and overhead) are fully assigned to the product.

Under the absorption-costing approach, expenses are separated according to function and then deducted from revenues to arrive at operating income. The two major functional categories of expense are cost of goods sold and operating expenses. These categories correspond to a firm's manufacturing and nonmanufacturing (marketing and administrative) expenses. **Cost of goods sold** is the cost of direct materials, direct labor, and overhead attached to the units sold. To compute the cost of goods sold, it is first necessary to determine the cost of goods manufactured.

Cost of Goods Manufactured The **cost of goods manufactured** represents the total manufacturing cost of goods completed during the current period. The only costs assigned to goods completed are the manufacturing costs of direct materials, direct labor, and overhead. The details of this cost assignment are given in a supporting schedule, called the *statement of cost of goods manufactured*. **Example 2.2** shows how to create the statement of cost of goods manufactured.

EXAMPLE 2.2

The HOW and WHY of Preparing the Statement of Cost of Goods Manufactured

Information:

Carreker Company manufactures cell phones. For next year, Carreker predicts that 30,000 units will be produced, with the following total costs:

Direct materials	$150,000
Direct labor	90,000
Variable overhead	30,000
Fixed overhead	450,000

Carreker expects to purchase $143,600 of direct materials next year. Projected beginning and ending inventories for direct materials and work in process are as follows:

	Direct Materials Inventory	Work-in-Process Inventory
Beginning	$53,400	$75,000
Ending	47,000	60,000

Why:
The primary use for the statement of cost of goods manufactured is for external financial reporting. It is a crucial input to the statement of cost of goods sold and to the income statement.

EXAMPLE 2.2

(Continued)

Required:

1. Prepare a statement of cost of goods manufactured in good form.

2. *What if* 32,000 cell phones were to be manufactured next year? Explain which lines of the statement of cost of goods manufactured would be affected and how.

Solution:

1.

Carreker Company
Statement of Cost of Goods Manufactured
for the Coming Year

Direct materials		
Beginning inventory	$ 53,400	
Add: Purchases	143,600	
Materials available	$197,000	
Less: Ending inventory	47,000	
Direct materials used in production		$150,000
Direct labor		90,000
Manufacturing (factory) overhead		480,000
Total manufacturing costs added		$720,000
Add: Beginning work in process		75,000
Less: Ending work in process		60,000
Cost of goods manufactured		$735,000

2. If the number of units produced increases, the cost of direct materials used in production will increase. Since there are sufficient direct materials in beginning inventory, it is not clear whether purchases would increase, or instead, if ending materials inventory would go down. Direct labor would increase to reflect the additional units. Overhead would increase due to the increase in variable overhead, but the fixed overhead component would remain the same. There is no clear need for changes in beginning and ending work in process as long as the additional 2,000 units come from current production.

Notice in Example 2.2 that the *total manufacturing costs* of the period are added to the manufacturing costs found in beginning work in process. The costs found in ending work in process are then subtracted to arrive at the cost of goods manufactured. If the cost of goods manufactured is for a single product, then the average unit cost can be computed by dividing the cost of goods manufactured by the number of units produced. For example, for Carreker Company, the average cost per unit of cell phones is about $24.50 ($735,000/30,000).

Work in process consists of all partially completed units found in production at a given point in time. Beginning work in process consists of the partially completed units on hand at the beginning of a period. Ending work in process consists of the incomplete units on hand at the period's end. In the statement of cost of goods manufactured, the cost of these partially completed units is reported as the cost of beginning work in process and the cost of ending work in process. The cost of beginning work in process represents the manufacturing costs carried over from the prior period; the cost of ending work in process represents the manufacturing costs that will be carried over to the next period. In both cases, additional manufacturing costs must be incurred to complete the units in work in process.

Cost of Goods Sold   Once the cost of goods manufactured statement is prepared, the cost of goods sold can be computed. The cost of goods sold is the manufacturing cost of the units that were sold during the period. It is important to remember that the cost of goods sold may or may not equal the cost of goods manufactured. In addition, we must remember that the cost of goods sold is an expense, and it belongs on the income statement. **Example 2.3** shows the cost of goods sold schedule for a manufacturing company.

Finally, we are ready to prepare an income statement for a manufacturing firm. **Example 2.4** shows how the results of the statement of cost of goods sold are included with

---

EXAMPLE 2.3

The HOW and WHY of Preparing the Statement of Cost of Goods Sold

Information:

Carreker Company manufactures cell phones. For next year, Carreker predicts that 30,000 units will be produced with the following total costs:

Direct materials	$150,000
Direct labor	90,000
Variable overhead	30,000
Fixed overhead	450,000

Carreker expects to purchase $143,600 of direct materials next year. Projected beginning and ending inventories for direct materials and work in process are as follows:

	Direct Materials Inventory	**Work-in-Process Inventory**
Beginning	$53,400	$75,000
Ending	47,000	60,000

Carreker Company expects to sell 34,000 units. Beginning inventory of finished goods is expected to be $151,000, and ending inventory of finished goods is expected to be $45,000.

> **Why:**
> The primary use for the statement of cost of goods sold is for external financial reporting. It is a crucial input to the income statement.

Required:

1. Prepare a statement of cost of goods sold in good form.

2. *What if* only 32,000 cell phones were to be sold next year? Explain which lines of the statement of cost of goods sold would be affected and how.

Solution:

1.

Carreker Company
Statement of Cost of Goods Sold
for the Coming Year

Cost of goods manufactured	$735,000
Add: Beginning finished goods	151,000
Cost of goods available for sale	$886,000
Less: Ending finished goods	45,000
Cost of goods sold	$841,000

2. If the number of units sold decreases, and production remains the same, then ending finished goods will be higher as the unsold units remain in inventory.

Information:

Carreker Company manufactures cell phones. For next year, Carreker predicts that 30,000 units will be produced with the following total costs:

Direct materials	$150,000
Direct labor	90,000
Variable overhead	30,000
Fixed overhead	450,000

EXAMPLE 2.4

The HOW and WHY of Preparing the Income Statement for a Manufacturing Firm

Carreker expects to purchase $143,600 of direct materials next year. Projected beginning and ending inventories for direct materials and work in process are as follows:

	Direct Materials Inventory	Work-in-Process Inventory
Beginning	$53,400	$75,000
Ending	47,000	60,000

Carreker Company expects to sell 34,000 units at a price of $35 each. Beginning inventory of finished goods is expected to be $151,000, and ending inventory of finished goods is expected to be $45,000. Total selling expense is projected at $62,000, and total administrative expense is projected at $187,000.

Why:

The primary use for the income statement is for external financial reporting. Investors and outside parties use it to determine the financial health of a firm.

Required:

1. Prepare an income statement in good form. Give percentages of sales for each major line item.

2. *What if* only 32,000 cell phones were to be sold next year? Explain which lines of the income statement would be affected and how.

Solution:

1.

Carreker Company
Income Statement
for the Coming Year

			%
Sales ($35 × 34,000)		$1,190,000	100.00
Less: Cost of goods sold		841,000	70.67
Gross margin		$ 349,000	29.33
Less operating expenses:			
Selling expenses	$ 62,000		
Administrative expenses	187,000	249,000	20.92
Operating income		$ 100,000	8.40*

*Difference is due to rounding.

2. If the number of units sold decreases, both sales and cost of goods sold will decrease, as will gross margin. Since no variable elements have been noted for selling and administrative expense, it is assumed that they are fixed and will not change if sales volume changes. Operating income will decrease.

nonmanufacturing expenses to calculate operating income. Gross margin, also called gross profit (the difference between sales and cost of goods sold), is an important number on the income statement. The gross margin and gross margin percentage (gross margin divided by sales) are important measures of profitability.

Often, the income statement includes a column showing each line item as a percent of sales. Clearly, sales is 100 percent of sales. Management can review these percentages and compare them with past history of the firm and with industry averages to see whether expenses are in line with expectations. If the industry generally spends 15 percent of sales on selling expense, then a company that spends significantly more or less than that amount may want to carefully consider whether its marketing strategy is appropriate.

Income Statement: Service Organization

The income statement for a service organization looks very similar to the one shown in Example 2.4 for a manufacturing organization. The cost of goods sold does, however, differ in some key ways. For one thing, the service firm has no finished goods inventories since services cannot be stored, although it is possible to have work in process for services. For example, an architect may have drawings in process and an orthodontist may have numerous patients in various stages of processing for braces. Additionally, some service firms add order fulfillment costs to the cost of goods sold.

An online retail company such as Lands' End does not manufacture the items it sells. Instead, it adds value by purchasing products, arranging for the manufacture of particular designs, and providing convenient Internet options. The cost of storing goods, picking and packing them, and shipping them to customers is shown as part of cost of goods sold.

OBJECTIVE

Explain the differences between traditional and contemporary cost management systems.

TRADITIONAL AND ACTIVITY-BASED COST MANAGEMENT SYSTEMS

Cost management systems can be broadly classified as *traditional* or *activity-based*. While both of these systems are found in practice, the traditional cost management systems are more widely used than the activity-based systems. As the need for highly accurate cost information increases, however, savvy cost accountants have learned to apply activity-based costing concepts to the determination of costs for management decision making. This is particularly true in organizations faced with increased product diversity, more product complexity, shorter product life cycles, increased quality requirements, and intense competitive pressures. These organizations often adopt a just-in-time manufacturing approach and implement advanced manufacturing technology (discussed in detail in Chapter 11). For firms operating in this advanced manufacturing environment, the traditional cost management system may not work well. More relevant and timely cost information is needed for these organizations to build a sustainable long-term competitive advantage. Organizations must improve the value received by their customers while increasing their own profits at the same time. Better assessment of cost behavior, increased accuracy in product costing, and an attempt to achieve continuous cost improvement are all critical for the advanced manufacturing environment.

Traditional Cost Management Systems: A Brief Overview

Cost management systems are made up of two subsystems: the cost accounting system and the operational control system. It is logical and convenient to discuss each subsystem separately. Of course, what is true for a subsystem is true for the overall cost management system.

Traditional Cost Accounting   A traditional cost accounting system assumes that all costs can be classified as fixed or variable with respect to changes in the *units* or *volume* of product produced. Thus, units of product or other drivers highly correlated with units produced, such as direct labor hours and machine hours, are the only drivers *assumed* to be of importance. These unit- or volume-based drivers are used to assign production costs to products. A cost accounting system that uses only unit-based activity drivers to assign costs to cost objects is called a **traditional cost system**. Since unit-based activity drivers usually are not the only drivers that explain causal relationships, much of the product cost assignment activity must be classified as allocation (recall that allocation is cost assignment based on *assumed* linkages or convenience). Therefore, traditional cost accounting systems tend to be allocation intensive.

The product costing objective of a traditional cost accounting system is typically satisfied by assigning production costs to inventories and cost of goods sold for purposes of financial reporting. More comprehensive product cost definitions, such as the value-chain and operating cost definitions illustrated in Exhibit 2.7, are not available for management use. Traditional cost accounting systems, however, often furnish useful variants of the product cost definitions. For example, prime costs and variable manufacturing costs per unit may be reported.

Traditional Cost Control   A **traditional operation control system** assigns costs to organizational units and then holds the organizational unit manager responsible for controlling the assigned costs. Performance is measured by comparing actual outcomes with standard or budgeted outcomes. The emphasis is on financial measures of performance; nonfinancial measures may be ignored. Managers are rewarded based on their ability to control costs. This approach traces costs to individuals who are responsible for the incurrence of costs. The reward system is used to motivate these individuals to manage costs. The approach assumes that maximizing the performance of the overall organization is achieved by maximizing the performance of individual organizational subunits (referred to as *responsibility centers*).

Activity-Based Cost Management Systems: A Brief Overview

Activity-based cost management systems have evolved in response to significant changes in the competitive business environment faced by both service and manufacturing firms. The overall objective of an activity-based cost management system is to manage activities to reduce costs and improve customer value. A well-designed activity-based cost management system helps managers achieve operational and strategic objectives. Operational activity-based management relates to efficiency or "doing things right." Thus, activity-based costing information is used to improve efficiency and lower cost while maintaining or improving customer value. Strategic activity-based management relates to effectiveness or "doing the right things." Thus, activity-based costing information helps managers choose which services or products to produce and which activities would be most appropriate to produce them.[21] Generally, more managerial objectives can be met with an activity-based system than with a traditional system.

Activity-Based Cost Accounting   An activity-based cost accounting system emphasizes tracing over allocation. The role of driver tracing is significantly expanded by identifying

---

21 R. S. Kaplan and R. Cooper, *Cost and Effect: Using Integrated Cost Systems to Drive Profitability and Performance* (Boston: Harvard Business School Press, 1998).

drivers unrelated to the volume of product produced (called *non-unit-based activity drivers*). The use of both unit- and non-unit-based activity drivers increases the accuracy of cost assignments and the overall quality and relevance of cost information. A cost accounting system that uses both unit- and non-unit-based activity drivers to assign activity costs to cost objects is called an **activity-based cost (ABC) system**. For example, consider the activity called "moving materials" (moving raw materials and partially finished goods from one point to another within a factory). The number of moves required for a product may be a much better measure of the product's demand for the materials handling activity than the number of units produced. In fact, the number of units produced may have little to do with measuring products' demands for materials handling. (A batch of 10 units of one product could require as much materials handling activity as a batch of 100 units of another product.) Thus, an activity-based cost accounting system tends to be tracing intensive.

Product costing in an activity-based system tends to be flexible. The activity-based cost management system is capable of producing cost information for a variety of managerial objectives, including the financial reporting objective. More comprehensive product costing definitions are emphasized for better planning, control, and decision making. Therefore, the maxim of "different costs for different purposes" takes on real meaning.

Activity-Based Cost Control The activity-based operational control subsystem also differs significantly from that of a traditional system. The emphasis of the traditional cost management accounting system is on managing costs. However, the management of activities —not costs—is the key to successful control in the advanced manufacturing environment, and *activity-based management* is at the heart of a contemporary operational control system. **Activity-based management (ABM)** focuses on the management of activities with the objective of improving the value received by the customer and the profit received by the company in providing this value. It includes driver analysis, activity analysis, and performance evaluation and draws on ABC as a major source of information.[22] In Exhibit 2.8, the vertical

Exhibit 2.8

Activity-Based Management Model

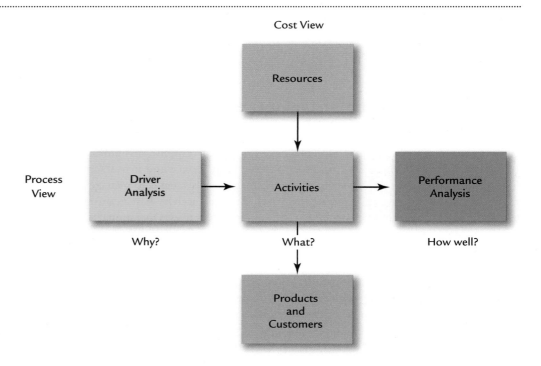

---

22 This definition of activity-based management and the illustrative model in Exhibit 2.8 are based on the following source: Norm Raffish and Peter B. B. Turney, "Glossary of Activity-Based Management," *Journal of Cost Management* (Fall 1991): 53–63. Other terms throughout the text relating to activity-based management are also drawn from this source.

dimension, or *cost view*, traces the cost of resources to activities and then to the cost objects. The cost view serves as an important input to the control dimension, which is called the *process view*. The process view identifies factors that cause an activity's cost (explains why costs are incurred), assesses what work is done (identifies activities), and evaluates the work performed and the results achieved (how well the activity is performed). Thus, an activity-based control system requires detailed information on activities.

This new approach focuses on accountability for activities rather than costs to maximize systemwide, rather than individual, performance. Activities cut across functional and departmental lines, are systemwide in focus, and require a global approach to control. Essentially, this form of control admits that maximizing the efficiency of individual subunits does not necessarily lead to maximum efficiency for the system as a whole. Another significant difference exists; in the ABM operational control information system, both financial and nonfinancial measures of performance are important. Exhibit 2.9 compares the characteristics of the traditional and activity-based cost management systems.

Big Data

Big data is increasingly important to companies today. Firms are looking for data analysts, data scientists, data specialists, and so on. What does this mean to you as an accounting student? The cost accountant plays a key role in a well-rounded data analysis team. The accountant has a deep understanding of types of costs and the data systems created to capture those costs. She or he can help to merge outside data sets (e.g., customer buying patterns, social media responses) with internal cost data sets to answer managerial concerns regarding needed production, purchases, staffing patterns, and so on. The management or cost accountant plays a key role in accumulating and analyzing big data. A wide variety of databases must be updated and merged in order to answer key management questions. For example, the accountant can amass data on resource usage to help managers determine what actions to take to effect savings while not degrading productivity or customer experience. Accountants work to find hidden patterns, correlations, and trends in costs and sales. They can bring their special expertise together with other professionals in sales and marketing, engineering, and product design to better meet customer expectations and provide a competitive advantage for their companies.

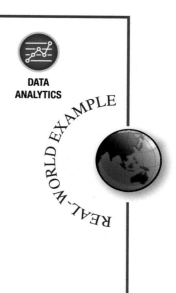

DATA ANALYTICS

REAL-WORLD EXAMPLE

Choice of a Cost Management System

An activity-based cost management system offers significant benefits, including greater product costing accuracy, improved decision making, enhanced strategic planning, and an increased ability to manage activities. These benefits, however, are expensive. An activity-based cost

Traditional	Activity-Based
Unit-based drivers	Unit- and non-unit-based drivers
Allocation intensive	Tracing intensive
Narrow and rigid product costing	Broad, flexible product costing
Focus on managing costs	Focus on managing activities
Sparse activity information	Detailed activity information
Maximization of individual unit performance	Systemwide performance maximization
Uses financial measures of performance	Uses both financial and nonfinancial measures of performance

Exhibit 2.9

Comparison of Traditional and Activity-Based Cost Management Systems

management system is more complex and requires considerably more measurement activity —and measurement can be costly. As Kaplan and Anderson point out, "ABC systems (are) expensive to build, complex to sustain, and difficult to modify."[23]

In deciding whether to implement an activity-based cost management system, a manager must assess the trade-off between the cost of measurement and the cost of errors.[24] **Measurement costs** are the costs associated with the measurements required by the cost management system. **Error costs** are the costs associated with making poor decisions based on bad cost information. Optimally, a cost management system would minimize the sum of measurement and error costs. Note, however, that the two costs conflict. More complex cost management systems produce lower error costs but have higher measurement costs. (Consider, for example, the number of activities that must be identified and analyzed, along with the number of drivers that must be used to assign costs to products.) The tradeoff between error and measurement costs is illustrated in Exhibit 2.10. The message is clear.

New approaches to activity-based costing are being developed. For example, time-driven activity-based costing streamlines the cost drivers and focuses on the time it takes to perform an activity.[25] Alternatively, for some organizations, the optimal cost system may not be an ABM system. Depending on the trade-offs, the optimal cost management system may very well be a simpler, traditional system. This could explain, in part, why most firms still maintain this type of system.

Recent changes in the manufacturing environment may increase the attractiveness of more accurate, yet complex, cost management systems. New information technology decreases measurement costs; computerized production planning systems and more powerful, less expensive computers make it easier to collect data and perform calculations. As measurement costs decrease, the measurement cost curve shown in Exhibit 2.10 shifts downward and to the right, causing the total cost curve to shift to the right. The optimal cost management system is now one that allows more accuracy.

Exhibit 2.10

Trade-Off between Measurement and Error Costs

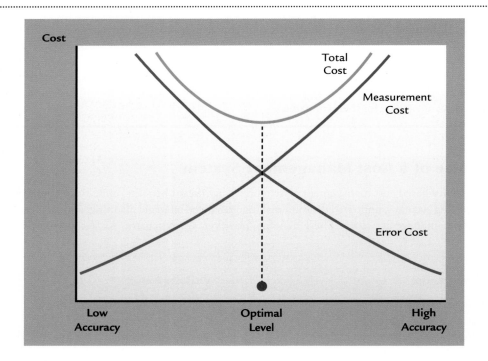

23 R. S. Kaplan and S. R. Anderson, "The Innovation of Time-Driven Activity-Based Costing," *Cost Management* 21, 2 (March/April 2007): 5–15.

24 The discussion of these issues is based on the following article: Robin Cooper, "The Rise of Activity-Based Costing — Part Two: When Do I Need an Activity-Based Cost System?" *Journal of Cost Management* (Summer 1988): 45–54.

25 R. S. Kaplan and S. R. Anderson, "Time-Driven Activity-Based Costing," *Harvard Business Review* (November 2004), http://oakforestventures.com/pdf/OFV_pdf005.pdf

As the cost of measurement has decreased, the cost of errors has increased. Basically, errors consist of over- or under-costing products. If competition heats up for an overcosted product, the firm may drop what *appears* to be an unprofitable product under a traditional system. If the nature of the competition changes, error costs can increase as well.

For example, if single-product-focused competitors emerge, then their pricing and marketing strategies will be based on more accurate cost information (since all costs are known to belong to the single product). Because of better cost information, the more focused firms may gain market share at the expense of multiple-product producers (whose cost systems may be allocating rather than tracing costs to individual products). Other factors such as deregulation and just-in-time manufacturing (which leads to a more focused production environment) can also increase the cost of errors. As the cost of errors increases, the error cost curve in Exhibit 2.10 shifts upward and to the right, causing the total cost curve to shift to the right, making a more accurate cost system the better choice.

Another cost, which is increasing for some firms, is the cost of unethical conduct.

ETHICS For example, Metropolitan Life Insurance Company paid over $20 million in fines and had to refund more than $50 million to policyholders because some of its agents illegally sold policies as retirement plans.[26] An ABM system that tracks policy sales by type, age of policyholder, agent, and policyholder's objective could give an early warning signal of problems. A key point is that companies are expected to exercise control over their operations. If there is room for ethical misconduct, the company must develop the means to identify and correct abuses. As the cost of measurement decreases and the cost of errors increases, the existing cost management system is no longer optimal. Exhibit 2.11 illustrates how changing error and measurement costs can make an existing cost management system obsolete. As the exhibit illustrates, a more accurate cost management system is mandated because of changes in error and measurement costs. Firms, then, should consider implementing an ABM system if they have experienced a decrease in measurement costs and an increase in error costs. Although the majority of firms still use a traditional cost management system, the use of activity-based costing and activity-based management is spreading, and interest in contemporary cost management systems is high. •

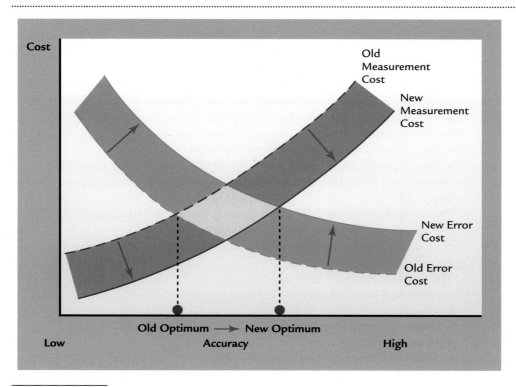

Exhibit 2.11

Shifting Measurement and Error Costs

26 Chris Roush, "Fields of Green—and Disaster Areas," *Business Week* (January 9, 1995): 94.

SUMMARY OF LEARNING OBJECTIVES

LO1. Describe a cost management information system, its objectives, and its major subsystems, and indicate how it relates to other operating and information systems.
- Cost management system, a subsystem of the accounting information system, designed to satisfy costing, controlling, and decision-making objectives
- Two major subsystems: cost accounting system and the operational control system

LO2. Define data analytics, and describe its role in cost management.
- Data analytics represents the process through which an organization utilizes various amounts and types of data to help connect strategy and other key goals to improved decision making.
- Effectively utilizing data analytics requires accountants to answer seven important questions—What, Why, How, Where, Which, When, and Who—in order to improve cost management decisions.

LO3. Explain the cost assignment process.
- Objective of the cost accounting system is assigning costs to cost objects
- Three methods of cost assignment:
  - Direct tracing—physical observation, most accurate
  - Driver tracing—more expensive, more accurate than allocation
  - Allocation—least accurate, easiest to apply

LO4. Define tangible and intangible products, and explain why there are different product cost definitions.
- Products are tangible
- Services are:
  - Intangible
  - Perishable (cannot be inventoried)
  - Inseparable (buyer and provider interact)
- Product cost definitions:
  - Value chain includes research and development, production, marketing, and customer service. Used for pricing decisions, product mix decisions, strategic profitability analysis.
  - Operating product costs include production, marketing, and customer service. Used for strategic design decisions, tactical profitability analysis.
  - Traditional product costs include only production (direct materials, direct labor, overhead) and are used for external financial reporting.

LO5. Prepare income statements for manufacturing and service organizations.
- Income statements rely on:
  - Cost of goods manufactured or services provided
  - Cost of goods sold or services sold (typically the same as services provided)
- Gross margin is the difference between sales revenue and the cost of goods (or services) sold.
- Operating income is the difference between gross margin and selling (or marketing) and administrative expense.

LO6. Explain the differences between traditional and contemporary cost management systems.
- Traditional systems characterized by:
  - Use of unit-based drivers
  - Allocation
  - Narrow and rigid product costing
  - Focus on managing costs
  - Maximization of individual unit performance
  - Use of financial measures of performance

- Activity-based systems characterized by:
  - Use of unit- and non-unit-based drivers
  - Tracing
  - Broad, flexible product costing
  - Focus on managing activities
  - Systemwide performance maximization
  - Use of both financial and nonfinancial measures of performance

EXAMPLE 2.1	The HOW and WHY of Calculating Prime Cost, Conversion Cost, Variable Product Cost, and Total Product Cost, page 48
EXAMPLE 2.2	The HOW and WHY of Preparing the Statement of Cost of Goods Manufactured, page 50
EXAMPLE 2.3	The HOW and WHY of Preparing the Statement of Cost of Goods Sold, page 52
EXAMPLE 2.4	The HOW and WHY of Preparing the Income Statement for a Manufacturing Firm, page 53

KEY TERMS

Absorption-costing income, 50

Accounting information system, 30

Activity, 41

Activity-based cost (ABC) system, 56

Activity-based management (ABM), 56

Administrative costs, 49

Allocation, 42

Assets, 40

Conversion cost, 47

Cost, 40

Cost accounting information system, 35

Cost management information system, 32

Cost objects, 40

Cost of goods manufactured, 50

Cost of goods sold, 50

Data analytics, 36

Direct costs, 41

Direct labor, 46

Direct materials, 46

Direct tracing, 42

Downstream costs, 45

Drivers, 42

Driver tracing, 42

Error costs, 58

Expenses, 40

Financial accounting information system, 32

Full-costing income, 50

Indirect costs, 41

Indirect materials, 46

Inseparability, 43

Intangibility, 43

Loss, 40

Marketing (selling) costs, 49

Measurement costs, 58

Nonproduction costs, 46

Operational control information system, 35

Overhead, 46

Period costs, 49

Perishability, 43

Prime cost, 47

Production (or product) costs, 46

Services, 43

Supplies, 46

System, 30

Tangible products, 43		Upstream costs, 45	
Traceability, 41		Value chain, 33	
Traditional cost system, 55		Work in process, 51	
Traditional operation control system, 55			

BRIEF EXERCISES

OBJECTIVE 4

Example 2.1

Brief Exercise 2-1 Product Costs

Bob's Bistro produces party-sized hoagie sandwiches. For next year, Bob's Bistro predicts that 50,000 units will be produced with the following total costs:

Direct materials	$200,000
Direct labor	100,000
Variable overhead	60,000
Fixed overhead	260,000

Required:

1. Calculate the prime cost per unit.
2. Calculate the conversion cost per unit.
3. Calculate the total variable cost per unit.
4. Calculate the total product (manufacturing) cost per unit.
5. *What if* the number of units decreased to 40,000 and all unit variable costs stayed the same? Explain what the impact would be on the following costs: total direct materials, total direct labor, total variable overhead, total fixed overhead, unit prime cost, and unit conversion cost. What would the product cost per unit be in this case?

OBJECTIVE 5

Example 2.2

Brief Exercise 2-2 Cost of Goods Manufactured

Refer to **Brief Exercise 2-1.** For next year, Bob's Bistro predicts that 50,000 units will be produced with the following total costs:

Direct materials	?
Direct labor	$ 100,000
Variable overhead	60,000
Fixed overhead	260,000

Next year, Bob's Bistro expects to purchase $195,500 of direct materials. Projected beginning and ending inventories for direct materials and work in process are as follows:

	Direct Materials Inventory	Work-in-Process Inventory
Beginning	$9,500	$4,500
Ending	5,000	2,500

Required:

1. Prepare a statement of cost of goods manufactured in good form.
2. *What if* the ending inventory of direct materials decreased by $3,000? Which line items on the statement of cost of goods manufactured would be affected and in what direction (increase or decrease)?

Brief Exercise 2-3 Cost of Goods Sold

OBJECTIVE ◀ 5
Example 2.3

Refer to **Brief Exercise 2-2.**

Bob's Bistro expects to produce 50,000 units and sell 50,500 units. Beginning inventory of finished goods is $13,000, and ending inventory of finished goods is expected to be $10,000.

Required:

1. Prepare a statement of cost of goods sold in good form.
2. *What if* the beginning inventory of finished goods increased by $4,000? What would be the effect on the cost of goods sold?

Brief Exercise 2-4 Income Statement

OBJECTIVE ◀ 5
Example 2.4

Refer to **Brief Exercises 2-2** and **2-3.** Next year, Bob's Bistro expects to produce 50,000 units and sell 50,500 units at a price of $20.00 each. Beginning inventory of finished goods is $13,000, and ending inventory of finished goods is expected to be $10,000. Total selling expense is projected at $130,000, and total administrative expense is projected at $154,000.

Required:

1. Prepare an income statement in good form. Be sure to include the percent of sales column. Round answers to two decimal places.
2. *What if* the operating expenses percentage for the past few years was 20 percent? Explain how management might react.

Brief Exercise 2-5 Costs of Services

OBJECTIVE ◀ 4
Example 2.1

Jean and Tom Perritz own and manage Happy Home Helpers, Inc. (HHH), a house-cleaning service. Each cleaning (cleaning one house one time) takes a team of three house cleaners about 1.5 hours. On average, HHH completes about 15,000 cleanings per year. The following total costs are associated with the total cleanings:

Direct materials	$ 27,000
Direct labor	472,500
Variable overhead	15,000
Fixed overhead	18,000

Required:

1. Calculate the prime cost per cleaning.
2. Calculate the conversion cost per cleaning.
3. Calculate the total variable cost per cleaning.
4. Calculate the total service cost per cleaning.
5. *What if* rent on the office that Jean and Tom use to run HHH increased by $1,500? Explain the impact on the following:
   a. Prime cost per cleaning
   b. Conversion cost per cleaning
   c. Total variable cost per cleaning
   d. Total service cost per cleaning

Brief Exercise 2-6 Cost of Services Produced

OBJECTIVE ◀ 5
Example 2.2

Jean and Tom Perritz own and manage Happy Home Helpers, Inc. (HHH), a house-cleaning service. Each cleaning (cleaning one house one time) takes a team of three house cleaners about 1.5 hours. On average, HHH completes about 15,000 cleanings per year. The following total costs are associated with the total cleanings:

Direct materials	?
Direct labor	$472,500
Variable overhead	15,000
Fixed overhead	18,000

Next year, HHH expects to purchase $25,600 of direct materials. Projected beginning and ending inventories for direct materials are as follows:

Direct Materials Inventory	
Beginning	$4,000
Ending	2,600

There is no work-in-process inventory; in other words, a cleaning is started and completed on the same day.

Required:

1. Prepare a statement of services produced in good form.
2. *What if* HHH planned to purchase $30,000 of direct materials? Assume there would be no change in beginning and ending inventories of materials. Explain which line items on the statement of services produced would be affected and how (increase or decrease).

OBJECTIVE 5
Example 2.3

Brief Exercise 2-7 Cost of Services Sold

Jean and Tom Perritz own and manage Happy Home Helpers, Inc. (HHH), a house-cleaning service. Each cleaning (cleaning one house one time) takes a team of three house cleaners about 1.5 hours. On average, HHH completes about 15,000 cleanings per year. The following total costs are associated with the total cleanings:

Direct materials	?
Direct labor	$472,500
Variable overhead	15,000
Fixed overhead	18,000

Next year, HHH expects to purchase $25,600 of direct materials. Projected beginning and ending inventories for direct materials are as follows:

Direct Materials Inventory	
Beginning	$4,000
Ending	2,600

There is no work-in-process inventory and no finished goods inventory; in other words, a cleaning is started and completed on the same day.

Required:

1. Prepare a statement of cost of services sold in good form.
2. How does this cost of services sold statement differ from the cost of goods sold statement for a manufacturing firm?

OBJECTIVE 5
Example 2.4

Brief Exercise 2-8 Income Statement

Jean and Tom Perritz own and manage Happy Home Helpers, Inc. (HHH), a house-cleaning service. Each cleaning (cleaning one house one time) takes a team of three house cleaners about 1.5 hours. On average, HHH completes about 15,000 cleanings per year. The following total costs are associated with the total cleanings:

Direct materials	?
Direct labor	$472,500
Variable overhead	15,000
Fixed overhead	18,000

Next year, HHH expects to purchase $25,600 of direct materials. Projected beginning and ending inventories for direct materials are as follows:

Direct Materials Inventory	
Beginning	$4,000
Ending	2,600

There is no work-in-process inventory and no finished goods inventory; in other words, a cleaning is started and completed on the same day. HHH expects to sell 15,000 cleanings at a price of $45 each next year. Total selling expense is projected at $22,000, and total administrative expense is projected at $53,000.

Required:

1. Prepare an income statement in good form.
2. *What if* Jean and Tom increased the price to $50 per cleaning and no other information was affected? Explain which line items in the income statement would be affected and how.

EXERCISES

Exercise 2-9 Systems Concepts

OBJECTIVE ◀ 1

In general, systems are described by the following pattern: (1) interrelated parts, (2) processes, and (3) objectives. Operational models of systems also identify inputs and outputs.

The dishwashing system of a college cafeteria consists of the following steps. First, students dispose of any waste paper (e.g., napkins) in a trash can; then they file by an opening to the dishwashing area and drop off their trays. Persons 1 and 2 take the trays; rinse the extra food down the disposal; and stack the dishes, glasses, and silverware in heavy-duty plastic racks. These racks slide along a conveyor into the automatic dishwasher. When the racks emerge from the other end of the dishwasher, they contain clean, germ-free items. Person 3 removes the racks and, with Person 4, empties them of clean items; stacking the dishes, silverware, glasses, and trays for future use. The empty racks are returned to the starting position in front of Persons 1 and 2. The following items are associated with this dishwashing system:

a. Automatic dishwasher
b. Racks to hold the dirty glasses, silverware, and dishes
c. Electricity
d. Water
e. Waste disposal
f. Sinks and sprayers
g. Dish detergent
h. Gas heater to heat water to 180 degrees Fahrenheit
i. Conveyor belt
j. Persons 1, 2, 3, and 4
k. Clean, germ-free dishes
l. Dirty dishes
m. Half-eaten dinner
n. Aprons

Required:

1. What is the objective of the dishwashing system? What processes can you identify?
2. Classify the items into one of the following categories:
   a. Interrelated parts
   b. Inputs
   c. Outputs
3. Draw an operational model for the dishwashing system.
4. Discuss how a cost management information system is similar to and different from the dishwashing system.

OBJECTIVE ▶ 1 ### Exercise 2-10 Cost Accounting Information System

The following items are associated with a cost accounting information system:
  a. Usage of direct materials
  b. Assignment of direct materials cost to each product
  c. Direct labor cost incurrence
  d. Depreciation on production equipment
  e. Cost accounting personnel
  f. Submission of a bid, using product cost plus 25 percent
  g. Power cost incurrence
  h. Materials handling cost incurrence
  i. Computer
  j. Assignment of direct labor costs to products
  k. Costing out of products
  l. Decision to continue making a part rather than buying it
  m. Printer
  n. Report detailing individual product costs
  o. Assignment of overhead costs to individual products

Required:

  1. Classify the preceding items into one of the following categories:
      a. Interrelated parts
      b. Processes
      c. Objectives
      d. Inputs
      e. Outputs
      f. User actions
  2. Draw an operational model that illustrates the cost accounting information system—with the preceding items used as examples for each component of the model.
  3. Based on your operational model, identify which product cost definition is being used: value chain, operating, or product (manufacturing).

OBJECTIVE ▶ 2 ### Exercise 2-11 Data Analytics and Cost Management

**DATA
ANALYTICS**

Consider the following data analytic types (1 through 4):
  1. Descriptive
  2. Diagnostic
  3. Predictive
  4. Prescriptive

Required:

Read the following brief descriptions (a through f) of various cost management analyses. Classify each description into the data analytic type (1 through 4) to which it most likely belongs (Note: A type can be used more than once):
  a. A multiple regression analysis finds that the number of orders requiring special handling activities represents a significant driver of overhead costs.
  b. A Monte Carlo simulation uses data from the accounting information system to forecast the incremental costs of different new store location scenarios under consideration.
  c. A linear programming optimization model shows the maximum profitability service mix for a spa and wellness center constrained by the number of certified professionals it can employ each year.
  d. A ratio analysis of historical data reveals an upward trend in warranty costs.
  e. An IBM Watson-based sentiment analysis of customer text messages provides insights regarding their willingness to pay for costly new product features.
  f. An Excel-based spreadsheet analysis of overhead costs demonstrates that a large favorable spending variance is outweighed by an even larger efficiency variance (refer to Exhibit 2.6, p. 40, for a review of data analytic types).

Exercise 2-12 Cost Assignment Methods

OBJECTIVE ▸ 3

Nizam Company produces speaker cabinets. Recently, Nizam switched from a traditional departmental assembly line system to a manufacturing cell in order to produce the cabinets. Suppose that the cabinet manufacturing cell is the cost object. Assume that all or a portion of the following costs must be assigned to the cell:

a. Depreciation on electric saws, sanders, and drills used to produce the cabinets
b. Power to heat and cool the plant in which the cell is located
c. Salary of cell supervisor
d. Wood used to produce the cabinet housings
e. Maintenance for the cell's equipment (provided by the maintenance department)
f. Labor used to cut the wood and to assemble the cabinets
g. Replacement sanding belts
h. Cost of janitorial services for the plant
i. Ordering costs for materials used in production
j. The salary of the industrial engineer (she spends about 20 percent of her time on work for the cell)
k. Cost of maintaining plant and grounds
l. Cost of plant's personnel office
m. Depreciation on the plant
n. Plant receptionist's salary and benefits

Required:

Identify which cost assignment method would likely be used to assign the costs of each of the preceding activities to the cabinet manufacturing cell: direct tracing, driver tracing, or allocation. When driver tracing is selected, identify a potential activity driver that could be used for the tracing.

Exercise 2-13 Product Cost Definitions

OBJECTIVE ▸ 4

Three possible product cost definitions were introduced: (1) value chain, (2) operating, and (3) product or manufacturing. Identify which of the three product cost definitions best fits the following situations (justify your choice):

a. Determining which of several potential new products should be developed, produced, and sold
b. Deciding whether to produce and sell a product whose design and development costs were higher than budgeted
c. Setting the price for a new product
d. Valuation of finished goods inventories for external reporting
e. Determining whether to add a complementary product to the product line
f. Choosing among competing product designs
g. Calculating cost of goods sold for external reporting
h. Deciding whether to increase the price of an existing product
i. Deciding whether to accept or reject a special order, where the price offered is lower than the normal selling price

Exercise 2-14 Cost Definitions

OBJECTIVE ▸ 4 5

SHOW ME HOW

Picante, Inc., provided the following information for the last calendar year:

Beginning inventory:	
Direct materials	$150,500
Work in process	95,300
Ending inventory:	
Direct materials	$145,300
Work in process	91,400

During the year, direct materials purchases amounted to $184,800, direct labor cost was $149,100, and overhead cost was $228,800. There were 20,000 units produced.

Required:

1. Calculate the total cost of direct materials used in production.
2. Calculate the cost of goods manufactured. Calculate the unit manufacturing cost.
3. Of the unit manufacturing cost calculated in Requirement 2, $9.50 is direct materials and $11.44 is overhead. What is the prime cost per unit? Conversion cost per unit?

OBJECTIVE  4 5

SHOW ME
HOW

Exercise 2-15 Cost Definitions and Calculations

For each of the following independent situations, calculate the missing values:

1. The Belen plant purchased $78,300 of direct materials during June. Beginning direct materials inventory was $2,500, and direct materials used in production were $73,500. What is ending direct materials inventory?
2. Forster Company produced 14,000 units at an average cost of $5.90 each. The beginning inventory of finished goods was $3,422. (The average unit cost was $5.90.) Forster sold 14,120 units. How many units remain in ending finished goods inventory?
3. Beginning work in process (WIP) was $116,000, and ending WIP was $117,300. If total manufacturing costs were $349,000, what was the cost of goods manufactured?
4. If the conversion cost is $84 per unit, the prime cost is $55, and the manufacturing cost per unit is $105, what is the direct materials cost per unit?
5. Total manufacturing costs for August were $412,000. Prime cost was $64,000, and beginning WIP was $76,000. The cost of goods manufactured was $434,000. Calculate the cost of overhead for August and the cost of ending WIP.

OBJECTIVE 5

SHOW ME   EXCEL
HOW

Exercise 2-16 Cost of Goods Manufactured and Sold

LeMans Company produces specialty papers at its Fox Run plant. At the beginning of June, the following information was supplied by its accountant:

Direct materials inventory	$62,400
Work-in-process inventory	33,900
Finished goods inventory	55,600

During June, direct labor cost was $143,000, direct materials purchases were $346,000, and the total overhead cost was $375,800. The inventories at the end of June were:

Direct materials inventory	$63,000
Work-in-process inventory	37,500
Finished goods inventory	50,800

Required:

1. Prepare a cost of goods manufactured statement for June.
2. Prepare a cost of goods sold schedule for June.

OBJECTIVE 4 5

SHOW ME   DATA   EXCEL
HOW   ANALYTICS

Exercise 2-17 Prime Cost, Conversion Cost, Preparation of Income Statement: Manufacturing Firm

Kildeer Company makes easels for artists. During the last calendar year, a total of 30,000 easels were made, and 31,000 were sold for $52 each. The actual unit cost is as follows:

Direct materials	$14.70
Direct labor	5.80
Variable overhead	3.25
Fixed overhead	15.25
Total unit cost	$39.00

The selling expenses consisted of a commission of $1.30 per unit sold and advertising co-payments totaling $95,000. Administrative expenses, all fixed, equaled $183,000. There were no beginning and ending work-in-process inventories. Beginning finished goods inventory was $132,600 for 3,400 easels.

Required:

1. Calculate the number and the dollar value of easels in ending finished goods inventory.
2. Prepare a cost of goods sold statement.
3. Prepare an absorption-costing income statement. Add a column for percentage of sales.
4. Briefly explain how Kildeer's accountants might utilize one or more data analytic types (descriptive, diagnostic, predictive, or prescriptive), along with its absorption-costing income statement, to improve various decisions involving its easels (refer to Exhibits 2.5 and 2.6, pp. 37, 40, for a review of data analytic types).

Exercise 2-18 Cost of Goods Manufactured and Sold

OBJECTIVE ◀ 5

EXCEL   SHOW ME HOW

Anglin Company, a manufacturing firm, has supplied the following information from its accounting records for the last calendar year:

Direct labor cost	$495,900
Purchases of direct materials	378,890
Freight-in on materials	7,500
Factory supplies used	18,500
Factory utilities	54,000
Commissions paid	78,983
Factory supervision and indirect labor	165,000
Advertising	145,600
Materials handling	16,900
Work-in-process inventory, January 1	201,000
Work-in-process inventory, December 31	117,400
Direct materials inventory, January 1	37,200
Direct materials inventory, December 31	34,600
Finished goods inventory, January 1	59,200
Finished goods inventory, December 31	62,700

Required:

1. Prepare a cost of goods manufactured statement.
2. Prepare a cost of goods sold statement.

Exercise 2-19 Income Statement, Direct and Indirect Cost Concepts, Service Company

OBJECTIVE ◀ 4 5

SHOW ME HOW

Lakeesha Barnett owns and operates a package mailing store in a college town. Her store, Send It Packing, helps customers wrap items and send them via UPS, FedEx, and the USPS. Send It Packing also rents mailboxes to customers by the month. In May, purchases of materials (stamps, cardboard boxes, tape, Styrofoam peanuts, bubble wrap, etc.) equaled $11,450; the beginning inventory of materials was $1,050, and the ending inventory of materials was $950. Payments for direct labor during the month totaled $25,570. Overhead incurred was $18,130 (including rent, utilities, and insurance, as well as payments of $14,050 to UPS and FedEx for the delivery services sold). Since Send It Packing is a franchise, Lakeesha owes a monthly franchise fee of 5 percent of sales. She spent $2,750 on advertising during the month. Other administrative costs (including accounting and legal services and a trip to Dallas for training) amounted to $3,650 for the month. Revenues for May were $102,100.

Required:

1. What was the cost of materials used for packaging and mailing services during May?
2. What was the prime cost for May?
3. What was the conversion cost for May?
4. What was the total cost of services for May?
5. Prepare an income statement for May.
6. Of the overhead incurred, is any of it direct? Indirect? Explain.

OBJECTIVE ▸ **1**

Exercise 2-20 Product Cost Definitions, Value Chain

Millennium Pharmaceuticals, Inc. (MPI), designs and manufactures a variety of drugs. One new drug, Glaxane, has been in development for seven years. FDA approval has just been received, and MPI is ready to begin production and sales.

Required:

Refer to Exhibit 2.7. Which costs in the value chain would be considered by each of the following managers in their decision regarding Glaxane?

1. Shelly Roberts is plant manager of the New Bern, North Carolina, plant where Glaxane will be produced. Shelly has been assured that Glaxane capsules will use well-understood processes and not require additional training or capital investment.
2. Leslie Bothan is vice president of marketing. Leslie's job involves pricing and selling Glaxane. Because Glaxane is the first drug in its "drug family" to be commercially produced, there is no experience with potential side effects. Extensive testing did not expose any real problems (aside from occasional heartburn and insomnia), but the company could not be sure that such side effects did not exist.
3. Dante Fiorello is chief of research and development. His charge is to ensure that all research projects, taken as a whole, eventually produce drugs that can support the R&D labs. He is assessing the potential for further work on drugs in the Glaxane family.

OBJECTIVE ▸ **6**

**DATA
ANALYTICS**

Exercise 2-21 Traditional versus Activity-Based Cost Management Systems

Jazon Manufacturing produces two different models of cameras. One model has an automatic focus, whereas the other requires the user to determine the focus. The two products are produced in batches. Each time a batch is produced, the equipment must be configured (set up) for the specifications of the camera model being produced. The manual-focus camera requires more parts than the automatic-focus model. The manual-focus model is also more labor intensive, requiring much more assembly time but less machine time. Although the manual model is more labor intensive, the machine configuration required for this product is more complex, causing the manual model to consume more of the setup activity resources than the automatic camera. Many, but not all, of the parts for the two cameras are purchased from external suppliers. Because it has more parts, the manual model makes more demands on the purchasing and receiving activities than does the automatic camera. Jazon currently assigns only manufacturing costs to the two products. Overhead costs are collected in one plantwide pool and are assigned to the two products in proportion to the direct labor hours used by each product. All other costs are viewed as period costs.

Jazon budgets costs for all departments within the plant—both support departments like maintenance and purchasing and production departments like machining and assembly. Departmental managers are evaluated and rewarded on their ability to control costs. Individual managerial performance is assessed by comparing actual costs with budgeted costs.

Required:

1. Is Jazon using a traditional or an activity-based cost management system? Explain.
2. Assume that you want to design a more accurate cost accounting system. What changes would you need to make? Be specific. Explain why the changes you make will improve the accuracy of cost assignments.
3. What changes would need to be made to implement an activity-based operational control system? Explain why you believe the changes will offer improved control.
4. Explain how implementing an activity-based operational control system could affect Jazon's ability to perform specific types (descriptive, diagnostic, predictive, or prescriptive) of data analytics for use in managing costs (see Exhibits 2.5 and 2.6, pp. 37, 40, for a review of data analytic types). Note: More than one analytic type might apply.

Exercise 2-22 Direct Materials Cost, Prime Cost, Conversion Cost, Cost of Goods Manufactured

  OBJECTIVE ◀ 4 5

SHOW ME
HOW

Ellerson Company provided the following information for the last calendar year:

Beginning inventory:	
Direct materials	$68,000
Work in process	29,400
Finished goods	43,200
Ending inventory:	
Direct materials	$70,400
Work in process	40,000
Finished goods	42,100

During the year, direct materials purchases amounted to $278,000, direct labor cost was $189,000, and overhead cost was $523,000. During the year, 100,000 units were completed.

Required:

1. Calculate the total cost of direct materials used in production.
2. Calculate the cost of goods manufactured. Calculate the unit manufacturing cost.
3. Of the unit manufacturing cost calculated in Requirement 2, $2.70 is direct materials and $5.30 is overhead. What is the prime cost per unit? Conversion cost per unit?

Exercise 2-23 Cost of Goods Sold, Income Statement

OBJECTIVE ◀ 2 5

DATA   SHOW ME
ANALYTICS   HOW

Refer to **Exercise 2-22**. Last calendar year, Ellerson recognized revenue of $1,312,000 and had selling and administrative expenses of $204,600.

Required:

1. What is the cost of goods sold for last year?
2. Prepare an income statement for Ellerson for last year.
3. Ellerson's chief accountant believes that conducting trend analyses into the company's cost of goods sold and net income figures over the past 10 years would provide helpful decision-making insights. Identify the data analytic type (descriptive, diagnostic, predictive, or prescriptive) that would be represented by these analyses (see Exhibits 2.5 and 2.6, pp. 37, 40, for a review of data analytic types). Also, briefly explain one decision-making insight that might be provided by these analyses.

PROBLEMS

OBJECTIVE 4 5

Problem 2-24 Cost Assignment Methods

Brody Company makes industrial cleaning solvents. Various chemicals, detergent, and water are mixed together and then bottled in 10-gallon drums. Brody provided the following information for last year:

Raw materials purchases	$250,000
Direct labor	140,000
Depreciation on factory equipment	45,000
Depreciation on factory building	30,000
Depreciation on headquarters building	50,000
Factory insurance	15,000
Property taxes:	
Factory	20,000
Headquarters	18,000
Utilities for factory	34,000
Utilities for sales office	1,800
Administrative salaries	150,000
Indirect labor salaries	156,000
Sales office salaries	90,000
Beginning balance, raw materials	124,000
Beginning balance, work in process	124,000
Beginning balance, finished goods	84,000
Ending balance, raw materials	102,000
Ending balance, work in process	130,000
Ending balance, finished goods	82,000

Last year, Brody completed 100,000 units. Sales revenue equaled $1,200,000, and Brody paid a sales commission of 5 percent of sales.

Required:

1. Calculate the direct materials used in production for last year.
2. Calculate total prime cost.
3. Calculate total conversion cost.
4. Prepare a cost of goods manufactured statement for last year. Calculate the unit product cost.
5. Prepare a cost of goods sold statement for last year.
6. Prepare an income statement for last year. Show the percentage of sales that each line item represents.

OBJECTIVE 6

Problem 2-25 Cost Information and Decision Making, Resource and Activity Drivers, Activity-Based versus Traditional Systems

Wright Plastic Products is a small company that specialized in the production of plastic dinner plates until several years ago. Although profits for the company had been good, they have been declining in recent years because of increased competition. Many competitors offer a full range of plastic products, and management felt that this created a competitive disadvantage. The output of the company's plants was exclusively devoted to plastic dinner plates. Three years ago, management made a decision to add additional product lines. They determined that existing idle capacity in each plant could easily be adapted to produce other plastic products. Each plant would produce one additional product line. For example, the Atlanta plant would add a line of plastic cups. Moreover, the variable cost of producing a package of cups (one dozen) was virtually identical to that of a package of plastic plates. (Variable costs referred to here are those that change in total as the units produced change. The costs include direct materials, direct labor, and unit-based variable overhead such as power and other machine costs.) Since the fixed expenses would not change, the new product was forecast to increase profits significantly (for the Atlanta plant).

Two years after the addition of the new product line, the profits of the Atlanta plant (as well as other plants) had not improved—in fact, they had dropped. Upon investigation, the president of the company discovered that profits had not increased as expected because the so-called fixed cost pool had increased dramatically. The president interviewed the manager of each support department at the Atlanta plant. Typical responses from four of those managers are given next.

Materials handling: The additional batches caused by the cups increased the demand for materials handling. We had to add one forklift and hire additional materials handling labor.

Inspection: Inspecting cups is more complicated than plastic plates. We only inspect a sample drawn from every batch, but you need to understand that the number of batches has increased with this new product line. We had to hire more inspection labor.

Purchasing: The new line increased the number of purchase orders. We had to use more resources to handle this increased volume.

Accounting: There were more transactions to process than before. We had to increase our staff.

Required:

1. Explain why the results of adding the new product line were not accurately projected.
2. Could this problem have been avoided with an activity-based cost management system? If so, would you recommend that the company adopt this type of system? Explain and discuss the differences between an activity-based cost management system and a traditional cost management system.

Problem 2-26 Systems Concepts, Traditional versus Activity-Based Cost Accounting Systems

OBJECTIVE 1 6

The following items are associated with a traditional cost accounting information system, an activity-based cost accounting information system, or both (i.e., some elements are common to the two systems):

a. Usage of direct materials
b. Direct materials cost assigned to products using direct tracing
c. Direct labor cost incurrence
d. Direct labor cost assigned to products using direct tracing
e. Setup cost incurrence
f. Setup cost assigned using number of setups as the activity driver
g. Setup cost assigned using direct labor hours as the activity driver
h. Cost accounting personnel
i. Submission of a bid, using product cost plus 25 percent
j. Purchasing cost incurrence
k. Purchasing cost assigned to products using direct labor hours as the activity driver
l. Purchasing cost assigned to products using number of orders as the activity driver
m. Materials handling cost incurrence
n. Materials handling cost assigned using the number of moves as the activity driver
o. Materials handling cost assigned using direct labor hours as the activity driver
p. Computer
q. Costing out of products
r. Decision to continue making a part rather than buying it
s. Printer
t. Customer service cost incurred

u. Customer service cost assigned to products using number of complaints as the activity driver
v. Report detailing individual product costs
w. Commission cost
x. Commission cost assigned to products using units sold as the activity driver
y. Plant depreciation
z. Plant depreciation assigned to products using direct labor hours

Required:

1. For each cost system, classify the relevant items into one of the following categories:
    a. Interrelated parts
    b. Processes
    c. Objectives
    d. Inputs
    e. Outputs
    f. User actions
2. Explain the choices that differ between the two systems. Which system will provide the best support for the user actions? Explain.
3. Draw an operational model that illustrates each cost accounting system—with the items that belong to the system used as examples for each component of the model.
4. Based on the operational models, comment on the relative costs and benefits of the two systems. Which system should be chosen?

OBJECTIVE `1` `6` **Problem 2-27 Activity-Based versus Traditional Operational Control Systems**

The actions listed next are associated with either an activity-based operational control system or a traditional operational control system:

a. Budgeted costs for the maintenance department are compared with the actual costs of the maintenance department.
b. The maintenance department manager receives a bonus for "beating" budget.
c. The costs of resources are traced to activities and then to products.
d. The purchasing department is set up as a responsibility center.
e. Activities are identified and listed.
f. Activities are categorized as adding or not adding value to the organization.
g. A standard for a product's material usage cost is set and compared against the product's actual materials usage cost.
h. The cost of performing an activity is tracked over time.
i. The distance between moves is identified as the cause of materials handling cost.
j. A purchasing agent is rewarded for buying parts below the standard price set by the company.
k. The cost of the materials handling activity is reduced dramatically by redesigning the plant layout.
l. An investigation is undertaken to find out why the actual labor cost for the production of 1,000 units is greater than the labor standard allowed.
m. The percentage of defective units is calculated and tracked over time.
n. Engineering has been given the charge to find a way to reduce setup time by 75 percent.
o. The manager of the receiving department lays off two receiving clerks so that the fourth-quarter budget can be met.

Required:

Classify the preceding actions as belonging to either an activity-based operational control system or a traditional control system. Explain why you classified each action as you did.

Problem 2-28 Income Statement, Cost of Goods Manufactured

OBJECTIVE ◀ 4 5

EXCEL **DATA ANALYTICS**

Spencer Company produced 200,000 cases of sports drinks during the past calendar year. Each case of 1-liter bottles sells for $36. Spencer had 2,500 cases of sports drinks in finished goods inventory at the beginning of the year. At the end of the year, there were 11,500 cases of sports drinks in finished goods inventory. Spencer's accounting records provide the following information:

Purchases of direct materials	$2,350,000
Direct materials inventory, January 1	290,000
Direct materials inventory, December 31	112,000
Direct labor	1,100,000
Indirect labor	334,000
Depreciation, factory building	525,000
Depreciation, factory equipment	416,000
Property taxes on factory	65,000
Utilities, factory	150,000
Insurance on factory	200,000
Salary, sales supervisor	85,000
Commissions, salespersons	216,000
Advertising	500,000
General administration	390,000
Work-in-process inventory, January 1	450,000
Work-in-process inventory, December 31	750,000
Finished goods inventory, January 1	107,500
Finished goods inventory, December 31	488,750

Required:

1. Prepare a cost of goods manufactured statement.
2. Compute the cost of producing one case of sports drink last year. (Round your answer to the nearest cent.)
3. Prepare an income statement on an absorption-costing basis. Include a column showing the percent of each line item of sales. (Round your percentage answers to two significant digits, e.g., 45.67%.)
4. Consider Step 4 "where" core issue described in Exhibit 2.5. Briefly explain why you would expect Spencer's accountants to find it easy or difficult to answer this "where" question with respect to conducting data analyses involving its cost of goods sold.

Problem 2-29 Cost of Goods Manufactured Cost Identification, Solving for Unknowns

OBJECTIVE ◀ 3 5

Allright Test Design Company creates, produces, and sells Internet-based CPA and CMA review courses for individual use. Davis Webber, head of human resources, is convinced that question development employees must have strong analytical and problem-solving skills. He asked Andrea Lee, controller for Allright Test Design, to help develop problems for use in screening applicants before they are interviewed. One of the problems Andrea developed is based on the following data for a mythical company (Mythic, Inc.) for the previous year:

a. Conversion cost was $140,000 and was four times the prime cost.
b. Direct materials used in production equaled $5,000.
c. Cost of goods manufactured was $154,000.
d. Ending work in process is 40 percent of the cost of beginning work in process.
e. There are no beginning or ending inventories for direct materials.
f. Cost of goods sold was 110 percent of cost of goods manufactured.
g. Beginning finished goods inventory was $22,400.

Required:

1. Using the given information, prepare a cost of goods manufactured statement.
2. Using the given information, prepare a cost of goods sold statement.

OBJECTIVE ▶ 4 5 **Problem 2-30 Income Statement, Cost of Services Provided, Service Attributes**

Mason, Durant, and Santos (MDS) is a tax services firm. The firm is located in Oklahoma City and employs 15 professionals and eight staff. The firm does tax work for small businesses and well-to-do individuals. The following data are provided for the last fiscal year. (The Mason, Durant, and Santos fiscal year runs from July 1 through June 30.)

Returns processed	$ 3,000
Returns in process, beginning of year	44,000
Returns in process, end of year	13,000
Cost of services sold	1,577,500
Beginning direct materials inventory	20,000
Purchases, direct materials	40,000
Direct labor	1,400,000
Overhead	100,000
Administrative expenses	257,000
Selling expenses	65,000

Required:

1. Prepare a statement of cost of services sold.
2. Refer to the statement prepared in Requirement 1. What is the dominant cost? Will this always be true of service organizations? If not, provide an example of an exception.
3. Assuming that the average fee for processing a return is $850, prepare an income statement for Mason, Durant, and Santos.
4. Discuss three differences between services and tangible products. Calculate the average cost of preparing a tax return for last year. How do the differences between services and tangible products affect the ability of MDS to use the last year's average cost of preparing a tax return in budgeting the cost of tax return services to be offered next year?

OBJECTIVE ▶ 4 5 **Problem 2-31 Cost of Goods Manufactured, Income Statement**

Vasani House Company produces numerous fabrics for use in automobile, airplane, and boat seats. For last year, Vasani House reported the following:

Work-in-process inventory, January 1	$ 28,750
Work-in-process inventory, December 31	23,250
Finished goods inventory, January 1	46,500
Finished goods inventory, December 31	49,000
Direct materials inventory, January 1	12,050
Direct materials inventory, December 31	13,550
Direct materials purchased	241,000
Direct labor	485,000
Plant depreciation	75,900
Salary, production supervisor	88,100
Indirect labor	58,800
Utilities, factory	40,700
Sales commissions	62,000
Salary, sales supervisor	75,000
Depreciation, factory equipment	28,000
Administrative expenses	288,600
Supplies (70% used in the factory, 30% used in the sales office)	80,000
Advertising expense	53,400

Last year, Vasani House produced 6,800 units and sold 7,000 units at $250 per unit.

Required:

1. Prepare a statement of cost of goods manufactured.
2. Prepare an absorption-costing income statement.

PRODUCT COST DEFINITIONS: ETHICS CASE

2-32 High drug costs are often in the news. Consumer groups contend that the pricing for some drugs (e.g., HIV anti-retrovirals, Betaseron for multiple sclerosis) is "too high" considering that the cost to manufacture each dose is so low. They talk of price gouging and excessive profits. Pharmaceutical companies defend the prices charged on the basis of research and development costs. They state that the percentage of successful drugs emanating from research efforts is low and that it may take years before a promising drug passes through Food and Drug Administration (FDA) requirements and becomes available for sale.

OBJECTIVE ◀ 4

Required:

1. Which cost definition from Exhibit 2.7 is being used by the consumer groups? The pharmaceutical companies? What items are included in the cost figures cited by consumer groups? What items are the pharmaceutical companies including in their discussion of product cost? Which costs do you think should be included when comparing the cost of a drug with its price?
2. Suppose that you are the accountant for the pharmaceutical company who is charged with the responsibility for compiling costs associated with your newest drug. The cost figures will be used in pricing and to determine profitability of the drug. What costs do you think you would include? Does the IMA Statement of Ethical Professional Practice have any bearing on your choice? Discuss.

3 Cost Behavior and Forecasting

After studying this chapter, you should be able to:

1 Define and describe fixed, variable, and mixed costs.

2 Explain the use of resources and activities and their relationship to cost behavior.

3 Explain how several methods of cost estimation can be used.

4 Separate mixed costs into their fixed and variable components using the high-low method, the scatterplot method, and the method of least squares.

5 Evaluate the reliability of the cost formula.

6 Explain how multiple regression can be used to assess cost behavior.

7 Recognize nonlinear cost behavior, and discuss its impact on cost forecasting.

8 Discuss the use of managerial judgment in determining cost behavior.

Flamingo Images/Shutterstock.com

USING COST BEHAVIOR KNOWLEDGE TO IMPROVE PROFITABILITY

at Airbnb

Have you ever wondered what it might be like to live along the Puget Sound in Seattle, among snow-packed mountain peaks in Montana, or in a centuries-old castle in Ireland? Or how about hosting your family's holiday get-together at a grand home with a designer kitchen? If so, you might want to rent your next vacation lodging through **Airbnb** by choosing from among its 7 million homes, boats, and treehouses—owned by 3 million hosts—in over 1,000 cities across 191 countries worldwide.[1]

Airbnb hosts have earned over $65 billion in revenues from renting out their homes since the company's founding in 2008 at San Francisco. It is understandable how a revenue number this high has grabbed the attention of so many hosts. However, before Airbnb hosts can make positive profits, they must carefully consider and understand the numerous associated costs, including how they behave in various and sometimes drastically changing business environments. For example, hosting involves variable costs, such as the time commitment for emailing guests (e.g., concerning restaurant and sightseeing recommendations and key pickup and drop-off procedures) and Airbnb management (e.g., about guest complaints or refunds). Additional variable costs include rental property upkeep, such as inspecting and fixing and replacing household furniture and other restocking items that wear out faster with increased guest usage. Other upkeep costs are fixed in nature, such as inspecting and fixing and replacing household appliances (e.g., toaster, dishwasher, washing machine, clothes dryer, HVAC units, and water heater), as well as other systems like landscape sprinklers, automatic garage doors, and high-tech security systems that do not vary as the number of guests increases or decreases. Another important fixed cost pertains to the provision of reliable high-speed internet access. However, perhaps the most critical fixed cost involves the administration of a timely and accurate reservation management process, as well as a reliable bookkeeping system to track the exchange of fees, deposits, and other financial items.

In addition, due to the often unexpectedly large time commitment to manage properties, some Airbnb hosts hire third-party property management services to help provide neighborhood-specific tips, assist with the guest check-in process, purchase and deliver cleaning and other supplies, and thoroughly clean the rental properties between guest stays, which during busy season might only provide a cleaning window of a day or even only a few hours. These third-party property management contracts can be structured such that the host pays the property manager a fixed monthly fee plus a commission for each assisted guest booking, which represents a mixed cost for the host. Finally, some home insurance policies call for the monthly premium to increase each time that cumulative monthly occupancy reaches a new level, which represents a step-function cost for the host.

---

1 See https://news.airbnb.com/airbnb-celebrates-half-a-billion-guest-arrivals/.

Beyond understanding cost behavior, hosts also need to grasp other important cost terminology. Some Airbnb hosts decide to purchase multiple properties in order to provide them with additional rental revenue. For example, roughly one-third of Airbnb hosts run between 2 and 24 properties, whereas another one-third of hosts run more than 25 properties. This leveraging strategy provides potential for considerable revenue generation. However, it also raises significant risks, such as the cost of making sizable mortgage payments on multiple properties regardless of whether or not guests rent the associated properties. In other words, these mortgage payments are nondiscretionary costs in nature because they will persist even when properties go unrented. For instance, one Airbnb host, Cheryl, experienced the reality of nondiscretionary costs hitting home during a significant and unexpected economic downturn that caused many typical Airbnb guests to stay home. During this time, Cheryl's Airbnb rental revenue fell to almost zero for an extended period. However, she still had to make her $22,000 in monthly mortgage payments during this downturn.[2]

Therefore, in addition to forecasting demand and rental revenues, profitably managing one or more Airbnb properties requires that hosts accurately estimate the various costs described earlier. Accurate cost estimates rely heavily on understanding cost behavior patterns, cost terminology, and various forecasting techniques studied in this chapter. With an informed cost management perspective, Cheryl and other Airbnb hosts are better prepared to manage and enjoy the additional net income that can arise from their participation in the challenging but exciting guest lodging industry.

Costs can display variable, fixed, or mixed behavior. Knowing how costs change as activity changes is essential to planning, controlling, and decision making. For example, budgeting, deciding to keep or drop a product line, and evaluating the performance of a segment all depend on an understanding of cost behavior. Not knowing and understanding cost behavior can lead to poor—and even disastrous—decisions. This chapter discusses cost behavior in depth so that a proper foundation is laid for its use in studying other cost management topics. Cost-volume-profit analysis (Chapter 16) and variable-costing systems (Chapter 18), for example, require that all costs be classified as fixed or variable. This chapter describes ways of separating costs into fixed and variable categories, discusses the assumptions and limitations underlying these methods, and assesses the reliability of these procedures.

OBJECTIVE 1 ▶
Define and describe fixed, variable, and mixed costs.

BASICS OF COST BEHAVIOR

Cost behavior is the term used to describe whether and how a cost changes when the level of output changes. A cost that in total does not change as output changes is a *fixed cost*. A *variable cost*, on the other hand, increases in total with an increase in output and decreases in total with a decrease in output. While economics may *assume* that fixed and variable costs are known, in the real world, management accountants must determine them. Let's first review the basics of cost and output measures. Then, we will look at fixed, variable, and mixed costs. Finally, we will assess the impact of time horizon on cost behavior.

---

2   T. Mickle and P. Rana, " 'A Bargain with the Devil'—Bill Comes Due for Overextended Airbnb Hosts," https://www.wsj .com/articles/a-bargain-with-the-devilbill-comes-due-for-overextended-airbnb-hosts-11588083336, accessed August 7, 2020.

Cost Objects

Recall from Chapter 2 that a cost object is the item for which managers want cost information. So the first step is to determine appropriate cost objects. This determination is relatively easy in a manufacturing firm; the cost object typically is a tangible product. For service firms, the logical cost object is a service. For example, hospitals may view particular services, such as blood tests or radiology services, as primary cost objects. There are, however, a variety of cost objects for which managers may need to know cost behavior.

The Internet has fundamentally changed the way companies do business with their suppliers and customers. Price competition is severe so firms cannot, typically, succeed using only a low-price strategy. Instead, they use a customer-service strategy. Internet-based companies strive to provide a shopping experience that is user friendly, with an abundance of information tailored to customer needs, and a secure payment system. Ideally, the company provides a seamless interface for customers, taking them from information search, through product/ service choice, payment, and post-sale follow-up. Software that tracks ongoing customer preferences is a large part of the enhanced customer shopping experience. Amazon.com is an excellent example of this enhanced customer focus, as it welcomes new and returning customers and makes the shopping experience fun and easy. For example, Amazon reacted quickly by adding 100,000 new warehouse workers plus 75,000 additional employees in roughly a one-month period to help fulfill surging customer orders.[3] This means that the customer is the appropriate cost object, and activities and drivers that are tied to customer service are important data to Internet-based firms.

Measures of Output

The terms *fixed cost* and *variable cost* only have meaning when related to some output measure or driver. Therefore, we must first determine the underlying activities and the associated drivers that measure the capacity of an activity and its output. For example, materials handling may be measured by the number of moves; shipping goods may be measured by the units sold; and laundering hospital linen may be measured by the pounds of laundry. The choice of driver is tailored not only to the particular firm but also to the particular activity or cost being measured.

Activity drivers explain changes in activity costs by measuring changes in activity output (usage). The two general categories of activity drivers are *unit-level drivers* and *non-unit-level drivers*. Recall that drivers are factors that *cause* changes in resource usage, activity usage, costs, and revenues. **Unit-level drivers** explain changes in cost as units produced change. Pounds of direct materials, kilowatt-hours used to run production machinery, and direct labor hours are examples of unit-based activity drivers. While none of these drivers is equal to the number of units produced, each does vary proportionately with the number of units produced. **Non-unit-level drivers** explain how costs change as factors other than the number of units produced changes. Examples of non-unit-based output measures include the number of setups, work orders, engineering change orders, number of product or service lines, inspection hours, and material moves.

In a traditional cost management system, cost behavior is assumed to be described by unit-based drivers only. In an activity-based cost management system, both unit- and non-unit-based drivers are used. Thus, the ABC system tends to produce a much richer view of cost behavior than would a traditional, unit-based, system. In turn, cost behavior patterns for a much broader set of activities must now be identified.

We now take a closer look at fixed, variable, and mixed costs. In each case, the cost is related to only one measure of output.

3 Taylor Soper, "Here's What Amazon Is Doing to Increase Capacity for Surging Online Grocery Demand Orders," (13 April 2020), https://www.geekwire.com/2020/heres-amazon-increase-capacity-surging-online-grocery-demand -orders/, accessed August 7, 2020.

Fixed Costs

Fixed costs are costs that *in total* are constant within the relevant range as the level of the associated driver varies. To illustrate fixed cost behavior, consider a plant operated by JCM Audio Systems, Inc., that produces speakers for home audio systems. One department in the plant produces a 3½-inch voice coil and inserts it into each speaker passing through the department. The activity is voice-coil production, and the activity driver is the number of voice coils produced. The department operates two production lines, and each can make up to 100,000 voice coils per year. The production workers of each line are supervised by a production-line manager who is paid $60,000 per year. For production up to 100,000 units, only one manager is needed; for production between 100,001 and 200,000 units, the second line is activated and two managers are needed. The cost of supervision for several levels of production for the plant is given as follows:

JCM Audio Systems, Inc.

Supervision Cost	Voice Coils Produced	Unit Cost
$ 60,000	40,000	$1.50
60,000	80,000	0.75
60,000	100,000	0.60
120,000	120,000	1.00
120,000	160,000	0.75
120,000	200,000	0.60

The first step in assessing cost behavior is defining an appropriate activity driver. In this case, the activity driver is the number of voice coils produced. The second step is defining what is meant by **relevant range**, the range over which the assumed cost relationship is valid for the normal operations of a firm. Suppose that the relevant range is 120,000 to 200,000 units processed. Notice that the *total* cost of supervision remains constant within this range as more voice coils are produced. JCM Audio Systems pays $120,000 for supervision regardless of whether it produces 120,000, 160,000, or 200,000 voice coils.

Pay particular attention to the words *in total* in the definition of fixed costs. While the total cost of supervision remains unchanged as more voice coils are produced, the unit cost does change as the number of units changes. As the example shows, within the relevant range, the unit cost of supervision decreases from $1.00 to $0.60. Because of the behavior of per-unit fixed costs, it is easy to get the impression that fixed costs are affected by changes in the level of the driver, when in reality they are not. Unit fixed costs can be misleading and may adversely affect some decisions. It is often safer to work with total fixed costs.

Exhibit 3.1 is a graph of fixed cost behavior. For the relevant range, fixed cost behavior is described by a horizontal line. Notice that for 120,000 voice coils produced, supervision cost is $120,000; for 160,000 voice coils produced, supervision cost is still $120,000. This line visually demonstrates that cost remains unchanged as the level of the activity driver varies. For the relevant range, total fixed costs can be represented by the following simple linear equation:

$$F = \text{Total fixed costs}$$

In the example for JCM Audio Systems, supervision cost amounted to $120,000 for any level of output between 100,001 and 200,000 voice coils produced. Thus, supervision is a fixed cost, and the fixed cost equation in this case is $F = \$120,000$. Strictly speaking, this equation assumes that the fixed costs are $120,000 for all levels (as if the line extends to the vertical axis as indicated by the dashed portion in Exhibit 3.1). Although this assumption is not true, it is harmless as long as the operating decisions are confined to the relevant range.

Can fixed costs change? Of course they can, but this does not make them variable. They are fixed at a new higher (or lower) level. Suppose that JCM Audio Systems gives a raise to the voice coil line supervisors. Instead of being paid $60,000 per year, they are paid $64,000 per

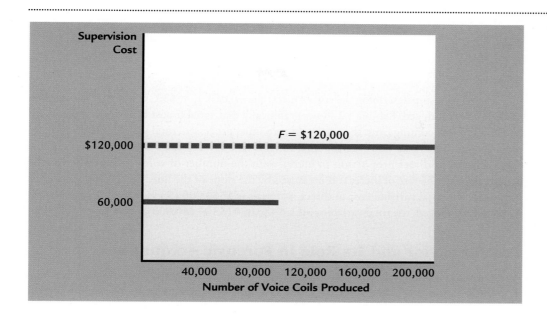

Exhibit 3.1

Fixed Cost Behavior

year. Now the cost of supervision is $128,000 per year (2 × $64,000). However, supervisory costs are still fixed with respect to the number of voice coils produced. Can you draw in the new fixed cost line on Exhibit 3.1?[4]

Variable Costs

Variable costs are defined as costs that, in total, vary in direct proportion to changes in an activity driver. To illustrate, let's expand the JCM Audio Systems example to examine the direct materials cost of the voice coils. The cost is the cost of direct materials for the voice coils, and the driver is the number of voice coils produced. Each voice coil requires direct materials costing $3. The total direct materials cost of voice coils for various levels of production is given as follows:

JCM Audio Systems, Inc.

Total Direct Materials Cost of Voice Coils	Voice Coils Produced	Unit Direct Materials Cost of Voice Coils
$120,000	40,000	$3
240,000	80,000	3
360,000	120,000	3
480,000	160,000	3
600,000	200,000	3

As more voice coils are produced, the total cost of direct materials increases in direct proportion. For example, as production doubles from 80,000 to 160,000 units, the *total* cost of voice coils doubles from $240,000 to $480,000. Notice also that the unit cost of direct materials is constant.

Variable costs can also be represented by a linear equation. Here, total variable costs depend on the level of activity driver. This relationship can be described by the following equation:

$$Y_v = VX$$

---

4   The new line is a horizontal line that intersects the y-axis at $128,000. Note that it is drawn parallel to and above the original fixed cost line.

where

$$Y_v = \text{Total variable costs}$$
$$V = \text{Variable cost per unit}$$
$$X = \text{Number of units of the driver}$$

The relationship describing the cost of direct materials is $Y_v = \$3X$, where $X =$ the number of voice coils produced. Exhibit 3.2 shows graphically that variable cost behavior is represented by a straight line coming from the origin. At zero units processed, total variable cost is zero. As units produced increase, however, the total variable cost also increases. Note that total variable cost increases in direct proportion to increases in the number of voice coils produced (the activity driver); the rate of increase is measured by the slope of the line. At 120,000 voice coils produced, the total variable cost of direct materials is $360,000 ($3 × 120,000); at 160,000 voice coils produced, the total variable cost is $480,000 ($3 × 160,000).

Cost Behavior and Its Role in Forensic Accounting

As mentioned in Chapter 1, virtually any area within accounting can play an important role in forensic accounting situations. Cost estimations, income measurement, income tax considerations, and incremental accounting analyses represent a few common examples of various accounting areas that play an essential role in the court's ability to intelligently and fairly resolve case issues. Perhaps the most frequently used accounting area in evaluating such disputed litigation case issues is that of cost behavior. Cost behavior often is used in determining whether liability exists and, if so, the amount of damages resulting from such liability.

As we discuss in this chapter, costs behave, or change, in different ways as the volume of activity changes. For example, as the volume of activity changes, some costs in total remain unchanged, other costs in total change directly and proportionately with the activity, and yet other costs in total change but not proportionately with the activity (see discussions regarding nonlinear cost behavior later in the chapter). Cost behavior patterns can be essential to the court in determining whether liability exists within a case. Federal antitrust cases provide one example of such a situation. A major determinant of liability in a federal antitrust case is whether the defendant has engaged in "predatory pricing". Predatory pricing is the act of pricing products or services so low that the only logical explanation is that the purpose is to drive competitors out of business and, once accomplished, to raise prices to monopolistic levels. Because the previous description of predatory pricing is not very useful in courts, typically the operational definition of predatory pricing is to price products or services below their average variable costs.

Exhibit 3.2

Variable Cost Behavior

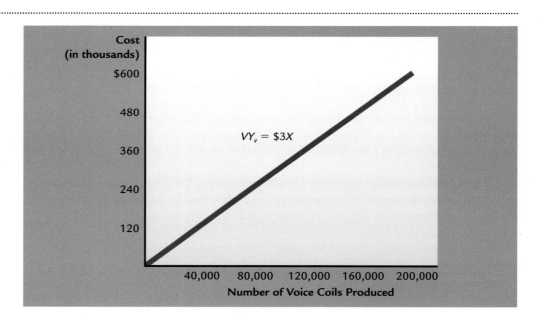

Most companies do not measure or report their costs by cost behavior pattern. As a result, both the plaintiff and the defendant usually must analyze the relevant costs and be prepared to defend them to the court. It should be noted that if a company is found to be engaged in predatory pricing, it is not an adequate defense to claim that the company was unaware that it was engaged in predatory pricing. There are other situations in forensic accounting in which cost behavior may play a role in determining whether a participant in a litigation has liability in a case. For example, a special area of fraud litigation under the Federal False Claims Act (FFCA) may utilize cost behavior and other accounting measurements in the court's assessment of liability.

As noted earlier, once the court has found that one side in a case has liability for its actions (or inactions), estimating the amount of damages becomes essential for final dispute resolution. Because almost all case disputes involve unexpected changes in activity (e.g., changes in sales or production quantities resulting from contract breaches or other disputed actions), the party claiming damages (i.e., the plaintiff) and the party defending against damages (i.e., the defendant) need to determine the amount of costs, lost profits, or other accounting measures of damages that occurred as the result of actions or lack of actions in the alleged case. The use of cost behavior knowledge and cost behavior estimation techniques is essential in estimating the damages and in explaining and defending those estimates to the court. Later in the book, we will discuss other cost concepts and actions that have relevance in forensic accounting cases.

Sustainability Cost Estimation and Management at FedEx

FedEx's annual Global Citizenship Report describes its intense aircraft modernization efforts across the entire fleet "to lower [aircraft fuel] costs through enhanced reliability, operational flexibility, reduced maintenance expenses, and improved fuel efficiency."[5] FedEx also pursues numerous additional cost-cutting innovations, including wake surfing flying techniques, which confirmed during formation flight tests that reduced jet fuel consumption was achieved by flying in the wingtip vortex of the lead aircraft. This "wake surfing" technique emulates the flying formation of birds and could potentially reduce fuel consumption by as much as 10 percent. In total, FedEx pursues over 70 different fuel-saving projects involving biofuels, modernized planes, and a simplified fuel policy (e.g., which encourages improved communication among the various teams that determine the amount of fuel added to each flight). Collectively, these efforts reduced FedEx's annual fuel consumption by 250 million gallons of fuel and avoided more than 2.41 million metric tons of CO_2 emissions, which resulted in annual cost savings to FedEx of over $553 million. These successful cost savings programs rely heavily on the ability of the company's accountants to understand the cost behaviors of the many costs involved with these numerous innovative programs, many of which are driven by unique or new activity drivers. Furthermore, accountants must be able to accurately forecast the amount of such costs, oftentimes without the benefit of having past historical data on which to base their estimates. These efforts represent an impressive partnership between accountants, designers, and engineers to bring ideas to fruition in a high-quality and cost-effective fashion.

REAL-WORLD EXAMPLE

Linearity Assumption

The definition of variable costs just given and the graph in Exhibit 3.2 imply a linear relationship between the cost of direct materials and the number of voice coils produced. How reasonable is the assumption that costs are linear? Do costs really increase in direct proportion to increases in the level of the activity driver? If not, then how well does this assumed linear cost function approximate the underlying cost function?

5 FedEx, "Multiplying Opportunities: 2020 Global Citizenship Report," 2020, http://sustainability.fedex.com /FedEx_2020_Global_Citizenship_Report.pdf, accessed August 7, 2020.

Economists usually assume that variable costs increase at a decreasing rate up to a certain volume, at which point they increase at an increasing rate. This type of *nonlinear behavior* is displayed in Exhibit 3.3. Here, variable costs increase as the number of units increases, but not in direct proportion. Given its importance, we examine nonlinear cost behavior in more detail later in the chapter.

If the nonlinear view more accurately portrays reality, what should we do? One possibility is to determine the actual cost function—but every activity could have a different cost function, and this approach could be very time consuming and expensive (if it can even be done). It is much simpler to assume a linear relationship.

If the linear relationship is assumed, then the main concern is how well this assumption approximates the underlying cost function. Exhibit 3.4 gives us some idea of the consequences of assuming a linear cost function. As with fixed costs, we can define the *relevant range* as the range of activity for which the assumed cost relationships are valid. Here, validity refers to how

Exhibit 3.3

Nonlinearity of Variable Costs

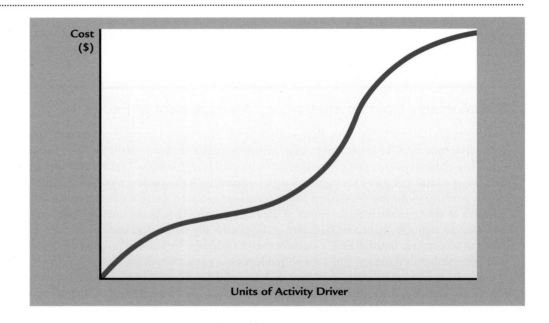

Exhibit 3.4

Relevant Range for Variable Costs

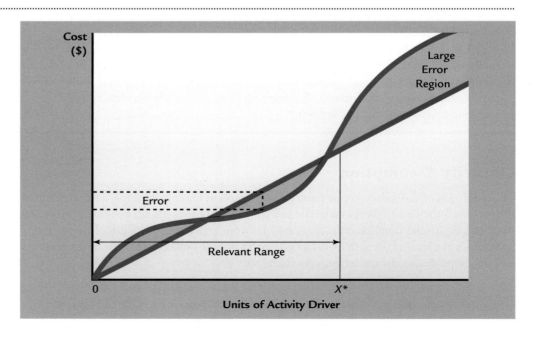

closely the linear cost function approximates the underlying cost function. Note that as units increase beyond X^*, the approximation appears to break down.

Mixed Costs

Mixed costs are costs that have both a fixed and a variable component. For example, sales representatives are often paid a salary plus a commission on sales. Suppose that JCM Audio Systems has 10 sales representatives, each earning a salary of $30,000 per year plus a commission of $5 per speaker sold. The activity is selling, and the activity driver is units sold. If 100,000 speakers are sold, then the total selling cost (associated with the sales representatives) is $800,000—the sum of the fixed salary cost of $300,000 (10 × $30,000) and the variable cost of $500,000 ($5 × 100,000). **Example 3.1** shows how and why the linear equation can be used to describe a mixed cost.

EXAMPLE 3.1

The HOW and WHY of Forming an Equation to Describe Mixed Cost

Information:
JCM Audio Systems has 10 sales representatives, each earning a salary of $30,000 per year plus a commission of $5 per speaker sold. Last year, 100,000 speakers were sold.

> **Why:**
> As long as 100,000 speakers is in the relevant range, then a straight line depicts the cost relationship well. If the cost function is known, sensitivity analysis can be used to see what the total selling cost would be at differing levels of sales.

Required:

1. Develop a cost equation for total selling cost.

2. Compute the total variable selling cost last year.

3. Compute the total selling cost last year.

4. Compute the unit selling cost for last year.

5. *What if* 110,000 speakers had been sold last year? What would be the total selling cost and the unit selling cost? Explain why the unit selling cost decreased.

Solution:

1. Total selling cost = Fixed selling cost + (Variable rate × Units sold)
   = $300,000 + ($5 × Units sold)

2. Total variable selling cost = Variable rate × Units sold
   = $5 × 100,000
   = $500,000

3. Total selling cost = $300,000 + ($5 × Units sold)
   = $300,000 + $500,000
   = $800,000

4. Unit selling cost = Total selling cost/Units sold
   = $800,000/100,000
   = $8

5. Total selling cost = $300,000 + ($5 × 110,000) = $850,000
   Unit selling cost = $850,000/110,000 = $7.73 (rounded)

   The unit selling cost went down because the fixed cost, which stays the same, is spread out over a greater number of units.

Exhibit 3.5

Mixed Cost Behavior

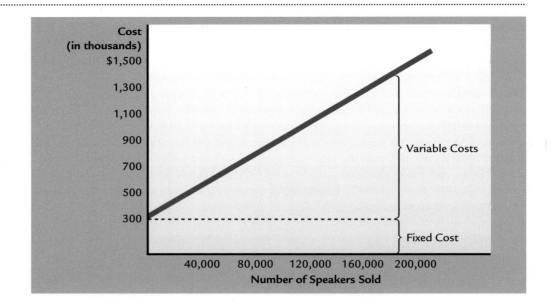

The graph for our mixed cost example is given in Exhibit 3.5. (The graph assumes that the relevant range is 0 to 200,000 units.) Mixed costs are represented by a line that intercepts the vertical axis (at $300,000, for this example). The intercept corresponds to the fixed cost component, and the slope of the line gives the variable cost per unit of activity driver (slope is $5 for the example portrayed).

Time Horizon

Determining whether a cost is fixed or variable depends on the time horizon. According to economics, in the **long run**, all costs are variable; in the **short run**, at least one cost is fixed. But how long is the short run? Different costs have short runs of different lengths. Direct materials, for example, are relatively easy to adjust. **Starbucks Coffee** may treat coffee beans (a direct material) as strictly variable, even though for the next few hours the amount already on hand is fixed. The lease of space for one of its coffee shops, however, is more difficult to adjust; it may run for one or more years. This cost is typically seen as fixed. The length of the short-run period depends to some extent on management judgment and the purpose for which cost behavior is being estimated. For example, submitting a bid on a one-time, special order may span only a month—long enough to create a bid and produce the order. Other types of decisions, such as product mix decisions, will affect costs over a much longer period of time. In this case, the costs that must be considered are long-run variable costs, including product design, product development, market development, and market penetration. Short-run costs often do not adequately reflect all the costs necessary to design, produce, market, distribute, and support a product.

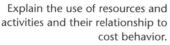 **OBJECTIVE 2**

Explain the use of resources and activities and their relationship to cost behavior.

RESOURCES, ACTIVITIES, AND COST BEHAVIOR

Resources are economic elements that enable one to perform activities. Common resources of a manufacturing plant include direct materials, direct labor, electricity, equipment, and so on. When a company spends money on resources, it is *acquiring* the ability or capacity to perform an activity. Recall from Chapter 2 that an activity is a task, such as setting up equipment, purchasing materials, assembling materials, and packing completed units in boxes. When a firm acquires the resources needed to perform an activity, it obtains **activity capacity**. Usually, the amount of activity capacity needed corresponds to the level where the activity is performed efficiently. This efficient level of activity performance is called **practical capacity**.

If all of the activity capacity acquired is not used, then there is **unused capacity**, which is the difference between the acquired capacity and the actual amount of the activity used. The relationship between resource spending and resource usage can be used to define variable and fixed cost behavior.

Flexible Resources

Resources can be categorized as (1) flexible and (2) committed. **Flexible resources** are supplied as used and needed. The organization is free to buy what it needs, when it needs it, so the quantity of the resource supplied equals the quantity demanded. There is no unused capacity for this category of resources (resources used equal resources supplied).

Since the cost of flexible resources equals the cost of resources used, the total cost of the resource increases as demand for the resource increases. The cost of a flexible resource is a variable cost. For example, in a just-in-time manufacturing environment, materials are purchased when needed and are used right away. Thus, as the units produced increase, the amount (and cost) of direct materials increases proportionately. Similarly, power is a flexible resource. Using kilowatt-hours as the driver, as the demand for power increases, the cost of power increases. Note that in each example, resource supply and usage are measured by an output measure, or driver.

Committed Resources

Committed resources are supplied in advance of usage. An explicit or implicit contract is used to obtain a given quantity of resource, regardless of whether that amount is fully used or not. Because the amount of committed resource supplied may exceed the firm's demand for it, unused capacity is possible.

Many resources are acquired before the actual demands for the resource are realized. There are two examples of this category of resource acquisition. First, organizations acquire *multi-period service capacities* by paying cash up front or by entering into an explicit contract that requires periodic cash payments. Buying or leasing buildings and equipment are examples of this form of advance resource acquisition. The annual expense associated with the multi-period category is independent of actual usage of the resource. Often, these expenses are referred to as **nondiscretionary (or committed) fixed expenses** because they essentially correspond to committed resources—costs incurred that provide long-term activity capacity. The chapter-opening feature illustrates the importance for **Airbnb** hosts to understand the nature of their nondiscretionary fixed mortgage payments as these sizable costs typically are committed and cannot be easily avoided in the short term when Airbnb guest demand decreases, such as during an unexpected economic downturn. The trend toward a more remote workforce presents another interesting example of companies managing their nondiscretionary fixed expenses. Specifically, as an increasing number of employees across many industries demonstrate their ability (and sometimes preference) to work effectively from home, companies such as **Barclays** and **Nationwide** are considering significant long-term office space downsizing initiatives to reduce building lease costs.[6]

ETHICS A second and more important example concerns organizations that acquire resources in advance through implicit contracts—usually with their employees.

These implicit contracts require an ethical focus, since they imply that the organization will maintain employment and salary levels even though there may be temporary downturns in the quantity of activity used. Hiring three sustaining engineers for $150,000 who can supply the capacity of processing 7,500 change orders (the driver) is an example of implicit contracting. (Often, in response to customer feedback and competitive pressures, products need to be

---

6 See https://www.cnbc.com/2020/05/01/major-companies-talking-about-permanent-work-from-home-positions
.html, accessed October 2, 2020.

redesigned or modified. An engineering change order is the document that initiates this process.) Certainly, none of the three engineers would expect to be laid off if only 7,000 change orders were actually processed—unless, of course, the downturn in demand is viewed as being permanent. •

Companies can manage economic ups and downs with lower-level salaries and then vary the level bonuses at the end of the year. In addition, many companies use a lower level of permanent employees and a fluctuating level of temporary, or contingent, workers. This practice includes both manufacturing and service industries as well as unskilled (e.g., day laborers) and skilled workers (e.g., nurses and information technology specialists).

REAL-WORLD EXAMPLE

Google, for example, has more temporary and contract workers (121,000) globally than full-time employees (102,000).[7] Differences in salary, benefits, and vacation plans represent common key financial differences between temporary workers and employees. When a new project begins, contract workers allow the company to staff up quickly, and when the projects are through, it is easy for the company to lay off those workers.

A key reason for the use of contingent workers is flexibility—in meeting demand fluctuations, in controlling downsizing, and in buffering core workers against job loss. Resource spending for this category essentially corresponds to **discretionary fixed expenses**—costs incurred for the acquisition of short-term activity capacity that can be avoided relatively easily in the short term if management decides to do so.

Implications for Control and Decision Making

The activity-based resource usage model just described can improve both managerial control and decision making. Operational control information systems encourage managers to pay more attention to controlling resource usage and spending. A well-designed operational system would allow managers to assess the changes in resource demands that will occur from new product mix decisions. Adding new, customized products may increase the demand for various overhead activities; if sufficient unused activity capacity does not exist, then resource spending must increase.

Similarly, if resource usage can be reduced, bringing about unused capacity, managers must carefully consider what to do with the excess capacity. Eliminating the excess capacity may decrease resource spending and thus improve overall profits. Alternatively, using the excess capacity to increase output could increase revenues without a corresponding increase in resource spending.

The activity-based resource usage model also allows managers to better calculate the changes in resource supply and demand resulting from decisions such as make or buy, accept or reject special orders, and keep or drop product lines. The model increases the power of a number of traditional management accounting decision-making models. These are explored in the decision-making chapters found in Part 4 (Chapters 16–20).

Step-Cost Behavior

So far, we have assumed that the cost function is continuous. In reality, some cost functions may be discontinuous. One such discontinuous function, a step function, is shown in Exhibit 3.6.

---

7 Daisuke Wakabayashi, "Google's Shadow Work Force: Temps Who Outnumber Full-Time Employees," (28 May 2019), https://www.nytimes.com/2019/05/28/technology/google-temp-workers.html, accessed August 7, 2020.

A **step-cost function** displays a constant level of cost for a range of output and then jumps to a higher level of cost at some point, where it remains for a similar range of activity. In Exhibit 3.6, the cost is $100, as long as output is between 0 and 20 units. If the volume is between 20 and 40 units, the cost jumps to $200.

Step-Variable Costs Items that display a step-cost behavior must be purchased in chunks. The width of the step defines the range of activity output for which a particular quantity of the resource must be acquired. The width of the step in Exhibit 3.6 is 20 units. If the width of the step is narrow, as in Exhibit 3.6, the cost of the resource changes in response to fairly small changes in resource usage. Costs that follow a step-cost behavior with narrow steps are defined as **step-variable costs**. If the width of the step is narrow, step-variable costs can be approximated by a strictly variable cost.

Step-Fixed Costs In reality, many so-called fixed costs may be best described by a step-cost function. Many committed resources—particularly those that involve implicit contracting—follow a step-cost function. Suppose, for example, that a company hires three sustaining engineers—engineers who are responsible for redesigning existing products to meet customer requirements. The salaries paid to the engineers represent the cost of acquiring the engineering redesign capacity. The number of engineering changes that can be *efficiently* processed by the three engineers is a measure of that capacity. The nature of this resource requires that the capacity be acquired in chunks (one engineer hired at a time). The cost function for this example is displayed in Exhibit 3.7. Notice that the width of the steps is 2,500 units, a much wider step than the cost function displayed in Exhibit 3.6. Costs that follow a step-cost behavior with wide steps are defined as **step-fixed costs**. Step-fixed costs are assigned to the fixed cost category, since most are fixed over the firm's normal operating range.

When resources are acquired in advance, there may be a difference between the *resources supplied* and the *resources used (demanded)*. This can only occur for costs that display fixed cost behavior (resources acquired in advance of usage). The traditional cost management system provides information only about the cost of the resources supplied. A contemporary cost management system, on the other hand, tells how much of the activity is used and the cost of its usage, based on the activity rate. The average unit cost, obtained by dividing the resource expenditure by the activity's practical capacity, is the **activity rate**. The activity rate is used to

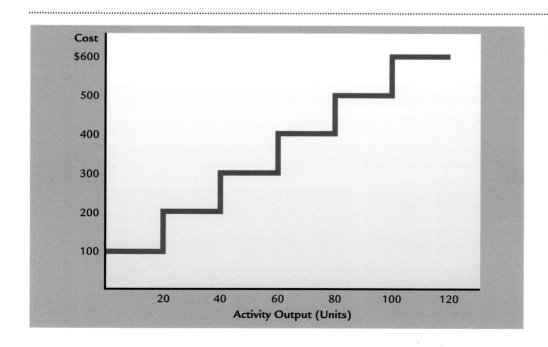

Exhibit 3.6

Step-Cost Function

Exhibit 3.7

Step-Fixed Costs

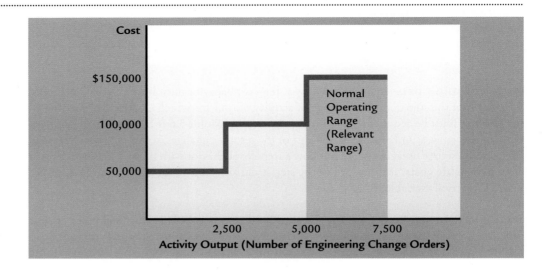

calculate the cost of resource usage and the cost of unused activity. The relationship between resources supplied and resources used is expressed by either of the following two equations:

$$\text{Activity availability} = \text{Activity output} + \text{Unused capacity}$$

$$\text{Cost of activity supplied} = \text{Cost of activity used} + \text{Cost of unused activity}$$

Example 3.2 illustrates the way a company may determine the cost of capacity used and unused capacity.

EXAMPLE 3.2

The HOW and WHY of Calculating Activity Availability, Capacity Used, and Unused Capacity

Information:

Davin Company has three sustaining engineers, each of whom is paid $50,000 per year and is able to process 2,500 change orders. Last year, 6,000 change orders were processed by the three engineers.

> **Why:**
> If managers know the total capacity available as well as the capacity used, they can better utilize the activity capacity and know when additional capacity must be acquired.

Required:

1. Calculate the activity rate per change order.

2. Calculate, in terms of change orders, the:
   a. total activity availability.
   b. unused capacity.

3. Calculate, in dollars, the:
   a. total activity availability.
   b. unused capacity.

4. Express total activity availability in terms of activity capacity used and unused capacity.

5. *What if* the number of change orders processed equaled 7,500? What would unused capacity be?

EXAMPLE 3.2

(Continued)

Solution:

1. Activity rate = Total cost of sustaining engineers/Number of change orders

    $$= (3 \times \$50,000)/(3 \times 2,500)$$
    $$= \$20/\text{change order}$$

2. a. Total activity availability = $3 \times 2,500 = 7,500$ change orders
    b. Unused capacity = $7,500 - 6,000 = 1,500$ change orders

3. a. Total activity availability = $\$20(3 \times 2,500) = \$150,000$
    b. Unused capacity = $\$20(7,500 - 6,000) = \$30,000$

4. Total activity availability = Activity capacity used + Unused capacity

    $$7,500 = 6,000 + 1,500$$
    or
    $$\$150,000 = \$120,000 + \$30,000$$

5. If the actual change orders processed equaled 7,500, then all three engineers would be working at capacity and there would be no unused capacity.

Notice that the cost of unused capacity shown in Example 3.2 occurs because the resource (engineering redesign) must be acquired in lumpy (whole) amounts. Even if the company had anticipated the need for only 6,000 change orders, it would have been difficult to hire the equivalent of 2.4 engineers (6,000/2,500).

Activities and Mixed Cost Behavior

When activities use a mix of resources that are acquired in advance and resources that are acquired as needed, they display mixed cost behavior. Suppose that a plant has its own power department; it has acquired long-term capacity for supplying power by investing in a building and equipment (resources acquired in advance). The plant also acquires fuel to produce power as needed (resources acquired as needed). The cost of the building and equipment is independent of the kilowatt-hours produced, but the cost of fuel increases as the demand for kilowatt-hours increases. The activity of supplying power has both a fixed cost component and a variable cost component, using kilowatt-hours as the output measure.

What the Accounting Records Reveal Sometimes it is easy to identify the variable and fixed components of a mixed cost, as in the example in Example 3.1 for the sales representatives. Many times, however, the only information available is the total cost of an activity and a measure of output (the variables Y and X). For example, the accounting system will usually record both the total cost of the maintenance activity for a given period and the number of maintenance hours provided during that period. The accounting records do not reveal the fixed and variable components of total maintenance cost.

Need for Cost Separation Since accounting records typically show only the total cost and the associated output of a mixed cost item, it is necessary to separate the total cost into its fixed and variable components. Only through a formal effort to separate costs can they be classified into the appropriate cost behavior categories. The next two sections describe ways of separating costs into fixed and variable components.

METHODS OF DETERMINING COST BEHAVIOR

In practice, companies use a variety of methods of estimating costs. Among these methods are the industrial engineering method, the account analysis method, and a variety of quantitative and statistical methods. The best cost estimators are individuals who thoroughly understand the process, the cost drivers, and the degree of variability between the driver, the activity, and the cost.

The **industrial engineering method** is a forward-looking method of determining, through physical observation and analysis, just what activities, in what amounts, are needed to complete a process. Time and motion studies may be used in conjunction with this method. Industrial engineers may literally stand behind production workers with a stop watch to determine precisely how many minutes it takes to produce a unit of product. Once completed, the engineering studies are very precise. They are expensive to implement, however, and seldom updated once they are done. This method is most frequently used for manufacturing processes where there is a direct link between materials and labor inputs with the output. An advantage of engineering methods is that they can be applied to new processes and designs. Industrial engineers determine the amount of each direct material needed and the amount of labor time each process will take. Then accountants and purchasing specialists can apply the appropriate unit costs. While this method is useful in determining the cost of manufactured items, where the process stays the same from unit to unit, it is less useful in services where different customers or circumstances may require varying amounts of time and types of service.

The **account analysis method** can be used to estimate costs by classifying accounts in the general ledger as fixed, variable, or mixed. In practice, accounts are usually put into either the fixed or variable category based on the predominant nature of the costs in the individual account. This method is often used in practice because it is simple and straightforward to apply. Accountants with a good knowledge of the cost behavior of the various accounts can create credible cost functions using the approach. As an alternative, some accountants have set up subaccounts in the chart of accounts that are designed to separate relatively fixed from relatively variable cost categories. If costs in each account are predominantly of one of the two types, this method will give reasonable results.

To use the account analysis method, the accountant uses judgment and experience to separate the accounts into two categories—fixed and variable. Once the fixed categories are known, the average monthly cost can be computed and this is the fixed amount. The variable categories need to be further separated into categories according to the driver the accountant wishes to associate with the account. For example, accounts that are variable with respect to direct labor hours can be separated, their average costs determined, and then that total divided by the average amount of direct labor hours to obtain the variable rate per direct labor hour. Similarly, accounts driven by machine hours, purchase orders, etc., can be averaged and then divided by their average amount of driver to obtain the rates. **Example 3.3** shows how the account analysis method can be used to separate fixed and variable costs, determine a cost function, and use that cost function in budgeting.

EXAMPLE 3.3

The HOW and WHY of Using Account Analysis to Determine Fixed and Variable Costs

Information:
The controller for Morrisey Company wants to determine the cost behavior of factory overhead. Based on observation and discussions with plant workers, she feels that five accounts are most relevant. Two are fixed—supervisory salaries and depreciation—and the remaining three are variable. Indirect labor is primarily used to move materials and varies with number of moves. The largest component of utilities is electricity to run production machinery, which is driven by machine hours. Purchasing seems to be driven by the number of purchase orders. The accounts and their balances for the past six months are as shown on the following page.

EXAMPLE 3.3

(Continued)

	Indirect Labor Cost	Utilities	Purchasing	Supervisory Salaries	Plant and Equipment Depreciation
July	$ 14,250	$12,000	$ 38,200	$ 20,000	$ 6,500
August	15,800	10,600	35,400	23,000	6,500
September	16,800	12,500	37,600	32,000	6,500
October	20,700	12,500	40,200	27,800	6,500
November	20,000	12,500	39,900	25,400	6,500
December	17,000	12,500	39,700	17,000	6,500
Total	$104,550	$72,600	$231,000	$145,200	$39,000

Information on machine hours, number of moves, and number of purchase orders for the six-month period follows:

	Number of Moves	Machine Hours (Mhr)	Purchase Orders (PO)
July	340	5,400	250
August	380	5,200	300
September	400	5,800	450
October	500	6,200	380
November	480	6,000	340
December	420	5,600	200
Total	2,520	34,200	1,920

> **Why:**
> By separating accounts with primarily fixed costs from those with primarily variable costs, and associating the variable costs with relevant drivers, it is possible to determine cost behavior and use it in budgeting, performance evaluation, and decision making.

Required:

1. Why did the controller decide that supervisory salaries and depreciation on the plant were fixed?

2. Calculate the average account balances for each of the five accounts. Calculate the average monthly amount of each of the three drivers.

3. Calculate the total fixed overhead for the month and the variable rates for indirect labor, utilities, and purchasing. Express the results in the form of an equation for total overhead cost.

4. In January, 490 moves, 4,375 machine hours, and 220 purchase orders are expected. What is the total overhead cost expected for the factory in January?

5. *What if* purchase orders predicted for January were 300? How would that affect the predicted overhead cost?

Solution:

1. Clearly, depreciation is fixed at $6,500 per month, and will not change unless equipment is bought or sold. While supervisory salaries did change during the six-month period, they were no doubt placed in the fixed category because they do not vary with the drivers under consideration: number of moves, machine hours, and purchase orders.

EXAMPLE 3.3

(Continued)

2.   Average indirect labor cost = $104,550/6 = $17,425
Average utilities = $72,600/6 = $12,100
Average purchasing = $231,000/6 = $38,500
Average supervisory salaries = $145,200/6 = $24,200
Average depreciation = $39,000/6 = $6,500
Average number of moves = 2,520/6 = 420
Average machine hours = 34,200/6 = 5,700
Average purchase orders = 1,920/6 = 320

3.   Total fixed overhead cost = $24,200 + $6,500 = $30,700
Variable rate for indirect labor = $17,425/420 = $41.49 per move (rounded)
Variable rate for utilities = $12,100/5,700 = $2.12 per Mhr (rounded)
Variable rate for purchasing = $38,500/320 = $120.31 per PO (rounded)
Total overhead cost = $30,700 + $41.49 (moves) + $2.12 (machine
hours) + 120.31 (purchase orders)

4.   Total overhead cost = $30,700 + ($41.49 × 490) + ($2.12 × 4,375)
+ ($120.31 × 220) = $86,773 (rounded)

5.   If purchase orders increase by 80, then predicted January overhead cost would increase by $9,624.80 ($120.31 × 80) to a total of $96,398 (rounded).

The industrial engineering method and the account analysis method are judgment-based methods of determining cost behavior. Quantitative methods also exist that rely on past data to generate a linear model that describes the variable and fixed portions of a cost. These are described in the next section.

OBJECTIVE 4

Separate mixed costs into their fixed and variable components using the high-low method, the scatterplot method, and the method of least squares.

QUANTITATIVE METHODS FOR SEPARATING MIXED COSTS INTO FIXED AND VARIABLE COMPONENTS

The three widely used quantitative methods of separating a mixed cost into its fixed and variable components are the high-low method, the scatterplot method, and the method of least squares. Each method requires us to make the simplifying assumption of a linear cost relationship. Therefore, before we examine each of these methods more closely, let's review the expression of cost as an equation for a straight line from Example 3.1.

$$Y = F + VX$$

where

Y = Total cost (the dependent variable)
F = Fixed cost component (the intercept parameter)
V = Variable cost per unit (the slope parameter)
X = Measure of output (the independent variable)

The **dependent variable** is a variable whose value depends on the value of another variable. In the preceding equation, total cost is the dependent variable; it is the cost we are trying to predict. The **independent variable** is a variable that measures output and explains changes in the cost. It is an activity driver. A good independent variable causes or is closely associated with the dependent variable. The **intercept parameter** corresponds to fixed cost. Graphically, the intercept parameter is the point at which the mixed cost line intercepts the cost (vertical) axis. The **slope parameter** corresponds to the variable cost per unit of output. Graphically, this represents the slope of the mixed cost line.

Since the accounting records reveal only X and Y, those values must be used to estimate the parameters F and V. With estimates of F and V, the fixed and variable components can be estimated, and the behavior of the mixed cost can be predicted as output changes.

Three methods will be described for estimating F and V: the high-low method, the scatter-plot method, and the method of least squares. The same data will be used with each method so that comparisons among them can be made. In the example, the plant manager for Anderson Company wants to determine the fixed and variable components of materials handling costs. He believes that the number of material moves is a good driver for the activity. Data for 10 months of materials handling costs and number of material moves are given in **Example 3.4**.

<table>
<tr><td colspan="2">

Information:

Anderson Company had the following 10 months of data on materials handling cost and number of moves:

</td><td>

EXAMPLE 3.4

</td></tr>
</table>

Month	Materials Handling Cost	Number of Moves
January	$2,000	100
February	3,090	125
March	2,780	175
April	1,990	200
May	7,500	500
June	5,300	300
July	4,300	250
August	6,300	400
September	5,600	475
October	6,240	425

The HOW and WHY of Using the High-Low Method to Determine Fixed Cost and Variable Rate

Why:
The high-low method gives managers a quick way of estimating cost behavior. Only two data points are needed, the high and low activity points, so this method is especially easy for companies without a long history.

Required:

1. Determine the high point and the low point.

2. Calculate the variable rate for materials handling based on the number of moves.

3. Calculate the fixed monthly cost of materials handling.

4. Write the cost formula for the materials handling activity showing the fixed cost and the variable rate.

5. If Anderson Company estimates that November will have 350 moves, what is the total estimated materials handling cost for that month?

6. *What if* Anderson wants to estimate materials handling cost for the coming year and expects 3,940 moves? What will estimated total materials handling cost be? What is the total fixed materials handling cost? Why doesn't it equal the fixed cost calculated in Requirement?

EXAMPLE 3.4

(Continued)

Solution:

1. The high number of moves is in May, and the low number of moves in January. *(Hint:* Did you notice that the low cost of $1,990 was for April, yet April is not the low point because its number of moves is not the lowest activity level?)

2. Variable rate = (High cost − Low cost)/(High moves − Low moves)
   = ($7,500 − $2,000)/(500 − 100) = $5,500/400
   = $13.75 per move

3. Fixed cost = Total cost − (Variable rate × Moves)
   Let's choose the high point with cost of $7,500 and 500 moves.
   Fixed cost = $7,500 − ($13.75 × 500)
      = $625
   (Hint: Check your work by computing fixed cost using the low point.)

4. If the variable rate is $13.75 per move and fixed cost is $625 per month, then the formula for monthly materials handling cost is Total materials handling cost = $625 + ($13.75 × Moves).

5. Materials handling cost = $625 + $13.75(350) = $5,437.50

6. Materials handling cost for the year = 12($625) + $13.75(3,940)

   = $7,500 + $54,175 = $61,675

   The fixed cost for the year is 12 times the fixed cost for the month. Thus, instead of $625, the yearly fixed cost is $7,500.

The High-Low Method

Basic geometry tells us that two points determine a line. F, the fixed cost component, is the intercept of the total cost line, and V, the variable cost per unit, is the slope of the line. Given two points, the slope and the intercept can be determined. The **high-low method** preselects the two points that are used to compute the parameters F and V. The *high point* is defined as the point with the *highest output or driver level.* The *low point* is defined as the point with the *lowest output or driver level.* Note that the high and low points are determined by the independent variable, not the dependent (typically cost) variable. Example 3.4 shows how and why the high-low method can be used to determine the fixed cost and variable rate.

Notice that the last requirement of Example 3.4 asks us to compute the materials handling cost for the year, not for a month. Since monthly data were used to determine the cost formula, fixed cost must be multiplied by 12 to get the fixed cost for the year instead of the month. If the materials handling cost for the quarter were desired, then fixed cost would be multiplied by three (the number of months in a quarter). If weekly data had been used to determine the cost formula, the fixed cost for the year would be the weekly fixed cost multiplied by 52, the number of weeks in a year.

The high-low method has two advantages. First, it is objective. That is, any two people using the high-low method on a particular data set will arrive at the same answer. Second, it is simple to calculate. The high-low method allows a manager to get a quick fix on a cost relationship using only two data points. For example, a manager may have only two years of data. Sometimes, this will be enough to get a crude approximation of the cost relationship.

The high-low method is usually not as good as the other methods for two reasons. First, the high or low points can be what are known as outliers, representing atypical cost-activity relationships. If so, the cost formula computed using these two points will not represent what usually takes place. The **scatterplot method** can help a manager avoid this trap by selecting two points that appear to be representative of the general cost-activity pattern. Second, even if these points are not outliers, other pairs of points may clearly be more representative. Again, the scatterplot method allows the choice of the more representative points.

   An important point must be made regarding the estimates of fixed and variable costs yielded by the high-low method. These estimates should "look reasonable" to the cost analyst. For example, suppose that the high-low method returns a negative fixed cost estimate. That cannot be right; a negative fixed cost implies that a zero amount of the driver would result in revenue to the company. This is another reason that the scatterplot method can be useful. Perhaps the high or the low point is an outlier, such that the line drawn through it is very different from a line that would be drawn if the outlier were thrown out and the second-highest (or lowest) point were selected.

Scatterplot Method

The first step in applying the scatterplot method is to plot the data points so that the relationship between materials handling costs and activity output can be seen. This plot is referred to as a **scattergraph** and is shown in Exhibit 3.8, Graph A. The vertical axis is total activity cost (materials handling cost), and the horizontal axis is the driver or output measure (number of moves). Looking at Exhibit 3.8, Graph A, we see that the relationship between materials handling costs and number of moves is reasonably linear; cost goes up as the number of moves goes up, and vice versa.

   Now let's examine Exhibit 3.8, Graph B, to see if the line determined by the high and low points is representative of the overall relationship. It does look relatively representative. Does that mean that the high-low line should be chosen? Not necessarily. Suppose that management believes the variable costs of materials handling will go down in the near future. In that case, the high-low line gives a somewhat higher variable cost (slope) than desired. The scatterplot line will be chosen with a shallower slope.

   Thus, one purpose of a scattergraph is to assess the validity of the assumed linear relationship. Additionally, inspecting the scattergraph may reveal several points that do not seem to fit the general pattern of behavior. Upon investigation, it may be discovered that these points (the outliers) were due to some irregular occurrences. This knowledge can provide justification for their elimination and perhaps lead to a better estimate of the underlying cost function.

   A scattergraph can provide insight concerning the relationship between cost and output by allowing one to visually fit a line to the points on the scattergraph. In doing so, the line should appear to best fit the points. In making that choice, a cost analyst is free to use past experience with the behavior of the cost item. Experience may provide the analyst with a good intuitive sense of how materials handling costs behave; the scattergraph then becomes a useful tool to quantify this intuition. Fitting a line to the points in this way is how the scatterplot method works. Keep in mind that the scattergraph and the other statistical aids are tools that help managers improve their judgment. Using the tools does not prevent the manager from using his or her own judgment to alter any of the estimates produced by formal methods.

   Examine Exhibit 3.8, Graph A, carefully. Based only on the information contained in the graph, how would you fit a line to the points in it? Of course, there are an infinite number of lines that might go through the data, but let's choose one that goes through the point for January (100, $2,000) and intersects the y-axis at $800. Now, we have the straight line shown in Exhibit 3.8, Graph C. The fixed cost is the intercept, $800. The high-low method can be used to determine the variable rate.

   The two chosen points are (100, $2,000) and (0, $800). These two points are used to compute the slope:

$$V = (Y_2 - Y_1)/(X_2 - X_1)$$
$$= (\$2{,}000 - \$800)/(100 - 0)$$
$$= \$1{,}200/100$$
$$= \$12$$

Exhibit 3.8

Scattergraph for Anderson Company's Materials Handling Costs

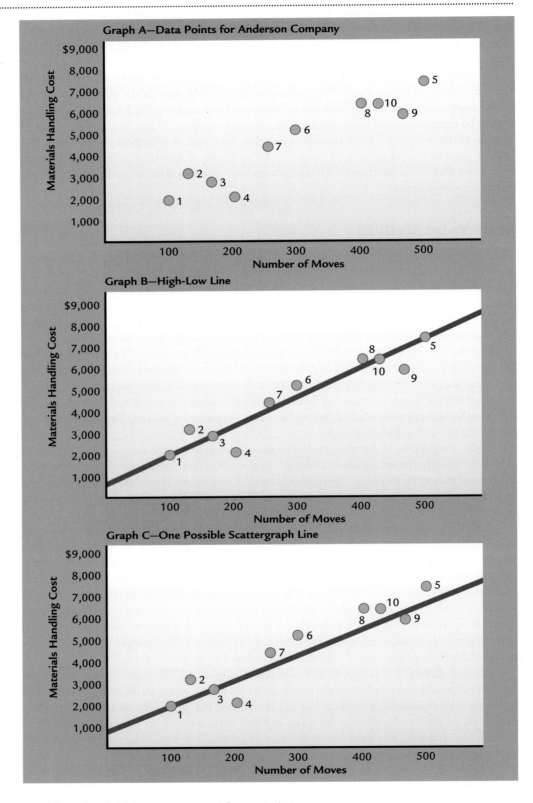

Thus, the variable cost per material move is $12.

The fixed and variable components of the materials handling cost have now been identified. The cost formula for the materials handling activity can be expressed as:

$$Y = \$800 + \$12X$$

Using this formula, the total cost of materials handling for moves between 100 and 500 can be predicted and then broken down into fixed and variable components. Assume that 350 moves are planned for November. Using the cost formula, the predicted cost is $5,000 [$800 + ($12 × 350)]. Of this total cost, $800 is fixed, and $4,200 is variable.

A significant advantage of the scatterplot method is that it allows a cost analyst to inspect the data visually. Exhibit 3.9 illustrates cost behavior situations that are not appropriate for the simple application of the high-low method. Graph A shows a nonlinear relationship between cost and output. An example of this is a volume discount given on direct materials or evidence of learning by workers (e.g., as more hours are worked, the total cost increases at a decreasing rate

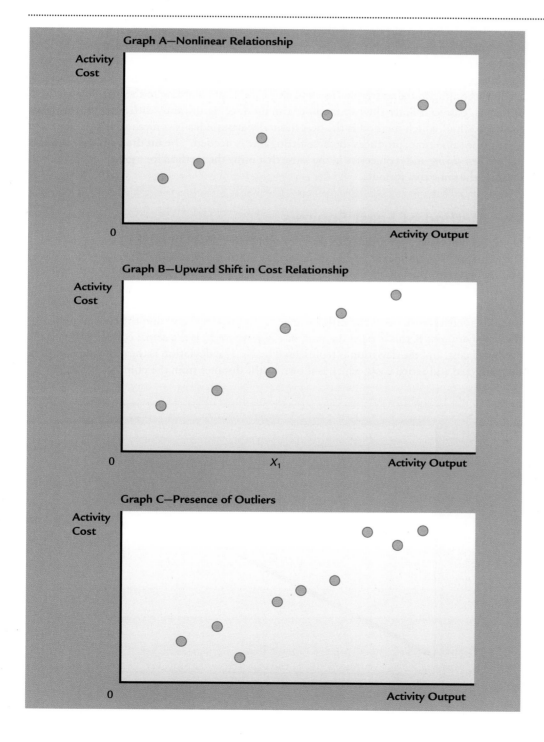

Exhibit 3.9

Scattergraphs for Various Cost Behavior Patterns

due to the increased efficiency of the workers). Graph B shows an upward shift in cost if more than X_1 units are made—perhaps due to the costs of paying an additional supervisor or running a second shift. Graph C shows outliers that do not represent the overall cost relationship.

The cost formula for materials handling was obtained by fitting a line to two points [(0, $800) and (100, $2,000)] in Exhibit 3.8, Graph C. We used our judgment to select the line. Whereas one person may decide that the best-fitting line is the one passing through those two points, others, using their own judgment, may decide that the best line passes through other pairs of points.

The scatterplot method suffers from the lack of any objective criterion for choosing the best-fitting line. The quality of the cost formula depends on the quality of the subjective judgment of the analyst. The high-low method removes the subjectivity in the choice of the line. Regardless of who uses the method, the same line will result.

Looking again at Exhibit 3.8, Graphs B and C, we can compare the results of the scatterplot method with those of the high-low method. There is a difference between the fixed cost components and the variable rates. The predicted materials handling cost for 350 moves is $5,000 according to the scatterplot method and $5,437.50 according to the high-low method. Which is "correct"? Since the two methods can produce significantly different cost formulas, the question of which method is the best naturally arises. Ideally, a method that is objective and, at the same time, produces the best-fitting line is needed. The **method of least squares** defines *best-fitting* and is objective in the sense that using the method for a given set of data will produce the same cost formula.

The Method of Least Squares

Up to this point, we have alluded to the concept of a line that best fits the points shown on a scattergraph. What is meant by a best-fitting line? Intuitively, it is the line to which the data points are closest. But what is meant by closest?

Consider Exhibit 3.10. Here, an arbitrary line ($Y = F + VX$) has been drawn. The closeness of each point to the line can be measured by the vertical distance of the point from the line. This vertical distance is the difference between the actual cost and the cost predicted by the line. For point 8, this is $E_8 = Y_8 - (F + VX_8)$, where Y_8 is the actual cost, $F + VX_8$ is the predicted cost, and the deviation is represented by E_8. The **deviation** is the difference between the predicted and actual costs, which is shown by the distance from the point to the line.

Exhibit 3.10

Deviations of Data from a Line

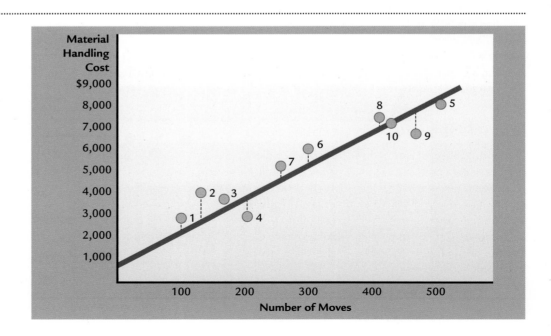

The vertical distance measures the closeness of a single point to the line, but we really need a measure of closeness of *all* points to the line. One possibility is to add all the single measures to obtain an overall measure. However, since the single measures can be positive or negative, this overall measure may not be very meaningful. For example, the sum of small positive deviations could result in an overall measure greater in magnitude than the sum of large positive deviations and large negative deviations because of the cancelling effect of positive and negative numbers. To correct this problem, each single measure of closeness is first squared, and then these squared deviations are summed as the overall measure of closeness. Squaring the deviations avoids the cancellation problem caused by a mix of positive and negative numbers.

To illustrate this concept, a measure of closeness will be calculated for the cost formula produced by the scatterplot method for Anderson Company's materials handling costs.

Actual Cost	Predicted Cost[a]	Deviation[b]	Deviation Squared
$2,000	$2,000	0	0
3,090	2,300	790	624,100
2,780	2,900	−120	14,400
1,990	3,200	−1,210	1,464,100
7,500	6,800	700	490,000
5,300	4,400	900	810,000
4,300	3,800	500	250,000
6,300	5,600	700	490,000
5,600	6,500	−900	810,000
6,240	5,900	340	115,600
Total measure of closeness			5,068,200

[a] Predicted cost = $800 + $12X, where X is the actual measure of activity output associated with the actual activity cost and cost is rounded to the nearest dollar.

[b] Deviation = Actual cost — Predicted cost.

Since the measure of closeness is the sum of the squared deviations of the points from the line, the smaller the measure, the better the line fits the points. For example, the scatterplot method line has a closeness measure of 5,068,200. A similar calculation produces a closeness measure of 5,402,013 for the high-low line. Thus, the scatterplot line fits the points better than the high-low line. This outcome supports the earlier claim that the use of judgment in the scatterplot method is superior to the high-low method.

In principle, comparing closeness measures can produce a ranking of all lines from best to worst. The line that fits the points better than any other line is called the *bestfitting line.* It is the line with the smallest (least) sum of squared deviations. The method of least squares identifies the best-fitting line. We rely on statistical theory to obtain the formulas that produce the best-fitting line.

Using Regression Programs

Computing the regression formula manually is tedious, even with only a few data points. As the number of data points increases, manual computation becomes impractical. (When multiple regression is used, manual computation is virtually impossible.) Fortunately, spreadsheet packages such as Alteryx, JMP, Microsoft Excel, Minitab, and R have regression routines that will perform the computations. All that you need to do is input the data. The spreadsheet regression program supplies more than the estimates of the coefficients. It also provides information that can be used to see how reliable the cost equation is, a feature that is not available for the scatterplot and high-low methods.

Exhibit 3.11

Spreadsheet Data for Anderson Company's Materials Handling Cost

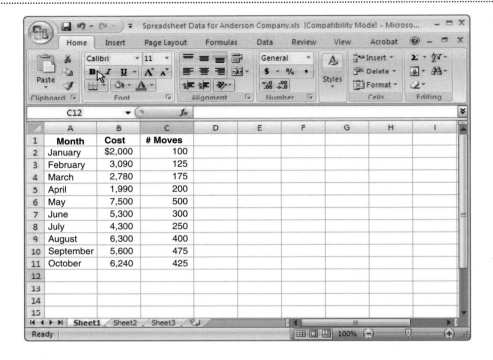

The first step in using the computer to calculate regression coefficients is to enter the data. Exhibit 3.11 shows the computer screen you would see if you entered the Anderson Company monthly data on materials handling cost and number of moves into a spreadsheet. It is a good idea to label your variables as is done in the exhibit: the months are labeled in column A, column B is labeled for materials handling cost, and column C is labeled for the number of moves. The next step is to run the regression. In Excel the regression routine is located under the "Tools" menu (toward the top left of the screen). When you pull down the "Tools" menu, you will see a number of menu possibilities. If you see "Data Analysis" just click on that and then click on "Regression." (If you don't see "Data Analysis," then choose "Add-Ins" and then select "Analysis ToolPak," which will add the data analysis tools. When the data analysis tools have been added, "Data Analysis" will appear at the bottom of the "Tools" menu; click on "Data Analysis," and then "Regression.")

When the "Regression" screen pops up, you can tell the program where the dependent and independent variables are located. In the box labeled "Input Y Range," place the cursor at the beginning of the rectangle, click, and then (again using the cursor) block the values under the dependent variable column, in this case, cells b2 through b11. Then, move the cursor to the beginning of the box for the "Input X Range," click, and block the values in cells c2 through c11. Finally, you need to tell the computer where to place the output. You can choose to put it on a separate worksheet or on the current worksheet. Let's assume you are going to save the output to the current worksheet. Click on the radio button by your choice, and then, using your cursor, block a nice-sized rectangle—for example, cells a13 through f20—and click on "OK." In less than the blink of an eye, the regression output is complete. The regression output is shown in Exhibit 3.12.

Example 3.5 takes the results of the regression program and uses them to construct a cost formula. That cost formula can then be used to determine the predicted cost given an estimate of the independent variable.

Exhibit 3.12

Regression Results for Anderson Company's Materials Handling Cost

	A	B	C	D	E	F	G
1	SUMMARY OUTPUT						
2	Regression Statistics						
3	Multiple R	0.928949080					
4	R Square	0.862946394					
5	Adjusted R Square	0.845814693					
6							
7	Square						
8	Standard Error	770.4987038					
9	Observations	10					
10							
11	ANOVA						
12		df	SS	MS	F	Significance F	
13	Regression	1	29903853.98	29903853.98	50.37132077	0.000102268	
14	Residual	8	4749346.021	593668.2526			
15	Total	9	34653200				
16							
17							
18		Coefficients	Standard Error	t Stat	P-value		
19	Intercept	854.4993582	569.7810263	1.499697811	0.172079925		
20	X Variable 1	12.3915276	1.745955536	7.097275588	0.000102268		
21							
22							
23							
24							

EXAMPLE 3.5

The HOW and WHY of Using the Regression Results for Fixed Cost and Variable Rate to Construct and Use a Cost Formula

Information:

Anderson Company had 10 months of data on materials handling cost and number of moves, as shown in Example 3.4. Regression was run on these data and the coefficients shown by the regression program results in Exhibit 3.12 are:

Intercept	854.4994
X variable 1	12.39153

Why:

Regression gives the best linear unbiased estimates of the intercept and slope for a set of data points. These can be used to find the fixed cost and variable rate in a cost scenario, and can be used to predict cost for a given amount of the independent variable.

Required:

1. Construct the cost formula for the materials handling activity showing the fixed cost and the variable rate.

2. If Anderson Company estimates that November will have 350 moves, what is the total estimated materials handling cost for that month?

3. *What if* Anderson wants to estimate materials handling cost for the coming year and expects 3,940 moves? What will estimated total materials handling cost be? What is the total fixed materials handling cost? Why doesn't it equal the fixed cost calculated in Requirement 2?

EXAMPLE 3.5

(Continued)

Solution:

1. Rounding the regression estimates to the nearest cent, the formula for monthly materials handling cost is as follows:

    Total materials handling cost = $854.50 + ($12.39 × Moves)

2. Materials handling cost = $854.50 + $12.39(350) = $5,191

3. Materials handling cost for the year = 12($854.50) + $12.39(3,940)

    $$= \$10,254 + \$48,816.60 = \$59,070.60$$

    The fixed cost for the year is 12 times the fixed cost for the month. Thus, instead of $854.50, the yearly fixed cost is $10,254.

Since the regression cost formula is the best-fitting line, it should produce better predictions of materials handling costs than either the high-low or scatterplot methods. From Example 3.5 for 350 moves, the estimate predicted by the least-squares line is $5,191 [$854.50 + ($12.39 × 350)], with a fixed component of $854.50 plus a variable component of $4,336.50. Using this prediction as a standard, the scatterplot line most closely approximates the least-squares line.

While the computer output in Exhibit 3.12 can give us the fixed and variable cost coefficients, its major usefulness lies in its ability to provide information about the reliability of the estimated cost formula.

OBJECTIVE **5**

Evaluate the reliability of the cost formula.

RELIABILITY OF COST FORMULAS

Regression routines provide information to help assess the reliability of the estimated cost formula. This is a feature not provided by either the scatterplot or high-low methods. Exhibit 3.12 serves as the point of reference for discussing three statistical assessments concerning the cost formula's reliability: *hypothesis test of cost parameters*, *goodness of fit*, and *confidence intervals*. The **hypothesis test of cost parameters** indicates whether the parameters are different from zero. For our setting, **goodness of fit** measures the degree of association between cost and activity output. This measure is important because the method of least squares identifies the best-fitting line, but it does not reveal how good the fit is. The best-fitting line may not be a good-fitting line. It may perform miserably when it comes to predicting costs. A confidence interval provides a range of values for the actual cost with a prespecified degree of confidence. Confidence intervals allow managers to predict a range of values instead of a single prediction. Of course, if the degree of association is perfect, then the confidence interval will consist of a single point and the actual cost will always coincide with the predicted cost. Thus, goodness of fit and confidence intervals are related, and they provide cost analysts some idea of how reliable the resulting cost equation is.

Hypothesis Test of Parameters

Refer once again to Exhibit 3.12. The fourth column of the bottom table, labeled "*t* Stat," presents the *t* statistics for each parameter. These *t* statistics are used to test the hypothesis that the parameters are different from zero. The fifth column, labeled "*P*-value," is the level of significance achieved. Generally, a *P*-value of 0.05 or less is needed for significance (to feel comfortable that the independent variable is indeed strongly associated with the dependent variable). The fixed cost parameter, the intercept, is significant at the 0.172 level. This is NOT significant at the 0.05 or even the 0.10 levels. Thus, the presence of fixed materials handling costs is questionable. The variable cost parameter is significant at the 0.0001 level, so the number of moves appears to be a highly significant explanatory variable—a good driver for materials handling costs. If the number of moves had been nonsignificant as well, then we would try to find another, better, independent variable to explain materials handling costs. The third column presents the standard error for each parameter. This value is used to compute the t statistic in column 4: the coefficient in column 2 is divided by the corresponding standard error.

Goodness of Fit Measures

Initially, we assume that a single activity driver (activity output variable) explains changes (variability) in activity cost. Our experience with the Anderson Company example suggests that the number of moves can explain changes in materials handling costs. The scattergraph shown back in Exhibit 3.8 confirms this belief because it reveals that materials handling cost and output (as measured by the number of moves) seem to move together. It is quite likely that a significant percentage of the total variability in cost is explained by our activity output variable.

The percentage of variability in the dependent variable explained by an independent variable (in this case, a measure of activity output) is called the **coefficient of determination** **(R^2)**. The higher the percentage of cost variability explained, the better job the independent variable does of explaining the dependent variable. Since R^2 is the percentage of variability explained, it always has a value between 0 and 1.00.

In the printout in Exhibit 3.12, there are two measures of R^2. They are "R Square" and "Adjusted R Square." Typically, we use the Adjusted R Square because this value has been adjusted for the number of variables included in the equation.[8] The value for Adjusted R Square is 0.85 (rounded), which means that 85 percent of the variability in the materials handling cost is explained by the number of moves. How good is this result? There is no cut-off point for a good versus a bad coefficient of determination. Clearly, the closer R^2 is to 1.00, the better. Is 85 percent good enough? How about 73 percent? Or even 46 percent? It depends. A cost equation with a coefficient of determination of 75 percent has an independent variable that explains three-fourths of the variability in cost. However, some other factor or combination of factors explains the remaining one-fourth. Depending on your tolerance for error, you may want to improve the equation by trying different independent variables (for example, materials handling hours worked rather than number of moves) or by trying multiple independent variables (or multiple regression, which is explained in a succeeding section of this chapter). As with almost any quantitative result, the particular context should be considered in interpreting its meaning and effect on subsequent decisions. For example, Apple management likely interprets an R^2 of .60 much differently on a first generation product than it would for a mature product that has been through numerous design, production, sales, and servicing cycles.

In summary, the computer output in Exhibit 3.12 shows that the fixed cost coefficient is not significant, and the R^2 for materials handling cost is 0.85. Anderson Company may want to consider other variables and perhaps use multiple regression.

Coefficient of Correlation   An alternative measure of goodness of fit is the **coefficient of correlation (r)**, which is the square root of the coefficient of determination when there is one independent variable. Since square roots can be negative, the value of the coefficient of correlation can range between −1 and +1. If the coefficient of correlation is positive, then the two variables (in the Anderson example, materials handling cost and number of moves) move together in the same direction; they are positively correlated. Perfect positive correlation would yield a value of 1.00 for the coefficient of correlation. If the coefficient of correlation is negative, then the two variables move in a predictable fashion but in opposite directions. Perfect negative correlation would yield a coefficient of correlation of −1.00. A coefficient of correlation value close to zero indicates no correlation. That is, knowledge of the movement of one variable gives us no clue as to the movement of the other variable. Exhibit 3.13 illustrates the concept of correlation.

---

8   Increasing the number of independent variables in the equation leads to an ever-increasing value of R Square. Therefore, the R Square value ideally should be adjusted for the number of variables in order to retain its meaning.

Exhibit 3.13

Correlation Illustrated

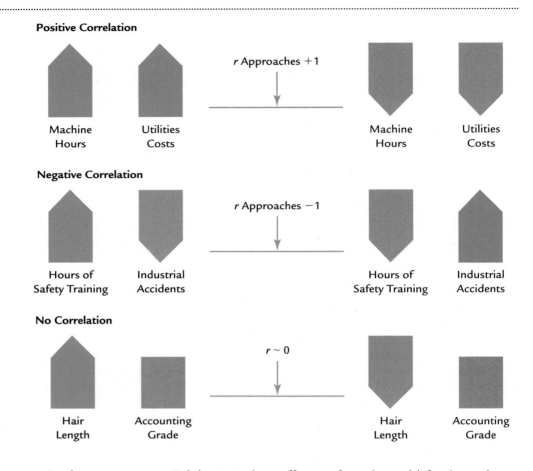

Positive Correlation

Machine Hours   Utilities Costs   *r* Approaches +1   Machine Hours   Utilities Costs

Negative Correlation

Hours of Safety Training   Industrial Accidents   *r* Approaches −1   Hours of Safety Training   Industrial Accidents

No Correlation

Hair Length   Accounting Grade   *r* ~ 0   Hair Length   Accounting Grade

Looking once again at Exhibit 3.12, the coefficient of correlation (r) for the Anderson Company example is given by "Multiple R" and is 0.929. Notice that r is the positive square root of R^2, computed previously. The square root is positive because the correlation between X and Y is positive. In other words, as the number of moves increases, the materials handling cost increases. This positive correlation is reflected by a positive value for V, the variable rate. If cost decreases as activity output increases, then the coefficient of correlation (and the value of V) is negative. The sign of V reveals the sign of the coefficient of correlation. The very high positive correlation between materials handling cost and the number of moves indicates that the number of moves represents a good choice for an activity driver.

Standard Errors

Goodness of fit can be further analyzed using the standard error of the regression and the standard errors of the estimates. Put simply, the standard error of the regression tells how tightly the data points cluster around the regression line. A smaller standard error indicates that the regression line more closely approximates the data. A larger standard error indicates the opposite and may be cause to search for more and better independent variables.

The Anderson Company regression results in Exhibit 3.12 show a standard error of the regression of $771 (rounded). What does this mean? On average, the actual cost of moving materials and the predicted cost differ by $771. The average monthly cost of moving materials is $4,510. Thus, a standard error of $771 seems large. A smaller standard error would give Anderson Company more confidence in the predicted value of moving costs. This may encourage the company to search for more and/or better independent variables.

Now we consider the standard errors of the estimated coefficients. From Exhibit 3.12, we see that the standard error for the independent variable, machine hours, is 1.75 compared with the coefficient of 12.39. We can test to see if the 12.39 is significantly different from zero by constructing a confidence interval around it. For a 95 percent degree of confidence, the t statistic is 2.306, and the confidence interval is $12.39 \pm (2.306 \times 1.75)$, or at 95 percent confidence, the true value of the coefficient of machine hours lies in the range of 8.3545 to 16.4255. We can say that it is likely that machine hours do affect materials handling cost. For the intercept term, however, the range is far larger. At a 95 percent confidence level, the range is $854 \pm (2.306 \times 570)$ or -460.42 to 2,168.42. This range does include zero, and we cannot be reasonably confident that the coefficient on the intercept term, fixed cost, is significantly different from zero.

**DATA
ANALYTICS**

Big Data and Sustainability—Using Smart Meters to Decrease Electrical Usage and CO_2 Emissions

Within the United States, almost 100 million utility meters (or half of all meters) have been switched from analog meters (the ones with the dials that whirl around madly every time you turn on the air conditioning) to smart meters. Smart meters are digital meters that connect people's houses with the electric grid. They have a number of features, including remote sensing, direct real-time communication with the utility company, the ability to adjust a house's electrical use during peak hours, and finally, the ability for individuals to switch energy suppliers without interrupting service.

Remote sensing means that a meter reader no longer has to stop and walk up to each house, mark down the reading, and then report to the utility. Instead, a utility vehicle travels slowly up and down streets taking readings remotely from each meter. Alternatively, if the smart meter is directly connected to the utility, no reader is needed at all. The meter "reports" directly to the utility every 15 to 30 minutes throughout the day. This capability produces vast amounts of data that the utility can use to determine oncoming peak usage, not to mention adjusting bills to reflect peak usage amounts.

One of the most important aspects of smart meters is that consumers may be able to log onto the utility's website to view their own electrical usage. The system allows individuals to view their hourly electric and daily gas energy usage, so they can see how much energy they use over the course of a day or a week. They can then use that information to adjust behavioral patterns of electrical usage and exercise greater control of electrical consumption. For example, running the dishwasher in the middle of the night rather than during peak usage evening hours. To the extent that utilities begin pricing electrical usage according to the time of day used, consumers' identification of their own peak usage can lead them to direct non–time-dependent electrical needs to off-peak hours. Of course, this also can lead to overall higher bills as some peak usage needs must occur during peak hours (e.g., air conditioning must occur during daylight hours and less so in the middle of the night).

The bottom line is that big data can be used to allow individuals to hone in on their own electrical usage and, to the extent possible and desired, decrease usage and carbon dioxide (CO_2) emissions. By viewing electrical usage frequently, what used to look like a fairly fixed cost for users can be seen to be more variable and more controllable.

REAL-WORLD EXAMPLE

MULTIPLE REGRESSION

OBJECTIVE 6

Explain how multiple regression can be used to assess cost behavior.

In the Anderson Company example, 85 percent of the variability in materials handling cost was explained by changes in the number of moves. As a result, the company may want to search for additional explanatory variables. For example, the weight of the items moved might be useful—particularly if forklifts and other heavy machinery are needed for moving parts and products from one location to another.

In the case of two explanatory variables, the linear equation is expanded to include the additional variable:

$$Y = F + V_1X_1 + V_2X_2$$

where

$$X_1 = \text{Number of moves}$$
$$X_2 = \text{Number of pounds moved}$$

With three variables (Y, X_1, X_2), a minimum of three points is needed to compute the parameters F, V_1, and V_2. Seeing the points becomes difficult because they must be plotted in three dimensions. Using the scatterplot method or the high-low method is not practical.

However, the extension of the method of least squares is straightforward. It is relatively simple to develop a set of equations that provides values for F, V_1, and V_2 that yields the best-fitting equation. Whenever least squares is used to fit an equation involving two or more independent variables, the method is called **multiple regression**. The computations required for multiple regression are far more complex than in simple (one independent variable) regression. In fact, any practical application of multiple regression requires use of a computer.

Let's return to the Anderson Company example. Recall that the R^2 is just 85 percent and that the fixed cost coefficient was not significant. Perhaps another variable can help explain materials handling costs. Suppose that Anderson Company's controller finds that in some months many more pounds of materials were moved than in other months. The heavier materials required additional equipment to handle the increased load.

The controller adds the variable "pounds moved" and gathers information on that variable for the 10 months. These data are shown below.

Month	Materials Handling Cost	Number of Moves	Pounds Moved
January	$2,000	100	6,000
February	3,090	125	15,000
March	2,780	175	7,800
April	1,990	200	600
May	7,500	500	29,000
June	5,300	300	23,000
July	4,300	250	17,000
August	6,300	400	25,000
September	5,600	475	12,000
October	6,240	425	22,400

Multiple regression can be run using the number of moves and the number of pounds moved as the independent variables.

Running multiple regression using the Excel program is no more difficult than using it to run simple regression. Going back to Exhibit 3.11, add the data for number of pounds moved in column D. Then, proceed to run regression as explained earlier. When the box for "Input X Range" appears, click, and block the values in cells c2 through d11. This will include both independent variables. Continue with the earlier instructions. The results that pop up will look like those shown for the computer screen shown in Exhibit 3.14.

The computer screen conveys some very interesting and useful information. The cost equation is defined by the first two columns of the lowest table. The first column identifies the individual cost components. The intercept is the fixed activity cost, X Variable 1 is the number of moves (because it was in the first column, column C, of the data input for the independent variables), and X Variable 2 is the number of pounds moved (because it was in the second column, column D, of the data input for the independent variables). The column labeled "Coefficients" identifies the estimated fixed cost and the variable cost per unit for each activity driver. **Example 3.6** shows how and why to construct a cost equation using the results of multiple regression.

Exhibit 3.14

Multiple Regression Results for Anderson Company's Materials Handling Cost

	A	B	C	D	E	F	G
1	SUMMARY OUTPUT						
2	*Regression Statistics*						
3	Multiple R	0.999420					
4	R Square	0.998841					
5	Adjusted R Square	0.998509					
6							
7	Square						
8	Standard Error	75.76272					
9	Observations	10					
10							
11	ANOVA						
12		*df*	*SS*	*MS*	*F*	*Significance F*	
13	Regression	2	34613020	17306510	3015.076722	5.30799E-11	
14	Residual	7	40179.93	5739.99			
15	Total	9	34653200				
16							
17							
18		*Coefficients*	*Standard Error*	*t Stat*	*P-value*		
19	Intercept	507.3097	57.3225	8.850098	4.7575E-05		
20	*X* Variable 1	7.835162	0.234048	33.47672	5.49745E-09		
21	*X* Variable 2	0.107181	0.003742	28.64286	1.62622E-08		
22							
23							
24							

EXAMPLE 3.6

The HOW and WHY of Constructing a Cost Equation Using the Results from Multiple Regression

Information:

Anderson Company had the following 10 months of data on materials handling cost, the number of moves, and the number of pounds moved.

Coefficients shown by the regression program results in Exhibit 3.14 are:

Intercept	507.3097
X variable 1	7.835162
X variable 2	0.107181

Why:
Multiple regression works well when a dependent variable can be explained by two or more independent variables. This may increase R^2 and decrease the confidence interval around the predicted value of the dependent variable.

Required:

1. Construct the cost formula for the materials handling activity showing the fixed cost and the variable rates for the two independent variables.

2. If Anderson Company estimates that November will have 350 moves and 17,000 pounds of materials moved, what is the total estimated materials handling cost for that month?

3. *What if* Anderson wants to estimate materials handling cost for the coming year and expects 3,940 moves with a total of 204,000 pounds moved? What will estimated total materials handling cost be? What is the total fixed materials handling cost? Why doesn't it equal the fixed cost calculated in Requirement 2?

EXAMPLE 3.6

(Continued)

Solution:

1. Rounding the regression estimates to the nearest cent, the formula for monthly materials handling cost is as follows:

   Total materials handling cost = \$507.31 + (\$7.84 × Moves) + (\$0.11 × Pounds)

2. Materials handling cost = \$507.31 + (\$7.84 × 350) + (\$0.11 × 17,000)

   = \$5,121 (rounded)

3. Materials handling cost for the year

   = (12 × \$507.31) + (\$7.84 × 3,940) + (\$0.11 × 204,000)

   = \$6,087.72 + \$30,889.60 + \$22,440 = \$59,417 (rounded)

   The fixed cost for the year is 12 times the fixed cost for the month. Thus, instead of \$507.31, the yearly fixed cost is \$6,088 (rounded).

Let's take another look at Exhibit 3.14. The Adjusted R Square (coefficient of determination) is 99 percent—a significant improvement in explanatory power is achieved by adding the pounds moved variable. In addition, all three coefficients are highly significant.

For multiple regression, R^2 is usually referred to as the multiple coefficient of determination. Notice also that the standard error of estimate, S_e, is available in a multiple regression setting. The standard error is now 75.76, indicating that the data points are more tightly clustered around the regression line and that the equation is better.

Refer once again to Exhibit 3.14. Columns 4 and 5 of the lowest table present some statistical data concerning the three parameters. The fourth column presents t statistics for each of these parameters. These t statistics are used to test the hypothesis that the parameters are different from zero. The fifth column presents the level of significance achieved. All parameters are significant at the 0.0001 level. Thus, we can have some confidence that the two drivers are good predictors of materials handling cost, and that the materials handling activity has a fixed cost component. This example illustrates very clearly that multiple regression can be a useful tool for identifying the behavior of activity costs.

OBJECTIVE 7

Recognize nonlinear cost behavior, and discuss its impact on cost forecasting.

NONLINEAR COST BEHAVIOR AND THE LEARNING CURVE

As noted earlier, some cost behaviors do not follow a linear pattern. Instead, they behave in a curvilinear fashion such that total costs can change in a significant and nonlinear manner as the output level changes. Understanding all types of cost behavior is critical for accurately estimating the costs and, thus, the net income expected to result from key business decisions. Given that nonlinear cost behavior is relatively less common, but more complex, than traditional variable and fixed cost behavior, managers often struggle to identify its existence and accurately forecast such behavior. If management fails to either recognize or accurately estimate the amount of nonlinear costs at critically different output volumes, the financial outcomes of resulting decisions can be disastrous. Therefore, we examine in this section two specific types of nonlinear cost behavior.

Semi-Variable Cost Behavior

Nonlinear cost behavior also is referred to as semi-variable in nature. A **semi-variable cost** is a cost that is variable in nature, but its rate of change is not constant. As shown in Exhibit 3.15,

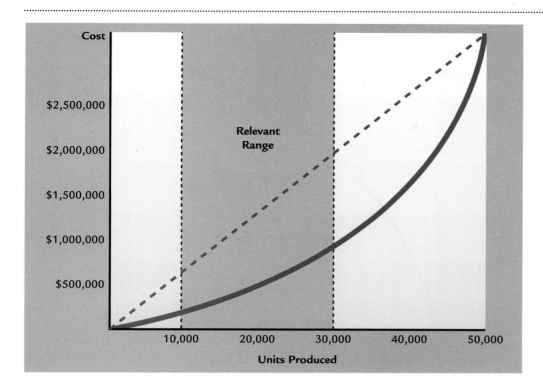

Exhibit 3.15
Semi-Variable Cost: Increasing Rate

a semi-variable cost might behave such that the total cost function is increasing at an *increasing* rate. A direct materials cost might behave in this manner when the supply of the raw material becomes increasingly scarce as the total industry output (or consumption) grows particularly large. For example, electric car battery production requires certain rare earth minerals, such as lithium and cobalt—which are extracted from relatively few geographic locations around the world—that have a per-unit cost that can increase significantly as output reaches high levels.[9] Geopolitical factors, including global trade wars, local protests around worker human rights, and environmental concerns, also can cause these rare earth mineral costs to increase at an increasing rate. When management fails to recognize that a cost behaves in this manner, total cost often is underestimated because management assumes that total cost increases at a constant rate (i.e., as a typical variable cost), when in reality total cost continues to spiral upward at an increasing rate as output increases (as shown in Exhibit 3.15). When total cost is underestimated, net income is overestimated. When actual total costs turn out to be greater than expected, and net income lower than expected, management is left to understand and explain this unexpected negative financial outcome.

Alternately, as shown in Exhibit 3.16, a semi-variable cost might behave such that the total cost function is increasing at a *decreasing* rate. An important example of this type of semi-variable cost behavior is the learning curve. The **learning curve** shows how the labor hours worked per unit decrease as the number of units produced increases. The basis of the learning curve is almost intuitive—as we perform an action repeatedly, we improve, and each additional performance takes less time than the preceding ones. We learn how to do the task, become more efficient, and smooth out the rough spots. In a manufacturing firm, learning takes place throughout the process; workers learn their tasks, and managers learn to schedule production more efficiently and to arrange the flow of work. Each time cumulative volume doubles, costs fall by a constant and predictable percentage. This effect was first documented in the aircraft industry and remains a significant cost for **GE Aviation**.[10]

9 Nicole Kobie, "As Electric Car Sales Soar, the Industry Faces a Cobalt Crisis," *Wired* (February 20, 2020), https://www .wired.co.uk/article/cobalt-battery-evs-shortage, accessed August 7, 2020.

10 Tomas Kellner, "The Art of Engineering: The World's Largest Jet Engine Shows Off Composite Curves" (April 28, 2016), https://www.ge.com/news/reports/the-art-of-engineering-the-worlds-largest-jet-engine-shows-off-composite -curves, accessed August 7, 2020.

Exhibit 3.16

Semi-Variable Cost: Decreasing Rate

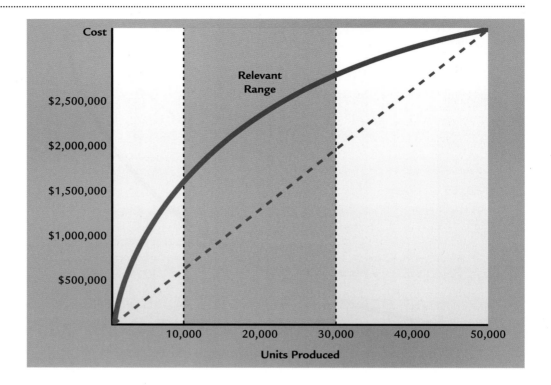

When management fails to recognize that a cost behaves in this manner, total cost often is overestimated because management assumes that total cost increases at a constant rate (i.e., as a typical variable cost), when in reality total cost continues to increase but at a decreasing rate as output increases (as shown in Exhibit 3.16). When total cost is overestimated, net income is underestimated. As a result of overestimating costs and underestimating net income, management might decide not to pursue the opportunity at hand, thereby foregoing a potentially profitable opportunity because of a failure to properly understand learning curve cost behavior patterns.

In addition to production, learning curve behavior also extends to other areas of the value chain, such as marketing, distribution, and customer service, as their per-unit costs can decrease as the number of units produced and sold increases. Learning curve behavior also applies to the service industry, such as students painting dorm rooms between academic terms. When used in this way, the learning curve often is referred to as the **experience curve**. The experience curve relates cost to increased efficiency such that the more often a task is performed, the lower will be the cost of doing it.

The learning curve model takes two common forms: the cumulative average-time learning curve model and the incremental unit-time learning curve model. The difference between the two lies in the assumption made about the speed of learning. Given their widespread prevalence in many businesses, we will examine these two learning curve forms in more detail.

Cumulative Average-Time Learning Curve

The **cumulative average-time learning curve model** states that the cumulative average time per unit decreases by a constant percentage, or learning rate, each time the cumulative quantity of units produced doubles. The **learning rate** is expressed as a percent, and it gives the percentage of time needed to make the next unit, based on the time it took to make the previous unit. The learning rate is determined through experience and must be between 50 and 100 percent. A 50 percent learning rate would eventually result in no labor time per unit—an absurd result. A 100 percent learning rate implies no learning (since the amount of decrease is zero). An 80 percent learning curve is often used to illustrate this model, possibly because the original learning curve work with the aircraft industry found an 80 percent learning curve. **Example 3.7** shows how to calculate the amount of time needed for producing successive units given an 80 percent learning rate and 100 direct labor hours for the first unit.

EXAMPLE 3.7

The HOW and WHY of Calculating the Cumulative Average-Time Learning Curve

Information:

Lindstrom Company installs computerized patient record systems in hospitals and medical centers. Lindstrom has noticed that each general type of system is subject to an 80 percent learning curve. The installation takes a team of professionals to set up and test the system. Assume that the first installation takes 1,000 hours, and the team of professionals is paid an average of $50 per hour.

Why:

As learning occurs, workers become more familiar with the task and can complete it more quickly. The first system installed takes the longest time, by the eighth to sixteenth time the task is performed, the workers have incorporated learning effects and the task takes much less time. Managers need to know how quickly the learning will occur and what effect that will have on labor cost for budgeting, bidding, and performance evaluation.

Required:

1. Set up a table with columns showing: the cumulative number of units, cumulative average time per unit in hours, and cumulative total time in hours. Show results by row for total production of one system, two systems, four systems, eight systems, sixteen systems, and thirty-two systems.

2. What is the total labor cost if Lindstrom installs the following number of systems: one, four, or sixteen? What is the average cost per installed system for the following number of systems: one, four, or sixteen?

3. *What if* Lindstrom is budgeting labor cost for next year based on the installation of 16 additional systems? Calculate total budgeted labor cost for a team that had previously completed 16 systems the prior year. Calculate total budgeted labor cost for a new team that had not completed any systems to date.

Solution:

1.

Cumulative Number of Systems (1)	Cumulative Average Time per System in Hours (2)	Cumulative Total Time: Labor Hours (3) = (1) × (2)
1	1,000	1,000.0
2	800.0 (0.8 × 1,000)	1,600.0
4	640.0 (0.8 × 800)	2,560.0
8	512.0 (0.8 × 640)	4,096.0
16	409.6 (0.8 × 512)	6,553.6
32	327.7 (0.8 × 409.6)	10,486.4

Notice that every time the number of systems installed doubles, the cumulative average time per unit (in column 2) is just 80 percent of the previous amount.

EXAMPLE 3.7

(Continued)

2. Cost for installing one system = 1,000 hours × $50 = $50,000

   Cost for installing four systems = 2,560 hours × $50 = $128,000

   Cost for installing sixteen systems = 6,553.6 hours × $50 = $327,680

   Average cost per system for one system = $50,000/1 = $50,000

   Average cost per system for four systems = $128,000/4 = $32,000

   Average cost per system for sixteen systems = $327,680/16 = $20,480

3. Budgeted labor cost for experienced team = (10,486.4 − 6,553.6) × $50

   = $196,640

   Budgeted labor cost for new team = 6,553.6 × $50 = $327,680

Example 3.7 shows the cumulative average time and cumulative total time according to the doubling formula. How do we obtain these amounts for units that are not doubles of the original amount? This task is accomplished by realizing that the cumulative average-time learning model takes a logarithmic relationship.

$$Y = pX^q$$

where

Y = Cumulative average time per unit

X = Cumulative number of units produced

p = Time in labor hours required to produce the first unit

q = Rate of learning

Therefore:

$$q = \ln (\text{percent learning})/\ln 2$$

For an 80 percent learning curve:

$$q = 0.2231/0.6931 = 0.3219$$

So, when $X = 3$, $p = 100$, and $q = 0.3219$, $Y = 100 \times 3^{-03219} = 70.21$ labor hours.

Excel can be used to calculate the number of hours required for units that are not doubles of the first. Exhibit 3.17 shows an Excel screenshot for the example from Example 3.7. The rows in bold are the cumulative number of units that obey the doubling rule. Example 3.7 tells how to calculate columns C and D for those rows. For row 7, corresponding to 3 units, follow the following steps:

Step 1: Cell F5: enter "=LN(0.8)/LN(2)". After the value "−0.32192809" appears, copy the cell and then paste it into cells F5 through F20.

Step 2: Cell A7: enter "3".

Step 3: Cell B7: enter " = 1000*POWER(A7,F7)". You are entering "1000" because that is the cumulative average time per unit for one unit. In different examples, you will enter a different cumulative average time per unit for one unit. That is, if the first unit had taken 78 hours, you would have entered "=78*POWER(A7,F7)".

Step 4: Cell C7: enter "=A7*B7".

Step 5: Cell D7: enter "=C7−C6".

You can now copy and paste cell B7 into cells B8 through B20, cell C7 into cells C8 through C20, and so on.

Let's take a closer look at the time for the last unit in Exhibit 3.17. See how the time it takes to complete the last unit drops from the first unit (1,000 hours) to the sixteenth unit

Exhibit 3.17

Spreadsheet for Cumulative Average-Time Learning Model

Cumulative Number of Units	Cumulative Average Time per Unit	Cumulative Total Time	Time for Last Unit	Value of q OR = ln(.8)/ln(2)
1	1000	1000	1000	−0.32192809
2	800	1600	600	−0.32192809
3	702.1037028	2106.31111	506.3111	−0.32192809
4	640	2560	453.6889	−0.32192809
5	595.6373436	2978.18672	418.1867	−0.32192809
6	561.6829622	3370.09777	391.9111	−0.32192809
7	534.4895247	3741.42667	371.3289	−0.32192809
8	512	4096	354.5733	−0.32192809
9	492.9496095	4436.54649	340.5465	−0.32192809
10	476.5098749	4765.09875	328.5523	−0.32192809
11	462.1111387	5083.22253	318.1238	−0.32192809
12	449.3463698	5392.15644	308.9339	−0.32192809
13	437.9155217	5692.90178	300.7453	−0.32192809
14	427.5916197	5986.28268	293.3809	−0.32192809
15	418.1991845	6272.98777	286.7051	−0.32192809
16	409.6	6553.6	280.6122	−0.32192809

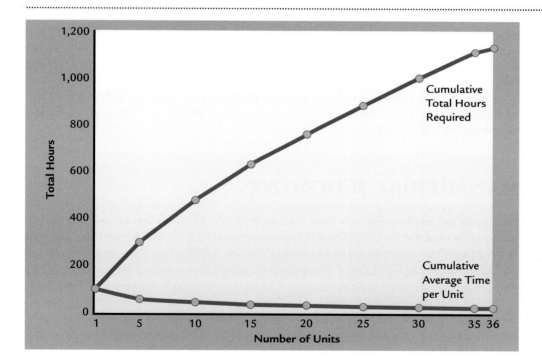

Exhibit 3.18

Graph of Cumulative Total Hours Required and the Cumulative Average Time per Unit

(just 280.6 hours). This learning helps companies realize efficiencies as more and more units are completed. Accountants can use this information in budgeting and preparing bids, as they realize that the time for the first unit of a new type of job will not be equal to the time it takes to complete the last unit. Cost goes down. Accountants can also use this information to advise managers on the need to keep experienced employees rather than having excessive turnover. The turnover requires more training and does not give the company the benefit of the experienced employee's ability to do the job more quickly and competently.

Exhibit 3.18 shows the graph of both the cumulative average time per unit (the bottom line) and the cumulative total hours required (top line). We can see that the time per unit decreases as output increases, but that it decreases at a decreasing rate. We also see that the total labor hours increase as output increases, but they increase at a decreasing rate. Again, the implication for costing is that average cost will decrease as more experience is gained.

Incremental Unit-Time Learning Curve

The **incremental unit-time learning curve model** decreases by a constant percentage each time the cumulative quantity of units produced doubles. The same general assumptions for the learning curve hold; however, the learning rate is assumed to apply to the last unit produced, not to the cumulative average of all units to date. For an 80 percent learning rate, the cumulative average-time learning model assumes that the cumulative *average* time for every unit produced is just 80 percent of the amount for the previous output level. Thus, when we look at the time to produce two units, the average time for each of the units is assumed to be 80 percent of the time for the first unit. However, the incremental unit-time learning model assumes that only the *last* (incremental) unit experiences the decrease in time, so the second unit takes 80 hours, but the first still takes 100 hours. Thus, the total time is 180 (100 + 80) hours. Further explanation of the incremental unit-time learning curve will be left for more advanced courses.

The use of the learning curve concepts permits management to be more accurate in budgeting and performance evaluation for processes in which learning occurs. While the learning curve was originally developed for manufacturing processes, it can also apply in service industries. For example, insurance companies develop new policies and new methods of selling policies. There is a learning component to each new policy as employees discover glitches that were unexpected in the development process and then learn how to fix those glitches and become more efficient.

Of course, it is important to note that the learning rate can differ for each process. Management must estimate the rate, usually on the basis of discussion with engineering and production personnel and past experience.

MANAGERIAL JUDGMENT

Managerial judgment is critically important in determining cost behavior and is by far the most widely used method in practice. Many managers simply use their experience and past observation of cost relationships to determine fixed and variable costs. This method, however, may take a number of forms. Some managers simply assign particular activity costs to the fixed category and others to the variable category. They ignore the possibility of mixed costs. Thus, a chemical firm may regard materials and utilities as strictly variable, with respect to pounds of chemical produced, and all other costs as fixed. Even labor, the textbook example of a unit-based variable cost, may be fixed for this firm. The appeal of this method is simplicity. Before opting for this course of action, management would do well to make sure that each cost is predominantly fixed or variable and that the decisions being made are not highly sensitive to errors in classifying costs as fixed or variable. Interestingly, psychology studies document how widespread powerful cognitive heuristics and biases can significantly affect how accountants process information, including various types of cost management data. The anchoring and adjustment heuristic and confirmation bias represent two heavily studied such phenomena that accountants and management might be wise to consider when making decisions based on cost management information. [11]

---

11   Daniel Kahneman, *Thinking, Fast and Slow* (New York: Farrar, Straus and Giroux, 2011).

To illustrate the use of judgment in assessing cost behavior, consider **Elgin Sweeper Company**, a leading manufacturer of motorized street sweepers with over 100 years of industry experience. Using production volume as the measure of activity output, Elgin revised its chart of accounts to organize costs into fixed and variable components. Elgin's accountants used their knowledge of the company to assign expenses to either a fixed or variable category, using a decision rule that categorized an expense as fixed if it were fixed 75 percent of the time and as variable if it were variable 75 percent of the time.

REAL-WORLD EXAMPLE

Management may instead identify mixed costs and divide these costs into fixed and variable components by deciding just what the fixed and variable parts are—that is, using experience to say that a certain amount of a cost is fixed and therefore that the rest must be variable. Then, the variable component can be computed using one or more cost/volume data points. This use of judgment has the advantage of accounting for mixed costs but is subject to a similar type of error as the strict fixed/variable dichotomy. That is, management may be wrong in its assessment.

The advantage of using managerial judgment to separate fixed and variable costs is its simplicity. In situations in which the manager has a deep understanding of the firm and its cost patterns, this method can give good results. If the manager does not have good judgment, however, errors will occur. Therefore, it is important to consider the experience of the manager, the potential for error, and the effect that error could have on related decisions. With the continuing advancement of data analytics and the increasing complexity of most business operations, some blend of managerial judgment and the quantitative approaches examined in this chapter likely represents the most logical and consistently effective approach to understanding cost behavior and forecasting costs.

SUMMARY OF LEARNING OBJECTIVES

LO1. Define and describe fixed, variable, and mixed costs.
- Variable costs change in total as activity usage changes.
- Usually, variable costs increase in total in direct proportion to increases in activity output.
- Fixed costs do not change in total as activity output changes.
- Mixed costs have both a variable and a fixed component.

LO2. Explain the use of resources and activities and their relationship to cost behavior.
- Flexible resources are acquired as used and needed.
  - Flexible resources have no excess capacity for these resources.
  - They are usually considered to be variable costs.
- Committed resources are acquired in advance of usage.
  - May have excess capacity
  - Frequently considered fixed
  - Can be discretionary or nondiscretionary
- Step costs are acquired in lumpy amounts.
  - Narrow steps approximated by a variable cost function
  - Wide steps approximated as fixed

LO3. Explain how several methods of cost estimation can be used.
- The industrial engineering method uses physical observation and analysis to determine what activities in what amounts are needed to complete a process.
  - Time and motion studies may be used
  - Typically expensive and seldom updated

- Account analysis requires the accountant to classify accounts as either fixed or variable.
  - Frequently used in practice
  - Gives good results if accounts are primarily fixed costs or variable costs
  - Average account values and average driver values are used to calculate fixed costs and variable rates

LO4. Separate mixed costs into their fixed and variable components using the high-low method, the scatterplot method, and the method of least squares.
- High-low method uses the high and the low data points to form a straight line.
  - Slope is variable rate.
  - Intercept is fixed cost.
  - Advantages: objective and easy
  - Disadvantage: nonrepresentative high or low point leads to misestimated cost function
- Scatterplot method plots data—two points chosen to determine a line.
  - Intercept is fixed cost.
  - Slope is variable rate.
  - Advantages: identify nonlinearity, outliers, shifts in the cost relationship
  - Disadvantage: subjectivity
- OLS (regression) produces a best-fitting line.

LO5. Evaluate the reliability of the cost formula.
- Coefficient of correlation shows degree to which two variables move together.
  - Perfect positive correlation is 1.0.
  - Perfect negative correlation is −1.0.
- Coefficient of determination (R^2) shows amount of cost variability explained by driver.
  - $0 \leq R^2 \leq 1.0$
  - Often multiplied by 100 and used as percent
- Smaller standard errors of estimate indicate better goodness of fit.

LO6. Explain how multiple regression can be used to assess cost behavior.
- Has two or more independent variables
- Useful when dependent variable is affected by more than one independent variable

LO7. Recognize nonlinear cost behavior, and discuss its impact on cost forecasting.
- Nonlinear costs, also referred to as *semi-variable costs*, are variable in nature, but their rate of change is not constant.
- Nonlinear costs can be challenging to identify and accurately estimate.
- A learning curve depicts a nonlinear relationship between labor hours and output.
- Doubling of output requires less than a doubling of labor time.
- Cumulative average-time learning curve assumes the cumulative average time per unit decreases by a constant percentage, or learning rate, each time the cumulative quantity of units produced doubles.
- Incremental unit-time learning curve assumes the incremental unit time decreases by a constant percentage each time the cumulative quantity of units produced doubles.

LO8. Discuss the use of managerial judgment in determining cost behavior.
- Used alone or in conjunction with the high-low, scatterplot, or least-squares methods
- Experienced managers use knowledge of cost and activity-level relationships to:
  - Identify outliers
  - Understand structural shifts
  - Adjust parameters due to anticipated changing conditions

EXAMPLE 3.1	The HOW and WHY of Forming an Equation to Describe Mixed Cost, page 87
EXAMPLE 3.2	The HOW and WHY of Calculating Activity Availability, Capacity Used, and Unused Capacity, page 92
EXAMPLE 3.3	The HOW and WHY of Using Account Analysis to Determine Fixed and Variable Costs, page 94
EXAMPLE 3.4	The HOW and WHY of Using the High-Low Method to Determine Fixed Cost and Variable Rate, page 97
EXAMPLE 3.5	The HOW and WHY of Using the Regression Results for Fixed Cost and Variable Rate to Construct and Use a Cost Formula, page 105
EXAMPLE 3.6	The HOW and WHY of Constructing a Cost Equation Using the Results from Multiple Regression, page 111
EXAMPLE 3.7	The HOW and WHY of Calculating the Cumulative Average-Time Learning Curve, page 115

KEY TERMS

Account analysis method, 94

Activity capacity, 88

Activity rate, 91

Coefficient of correlation (r), 107

Coefficient of determination (R^2), 107

Committed resources, 89

Cost behavior, 80

Cumulative average-time learning curve model, 114

Dependent variable, 96

Deviation, 102

Discretionary fixed expenses, 90

Experience curve, 114

Fixed costs, 82

Flexible resources, 89

Goodness of fit, 106

High-low method, 98

Hypothesis test of cost parameters, 106

Incremental unit-time learning curve model, 118

Independent variable, 96

Industrial engineering method, 94

Intercept parameter, 96

Learning curve, 113

Learning rate, 114

Long run, 88

Method of least squares, 102

Mixed costs, 87

Multiple regression, 110

Nondiscretionary (committed) fixed expense, 89

Non-unit-level drivers, 81

Practical capacity, 89

Relevant range, 82

Scattergraph, 99

Scatterplot method, 99

Semi-variable cost, 112

Short run, 88

Slope parameter, 97

Step-cost function, 91

Step-fixed costs, 91

Step-variable costs, 91

Unit-level drivers, 81

Unused capacity, 89

Variable costs, 83

BRIEF EXERCISES

OBJECTIVE ▶ 1
Example 3.1

Brief Exercise 3-1 Mixed Costs and Cost Formula

Callie's Gym is a complete fitness center. Owner Callie Ducain employs various fitness trainers who are expected to staff the front desk and to teach fitness classes. While on the front desk, trainers answer the phone, handle walk-ins and show them around the gym, answer member questions about the weight machines, and do light cleaning (wiping down the equipment, vacuuming the floor). The trainers also teach fitness classes (e.g., pilates, spinning, body pump) according to their own interest and training level. The cost of the fitness trainers is $600 per month and $20 per class taught. Last month, 100 classes were taught.

Required:

1. Develop a cost equation for total cost of labor.
2. What was total variable labor cost last month?
3. What was total labor cost last month?
4. What was the unit cost of labor (per class) for last month?
5. *What if* Callie increased the number of classes offered by 50 percent? What would be the total labor cost? The unit labor cost? Explain why the unit labor cost decreased.

OBJECTIVE ▶ 2
Example 3.2

Brief Exercise 3-2 Activity Availability, Capacity Used, Unused Capacity

Noel's Mobile Pet Services Company has a grooming department staffed by 10 professional pet groomers. Each groomer is paid $75,000 per year and is able to process 5,000 grooming orders. Last year, 46,000 grooming orders were processed by the 10 groomers.

Required:

1. Calculate the activity rate per grooming order.
2. Calculate, in terms of grooming orders, the:

   a. total activity availability
   b. unused capacity

3. Calculate the dollar cost of:

   a. total activity availability
   b. unused capacity

4. Express total activity availability in terms of activity capacity used and unused capacity.
5. *What if* one of the professional groomers agreed to work half time for $14,000? How many grooming orders could be processed by four and a half professional groomers? What would unused capacity be in grooming orders?

OBJECTIVE ▶ 3
Example 3.3

**DATA
ANALYTICS**

Brief Exercise 3-3 Account Analysis to Determine Cost Behavior

J. Q. Higgins, owner of Robin's Nest, wants to determine the cost behavior of labor and overhead. Higgins pays his workers a salary; during busy times, everyone works to get the orders out. Temps (temporary workers hired through an agency) may be hired to pack and prepare completed orders for shipment. During slower times, Higgins catches up on bookkeeping and administrative tasks while the salaried workers do preventive maintenance, clean the lines and building, etc. Temps are not hired during slow times. Higgins found that workers' salaries, temp agency payments, rentals, utilities, and plant and equipment depreciation are the largest dollar accounts. He believes that workers' salaries and plant and equipment depreciation are fixed, temp agency payments are associated with the number of orders (since temp workers are used to pack and prepare completed orders for shipment), and electricity is associated with the number of machine hours. When the number of different parts stored by Robin's Nest exceeds the space in the materials storeroom, Higgins rents nearby warehouse space. He can rent as much or as little space as he wants on a month-to-month basis. Therefore, he believes warehouse rental payments are variable with the number of parts purchased and stored. The account balances for the past six months as well as the six-month total are as follows:

	Workers' Salaries	Temp Agency Payments	Warehouse Rental	Electricity	Plant and Equipment Depreciation
January	$ 9,800	$ 0	$ 350	$ 880	$ 3,100
February	9,800	900	460	910	3,100
March	9,800	1,650	395	850	3,100
April	9,800	2,050	390	890	3,100
May	9,800	2,150	440	750	3,100
June	9,800	2,100	365	820	3,100
Total	$58,800	$8,850	$2,400	$5,100	$18,600

Information on number of machine hours, orders, and parts for the six-month period follows:

	Machine Hours	Number of Orders	Number of Parts
January	3,500	250	510
February	5,700	350	730
March	6,600	425	820
April	7,100	580	890
May	7,000	550	900
June	7,300	545	950
Total	37,200	2,700	4,800

Required:

1. Calculate the monthly average account balance for each account. Calculate the average monthly amount for each of the three drivers.
2. Calculate fixed monthly cost and the variable rates for temp agency payments, warehouse rent, and electricity. Express the results in the form of an equation for total cost. (Round your answers to the nearest cent.)
3. In July, Higgins predicts there will be 475 orders, 850 parts, and 6,700 machine hours. What is the total labor and overhead cost for July?
4. *What if* Higgins buys a new machine in July for $60,000? The machine is expected to last 20 years and will have no salvage value at the end of that time. What part of the cost equation will be affected? How? What is the new expected cost in July?
5. Briefly explain how your responses to Requirements 3 and 4 represent examples of predictive data analytics (see Exhibits 2.5 and 2.6, pp. 37, 40 for a review of data analytic types).

Brief Exercise 3-4 High-Low Method to Determine Fixed Cost and Variable Rate

OBJECTIVE ◀ 4

Example 3.4

McGarvey Manufacturing Company had the following 12 months of data on purchasing cost and number of purchase orders.

Month	Purchasing Cost	Number of Purchase Orders
January	$19,250	370
February	18,050	330
March	18,200	320
April	18,050	410
May	19,345	400
June	19,500	450
July	19,670	460
August	20,940	560

September	19,430	440
October	20,020	600
November	18,800	470
December	19,340	480

Required:

1. Determine the high point and the low point.
2. Calculate the variable rate for purchasing cost based on the number of purchase orders. (Round to nearest cent.)
3. Calculate the fixed monthly cost of purchasing. (Round to nearest dollar.)
4. Write the cost formula for the purchasing activity showing the fixed cost and the variable rate.
5. If McGarvey Manufacturing Company estimates that next month will have 480 purchase orders, what is the total estimated purchasing cost for that month? (Round to nearest dollar.)
6. *What if* McGarvey Manufacturing wants to estimate purchasing cost for the coming year and expects 6,000 purchase orders? What will estimated total purchasing cost be? What is the total fixed purchasing cost? Why doesn't it equal the fixed cost calculated in Requirement 3? (Round to nearest dollar.)

OBJECTIVE 5
Example 3.5

Brief Exercise 3-5 Using Regression Results to Construct and Apply a Cost Formula

Refer to Brief Exercise 3-4 for data on McGarvey Manufacturing Company's purchasing cost and number of purchase orders.

The controller for McGarvey Manufacturing ran regression on the data, and the coefficients shown by the regression program are:

| Intercept | 15,676 (rounded to the nearest dollar) |
| X variable 1 | 8.03 (rounded to the nearest cent) |

Required:

1. Construct the cost formula for the purchasing activity showing the fixed cost and the variable rate.
2. If McGarvey Manufacturing Company estimates that next month will have 480 purchase orders, what is the total estimated purchasing cost for that month? (Round your answer to the nearest dollar.)
3. *What if* McGarvey Manufacturing wants to estimate purchasing cost for the coming year and expects 6,000 purchase orders? What will estimated total purchasing cost be? (Round your answer to the nearest dollar.) What is the total fixed purchasing cost? Why doesn't it equal the fixed cost calculated in Requirement 1?

OBJECTIVE 6
Example 3.6

Brief Exercise 3-6 Using Multiple Regression Results to Construct and Apply a Cost Formula

The controller for McGarvey Manufacturing Company felt that the number of purchase orders alone did not explain the monthly purchasing cost. He knew that nonstandard orders (for example, one requiring an overseas supplier) took more time and effort. He collected data on the number of nonstandard orders for the past 12 months and added that information to the data on purchasing cost and total number of purchase orders.

Month	Purchasing Cost	Number of Purchase Orders	Number of Nonstandard Orders
January	$19,250	370	61
February	18,050	330	40
March	18,200	320	35
April	18,050	410	14
May	19,345	400	73
June	19,500	450	55
July	19,670	460	30
August	20,940	560	80
September	19,430	440	51
October	20,020	600	75
November	18,800	470	12
December	19,340	480	27

Multiple regression was run on the above data; the coefficients shown by the regression program are:

Intercept	15,626 (rounded to the nearest dollar)
X variable 1	6.38 (rounded to the nearest cent)
X variable 2	16.90 (rounded to the nearest cent)

Required:

1. Construct the cost formula for the purchasing activity showing the fixed cost and the variable rate.
2. If McGarvey Manufacturing Company estimates that next month will have 480 total purchase orders and 42 nonstandard orders, what is the total estimated purchasing cost for that month? (Round your answer to the nearest dollar.)
3. *What if* McGarvey Manufacturing wants to estimate purchasing cost for the coming year and expects 6,000 purchase orders and 550 nonstandard orders? What will estimated total purchasing cost be? What is the total fixed purchasing cost? Why doesn't it equal the fixed cost calculated in Requirement 2? (Round your answers to the nearest dollar.)

Brief Exercise 3-7 Cumulative Average-Time Learning Curve

OBJECTIVE ◀ 7
Example 3.7

Pohlman Company makes aircraft engines. Pohlman has noticed that, in general, each new engine design is subject to an 80 percent learning rate. Assume that the first unit produced takes 500 hours, and direct labor is paid an average of $30 per hour.

Required:

1. Set up a table with columns showing: the cumulative number of units, cumulative average time per unit in hours, and cumulative total time in hours. Show results by row for total production of: one engine, two engines, four engines, eight engines, sixteen engines, and thirty-two engines. (Round hour answers to two significant digits.)
2. What is the total labor cost if Pohlman manufactures the following number of engines: one, four, or sixteen? What is the average cost per engine for the following number of engines: one, four, or sixteen? (Round your answers to the nearest dollar.)
3. *What if* Pohlman is preparing a bid to build 16 engines? Calculate budgeted labor cost for an engine design which Pohlman has built before (assume that 16 of these engines had been made previously and the first unit took 500 hours). Calculate budgeted labor cost for a new engine design that Pohlman's workers have never made before (assume the first unit will take 500 hours).

EXERCISES

OBJECTIVE ▐1▌ ▐2▌ ▶
Exercise 3-8 Cost Behavior, Flexible and Committed Resources

State University's football team just received a bowl game invitation, and the students and alumni are excited. Holiday Travel Agency, located close to campus, decided to put together a bowl game package. For $50,000, a 737 jet could be chartered to take up to 170 people to and from the bowl city. A block of 85 hotel rooms could be confirmed for $400 each (a three-night commitment); Holiday Travel must pay for all the rooms in advance and cannot cancel any of them. The day of the game, a pregame buffet will be catered at $30 per person, and each person will receive a game favor package (consisting of a sweatshirt, a T-shirt, a commemorative pin with the school and bowl logos, and two pompons in the school's colors). All items in the favor package can be purchased by Holiday Travel on December 21 and will cost the agency $25 per set. Buses will be chartered in the bowl city to transport participants to and from the airport and the game. Each bus holds 50 people and can be chartered for $500. The bowl game is scheduled for December 28, and the trip will span three nights—December 26, 27, and 28. Purchasers must reserve their package and pay in full by December 20.

Required:

1. List the resources that are mentioned in the above scenario.
2. For each resource, determine (a) whether it is a flexible or committed resource and (b) the type of cost behavior displayed (variable, fixed, mixed, or step cost).

OBJECTIVE ▐1▌ ▶
Exercise 3-9 Variable, Fixed, and Mixed Costs

Classify the following costs of activity inputs as variable, fixed, or mixed. Identify the activity and the associated activity driver that allow you to define the cost behavior. For example, assume that the resource input is "cloth in a shirt." The activity would be "sewing shirts," the cost behavior "variable," and the activity driver "units produced." Prepare your answers in the following format:

Activity	Cost Behavior	Activity Driver
Sewing shirts	Variable	Units produced

a. Flu vaccine
b. Salaries, equipment, and materials used for moving materials in a factory
c. Forms used to file insurance claims
d. Salaries, forms, and postage associated with purchasing
e. Printing and postage for advertising circulars
f. Equipment, labor, and parts used to repair and maintain production equipment
g. Power to operate sewing machines in a clothing factory
h. Wooden cabinets enclosing audio speakers
i. Advertising
j. Sales commissions
k. Fuel for a delivery van
l. Depreciation on a warehouse
m. Depreciation on a forklift used to move partially completed goods
n. X-ray film used in the radiology department of a hospital
o. Rental car provided for a client

OBJECTIVE ▐1▌ ▶
Exercise 3-10 Cost Behavior

Fresh Powder, Inc., manufactures snowboards. Based on past experience, Fresh Powder has found that its total annual overhead costs can be represented by the following formula: Overhead cost = $2,500,000 + $125X, where X equals number of snowboards. Last year, Fresh Powder produced 50,000 snowboards. Actual overhead costs for the year were as expected.

Required:

1. What is the driver for the overhead activity?
2. What is the total overhead cost incurred by Fresh Powder last year?
3. What is the total fixed overhead cost incurred by Fresh Powder last year?
4. What is the total variable overhead cost incurred by Fresh Powder last year?
5. What is the overhead cost per unit produced?
6. What is the fixed overhead cost per unit?
7. What is the variable overhead cost per unit?
8. Recalculate Requirements 5, 6, and 7 for the following levels of production: (a) 49,000 units and (b) 52,000 units. (Round your answers to the nearest cent.) Explain this outcome.

Exercise 3-11 Types of Costs

OBJECTIVE ◀ 1

Cashion Company produces chemical mixtures for veterinary pharmaceutical companies. Its factory has four mixing lines that mix various powdered chemicals together according to specified formulas. Each line can produce up to 5,000 barrels per year. Each line has one supervisor who is paid $34,000 per year. Depreciation on equipment averages $16,000 per year. Direct materials and power cost about $4.50 per unit.

Required:

1. Prepare a graph for each of these three costs: equipment depreciation, supervisors' wages, and direct materials and power. Use the vertical axis for cost and the horizontal axis for units (barrels). Assume that sales range from 0 to 20,000 units.
2. Assume that the normal operating range for the company is 16,000 to 19,000 units per year. How would you classify each of the three types of cost?

Exercise 3-12 Cost Behavior and Forensic Accounting

OBJECTIVE ◀ 1

Washington Theater System entered into a three-year agreement with a local civic organization such that the organization would provide 5,000 of its patrons each month with a special ticket to attend a movie at Washington's theaters. Each special ticket provides the patron with a ticket to the movie of their choice, a small bag of popcorn, and a small soft drink. After one year of utilizing this special movie ticket program, the civic organization decided that it would no longer continue with it. Washington Theater System sued the civic organization for damages. The court agreed that the civic organization was liable under the agreement for damages the theater incurred regarding the second and third year of the agreement. The following information items pertain to Washington's alleged damages it suffered as a result of the civic organization's action:

- The unit (i.e., per ticket) ticket price to the civic organization in the special movie program was $7.00 for each month during the life of the contract.
- Thirty percent of the ticket price must be paid by Washington to the movie distributor for viewing each movie.
- Five percent of ticket sales went to a marketing firm that sold the special ticket program to the civic organization.
- The unit material and container cost of the popcorn was $0.40.
- The unit material and container cost for each soft drink was $0.45.
- The monthly salary for a Washington Theater System manager hired to oversee the servicing of the special ticket program activities was $5,000.

Required:

1. Which of the items represents a variable cost? Which of the items represents a fixed cost? Estimate the amount of monthly and total damages suffered by Washington Theater System as a result of the civic organization's unilateral contract cancellation.
2. Briefly explain one or more challenges that Washington Theater System's accounting team might face in this forensic scenario after estimating the amount of damages.

OBJECTIVE   **Exercise 3-13 Resource Usage Model and Cost Behavior**

For the following activities and their associated resources, identify the following: (1) a cost driver, (2) flexible resources, and (3) committed resources. Also, label each resource as one of the following with respect to the cost driver: (a) variable and (b) fixed.

Activity	Resource Description
Maintenance	Equipment, labor, and parts
Inspection	Test equipment, inspectors (each inspector can inspect five batches per day), and units inspected (process requires destructive sampling)*
Packing	Materials, labor (each packer places five units in a box), and conveyor belt
Payable processing	Clerks, materials, equipment, and facility
Assembly	Conveyor belt, supervision (one supervisor for every three assembly lines), direct labor, and materials

*Destructive sampling occurs whenever it is necessary to destroy a unit as inspection occurs.

OBJECTIVE   **Exercise 3-14 Resource Usage and Supply, Activity Rates, Service Organization**

**SHOW ME
HOW**

EcoBrite Labs performs tests on water samples supplied by outside companies to ensure that their waste water meets environmental standards. Customers deliver water samples to the lab and receive the lab reports via the Internet. The EcoBrite Labs facility is built and staffed to handle the processing of 100,000 tests per year. The lab facility cost $160,000 to build and is expected to last 10 years and will have no salvage value. Processing equipment cost $250,000 and has a life expectancy of five years and will have no salvage value. Both facility and equipment are depreciated on a straight-line basis. EcoBrite Labs has six salaried laboratory technicians, each of whom is paid $30,000. In addition to the salaries, facility, and equipment, EcoBrite Labs expects to spend $50,000 for chemicals and other supplies (assuming 100,000 tests are performed). Last year, 86,000 tests were performed.

Required:

1. Classify the resources associated with the water testing activity into one of the following types: (1) committed resources and (2) flexible resources.
2. Calculate the total annual activity rate for the water testing activity. Break the activity rate into fixed and variable components. (Round your answers to three significant digits.)
3. Compute the total activity availability, and break this into activity output and unused activity.
4. Calculate the total cost of resources supplied, and break this into the cost of activity used and the cost of unused activity.

OBJECTIVE   **Exercise 3-15 Step Costs, Relevant Range**

**DATA
ANALYTICS**

J. Klompus, Inc., produces industrial machinery. J. Klompus has a machining department and a group of direct laborers called machinists. Each machinist is paid $25,000 and can machine up to 500 units per year. Klompus also hires supervisors to develop machine specification plans and to oversee production within the machining department. Given the planning and supervisory work, a supervisor can oversee three machinists, at most. Klompus's accounting and production history reveal the following relationships between units produced and the costs of direct labor and supervision (measured on an annual basis):

Units Produced	Direct Labor	Supervision
0–500	$ 25,000	$ 40,000
501–1,000	50,000	40,000
1,001–1,500	75,000	40,000
1,501–2,000	100,000	80,000
2,001–2,500	125,000	80,000
2,501–3,000	150,000	80,000
3,001–3,500	175,000	120,000
3,501–4,000	200,000	120,000

Required:

1. Prepare two graphs: one that illustrates the relationship between direct labor cost and units produced, and one that illustrates the relationship between the cost of supervision and units produced. Let cost be the vertical axis and units produced the horizontal axis.
2. How would you classify each cost? Why?
3. Suppose that the normal range of activity is between 2,400 and 2,450 units and that the exact number of machinists is currently hired to support this level of activity. Further suppose that production for the next year is expected to increase by an additional 400 units. How much will the cost of direct labor increase (and how will this increase be realized)? Cost of supervision?
4. Briefly explain how data visualization methods (e.g., tabular, graphical, and textual) affect a person's ability to detect or interpret cost behavior patterns in a set of data.

Exercise 3-16 Account Analysis Method

OBJECTIVE 3

SHOW ME
HOW

Penny Hassan runs the Shear Beauty Salon near a college campus. Several months ago, Penny used some unused space at the back of the salon and bought two used tanning beds. She hired a receptionist and kept the salon open for extended hours each week so that tanning clients would be able to use the benefits of their tanning packages. After three months, Penny wanted additional information on the costs of the tanning area. She accumulated the following data on four accounts:

	Wages	Supplies and Maintenance	Equipment Depreciation	Electricity	Tanning Minutes	Number of Visits
January	$1,750	$1,450	$150	$300	4,100	410
February	1,670	1,900	150	410	3,890	380
March	1,800	4,120	150	680	6,710	560

Penny decided that wages and equipment depreciation were fixed. She thought supplies and maintenance would vary with the number of tanning visits and that electricity would vary with the number of tanning minutes.

Required:

1. Calculate the average account balance for each account. Calculate the average monthly amount for each of the two drivers. (Round all answers to the nearest dollar or the nearest whole unit.)
2. Calculate fixed monthly cost and the variable rates for the account averages. (Round to the nearest cent.) Express the results in the form of an equation for total cost.
3. In April, Penny predicts there will be 360 visits for a total of 3,700 minutes. What is the total cost for April?
4. Suppose that Penny decides to buy a new tanning bed at the beginning of April for $6,960. The tanning bed is expected to last four years and will have no salvage value at the end of that time. What part of the cost equation will be affected? How? What is the new expected cost in April?

Exercise 3-17 Account Analysis Method

OBJECTIVE 3

SHOW ME
HOW

Shirrell Blackthorn is the accountant for several pizza restaurants based in a tri-city area. The president of the chain wanted some help with budgeting and cost control, so Shirrell decided to analyze the accounts for the past year. She divided the accounts into four different categories, depending on whether they appeared to be primarily fixed or to vary with one of three different drivers. Food and wage costs appeared to vary with the total sales dollars. Delivery costs varied with the number of miles driven (workers were required to use their own cars and were reimbursed for miles driven). A group of other costs, including purchasing, materials handling, and purchases of kitchen equipment, dishes, and pans, appeared to vary with the number of different product types (e.g., pizza, salad, and lasagna). Shirrell came up with the following monthly averages:

Food and wage costs	$175,000
Delivery costs	$18,000
Other costs	$9,520
Fixed costs	$255,000
Sales revenue	$560,000
Delivery mileage in miles	8,000
Number of product types	14

Required:

1. Calculate the average variable rate for the following costs: food and wages, delivery costs, and other costs.
2. Form an equation for total cost based on the fixed costs and your results from Requirement 1.
3. The president is considering expanding the restaurant menu and plans to add one new offering to the menu. According to the cost equation, what is the additional monthly cost for the new menu offering?

OBJECTIVE 4

SHOW ME HOW   **EXCEL**

Exercise 3-18 Scattergraph Method, High-Low Method

Deepa Dalal opened a free-standing radiology clinic. She had anticipated that the costs for the radiological tests would be primarily fixed, but she found that costs increased with the number of tests performed. Costs for this service over the past nine months are as follows:

Month	Radiology Tests	Total Cost
January	2,800	$133,500
February	2,600	135,060
March	3,100	175,000
April	3,500	170,600
May	3,400	176,900
June	3,700	186,600
July	3,840	174,450
August	4,100	195,510
September	3,450	185,300

Required:

1. Prepare a scattergraph based on the preceding data. Use cost for the vertical axis and number of radiology tests for the horizontal axis. Based on an examination of the scattergraph, does there appear to be a linear relationship between the cost of radiology service and the number of tests?
2. Compute the cost formula for radiology services using the high-low method.
3. Calculate the predicted cost of radiology services for October for 3,500 tests using the formula found in Requirement 2.

OBJECTIVE 4 5

SHOW ME HOW

Exercise 3-19 Method of Least Squares, Goodness of Fit

Refer to the data in **Exercise 3-18**.

Required:

1. Compute the cost formula for radiology services using the method of least squares.
2. Using the formula computed in Requirement 1, what is the predicted cost of radiology services for October for 3,500 appointments? (Round the answer to the nearest dollar.)

3. What does the coefficient of determination tell you about the cost formula computed in Requirement 1? What are the *t* statistics for the number of tests and the intercept term? What do these statistics tell you about the choice of number of tests as the independent variable and the probability that there are fixed costs?

Exercise 3-20 High-Low Method, Cost Formulas

OBJECTIVE ◄ 4

SHOW ME
HOW

The controller of the South Charleston plant of Ravinia, Inc., monitored activities associated with materials handling costs. The high and low levels of resource usage occurred in September and March for three different resources associated with materials handling. The number of moves is the driver. The total costs of the three resources and the activity output, as measured by moves for the two different levels, are presented as follows:

Resource	Number of Moves	Total Cost
Forklift depreciation:		
Low	6,500	$ 1,800
High	20,000	1,800
Indirect labor:		
Low	6,500	$ 74,250
High	20,000	135,000
Fuel and oil for forklift:		
Low	6,500	$ 4,940
High	20,000	15,200

Required:

1. Determine the cost behavior formula of each resource. Use the high-low method to assess the fixed and variable components.
2. Using your knowledge of cost behavior, predict the cost of each item for an activity output level of 9,000 moves.
3. Construct a cost formula that can be used to predict the total cost of the three resources combined. Using this formula, predict the total materials handling cost if activity output is 9,000 moves. In general, when can cost formulas be combined to form a single cost formula?

Exercise 3-21 Method of Least Squares, Evaluation of Cost Equation

OBJECTIVE ◄ 4 5

EXCEL   SHOW ME
HOW

Lassiter Company used the method of least squares to develop a cost equation to predict the cost of moving materials. There were 80 data points for the regression, and the following computer output was generated:

Intercept	$17,350
Slope	12.00
Coefficient of correlation	0.92
Standard error	$220

The activity driver used was the number of moves.

Required:

1. What is the cost formula?
2. Using the cost formula, predict the cost of moving materials if 340 moves are made. (Round to the nearest dollar.)
3. What percentage of the variability in moving cost is explained by the number of moves? Do you think the equation will predict well? Why or why not?

OBJECTIVE 6

SHOW ME
HOW

EXCEL

Exercise 3-22 Multiple Regression

Sweet Dreams Bakery was started five years ago by Della Fontera who was known for her breads, sweet rolls, and personalized cakes. Della had kept her accounting system simple, believing that she had a good intuitive handle on costs. She had been using the following formula to describe her monthly overhead costs:

$$\text{Overhead cost} = \$7,800 + \$7.50 \text{ (direct labor hours)}$$

For breads and sweet rolls that were available in the bakery case each day, she applied a standard pricing system. For special orders, however, Della needed her cost formula to help her come up with an estimated cost for the personalized cake or wedding cake. To that cost, she applied a markup percentage.

Lately, however, the increase in the variety of orders and the elaborateness of the wedding cakes made her wonder if a more sophisticated view of costs would help her in planning, budgeting, and pricing.

After some late-night discussions with her workers, Della determined that Sweet Dreams' expansion into wedding cakes and gift baskets had made special orders a more complex operation. The various shapes of the wedding cake tiers had required Della's investing in different-sized cake pans, as well as decorating tips for icing. The different icing patterns and elaborate designs took much more time for icing, as well. In addition, while a five-year-old's birthday cake just requires that the child's name and (possibly) the superhero's name are spelled correctly, a wedding cake is a once-in-a-lifetime item that must achieve perfection. Gift baskets required Della to stock baskets, cellophane, and bows. Then when an order came in, a worker had to stop baking to arrange the muffins and breads artfully in the basket, wrap it, and tie the bow. While it seemed simple enough, this took time and thought. Thus, the number of direct labor hours was still an important variable, but so were the number of wedding cakes and gift baskets. Della rummaged through her college textbooks and found information on regression. Then, with help from one of her computer savvy workers, she ran multiple regression tables for the past 24 months of data for Sweet Dreams for three independent variables: number of direct labor hours, the number of wedding cakes, and the number of gift baskets. The following printout was obtained:

Parameter	Estimate	t for H_o Parameter $= 0$	$Pr > t$	Standard Error of Parameter
Intercept	1,980	93.00	0.0001	264.00
Number of direct labor hours	2.56	3.60	0.0050	0.89
Number of wedding cakes	67.40	5.58	0.0050	3.19
Number of gift baskets	2.20	2.96	0.0250	0.75

$R^2 = 0.92$

$S_e = 65$

Observations: 24

Required:

1. Write out the cost equation for Sweet Dreams' monthly overhead cost.
2. Suppose that next month Sweet Dreams expects to have 550 direct labor hours, 35 wedding cakes, and 20 gift baskets. What is the expected overhead? (Round to the nearest dollar.)
3. What does R^2 mean in this equation? Overall, what is your evaluation of the cost equation that was developed for the cost of overhead? Suppose that Sweet Dreams charges an extra $2.50 to prepare a gift basket. This charge is in addition to the price charged for the items (e.g., muffins) that the customer chooses to put into the basket. How might Della use the results of the regression equation to see whether or not the $2.50 charge is appropriate?

Exercise 3-23 Multiple Regression

Ginnian and Fitch, a regional accounting firm, performs yearly audits on a number of different for-profit and not-for-profit entities. Two years ago, Luisa Mellina, Ginnian's partner in charge of operations, became concerned about the amount of audit time required by not-for-profit entities. As a result, she instituted a series of training programs focusing on the auditing of not-for-profit entities. Now, she would like to see if the training seemed to work. So, she ran a multiple regression on 22 months of data for Ginnian for three variables: the total monthly cost of audit professional time, the number of not-for-profit audits, and the hours of training in the audit of not-for-profit entities. The following printout was obtained:

Parameter	Estimate	t for H_o Parameter $= 0$	$Pr > t$	Standard Error of Parameter
Intercept	286,700	70.00	0.0001	345.00
Number of not-for-profit audits	790	3.60	0.0050	27.45
Hours of training	−45.50	−1.96	0.0250	5.13

$R^2 = 0.79$

$S_e = 12,030$

Observations: 22

Required:

1. Write out the cost equation for Ginnian's audit professional time.
2. If Ginnian expects to have 9 audits of not-for-profits next month and expects that audit professionals will have a total of 130 hours of not-for-profit training, what is the anticipated cost of professional time?
3. Are the hours spent auditing not-for-profit entities positively or negatively correlated with audit professional costs? Is percentage of experienced team members positively or negatively correlated with audit professional cost?
4. What does R^2 mean in this equation? Overall, what is your evaluation of the cost equation that was developed for the cost of audit professionals?

Exercise 3-24 Learning Curve

Bordner Company manufactures HVAC (heating, ventilation, and air conditioning) systems for commercial buildings. For each new design, Bordner faces a 90 percent learning rate. On average, the first unit of a new design takes 600 hours. Direct labor is paid $25 per hour.

Required:

1. Set up a table with columns showing: the cumulative number of units, cumulative average time per unit in hours, and cumulative total time in hours. Show results by row for total production of one unit, two units, four units, eight units, and sixteen units. (Round hour answers to two significant digits.)
2. What is the total labor cost if Bordner makes the following number of units: one, four, sixteen? What is the average cost per system for the following number of systems: one, four, or sixteen? (Round your answers to the nearest dollar.)
3. Using the logarithmic function, set up a table with columns showing: the cumulative number of units, cumulative average time per unit in hours, cumulative total time in hours, and the time for the last unit. Show results by row for each of units one through eight. (Round answers to two significant digits.)

Exercise 3-25 Learning Curve

Sharon Glessing, controller for Janson Company, has noticed that the company faces a 75 percent learning rate for its specialty design line. In planning the cost of the latest design, Sharon assumed that the first set of units would take 1,000 direct labor hours. She decided to use this information in budgeting for the cost of the total project, which would involve the manufacture of 16 sets. Direct labor is paid $40 per hour.

OBJECTIVE 6 SHOW ME HOW

OBJECTIVE 7 SHOW ME HOW

OBJECTIVE 7 SHOW ME HOW

Required:

1. Set up a table with columns showing the cumulative number of units, cumulative average time per unit in hours, and cumulative total time in hours. Show results by row for total production of one unit, two units, four units, eight units, and sixteen units. (Round hour answers to two significant digits.)
2. What is the total labor cost if Janson Company makes eight sets? Sixteen sets? (Round your answers to the nearest dollar.)
3. Using the logarithmic function, set up a table with columns showing: the cumulative number of units, cumulative average time per unit in hours, cumulative total time in hours, and the time for the last unit. Show results by row for each of unit sets one through eight. (Round hour answers to two significant digits.) What is the direct labor cost for the eighth set?

OBJECTIVE **1** **2** **7**

DATA ANALYTICS

Exercise 3-26 Cost Behavior Patterns

The graphs below represent cost behavior patterns that might occur in a company's cost structure. The vertical axis represents total cost, and the horizontal axis represents activity output.

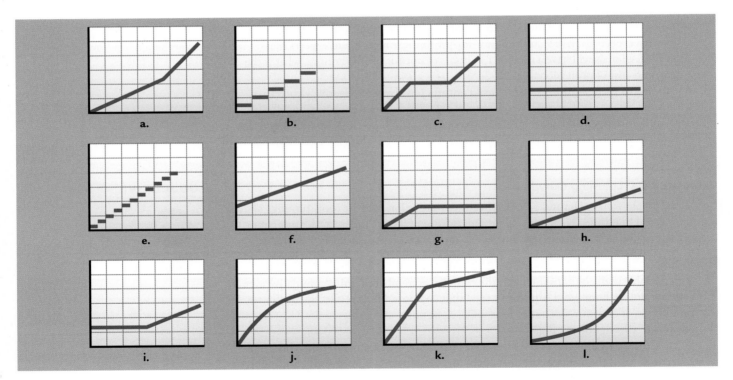

Required:

Part 1: For each of the following situations, choose the graph from the group a–l that best illustrates the cost pattern involved. Also, for each situation, identify the driver that measures activity output.

1. The cost of power when a fixed fee of $500 per month is charged plus an additional charge of $0.12 per kilowatt-hour used.
2. Commissions paid to sales representatives. Commissions are paid at the rate of 5 percent of sales made up to total annual sales of $500,000, and 7 percent of sales above $500,000.
3. A part purchased from an outside supplier costs $12 per part for the first 3,000 parts and $10 per part for all parts purchased in excess of 3,000 units.
4. The cost of surgical gloves, which are purchased in increments of 100 units (gloves come in boxes of 100 pairs).

5. The cost of tuition at a local college that charges $250 per credit hour up to 15 credit hours. Hours taken in excess of 15 are free.

6. The cost of tuition at another college that charges $4,500 per semester for any course load ranging from 12 to 16 credit hours. Students taking fewer than 12 credit hours are charged $375 per credit hour. Students taking more than 16 credit hours are charged $4,500 plus $300 per credit hour in excess of 16.

7. A beauty shop's purchase of soaking solution to remove artificial nails. Each jar of solution can soak off approximately 50 nails before losing its effectiveness.

8. Purchase of diagnostics equipment by a company for inspection of incoming orders.

9. Use of disposable gowns by patients in a hospital.

10. Cost of labor at a local fast-food restaurant. Three employees are always on duty during working hours; more employees can be called in during periods of heavy demand to work on an "as-needed" basis.

11. A manufacturer found that the maintenance cost of its heavy machinery was tied to the age of the equipment. Experience indicated that the maintenance cost increased at an increasing rate as the equipment aged.

Part 2: Briefly explain why the use of graphs (such as the ones depicted in a. through l. of Part 1) could be considered a form of descriptive data analytics (see Exhibits 2.5 and 2.6, pp. 37, 40 for a review of data analytic types).

Exercise 3-27 Interpreting Cost Behavior Graphs

OBJECTIVE ◀ 1 2 7

Examine the graphs in Exercise 3-26.

Required:

As explained in this chapter, cost behavior patterns can be described as fixed, variable, semi-variable, mixed, or step function in nature. Explain the exact type of cost behavior pattern represented by each of the cost curves shown in graphs a. through l. Note that some of the graphs might represent a combination of multiple cost behavior patterns.

PROBLEMS

Problem 3-28 Cost Behavior, Resource Usage, Excess Capacity

OBJECTIVE ◀ 1 2

Rolertyme Company manufactures roller skates. With the exception of the rollers, all parts of the skates are produced internally. Neeta Booth, president of Rolertyme, has decided to make the rollers instead of buying them from external suppliers. The company needs 100,000 sets per year (currently it pays $1.90 per set of rollers).

The rollers can be produced using an available area within the plant. However, equipment for production of the rollers would need to be leased ($30,000 per year lease payment). Additionally, it would cost $0.50 per machine hour for power, oil, and other operating expenses. The equipment will provide 60,000 machine hours per year. Direct material costs will average $0.75 per set, and direct labor will average $0.25 per set. Since only one type of roller would be produced, no additional demands would be made on the setup activity. Other overhead activities (besides machining and setups), however, would be affected. The company's cost management system provides the following information about the current status of the overhead activities that would be affected. (The supply and demand figures do not include the effect of roller production on these activities.) The lumpy quantity indicates how much capacity must be purchased should any expansion of activity supply be needed. The purchase price is the cost of acquiring the capacity represented by the lumpy quantity. This price also represents the cost of current spending on existing activity supply (for each block of activity).

Activity Price	Cost Driver	Supply	Usage	Lumpy Quantity	Purchase
Purchasing	Orders	25,000	23,000	5,000	$25,000
Inspection	Hours	10,000	9,000	2,000	30,000
Materials handling	Moves	4,500	4,300	500	15,000

Production of rollers would place the following demands on the overhead activities:

Activity	Resource Demands
Machining	50,000 machine hours
Purchasing	2,000 purchase orders (associated with raw materials used to make the rollers)
Inspection	750 inspection hours
Materials handling	500 moves

Producing the rollers also means that the purchase of outside rollers will cease. Thus, purchase orders associated with the outside acquisition of rollers will drop by 5,000. Similarly, the moves for the handling of incoming orders will decrease by 200. The company has not inspected the rollers purchased from outside suppliers.

Required:

1. Classify all resources associated with the production of rollers as flexible resources and committed resources. Label each committed resource as a short- or long-term commitment. How should we describe the cost behavior of these short- and long-term resource commitments? Explain.
2. Calculate the total annual resource spending (for all activities except for setups) that the company will incur after production of the rollers begins. Break this cost into fixed and variable activity costs. In calculating these figures, assume that the company will spend no more than necessary. What is the effect on resource spending caused by production of the rollers?
3. Refer to Requirement 2. For each activity, break down the cost of activity supplied into the cost of activity output and the cost of unused activity.

OBJECTIVE ▸ 4 ▸ 1 ▸   **Problem 3-29 Cost Behavior, High-Low Method, Pricing Decision**

St. Teresa's Medical Center (STMC) offers a number of specialized medical services, including neuroscience, cardiology, and oncology. STMC's strong reputation for quality medical care allowed it to branch out into other services. It is now ready to expand its orthopedic services and has just added a free-standing orthopedic clinic offering a full range of outpatient, surgical, and physical therapy services. The cost of the orthopedic facility is depreciated on a straight-line basis. All equipment within the facility is leased.

Since the clinic had no experience with in-patient orthopedic services (for patients recovering from hip and knee replacements, for example), it decided to operate the orthopedic center for two months before determining how much to charge per patient day on an ongoing basis. As a temporary measure, the clinic adopted a patient-day charge of $190, an amount equal to the fees charged by a hospital specializing in orthopedic care in a nearby city.

This initial per-day charge was quoted to patients entering the orthopedic center during the first two months with assurances that if the actual operating costs of the new center justified it, the charge could be less. In no case would the charges be more. A temporary policy of billing after 60 days was adopted so that any adjustments could be made.

The orthopedic center opened on January 1. During January, the center had 4,200 patient days of activity. During February, the activity was 4,500 patient days. Costs for these two levels of activity output are as follows:

	4,200 Patient Days	4,500 Patient Days
Salaries, nurses	$ 55,000	$ 55,000
Aides	32,000	32,000
Pharmacy	235,700	251,300
Laboratory	120,300	127,200
Depreciation	25,000	25,000
Laundry	20,160	21,600
Administration	27,000	27,000
Lease (equipment)	36,000	36,000

Required:

1. Classify each cost as fixed, variable, or mixed, using patient days as the activity driver.
2. Use the high-low method to separate the mixed costs into fixed and variable.
3. The administrator of the orthopedic center estimated that the center will average 4,300 patient days per month. If the center is to be operated as a nonprofit organization, how much will it need to charge per patient day? How much of this charge is variable? How much is fixed?
4. Suppose the orthopedic center averages 4,800 patient days per month. How much would need to be charged per patient day for the center to cover its costs? Explain why the charge per patient day decreased as the activity output increased.

Problem 3-30 High-Low Method, Method of Least Squares, Correlation

OBJECTIVE ◄ 2 4 5

Big Mike's, a large hardware store, has gathered data on its overhead activities and associated costs for the past 10 months. Nizam Sanjay, a member of the controller's department, believes that overhead activities and costs should be classified into groups that have the same driver. He has decided that unloading incoming goods, counting goods, and inspecting goods can be grouped together as a more general receiving activity, since these three activities are all driven by the number of receiving orders. The 10 months of data shown below have been gathered for the receiving activity.

Month	Receiving Orders	Receiving Cost
1	1,000	$12,170
2	1,340	12,940
3	1,150	13,750
4	900	9,930
5	1,350	15,070
6	1,400	14,145
7	1,600	16,640
8	1,490	14,800
9	1,800	17,940
10	1,700	15,000

Required:

1. Prepare a scattergraph, plotting the receiving costs against the number of purchase orders. Use the vertical axis for costs and the horizontal axis for orders.
2. Select two points that make the best fit, and compute a cost formula for receiving costs.
3. Using the high-low method, prepare a cost formula for the receiving activity.
4. Using the method of least squares, prepare a cost formula for the receiving activity. What is the coefficient of determination?

OBJECTIVE 6 5 4 1

Problem 3-31 Cost Formulas, Single and Multiple Activity Drivers, Coefficient of Correlation

Kimball Company has developed the following cost formulas:

$$\text{Material usage: } Y_m = \$80X; r = 0.95$$
$$\text{Labor usage (direct): } Y_l = \$20X; r = 0.96$$
$$\text{Overhead activity: } Y_o = \$350{,}000 + \$100X; r = 0.75$$
$$\text{Selling activity: } Y_s = \$50{,}000 + \$10X; r = 0.93$$

where

$$X = \text{Direct labor hours}$$

The company has a policy of producing on demand and keeps very little, if any, finished goods inventory (thus, units produced equals units sold). Each unit uses one direct labor hour for production.

The president of Kimball Company has recently implemented a policy that any special orders will be accepted if they cover the costs that the orders cause. This policy was implemented because Kimball's industry is in a recession and the company is producing well below capacity (and expects to continue doing so for the coming year). The president is willing to accept orders that minimally cover their variable costs so that the company can keep its employees and avoid layoffs. Also, any orders above variable costs will increase overall profitability of the company.

Required:

1. Compute the total unit variable cost. Suppose that Kimball has an opportunity to accept an order for 20,000 units at $220 per unit. Should Kimball accept the order? (The order would not displace any of Kimball's regular orders.)
2. Explain the significance of the coefficient of correlation measures for the cost formulas. Did these measures have a bearing on your answer in Requirement 1? Should they have a bearing? Why or why not?
3. Suppose that a multiple regression equation is developed for overhead costs: $Y = \$100{,}000 + \$100X_1 + \$5{,}000X_2 + \$300X_3$, where $X_1 = $ direct labor hours, $X_2 = $ number of setups, and $X_3 = $ engineering hours. The coefficient of determination for the equation is 0.94. Assume that the order of 20,000 units requires 12 setups and 600 engineering hours. Given this new information, should the company accept the special order referred to in Requirement 1? Is there any other information about cost behavior that you would like to have? Explain.

OBJECTIVE 6 5 4

Problem 3-32 Scatterplot, High-Low Method, Regression

The management of Wheeler Company has decided to develop cost formulas for its major overhead activities. Wheeler uses a highly automated manufacturing process, and power costs are a significant manufacturing cost. Cost analysts have decided that power costs are mixed; thus, they must be broken into their fixed and variable elements so that the cost behavior of the power usage activity can be properly described. Machine hours have been selected as the activity driver for power costs. The following data for the past eight quarters have been collected:

Quarter	Machine Hours	Power Cost
1	20,000	$26,000
2	25,000	38,000
3	30,000	42,500
4	22,000	35,000
5	21,000	34,000
6	18,000	31,400
7	24,000	36,000
8	28,000	42,000

Required:

1. Prepare a scattergraph by plotting power costs against machine hours. Does the scatter-graph show a linear relationship between machine hours and power cost?
2. Using the high and low points, compute a power cost formula.
3. Use the method of least squares to compute a power cost formula. Evaluate the coefficient of determination.
4. Rerun the regression and drop the point (20,000; $26,000) as an outlier. Compare the results from this regression to those for the regression in Requirement 3. Which is better?

Problem 3-33 Method of Least Squares

OBJECTIVE ◀ 1 4 5 6

DeMarco Company is developing a cost formula for its packing activity. Discussion with the workers in the Packing Department has revealed that packing costs are associated with the number of customer orders, the size of the orders, and the relative fragility of the items (more fragile items must be specially wrapped in bubble wrap and Styrofoam). Data for the past 20 months have been gathered:

Month	Packing Cost	Number of Orders	Weight of Orders	Number of Fragile Items
1	$ 45,000	11,200	24,640	1,120
2	58,000	14,000	31,220	1,400
3	39,000	10,500	18,000	1,000
4	35,600	9,000	19,350	850
5	90,000	21,000	46,200	4,000
6	126,000	31,000	64,000	5,500
7	90,600	20,000	60,000	1,800
8	63,000	15,000	40,000	750
9	79,000	16,000	59,000	1,500
10	155,000	40,000	88,000	2,500
11	450,000	113,500	249,700	11,800
12	640,000	150,000	390,000	14,000
13	41,000	10,000	23,000	900
14	54,000	14,000	29,400	890
15	58,000	15,000	30,000	1,500
16	58,090	14,500	31,900	1,340
17	80,110	18,000	50,000	3,000
18	123,000	30,000	75,000	2,000
19	108,000	27,000	63,450	1,900
20	76,000	18,000	41,400	1,430

Required:

1. Using the method of least squares, run a regression using the number of orders as the independent variable.
2. Run a multiple regression using three independent variables: the number of orders, the weight of orders, and the number of fragile items. Which regression equation is better? Why?
3. Predict the total packing cost for 25,000 orders, weighing 40,000 pounds, with 4,000 fragile items.
4. How much would the cost estimated for Requirement 3 change if the 25,000 orders weighed 40,000 pounds, but only 2,000 were fragile items?

OBJECTIVE 6 5 4 2 ▶   **Problem 3-34 High-Low Method, Scatterplot, Regression**

Weber Valley Regional Hospital has collected data on all of its activities for the past 16 months. Data for cardiac nursing care follow:

	Y Cost	X Hours of Nursing Care
May Year 1	$59,600	1,400
June Year 1	57,150	1,350
July Year 1	61,110	1,460
August Year 1	65,800	1,600
September Year 1	69,500	1,700
October Year 1	64,250	1,550
November Year 1	52,000	1,200
December Year 1	66,000	1,600
January Year 2	83,000	1,800
February Year 2	66,550	1,330
March Year 2	79,500	1,700
April Year 2	76,000	1,600
May Year 2	68,500	1,400
June Year 2	73,150	1,550
July Year 2	73,175	1,505
August Year 2	66,150	1,290

Required:

1. Using the high-low method, calculate the variable rate per hour and the fixed cost for the nursing care activity.
2. Run a regression on the data, using hours of nursing care as the independent variable. Predict cost for the cardiac nursing care for September Year 2 if 1,400 hours of nursing care are forecast. Evaluate the regression equation. How comfortable are you with the predicted cost for September Year 2?
3. Upon looking into the events that happened at the end of Year 1, you find that the cardiology ward bought a cardiac-monitoring machine for the nursing station. Administrators also decided to add a new supervisory position for the evening shift. Monthly depreciation on the monitor and the salary of the new supervisor together total $10,000. Now, run two regression equations, one for the observations from Year 1 and the second using only the observations for the eight months in Year 2. Discuss your findings. What is your predicted cost of the cardiac nursing care activity for September Year 2?

OBJECTIVE 6 5 4 1 ▶   **Problem 3-35 Comparison of Regression Equations**

Friendly Bank is attempting to determine the cost behavior of its small business lending operations. One of the major activities is the application activity. Two possible activity drivers have been mentioned: application hours (number of hours to complete the application) and number of applications. The bank controller has accumulated the following data for the setup activity:

Month	Application Costs	Application Hours	Number of Applications
February	$ 7,700	2,000	70
March	7,650	2,100	50
April	10,052	3,000	50
May	9,400	2,700	60
June	9,584	3,000	20
July	8,480	2,500	40
August	8,550	2,400	60
September	9,735	2,900	50
October	10,500	3,000	90

Required:

1. Estimate a regression equation with application hours as the activity driver and the only independent variable. If the bank forecasts 2,600 application hours for the next month, what will be the budgeted application cost?
2. Estimate a regression equation with number of applications as the activity driver and the only independent variable. If the bank forecasts 80 applications for the next month, what will be the budgeted application cost?
3. Which of the two regression equations do you think does a better job of predicting application costs? Explain.
4. Run a multiple regression to determine the cost equation using both activity drivers. What are the budgeted application costs for 2,600 application hours and 80 applications?

Problem 3-36 Multiple Regression, Confidence Intervals, Reliability of Cost Formulas

OBJECTIVE ◄ 2 5 6

Randy Harris, controller, has been given the charge to implement an advanced cost management system. As part of this process, he needs to identify activity drivers for the activities of the firm. During the past four months, Randy has spent considerable effort identifying activities, their associated costs, and possible drivers for the activities' costs.

Initially, Randy made his selections based on his own judgment using his experience and input from employees who perform the activities. Later, he used regression analysis to confirm his judgment. Randy prefers to use one driver per activity, provided that an R^2 of at least 80 percent can be produced. Otherwise, multiple drivers will be used, based on evidence provided by multiple regression analysis. For example, the activity of inspecting finished goods produced an R^2 of less than 80 percent for any single activity driver. Randy believes, however, that a satisfactory cost formula can be developed using two activity drivers: the number of batches and the number of inspection hours. Data collected for a 14-month period are as follows:

Inspection Costs	Hours of Inspection	Number of Batches
$17,689	100	10
18,350	120	20
13,125	60	15
28,000	320	30
30,560	240	25
31,755	200	40
40,750	280	35
29,500	230	22
47,570	350	50
36,740	270	45
43,500	350	38
26,780	200	18
28,500	140	28
17,000	160	14

Required:

1. Calculate the cost formula for inspection costs using the two drivers, inspection hours and number of batches. Are both activity drivers useful? What does the R^2 indicate about the formula?
2. Using the formula developed in Requirement 1, calculate the inspection cost when 300 inspection hours are used and 30 batches are produced. Prepare a 90 percent confidence interval for this prediction.

OBJECTIVE 5 4 2

Problem 3-37 Simple and Multiple Regression, Evaluating Reliability of an Equation

The Lockit Company manufactures door knobs for residential homes and apartments. Lockit is considering the use of simple (single-driver) and multiple regression analyses to forecast annual sales because previous forecasts have been inaccurate. The new sales forecast will be used to initiate the budgeting process and to identify more completely the underlying process that generates sales.

Larry Abram, the controller of Lockit, has considered many possible independent variables and equations to predict sales and has narrowed his choices to four equations. Abram used annual observations from 20 prior years to estimate each of the four equations.

Following are definitions of the variables used in the four equations and a statistical summary of these equations:

Statistical Summary of Four Equations

Equation	Dependent Variable	Independent Variable (s)	Intercept	Independent Variable (Rate)	Standard Error	R Square	t-Value
1	S_t	S_{t-1}	$ 500,000	$ 1.10	$500,000	0.94	5.50
2	S_t	G_t	1,000,000	0.00001	510,000	0.90	10.00
3	S_t	G_{t-1}	900,000	0.000012	520,000	0.81	5.00
4	S_t		600,000		490,000	0.96	
		N_{t-1}		10.00			4.00
		G_t		0.000002			1.50
		G_{t-1}		0.000003			3.00

S_t = Forecasted sales in dollars for Lockit in period t
S_{t-1} = Actual sales in dollars for Lockit in period $t - 1$
G_t = Forecasted U.S. gross domestic product in period t
G_{t-1} = Actual U.S. gross domestic product in period $t - 1$
N_{t-1} = Lockit's net income in period $t - 1$

Required:

1. Write Equations 2 and 4 in the form $Y = a + bx$.
2. If actual sales are $1,500,000 in the current year, what would be the forecasted sales for Lockit in the coming year?
3. Explain why Larry Abram might prefer Equation 3 to Equation 2.
4. Explain the advantages and disadvantages of using Equation 4 to forecast sales.

(CMA adapted)

OBJECTIVE 7

DATA ANALYTICS

Problem 3-38 Learning Curve

Harriman Industries manufactures engines for the aerospace industry. It has completed manufacturing the first unit of the new ZX-9 engine design. Management believes that the 1,000 labor hours required to complete this unit are reasonable and is prepared to go forward with the manufacture of additional units. An 80 percent cumulative average-time learning curve model for direct labor hours is assumed to be valid. Data on costs are as follows:

Direct materials	$10,500
Direct labor	$30 per direct labor hour
Variable manufacturing overhead	$40 per direct labor hour

Required:

1. Set up a table with columns for cumulative number of units, cumulative average time per unit in hours, and the cumulative total time in hours. Complete the table for 1, 2, 4, 8, 16, and 32 units. (Round hours to one significant digit.)

2. What are the total variable costs of producing 1, 2, 4, 8, 16, and 32 units? What is the variable cost per unit for 1, 2, 4, 8, 16, and 32 units?

3. Briefly describe a decision scenario for Harriman's management in which the use of its learning curve insights would be considered a predictive data analytics (see Exhibits 2.5 and 2.6, pp. 37, 40 for a review of data analytic types).

4. Briefly describe a decision scenario for Harriman's management in which the use of its learning curve insights would be considered a prescriptive data analytics (see Exhibits 2.5 and 2.6, pp. 37, 40 for a review of data analytic types).

Problem 3-39 Learning Curve

OBJECTIVE ◀ 7

Thames Assurance Company sells a variety of life and health insurance products. Recently, Thames developed a long-term care policy for sale to members of university and college alumni associations. Thames estimated that the sale and service of this type of policy would be subject to a 90 percent cumulative average-time learning curve model. Each unit consists of 350 policies sold. The first unit is estimated to take 1,000 hours to sell and service.

Required:

1. Set up a table with columns for cumulative number of units, cumulative average time per unit in hours, and the cumulative total time in hours. Complete the table for 1, 2, 4, 8, 16, and 32 units.

2. Suppose that Thames revises its assumption to an 80 percent learning curve. How will this affect the amount of time needed to sell and service eight units? How do you suppose that Thames estimates the percent learning rate?

4

Activity-Based Costing

After studying this chapter, you should be able to:

1 Describe the basics of plantwide and departmental overhead costing.

2 Explain why plantwide and departmental overhead costing may not be accurate.

3 Provide a detailed description of activity-based product costing.

4 Explain how ABC can be simplified.

iStockphoto.com/bgwalker

ACTIVITY-BASED COSTING

at the University of Pittsburg Medical Center

Health-care systems are characterized by service variety and complexity. As the rate of health-care spending continues to grow, there is an increasing need for hospitals to understand what it costs to provide health-care services. Understanding costs can help reduce waste and eliminate inefficiency. It can also help establish accurate pricing for the various health-care services offered.

The **University of Pittsburg Medical Center** (UPMC) recognized these concerns and proactively implemented an activity-based costing system. UPMC has more than $21 billion in revenue, with 40 hospitals and 8,400 licensed beds. Clearly, knowing its costs and managing them was critical for its long-term sustainability. The traditional hospital costing methods, relative value units (RVU), and ratio of cost to charges (RCC) did not provide the needed information, accuracy, and detail to allow UPMC to improve its processes, eliminate waste, and increase efficiency. UPMC found that the activity-based accounting system provided accurate, actionable, and defensible data that allowed them to improve quality and reduce costs.[1]

To improve care and enhance their competitive position, UPMC decided to adopt a service-line approach, formally considering the services they offered from a patient perspective rather than a departmental perspective. Activity-based costing allowed UPMC to identify the activities and costs associated with service lines, enabling them to improve quality and lower costs of the various patient-care services offered. Armed with this information, managers could then take actions needed to realize significant savings. Using accurate and timely cost information, UPMC has produced process improvements and millions in savings for surgical services, orthopedics, women's health (deliveries and hysterectomies), and neurosurgery.[2]

UPMC has used its new activity-based costing system to study differences in procedure costs. For example, physician supply costs for postural lateral lumbar fusion (a type of spinal surgery) ranged from as much as 49 percent above the median to 87 percent below it.[3] Using the

---

1　"Activity-Based Costing and Clinical Service Lines Team up to Improve Financial and Clinical Outcomes," *Health Catalyst Success Stories* (February 15, 2018), https://www.healthcatalyst.com/success_stories/activity-based-costing-in-healthcare-service-lines-upmc, accessed March 31, 2020.

2　"Service Lines and Activity-Based Costing Reveal True Cost of Care for UPMC," *Health Catalyst Success Stories* (September 1, 2016), https://www.healthcatalyst.com/success_stories/activity-based-costing-in-healthcare-upmc, accessed March 31, 2020.

3　Tara Bannow, "More Hospitals Calculating Actual Cost of Care," *Modern Healthcare* (May 18, 2019), https://www.modernhealthcare.com/finance/more-hospitals-calculating-actual-cost-care, accessed March 31, 2020.

results of studies like those for the spinal surgery, UPMC then explored ways to reduce the variation. Other health-care systems are following the example of UPMC and are implementing activity-based costing and time-driven activity-based costing. For example, **Owensboro Health**, Kentucky, has used activity-based costing to determine the cost of each procedure and is using the information to reduce the amount patients are charged for certain services.[4] Similarly, the 11-hospital **Baptist Health** in Little Rock, Arkansas, has used its new activity-based cost information in its negotiations with payers; at times, Baptist has even offered to lower its rates for some services because they can be performed at a lower cost.[5] The executive vice president and chief financial officer of UPMC predicted that over the next five to seven years, every health-care system will be using activity-based costing tools.[6]

As the UPMC example illustrates, an organization must understand what it costs to offer a service or manufacture a product. Accurate cost information for products and services is needed to identify waste and inefficiency, which then enables managers to improve efficiency and price products and services more competitively. Clearly, data analytics play a vital role in this process of determining what it costs to produce a unit of output. The questions of what is being measured, why it is being measured, where the data are, how it is being measured, and which measurement model should be used are all vital. Also, it should be noted that calculating a unit cost certainly describes what is happening. Moreover, calculating a unit cost is necessary but not sufficient. Understanding why a unit of product costs an indicated amount is also critical. Furthermore, unit cost information can be used to predict the level of resources needed for producing a given number of products or services. Finally, based on the diagnostic evaluation of unit cost, inefficiencies and waste can be identified and managers can determine what it should cost to produce a unit of output.

DATA ANALYTICS

In Chapter 2, we mentioned that cost management information systems can be divided into two types: unit-based and activity-based. The unit-based costing systems use traditional product cost definitions and use only unit-based activity drivers to assign overhead to products or services. Based on the experience of UPMC and other hospitals, traditional costing may not provide the information and accuracy needed to improve quality, efficiency, and maintain competitiveness. This chapter begins by describing how unit-based costing is used for computing traditional product costs. This enables us to compare and contrast unit-based and activity-based costing approaches. In the chapter, we consider two unit-based analytic models and five activity-based analytic models. An activity-based cost accounting system offers greater product-costing accuracy but at an increased cost. All the analytical variations of activity-based costing have the objective of preserving the benefits of activity-based costing while reducing the measurement cost. The justification for adopting an activity-based costing approach must rely on the benefits of improved decisions resulting from materially different product or service costs. It is important to understand that a necessary condition for improved decisions is that the accounting numbers produced by an activity-based costing system must be significantly different from those produced by a unit-based costing system. When will this be the case? Are there any signals that management might receive which would indicate that unit-based costing is no longer working? Finally, assuming that an activity-based cost accounting model is called for, how does it work? What are its basic features? Detailed features? What steps must be followed for successful implementation of an activity-based costing (ABC) system? This chapter addresses these questions and other related issues.

---

4 Ibid.
5 Ibid.
6 Ibid.

UNIT-LEVEL PRODUCT COSTING

OBJECTIVE 1

Describe the basics of plantwide and departmental overhead costing.

Unit-based product costing assigns only manufacturing costs to products. Exhibit 4.1 shows the general unit-based product-costing model. Assigning the cost of direct materials and direct labor to products poses no particular challenge. These costs can be assigned to products using direct tracing, and most unit-based costing systems are designed to ensure that this tracing takes place. Overhead costs, on the other hand, pose a different problem. The physically observable input-output relationship that exists between direct labor, direct materials, and products is simply not available for overhead. Thus, assignment of overhead must rely on driver tracing and perhaps allocation. Unit-based costing first assigns overhead costs to a functional unit, creating either plant or departmental cost pools. Next, these pooled costs are assigned to products using *predetermined overhead rates* based on unit-level drivers.

A **predetermined overhead rate** is calculated at the beginning of the year using the following formula:

Overhead rate = Budgeted annual overhead/Budgeted annual driver level

Predetermined rates are used because overhead and production often are incurred non-uniformly throughout the year, and it is not possible to wait until the end of the year to calculate the actual overhead cost assignments (managers need unit product cost information throughout the year). A cost system that uses predetermined overhead rates and actual costs for direct materials and direct labor is referred to as a **normal cost system**. Budgeted overhead is simply the firm's best estimate of the amount of overhead (utilities, indirect labor, depreciation, etc.) to be incurred in the coming year. The estimate is often based on last year's figures, adjusted for anticipated changes in the coming year. The second input requires that the predicted level for an activity driver be specified. Assignment of overhead costs should follow, as nearly as possible, a cause-and-effect relationship. Drivers are simply causal factors that measure the consumption of overhead by products. In unit-based costing, only *unit-level drivers* are used to calculate overhead rates.

Unit-level drivers are factors that measure the demands placed on unit-level activities by products. Unit-level activities are activities performed each and every time a unit of a product is produced. The five most commonly used unit-level drivers are:

1. Units produced
2. Direct labor hours
3. Direct labor dollars
4. Machine hours
5. Direct material dollars

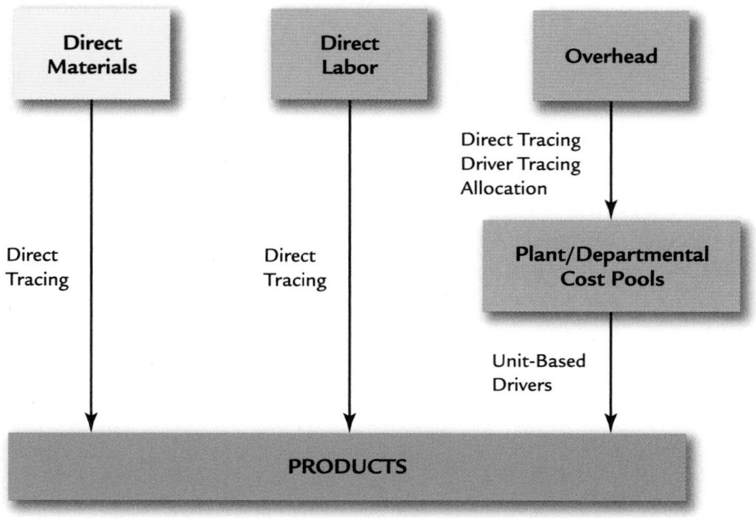

Exhibit 4.1

Unit-Based Product-Costing Model

Unit-level drivers increase as units produced increase. Thus, the use of only unit-based drivers to assign overhead costs to products assumes that all overhead consumed by products is highly correlated with the number of units produced. To the extent that this assumption is true, unit-based costing can produce accurate cost assignments.

Plantwide or departmental predetermined overhead rates are used to assign or apply overhead costs to production as the actual production activity unfolds. The total overhead assigned to actual production at any point in time is called **applied overhead**. Applied overhead is computed using the following formula:

Applied overhead = Overhead rate × Actual driver usage

Once the applied overhead is assigned, the unit cost is calculated by dividing the total applied overhead by the units produced.

Overhead Assignment: Plantwide Rates

For plantwide rates, all budgeted overhead costs are assigned to a plantwide pool (first-stage cost assignment). Next, a plantwide rate is computed using a single unit-level driver, which is usually direct labor hours. Finally, overhead costs are assigned to products by multiplying the rate by the actual total direct labor hours used by each product (second-stage assignment). The corresponding calculations and their rationale are illustrated in **Example 4.1**.

EXAMPLE 4.1

The HOW and WHY of Applied Overhead and Unit Overhead Cost: Plantwide Rates

Information:
The Boise plant of Juguette, Inc., produces two types of battery-operated toys: robots and race cars. The Boise plant uses a plantwide rate based on direct labor hours to assign its overhead costs. The company has the following estimated and actual data for the coming year:

Estimated overhead	$350,000
Expected activity	50,000
Actual activity (direct labor hours):	
Robots	10,000
Race cars	40,000
Units produced:	
Robots	50,000
Race cars	250,000

Why:
Product cost information is needed for such things as financial statement preparation, pricing decisions, and keep-or-drop decisions. Predetermined overhead rates (based on expected overhead and expected activity) are used because overhead and production are incurred nonuniformly and managers cannot wait until the end of the year to obtain product cost information. A plantwide rate is used under the assumption that all overhead costs are largely caused by a single, unit-level cost driver such as direct labor hours or machine hours.

EXAMPLE 4.1

(*Continued*)

Required:

1. Calculate the predetermined plantwide overhead rate and the applied overhead for each product, using direct labor hours.

2. Calculate the overhead cost per unit for each product.

3. *What if* robots used 5,000 hours (to produce 50,000 units) instead of 10,000 hours? Calculate the effect on the profitability of this product line if all 50,000 units are sold, and then discuss the implications of this outcome.

Solution:

1. Plantwide rate = $350,000/50,000 = $7.00 per hour

   Applied overhead:

	Robots	Race Cars
$7.00 × 10,000	$70,000	
$7.00 × 40,000		$280,000

2. Overhead per unit (robots) = $70,000/50,000 = $1.40

   Overhead per unit (race cars) = $280,000/250,000 = $1.12

3. There would be a reduction of $35,000 ($7.00 × 5,000) of overhead assigned to the robots, and so profitability for this product line would increase by this amount. Overhead assignments affect product cost and profitability and thus can affect many decisions (e.g., pricing). This conclusion, in turn, implies that the way overhead is assigned is important.

Calculation and Disposition of Overhead Variances

From Example 4.1, the initial calculation of applied overhead is $350,000. It is possible (and likely) that the applied amount in a period differs from the actual overhead incurred for the period. Since the predetermined overhead rate is based on estimated data, applied overhead will rarely equal actual overhead. The difference between actual overhead and applied overhead is an **overhead variance**. If actual overhead is greater than applied overhead, then the variance is called **underapplied overhead**. If applied overhead is greater than actual overhead, then the variance is called **overapplied overhead**.

Overhead variances occur because it is impossible to perfectly estimate future overhead costs and production activity. Costs reported on the financial statements must be actual—not estimated—amounts. Accordingly, at the end of a reporting period, procedures must exist to dispose of any overhead variance. An overhead variance is disposed of in one of two ways:

1. If immaterial, it is assigned to cost of goods sold.

2. If material, it is allocated among work-in-process inventory, finished goods inventory, and cost of goods sold.

The most common practice is simply to assign the entire overhead variance to cost of goods sold. This practice is justified on the basis of materiality, the same principle used to justify expensing the entire cost of a pencil sharpener in the period acquired rather than allocating (through depreciation) its cost over the life of the sharpener. Thus, the overhead variance is added to cost of goods sold if underapplied and subtracted from cost of goods sold if overapplied. A journal entry is the mechanism for adding or subtracting the overhead variance. Assuming that both actual and applied overhead are accumulated in the overhead control account, Cost of Goods Sold would be debited (credited) if under- (over-) applied.

If the overhead variance is material, it should be allocated to the period's production. Conceptually, the overhead costs of a period belong to goods started but not completed (work-in-process inventory), goods finished but not sold (finished goods inventory), and goods finished and sold (cost of goods sold). The recommended way to achieve this allocation is to prorate the overhead variance based on the ending applied overhead balances in each account. Using applied overhead captures the original cause-and-effect relationships used to assign overhead. Using another balance to prorate, such as total manufacturing costs, may result in an unfair assignment of the additional overhead. For example, two products identical on all dimensions except for the cost of direct material inputs should receive the same overhead assignment. Yet, if total manufacturing costs were used to allocate an overhead variance, then the product with the more expensive direct materials would receive a higher overhead assignment. The prorating adds the amount to each account if underapplied and subtracts an amount from each account if overapplied. Again, a journal entry is the mechanism used. **Example 4.2** illustrates the calculation and disposal of overhead variances.

Overhead Application: Departmental Rates

For departmental rates, overhead costs are assigned to individual production departments, creating departmental overhead cost pools. In the first stage, producing departments are cost objects, and budgeted overhead costs are assigned using direct tracing, driver tracing, and allocation. Once costs are assigned to individual production departments, then unit-level drivers such as direct labor hours (for labor-intensive departments) and machine hours (for machine-intensive departments) are used to compute predetermined overhead rates for each department. Products passing through the departments are assumed to consume overhead resources in proportion to the departments' unit-based drivers (machine hours or direct labor hours used). Thus, in the second stage, overhead is assigned to products by multiplying the

---

EXAMPLE 4.2

The HOW and WHY of Overhead Variances and Their Disposal

Information:

Juguette's Boise plant produces two types of battery-operated toys: robots and race cars. The company has the following data for the past year:

		Prorate percentage
Actual overhead	$380,000	
Applied overhead:		
Work-in-process inventory	$ 70,000	20% ($70,000/$350,000)
Finished goods inventory	105,000	30% ($105,000/$350,000)
Cost of goods sold	175,000	50% ($175,000/$350,000)
Total	$350,000	100%

The Boise plant uses the overhead control account to accumulate both actual and applied overhead.

Why:

At the end of the period, the total actual amount of overhead incurred must be reported as a product cost. Financial reports use actual production costs and, thus, applied and actual overhead must be reconciled. First, the difference is calculated: Actual overhead – Applied overhead (called an overhead variance). Next, the variance balance, which is either under- or overapplied overhead, must be removed through an adjustment at the end of the period. If the amount of the overhead variance is not material, then it is typically closed out to cost of goods sold. If material, the variance is prorated among Work in Process, Finished Goods, and Cost of Goods Sold.

EXAMPLE 4.2

(Continued)

Required:

1. Calculate the overhead variance for the year and close it to Cost of Goods Sold.

2. Assume the variance calculated is material. After prorating, close the variances to the appropriate accounts and provide the final ending balances of these accounts.

3. *What if* the variance is overapplied instead of underapplied? Provide the appropriate adjusting journal entries (if immaterial and then if material).

Solution:

1. Overhead variance = $380,000 − $350,000 = $30,000 underapplied

Cost of Goods Sold	30,000	
Overhead Control		30,000

2. Proration: (0.20 × $30,000; 0.30 × $30,000; 0.50 × $30,000)

Work-in-Process Inventory	6,000	
Finished Goods Inventory	9,000	
Cost of Goods Sold	15,000	
Overhead Control		30,000

	Unadjusted Balance	Prorated Underapplied Overhead	Adjusted Balance
Work-in-Process Inventory	$ 70,000	$ 6,000	$ 76,000
Finished Goods Inventory	105,000	9,000	114,000
Cost of Goods Sold	175,000	15,000	190,000

3.

Overhead Control	30,000	
Cost of Goods Sold		30,000

Overhead Control	30,000	
Cost of Goods Sold		15,000
Work-in-Process Inventory		6,000
Finished Goods Inventory		9,000

departmental rates by the amount of the driver used in the respective departments. The total overhead assigned to products is simply the sum of the amounts received in each department. Increased accuracy is the usual justification offered for the use of departmental rates.

The Juguette example will again be used to illustrate departmental rates. Assume that the Boise plant of Juguette has two producing departments: Molding and Assembly. Machine hours are used to assign the overhead of molding, and direct labor hours are used to assign the overhead of assembly. **Example 4.3** illustrates the calculations and discusses their rationale.

EXAMPLE 4.3

The HOW and WHY of Departmental Overhead Rates: Their Assignment and Rationale

Information:

The data for the two producing departments of the Boise plant are given below.

	Molding	Assembly	Total
Estimated overhead	$250,000	$100,000	$350,000
Direct labor hours (expected and actual):			
Robots	5,000	5,000	10,000
Race cars	5,000	35,000	40,000
Total	10,000	40,000	50,000
Machine hours:			
Robots	17,000	3,000	20,000
Race cars	3,000	7,000	10,000
Total	20,000	10,000	30,000

Machine hours are used to assign the overhead of the Molding Department, and direct labor hours are used to assign the overhead of the Assembly Department. There are 50,000 robots produced and sold and 250,000 race cars.

Why:

Product costs that reflect the consumption of resources actually used are relatively more accurate and improve decision making and control. Overhead intensity and patterns of consumption by products can differ from department to department. The argument is that departmental overhead rates will better reflect each product's use of resources and thus will be more accurate than a single plantwide rate.

Required:

1. Calculate the overhead rates for each department.

2. Assign overhead to the two products and calculate the overhead cost per unit. How does this compare with the plantwide rate unit cost of Example 4.1?

3. *What if* the machine hours in Molding were 5,000 for robots and 15,000 for race cars and the direct labor hours used in Assembly were 4,000 and 36,000, respectively? Calculate the overhead cost per unit for each product, and compare with the plantwide rate unit cost of Example 4.1. What can you conclude from this outcome?

Solution:

1. Molding: $250,000/20,000 = $12.50 per machine hour

    Assembly: $100,000/40,000 = $2.50 per direct labor hour

2. Overhead assignment:

	Robots	Race Cars
($12.50 × 17,000) + ($2.50 × 5,000)	$225,000	
($12.50 × 3,000) + ($2.50 × 35,000)		$125,000
Total applied overhead	$225,000	$125,000
Units of production	÷50,000	÷250,000
Unit overhead cost	$ 4.50	$ 0.50

EXAMPLE 4.3

(Continued)

The cost increased dramatically for robots (from $1.40 to $4.50) and decreased significantly for race cars (from $1.12 to $0.50).

3. Overhead assignment:

	Robots	Race Cars
($12.50 × 5,000) + ($2.50 × 4,000)	$72,500	
($12.50 × 15,000) + ($2.50 × 36,000)		$277,500
Total applied overhead	$72,500	$277,500
Units of production	÷50,000	÷250,000
Unit overhead cost	$ 1.45	$ 1.11

Compared to the plantwide unit overhead costs, the cost is $0.05 more for robots and $0.01 less for racing cars. The message is that departmental rates may not necessarily cause a significant change in the assignments. It depends on the complexity of each product and how the resource demands are made in each department. However, implementation of departmental rates would probably be done based on the observation that significant differences in resource consumption do exist, justifying the decision.

LIMITATIONS OF PLANTWIDE AND DEPARTMENTAL RATES

OBJECTIVE ◀ 2
Explain why plantwide and departmental overhead costing may not be accurate.

Plantwide and departmental rates have been used for decades and continue to be used successfully by many organizations. In some settings, however, they do not work well and may actually cause severe product cost distortions. Of course, to cause a significant cost distortion, overhead costs must be a significant percentage of total manufacturing costs. For some manufacturers, overhead costs are a small percentage (e.g., 5 percent or less), and the system in which these costs are assigned is not a major issue. In this case, using a very simple, uncomplicated approach such as plantwide rates is appropriate. Assuming, however, that the overhead costs are a significant percentage of total manufacturing costs, at least two major factors can impair the ability of the unit-based plant-wide and departmental rates to assign overhead costs accurately: (1) the proportion of non-unit-related overhead costs to total overhead costs is large, and (2) the degree of product diversity is great.

Non-Unit-Related Overhead Costs

The use of either plantwide rates or departmental rates assumes that a product's consumption of overhead resources is related strictly to the units produced. But what if there are overhead activities that are unrelated to the number of units produced? Setup costs, for example, are incurred each time a batch of products is produced. A batch may consist of 1,000 or 10,000 units, and the cost of setup is the same. Yet, as more setups are done, setup costs increase. The number of setups, not the number of units produced, is the cause of setup costs. Furthermore, product engineering costs may depend on the number of different engineering work orders rather than the units produced of any given product. Both these examples illustrate the existence of non-unit-based drivers. **Non-unit-based drivers** are factors, other than the number of units produced, that measure the demands that cost objects place on activities. Thus, unit-level drivers cannot assign these costs accurately to products. In fact, using only unit-level drivers to assign non-unit-related overhead costs can create distorted product costs. The severity of this distortion depends on what proportion of total overhead costs these non-unit-based costs represent. For many companies, this percentage can be significant—reaching more than 40 or 50 percent of the total. Clearly, as this percentage decreases, the acceptability of using unit-based drivers for assigning costs increases.

Product Diversity

Significant non-unit overhead costs will not cause product cost distortions provided products consume the non-unit overhead activities in the same proportion as the unit-level overhead activities. Product diversity, on the other hand, can cause product cost distortion. **Product diversity** simply means that products consume overhead activities in different proportions. Product diversity is caused by such things as differences in product size, product complexity, setup time, and size of batches. The proportion of each activity consumed by a product is defined as the **consumption ratio**. The way that non-unit overhead costs and product diversity can produce distorted product costs (when only unit-level drivers are used to assign overhead costs) will be illustrated by providing detailed data for the Boise plant of Juguette, Inc.

The Failure of Unit-Based Overhead Rates

To illustrate the failure of plantwide and departmental rates, let's once again consider Juguette's Boise plant, which produces battery-operated toy robots and race cars. The two producing departments are Molding and Assembly. Molding is responsible for shaping the plastic components of each product, and assembly is responsible for assembling the internally produced plastic components with outside purchased electronic parts. Expected product-costing data are given in Exhibit 4.2. Because the quantity of race cars produced is five times greater than that of robots, we can label the race cars a high-volume product and robots a low-volume product. Because different molds are needed, the products are produced in batches. The molds for robots are larger and more varied than those for race cars; thus, batches for robots tend to be smaller and take longer to process.

Exhibit 4.2

Product-Costing Data

I. Activity Usage Measures (expected and actual)

	Robots	Race Cars	Total
Units produced	50,000	250,000	—
Prime costs	$200,000	$750,000	$950,000
Direct labor hours	10,000	40,000	50,000
Machine hours	20,000	10,000	30,000
Number of setups	25	75	100
Inspection hours	1,200	2,800	4,000
Number of moves	140	210	350

II. Departmental Data (expected and actual)

	Molding	Assembly	Total
Direct labor hours:			
Robots	5,000	5,000	10,000
Race cars	5,000	35,000	40,000
Total	10,000	40,000	50,000
Machine hours:			
Robots	17,000	3,000	20,000
Race cars	3,000	7,000	10,000
Total	20,000	10,000	30,000
Overhead costs:			
Machining	$120,000	$ 30,000	$150,000
Moving materials	40,000	30,000	70,000
Setting up	70,000	10,000	80,000
Inspecting products	20,000	30,000	50,000
Total	$250,000	$100,000	$350,000

For ease of presentation, only four types of overhead activities, performed by four distinct support departments, are assumed: setting up the equipment for each batch, machining, inspecting, and moving a batch. Each batch of products is inspected after each department's operations. After molding, a sample of the components is inspected to ensure correct size and shape. After assembly, a sample is also tested to ensure that each unit works as expected. Overhead costs are assigned to the two production departments using the direct method (described in Chapter 7). Effectively, costs are assigned using direct and driver tracing.

Unit Cost Computation: Plantwide and Departmental Overhead Rates

The traditional unit product cost is the unit overhead cost plus the unit prime cost. Prime costs are assigned to each of the products using direct tracing. From Exhibit 4.2, the unit prime cost for robots is $4.00 ($200,000/50,000), and the unit prime cost for race cars is $3.00 ($750,000/250,000). Examples 4.1 and 4.3 provide the unit overhead cost calculations for plantwide and overhead rates. Adding the unit prime costs to the unit overhead costs produces the desired unit product cost. Exhibit 4.3 summarizes and provides the details of these calculations.

Problems with Costing Accuracy   The accuracy of the overhead cost assignment can be challenged regardless of whether plantwide or departmental rates are used. The main problem with either procedure is the assumption that machine hours and/or direct labor hours drive or cause all overhead costs.

From Exhibit 4.2, we know that race cars, the high-volume product, use four times the direct labor hours used by robots, the low-volume product (40,000 hours versus 10,000 hours). Thus, if a plantwide rate is used, the race cars will receive four times more overhead cost than will the robots. But is this reasonable? Do unit-based activity drivers explain the consumption of all overhead activities? In particular, can we reasonably assume that each product's consumption of overhead increases in direct proportion to the direct labor hours used? Let's look at the four overhead activities and see if unit-based drivers accurately reflect the demands of the two products for overhead resources.

Of the four activities, only machining appears to be a unit-level cost, since machining will occur each time a unit is produced. Thus, using direct labor hours or machine hours on the surface appears reasonable. However, the data in Exhibit 4.2 suggest that a significant portion of overhead costs is not driven or caused by the units produced (measured by direct labor hours). For example, each product's demands for the setup, material-moving, and inspection activities are more logically related to the number of setups, number of moves, and inspection hours, respectively. These non-unit-level activities represent more than 50 percent ($200,000/$350,000) of the total overhead

---

I. Plantwide

	Robots	Race Cars
Prime cost[a]	$4.00	$3.00
Overhead cost[b]	1.40	1.12
Unit cost	$5.40	$4.12

II. Departmental

	Robots	Race Cars
Prime cost[a]	$4.00	$3.00
Overhead cost[c]	4.50	0.50
Unit cost	$8.50	$3.50

[a]$200,000/50,000; $750,000/250,000.
[b]From Example 4.1.
[c]From Example 4.3.

Exhibit 4.3

Unit Product Cost: Plantwide and Departmental Rates

costs—a significant percentage. Notice that the high-volume product, race cars, uses three times the number of setups of robots, about 2.33 times as many inspection hours, and only one and one-half times as many moves. However, use of direct labor hours, a unit-based activity driver, and a plantwide rate assigns four times more setup, inspection, and materials handling costs to the race cars than to the robots. Thus, we have product diversity, and we should expect product cost distortion because the quantity of unit-based overhead that each product consumes does not vary in direct proportion to the quantity consumed of non-unit-based overhead. How to calculate the consumption ratios for the various activities is shown in Example 4.4. Consumption ratios are simply the proportion of each activity consumed by a product. Activity drivers are a measure of activity output and thus can be used as measures of activity consumption. The *assumed* consumption ratios can also be calculated for the plantwide and overhead rates. Comparing the consumption ratios with the assumed consumption pattern of a plantwide rate suggests that using only direct labor hours to assign costs will overcost the race cars and under-cost the robots. Comparing the departmental consumption ratios with the plantwide ratios (in **Example 4.4**) and the product costs illustrated in Exhibit 4.3 indicates that the departmental rates are likely making a correction in the right direction (more overhead is being assigned to the robots and less to the race cars), but whether the correction is about right, too little, or too much can be assessed by calculating activity-based costs.

EXAMPLE 4.4

The HOW and WHY of Consumption Ratios

Information:
Product-costing data from Exhibit 4.2.

> **Why:**
> Consumption ratios reflect the proportion of an activity consumed by the individual products. They are especially useful to assign costs of a shared resource. For example, two individuals sharing the cost of a pizza would logically do so in proportion to the amount of the pizza consumed. In a multiple-product firm, there are many shared resources, and it is reasonable to assign the costs of shared resources in proportion to the resource consumed. Activity drivers are a measure of activity output and thus can be used as measures of activity consumption.

Required:

1. Calculate the activity consumption ratios for each product.

2. Calculate the *assumed* consumption ratios for plantwide (direct labor hours) and departmental rates.

3. *What if* the activity consumption ratios were approximately equal to the consumption ratio associated with direct labor hours? What does this tell you?

Solution:

1.

| | Consumption Ratios | | |
Overhead Activity	Robots	Race Cars	Activity Driver
Machining	0.67[a]	0.33[a]	Machine hours
Setups	0.25[b]	0.75[b]	Number of setups
Inspecting products	0.30[c]	0.70[c]	Inspection hours
Moving materials	0.40[d]	0.60[d]	Number of moves

[a]20,000/30,000 (robots) and 10,000/30,000 (race cars).
[b]25/100 (robots) and 75/100 (race cars).
[c]1,200/4,000 (robots) and 2,800/4,000 (race cars).
[d]140/350 (robots) and 210/350 (race cars).

2.

	Consumption Ratios		
Overhead Activity	**Robots**	**Race Cars**	**Activity Driver**
Plantwide:			
Manufacturing	0.20[a]	0.80[a]	Direct labor hours
Departmental:			
Molding	0.85[b]	0.15[b]	Machine hours
Assembly	0.13[c]	0.87[c]	Direct labor hours

[a] 10,000/50,000 (robots) and 40,000/50,000 (race cars).
[b] 17,000/20,000 (robots) and 3,000/20,000 (race cars).
[c] 5,000/40,000 (robots) and 35,000/40,000 (race cars).

3. If the activity ratios were approximately the same (all about 0.20 and 0.80 for each product, respectively), it would indicate that there is little product diversity—that the products are consuming all activities in the same ratio as direct labor hours. This outcome would signal that a plantwide rate is functioning quite well in assigning overhead costs to products. There would be no need to use either departmental or activity rates.

EXAMPLE 4.4

(*Continued*)

Activity Rates: A Better Approach The most direct method of overcoming the distortions caused by the unit-level rates is to expand the number of rates used so that the rates reflect the actual consumption of overhead costs by the various products. Thus, instead of pooling the overhead costs in plant or departmental pools, rates are calculated for each individual overhead activity. The rates are based on causal factors that measure consumption (unit- and non-unit-level activity drivers). Costs are assigned to each product by multiplying the activity rates by the amount consumed by each activity (as measured by the activity driver). **Example 4.5** illustrates the calculations and summarizes the rationale for activity-based costing.

EXAMPLE 4.5

The HOW and WHY of Activity-Based Costing

Information:
Activity usage and costs from Exhibit 4.2:

	Robots	Race Cars	Total
Units produced	50,000	250,000	—
Prime costs	$200,000	$750,000	$950,000
Machine hours	20,000	10,000	30,000
Number of setups	25	75	100
Number of moves	140	210	350
Inspection hours	1,200	2,800	4,000

Overhead costs:	
Machining	$150,000
Setting up	80,000
Moving materials	70,000
Inspecting products	50,000

EXAMPLE 4.5

(Continued)

Why:
An activity rate is calculated for each activity and the activity cost is assigned to products based on how much they use of each activity. The assignment is done using cause-and-effect relationships. Causal factors, called activity drivers, measure the amount of activity consumed by a product. The activity rate multiplied by the amount used of the activity determines the amount of activity cost assigned to a particular product. The total of all the assigned activity costs is the amount of overhead consumed by a product. Because the assignment uses causal factors, it tends to be *relatively* more accurate than assignments that use only unit-level drivers.

Required:

1. Calculate the four activity rates.

2. Calculate the unit costs using activity rates. Also, calculate the overhead cost per unit (see Exhibit 4.3 for unit prime costs).

3. *What if* consumption ratios instead of activity rates were used to assign costs instead of activity rates? Show the cost assignment for moving materials.

Solution:

1.   Machining rate: $150,000/30,000 = $5.00 per machine hour
               Setup rate: $80,000/100 = $800 per setup
        Moving materials rate: $70,000/350 = $200 per move
           Inspecting rate: $50,000/4,000 = $12.50 per hour

2.

	Robots	Race Cars
Prime costs	$200,000	$750,000
Overhead costs:		
Machining:		
$5 × 20,000	100,000	
$5 × 10,000		50,000
Setting up:		
$800 × 25	$ 20,000	
$800 × 75		$ 60,000
Moving materials:		
$200 × 140	28,000	
$200 × 210		42,000
Inspecting products:		
$12.50 × 1,200	15,000	
$12.50 × 2,800		35,000
Total manufacturing costs	$363,000	$937,000
Units of production	÷50,000	÷250,000
Unit cost	$ 7.26	$ 3.75

Overhead cost per unit: Robots: $7.26 − $4.00* = $3.26
                                  Cars: $3.75 − $3.00* = $0.75

*Prime cost per unit:
  Robots = $200,000 ÷ 50,000 = $4.00
  Cars = $750,000 ÷ 250,000 = $3.00

EXAMPLE 4.5

(Continued)

3. Using consumption ratios will yield exactly the same overhead assignments as activity rates, if the actual activity usage is the same as the expected usage (assuming no rounding error for the ratios). For moving materials, the consumption ratio is 0.40 for robots and 0.60 for race cars. Thus, the assignment is 0.40 × $70,000 = $28,000 (robots) and 0.60 × $70,000 = $42,000 (race cars), which is the same assignment obtained using activity rates.

Comparison of Different Product-Costing Methods In Exhibit 4.4, the unit costs and unit overhead costs from activity-based costing are compared with the unit costs produced by unit-based costing using either a plantwide or departmental rate. This comparison clearly illustrates the effects of using only unit-based activity drivers to assign overhead costs. The activity-based cost assignment follows a cause-and-effect pattern of overhead consumption and is therefore the most accurate of the three costs shown in Exhibit 4.4. Using a plantwide overhead rate undercosts the robots and over-costs the race cars. In fact, relative to the ABC cost, the plantwide assignment decreases the total unit cost of the robots by at least 25 percent [($7.26 − $5.40)/$7.26] and increases the unit cost of the race cars by about 10 percent [($4.12 − $3.75)/$3.75]. The effect is even more dramatic when comparing only unit overhead costs. Departmental overhead rates overcorrect and produce distortions as well, although, in this example, the distortion is reduced (about a 17 percent error for robots and 7 percent for race cars, relative to ABC assignments). Thus, in the presence of significant non-unit overhead costs and product diversity, using only unit-based activity drivers can lead to one product subsidizing another (for plantwide rates, the race cars subsidize the robots). This subsidy could create the appearance that one group of products is highly profitable and can adversely impact the pricing and competitiveness of another group of products. In a highly competitive environment, the more accurate the cost information, the better the planning and decision making.

ABC Users The Juguette, Inc., example also helps us understand when ABC may be useful for a firm. First, multiple products are needed. ABC offers no increase in product-costing accuracy for a single-product setting. Second, there must be product diversity. If products consume non-unit-level activities in the same proportion as unit-level activities, then ABC assignments will be the same as unit-based assignments. Third, non-unit-level overhead must be a significant percentage of production cost. If it is not, then it hardly matters how it is assigned. Thus, firms that have plants with multiple products, high product diversity, and significant non-unit-level overhead are candidates for an ABC system.

A survey published in 1998 studied this concept.[7] Of those firms surveyed, 49 percent had adopted ABC. When compared with non-adopting firms, it was found that adopting firms

Exhibit 4.4 Comparison of Unit Costs

	Total Unit Cost			Unit Overhead Cost		
	Robots	**Race Cars**		**Robots**	**Race Cars**	
Activity-based cost	$7.26	$3.75	Example 4.5	$3.26	$0.75	Example 4.5
Unit-based cost:						
Plantwide rate	5.40	4.12	Exhibit 4.3	1.40	1.12	Example 4.1
Departmental rates	8.50	3.50	Exhibit 4.3	4.50	0.50	Example 4.3

---

7 Kip Krumwiede, "ABC: Why It's Tried and How It Succeeds," *Management Accounting* (April 1998): 32–38.

reported a higher potential for distorted costs and a higher level of overhead when expressed as a percentage of total production costs. Adopting firms also reported a greater need or utility for accurate cost information for decision making. These conclusions continue to be supported by more recent studies. A survey of 348 manufacturing and service companies worldwide (about half were North American firms) found that ABC is used across the entire value chain at approximately the same rate.[8] ABC had an overall usage rate of about 50 percent; however, more than 87 percent of the organizations indicated that an ideal costing system involves some form of ABC, indicating some potential for growth in the adoption of ABC. Only 2.8 percent of non-ABC users previously used ABC but no longer use it. Another study found that product diversity is positively related to ABC adoption and use.[9] In a survey conducted by the Healthcare Financial Management Association and the Institute of Management Accountants, it was found that hospitals and other health organizations were increasing their usage of ABC and that there was general agreement that ABC provided more useful product cost information than conventional accounting.[10]

OBJECTIVE **3**

Provide a detailed description of activity-based product costing.

ACTIVITY-BASED COSTING SYSTEM

The Juguette, Inc., example shows quite clearly that prime costs are assigned in the same way for functional or activity-based costing. The example also demonstrates that the total amount of overhead costs is assigned under either approach. The amount assigned to each product, though, can differ significantly, depending on which method is used. The theoretical premise of activity-based costing is that it assigns costs according to the resource consumption pattern of products. If this is true, then activity-based costing should produce more accurate product costs if there is product diversity simply because unit-based drivers cannot capture the full consumption pattern of products. The Juguette, Inc., example suggests that we simply need to choose among a plant-wide cost pool, departmental cost pools, or activity cost pools. While this is true, it is also true that we are talking about different levels of aggregation. In reality, if there is no product diversity and a plantwide cost pool is chosen, all we need is the cost of overhead resources taken from the general ledger accounts: depreciation, salaries, utilities, rent, etc. On the other hand, departmental cost pools require more detail and less aggregation because costs must be assigned to every producing department. Finally, activity-based costing requires the most detail and the least aggregation because each activity performed and its associated costs must be identified.

As Exhibit 4.5 illustrates, an **activity-based costing (ABC) system** first traces costs to activities and then to products and other cost objects. The underlying assumption is that activities consume resources, and products and other cost objects consume activities. In designing an ABC system, there are six essential steps, as listed in Exhibit 4.6.

Activity Identification, Definition, and Classification

Identifying activities is a logical first step in designing an activity-based costing system. Activities represent actions taken or work performed by equipment or people for other people. Identifying an activity is equivalent to describing action taken—usually by using an action verb and an object that receives the action. A simple list of the activities identified is called an **activity inventory**. A sample activity inventory for an electronics manufacturer is listed in Exhibit 4.7.

---

8   William Stratton, Dennis Desrouches, Raeh A. Lawson, and Toby Hatch, "Activity-Based Costing: Is It Still Relevant?" *Management Accounting Quarterly* (Spring 2009): 31–40.

9   Martjin Schoute, "The Relationship Between Product Diversity, Usage of Advanced Manufacturing Technologies and Activity-Based Costing Adoption," *The British Accounting Review* (June 2011): 120–134.

10 Raef Lawson, "Costing Practices in Healthcare Organizations: A Look at Adoption of ABC" (December 5, 2017), https://www.hfma.org/topics/article/57198.html, accessed March 12, 2020.

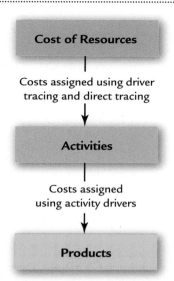

Exhibit 4.5
Activity-Based Costing Model

Of course, the actual inventory of activities for most organizations would list more than 12 activities (220 to 300 are not uncommon).

Activity Definition Once an inventory of activities exists, then activity attributes are used to define activities. **Activity attributes** are nonfinancial and financial information items that describe individual activities. An **activity dictionary** lists the activities in an organization along with desired attributes. The attributes selected depend on the purpose being served. Examples of activity attributes with a product-costing objective include tasks that describe the activity, types of resources consumed by the activity, amount (percentage) of time spent on an activity by workers, cost objects that consume the activity, and a measure of activity consumption (activity driver). Activities are the building blocks for both product costing and continuous improvement. An activity dictionary provides crucial information for activity-based costing as well as activity management. It is a key source of information for building an activity-based database that is discussed later in the chapter.

Activity Classification Attributes define and describe activities and, at the same time, become the basis for activity classification. Activity classification facilitates the achievement of key managerial objectives such as product or customer costing, continuous improvement, total quality management, and environmental cost management. For example, for costing purposes, activities can be classified as primary or secondary. A **primary activity** is an activity that is consumed by a final cost object such as a product or customer. A **secondary activity** is one that is consumed by intermediate cost objects such as primary activities, materials, or other secondary activities. Recognizing the difference between the two types of activities facilitates product costing. Exhibit 4.5 indicates that activities consume resources. Thus, in the first stage of

---

1. Identify, define, and classify activities and key attributes.
2. Assign the cost of resources to activities.
3. Assign the cost of secondary activities to primary activities.
4. Identify cost objects and specify the amount of each activity consumed by specific cost objects.
5. Calculate primary activity rates.
6. Assign activity costs to cost objects.

Exhibit 4.6
Design Steps for an ABC System

Exhibit 4.7

Sample Activity Inventory

1. Developing test programs
2. Making probe cards
3. Testing products
4. Setting up lots
5. Collecting engineering data
6. Handling wafer lots
7. Inserting dies
8. Providing utilities
9. Providing space
10. Purchasing materials
11. Receiving materials
12. Paying for materials

activity-based costing, the cost of resources is assigned to activities. Exhibit 4.5 also reveals that products consume activities—but only primary activities. Thus, before assigning the costs of primary activities to products, the costs of the secondary activities consumed by primary activities must be assigned to the primary activities. Many other useful activity classifications exist. For example, activities can be classified as *value-added* or *non-value-added* (defined and discussed in detail in Chapter 12) and as *quality-related* or as *environmental* (discussed in Chapter 14). In designing an activity costing system, the desired attributes and essential classifications need to be characterized up front so that the necessary data can be collected for the activity dictionary.

Gathering the Necessary Data   Interviews, questionnaires, surveys, and observation are means of gathering data for an ABC system. Interviews with managers or other knowledgeable representatives of functional departments are perhaps the most common approach for gathering the needed information. Interview questions can be used to identify activities and activity attributes needed for costing or other managerial purposes. The information derived from interview questions serves as the basis for constructing an activity dictionary and provides data helpful for assigning resource costs to individual activities. In structuring an interview, the questions should reveal certain key attributes. Interview questions should be structured to provide answers that allow the desired attributes to be identified and measured. An example is perhaps the best way to show how an interview can be used to collect the data for an activity dictionary.

Illustrative Example   Suppose that a hospital is carrying out an ABC pilot study to determine the nursing cost for different types of cardiology patients. The cardiology unit is located on one floor of the hospital. The interview with the unit's nursing supervisor is provided below. Questions are given along with their intended purposes and the supervisor's responses. The interview is not intended to be viewed as an exhaustive analysis but rather represents a sample of what could occur.

Question 1 (Activity Identification): Can you describe what your nurses do for patients in the cardiology unit? (Activities are people doing things for other people.)

Response: There are four major activities: treating patients (administering medicine and changing dressings), monitoring patients (checking vital signs and posting patient information), providing hygienic and physical care for patients (bathing, changing bedding and clothes, walking the patient, etc.), and responding to patient requests (counseling, providing snacks, and answering calls).

Question 2 (Activity Identification): Do any patients use any equipment? (Activities also can be equipment doing work for other people.)

Response: Yes. In the cardiology unit, monitors are used extensively. Monitoring is an important activity for this type of patient.

Question 3 (Activity Identification): What role do you have in the cardiology unit? (Activities are people doing things for other people.)

Response: I have no direct contact with the patients. I am responsible for scheduling, evaluations, and resolving problems with the ward's nurses.

Question 4 (Resource Identification): What resources are used by your nursing care activities (equipment, materials, energy)? (Activities consume resources in addition to labor.)

Response: Uniforms (which are paid for by the hospital), computers, nursing supplies such as scissors and instruments (supplies traceable to a patient are charged to the patient), and monitoring equipment at the nursing station.

Question 5 (Resource Driver Identification): How much time do nurses spend on each activity? How much equipment time is spent on each activity? (Information is needed to assign the cost of labor and equipment to activities.)

Response: We recently completed a work survey. About 25 percent of a nurse's time is spent treating patients, 20 percent providing hygienic care, 40 percent responding to patient requests, and 15 percent on monitoring patients. My time is 100 percent supervision. The monitoring equipment is used 100 percent for monitoring activity. Use of the computer is divided between 40 percent for supervisory work and 60 percent for monitoring. (Posting readings to patient records is viewed as a monitoring task.)

Question 6 (Potential Activity Drivers): What are the outputs of each activity? That is, how would you measure the demands for each activity? (This question helps identify activity drivers.)

Response: Treating patients: number of treatments; providing hygienic care: hours of care; responding to patient requests: number of requests; and monitoring patients: monitoring hours.

Question 7 (Potential Cost Objects Identified): Who or what uses the activity output? (Identifies the cost object: products, other activities, customers, etc.)

Response: Well, for supervising, I schedule, evaluate performance, and try to ensure that the nurses carry out their activities efficiently. Nurses benefit from what I do. Patients receive the benefits of the nursing care activities. We have three types of cardiology patients: intensive care, intermediate care, and normal care. These patients make quite different demands on the nursing activities. For example, intensive care patients rarely have walking time but use a lot of treatments and need more monitoring time.

Activity Dictionary Based on the answers to the interview, an activity dictionary can now be prepared. Exhibit 4.8 illustrates the dictionary for the cardiology unit. The activity dictionary names the activity (typically by using an action verb and an object that receives the action), describes the tasks that make up the activity, classifies the activity as primary or secondary, lists the users (cost objects), and identifies a measure of activity output (activity driver). For example, the supervising activity is consumed by the following primary activities: treating patients, providing hygienic care, responding to patient requests, and monitoring patients. The three products—intensive care patients, intermediate care patients, and normal care patients—in turn consume the primary activities.

Assigning Costs to Activities

After identifying and describing activities, the next task is determining how much it costs to perform each activity. The cost of an activity is simply the cost of the resources consumed by each activity. Activities consume resources such as labor, materials, energy, and capital. The cost of these resources is found in the general ledger, but how much is spent on each activity is not revealed. Resource costs must be assigned to activities using direct and driver tracing. For example, consider the labor resource. The time spent on each activity is the driver used to assign the labor costs to the activity. If the time spent is 100 percent, then labor is exclusive to the activity, and direct tracing is the cost assignment method (such as the labor cost of nursing supervision). On the other hand, if the nursing resource is shared by several activities, then driver tracing is used for the cost assignment. These drivers are called resource drivers. **Resource drivers** are factors that measure the consumption of resources by activities. For labor resources, a *work distribution matrix* is often used. A work distribution matrix simply identifies the amount of labor consumed by each activity and is derived from the interview process (or a written survey). Interviews, survey forms, questionnaires, and timekeeping systems are examples of tools that can be used to collect data on resource drivers. Notice that tracking the effort spent on different activities is similar to tracking the time that laborers spend on different jobs. However, there is one critical difference. The percent of effort spent on various activities is usually fairly constant and may only need to be measured periodically (perhaps annually). The same constancy property also exists for other types of resource drivers. In effect, the labor time is a standard used to assign the cost of resources. Actual times need not be constantly measured and used to achieve the desired cost assignment.

Labor is only one of many resources consumed by activities. Activities also consume materials, capital, and energy. The interview, for example, reveals that cardiology care activities also include the use of monitors (capital), a computer (capital), uniforms (materials), and supplies (materials). The cost of these other resources is also assigned to activities using direct tracing and resource drivers. Assigning costs to activities completes the first stage of activity-based costing. In this first stage, activities are classified as primary and secondary. If there are secondary activities, then intermediate stages exist. In an intermediate stage, the cost of secondary activities is assigned to those activities (or other intermediate cost objects) that consume their output. These calculations and concepts are illustrated in **Example 4.6**.

The assignment of resource costs to activities requires that the resource costs described in the general ledger be unbundled and reassigned. In a traditional accounting system, the general ledger reports costs by department and by spending account (based on a chart of accounts). The $340,000 of nursing salaries, for example, would be recorded as part of the total salaries of the cardiology unit. The general ledger indicates what is spent, but it does not reveal how the resources are spent. Of course, the resources are spent on the basic work (activities) performed in the department. In an activity-based cost system, costs must be reported by activity. Thus, an ABC system must restate the general ledger costs so that the new system reveals how the resources are being consumed. Exhibit 4.9 illustrates the unbundling concept for nursing care activities in the cardiology unit. As the exhibit indicates, the reassignment of resource costs to individual activities contributes to the creation of an ABC database for the organization.

Exhibit 4.8

Activity Dictionary: Cardiology Unit

Activity Name	Activity Description	Activity Type	Cost Object(s)	Activity Driver
Supervising nurses	Scheduling, coordinating, and performance evaluation	Secondary	Activities within department	Percentage of time nurses spend on each activity
Treating patients	Administering medicine and changing dressings	Primary	Patient types	Number of treatments
Providing hygienic care	Bathing, changing bedding and clothes, and walking patients	Primary	Patient types	Labor hours
Responding to patient requests	Answering calls, counseling, providing snacks, etc.	Primary	Patient types	Number of requests
Monitoring patients	Checking vital signs and posting patient information	Primary	Patient types	Monitoring hours

EXAMPLE 4.6

Information:

Resources		Activities	Nursing Hours	
Supervision	$ 50,000	Supervising nurses	2,000	10.0%
Supplies and uniforms	60,000	Treating patients	4,500	22.5
Salaries	340,000	Providing hygienic care	3,600	18.0
Computer	10,000	Responding to requests	4,500	22.5
Monitor	26,000	Monitoring patients	5,400	27.0
Total	$486,000	Total	20,000	100.0%
		Total without supervising	18,000	

The HOW and WHY of Assigning Resource Costs to Activities

- Monitors are used only by the monitoring activity.

- The one computer is used 800 hours for supervisory work (40 percent) and 1,200 hours for monitoring work (60 percent).

- The nursing resources (supplies, uniforms, and labor) are assigned to activities using nursing hours. The supervisor spends 100 percent of her time on supervision.

> **Why:**
> Activities consume resources, and other cost objects consume activities. The cost of each activity must therefore be determined. The cost of resources is assigned to activities using direct tracing and driver tracing. Resource drivers are used to assign shared resources. After this initial assignment, the costs of secondary activities are assigned to primary activities.

Required:

1. Prepare a work distribution matrix for the five activities.

2. Calculate the cost of each activity.

3. *What if* the cost of the supervising activity is assigned to the other four activities? Why would this be done? If it is done, what is the final cost of these four primary activities?

Solution:

1.

Percentage of Time on Each Activity

Activity	Supervisor	Nurses	Supporting Calculation
Supervising nurses	100%	0%	(2,000/2,000)
Treating patients	0	25	(4,500/18,000)
Providing hygienic care	0	20	(3,600/18,000)
Responding to requests	0	25	(4,500/18,000)
Monitoring patients	0	30	(5,400/18,000)

EXAMPLE 4.6

(Continued)

2.

Activities	Monitor[a]	Computer[b]	Nursing Resources[c]	Total
Supervising nurses		$4,000	$ 56,000	$ 60,000
Treating patients			98,500	98,500
Providing hygienic care			78,800	78,800
Responding to requests			98,500	98,500
Monitoring patients	$26,000	6,000	118,200	150,200

[a]Exclusive use by monitoring (100% × $26,000).
[b]0.40 × $10,000; 0.60 × 10,000.
[c]$50,000 + (0.10 × $60,000); [(0.25 × $340,000) + (0.225 × $60,000)]; [(0.20 × $340,000) + (0.18 × $60,000)];
[(0.25 × $340,000) + (0.225 × $60,000)]; [(0.30 × $340,000) × (0.27 × $60,000)].

3. Supervising is a secondary activity, and its costs are consumed by primary activities (assigned in proportion to the labor content of each activity).

Treating patients	$113,500[a]
Providing hygienic care	90,800[b]
Responding to requests	113,500[c]
Monitoring patients	168,200[d]

[a]$98,500 + (0.25 × $60,000).
[b]$78,800 + (0.20 × $60,000).
[c]$98,500 + (0.25 × $60,000).
[d]$150,200 + (0.30 × $60,000).

REAL-WORLD EXAMPLE

Big Data and ABC

DHL Express is the world's leader in the logistics industry. To maintain competitiveness, DHL felt it critical that the costs be accurately allocated to facilitate aggressive pricing decisions. Not long after the appearance of ABC, DHL adopted an ABC approach to ensure accurate costing and margin calculations. For more than a decade, DHL used Microsoft Access as the costing tool and allowed local country managers to allocate costs using ABC. Detailed employee interviews were conducted annually to obtain the data needed (e.g., time spent picking up shipments and time spent making deliveries) that allowed the system to work; however, DHL found that the data collected was subjective, very time consuming, and dated by the time it was made available. The data itself and its limitations were often the focus of the discussion rather than the strategic ramifications and profitability of a customer, product, or trade lane.

DHL realized that it had a large data warehouse because it routinely tracked customer shipments. Each shipment is scanned at pickup, at arrival and departure from collection facilities, at customs, and at delivery. The key was making this operational data available for costing. DHL created a single, global system that allowed the company to have a unified costing and pricing system. The global activity-based costing system is easily and efficiently update and provides timely and accurate information.[11]

---

11   Bill Tobey, "Get Precise on Cost," http://www.teradatamagazine.com/v11n01/Features/Get-Precise-on-Cost/, accessed April 10, 2016; Taylor Provost, "How DHL's Big Data Boosts Performance," http://ww2.cfo.com /management-accounting/2013/01/how-dhls-big-data-boosts-performance/, accessed April 10, 2016.

General Ledger ───→ ABC Database			
Cardiology Unit			
Chart of Accounts View		**ABC View**	
Supervision	$ 50,000	Supervising nurses	$ 60,000
Supplies and uniforms	60,000	Treating patients	98,500
Salaries	340,000	Providing hygienic care	78,800
Computer	10,000	Responding to requests	98,500
Monitor	26,000	Monitoring patients	150,200
Total	$486,000	Total	$486,000

Exhibit 4.9

Unbundling of General Ledger Costs

Cost Objects and Bills of Activities

Once the costs of primary activities are determined, these costs can then be assigned to products or other cost objects in proportion to their usage of the activity, as measured by activity drivers. However, before any assignment is made, the cost objects must be identified and the demands these objects place on the activities must be measured. Many different cost objects are possible: products, materials, customers, distribution channels, suppliers, and geographical regions are some examples. For our example, the cost objects are products (services): intensive cardiology care, intermediate cardiology care, and normal cardiology care. How to deal with cost assignment for other cost objects is discussed in a later section. **Activity drivers** measure the demands that cost objects place on activities. Most ABC system designs choose between one of two types of activity drivers: transaction drivers and duration drivers. **Transaction drivers** measure the number of times an activity is performed, such as the number of treatments and the number of requests. **Duration drivers** measure the demands in terms of the time it takes to perform an activity, such as hours of hygienic care and monitoring hours. Duration drivers should be used when the time required to perform an activity varies from transaction to transaction. If, for example, treatments for normal care patients average 10 minutes but for intensive care patients average 45 minutes, then treatment hours may be a much better measure of the demands placed on the activity of treating patients than the number of treatments.

With the drivers defined, a bill of activities can be created. A **bill of activities** specifies the product, expected product quantity, activities, and amount of each activity expected to be consumed by each product. Exhibit 4.10 presents a bill of activities for the cardiology care example.

Activity Rates and Product Costing Primary activity rates are computed by dividing the budgeted activity costs by practical activity capacity, where activity capacity is the amount of activity output (as measured by the activity driver). Practical capacity is the activity output that can be produced if the activity is performed efficiently. Using data from Example 4.6 and Exhibit 4.10, the activity rates for the cardiology unit nursing care example can now be calculated:

Rate Calculations:
Treating patients: $113,500/3,000 = $37.83 per treatment
Providing hygienic care: $90,800/3,600   = $25.22 per hour of care
Responding to requests: $113,500/8,000 = $14.19 per request
Monitoring patients: $168,200/5,400 = $31.15 per monitoring hour

Note: Rates are rounded to the nearest cent.

Activity	Driver	Normal	Intermediate	Intensive	Total
Production (output)	Patient days	10,000	5,000	3,000	
Treating patients	Treatments	500	1,000	1,500	3,000
Providing hygienic care	Hygienic hours	1,125	562	1,913	3,600
Responding to requests	Requests	3,000	4,000	1,000	8,000
Monitoring patients	Monitoring hours	540	1,620	3,240	5,400

Exhibit 4.10

Bill of Activities: Cardiology Unit

These rates provide the price charged for activity usage. Using these rates, costs are assigned as shown in Exhibit 4.11. As should be evident, the assignment process is the same as that for the Juguette example illustrated earlier in Example 4.5 (see page 157). However, we now know the details behind the development of the activity rates and usage measures. Furthermore, the hospital setting emphasizes the utility of activity-based costing in service organizations.

Classifying Activities

To help identify activity drivers and enhance the management of activities, activities are often classified into one of the following four general activity categories: (1) unit-level, (2) batch-level, (3) product-level, and (4) facility-level. **Unit-level activities** are those that are performed each time a unit is produced. Grinding, polishing, and assembly are examples of unit-level activities. **Batch-level activities** are those that are performed each time a batch is produced. The costs of batch-level activities vary with the number of batches but are fixed (and, therefore, independent) with respect to the number of units in each batch. Setups, inspections (if done by sampling units from a batch), purchasing, and materials handling are examples of batch-level activities. **Product-level activities** are those activities performed that enable the various products of a company to be produced. These activities and their costs tend to increase as the number of different products increases. Engineering changes (to products), developing product-testing procedures, introducing new products, and expediting goods are examples of product-level activities. **Facility-level activities** are those that sustain a factory's general manufacturing processes. Providing facilities, maintaining grounds, and providing plant security are examples.

Classifying activities into these general categories facilitates product costing because the costs of activities associated with the different levels respond to different types of activity drivers. (Cost behavior differs by level.) Knowing the activity level is important because it helps management identify the activity drivers that measure the amount of each activity output being consumed by individual products. Activity-based costing systems improve product-costing accuracy by recognizing that many of the so-called fixed overhead costs vary in proportion to changes other than production volume. Level classification also provides insights concerning the root causes of activities and thus can help managers in their efforts to improve activity performance.

By understanding what causes these costs to increase or decrease, they can be traced to individual products. This cause-and-effect relationship allows managers to improve

Exhibit 4.11

Assigning Costs: Final Cost Objects

	Normal	Intermediate	Intensive
Treating patients:			
$37.83 × 500	$ 18,915		
$37.83 × 1,000		$ 37,830	
$37.83 × 1,500			$ 56,745
Providing hygienic care:			
$25.22 × 1,125	28,373		
$25.22 × 562		14,174	
$25.22 × 1,913			48,246
Responding to requests:			
$14.19 × 3,000	42,570		
$14.19 × 4,000		56,760	
$14.19 × 1,000			14,190
Monitoring patients:			
$31.15 × 540	16,821		
$31.15 × 1,620		50,463	
$31.15 × 3,240			100,926
Total costs	$ 106,679	$159,227	$220,107
Units	÷10,000	÷5,000	÷3,000
Nursing cost per patient day*	$ 10.67	$ 31.85	$ 73.37

*Rounded to nearest cent.

product-costing accuracy, which can significantly improve decision making. Additionally, this large pool of fixed overhead costs is no longer so mysterious. Knowing the underlying behavior of many of these costs allows managers to exert more control over the activities that cause the costs. It also allows managers to identify which of the activities add value and which do not. Value analysis is the heart of activity-based management and is the basis for continuous improvement. Activity-based management and continuous improvement are explored in later chapters.

Reducing the Size and Complexity of an ABC System

OBJECTIVE 4

Explain how ABC can be simplified.

As should be evident from the discussion up to this point, ABC systems are expensive to create and implement, complex to operate, and difficult to modify or update. You may wish to review Exhibit 4.6, which listed six steps for the process of creating, implementing, and operating an ABC system. The first three steps correspond to the first stage of ABC (Stage 1), and the last three steps correspond to the second stage of ABC (Stage 2). Stage 1 requires time-consuming and costly interviewing and surveying with the objective of identifying and classifying activities and then determining the cost of each activity. This Stage 1 process produces results that are subjective and difficult to validate. Stage 2 requires an activity rate for each activity. An organization may have hundreds of different activities and, thus, hundreds of activity rates. Activity rates require the identification of activity drivers that measure the consumption of activities by cost objects. Both Stage 1 and Stage 2 are complex and costly. Efforts to simplify ABC have been proposed that involve either before-the-fact simplification or after-the-fact simplification. One prominent before-the-fact simplification approach is *Time-Driven ABC (TDABC)* and is concerned with simplifying Stage 1. Another emerging before-the-fact simplification method is *Duration-Based Costing*. Two after-the-fact simplification approaches that simplify Stage 2 are the *Approximately Relevant ABC System* and the *Equally Accurate ABC System*.

Before-the-Fact Simplification: TDABC

Time-Driven Activity-Based Costing (TDABC) is a before-the-fact simplification method that simplifies Stage 1 by eliminating the need for detailed interviewing and surveying to determine resource drivers.[12] Activities still must be identified. However, TDABC drives the resource cost directly to products without the need to formally calculate the activity cost. This outcome is accomplished in a very simple and straightforward way. First, it calculates the total cost of resources supplied by a department or process (resources such as equipment, personnel, materials, etc.). Second, the practical capacity, measured in time, is estimated for all personnel and/or equipment that actually perform work. Administrative and staff time are not included. Third, a capacity cost rate is calculated by dividing the total resource cost by the practical capacity (as measured by resource time used in the department) of the resources supplied:

Capacity cost rate = Cost of resources supplied/Practical capacity of resources supplied

Fourth, the time to perform one unit of activity is estimated. One unit of activity is one unit of an activity driver. Finally, multiplying the capacity cost rate by the time to perform one unit of activity yields the activity rate:

Activity rate = Capacity cost rate × Time to perform one unit of activity

Using the activity rates, resource costs are assigned to a product simply by multiplying the activity rate for each activity by the amount of activity consumed by the product and then summing,

---

12 TDABC is described in Robert S. Kaplan and Steven R. Anderson, "Time-Driven Activity-Based Costing," *Harvard Business Review* (November 2004): 131–138; and "The Innovation of Time-Driven Activity-Based Costing," *Cost Management* 21, 2 (March/April): 5–15.

just as done in traditional ABC. The resource or overhead cost per unit is then obtained by dividing this total assigned resource cost by the units produced for the product.

However, TDABC usually calculates this same outcome using *time equations*. Multiplying the time to perform one unit of activity by the total activity transactions effectively converts transaction drivers to duration drivers. Thus, the total time for servicing or producing a product j that uses n activities can be expressed as follows:

$$T_j = t_1q_{1j} + t_2q_{2j} + ... t_nq_{nj} \qquad (4.1)$$

where:
T_j = the total time used by Product j
t_i = the time per unit of activity i, i = 1, 2, ..., n
q_{ij} = the amount of activity i consumed by Product j, i = 1, 2, ..., n

Multiplying T_j by the capacity cost rate gives the total resource cost assigned to Product j. Dividing this total by the units produced of Product j gives the overhead cost per unit.

Thus, in practical terms, the resource cost can be driven directly to products without formally calculating the activity cost. However, activity cost can be calculated, if desired, as follows:

$$\text{Activity cost} = \text{Activity rate} \times \text{Total activity output}$$

Example 4.7 illustrates the basic concepts of TDABC.

EXAMPLE 4.7

The HOW and WHY of TDABC

Information:
Exhibit 4.10 and the following information on a cardiology unit:

Resources		Activities	Time/Unit of Activity
Supervision	$ 50,000	Treating patients	1.40 hrs. per treatment
Supplies and uniforms	60,000	Providing hygienic care	1.00 hr.
Salaries	340,000	Responding to requests	0.60 hr. per request
Computer	10,000	Monitoring patients	1.00 hr.
Monitor	26,000		
Total	$486,000		
Total nursing hours	18,000	(practical capacity)	

Why:
TDABC avoids detailed interviewing, surveying, and timekeeping systems required for assessing resource drivers to assign resource costs to activities. All that is needed is the total productive time supplied by personnel or equipment in a department or process (measured at practical capacity), the total resource costs, and the time required to perform one unit of activity. The first two data items are readily obtained through objective estimates. For transaction drivers, the amount of time required to perform one transaction (such as a setup) is obtained by observation or interview. For duration drivers, the time per unit of activity is simply a unit of time. The capacity cost rate is total resource cost/total time at practical capacity. This rate is multiplied by the time per unit of an activity to obtain the activity rate. This rate multiplied by the total activity output provides the activity cost.

EXAMPLE 4.7

(Continued)

Required:

1. Calculate the capacity cost rate for the cardiology unit, and then calculate the activity rate for each activity.

2. Calculate the cost per patient day for the intermediate care patients.

3. *What if* management decided to use time equations for assigning resource costs to patients. Develop a time equation that expresses the time required to service intermediate care patients. Next, using this time equation, show that the cost per patient day is the same as that calculated in Requirement 2.

Solution:

1. Capacity cost rate = $486,000/18,000 = $27 per hour

    Treating patients: $27 × 1.40 = $37.80 per treatment
    Providing hygienic care: $27 × 1 = $27 per care hour
    Responding to requests: $27 × 0.60 = $16.20 per request
    Monitoring patients: $27 × 1 = $27 per monitoring hour

2. Using the activity rates from Requirement 1 and the activity quantities and patient days from Exhibit 4.10:

    Cost per patient day = [($37.80 × 1,000) + ($27 × 562) + ($16.20 × 4,000) + ($27 × 1,620)]/5,000 = $32.30

    Note that activity costs never had to be calculated. TDABC drives resource costs directly to the cost object.

3. The time to service intermediate care patients can be expressed by the following time equation:

    Time to service intermediate care patients (hours) = 1.4 × (number of treatments) + 1 × (hygienic care hours) + 0.6 × (number of requests) + 1 × (monitoring hours)

    Next, inputting activity data from Exhibit 4.10 into the preceding equation, the total service time for intermediate care patients can be calculated as follows:

    Time to service = (1.4 × 1,000) + 563 + (0.6 × 4,000) + 1,620
    = 5,982 hours

    Using the capacity cost rate of $27 per hour, the total cost assigned to intermediate care patients would be:

    Total cost assigned = $27 × 5,982
    = $161,514

    which when divided by the 5,000 patient days for intermediate care patients yields the expected per patient cost of $32.30.

Model Updating Example 4.7 illustrates that the detailed requirements typically found in Stage 1 are not needed. TDABC also has a significant advantage when it comes to updating requirements. If new activities are added or identified, there is no need to engage in detailed interviews as with traditional ABC. Instead, all that is needed is observation to determine how long it takes to produce one unit of output for each new activity. Other changes in operations such as changes in resource costs or time (e.g., resource price increases, acquisition of new equipment, process improvements, increase in activity efficiency, etc.) are easily updated by adjusting the capacity cost rate. This then produces new activity rates. Updates are easily obtained as changes occur. This can be illustrated using the data from Example 4.7. Assume that at mid-year, the nursing supervisor resigns and a new supervisor is hired for a salary of $63,200 (an increase of $13,200) and that the remaining cardiology nurses received a salary increase of 12 percent (an increase of $40,800). Thus, resource costs increase by $54,000 due to these salary changes. Updating is easily accomplished. First, the new capacity cost rate = $540,000/18,000 = $30 per hour. New activity rates can then be calculated as follows:

$$\text{Treating patients: } \$30 \times 1.40 = \$42 \text{ per patient}$$
$$\text{Providing hygienic care: } \$30 \times 1 = \$30 \text{ per care hour}$$
$$\text{Responding to requests: } \$30 \times 0.60 = \$18 \text{ per request}$$
$$\text{Monitoring patients: } \$30 \times 1 = \$30 \text{ per monitoring hour}$$

Measuring Unused Capacity Although not illustrated in Example 4.7, another feature of TDABC is its ability to calculate the cost of unused capacity. The unit time multiplied by the activity output is the total time used by an activity. If the actual activity quantities differ from the practical capacity quantities (practical capacity ranges from 80 to 90 percent of theoretical capacity), then the cost assigned to products will be less than the cost of the total resources. The difference is the cost of unused capacity.

Cost of unused capacity = Total cost of resources − Total resource cost assigned to products

For example, if the total cost of resources is $486,000 and the total cost of resources assigned to products is $476,000, then the cost of unused capacity is $10,000 ($486,000 − $476,000).

Time Equations Time equations offer considerable flexibility for dealing with product and activity complexities. In Example 4.7, it was assumed that the time required to perform one unit of activity was the same for each patient type. Obviously, this is unlikely for certain activities and products. For example, more critical patients may need more treatment time or monitoring time. TDABC handles this additional complexity in a very simple, straightforward way. TDABC estimates the differing resource demands by using time equations. To illustrate, if treatment time differs by patient category, the unit time variation can be captured by a time equation such as the following:

Unit treatment time = 1.4 + 0.1 (if immediate care patient) + 0.2 (if intensive care patient)

Thus, the unit times for a treatment would be 1.4 for normal care patients, 1.5 for intermediate care patients, and 1.6 for intensive care patients. Using a capacity rate of $30, the activity rate for the treatment activity is $42 ($30 × 1.4) for normal patients, $45 ($30 × 1.5) for intermediate patients, and $48 ($30 × 1.6) for intensive care patients.

Time equations can also be used to capture the complexity of activity characteristics. For example, treating patients is made up of a number of subtasks, not all of which may be present in a given treatment. All patients may require such treatment tasks as changing dressings and taking certain medications by mouth. However, some patients at risk (e.g., those with a heart valve lesion or a prosthetic valve) may need IV administration of antibiotics. This additional treatment task would increase the unit time for some patients in each patient category. The earlier time equation can be modified to take into account this activity complexity (which holds across the three patient categories):

Unit treatment time = 1.4 + 0.1 (if immediate care patient)
+ 0.2 (if intensive care patient) + 0.3 (if IV patient).

Thus, a normal care patient without IV would have a unit treatment time of 1.4, but with IV, the unit time would be 1.7. Similar adjustments would be made for the other two patient categories. The effect is to double the number of cost objects—moving from three types of patients to six types.

An interesting application of time equations is reported for the inter-library loan service of the **KU Leuven Arenberg Library**.[13] The initial activity for a requested book or article from another library is defined as *processing the request*. The transaction driver is defined as the number of requests processed. Thus, TDABC must estimate the time required to process one request. The estimated time required to process one request is 6.8 minutes and is the sum of the following tasks: receive the request, select the library that has the requested book or article, print a hard copy of the request, enter data in an Excel™ file, and classify all printouts. The time for processing a request can be increased or decreased depending on two additional complexities. First, if the library patron asks for feedback, then an additional 6.3 minutes are required to provide the feedback via email, telephone, or personal contact at the library desk. Second, the lending library may respond negatively and indicate that the book or article is not available. In this case, the process needs to be repeated with a new potential lending library, which adds an additional 6.6 minutes. The resulting time equation for this initial activity is given as:

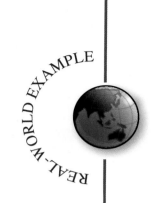

REAL-WORLD EXAMPLE

Process time = 6.8 + 6.3 (if feedback is requested) + 6.6 (if negative response)

Duration-Based Costing (DBC)

Duration-Based Costing (DBC) is a before-the-fact simplification method that eliminates the need for Stage 1 of ABC and dramatically simplifies Stage 2. In fact, DBC is as simple as a traditional unit-based costing approach but has the same accuracy as a comprehensive ABC system that uses duration-based drivers.[14] The cost assignment under DBC requires four items of information: (1) the cycle time for each product (cost object); (2) the practical capacity for each product; (3) the total overhead (resource) cost; and (4) the total time of all primary activities. The first three items are observable and found within an organization's cost accounting information system. Total time of all primary activities is derived from the cycle time and practical capacity for each product.

Cycle time is the length of time between the beginning and completion of a process. Operationally, it is time required to produce one unit of product for a continuous process (**time/units**) or one batch for a batch process (**time/batches**). A batch can be made up of numerous homogeneous units. Every activity consumed by a product contributes to its cycle time. Thus, the expected total time spent with primary activities *for a* single product (product *i*) is its *cycle time* multiplied by the *units of product produced at practical capacity*:

$$T_i = C_i \times P_i \tag{4.2}$$

where
T_i = Product *i*'s total time used for all primary activities
C_i = Cycle time for product *i*
P_i = Units of product *i* produced at practical capacity

Thus, the total time (T) in the system for all primary activities is simply the sum of all products' total primary activity times:

$$T = \Sigma_i T_i \tag{4.3}$$

Once the total time is known, then a single predetermined overhead (OH) rate for DBC is computed as follows:

$$\text{OH rate} = (\text{Total overhead or resource cost})/T \tag{4.4}$$

13 Eli Pernot, Filip Roodhooft, and Alexandria Van den Abbeele, "Time-Driven Activity-Based Costing for Inter-Library Services: A Case Study in a University," *The Journal of Academic Librayship* 33, 5 (September 2007): 551–560.

14 This section and the rationale in the corresponding Example are based on the following article: Anne-Marie T. Lelkes and Donald R. Deis, "Using the Production Cycle Time to Reduce the Complexity of ABC," *Journal of Theoretical Accounting Research* (Fall 2013): 57–84.

Using this rate, the overhead costs assigned to each product are calculated as follows:

$$\text{OH cost per unit} = \text{OH rate} \times C_i \qquad (4.5)$$

$$\text{Total overhead cost assigned} = \text{OH rate} \times C_i \times P_i \qquad (4.6)$$

Under some reasonable assumptions, these overhead assignments match those of an ABC system that uses only duration drivers. **Example 4.8** illustrates DBC and shows that DBC assignments are the same as those under ABC.

EXAMPLE 4.8

The HOW and WHY of DBC

Information:
Jackson Company produces cylinders and currently uses an ABC system. The following data were provided for the coming year:

A. Activities with duration drivers (setup hours, welding hours, etc.):

	Activities				
Products	**Setups**	**Welding**	**Machining**	**Inspecting**	**Total Hours**
Cylinder 1	250	1,600	2,400	750	5,000
Cylinder 2	750	2,400	1,600	250	5,000
Total hours	1,000	4,000	4,000	1,000	10,000

B. Activities with consumption ratios and costs:

	Activities				Cost
Products	**Setups**	**Welding**	**Machining**	**Inspecting**	**Assignment**
Cylinder 1	0.25	0.40	0.60	0.75	$18,000
Cylinder 2	0.75	0.60	0.40	0.25	$18,000
Activity costs	$10,000	$5,000	$15,000	$6,000	$36,000

C. Products with cycle time and practical capacity:

Product	Cycle Time	Practical Capacity
Cylinder 1	0.4 hours	12,500 units
Cylinder 2	1.25 hours	4,000 units

Why:
DBC uses a single overhead rate that produces overhead product cost assignments that essentially match those of ABC when all activity drivers are duration drivers. (See Equations 4.2 through 4.6.) DBC has the same updating simplicity as TDABC but has significantly less complexity as it eliminates the data gathering intensity of Stage 2. Furthermore, DBC can calculate the cost of unused capacity by multiplying the OH rate by the difference between the actual units produced and the units at practical capacity. DBC matches ABC whenever there is no correlation between (1) the consumption ratios and total activity time and (2) the consumption ratios and activity cost. For example, as the consumption ratio for Cylinder A increases from 0.25 for Setups to 0.40 for Welding, 0.60 for Machining, and 0.75 for Inspecting, there is no logical reason that the activity cost (or time) should increase (or decrease). The assumption of no correlation seems quite reasonable.

EXAMPLE 4.8

(Continued)

Required:

1. Using cycle time and practical capacity for each product, calculate the total time for all primary activities (see Equations 4.2 and 4.3). Comment on the relationship to ABC.

2. Calculate the overhead rate that DBC uses to assign costs (see Equation 4.4). Comment on the relationship to a unit-based plantwide overhead rate.

3. Use the overhead rate calculated in Requirement 2 to calculate (a) the overhead cost per unit for each product, and (b) the total overhead assigned to each product. How does this compare to the ABC assignments shown in Part B of the Information set?

4. *What if* the units actually produced were 10,000 for Cylinder 1 and 4,000 for Cylinder 2. Using DBC, calculate the cost of unused capacity.

Solution:

1. Cylinder 1: $T_1 = 0.40 \times 12,500 = 5,000$ hours

   Cylinder 2: $T_2 = 1.25 \times 4,000 = 5,000$ hours

   Thus, $T = T_1 + T_2$

   $$= 5,000 + 5,000$$
   $$= 10,000 \text{ hours}$$

   T represents the total hours of all activities spent producing the two products. However, the total time can be calculated without knowing the detailed information found in the ABC system.

2. OH rate = (Total overhead costs)$/T$

   $$= \$36,000/10,000$$
   $$= \$3.60 \text{ per labor hour}$$

   Both unit-based costing and DBC use a single overhead rate to assign overhead costs to products. However, a unit-based overhead rate uses only direct labor hours in the denominator. The DBC overhead rate uses total production hours needed—including direct labor hours, indirect labor hours, and machine hours.

3. Overhead cost per unit:

   Cylinder 1: $0.40 \times \$3.60 = \$1.44$
   Cylinder 2: $1.25 \times \$3.60 = \$4.50$

   Total overhead cost assigned to each product:

   Cylinder 1: $\$1.44 \times 12,500 = \$18,000$
   Cylinder 2: $\$4.50 \times 4,000 = \$18,000$

   Note that the costs assigned to each cylinder are identical to ABC assignments.

4. Cost of unused capacity = (OH rate) $\times$ (P_1 − Actual units produced)
   $$= \$1.44 \times (12,500 - 10,000)$$
   $$= \$1.44 \times 2,500$$
   $$= \$3,600$$

DBC Compared to TDABC From Example 4.8, the simplicity of DBC compared to TDABC is striking. Both TDABC and DBC calculate a capacity cost rate, which is Total Resources/Total Time. Conceivably, DBC could calculate total time in the same way as TDABC rather than derive it using cycle time and units produced; however, a derived calculation is simpler. TDABC requires that the time to perform one unit of activity be estimated for

DATA ANALYTICS

each activity. Using the unit activity time, activity transaction data, and the capacity cost rate, TDABC calculates the resource cost assigned to a product or cost object. DBC only requires that the cycle time for each product or cost object be measured. The cycle time and the capacity cost rate are all that is needed to calculate the resource cost assigned to products or cost objects.

DBC thus simplifies not only Stage 1 but Stage 2 of ABC. In fact, DBC simplifies TDABC by using cycle time, eliminating the need for time equations. To illustrate the nature of this simplification, consider Equation 4.1 of TDABC once again:

$$T_j = t_1q_{1j} + t_2q_{2j} + ... t_nq_{nj} \qquad (4.1)$$

If both sides of the time equation are divided by P_j, the number of units of Product j, the following result is obtained:

$$T_j/P_j = (t_1q_{1j} + t_2q_{2j} +... t_nq_{nj})/P_j$$

Notice that the left side of this new equation, T_j/P_j, is time/units, which is the measure of cycle time for Product j. Multiplying cycle time by the capacity rate (or OH rate of DBC) drives the resource cost to products and yields the resource cost per unit. Cycle time, however, can be obtained independently of the time equation, and so the detailed unit activity times and transaction data required of TDABC are no longer needed.

To illustrate, suppose that the time equation for Cylinder 1 of Example 4.8 uses 50 setups, 1,600 welding hours, 2,400 machine hours, and 50 inspections. The time equation for Cylinder 1 is given as follows (t_i's are expressed in hours per unit of activity):

$T_1 = 5 \times$ (number of setups) $+ 1 \times$ (welding hours) $+ 1 \times$ (machine hours) $+ 15 \times$ (number of inspections)

Thus, the total hours used to service Cylinder 1 is 5,000 [$T_1 = (5 \times 50) + 1,600 + 2,400 + (15 \times 50)$]. The total amount of cost TDABC assigns to Cylinder 1 would be $3.60 \times 5,000 = \$18,000$, which when divided by 12,500 units yields a unit cost of $1.44, the same value obtained by multiplying the cycle time of 0.4 (5,000/12,500) by $3.60.

After-the-Fact Simplification

DATA
ANALYTICS

Although TDABC simplifies Stage 1, Stage 2 still has to deal with hundreds of different activity rates. While information technology is capable of handling this volume, there is merit to reducing the number of rates if it can be done without suffering a significant decrease in the accuracy of the cost assignments. After all, increased accuracy of cost assignments is the source of the decision benefits and the justification for using TDABC. Fewer activity rates may produce more readable and manageable product cost reports, reducing the perceived complexity of an activity-based costing system and increasing its likelihood of managerial acceptance. For example, if there are a large number of activities on a bill of activities, managers are likely to find it too complex to read, interpret, and use. In this case, the more complex ABC or TDABC system may not be sustained. One of the oft-cited reasons for refusing to implement an ABC system or for abandoning it, once implemented, is the perceived complexity of the system. Fewer rates may also reduce the ongoing cost of operating an ABC system. Predetermined rates require that actual activity data be collected so that overhead can be applied. Fewer rates thus reduce the ongoing data collection activity required. In practical terms, a complex ABC system may not be sustainable simply because there is too much actual driver data to collect effectively.

Consider the data presented in Exhibit 4.12 for Patterson Company, a manufacturer of wafers for integrated circuits. Patterson produces two types of wafers: Wafer A and Wafer B. A wafer is a thin slice of silicon used as a base for integrated circuits or other electronic components. The dies on each wafer represent a particular configuration—a configuration designed for use by a particular end product. Patterson produces wafers in batches, where each batch corresponds to a particular type of wafer (A or B). In the wafer inserting and sorting process, dies are inserted, and the wafers are tested to ensure that the dies are not defective. From Exhibit 4.12, we see that the activity-based costs for Wafer A and Wafer B are $800,000 and $1,200,000, respectively.

Exhibit 4.12 Data for Patterson Company

Activity	Budgeted Activity Cost	Driver	Quantity[a]	Expected Consumption Ratios	
				Wafer A	Wafer B
Inserting and sorting process:					
1. Developing test programs	$ 400,000	Engineering hours	10,000	0.25	0.75
2. Making probe cards	58,750	Development hours	4,000	0.10	0.90
3. Testing products	300,000	Test hours	20,000	0.60	0.40
4. Setting up batches	40,000	Number of batches	100	0.55	0.45
5. Engineering design	80,000	Number of change orders	50	0.15	0.85
6. Handling wafer lots	90,000	Number of moves	200	0.45	0.55
7. Inserting dies	350,000	Number of dies	2,000,000	0.70	0.30
Procurement process:					
8. Purchasing materials	450,000	Number of purchase orders	2,500	0.20	0.80
9. Unloading materials	60,000	Number of receiving orders	3,000	0.35	0.65
10. Inspecting materials	75,000	Inspection hours	5,000	0.65	0.35
11. Moving materials	30,000	Distance moved	3,000	0.50	0.50
12. Paying suppliers	66,250	Number of invoices	3,500	0.30	0.70
Total activity cost	$2,000,000				
Unit-level (plantwide) cost assignment[b]				$1,400,000	$ 600,000
Activity cost assignment[c]				$ 800,000	$1,200,000

[a]Total amount of the activity expected to be used by both products.
[b]Calculated using *number of dies* as the single unit-level driver: Wafer A = 0.7 × $2,000,000; Wafer B = 0.3 × $2,000,000.
[c]Calculated using *each* activity cost and either the associated consumption ratios or activity rates. For example, the cost assigned to Wafer A using the consumption ratio for *developing testing programs* is 0.25 × $400,000 = $100,000. Repeating this for each activity and summing yields a total of $800,000 assigned to Wafer A.

These activity-based costs are calculated using the 12 drivers. A key question is whether or not the benefits of an ABC system can essentially be captured with a system using a significantly reduced number of drivers. We will consider two approaches for simplification: (1) Approximately Relevant ABC Systems, and (2) Equally Accurate Reduced ABC Systems.

Approximately Relevant ABC Systems It is possible that an organization is better off having an approximately relevant ABC system rather than a precisely useless one.[15] One intriguing suggestion for obtaining an approximately relevant ABC system is to do an analysis of the activity accounting system and to use only the most expensive activities for ABC assignment.[16] The costs of all other activities can be added to the cost pools of the expensive activities. For example, the costs of the less expensive activities could be allocated in proportion to the costs in each of the expensive activities. In this way, most costs are assigned to the products accurately. The costs of the most expensive activities are still assigned using appropriate cause-and-effect drivers, while the added costs are assigned somewhat arbitrarily. The advantages of this approach are that it is simple, easy to understand, and easy to implement. It also often provides a good approximation of the ABC costs. **Example 4.9** illustrates this approach.

   Example 4.9 illustrates that the ABC costs are approximated quite well by the reduced system of four drivers. Furthermore, it seems that the cost is much better than the plantwide rate, even when the system has significant error relative to the ABC assignments. If activity

---

15   Tom Pryor, "Simplify Your ABC," *Cost Management Newsletter* 15 (June 2004): accessed online at http://www.icms .net/news-21.htm.
16   Ibid.

EXAMPLE 4.9

The HOW and WHY of Approximately Relevant ABC Systems

Information:
Exhibit 4.12.

> **Why:**
> The number of drivers used to assign costs can be reduced by using only the drivers associated with the most expensive activities. Costs of the less expensive activities are allocated to the more expensive activities in proportion to their original cost. This provides a cost system that assigns most of the costs using causal relationships and yet is simple to understand and easy to use. For this method to be of value, a high percentage of the overhead costs must be attributable to a relatively small number of activities.

Required:

1. Using the four most expensive activities, calculate the overhead cost assigned to each product.

2. Calculate the error relative to the fully specified ABC product cost and comment on the outcome.

3. *What if* activities 1, 5, 8, and 12 each had a cost of $400,000 and the remaining activities had a cost of $50,000? Calculate the cost assigned to Wafer A by a fully specified ABC system and then by an approximately relevant ABC approach. Comment on the implications for the approximately relevant approach.

Solution:
1.

Activity	Budgeted Activity Cost[a]	Driver	Quantity	Expected Consumption Ratios	
				Wafer A	Wafer B
1. Developing test programs	$ 533,333	Engineering hours	10,000	0.25	0.75
3. Testing products	400,000	Test hours	20,000	0.60	0.40
7. Inserting dies	466,667	Number of dies	2,000,000	0.70	0.30
8. Purchasing materials	600,000	Purchase orders	2,500	0.20	0.80
Total activity cost	$2,000,000				
Approximate ABC cost[b]				$820,000	$1,180,000

[a]Original activity cost plus share of the costs of the remaining "inexpensive" activities (allocated in proportion to the original costs of the expensive activities (as shown in Exhibit 4.12): For example, the cost pool for purchasing materials is $450,000 + [($450,000/$1,500,000) × $500,000] = $600,000.
[b]Reduced system ABC assignment (using consumption ratios): Wafer A: [(0.25 × $533,333) + (0.60 × $400,000) + (0.70 × $466,667) + (0.20 × $600,000)]; Wafer B: [(0.75 × $533,333) + (0.40 × $400,000) + (0.30 × $466,667) + (0.80 × $600,000)].

2. Relative error, Wafer A: ($820,000 − $800,000)/$800,000 = 0.025 (2.5%)

Relative error, Wafer B: ($1,180,000 − $1,200,000)/$1,200,000 = − 0.017 (−1.7%)

The maximum error is a 2.5 percent overstatement of the ABC cost of Exhibit 4.12, when 12 drivers are used. This is a very good approximation indicating that the approach has merit.

EXAMPLE 4.9

(Continued)

3. Using consumption ratios, the ABC cost of Wafer A is $400,000(0.25 + 0.15 + 0.20 + 0.30) + $50,000(0.10 + 0.60 + 0.55 + 0.45 + 0.70 + 0.35 + 0.65 + 0.50) = $555,000. Since the cost is the same for each of the four most expensive activities, the reassigned cost for each of the four activities is $500,000 (each receives the same amount of the less expensive activities). Thus, using consumption ratios, the approximately relevant cost is $500,000(0.25 + 0.15 + 0.20 + 0.30) = $450,000. The difference between the ABC cost and the approximately relevant cost is −$105,000 ($450,000 − $555,000) or a relative error of about −19 percent. It appears that a significant error can occur even when the expensive activities account for about 80 percent of the total overhead. However, this is still a vast improvement over the plantwide rate assignment (which is $1,400,000 vs. $555,000).

costs roughly follow the Pareto principle or 80/20 rule (80 percent of the overhead costs are caused by 20 percent of the activities), then this approach for reducing the size of the system has considerable promise. For example, if a system has 100 activities, then the top 20 activities (as measured by their cost) need to account for a very high percentage of the total costs. In those cases where this holds, a reduced system may work reasonably well because *most* of the costs are assigned using cause-and-effect relationships. Even so, there may be some who would balk at the notion of using 15–20 drivers. The approach also loses its usefulness for those companies where a small number of activities do not account for a large share of the overhead costs.

Equally Accurate Reduced ABC Systems   Another approach is to use expected consumption ratios to reduce the number of drivers. Although the theoretical motivation for this approach is beyond the scope of the text, the methodology is straightforward. Consider again the 12 activities of Exhibit 4.12. The product costs assigned to Wafer A and Wafer B were $800,000 and $1,200,000, respectively. Thus, Wafer A is expected to consume 40 percent ($800,000/$2,000,000) of the total cost being assigned, and Wafer B is expected to consume 60 percent ($1,200,000/$2,000,000) of the total cost being assigned. Wafer A has an *expected global consumption ratio* of 0.40, and Wafer B has an *expected global consumption ratio* of 0.60. The **expected global consumption ratio** is the proportion of the total activity costs consumed by a given product (cost object). The expected global consumption ratio pattern for Patterson Company is (0.40, 0.60). Each activity also has a consumption ratio pattern.

For a two-product firm, the activity consumption ratio patterns are always described by an array (vector) of two components. For the Patterson Company example, the first ratio in the array is the proportion of the activity consumed by Wafer A, and the second ratio is the proportion consumed by Wafer B. For example, the activity, developing test programs, has a consumption pattern of (0.25, 0.75), where Wafer A consumes 25 percent of the activity cost and Wafer B consumes 75 percent of the activity cost. Similarly, the activity, inserting dies, has a consumption pattern of (0.70, 0.30), where Wafer A consumes 70 percent of the activity cost and Wafer B consumes 30 percent. As the number of products increases, the number of consumption ratio components also increases. The dimension of the consumption ratio pattern array corresponds to the number of products. When the number of activities is more than the number of products, it is always possible to find a reduced system that *duplicates* the cost assignments of the larger system. To achieve this duplication, the number of drivers needed is *at most* equal to the number of products (two drivers for our example). Thus, two drivers can be used to match the larger 12-driver system cost assignments. A key step in the reduction process is expressing each global consumption ratio as a weighted combination of the consumption ratios for each product. For example, using the activities, developing test programs and inserting dies, the weighted combination for Wafer A is $0.25w_1 + 0.70w_2 = 0.40$. A similar equation can be developed for Wafer B: $0.75w_1 + 0.30w_2 = 0.60$. Solving these two equations yields values for

w_1 and w_2. These values are *allocation ratios* and when multiplied by the total overhead costs define two cost pools (one for the first activity and one for the second activity). Using the consumption ratios or drivers for each activity then assigns the appropriate amount of cost to each product. How this is achieved and the motivation are summarized in **Example 4.10**.

EXAMPLE 4.10

The HOW and WHY of Equally Accurate Reduced ABC Systems

Information:

From Exhibit 4.12, the following data are extracted:

Activity	Driver	Quantity	Expected Consumption Ratios Wafer A	Wafer B
3. Testing products	Test hours	20,000	0.60	0.40
8. Purchasing materials	Purchase orders	2,500	0.20	0.80
1. Developing test programs	Number of engineering hours	10,000	0.25	0.75
7. Inserting dies	Number of dies	2,000,000	0.70	0.30
ABC assignment			$ 800,000	$1,200,000
Total overhead cost			$2,000,000	

Why:

It is always possible to find a reduced system that matches the accuracy of the larger ABC system. Using fewer drivers facilitates acceptance and use of an ABC system. The steps that should be followed to achieve the desired simplification are as follows: (1) calculate the expected global consumption ratio (ABC product cost/total overhead cost); (2) select the needed number of activities (equal to the number of products); (3) form equations for each product by multiplying the consumption ratios of each product by the allocation weights and setting the result equal to the product's global consumption ratio; (4) solve the simultaneous set of equations; and (5) use the weights to form the cost pools that will duplicate the larger ABC system cost assignments; and (6) use the consumption ratios (or drivers) to assign the cost pools to individual products.

Required:

1. Form reduced system cost pools for activities 3 and 8.

2. Assign the costs of the reduced system cost pools to Wafer A and Wafer B.

3. *What if* the two activities were 1 and 7? Repeat Requirements 1 and 2. What does this imply?

Solution:

1. Global ratios = 0.40 ($800,000/$2,000,000) for Wafer A and 0.60 ($1,200,000/$2,000,000) for Wafer B.

   Equations:

   $0.60w_1 + 0.20w_2 = 0.40$ (Wafer A)

   $0.40w_1 + 0.80w_2 = 0.60$ (Wafer B)

EXAMPLE 4.10

(*Continued*)

Multiplying both sides of the first equation by 4, subtracting the second from the first, and solving, we obtain:

Solving: $w_1 = 1/2$ and $w_2 = 1/2$

Testing products cost pool: $0.5 \times \$2,000,000 = \$1,000,000$
Purchasing cost pool: $0.5 \times \$2,000,000 = \$1,000,000$

2. Using the consumption ratios, the same cost assignment is realized with two drivers:

   Wafer A: $(0.60 \times \$1,000,000) + (0.20 \times \$1,000,000) = \$800,000$
   Wafer B: $(0.40 \times \$1,000,000) + (0.80 \times \$1,000,000) = \$1,200,000$

3. Equations:

   $0.25w_1 + 0.70w_2 = 0.40$ Wafer A

   $0.75w_1 + 0.30w_2 = 0.60$ Wafer B

   Solving: $w_1 = 2/3$ and $w_2 = 1/3$

   Cost pool (test programs): $(2/3) \times \$2,000,000 = \$1,333,333$
   Cost pool (inserting dies): $(1/3) \times \$2,000,000 = \$666,667$

   Wafer A: $(0.25 \times \$1,333,333) + (0.70 \times \$666,667) = \$800,000$ (rounded)
   Wafer B: $(0.75 \times \$1,333,333) + (0.30 \times \$666,667) = \$1,200,000$ (rounded)

The implication is that any two activities will work—but negative allocations may occur if the global ratio on the right-hand side does not lie between the coefficients of the two allocation weights.

Example 4.10 shows that an equally accurate simplified system can be derived from the more complex ABC system. Instead of using 12 drivers, it is possible to use only two drivers and achieve the same cost assignment of the more complex system. This reduced system represents an *after-the-fact* simplification. The reduced system is derived from an *existing* complex ABC data set. Of course, the same is true for the approximately relevant reduced system that uses the Pareto principle to achieve the reduction. The value of after-the-fact simplification is based on two key justifications. First, the reduced system eliminates the perceived complexity of the system. For example, it is much easier for nonfinancial users to read, interpret, and use a 2-driver system compared to a 12-driver system. Second, the reduced ABC system needs to collect actual driver data only for the drivers being used to assign the costs to products. For example, in the case of Patterson Company, only actual data for testing hours and number of purchase orders need to be collected so that overhead costs can be assigned (applied) to the two products. This is much less costly than collecting actual data for 12 drivers. Finally, it should also be pointed out that the two drivers in Exhibit 4.12 are only one of many 2-driver combinations that can be used to reduce the ABC system without sacrificing the assignment accuracy of the more complex system.

SUMMARY OF LEARNING OBJECTIVES

LO1. Describe the basics of plantwide and departmental overhead costing.
- Budgeted overhead costs are accumulated into plantwide or departmental pools and predetermined overhead rates are calculated.
- Predetermined rates use unit-level drivers such as direct labor hours and machine hours.
- Overhead is assigned by multiplying the rate by the actual total amount of unit-level driver (e.g., direct labor hours).
- The difference between the actual overhead and applied overhead is an overhead variance and is either under- or overapplied. If the variance is immaterial, it is closed to Cost of Goods Sold; otherwise, it is allocated among work-in-process inventory, finished goods, and cost of good sold.

LO2. Explain why plantwide and departmental overhead costing may not be accurate.
- Overhead assignments should reflect the amount of overhead demanded (consumed) by each product.
- Many overhead activities are unrelated to the units produced, and assigning overhead using unit-level drivers may distort product costs.
- If overhead is a significant proportion of total manufacturing costs, this distortion can be serious.
- Activity-based costing uses both unit-level and non-unit-level drivers and thus reflects a more accurate picture of the actual overhead consumed by products.

LO3. Provide a detailed description of activity-based product costing.
- Identify, define, and classify activities and key attributes.
- Assign the cost of resources to activities.
- Assign the cost of secondary activities to primary activities.
- Identify cost objects and specify the amount of each activity consumed by specific cost objects.
- Calculate primary activity rates.
- Assign activity costs to cost objects.

LO4. Explain how ABC can be simplified.
- TDABC, a before-the-fact simplification approach, eliminates the need to identify resource drivers to assign resource costs to activities, eliminating the need for much of the detailed implementation interviews.
- TDABC also makes it easier to update ABC when changes occur.
- DBC is a before-the-fact simplification approach that is as simple as using a plantwide rate but has the same accuracy as ABC.
- Simplified ABC systems can be derived from complex ABC systems.
- Simplified systems facilitate the presentation and use of ABC information and reduce the cost of collecting actual driver data.
- Two after-the-fact approaches were discussed: the approximately relevant reduced ABC system and the equally accurate reduced ABC system. The first approach may be useful for those firms where a few activities account for most of the overhead costs. The second system is useful whenever the number of activities is greater than the number of products (which is usually the case).

EXAMPLE 4.1	The HOW and WHY of Applied Overhead and Unit Overhead Cost: Plantwide Rates, page 148
EXAMPLE 4.2	The HOW and WHY of Overhead Variances and Their Disposal, page 150
EXAMPLE 4.3	The HOW and WHY of Departmental Overhead Rates: Their Assignment and Rationale, page 152
EXAMPLE 4.4	The HOW and WHY of Consumption Ratios, page 156

EXAMPLE 4.5   The HOW and WHY of Activity-Based Costing, page 157

EXAMPLE 4.6   The HOW and WHY of Assigning Resource Costs to Activities, page 165

EXAMPLE 4.7   The HOW and WHY of TDABC, page 170

EXAMPLE 4.8   The HOW and WHY of DBC, page 174

EXAMPLE 4.9   The HOW and WHY of Approximately Relevant ABC Systems, page 178

EXAMPLE 4.10 The HOW and WHY of Equally Accurate Reduced ABC Systems, page 180

KEY TERMS

Activity attributes, 161

Activity dictionary, 161

Activity drivers, 167

Activity inventory, 160

Activity-based costing (ABC) system, 160

Applied overhead, 148

Batch-level activities, 168

Bill of activities, 167

Consumption ratio, 154

Cycle time, 173

Duration-Based Costing (DBC), 173

Duration drivers, 167

Expected global consumption ratio, 179

Facility-level activities, 168

Non-unit-based drivers, 153

Normal cost system, 147

Overapplied overhead, 149

Overhead variance, 149

Predetermined overhead rate, 147

Primary activity, 161

Product diversity, 154

Product-level activities, 168

Resource drivers, 164

Secondary activity, 161

Time/batches, 173

Time-Driven Activity-Based Costing (TDABC), 169

Time/units, 173

Transaction drivers, 167

Underapplied overhead, 149

Unit-level activities, 168

Unit-level drivers, 147

BRIEF EXERCISES

Brief Exercise 4-1 Applied Overhead and Unit Overhead Cost: Plantwide Rates

OBJECTIVE ◄ 1
Example 4.1

Imprimo, Inc., produces two types of ink-jet printers: business and home. Imprimo uses a plantwide rate based on direct labor hours to assign its overhead costs. The company has the following estimated and actual data for the coming year:

Estimated overhead	$3,000,000
Expected activity	75,000
Actual activity (direct labor hours):	
Business printer	15,000
Home printer	60,000
Units produced:	
Business printer	30,000
Home printer	300,000

Required:

1. Calculate the predetermined plantwide overhead rate and the applied overhead for each product, using direct labor hours.
2. Calculate the overhead cost per unit for each product.
3. *What if* the home printer business used 30,000 hours (to produce 30,000 units) instead of 15,000 hours (total expected hours remain the same)? Calculate the effect on the profitability of this product line if all 30,000 units are sold, and then discuss the implications of this outcome.

OBJECTIVE ▶1
Example 4.2

Brief Exercise 4-2 Overhead Variances and Their Disposal

Warner Company has the following data for the past year:

Actual overhead	$470,000
Applied overhead:	
Work-in-process inventory	$100,000
Finished goods inventory	200,000
Cost of goods sold	200,000
Total	$500,000

Warner uses the overhead control account to accumulate both actual and applied overhead.

Required:

1. Calculate the overhead variance for the year and close it to cost of goods sold.
2. Assume the variance calculated is material. After prorating, close the variances to the appropriate accounts and provide the final ending balances of these accounts.
3. *What if* the variance is of the opposite sign calculated in Requirement 1? Provide the appropriate adjusting journal entries for Requirements 1 and 2.

OBJECTIVE ▶1
Example 4.3

Brief Exercise 4-3 Departmental Overhead Rates

Lansing, Inc., provided the following data for its two producing departments:

	Molding	Polishing	Total
Estimated overhead	$400,000	$80,000	$480,000
Direct labor hours (expected and actual):			
Form A	1,000	5,000	6,000
Form B	4,000	15,000	19,000
Total	5,000	20,000	25,000
Machine hours:			
Form A	3,500	3,000	6,500
Form B	1,500	2,000	3,500
Total	5,000	5,000	10,000

Machine hours are used to assign the overhead of the Molding Department, and direct labor hours are used to assign the overhead of the Polishing Department. There are 30,000 units of Form A produced and sold and 50,000 of Form B.

Required:

1. Calculate the overhead rates for each department.
2. Using departmental rates, assign overhead to the two products and calculate the overhead cost per unit. How does this compare with the plantwide rate unit cost, using direct labor hours?
3. *What if* the machine hours in Molding were 1,200 for Form A and 3,800 for Form B and the direct labor hours used in Polishing were 5,000 and 15,000, respectively? Calculate the overhead cost per unit for each product using departmental rates, and compare with the plantwide rate unit costs calculated in Requirement 2. What can you conclude from this outcome?

Brief Exercise 4-4 Consumption Ratios

Larsen, Inc., produces two types of electronic parts and has provided the following data:

	Part X12	Part YK7	Total
Units produced	100,000	600,000	—
Direct labor hours	30,000	70,000	100,000
Machine hours	50,000	300,000	350,000
Number of setups	40	80	120
Testing hours	1,000	9,000	10,000
Number of purchase orders	500	3,500	4,000

There are four activities: machining, setting up, testing, and purchasing.

Required:

1. Calculate the activity consumption ratios for each product.
2. Calculate the consumption ratios for the plantwide rate (direct labor hours). When compared with the activity ratios, what can you say about the relative accuracy of a plantwide rate? Which product is undercosted?
3. *What if* the machine hours were used for the plantwide rate? Would this remove the cost distortion of a plantwide rate?

Brief Exercise 4-5 Activity-Based Product Costing

Davis Company produces two hair dryers: regular and deluxe. The company has four activities: machining, engineering, receiving, and inspection. Information on these activities and their drivers is given below.

	Regular	Deluxe	Total
Units produced	100,000	200,000	—
Prime costs	$16,000,000	$60,000,000	$76,000,000
Machine hours	200,000	1,000,000	1,200,000
Engineering hours	800	7,200	8,000
Receiving orders	800	2,400	3,200
Inspection hours	1,600	3,200	4,800

Overhead costs:

Machining	$24,000,000
Engineering	8,000,000
Receiving	2,240,000
Inspecting products	1,440,000

Required:

1. Calculate the four activity rates.
2. Calculate the unit costs using activity rates. Also, calculate the overhead cost per unit.
3. *What if* consumption ratios instead of activity rates were used to assign costs instead of activity rates? Show the cost assignment for the inspection activity.

OBJECTIVE 3

Example 4.6

Brief Exercise 4-6 Assigning Cost of Resources to Activities, Unbundling the General Ledger

Golding Bank provided the following data about its resources and activities for its checking account process:

Resources		Activities	Clerical Hours
Supervision	$ 70,000	Processing accounts	10,000
Phone and supplies	90,000	Issuing statements	5,000
Salaries	275,000	Processing transactions	7,000
Computer	25,000	Answering customer inquiries	3,000
Total	$460,000	Total	25,000

- Computers are used only by the issuing (30 percent) and processing transaction (70 percent) activities.
- Phone and supplies are 60 percent customer inquiries with the other 40 percent divided equally among the remaining activities, including supervising the checking operation.
- The supervisor spends 100 percent of her time on supervision. In addition to the 25,000 clerical hours, there are 2,000 hours of supervision used (the hours used by the supervising clerks activity, which is not listed above).

Required:

1. Prepare a work distribution matrix for the five primary activities.
2. Calculate the cost of each activity.
3. *What if* the cost of the supervising activity is assigned to the other four activities? Why would this be done? If it is done, what is the final cost of these four primary activities?

OBJECTIVE 4

Example 4.7

Brief Exercise 4-7 Simplifying the ABC System: TDABC

Golding Bank provided the following data about its two checking account products and their associated resources and activities:

Resources		Activities	Driver	Time per Unit of Activity	Traditional Account	Interest-Bearing Account
Supervision	$ 70,000	Processing accounts	No. of accounts	0.20 hr.	2,000	1,000
Phone and supplies	90,000	Issuing statements	No. of statements	0.10 hr.	60,000	10,000
Salaries	275,000	Processing transactions	No. of transactions	0.05 hr.	160,000	120,000
Computer	25,000	Answering customer inquiries	No. of inquiries	0.15 hr.	1,500	1,500
Total	$460,000					

At practical capacity, Golding uses 25,000 check processing hours.

Required:

1. Calculate the capacity cost rate for the checking account process, and then calculate the activity rate for each activity.
2. Assuming there are 2,000 interest-bearing checking accounts, calculate the cost per account using the activity rates from Requirement 1.
3. A time equation is used to assign resource costs to checking accounts. Develop a time equation for the interest-bearing checking account product. Again, assuming that there are 2,000 interest bearing accounts, show that the resource cost per account is the same as calculated in Requirement 2.
4. *What if* process improvements decreased the number of customer inquiries, leading to a 10 percent reduction in check processing hours and a $10,000 reduction in total resource costs? Update all the activity rates for these changes in operating conditions.

Brief Exercise 4-8 Simplifying the ABC System: DBC

OBJECTIVE ◄ 4
Example 4.8

Electan Company produces two types of printers. The company uses ABC, and all activity drivers are duration drivers. Electan Company is considering using DBC and has gathered the following data to help with its decision.

A. Activities with duration drivers:

	Activities				
Products	Changeover	Assembly	Testing	Rework	Total Hours
Printer A	1,000	12,000	8,000	8,000	25,000
Printer B	4,000	8,000	12,000	12,000	25,000
Total hours	5,000	20,000	20,000	20,000	50,000

B. Activities with consumption ratios and costs:

	Activities				Cost
Products	Changeover	Assembly	Testing	Rework	Assignment
Printer A	0.20	0.60	0.40	0.80	$155,000
Printer B	0.80	0.40	0.60	0.20	$155,000
Activity costs	$75,000	$120,000	$60,000	$55,000	$310,000

C. Products with cycle time and practical capacity:

Product	Cycle Time	Practical Capacity
Printer A	2.5 hours	10,000 units
Printer B	1.25 hours	20,000 units

Required:

1. Using cycle time and practical capacity for each product, calculate the total time for all primary activities. Comment on the relationship to ABC.
2. Calculate the overhead rate that DBC uses to assign costs. Comment on the relationship to a unit-based plantwide overhead rate.
3. Use the overhead rate calculated in Requirement 2 to calculate (a) the overhead cost per unit for each product, and (b) the total overhead assigned to each product. How does this compare to the ABC assignments shown in Part B of the Information set?
4. *What if* the units actually produced were 10,000 for Printer A and 18,000 for Printer B. Using DBC, calculate the cost of unused capacity.

Brief Exercise 4-9 Simplifying the ABC System: Approximately Relevant ABC Systems

OBJECTIVE ◄ 4
Example 4.9

Patterson Company produces wafers for integrated circuits. Data for the most recent year are provided:

			Expected Consumption Ratios	
Activity		Driver	Wafer A	Wafer B
Inserting and sorting process activities:				
1. Developing test programs	$ 50,000	Engineering hours	0.25	0.75
2. Making probe cards	60,000	Development hours	0.10	0.90
3. Testing products	600,000	Test hours	0.60	0.40
4. Setting up batches	135,000	Number of batches	0.55	0.45
5. Engineering design	90,000	Number of change orders	0.15	0.85
6. Handling wafer lots	300,000	Number of moves	0.45	0.55
7. Inserting dies	700,000	Number of dies	0.70	0.30

(continued)

Procurement process activities:

8. Purchasing materials	400,000	Number of purchase orders	0.20	0.80
9. Unloading materials	60,000	Number of receiving orders	0.35	0.65
10. Inspecting materials	75,000	Inspection hours	0.65	0.35
11. Moving materials	500,000	Distance moved	0.50	0.50
12. Paying suppliers	30,000	Number of invoices	0.30	0.70
Total activity cost	$3,000,000			

Unit-level (plantwide) cost assignment[a]	$2,100,000	$ 900,000
Activity cost assignment[b]	$1,500,000	$1,500,000

[a]Calculated using number of dies as the single unit-level driver.
[b]Calculated by multiplying the consumption ratio of each product by the cost of each activity.

Required:

1. Using the five most expensive activities, calculate the overhead cost assigned to each product. Assume that the costs of the other activities are assigned in proportion to the cost of the five activities.
2. Calculate the error relative to the fully specified ABC product cost and comment on the outcome.
3. *What if* activities 1, 2, 5, and 8 each had a cost of $650,000 and the remaining activities had a cost of $50,000? Calculate the cost assigned to Wafer A by a fully specified ABC system and then by an approximately relevant ABC approach. Comment on the implications for the approximately relevant approach.

OBJECTIVE **4**
Example 4.10

Brief Exercise 4-10 Simplifying the ABC System: Equally Accurate Reduced ABC Systems

Selected activities and other information are provided for Patterson Company for its most recent year of operations.

			Expected Consumption Ratios	
Activity	**Driver**	**Quantity**	**Wafer A**	**Wafer B**
7. Inserting dies	Number of dies	2,000,000	0.70	0.30
8. Purchasing materials	Number of purchase orders	2,500	0.20	0.80
1. Developing test programs	Engineering hours	10,000	0.25	0.75
3. Testing products	Test hours	20,000	0.60	0.40
ABC assignment			$1,500,000	$1,500,000
Total overhead cost				$3,000,000

Required:

1. Form reduced system cost pools for activities 7 and 8.
2. Assign the costs of the reduced system cost pools to Wafer A and Wafer B.
3. *What if* the two activities were 1 and 3? Repeat Requirements 1 and 2. What does this imply?

EXERCISES

OBJECTIVE **1**

SHOW ME
HOW

Exercise 4-11 Predetermined Overhead Rate, Applied Overhead, Unit Cost

Gomez, Inc., costs products using a normal costing system. The following data are available for last year:

Budgeted:

Overhead	$ 285,600
Machine hours	84,000
Direct labor hours	10,200

Actual:

Overhead	$ 285,000
Machine hours	82,200
Direct labor hours	9,930
Prime cost	$1,050,000
Number of units	150,000

Overhead is applied on the basis of direct labor hours.

Required:

1. What was the predetermined overhead rate?
2. What was the applied overhead for last year?
3. Was overhead over- or underapplied, and by how much?
4. What was the total cost per unit produced (carry your answer to four significant digits)?

Exercise 4-12 Predetermined Overhead Rate, Application of Overhead

OBJECTIVE 1

Findley Company and Lemon Company both use predetermined overhead rates to apply manufacturing overhead to production. Findley's is based on machine hours, and Lemon's is based on materials cost. Budgeted production and cost data for Findley and Lemon are as follows:

SHOW ME
HOW

	Findley	Lemon
Manufacturing overhead	$912,000	$ 990,000
Units	20,000	60,000
Machine hours	48,000	33,750
Materials cost	$450,000	$1,800,000

At the end of the year, Findley Company had incurred overhead of $915,000 and had produced 19,600 units using 47,780 machine hours and materials costing $445,000. Lemon Company had incurred overhead of $972,000 and had produced 61,500 units using 32,650 machine hours and materials costing $1,777,500.

Required:

1. Compute the predetermined overhead rates for Findley Company and Lemon Company.
2. Was overhead over- or underapplied for each company, and by how much?

Exercise 4-13 Predetermined Overhead Rate, Overhead Variances, Journal Entries

OBJECTIVE 1

SHOW ME
HOW

Craig Company uses a predetermined overhead rate to assign overhead to jobs. Because Craig's production is machine intensive, overhead is applied on the basis of machine hours. The expected overhead for the year was $5.7 million, and the practical level of activity is 375,000 machine hours.

During the year, Craig used 382,500 machine hours and incurred actual overhead costs of $5.73 million. Craig also had the following balances of applied overhead in its accounts:

Work-in-process inventory	$ 576,000
Finished goods inventory	624,000
Cost of goods sold	1,800,000

Required:

1. Compute a predetermined overhead rate for Craig.
2. Compute the overhead variance, and label it as under- or overapplied.

3. Assuming the overhead variance is immaterial, prepare the journal entry to dispose of the variance at the end of the year.
4. Assuming the overhead variance is material, prepare the journal entry that appropriately disposes of the overhead variance at the end of the year.

OBJECTIVE 1

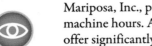

SHOW ME
HOW

Exercise 4-14 Departmental Overhead Rates

Mariposa, Inc., produces machine tools and currently uses a plantwide overhead rate, based on machine hours. Alice Chen, the plant manager, has heard that departmental overhead rates can offer significantly better cost assignments than can a plantwide rate.

Mariposa has the following data for its two departments for the coming year:

	Department A	Department B
Overhead costs (expected)	$720,000	$180,000
Normal activity (machine hours)	120,000	60,000

Required:

1. Compute a predetermined overhead rate for the plant as a whole based on machine hours.
2. Compute predetermined overhead rates for each department using machine hours.
3. Suppose that a machine tool (Product X75) used 60 machine hours from Department A and 150 machine hours from Department B. A second machine tool (Product Y15) used 150 machine hours from Department A and 60 machine hours from Department B. Compute the overhead cost assigned to each product using the plantwide rate computed in Requirement 1. Repeat the computation using the departmental rates found in Requirement 2. Which of the two approaches gives the fairest assignment? Why?
4. Repeat Requirement 3 assuming the expected overhead cost for Department B is $360,000. Now would you recommend departmental rates over a plantwide rate?

OBJECTIVE 2

SHOW ME
HOW

Exercise 4-15 Drivers and Product-Costing Accuracy

McCourt Company produces two types of leather purses: standard and handcrafted. Both purses use equipment for cutting and stitching. The equipment also has the capability of creating standard designs. The standard purses use only these standard designs. They are all of the same size to accommodate the design features of the equipment. The handcrafted purses can be cut to any size because the designs are created manually. Many of the manually produced designs are in response to specific requests of retailers. The equipment must be specially configured to accommodate the production of a batch of purses that will receive a handcrafted design. McCourt Company assigns overhead using direct labor dollars. Muggs Clark, sales manager, is convinced that the purses are not being costed correctly.

To illustrate his point, he decided to focus on the expected annual setup and machine-related costs, which are as follows:

Setup equipment	$45,000
Depreciation	50,000*
Operating costs	55,000

* Computed on a straight-line basis; book value at the beginning of the year was $250,000.

The machine has the capability of supplying 250,000 machine hours over its remaining life.

Muggs also collected the expected annual prime costs for each purse, the machine hours, and the expected production (which is the normal output for the company).

	Standard Purse	Handcrafted Purse
Direct labor	$30,000	$90,000
Direct materials	$30,000	$30,000
Units	7,500	7,500
Machine hours	45,000	5,000
Number of setups	100	100
Setup time	1,000 hrs.	500 hrs.

Required:

1. Do you think that the direct labor costs and direct materials costs are accurately traced to each type of purse? Explain.
2. The controller has suggested that overhead costs be assigned to each product using a plant-wide rate based on direct labor dollars. Machine costs and setup costs are overhead costs. Assume that these are the only overhead costs. For each type of purse, calculate the overhead per unit that would be assigned using a direct labor dollars overhead rate. Do you think that these costs are traced accurately to each purse? Explain.
3. Now calculate the overhead cost per unit per purse using two overhead rates: one for the setup activity and one for the machining activity. In choosing a driver to assign the setup costs, did you use number of setups or setup hours? Why? As part of your explanation, define transaction and duration drivers. Do you think machine costs are traced accurately to each type of purse? Explain.

Exercise 4-16 Multiple versus Single Overhead Rates, Activity Drivers

Deoro Company has identified the following overhead activities, costs, and activity drivers for the coming year:

Activity	Expected Cost	Activity Driver	Activity Capacity
Setting up equipment	$480,000	Number of setups	600
Ordering costs	360,000	Number of orders	18,000
Machine costs	840,000	Machine hours	42,000
Receiving	400,000	Receiving hours	10,000

Deoro produces two models of dishwashers with the following expected prime costs and activity demands:

	Model A	Model B
Direct materials	$600,000	$800,000
Direct labor	$480,000	$480,000
Units completed	16,000	8,000
Direct labor hours	6,000	2,000
Number of setups	400	200
Number of orders	6,000	12,000
Machine hours	24,000	18,000
Receiving hours	3,000	7,000

The company's normal activity is 8,000 direct labor hours.

Required:

1. Determine the unit cost for each model using direct labor hours to apply overhead.
2. Determine the unit cost for each model using the four activity drivers.
3. Which method produces the more accurate cost assignment? Why?

Exercise 4-17 Activity-Based Costing, Activity Identification, Activity Dictionary

Golding Bank is in the process of implementing an activity-based costing system. A copy of an interview with the manager of Golding's Credit Card Department follows.

QUESTION 1: How many employees are in your department?

RESPONSE: There are eight employees, including me.

QUESTION 2: What do they do (please describe)?

RESPONSE: There are four major activities: supervising employees, processing credit card transactions, issuing customer statements, and answering customer questions.

QUESTION 3: Do customers outside your department use any equipment?

RESPONSE: Yes. Automatic bank tellers service customers who require cash advances.

QUESTION 4: What resources are used by each activity (equipment, materials, energy)?

RESPONSE: We each have our own computer, printer, and desk. Paper and other supplies are needed to operate the printers. Of course, we each have a telephone as well.

QUESTION 5: What are the outputs of each activity?

RESPONSE: Well, for supervising, I manage employees' needs and try to ensure that they carry out their activities efficiently. Processing transactions produces a posting for each transaction in our computer system and serves as a source for preparing the monthly statements. The number of monthly customer statements has to be the product for the issuing activity, and I suppose that the number of customers served is the output for the answering activity. And I guess that the number of cash advances would measure the product of the automatic teller activity, although the teller really generates more transactions for other products such as checking and savings accounts. So, perhaps the number of teller transactions is the real output.

QUESTION 6: Who or what uses the activity output?

RESPONSE: We have three products: classic, gold, and platinum credit cards. Transactions are processed for these three types of cards, and statements are sent to clients holding these cards. Similarly, answers to questions are all directed to clients who hold these cards. As far as supervising, I spend time ensuring the proper coordination and execution of all activities except for the automatic teller. I really have no role in managing that particular activity.

QUESTION 7: How much time do workers spend on each activity? By equipment?

RESPONSE: I just completed a work survey and have the percentage of time calculated for each worker. All seven clerks work on each of the three departmental activities. About 40 percent of their time is spent processing transactions, with the rest of their time split evenly between issuing statements and answering questions. Phone time for all seven workers is used only for answering client questions. Computer time is 70 percent transaction processing, 20 percent statement preparation, and 10 percent question answering. Furthermore, my own time and that of my computer and telephone are 100 percent administrative. Credit card transactions represent about 20 percent of the total automatic teller transactions.

Required:

Prepare an activity dictionary using five columns: activity name, activity description, activity type (primary or secondary), cost object(s), and activity driver.

OBJECTIVE 3

SHOW ME HOW

Exercise 4-18 Assigning Resource Costs to Activities, Resource Drivers, Primary and Secondary Activities

Refer to the interview in **Exercise 4-17** (especially to Questions 4 and 7). The general ledger reveals the following annual costs:

Supervisor's salary	$ 64,600
Clerical salaries	210,000
Computers, desks, and printers	32,000
Computer supplies	7,200
Telephone expenses	4,000
ATM	1,250,000

All nonlabor resources, other than the ATM, are spread evenly among the eight credit department employees (in terms of assignment and usage). Credit department employees have no contact with ATMs. Printers and desks are used in the same ratio as computers by the various activities.

Required:

1. Determine the cost of all primary and secondary activities.
2. Assign the cost of secondary activities to the primary activities.

Exercise 4-19 Assigning Resource Costs to Activities, Resource Drivers, Primary and Secondary Activities

OBJECTIVE ◄ 3

SHOW ME
HOW

Bob Russo, cost accounting manager for Hemple Products, was asked to determine the costs of the activities performed within the company's Manufacturing Engineering Department. The department has the following activities: creating bills of materials (BOMs), studying manufacturing capabilities, improving manufacturing processes, training employees, and designing tools. The general ledger accounts reveal the following expenditures for Manufacturing Engineering:

Salaries	$500,000
Equipment	100,000
Supplies	30,000
Total	$630,000

The equipment is used for two activities: improving processes and designing tools. The equipment's time is divided by two activities: 40 percent for improving processes and 60 percent for designing tools. The salaries are for nine engineers, one who earns $100,000 and eight who earn $50,000 each. The $100,000 engineer spends 40 percent of her time training employees in new processes and 60 percent of her time on improving processes. One engineer spends 100 percent of her time on designing tools, and another engineer spends 100 percent of his time on improving processes. The remaining six engineers spend equal time on all activities. Supplies are consumed in the following proportions:

Creating BOMs	10%
Studying capabilities	5
Improving processes	35
Training employees	20
Designing tools	30

After determining the costs of the engineering activities, Bob was then asked to describe how these costs would be assigned to jobs produced within the factory. (The company manufactures machine parts on a job-order basis.) Bob responded by indicating that creating BOMs and designing tools were the only primary activities. The remaining were secondary activities. After some analysis, Bob concluded that studying manufacturing capabilities was an activity that enabled the other four activities to be realized. He also noted that all of the employees being trained are manufacturing workers—employees who work directly on the products. The major manufacturing activities are cutting, drilling, lathing, welding, and assembly. The costs of these activities are assigned to the various products using hours of usage (grinding hours, drilling hours, etc.). Furthermore, tools were designed to enable the production of specific jobs. Finally, the process improvement activity focused only on the five major manufacturing activities.

Required:

1. What is meant by unbundling general ledger costs? Why is it necessary?
2. What is the difference between a general ledger database system and an activity-based database system?
3. Using the resource drivers and direct tracing, calculate the costs of each manufacturing engineering activity. What are the resource drivers?
4. Describe in detail how the costs of the engineering activities would be assigned to jobs using activity-based costing. Include a description of the activity drivers that might be used. Where appropriate, identify both a possible transaction driver and a possible duration driver.

OBJECTIVE **Exercise 4-20 Process Identification and Activity Classification**

Calzado Company produces leather shoes in batches. The shoes are produced in one plant located on 20 acres. The plant operates two shifts, five days per week. Each time a batch is produced, just-in-time suppliers deliver materials to the plant. When the materials arrive, a worker checks the quantity and type of materials with the bill of materials for the batch. The worker then makes an entry at a PC terminal near the point of delivery acknowledging receipt of the material. An accounts payable clerk reviews all deliveries at the end of each day and then prints and mails checks the same day materials are received. Prior to producing a batch, the equipment must be configured to reflect style and size features. Once configured, the batch is produced passing through three operations: cutting, sewing, and attaching buckles and other related parts such as heels. At the end of the production process, a sample of shoes is inspected to ensure the right level of quality.

After inspection, the batch is divided into lots based on the customer orders for the shoes. The lots are packaged in boxes and then transferred to a staging area to await shipment. After a short wait (usually within two hours), the lots are loaded onto trucks and delivered to customers (retailers).

Within the same plant, the company also has a team of design engineers who respond to customer feedback on style and comfort issues. This department modifies existing designs, develops new shoe designs, builds prototypes, and test markets the prototypes before releasing the designs for full-scale production.

Required:

1. Identify Calzado's processes and their associated activities.
2. Classify each activity within each process as unit level, batch level, product level, or facility level.

OBJECTIVE **Exercise 4-21 TDABC**

Bob Russo, cost accounting manager for Hemple Products, was asked to determine the costs of the activities performed within the company's Manufacturing Engineering Department. The department has the following activities: creating bills of materials (BOMs), studying manufacturing capabilities, improving manufacturing processes, training employees, and designing tools. The resource costs (from the general ledger) and the times to perform one unit of each activity are provided below.

Resource Costs		Activities	Unit Time	Driver
Salaries	$500,000	Creating BOMs	0.5 hr.	No. of BOMs
Equipment	100,000	Designing tools	5.4 hrs.	No. of tool designs
Supplies	30,000	Improving processes	1.0 hr.	Process improvement hrs.
Total	$630,000	Training employees	2.0 hrs.	No. of training sessions
		Studying capabilities	1.0 hrs.	Study hrs.

Total machine and labor hours (at practical capacity):

Machine hours	2,000
Engineering hours	18,000
Total hours	20,000

The activity, designing tools, uses the number of tools designed as the activity driver. Using a traditional approach, the cost of the designing tools activity was determined to be $179,000 (see Exercise 4-19) with an expected activity output of 1,000 for the coming year. During the first week of the year, two jobs (Job 150 and Job 151) had a demand for 10 and 20 new tools, respectively.

Required:

1. Calculate the capacity cost rate for the Manufacturing Engineering Department.
2. Using the capacity cost rate, determine the activity rates for each activity.
3. Calculate the cost of designing tools that would be assigned to each job using the TDABC-derived activity rate and then repeat using the traditional ABC rate. What might be the cause or causes that would explain the differences in the two approaches?
4. Now suppose that time for creating BOMs is 0.50 for a standard product but that creating a BOM for a custom product adds an additional 0.3 hour. Express the time equation for this added complexity and then calculate the activity rate for the activity of creating a BOM for custom products.

Exercise 4-22 Approximately Relevant ABC

Silven Company has identified the following overhead activities, costs, and activity drivers for the coming year:

Activity	Expected Cost	Activity Driver	Activity Capacity
Setting up equipment	$126,000	Number of setups	150
Ordering materials	18,000	Number of orders	900
Machining	126,000	Machine hours	10,500
Receiving	30,000	Receiving hours	1,250

Silven produces two models of cell phones with the following expected activity demands:

	Model X	Model Y
Units completed	5,000	10,000
Number of setups	100	50
Number of orders	300	600
Machine hours	6,000	4,500
Receiving hours	375	875

Required:

1. Determine the total overhead assigned to each product using the four activity drivers.
2. Determine the total overhead assigned to each model using the two most expensive activities. The costs of the two relatively inexpensive activities are allocated to the two expensive activities in proportion to their costs.
3. Using ABC as the benchmark, calculate the percentage error and comment on the accuracy of the reduced system. Explain why this approach may be desirable.

Exercise 4-23 Equally Accurate Reduced ABC System

Refer to **Exercise 4-22**.

Required:

1. Calculate the global consumption ratios for the two products.
2. Using the activity consumption ratios for number of orders and number of setups, show that the same cost assignment can be achieved using these two drivers as that of the complete, four-driver ABC system.

OBJECTIVE 4

SHOW ME
HOW

Exercise 4-24 Duration-Based Costing

Gee Manufacturing produces two models of camshafts used in the production of automobile engines: Regular and High Performance. Gee currently uses an ABC system to assign costs to the two products. For the coming year, the company has the following overhead activities, costs, and activity drivers:

Activity	Expected Cost	Activity Driver	Activity Capacity
Setups	$214,612	Setup hours	10,000
Machining	$420,000	Machine hours	20,000
Moving	$112,500	Move hours	5,000
Total OH	$747,112		

At practical capacity, the expected activity demands for each product are as follows:

	Regular Performance Model	High Performance Model
Units completed	30,000	8,000
Setup hours	8,000	2,000
Machine hours	6,000	14,000
Moving hours	1,000	4,000

The production cycle time for the regular performance camshaft is 0.50 (hours per unit) and that of the high performance camshaft is 2.5 (hours per unit).

Required:

1. Calculate the consumption ratios for each activity. Use these consumption ratios to assign the total overhead to each camshaft model and then calculate the overhead cost per unit for each model (round unit cost to two decimal places).
2. Calculate the total and per unit overhead assigned to each model using DBC (assume you only know cycle time, total overhead costs, and units at practical capacity). Round the overhead rate to four decimal places and the per unit overhead cost to two decimal places. How do the cost assignments compare to those of ABC?
3. Explain to Gee why DBC might be a better choice for assigning overhead costs.

OBJECTIVE 4

SHOW ME   DATA
HOW   ANALYTICS

Exercise 4-25 TDABC

A consulting firm has recently installed a TDABC system for the Shawnee University Library. The consulting firm identified four major processes or departments for the library: Acquisition, Cataloging, Circulation, and Document Delivery. The Acquisition Department is responsible for acquiring new books and new journal subscriptions. Information for the Acquisition Department is given as follows:

Resource Costs		Activities	Unit Time (Minutes)	Driver	Books	Journals
Salaries	$130,000	Selecting or notifying	6	No. of selections	12,000	2,000
Computer maintenance	10,000	Processing requests	5	No. of requests	6,000	700
Library management system	30,000	Ordering	15	No. of orders	4,000	500
Supplies	10,000	Processing invoices	12	No. of invoices	3,000	250
Total	$180,000	Receiving books or journals	11	No. of units received	5,000	500

Periodically, the library is notified of new books and journals by publishers. The Acquisition Department reviews the publishers' list to see if any items are already in the library's collection and also checks the demand for particular books or journals. After this selection process is complete, a list of potential acquisitions is sent to the professors of the university. Professors respond by sending a request for books or journals to the Acquisition Department. These requests are filtered, processed, and transferred to the person responsible for placing orders. When an invoice is received, it is compared with the order and payment is arranged. When the product is received, the product is verified and the requesting person is informed.

In the Acquisition Department, there are two full-time librarians and several student employees that provide 4,500 total labor hours (practical capacity). In addition, there are 500 machine hours used in the acquisition process (also at practical capacity). Thus, the total practical capacity of the Acquisition Department is 5,000 hours or 300,000 minutes per year. The library orders 5,000 new books per year and acquires 500 new journal subscriptions.

1. Calculate the capacity cost rate for the Acquisition Department of the Shawnee University Library.
2. Using the capacity rate, determine the activity rates for each activity.
3. Using the activity rates, calculate the cost per unit for acquiring books and journals. What is the cost of unused capacity?
4. Prepare a time equation for acquiring books and one for acquiring journals. Using the time equations, calculate the unit costs for acquiring books and journals.
5. Suppose that some professors respond with a request for a book or journal that is not on the list provided by the library. In such cases, it takes an additional two minutes to read and reply. How would you modify the time equations in Requirement 4 to deal with this additional complexity? What will be the unit cost for books if out of the 6,000 requests for books, 500 are for books not on the list provided? Identify the data analytic type (descriptive, diagnostic, predictive, or prescriptive) that will help the library answer these questions. *Note:* More than one analytic type might apply.

Exercise 4-26 DBC

Refer to the information in **Exercise 4-25**.

For each of the following requirements, identify the data analytic type (descriptive, diagnostic, predictive, or prescriptive) that will help provide the needed answers. *Note:* More than one data analytic type might appear in any requirement.

OBJECTIVE 4

DATA ANALYTICS   SHOW ME HOW

Required:

1. Based on interviews and observations, the consulting firm noted that 90 percent of the practical capacity of the Acquisition Department is used for book acquisition and 10 percent for journal acquisition. Using this information, calculate the cycle time for book acquisition and the cycle time for journal acquisition.
2. Calculate the OH or capacity cost rate for the library. Using this rate and the cycle times from Requirement 1, calculate the unit cost of book acquisition and the unit cost of journal acquisition. Predict what the unit costs for books and journals would be if computer maintenance cost is budgeted to increase by 50 percent and salaries are budgeted to increase by $25,000.
3. For each activity, use the TDABC information to convert the transaction drivers to duration drivers. Using the time values provided for each activity, estimate the cycle time for book acquisition and journal acquisition. Using these cycle time values, calculate the unit cost of book acquisition and the unit cost of journal acquisition. Explain why the DBC unit cost would be the same as the TDABC unit cost, using the time values provided by TDABC.

PROBLEMS

OBJECTIVE **Problem 4-27 Predetermined Overhead Rates, Overhead Variances, Unit Costs**

Primera Company produces two products and uses a predetermined overhead rate to apply overhead. Primera currently applies overhead using a plantwide rate based on direct labor hours. Consideration is being given to the use of departmental overhead rates where overhead would be applied on the basis of direct labor hours in Department 1 and on the basis of machine hours in Department 2. At the beginning of the year, the following estimates are provided:

	Department 1	Department 2
Direct labor hours	640,000	128,000
Machine hours	16,000	192,000
Overhead cost	$384,000	$1,152,000

Actual results reported by department and product during the year are as follows:

	Department 1	Department 2
Direct labor hours	627,200	134,400
Machine hours	17,600	204,800
Overhead cost	$400,000	$1,232,000

	Product 1	Product 2
Direct labor hours:		
Department 1	480,000	147,200
Department 2	96,000	38,400
Machine hours:		
Department 1	8,000	9,600
Department 2	24,800	180,000

Required:

1. Compute the plantwide predetermined overhead rate and calculate the overhead assigned to each product.
2. Calculate the predetermined departmental overhead rates and calculate the overhead assigned to each product.
3. Using departmental rates, compute the applied overhead for the year. What is the under- or overapplied overhead for the firm?
4. Prepare the journal entry that disposes of the overhead variance calculated in Requirement 3, assuming it is not material in amount. What additional information would you need if the variance is material to make the appropriate journal entry?

OBJECTIVE **Problem 4-28 Unit-Based versus Activity-Based Costing**

EXCEL

Fisico Company produces exercise bikes. One of its plants produces two versions: a standard model and a deluxe model. The deluxe model has a wider and sturdier base and a variety of electronic gadgets to help the exerciser monitor heartbeat, calories burned, distance traveled, etc. At the beginning of the year, the following data were prepared for this plant:

	Standard Model	Deluxe Model
Expected quantity	30,000	15,000
Selling price	$370	$700
Prime costs	$4.5 million	$5.25 million
Machine hours	37,500	37,500
Direct labor hours	75,000	75,000
Engineering support (hours)	13,500	31,500
Receiving (orders processed)	3,000	4,500
Materials handling (number of moves)	15,000	45,000
Purchasing (number of requisitions)	750	1,500
Maintenance (hours used)	6,000	24,000
Paying suppliers (invoices processed)	3,750	3,750
Setting up batches (number of setups)	60	540

Additionally, the following overhead activity costs are reported:

Maintenance	$ 600,000
Engineering support	900,000
Materials handling	1,200,000
Setups	750,000
Purchasing	450,000
Receiving	300,000
Paying suppliers	300,000
	$4,500,000

Required:

1. Calculate the cost per unit for each product using direct labor hours to assign all overhead costs.

2. Calculate activity rates and determine the cost per unit. Compare these costs with those calculated using the unit-based method. Which cost is the most accurate? Explain.

Problem 4-29 ABC, Resource Drivers, Service Industry

OBJECTIVE ◀ 2 3

Glencoe Medical Clinic operates a cardiology care unit and a maternity care unit. Cara Abadi, the clinic's administrator, is investigating the charges assigned to cardiology patients. Currently, all cardiology patients are charged the same rate per patient day for daily care services. Daily care services are broadly defined as occupancy, feeding, and nursing care. A recent study, however, revealed several interesting outcomes. First, the demands patients place on daily care services vary with the severity of the case being treated. Second, the occupancy activity is a combination of two activities: lodging and use of monitoring equipment. Since some patients require more monitoring than others, these activities should be separated. Third, the daily rate should reflect the difference in demands resulting from differences in patient type. Separating the occupancy activity into two separate activities also required the determination of the cost of each activity. Determining the costs of the monitoring activity was fairly easy because its costs were directly traceable. Lodging costs, however, are shared by two activities: lodging cardiology patients and lodging maternity care patients. The total lodging costs for the two activities were $5,700,000 per year and consisted of such items as building depreciation, building maintenance, and building utilities. The cardiology floor and the maternity floor each occupy 20,000 square feet. Abadi determined that lodging costs would be assigned to each unit based on square feet.

To compute a daily rate that reflected the difference in demands, patients were placed in three categories according to illness severity, and the following annual data were collected:

Activity	Cost of Activity	Activity Driver	Quantity
Lodging	$2,850,000	Patient days	22,500
Monitoring	2,100,000	Monitoring hours used	30,000
Feeding	450,000	Patient days	22,500
Nursing care	4,500,000	Nursing hours	225,000
Total	$9,900,000		

The demands associated with patient severity are also provided:

Severity	Patient Days	Monitoring Hours	Nursing Hours
High	7,500	15,000	135,000
Medium	11,250	12,000	75,000
Low	3,750	3,000	15,000

Required:

1. Suppose that the costs of daily care are assigned using only patient days as the activity driver (which is also the measure of output). Compute the daily rate using this unit-based approach of cost assignment.
2. Compute activity rates using the given activity drivers (combine activities with the same driver).
3. Compute the charge per patient day for each patient type using the activity rates from Requirement 2 and the demands on each activity.
4. Suppose that the product is defined as "stay and treatment" where the treatment is bypass surgery. What additional information would you need to cost out this newly defined product?
5. Comment on the value of activity-based costing in service industries.

OBJECTIVE 2 3

Problem 4-30 Activity-Based Costing: Service Firm

Glencoe First National Bank operated for years under the assumption that profitability can be increased by increasing dollar volumes. Historically, First National's efforts were directed toward increasing total dollars of sales and total dollars of account balances. In recent years, however, First National's profits have been eroding. Increased competition, particularly from savings and loan institutions, was the cause of the difficulties. As key managers discussed the bank's problems, it became apparent that they had no idea what their products were costing. Upon reflection, they realized that they had often made decisions to offer a new product which promised to increase dollar balances without any consideration of what it cost to provide the service.

After some discussion, the bank decided to hire a consultant to compute the costs of three products: checking accounts, personal loans, and the gold VISA. The consultant identified the following activities, costs, and activity drivers (annual data):

Activity	Activity Cost	Activity Driver	Activity Capacity
Providing ATM service	$ 100,000	No. of transactions	200,000
Computer processing	1,000,000	No. of transactions	2,500,000
Issuing statements	800,000	No. of statements	500,000
Customer inquiries	360,000	Telephone minutes	600,000

The following annual information on the three products was also made available:

	Checking Accounts	Personal Loans	Gold VISA
Units of product	30,000	5,000	10,000
ATM transactions	180,000	0	20,000
Computer transactions	2,000,000	200,000	300,000
Number of statements	300,000	50,000	150,000
Telephone minutes	350,000	90,000	160,000

In light of the new cost information, Dana Kowalski, the bank president, wanted to know whether a decision made two years ago to modify the bank's checking account product was sound. At that time, the service charge was eliminated on accounts with an average annual balance greater than $1,000. Based on increases in the total dollars in checking, Dana was pleased with the new product. The checking account product is described as follows: (1) checking account balances greater than $500 earn interest of 2 percent per year, and (2) a service charge of $5 per month is charged for balances less than $1,000. The bank earns 4 percent on checking account deposits. Fifty percent of the accounts are less than $500 and have an average balance of $400 per account. Ten percent of the accounts are between $500 and $1,000 and average $750 per account. Twenty-five percent of the accounts are between $1,000 and $2,767; the average balance is $2,000. The remaining accounts carry a balance greater than $2,767. The average balance for these accounts is $5,000. Research indicates that the $2,000 category was by far the greatest contributor to the increase in dollar volume when the checking account product was modified two years ago.

Required:

1. Calculate rates for each activity.
2. Using the rates computed in Requirement 1, calculate the cost of each product.
3. Evaluate the checking account product. Are all accounts profitable? Compute the average annual profitability per account for the four categories of accounts described in the problem. What recommendations would you make to increase the profitability of the checking account product? (Break-even analysis for the unprofitable categories may be helpful.)

Problem 4-31 Product-Costing Accuracy, Corporate Strategy, ABC

OBJECTIVE ◀ 2 3

EXCEL

Autotech Manufacturing is engaged in the production of replacement parts for automobiles. One plant specializes in the production of two parts: Part #127 and Part #234. Part #127 produced the highest volume of activity, and for many years it was the only part produced by the plant. Five years ago, Part #234 was added. Part #234 was more difficult to manufacture and required special tooling and setups. Profits increased for the first three years after the addition of the new product. In the last two years, however, the plant faced intense competition, and its sales of Part #127 dropped. In fact, the plant showed a small loss in the most recent reporting period. Much of the competition was from foreign sources, and the plant manager was convinced that the foreign producers were guilty of selling the part below the cost of producing it. The following conversation between Patty Goodson, plant manager, and Joseph Fielding, divisional marketing manager, reflects the concerns of the division about the future of the plant and its products.

JOSEPH: You know, Patty, the divisional manager is real concerned about the plant's trend. He indicated that in this budgetary environment, we can't afford to carry plants that don't show a profit. We shut one down just last month because it couldn't handle the competition.

PATTY: Joe, you and I both know that Part #127 has a reputation for quality and value. It has been a mainstay for years. I don't understand what's happening.

JOSEPH: I just received a call from one of our major customers concerning Part #127. He said that a sales representative from another firm offered the part at $20 per unit—$11 less than what we charge. It's hard to compete with a price like that. Perhaps the plant is simply obsolete.

PATTY: No. I don't buy that. From my sources, I know we have good technology. We are effi-cient. And it's costing a little more than $21 to produce that part. I don't see how these companies can afford to sell it so cheaply. I'm not convinced that we should meet the price. Perhaps a better strategy is to emphasize producing and selling more of Part #234. Our margin is high on this product, and we have virtually no competition for it.

JOSEPH: You may be right. I think we can increase the price significantly and not lose business. I called a few customers to see how they would react to a 25 percent increase in price, and they all said that they would still purchase the same quantity as before.

PATTY: It sounds promising. However, before we make a major commitment to Part #234, I think we had better explore other possible explanations. I want to know how our production costs compare to those of our competitors. Perhaps we could be more efficient and find a way to earn our normal return on Part #127. The market is so much bigger for this part. I'm not sure we can survive with only Part #234. Besides, my production people hate that part. It's very difficult to produce.

After her meeting with Joseph, Patty requested an investigation of the production costs and comparative efficiency. She received approval to hire a consulting group to make an independent investigation. After a three-month assessment, the consulting group provided the following information on the plant's production activities and costs associated with the two products:

	Part #127	Part #234
Production	500,000	100,000
Selling price	$31.86	$24.00
Overhead per unit*	$12.83	$5.77
Prime cost per unit	$8.53	$6.26
Number of production runs	100	200
Receiving orders	400	1,000
Machine hours	125,000	60,000
Direct labor hours	250,000	22,500
Engineering hours	5,000	5,000
Material moves	500	400

*Calculated using a plantwide rate based on direct labor hours. This is the current way of assigning the plant's overhead to its products.

The consulting group recommended switching the overhead assignment to an activity-based approach. It maintained that activity-based cost assignment is more accurate and will provide better information for decision making. To facilitate this recommendation, it grouped the plant's activities into homogeneous sets with the following costs:

Overhead:	
Setup costs	$ 240,000
Machine costs	1,750,000
Receiving costs	2,100,000
Engineering costs	2,000,000
Materials-handling costs	900,000
Total	$6,990,000

Required:

1. Verify the overhead cost per unit reported by the consulting group using direct labor hours to assign overhead. Compute the per-unit gross margin for each product.
2. After learning of activity-based costing, Patty asked the controller to compute the product cost using this approach. Recompute the unit cost of each product using activity-based costing. Compute the per-unit gross margin for each product.
3. Should the company switch its emphasis from the high-volume product to the low-volume product? Comment on the validity of the plant manager's concern that competitors are selling below the cost of making Part #127.
4. Explain the apparent lack of competition for Part #234. Comment also on the willingness of customers to accept a 25 percent increase in price for Part #234.
5. Assume that you are the manager of the plant. Describe what actions you would take based on the information provided by the activity-based unit costs.

Problem 4-32 Time-Driven Activity-Based Costing Compared to ABC: Stage 1

OBJECTIVE ▶ 4

The Bienestar Cardiology Clinic has two major activities: diagnostic and treatment. The two activities use four resources: nursing, medical technicians, cardiologists, and equipment. Detailed interviews have provided the work distribution matrix shown below.

Activity	Resources				Total Activity Time
	Nursing	Technicians	Cardiologists	Equipment	
Diagnosing patients	0.70	0.80	0.40	0.60	12,000 hrs.
Treating patients	0.30	0.20	0.60	0.40	8,000 hrs.
Total time (hrs.)	4,000	4,000	6,000	6,000	20,000
Cost	$80,000	$80,000	$320,000	$320,000	

The total time estimated corresponds to practical capacity (interviewers adjusted the total time to about 80 percent of the available time). The equipment time is measured in machine hours. Thus, the total time (at practical capacity) in the system is 20,000 hours. In considering the implementation of a TDABC model, the following unit times and transaction information are also provided:

	Unit Time	Driver	Expected Activity Driver Quantity
Diagnosing patients	3 hrs.	No. of patients	4,000
Treating patients	0.8 hr.	No. of treatments	10,000

Required:

1. Calculate the cost of each activity using the indicated values of the resource drivers.
2. Calculate the capacity cost rate for TDABC. Using the capacity cost rate, calculate the cost of each activity under TDABC. Compare these values with those obtained in Requirement 1 and discuss possible reasons for any differences.
3. Suppose that the actual activity driver quantities are 3,500 and 9,000. Calculate the cost of unused capacity.
4. Suppose that the clinic acquires new equipment that reduces the total time required for the two activities from 6,000 to 4,000 hours. The equipment cost remains the same. Explain how the ABC system would be updated and then describe how TDABC would provide updates.
5. Suppose that diagnosing patients without any cardiac disease takes two hours while diagnosing patients with mildly diseased hearts takes an additional 1.5 hours and those with more severe problems takes an additional two hours. Prepare a time equation and, using the capacity cost rate from Requirement 2, calculate the activity rate for each of the three types of patients.

Problem 4-33 DBC, TDABC, and ABC

Refer to the data in **Problem 4-32**. The clinic has identified three types of patients: those with no heart disease, those with mild heart disease, and those with severe heart disease. The following additional data are provided:

Patient Type	Diagnosing Patients	Treating Patients	Average Time Spent Servicing Each Patient Type (Cycle Time)
No disease	2,000	0	3 hrs.
Mild disease	1,500	5,000	5.6 hrs.
Severe disease	500	5,000	11.0 hrs.
Activity cost	?	?	

Required:

1. Using the activity costs calculated from Requirement 1 of Problem 4-32 (or calculate them if necessary), calculate the unit cost of servicing each type of patient using traditional ABC.
2. Using TDABC-derived activity rates, calculate the unit cost of servicing each type of patient.
3. Using DBC, calculate the unit cost of servicing each type of patient.
4. Suppose that a medical consultant proposes a new patient-processing system that will shorten diagnostic and treatment times but would require more skilled nurses and technicians as well as an equipment upgrade. However, the total practical capacity would remain the same, at 20,000 hours. Total resource costs are predicted to increase by $100,000. The consultant estimates that the cycle times for each patient type would be reduced from 3 to 2 hours, 5.6 to 4.5 hours, and 11 to 9 hours. The physicians that own the clinic have expressed a willingness to implement the changes, provided that the unit cost of servicing each patient type decreases. Use DBC to estimate the new unit costs. Should the clinic implement the new system? Discuss the advantages of DBC for this analysis over ABC and TDABC. Finally, identify the data analytic types (descriptive, diagnostic, predictive, or prescriptive) that apply for this analysis (see Exhibits 2.5 and 2.6, pp. 37, 40, for a review of data analytic types). *Note:* More than one analytic type might apply.

OBJECTIVE 2 4

Problem 4-34 Activity-Based Costing, Reducing the Number of Drivers and Equal Accuracy

Reducir, Inc., produces two different types of hydraulic cylinders. Reducir produces a major subassembly for the cylinders in the Cutting and Welding Department. Other parts and the subassembly are then assembled in the Assembly Department. The activities, expected costs, and drivers associated with these two manufacturing processes are given below.

Process	Activity	Cost	Activity Driver	Expected Quantity
Cutting and Welding	Welding	$ 776,000	Welding hours	4,000
	Machining	450,000	Machine hours	10,000
	Inspecting	448,250	No. of inspections	1,000
	Materials handling	300,000	No. of moves	12,000
	Setups	240,000	No. of setups	100
		$2,214,250		
Assembly	Changeover	$ 180,000	Changeover hours	1,000
	Rework	61,750	Rework orders	50
	Testing	300,000	No. of tests	750
	Materials handling	380,000	No. of parts	50,000
	Engineering support	130,000	Engineering hours	2,000
		$1,051,750		

Note: In the assembly process, the materials-handling activity is a function of product characteristics rather than batch activity.

Other overhead activities, their costs, and drivers are listed below.

Activity	Cost	Activity Driver	Quantity
Purchasing	$135,000	Purchase requisitions	500
Receiving	274,000	Receiving orders	2,000
Paying suppliers	225,000	No. of invoices	1,000
Providing space and utilities	100,000	Machine hours	10,000
	$734,000		

Other production information concerning the two hydraulic cylinders is also provided:

	Cylinder A	Cylinder B
Units produced	15,000	30,000
Welding hours	1,600	2,400
Machine hours	3,000	7,000
Inspections	500	500
Moves	7,200	4,800
Setups	45	55
Changeover hours	540	460
Rework orders	5	45
No. of tests	500	250
Parts	40,000	10,000
Engineering hours	1,500	500
Requisitions	425	75
Receiving orders	1,800	200
Invoices	650	350

Required:

1. Using a plantwide rate based on machine hours, calculate the total overhead cost assigned to each product and the unit overhead cost.
2. Using activity rates, calculate the total overhead cost assigned to each product and the unit overhead cost. Comment on the accuracy of the plantwide rate.
3. Calculate the global consumption ratios.
4. Calculate the consumption ratios for welding and materials handling (Assembly) and show that two drivers, welding hours and number of parts, can be used to achieve the same ABC product costs calculated in Requirement 2. Explain the value of this simplification.
5. Calculate the consumption ratios for inspection and engineering, and show that the drivers for these two activities also duplicate the ABC product costs calculated in Requirement 2.

Problem 4-35 TDABC and DBC

Refer to the data in **Problem 4-34** for Reducir, Inc. Based on a recent internal study, the following information was also gathered and made available. The unit time information was gathered to allow the company to use TDABC. Cycle time was also calculated using historical production data. Practical capacity is 30,200 hours.

OBJECTIVE ◀ 4

DATA
ANALYTICS

Activity Drivers	Cylinder A Transactions	Time per Transaction (hrs.)	Cylinder B Transactions	Time per Transaction (hrs.)
1. Welding hours	1,600	1.00	2,400	1.00
2. Machine hours	3,000	1.00	7,000	1.00
3. Inspections	500	0.75	500	0.60
4. Moves	7,200	0.80	4,800	0.50
5. Setups	45	0.70	55	0.55
6. Changeover hours	540	1.00	460	1.00
7. Rework orders	5	0.80	45	0.45
8. No. of tests	500	0.20	250	0.20
9. No. of parts	40,000	0.06	10,000	0.04
10. Engineering hours	1,500	1.00	500	1.00
11. Requisitions	425	0.15	75	0.10
12. Receiving orders	1,800	0.35	200	0.20
13. No. of Invoices	650	0.30	350	0.30

Reducir, Inc. produced 15,000 units of Cylinder A and 30,000 units of Cylinder B. Cylinder A has a cycle time of 1.1 hours, and Cylinder B has a cycle time of 0.45 hours.

Required:

1. Calculate the capacity cost rate that would be used for either TDABC or DBC.
2. Using DBC, calculate the resource or overhead cost per unit for each cylinder. Now assume that 30,000 actual hours were used to produce the indicated output. What is the cost of unused capacity?
3. Using TDABC, calculate the activity rates and use these rates to calculate the unit overhead cost for each cylinder (round each calculation to the nearest dollar). Calculate the cost of unused capacity.
4. Using TDABC, the total time used by Cylinder A is 16,199 hours (rounded) and the total time used by Cylinder B is 13,713 hours. Explain how these values would be calculated. Can you use this information to calculate the unit costs for each cylinder? Did you need any activity rates? Explain.
5. Using the total time calculated for each product by TDABC from Requirement 4, estimate the cycle time for each product (round to three decimal places). Using these cycle time estimates, calculate the unit costs for each product using DBC. How do they compare to the TDBAC unit costs? Offer some explanations as to why the cycle time estimate from using the unit activity times of TDABC would differ from a more macro estimate of cycle time.
6. Reducir, Inc., can reduce the cycle time for Cylinder A by 0.20 hours and that of Cylinder B by 0.05 hours by rearranging the production layout of its plant. Assume practical capacity decreases to 30,000 hours. By changing the plant layout, the total cost of material handling in the Cutting and Welding Department would be reduced by $200,000. Using DBC, predict what the new overhead cost per unit would be if this improvement is implemented. Identify the data analytic types (descriptive, diagnostic, predictive, or prescriptive) that apply for this analysis (see Exhibits 2.5 and 2.6, pp. 37, 40, for a review of data analytic types). *Note:* More than one analytic type might apply.

Problem 4-36 Approximately Relevant ABC

Refer to the data given in **Problem 4-34** and suppose that the expected activity costs are reported as follows (all other data remain the same):

Process	Activity	Cost
Cutting and Welding	Welding	$2,000,000
	Machining	1,000,000
	Inspecting	50,000
	Materials handling	72,000
	Setups	400,000
		$3,522,000
Assembly	Changeover	$ 28,000
	Rework	50,000
	Testing	40,000
	Materials handling	60,000
	Engineering support	70,000
		$ 248,000

Other overhead activities:

Activity	Cost
Purchasing	$ 50,000
Receiving	70,000
Paying suppliers	80,000
Providing space and utilities	30,000
	$230,000

The per unit overhead cost using the 14 activity-based drivers is $110.80 and $77.90 for Cylinder A and Cylinder B, respectively.

Required:

1. Determine the percentage of total costs represented by the three most expensive activities.
2. Allocate the costs of all other activities to the three activities identified in Requirement 1. Allocate the other activity costs to the three activities in proportion to their individual activity costs (round each calculation to nearest dollar). Now assign these total costs to the products using the drivers of the three chosen activities.
3. Using the costs assigned in Requirement 2, calculate the percentage error using the ABC costs as a benchmark. Comment on the value and advantages of this ABC simplification.

Problem 4-37 Product-Costing Accuracy, Plantwide and Departmental Rates, ABC

Escuha Company produces two type of calculators: scientific and business. Both products pass through two producing departments. The business calculator is by far the most popular. The following data have been gathered for these two products:

	Product-Related Data	
	Scientific	Business
Units produced per year	75,000	750,000
Prime costs	$250,000	$2,500,000
Direct labor hours	100,000	1,000,000
Machine hours	50,000	500,000
Production runs	100	150
Inspection hours	2,000	3,000
Maintenance hours	2,250	9,000

	Department Data	
	Department 1	**Department 2**
Direct labor hours:		
Scientific calculator	75,000	25,000
Business calculator	112,500	887,500
Total	187,500	912,500
Machine hours:		
Scientific calculator	25,000	25,000
Business calculator	400,000	100,000
Total	425,000	125,000
Overhead costs:		
Setup costs	$225,000	$225,000
Inspection costs	175,000	175,000
Power	250,000	150,000
Maintenance	200,000	250,000
Total	$850,000	$800,000

Required:

1. Compute the overhead cost per unit for each product using a plantwide, unit-based rate using direct labor hours.
2. Compute the overhead cost per unit for each product using departmental rates. In calculating departmental rates, use machine hours for Department 1 and direct labor hours for Department 2. Repeat using direct labor hours for Department 1 and machine hours for Department 2.
3. Compute the overhead cost per unit for each product using activity-based costing.
4. Comment on the ability of departmental rates to improve the accuracy of product costing.

DATA ANALYTICS

CableTech Bell Corporation (CTB) operates in the telecommunications industry. CTB has two divisions: the Phone Division and the Cable Service Division. The Phone Division manufactures telephones in several plants located in the Midwest. The product lines run from relatively inexpensive touch-tone wall and desk phones to expensive, high-quality cellular phones. CTB also operates a cable TV service in Ohio. The Cable Service Division offers three products: a basic package with 25 channels; an enhanced package, which is the basic package plus 35 additional channels and two movie channels; and a premium package, which is the basic package plus 55 additional channels and six movie channels.

The Cable Service Division reported the following activity for the month of March:

	Basic	**Enhanced**	**Premium**
Sales (units)	50,000	500,000	300,000
Price per unit	$32	$60	$90
Unit costs:			
Directly traced	$ 6	$18	$36
Driver traced	$ 4	$ 8	$12
Allocated	$20	$26	$30

The unit costs are divided as follows: 70 percent production and 30 percent marketing and customer service. Direct labor cost is the only driver used for tracing. Typically, the division uses only production costs to define unit costs. The preceding unit product cost information was provided at the request of the marketing manager and was the result of a special study.

Bryce Youngers, the president of CTB, is reasonably satisfied with the performance of the Cable Service Division. March's performance is fairly typical of what has been happening over the past two years. The Phone Division, however, is another matter. Its overall profit performance has been declining. Two years ago, income before income taxes had been about 25 percent of sales. March's dismal performance was also typical for what has been happening this year and is expected to continue— unless some action by management is taken to reverse the trend. During March, the Phone Division reported the following results:

Inventories:	
Materials, March 1	$ 23,000
Materials, March 31	40,000
Work in process, March 1	130,000
Work in process, March 31	45,000
Finished goods, March 1	480,000
Finished goods, March 31	375,000
Costs:	
Direct labor	$117,000
Plant and equipment depreciation	50,000
Materials handling	85,000
Inspections	60,000
Scheduling	30,000
Power	30,000
Plant supervision	12,000
Manufacturing engineering	21,000
Sales commissions	120,000
Salary, sales supervisor	10,000
Supplies	17,000
Warranty work	40,000
Rework	30,000

During March, the Phone Division purchased materials totaling $312,000. There are no significant inventories of supplies (beginning or ending). Supplies are accounted for separately from materials. CTB's Phone Division had sales totaling $1,170,000 for March.

Based on March's results, Bryce decided to meet with three of the Phone Division's managers: Kim Breashears, divisional manager; Jacob Carder, divisional controller; and Larry Hartley, sales manager. A transcript of their recorded conversation is given next:

Bryce: "March's profit performance is down once again, and I think we need to see if we can identify the problem and correct it—before it's too late. Kim, what's your assessment of the situation?"

Kim: "Foreign competition is eating us alive—selling phones at a lower price and high quality. If we could lower our prices by 10 to 15 percent, I think that we'd regain most of our lost market share. But we also need to make sure that the quality of our products meets that of our competitors. We are spending a lot of money each month on inspection, rework, and warranties. I'd like to see these costs cut by at least 50 percent. If we could do that by improving quality, then customers would be more satisfied with our products, and we would not only regain our market share but increase it."

Larry: "They're right. If we could lower our prices by 10 to 15 percent, I think that we'd regain most of our lost market share. But we also need to make sure that the quality of our products meets that of our competitors. As you know, we are spending a lot of money each month on rework and warranties. That worries me. I'd like to see that warranty cost cut by 70 to 80 percent. If we could do that, then customers would be more satisfied with our products, and I bet that we would not only regain our market share but increase it."

Jacob: "Lowering prices without lowering per-unit costs will not help us increase our profitability. I think we need to improve our cost accounting system. I am not confident that we really know how much each of our product lines is costing us. It may be that we are overpricing some of our units because we are overcosting them. We may be underpricing other units."

Larry: "This sounds promising—especially if the overcosting is for some of our high-volume lines. A price decrease for these products would make the biggest difference—and if we knew they were over-costed, then we could offer immediate price reductions."

Bryce: "Jacob, I need more explanation. We have been using the same cost accounting system for the last 10 years. Why would it be a problem?"

Jacob: "I think that our manufacturing environment has changed. Over the years, we have added a lot of different product lines. Some of these products make very different demands on our manufacturing overhead resources. We trace—or attempt to trace—overhead costs to the different products using direct labor cost, a unit-based cost driver. We may be doing more allocation than tracing. If so, then we probably don't have a very good idea of our actual product costs. Also, as you know, with the way computer technology has changed over time, it is easier and cheaper to collect and use detailed information—information that will allow us to assign costs more accurately."

Bryce: "This may be something we should explore. Jacob, what do you suggest?"

Jacob: "If we want more accurate product costs and if we really want to get in the cost reduction business, then we need to understand how costs behave. In particular, we need to understand activity cost behavior. Knowing what activities we perform, why we perform them, and how well we perform them will help us identify areas for improvement. We also need to know how the different products consume activity resources. What this boils down to is the need to use an activity-based management system. But before we jump into this, we need some idea of whether non-unit-based drivers add anything. Activity-based management is not an inexpensive undertaking. So I suggest that we do a preliminary study to see if direct labor cost is adequate for tracing. If not, then maybe some non-unit-drivers might be needed. In fact, if you would like, I can gather some data that will provide some evidence on the usefulness of the activity-based approach."

Bryce: "What do you think, Kim? It's your division."

Kim: "What Jacob has said sounds promising. I think he should pursue it and do so quickly. I also think that we need to look at improving our quality. It sounds like we have a problem there. If quality could be improved, then our costs will drop. I'll talk to our quality people. Jacob, in the meantime, find out for us if moving to an activity-based system is the way to go. How much time do you need?"

Jacob: "I have already been gathering data. I could probably have a report within two weeks."

MEMO

TO: Kim Breashears
FROM: Jacob Carder
SUBJECT: Preliminary Analysis

Based on my initial analysis, I am confident that an ABC system will offer significant improvement. For one of our conventional phone plants, I regressed total monthly overhead cost on monthly direct labor cost using the following 15 months of data:

Overhead	Direct Labor Cost
$360,000	$110,000
300,000	100,000
350,000	90,000
400,000	100,000
320,000	90,000
380,000	100,000
300,000	90,000
280,000	90,000
340,000	95,000
410,000	115,000
375,000	100,000
360,000	85,000
340,000	85,000
330,000	90,000
300,000	80,000

The results were revealing. Although direct labor cost appears to be a driver of overhead cost, it really doesn't explain a lot of the variation. I then searched for other drivers—particularly non-unit drivers—that might offer more insight into overhead cost behavior. Every time a batch is produced, material movement occurs, regardless of the size of the batch. The number of moves seemed like a more logical driver. I was able to gather only 10 months of data for this. (Our information system doesn't provide the number of moves, so I had to build the data set by interviewing production personnel.) This information is provided next:

Materials-Handling Cost	Number of Moves
$80,000	1,500
60,000	1,000
70,000	1,250
72,000	1,300
65,000	1,100
85,000	1,700
67,000	1,200
73,500	1,350
83,000	1,400
84,000	1,700

The regression results were impressive. There is no question in my mind that the number of moves is a good driver of materials-handling costs. Using the number of moves to assign materials-handling costs to products would likely be better than the cost assignment using direct labor cost. Furthermore, since small batches use the same number of moves as large batches, we have some evidence that we may be overcosting our high-volume products.

Kim, you expressed the desire of reducing the costs of inspection, reworking, and warranties. In addition to the pilot study for one plant, I also collected information about these three activities for the division. For the inspection activity, we have 15 inspectors who are paid an average of $4,000 per month. Each inspector offers a practical inspection capacity of 2,000 hours per year. However, it appears that inspectors actually work only about

80 percent of those hours. Rework cost is simply the cost of replacing some faulty components and the associated direct labor. The rework cost per unit is predictable and *constant per unit regardless of the product model.* Warranty cost, on the other hand, involves the salaries of two technicians, with the remaining cost, the cost of replacement components, which is relatively constant per unit repaired. The technicians are paid $5,000 per month and provide 2,000 hours of service per year. Warranty service usually requires 3,600 technician hours per year.

After receiving the memo, Kim was intrigued, both by the activity-based costing pilot study and by the potential savings for the division by improving quality. She then asked Jacob to use the same phone plant as a pilot for a preliminary ABC analysis. She instructed him to assign all overhead costs to the plant's two products (Regular and Deluxe models), using only four activities. The four activities were rework, moving materials, inspecting products, and a general catch-all activity labeled "other manufacturing activities." From the special study already performed, she knew that materials handling and inspecting involved significant cost; from production reports, she also knew that the rework activity involved significant cost. If the ABC and unit-based cost assignments did not differ by breaking out these three major activities, then ABC may not matter.

Pursuant to the request, Jacob produced the following cost and driver information:

Activity	Expected Cost	Driver	Activity Capacity
Other activities	$2,000,000	Direct labor dollars	$1,250,000
Moving materials	900,000	Number of moves	18,000
Inspecting	720,000	Inspection hours	24,000
Reworking	380,000	Rework hours	3,800
Total overhead cost	$4,000,000		

Expected activity demands:

	Regular Model	Deluxe Model
Units completed	100,000	40,000
Direct labor dollars	$875,000	$375,000
Number of moves	7,200	10,800
Inspection hours	6,000	18,000
Rework hours	1,900	1,900

Required:

1. Answer the following regarding the product costing system of the Cable Service Division:

   a. Complete the following table with the appropriate product costs for the Cable Service Division:

	Basic	Enhanced	Premium
Product cost for pricing	?	?	?
Product cost for cost of services sold	?	?	?

   b. Allocation relies on:
      a. exclusive physically observable causal relationships to assign costs.
      b. causal factors to assign costs.
      c. assumed linkages or convenience to assign costs.
      d. none of the above.

   c. Direct tracing relies on:
      a. exclusive physically observable causal relationships to assign costs.
      b. causal factors to assign costs.
      c. assumed linkages or convenience to assign costs.
      d. none of the above.

    d. Driver tracing relies on:

      a. exclusive physically observable causal relationships to assign costs.

      b. causal factors to assign costs.

      c. assumed linkages or convenience to assign costs.

      d. none of the above.

    e. Based on how costs are assigned, do you think that the Cable Service Division is using a functional-based or an activity-based costing system? Explain and discuss other differences between functional- and activity-based costing.

2. Prepare income statements for the Cable Service Division and for the Phone Division for March. For the income statement associated with the Phone Division, include a supporting cost of goods manufactured statement. Discuss the differences between the products of the two divisions.

3. Review Exhibit 2.5, p. 37. Now consider the concern that Jacob has expressed about the costing practices of the Phone Division. Also consider the directives that Kim gave Jacob and his resulting actions. Now answer the following:

    a. What is Jacob attempting to measure?

    b. Why is he attempting to measure it?

    c. How is it currently being measured, and how will the measurement approach change?

    d. Where did Jacob get the data needed to carry out the proposed analyses?

    e. Which analytic methods did Jacob use or propose to be used?

    f. When will the analysis be completed and ready for decision making?

    g. Who needs to understand the analysis done by Jacob, and how was it or will it be communicated?

4. Using a regression program such as Microsoft Excel, calculate two cost formulas: (1) overhead using direct labor cost as the driver and (2) materials handling cost using number of moves as the driver. Based on the outcomes, answer the following:

    a. Direct labor cost formula:
      Intercept (rounded to nearest dollar)
      Slope (Coefficient 1, rounded to the nearest cent)
      R Square (rounded to two decimal places)

    b. Formula for material handling cost (based on number of moves):
      Intercept (rounded to nearest dollar)
      Slope (Coefficient 1, rounded to the nearest cent)
      R Square (rounded to two decimal places

    c. The intercept can be interpreted as:
      a. fixed cost.
      b. variable cost per unit.
      c. total cost.
      d. mixed cost.

    d. Coefficient 1 can be interpreted as:
      a. fixed cost.
      b. variable cost per unit.
      c. total cost.
      d. mixed cost.

    e. Comment on Jacob's observations concerning the outcomes.

5. Answer the following:

    a. Inspection is a (**select**: variable, fixed, mixed, step-fixed) cost, with each (**select**: unit, step) being defined by ____?_____ inspection hours per year. Each (**select**: unit, step) costs $____?_____. Current activity capacity for inspection is _____?_____ hours. Current demand for the inspection activity is ____?_____ hours.

   b. Rework is a:
     a. variable cost.
     b. fixed cost.
     c. mixed cost.
     d. step-fixed cost.

   c. Warranty is a:
     a. variable cost.
     b. fixed cost.
     c. mixed cost.
     d. step-fixed cost.

   d. Assume that quality improves so that the current demand for the output of the inspection, rework, and warranty activities drops by 50 percent (with the Phone Division capturing all savings possible by reducing the resources currently used by the activities). Calculate the increase in March's pre-tax operating income produced by the savings.

6. Using the data generated by Jacob's pilot for a preliminary ABC analysis, answer the following:

   a. Calculate the overhead cost per unit for each phone model using direct labor cost to assign all overhead costs to products (round overhead rate to two decimal places).
   b. Calculate the overhead cost per unit for each phone model using the four activities and drivers identified by Jacob (round activity rates to two decimal places).
   c. Using the ABC assignments as the benchmark, the unit manufacturing cost for the Regular model is currently (**select**: understated, overstated) by $____.
   d. If the unit product cost of the Regular model is (**select**: understated, overstated), then the selling price could be (**select**: increased, decreased), making the company (**select**: more, less) competitive.

7. Suppose that Jacob learned about duration-based costing after completing the pilot study. According to the plant manager of the phone plant used for the pilot study, the cycle time for the Regular model is 0.50 hours and that of the Deluxe model is one hour. Calculate the unit cost for each model using duration-based costing. How do unit costs compare to the ABC costs? Which approach would you recommend to Kim?

8. Review Exhibit 2.6, p. 40. Now consider the use of the regression model in the memo submitted by Jacob. Which of the four data analytic types (descriptive, diagnostic, predictive, and prescriptive) apply to the use of the regression model? *Note:* More than one may apply. Explain your choice(s).

5   Product and Service Costing: Job-Order System

After studying this chapter, you should be able to:

1 ▶ Differentiate the cost accounting systems of service and manufacturing firms and of unique and standardized products.

2 ▶ Discuss the interrelationship of cost accumulation, cost measurement, and cost assignment.

3 ▶ Identify the source documents used in job-order costing.

4 ▶ Describe the cost flows associated with job-order costing, and prepare the journal entries.

5 ▶ Explain how activity-based costing is applied to job-order costing.

6 ▶ Explain how spoiled units are accounted for in a job-order costing system.

Faiz Zaki/Shutterstock.com

USING JOB-ORDER COSTING

at Marvel Studios

What do **Boeing**, with sales of $76.56 billion; the **Conlan Company**, an Atlanta, Georgia–based construction company with estimated revenue of $36.8 million; and **Susan's Fine Catering**, a Denver catering firm with estimated revenue of $250,000, have in common?[1] Each one makes custom products or services that have differing costs and uses job-order costing.

Marvel Studios, with estimated revenue of $5 billion in 2019, accounts for the costs of each movie separately. *Avengers Endgame* had budgeted costs of $356 million, making it the third most expensive movie of all time.[2] Production accountants kept track of all costs associated with making the movie. (Separate accountants kept track of the costs of selling and distribution.) A large proportion went to the cast. Five stars, Scarlet Johansson, Chris Evans, Chris Hemsworth, Jeremy Renner, and Mark Ruffalo, received about $15 million each. Robert Downey, Jr., was rumored to have been paid about $75 million. Other costs included visual effects artists as well as outside contractors, such as **Industrial Light & Magic**. Finally, myriad other production costs, such as directing, cinematography, writing, editing, several months of using Pinewood Studios, daily catering, and so on, were assigned to the movie. Revenues are also kept track of on a per movie basis. By summer 2019, *Avengers Endgame* had earned $2.7 billion in revenue.

CHARACTERISTICS OF THE PRODUCTION PROCESS

Now that we have an understanding of basic cost terminology and the ways of applying overhead to production, we need to look more closely at the system that the firm sets up to account for costs. In general, a firm's cost management system mirrors the production process. A cost management system modeled after the production process allows managers to better monitor the economic performance of the firm. A production process may yield a tangible product or a service. Those products or services may be similar in nature or unique. These characteristics of the production process determine the best approach for developing a cost management system.

---

1 https://investors.boeing.com/investors/investor-news/press-release-details/2020/Boeing-Reports-Fourth-Quarter-Results/default.aspx; https://growjo.com/company/The_Conlan_Company#revenue-financials; and Susan's Fine Catering based on interview by the author with the owner, May 27, 2020.

2 Mark Hughes, "Marvel Studios Could Top $5 Billion in 2019," *Forbes* (April 30, 2019), https://www.forbes.com/sites/markhughes/2019/04/30/marvel-studios-could-top-5-billion-in-2019/#10bfab237a30; and Information on *Avengers Endgame* taken from "Why Avengers Endgame Cost $400 Million to Make" (June 11, 2019), https://www.youtube.com/watch?v=5yTtA21F6Tk.

OBJECTIVE

Differentiate the cost accounting systems of service and manufacturing firms and of unique and standardized products.

Manufacturing Firms versus Service Firms

Manufacturing involves combining direct materials, direct labor, and overhead to produce a new product. The good produced is tangible and can be inventoried and transported from the plant to the customer. A service is characterized by its intangible nature. It is not separable from the customer and cannot be inventoried. Traditional cost accounting has emphasized manufacturing and virtually ignored services. Now, more than ever, that approach will not do. Our economy has become increasingly service oriented. Managers must be able to track the costs of services rendered just as precisely as they track the costs of goods manufactured. In fact, a company's controller may find it necessary to cost both goods and services as managers take an internal customer approach.

The range of manufacturing and service firms can be represented by a continuum as shown in Exhibit 5.1. The pure service, shown at the left, involves no raw materials and no tangible item for the customer. There are few pure services. Perhaps an example would be an Internet cafe. In the middle of the continuum, and still very much a service, is a beauty salon, which uses direct materials such as hair dye and styling gel. At the other end of the continuum is the manufactured product. Examples include automobiles, cereals, cosmetics, and drugs. Even these often have a service component. For example, a prescription drug must be prescribed by a physician and dispensed by a licensed pharmacist. Automobile dealers stress the continuing service associated with their cars. And what about fast food? Does Taco Bell provide a product or a service? There are elements of both.

Four areas in which services differ from products are intangibility, inseparability, heterogeneity, and perishability. **Intangibility** refers to the nonphysical nature of services as opposed to products. **Inseparability** means that production and consumption take place at the same time. **Heterogeneity** refers to the greater chances for variation in the performance of services than in the production of products. **Perishability** means that services cannot be inventoried but must be consumed when performed. These differences affect the types of information needed for planning, control, and decision making in the production of services. Exhibit 5.2 illustrates the features associated with the production of services and their interface with the cost management system.

Intangibility of services leads to a major difference in the accounting for services as opposed to products. A service company cannot inventory the service and therefore has a minimal to moderate inventory of supplies. A manufacturing company has inventories of raw materials, supplies, work in process, and finished goods. Because of the significance and complexity of inventories in manufacturing, we will spend more time on manufacturing companies in accounting for the cost of inventories.

Service firms are keenly aware of the importance of human resources; the service is provided by people. A key assumption of microeconomics is the homogeneity of labor. That is, one direct laborer is assumed to be identical to another. This assumption is the basis of labor standards in standard costing. Service companies know that one worker is not identical to another.

Exhibit 5.1

Continuum of Services and Manufactured Products

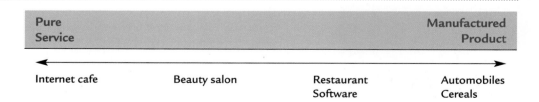

Exhibit 5.2

Features of Service Firms and Their Interface with the Cost Management System

Feature	Relationship to Business	Impact on Cost Management System
Inseparability	Consumer is involved in service process. Services are difficult to mass produce.	Costs are accounted for by customer type. System must be generated to encourage consistent quality.
Intangibility	Services cannot be stored. Services cannot be patented. Pricing is complicated.	There are no inventory accounts. There is a strong ethical code. Costs must be related to entire organization.
Heterogeneity	Services are difficult to standardize. It is difficult to ensure quality control of services.	A strong systems approach is needed. Productivity measurement is ongoing. Total quality management is critical.
Perishability	Service benefits expire quickly. Service may be repeated often for one customer.	There are no inventories. There system needs to be a standardized to handle repeat customers.

Source: First two columns based on Valarie Zeithamel, A. Parsuraman, and Leonard L. Berry, "Problems and Strategies in Services Marketing," *Journal of Marketing* 49 (Spring 1985): 33–46.

REAL-WORLD EXAMPLE

For example, Walt Disney World hires "backstage employees" and "on-stage employees." The backstage employees may do maintenance, sew costumes, and work in personnel (called "central casting"), but they do not work with the paying public (called "guests"). On-stage employees, hired for both their particular skills and their ability to interact well with people, work directly with the guests.

A further aspect of labor heterogeneity is that a worker is not the same from one day to the next. Workers can be affected by the job undertaken, the mix of other individuals with whom they work, their education and experience, and personal factors such as health and home life. These factors make the provision of a consistent level of service difficult. The measurement of productivity and quality in a service company must be ongoing and sensitive to these factors.

Inseparability means that differences in customers affect the service firm more than the manufacturing firm. When Proctor-Silex® sells a toaster, the mood and personal qualities of the customer are irrelevant. When Memorial Sloan-Kettering Cancer Center sells a service to a customer, however, the disposition of the customer may affect the amount of service required as well as the quality of the service rendered. Inseparability also means that customers evaluate services differently from products. As a result, service companies may need to spend more money on some resources and less on others than would be necessary in a manufacturing plant. For example, consumers may use price and physical facilities as the major cues to service quality. Service firms, then, tend to incur higher costs for attractive places of business than do manufacturing firms. Your initial impression of a manufacturing plant may be how large, noisy, and dingy it is. Floors are concrete; the ceiling is typically unfinished. In short, it is not a pretty sight. However, as long as a high-quality product is made, the consumer does not care. This is very different from most consumers' attitudes toward the service environment. Banks, doctors' offices, and restaurants are pleasant places, tastefully decorated, and filled with plants. This is cost effective to the extent that customers are drawn to such an environment to conduct business. In addition, the environment may allow the service firm to charge a higher price—signaling its higher quality.

Perishability of services is very similar to intangibility, but there is a subtle distinction. A service is perishable if the effects are short term. Not all services fall into this category. Plastic surgery is not perishable, but haircuts are. The impact on cost management is that perishable services require systems to easily handle repeat customers. The repetitive nature of the service also leads us to the use of standardized processes and costing. Examples are financial services (e.g., check clearing by banks), janitorial services, and beauty and barber shops.

ETHICS   Customers may perceive greater risk when buying services than when buying products. Ethics are important here. The internal accountant who is responsible for gathering data on service quality must accurately report the bad news as well as the good. A customer who has been stung once by misleading advertising or a firm's failure to deliver the promised performance will be loathe to try that firm again. A manufacturer can offer a warranty or product replacement. But the service firm must consider the customer's wasted time. Therefore, the service firm must be especially careful to avoid promising more than can or will be delivered. •

Consider the example of **Lexus**, which discovered a defect shortly after introducing the Lexus 400 sedan into the United States. Lexus dealers contacted each buyer personally and arranged for loaner cars while the defect was being fixed. In the case of buyers who lived far from a dealership, Lexus brought the repair people to the buyers. More recently, Lexus discovered a larger transmission problem and immediately swapped out the affected cars for new cars. These efforts explain Lexus continuing ranking at the top of the luxury car brands in J. D. Powers surveys, including number one in 2020.[3] Contrast this experience with service issues experienced by many GM buyers who must deal with several layers of automotive hierarchy in order to get a defect repaired. Clearly, Lexus understood the value of customers' time in arranging the service.

Service companies are particularly interested in planning and control techniques that apply to their special types of firms. Productivity measurement and quality control are very important. Pricing may involve different considerations for the service firm.

The important point is that service and manufacturing companies may have different needs for accounting data and techniques. It is important for the accountant to be aware of relevant differences in order to provide appropriate support, and to be cross-functionally trained.

McDonald's is an example of both a manufacturing and a service company. In the kitchen, McDonald's runs a production line. The product is rigidly consistent. Each hamburger contains the same amount of meat, mustard, ketchup, and pickles. The buns are identical. The burgers are cooked the prescribed amount of time to the right temperature. They are wrapped in a methodical manner and join other burgers in the warming bin. Standard cost accounting techniques work well for this phase, and McDonald's uses them. At the counter, however, the company becomes a service organization. Customers want their orders taken and filled quickly and correctly. In addition, they want pleasant service and maybe some help finding certain items on the menu. Clean restrooms are critical. McDonald's emphasizes nonfinancial measures of performance for service areas: counter customers are to be served within 60 seconds; drive-through customers are to be served within 90 seconds; restrooms are to be checked and cleaned at least once an hour.

3   Bill Taylor, "More Lessons from Lexus—Why It Pays to Do the Right Thing," *Harvard Business Publishing* (December 12, 2007), http://blogs.harvardbusiness.org/taylor/2007/12/more_lessons_from_lexuswhy_it.html, accessed January 10, 2012; J. D. Power Press Release, "Coronavirus Fallout: Vehicle Service Customer Satisfaction Improves, but Dealers Should Prepare for Parts Shortages and Dissatisfied Owners, J.D. Power Finds," March 12, 2020, https://www.jdpower.com/business/press-releases/2020-customer-service-index-csi-study, accessed October 7, 2020.

Unique versus Standardized Products and Services

A second way of characterizing products and services is according to the degree of uniqueness. If a firm produces unique products in small batches, and if those products incur different costs, then the firm must keep track of the costs of each product or batch. This is referred to as a job-order costing system, the focus of this chapter. At the other extreme, the company may make many identical units of the same product. Since the units are the same, the costs of each unit are also the same. Accounting for the costs of the identical units is relatively simple and is referred to as a process-costing system, examined in Chapter 6.

The uniqueness of the products (or units) for cost accounting purposes relates to unique costs. Consider a large construction company that builds houses in developments across the Midwest. While the houses are based on several standard models, buyers can customize their houses by selecting different types of brick, tile, carpet, and so on, from a set menu of choices. While one house is painted white and its neighbor house is painted green, the cost is the same. However, if different selections have different costs, then those costs must be accounted for separately. Thus, if one home buyer selects a whirlpool tub while another selects a standard model, the different cost of the two tubs must be tracked to the correct house. A production process that appears to produce similar products may incur different costs for each product. In this type of situation, the firm should track costs using a job-order costing system.

Both service and manufacturing firms use the job-order costing approach. Custom cabinet makers and home builders manufacture unique products, which must be accounted for using a job-order costing approach. Dental and medical services also use job-order costing. The costs associated with a simple dental filling clearly differ from those associated with a root canal. Printing, automotive repair, and appliance repair are services using job-order costing.

Firms in process industries mass-produce large quantities of similar, or homogeneous, products. Each product is essentially indistinguishable from its companion product. Examples of process manufacturers include food, cement, petroleum, and chemical firms. The important point here is that the cost of one unit of product is identical to the cost of another. Therefore, service firms can also use a process-costing approach. Discount stockbrokers, for example, incur much the same cost to execute a customer order for one stock as for another; check-clearing departments of banks incur a uniform cost to clear a check, no matter the value of the check or to whom it is written.

A third type of costing system is operation costing. **Operation costing** is a hybrid of job-order and process costing. Units within a batch are the same and can be accounted for using a process approach. However, each batch is different from other batches and the costs of the batches are handled separately in a job-order costing manner. Some clothing and electronic firms use operation costing.

Interestingly, companies are gravitating toward job-order costing because of the increased variety of products and increased demand for small orders and prototypes.

An excellent example is Austin, Texas–based apparel company **Sew Sister Fabrics**. The company specializes in small orders (as few as 16 pieces per design) for designers and small specialty lingerie companies. Able to complete an order in less than three to four weeks, Sew Sister Fabrics easily competes against companies outsourcing their production overseas. The company's founder says, "These clients were tired of wait times in port, high minimum orders, and samples that were far superior to the actual product received."[4] Thus, a combination of customer demand for specialized products, flexible manufacturing, and improved information technology has led world-class manufacturers to approximate a job-order environment.

REAL-WORLD EXAMPLE

---

4 Phaedra Hise, "Feisty Factories," *Fortune Small Business* (June 2007): 22–32, http://money.cnn.com/2007/05/11 / magazines/fsb/fiesty_factories.fsb/index.htm?postversion=2007051511, accessed January 10, 2012.

OBJECTIVE 2

Discuss the interrelationship of cost accumulation, cost measurement, and cost assignment.

SETTING UP THE COST ACCOUNTING SYSTEM

Once the characteristics of a firm's production process are understood, the accountant can set up a system for generating appropriate cost information. A good cost accounting information system is flexible and reliable. It provides information for a variety of purposes and can be used to answer different types of questions. In general, the system is used to satisfy the needs for cost accumulation, cost measurement, and cost assignment. **Cost accumulation** is the recognition and recording of costs. **Cost measurement** involves determining the dollar amounts of direct materials, direct labor, and overhead used in production. **Cost assignment** is the association of production costs with the units produced. Exhibit 5.3 illustrates the relationship of cost accumulation, cost measurement, and cost assignment.

Cost Accumulation

Cost accumulation refers to the recognition and recording of costs. The cost accountant needs to develop source documents that keep track of costs as they occur. A **source document** describes a transaction. Data from these source documents can then be recorded in a database. The recording of data in a database allows accountants and managers the flexibility to analyze subsets of the data as needed to aid in management decision making. The cost accountant can also use the database to see that the relevant costs are recorded in the general ledger and posted to appropriate accounts for purposes of external financial reporting.

Well-designed source documents can supply information in a flexible way. In other words, the information can be used for multiple purposes. For example, the sales receipt written up or input by a clerk when a customer buys merchandise lists the date, the items purchased, the quantities, the prices, the sales tax paid, and the total dollar amount received. Just this one source document can be used in determining sales revenue for the month, the sales by each product, the tax owed to the state, and the cash received or the accounts receivable recorded. Similarly, employees often fill in labor time tickets, indicating which jobs they worked on, on what date, and for how long. Data from the labor time ticket can be used in determining direct labor cost used in production, the amount to pay the worker, the degree of productivity improvement achieved over time, and the amount to budget for direct labor for an upcoming job.

Exhibit 5.3

Relationship of Cost Accumulation, Cost Measurement, and Cost Assignment

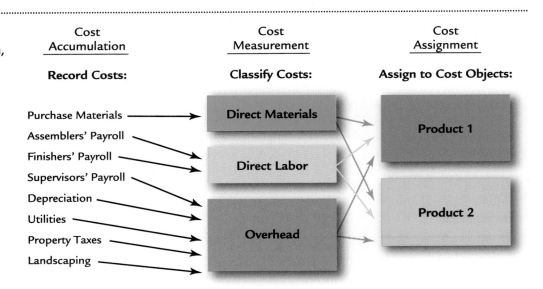

Cost Measurement

Once costs are accumulated (recorded), they can be classified or organized in a meaningful way and then associated with the units produced. Cost measurement refers to classifying the costs. For example, in manufacturing it may consist of determining the dollar amounts of direct materials, direct labor, and overhead used in production. The dollar amounts may be the actual amounts expended for the manufacturing inputs or they may be estimated amounts. Often, bills for overhead items arrive after the unit cost must be calculated; therefore, estimated amounts are used to ensure timeliness of cost information and to control costs.

There are two commonly used ways to *measure* the costs associated with production: actual costing and normal costing. Actual costing requires the firm to use the actual cost of all resources used in production to determine unit cost. While intuitively reasonable, this method has drawbacks, as we shall see. The second method, normal costing, requires the firm to apply actual costs of direct materials and direct labor to units produced. Overhead, however, is applied based on a predetermined estimate. Normal costing, introduced in Chapter 4, is more widely used in practice; it will be further discussed in this chapter.

Actual versus Normal Costing An **actual cost system** uses actual costs for direct materials, direct labor, and overhead to determine unit cost. In practice, strict actual cost systems are rarely used because they cannot provide accurate unit cost information on a timely basis. Per-unit computation of the direct materials and direct labor costs is not the problem. Direct materials and direct labor can be traced to units produced. The main problem with using actual costs for calculation of unit cost is with manufacturing overhead. There are two reasons why this is so.

First, many overhead costs are not incurred uniformly throughout the year; they can change significantly from one month to the next. For example, a factory located in the Northeast may incur higher utilities costs in the winter as it heats the factory. Even if the factory always produced 10,000 units a month, the per-unit overhead cost in December would be higher than the per-unit overhead cost in June. As a result, one unit of product costs more in one month than another, even though the units are identical, and the production process is the same. The difference in the per-unit overhead cost is due to actual overhead costs that were incurred nonuniformly.

The second reason is that per-unit overhead costs fluctuate dramatically because of nonuniform production levels. Suppose a factory has seasonal production; it may produce 10,000 units in March, but 30,000 units in September as it gears up for the holiday buying season. Then, if all other costs remain the same, month to month, the per-unit overhead of the product would be approximately three times as high in March as in September. Again, the units are identical, and the production process is the same.

The problem of fluctuating per-unit overhead costs can be avoided if the firm waits until the end of the year to assign the overhead costs. Unfortunately, waiting until the end of the year to determine overhead costs per unit is unacceptable. A company needs timely unit cost information throughout the year, both for interim financial statements and to help managers make decisions such as pricing. Most decisions requiring unit cost information simply cannot wait until the end of the year. Managers must react to day-to-day conditions in the marketplace in order to maintain a sound competitive position.

Normal costing solves the problems associated with actual costing. A cost system that measures overhead costs on a predetermined basis and uses actual costs for direct materials and direct labor is called a **normal costing system**. As explained in Chapter 4, predetermined overhead or activity rates are calculated at the beginning of the year, and are used to apply overhead to production as the year goes on. Any difference between actual and applied overhead is handled as an overhead variance.

Virtually all firms assign overhead to production on a predetermined basis. This fact seems to suggest that most firms successfully approximate the end-of-the-year overhead rate. Thus, the measurement problems associated with the use of actual overhead costs are solved by the use of estimated overhead costs. A job-order costing system that uses actual costs for direct materials and direct labor and estimated costs for overhead is called a *normal job-order costing system*.

Cost Assignment

Once costs have been accumulated and measured, they are assigned to units of product manufactured or units of service delivered. Unit costs are important for a wide variety of purposes. For example, bidding is a common requirement in markets for custom homes and industrial buildings. It is virtually impossible to submit a meaningful bid without knowing the costs associated with the units to be produced. Product cost information is vital in a number of other areas as well. Decisions concerning product design and introduction of new products are affected by expected unit costs. Decisions to make or buy a product, to accept or reject a special order, or to keep or drop a product line require unit cost information.

In its simplest form, computing the unit manufacturing or service cost is easy. The unit cost is the total product cost associated with the units produced divided by the number of units produced. For example, if a toy company manufactures 100,000 tri-cycles and the total cost of direct materials, direct labor, and overhead for these tricycles is $1,500,000, then the cost per tricycle is $15 ($1,500,000/100,000). Although the concept is simple, the practical reality of the computation is more complex and breaks down when there are products that differ from one another or when the company needs to know the cost of the product before all of the actual costs associated with its production are known.

Importance of Unit Costs to Manufacturing Firms   Unit cost is a critical piece of information for a manufacturer. Unit costs are essential for valuing inventory, determining income, and making a number of important decisions.

Disclosing the cost of inventories and determining income are financial reporting requirements that a firm faces at the end of each period. In order to report the cost of its inventories, a firm must know the number of units on hand and the unit cost. The cost of goods sold, used to determine income, also requires knowledge of the units sold and their unit cost.

Whether or not the unit cost information should include all manufacturing costs depends on the purpose for which the information is going to be used. For financial reporting, full or absorption unit cost information is required. If a firm is operating below its production capacity, however, variable cost information may be much more useful in a decision to accept or reject a special order. Thus, unit cost information needed for external reporting may not supply the information necessary for a number of internal decisions, especially those decisions that are short run in nature. Different costs are needed for different purposes.

Full cost information is useful as an input for a number of important internal decisions as well as for financial reporting. In the long run, for any product to be viable, its price must cover its full cost. Decisions to introduce a new product, to continue a current product, and to analyze long-run prices are examples of important internal decisions that rely on full unit cost information.

Importance of Unit Costs to Nonmanufacturing Firms   Service and nonprofit firms also require unit cost information. Conceptually, the way companies accumulate and assign costs is the same whether or not the firm is a manufacturing firm. The service firm must first identify the service "unit" being provided. In an auto repair shop, the service unit would be the work performed on an individual customer's car. Because each car is different in terms of the work required (an oil change versus a transmission overhaul, for example), the costs must be assigned individually to each job. A hospital would accumulate costs by patient, patient day, and type of procedure (e.g., X-ray, complete blood count test). A governmental agency must also identify the service provided. For example, city government might provide household trash collection and calculate the cost by truck run or by collection per house.

Service firms use cost data in much the same way that manufacturing firms do. They use costs to determine profitability, the feasibility of introducing new services, and so on. However, because service firms do not produce physical products, they do not need to value work-in-process and finished goods inventories. Of course, they may have supplies, and the inventory of supplies is simply valued at historical cost.

Nonprofit firms must track costs to be sure that they provide their services in a cost-efficient way. Governmental agencies have a fiduciary responsibility to taxpayers to use funds wisely. This requires accurate accounting for costs.

Production of Unit Cost Information To produce unit cost information, both cost measurement and cost assignment are required. We have already considered two types of cost measurement systems, actual costing and normal costing. We have seen that normal costing is preferred because it provides information on a more timely basis. Shortly, we will address the cost assignment method of job-order costing. Let's review the determination of per-unit cost.

Direct materials and direct labor costs are traced to units of production. There is a clear relationship between the amount of materials and labor used and the level of production. Actual costs can be used because the actual costs of materials and labor are known reasonably well at any point in time.

Overhead is applied using a predetermined rate based on budgeted overhead costs and budgeted amount of driver. Two considerations arise. One is the choice of the activity base or driver. The other is the activity level. Chapter 4 discussed the choice of activity base or driver for plantwide, departmental, and activity-based overhead rates. We now turn to the choice of the activity level for the denominator of the overhead rate.

Sustainability through Additive Manufacturing[5]

A key avenue to greater sustainability is through the reduction of resources used, whether those are raw materials, supplies, energy, or transportation/distribution. A new technology that promises to help reduce raw material and transportation usage is additive manufacturing (AM). AM is defined as the process of joining materials to make objects from three-dimensional (3D) model data, usually layer upon layer, as opposed to subtractive manufacturing methodologies. In other words, instead of taking a piece of metal and machining it or joining separate components together, 3D printers are used to deposit layer on layer of material to generate the final design. This is no longer science fiction or a fun way to make toys; large-scale components can also be made.

For example, **GE** makes aircraft engines for a wide variety of commercial and military aircraft manufacturers. The company is investing heavily in additive manufacturing and is using it to make fuel nozzles for its new Leap engine. "Every Leap engine contains 19 nozzles, each of which has to withstand temperatures up to 3,000 degrees Fahrenheit. And where 20 separate parts were once machined together to construct the nozzle's interior passageways, there is now only one piece built up by a layering of powdered metals melted and fused together through a direct metal laser melting, or DMLM, process—making each nozzle five times stronger than those made through milling, welding, and other subtractive manufacturing processes."

But does AM really improve sustainability? No, if it just increases overconsumption and causes an increase in printing. Yes, if it can increase manufacturing efficiency, decrease materials usage, and decrease the transportation needed to ferry raw materials to the job sites.[6] GE uses AM to develop and test designs quickly. If the design fails, a new design can be tested and the process becomes much faster. For example, it took about fifty different designs to come up with a workable fuel nozzle design for the new engine. This not only saves on time to market, but also results in less raw material and energy use. As GE's business development manager of additive technologies at GE Aviation put it, "the real power of additive is taking six parts and designing it into one. You can create geometry that you can't make it any other way." So not only are costs reduced, but the quality of the final product is improved.

5 Much of this material is taken from Andrew Zaleski, "GE's Bestselling Jet Engine Makes 3-D Printing a Core Component," (March 5, 2015), http://fortune.com/2015/03/05/ge-engine-3d-printing/, accessed May 27, 2016.

6 Ella Rose, "Can Additive Manufacturing be a Vehicle to a More Sustainable Future?" (July 22, 2014), https://www.forum-forthefuture.org/blog/can-additive-manufacturing-be-vehicle-more-sustainable-future, accessed May 27, 2016.

Choosing the Activity Level

Once the measure(s) of activity are chosen, we still need to predict the level of activity usage that applies to the coming year. Although any reasonable level of activity could be chosen, the two leading candidates are expected actual activity and normal activity. **Expected activity level** is simply the production level the firm expects to attain for the coming year. **Normal activity level** is the average activity usage that a firm experiences in the long term (normal volume is computed over more than one year).

For example, assume that Paulos Manufacturing expects to produce 18,000 units next year and has budgeted overhead for the year at $216,000. Over the past four years, Paulos Manufacturing produced the following number of units:

Year 1	22,000
Year 2	17,000
Year 3	21,000
Year 4	20,000

If expected actual capacity is used, Paulos Manufacturing will apply overhead using a predetermined rate of $12 ($216,000/18,000). However, if normal capacity is used, then the denominator of the equation for predetermined overhead is the average of the past four years of activity, or 20,000 units [(22,000 + 17,000 + 21,000 + 20,000)/4]. Then the predetermined overhead rate to be used for the coming year is $10.80 ($216,000/20,000).

Which choice is better? Of the two, normal activity has the advantage of using much the same activity level year after year. As a result, it produces less fluctuation from year to year in the assignment of per-unit overhead cost. Of course, if activity stays fairly stable, then the normal capacity level is roughly equal to the expected actual capacity level.

Other activity levels used for computing **predetermined overhead rates** are those corresponding to the theoretical and practical levels. **Theoretical activity level** is the absolute maximum production activity of a manufacturing firm. It is the output that can be realized if everything operates perfectly. **Practical activity level** is the maximum output that can be realized if everything operates efficiently. Efficient operation allows for some imperfections such as normal equipment breakdowns, some shortages, and workers operating at less than peak capability. Normal and expected actual activities tend to reflect consumer demand, while theoretical and practical activities reflect a firm's production capabilities. Exhibit 5.4 illustrates these four measures of activity level.

Exhibit 5.4

Measures of Activity Level

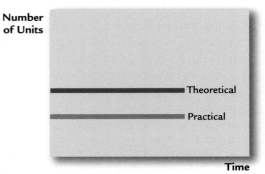

Consumer Demand–
Oriented Measures of
Activity Level

Productive Capability
Measures of Activity Level

THE JOB-ORDER COSTING SYSTEM: GENERAL DESCRIPTION

As we have seen, manufacturing and service firms can be divided into two major industrial types based on the uniqueness of their product. The degree of product or service heterogeneity affects the way in which we track costs. As a result, three different cost assignment systems have been developed: job-order costing, operation costing, and process costing. Job-order costing systems will be described in this chapter.

Overview of the Job-Order Costing System

Firms operating in job-order industries produce a wide variety of products or jobs that are usually quite distinct from each other. Customized or built-to-order products fit into this category, as do services that vary from customer to customer. Examples of job-order processes include printing, construction, furniture making, automobile repair, and beautician services. In manufacturing, a job may be a single unit such as a house, or it may be a batch of units such as eight tables. Job-order systems may be used to produce goods for inventory that are subsequently sold in the general market. Often, however, a job is associated with a particular customer order. The key feature of job-order costing is that the cost of one job differs from that of another job and must be monitored separately.

For job-order production systems, costs are accumulated by *job*. This approach to assigning costs is called a **job-order costing system**. In a job-order firm, collecting costs by job provides vital information for management. Once a job is completed, the unit cost can be obtained by dividing the total manufacturing costs by the number of units produced. For example, if the production costs for printing 100 wedding announcements total $350, then the unit cost for this job is $3.50. The manager of the printing firm can compare the unit cost information with the prevailing market price to see if there is a reasonable profit margin. If there is not, then this may signal that the costs are out of line with those of other printing firms, and the manager might work to reduce costs or, alternatively, seek to emphasize other types of jobs for which the firm can earn a reasonable profit margin. In fact, the profit contributions of different printing jobs offered by the firm can be computed, and this information can then be used to select the most profitable mix of printing services to offer.

In illustrating job-order costing, we will assume a normal costing measurement approach. The actual costs of direct materials and direct labor are assigned to jobs along with overhead applied using a predetermined overhead rate. *How* these costs are actually assigned to the various jobs, however, is the central issue. In order to assign these costs, we must identify each job and the direct materials and direct labor associated with it. Additionally, some mechanism must exist to allocate overhead costs to each job.

The document that identifies each job and accumulates its manufacturing costs is the **job-order cost sheet**. An example is shown in Exhibit 5.5. The cost accounting department creates such a cost sheet upon receipt of a production order. Orders are written up in response to a specific customer order or in conjunction with a production plan derived from a sales forecast. Each job-order cost sheet has a job-order number that identifies the new job. In a small company, with relatively few jobs, the name of the customer may be used to identify the job. For example, a housing contractor may identify jobs as the "Oltman's house" or the "Rhea's house." A firm with many jobs may set up a system in which the first four numbers are the year, and the succeeding numbers identify the job in that year. Jobs in this example might be labeled "20x1-001" or "20x1-089." The key point is that each job is unique and its costs must be recorded separately from the costs of other jobs. Every job in process at any point in time should have a job-order cost sheet in which all costs associated with the job are entered.

Exhibit 5.5

The Job-Order Cost Sheet

			Job Number		16	
For	Benson Company		Date Ordered		April 2, 20x1	
Item Description	Valves		Date Completed		April 24, 20x1	
Quantity Completed	100		Date Shipped		April 25, 20x1	

Direct Materials		Direct Labor				Overhead			
Requisition Number	Amount	Ticket Number	Hours	Rate	Amount	Hours	Rate	Amount
12	$300	68	4	$12	$ 48	8	$10	$ 80
18	450	72	7	10	70	10	10	100
	$750				$118			$180

Cost Summary

Direct Materials $ 750

Direct Labor   118

Overhead   180

Total Cost $1,048

Unit Cost $10.48

In a manual accounting system, the job-order cost sheet is a document. Today, however, most accounting systems are automated. The cost sheet usually corresponds to a record in a work-in-process inventory master file. The collection of all job cost sheets defines a **work-in-process inventory file**. In a manual system, the file would be located in a filing cabinet, whereas in an automated system, it is stored electronically. In either system, the file of job-order cost sheets serves as a subsidiary work-in-process inventory ledger.

Both manual and automated systems require the same kind of data in order to accumulate costs and track the progress of a job. A job-order costing system must be able to identify the quantity of direct materials, direct labor, and overhead used by each job. Documentation and procedures are needed to associate the resources used by a job with the job itself. This need is satisfied through the use of materials requisitions for direct materials, time tickets for direct labor, and predetermined rates for overhead.

Materials Requisitions

The cost of direct materials is assigned to a job by the use of a source document known as a **materials requisition form**, illustrated in Exhibit 5.6. Notice that the form asks for the description, quantity, and unit cost of the direct materials issued and, most importantly, for the job number. Using this form, the Cost Accounting Department can enter the total cost of direct materials right onto the job-order cost sheet. If the accounting system is automated, the data are entered directly at a computer terminal, using the materials requisition forms as source documents. A program then enters the cost of direct materials onto the record for each job.

In addition to providing essential information for assigning direct materials costs to jobs, the materials requisition form may also have other data items such as requisition number, date, and signature. These items are used to maintain proper control over a firm's inventory of direct materials. The signature, for example, transfers responsibility for the materials from the storage area to the person receiving the materials, usually a production supervisor.

Exhibit 5.6
Materials Requisition Form

Date _____ April 8, 20x1 _____

Department _____ Grinding _____

Job Number _____ 62 _____

Materials Requisition
Number 678

Description	Quantity	Cost/Unit	Total Cost
Casing	100	$3	$300

Authorized Signature ____ Jim Lawson ____

No attempt is made to trace the cost of other materials, such as supplies, lubricants, and so on, to a particular job. These indirect materials are part of overhead and are assigned to jobs through the predetermined overhead rate.

Job Time Tickets

Direct labor must be assigned to each particular job. This is done using a source document known as a **time ticket** (see Exhibit 5.7). When an employee works on a particular job, she fills out a time ticket that identifies her name, wage rate, hours worked, and job number. These time tickets are collected daily and transferred to the Cost Accounting Department, where the

Exhibit 5.7
Time Ticket

Employee Number _____ 45 _____

Name _____ Ann Wilson _____

Date _____ April 12, 20x1 _____

Time Ticket
Number 68

20x1 Start Time	Stop Time	Total Time	Hourly Rate	Amount	Job Number
8:00	10:00	2	$14	$28	16
10:00	11:00	1	14	14	17
11:00	12:00	1	14	14	16
1:00	6:00	5	14	70	16

Approved by ____ Jim Lawson ____
              Department Supervisor

information is used to post the cost of direct labor to individual jobs. Again, in an automated system, posting involves entering the data onto the computer.

Time tickets are used only for direct laborers. Since indirect labor is common to all jobs, these costs belong to overhead and are allocated using the predetermined overhead rate.

Overhead Application

Jobs are assigned overhead costs with the predetermined overhead rate. Typically, direct labor hours is the measure used to calculate overhead. For example, assume a firm has estimated overhead costs for the coming year of $900,000, and expected activity is 90,000 direct labor hours. The predetermined overhead rate is $900,000/90,000 direct labor hours = $10 per direct labor hour.

Since the number of direct labor hours charged to a job is known from time tickets, the assignment of overhead costs to jobs is simple once the predetermined rate has been computed. For instance, Exhibit 5.7 reveals that Ann Wilson worked a total of eight hours on Job 16. From this time ticket, overhead totaling $80 ($10 × 8 hours) would be assigned to Job 16.

What if overhead is assigned to jobs based on something other than direct labor hours? Then the other driver must be accounted for as well. That is, the actual amount used of the other driver (for example, machine hours) must be collected and posted to the job cost sheets. Employees must create a source document that will track the machine hours used by each job. A machine time ticket could easily accommodate this need.

Unit Cost Calculation

Once a job is completed, its total manufacturing cost is computed by first totaling the costs of direct materials, direct labor, and overhead, and then summing these individual totals. If there are multiple units in a job, the grand total can be divided by the number of units produced to obtain the unit cost. **Example 5.1** shows how and why to set up a simplified job-order cost sheet. Notice that the simplified sheet illustrated in Example 5.1 leaves out the detail of the job-order cost sheet illustrated in Exhibit 5.5. This simplified sheet will be useful in organizing the information for homework problems and test problems.

EXAMPLE 5.1

The HOW and WHY of Setting Up a Simplified Job-Order Cost Sheet

Information:
All-Round Fence Company installs fences for homeowners and small commercial firms. During March, All-Round worked on three jobs. Data relating to these three jobs follow:

	Job 62	Job 63	Job 64
Beginning balance	$ 620	$ 0	$ 0
Materials requisitioned	4,900	4,600	3,000
Direct labor cost	2,500	1,740	1,600

Overhead is assigned at the rate of 60 percent of direct labor cost. During March, Job 62 was completed and sold at 125 percent of cost. Jobs 63 and 64 remain unfinished at the end of the month.

Why:
Because each job is unique in terms of the cost of materials and labor, costs must be tracked separately by job.

EXAMPLE 5.1

(Continued)

Required:

1. What is the meaning of the beginning balance for Job 62? Why is there no beginning balance for Jobs 63 and 64?

2. Set up a simple job-order cost sheet for Jobs 62, 63, and 64.

3. Calculate the price and the gross margin for Job 62.

4. **What if** the overhead rate was 80 percent of direct labor cost? How would the costs added to the three jobs be affected?

Solution:

1. Job 62 had a beginning balance on March 1, so it must have been started earlier (in February, say). The job was clearly not finished since more cost was added in March. Jobs 63 and 64 must have been started in March.

2.

	Job 62	**Job 63**	**Job 64**
Beginning balance	$ 620	$ 0	$ 0
Materials requisitioned	4,900	4,600	3,000
Direct labor cost	2,500	1,740	1,600
Applied overhead*	1,500	1,044	960
Total cost	$9,520	$7,384	$5,560

*Applied overhead is 0.6 × Direct labor cost.

3. Job 62 price = $9,520 + (0.25 × $9,520) = $11,900

   Job 62 gross margin = $11,900 − $9,520 = $2,380

4. If the overhead rate was 80 percent of direct labor cost, rather than 60 percent, the applied overhead for each job would be higher and the total cost would be higher. Since cost is used as the basis of price, the bid prices would also be higher.

All completed job-order cost sheets of a firm can serve as a subsidiary ledger for the finished goods inventory. In a manual accounting system, the completed sheets would be transferred from the work-in-process inventory files to the finished goods inventory file. In an automated accounting system, an updating run would delete the finished job from the work-in-process inventory master file and add it to the finished goods inventory master file. In either case, adding the totals of all completed job-order cost sheets gives the cost of finished goods inventory at any point in time. In a more sophisticated relational database, the file would consist of all jobs, and a column or attribute within the file would note the status of the job—in process, completed, or sold.

As finished goods are sold and shipped, the cost records would be pulled (or deleted) from the finished goods inventory file. These records then form the basis for calculating a period's cost of goods sold.

JOB-ORDER COSTING: SPECIFIC COST FLOW DESCRIPTION

OBJECTIVE 4

Describe the cost flows associated with job-order costing, and prepare the journal entries.

Recall that cost flow follows costs from the point at which they are incurred to the point at which they are recognized as an expense on the income statement. Of principal interest in a job-order costing system is the flow of manufacturing costs. Accordingly, we begin with a description of exactly how we account for the three manufacturing cost elements (direct materials, direct labor, and overhead).

A simplified job shop environment is used as the framework for this description. All Signs Company, recently formed by Bob Fredericks, produces a wide variety of customized signs. Bob leased a small building and bought the necessary production equipment. For the first month of operation (January), Bob has finalized two orders: one for 20 street signs for a new housing development and a second for 10 laser-carved wooden signs for a golf course. Both orders must be delivered by January 31 and will be sold for manufacturing cost plus 50 percent. Bob expects to average two orders per month for the first year of operation.

Bob created two job-order cost sheets and assigned a number to each job. Job 101 is the street signs, and Job 102 is the golf course signs.

Accounting for Direct Materials

Since the company is beginning its business, it has no beginning inventories. To produce the 30 signs in January and retain a supply of direct materials on hand at the beginning of February, Bob purchases, on account, $2,500 of direct materials. This purchase is recorded as follows:

1. Materials Inventory   2,500
        Accounts Payable   2,500

Materials Inventory is an inventory account. It also is the controlling account for all raw materials. When materials are purchased, the cost of these materials "flows" into the materials inventory account.

From January 2 to January 19, the production supervisor used three requisition forms to remove $1,000 of direct materials from the storeroom. From January 20 to January 31, two additional requisition forms for $500 of direct materials were used. The first three forms revealed that the direct materials were used for Job 101; the last two requisitions were for Job 102. Thus, for January, the cost sheet for Job 101 would have a total of $1,000 in direct materials posted, and the cost sheet for Job 102 would have a total of $500 in direct materials posted. In addition, the following entry would be made:

2. Work-in-Process Inventory   1,500
        Materials Inventory   1,500

Exhibit 5.8

Summary of Direct Materials Cost Flows

Materials Inventory		Work-in-Process Inventory	
(1) 2,500	(2) 1,500	(2) 1,500	
Purchase of Materials		Issue of Direct Materials	

Subsidiary Accounts (Cost Sheets)

Job 101 Direct Materials	
Req. No.	Amount
1	$ 300
2	200
3	500
	$1,000

Job 102 Direct Materials	
Req. No.	Amount
4	$250
5	250
	$500

Source Documents: Materials Requisitions Forms

This second entry captures the flow of direct materials flowing from the storeroom to work in process. All such flows are summarized in the work-in-process inventory account and are posted individually to the respective jobs. Work-in-Process Inventory is a controlling account, and the job cost sheets are the subsidiary accounts. Exhibit 5.8 summarizes the direct materials cost flows. Notice that the source document that drives the direct materials cost flows is the materials requisition form.

Accounting for Direct Labor Cost

Since two jobs were in progress during January, time tickets filled out by direct laborers must be sorted by each job. Once the sorting is completed, the hours worked and the wage rate of each employee are used to assign the direct labor cost to each job. For Job 101, the time tickets showed 60 hours at an average wage rate of $10 per hour, for a total direct labor cost of $600. For Job 102, the total was $250, based on 25 hours at an average hourly wage of $10. In addition to the postings to each job's cost sheet, the following summary entry would be made:

3.   Work-in-Process Inventory   850
      Wages Payable   850

The summary of the direct labor cost flows is given in Exhibit 5.9. Notice that the direct labor costs assigned to the two jobs exactly equal the total assigned to Work-in-Process Inventory. Note also that the time tickets filled out by the individual laborers are the source of information for posting the labor cost flows. Remember that the labor cost flows reflect only direct labor cost. Indirect labor is assigned as part of overhead.

Accounting for Overhead

Under a normal costing approach, actual overhead costs are *never* assigned to jobs. Overhead is applied to each individual job using a predetermined overhead rate. Recall, however, that a company must still account for *actual overhead costs* incurred. We will first describe how to account for applied overhead and then discuss accounting for actual overhead.

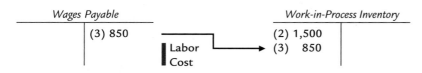

Wages Payable		Work-in-Process Inventory	
	(3) 850	(2) 1,500	
		(3) 850	

Labor Cost

Exhibit 5.9

Summary of Direct Labor Cost Flows

Work-in-Process Inventory Subsidiary Accounts (Cost Sheets)

Job 101
Labor

Ticket	Hours	Rate	Amount
1	15	$10	$150
2	20	10	200
3	25	10	250
	60		$600

Job 102
Labor

Ticket	Hours	Rate	Amount
4	15	$10	$150
5	10	10	100
	25		$250

Source Documents: Time Tickets

Accounting for Overhead Application   Assume that Bob has estimated overhead costs for the year at $9,600. Additionally, since he expects business to increase throughout the year as he becomes established, he estimates 2,400 total direct labor hours. Accordingly, the predetermined overhead rate is as follows:

$$\text{Overhead rate} = \$9,600/2,400 = \$4 \text{ per direct labor hour}$$

Overhead costs flow into Work-in-Process Inventory via the predetermined rate.

Since direct labor hours are used to assign overhead into production, the time tickets serve as the source documents for assigning overhead to individual jobs and to the controlling work-in-process inventory account.

For Job 101, with a total of 60 hours worked, the amount of overhead cost posted is $240 ($4 × 60). For Job 102, the overhead cost is $100 ($4 × 25). A summary entry reflects a total of $340 (i.e., all overhead applied to jobs worked on during January) in applied overhead.

4.	Work-in-Process Inventory	340	
	Overhead Control		340

The credit balance in the overhead control account equals the total applied overhead at a given point in time. In normal costing, only applied overhead ever enters the work-in-process inventory account.

Accounting for Actual Overhead Costs   To illustrate how actual overhead costs are recorded, assume that All Signs Company incurred the following indirect costs for January:

Lease payment	$200
Utilities	50
Equipment depreciation	100
Indirect labor	65
Total overhead costs	$415

As indicated earlier, actual overhead costs never enter the work-in-process inventory account. The usual procedure is to record actual overhead costs on the debit side of the overhead control account. For example, the actual overhead costs would be recorded as follows:

5.	Overhead Control	415	
	Lease Payable		200
	Utilities Payable		50
	Accumulated Depreciation—Equipment		100
	Wages Payable		65

Thus, the debit balance in Overhead Control gives the total actual overhead costs at a given point in time. Since actual overhead costs are on the debit side of this account and applied overhead costs are on the credit side, the balance in Overhead Control is the overhead variance at a given point in time. For All Signs Company at the end of January, the actual overhead of $415 and applied overhead of $340 produce underapplied overhead of $75 ($415 − $340).

The flow of overhead costs is summarized in Exhibit 5.10. To apply overhead to work-in-process inventory, a company needs information from the time tickets and a predetermined overhead rate based on direct labor hours.

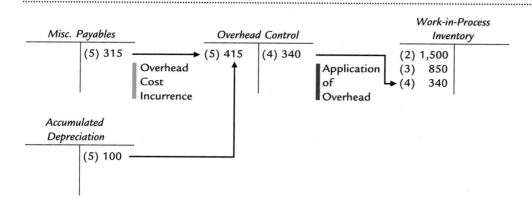

Exhibit 5.10

Summary of Overhead Cost Flows

Work-in-Process Inventory Subsidiary Accounts (Cost Sheets)

Job 101 Applied Overhead		
Hours	Rate	Amount
60	$4	$240

Job 102 Applied Overhead		
Hours	Rate	Amount
25	$4	$100

Note: Information from time tickets; predetermined rate used.

Accounting for Finished Goods Inventory

We have already seen what takes place when a job is completed. The columns for direct materials, direct labor, and applied overhead are totaled. These totals are then transferred to another section of the cost sheet where they are summed to yield the manufacturing cost of the job. This job cost sheet is then transferred to a finished goods inventory file. Simultaneously, the costs of the completed job are transferred from the work-in-process inventory account to the finished goods inventory account.

For example, assume that Job 101 was completed in January with the completed job-order cost sheet shown in Exhibit 5.11. Since Job 101 is completed, the total manufacturing costs of $1,840 must be transferred from the work-in-process inventory account to the finished goods inventory account. This transfer is described by the following entry:

6.   Finished Goods Inventory   1,840
         Work-in-Process Inventory   1,840

Exhibit 5.12 shows a summary of the cost flows that occur when a job is finished.

Completion of goods in a manufacturing process represents an important step in the flow of manufacturing costs. Because of the importance of this stage in a manufacturing operation, a schedule of the cost of goods manufactured is prepared periodically to summarize the cost flows of all production activity. This report is an important input for a firm's income statement and can be used to evaluate a firm's manufacturing effort. The statement of cost of goods manufactured was first introduced in Chapter 2. However, in a normal costing system, the report is somewhat different from the actual cost report presented in that chapter.

Exhibit 5.11

Completed Job-Order Cost Sheet

Job Number _____ 101 _____

For _____ Housing Development _____   Date Ordered ___ Jan. 1, 20x1 ___

Item Description ___ Street Signs ___   Date Started ___ Jan. 2, 20x1 ___

Quantity Completed ___ 20 ___   Date Finished ___ Jan. 15, 20x1 ___

Direct Materials		Direct Labor				Applied Overhead		
Requisition Number	Amount	Ticket Number	Hours	Rate	Amount	Hours	Rate	Amount
1	$ 300	1	15	$10	$150	15	$4	$ 60
2	200	2	20	10	200	20	4	80
3	500	3	25	10	250	25	4	100
	$1,000				$600			$240

Cost Summary

Direct Materials ___ $1,000 ___

Direct Labor _____ 600 _____

Overhead _____ 240 _____

Total Cost _____ $1,840 _____

Unit Cost _____ $92 _____

Exhibit 5.12

Summary of Finished Goods Cost Flow

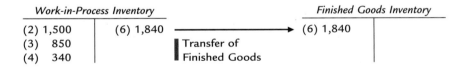

Work-in-Process Inventory		Finished Goods Inventory	
(2) 1,500	(6) 1,840	(6) 1,840	
(3) 850	Transfer of		
(4) 340	Finished Goods		

The statement of cost of goods manufactured presented in Exhibit 5.13 summarizes the production activity of All Signs Company for January. The key difference between this report and the one appearing in Chapter 2 is the use of applied overhead to arrive at the cost of goods manufactured. Finished goods inventories are carried at *normal cost* rather than the *actual cost*.

Notice that ending work-in-process inventory is $850. Where did we obtain this figure? Of the two jobs, Job 101 was finished and transferred to Finished Goods Inventory at a cost of $1,840. This amount is credited to Work-in-Process Inventory, leaving an ending balance of $850. Alternatively, we can add up the amounts debited to Work-in-Process Inventory for all remaining unfinished jobs. Job 102 is the only job still in process. The manufacturing costs assigned thus far are direct materials, $500; direct labor, $250; and overhead applied, $100. The total of these costs gives the cost of ending work-in-process inventory.

Exhibit 5.13

Statement of Cost of Goods
Manufactured

All Signs Company
Statement of Cost of Goods Manufactured
For the Month Ended January 31, 20x1

Direct materials:		
Beginning direct materials inventory	$ 0	
Add: Purchases of direct materials	2,500	
Total direct materials available	$2,500	
Less: Ending direct materials	1,000	
Direct materials used		$1,500
Direct labor		850
Manufacturing overhead:		
Lease	$ 200	
Utilities	50	
Depreciation	100	
Indirect labor	65	
	$ 415	
Less: Underapplied overhead	75	
Overhead applied		340
Current manufacturing costs		$2,690
Add: Beginning work-in-process inventory		0
Less: Ending work-in-process inventory		(850)
Cost of goods manufactured		$1,840

Accounting for Cost of Goods Sold

In a job-order firm, units can be produced for a particular customer or they can be produced with the expectation of selling the units as market conditions warrant.

When the job is shipped to the customer, the cost of the finished job becomes the cost of the goods sold. When Job 101 is shipped, the following entries would be made. (Recall that a markup of 50 percent is used, so the selling price is 150 percent of manufacturing cost.)

7a.	Cost of Goods Sold	1,840	
	Finished Goods Inventory		1,840
7b.	Accounts Receivable	2,760	
	Sales Revenue		2,760

In addition to these entries, a statement of cost of goods sold usually is prepared at the end of each reporting period (e.g., monthly and quarterly). Exhibit 5.14 presents such a statement for All Signs Company for January. Typically, the overhead variance is not material and is therefore closed to the cost of goods sold account. Cost of goods sold *before* adjustment for an overhead variance is called **normal cost of goods sold**. After adjustment for the period's overhead variance takes place, the result is called the **adjusted cost of goods sold**. It is this latter figure that appears as an expense on the income statement. **Example 5.2** shows how and why the job-order cost sheet can be used in determining the ending balances of Work in Process, Finished Goods, and Cost of Goods Sold.

Exhibit 5.14

Statement of Cost of Goods Sold

All Signs Company Statement of Cost of Goods Sold For the Month Ended January 31, 20x1	
Beginning finished goods inventory	$ 0
Cost of goods manufactured	1,840
Goods available for sale	$1,840
Less: Ending finished goods inventory	0
Normal cost of goods sold	$1,840
Add: Underapplied overhead	75
Adjusted cost of goods sold	$1,915

EXAMPLE 5.2

The HOW and WHY of Using a Job-Order Cost Sheet to Determine the Balances of Work in Process, Finished Goods, and Cost of Goods Sold

Information:

(We use the same data as Example 5.1.) All-Round Fence Company installs fences for homeowners and small commercial firms. During March, All-Round worked on three jobs. Completed job-order cost sheets for March (from Example 5.1) follow:

	Job 62	Job 63	Job 64
Beginning balance	$ 620	$ 0	$ 0
Materials requisitioned	4,900	4,600	3,000
Direct labor cost	2,500	1,740	1,600
Applied overhead	1,500	1,044	960
Total cost	$9,520	$7,384	$5,560

During March, Job 62 was completed and sold at 125 percent of cost. Jobs 63 and 64 remain unfinished at the end of the month.

> **Why:**
> Since all costs are tracked by job, the balance in Work in Process can be computed by summing the costs of all incomplete jobs. The amount added to Finished Goods is the sum of jobs completed but not sold. Cost of Goods Sold must be the total cost of all jobs sold during the month.

Required:

1.   What is the ending balance of Work in Process for March?

2.   Assume that the March 1 balance of Finished Goods was zero. What is the ending balance of Finished Goods for March?

3.   What is the cost of goods sold for March?

4.   *What if* the March 1 balance of Finished Goods was $4,560 (consisting of Job 61)? What is the ending balance of Finished Goods in March?

Solution:

1.   Since Jobs 63 and 64 are unfinished by March 31, their total cost must be the balance in Work in Process.

$$\text{March 31 Work in Process} = \$7,384 + \$5,560 = \$12,944$$

EXAMPLE 5.2

(*Continued*)

2. Since no jobs were completed but not sold, nothing is added to Finished Goods during March. Since the beginning balance in Finished Goods was zero, the ending balance must also be zero.

3. Cost of goods sold = Job 62 = $9,520

4. If the beginning balance of Finished Goods was $4,560, any newly completed jobs were sold by the end of March, and Job 61 was not sold during March, the ending balance would remain at $4,560.

Exhibit 5.15

All Signs Company Summary of Manufacturing Cost Flows

Materials Inventory					Wages Payable				Overhead Control		
(1)	2,500	(2)	1,500		(3)	850	(5)	415	(4)	340
									(8)	75

Work-in-Process Inventory					Finished Goods Inventory				Cost of Goods Sold	
(2)	1,500	(6)	1,840	(6)	1,840	(7a)	1,840	(7a)	1,840	
(3)	850							(8)	75	
(4)	340									

(1)	Purchase of direct materials	$2,500
(2)	Issue of direct materials	1,500
(3)	Incurrence of direct labor cost	850
(4)	Application of overhead	340
(5)	Incurrence of actual overhead cost	415
(6)	Transfer of Job 101 to finished goods	1,840
(7a)	Cost of goods sold of Job 101	1,840
(8)	Closing out underapplied overhead	75

Closing the overhead variance to the cost of goods sold account is done once, at the end of the year. Variances are expected each month because of nonuniform production and nonuniform actual overhead costs. As the year unfolds, these monthly variances should, by and large, offset each other so that the year-end variance is small. Nonetheless, to illustrate how the year-end overhead variance would be treated, we will close out the overhead variance experienced by All Signs Company in January.

Closing the underapplied overhead to cost of goods sold requires the following entry:

8.   Cost of Goods Sold   75
          Overhead Control   75

Notice that debiting Cost of Goods Sold is equivalent to adding the underapplied amount to the normal cost of goods sold figure. If the overhead variance had been over-applied, then the entry would reverse, and Cost of Goods Sold would be credited.

If Job 101 had not been ordered by a customer but had been produced with the expectation that the signs could be sold to various other developers, then all 20 units may not be sold at the same time. Assume that on January 31, 15 signs were sold. In this case, the cost of goods sold figure is the unit cost times the number of units sold ($92 × 15, or $1,380). The unit cost figure is found on the job-order cost sheet in Exhibit 5.11.

Closing out the overhead variance to Cost of Goods Sold completes the description of manufacturing cost flows. To facilitate a review of these important concepts, Exhibit 5.15 shows a complete summary of the manufacturing cost flows for All Signs Company. Notice that these entries summarize information from the underlying job-order cost sheets.

Although the description in this exhibit is specific to the example, the pattern of cost flows shown would be found in any manufacturing firm that uses a normal job-order costing system.

Manufacturing cost flows, however, are not the only cost flows experienced by a firm. Non-manufacturing costs are also incurred. A description of how we account for these costs follows, after Exhibit 5.15.

Accounting for Nonmanufacturing Costs

Recall that costs associated with selling and general administrative activities are classified as nonmanufacturing costs. These costs are period costs and are never assigned to the product in a traditional costing system. They are not part of the manufacturing cost flows. They do not belong to the overhead category and are treated as a totally separate category.

To illustrate how these costs are accounted for, assume All Signs Company had the following additional transactions in January:

Advertising circulars	$ 75
Sales commission	125
Office salaries	500
Depreciation, office equipment	50

The following compound entry could be used to record the preceding costs:

Selling Expense Control	200	
Administrative Expense Control	550	
Accounts Payable		75
Wages Payable		625
Accumulated Depreciation—Office		
Equipment		50

Controlling accounts accumulate all of the selling and administrative expenses for a period. At the end of the period, all of these costs flow to the period's income statement. An income statement for All Signs Company is shown in Exhibit 5.16.

With the description of the accounting procedures for selling and administrative expenses completed, the basic essentials of a normal job-order costing system are also complete. This description has assumed that a single plantwide overhead rate was being used.

**DATA
ANALYTICS**

Data Analytics in Job-Order Costing

All-Signs Company has accumulated much data through the job-order costing process. The owner, Bob Fredericks, can use these data descriptively, as he learns about the costs of the particular jobs and the amount of time it takes to complete them. He can use the data diagnostically if a later job does not go the way he expects—then he can examine each type of cost and compare it with what has happened before. He can use the data predictively, as he budgets the cost of similar future jobs. Finally, he can use the data prescriptively if, for example, he wants to decrease certain costs. Going through each step of the job-order costing procedure ensures that he has a deep understanding of his production process and how to improve it in the future.

Using Big Data and Data Analytics in Construction

Huge construction firms, the ones responsible for constructing skyscrapers, airports, and office buildings, are classic examples of job-order costing firms. Each project requires huge amounts of resources and work, leading to enormous amounts of data. In fact, an often used phrase in the industry is that construction companies are accounting companies that happen to erect buildings. In this industry, 35 percent of costs are for material waste and rework. Rigidly accounting for raw materials can mean the difference between delivering on budget and bankrupting the company. Unfortunately, much of the data is kept in individual departmental databases, not seen or used by other departments. Big data analysis is starting to change that.

JE Dunn Construction, builder of large corporate offices, college dormitories, and military and government projects, partnered with Autodesk ADSK to build systems allowing real-time data-driven predictive modeling. They integrated the model into their own cost estimation system. This allows them to help an owner see the concept model from the architect and see the dollars tied to it. As the JE Dunn CIO reported, "The owner can say 'Show me what it would be like if we added another floor' or 'what if we made this part bigger?' Every element in the design is tied to (JE Dunn's) cost estimate. It is completely integrated so the solution changes visually, on the fly. This changes everything—the owner can see that we understand what they want, and see that our numbers are right. That level of reliability is really changing the industry and effectiveness of our early pricing."

The result is that big data analysis linkages speed up the design process. One $60 million civic center construction project benefited to the tune of $11 million of cost reduction and twelve weeks of reduced preconstruction planning.[7] Thus data analytics were used both to predict the impact of design changes on cost and to prescribe potential changes to reduce costs and time.

REAL-WORLD EXAMPLE

Exhibit 5.16
Income Statement

All Signs Company
Income Statement
For the Month Ended January 31, 20x1

Sales		$2,760
Less: Cost of goods sold		1,915
Gross margin		$ 845
Less selling and administrative expenses:		
Selling expenses	$200	
Administrative expenses	550	750
Operating income		$ 95

JOB-ORDER COSTING WITH ACTIVITY-BASED COSTING

OBJECTIVE 5
Explain how activity-based costing is applied to job-order costing.

As Chapter 4 pointed out, using a single rate based on direct labor hours to assign overhead may lead to inaccurate cost assignments, in that too much or too little overhead is assigned. Departmental overhead rates and activity-based costing were suggested as ways of solving this problem. In job-order costing, departmental overhead rates and activity-based costing affect

---

7 Taken from Bernard Marr, "How Big Data and Analytics Are Transforming the Construction Industry," (April 19, 2016), http://www.forbes.com/sites/bernardmarr/2016/04/19/how-big-data-and-analytics-are-transforming-the -construction-industry/#4793d1f05cd0, accessed May 27, 2016.

only the application of overhead. Thus, the job-order costing sheet has additional lines for overhead application, and the source documents must include all drivers for which overhead is applied. **Example 5.3** shows how and why to set up a job-order cost sheet for a company using activity-based costing.

EXAMPLE 5.3

The HOW and WHY of Using Activity-Based Costing in Job-Order Costing

Information:

Glover Company is a job-order costing firm that uses activity-based costing to apply overhead to jobs. Glover identified three overhead activities and related drivers. Budgeted information for the year is as follows:

Activity	Cost	Driver	Amount of Driver
Engineering design	$120,000	Engineering hours	3,000
Purchasing	80,000	Number of parts	10,000
Other overhead	250,000	Direct labor hours	40,000

Glover worked on four jobs in July. Data are as follows:

	Job 60	Job 61	Job 62	Job 63
Balance, 7/1	$32,450	$40,770	$29,090	$ 0
Direct materials	$26,000	$37,900	$25,350	$11,000
Direct labor	$40,000	$38,500	$43,000	$20,900
Engineering hours	20	10	15	100
Number of parts	150	180	200	500
Direct labor hours	2,500	2,400	2,600	1,200

By July 31, Jobs 60 and 62 were completed and sold. The remaining jobs were in process.

> **Why:**
> ABC requires data to be collected on each activity cost and driver. Then the activity cost is assigned to each job since it is unique in its use of activity drivers.

Required:

1. Calculate the activity rates for each of the three overhead activities.

2. Prepare job-order cost sheets for each job showing all costs through July 31.

3. Calculate the balance in Work in Process on July 31.

4. Calculate cost of goods sold for July.

5. *What if* Job 61 required no engineering hours? What is the new cost of Job 61? How would the cost of the other jobs be affected?

Solution:

1. Engineering design rate = $120,000/3,000 = $40 per engineering hour
   Purchasing rate = $80,000/10,000 = $8 per part
   Other overhead = $250,000/40,000 = $6.25 per direct labor hour

EXAMPLE 5.3

(*Continued*)

2.

	Job 60	Job 61	Job 62	Job 63
Balance, 7/1	$ 32,450	$ 40,770	$ 29,090	$ 0
Direct materials	26,000	37,900	25,350	11,000
Direct labor	40,000	38,500	43,000	20,900
Engineering design	800	400	600	4,000
Purchasing	1,200	1,440	1,600	4,000
Other overhead	15,625	15,000	16,250	7,500
Total cost	$116,075	$134,010	$115,890	$47,400

3. Work in Process = Job 61 + Job 63 = $134,010 + $47,400 = $181,410

4. Cost of goods sold = Job 60 + Job 62 = $116,075 + $115,890 = $231,965

5. If Job 61 required no engineering time, then the engineering applied to Job 61 would be zero and the cost of Job 61 would decrease by $400. The new Job 61 cost would be $133,610. The cost of the other three jobs would not be affected.

ACCOUNTING FOR SPOILED UNITS IN A TRADITIONAL JOB-ORDER COSTING SYSTEM

OBJECTIVE ◄ 6

Explain how spoiled units are accounted for in a job-order costing system.

Throughout this chapter, we have assumed that all units produced are good units. In this case, all manufacturing costs are associated with good units and flow into cost of goods sold. However, on occasion, mistakes are made; defective units are produced and are either thrown away or reworked and sold. How do we account for those costs?

First, we must distinguish between normal and abnormal spoilage. **Normal spoilage** is expected due to the nature of the production process. If the spoilage is not caused by any particular job, it is subsumed in the overhead rate and spread across all jobs through applied overhead. For example, when maintenance workers oil the sewing machines in a clothing factory, the next item to be sewn may pick up some drops of the machine oil and must be discarded. This is normal spoilage and the cost is included in overhead that is then applied to all units produced. Sometimes, normal spoilage is due to the exacting nature of the job, perhaps materials that are more difficult to work with or that break easily. In this case, the extra cost is added to that job's cost. **Abnormal spoilage** is unexpected and not part of normal operations. It may result from electrical surges, or by a leaky roof that allows rain to spoil the jobs beneath. This type of spoilage is not charged to the production accounts (Work in Process, Finished Goods and Cost of Goods Sold), but instead is charged to Loss from Abnormal Spoilage. **Example 5.4** tells how to treat spoilage and why the distinction between normal and abnormal spoilage is made.

EXAMPLE 5.4

The HOW and WHY of Accounting for Normal and Abnormal Spoilage in a Job-Order Environment

Information:
Petris, Inc., manufactures cabinets on a job-order basis. Job 98-12 calls for 100 units with direct materials of $2,000 and direct labor of $1,000. Overhead is applied at the rate of 150 percent of direct labor dollars. At the end of the job, 100 units are produced; however, three of the cabinets required rework which cost an additional $50 of material and $60 of direct labor.

Why:
Normal spoilage requires that the additional cost of any rework be charged to Overhead Control unless it was due to requirements of the job itself, then it is added to that job's cost. If the spoilage is abnormal, any additional cost is assigned to Loss from Abnormal Spoilage.

EXAMPLE 5.4

(Continued)

Required:

1. Assume that the spoilage was due to assigning new, untrained workers to the job and was not caused by Job 98-12.

    a. Calculate the cost of Job 98-12.

    b. Make any needed journal entry to the overhead control account.

2. Assume that the spoilage is a result of exacting specifications for Job 98-12.

    a. Calculate the cost of Job 98-12.

    b. Make any needed journal entry to the overhead control account.

3. Now suppose that the spoilage was due to an unexpected machine breakdown. What is the cost of Job 98-12? How would the spoilage be accounted for?

4. ***What if*** three of the cabinets in Job 98-12 were not completely up to specifications due to unevenly applied stain? The stain could not be reworked, but the customer was willing to accept those three for a $20 per cabinet discount in the price. What is the total cost of the job? Would there be any additional entries to Overhead Control?

Solution:

1. a.

Job 98-12		Overhead Control	
Direct materials	$2,000	Direct materials	$ 50
Direct labor	1,000	Direct labor (6 × $10)	60
Overhead ($1,000 × 150%)	1,500	Overhead ($60 × 150%)	90
Total job cost	$4,500	Total	$200

b. Since the spoilage is normal and the rework is not assignable to the job, the cost must be charged (debited) to Overhead Control.

Overhead Control	110	
Materials		50
Payroll		60

2. a.

Direct materials ($2,000 + $50)	$2,050
Direct labor [$1,000 + (6 × $10)]	1,060
Overhead ($1,060 × 150%)	1,590
Total job cost	$4,700

b. No additional entry is needed to Overhead Control since all costs of the job are added to the job-order cost sheet and flow through Work in Process.

3. The cost of the job is $4,500, the same as calculated in Requirement 1. However, the spoilage is abnormal and would be charged to the Loss from Abnormal Spoilage account.

4. If no rework is done, then the job-order cost sheet will look like the one in Requirement 1. Total cost is $4,500, and no additional entries are made to Overhead Control. The price discount will affect the price charged; it will be lower than it otherwise would be.

SUMMARY OF LEARNING OBJECTIVES

LO1. Differentiate the cost accounting systems of service and manufacturing firms and of unique and standardized products.
- Manufacturing firms produce tangible products and need costs for:
  - Inventory measurement on the balance sheet (Materials, Work in Process, Finished Goods)
  - Cost of Goods Sold on the income statement
- Service firms produce intangible products with the following characteristics:
  - Intangibility
  - Inseparability
  - Heterogeneity
  - Perishability
- Uniqueness of units of service or production affects costing method.
  - Job-order costing is used for unique units with unique costs of production.
  - Operation costing is a hybrid of job-order and process costing. Batches consist of unique units.
  - Process costing is used when units are homogeneous.

LO2. Discuss the interrelationship of cost accumulation, cost measurement, and cost assignment.
- Cost accumulation is the recording of costs in the general ledger.
- Cost measurement refers to the classification and organization of costs.
- Cost assignment determines the cost of particular cost objects (such as units).

LO3. Identify the source documents used in job-order costing.
- Job-order cost sheets summarize all costs assigned to a job.
  - Subsidiary to work-in-process account
  - Includes direct materials, direct labor, and applied overhead
- Materials requisition forms record materials signed out for use on a job.
- Time tickets are used to keep track of direct labor time used on each job.
- Other source documents track the amount of activity drivers used by each job.

LO4. Describe the cost flows associated with job-order costing, and prepare the journal entries.
- Costs flow into Work in Process as debits for:
  - Direct materials (credit the materials account)
  - Direct labor (credit the payroll account)
  - Applied overhead (credit the overhead control account)
- Cost of completed jobs is:
  - Debited to Finished Goods (if inventoried) or Cost of Goods Sold (if sold immediately upon completion)
  - Credited to Work in Process
- Cost of Goods Sold is:
  - Debited to Cost of Goods Sold
  - Credited to Finished Goods (if removed from inventory) or Work in Process (if sold immediately upon completion)
- Jobs sold are:
  - Debited to Accounts Receivable or Cash
  - Credited to Sales Revenue

LO5. Explain how activity-based costing is applied to job-order costing.
- Use of activity drivers must be tracked by job.
- Activity cost is applied to each job by multiplying the activity rate by the job's use of the associated driver.

LO6. Explain how spoiled units are accounted for in a job-order costing system.
- Normal spoilage is expected.
  - Cost of normal spoilage not caused by particular job is included in the overhead rate.
  - Cost of normal spoilage caused by particular job is added to that job's cost.
- Abnormal spoilage is unexpected and not part of normal production. It is charged to Loss from Abnormal Spoilage.

EXAMPLE 5.1	The HOW and WHY of Setting Up a Simplified Job-Order Cost Sheet, page 230
EXAMPLE 5.2	The HOW and WHY of Using a Job-Order Cost Sheet to Determine the Balances of Work in Process, Finished Goods, and Cost of Goods Sold, page 238
EXAMPLE 5.3	The HOW and WHY of Using Activity-Based Costing in Job-Order Costing, page 242
EXAMPLE 5.4	The HOW and WHY of Accounting for Normal and Abnormal Spoilage in a Job-Order Environment, page 243

KEY TERMS

Abnormal spoilage, 243	**Normal activity level**, 226
Actual cost system, 223	**Normal cost of goods sold**, 237
Adjusted cost of goods sold, 237	**Normal costing system**, 223
Cost accumulation, 222	**Normal spoilage**, 243
Cost assignment, 222	**Operation costing**, 221
Cost measurement, 222	**Perishability**, 218
Expected activity level, 226	**Practical activity level**, 226
Heterogeneity, 218	**Predetermined overhead rates**, 226
Inseparability, 218	**Source document**, 222
Intangibility, 218	**Theoretical activity level**, 226
Job-order cost sheet, 227	**Time ticket**, 229
Job-order costing system, 227	**Work-in-process inventory file**, 228
Materials requisition form, 228	

BRIEF EXERCISES

Example 5.1

Brief Exercise 5-1 Job Costs Using a Plantwide Overhead Rate

Perrin Company designs industrial prototypes for outside companies. Budgeted overhead for the year was $242,000, and budgeted direct labor hours were 20,000. The average wage rate for direct labor is expected to be $22 per hour. During June, Perrin Company worked on four jobs. Data relating to these four jobs follow:

	Job 39	Job 40	Job 41	Job 42
Beginning balance	$28,900	$37,400	$15,000	$ 0
Materials requisitioned	19,800	24,300	7,000	16,700
Direct labor cost	9,900	13,200	11,000	4,000

Overhead is assigned as a percentage of direct labor cost. During June, Jobs 39 and 40 were completed; Job 39 was sold at 130 percent of cost. Job 40 is the only job in Finished Goods Inventory and will remain there until the customer accepts delivery and pays. Jobs 41 and 42 remain unfinished at the end of the month.

Required:

1. Calculate the overhead rate based on direct labor cost.
2. Set up a simple job-order cost sheet for all jobs in process during June.
3. *What if* the expected direct labor rate at the beginning of the year was $24.20 instead of $22? What would the overhead rate be? How would the cost of the jobs be affected?

Brief Exercise 5-2 Job Costs Using a Plantwide Overhead Rate

Refer to **Brief Exercise 5-1** for data.

OBJECTIVE ◄ 3 4
Example 5.2

Required:

1. Calculate the balance in Work in Process as of June 30.
2. Calculate the balance in Finished Goods as of June 30.
3. Calculate the cost of goods sold for June.
4. Calculate the price charged for Job 39.
5. *What if* the customer for Job 40 was able to pay for the job by June 30? What would happen to the balance in Finished Goods? What would happen to the balance of Cost of Goods Sold?

Brief Exercise 5-3 Job Costs Using Activity-Based Costing

Reider Company is a job-order costing firm that uses activity-based costing to apply overhead to jobs. Reider identified three overhead activities and related drivers. Budgeted information for the year is as follows:

OBJECTIVE ◄ 5
Example 5.3

Activity	Cost	Driver	Amount of Driver
Materials handling	$ 72,000	Number of moves	3,000
Engineering	165,000	Number of change orders	10,000
Other overhead	280,000	Direct labor hours	50,000

Reider worked on four jobs in July. Data are as follows:

	Job 13-43	Job 13-44	Job 13-45	Job 13-46
Beginning balance	$20,300	$19,800	$ 2,300	$ 0
Direct materials	$ 6,500	$8,900	$12,700	$9,800
Direct labor cost	$18,000	$20,000	$32,000	$2,400
Number of moves	44	52	29	5
Number of change orders	30	40	20	20
Direct labor hours	900	1,000	1,600	120

By July 31, Jobs 13-43 and 13-44 were completed and sold. Jobs 13-45 and 13-46 were still in process.

Required:

1. Calculate the activity rates for each of the three overhead activities.
2. Prepare job-order cost sheets for each job showing all costs through July 31.
3. Calculate the balance in Work in Process on July 31.
4. Calculate the cost of goods sold for July.
5. *What if* Job 13-46 required no engineering change orders? What is the new cost of Job 13-46? How would the cost of the other jobs be affected?

OBJECTIVE 6
Example 5.4

Brief Exercise 5-4 Cost of Normal Spoilage

Stanley Company installs granite countertops in customers' homes. First, the customer chooses the particular granite slab, and then Stanley measures the countertop area at the customer's home, cuts the granite to that shape, and installs it. The Flores job calls for direct materials of $2,600 and direct labor of $700. Overhead is applied at the rate of 160 percent of direct labor cost. Unfortunately, one small countertop breaks during installation and Stanley must cut another piece and install it to properly complete the job. The additional rework required direct materials costing $900 and direct labor costing $250. Assume that the spoilage was due to carelessness by a Stanley worker and it is considered to be normal spoilage.

Required:

1. Calculate the cost of the Flores job.
2. Make any needed journal entry to the overhead control account.
3. *What if* the additional rework required $200 of direct labor? What would be the effect on the cost of the Tramel job?

OBJECTIVE 6
Example 5.4

Brief Exercise 5-5 Cost of Normal Spoilage Caused by Nature of Job

Refer to the data in **Brief Exercise 5-4**. Now assume that the spoilage was due to the inherently fragile nature of the piece of stone picked out by the Flores family. Stanley had warned them that the chosen piece could require much more care and potentially additional work. As a result, Stanley considers this spoilage to be caused by the Flores' job.

Required:

1. Calculate the cost of the Flores job.
2. Make any needed journal entry to the overhead control account.
3. *What if* the additional rework required $200 of direct labor? What would be the effect on the cost of the Flores job?

EXERCISES

OBJECTIVE 1

Exercise 5-6 Classifying Firms as Either Manufacturing or Service

Classify the following types of firms as either manufacturing or service. Explain the reasons for your choice in terms of the four features of service firms (heterogeneity, inseparability, intangibility, and perishability).

   a. Bicycle production
   b. Pharmaceuticals
   c. Income tax preparation
   d. Application of artificial nails
   e. Glue production
   f. Child care

Exercise 5-7 Characteristics of Production Process, Cost Measurement

OBJECTIVE 1 2

SHOW ME
HOW

Vince Kim, of EcoScape Company, designs and installs custom lawn and garden irrigation systems for homes and businesses throughout the state. Each job is different, requiring different materials and labor for installing the systems. EcoScape estimated the following for the year:

Number of direct labor hours	6,720
Direct labor cost	$67,200
Overhead cost	$50,400

During the year, the following actual amounts were experienced:

Number of direct labor hours	6,045
Direct labor incurred	$66,495
Overhead incurred	$50,500

Required:

1. Should EcoScape use process costing or job-order costing? Explain.
2. If EcoScape uses a normal costing system and overhead is applied on the basis of direct labor hours, what is the overhead rate? What is the average actual wage rate? What is the cost of an installation that takes $3,500 of direct materials and 20 direct labor hours?
3. Explain why EcoScape would have difficulty using an actual costing system.

Exercise 5-8 Characteristics of Production Process, Cost Measurement

OBJECTIVE 1 2

Refer to the data in **Exercise 5-7**. Vince Kim, owner of EcoScape, noticed that the watering systems for many houses in a local subdivision had the same layout and required virtually identical amounts of prime cost. Vince met with the subdivision builders and offered to install a basic watering system in each house. The idea was accepted enthusiastically, so Vince created a new company, Irrigation Specialties, to handle the subdivision business. In its first three months in business, Irrigation Specialties experienced the following:

	June	July	August
Number of systems installed	60	80	120
Direct materials used	$18,000	$24,000	$36,000
Direct labor incurred	$12,000	$16,000	$24,000
Overhead	$10,900	$12,340	$14,500

Required:

1. Should Irrigation Specialties use process costing or job-order costing? Explain.
2. If Irrigation Specialties uses an actual costing system, what is the cost of a single system installed in June? In July? In August? Round your answers to the nearest dollar.
3. Now assume that Irrigation Specialties uses a normal costing system. Estimated overhead for the year is $54,000, and estimated production is 600 watering systems. What is the predetermined overhead rate per system? What is the cost of a single system installed in June? In July? In August?

Exercise 5-9 Activity Levels Used to Compute Overhead Rates

OBJECTIVE 2

Reggie Wilmore has just started a new business—building and installing custom garage organization systems. Reggie builds the cabinets and work benches in his workshop, then installs them in clients' garages. Reggie figures his overhead for the coming year will be $12,000. Since his business is labor intensive, he plans to use direct labor hours as his overhead driver. For the coming year, he expects to complete 100 jobs, averaging 25 direct labor hours each. However, he has the capacity to complete 125 jobs averaging 25 direct labor hours each.

Required:

1. Four measures of activity level were mentioned in the text. Which two measures is Reggie considering in computing a predetermined overhead rate?
2. Compute the predetermined overhead rates using each of the measures in your answer to Requirement 1.
3. Which one would you recommend that Reggie use? Why?

OBJECTIVE **3** **4**

DATA ANALYTICS

Exercise 5-10 Source Documents, Job Cost Flows

Refer to **Exercise 5-9**.

Required:

1. What source documents will Reggie need to account for costs in his new business?
2. Suppose Reggie's business grows, and he expands his workshop and hires three additional carpenters to help him. What source documents will he need now?
3. Which of the data analytic types—descriptive, diagnostic, predictive, or prescriptive—is Reggie using to develop the new source documents? Explain. (See Exhibits 2.5 and 2.6, pp. 37, 40, for a review of data analytic types.)

OBJECTIVE **4**

SHOW ME HOW

Exercise 5-11 Job Costs, Ending Work in Process

During March, Estes Company worked on three jobs. Data relating to these three jobs follow:

	Job 86	Job 87	Job 88
Units in each order	200	180	220
Units sold	—	180	—
Materials requisitioned	$3,560	$ 950	$2,400
Direct labor hours	220	180	400
Direct labor cost	$4,400	$3,600	$8,000

Overhead is assigned on the basis of direct labor hours at a rate of $8.40 per direct labor hour. During March, Jobs 86 and 87 were completed and transferred to Finished Goods Inventory. Job 87 was sold by the end of the month. Job 88 was the only unfinished job at the end of the month.

Required:

1. Calculate the per-unit cost of Jobs 86 and 87.
2. Compute the ending balance in the work-in-process inventory account.
3. Prepare the journal entries reflecting the completion of Jobs 86 and 87 and the sale of Job 87. The selling price is 150 percent of cost.

OBJECTIVE **3** **4**

SHOW ME HOW

Exercise 5-12 Predetermined Overhead Rate, Application of Overhead to Jobs, Job Cost

On April 1, Sangvikar Company had the following balances in its inventory accounts:

Materials Inventory	$12,730
Work-in-Process Inventory	21,340
Finished Goods Inventory	8,700

Work-in-process inventory is made up of three jobs with the following costs:

	Job 114	Job 115	Job 116
Direct materials	$2,411	$2,640	$3,650
Direct labor	1,800	1,560	4,300
Applied overhead	1,170	1,014	2,795

During April, Sangvikar experienced the transactions listed below.

a. Materials purchased on account, $29,000.

b. Materials requisitioned: Job 114, $16,500; Job 115, $12,200; and Job 116, $5,000.

c. Job tickets were collected and summarized: Job 114, 150 hours at $12 per hour; Job 115, 220 hours at $14 per hour; and Job 116, 80 hours at $18 per hour.

d. Overhead is applied on the basis of direct labor cost.

e. Actual overhead was $4,415.

f. Job 115 was completed and transferred to the finished goods warehouse.

g. Job 115 was shipped, and the customer was billed for 125 percent of the cost.

Required:

1. Calculate the predetermined overhead rate based on direct labor cost.
2. Calculate the ending balance for each job as of April 30.
3. Calculate the ending balance of Work in Process as of April 30.
4. Calculate the cost of goods sold for April.
5. Assuming that Sangvikar prices its jobs at cost plus 25 percent, calculate the price of the one job that was sold during April. (Round to the nearest dollar.)

Exercise 5-13 Job Cost Flows, Journal Entries

Refer to **Exercise 5-12**.

Required:

1. Prepare journal entries for the April transactions.
2. Calculate the ending balances of each of the inventory accounts as of April 30.

Exercise 5-14 Predetermined Overhead Rate, Application of Overhead to Jobs, Job Cost, Unit Cost

On August 1, Cairle Company's work-in-process inventory consisted of three jobs with the following costs:

	Job 70	Job 71	Job 72
Direct materials	$1,600	$2,000	$850
Direct labor	1,900	1,300	900
Applied overhead	1,425	975	675

During August, four more jobs were started. Information on costs added to the seven jobs during the month is as follows:

	Job 70	Job 71	Job 72	Job 73	Job 74	Job 75	Job 76
Direct materials	$800	$1,235	$3,550	$5,000	$300	$560	$ 80
Direct labor	1,000	1,400	2,200	1,800	600	860	172

Before the end of August, Jobs 70, 72, 73, and 75 were completed. On August 31, Jobs 72 and 75 were sold.

Required:

1. Calculate the predetermined overhead rate based on direct labor cost.
2. Calculate the ending balance for each job as of August 31.
3. Calculate the ending balance of Work in Process as of August 31.
4. Calculate the cost of goods sold for August.
5. Assuming that Cairle prices its jobs at cost plus 20 percent, calculate Cairle's sales revenue for August.

OBJECTIVE 4

Exercise 5-15 Income Statement

Refer to **Exercise 5-14**. Cairle's selling and administrative expenses for August were $1,200.

Required:

Prepare an income statement for Cairle Company for August.

OBJECTIVE 4

SHOW ME
HOW

EXCEL

Exercise 5-16 Journal Entries, T-Accounts

Lincoln Brothers Company makes jobs to customer order. During the month of May, the following occurred:

a. Materials were purchased on account for $51,200.
b. Materials totaling $43,600 were requisitioned for use in producing various jobs.
c. Direct labor payroll for the month was $26,100 with an average wage of $18 per hour.
d. Actual overhead of $12,450 was incurred and paid in cash.
e. Manufacturing overhead is charged to production at the rate of $6.20 per direct labor hour.
f. Completed jobs costing $61,750 were transferred to Finished Goods.
g. Jobs costing $64,200 were sold on account for $80,250.

Beginning balances as of July 1 were:

Materials Inventory	$2,200
Work-in-Process Inventory	3,800
Finished Goods Inventory	3,460

Required:

1. Prepare the journal entries for the preceding events.
2. Calculate the ending balances of:
   a. Materials Inventory
   b. Work-in-Process Inventory
   c. Overhead Control
   d. Finished Goods Inventory

OBJECTIVE 4 5

SHOW ME
HOW

Exercise 5-17 Unit Cost, Ending Work-in-Process Inventory, Journal Entries

During August, Skyler Company worked on three jobs. Data relating to these three jobs follow:

	Job 39	Job 40	Job 41
Units in each order	60	100	80
Units sold	—	100	—
Materials requisitioned	$ 700	$ 680	$ 800
Direct labor hours	360	400	200
Direct labor cost	$1,980	$2,480	$1,240

Overhead is assigned on the basis of direct labor hours at a rate of $2.30 per direct labor hour. During August, Jobs 39 and 40 were completed and transferred to Finished Goods Inventory. Job 40 was sold by the end of the month. Job 41 was the only unfinished job at the end of the month.

Required:

1. Calculate the per-unit cost of Jobs 39 and 40. (Round unit costs to nearest cent.)
2. Compute the ending balance in the work-in-process inventory account.
3. Prepare the journal entries reflecting the completion of Jobs 39 and 40 and the sale of Job 40. The selling price is 140 percent of cost.

Exercise 5-18 Activity-Based Costing, Unit Cost, Ending Work-in-Process Inventory, Journal Entries

OBJECTIVE 4 5

DATA ANALYTICS **SHOW ME HOW**

Feldspar Company uses an ABC system to apply overhead. There are three activity rates:

Setting up	$20 per setup
Machining	$5.10 per machine hour
Other overhead	80% of direct labor cost

During September, Feldspar worked on three jobs. Data relating to these jobs follow:

	Job 13-280	Job 13-281	Job 13-282
Units in each order	200	500	100
Units sold	200	—	100
Materials requisitioned	$4,730	$3,800	$5,600
Direct labor cost	$2,000	$4,600	$ 800
Machine hours	80	100	40
Number of setups	20	15	25

During September, Jobs 13-280 and 13-282 were completed and transferred to Finished Goods Inventory. Job 13-280 was sold by the end of the month. Job 13-281 was the only unfinished job at the end of the month.

Required:

1. Calculate the per-unit cost of Jobs 13-280 and 13-282. (Round unit cost to nearest cent.)
2. Compute the ending balance in the work-in-process inventory account.
3. Prepare the journal entries reflecting the completion of Jobs 13-280 and 13-282 and the sale of Job 13-280 on account. The selling price is 150 percent of cost.
4. Suppose Feldspar has secured contracts for two new jobs in October that have simpler designs and will require fewer setups than average. How can the activity-based rates help the company anticipate costs in October and revenue and income when the new jobs are complete? Identify the data analytic types (descriptive, diagnostic, predictive, or prescriptive) that will help Feldspar answer these questions. (See Exhibits 2.5 and 2.6, pp. 37, 40, for a review of data analytic types. *Note:* More than one analytic type might apply.)

Exercise 5-19 Journal Entries, T-Accounts

OBJECTIVE 4

SHOW ME HOW

Kapoor Company uses job-order costing. During January, the following data were reported:

a. Materials purchased on account: direct materials, $98,500; indirect materials, $14,800.
b. Materials issued: direct materials, $82,500; indirect materials, $8,800.
c. Labor cost incurred: direct labor, $67,000; indirect labor, $18,750.
d. Other manufacturing costs incurred (all payables), $46,200.
e. Overhead is applied on the basis of 110 percent of direct labor cost.
f. Work finished and transferred to Finished Goods Inventory cost $230,000.
g. Finished goods costing $215,000 were sold on account for 140 percent of cost.
h. Any over- or underapplied overhead is closed to Cost of Goods Sold.

Required:

1. Prepare journal entries to record these transactions.
2. Prepare a T-account for Overhead Control. Post all relevant information to this account. What is the ending balance in this account?
3. Prepare a T-account for Work-in-Process Inventory. Assume a beginning balance of $10,000, and post all relevant information to this account. Did you assign any actual overhead costs to Work-in-Process Inventory? Why or why not?

OBJECTIVE 4 5

SHOW ME
HOW

EXCEL

Exercise 5-20 Activity-Based Costing, Unit Cost, Ending Work-in-Process Inventory

Salazar Company is a job-order costing firm that uses activity-based costing to apply overhead to jobs. Salazar identified three overhead activities and related drivers. Budgeted information for the year is as follows:

Activity	Cost	Driver	Amount of Driver
Setting up design	$156,000	Setups	1,200
Purchasing	187,500	Number of parts	15,000
Other overhead	420,000	Direct labor hours	50,000

Salazar worked on five jobs in March. Data are as follows:

	Job 15	Job 16	Job 17	Job 18	Job 19
Balance, March 1	$34,500	$39,890	$24,090	$ 0	$ 0
Direct materials	$28,000	$37,900	$25,350	$11,000	$13,560
Direct labor	$10,000	$ 8,500	$23,000	$12,900	$ 8,000
Setups	20	14	35	8	15
Number of parts	150	180	200	500	300
Direct labor hours	650	580	1,600	870	520

By March 31, Jobs 15, 16, and 17 were completed and sold. The remaining jobs were in process.

Required:

1. Calculate the activity rates for each of the three overhead activities.
2. Prepare job-order cost sheets for each job showing all costs through March 31. What is the cost of each job by the end of March?
3. Calculate the balance in Work in Process on March 31.
4. Calculate the cost of goods sold for March.

PROBLEMS

OBJECTIVE 4 5

EXCEL

Problem 5-21 Journal Entries, T-Accounts, Cost of Goods Manufactured and Sold

During May, the following transactions were completed and reported by Sylvana Company:
   a. Materials purchased on account, $60,100.
   b. Materials issued to production to fill job-order requisitions: direct materials, $51,000; indirect materials, $8,950.
   c. Payroll for the month: direct labor, $85,500; indirect labor, $37,800; administrative, $35,000; sales, $24,500.
   d. Depreciation on factory plant and equipment, $9,400.
   e. Property taxes on the factory accrued during the month, $2,750.
   f. Insurance on the factory expired with a credit to the prepaid insurance account, $6,240.
   g. Factory utilities, $5,500.
   h. Advertising paid with cash, $7,900.
   i. Depreciation on office equipment, $700; on sales vehicles, $1,600.
   j. Legal fees incurred but not yet paid for preparation of lease agreements, $750.
   k. Overhead is charged to production at a rate of $16 per direct labor hour. Records show 4,500 direct labor hours were worked during the month.
   l. Cost of jobs completed during the month, $160,000.

The company also reported the following beginning balances in its inventory accounts:

Materials Inventory	$ 8,000
Work-in-Process Inventory	38,900
Finished Goods Inventory	48,200

Required:

1. Prepare journal entries to record the transactions occurring in May.
2. Prepare T-accounts for Materials Inventory, Overhead Control, Work-in-Process Inventory, and Finished Goods Inventory. Post all relevant entries to these accounts.
3. Prepare a statement of cost of goods manufactured.
4. If the overhead variance is all allocated to cost of goods sold, by how much will cost of goods sold decrease or increase?

Problem 5-22 Overhead Application, Activity-Based Costing, Bid Prices

OBJECTIVE ◀ 4 5

Firenza Company manufactures specialty tools to customer order. Budgeted overhead for the coming year is:

Purchasing	$40,000
Setups	37,500
Engineering	45,000
Other	40,000

Previously, Sanjay Bhatt, Firenza Company's controller, had applied overhead on the basis of machine hours. Expected machine hours for the coming year are 50,000. Sanjay has been reading about activity-based costing, and he wonders whether or not it might offer some advantages to his company. He decided that appropriate drivers for overhead activities are purchase orders for purchasing, number of setups for setup cost, engineering hours for engineering cost, and machine hours for other. Budgeted amounts for these drivers are 5,000 purchase orders, 500 setups, and 2,500 engineering hours.

Sanjay has been asked to prepare bids for two jobs with the following information:

	Job 1	Job 2
Direct materials	$4,500	$9,340
Direct labor	$1,200	$2,100
Number of purchase orders	15	20
Number of setups	3	4
Number of engineering hours	45	10
Number of machine hours	200	200

The typical bid price includes a 40 percent markup over full manufacturing cost.

Required:

1. Calculate a plantwide rate for Firenza Company based on machine hours. What is the bid price of each job using this rate?
2. Calculate activity rates for the four overhead activities. What is the bid price of each job using these rates?
3. Which bids are more accurate? Why?

Problem 5-23 Plantwide Overhead Rate, Activity-Based Costing, Job Costs

OBJECTIVE ◀ 3 5

Foto-Fast Copy Shop provides a variety of photocopying and printing services. On June 5, the owner invested in some computer-aided photography equipment that enables customers to reproduce a picture or illustration, input it digitally into the computer, enter text into the computer, and then print out a four-color professional quality brochure. Prior to the purchase of this equipment, Foto-Fast Copy Shop's overhead averaged $37,500 per year. After the installation of the new equipment, the total overhead increased to $90,000 per year. Foto-Fast Copy Shop has always costed jobs on the basis of actual materials and labor plus overhead assigned using a predetermined overhead rate based on direct labor hours. Budgeted direct labor hours for the year are 7,500, and the wage rate is $8 per hour.

Required:

1. What was the predetermined overhead rate prior to the purchase of the new equipment?
2. What was the predetermined overhead rate after the new equipment was purchased?
3. Suppose Rick Anselm brought in several items he wanted photocopied. The job required 600 sheets of paper at $0.02 each and 45 minutes of direct labor time. What would have been the cost of Rick's job on May 20? On June 20?
4. Suppose that the owner decides to calculate two overhead rates, one for the photocopying area based on direct labor hours as before, and one for the computer-aided printing area based on machine time. Estimated overhead applicable to the computer-aided printing area is $52,500, and forecasted usage of the machines is 2,000 hours. What are the two overhead rates? Which overhead rate system is better—one rate or two?

OBJECTIVE ▶ 5 | **Problem 5-24 Plantwide Overhead Rate versus Departmental Rates, Effects on Pricing Decisions**

Cherise Ortega, marketing manager for Romer Company, was puzzled by the outcome of two recent bids. The company's policy was to bid 150 percent of the full manufacturing cost. One job (labeled Job 97-28) had been turned down by a prospective customer, who had indicated that the proposed price was $3 per unit higher than the winning bid. A second job (Job 97-35) had been accepted by a customer, who was amazed that Romer could offer such favorable terms. This customer revealed that Romer's price was $43 per unit lower than the next lowest bid.

Cherise has been informed that the company was more than competitive in terms of cost control. Accordingly, she began to suspect that the problem was related to cost assignment procedures. Upon investigating, Cherise was told that the company uses a plantwide overhead rate based on direct labor hours. The rate is computed at the beginning of the year using budgeted data. Selected budgeted data are given below.

	Department A	Department B	Total
Overhead	$500,000	$2,000,000	$2,500,000
Direct labor hours	200,000	50,000	250,000
Machine hours	20,000	120,000	140,000

Cherise also discovered that the overhead costs in Department B were higher than those in Department A because B has more equipment, higher maintenance, higher power consumption, higher depreciation, and higher setup costs. In addition to the general procedures for assigning overhead costs, Cherise was supplied with the following specific manufacturing data on Jobs 97-28 and 97-35:

	Job 97-28		
	Department A	Department B	Total
Direct labor hours	5,000	1,000	6,000
Machine hours	200	500	700
Prime costs	$100,000	$20,000	$120,000
Units produced	14,400	14,400	14,400

Job 97-35

	Department A	Department B	Total
Direct labor hours	400	600	1,000
Machine hours	200	3,000	3,200
Prime costs	$10,000	$40,000	$50,000
Units produced	1,500	1,500	1,500

Required:

1. Using a plantwide overhead rate based on direct labor hours, develop the bid prices for Jobs 97-28 and 97-35 (express the bid prices on a per-unit basis).
2. Using departmental overhead rates (use direct labor hours for Department A and machine hours for Department B), develop per-unit bid prices for Jobs 97-28 and 97-35.
3. Compute the difference in gross profit that would have been earned had the company used departmental rates in its bids instead of the plantwide rate.
4. Explain why the use of departmental rates in this case provides a more accurate product cost.

Problem 5-25 Cost of Spoiled Units

OBJECTIVE ◀ 6

Lieu Company is a specialty print shop. Usually, printing jobs are priced at standard cost plus 50 percent. Job 631 involved printing 400 wedding invitations with the following standard costs:

Direct materials	$240
Direct labor	60
Overhead	80
Total	$380

Normally, the invitations would be taken from the machine, the top one inspected for correct wording, spelling, and quality of print, and all of the invitations wrapped in plastic and stored on shelves designated for completed jobs. In this case, however, the technician decided to go to lunch before inspecting and wrapping the job. He stacked the unwrapped invitations beside the printing press and left. One hour later, he returned and found the invitations had fallen on the floor and been stepped on. It turned out that about 50 invitations were ruined and had to be discarded. An additional 50 invitations were then printed to complete the job.

Required:

1. Calculate the cost of the spoiled invitations. How should the spoilage cost be accounted for?
2. What is the price of Job 631?
3. Suppose that another job, 705, also required 400 wedding invitations. The standard costs are identical to those of Job 631. However, Job 705 required an unusual color of ink that could only be obtained in a formula that was difficult to use. Lieu printers know from experience that getting this ink color to print correctly requires trial and error. In the case of Job 705, the first 50 invitations had to be discarded due to inconsistencies in the color of ink. What is the cost of the spoilage, and how would it be treated?
4. What is the price of Job 705?

Problem 5-26 Cost of Reworked Units

OBJECTIVE ◀ 6

Warren's Sporting Goods Store sells a variety of sporting goods and clothing. In a back room, Warren's has set up heat transfer equipment to personalize T-shirts for Little League teams. Typically, each team has the name of the individual player put on the back of the T-shirt. Last week, Shona Kohlmia, coach of the Terrors, brought in a list of names for her team. Her team consisted of 12 players with the following names: Mary Kate, Kayla, Katie, Tara, Heather, Emma, Kimberleigh, Jennifer, Dayna, Elizabeth, Kyle, and Wendy. Shona was quoted a price of $0.60 per letter.

Chip Russell, Warren's newest employee, took Shona's order and worked on the job. He selected the appropriate letters, arranged the letters in each name carefully on a shirt, and heat-pressed them on. When Shona returned, she was appalled to see that the names were on the front of the shirts. Jim Warren, owner of the sporting goods store, assured Shona that the letters could easily be removed by applying more heat and lifting them off. This process ruins the old letters, so new letters must then be placed correctly on the shirt backs. He promised to correct the job immediately and have it ready in an hour and a half.

Costs for heat transferring are as follows:

Letters (each)	$0.45
Direct labor (per hour)	8.00
Overhead (per direct labor hour)	4.00

Shona's job originally took one hour and 12 minutes of direct labor time. The removal process goes more quickly and should take only 30 minutes.

Required:

1. What was the original cost of Shona's job?
2. What is the cost of rework on Shona's job? Assume that Chip failed to ask whether the names should be placed on the back or the front of the shirts. How should the rework cost be treated?
3. Now assume that Shona had mistakenly told Chip to put the names on the front of the shirts. In an effort to keep his customer happy, Jim suggested that Shona pay only for the new letters and the firm would pay for the labor cost. How much did Jim charge Shona in addition to the original price of the job?

OBJECTIVE 3 4

DATA ANALYTICS

Problem 5-27 Job-Order Costing: Housing

Sutton Construction Inc. is a privately held, family-founded corporation that builds single- and multiple-unit housing. Most projects Sutton Construction undertakes involve the construction of multiple units. Sutton Construction has adopted a job-order costing system for determining the cost of each unit. The costing system is fully computerized. Each project's costs are divided into the following five categories:

1. *General conditions*, including construction site utilities, project insurance permits and licenses, architect's fees, decorating, field office salaries, and cleanup costs.
2. *Hard costs*, such as subcontractors, direct materials, and direct labor.
3. *Finance costs*, including title and recording fees, inspection fees, and taxes and discounts on mortgages.
4. *Land costs*, which refer to the purchase price of the construction site.
5. *Marketing costs*, such as advertising, sales commissions, and appraisal fees.

Recently, Sutton Construction purchased land for the purpose of developing 20 new single-family houses. The cost of the land was $250,000. Lot sizes vary from ¼ to ½ acre. The 20 lots occupy a total of eight acres.

General conditions costs for the project totaled $120,000. This $120,000 is common to all 20 units that were constructed on the building site.

Job 3, the third house built in the project, occupied a ¼-acre lot and had the following hard costs:

Direct materials	$ 8,000
Direct labor	6,000
Subcontractor	14,000

For Job 3, finance costs totaled $4,765 and marketing costs, $800. General conditions costs are allocated on the basis of units produced. Each unit's selling price is determined by adding 40 percent to the total of all costs.

Required:

1. Identify all production costs that are directly traceable to Job 3. Are all remaining production costs equivalent to overhead found in a manufacturing firm? Are there nonproduction costs that are directly traceable to the housing unit? Which ones?

2. Develop a job-order cost sheet for Job 3. What is the cost of building this house? Did you include finance and marketing costs in computing the unit cost? Why or why not? How did you determine the cost of land for Job 3?

3. Which of the five cost categories corresponds to overhead? Do you agree with the way in which this cost is allocated to individual housing units? Can you suggest a different allocation method?

4. Calculate the selling price of Job 3. Calculate the profit made on the sale of this unit.

5. Review the five cost categories. Describe how each category might be used in terms of data analytics—descriptive, diagnostic, predictive, or prescriptive. (See Exhibits 2.5 and 2.6, pp. 37, 40, for a review of data analytic types.)

Problem 5-28 Case on Job-Order Costing: Dental Practice

OBJECTIVE ◀ 3 4

Dr. Alyx Hemmings is employed by Mesa Dental. Mesa Dental recently installed a computerized job-order costing system to help monitor the cost of its services. Each patient is assigned a job number when he or she checks in with the receptionist. The receptionist-bookkeeper notes the time the patient enters the treatment area and when the patient leaves the area. This difference between the entry and exit times is the number of patient hours used and the direct labor time assigned to the dental assistant. (A dental assistant is constantly with the patient.) The direct labor time assigned to the dentist is 50 percent of the patient hours. (The dentist typically splits her time between two patients.)

The chart filled out by the dental assistant provides additional data that is entered into the computer. For example, the chart contains service codes that identify the nature of the treatment, such as whether the patient received a crown, a filling, or a root canal. The chart not only identifies the type of service but its level as well. For example, if a patient receives a filling, the dental assistant indicates (by a service-level code) whether the filling was one, two, three, or four surfaces. The service and service-level codes are used to determine the rate to be charged to the patient. The costs of providing different services and their levels also vary.

Costs assignable to a patient consist of materials, labor, and overhead. The types of materials used—and the quantity—are identified by the assistant and entered into the computer by the bookkeeper. Material prices are kept on file and accessed to provide the necessary cost information. Overhead is applied on the basis of patient hours. The rate used by Mesa Dental is $32 per patient hour. Direct labor cost is also computed using patient hours and the wage rates of the direct laborers. Dr. Hemmings is paid an average of $60 per hour for her services. Dental assistants are paid an average of $20 per hour. Given the treatment time, the software program calculates and assigns the labor cost for the dentist and her assistant; overhead cost is also assigned using the treatment time and the overhead rate.

The overhead rate does not include a charge for any X-rays. The X-Ray Department is separate from dental services; X-rays are billed and costed separately. The cost of an X-ray is $12 per film; the patient is charged $15 per film. If cleaning services are required, cleaning labor costs $35 per patient hour.

Glen Johnson, a patient (Job 267), spent 30 minutes in the treatment area and had a two-surface filling. He received two Novocaine shots and used three ampules of amalgam. The cost of the shots was $14 ($7 each). The cost of the amalgam was $6 per ampule. Other direct materials used are insignificant in amount and are included in the overhead rate. The rate charged to the patient for a two-surface filling is $110. One X-ray was taken.

Required:

1. Prepare a job-order cost sheet for Glen Johnson. What is the cost for providing a two-surface filling? What is the gross profit earned? Is the X-ray a direct cost of the service? Why are the X-rays costed separately from the overhead cost assignment?

2. Suppose that the patient time and associated patient charges are given for the following fillings:

	1-Surface	2-Surface	3-Surface	4-Surface
Time	20 minutes	30 minutes	40 minutes	50 minutes
Charge	$90	$110	$150	$175

Compute the cost for each filling and the gross profit for each type of filling. Assume that the cost of Novocaine is $14 for all fillings. Ampules of amalgam start at two and increase by one for each additional surface. Assume also that only one X-ray film is needed for all four cases. Does the increase in billing rate appear to be fair to the patient? Is it fair to the dental corporation?

OBJECTIVE 3 4

DATA ANALYTICS

Problem 5-29 Case on Job-Order Costing and Pricing Decisions

Nutratask, Inc., is a pharmaceutical manufacturer of amino-acid-chelated minerals and vitamin supplements. The company was founded in 1974 and is capable of performing all manufacturing functions, including packaging and laboratory functions. Currently, the company markets its products in the United States, Canada, Australia, Japan, and Belgium.

Mineral chelation enhances the mineral's availability to the body, making the mineral a more effective supplement. Most of the chelates supplied by Nutratask are in powder form, but the company has the capability to make tablets or capsules.

The production of all chelates follows a similar pattern. Upon receiving an order, the company's chemist prepares a load sheet (a bill of materials that specifies the product, the theoretical yield, and the quantities of materials that should be used). Once the load sheet is received by production, the materials are requisitioned and sent to the blending room. The chemicals and minerals are added in the order specified and blended together for two to eight hours, depending on the product. After blending, the mix is put on long trays and sent to the drying room, where it is allowed to dry until the moisture content is 7 to 9 percent. Drying time for most products is from one to three days.

After the product is dry, several small samples are taken and sent to a laboratory to be checked for bacterial level and to determine whether the product meets customer specifications. If the product is not fit for human consumption or if it fails to meet customer specifications, additional materials are added under the direction of the chemist to bring the product up to standard. Once the product passes inspection, it is ground into a powder of different meshes (particle sizes) according to customer specifications. The powder is then placed in heavy cardboard drums and shipped to the customer (or, if requested, put in tablet or capsule form and then shipped).

Since each order is customized to meet the special needs of its customers, Nutratask uses a job-order costing system. Recently, Nutratask received a request for a 300-kilogram order of potassium aspartate. The customer offered to pay $8.80/kg. Upon receiving the request and the customer's specifications, Lanny Smith, the marketing manager, requested a load sheet from the company's chemist. The load sheet prepared showed the following material requirements:

Material	Amount Required
Aspartic acid	195.00 kg
Citric acid	15.00 kg
K_2CO_3 (50%)	121.50 kg
Rice	30.00 kg

The theoretical yield is 300 kg.

Lanny also reviewed past jobs that were similar to the requested order and discovered that the expected direct labor time was 16 hours. The production workers at Nutratask earn an average of $12.50 per hour.

Purchasing sent Lanny a list of prices for the materials needed for the job.

Material	Price/kg
Aspartic acid	$5.75
Citric acid	2.02
K_2CO_3	4.64
Rice	0.43

Overhead is applied using a companywide rate based on direct labor dollars. The rate for the current period is 110 percent of direct labor dollars.

Whenever a customer requests a bid, Nutratask usually estimates the manufacturing costs of the job and then adds a markup of 30 percent. This markup varies depending on the competition and general economic conditions. Currently, the industry is thriving, and Nutratask is operating at capacity.

Required:

1. Prepare a job-order cost sheet for the proposed job. What is the expected per-unit cost? Should Nutratask accept the price offered by the prospective customer? Why or why not?
2. Suppose Nutratask and the prospective customer agree on a price of cost plus 30 percent. What is the gross profit that Nutratask expects to earn on the job?
3. Suppose that the actual costs of producing 300 kg of potassium aspartate were as follows:

Direct materials:	
Aspartic acid	$1,170.00
Citric acid	30.00
K_2CO_3	577.00
Rice	13.00
Total materials cost	$1,790.00
Direct labor	$ 225.00
Overhead	247.50

What is the actual per-unit cost? The bid price is based on expected costs. How much did Nutratask gain (or lose) because of the actual costs differing from the expected costs? Suggest some possible reasons why the actual costs differed from the projected costs.

4. Assume that the customer had agreed to pay *actual* manufacturing costs plus 30 percent. Suppose the actual costs are as described in Requirement 3 with one addition: an under-applied overhead variance is allocated to Cost of Goods Sold and spread across all jobs sold in proportion to their total cost (unadjusted cost of goods sold). Assume that the underapplied overhead cost added to the job in question is $30. Upon seeing the addition of the underapplied overhead in the itemized bill, the customer calls and complains about having to pay for Nutratask's inefficient use of overhead costs. If you were assigned to deal with this customer, what kind of response would you prepare? How would you explain and justify the addition of the underapplied overhead cost to the customer's bill?
5. Lanny reviewed past jobs that were similar to determine the expected cost per unit. Which of the data analytic types—descriptive, diagnostic, predictive, or prescriptive—is he using to get the per-unit cost? (See Exhibits 2.5 and 2.6, pp. 37, 40, for a review of data analytic types.)

RESEARCH ASSIGNMENT

5-30 Interview an accountant who works for a service organization that uses job-order costing. For a small firm, you may need to talk to an owner/manager. Examples are a funeral home, insurance firm, repair shop, medical clinic, and dental clinic. Write a paper that describes the job-order costing system used by the firm. Some of the questions that the paper should address are:

OBJECTIVE ◄ 1 2 3 4

a. What service(s) does the firm offer?
b. What document or procedure do you use to collect the costs of the services performed for each customer?
c. How do you assign the cost of direct labor to each job?
d. How do you assign overhead to individual jobs?
e. How do you assign the cost of direct materials to each job?
f. How do you determine what to charge each customer?
g. How do you account for a completed job?

As you write the paper, state how the service firm you investigated adapted the job-order accounting procedures described in this chapter to its particular circumstances. Were the differences justified? If so, explain why. Also, offer any suggestions you might have for improving the approach that you observed.

6

Process Costing

After studying this chapter, you should be able to:

1 Describe the basic characteristics of process costing, including cost flows, journal entries, and the cost of production report.

2 Describe process costing for settings without work-in-process inventories.

3 Describe process costing for settings with ending work-in-process inventories.

4 Prepare a departmental production report using the FIFO method.

5 Prepare a departmental production report using the weighted average method.

6 Prepare a departmental production report with transferred-in goods and changes in output measures.

7 Describe the basic features of operation costing.

8 Explain how spoilage is treated in a process-costing system.

Parmna/Shutterstock.com

PROCESS COSTING

at LafargeHolcim

LafargeHolcim is the largest producer of cement in the world. LafargeHolcim is headquartered in Switzerland and operates in 90 countries. The company has 380 plants with an annual production capacity of 386 million tons of cement.[1] Recently, LafargeHolcim has embarked on technological upgrades for hundreds of its plants found in more than 50 countries. These upgrades include the use of artificial intelligence, robotics, and preventive maintenance. The objective of LafargeHolcim's technological upgrade initiative is to obtain a 15 to 20 percent operational efficiency gain compared to a conventional cement plant.[2]

Cement production is a prominent example of process manufacturing. The manufacture of cement begins with the *extraction process*. In the extraction process, important raw materials such as limestone and shale (or clay) are obtained by blasting. Wheel loaders and large dump trucks are then used to load and transport these materials to the *crushing process*. In the crushing process, the mined rock is crushed to marble size. After crushing, the materials go through a *blending process* where the limestone, clays, and additional components are mixed to form a blended mix. This blended mix is then fed to a mill where it is ground into a fine powder (the *milling process*). After milling, the raw meal is sent to the *clinkerization process*. In the clinkerization process, the raw meal or kiln feed is preheated and then fed into a rotary kiln that uses temperatures of 1,300 to 1,400°C. The high temperature converts the kiln feed into clinkers. Clinkers are then sent to the last production process, *final grinding*, where clinkers are ground into a powder that we all know as cement.

Although LafargeHolcim needs to understand the preceding processes to increase efficiency, the company also needs to know how much it costs to produce its product to measure the value of any efficiency gains. Knowing how much it costs to produce cement involves more than what might seem apparent at first glance. For one thing, the output of each process is physically different. Moreover, even if the output of each process is measured by weight, the *amount* of product can change from one process to the next because of adding materials and losing materials through heating and chemical reactions. Furthermore, the cost of the final product must include the cost of producing the output of each process. How those costs are transferred from one process to the next to produce the final product cost is a critical issue. Additionally, at a given point in time, there will be product in process in each of the processes. LafargeHolcim must have a means to determine how much of a period's cost is assigned to the work in process (for each process) and how much of that cost belongs to the actual finished goods produced during that period. Clearly, process costing is a fundamental costing model that must be understood.

1 Janet Mutegi, "World's 10 Largest Cement Companies" (September 2, 2019), https://www.constructionkenya
.com/5390/largest-cement-companies-world/, accessed May 20, 2020.
2 "LafargeHolcim launch 'Plants of Tomorrow,' " *AggNet* (July 9, 2019), https://www.agg-net.com/news
/lafargeholcim-launch-plants-of-tomorrow, accessed May 25, 2020.

BASIC OPERATIONAL AND COST CONCEPTS

LafargeHolcim illustrates the nature of process manufacturing and reveals the complexity of process costing. The ultimate objective of process costing for LafargeHolcim is to determine how much it costs to produce cement. Yet there are vast amounts of data involved—tons of limestone, tons of shale or clay, tons of crushed limestone, fleets of loaders and trucks, hundreds of workers and managers, buildings, rotary kilns, fuel for kilns, material additives, and so forth. For some processes, the amount of output coming out will be greater than the output transferred in from a prior process. For others, such as the clinkerization process, the output will be less than the amount transferred in from the milling process. Clearly, a data analytic model is needed to convert all these data into usable information. Each process must define and measure its output. Costs of resources for the process must also be measured. Unit costs must be calculated. Goods completed and goods in process must be valued. How all this is done is described by the data analytic model known as *process costing*.

To understand a process-costing system, it is necessary to understand the underlying operational system. An operational process system is characterized by a large number of homogeneous products passing through a series of *processes*, where each process is responsible for one or more operations that bring a product one step closer to completion. Thus, a **process** is a series of activities (operations) that are linked to perform a specific objective. Bienestar Company, a manufacturer of a wide variety of over-the-counter medications and vitamins, uses process costing in all of its plants. For example, its Wichita plant produces an antihistamine and uses three processes: blending, encapsulating, and bottling. The blending process consists of four linked activities: selecting, sifting, measuring, and mixing. Direct laborers select the appropriate chemicals (active and inert ingredients) and sift the materials to remove any foreign substances, and then the materials are *measured* and *combined* in a mixer to blend them thoroughly in the prescribed proportions.

In each process, materials, labor, and overhead inputs may be needed (typically in equal amounts for each unit of product). Upon completion of a particular process, the partially completed goods are transferred to another process. For example, when the mix prepared by the Blending Department is finished, the resulting mixture is sent to the encapsulating process. The encapsulating process consists of four linked activities: loading, filling, sealing, and drying. Initially, the blend and a gelatin mass are loaded into a machine. Two thin ribbons of gel are formed, one on each side of the machine. The mix is fed to a positive displacement pump, which inserts an accurate dose between the two ribbons of gel. The two ribbons are then sealed together using heat and pressure. Finally, the capsules are placed in tumble dryers and then conveyed to a drying room. Once sufficiently dry, they can be sent to bottling. The final process is bottling. It has four linked activities: loading, counting, capping, and packing. Capsules are transferred to this department, loaded into a hopper, and automatically counted into bottles. Filled bottles are mechanically capped, and direct labor then manually packs the correct number of bottles into boxes that are transferred to the warehouse. Exhibit 6.1 summarizes the operational process system for antihistamine manufacturing.

Cost Flows

The cost flows for a process-costing system are basically similar to those of a job-order costing system. There are two key differences. First, a job-order costing system accumulates production costs by job, and a process-costing system accumulates production costs by process. Second, for manufacturing firms, the job-order costing system uses a single work-in-process (WIP) account, while the process-costing system has a WIP account for every process. Exhibit 6.2 illustrates the first key difference: the different approaches to cost accumulation. Notice that job systems assign manufacturing costs to jobs (which act as subsidiary work-in-process accounts) and transfer these costs directly to the finished goods account when the job is completed. When units are finished for a process, manufacturing costs are transferred from one process department's

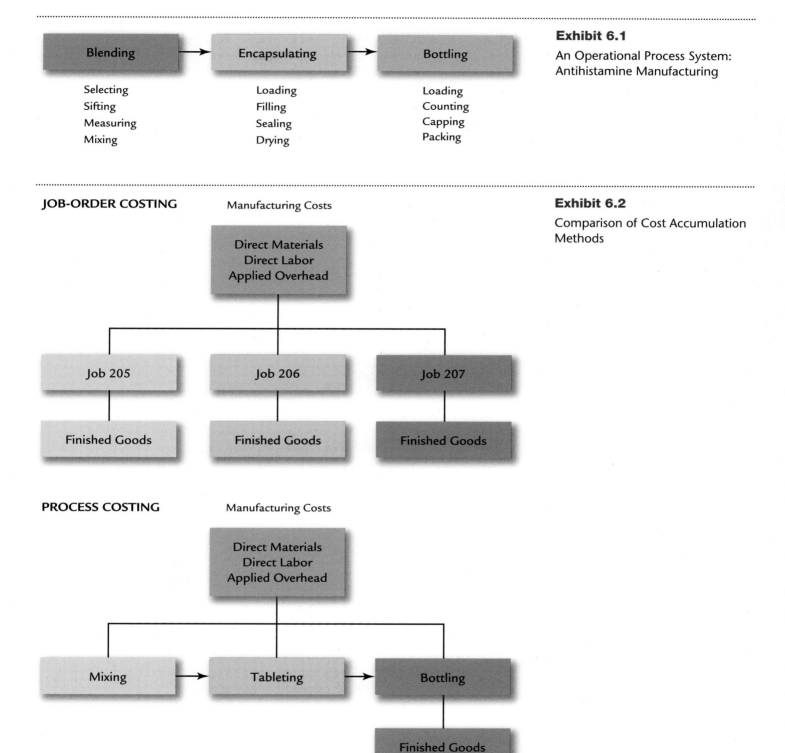

Exhibit 6.1

An Operational Process System: Antihistamine Manufacturing

Exhibit 6.2

Comparison of Cost Accumulation Methods

account to the next. A cost transferred from a prior process to a subsequent process is referred to as a **transferred-in cost**. The last process transfers the costs to Finished Goods. **Example 6.1** reviews the rationale for process cost flows, shows how the cost flows are calculated (without WIP inventories), and shows how journal entries are made.

Example 6.1 illustrates that when goods are completed in one process, they are transferred with their costs to the subsequent process. Exhibit 6.3, on page 267, illustrates this transfer of costs using T-accounts. For example, Blending transferred $15,000 of its costs to Encapsulating, and Encapsulating (after further processing) transferred $22,500 of costs to Bottling. These transferred-in are (from the viewpoint of the process receiving them) a type of direct materials cost. This is true because the subsequent process receives a partially completed unit that must be subjected to additional manufacturing activity, which includes more direct labor, more overhead, and, in some cases, additional direct materials. For example, the second journal entry for the Encapsulating Department reveals that $7,500 of additional manufacturing costs were added after receiving the transferred-in goods from Blending. Thus, while Blending sees the active and inert powders as a combination of direct materials, direct labor, and overhead costs, Encapsulating sees only the powder—a direct material, costing $15,000.

EXAMPLE 6.1

The HOW and WHY of Cost Flows: Process Costing

Information:

Bienestar's Wichita plant produced 10,000 bottles of antihistamine with the following costs:

	Blending Process	Encapsulating Process	Bottling Process
Direct materials	$7,500	$1,400	$3,000
Direct labor	3,500	2,700	2,000
Applied overhead	4,000	3,400	2,500

> **Why:**
>
> In process costing, each department (process) accumulates its costs in a WIP account. As the work is finished in a process, the partially completed units and all their associated costs are transferred to the next process. Costs are transferred by debiting the WIP account of the process receiving the units while the WIP account of the transferring department is credited.

Required:

1. Calculate the costs transferred out of each department. Assume no WIP inventories.

2. Prepare the journal entries corresponding to these transfers. Also, prepare the journal entry for Encapsulating that reflects the costs added to the transferred-in goods received from Blending.

3. *What if* the Blending Department had an ending WIP of $5,000? Calculate the cost transferred out and provide the journal entry that would reflect this transfer. What is the effect on finished goods calculated in the first requirement, assuming the other two departments have no ending WIP?

Solution:

1.

	Blending	Encapsulating	Bottling
Direct materials	$ 7,500	$ 1,400	$ 3,000
Direct labor	3,500	2,700	2,000
Applied overhead	4,000	3,400	2,500
Costs added	$15,000	$ 7,500	$ 7,500
Costs transferred in	0	15,000	22,500
Costs transferred out	$15,000	$22,500	$30,000

2. Transfer entries:

EXAMPLE 6.1

(Continued)

Work in Process—Encapsulating	15,000	
Work in Process—Blending		15,000
Work in Process—Bottling	22,500	
Work in Process—Encapsulating		22,500
Finished Goods	30,000	
Work in Process—Bottling		30,000

Cost-added entry (Encapsulating only):

Work in Process—Encapsulating	7,500	
Materials		1,400
Payroll		2,700
Overhead Control		3,400

3. The cost transferred out would be $10,000 ($15,000 – $5,000). The journal entry is:

Work in Process—Encapsulating	10,000	
Work in Process—Blending		10,000

Finished goods is reduced by $5,000.

Although a process-costing system has more work-in-process accounts than a job-order costing system, it is a simpler and less expensive system to operate. In a process-costing system, there are no individual jobs, no job-order cost sheets, and no need to track materials to individual jobs. Materials are tracked to processes, but there are far fewer processes than jobs. Further, there is no need to use time tickets for assigning labor costs to processes. Since laborers typically work their entire shift within a particular process, no detailed tracking of labor is needed. In fact, in many firms, labor costs are such a small percentage of total process costs that they are simply combined with overhead costs, creating a conversion cost category.

The Production Report

In process-costing systems, costs are accumulated by department for a period of time. The **production report** is the document that summarizes the manufacturing activity that takes place in a process department for a given period of time. The production report also serves as a source document for transferring costs from the work-in-process account of a prior department to the work-in-process account of a subsequent department. In the department that handles the final stage of processing, it serves as a source document for transferring costs from the work-in-process account to the finished goods account.

A production report provides information about the physical units processed in a department and also about the manufacturing costs associated with them. Thus, a production report is divided into a unit information section and a cost information section. The unit information section has two major subdivisions: (1) units to account for and (2) units accounted for.

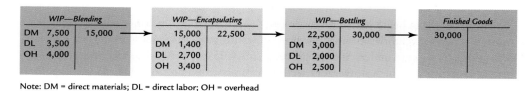

WIP—Blending		WIP—Encapsulating		WIP—Bottling		Finished Goods
DM 7,500	15,000 →	15,000	22,500 →	22,500	30,000 →	30,000
DL 3,500		DM 1,400		DM 3,000		
OH 4,000		DL 2,700		DL 2,000		
		OH 3,400		OH 2,500		

Note: DM = direct materials; DL = direct labor; OH = overhead

Exhibit 6.3

Process Cost Flows Illustrated Using T-Accounts: No Ending WIP

Exhibit 6.4

Basic Features of a Process-Costing System

1. Homogeneous units pass through a series of similar processes.
2. Each unit in each process receives a similar dose of manufacturing costs.
3. Manufacturing costs are accumulated by a process for a given period of time.
4. There is a work-in-process account for each process.
5. Manufacturing cost flows and the associated journal entries are generally similar to job-order costing.
6. The departmental production report is the key document for tracking manufacturing activity and costs.
7. Unit costs are computed by dividing the departmental costs of the period by the output of the period.

Similarly, the cost information section has two major subdivisions: (1) costs to account for and (2) costs accounted for. In summary, a production report traces the flow of units through a department, identifies the costs charged to the department, shows the computation of unit costs, and reveals the disposition of the department's costs for the reporting period.

Unit Costs

A key input to the cost of production report is unit costs. In principle, calculating unit costs in a process-costing system is very simple. First, measure the manufacturing costs for a process department for a given period of time. Second, measure the output of the process department for the same period of time. Finally, the unit cost for a process is computed by dividing the costs of the period by the output of the period. With the exception of the final process, the unit cost calculated is for a *partially completed unit*. The unit cost for the final process is the cost of the fully completed product. Exhibit 6.4 summarizes the basic features of a process-costing system.

While the basic features seem relatively simple, the actual details of process-costing systems are somewhat more complicated. A major source of difficulty is dealing with how costs and output of the period are defined when calculating the unit cost of each process. The presence of significant work-in-process inventories complicates the cost and output definitions needed for the unit cost calculation. For example, partially finished units in the beginning work-in-process inventory carry with them work and costs associated with a prior period. Yet, these units must be finished this period, and they will also have current-period costs and work associated with them. A fundamental question is how to deal with the prior-period costs and work. Another important and related complicating factor is nonuniform application of production costs (i.e., units half completed may not have half of each input needed). Much of our discussion of process-costing systems will deal with the approaches taken to deal with these complicating factors.

Perhaps it is best to begin with a discussion of process costing in settings where there are no work-in-process inventories. Seeing how process costing works without work-in-process inventories makes it easier to understand the procedures that are needed to deal with work-in-process inventories. Study of the no-inventory setting is also justified because many firms operate in such a setting.

 OBJECTIVE 2

Describe process costing for settings without work-in-process inventories.

PROCESS COSTING WITH NO WORK-IN-PROCESS INVENTORIES

Perhaps it is best to begin with a discussion of process costing in settings where there are no work-in-process inventories. Seeing how process costing works without work-in-process inventories makes it easier to understand the procedures that are needed to deal with work-in-process inventories. Study of the no-inventory setting is also justified because many service organizations and just-in-time (JIT) manufacturing firms operate in such a setting.

Service Organizations

Services that are basically homogeneous and repetitively produced can take advantage of a process-costing approach. Processing tax returns, sorting mail by zip code, check processing in a bank, changing oil, air travel between Dallas and New York City, checking baggage, and laundering and pressing shirts are all examples of homogeneous services that are repetitively produced. Although many services consist of a single process, some services require a sequence of processes. Air travel between Dallas and New York City, for example, involves the following sequence of services: reservation, ticketing, baggage checking and seat confirmation, flight, and baggage delivery and pickup. Although services cannot be stored, it is possible for firms engaged in service production to have work-in-process inventories. For example, a batch of tax returns can be partially completed at the end of a period. However, many services are provided in such a way that there are no work-in-process inventories. Teeth cleaning, funerals, surgical operations, sonograms, and carpet cleaning are a few examples where work-in-process inventories would be virtually nonexistent. **Example 6.2** illustrates the costing of services using a process-costing approach with no ending work in process (EWIP).

The calculation in Example 6.2 illustrates the process-costing principle, a concept that applies in settings that are more complicated.

EXAMPLE 6.2

The HOW and WHY of Process Costing: Services with No WIP Inventories

Information:
Warin Wecare specializes in 3D pregnancy sonograms. During the month of April, Warin had the following cost and output information:

Direct materials	$ 4,000
Direct labor	$ 8,000
Overhead	$16,000
Number of sonograms	400

Why:
Theoretically, the current-period unit cost for process costing should use only costs and output that belong to the period. This is expressed as the **process-costing principle**: *To calculate the period's unit cost, divide the costs of the period by the output of the period.*

Required:

1. Calculate the cost per sonogram for April.

2. Calculate the cost of services sold for April.

3. *What if* Warin found a way to reduce material costs by 50 percent? How would this affect the profit per sonogram?

Solution:

1. Unit cost = Costs of the period/Output of the period = $28,000/400 = $70 per sonogram

2. Cost of services sold = Unit cost × Output produced = $70 × 400 = $28,000

3. Reduction in unit cost (profit change) = Savings of the period/Output of the period = $2,000/400 = $5 per sonogram increase in profitability

JIT Manufacturing Firms

Many firms have adopted a just-in-time (JIT) manufacturing approach. The overall thrust of JIT manufacturing is supplying a product that is needed, when it is needed, and in the quantity that is needed. JIT manufacturing emphasizes continuous improvement and the elimination of waste. Since carrying unnecessary inventory is viewed as wasteful, JIT firms strive to minimize inventories. *Successful* implementation of JIT policies tends to reduce work-in-process inventories to insignificant levels. Furthermore, the way manufacturing is carried out in a JIT firm usually is structured so that process costing can be used to determine product costs. Essentially, work cells are created that produce a product or subassembly from start to finish.

Costs are collected by cell for a period of time, and output for the cell is measured for the same period. Unit costs are computed by dividing the costs of the period by output of the period (following the process-costing principle). The computation is identical to that used by service organizations, as illustrated by the sonogram example in Example 6.2. Why? Because there is no ambiguity concerning what costs belong to the period and how output is measured. One of the objectives of JIT manufacturing is simplification. Keep this in mind as you study the process-costing requirements of manufacturing firms that carry work-in-process inventories. The difference between the two settings is impressive and demonstrates one of the significant benefits of JIT.

The Role of Activity-Based Costing

Activity-based costing (ABC) can have a role in process settings provided multiple products are being produced. The role of ABC for both cellular and independent process manufacturing is to assign overhead shared by processes or cells to the individual processes and cells. Since each process (cell) is dedicated to the production of a single product, the overhead located within the cell belongs exclusively to the product. However, activities may be shared by processes (cells) such as moving materials, inspecting output, ordering materials, and so on. Activity rates are used to assign overhead to individual processes, and this overhead is assigned to process output using the usual approaches.

OBJECTIVE 3

Describe process costing for settings with ending work-in-process inventories.

PROCESS COSTING WITH ENDING WORK-IN-PROCESS INVENTORIES

Whenever work-in-process inventories are present, the calculations for process costing become more complicated. The presence of work-in-process inventories creates a need to define more carefully what is meant by a period's output. By definition, ending work in process is not complete. Thus, a unit completed and transferred out during the period is not identical (or equivalent) to one in ending work-in-process inventory, and the cost attached to the two units should not be the same. In computing the unit cost, the output of the period must be defined, taking into consideration both completed units and partially completed units. For example, consider Richardson Testing Center, a medical laboratory (a service organization) that serves a metropolitan area and several of its outlying communities. The laboratory has several departments, one of which specializes in CBC (complete blood count) tests. Physicians in the region send blood samples to the laboratory. The CBC Department runs the test and inputs the resulting data into the computer so that a statistical analysis can be conducted and a report prepared. During the month of January, 30,000 blood tests were run and analyzed, and reports for completed tests were sent to the referring physicians. These completed tests ("units") were finished and transferred out by mailing the results of the tests to the physicians. Because of the holiday season, the CBC Department rarely has any work in process at the beginning of January. However, at the end of January, there were units (blood samples) that were worked on but not finished, producing an ending work-in-process inventory of 6,000 units, 25 percent complete with respect to all production costs in ending work in process. What is the output in January? 30,000 units? 36,000 units? If we say 30,000 units, then we ignore the effort expended on the units in ending work in process. Furthermore, the production costs incurred in January belong both to the units completed and to the partially completed units in ending work in process. On the other hand, if we say 36,000 units, we ignore the fact that the 6,000 units in ending work in process are only partially completed. Somehow, output must be measured so that it reflects the effort expended on both completed and partially completed units.

Physical Flow and Equivalent Units

The solution is to calculate equivalent units of output. **Equivalent units of output** are the complete units that could have been produced given the total amount of productive effort expended for the period under consideration. Determining equivalent units of output for transferred-out units is easy; a unit would not be transferred out unless it were complete. Thus, every transferred-out unit is an equivalent unit. Units remaining in ending work-in-process inventory, however, are not complete. Someone in production must "eyeball" ending work in process to estimate its degree of completion.

In reality, how the completion rate is calculated is not well documented. In a survey of large Brazilian companies, only about 26 percent indicated that they used the concepts of completion rates and degree of completion. Interestingly, the accounting department was identified as the most frequently specified unit responsible for determining completion levels, followed by production and manufacturing. The survey did not reveal any objective method used for calculating completion levels.[3]

Knowing the physical units in beginning and ending work in process, their stage of completion, and the units completed and transferred out provides essential information for the computation of the period's equivalent units of output. Thus, the first two steps in building a production report for process costing are (1) the preparation of a **physical flow schedule**, which provides an analysis of the physical flow units; and (2) the calculation of the period's equivalent units. These two steps make up the unit information section of the report. **Example 6.3** illustrates these first two steps.

EXAMPLE 6.3

The HOW and WHY of Physical Flow Analysis and Equivalent Units: EWIP Only

Information:
Richardson Testing Center had the following data for CBC production for January (output is measured in number of tests):

Units, beginning work in process	—
Units started	36,000
Units completed	30,000
Units, ending work in process (25% complete)	6,000

---

3 Reinaldo Guerreiro, Edgard Br. Cornachione, and Armando Cartelli, "Equivalent Units of Production: A New Look at an Old Issue," *Managerial Auditing Journal*, Vol. 21, No. 3 (2006): 303–316.

EXAMPLE 6.3

(*Continued*)

> **Why:**
> A physical flow schedule shows the units to account for and what happened to them. The equivalent units schedule measures the output of the period. A fully completed unit is counted as a unit of output. Output for a unit in ending work in process is counted by its degree of completion. Units completed plus the equivalent units in EWIP (Degree of completion × Units in EWIP) provide a total measure of output for the period.

Required:

1. Prepare a physical flow schedule.

2. Prepare an equivalent units schedule. Explain why output is measured in equivalent units.

3. *What if* EWIP is 75 percent complete? How would this change affect the physical flow schedule? The equivalent units schedule?

Solution:

1. Units started and completed = Units completed Units, BWIP

$$= 30,000 - 0 = 30,000$$

Units started = Units, EWIP + Units started and completed

$$= 6,000 + 30,000 = 36,000$$

Physical flow schedule:		
Units to account for:		
Units in BWIP		0
Units started		36,000
Total units to account for		36,000
Units accounted for:		
Units completed:		
From BWIP	0	
Started and completed	30,000	30,000
Units in EWIP		6,000
Total units accounted for		36,000

2.

Equivalent units schedule:	
Units completed	30,000
Units in EWIP × Fraction complete:	
6,000 × 0.25	1,500
Equivalent units	31,500

Output for the period must take into consideration the work done on units fully completed as well as the work done on partially completed units. Thus, equivalent units become the relevant output measure.

3. Changing the degree of completion does not affect the physical flow schedule. This schedule measures the flow of the units, regardless of their stage of completion. However, the equivalent units' schedule is affected. There would now be 4,500 (0.75 × 6,000) equivalent units for EWIP, increasing the total output for the period to 34,500.

Calculating Unit Costs, Assigning Costs to Inventories, and Reconciliation

The physical flow and equivalent units schedules are prerequisites to computing the unit cost. Unit cost information and information from the output schedule are both needed to value goods transferred out and goods in ending work in process. Finally, the costs in beginning work in process and the costs incurred during the current period should equal the total costs assigned to goods transferred out and to goods in ending work in process (**cost reconciliation**). Thus, the final three steps needed for a production report are (3) unit cost calculation, (4) valuation of inventories, and (5) cost reconciliation. These last three steps make up the cost information section of the production report. **Example 6.4** illustrates these final three steps.

EXAMPLE 6.4

The HOW and WHY of Unit Cost, Inventory Valuation, and Cost Reconciliation: EWIP Only

Information:
For the month of January, Richardson Testing Center incurred total production costs of $787,500 for processing CBC tests and had the equivalent units schedule:

Units completed	30,000
Units in EWIP × Fraction complete:	
6,000 × 0.25	1,500
Equivalent units	31,500

Why:
Unit cost is calculated by dividing the cost of the period by the output of the period. The cost of goods (services) transferred out is the unit cost multiplied by the units completed. The cost of EWIP is the unit cost multiplied by the *equivalent units* found in EWIP. Reconciliation is making sure that the costs assigned to goods or services completed and EWIP are equal to the costs to account for.

Required:

1. Calculate the cost of preparing one CBC test for January.

2. Assign costs to tests completed and to EWIP, and then do a cost reconciliation.

3. *What if* the costs assigned to tests completed and EWIP total $800,000? What are possible reasons for the discrepancy between the costs assigned and the costs to account for?

Solution:

1. Unit cost = $787,500/31,500 = $25 per test

2. Costs assigned:

Tests completed ($25 × 30,000)	$750,000
EWIP ($25 × 1,500)	37,500
Total assigned	$787,500

Reconciliation: The costs assigned equal the costs to account for of $787,500.

3. Since the $800,000 is different than the costs to account for, an error has been made somewhere. Possibilities include calculating the wrong output, using the wrong costs to calculate the unit cost, using the wrong number to calculate the units transferred out or to value EWIP, and simple arithmetic errors.

The Five Steps of the Production Report

Recall that the cost of production report has a unit information section and a cost information section. The unit information section is concerned with output measurement, and the cost information section is concerned with identifying all costs and accounting for them.

As we have shown with the Richardson Testing Center example, five steps must be followed in preparing a cost of production report:

1. Analysis of the flow of physical units
2. Calculation of the period's output (equivalent units)
3. Computation of unit cost
4. Valuation of inventories (goods transferred out and ending work in process)
5. Cost reconciliation

The method and format for preparing this cost of production report are shown in **Example 6.5**.

EXAMPLE 6.5

The HOW and WHY of a Production Report

Information:

Steps 1–5 of the Richardson Testing Center example, found in Examples 6.3 and 6.4.

> **Why:**
> The production report summarizes process manufacturing and costing activity for a given period of time. It is the counterpart of the job-order cost sheet and acts as a subsidiary to the WIP account. The unit information section provides the physical flow and equivalent units schedules. The cost information section shows the unit cost calculation as well as the amounts assigned to goods transferred out and ending work in process, and provides a cost reconciliation.

Required:

1. What is the purpose of a production report?

2. Prepare a production report for Richardson.

3. *What if* the degree of completion is 75 percent for ending work in process? Explain how this would change the production report.

Solution:

1. Since a production report summarizes the manufacturing and costing activity for a given period, it provides information for decision making and control. For example, successive production reports can be used to measure trends in unit costs.

2.

Richardson Testing Center
Production Report for January

UNIT INFORMATION		
Units to account for:		
Units in beginning work in process	0	
Units started	36,000	
Total units to account for	36,000	
	Physical Flow	*Equivalent Units*
Units accounted for:		
Units completed	30,000	30,000
Units in ending work in process (25% complete)	6,000	1,500
Total units accounted for	36,000	
Work completed		31,500

EXAMPLE 6.5

(*Continued*)

COST INFORMATION	
Costs to account for:	
Beginning work in process	$ 0
Incurred during the period	787,500
Total costs to account for	$787,500
Divided by equivalent units	÷ 31,500
Cost per equivalent unit	$ 25
Costs accounted for:	
Goods transferred out ($25 × 30,000)	$750,000
Ending work in process ($25 × 1,500)	37,500
Total costs accounted for	$787,500

3. If the degree of completion is 75 percent, the equivalent units in EWIP are 4,500, changing the total equivalent units to 34,500. This, in turn, will change the unit cost from $25 to $22.83 (rounded). The new unit cost will then be used to calculate a new cost of goods transferred out and EWIP.

Nonuniform Application of Productive Inputs

Up to this point, we have assumed that work in process being 25 percent complete meant that 25 percent of direct materials, direct labor, and overhead needed to complete the process have been used and that another 75 percent are needed to finish the units. In other words, we have assumed that the productive inputs are applied uniformly as the manufacturing process unfolds.

Assuming uniform application of conversion costs (direct labor and overhead) is not unreasonable. Direct labor input is usually needed throughout the process, and overhead is normally assigned on the basis of direct labor hours. Direct materials, on the other hand, are not as likely to be applied uniformly. In many instances, direct materials are added at either the beginning or the end of the process.

For example, consider the Richardson Testing Center example. It is more likely that materials (e.g., special chemicals) would be added at the beginning of the process rather than uniformly throughout the process. If so, then ending work in process that is 25 percent complete with respect to conversion inputs would be 100 percent complete with respect to material inputs.

Different percentage completion figures for productive inputs at the same stage of completion pose a problem for the calculation of equivalent units. Fortunately, the solution is relatively simple. Equivalent units calculations are done for each category of input. Thus, there are equivalent units calculated for *each* category of direct materials and for conversion costs. Unit costs are also calculated for each category, with the total unit cost being the sum of the categories. **Example 6.6** summarizes the rationale and shows how the calculations are done for multiple inputs.

Information:
For the CBC blood tests, Richardson adds materials at the beginning of the process. Conversion costs are added uniformly. For January, EWIP is 25 percent complete with respect to conversion costs. The following information is provided for January:

EXAMPLE 6.6

(Continued)

Physical flow schedule:

Units to account for:		
Units in BWIP		0
Units started		36,000
Total units to account for		36,000
Units accounted for:		
Units completed:		
From BWIP	0	
Started and completed	30,000	30,000
Units in EWIP		6,000
Total units accounted for		36,000

	Inputs	
	Direct Materials	**Conversion**
Costs	$72,000	$715,500

> **Why:**
> If materials are added at the beginning or end of a process, then there will be different completion percentages for materials and conversion costs. Typically, conversion costs are added uniformly and materials are added at discrete points in the production process. Assuming conversion is less than 100 percent at a given point in time, then materials added at the beginning are 100 percent complete and materials added at the end are 0 percent complete. Accordingly, equivalent units are calculated for each type of input, and a unit cost is calculated for each input. To calculate the unit cost for each category also requires that costs be accounted for by input category. The unit cost is the sum of the input category unit costs.

Required:

1. Calculate the equivalent units for each input category.

2. Calculate the unit cost for each category and in total.

3. ***What if*** materials are also added at the end of the process, costing $30,000? Let materials added at the beginning be Type 1 materials and those at the end be Type 2 materials. Calculate the new unit cost.

Solution:

1.	**Direct Materials**	**Conversion**
Units completed	30,000	30,000
Units EWIP × Fraction complete:		
6,000 × 100%	6,000	
6,000 × 25%	—	1,500
Equivalent units	36,000	31,500

2. Unit direct materials cost = $72,000/36,000 = $2.00

Unit conversion cost = $715,500/31,500 = $22.71 (rounded)

Total unit cost = Unit direct materials cost + Unit conversion cost = $2.00 + $22.71 = $24.71

EXAMPLE 6.6

(*Continued*)

3. Now there would be another materials category and a third column of equivalent units:

	Direct Materials (Type 2)
Units completed	30,000
Units EWIP × Fraction complete: 6,000 × 0%	0
Equivalent units	30,000

Unit materials cost (Type 2) = $30,000/30,000 = $1.00, and the total unit cost would now become $25.71.

Beginning Work-in-Process Inventories

The Richardson example only showed the effect of ending work-in-process inventories on output measurement. The presence of beginning work-in-process inventories also complicates output measurement. Since many firms have partially completed units in process at the beginning of a period, there is a clear need to address the issue. The work done on these partially completed units represents prior-period work, and the costs assigned to them are prior-period costs. In computing a *current-period* unit cost for a department, two approaches have evolved for dealing with the prior-period output and prior-period costs found in beginning work in process: the *first-in, first-out (FIFO) costing method* and the *weighted average method*. Both methods follow the same five steps described for preparing a cost of production report. The two methods, however, usually only produce the same result for Step 1. The two methods are best illustrated by example. The FIFO method is discussed first, followed by a discussion of the weighted average method.

Big Data

Big data can improve the yield (good output) and increase quality for process manufacturers. Large historical process datasets can be analyzed using such tools as data visualizations, correlation analyses, significance testing, and artificial neural networks to reveal insights that allow significant process improvements. Using advanced statistical analyses, one of the leading biopharmaceutical companies managed to increase the good output (yield) of one its vaccines by more than 50 percent and, in the process, produced an annual savings of $5 to $10 million (and this was for just one of its hundreds of products).[4]

REAL-WORLD EXAMPLE

FIFO COSTING METHOD

The process-costing principle requires that the costs of the period be divided by the output of the period. Thus, theoretically, only *current*-period costs and *current*-period output should be used to compute *current*-period unit costs. The FIFO method attempts to follow this theoretical guideline. Under the **FIFO costing method**, the equivalent units and manufacturing costs in beginning work in process are *excluded* from the current-period unit cost calculation. Thus, the FIFO method recognizes that the work and costs carried over from the prior period legitimately belong to that period.

OBJECTIVE 4

Prepare a departmental production report using the FIFO method.

---

4 Eric Auschitzky, Markus Hammer, and Agesan Rajagopaul, "How Big Data Can Improve Manufacturing," July, 2014, http://www.mckinsey.com/business-functions/operations/our-insights/how-big-data-can-improve-manufacturing (accessed April 23, 2016).

Since FIFO excludes prior-period work and costs, we need to create two categories of completed units. FIFO assumes that units in beginning work in process are completed first, before any new units are started. Thus, one category of completed units is that of beginning work-in-process units. The second category is for those units started *and* completed during the current period.

These two categories of completed units are needed in the FIFO method so that each category can be costed correctly. For the units started and completed, the unit cost is obtained by dividing total current manufacturing costs by the current-period equivalent output. However, for the beginning work-in-process units, the total associated manufacturing costs are the sum of the prior-period costs plus the costs incurred in the current period to finish the units. Thus, the unit cost is this total cost divided by the units in beginning work in process.

To illustrate the FIFO method, let's return to the Wichita plant of Bienestar Company, a plant that mass produces a widely used antihistamine medication (see discussion on page 264). Recall that this plant uses three processes: blending, encapsulating, and bottling. Given the May data for the plant's blending operation, the five steps of the FIFO method can be illustrated. The first two steps concern unit-level information and are shown in **Example 6.7**. Steps 3 through 5 are concerned with cost information and are illustrated in **Example 6.8**.

EXAMPLE 6.7

The HOW and WHY of Physical Flow Analysis and Equivalent Units: FIFO Method

Information:

The production of Bienestar's antihistamine product begins in the Blending Department. All materials are added at the *beginning* of the blending process. Output is measured in ounces. The production data for May are as follows:

Production:	
Units in process, May 1, 70% complete*	15,000
Units completed and transferred out	90,000
Units in process, May 31, 40% complete*	30,000

*With respect to conversion costs.

> **Why:**
> The physical flow schedule traces the units in process regardless of their stage of completion and provides the information needed for preparing the equivalent units schedule. FIFO uses only current output to calculate the current-period unit cost. Thus, FIFO treats the work (equivalent output) in BWIP as belonging to the prior period and only counts the work (equivalent output for each input) done this period as part of this period's output.

Required:

1. Prepare a physical flow schedule for May (Step 1).

2. Prepare an equivalent units schedule for May using the FIFO method (Step 2).

3. *What if* 80 percent of the materials were added at the beginning of the process and 20 percent were added at the end of the process (assume the same type of materials)? How many equivalent units of materials would there be?

Solution:

1. First, two calculations are needed:

$$\text{Units started and completed} = \text{Units completed} - \text{Units, BWIP}$$
$$= 90,000 - 15,000 = 75,000$$
$$\text{Units started} = \text{Units started and completed} + \text{Units, EWIP}$$
$$= 75,000 + 30,000 = 105,000$$

EXAMPLE 6.7

(*Continued*)

Step 1: Physical Flow Schedule: Blending Department

Units to account for:		
Units, beginning work in process (70% complete)		15,000
Units started during May		105,000
Total units to account for		120,000
Units accounted for:		
Units completed and transferred out:		
Started and completed	75,000	
From beginning work in process	15,000	90,000
Units in ending work in process (40% complete)		30,000
Total units accounted for		120,000

2.

Step 2: Equivalent Units Schedule: Blending Department

	Direct Materials	Conversion Costs
Units started and completed	75,000	75,000
Add: Units in beginning work in process × Percentage complete:		
15,000 × 0% direct materials	—	
15,000 × 30% conversion costs		4,500
Add: Units in ending work in process × Percentage complete:		
30,000 × 100% direct materials	30,000	—
30,000 × 40% conversion costs	—	12,000
Equivalent units of output	105,000	91,500

3. Equivalent units of materials = 75,000 + (0.20 × 15,000) + (0.80 × 30,000) = 102,000

Example 6.8 takes the unit information found in Step 2 of Example 6.7 and combines it with costs incurred in May to calculate a unit cost for May. This unit cost is then used to value ending work in process and calculate the cost of goods transferred out to the Encapsulating Department.

EXAMPLE 6.8

The HOW and WHY of Unit Cost and Cost Assignment: FIFO

Information:
The equivalent units schedule of Example 6.7 (Step 2) and the following cost data from the Wichita plant's Blending Department for the month of May:

Costs:	
Work in process, May 1:	
Direct materials	$ 1,500
Conversion costs	525
Total work in process	$ 2,025
Current costs:	
Direct materials	$18,900
Conversion costs	4,575
Total current costs	$23,475

EXAMPLE 6.8

(Continued)

> **Why:**
> Under FIFO, the costs in BWIP from the prior period are excluded in calculating the unit cost. The unit cost is the costs of the period divided by the output of the period. *The cost of units transferred out is the sum of three different items:* (1) the costs incurred in the prior period found in BWIP, (2) the costs of completing the BWIP incurred this period, and (3) the costs of the units started and completed this period. Finally, the ending value of EWIP must also be determined.

Required:

1. Calculate the unit cost for May, using the FIFO method (Step 3).

2. Calculate the cost of goods transferred out and the cost of EWIP (Step 4). Also, reconcile the costs assigned with the costs to account for (Step 5).

3. *What if* you were asked for the unit cost from the month of April? Calculate April's unit cost and explain why this might be of interest to management.

Solution:

1. **Step 3: Unit Cost Calculation**

    Unit cost = Unit materials cost + Unit conversion cost

    $\qquad$ = \$18,900/105,000 + \$4,575/91,500

    $\qquad$ = \$0.18 + \$0.05 = \$0.23 per ounce

2. **Step 4: Valuation of Inventories**
    Using unit cost information and the information from the equivalent units schedule (Step 2 of Example 6.7):

Cost of goods transferred out:	
From BWIP	\$ 2,025
To complete BWIP (\$0.05 × 4,500)	225
Started and completed (\$0.23 × 75,000)	17,250
Total	\$19,500
EWIP:	
(\$0.18 × 30,000) + (\$0.05 × 12,000)	\$ 6,000
Total costs assigned (accounted for)	\$25,500

    Step 5: Reconciliation (comparing costs assigned to costs to account for)

Cost to account for:		
BWIP	\$ 2,025	
Current (May)	23,475	
Total	\$25,500	

3. Since materials are added at the beginning, there are 15,000 equivalent units of materials (100% complete); there are 10,500 equivalent units of conversion (0.70 × 15,000). Thus, April unit cost = \$1,500/15,000 + \$525/10,500 = \$0.10 + \$0.05 = \$0.15. Knowing last month's unit cost allows managers to assess trends in cost and thus exercise better control over costs. If costs are increasing, it may reveal problems that can be corrected. If decreasing, it may reveal that continuous improvement efforts are succeeding.

Step 4 of FIFO Revisited

The FIFO method unit costs are used to value output that is related to the *current period*. There are three categories of current-period output: equivalent units in ending work in process, units started and completed, and the equivalent units of work necessary to *finish* the units in beginning work in process.

Since all equivalent units in ending work in process are current-period units, the cost of ending work in process is computed by multiplying the unit cost of each input category by the equivalent units of output for each category: direct materials ($0.18 × 30,000) and conversion costs ($0.05 × 12,000).

When it comes to valuing goods transferred out, two categories of completed units must be considered: those that were started and completed and those that were completed from beginning work in process. Of the 90,000 completed units, 75,000 are units started and completed in the current period, and 15,000 are units completed from beginning work in process. The 75,000 units that were started and completed in the current period represent current output and are valued at $0.23 per unit (yielding a cost of $17,250). For these units, the use of the current-period unit cost is entirely appropriate. However, the cost of the 15,000 beginning work-in-process units that were transferred out is another matter. These units started the period with $2,025 of manufacturing costs already incurred (cost taken from Example 6.8), 10,000 equivalent units of direct materials already added, and 10,500 equivalent units of conversion activity already completed. To these beginning costs, additional costs were needed to finish the units. As we saw in Example 6.7, the effort expended to complete these units required an additional 4,500 equivalent units of conversion activity. These 4,500 equivalent units of conversion activity were produced this period at a cost of $0.05 per equivalent unit. Thus, the total cost of finishing the units in beginning work in process is $225 ($0.05 × 4,500). Adding this $225 to the $2,025 in cost carried over from the prior period gives a total manufacturing cost for these units of $2,250. Adding the cost of BWIP units to the units started and completed results in the total cost of goods transferred out.

Production Report and Journal Entries

Steps 1 through 5 of Examples 6.7 and 6.8 provide the information for the May production report based on the FIFO method. This report is shown in Exhibit 6.5. The journal entries associated with the Blending Department (Wichita plant) example for the month of May are as shown on page 282.

1. Work in Process—Blending   18,900
       Materials   18,900
   To record requisitions of materials for May.
2. Work in Process—Blending   4,575
       Conversion Costs—Control   4,575
   To record the application of overhead and the incurrence of direct labor.
3. Work in Process—Encapsulating   19,500
       Work in Process—Blending   19,500
   To record the transfer of cost of goods completed from Blending to Encapsulating.

Exhibit 6.5

Production Report: Blending
Department

Bienestar Company, Wichita Plant			
Blending Department			
Production Report for May			
(FIFO Method)			

UNIT INFORMATION

Units to account for:		Units accounted for:	
Units, beginning work in process	15,000	Units completed	90,000
Units started	105,000	Units, ending work in process	30,000
Total units to account for	120,000	Total units accounted for	120,000

	Equivalent Units	
	Direct Materials	Conversion Costs
Units started and completed	75,000	75,000
Units, beginning work in process	—	4,500
Units, ending work in process	30,000	12,000
Equivalent units of output	105,000	91,500

COST INFORMATION

	Direct Materials	Conversion Costs	Total
Costs to account for:			
Beginning work in process	$ 1,500	$ 525	$ 2,025
Incurred during the period	18,900	4,575	23,475
Total costs to account for	$ 20,400	$ 5,100	$25,500
Cost per equivalent unit:			
Current costs	$ 18,900	$ 4,575	
Divided by equivalent units	÷105,000	÷91,500	
Cost per equivalent unit	$ 0.18	$ 0.05	$ 0.23
Costs accounted for:			
Units transferred out:			
Units, beginning work in process:			
From prior period		$ 2,025	
From current period ($0.05 × 4,500)		225	
Units started and completed ($0.23 × 75,000)		17,250	$19,500
Ending work in process:			
Direct materials ($0.18 × 30,000)		$ 5,400	
Conversion costs ($0.05 × 12,000)		600	6,000
Total costs accounted for			$25,500

OBJECTIVE **5**

Prepare a departmental production
report using the weighted average
method.

WEIGHTED AVERAGE COSTING METHOD

Excluding prior-period work and costs creates some bookkeeping and computational complexity that can be avoided if certain conditions are satisfied. Specifically, if the costs of production remain very stable from one period to the next, then it may be possible to use the weighted average method. This method does not track prior-period output and costs separately from current-period output and costs. The **weighted average costing method** picks up beginning inventory costs and the accompanying equivalent output and treats them as if they belong to the current period. Prior-period output and manufacturing costs found in beginning work in process are merged with the current-period output and manufacturing costs.

The merging of beginning inventory output and current-period output is accomplished by the way in which equivalent units are calculated. Under the weighted average method, equivalent units of output are computed by adding units completed to equivalent units in ending work in process. The equivalent units in beginning work in process are included in the computation. Thus, these units are counted as part of the current period's equivalent units of output.

The weighted average method merges prior-period costs with current-period costs by simply adding the manufacturing costs in beginning work in process to the manufacturing costs incurred during the current period. The total cost is treated as if it were the current period's total manufacturing cost.

The illustration of the weighted average method is based on the same Bienestar Company data that were used to illustrate the FIFO method. Using the same data highlights the differences between the two methods. The five steps for costing out production follow. **Example 6.9** shows the first two steps for the weighted average method, and **Example 6.10** illustrates Steps 3 to 5.

EXAMPLE 6.9

The HOW and WHY of Physical Flow Analysis and Equivalent Units: Weighted Average Method

Information:

The production of Bienestar's antihistamine product begins in the Blending Department. All materials are added at the **beginning** of the blending process. Output is measured in ounces. The production data for May are as follows:

Production:	
Units in process, May 1, 70% complete*	15,000
Units completed and transferred out	90,000
Units in process, May 31, 40% complete*	30,000

*With respect to conversion costs.

Why:

The physical flow schedule traces the units in process regardless of their stage of completion. To calculate equivalent units, weighted average counts prior-period output in BWIP as belonging to the current period. Thus, all completed units are treated as output of the current period. There is no requirement to calculate the work needed to complete the units in BWIP. Once weighted average equivalent units are calculated, the FIFO equivalent units can be obtained by subtracting out the prior-period output found in BWIP.

Required:

1. Prepare a physical flow schedule for May (Step 1).

2. Prepare an equivalent units schedule for May using the weighted average method (Step 2).

3. *What if* a need surfaced to know the FIFO equivalent units? Calculate the FIFO equivalent units starting with the weighted average equivalent units.

Solution:

1. First, two calculations are needed:

   Units started and completed = Units completed − Units, BWIP
   $$= 90,000 - 15,000 = 75,000$$
   Units started = Units started and completed + Units, EWIP
   $$= 75,000 + 30,000 = 105,000$$

EXAMPLE 6.9

(Continued)

Step 1: Physical Flow Schedule: Blending Department

Units to account for:		
Units, beginning work in process (70% complete)		15,000
Units started during May		105,000
Total units to account for		120,000
Units accounted for:		
Units completed and transferred out:		
Started and completed	75,000	
From beginning work in process	15,000	90,000
Units in ending work in process (40% complete)		30,000
Total units accounted for		120,000

2. **Step 2: Equivalent Units Schedule: Blending Department**

	Direct Materials	Conversion Costs
Units completed	90,000	90,000
Add: Units in ending work in process × Percentage complete:		
30,000 × 100% direct materials	30,000	—
30,000 × 40% conversion costs	—	12,000
Equivalent units of output	120,000	102,000

3.

	Direct Materials	Conversion Costs
Weighted average equivalent units of output	120,000	102,000
Less equivalent units in BWIP	15,000	10,500
FIFO equivalent units	105,000	91,500

EXAMPLE 6.10

The HOW and WHY of Unit Cost and Cost Assignment: Weighted Average Method

Information:

The equivalent units schedule of Example 6.9 (Step 2) and the following cost information from the Wichita plant's Blending Department for the month of May:

Costs:	
Work in process, May 1:	
Direct materials	$ 1,500
Conversion costs	525
Total work in process	$ 2,025
Current costs:	
Direct materials	$18,900
Conversion costs	4,575
Total current costs	$23,475

EXAMPLE 6.10

(*Continued*)

> **Why:**
> The weighted average method counts prior-period work and costs in BWIP as if they belong to the current period; thus, the unit cost is obtained by dividing the sum of the costs in BWIP and the current-period costs by the weighted average equivalent output. The resulting unit cost is a blend of the prior-period unit cost and the actual current-period unit cost. The valuation of cost of goods transferred out is simplified as it is the total unit cost multiplied by the units completed.

Required:

1. Calculate the unit cost for May, using the weighted average method (Step 3).

2. Calculate the cost of goods transferred out and the cost of EWIP (Step 4). Also, reconcile the costs assigned with the costs to account for (Step 5).

3. ***What if*** you were asked to show that the weighted average unit cost for materials is the blend of the April unit materials cost and the May unit materials cost? From Example 6.8, we know that the April unit materials cost is $0.10 and the May unit materials cost is $0.18. The equivalent units in BWIP are 15,000, and the FIFO equivalent units are 105,000. Calculate the weighted average unit materials cost using weights defined as the proportion of total units completed from each source (BWIP output and current output).

Solution:

1. **Step 3: Unit Cost Calculation**

    Unit cost = Unit materials cost + Unit conversion cost

    $\quad\quad$ = ($1,500 + $18,900)/120,000 + ($525 + $4,575)/102,000

    $\quad\quad$ = $0.17 + $0.05 = $0.22 per ounce

2. **Step 4: Valuation of Inventories**

    Using unit cost information and the information from the equivalent units schedule (Step 2 of Example 6.9):

Cost of goods transferred out:	
$\quad$ Units completed ($0.22 × 90,000)	$19,800
EWIP:	
$\quad$ ($0.17 × 30,000) + ($0.05 × 12,000)	5,700
$\quad\quad$ Total costs assigned (accounted for)	$25,500

    Step 5: Reconciliation (comparing costs assigned to costs to account for)

Cost to account for:	
$\quad$ BWIP	$ 2,025
$\quad$ Current (May)	23,475
$\quad\quad$ Total	$25,500

3. Unit materials cost = (15,000/120,000)$0.10 + (105,000/120,000)$0.18

    $\quad\quad\quad\quad\quad\quad$ = $0.17

Production Report

Steps 1 through 5 shown in Examples 6.9 and 6.10 provide all of the information needed to prepare a production report for the Blending Department for May. This report is given in Exhibit 6.6. The journal entries for the weighted average method follow the same pattern shown for the FIFO method. Thus, there is no reason to repeat the entries.

FIFO Compared with Weighted Average

The FIFO and weighted average methods differ on two key dimensions: (1) how output is computed and (2) what costs are used for calculating the period's unit cost. The unit cost computation for the Blending Department is as follows:

| | FIFO | | Weighted Average | |
	Direct Materials	Conversion Costs	Direct Materials	Conversion Costs
Costs	$ 18,900	$ 4,575	$ 20,400	$ 5,100
Output (units)	÷105,000	÷91,500	÷120,000	÷102,000
Unit cost	$ 0.18	$ 0.05	$ 0.17	$ 0.05

The two methods use different total costs and different measures of output. The FIFO method is the more theoretically appealing because it divides the cost of the period by the output of the period. The weighted average method, however, merges costs in beginning work in process with current-period costs and merges the output found in beginning work in process with current-period output. This creates the possibility for errors—particularly if the weighted average method is used for settings where input costs are changing significantly from one period to the next.

In the Blending Department example, the FIFO method unit cost and the weighted average method unit cost for conversion costs are the same; evidently, the cost of this input remained the same for the two periods being considered. The unit direct materials cost for the FIFO method, however, is $0.18 versus $0.17 for the weighted average method. Apparently, the cost of direct materials has increased, and merging the lower direct materials cost of the prior period with that of the current period creates a weighted average direct materials cost that underestimates the current-period direct materials cost. The resulting difference in the cost of a fully completed unit is only $0.01 ($0.23 − $0.22). On the surface, this seems harmless.

Exhibit 6.6

Production Report: Blending Department

Bienestar Company Blending Department, Wichita Plant Blending Department Production Report for May (Weighted Average Method)			
UNIT INFORMATION			
Units to account for:		Units accounted for:	
Units, beginning work in process	15,000	Units completed	90,000
Units started	105,000	Units, ending work in process	30,000
Total units to account for	120,000	Total units accounted for	120,000

| | Equivalent Units | |
	Direct Materials	Conversion Costs
Units completed	90,000	90,000
Units, ending work in process	30,000	12,000
Equivalent units of output	120,000	102,000

COST INFORMATION			
	Direct Materials	**Conversion Costs**	**Total**
Costs to account for:			
Beginning work in process	$ 1,500	$ 525	$ 2,025
Incurred during the period	18,900	4,575	23,475
Total costs to account for	$ 20,400	$ 5,100	$25,500
Divided by equivalent units	÷120,000	÷102,000	
Cost per equivalent unit	$ 0.17	$ 0.05	$ 0.22
Costs accounted for:			
Units transferred out ($0.22 × 90,000)			$19,800
Ending work in process:			
Direct materials ($0.17 × 30,000)		$ 5,100	
Conversion costs ($0.05 × 12,000)		600	5,700
Total costs accounted for			$25,500

Exhibit 6.6

(Continued)

The difference in the costs reported under each method for goods transferred out and the ending work-in-process inventories is only $300 (see Exhibits 6.5 and 6.6). This is a less than 2 percent difference for goods transferred out and only about a 5 percent difference for ending work in process. The $0.01 unit cost difference does not appear to be material. Yet, if the final product is considered, even a $0.01 difference may be significant. Recall that Bienestar passes the powder from the Blending Department to the Encapsulating Department, where the powder is converted to capsules. Next, the capsules are sent to the Bottling Department where eight tablets are placed in small metal boxes. The output of the Mixing Department is measured in ounces. Suppose that four ounces of powder convert to eight tablets. The difference in the cost of the final product would be understated by $0.04—not $0.01. Using this unit cost information may produce erroneous decisions such as under- or overpricing. Furthermore, if the other two departments also use the weighted average method, the costs in those departments could also be understated. The cumulative effect could produce a significant distortion in cost for the final product—magnifying the effect.

A second disadvantage of weighted average costing should be mentioned as well. The weighted average method also combines the performance of the current period with that of a prior period. Often, it is desirable to exercise control by comparing the actual costs of the current period with the budgeted or standard costs for the period. The weighted average method makes this comparison suspect because the performance of the current period is not independent of the prior period.

The major benefit of the weighted average method is simplicity. By treating units in beginning work in process as belonging to the current period, all equivalent units belong to the same time period when it comes to calculating unit costs. As a consequence, the requirements for computing unit cost are greatly simplified. Yet, as has been discussed, accuracy and performance measurement are impaired. The FIFO method overcomes both of these disadvantages. It should be mentioned, however, that both methods are widely used. Perhaps we can conclude that there are many settings in which the distortions caused by the weighted average method are not serious enough to be of concern.

TREATMENT OF TRANSFERRED-IN GOODS

In process manufacturing, some departments invariably receive partially completed goods from prior departments. For example, under the FIFO method, the transfer of goods from Blending to Encapsulating is valued at $19,500. These transferred-in goods are a type of

OBJECTIVE  6

Prepare a departmental production report with transferred-in goods and changes in output measures.

direct material for the subsequent process—materials that are added at the beginning of the subsequent process. The usual approach is to treat transferred-in goods as a separate material category when calculating equivalent units (the what-if question of Example 6.6 illustrates the possibility of multiple material categories). Thus, we now have three categories of manufacturing inputs: transferred-in materials, direct materials added, and conversion costs. For the Bienestar Company example, Encapsulating receives transferred-in materials, a powdered mixture, from Mixing, loads the powder into gelatin capsules (a material added), seals the capsules, and dries them. The process uses labor and overhead to convert the powder into capsules.

In dealing with transferred-in goods, three important points should be remembered. First, the cost of this material is the cost of the goods transferred out computed in the prior department. Second, the units started in the subsequent department correspond to the units transferred out from the prior department, assuming that there is a one-to-one relationship between the output measures of both departments. Third, the units of the transferring department may be measured differently than the units of the receiving department. If this is the case, then the goods transferred in must be converted to the units of measure used by the second department.

To illustrate how process costing works for a department that receives transferred-in work, we will use the Encapsulating Department of the Bienestar Company's Wichita plant. The Encapsulating Department receives a powder from Blending and fills capsules with the powder. The units of the Blending Department are measured in ounces, and the units of the Encapsulating Department are measured in capsules. To convert ounces to capsules, we need to know the relationship between ounces and capsules. Every ounce of the transferred-in mix converts to 4.4 capsules. Thus, to convert the transferred-in materials to the new output measure, multiply the transferred-in units by 4.4.

Now let's consider the month of May for the Wichita plant and focus our attention on the Encapsulating Department. We will assume that the Wichita plant uses the weighted average method. May's cost and production data for the Tableting Department are given in Exhibit 6.7. Notice that the transferred-in cost for May is the Mixing Department's transferred-out cost. (Exhibit 6.6 shows that the Mixing Department transferred out 90,000 ounces of powder, costing $19,800.) Also notice that output for the Encapsulating Department is measured in capsules. Given the data in Exhibit 6.7, the five steps of process costing can be illustrated for the Tableting Department.

Step 1: Physical Flow Schedule   In constructing a physical flow schedule for the Encapsulating Department, its dependence on the Blending Department must be considered:

Units to account for:		
Units, beginning work in process		24,000
Units transferred in during May		396,000*
Total units to account for		420,000
Units accounted for:		
Units completed and transferred out:		
Started and completed	351,000	
From beginning work in process	24,000	375,000
Units, ending work in process		45,000
Total units accounted for		420,000

*90,000 × 4.4 (converts transferred-in units from ounces to capsules).

Exhibit 6.7

Production and Cost Data:
Encapsulating Department

Bienestar Company, Wichita Plant
Encapsulating Department
Production and Cost Data for May

Production:

Units in process, May 1, 80% complete[a]	24,000 (capsules)
Units completed and transferred out	375,000
Units in process, May 31, 30% complete[a]	45,000

Costs:

Work in process, May 1:

Transferred-in costs	$ 1,200
Direct materials (gelatin capsules)	450
Conversion costs	270
Total work in process	$ 1,920

Current costs:

Transferred-in costs	$ 19,800
Direct materials (gelatin capsules)[b]	3,750
Conversion costs	7,500
Total current costs	$ 31,050

[a] With respect to conversion costs. Direct materials are 100 percent complete because they are added at the beginning of the process.
[b] The cost of capsule coating materials is insignificant and therefore added to the conversion costs category.

Exhibit 6.8

Equivalent Units of Production:
Weighted Average Method

	Transferred-In Materials	Direct Materials Added	Conversion Costs
Units completed	375,000	375,000	375,000
Add: Units in ending work in process × Percentage complete:			
45,000 × 100%	45,000	—	—
45,000 × 100%	—	45,000	—
45,000 × 30%	—	—	13,500
Equivalent units of output	420,000	420,000	388,500

Step 2: Calculation of Equivalent Units The calculation of equivalent units of production using the weighted average method is shown in Exhibit 6.8. Notice that the transferred-in goods from Mixing are treated as materials added at the beginning of the process. Transferred-in materials are always 100 percent complete, since they are added at the beginning of the process.

Step 3: Computation of Unit Costs The unit cost is computed by calculating the unit cost for each input category:

$$\text{Unit transferred-in cost} = (\$1,200 + \$19,800)/\,420,000 = \$0.05$$
$$\text{Unit direct materials cost} = (\$450 + \$3,750)/\,420,000 = \$0.01$$
$$\text{Unit conversion costs} = (\$270 + \$7,500)/\,388,500 = \$0.02$$
$$\text{Total unit cost} = \$0.05 + \$0.01 + \$0.02$$
$$= \$0.08$$

Step 4: Valuation of Inventories The cost of goods transferred out is simply the unit cost multiplied by the goods completed:

$$\text{Cost of goods transferred out} = \$0.08 \times 375,000 = \$30,000$$

Costing out ending work in process is done by computing the cost of each input and then adding to obtain the total:

Transferred-in materials: $0.05 × 45,000	$2,250
Direct materials added: $0.01 × 45,000	450
Conversion costs: $0.02 × 13,500	270
Total	$2,970

The cost of production report for the Encapsulating Department for the month of May, including Step 5 (which was skipped), is shown in Exhibit 6.9.

The only additional complication introduced in the analysis for a subsequent department is the presence of the transferred-in category. As we have just shown, dealing with this category is similar to handling any other category. However, remember that the current cost of this special type of material is the cost of the units transferred in from the prior process and that the units transferred in are the units started (adjusted for any differences in output measurement).

OBJECTIVE 7

Describe the basic features of operation costing.

OPERATION COSTING

Not all manufacturing firms have a pure job production environment or a pure process production environment. Some manufacturing firms have characteristics of both job and process environments. Firms in these *hybrid* settings often use *batch production processes*. **Batch production processes** produce batches of different products which are identical in many ways but differ in others. In particular, many firms produce products that make virtually the same demands on conversion inputs but different demands on direct materials inputs. Thus, the conversion activities are similar or identical, but the direct materials used are significantly different. For example, the conversion activities required to produce cans of pie filling are essentially identical for apple or cherry pie filling, but the cost of the direct materials can differ significantly. Similarly, the conversion activities for skirts may be identical, but the cost of direct materials can differ dramatically, depending on the nature of the fabric used (wool versus polyester, for example). Clothes, textiles, shoes, and food industries are examples where batch production may take place. For these firms, a costing system known as *operation costing* is often adopted.

Exhibit 6.9

Production Report: Encapsulating Department

Bienestar Company, Wichita Plant
Encapsulating Department
Production Report for May
(Weighted Average Method)

UNIT INFORMATION

Units to account for:		Units accounted for:	
Units, beginning work in process	24,000	Units completed	375,000
Units started	396,000	Units, ending work in process	45,000
Total units to account for	420,000	Total units accounted for	420,000

	Equivalent Units		
	Transferred-In Materials	**Direct Materials**	**Conversion Costs**
Units completed	375,000	375,000	375,000
Units, ending work in process	45,000	45,000	13,500
Equivalent units of output	420,000	420,000	388,500

COST INFORMATION				
	Transferred-In Materials	**Direct Materials**	**Conversion Costs**	**Total**
Costs to account for:				
Beginning work in process	$ 1,200	$ 450	$ 270	$ 1,920
Incurred during the period	19,800	3,750	7,500	31,050
Total costs to account for	$ 21,000	$ 4,200	$ 7,770	$32,970
Divided by equivalent units	÷420,000	÷420,000	÷388,500	
Cost per equivalent unit	$ 0.05	$ 0.01	$ 0.02	$ 0.08
Costs accounted for:				
Units transferred out ($0.08 × 375,000)				$30,000
Ending work in process:				
Transferred-in materials ($0.05 × 45,000)		$2,250		
Direct materials ($0.01 × 45,000)		450		
Conversion costs ($0.02 × 13,500)		270		2,970
Total costs accounted for				$32,970

Exhibit 6.9

(Continued)

Basics of Operation Costing

Operation costing is a blend of job-order and process-costing procedures applied to batches of homogeneous products. This costing system uses *job-order procedures* to assign direct materials costs to batches and *process procedures* to assign conversion costs. A hybrid costing approach is used because each batch uses different doses of direct materials but makes the same demands on the conversion resources of individual processes (usually called operations). Although different batches may pass through different operations, the demands for conversion activities for the *same* process do not differ among batches.

Work orders are used to collect production costs for each batch. Work orders also are used to initiate production. Using work orders to initiate and track costs to each batch is a job-costing characteristic. However, since individual products of different batches consume the same conversion resources as they pass through the same operation, then each product (regardless of batch membership) can be treated as a single homogeneous unit. This last trait is a process-costing characteristic and can be exploited to simplify the assignment of conversion costs.

Materials requisition forms are used to identify the direct materials, quantity and prices, and work order number. Using the materials requisition form as the source document, the cost of direct materials is posted to the work order sheet. Conversion costs are collected by *process* and assigned to products using a *predetermined conversion rate* (identical in concept to predetermined overhead rates). Conversion costs are budgeted for each department, and a single conversion rate is computed for each department (process) using a unit-based activity driver such as direct labor hours or machine hours. For example, assume that the budgeted conversion costs for a sewing operation are $100,000 (consisting of items such as direct labor, depreciation, supplies, and power), and the practical capacity of the operation is 10,000 machine hours. The conversion rate is computed as follows:

$$\text{Conversion rate} = \$100,000/10,000 \text{ machine hours}$$
$$= \$10 \text{ per machine hour}$$

Now consider two batches of shoes that pass through the sewing operation: one batch consists of 50 pairs of leather boots, and the second batch consists of 50 pairs of leather sandals. First, it should be clear that the batches have different direct material requirements so the cost of direct materials should be tracked separately (job-costing feature). Second, it should also be obvious that the sewing activity is the same for each in the sense that one hour of sewing time should consume the same resources regardless of whether the product is boots or sandals (the process-costing feature). If the batch of boots takes 25 machine hours, the batch will be assigned $250 of conversion costs ($10 × 25 hours). If the batch of sandals takes 12 machine hours, it will be assigned $120 of conversion costs ($10 × 12). Again, even though the products consume the same resources per machine hour, the batches can differ in total amount of resources consumed in an operation. So it is necessary to use a work order for each batch to collect costs.

Exhibit 6.10 illustrates the physical flow and cost flow features of operation costing. The illustration is for two batches and three processes. Panel A illustrates the physical flows, and Panel B shows the cost flows. The letters *a* and *f* represent the assignment of direct materials cost to the two batches. This example assumes that all direct materials are issued at the very beginning. Thus, direct materials cost would be assigned to the work-in-process account for the beginning process for each batch. The example also illustrates that batches do not have to participate in every process. Batch A uses Processes 2 and 3, while Batch B uses Processes 1 and 2. The letters immediately following the process represent the application of conversion costs to the respective batches.

Exhibit 6.10

Basic Features of Operation Costing

Panel A: Physical Flows

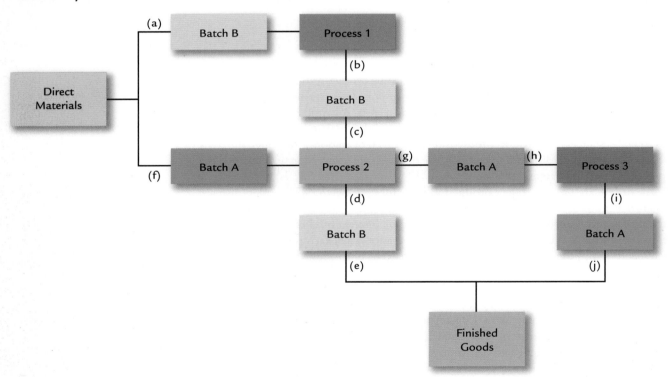

Panel B: Cost Flows (shown by letter in Panel A and in dollars below)

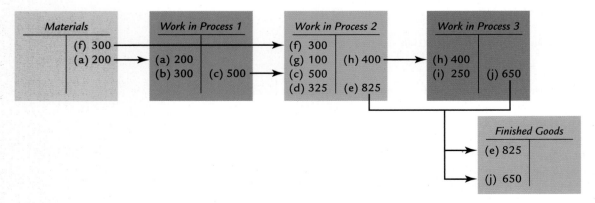

Operation Costing Example

To illustrate operation costing, consider the Des Moines plant of Bienestar Company. The Des Moines plant produces a variety of vitamin and mineral products. The company produces a multivitamin and mineral product as well as single vitamin and mineral products, e.g., bottles of vitamins C and E, calcium, and so on. Assume that the company also produces different strengths of vitamins (for example, 200 mg and 1,000 mg doses of vitamin C). The company also uses different sizes of bottles (for example, 60 and 120 capsules). There are four operations: picking, encapsulating, tableting, and bottling. Consider the following two work orders:

	Work Order 100	**Work Order 101**
Direct materials	Ascorbic acid	Vitamin E
	Capsules	Vitamin C
	Bottle (100 capsules)	Vitamin B1
	Cap and labels	Vitamin B2
		Vitamin B4
		Vitamin B12
		Biotin
		Zinc
		Bottle (60 tablets)
		Cap and labels
Operations	Picking	Picking
	Encapsulating	Tableting
	Bottling	Bottling
Number in batch	5,000 bottles	10,000 bottles

Notice how the work order specifies the direct materials needed, the operation required, and the size of the batch. Assume the following costs are collected by work order:

	Work Order 100	**Work Order 101**
Direct materials	$4,000	$15,000
Conversion costs:		
Picking	1,000	3,000
Encapsulating	3,000	—
Tableting	—	4,000
Bottling	1,500	2,000
Total production costs	$9,500	$24,000

The journal entries associated with Work Order 100 are illustrated below. The first entry assumes that all materials needed for the batch are requisitioned at the start. Another possibility is to requisition the materials needed for the batch in each process as the batch enters that process.

1.	Work in Process—Picking	4,000	
	Materials		4,000
2.	Work in Process—Picking	1,000	
	Conversion Costs Applied		1,000
3.	Work in Process—Encapsulating	5,000	
	Work in Process—Picking		5,000
4.	Work in Process—Encapsulating	3,000	
	Conversion Costs Applied		3,000
5.	Work in Process—Bottling	8,000	
	Work in Process—Encapsulating		8,000
6.	Work in Process—Bottling	1,500	
	Conversion Costs Applied		1,500
7.	Finished Goods	9,500	
	Work in Process—Bottling		9,500

The journal entries for the other work order are not shown but would follow a similar pattern.

SUMMARY OF LEARNING OBJECTIVES

LO1. Describe the basic characteristics of process costing, including cost flows, journal entries, and the cost of production report.
- Process systems are characterized by a larger number of homogeneous products passing through a series of processes.
- Materials, labor, and overhead are applied in each process.
- Costs are accumulated by process and are transferred from one process to another by debiting WIP of the receiving process and crediting the WIP of the transferring process.
- The production report summarizes manufacturing activity and costs for a process for a given period of time.

LO2. Describe process costing for settings without work-in-process inventories.
- No WIP inventories can occur in service organizations and JIT manufacturing firms.
- The unit cost is the costs of the period divided by the output of the period.
- ABC can be used to assign shared overhead to processes.

LO3. Describe process costing for settings with ending work-in-process inventories.
- With EWIP, output is measured using equivalent units.
- Equivalent units are the complete units that could have been produced given the total amount of effort expended.
- Five steps are followed to prepare a cost of production report:
  - Physical flow analysis
  - Equivalent unit calculation
  - Calculation of unit cost
  - Valuation of inventories
  - Cost reconciliation
- If materials are not added uniformly, multiple calculations of equivalent units are needed, one for each type of input.

LO4. Prepare a departmental production report using the FIFO method.
- The FIFO method excludes the equivalent output and costs in BWIP when the current-period unit cost is calculated.
- FIFO follows the process-costing principle.
- When calculating costs of goods transferred out, two categories of completed units are needed:
  - Units completed from BWIP
  - Units started and completed
- For the BWIP category, the cost is the sum of the prior-period cost and the current cost to complete the BWIP.

LO5. Prepare a departmental production report using the weighted average method.
- The weighted average method treats the equivalent output and costs in BWIP as if they belong to the current period when calculating unit cost.
- The costing of goods transferred out is simplified as there is only one category of completed units.

LO6. Prepare a departmental production report with transferred-in goods and changes in output measures.
- Partially completed goods (transferred-out goods) received by a prior department are transferred-in goods.
- For the receiving department, transferred-in goods are materials that are added at the beginning of the process.
- Transferred-in goods may need to be remeasured to reflect the output measure of the receiving department.

LO7. Describe the basic features of operation costing.
- Operation costing is a blend of job-order and process-costing procedures and can be used whenever batches of homogeneous products are produced.
- Job-order procedures are used to assign direct materials costs.
- Process procedures are used to assign conversion costs.

EXAMPLE 6.1	The HOW and WHY of Cost Flows: Process Costing, page 266
EXAMPLE 6.2	The HOW and WHY of Process Costing: Services with No WIP Inventories, page 269
EXAMPLE 6.3	The HOW and WHY of Physical Flow Analysis and Equivalent Units: EWIP Only, page 271
EXAMPLE 6.4	The HOW and WHY of Unit Cost, Inventory Valuation, and Cost Reconciliation: EWIP Only, page 273
EXAMPLE 6.5	The HOW and WHY of a Production Report, page 274
EXAMPLE 6.6	The HOW and WHY of Equivalent Units and Unit Costs with Nonuniform Inputs, page 275
EXAMPLE 6.7	The HOW and WHY of Physical Flow Analysis and Equivalent Units: FIFO Method, page 278
EXAMPLE 6.8	The HOW and WHY of Unit Cost and Cost Assignment: FIFO, page 279
EXAMPLE 6.9	The HOW and WHY of Physical Flow Analysis and Equivalent Units: Weighted Average Method, page 283
EXAMPLE 6.10	The HOW and WHY of Unit Cost and Cost Assignment: Weighted Average Method, page 284

KEY TERMS

Batch production processes, 290	**Process**, 264
Cost reconciliation, 273	**Process-costing principle**, 269
Equivalent units of output, 271	**Production report**, 267
FIFO costing method, 277	**Transferred-in cost**, 265
Operation costing, 291	**Weighted average costing method**, 282
Physical flow schedule, 271	**Work orders**, 291

APPENDIX: SPOILED UNITS

OBJECTIVE ◀ **8**

Explain how spoilage is treated in a process-costing system.

When spoilage takes place in a process-costing situation, its effects ripple through the cost of production report. Let's take Payson Company as an example. Payson Company produces a product that passes through two departments: Mixing and Cooking. In the Mixing Department, all direct materials are added at the beginning of the process. All other manufacturing inputs are added uniformly. The following information pertains to the Mixing Department for February:

a. Beginning work in process (BWIP), February 1: 100,000 pounds, 40 percent complete with respect to conversion costs. The costs assigned to this work are as follows:

Direct materials	$20,000
Direct labor	10,000
Overhead	30,000

b. Ending work in process (EWIP), February 28: 50,000 pounds, 60 percent complete with respect to conversion costs.

c. Units completed and transferred out: 360,000 pounds. The following costs were added during the month:

Direct materials	$211,000
Direct labor	100,000
Overhead	270,000

d. All units are inspected at the 80 percent point of completion, and any spoiled units identified are discarded. During February, 10,000 pounds were spoiled.

We can look at the five steps of the cost of production report. First, we must create a physical flow schedule.

Units to account for:	
Units, beginning work in process	100,000
Units started	320,000
Total units to account for	420,000
Units accounted for:	
Units transferred out	360,000
Units spoiled	10,000
Units, ending work in process	50,000
Total units accounted for	420,000

The second step is the creation of a schedule of equivalent units, shown below.

	Direct Materials	Conversion Costs
Units completed	360,000	360,000
Units spoiled × Percentage complete:		
Direct materials (10,000 × 100%)	10,000	
Conversion costs (10,000 × 80%)		8,000
Units in ending work in process × Percentage complete:		
Direct materials (50,000 × 100%)	50,000	—
Conversion costs (50,000 × 60%)	—	30,000
Equivalent units of output	420,000	398,000

The cost per equivalent unit is as follows:

DM unit cost ($20,000 + $211,000)/420,000	$0.55
CC unit cost ($40,000 + $370,000)/398,000	1.03*
Total cost per equivalent unit	$1.58

*Rounded.

Now we must calculate the cost of goods transferred out and the cost of ending work in process. If the spoilage is normal (expected), the cost of spoiled units is added to the cost of the good units. In this case, the inspection occurred at the 80 percent point of completion. Therefore, none of the spoiled units are from ending work in process (as these units are only 60 percent complete and have not yet been inspected). Thus, all spoilage cost is assigned to the good units transferred out.

Cost of goods transferred out:	
Good units ($1.58 × 360,000)	$568,800
Spoiled units ($0.55 × 10,000) + ($1.03 × 8,000)	13,740
	$582,540

$$\text{Cost of ending work in process} = (\$0.55 \times 50,000) + (\$1.03 \times 30,000)$$
$$= \$58,400$$

Costs are reconciled as follows:

Costs to account for:	
Beginning work in process	$ 60,000
Costs added	581,000
Total costs to account for	$641,000
Costs accounted for:	
Goods transferred out	$582,540
Ending work in process	58,400
Total costs accounted for	$640,940*

*$60 difference is due to rounding.

Suppose that the spoilage was abnormal. Then the spoilage cost is assigned to a spoilage loss account. The costs are accounted for as follows:

$$\text{Cost of good units transferred out} = \$1.58 \times 360,000 = \$568,800$$
$$\text{Spoiled units} = (\$0.55 \times 10,000) + (\$1.03 \times 8,000)$$
$$= \$13,740$$
$$\text{Cost of ending work in process} = (\$0.55 \times 50,000) + (\$1.03 \times 30,000)$$
$$= \$58,400$$

Costs are reconciled as follows:

Costs to account for:	
Beginning work in process	$ 60,000
Costs added	581,000
Total costs to account for	$641,000
Costs accounted for:	
Goods transferred out	$568,800
Loss from abnormal spoilage	13,740
Ending work in process	58,400
Total costs accounted for	$640,940*

*$60 difference is due to rounding.

Notice the difference between the treatment of normal and abnormal spoilage. When spoilage is assumed to be normal, it is not tracked separately but is embedded in the total cost of good units. As a result, no one knows precisely how much spoilage adds to total manufacturing costs and whether an effort should be made to reduce it. The treatment of spoilage as abnormal is more in keeping with an emphasis on total quality management where there is no tolerance allowed for waste. At least the product cost of spoiled goods is tracked in a separate account. Of course, a factory engaged in total quality management would not stop at classifying spoilage as abnormal. It would also identify the activities that are associated with these spoiled goods in an effort to discover the root causes of poor quality.

BRIEF EXERCISES

Brief Exercise 6-1 Cost Flows

OBJECTIVE 1
Example 6.1

Lamont Company produced 80,000 machine parts for diesel engines. There were no beginning or ending work-in-process inventories in any department. Lamont incurred the following costs for May:

	Molding Department	Grinding Department	Finishing Department
Direct materials	$13,000	$ 5,200	$ 8,000
Direct labor	10,000	8,800	12,000
Applied overhead	17,000	14,000	11,000

Required:

1. Calculate the costs transferred out of each department.
2. Prepare the journal entries corresponding to these transfers. Also, prepare the journal entry for Grinding that reflects the costs added to the transferred-in goods received from Molding.
3. *What if* the Grinding Department had an ending WIP of $12,000? Calculate the cost transferred out and provide the journal entry that would reflect this transfer. What is the effect on finished goods calculated in Requirement 1, assuming the other two departments have no ending WIP?

OBJECTIVE 2
Example 6.2

Brief Exercise 6-2 Unit Cost, No Work-in-Process Inventories

Lising Therapy has a physical therapist who performs electro-mechanical treatments for its patients. During April, Lising had the following cost and output information:

Direct materials	$ 750
Hygienist's salary	$4,250
Overhead	$5,000
Number of treatments	100

Required:

1. Calculate the cost per treatment for April.
2. Calculate the cost of services sold for April.
3. *What if* Lising found a way to reduce overhead costs by 20 percent? How would this affect the profit per treatment?

OBJECTIVE 3
Example 6.3

Brief Exercise 6-3 Physical Flow and Equivalent Units with EWIP

Fleming, Fleming, and Garcia, a local CPA firm, provided the following data for individual returns processed for March (output is measured in number of returns):

Units, beginning work in process	—
Units started	6,000
Units completed	5,000
Units, ending work in process (50% complete)	1,000
Total production costs	$5,500

Required:

1. Prepare a physical flow schedule.
2. Prepare an equivalent units schedule. Explain why output is measured in equivalent units.
3. *What if* EWIP is 80 percent complete? How would this change affect the physical flow schedule? The equivalent units schedule?

OBJECTIVE 3
Example 6.4

Brief Exercise 6-4 Cost Information

During October, McCourt Associates incurred total production costs of $60,000 for copyediting manuscripts and had the following equivalent units schedule:

Units completed	285
Units in EWIP × Fraction complete: 25 × 0.60	15
Equivalent units	300

Required:

1. Calculate the cost of copyediting one manuscript for October.
2. Assign costs to manuscripts completed and to EWIP and then do a cost reconciliation.
3. *What if* the costs assigned to units completed and EWIP total were calculated using a unit cost of $225? What is the discrepancy between the costs assigned and the costs to account for? What could have caused an incorrect unit cost?

OBJECTIVE 3
Example 6.5

Brief Exercise 6-5 Production Report

Limpiar Company produces a liquid household cleaning product. The Mixing Department, the first process department, mixes the ingredients required for the cleaning product. The following data are for May:

Work in process, May 1	—
Quarts started	270,000
Quarts transferred out	225,000
Quarts in EWIP	45,000
Direct materials cost	$105,000
Direct labor cost	$210,000
Overhead applied	$441,000

Direct materials are added throughout the process. Ending inventory is 60 percent complete with respect to direct labor and overhead.

Required:

1. Why would a manager want a production report?
2. Prepare a production report for the Mixing Department for May.

Brief Exercise 6-6   Nonuniform Inputs

OBJECTIVE ▶ 3
Example 6.6

Dulce Company produces 70 percent dark chocolate truffles. Conversion costs are added uniformly. For the first week in March, EWIP is 80 percent complete with respect to conversion costs. Materials are added at the beginning of the process. The following information is provided for the first week in March:

Physical flow schedule:

Units to account for:		
Units in BWIP		0
Units started		150,000
Total units to account for		150,000
Units accounted for:		
Units completed:		
From BWIP	0	
Started and completed	120,000	120,000
Units in EWIP		30,000
Total units accounted for		150,000

Inputs	
Direct Materials	**Conversion Costs**
$22,500	$14,400

Required:

1. Calculate the equivalent units for each input category.
2. Calculate the unit cost for each category and in total.
3. *What if* a different type of material is *also* added at the end of the process (an individual wrapper for each truffle), costing $6,000? Calculate the new unit cost.

Brief Exercise 6-7   Unit Information with BWIP, FIFO Method

OBJECTIVE ▶ 4
Example 6.7

Jackson Products produces a barbeque sauce using three departments: Cooking, Mixing, and Bottling. In the Cooking Department, all materials are added at the *beginning* of the process. Output is measured in ounces. The production data for July are as follows:

Production:	
Units in process, July 1, 60% complete*	10,000
Units completed and transferred out	80,000
Units in process, July 31, 80% complete*	15,000

*With respect to conversion costs.

Required:

1. Prepare a physical flow schedule for July.
2. Prepare an equivalent units schedule for July using the FIFO method.
3. ***What if*** 60 percent of the materials were added at the beginning of the process and 40 percent were added at the end of the process (all ingredients used are treated as the same type or category of materials)? How many equivalent units of materials would there be?

OBJECTIVE 4

Example 6.8

Brief Exercise 6-8 Cost Information and FIFO

Gunnison Company had the following equivalent units schedule and cost information for its Sewing Department for the month of December:

	Direct Materials	Conversion Costs
Units started and completed	40,000	40,000
Add: Units in beginning work in process ×		
Percentage complete:		
5,000 × 0% direct materials	—	
5,000 × 50% conversion costs		2,500
Add: Units in ending work in process ×		
Percentage complete:		
10,000 × 100% direct materials	10,000	—
10,000 × 35% conversion costs	—	3,500
Equivalent units of output	50,000	46,000
Costs:		
Work in process, December 1:		
Direct materials		$ 35,000
Conversion costs		10,000
Total work in process		$ 45,000
Current costs:		
Direct materials		$400,000
Conversion costs		184,000
Total current costs		$584,000

Required:

1. Calculate the unit cost for December, using the FIFO method.
2. Calculate the cost of goods transferred out, calculate the cost of EWIP, and reconcile the costs assigned with the costs to account for.
3. ***What if*** you were asked for the unit cost from the month of November? Calculate November's unit cost and explain why this might be of interest to management.

OBJECTIVE 5

Example 6.9

Brief Exercise 6-9 Unit Information with BWIP, Weighted Average Method

Jackson Products produces a barbeque sauce using three departments: Cooking, Mixing, and Bottling. In the Cooking Department, all materials are added at the *beginning* of the process. Output is measured in ounces. The production data for July are as follows:

Production:	
Units in process, July 1, 60% complete*	10,000
Units completed and transferred out	80,000
Units in process, July 31, 80% complete*	15,000

*With respect to conversion costs.

Required:

1. Prepare a physical flow schedule for July.
2. Prepare an equivalent units schedule for July using the weighted average method.
3. *What if* you were asked to calculate the FIFO units beginning with the weighted average equivalent units? Calculate the weighted average equivalent units by subtracting out the prior-period output found in BWIP.

Brief Exercise 6-10 Cost Information and the Weighted Average Method

OBJECTIVE 5

Example 6.10

Morrison Company had the equivalent units schedule and cost information for its Sewing Department for the month of December, as shown below.

	Direct Materials	Conversion Costs
Units completed	45,000	45,000
Add: Units in ending work in process ×		
Percentage complete:		
10,000 × 100% direct materials	10,000	—
10,000 × 45% conversion costs	—	4,500
Equivalent units of output	55,000	49,500
Costs:		
Work in process, December 1:		
Direct materials		$ 66,000
Conversion costs		14,000
Total work in process		$ 80,000
Current costs:		
Direct materials		$550,000
Conversion costs		184,000
Total current costs		$734,000

Required:

1. Calculate the unit cost for December, using the weighted average method.
2. Calculate the cost of goods transferred out, calculate the cost of EWIP, and reconcile the costs assigned with the costs to account for.
3. *What if* you were asked to show that the weighted average unit cost for materials is the blend of the November unit materials cost and the December unit materials cost? The November unit materials cost is $6.60 ($66,000/10,000), and the December unit materials cost is $12.22 ($550,000/45,000). The equivalent units in BWIP are 10,000, and the FIFO equivalent units are 45,000. Calculate the weighted average unit materials cost using weights defined as the proportion of total units completed from each source (BWIP output and current output).

EXERCISES

Exercise 6-11 Journal Entries

OBJECTIVE 1 2

EXCEL

Sharma Company has three process departments: Mixing, Encapsulating, and Bottling. At the beginning of the year, there were no work-in-process or finished goods inventories. The following data are available for the month of July:

Department	Manufacturing Costs Added*	Ending Work in Process
Mixing	$86,400	$21,600
Encapsulating	79,200	18,000
Bottling	72,000	3,600

*Includes only the direct materials, direct labor, and the overhead used to process the partially finished goods received from the prior department. The transferred-in cost is not included.

Required:

1. Prepare journal entries that show the transfer of costs from one department to the next (including the entry to transfer the costs of the final department).
2. Prepare T-accounts for the entries made in Requirement 1. Use arrows to show the flow of costs.

OBJECTIVE 2

**SHOW ME
HOW**

Exercise 6-12 Process Costing, Service Organization

A local barbershop cuts the hair of 1,200 customers per month. The clients are men, and the barbers offer no special styling. During the month of May, 1,200 customers were serviced. The cost of haircuts includes the following:

Direct labor	$ 9,000
Direct materials	1,000
Overhead	2,000
Total	$12,000

Required:

1. Explain why process costing is appropriate for this haircutting operation.
2. Calculate the cost per haircut.
3. Can you identify some possible direct materials used for this haircutting service? Is the usage of direct materials typical of services? If so, provide examples of services that use direct materials. Can you think of some services that would not use direct materials?

OBJECTIVE 1 2

Exercise 6-13 JIT Manufacturing and Process Costing

Friedman Company uses JIT manufacturing. There are several manufacturing cells set up within one of its factories. One of the cells makes stands for flat-screen televisions. The cost of production for the month of April is given below.

Cell labor	$ 60,000
Direct materials	150,000
Overhead	120,000
Total	$330,000

During May, 30,000 stands were produced and sold.

Required:

1. Explain why process costing can be used for computing the cost of production for the stands.
2. Calculate the cost per unit for a stand.
3. Explain how activity-based costing can be used to determine the overhead assigned to the cell.

OBJECTIVE 2 3

**SHOW ME
HOW**   **DATA
ANALYTICS**

Exercise 6-14 Physical Flow, Equivalent Units, Unit Costs, No Beginning WIP Inventory, Activity-Based Costing, DBC

McKay, Inc., produces a subassembly used in the production of hydraulic cylinders. The subassemblies are produced in three departments: Plate Cutting, Rod Cutting, and Welding. Materials are added at the beginning of the process. Overhead is applied using the following drivers and activity rates:

Driver	Rate	Actual Usage (by Plate Cutting)
Direct labor cost	120% of direct labor	$ 330,000
Inspection hours	$40 per hour	4,002 hours
Purchase orders	$100 per move	1,680 moves

During the first quarter, the Plate Cutting Department used 20,000 hours (direct, indirect, and machine hours) to produce the quarter's output. Other quarterly data for the Plate Cutting Department are as follows:

Beginning work in process , January 1	—
Units started	90,000
Direct materials cost	$720,000
Units, ending work in process (100% materials; 64% conversion), March 31	6,000

Required:

1. Prepare a physical flow schedule.
2. Calculate equivalent units of production for:
   a. Direct materials
   b. Conversion costs
3. Calculate unit costs for:
   a. Direct materials
   b. Conversion costs
   c. Total manufacturing
4. Provide the following information:
   a. The total cost of units transferred out
   b. The journal entry for transferring costs from Plate Cutting to Welding
   c. The cost assigned to units in ending inventory
5. Suppose the plant manager asked the following questions:
   a. What is the actual cycle time for the conversion cost output for the plate subassembly (round to four decimal places)?
   b. What is the conversion cost rate for the first quarter, using total conversion costs and total time (round to the nearest cent)?
   c. What is the conversion cost per unit, using duration-based costing (round to the nearest cent)?
   d. According to production engineering, if efficiency were increased to an ideal level, then the cycle time should be 0.20 hours. If this were to occur, what would the cost per plate be?

Identify the data analytic types (descriptive, diagnostic, predictive, or prescriptive) that apply to parts a. through d. (see Exhibits 2.5 and 2.6, pp. 37, 40, for a review of data analytic metrics). *Note:* More than one data analytic type might apply.

Exercise 6-15 Production Report, No Beginning Inventory

OBJECTIVE ◀ 1 3

SHOW ME
HOW

Softkin Company manufactures sun protection lotion. The Mixing Department, the first process department, mixes the chemicals required for the repellant. The following data are for the current year:

Work in process, January 1	—
Gallons started	450,000
Gallons transferred out	378,000
Direct materials cost	$ 900,000
Direct labor cost	$1,785,600
Overhead applied	$2,678,400

Direct materials are added at the beginning of the process. Ending inventory is 95 percent complete with respect to direct labor and overhead.

Required:

Prepare a production report for the Mixing Department for the current year.

Exercise 6-16 Weighted Average Method, FIFO Method, Physical Flow, Equivalent Units

Middelton Company manufactures a product that passes through two processes: Fabrication and Assembly. The following information was obtained for the Fabrication Department for October:

a. All materials are added at the beginning of the process.
b. Beginning work in process had 125,000 units, 40 percent complete with respect to conversion costs.
c. Ending work in process had 25,000 units, 20 percent complete with respect to conversion costs.
d. Started in process, 175,000 units.

Required:

1. Prepare a physical flow schedule.
2. Compute equivalent units using the weighted average method.
3. Compute equivalent units using the FIFO method.
4. Suppose that the cost of direct materials in beginning work in process is $560,000 and that the direct materials cost incurred for October is $700,000. With these changes, answer the following:

    a. What is the unit materials cost for the units in BWIP?
    b. What is the unit materials cost for units produced in October? Which method, weighted average or FIFO, should be used to answer this question? Explain why the unit materials cost is not the same for weighted average and FIFO. As part of your explanation, show that the weighted average unit cost for materials is the blend of the September unit materials cost and the October unit materials cost.
    c. Which data analytic types (descriptive, diagnostic, predictive, or prescriptive) apply for 4a and 4b? *Note:* More than one data analytic type might apply. (See Exhibits 2.5 and 2.6, pp. 37, 40, for a review of data analytic metrics.)

Exercise 6-17 FIFO Method, Valuation of Goods Transferred Out and Ending Work in Process

McCourt Company uses the FIFO method to account for the costs of production. For the first processing department, the following equivalent units schedule has been prepared:

	Direct Materials	Conversion Costs
Units started and completed	14,000	14,000
Units, beginning work in process:		
5,000 × 0%	—	—
5,000 × 40%	—	2,000
Units, ending work in process:		
3,000 × 100%	3,000	—
3,000 × 75%	—	2,250
Equivalent units of output	17,000	19,250

The cost per equivalent unit for the period was as follows:

Direct materials	$ 4.00
Conversion costs	12.00
Total	$16.00

The cost of beginning work in process was direct materials, $80,000; and conversion costs, $60,000.

Required:

1. Determine the cost of ending work in process and the cost of goods transferred out.
2. Prepare a physical flow schedule.

Exercise 6-18 Equivalent Units: Weighted Average Method

OBJECTIVE ◀ 5

SHOW ME
HOW

The following data are for four independent process-costing departments. Inputs are added continuously.

	A	B	C	D
Beginning inventory	5,000	4,000	—	45,000
Percent completion	30%	75%	—	60%
Units started	24,000	20,000	49,000	35,000
Ending inventory	4,000	—	9,000	10,000
Percent completion	20%	—	30%	20%

Required:

Compute the equivalent units of production for each of the preceding departments using the weighted average method.

Exercise 6-19 Equivalent Units: FIFO Method

OBJECTIVE ◀ 4

Using the data from **Exercise 6-18**, compute the equivalent units of production for each of the four departments using the FIFO method.

Exercise 6-20 Weighted Average Method, Unit Cost, Valuation of Goods Transferred Out and Ending Work in Process

OBJECTIVE ◀ 5

SHOW ME
HOW

Holmes Products, Inc., produces plastic cases used for video cameras. The product passes through three departments. For April, the following equivalent units schedule was prepared for the first department:

	Direct Materials	**Conversion Costs**
Units completed	25,000	25,000
Units, ending work in process ×		
Percentage complete:		
8,000 × 100%	8,000	—
8,000 × 50%	—	4,000
Equivalent units of output	33,000	29,000

Costs assigned to beginning work in process: direct materials, $90,000; conversion costs, $33,750. Manufacturing costs incurred during April: direct materials, $75,000; conversion costs, $220,000. Holmes uses the weighted average method.

Required:

1. Compute the unit cost for April.
2. Determine the cost of ending work in process and the cost of goods transferred out.

Exercise 6-21 FIFO Method, Unit Cost, Valuation of Goods Transferred Out, and Ending Work in Process

OBJECTIVE ◀ 4

SHOW ME
HOW

Dama Company produces women's blouses and uses the FIFO method to account for its manufacturing costs. The product Dama makes passes through two processes: Cutting and Sewing. During April, Dama's controller prepared the following equivalent units schedule for the Cutting Department:

	Direct Materials	**Conversion Costs**
Units started and completed	40,000	40,000
Units, beginning work in process:		
10,000 × 0%	—	—
10,000 × 50%	—	5,000
Units, ending work in process:		
20,000 × 100%	20,000	—
20,000 × 25%	—	5,000
Equivalent units of output	60,000	50,000

Costs in beginning work in process were direct materials, $20,000; conversion costs, $80,000. Manufacturing costs incurred during April were direct materials, $240,000; conversion costs, $320,000.

Required:

1. Prepare a physical flow schedule for April.
2. Compute the cost per equivalent unit for April.
3. Determine the cost of ending work in process and the cost of goods transferred out.
4. Prepare the journal entry that transfers the costs from Cutting to Sewing.

OBJECTIVE 5 6

SHOW ME HOW

Exercise 6-22 Weighted Average Method, Equivalent Units, Unit Cost, Multiple Departments

Brown Company has a product that passes through two processes: Grinding and Polishing. During December, the Grinding Department transferred 20,000 units to the Polishing Department. The cost of the units transferred into the second department was $40,000. Direct materials are added uniformly in the second process. Units are measured the same way in both departments.

The second department (Polishing) had the following physical flow schedule for December:

Units to account for:	
Units, beginning work in process	4,000 (40% complete)
Units started	?
Total units to account for	?
Units accounted for:	
Units, ending work in process	8,000 (50% complete)
Units completed	?
Units accounted for	?

Costs in beginning work in process for the Polishing Department were direct materials, $5,000; conversion costs, $6,000; and transferred in, $8,000. Costs added during the month: direct materials, $32,000; conversion costs, $50,000; and transferred in, $40,000.

Required:

1. Assuming the use of the weighted average method, prepare a schedule of equivalent units.
2. Compute the unit cost for the month.

OBJECTIVE 4 6

Exercise 6-23 FIFO Method, Equivalent Units, Unit Cost, Multiple Departments

Using the same data found in **Exercise 6-22**, assume the company uses the FIFO method.

SHOW ME HOW

Required:

Prepare a schedule of equivalent units, and compute the unit cost for the month of December.

OBJECTIVE 1 3

Exercise 6-24 Journal Entries, Cost of Ending Inventories

Baxter Company has two processing departments: Assembly and Finishing. A predetermined overhead rate of $10 per DLH is used to assign overhead to production. The company experienced the following operating activity for April:

SHOW ME HOW

a. Materials issued to Assembly, $24,000
b. Direct labor cost: Assembly, 500 hours at $9.20 per hour; Finishing, 400 hours at $8 per hour
c. Overhead applied to production
d. Goods transferred to Finishing, $32,500
e. Goods transferred to finished goods warehouse, $20,500
f. Actual overhead incurred, $10,000

Required:

1. Prepare the required journal entries for the preceding transactions.
2. Assuming Assembly and Finishing have no beginning work-in-process inventories, determine the cost of each department's ending work-in-process inventories.

Exercise 6-25 Operation Costing: Bread Manufacturing

OBJECTIVE ◀ 7

Tasty Bread makes and supplies bread throughout the state of Kansas. Three types of bread are produced: loaves, rolls, and buns. Seven operations describe the production process.

a. Mixing: Flour, milk, yeast, salt, butter, and so on, are mixed in a large vat.

b. Shaping: A conveyor belt transfers the dough to a machine that weighs it and shapes it into loaves, rolls, or buns, depending on the type being produced.

c. Rising: The individually shaped dough is allowed to sit and rise.

d. Baking: The dough is moved to a 100-foot-long funnel oven. (The dough enters the oven on racks and spends 20 minutes moving slowly through the oven.)

e. Cooling: The bread is removed from the oven and allowed to cool.

f. Slicing: For loaves and buns (hamburger and hot dog), the bread is sliced.

g. Packaging: The bread is wrapped (packaged).

Tasty produces its products in batches. The size of the batch depends on the individual orders that must be filled (orders come from retail grocers throughout the state). Usually, as soon as one batch is mixed, a second batch begins the mixing operation.

Required:

1. Identify the conditions that must be present for operation costing to be used in this setting. If these conditions are not met, explain how process costing would be used. If process costing is used, would you recommend the weighted average method or the FIFO method? Explain.

2. Assume that operation costing is the best approach for this bread manufacturer. Describe in detail how you would use operation costing. Use a batch of dinner rolls (consisting of 1,000 packages of 12 rolls) and a batch of whole wheat loaves (consisting of 5,000, 24-oz. sliced loaves) as examples.

PROBLEMS

Problem 6-26 Weighted Average Method, Physical Flow, Equivalent Units, Unit Costs, Cost Assignment, ABC

OBJECTIVE ◀ 3 5

Swasey Fabrication, Inc., manufactures frames for bicycles. Each frame passes through three processes: Cutting, Welding, and Painting. In September, the Cutting Department of the Tulsa, Oklahoma, plant reported the following data:

a. In Cutting, all direct materials are added at the beginning of the process.

b. Beginning work in process consisted of 40,500 units, 20 percent complete with respect to direct labor and overhead. Costs in beginning inventory included direct materials, $1,215,000; direct labor, $222,600; and applied overhead, $150,000.

c. Costs added to production during the month were direct materials, $2,565,000; direct labor, $3,471,150. Overhead was assigned using the following information:

Activity	Rate	Actual Driver Usage
Inspection	$150 per inspection hour	4,000 inspection hours
Maintenance	$750 per maintenance hour	1,600 maintenance hours
Receiving	$300 per receiving order	2,000 receiving orders

d. At the end of the month, 121,500 units were transferred out to Welding, leaving 13,500 units in ending work in process, or 25 percent complete.

Required:

1. Prepare a physical flow schedule.

2. Calculate equivalent units of production for direct materials and conversion costs.

3. Compute unit cost under weighted average.
4. Calculate the cost of goods transferred to Welding at the end of the month. Calculate the cost of ending inventory.
5. Prepare the journal entry that transfers the goods from Cutting to Welding.

OBJECTIVE 3 4

Problem 6-27 FIFO Method, Physical Flow, Equivalent Units, Unit Costs, Cost Assignment

Refer to the data in **Problem 6-26**. Assume that the FIFO method is used.

Required:

1. Prepare a physical flow schedule.
2. Calculate equivalent units of production for direct materials and conversion costs.
3. Compute unit cost. Round to three decimal places.
4. Calculate the cost of goods transferred to Welding at the end of the month. Calculate the cost of ending inventory.

OBJECTIVE 5

Problem 6-28 Weighted Average Method, Single Department Analysis, Uniform Costs

Hatch Company produces a product that passes through three processes: Fabrication, Assembly, and Finishing. All manufacturing costs are added uniformly for all processes. The following information was obtained for the Fabrication Department for December:

a. Work in process, June 1, had 90,000 units (40 percent completed) and the following costs:

Direct materials	$ 72,720
Direct labor	108,000
Overhead	36,000

b. During the month of June, 180,000 units were completed and transferred to the Assembly Department, and the following costs were added to production:

Direct materials	$216,000
Direct labor	144,000
Overhead	162,000

c. On June 30, there were 45,000 partially completed units in process. These units were 80 percent complete.

Required:

Prepare a cost of production report for the Fabrication Department for June using the weighted average method of costing. The report should disclose the physical flow of units, equivalent units, and unit costs and should track the disposition of manufacturing costs.

OBJECTIVE 4

Problem 6-29 FIFO Method, Single Department Analysis, One Cost Category

Refer to the data in **Problem 6-28**.

Required:

Prepare a cost of production report for the Fabrication Department for December using the FIFO method of costing.

OBJECTIVE 3 4 6

Problem 6-30 Service Organization with Work-in-Process Inventories, Multiple Departments, FIFO Method, Unit Cost

Hepworth Credit Corporation is a wholly owned subsidiary of a large manufacturer of computers. Hepworth is in the business of financing computers, software, and other services that the parent corporation sells. Hepworth has two departments that are involved in financing services: the Credit

Department and the Business Practices Department. The Credit Department receives requests for financing from field sales representatives, records customer information on a preprinted form, and then enters the information into the computer system to check the creditworthiness of the customer. (Other actions may be taken if the customer is not in the database.) Once creditworthiness information is known, a printout is produced with this information plus other customer-specific information. The completed form is transferred to the Business Practices Department.

The Business Practices Department modifies the standard loan covenant as needed (in response to customer request or customer risk profile). When this activity is completed, the loan is priced. This is done by keying information from the partially processed form into a personal computer spreadsheet program. The program provides a recommended interest rate for the loan. Finally, a form specifying the loan terms is attached to the transferred-in document. A copy of the loan-term form is sent to the sales representative and serves as the quote letter.

The following cost and service activity data for the Business Practices Department are provided for the month of May:

Transferred-in applications	11,200
Applications in process, May 1, 40% complete*	2,000
Applications in process, May 31, 25% complete*	3,200

*All materials and supplies are used at the end of the process.

	Transferred In	Direct Materials	Conversion Costs
Costs:			
Beginning work in process	$ 18,000	—	$ 11,200
Costs added	112,000	$5,000	150,000

Required:

1. How would you define the output of the Business Practices Department?
2. Using the FIFO method, prepare the following for the Business Practices Department:
   a. A physical flow schedule
   b. An equivalent units schedule
   c. Calculation of unit costs
   d. Cost of ending work in process and cost of units transferred out
   e. A cost reconciliation

Problem 6-31 Weighted Average Method, Journal Entries

OBJECTIVE  1 5 6

Muskoge Company uses a process-costing system. The company manufactures a product that is processed in two departments: Molding and Assembly. In the Molding Department, direct materials are added at the beginning of the process; in the Assembly Department, additional direct materials are added at the end of the process. In both departments, conversion costs are incurred uniformly throughout the process. As work is completed, it is transferred out. The following table summarizes the production activity and costs for February:

	Molding	Assembly
Beginning inventories:		
Physical units	10,000	8,000
Costs:		
Transferred in	—	$ 45,200
Direct materials	$ 22,000	—
Conversion costs	$ 13,800	$ 16,800
Current production:		
Units started	25,000	?
Units transferred out	30,000	35,000

Costs:		
Transferred in	—	?
Direct materials	$ 56,250	$ 39,550
Conversion costs	$103,500	$136,500
Percentage of completion:		
Beginning inventory	40%	50%
Ending inventory	80	50

Required:

1. Using the weighted average method, prepare the following for the Molding Department:
   a. A physical flow schedule
   b. An equivalent units calculation
   c. Calculation of unit costs. Round to four decimal places.
   d. Cost of ending work in process and cost of goods transferred out
   e. A cost reconciliation
2. Prepare journal entries that show the flow of manufacturing costs for the Molding Department. Materials are added at the beginning of the process.
3. Repeat Requirements 1 and 2 for the Assembly Department.

OBJECTIVE 2 4 6 ▶ **Problem 6-32 FIFO Method, Two-Department Analysis**

Refer to the data in **Problem 6-31**.

Required:

Repeat the requirements in **Problem 6-31** using the FIFO method.

OBJECTIVE 5 6 ▶ **Problem 6-33 Weighted Average Method, Two-Department Analysis, Change in Output Measure**

Healthway uses a process-costing system to compute the unit costs of the minerals that it produces. It has three departments: Mixing, Tableting, and Bottling. In Mixing, at the beginning of the process all materials are added and the ingredients for the minerals are measured, sifted, and blended together. The mix is transferred out in gallon containers. The Tableting Department takes the powdered mix and places it in capsules. One gallon of powdered mix converts to 1,600 capsules. After the capsules are filled and polished, they are transferred to Bottling where they are placed in bottles, which are then affixed with a safety seal and a lid and labeled. Each bottle receives 50 capsules.

During July, the following results are available for the first two departments (direct materials are added at the beginning in both departments):

	Mixing	Tableting
Beginning inventories:		
Physical units	5 gallons	4,000 capsules
Costs:		
Direct materials	$ 120	$ 32
Direct labor	128	20
Overhead	?	?
Transferred in	—	140
Current production:		
Transferred out	125 gallons	198,000 capsules
Ending inventory	6	6,000
Costs:		
Direct materials	$ 3,144	$ 1,584
Transferred in	—	?
Direct labor	4,096	1,944
Overhead	?	?
Percentage of completion:		
Beginning inventory	40%	50%
Ending inventory	50	40

Overhead in both departments is applied as a percentage of direct labor costs. In the Mixing Department, overhead is 200 percent of direct labor. In the Tableting Department, the overhead rate is 150 percent of direct labor.

Required:

1. Prepare a production report for the Mixing Department using the weighted average method. Follow the five steps outlined in the chapter. Round unit cost to three decimal places.
2. Prepare a production report for the Tableting Department. Materials are added at the beginning of the process. Follow the five steps outlined in the chapter. Round unit cost to four decimal places.

Problem 6-34 FIFO Method, Two-Department Analysis

Refer to the data in **Problem 6-33**.

OBJECTIVE ◄ 4 6

Required:

Prepare a production report for each department using the FIFO method.

Problem 6-35 Operation Costing: Unit Costs and Journal Entries

OBJECTIVE ◄ 7

Jacson Company produces two brands of a popular pain medication: regular strength and extra strength. Regular strength is produced in tablet form, and extra strength is produced in capsule form. All direct materials needed for each batch are requisitioned at the start. The work orders for two batches of the products are shown below, along with some associated cost information:

	Work Order 121 (Regular Strength)	Work Order 122 (Extra Strength)
Direct materials (actual costs):	$ 9,000	$15,000
Applied conversion costs:		
Mixing	?	?
Tableting	$ 5,000	—
Encapsulating	—	$ 6,000
Bottling	?	?
Batch size (bottles of 100 units)	12,000	18,000

In the Mixing Department, conversion costs are applied on the basis of direct labor hours. Budgeted conversion costs for the department for the year were $60,000 for direct labor and $190,000 for overhead. Budgeted direct labor hours were 5,000. It takes one minute of labor time to mix the ingredients needed for a 100-unit bottle (for either product).

In the Bottling Department, conversion costs are applied on the basis of machine hours. Budgeted conversion costs for the department for the year were $400,000. Budgeted machine hours were 20,000. It takes one-half minute of machine time to fill a bottle of 100 units.

Required:

1. What are the conversion costs applied in the Mixing Department for each batch? The Bottling Department?
2. Calculate the cost per bottle for the regular and extra strength pain medications.
3. Prepare the journal entries that record the costs of the 12,000 regular strength batch as it moves through the various operations.
4. Suppose that the direct materials are requisitioned by each department as needed for a batch. For the 12,000 regular strength batch, direct materials are requisitioned for the Mixing and Bottling departments. Assume that the amount of cost is split evenly between the two departments. How will this change the journal entries made in Requirement 3?

OBJECTIVE `3` `5` `7`

**DATA
ANALYTICS**

Problem 6-36 Case on Process Costing, Operation Costing, Impact on Resource Allocation Decision

Golding Manufacturing, a division of Farnsworth Sporting, Inc., produces two different models of bows and eight models of knives. The bow-manufacturing process involves the production of two major subassemblies: the limbs and the handle. The limbs pass through four sequential processes before reaching final assembly: lay-up, molding, fabricating, and finishing. In the Lay Up Department, limbs are created by laminating layers of wood. In Molding, the limbs are heat treated, under pressure, to form a strong resilient limb. In the Fabricating Department, any protruding glue or other processing residue is removed. Finally, in Finishing, the limbs are cleaned with acetone, dried, and sprayed with the final finishes.

The handles pass through two processes before reaching final assembly: pattern and finishing. In the Pattern Department, blocks of wood are fed into a machine that is set to shape the handles. Different patterns are possible, depending on the machine's setting. After coming out of the machine, the handles are cleaned and smoothed. They then pass to the Finishing Department where they are sprayed with the final finishes. In Final Assembly, the limbs and handles are assembled into different models using purchased parts such as pulley assemblies, weight adjustment bolts, side plates, and string.

Golding, since its inception, has been using process costing to assign product costs. A predetermined overhead rate is used based on direct labor dollars (80 percent of direct labor dollars). Recently, Golding has hired a new controller, Karen Jenkins. After reviewing the product costing procedures, Karen requested a meeting with the divisional manager, Aaron Suhr. The following is a transcript of their conversation:

KAREN: Aaron, I have some concerns about our cost accounting system. We make two different models of bows and are treating them as if they were the same product. Now I know that the only real difference between the models is the handle. The processing of the handles is the same, but the handles differ significantly in the amount and quality of wood used. Our current costing does not reflect this difference in direct material input.

AARON: Your predecessor is responsible. He believed that tracking the difference in direct material cost wasn't worth the effort. He simply didn't believe that it would make much difference in the unit cost of either model.

KAREN: Well, he may have been right, but I have my doubts. If there is a significant difference, it could affect our views of which model is more important to the company. The additional bookkeeping isn't very stringent. All we have to worry about is the Pattern Department. The other departments fit what I view as a process-costing pattern.

AARON: Why don't you look into it? If there is a significant difference, go ahead and adjust the costing system.

After the meeting, Karen decided to collect cost data on the two models: the Deluxe model and the Econo model. She decided to track the costs for one week. At the end of the week, she had collected the following data from the Pattern Department:

a. There were a total of 3,750 bows completed: 1,500 Deluxe Models and 2,250 Econo models.
b. There was no beginning work in process; however, there were 450 units in ending work in process: 350 Deluxe and 150 Econo models. Both models were 80 percent complete with respect to conversion costs and 100 percent complete with respect to direct materials.
c. The Pattern Department experienced the following costs:

Direct materials	$171,000
Direct labor	68,500

d. On an experimental basis, the requisition forms for direct materials were modified to identify the dollar value of the direct materials used by the Econo and Deluxe models:

Econo model	$ 45,000
Deluxe model	126,000

Required:

1. Compute the unit cost for the handles produced by the Pattern Department, assuming that process costing is totally appropriate.
2. Compute the unit cost of each handle, using the separate cost information provided on materials.
3. Compare the unit costs computed in Requirements 1 and 2. Is Karen justified in her belief that a pure process-costing relationship is not appropriate? Describe the costing system that should be used.
4. In the past, the marketing manager has requested more money for advertising the Econo line. Aaron has repeatedly refused to grant any increase in this product's advertising budget because its per-unit profit (selling price less manufacturing cost) is so low. Given the results in Requirements 1 through 3, should Aaron reconsider the request for additional advertising money for the Econo line?
5. Which data analytic types (descriptive, diagnostic, predictive, or prescriptive) would apply when (see Exhibits 2.5 and 2.6, pp. 37, 40, for a review data analytic metrics):
   a. unit costs were computed in Requirements 1 and 2?
   b. unit costs were compared and Karen's suggestion was evaluated?
   c. a recommendation was made for a costing system for the Pattern Department?
   d. Aaron's position on advertising money was evaluated?

Note: More than one data analytic type might apply.

Problem 6-37 Appendix: Normal and Abnormal Spoilage

OBJECTIVE ◀ 5 8

DATA ANALYTICS

Cuero Company produces leather strips for western belts using three processes: cutting, design and coloring, and punching. The weighted average method is used for all three departments. The following information pertains to the Design and Coloring Department for the month of June:
   a. There was no beginning work in process.
   b. There were 560,000 units transferred in from the Cutting Department.
   c. Ending work in process, June 30: 70,000 strips, 80 percent complete with respect to conversion costs.
   d. Units completed and transferred out: 462,000 strips. The following costs were added during the month:

Transferred in	$2,800,000
Direct materials	840,000
Conversion costs	1,092,000

   e. Direct materials are added at the beginning of the process.
   f. Inspection takes place at the end of the process. All spoilage is considered normal.

Required:

1. Calculate equivalent units of production for transferred-in materials, direct materials added, and conversion costs.
2. Calculate unit costs for the three categories of Requirement 1.
3. What is the total cost of units transferred out? What is the cost of ending work-in-process inventory? How is the cost of spoilage treated?
4. Assume that all spoilage is considered abnormal. How should abnormal spoilage be treated? Give the journal entry to account for the cost of the spoiled units. Some companies view all spoilage as abnormal. Explain why. Assume that abnormal spoilage is anything more than 1 percent of units completed and transferred out. Show the spoilage treatment for this scenario.
5. For Requirement 4, provide an example of each data analytic type (descriptive, diagnostic, predictive, and prescriptive) with a brief justification (see Exhibits 2.5 and 2.6, pp. 37, 40, for a review of data analytic types).

Problem 6-38 Appendix: Normal and Abnormal Spoilage in Process Costing

Mojada Toys, Inc., manufactures plastic water guns. Each gun's left and right frames are produced in the Molding Department. The left and right frames are then transferred to the Assembly Department where the trigger mechanism is inserted and the halves are glued together. (The left and right halves together define the unit of output for the Molding Department.) In June, the Molding Department reported the following data:

a. In the Molding Department, all direct materials are added at the beginning of the process.

b. Beginning work in process consisted of 5,400 units, 20 percent complete with respect to direct labor and overhead. Costs in beginning inventory included direct materials, $810; and conversion costs, $249.

c. Costs added to production during the month were direct materials, $1,710; and conversion costs, $3,747.

d. Inspection takes place at the end of the process. Malformed units are discarded. All spoilage is considered abnormal.

e. During the month, 12,600 units were started, and 14,400 good units were transferred out to Finishing. All other units finished were malformed and discarded. There were 1,800 units that remained in ending work in process, 25 percent complete.

Required:

1. Prepare a physical flow schedule.
2. Calculate equivalent units of production using the weighted average method.
3. Calculate the unit cost.
4. What is the cost of goods transferred out? Ending work in process? Loss due to spoilage?
5. Prepare the journal entry to remove spoilage from the Molding Department.

Problem 6-39 Appendix: Normal and Abnormal Spoilage in Process Costing, Changes in Output Measures, Multiple Departments

Grayson Company produces an industrial chemical used for cleaning and lubricating machinery. In the Mixing Department, liquid and dry chemicals are blended to form slurry. Output is measured in gallons. In the Baking Department, the slurry is subjected to high heat, and the residue appears in irregular lumps. Output is measured in pounds. In the Grinding Department, the irregular lumps are ground into a powder, and this powder is placed in 50-pound bags. Output is measured in bags produced. In April, the company reported the following data:

a. The Mixing Department transferred 50,000 gallons to the Baking Department, costing $250,000. Each gallon of slurry weighs two pounds.

b. The Baking Department transferred 100,000 pounds (irregular lumps) to the Grinding Department. At the beginning of the month, there were 5,000 gallons of slurry in process, 25 percent complete, costing $35,000 (transferred-in cost of $25,000 plus conversion cost of $10,000). No additional direct materials are added in the Baking Department. At the end of April, there was no ending work in process. Conversion costs for the month totaled $205,000. Normal loss during baking is 5 percent of good output. All transferred-in materials are lost, but since loss occurs uniformly throughout the process, only 50 percent of the conversion units are assumed to be lost.

c. The Grinding Department transferred 2,500 bags of chemicals to its finished goods warehouse. Beginning work in process for this department was 25,000 pounds, 40 percent complete with the following costs: transferred-in cost, $132,500; conversion cost, $15,000. Bags are used at the end of the process and cost $1.50 each. During bagging, normally one out of every 11 bags is torn and must be discarded. No powder is lost (the tearing occurs when the bag is being attached to a funnel). Conversion costs for the month's production are $172,500. There is no ending work in process.

Required:

1. Using FIFO, calculate the cost per bag of chemicals transferred to the finished goods warehouse. Show all work necessary for the calculation.
2. Prepare the journal entries needed to remove spoilage from the Baking and Grinding departments.

7 Allocating Costs of Support Departments and Joint Products

After studying this chapter, you should be able to:

1. Describe the difference between support departments and producing departments.

2. Calculate charging rates, and distinguish between single and dual charging rates.

3. Allocate support center costs to producing departments using the direct method, the sequential method, and the reciprocal method.

4. Calculate departmental overhead rates.

5. Identify the characteristics of the joint production process, and allocate joint costs to products.

DR MANAGER/Shutterstock.com

SUPPORT DEPARTMENT COST ALLOCATION

at Hewlett-Packard, IBM, and Dow Chemical

Over the past 20 or so years, companies such as **Hewlett-Packard**, **IBM**, and **Dow Chemical** have taken certain support departments and formed shared services centers (SSCs). The SSC performs activities that are used across a wide array of the company's divisions and departments. Payroll, receiving, customer billing, and accounts receivable processing are examples of SSCs. The company reaps the savings from economies of scale and standardized process design. Tools to measure performance are also incorporated into the SSC design. The SSC is faced with three important cost questions:

- What causes costs in our operation?
- How much should be charged back to the customers and producing departments?
- How do our costs compare with those of outsourcing firms that perform the same service?

The drivers used to develop charging rates are seldom unit-based drivers (based on production). Instead, they might include the number of transactions processed and the percentage of errors in customer-provided information. Because activity-based costing (ABC) provides a better understanding of costs and their related drivers, it provides a better framework for managing SSC costs than traditional cost accounting systems.[1]

Today, large corporations are using SSCs across a multidivision company. These SSCs think globally and standardize high-volume services through the corporation. They use "robotic process automation to automate routine, repetitive, rule-based activities."[2] The result is increased productivity and reduced cost across the corporation.

AN OVERVIEW OF COST ALLOCATION

Mutually beneficial costs, which occur when the same resource is used in the output of two or more services or products, are known as **common costs**. These common costs may pertain to periods of time, individual responsibilities, sales territories, and classes of customers. A special case of common costs is that of the joint production process. This chapter will first focus on the costs common to departments and to products, and then on the common costs of the joint production process.

The complexity of many modern firms leads the accountant to allocate costs of support departments to producing departments and individual product lines. Allocation is simply a means of dividing a pool of costs and assigning those costs to various subunits. While allocation does not increase or decrease the total cost, the amounts of cost assigned to the subunits can be affected by the allocation procedure chosen.

1 Ann Triplett and Jon Scheumann, "Managing Shared Services with ABM," *Strategic Finance* (February 2000): 40–45.
2 Jordan Bryan, "Five Characteristics of the Best Shared Services Centers" (February 22, 2019), https://www.gartner.com/smarterwithgartner/five-characteristics-of-the-best-shared-service-centers/

Because cost allocation can affect bid prices, the profitability of individual products, and the behavior of managers, it is an important topic.

Types of Departments

The first step in cost allocation is to determine what the cost objects are. Usually, they are departments. There are two categories of departments: producing departments and support departments. **Producing departments** are directly responsible for creating the products or services sold to customers. In a large public accounting firm, examples of producing departments are auditing, tax, and management advisory services (computer systems services). In a manufacturing setting such as Volkswagen (VW), producing departments are those that work directly on the products being manufactured (e.g., assembly and painting). **Support departments** provide essential services for producing departments. These departments are indirectly connected with an organization's services or products. At VW, those departments might include engineering, maintenance, personnel, and building and grounds.

Once the producing and support departments have been identified, the overhead costs traceable to each department can be determined. A factory cafeteria, for example, would have food costs, wages of cooks and servers, depreciation on dishwashers and stoves, and supplies (e.g., napkins and plastic forks). Overhead directly associated with a producing department, such as assembly in a furniture-making plant, would include supplies used by that department, supervisory salaries, and depreciation on departmental equipment. Overhead that cannot be easily assigned to a producing or support department is assigned to a catchall department such as general factory. General factory might include depreciation on the factory building, rental of a Santa Claus suit for the factory Christmas party, the cost of restriping the parking lot, the plant manager's salary, and telephone service. In this way, all costs are assigned to a department.

Exhibit 7.1 shows how a manufacturing firm and a service firm can be divided into producing and support departments. The manufacturing plant, which makes furniture, may be departmentalized into two producing departments (Assembly and Finishing) and four support departments (Materials Storeroom, Cafeteria, Maintenance, and General Factory). The service firm, a bank, might be departmentalized into three producing departments (Auto Loans, Commercial Lending, and Personal Banking) and three support departments (Drive Through, Data Processing, and Bank Administration). Overhead costs are traced to each department. Note that each factory or service company overhead cost must be assigned to one, and only one, department.

Once the company is departmentalized and all overhead costs are traced to the individual departments, support department costs are assigned to producing departments, and overhead rates are developed to cost products. Although support departments do not work directly on the products or services that are sold, the costs of providing these support services are part of the total product cost and must be assigned to the products. This assignment of costs consists of a two-stage allocation: (1) allocation of support department costs to producing departments and (2) assignment of these allocated costs to individual products. The second-stage allocation, achieved through the use of departmental overhead rates, is necessary because there are multiple products being worked on in each producing department. If there were only one product within a producing department, all the support costs allocated to that department would belong to that product. Recall that a predetermined overhead rate is computed by taking total estimated overhead for a department and dividing it by an estimate of an appropriate base. Now we see that a producing department's overhead consists of two parts: overhead directly associated with a producing department and overhead allocated to the producing department from the support departments. A support department cannot have an overhead rate that assigns overhead costs to units produced, because products are not produced in support departments. The nature of support departments is to service producing departments, not the products that pass through the producing departments. For example, maintenance personnel repair and maintain the equipment in the Assembly Department, not the furniture that is assembled in that department. Exhibit 7.2 summarizes the steps involved.

Manufacturing Firm: Furniture Maker	
Producing Departments	**Support Departments**
Assembly:	Materials Storeroom:
Supervisors' salaries	Clerk's salary
Small tools	Depreciation on forklift
Indirect materials	Cafeteria:
Depreciation on machinery	Food
Finishing:	Cooks' salaries
Sandpaper	Depreciation on stoves
Depreciation on sanders and buffers	Maintenance:
	Janitors' salaries
	Cleaning supplies
	Machine oil and lubricants
	General Factory:
	Depreciation on building
	Security
	Utilities
Service Firm: Bank	
Producing Departments	**Support Departments**
Auto Loans:	Drive Through:
Loan processors' salaries	Tellers' salaries
Forms and supplies	Depreciation on equipment
Commercial Lending:	Data Processing:
Lending officers' salaries	Personnel salaries
Depreciation on office equipment	Software
Bankruptcy prediction software	Depreciation on hardware
Personal Banking:	Bank Administration:
Supplies and postage for statements	Salary of CEO
	Receptionist's salary
	Telephone costs
	Depreciation on bank and vault

Exhibit 7.1

Examples of Departmentalization for a Manufacturing Firm and a Service Firm

1. Departmentalize the firm.
2. Classify each department as a support department or a producing department.
3. Trace all overhead costs in the firm to a support or producing department.
4. Allocate support department costs to the producing departments.
5. Calculate predetermined overhead rates for producing departments.
6. Allocate overhead costs to the units of individual product through the predetermined overhead rates.

Exhibit 7.2

Steps in Allocating Support Department Costs to Producing Departments

Exhibit 7.3

Examples of Possible Activity
Drivers for Support Departments

Accounting:
  Number of transactions
Cafeteria:
  Number of employees
Data Processing:
  Number of lines entered
  Number of hours of service
Engineering:
  Number of change orders
  Number of hours
Maintenance:
  Machine hours
  Maintenance hours
Materials Storeroom:
  Number of material moves
  Pounds of material moved
  Number of different parts

Payroll:
  Number of employees
Personnel:
  Number of employees
  Number of firings or layoffs
  Number of new hires
  Direct labor cost
Power:
  Kilowatt-hours
  Machine hours
Purchasing:
  Number of orders
  Cost of orders
Shipping:
  Number of orders

Types of Allocation Bases

In effect, producing departments *cause* support activities. **Causal factors** are variables or activities within a producing department that provoke the incurrence of support costs. In choosing a basis for allocating support department costs, appropriate causal factors (activity drivers) should be identified. Using causal factors results in more accurate product costs. Furthermore, if the causal factors are known, managers are more able to control the consumption of services.

To illustrate the types of causal factors, or activity drivers, that can be used, consider the following three support departments: Power, Personnel, and Materials Handling. For power costs, a logical allocation base is kilowatt-hours, which can be measured by separate meters for each department. If separate meters do not exist, perhaps machine hours used by each department would be a good proxy, or a means of approximating power usage. For personnel costs, both the number of producing department employees and the labor turnover (e.g., number of new hires) are possible activity drivers. For materials handling, the number of material moves, the hours of materials handling used, and the quantity of material moved are all possible activity drivers. Exhibit 7.3 lists some possible activity drivers for allocating support department costs. When competing activity drivers exist, managers choose the factor that is most easily measured and provides the most convincing relationship.

While the use of a causal factor to allocate common cost is the best solution, sometimes an easily measured causal factor cannot be found. In that case, the accountant looks for a good proxy. For example, the common cost of plant depreciation may be allocated to producing departments on the basis of square footage. Though square footage does not cause depreciation, it can be argued that the number of square feet a department occupies is a good proxy for the services provided to it by the factory building. The choice of a good proxy to guide allocation is dependent upon the company's objectives for allocation.

Objectives of Allocation

A number of important objectives are associated with the allocation of support department costs to producing departments and ultimately to specific products. The following major objectives have been identified by the IMA: [3]

1. To obtain a mutually agreeable price
2. To compute product-line profitability

[3] NAA, "Allocation of Service and Administrative Costs," *Statements of Management Accounting (Statement 4B)* (Montvale, NJ: NAA, 1985). The NAA is now known as the Institute of Management Accountants (IMA).

3. To predict the economic effects of planning and control
4. To value inventory
5. To motivate managers

Competitive pricing requires a good understanding of costs. If costs are not accurately allocated, some costs could be overstated, resulting in prices, or bids, that are too high and a loss of potential business. Alternatively, if the costs are understated, bids could be too low, producing losses on these products.

Good estimates of individual product costs also allow managers to assess the profitability of individual products and services. Multiproduct companies need to be sure that all products are profitable and that the overall profitability of the firm is not disguising the poor performance of individual products. This meets the profitability objective identified by the IMA.

By assessing the profitability of various support services, a manager may evaluate the mix of support services offered by the firm. From this evaluation, executives may decide to drop some support services, reallocate resources from one to another, reprice certain support services, or exercise greater cost control in some areas. These steps would meet the IMA's planning and control objective.

For a service organization such as a law firm, the IMA objective of inventory valuation is not relevant. For manufacturing organizations, however, this objective requires special attention. Rules of financial reporting or Generally Accepted Accounting Principles (GAAP) require that all direct and indirect manufacturing costs be assigned to the products produced. Since support department costs are indirect manufacturing costs, they must be assigned to products. This is accomplished through support department cost allocation. Inventories and cost of goods sold, then, include direct materials, direct labor, and all manufacturing overhead, including the cost of support departments.

Allocations can be used to motivate managers. If support department costs are not allocated to producing departments, managers tend to overuse these services. Consumption of a support service may continue until the marginal benefit of the service equals zero. Of course, the marginal cost of a service is greater than zero. By allocating the costs and holding managers of producing departments responsible for the economic performance of their units, the organization ensures that managers will use a support service until the marginal benefit of that service equals its marginal cost. Thus, allocation of support department costs helps each producing department select the correct level of support service use.

There are other behavioral benefits. Allocation of support department costs to producing departments encourages managers of those departments to monitor the performance of support departments. Since support department costs affect the economic performance of their own departments, those managers have an incentive to control these costs through means other than simple usage of the support service. For instance, the managers can compare the internal costs of the support service with the costs of acquiring it externally. If a support department is not as cost effective as an outside source, perhaps the company should not continue to supply the service internally.

Many university libraries have long used outside contractors for photocopying services. These contractors were more cost efficient and provided a higher level of service to library users than the previous method of using professional librarians to make change, keep the copy machines supplied with paper, fix paper jams, and so forth. Now many university libraries provide even more services, such as coffee shops and cafes, inside the building. They may arrange the services through the university dining halls or through outside companies such as **Starbucks**.[4]

REAL-WORLD EXAMPLE

4 Troy Lambert, "Retail Co-Location: Coffee at the Library" (June 12, 2017), publiclibrariesonline.org/2017/06
/retail-co-location-coffee-at-the-library/

Monitoring by managers of producing departments will also encourage managers of support departments to be more sensitive to the needs of the producing departments.

Clearly, there are good reasons for allocating support department costs. The validity of these reasons depends, however, on the accuracy and fairness of the cost assignments made. Although it may not be possible to identify a single method of allocation that simultaneously satisfies all of these objectives, several guidelines have been developed to assist in determining the best allocation method. These guidelines are cause and effect, benefits received, fairness, and ability to bear. Another guideline to be used in conjunction with any of the others is cost-benefit. That is, the method used must provide sufficient benefits to justify any effort involved.

Cause and effect require the determination of causal factors to guide allocation. For example, a corporate legal department may track the number of hours spent on legal work for its various divisions (e.g., handling patent applications, lawsuits, etc.). The number of hours worked by lawyers and paralegals has a clear cause-and-effect relationship with the overall cost of the Legal Department and may be used to allocate these costs to the various company divisions.

The benefits-received guideline associates the cost with perceived benefits. Research and development (R&D) costs, for example, may be allocated on the basis of the sales of each division. While some R&D efforts may be unsuccessful and the successful efforts may happen to benefit one division in one year, all divisions have a stake in corporate R&D and will at some point have increased sales because of it.

Fairness or equity is a guideline often mentioned in government contracting. In the case of cost allocation methods, fairness usually means that the government contract should be costed in a method similar to nongovernmental contracts. For example, an airplane engine manufacturer may allocate a portion of corporate Legal Department costs to the government contract if these costs are usually allocated to private contracts.

Ability to bear is the least desirable guideline. It tends to "penalize" the most profitable division by allocating to it the largest proportion of a support department cost—regardless of whether the profitable division receives any services from the allocated department. As a result, no motivational benefits of allocation are realized.

In determining how to allocate support department costs, the guideline of cost-benefit must be considered. In other words, the costs of implementing a particular allocation scheme must be compared to the benefits expected to be derived. As a result, companies try to use easily measured and understood bases for allocation.

OBJECTIVE ▶2▶

Calculate charging rates, and distinguish between single and dual charging rates.

ALLOCATING ONE DEPARTMENT'S COSTS TO OTHER DEPARTMENTS

Frequently, the costs of a support department are allocated to other departments through the use of a charging rate. For example, a company's Data Processing Department may serve various other departments. The cost of operating the Data Processing Department is then allocated to the user departments. While this seems simple and straightforward, a number of considerations go into determining an appropriate charging rate. The two major factors are (1) the choice of a single or a dual charging rate and (2) the use of budgeted versus actual support department costs.

A Single Charging Rate

Some companies prefer to develop a single charging rate. This is conceptually similar to a plant-wide overhead rate in that all support department costs are accumulated in the numerator and some measure of usage is in the denominator. There is only one rate, and it is relatively simple to apply. Suppose, for example, that Parminder and Lopez, a large regional public accounting firm, develops an in-house Photocopying Department to serve its three producing departments (Audit, Tax, and Management Advisory Services, or MAS). The firm wants to charge the using departments for their use of the photocopying service. **Example 7.1** illustrates the calculation and use of the single charging rate when it is applied to budgeted amounts.

Information:

The expected (budgeted) cost of Parminder and Lopez's Photocopying Department for the coming year includes:

Fixed costs (machine rental, salaries): $26,190 per year
Variable costs (paper and toner): $0.023 per page copied

Estimated (budgeted) usage by:

Audit Department	94,500
Tax Department	67,500
MAS Department	108,000
Total pages	270,000

Actual usage by:

Audit Department	92,000
Tax Department	65,000
MAS Department	115,000
Total pages	272,000

Why:

Many companies want to charge the costs of using support departments to the using departments. This makes the using departments responsible for their usage and helps to prevent overuse of resources.

Required:

1. Calculate a single charging rate for the Photocopying Department.

2. Use this rate to assign the costs of the Photocopying Department to the user departments based on actual usage. Calculate the total amount charged for photocopying for the year.

3. *What if* the Audit and Tax departments used 92,000 and 65,000 pages, respectively, but the MAS Department only used 111,000 pages? How much would have been charged out to the three departments?

Solution:

1. Total expected costs of the Photocopying Department:

Fixed costs	$26,190
Variable costs ($0.023 × 270,000 pages)	6,210
Total costs	$32,400

Single charging rate = $32,400/270,000 = $0.12 per page

2. Charge based on actual usage = Charging rate × Actual pages
    Audit Department charge = $0.12 × 92,000 = $11,040
    Tax Department charge = $0.12 × 65,000 = $7,800
    MAS Department charge = $0.12 × 115,000 = $13,800
    Total amount charged = $11,040 + $7,800 + $13,800
    = $32,640

3. Audit Department charge = $0.12 × 92,000 = $11,040
    Tax Department charge = $0.12 × 65,000 = $7,800
    MAS Department charge = $0.12 × 111,000 = $13,320
    Total amount charged = $11,040 + $7,800 + $13,320 = $32,160

Under the single charging rate, the amount charged to the producing departments is based solely on the number of pages copied. Example 7.1 shows that the amount charged to the three using departments for their actual usage—272,000 pages copied— is $32,640. A single rate treats the fixed cost as if it were variable. In fact, to the producing departments, photocopying is strictly variable. Did the Photocopying Department need $32,640 to copy 272,000 pages? No, it needed only $32,446 [$26,190 + (272,000 × $0.023)]. The extra amount charged is due to the treatment of a fixed cost in a variable manner. Similarly, if the total number of pages is less than the amount budgeted, the single rate has the effect of undercompensating the Photocopying Department. Example 7.1 shows that if the actual pages copied had been 268,000, then $32,160 would be charged. However, the Photocopying Department needed $32,354 [$26,190 + (268,000 × $0.023)]. Again, the culprit is the treatment of fixed costs as if they were variable.

Multiple Charging Rates

Sometimes a single charging rate masks the variety of causal factors that lead to a support department's total costs. The Parminder and Lopez Photocopying Department is a good example. We saw that a single charging rate was based on the number of pages copied, making it look like every page copied cost $0.12. But this is not true. A large portion of the costs of the Photocopying Department are fixed; they are not affected by the number of pages copied. Recall that $26,190 per year is spent on wages and rental of the photocopier. Why is this cost incurred? A talk with the photocopying company representative quickly yields the information that the size of the machine rented depends not on the number of pages copied per year, but on monthly peak usage. When Parminder and Lopez established the Photocopying Department, it surveyed the Audit, Tax and MAS departments to determine each one's highest monthly usage. The Audit and MAS departments have fairly even copying needs throughout the year. The Tax Department, however, expects to need one-third of its yearly estimate in the month of April. Given this information, it appears that two charging rates are needed—one for variable costs based on the number of pages copied, and one for fixed costs based on estimated peak usage.

Developing a Variable Rate   The variable costs of the Photocopying Department are for paper and toner; these equal $0.023 per page. That is the variable rate to be used.

Developing a Fixed Rate   Fixed service costs are incurred to provide the capacity needed to deliver the service required by the producing departments. When the support department was established, its capacity was designed to serve the long-term needs of the producing departments. Since the original support needs caused the creation of the support service capacity, it seems reasonable to allocate fixed costs based on those needs.

Either the normal or peak activity of the producing departments provides a reasonable measure of original support service needs. Normal capacity is the average capacity achieved over more than one fiscal period. If service is required uniformly over the time period, normal capacity is a good measure of activity. Peak capacity allows for variation in the need for the support department, and the size of the department is structured to allow for maximum need. In our example, the Tax Department may need much more photocopying during the first four months of the year, and its usage may be based on that need. The choice of normal or peak capacity in allocating budgeted fixed service costs depends on the needs of the individual firm. Budgeted fixed costs are allocated in this way regardless of whether the purpose is product costing or performance evaluation.

The allocation of fixed costs follows a three-step procedure:

1. *Determination of budgeted fixed support service costs.* The fixed support service costs that should be incurred for a period need to be identified.
2. *Computation of the allocation ratio.* The practical or normal capacity of each producing department is used to compute an allocation ratio. The allocation ratio gives a producing department's share or percentage of the total capacity of all producing departments.

Allocation ratio = Producing department capacity/Total capacity

3. *Allocation.* The fixed support service costs are allocated in proportion to each producing department's original support service needs.

Allocation = Allocation ratio × Budgeted fixed support service costs

Example 7.2 shows how and why to calculate two charging rates—one for the variable costs of the support department, and the other rate for the fixed costs.

EXAMPLE 7.2

The HOW and WHY of Calculating and Using Multiple Charging Rates

Information:
The expected (budgeted) cost of Parminder and Lopez's Photocopying Department for the coming year include:

Fixed costs (machine rental, salaries): $26,190 per year
Variable costs (paper and toner): $0.023 per page copied

The Audit and MAS departments expect to use photocopying services evenly throughout the year. The Tax Department expects that one-third of its annual usage will occur in April.

Estimated (budgeted) usage:

	Yearly Pages	Monthly Peak Pages
Audit Department	94,500	7,875
Tax Department	67,500	22,500
MAS Department	108,000	9,000
Total pages	270,000	39,375

Actual usage in year:

Audit Department	92,000
Tax Department	65,000
MAS Department	115,000
Total pages	272,000

Why:
Two rates are calculated; the variable rate is based on number of pages and the fixed rate is based on peak usage. These rates more accurately assign support department costs to the using departments.

Required:

1. Calculate a variable rate for the Photocopying Department. Calculate the allocated fixed cost for each using department based on its budgeted monthly peak usage in pages.

2. Use the two rates to assign the costs of the Photocopying Department to the user departments based on actual usage. Calculate the total amount charged for photocopying for the year.

3. *What if* the Audit and Tax departments actually used 92,000 and 65,000 pages, respectively, but the MAS Department only used 111,000 pages? How much would have been charged out to the three departments?

EXAMPLE 7.2

(Continued)

Solution:

1.   Variable rate = $0.023 per page

The fixed allocation is calculated for each department based on budgeted monthly peak usage. Monthly peak usage for Audit and MAS is one-twelfth of the yearly amount. The monthly peak usage for Tax is one-third of the yearly amount (the amount for April). The allocation is given in the following table:

Department	Peak Number of Copies	Percent*	Budgeted Fixed Cost	Allocated Fixed Cost
Audit	7,875	20%	$26,190	$ 5,238
Tax	22,500	57	26,190	14,928
MAS	9,000	23	26,190	6,024
Total	39,375	100%		$26,190

*Percent for Audit = $7,875/$39,375 = 0.20, or 20%
Percent for Tax = $22,500/$39,375 = 0.57, or 57% (rounded)
Percent for MAS = $9,000/$39,375 = 0.23, or 23% (rounded)

2.

Department	Actual Number of Copies	Variable Rate	Variable Amount	Fixed Amount	Total Charge
Audit	92,000	$0.023	$2,116	$ 5,238	$ 7,354
Tax	65,000	0.023	1,495	14,928	16,423
MAS	115,000	0.023	2,645	6,024	8,669
Total	272,000		$6,256	$26,190	$32,446

3.

Department	Actual Number of Copies	Variable Rate	Variable Amount	Fixed Amount	Total Charge
Audit	92,000	$0.023	$2,116	$ 5,238	$ 7,354
Tax	65,000	0.023	1,495	14,928	16,423
MAS	111,000	0.023	2,553	6,024	8,577
Total	268,000		$6,164	$26,190	$32,354

Total Allocation Under the dual charging rates, the fixed photocopying rates are charged to the departments in accordance with their original capacity needs. Especially in a case like the Photocopying Department example, in which fixed costs are such a high proportion of total costs, the additional effort needed to develop the dual rates may be worthwhile.

Comparing Example 7.1 results with those of Example 7.2, we see that the allocation of Photocopying Department costs is very different when the two charging rates are used. In this case, the Tax Department absorbs a larger proportion of the cost, because its peak usage is responsible for the size of the department. Notice, too, that the total amount charged of $32,446 is very close to the actual cost of running the department. With the two charging rates, each based on a strong causal factor, the allocation of cost to the using departments is close to the amount of cost that they actually cause the support department. The development of dual charging rates (which are used as the basis for pricing) is particularly important in companies such as public utilities.

The dual-rate method has the benefit of sending the correct signal regarding increased usage of the support department. Suppose that the Tax Department wants to have several research articles on tax law changes photocopied for clients. Should this be done "in house" by the Photocopying Department or sent to a private photocopying firm that charges $0.06 per page? Under the single-rate method, the in-house charge would be too high because it wrongly assumes that fixed cost will increase as pages copied increase. However, under the dual-rate method, the additional cost would be only $0.023 per page, which correctly approximates the additional cost of the job.

Could there be more than two charging rates? Definitely. However, as a company breaks down support department resources and causal factors more finely, it may be approaching activity-based costing. The extra precision of charging rates must be balanced against the cost of determining and applying those rates. As always, the company must consider costs and benefits.

Budgeted versus Actual Usage

In Example 7.1 and 7.2, the allocation bases for determining the charging rates were based on budgeted amounts, not actual amounts. This is valuable for two reasons. First, the use of budgeted data permits producing departments to use the support department allocations in developing overhead rates that are used for product or service costing. Recall that the overhead rate is calculated at the beginning of the period, when actual costs are unknown. Thus, budgeted costs must be used. The second usage of allocated support department costs is for performance evaluation. In this case, too, budgeted support department costs are allocated to producing departments.

Managers of support and producing departments usually are held accountable for the performance of their departments. Their ability to control costs is an important factor in their performance evaluations. This ability is usually measured by comparing actual costs with planned or budgeted costs. If actual costs exceed budgeted costs, the department may be operating inefficiently, with the difference between the two costs serving as the measure of that inefficiency. Similarly, if actual costs are less than budgeted costs, the department may be operating efficiently.

A general principle of performance evaluation is that managers should be held responsible for costs or activities over which they have control. Since managers of producing departments have significant input regarding the level of support service consumed, they should be held responsible for their share of support service costs. This statement, however, has an important qualification: a department's evaluation should not be affected by the degree of efficiency achieved by another department.

This qualifying statement has an important implication for the allocation of support department costs. *Actual* costs of a support department should not be allocated to producing departments because they include efficiencies or inefficiencies achieved by the support department. Managers of producing departments do not control the degree of efficiency achieved by a support department manager. By allocating *budgeted* costs instead of actual costs, no inefficiencies or efficiencies are transferred from one department to another.

Whether budgeted usage or actual usage is employed depends on the purpose of the allocation. For *product costing*, the allocation is done at the beginning of the year on the basis of budgeted usage so that a predetermined overhead rate can be computed. If the purpose is *performance evaluation*, however, the allocation is done at the end of the period and is based on actual usage. The use of cost information for performance evaluation is covered in more detail in Chapter 9.

Let's return to our photocopying example. Recall that annual budgeted fixed costs were $26,190 and the budgeted variable cost per page was $0.023. The three producing departments—Audit, Tax, and MAS—estimated usage at 94,500 copies, 67,500 copies, and 108,000 copies, respectively. Given these data, the costs allocated to each department at the *beginning* of the year are shown in Exhibit 7.4.

Exhibit 7.4

Use of Budgeted Data for Product Costing: Comparison of Single- and Dual-Rate Methods

Single-Rate Method				
	Number of Copies	× Total Rate	=	Allocated Cost
Audit	94,500	$0.12		$11,340
Tax	67,500	0.12		8,100
MAS	108,000	0.12		12,960
Total	270,000			$32,400

Dual-Rate Method				
	Number of Copies	× Variable Rate	+ Fixed Allocation	= Allocated Cost
Audit	94,500	$0.023	$ 5,238	$ 7,412*
Tax	67,500	0.023	14,928	16,481*
MAS	108,000	0.023	6,024	8,508
Total	270,000			$32,401*

*Rounded.

When the allocation is done for the purpose of budgeting the producing departments' costs, then, of course, the budgeted support department costs are used. The photocopying costs allocated to each department would be added to other producing department costs—including those directly traceable to each department plus other support department allocations—to compute each department's anticipated spending. In a manufacturing plant, the allocation of budgeted support department costs to the producing departments would precede the calculation of the predetermined overhead rate.

During the year, each producing department would also be responsible for actual charges incurred based on the actual number of pages copied. Going back to the actual usage assumed previously, a second allocation is now made to measure the actual performance of each department against its budget. The actual photocopying costs allocated to each department for performance evaluation purposes are shown in Exhibit 7.5.

Exhibit 7.5

Use of Actual Data for Performance Evaluation Purposes: Comparison of Single- and Dual-Rate Methods

Single-Rate Method				
	Number of Copies	× Total Rate	=	Allocated Cost
Audit	92,000	$0.12		$11,040
Tax	65,000	0.12		7,800
MAS	115,000	0.12		13,800
Total	272,000			$32,640

Dual-Rate Method				
	Number of Copies	× Variable Rate	+ Fixed Allocation	= Allocated Cost
Audit	92,000	$0.023	$ 5,238	$ 7,354
Tax	65,000	0.023	14,928	16,423
MAS	115,000	0.023	6,024	8,669
Total	272,000			$32,446

Fixed versus Variable Bases: A Note of Caution

Using normal or practical capacity to allocate fixed support service costs provides a *fixed* base. As long as the capacities of the producing departments remain at the original level, there is no reason to change the allocation ratios. Thus, each year, the Audit Department receives 35 percent of the budgeted fixed photocopying costs, the Tax Department 25 percent, and the MAS Department 40 percent, no matter what their actual usage is. If the capacities of the departments change, the ratios should be recalculated.

In practice, some companies choose to allocate fixed costs in proportion to actual usage or expected actual usage. Since usage may vary from year to year, allocation of fixed costs would then use a variable base. Variable bases, however, have a significant drawback: they allow the actions of one department to affect the amount of cost allocated to another department.

To see how this is demonstrated, let's return to Parminder and Lopez's Photocopying Department and assume that fixed costs are allocated on the basis of anticipated usage for the coming year. The Audit and Tax departments budget the same number of copies as before. However, the MAS Department anticipates much less activity due to a regional recession, which will cut down the number of new clients served; the anticipated number of photocopies for this department falls to 68,000. The adjusted fixed cost allocation ratios and allocated fixed cost based on the newly budgeted usage are as follows:

Department	Number of Copies	Percent	Allocated Fixed Cost
Audit	94,500	41.1%	$10,764
Tax	67,500	29.3	7,674
MAS	68,000	29.6	7,752
Total	230,000	100.0%	$26,190

Notice that both the Audit and Tax departments' allocation of fixed costs increased even though the fixed costs of the Photocopying Department remained unchanged. This increase is caused by a decrease in the MAS Department's use of photocopying. In effect, the Audit and Tax departments are penalized by MAS's decision to reduce the number of pages copied for its department. Imagine the feelings of the first two managers when they realize that their copying charges have increased due to the increase in allocated fixed costs! The penalty occurs because a variable base is used to allocate fixed support service costs; it can be avoided by using a fixed base.

CHOOSING A SUPPORT DEPARTMENT COST ALLOCATION METHOD

OBJECTIVE ◀ 3

Allocate support center costs to producing departments using the direct method, the sequential method, and the reciprocal method.

So far, we have considered cost allocation from a single support department to several producing departments. We used the direct method of support department cost allocation, in which support department costs are allocated only to producing departments. This was appropriate in the earlier example because no other support departments existed. This would also be appropriate when there is no possibility of interaction among support departments. Many companies do have multiple support departments and they frequently interact. For example, in a factory, Personnel and Cafeteria serve each other, other support departments, and the producing departments.

Ignoring these interactions and allocating support costs directly to producing departments may produce unfair and inaccurate cost assignments. For example, Power, although a support department, may use 30 percent of the services of the Maintenance Department. The maintenance costs caused by the Power Department belong to the Power Department. By not assigning these costs to the Power Department, its costs are understated. In effect, some of the costs caused by Power are "hidden" in the Maintenance Department because maintenance costs

Exhibit 7.6

Data for Support and Producing Departments

	Support Departments		Producing Departments	
	Power	**Maintenance**	**Grinding**	**Assembly**
Direct costs	$250,000	$160,000	$100,000	$ 60,000
Normal activity:				
Kilowatt-hours	—	200,000	600,000	200,000
Maintenance hours	1,000	—	4,500	4,500

would be lower if the Power Department did not exist. As a result, a producing department that is a heavy user of power and an average or below-average user of maintenance may then receive, under the direct method, a cost allocation that is understated.

In determining which support department cost allocation method to use, companies must determine the extent of support department interaction. In addition, they must weigh the costs and benefits associated with the three methods described and illustrated in the following sections: the direct, sequential, and reciprocal methods. Exhibit 7.6 presents data for a factory with two support departments, Power and Maintenance, and two producing departments—Grinding and Assembly. The activity drivers for the support departments are kilowatt-hours (for Power) and maintenance hours (for Maintenance). The direct overhead costs for each department are listed first. For the support departments, direct overhead costs include all costs of running the support departments. For the producing departments, the direct overhead costs are those overhead costs that are traced directly to those departments such as supervisory salaries and equipment depreciation. A final point should be made regarding the dashes for kilowatt-hours for Power and for maintenance hours for Maintenance. Doesn't the Power Department use power? Absolutely, however, it does not matter how many kilowatt-hours are used by Power for the purposes of allocating Power Department cost. Similarly for Maintenance, for allocation purposes, it does not matter how many hours the Maintenance Department spends on maintaining its own department.

Direct Method of Allocation

When companies allocate support department costs only to the producing departments, they are using the **direct method** of allocation. The direct method is the simplest and most straightforward way to allocate support department costs. All costs of the support departments are allocated directly to producing departments in proportion to each producing department's usage of the service. This method does not allocate any support department costs to another support department, even if other support departments use the services of a support department. This usage of one support department by another is called support department reciprocity. Under the direct method, no support department reciprocity or interaction is recognized. Exhibit 7.7 illustrates the direct method's lack of support department reciprocity. In Exhibit 7.7, we see that the direct method allocates support department costs only to the producing departments.

Example 7.3 shows how and why to allocate support department costs to producing departments using the direct method.

Examine Example 7.3 carefully. Notice that Requirement 1 shows how to calculate the allocation ratios. Since no support department cost is allocated to another support department, there are no percentages shown for Power or Maintenance. It is as if neither support department used the output of another support department. All of the support department output is assigned to the producing departments. In Requirement 2, the costs of Power and Maintenance are allocated to the producing departments. We see that all cost in each support department is divided up between the producing departments. Once those costs are allocated, there is zero cost remaining in the support departments.

Finally, it is a good idea to check the pre- and post-allocation totals. Before allocation, the total overhead in the factory is $570,000 ($250,000 + $160,000 + $100,000 + $60,000). After allocation is complete, total factory overhead is still $570,000 ($367,500 + $202,500).

Exhibit 7.7 Allocation of Support Department Costs to Producing Departments Using the Direct Method

Suppose there are two support departments, Power and Maintenance, and two producing departments, Grinding and Assembly, each with a "bucket" of directly traceable overhead cost.

Objective: Distribute all power and maintenance costs to Grinding and Assembly using the direct method.

Support Departments

Power   Maintenance

Producing Departments

Grinding   Assembly

Direct Method—allocate power and maintenance costs only to Grinding and Assembly.

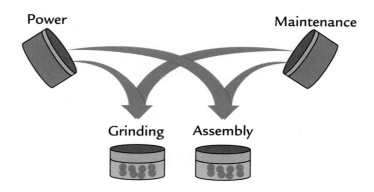

Power   Maintenance

Grinding   Assembly

After allocation—zero cost in Power and Maintenance; all overhead cost in Grinding and Assembly.

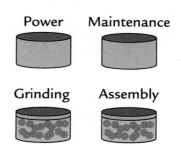

Power   Maintenance

Grinding   Assembly

EXAMPLE 7.3

The HOW and WHY of Allocating Support Department Costs to Producing Departments Using the Direct Method

Information:

Refer to Exhibit 7.6 for data on the two support and two producing departments. The costs of the Power Department are allocated on the basis of kilowatt-hours, and the costs of the Maintenance Department are allocated on the basis of maintenance hours. The factory uses the direct method of support department cost allocation.

Why:

Support department costs must be allocated to the producing departments so that the producing departments can calculate their overhead rates. The direct method is simple and easy to use. If there is relatively little support department reciprocity, it does a fairly good job.

EXAMPLE 7.3

(Continued)

Required:

1. Calculate the allocation ratios for the four departments using the direct method.

2. Using the direct method, allocate the costs of the Power and Maintenance departments to the Grinding and Assembly departments.

3. ***What if*** the Maintenance Department used only 100,000 kilowatt-hours? How would that affect the allocation of Power Department costs to the Grinding and Assembly departments?

Solution:

1. Allocation ratios:

	Proportion of Driver Used by			
	Power	**Maintenance**	**Grinding**	**Assembly**
Power	—	—	0.75^1	0.25^2
Maintenance	—	—	0.50^3	0.50^4

^{1}Proportion of kilowatt-hours used by Grinding = 600,000/(600,000 + 200,000) = 0.75
^{2}Proportion of kilowatt-hours used by Assembly = 200,000/(600,000 + 200,000) = 0.25
^{3}Proportion of maintenance hours used by Grinding = 4,500/(4,500 + 4,500) = 0.50
^{4}Proportion of maintenance hours used by Assembly = 4,500/(4,500 + 4,500) = 0.50

2.

	Support Departments		Producing Departments	
	Power	**Maintenance**	**Grinding**	**Assembly**
Direct costs	$250,000	$160,000	$100,000	$ 60,000
Allocate:				
Power^1	(250,000)	—	187,500	62,500
Maintenance^2	—	(160,000)	80,000	80,000
Total after allocation	$ 0	$ 0	$367,500	$202,500

^{1}Grinding = 0.75 × $250,000 = $187,500; Assembly = 0.25 × $250,000 = $62,500
^{2}Grinding = 0.50 × $160,000 = $80,000; Assembly = 0.50 × $160,000 = $80,000

3. Since none of the Power cost is allocated to Maintenance, it does not matter how many kilowatt-hours are used by Maintenance.

These totals will always be the same (except for rounding error). Allocation does not increase or decrease total overhead, it just redistributes it to the producing departments.

Sequential Method of Allocation

The **sequential (or step) method** of allocation recognizes that interactions among the support departments do occur; however, the sequential method takes only partial account of this interaction. Cost allocations are performed in step-down fashion, following a predetermined ranking procedure. This ranking can be performed in various ways. One possibility is to rank the support departments in order of the percentage of service provided to other support departments. Another possibility is to rank the support departments in order of their total cost, from highest cost department to lowest.

Exhibit 7.8 illustrates the sequential method. In it, Power is ranked first, then Maintenance. Next, power costs are allocated to Maintenance and the two producing departments. Finally, the costs of maintenance are allocated only to the producing departments.

Once the support departments have been ranked, the top ranking department is allocated to lower ranking support departments and the producing departments. It is then closed out

Exhibit 7.8 Allocation of Support Department Costs to Producing Departments Using the Sequential Method

Suppose there are two support departments, Power and Maintenance, and two producing departments, Grinding and Assembly, each with a "bucket" of directly traceable overhead cost.

Objective: Distribute all power and maintenance costs to Grinding and Assembly using the sequential method.

Support Departments
Power   Maintenance

Producing Departments
Grinding   Assembly

Step 1: Rank support departments—
#1 Power, #2 Maintenance.

Step 2: Distribute power costs to Maintenance, Grinding, and Assembly.

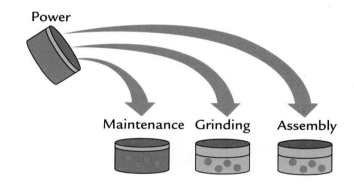

Then, distribute maintenance costs to Grinding and Assembly.

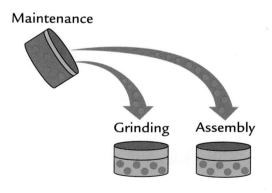

After allocation—zero cost in Power and Maintenance; all overhead cost in Grinding and Assembly.

Power   Maintenance

Grinding   Assembly

(has a total cost remaining of zero) and the remaining support departments cannot allocate cost back to it. Then, the costs of the support department next in sequence are similarly allocated, and so on. In the sequential method, once a support department's costs are allocated, it never receives a subsequent allocation from another support department. In other words, costs of a support department are never allocated to support departments *above* it in the sequence. Also note that the costs allocated from a support department are its direct costs *plus* any costs it receives in allocations from other support departments. The direct costs of a department are those that are directly traceable to the department.

Example 7.4 shows how and why to use the sequential method. The data originally given in Exhibit 7.6 are used. First, the support departments are ranked. Power provides relatively more service to Maintenance than Maintenance provides to Power. In addition, the cost of Power is higher than the cost of Maintenance. So, no matter which ranking system is used, Power is allocated first, then Maintenance.

As before, it is a good idea to check the pre- and post-allocation totals. Before allocation, the total overhead in the factory is $570,000 ($250,000 + $160,000 + $100,000 + $60,000). After allocation is complete, total factory overhead is $570,001 ($360,563 + $209,438); the dollar difference is due to rounding error. These totals will always be the same (except for rounding error). Allocation does not increase or decrease total overhead, it just redistributes it to the producing departments.

EXAMPLE 7.4

The HOW and WHY of Allocating Support Department Costs to Producing Departments Using the Sequential (Step) Method

Information:

Refer to Exhibit 7.6 for data on the two support and two producing departments. The costs of the Power Department are allocated on the basis of kilowatt-hours, and the costs of the Maintenance Department are allocated on the basis of maintenance hours. The factory uses the sequential method of support department cost allocation.

> **Why:**
> Support department costs must be allocated to the producing departments so that the producing departments can calculate their overhead rates. The sequential method takes some account of support department reciprocity and is, therefore, somewhat better than the direct method.

Required:

1. Calculate the allocation ratios for the four departments using the sequential method.

2. Using the sequential method, allocate the costs of the Power and Maintenance departments to the Grinding and Assembly departments.

3. *What if* the Maintenance Department used only 100,000 kilowatt-hours? How would that affect the allocation of Power Department costs to the Grinding and Assembly departments?

Solution:

1. Power is allocated first because 20 percent of its service [200,000/(200,000 + 600,000 + 200,000) = 20%] is used for other support departments (in this case, Maintenance). Only 10 percent [1,000/(1,000 + 4,500 + 4,500) = 10%]

EXAMPLE 7.4

(Continued)

of Maintenance services are used by other support departments (i.e., Power). Allocation ratios:

		Proportion of Driver Used by		
	Power	**Maintenance**	**Grinding**	**Assembly**
Power	—	0.20[1]	0.60[2]	0.20[3]
Maintenance	—	—	0.50[4]	0.50[5]

[1]Proportion of kilowatt-hours used by Maintenance = 200,000/(200,000 + 600,000 + 200,000) = 0.20
[2]Proportion of kilowatt-hours used by Grinding = 600,000/(200,000 + 600,000 + 200,000) = 0.60
[3]Proportion of kilowatt-hours used by Assembly = 200,000/(200,000 + 600,000 + 200,000) = 0.20
[4]Proportion of maintenance hours used by Grinding = 4,500/(4,500 + 4,500) = 0.50
[5]Proportion of maintenance hours used by Assembly = 4,500/(4,500 + 4,500) = 0.50

2.

	Support Departments		Producing Departments	
	Power	**Maintenance**	**Grinding**	**Assembly**
Direct costs	$ 250,000	$ 160,000	$100,000	$ 60,000
Allocate:				
Power[1]	(250,000)	50,000	150,000	50,000
Maintenance[2]	—	(210,000)	105,000	105,000
Total after allocation	$ 0	$ 0	$355,000	$215,000

[1]Maintenance = 0.2 × $250,000 = $50,000; Grinding = 0.60 × $250,000 = $150,000; Assembly = 0.20 × $250,000 = $50,000
[2]Grinding = 0.50 × ($160,000 + $50,000) = $105,000; Assembly = 0.50 × ($160,000 + $50,000) = $105,000

3. If Maintenance used only 100,000 kilowatt-hours, then the proportion of service it uses would drop to 11.11% [100,000/(100,000 + 600,000 + 200,000)]. Power would still be allocated first; however, the allocation ratios for Power would change to Maintenance, 11.11%; Grinding, 66.67%; and Assembly, 22.22% (rounded). Thus, relatively fewer dollars would be allocated to Maintenance, and relatively more to Grinding and Assembly. The new allocations would be as follows:

	Support Departments		Producing Departments	
	Power	**Maintenance**	**Grinding**	**Assembly**
Direct costs	$ 250,000	$ 160,000	$100,000	$ 60,000
Allocate:				
Power[1]	(250,000)	27,775	166,675	55,550
Maintenance[2]	—	(187,775)	93,888	93,888
Total after allocation	$ 0	$ 0	$360,563	$209,438

[1]Maintenance = 0.1111 × $250,000 = $27,775; Grinding = 0.6667 × $250,000 = $166,675; Assembly = 0.2222 × $250,000 = $55,550
[2]Grinding = 0.50 × ($160,000 + $27,775) = $93,888; Assembly = 0.50 × ($160,000 + $27,775) = $93,888

Note: The totals after allocation do not precisely sum to the before allocation totals due to rounding.

The sequential method may be more accurate than the direct method because it recognizes some interactions among the support departments. It does not recognize all interactions, however; no maintenance costs were assigned to the Power Department even though it used 10 percent of the Maintenance Department's output. The reciprocal method corrects this deficiency.

Reciprocal Method of Allocation

The **reciprocal method** of allocation recognizes all interactions of support departments. Under the reciprocal method, the usage of one support department by another is used to determine the total cost of each support department, where the total cost reflects interactions among the support departments. Then, the new total of support department costs is allocated to the producing departments. This method fully accounts for support department interaction.

Total Cost of Support Departments

To determine the total cost of a support department so that this total cost reflects interactions with other support departments, a system of simultaneous linear equations must be solved. Each equation, which is a cost equation for a support department, is the sum of the department's direct costs plus the proportion of service received from other support departments.

$$\text{Total cost} = \text{Direct costs} + \text{Allocated costs}$$

The same data set contained in Exhibit 7.6 used to illustrate the direct and sequential methods will be used to illustrate the reciprocal method. **Example 7.5** shows how and why the reciprocal method is used to allocate support department costs.

EXAMPLE 7.5

The HOW and WHY of Allocating Support Department Costs to Producing Departments Using the Reciprocal Method

Information:
Refer to Exhibit 7.6 for data on the two support and two producing departments. The costs of the Power Department are allocated on the basis of kilowatt-hours, and the costs of the Maintenance Department are allocated on the basis of maintenance hours. The factory uses the reciprocal method of support department cost allocation.

Why:
Support department costs must be allocated to the producing departments so that the producing departments can calculate their overhead rates. The reciprocal method takes full account of support department reciprocity and is, therefore, the theoretically best method.

Required:

1. Calculate the allocation ratios for the four departments in preparation for the reciprocal method.

2. Develop a simultaneous equations system of total costs for the support departments. Solve for the total reciprocated costs of each support department.

3. Using the reciprocal method, allocate the fully reciprocated costs of the Power and Maintenance departments to the Grinding and Assembly Departments.

4. ***What if*** the Maintenance Department used only 100,000 kilowatt-hours? How would that affect the allocation of Power Department costs to the Grinding and Assembly departments?

EXAMPLE 7.5

Solution:

(*Continued*)

1. Allocation ratios:

	Proportion of Driver Used by			
	Power	**Maintenance**	**Grinding**	**Assembly**
Power	—	0.20[1]	0.60[2]	0.20[3]
Maintenance	0.10[4]	—	0.45[5]	0.45[6]

[1]Proportion of kilowatt-hours used by Maintenance = 200,000/(200,000 + 600,000 + 200,000) = 0.20
[2]Proportion of kilowatt-hours used by Grinding = 600,000/(200,000 + 600,000 + 200,000) = 0.60
[3]Proportion of kilowatt-hours used by Assembly = 200,000/(200,000 + 600,000 + 200,000) = 0.20
[4]Proportion of maintenance hours used by Power = 1,000/(1,000 + 4,500 + 4,500) = 0.10
[5]Proportion of maintenance hours used by Grinding = 4,500/(1,000 + 4,500 + 4,500) = 0.45
[6]Proportion of maintenance hours used by Assembly = 4,500/(1,000 + 4,500 + 4,500) = 0.45

2. Let P = Fully reciprocated costs for Power; and
   M = Fully reciprocated costs for Maintenance
   $$P = \$250,000 + 0.1M$$
   $$M = \$160,000 + 0.2P$$

Solve for P by substituting ($\$160,000 + 0.2P$) for M:
$$P = \$250,000 + 0.1 (\$160,000 + 0.2P)$$
$$P - 0.02P = \$250,000 + \$16,000$$
$$0.98P = \$266,000$$
$$P = \$271,429 \text{ (rounded)}$$

Solve for M:

$$M = \$160,000 + 0.2(\$271,429) = \$214,286 \text{ (rounded)}$$

3.

	Support Departments		Producing Departments	
	Power	**Maintenance**	**Grinding**	**Assembly**
Direct costs	$ 250,000	$ 160,000	$100,000	$ 60,000
Allocate:				
Power[1]	(271,429)	54,286	162,857	54,286
Maintenance[2]	21,429	(214,286)	96,429	96,429
Total after allocation	$ 0	$ 0	$359,286	$210,715

[1]Maintenance = 0.20 × $271,429 = $54,286; Grinding = 0.60 × $271,429 = $162,857; Assembly = 0.20 × $271,429 = $54,286
[2]Power = 0.10 × $214,286 = $21,429; Grinding = 0.45 × $214,286 = $96,429; Assembly = 0.45 × $214,286 = $96,429

Note: The totals after allocation do not precisely sum to the before allocation totals due to rounding.

4. If Maintenance used only 100,000 kilowatt-hours, then the proportion of service it uses would drop to 11.11% [100,000/(100,000 + 600,000 + 200,000)]. The allocation ratios for Power would change to Maintenance, 11.11%; Grinding, 66.67%; and Assembly, 22.22% (rounded). This would affect the simultaneous equations and the subsequent allocation.
$$P = \$250,000 + 0.1M$$
$$M = \$160,000 + 0.1111P$$

Solve for P by substituting ($\$160,000 + 0.1111P$) for M:
$$P = \$250,000 + 0.1(\$160,000 + 0.1111P)$$
$$P - 0.01111P = \$250,000 + \$16,000$$
$$0.98889P = \$266,000$$
$$P = \$268,988 \text{ (rounded)}$$

EXAMPLE 7.5

(Continued)

Solve for M:

$$M = \$160{,}000 + 0.1111(\$268{,}988) = \$189{,}885 \text{ (rounded)}$$

The new allocations would be as follows:

| | Support Departments | | Producing Departments | |
	Power	Maintenance	Grinding	Assembly
Direct costs	$ 250,000	$ 160,000	$100,000	$ 60,000
Allocate:				
Power[1]	(268,988)	29,885	179,334	59,769
Maintenance[2]	18,989	(189,885)	85,448	85,448
Total after allocation	$ (1)	$ 0	$364,782	$205,217

[1]Maintenance = 0.1111 × $268,988 = $29,885; Grinding = 0.6667 × $268,988 = $179,334; Assembly = 0.2222 × $268,988 = $59,769
[2]Power = 0.10 × $189,885 = $18,989; Grinding = 0.45 × $189,885 = $85,448; Assembly = 0.45 × $189,885 = $85,448

Note: The totals after allocation do not precisely sum to the before allocation totals due to rounding.

As Example 7.5 shows, the steps for the reciprocal method are:
1. Compute the allocation ratios for all support and producing departments.
2. Form a simultaneous equations system with one equation for each support department. The interpretation of each equation is that the total reciprocated cost of the support department equals its original cost plus any cost that it imposes on any other support departments.
3. Solve the simultaneous equations system for each unknown to obtain the total reciprocated cost of each support department.
4. Allocate the total reciprocated costs of the support departments to other support departments and to the producing departments based on the allocation ratios developed in Step 1.

After the equations are solved, the total costs of each support department are known. These total costs, unlike the direct or sequential methods, reflect all interactions between support departments. As a result, the reciprocal method is the best method in terms of accounting for all interactions among the support departments.

Comparison of the Three Methods

Exhibit 7.9 gives the cost allocations from the Power and Maintenance departments to the Grinding and Assembly departments using the three support department cost allocation methods. How different are the results? Does it really matter which method is used? Depending on the degree of support department interaction, the three allocation methods can give quite different results. In this particular example, the direct method (as compared to the sequential method) allocated $12,500 more to the Grinding Department (and $12,500 less to the Assembly Department). Surely, the manager of the Assembly Department would prefer the direct method, and the manager of the Grinding Department would prefer the sequential method. Because allocation methods do affect the cost responsibilities of managers, it is important for the accountant to understand the consequences of the different methods and to have good reasons for the eventual choice.

It is important to keep a cost-benefit perspective in choosing an allocation method. The accountant must weigh the advantages of better allocation against the increased cost using a more theoretically preferred method, such as the reciprocal method. For example, about 30 years ago, the controller for the **IBM** Poughkeepsie plant decided that the reciprocal method of cost allocation would do a better job of allocating support department costs. He identified over

Exhibit 7.9 Comparison of Support Department Cost Allocations Using the Direct, Sequential, and Reciprocal Methods

	Direct Method		Sequential Method		Reciprocal Method	
	Grinding	**Assembly**	**Grinding**	**Assembly**	**Grinding**	**Assembly**
Direct costs	$100,000	$ 60,000	$100,000	$ 60,000	$100,000	$ 60,000
Allocated from						
power	187,500	62,500	150,000	50,000	162,857	54,286
Allocated from						
maintenance	80,000	80,000	105,000	105,000	96,429	96,429
Total cost	$367,500	$202,500	$355,000	$215,000	$359,286	$210,715

700 support departments and solved the system of equations using a computer. Computationally, he had no problems. The producing department managers, however, did not understand the reciprocal method. They were sure that extra cost was being allocated to their departments, but they were not sure just how. After months of meetings with the line managers, the controller threw in the towel and returned to the sequential method—which everyone did understand.[5]

Another factor to be considered in allocating support department cost is the rapid change in technology. Many firms currently find that support department cost allocation is useful for them. However, the move toward activity-based costing and just-in-time manufacturing can virtually eliminate the need for support department cost allocation. In the case of the just-in-time factory with manufacturing cells, much of the service (e.g., maintenance, materials handling, and setups) is performed by cell workers. Allocation is not necessary.

DEPARTMENTAL OVERHEAD RATES AND PRODUCT COSTING

OBJECTIVE ◀ 4
Calculate departmental overhead rates.

Upon allocating all support service costs to producing departments, an overhead rate can be computed for each department. This rate is computed by adding the allocated service costs to the overhead costs that are directly traceable to the producing department and dividing this total by some measure of activity, such as direct labor hours or machine hours. **Example 7.6** shows how and why to use the allocated support department costs to develop departmental overhead rates.

One might wonder, however, just how accurate are the job costs calculated in Example 7.6? Is this amount the true cost of the product in question? Since materials and labor are directly traceable to products, the accuracy of product costs depends largely on the accuracy of the assignment of overhead costs. This in turn depends on the degree of correlation between the

EXAMPLE 7.6

The HOW and WHY of Using Allocated Support Department Costs to Calculate Departmental Overhead Rates

Information:
Assume that the factory in our example uses the sequential method to allocate support department costs. The cost allocation is shown in Example 7.4. The Grinding Department overhead rate is based on normal activity of 71,000 machine hours. The Assembly Department overhead rate is based on normal activity of 107,500 direct labor hours.

Job 189 required 20 machine hours in Grinding and five direct labor hours in Assembly. Total direct materials cost was $465, and total direct labor cost was $370.

---

5 This is based on conversations between the author and the IBM controller.

EXAMPLE 7.6

(Continued)

> **Why:**
> One reason for support department cost allocation is to allow producing departments to calculate overhead rates. The overhead rates are then used to cost product.

Required:

1. Calculate the overhead rate for Grinding based on machine hours and the overhead rate for Assembly based on direct labor hours.

2. Using the overhead rates calculated in Requirement 1, calculate the cost of Job 189.

3. **What if** Job 189 had required five machine hours in Grinding and 20 direct labor hours in Assembly? Direct labor and direct materials costs remained the same. Calculate the new cost of Job 189.

Solution:

1. Grinding Department overhead rate = $355,000/71,000
   $$= \$5 \text{ per machine hour}$$
   Assembly Department overhead rate = $215,000/107,500
   $$= \$2 \text{ per direct labor hour}$$

2. Cost of Job 189:

Direct materials	$465
Direct labor cost	370
Applied overhead:	
Grinding (20 × $5)	100
Assembly (5 × $2)	10
Total cost	$945

3. New Cost of Job 189:

Direct materials	$465
Direct labor cost	370
Applied overhead:	
Grinding (5 × $5)	25
Assembly (20 × $2)	40
Total cost	$900

factors used to allocate support service costs to departments and the factors used to allocate the department's overhead costs to the products. For example, if power costs are highly correlated with kilowatt-hours and machine hours are highly correlated with a product's consumption of the Grinding Department's overhead costs, then we can have some confidence that the $5 overhead rate accurately assigns costs to individual products. However, if the allocation of support service costs to the Grinding Department or the use of machine hours is faulty—or both—then product costs will be distorted. The same reasoning can be applied to the Assembly Department. To ensure accurate product costs, great care should be used in identifying and using causal factors for both stages of overhead assignment.

Support Department Cost Allocation Benefits

Given the effort involved in support department cost allocation, one might ask whether the benefits outweigh the costs. Many companies say "yes." The following paragraphs give an example.

Using Big Data

"Did you get my order? Did you ship it? If not, when are you going to?" These are the three big questions that **Mott's** North America customers want answered—and they want them answered in real time. Mott's, which sells juices and processed fruit products (including applesauce, Clamato, Mr. and Mrs. T drink mixer, Rose's, and Holland House) to food brokers, uses SAP R/3 integrated applications to provide customer service and support. While many companies assign customer service to a support department, Mott's believes that customer service is the most critical issue in its business. The company wants to provide more timely information about order status, the availability of products, and production schedules and delivery. This requires big data analysis to integrate data files containing information on order taking, billing, accounts receivable, production, and shipping.

"Orders come in through EDI, telephone, or fax," says Jeff Morgan, senior vice president of information technology. "Customer service takes the order and checks availability to confirm delivery date. If there is insufficient product in inventory, the service representative checks the production plan. This automatically calculates lead times to determine delivery of the entire order or partial shipment and balance delivery date. The order is launched, financials are updated as it works its way through the system, and an invoice is generated. As soon as any data are entered into the system, they are immediately available for access by other users throughout the system."

Further benefits are gained through the elimination of duplicate data entry and the need to reconcile transactions between the formerly "siloed" support departments. The end results are a reduction in cost, improvement in customer service, and better understanding of the relationship between production and support costs.[6]

REAL-WORLD EXAMPLE

Careful management of support departments and the use of cost allocation methods can provide behavioral benefits to give companies a competitive edge. The choice of which allocation method to choose depends on the circumstances and an evaluation of costs and benefits.

ACCOUNTING FOR JOINT PRODUCTION PROCESSES

OBJECTIVE 5

Identify the characteristics of the joint production process, and allocate joint costs to products.

Joint products are two or more products produced simultaneously by the same process up to a "split-off" point. The **split-off point** is the point at which the joint products become separate and identifiable. For example, oil and natural gas are joint products. When a company drills for oil, it gets natural gas as well. As a result, the costs of exploration, acquisition of mineral rights, and drilling are incurred to the initial split-off point. Such costs are necessary to bring crude oil and natural gas out of the ground, and they are common costs to both products. Of course, some joint products may require processing beyond the split-off point. For example, crude oil can be processed further into aviation fuel, gasoline, kerosene, naphtha, and other petrochemicals. The key point, however, is that the direct materials, direct labor, and overhead costs incurred up to the initial split-off point are joint costs that can be allocated to the final product only in some arbitrary manner. Joint products are so enmeshed that once the decision to produce has been made, management decision has little effect on the output, at least to the initial split-off point. Exhibit 7.10 depicts the joint production process. Exhibit 7.11 depicts the usual production process in which two products are manufactured independently from a common material. For example, a Taurus and a Mustang require steel, but the purchase of steel by **Ford Motor Company** does not require the manufacture of either model of car.

---

6   Taken from SAP materials and the website: http://www.sap.com/usa.

Exhibit 7.10   Joint Production Process

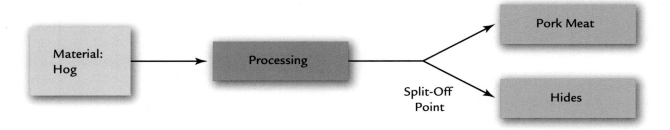

Joint products are related to each other such that an increase in the output of one increases the output of the others, although not necessarily in the same ratio. Up to the split-off point, you cannot get more of one product without getting more of the other(s). Whether considering the direct materials and conversion costs incurred prior to the initial split-off point as depicted in Exhibit 7.10, or the costs of heat, fuel, and depreciation incurred in the type of multiple-product production depicted in Exhibit 7.11, one characteristic stands out. They are all indirect costs in the sense that allocation among the various products is necessary: that is, such costs cannot be traced directly to the ultimate products they benefit.

Cost Separability and the Need for Allocation

Costs are either separable or not. **Separable costs** are easily traced to individual products and offer no particular problem. If not separable, they are allocated to various products for various reasons. Cost allocations are arbitrary. That is, there is no well-accepted theoretical way to determine which product incurs what part of the joint cost. In reality, all joint products benefit from the entire joint cost. The objective in joint cost allocation is to determine the most appropriate way to allocate a cost that is not really separable. The primary reason for joint cost allocation is that financial reporting (GAAP) and federal income tax law require it. In addition, these product costs are somewhat useful in calculating the cost of special lots or orders, including government cost-type contracts, and in justifying prices for legislative or administrative regulations. It is important to note that the allocation of joint costs is not appropriate for certain types of management decisions. The impact of joint costs on decision making is reserved for Chapter 17.

There are two important differences between costs incurred up to the split-off point in joint product situations and those indirect costs incurred for products that are produced independently. First, certain costs such as direct materials and direct labor, which are directly

Exhibit 7.11

Independent Multiple-Product Production Using the Same Material

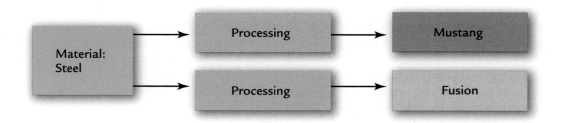

traceable to products when two or more products are separately produced, become indirect and indivisible when used prior to the split-off point. For example, if ore contains both iron and zinc, the direct material itself is a joint product. Since neither zinc nor iron can be produced alone prior to the split-off point, the related processing costs of mining, crushing, and splitting the ore are also joint costs. Second, manufacturing overhead becomes even more indirect in joint product situations. Consider the purchase of pineapples. A pineapple, in and of itself, is not a joint product. When pineapples are purchased for canning, however, the initial processing or trimming of the fruit results in a variety of products (skin for animal feed, trimmed core for further slicing and dicing, and juice). The processing costs to the point of split-off, as well as the cost of the original pineapples, are mutually beneficial to all products produced to that point. Both of these phenomena are caused either because the material itself is a joint product or because processing results in the simultaneous output of more than one product.

Accounting for Joint Product Costs

The accounting for overall joint costs of production (direct materials, direct labor, and overhead) is no different from the accounting for product costs in general. It is the *allocation* of joint costs to the individual products that is the source of difficulty. Still, the allocation must be done for financial reporting purposes—to value inventory carried on the balance sheet and to determine income. Thus, an allocation method must be found that, though arbitrary, allocates the costs on as reasonable a basis as possible. Because judgment is involved, equally competent accountants can arrive at different costs for the same product. There are a variety of methods for allocating joint costs. These methods include the physical units method, the weighted average method, the sales-value-at-split-off method, the net realizable value method, and the constant gross margin percentage method. These are covered in the following sections.

Physical Units Method   Under the **physical units method**, joint costs are distributed to products on the basis of some physical measure. These physical measures may be expressed in units such as pounds, tons, gallons, board feet, atomic weight, or heat units. If the joint products do not share the same physical measure (e.g., one product is measured in gallons, another in pounds), some common denominator may be used. For example, a producer of fuels may take gallons, barrels, and tons and convert each one into BTUs (British thermal units) of energy.

Computationally, the physical units method allocates the same proportion of joint cost to each product as the underlying proportion of units. So, if a joint process yields 300 pounds of Product A and 700 pounds of Product B, Product A receives 30 percent of the joint cost and Product B receives 70 percent. Alternatively, one can divide total joint costs by total output to find an average unit cost. The average unit cost is then multiplied by the number of units of each product. **Example 7.7** shows how and why the physical units method is used to allocate joint cost.

Although the physical units method is not wholly satisfactory, it has a measure of logic behind it. Since all products are manufactured by the same process, it is impossible to say that one costs more per unit to produce than the other. For example, manufacturers of forest products may add the average cost of logs entering the mill to the average conversion cost to arrive at an average finished product cost. This cost is applied to all finished products, no matter their type, grade, or market value. This method serves the purpose of product costing.

The physical units method may be used in any industry that processes joint products of differing grades (e.g., flour milling, tobacco, and lumber). However, a disadvantage of the physical units method is that high profits may be reflected from the sale of the high grades, with low profits or losses reflected on the sale of lower grades. This may result in incorrect managerial decisions if the data are not properly interpreted.

EXAMPLE 7.7

The HOW and WHY of Using the Physical Units Method to Allocate Joint Product Costs

Information:

A sawmill processes logs into four grades of lumber totaling 3,000,000 board feet as follows:

Grades	Board Feet
First and second	450,000
No. 1 common	1,200,000
No. 2 common	600,000
No. 3 common	750,000
Total	3,000,000

Total joint cost is $186,000.

Why:
The joint cost must be allocated to the various grades of lumber in order to cost product and value inventory. The physical units method allocates the cost in proportion to the number of units and is useful when the value of one product (here, grade) is close to the value of another product.

Required:

1. Allocate the joint cost to the four grades of lumber using the physical units method.

2. Allocate the joint cost to the four grades of lumber by finding the average joint cost per board foot and multiplying it by the number of board feet in the grade.

3. *What if* First and second and No. 1 common each had 825,000 board feet? How would that affect the allocation of cost to these two grades? How would it affect the allocation of cost to the No. 2 and No. 3 common grades?

Solution:

1.

Grades	Board Feet	Percent of Units*	Joint Cost Allocation
	(2)	(3)	(3) × $186,000
First and second	450,000	15%	$ 27,900
No. 1 common	1,200,000	40	74,400
No. 2 common	600,000	20	37,200
No. 3 common	750,000	25	46,500
Total	3,000,000	100%	$186,000

*Percent for First and second = 450,000/3,000,000 = 0.15, or 15%
Percent for No. 1 common = 1,200,000/3,000,000 = 0.40, or 40%
Percent for No. 2 common = 600,000/3,000,000 = 0.20, or 20%
Percent for No. 3 common = 750,000/3,000,000 = 0.25, or 25%

2. Average joint cost = $186,000/3,000,000 board feet = $0.062
    First and second joint cost allocation = $0.062 × 450,000 = $27,900
    No. 1 common joint cost allocation = $0.062 × 1,200,000 = $74,400
    No. 2 common joint cost allocation = $0.062 × 600,000 = $37,200
    No. 3 common joint cost allocation = $0.062 × 750,000 = $46,500
    (*Note:* Either method gives the same allocation results.)

3. If First and second and No. 1 common each had 825,000 board feet, then each would receive 27.5 percent (825,000/3,000,000) of the joint cost, or $51,150 (27.5% × $186,000). There would be no impact on the allocation to No. 2 common and No. 3 common since their proportion of total board feet did not change.

The physical units method presumes that each unit of material in the final product costs just as much to produce as any other. This is especially true where the dominant element can be traced to the product. Many feel this method often is unsatisfactory because it ignores the fact that not all costs are directly related to physical quantities. Also, the product might not have been handled at all if it had been physically separable before the split-off point from the part desired.

Weighted Average Method Some difficulties encountered under the physical units method can be overcome by using weight factors. These weight factors may include such diverse elements as amount of material used, difficulty to manufacture, time consumed, difference in type of labor used, and size of unit. These factors and their relative weights are usually combined in a single value, called the **weight factor**.

An example of the use of weight factors is found in the canning industry.[7] One type of weight factor is used to convert different-size cases of peaches into a uniform size for purposes of allocating joint costs to each case. Thus, if a basic case contains 24 cans of peaches in size 2½ cans, that case is assigned a weight factor of 1.0. A case with 24 cans in size 303 (a can roughly half the size of the size 2½ can) receives a weight of 0.57, and so on. Once all types of cases have been converted into basic cases using the weight factors, joint costs can be allocated according to the physical units method. Peaches can also be assigned weight factors according to grade (e.g., fancy, choice, standard, and pie). If the standard grade is weighted at 1.00, then the better grades are weighted more heavily and the pie grade less heavily. **Example 7.8** shows how and why the weighted average method can be used to allocate joint costs to different products.

As Example 7.8 shows, once the weight factors are applied, the physical units can be applied to obtain the percentage of weighted cases for each grade. These percentages are then multiplied by the joint cost to yield the allocated joint cost. The effect is to allocate relatively more of the joint cost to the fancy and choice grades because they represent more desirable peaches. The pie grade peaches, the good bits and pieces from bruised peaches, are relatively less desirable and are assigned a lower weight.

EXAMPLE 7.8

The HOW and WHY of Using the Weighted Average Method to Allocate Joint Product Costs

Information:
A peach-canning factory purchases $5,000 of peaches; grades them into fancy, choice, standard, and pie quality; and then cans each grade. The following data on grade, number of cases, and weight factor follow:

	Number of Cases	Weight Factor
Fancy	100	1.30
Choice	120	1.10
Standard	303	1.00
Pie	70	0.50
Total	593	

Why:
The joint cost must be allocated to the various grades of peaches in order to cost the product and value inventory. The weighted average method allows firms to place relatively more value on certain types or grades of units than on others.

Required:

1. Allocate the joint cost to the four grades of peaches using the weighted average method.

---

7 The peach-canning example is adapted from K. E. Jankowski, "Cost and Sales Control in the Canning Industry," N.A. *C.A. Bulletin* 36 (November 1954): 376.

EXAMPLE 7.8

(Continued)

2. *What if* the factory found that peaches for pie were being valued more by customers and decided to increase the weight factor for pie peaches to 1.00? How would that affect the allocation of cost to pie peaches? How would it affect the allocation of cost to the remaining grades?

Solution:

1.

Grades	Number of Cases	Weight Factor	Weighted Number of Cases	Percent	Allocated Joint Cost
Fancy	100	1.30	130	0.21667	$1,083
Choice	120	1.10	132	0.22000	1,100
Standard	303	1.00	303	0.50500	2,525
Pie	70	0.50	35	0.05833	292
Total			600		$5,000

2. If the pie grade weight factor is increased to 1.00, then the weighted number of cases would double and pie peaches would receive a relatively larger amount of joint cost. However, the allocation of cost to all other grades will decrease since the increased weighted cases for pie will impact all percentages. The following table shows what would happen:

Grades	Number of Cases	Weight Factor	Weighted Number of Cases	Percent	Allocated Joint Cost
Fancy	100	1.30	130	0.2047	$1,024
Choice	120	1.10	132	0.2079	1,040
Standard	303	1.00	303	0.4772	2,386
Pie	70	1.00	70	0.1102	551
Total			635		$5,001

(*Note:* The joint cost allocation total is not equal to $5,000 due to rounding.)

Frequently, weight factors are predetermined and set up as part of either an estimated cost or a standard cost system. The use of carefully constructed weight factors enables the cost accountant to give more attention to several influences and, therefore, results in more reasonable allocations. The real danger, of course, is that weights may be used that are either inappropriate in the first place or become so through the passage of time. Obviously, if arbitrary rates are used, the resulting costs of individual products will be arbitrary.

Allocation Based on Relative Market Value

Many accountants believe that joint costs should be allocated to individual products according to their ability to absorb joint costs. The advantage of this approach is that joint cost allocation will not produce consistently profitable or unprofitable items. The rationale for using ability to bear is the assumption that costs would not be incurred unless the jointly produced products together would yield enough revenue to cover all costs plus a reasonable return. On the other hand, fluctuations in the market value of any one or more of the end products automatically change the apportionment of the joint costs, though actually it costs no more or no less to produce than before.

The relative market value approach to joint cost allocation is better than the physical units approach if two conditions hold: (1) the physical mix of output can be altered by incurring more (less) total joint costs and (2) this alteration produces more (less) total market value.[8] Several variants of the relative market value method are found in practice.

---

8 William Cats-Baril, James F. Gatti, and D. Jacque Grinnell, "Joint Product Costing in the Semiconductor Industry," *Management Accounting* (February 1986): 29.

Sales-Value-at-Split-Off Method

The **sales-value-at-split-off method** allocates joint cost based on each product's proportionate share of market or sales value at the split-off point. Under this method, the higher the market value, the greater the share of joint cost charged against the product. As long as the prices at split-off are stable, or the fluctuations in prices of the various products are synchronized (not necessarily in amount, but in the rate of change), their respective allocated costs remain constant. **Example 7.9** shows how and why to allocate joint costs using the sales-value-at-split-off method.

EXAMPLE 7.9

The HOW and WHY of Using the Sales-Value-at-Split-Off Method to Allocate Joint Product Costs

Information:

A sawmill processes logs into four grades of lumber totaling 3,000,000 board feet as follows:

Grades	Board Feet	Price at Split-Off
First and second	450,000	$0.300
No. 1 common	1,200,000	0.200
No. 2 common	600,000	0.121
No. 3 common	750,000	0.070
Total	3,000,000	

Total joint cost is $186,000.

Why:
The joint cost must be allocated to the various grades of lumber in order to cost product and value inventory. The sales-value-at-split-off method allocates the joint cost in proportion to each product's sales value at the split-off point.

Required:

1. Allocate the joint cost to the four grades of lumber using the sales-value-at-split-off method.

2. *What if* First and second and No. 1 common each had 825,000 board feet? How would that affect the allocation of cost to these two grades? How would it affect the allocation of cost to the No. 2 and No. 3 common grades?

Solution:

1.

Grades	Board Feet Produced	Price at Split-Off	Sales Value at Split-Off	Percent of Total Market Value	Allocated Joint Cost
First and second	450,000	$0.300	$135,000	0.2699	$ 50,201
No. 1 common	1,200,000	0.200	240,000	0.4799	89,261
No. 2 common	600,000	0.121	72,600	0.1452	27,007
No. 3 common	750,000	0.070	52,500	0.1050	19,530
Total	3,000,000		$500,100		$185,999

Sales value at split-off for First and second = 450,000 × $0.300 = $135,000
Sales value at split-off for No. 1 common = 1,200,000 × $0.200 = $240,000
Sales value at split-off for No. 2 common = 600,000 × $0.121 = $72,600
Sales value at split-off for No. 3 common = 750,000 × $0.070 = $52,500

EXAMPLE 7.9

(Continued)

Percent for First and second = $135,000/$500,100 = 0.2699, or 26.99%
Percent for No. 1 common = $240,000/$500,100 = 0.4799, or 47.99%
Percent for No. 2 common = $72,600/$500,100 = 0.1452, or 14.52%
Percent for No. 3 common = $52,500/$500,100 = 0.1050, or 10.50%

First and second joint cost allocation = 0.2699 × $186,000 = $50,201
No. 1 common joint cost allocation = 0.4799 × $186,000 = $89,261
No. 2 common joint cost allocation = 0.1452 × $186,000 = $27,007
No. 3 common joint cost allocation = 0.1050 × $186,000 = $19,530
(*Note:* The total joint cost allocation does not equal $186,000 due to rounding.)

2. If First and second and No. 1 common each had 825,000 board feet, then First and second would have a much higher sales value at split-off and would receive a higher percentage of joint cost. No. 1 common would have a lower sales value at split-off and receive a lower joint cost allocation. While the sales value at split-off of No. 2 common and No. 3 common would not be affected, their sales value as a percent of the total would go down since the increased value for First and second went up. Results of this change follow:

Grades	Board Feet Produced	Price at Split-Off	Sales Value at Split-Off	Percent of Total Market Value	Allocated Joint Cost
First and second	825,000	$0.300	$247,500	0.4604	$ 85,634
No. 1 common	825,000	0.200	165,000	0.3069	57,083
No. 2 common	600,000	0.121	72,600	0.1350	25,110
No. 3 common	750,000	0.070	52,500	0.0977	18,172
Total	3,000,000		$537,600		$185,999

(*Note:* The total joint cost allocation does not equal $186,000 due to rounding.)

The sales-value-at-split-off method can be approximated through the use of weighting factors based on price. The advantage is that the price-based weights do not change as market prices do. An example of this method is found in the glue industry. Material is put into process in the Cooking Department. The products resulting from the cooking operations are the several "runs of glue." The first run is of the highest grade, has the highest market value, and costs the least. Successive runs require higher temperatures, cost more, and produce lower grades of products. Glue factories do not attempt to determine the actual cost of each skimming because the effect would be to show the lowest cost on the first grade of product and the highest cost on the lowest grade. Instead, the cost of all glue produced is determined, and this total cost is spread over the various grades on the basis of their respective tests of purity. The relative degree of purity is an indicator of the quality and, therefore, of the market value of each run or grade produced. Hence, multiplying the yield for each run by its relative purity is equivalent to multiplying it by the market value. The amounts weighted by purity are used to allocate the joint costs to each run. Additional runs would be undertaken, of course, only as long as the incremental revenue of the additional run is equal to or exceeds the incremental costs incurred.

The weighting factor based on market value at split-off is conceptually the same as the weighting factor method under physical units. However, in this case, the weighting factor is based on sales value, while the weighting factor described in the physical units section could be based on other considerations such as processing difficulty, size, and so on that may or may not be related to market value.

Net Realizable Value Method When market value is used to allocate joint costs, we are talking about market value *at the split-off point*. However, on occasion, there is no ready market price for the individual products at the split-off point. In this case, the net realizable value method can be used. First, we obtain a **hypothetical sales value** for each joint product by subtracting all separable (or further) processing costs from the eventual market value. This approximates the sales value at split-off. Then, the **net realizable value method** can be used to prorate the joint costs based on each product's share of hypothetical sales value. **Example 7.10** shows how and why to use the net realizable value method to allocate joint costs.

The net realizable value method is particularly useful when one or more products cannot be sold at the split-off point but must be processed further.

EXAMPLE 7.10

The HOW and WHY of Using the Net Realizable Value Method to Allocate Joint Product Costs

Information:

A company manufactures two products, Alpha and Beta, from a joint process. Each production run costs $5,750 and results in 1,000 gallons of Alpha and 3,000 gallons of Beta. Neither product is salable at split-off, but must be further processed such that the separable cost for Alpha is $1 per gallon and for Beta is $2 per gallon. The eventual market price for Alpha is $5 and for Beta is $4.

> **Why:**
> The net realizable value method is used when one or more of the joint products cannot be sold at split-off. In this case, a hypothetical market value is constructed so that joint cost allocation can be done as close to the split-off point as possible.

Required:

1. Allocate the joint cost to Alpha and Beta using the net realizable value method.

2. **What if** it cost $2 to process each gallon of Alpha beyond the split-off point? How would that affect the allocation of joint cost to these two products?

Solution:

1.

Product	Market Price (1)	−	Further Processing Cost (2)	=	Hypothetical Market Price (3)	×	Number of Units (4)	=	Hypothetical Market Value (5)	Percent*	Allocated Joint Cost**
Alpha	$5.00		$1.00		$4.00		1,000		$ 4,000	0.40	$2,300
Beta	4.00		2.00		2.00		3,000		6,000	0.60	3,450
Total									$10,000		$5,750

*Percent for Alpha = $4,000/$10,000 = 0.40, or 40%
 Percent for Beta = $6,000/$10,000 = 0.60, or 60%?
**Alpha joint cost allocation = 0.40 × $5,750 = $2,300
 Beta joint cost allocation = 0.60 × $5,750 = $3,450?

2. If it cost $2 to process each gallon of Alpha, the hypothetical market price would be less, the hypothetical market value would be less, and Alpha would receive a smaller allocation of joint cost. The following table shows the results:

Product	Market Price (1)	−	Further Processing Cost (2)	=	Hypothetical Market Price (3)	×	Number of Units (4)	=	Hypothetical Market Value (5)	Percent*	Allocated Joint Cost**
Alpha	$5.00		$2.00		$3.00		1,000		$3,000	0.3333	$1,916
Beta	4.00		2.00		2.00		3,000		6,000	0.6667	3,834
Total									$9,000		$5,750

*Percent for Alpha = $3,000/$9,000 = 0.3333, or 33.33% (rounded)
 Percent for Beta = $6,000/$9,000 = 0.6667, or 66.67% (rounded)?
**Alpha joint cost allocation = 0.3333 × $5,750 = $1,916 (rounded)
 Beta joint cost allocation = 0.6667 × $5,750 = $3,834 (rounded)

Constant Gross Margin Percentage Method   The net realizable value method is easy to apply. However, it assigns all profit to the hypothetical market value. In other words, the further processing costs are assumed to have no profit value even though they are critical to selling the products. The **constant gross margin percentage method** corrects for this by recognizing that costs incurred after the split-off point are part of the cost total on which profit is expected to be earned, and it allocates joint cost such that the gross margin percentage is the same for each product. **Example 7.11** shows how and why to apply the constant gross margin percentage method in joint cost allocation.

EXAMPLE 7.11

The HOW and WHY of Using the Constant Gross Margin Percentage Method to Allocate Joint Product Costs

Information:

A company manufactures two products, Alpha and Beta, from a joint process. Each production run costs $5,750 and results in 1,000 gallons of Alpha and 3,000 gallons of Beta. Neither product is salable at split-off, but must be further processed such that the separable cost for Alpha is $1 per gallon and for Beta is $2 per gallon. The eventual market price for Alpha is $5 and for Beta is $4.

> **Why:**
> The constant gross margin percentage method is used to avoid assuming that all profit occurs at the split-off point. It allocates joint cost to ensure that the same gross profit is applicable to all products.

Required:

1. Calculate the total revenue, total costs, and total gross profit the company will earn on the sale of Alpha and Beta.

2. Allocate the joint cost to Alpha and Beta using the constant gross margin percentage method.

3. *What if* it cost $2 to process each gallon of Alpha beyond the split-off point? How would that affect the allocation of joint cost to these two products?

Solution:

1.

Total revenue [($5 × 1,000) + ($4 × 3,000)]		$17,000
Further processing costs [($1 × 1,000) + ($2 × 3,000)]	$7,000	
Joint processing costs	5,750	12,750
Total gross margin		$ 4,250

2. Gross margin percentage = Gross margin/Total revenue
    = $4,250/$17,000 = 0.25, or 25%

	Alpha	Beta
Eventual market value	$5,000	$12,000
Less: Gross margin at 25% of market value	1,250	3,000
Cost of goods sold	$3,750	$ 9,000
Less separable costs:		
Alpha = $1 × 1,000 units	1,000	
Beta = $2 × 3,000 units		6,000
Allocated joint cost	$2,750	$ 3,000

EXAMPLE 7.11

(Continued)

3. An increase in the further processing cost of Alpha will reduce the gross margin percentage and will decrease the joint cost allocated to Alpha.

Total revenue [($5 × 1,000) + ($4 × 3,000)]		$17,000
Further processing costs [($2 × 1,000) + ($2 × 3,000)]	$8,000	
Joint processing costs	5,750	13,750
Total gross margin		$ 3,250

$$\text{Gross margin percentage} = \text{Gross margin/Total revenue}$$
$$= \$3,250/\$17,000$$
$$= 0.1912, \text{ or } 19.12\% \text{ (rounded)}$$

	Alpha	Beta
Eventual market value	$5,000	$12,000
Less: Gross margin at 19.12% of market value	956	2,294
Cost of goods sold	$4,044	$ 9,706
Less separable costs:		
Alpha = $2 × 1,000 units	2,000	
Beta = $2 × 3,000 units		6,000
Allocated joint cost	$2,044	$ 3,706

Notice that the constant gross margin percentage method allocates more joint cost to Alpha than did the net realizable value method. This is due to the assumption of a relationship between cost and the cost-created value. That is, the net realizable value assumed no gross margin attributable to further processing costs, while the constant gross margin percentage method assumed not only that further processing yields profit but also that it yields an identical profit percentage across products. Which assumption is correct? There are two important questions: first, whether there is a "direct relationship" between cost and value and, second, whether the relationship is necessarily the same for all products jointly produced before and after the split-off point. The practice of product-line pricing to meet competition tends to make such assumptions invalid. Although exceptions exist, many companies do not try to maintain more-or-less equal margins between prices and full costs on their various products.

Accounting for By-Products

The distinction between joint products and **by-products** rests solely on the relative importance of their sales value. A by-product is a secondary product recovered in the course of manufacturing a primary product. It is a product whose total sales value is relatively minor in comparison with the sales value of the main product(s). This is not a sharp distinction, but rather one of degree. The first distinction is whether the operation is characterized by joint production. Then any by-products must be distinguished from main or joint products. By-products can be characterized by their relationship to the main products in the following manner:

1. By-product resulting from scrap, trimmings, and so forth, of the main products in essentially non-joint product types of undertakings (e.g., fabric trimmings from clothing pieces)
2. Scrap and other residue from essentially joint product types of processes (e.g., fat trimmed from beef carcasses)
3. A minor joint product situation (fruit skins and trimmings used as animal feed)

Relationships between joint products and by-products change, as do the classes of products within each of these classifications. When the relative importance of the individual products changes, the products need to be reclassified and the costing procedures changed. In fact, many by-products begin as waste materials, become economically significant (and thus become by-products), and grow in importance to finally become full-fledged joint products. For example, sawdust and wood chips in sawmill operations were originally waste, but over the years, they have gained value as a major component of particle board. The various methods of accounting for by-products reflect this development. Generally, accounting for by-products began as an extension of accounting for waste material. Revenue from the sale of the by-products is recorded as separate income, when the amount of income is so small that it has little impact on either overall cost or sales. As the value of by-product revenues becomes more significant, the cost of the main product is reduced by recoveries, and finally the by-products achieve near main product status and are allocated a share of the joint cost incurred prior to split-off.

Pork production offers examples of different types of by-products. Of course, the joint (main) products include pork roasts, bacon, ribs, sausage, and so on. Many different by-products are also produced during the meat-packing process.

Sustainability

Seaboard Foods, for example, thoroughly washes its production facility at the end of each day's shift. The waste water, which contains blood and small trimmings, sluices down drains in the floor. These lead to pipes which channel the waste water into covered containment ponds where anaerobic bacteria get to work breaking down the proteins and producing methane. Seaboard then recovers the methane for use in utility production for the plant. There is no accounting needed for the use of the methane. It is used solely within the plant and is not resold to outside users. This is an example of the use of by-products to reduce waste and create energy. Seaboard Foods relies less on the electrical grid and takes waste product out of the environment.

Another pork by-product is heart valves for use in transplantation. These valves are sold to heart valve manufacturers who take up to four weeks to process the bovine or porcine valves into medical grade valves. Since no further processing occurs in the packing plant, this use can be accounted for as revenue from the sale of by-products, or as an offset against the cost of the main product(s).

Treatment of the By-Product as Other Revenue   If the by-product can be sold, the company can choose to credit the sale to "Other Income" or to set up an account for "Sale of By-Product." Then, the revenue from the sale of the by-product would be credited to that account. Under this method, no cost is assigned to the by-product. All joint cost is allocated to the main products. Suppose that Edwards Company manufactures several main products and one by-product from a joint production process. One production run has the following costs:

Direct materials	$15,000
Direct labor	6,500
Applied overhead	4,550
Total joint production cost	$26,050

From each production run, Edwards obtains 1,600 pounds of Product A, 400 pounds of Product B, and 30 pounds of a by-product. The by-product can be sold for $5 per pound. When the 30 pounds of by-product are sold, the following journal entry would be made:

Accounts Receivable	150	
Sale of By-Product		150

Notice that under this method, no cost is assigned to the by-product and it is not carried in inventory. All joint production cost ($26,050 per batch) is allocated to the main products.

Treatment of the By-Product as a Reduction in the Cost of the Main Products An alternative method is to account for any revenue received from sale of the by-product as a reduction in the joint costs of the main products. In the Edwards example, the joint cost of $26,050 would be reduced by $150 from the sale of the byproduct. Then, $25,900 would be the joint cost allocated to the main products, Product A and Product B. If Edwards used the physical units method of joint cost allocation, then the following allocations would be made:

	Units	Percent	Joint Cost Allocation
Product A	1,600	80%	$20,720
Product B	400	20	5,180
Total	2,000		$25,900

In summary, there are a number of ways to account for by-products. The treatments of by-product revenue as other income or as a deduction in the cost of the main products are the most commonly used accounting methods. By definition, by-product is immaterial. Thus, the accounting treatment focuses on methods that are relatively quick and simple.

Ethical Implications of Cost Allocation

ETHICS This chapter has dealt with the subject of cost allocation, that is, moving cost from one department or product to another department or product. There are good reasons for real-locating costs and many widely accepted and used ways of doing this. However, the ability to allocate costs among various cost objects gives management a fair amount of discretion as to how the allocation is done. We have seen that some ways of allocating costs give relatively more cost to a particular support department or joint product than another way of allocating costs. The question arises, is this cost allocation ethical? As always, we return to the fundamentals of business. The business is ethical if it treats all parties fairly and does not attempt to mislead or misstate results. ●

SUMMARY OF LEARNING OBJECTIVES

LO1. Describe the difference between support departments and producing departments.
- Producing departments create the products or services that the firm is in business to make and sell.
- Support departments serve producing departments but do not create a salable product.
- The costs of the support departments must be allocated to producing departments for:
  - Inventory valuation
  - Product-line profitability
  - Pricing
  - Planning and control (allocation can also be used to encourage favorable managerial behavior)

LO2. Calculate charging rates, and distinguish between single and dual charging rates.
- Single charging rate combines variable and fixed costs of the support department.
  - Budgeted fixed and variable costs are in the numerator and budgeted usage is in the denominator.
  - Actual usage by using departments is multiplied by the charging rate to get the amount charged.

- Dual rates separate the fixed and variable costs.
  - Fixed support department costs are allocated on the basis of original capacity.
  - Variable rate is based on budgeted usage.
- Budgeted costs, not actual costs, should be allocated.
  - Efficiencies or inefficiencies of the support departments are not passed on to the producing departments.
  - Because the causal factors can differ for fixed and variable costs, these types of costs should be allocated separately.

LO3. Allocate support center costs to producing departments using the direct method, the sequential method, and the reciprocal method.
- All three methods allocate all support department costs to the producing departments.
- The three methods differ in the degree of support department interaction considered.
  - The direct method allocates from support to producing departments. No reciprocity is recognized.
  - The sequential (or step) method ranks support departments and allocates from top ranking to lower ranking. Some reciprocity is recognized.
  - The reciprocal method takes full account of support department reciprocity.
- After allocation, zero cost remains in the support departments.
- Pre-allocation total overhead must equal post-allocation overhead.

LO4. Calculate departmental overhead rates.
- After allocation, total overhead in producing department is divided by budgeted base to obtain departmental overhead rate.
- Departmental overhead is applied to products passing through the department.

LO5. Identify the characteristics of the joint production process, and allocate joint costs to products.
- Joint production processes result in the output of two or more products that are produced simultaneously.
- Joint or main products have relatively significant sales value.
- Joint costs must be allocated to the individual products for purposes of financial reporting.
- Several methods have been developed to allocate joint costs.
  - Physical units method
  - Weighted average method
  - Sales-value-at-split-off method
  - Net realizable value method
  - Constant gross margin method
- Allocated joint costs are not useful for output and pricing decisions. Further processing costs, or separable costs, are used in management decision making.
- By-products are products obtained from joint production processes that have relatively little sales value. Two methods of accounting for by-product sales are:
  - Credit of by-product revenue to "Other Income" or "Sale of By-Product"
  - Reduction of the joint costs allocated to the main products by the amount of by-product revenue

EXAMPLE 7.1	The HOW and WHY of Calculating and Using a Single Charging Rate, page 323
EXAMPLE 7.2	The HOW and WHY of Calculating and Using Multiple Charging Rates, page 325
EXAMPLE 7.3	The HOW and WHY of Allocating Support Department Costs to Producing Departments Using the Direct Method, page 331

EXAMPLE 7.4	The HOW and WHY of Allocating Support Department Costs to Producing Departments Using the Sequential (Step) Method, page 334
EXAMPLE 7.5	The HOW and WHY of Allocating Support Department Costs to Producing Departments Using the Reciprocal Method, page 336
EXAMPLE 7.6	The HOW and WHY of Using Allocated Support Department Costs to Calculate Departmental Overhead Rates, page 339
EXAMPLE 7.7	The HOW and WHY of Using the Physical Units Method to Allocate Joint Product Costs, page 344
EXAMPLE 7.8	The HOW and WHY of Using the Weighted Average Method to Allocate Joint Product Costs, page 345
EXAMPLE 7.9	The HOW and WHY of Using the Sales-Value-at-Split-Off Method to Allocate Joint Product Costs, page 347
EXAMPLE 7.10	The HOW and WHY of Using the Net Realizable Value Method to Allocate Joint Product Costs, page 349
EXAMPLE 7.11	The HOW and WHY of Using the Constant Gross Margin Percentage Method to Allocate Joint Product Costs, page 350

KEY TERMS

By-products, 351

Causal factors, 320

Common costs, 317

Constant gross margin percentage method, 350

Direct method, 330

Hypothetical sales value, 348

Joint products, 341

Net realizable value method, 349

Physical units method, 343

Producing departments, 318

Reciprocal method, 336

Sales-value-at-split-off method, 347

Separable costs, 342

Sequential (or step) method, 332

Split-off point, 341

Support departments, 318

Weight factor, 345

BRIEF EXERCISES

Brief Exercise 7-1 Calculating and Using a Single Charging Rate

OBJECTIVE ▸ 2
Example 7.1

The expected costs for the Maintenance Department of Stazler, Inc., for the coming year include:

Fixed costs (salaries, tools): $64,900 per year
Variable costs (supplies): $1.35 per maintenance hour

Estimated usage by:

Assembly Department	4,500
Fabricating Department	6,700
Packaging Department	10,800
Total maintenance hours	22,000

Actual usage by:

Assembly Department	3,960
Fabricating Department	6,800
Packaging Department	10,000
Total maintenance hours	20,760

Required:

1. Calculate a single charging rate for the Maintenance Department.
2. Use this rate to assign the costs of the Maintenance Department to the user departments based on actual usage. Calculate the total amount charged for maintenance for the year.
3. *What if* the Assembly Department used 4,000 maintenance hours in the year? How much would have been charged out to the three departments?

OBJECTIVE 2

EXAMPLE 7.2

Brief Exercise 7-2 Calculating and Using Dual Charging Rates

The expected costs for the Maintenance Department of Stazler, Inc., for the coming year include:

Fixed costs (salaries, tools): $64,900 per year
Variable costs (supplies): $1.35 per maintenance hour

The Assembly and Packaging departments expect to use maintenance hours relatively evenly throughout the year. The Fabricating Department typically uses more maintenance hours in the month of November. Estimated usage in hours for the year and for the peak month is as follows:

	Yearly Hours	Monthly Peak Hours
Assembly Department	4,500	390
Fabricating Department	6,700	1,300
Packaging Department	10,800	910
Total maintenance hours	22,000	2,600

Actual usage for the year by:

Assembly Department	3,960
Fabricating Department	6,800
Packaging Department	10,000
Total maintenance hours	20,760

Required:

1. Calculate a variable rate for the Maintenance Department. Calculate the allocated fixed cost for each using department based on its budgeted peak month usage in maintenance hours.
2. Use the two rates to assign the costs of the Maintenance Department to the user departments based on actual usage. Calculate the total amount charged for maintenance for the year.
3. *What if* the Assembly Department used 4,000 maintenance hours in the year? How much would have been charged out to the three departments?

Brief Exercise 7-3 Direct Method of Support Department Cost Allocation

OBJECTIVE ▸3
EXAMPLE 7.3

Chekov Company has two support departments, Human Resources and General Factory, and two producing departments, Fabricating and Assembly.

	Support Departments		Producing Departments	
	Human Resources	General Factory	Fabricating	Assembly
Direct costs	$150,000	$360,000	$120,900	$86,000
Normal activity:				
Number of employees	—	60	45	80
Square footage	1,500	—	6,000	14,000

The costs of the Human Resources Department are allocated on the basis of number of employees, and the costs of General Factory are allocated on the basis of square footage. Chekov Company uses the direct method of support department cost allocation.

Required:

1. Calculate the allocation ratios for the four departments using the direct method.
2. Using the direct method, allocate the costs of the Human Resources and General Factory departments to the Fabricating and Assembly departments.
3. *What if* the General Factory Department had 40 employees? How would that affect the allocation of Human Resources Department costs to the Fabricating and Assembly departments?

Brief Exercise 7-4 Sequential (Step) Method of Support Department Cost Allocation

OBJECTIVE ▸3
EXAMPLE 7.4

Refer to **Brief Exercise 7-3**. Now assume that Chekov Company uses the sequential method to allocate support department costs. The support departments are ranked in order of highest cost to lowest cost.

Required:

1. Calculate the allocation ratios (rounded to four significant digits) for the four departments using the sequential method.
2. Using the sequential method, allocate the costs of the Human Resources and General Factory departments to the Fabricating and Assembly departments. (Round all allocated costs to the nearest dollar.)
3. *What if* the allocation ratios in Requirement 1 were rounded to six significant digits rather than four? How would that affect any rounding error in the allocation of costs?

Brief Exercise 7-5 Reciprocal Method of Support Department Cost Allocation

OBJECTIVE ▸3
EXAMPLE 7.5

Refer to **Brief Exercise 7-3**. Now assume that Chekov Company uses the reciprocal method to allocate support department costs.

Required:

1. Calculate the allocation ratios (rounded to four significant digits) for the four departments using the reciprocal method.
2. Develop a simultaneous equations system of total costs for the support departments. Solve for the total reciprocated costs of each support department. (Round reciprocated total costs to the nearest dollar.)
3. Using the reciprocal method, allocate the costs of the Human Resources and General Factory departments to the Fabricating and Assembly departments. (Round all allocated costs to the nearest dollar.)
4. *What if* the square footage in Fabricating were 14,000 and the square footage in Assembly were 6,000. How would that affect the allocation of support department costs?

OBJECTIVE **4**
EXAMPLE 7.6

Brief Exercise 7-6 Calculating Departmental Overhead Rates Using Post-Allocation Costs

Refer to **Brief Exercise 7-3** and solve for the allocated costs to Fabricating and Assembly using the direct method of support department cost allocation. The Fabricating Department overhead rate is based on normal activity of 82,000 machine hours. The Assembly Department overhead rate is based on normal activity of 160,000 direct labor hours.

Job 316 required six machine hours in Fabricating and four direct labor hours in Assembly. Total direct materials cost $120, and total direct labor cost was $80.

Required:

1. Calculate the overhead rate for Fabricating based on machine hours and the overhead rate for Assembly based on direct labor hours. (Round overhead rates to the nearest cent.)
2. Using the overhead rates calculated in Requirement 1, calculate the cost of Job 316.
3. *What if* Job 316 had required one machine hour in Fabricating and four direct labor hours in Assembly? Direct labor and direct materials costs remained the same. Calculate the new cost of Job 316.

OBJECTIVE **5**
EXAMPLE 7.7

Brief Exercise 7-7 Allocating Joint Costs Using the Physical Units Method

Sunny Lane, Inc., purchases peaches from local orchards and sorts them into four categories. Grade A are large blemish-free peaches that can be sold to gourmet fruit sellers. Grade B peaches are smaller and may be slightly out of proportion. These are packed in boxes and sold to grocery stores. Peaches to be sliced for canned peaches are even smaller than Grade B peaches and have blemishes. Peaches to be pureed for use in sauces are of lower grade than peaches for slices, yet still food grade for canning. Information on a recent purchase of 20,000 pounds of peaches is as follows:

Grades	Pounds
Grade A	1,500
Grade B	5,000
Slices	8,000
Pureed	5,500
Total	20,000

Total joint cost is $18,000.

Required:

1. Allocate the joint cost to the four grades of peaches using the physical units method. (Carry out the percent calculations to four significant digits.)
2. Allocate the joint cost to the four grades of peaches by finding the average joint cost per pound and multiplying it by the number of pounds in the grade. (Round all cost allocations to the nearest dollar.)
3. *What if* there were 2,000 pounds of Grade A peaches and 4,600 pounds of Grade B? How would that affect the allocation of cost to these two grades? How would it affect the allocation of cost to the remaining common grades?

OBJECTIVE **5**
EXAMPLE 7.8

Brief Exercise 7-8 Allocating Joint Costs Using the Weighted Average Method

Refer to **Brief Exercise 7-7**. Assume that Sunny Lane, Inc., uses the weighted average method of joint cost allocation and has assigned the following weights to the four grades of peaches:

Grades	Pounds	Weight Factor
Grade A	1,500	3.0
Grade B	5,000	2.0
Slices	8,000	0.5
Pureed	5,500	1.0
Total	20,000	

Total joint cost is $18,000.

Required:

1. Allocate the joint cost to the four grades of peaches using the weighted average method. (Carry out the percent calculations to four significant digits. Round all cost allocations to the nearest dollar.)
2. *What if* the factory found that Grade A peaches were being valued less by customers and decided to decrease the weight factor for Grade A peaches to 2.0? How would that affect the allocation of cost to Grade A peaches? How would it affect the allocation of cost to the remaining grades?

Brief Exercise 7-9 Allocating Joint Costs Using the Sales-Value-at-Split-Off Method

OBJECTIVE 5
EXAMPLE 7.9

Refer to **Brief Exercise 7-7**. Assume that Sunny Lane, Inc., uses the sales-value-at-split-off method of joint cost allocation and has provided the following information about the four grades of peaches:

Grades	Pounds	Price at Split-Off (per lb.)
Grade A	1,500	$6.00
Grade B	5,000	2.00
Slices	8,000	1.30
Pureed	5,500	0.80
Total	20,000	

Total joint cost is $18,000.

Required:

1. Allocate the joint cost to the four grades of peaches using the sales-value-at-split-off method. (Carry out the percent calculations to four significant digits. Round all cost allocations to the nearest dollar.)
2. *What if* the price at split-off of Grade B peaches decreased to $1.60 per pound? How would that affect the allocation of cost to Grade B peaches? How would it affect the allocation of cost to the remaining grades?

Brief Exercise 7-10 Allocating Joint Costs Using the Net Realizable Value Method

OBJECTIVE 5
EXAMPLE 7.10

A company manufactures three products, L-Ten, Triol, and Pioze, from a joint process. Each production run costs $12,900. None of the products can be sold at split-off, but must be processed further. Information on one batch of the three products is as follows:

Product	Gallons	Further Processing Cost per Gallon	Eventual Market Price per Gallon
L-Ten	3,500	$0.50	$2.00
Triol	4,000	1.00	5.00
Pioze	2,500	1.50	6.00

Required:

1. Allocate the joint cost to L-Ten, Triol, and Pioze using the net realizable value method. (Round the percentages to four significant digits. Round all cost allocations to the nearest dollar.)
2. *What if* it cost $2 to process each gallon of Triol beyond the split-off point? How would that affect the allocation of joint cost to the three products?

OBJECTIVE ▸5
EXAMPLE 7.11

Brief Exercise 7-11 Allocating Joint Costs Using the Constant Gross Margin Method

Refer to **Brief Exercise 7-10**. (Round percentages to four significant digits and cost allocations to the nearest dollar.)

Required:

1. Calculate the total revenue, total costs, and total gross profit the company will earn on the sale of L-Ten, Triol, and Pioze.
2. Allocate the joint cost to L-Ten, Triol, and Pioze using the constant gross margin percentage method.
3. *What if* it cost $2 to process each gallon of Triol beyond the split-off point? How would that affect the allocation of joint cost to these three products?

EXERCISES

OBJECTIVE ▸1

Exercise 7-12 Classifying Departments as Producing or Support— Manufacturing Firm

Classify each of the following departments in a factory that produces crème-filled snack cakes as a producing department or a support department.

a. Janitorial
b. Baking
c. Inspection
d. Mixing
e. Engineering
f. Grounds
g. Purchasing
h. Packaging
i. Icing (frosts top of snack cakes and adds decorative squiggle)
j. Filling (injects crème mixture into baked snack cakes)
k. Personnel
l. Cafeteria
m. General factory
n. Machine maintenance
o. Bookkeeping

OBJECTIVE ▸1

Exercise 7-13 Classifying Departments as Producing or Support—Service Firm

Classify each of the following departments in a large metropolitan law firm as a producing department or a support department.

a. Copying
b. WESTLAW computer research
c. Tax planning
d. Environmental law
e. Oil and gas law
f. Custodians
g. Word processing
h. Corporate law
i. Small business law
j. Personnel

OBJECTIVE ▸1

Exercise 7-14 Identifying Causal Factors for Support Department Cost Allocation

Identify some possible causal factors for the following support departments:

a. Cafeteria
b. Custodial services
c. Laundry
d. Receiving, shipping, and stores
e. Maintenance
f. Personnel
g. Accounting
h. Power
i. Building and grounds

Exercise 7-15 Objectives of Cost Allocation

OBJECTIVE ◀ 1

Dr. Fred Poston, "Dermatologist to the Stars," has a practice in southern California. The practice includes three dermatologists, three medical assistants, an office manager, and a receptionist. The office space, which is rented for $5,000 per month, is large enough to accommodate four dermatologists, but Dr. Poston has not yet found the right physician to fill the fourth spot. Dr. Poston developed a skin cleanser for his patients that is nongreasy and does not irritate skin that is still recovering from the effects of chemical peels and dermabrasion. The cleanser requires $0.50 worth of ingredients per eight-ounce bottle. A medical assistant mixes up several bottles at a time during lulls in her schedule. She waits until she has about 15 minutes free and then mixes 10 bottles of cleanser. She is paid $2,250 per month. Dr. Poston charges $5.00 per bottle and sells approximately 5,000 bottles annually. His accountant is considering various ways of costing the skin cleanser.

Required:

1. Give two reasons for allocating overhead cost to the cleanser. How should the cost of the office space and the medical assistant's salary be allocated to the cleanser? Explain.
2. Suppose that *Healthy You* magazine runs an article on Dr. Poston and his skin cleanser, which causes demand to skyrocket. Consumers across the country buy the cleanser via phone or internet order. Now, Dr. Poston believes that he can sell about 40,000 bottles annually. He can hire someone part time, for $1,000 per month, to mix and bottle the cleanser and to handle the financial business of the cleanser. An unused office and examining room can be dedicated to the production of the cleanser. Would your allocation choice for Requirement 1 change in this case? Explain.

Exercise 7-16 Objectives of Allocation

OBJECTIVE ◀ 1

Samantha and Rashida are planning a trip to Padre Island, Texas, during spring break. Members of the varsity volleyball team, they are looking forward to four days of beach volleyball and parasailing. They will drive Samantha's car and estimate that they will pay the following costs during the trip:

Motel (4 nights at $145)	$580
Food (each)	150
Gas in total	120
Parasailing and equipment rental (each)	125

They have reservations at the SeaScape Motel, which charges $120 per night for a single, $145 per night for a double, and an additional $15 per night if a rollaway bed is added to a double room.

Samantha's little sister, Kallie, wants to go along. She isn't into sports but thinks that four days of partying and relaxing on the beach would be a great way to unwind from the rigors of school. She figures that she could ride with Samantha and Rashida and share their room.

Required:

1. Using incremental costs only, what would it cost Kallie to accompany Samantha and Rashida?
2. Using the benefits-received method, what would it cost Kallie to go on the trip?

Exercise 7-17 Single and Dual Charging Rates

OBJECTIVE ◀ 2

SHOW ME HOW

Jeff McMillan owns a small neighborhood shopping mall. Of the 10 store spaces in the building, seven are rented by boutique owners and three are vacant. Jeff has decided that offering more services to stores in the mall would enable him to increase occupancy. He has decided to use one of the vacant spaces to provide, at cost, a gift-wrapping service to shops in the mall. The boutiques are enthusiastic about the new service. Most of them are staffed minimally, which means that every time they have to wrap a gift, phones go unanswered and other customers in line grow impatient. Jeff figured that the gift-wrapping service would incur the following costs:

the store space would normally rent for $1,800 per month, part-time gift wrappers could be hired for $1,500 per month, and wrapping paper and ribbon would average $1.20 per gift. The boutique owners estimated the following number of gifts to be wrapped per month.

Store	Number of Gifts Wrapped per Month
The Stationery Station	175
Arts & Collectibles	400
Kid-Sports	100
Java Jim's	75
Designer Shoes	20
Cristina's Closet	130
Alan's Drug and Sundries	100

After the service had been in effect for six months, Jeff calculated the following actual average monthly number of gifts wrapped for each of the stores.

Store	Actual Average Number of Gifts Wrapped per Month
The Stationery Station	160
Arts & Collectibles	420
Kid-Sports	240
Java Jim's	10
Designer Shoes	50
Cristina's Closet	200
Alan's Drug and Sundries	450

Required:

1. Calculate a single charging rate, on a per-gift basis, to be charged to the shops. Based on the shops' actual number of gifts wrapped, how much would be charged to each shop using the single charging rate?
2. Based on the shops' actual number of gifts wrapped, how much would be charged to each shop using the dual charging rate?
3. Which shops would prefer the single charging rate? Why? Which would prefer the dual charging rate, and why?
4. Several of the shop owners were angry about their bill for the gift-wrapping service. They pointed out that they were to be charged only for the cost of the service. How could you make a case for them?

OBJECTIVE 2

SHOW ME HOW   EXCEL

Exercise 7-18 Actual versus Budgeted Costs

Kumar, Inc., evaluates managers of producing departments on their ability to control costs. In addition to the costs directly traceable to their departments, each production manager is held responsible for a share of the costs of a support center, the Human Resources (HR) Department. The total costs of HR are allocated on the basis of actual direct labor hours used. The total costs of HR and the actual direct labor hours worked by each producing department are as follows:

	Year 1	Year 2
Direct labor hours worked:		
Department A	24,000	25,000
Department B	36,000	25,000
Total hours	60,000	50,000
Actual HR cost	$120,000	$120,000
Budgeted HR cost	115,000*	112,500*

*$0.25 per direct labor hour plus $100,000.

Required:

1. Allocate the HR costs to each producing department for Year 1 and Year 2 using the direct method with actual direct labor hours and actual HR costs.
2. Discuss the following statement: "The costs of human resource-related matters increased by 25 percent for Department A and decreased by over 16 percent for Department B. Thus, the manager of Department B must be controlling HR costs better than the manager of Department A." Which of the four data analytic types—descriptive, diagnostic, predictive, or prescriptive—is used to determine how well the managers are controlling human resources costs. (See Exhibits 2.5 and 2.6, pp. 37, 40, for a review of data analytic types.)
3. Can you think of a way to allocate HR costs so that a more reasonable and fair assessment of cost control can be made? Explain.

DATA ANALYTICS

Exercise 7-19 Fixed and Variable Cost Allocation

Refer to the data in **Exercise 7-18**. When the capacity of the HR Department was originally established, the normal usage expected for each department was 20,000 direct labor hours. This usage is also the amount of activity planned for the two departments in Year 1 and Year 2.

OBJECTIVE 2

EXCEL **SHOW ME HOW**

Required:

1. Allocate the costs of the HR Department using the direct method and assuming that the purpose is product costing.
2. Allocate the costs of the HR Department using the direct method and assuming that the purpose is to evaluate performance.

Exercise 7-20 Direct Method and Overhead Rates

Belami Company manufactures shampoo and hair conditioner, with each product manufactured in separate departments. Three support departments support the production departments: Power, General Factory, and Purchasing. Budgeted data on the five departments are as follows:

OBJECTIVE 3

EXCEL **SHOW ME HOW**

	Support Departments			**Producing Departments**	
	Power	**General Factory**	**Purchasing**	**Shampoo**	**Conditioner**
Overhead	$94,000	$430,000	$150,000	$146,000	$170,000
Square feet	3,000	—	3,000	9,600	8,400
Machine hours	—	1,403	1,345	8,000	24,000
Purchase orders	20	40	7	60	120

The company does not break overhead into fixed and variable components. The bases for allocation are power—machine hours; general factory—square feet; and purchasing—purchase orders.

Required:

1. Allocate the overhead costs to the producing departments using the direct method. (Take allocation ratios out to four significant digits. Round allocated costs to the nearest dollar.)
2. Using machine hours, compute departmental overhead rates. (Round the overhead rates to the nearest cent.)

Exercise 7-21 Sequential Method

Refer to the data in **Exercise 7-20**. The company has decided to use the sequential method of allocation instead of the direct method. The support departments are ranked in order of highest cost to lowest cost.

OBJECTIVE 3

EXCEL **SHOW ME HOW**

Required:

1. Allocate the overhead costs to the producing departments using the sequential method. (Take allocation ratios out to four significant digits. Round allocated costs to the nearest dollar.)
2. Using machine hours, compute departmental overhead rates. (Round the overhead rates to the nearest cent.)

Exercise 7-22 Reciprocal Method

Eilers Company has two producing departments and two support departments. The following budgeted data pertain to these four departments:

| | Support Departments | | Producing Departments | |
	General Factory	Receiving	Assembly	Finishing
Direct overhead	$400,000	$160,000	$43,000	$74,000
Square footage	—	2,700	5,400	5,400
Number of receiving orders	300	—	1,680	1,020
Direct labor hours	—	—	25,000	40,000

Required:

1. Allocate the overhead costs of the support departments to the producing departments using the reciprocal method. (Round allocation ratios to four significant digits. Round allocated costs to the nearest dollar.)
2. Using direct labor hours, compute departmental overhead rates. (Round to the nearest cent.)

Exercise 7-23 Direct Method

Refer to the data in **Exercise 7-22**. The company has decided to simplify its method of allocating support service costs by switching to the direct method.

Required:

1. Allocate the costs of the support departments to the producing departments using the direct method. (Round allocation ratios to four significant digits. Round allocated costs to the nearest dollar.)
2. Using direct labor hours, compute departmental overhead rates. (Round to the nearest cent.)

Exercise 7-24 Sequential Method

Refer to the data in **Exercise 7-22**. The support departments are ranked in order of highest cost to lowest cost.

Required:

1. Allocate the costs of the support departments using the sequential method. (Round allocation ratios to four significant digits. Round allocated costs to the nearest dollar.)
2. Using direct labor hours, compute departmental overhead rates. (Round to the nearest cent.)

Exercise 7-25 Physical Units Method

Alomar Company manufactures four products from a joint production process: barlon, selene, plicene, and corsol. The joint costs for one batch are as follows:

Direct materials	$67,900
Direct labor	34,000
Overhead	25,500

At the split-off point, a batch yields 1,400 barlon, 2,600 selene, 2,500 plicene, and 3,500 corsol. All products are sold at the split-off point: barlon sells for $15 per unit, selene sells for $20 per unit, plicene sells for $26 per unit, and corsol sells for $35 per unit. Carry out all percent calculations to four significant digits.

Required:

1. Allocate the joint costs using the physical units method.
2. Suppose that the products are weighted as shown on the next page.

Barlon	1.0
Selene	2.0
Plicene	1.5
Corsol	2.5

Allocate the joint costs using the weighted average method.

Exercise 7-26 Sales-Value-at-Split-off Method

Refer to **Exercise** 7-25 and allocate the joint costs using the sales-value-at-split-off method.

OBJECTIVE ◄ 5

SHOW ME
HOW

Exercise 7-27 Net Realizable Value Method, Decision to Sell at Split-off or Process Further

Arvin, Inc., produces two products, ins and outs, in a single process. The joint costs of this process were $77,300, and 14,000 units of ins and 36,000 units of outs were produced. Separable processing costs beyond the split-off point were as follows: ins, $17,500; outs, $9,000. Ins sell for $8.00 per unit; outs sell for $15.00 per unit.

OBJECTIVE ◄ 5

DATA
ANALYTICS

SHOW ME
HOW

Required:

1. Allocate the $77,300 joint costs using the estimated net realizable value method.
2. Suppose that ins could be sold at the split-off point for $7.00 per unit. Should Arvin sell ins at split-off or process them further? Show supporting computations. Which of the four data analytic types—descriptive, diagnostic, predictive, or prescriptive—is used to determine whether Arvin should process further or sell at the split-off point? (See Exhibits 2.5 and 2.6, pp. 37, 40, for a review of data analytic types.)

PROBLEMS

Problem 7-28 Allocation: Fixed and Variable Costs, Budgeted Fixed and Variable Costs

OBJECTIVE ◄ 2

Biotechtron, Inc., has two research laboratories in the Southwest, one in Yuma, Arizona, and the other in Bernalillo, New Mexico. The owner of Biotechtron centralized the legal services function in the Yuma office and had both laboratories send any legal questions or issues to the Yuma office. The legal services support center has budgeted fixed costs of $160,000 per year and a budgeted variable rate of $65 per hour of professional time. The normal usage of the legal services center is 2,600 hours per year for the Yuma office and 1,400 hours per year for the Bernalillo office. This corresponds to the expected usage for the coming year.

Required:

1. Determine the amount of legal services support center costs that should be assigned to each office.
2. Since the offices produce services, not tangible products, what purpose is served by allocating the budgeted costs?
3. Now, assume that during the year, the legal services center incurred actual fixed costs of $163,000 and actual variable costs of $272,400. It delivered 4,180 hours of professional time—2,580 hours to Yuma and 1,600 hours to Bernalillo. Determine the amount of the legal services center's costs that should be allocated to each office. Explain the purposes of this allocation.
4. Did the costs allocated in Requirement 3 differ from the costs incurred by the legal services center? If so, why?

OBJECTIVE ▶ **2** **3**

EXCEL

Problem 7-29 Direct Method, Variable versus Fixed Costing and Performance Evaluation

AirBorne is a small airline operating out of Boise, Idaho. Its three flights travel to Salt Lake City, Reno, and Portland. The owner of the airline wants to assess the full cost of operating each flight. As part of this assessment, the costs of two support departments (maintenance and baggage) must be allocated to the three flights. The two support departments that support all three flights are located in Boise (any maintenance or baggage costs at the destination airports are directly traceable to the individual flights). Budgeted and actual data for the year are as follows for the support departments and the three flights:

	Support Centers		Flights		
	Maintenance	Baggage	Salt Lake City	Reno	Portland
Budgeted data:					
Fixed overhead	$240,000	$150,000	$20,000	$18,000	$30,000
Variable overhead	$ 30,000	$ 64,000	$ 5,000	$10,000	$ 6,000
Hours of flight time*	—	—	2,000	4,000	2,000
Number of passengers	—	—	10,000	15,000	5,000
Actual data:					
Fixed overhead	$235,000	$156,000	$22,000	$17,000	$29,500
Variable overhead	$ 80,000	$ 33,000	$ 6,200	$11,000	$ 5,800
Hours of flight time	—	—	1,800	4,200	2,500
Number of passengers	—	—	8,000	16,000	6,000

*Normal activity levels.

Round all allocation ratios and variable rates to four significant digits. Round all allocated amounts to the nearest dollar.

Required:

1. Using the direct method, allocate the support service costs to each flight, assuming that the objective is to determine the cost of operating each flight.
2. Using the direct method, allocate the support service costs to each flight, assuming that the objective is to evaluate performance. Do any costs remain in the two support departments after the allocation? If so, how much? Explain how data analytics are used to improve business practices. (See Exhibits 2.5 and 2.6, pp. 37, 40, for a review of data analytic types.)

DATA ANALYTICS

OBJECTIVE ▶ **3**

Problem 7-30 Comparison of Methods of Allocation

Duweynie Pottery, Inc., is divided into two operating divisions: Pottery and Retail. The company allocates Power and General Factory department costs to each operating division. Power costs are allocated on the basis of the number of machine hours and general factory costs on the basis of square footage. No effort is made to separate fixed and variable costs; however, only budgeted costs are allocated. Allocations for the coming year are based on the following data:

	Support Departments		Operating Divisions	
	Power	General Factory	Pottery	Retail
Overhead costs	$150,000	$160,000	$98,000	$56,000
Machine hours	2,000	1,000	6,900	3,100
Square footage	2,000	1,700	4,000	6,000

Round all allocation ratios to four significant digits. Round all allocated amounts to the nearest dollar.

Required:

1. Allocate the support service costs using the direct method.
2. Allocate the support service costs using the sequential method. The support departments are ranked in order of highest cost to lowest cost.
3. Allocate the support service costs using the reciprocal method.

Problem 7-31 Direct Method, Reciprocal Method, Overhead Rates

OBJECTIVE 3 4

CMA

Macalister Corporation is developing departmental overhead rates based on direct labor hours for its two production departments—Molding and Assembly. The Molding Department employs 20 people, and the Assembly Department employs 80 people. Each person in these two departments works 2,000 hours per year. The production-related overhead costs for the Molding Department are budgeted at $190,000, and the Assembly Department costs are budgeted at $80,000. Two support departments—Engineering and General Factory—directly support the two production departments and have budgeted costs of $216,000 and $370,000, respectively. The production departments' overhead rates cannot be determined until the support departments' costs are properly allocated. The following schedule reflects the use of the Engineering Department's and General Factory Department's output by the various departments.

	Engineering	General Factory	Molding	Assembly
Engineering hours	—	2,000	2,000	8,000
Square feet	120,000	—	420,000	60,000

For all requirements, round allocation ratios to four significant digits and round allocated costs to the nearest dollar.

Required:

1. Calculate the overhead rates per direct labor hour for the Molding Department and the Assembly Department using the direct allocation method to charge the production departments for support department costs.
2. Calculate the overhead rates per direct labor hour for the Molding Department and the Assembly Department using the reciprocal method to charge support department costs to each other and to the production departments.
3. Explain the difference between the methods, and indicate the arguments generally presented to support the reciprocal method over the direct allocation method. *(CMA adapted)*

Problem 7-32 Physical Units Method, Relative Sales Value Method

OBJECTIVE 5

Farleigh Petroleum, Inc., is a small company that acquires high-grade crude oil from low-volume production wells owned by individuals and small partnerships. The crude oil is processed in a single refinery into Two Oil, Six Oil, and impure distillates. Farleigh Petroleum does not have the technology or capacity to process these products further and sells most of its output each month to major refineries. There were no beginning finished goods or work-in-process inventories on April 1. The production costs and output of Farleigh Petroleum for April are as follows:

Crude oil placed into production	$6,500,000
Direct labor and related costs	1,400,000
Manufacturing overhead	3,000,000

Data on barrels produced and selling price:

Two Oil, 300,000 barrels produced; sales price, $45 per barrel
Six Oil, 170,000 barrels produced; sales price, $25 per barrel
Distillates, 80,000 barrels produced; sales price, $14 per barrel

Required:

1. Calculate the amount of joint production cost that Farleigh Petroleum would allocate to each of the three joint products by using the physical units method. (Carry out the ratio calculation to four decimal places. Round allocated costs to the nearest dollar.)
2. Calculate the amount of joint production cost that Farleigh Petroleum would allocate to each of the three joint products by using the relative sales value method. (Carry out the ratio calculation to four decimal places. Round allocated costs to the nearest dollar.)

OBJECTIVE **2**

Problem 7-33 Fixed and Variable Cost Allocation

Welcome Inns is a chain of motels serving business travelers in New Mexico and southwest Texas. The chain has grown from one motel several years ago to five motels. In 20x1, the owner of the company decided to set up an internal Accounting Department to centralize control of financial information. (Previously, local CPAs handled each motel's bookkeeping and financial reporting.) The accounting office was opened in January 20x1 by renting space adjacent to corporate headquarters in Ruidoso, New Mexico. All motels have been supplied with personal computers and internet access to transfer information to central accounting on a daily basis.

The Accounting Department has budgeted fixed costs of $135,000 per year. Variable costs are budgeted at $20 per hour. In 20x1, actual cost for the Accounting Department was $223,000. Further information is as follows:

	Actual Revenues		Actual Hours of Accounting
	20×0	20×1	20×1
Ruidoso	$405,000	$420,000	1,475
Roswell	540,000	588,000	410
Santa Rosa	432,000	364,000	620
El Paso	648,000	728,000	890
Albuquerque	675,000	700,000	450

Required:

1. Suppose the total actual costs of the Accounting Department are allocated on the basis of 20x1 sales revenue. How much will be allocated to each motel?
2. Suppose that Welcome Inns views 20x0 sales figures as a proxy for budgeted capacity of the motels. Thus, fixed Accounting Department costs are allocated on the basis of 20x0 sales, and variable costs are allocated according to 20x1 usage multiplied by the variable rate. How much Accounting Department cost will be allocated to each motel?
3. Comment on the two allocation schemes. Which motels would prefer the method in Requirement 1? The method in Requirement 2? Explain.

OBJECTIVE **5**

DATA ANALYTICS

Problem 7-34 Physical Units Method, Relative Sales-Value-at-Split-off Method, Net Realizable Value Method, Decision Making

Sonimad Sawmill, Inc. (SSI), purchases logs from independent timber contractors and processes them into the following three types of lumber products:

1. Studs for residential construction (e.g., walls and ceilings)
2. Decorative pieces (e.g., fireplace mantels and beams for cathedral ceilings)
3. Posts used as support braces (e.g., mine support braces and braces for exterior fences around ranch properties)

These products are the result of a joint sawmill process that involves removing bark from the logs, cutting the logs into a workable size (ranging from 8 to 16 feet in length), and then cutting the individual products from the logs, depending upon the type of wood (pine, oak, walnut, or maple) and the size (diameter) of the log.

The joint process results in the following costs and output of products during a typical month:

Joint production costs:	
Materials (rough timber logs)	$ 500,000
Debarking (labor and overhead)	50,000
Sizing (labor and overhead)	200,000
Product cutting (labor and overhead)	250,000
Total joint costs	$1,000,000

Product yield and average sales value on a per-unit basis from the joint process are as follows:

Product	Monthly Output	Fully Processed Sales Price
Studs	75,000	$ 8
Decorative pieces	5,000	100
Posts	20,000	20

The studs are sold as rough-cut lumber after emerging from the sawmill operation without further processing by SSI. Also, the posts require no further processing. The decorative pieces must be planed and further sized after emerging from the SSI sawmill. This additional processing costs SSI $100,000 per month and normally results in a loss of 10 percent of the units entering the process. Without this planing and sizing process, there is still an active intermediate market for the unfinished decorative pieces where the sales price averages $60 per unit.

Required:

1. Based on the information given for Sonimad Sawmill, Inc., allocate the joint processing costs of $1,000,000 to each of the three product lines using the:
   a. Relative sales-value-at-split-off method
   b. Physical units method at split-off
   c. Estimated net realizable value method

2. Prepare an analysis for Sonimad Sawmill, Inc., to compare processing the decorative pieces further as it presently does, with selling the rough-cut product immediately at split-off. Be sure to provide all calculations.

3. Assume Sonimad Sawmill, Inc., announced that in six months it will sell the rough-cut product at split-off due to increasing competitive pressure. Identify at least three types of likely behavior that will be demonstrated by the skilled labor in the planing and sizing process as a result of this announcement. Explain how this behavior could be improved by management. *(CMA adapted)*

Problem 7-35 Single Charging Rates

OBJECTIVE ◀ 2

House Corporation Board (HCB) of Tri-Gamma Sorority is responsible for the operation of a two-story sorority house on the State University campus. HCB has set a normal capacity of 60 women. At any given point in time, there are 100 members of the chapter: 60 living in the house and 40 living elsewhere (e.g., in the freshman dorms on campus). HCB needs to set rates for the use of the house for the coming year. The following costs are budgeted: $240,000 fixed and $34,800 variable. The fixed costs are fairly insensitive to the number of women living in the house. Food is budgeted at $40,000 and is included in the fixed costs; food does not seem to vary greatly given the stated capacity. The variable expenses consist of telephone bills and some of the utilities. HCB is not responsible for chapter dues, party fees, pledging and initiation fees, and other social expenditures. Women living in the house eat 20 meals per week there and live in a two-person room. (All in-house members' rooms, bathroom facilities, etc., are on the second floor.) All members eat Monday dinner at the house and have full use of house facilities (e.g., the two TV lounges, kitchens, access to milk and cereal at any time, study facilities, and so on).

HCB has traditionally set two rates: one for in-house members and one for out-of-house members. There are 32 weeks in a school year.

Required:

1. Discuss the factors that might go into determining the charging rate for the two types of sorority members.
2. Set charging rates for the in-house and out-of-house members.

The items that appear within this chapter that are from the CMA are Problems 7-31 and 7-34. Source: Materials from the Certified Management Accountant Examination, Copyright 1981, 1982, 1983, 1984, 1985, 1989, 1990, 1991, 1992, 1995, 1996 by the Institute of Certified Management Accountants are reprinted and/or adapted with permission.

8 Budgeting for Planning and Control

Dmitry Kalinovsky/Shutterstock.com

BUDGETING

at PPG Industries

The onset of the coronavirus in early 2020 blindsided business, and corporate financial officers (CFOs) scrambled to readjust their budgets and ensure that cash would be readily available throughout the rest of the year. **Lufthansa AG**, **Cathay Pacific Airways Ltd.**, and **Singapore Airlines Ltd.** began slashing costs in anticipation of falling revenue and profits. **Citrix Systems, Inc.**, a Florida-based software company, "keeps a business continuity plan for natural disasters, credit-market challenges and health issues." This plan is designed to prepare them for unexpected situations. To implement it, their financial chief meets regularly with the company's internal audit team to evaluate sales and cash forecasts.[1] Thus, budgeting is moved to the forefront of business decision making.

    PPG Industries, a maker of paint, coatings, and specialty materials, found that demand for their products dropped and the inventory of raw materials increased. That helps them with cash flow, as they do not need to restock and pay for new inventory. This also impacts their purchases budgets that will be timed to potential increased sales later on. PPG is cutting discretionary spending and reducing production levels to respond to lower demand. Vince Morales, CFO of PPG, said, "Managing your cash and your liquidity—that's the primary objective for CFOs these days."[2]

THE ROLE OF BUDGETING IN PLANNING AND CONTROL

Careful planning, whether formal or informal, is vital to the health of any organization. Business managers must know their resource capabilities and have a plan that shows how those resources will be used. In this chapter, the basics of budgeting are discussed, and traditional master budgets are developed. Flexible and activity-based budgeting are also presented, along with extensive discussion of the behavioral aspects of budgeting and its use in control.

---

1 Nina Trentmann, "CFOs Look to Boost Cash holdings, Cut Costs Amid Coronavirus Outbreak," *The Wall Street Journal* (March 5, 2020), https://www.wsj.com/articles/cfos-look-to-boost-cash-holdings-cut-costs-amid-coronavirus-outbreak-11583447858, accessed May 23, 2020.

2 Nina Trentmann, "Inventory Buildup Helps, Hurts Paints and Coatings Maker PPG Industries," *The Wall Street Journal* (April 29, 2020), https://www.wsj.com/articles/inventory-buildup-helps-hurts-paints-and-coatings-maker-ppg-industries-11588194117, accessed May 23, 2020.

Budgeting is critically important to both planning and control. **Budgets** are quantitative plans for the future, stated in either physical or financial terms or both. When used for planning, a budget is a method for translating the goals and strategies of an organization into operational terms. Budgets are also used in control. **Control** is the process of setting standards, receiving feedback on actual performance, and taking corrective action whenever actual performance deviates significantly from planned performance. Thus, budgets can be used to compare actual outcomes with planned outcomes, and they can steer operations back on course, if necessary.

Exhibit 8.1 illustrates the relationship of budgets to planning, operating, and control. Budgets evolve from the long-run objectives of the firm; they form the basis for operations. Actual results are compared with budgeted amounts through control. This comparison provides feedback both for operations and for future budgets.

Purposes of Budgeting

Budgets are usually prepared for areas within an organization (departments, plants, divisions, and so on) and for activities (sales, production, research, and so on). This system of budgets serves as the comprehensive financial plan for the organization as a whole and gives an organization several advantages.

1. It forces managers to plan.
2. It provides resource information that can be used to improve decision making.
3. It aids in the use of resources and employees by setting a benchmark that can be used for the subsequent evaluation of performance.
4. It improves communication and coordination.

Budgeting forces management to plan for the future—to develop an overall direction for the organization, foresee problems, and develop future policies. When managers plan, they grow to understand the capabilities of their businesses and where the resources of the business should be used. All businesses and not-for-profit entities should budget. All large businesses

---

Exhibit 8.1

The Master Budget and Its
Interrelationships

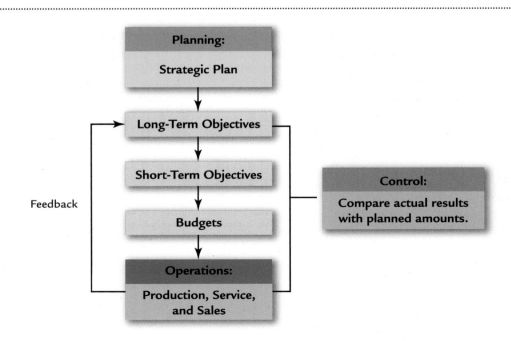

do budget. In fact, the budgeting activity of a company such as **ConocoPhillips** or **IBM** takes significant amounts of time and involves many managers at a variety of levels. Some small businesses do not budget, and many of those go out of business in short order.

Budgets help managers make better decisions. For example, a cash budget points out potential shortfalls. If a company foresees a cash deficiency, it may want to improve accounts receivable collection or postpone plans to purchase new assets.

Budgets set standards for the use of a company's resources and help control and motivate employees. Businesses with successful budgets ensure that steps are taken to achieve the objectives outlined in an organization's master plan.

Budgets are also used for communication and coordination of employee efforts, so that all employees can be aware of their role in achieving the organization's objectives. This is why explicitly linking the budget to the long-run plans of the organization is so important. The budget is not a series of vague, rosy scenarios, but a set of specific plans to achieve those objectives. Budgets encourage coordination because the various areas and activities of the organization must all work together to achieve the stated objectives. The role of communication and coordination becomes more important as an organization grows larger.

The Budgeting Process

The budgeting process can range from the fairly informal process undergone by a small firm, to an elaborately detailed, several-month procedure employed by large firms. Key features of the process include directing and coordinating the overall budget.

Directing and Coordinating Every organization must have someone responsible for directing and coordinating the overall budgeting process. This **budget director** works under the direction of the budget committee and is usually the controller or someone who reports to the controller. The **budget committee** is responsible for reviewing the budget, providing policy guidelines and budgetary goals, resolving differences that may arise as the budget is prepared, approving the final budget, and monitoring the actual performance of the organization as the year unfolds. The budget committee ensures that the budget is linked to the strategic plan of the organization. The president of the organization appoints the members of the committee, who are usually the president, the vice presidents, and the controller.

Types of Budgets The **master budget** is a comprehensive financial plan for the year made up of various individual departmental and activity budgets. A master budget can be divided into *operating* and *financial* budgets. **Operating budgets** are concerned with the income-generating activities of a firm: sales, production, and finished goods inventories. The ultimate outcome of the operating budgets is a pro forma or budgeted income statement. Note that "pro forma" is synonymous with "budgeted" and "estimated." In effect, the pro forma income statement is done "according to form" but with estimated, not historical, data. **Financial budgets** are concerned with the inflows and outflows of cash and with financial position. Planned cash inflows and outflows are detailed in a cash budget, and expected financial position at the end of the budget period is shown in a budgeted, or pro forma, balance sheet. Exhibit 8.2 illustrates the components of the master budget.

The master budget is usually prepared for a one-year period corresponding to the company's fiscal year. The yearly budgets are broken down into quarterly and monthly budgets. Using shorter time periods helps managers to compare actual data with budgeted data as the year unfolds. Because progress can be checked more frequently, problems can be identified and handled before they become serious.

Most organizations prepare the budget for the coming year during the last four or five months of the current year. However, some organizations use continuous budgeting. A **continuous** (or **rolling**) **budget** is a moving 12-month budget. As one month ends, an

Exhibit 8.2

Components of the Master Budget

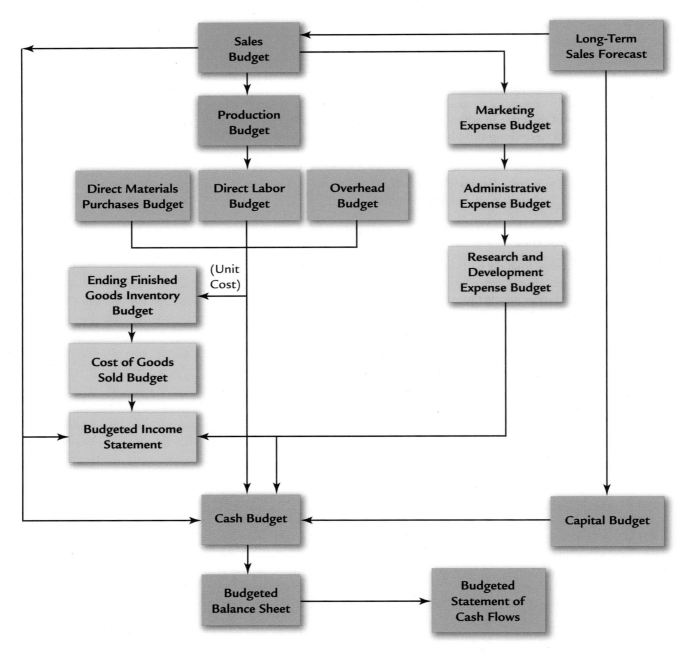

additional month in the future is added so that the company always has a 12-month plan on hand. Proponents of continuous budgeting maintain that it forces managers to plan ahead constantly. The majority of CFOs believe that rolling forecasts are very valuable, and companies that do use them typically roll out the forecasts for five or six quarters rather than four.[3]

---

3   Omar Aguilar, "How Strategic Performance Management Is Helping Companies Create Business Value," *Strategic Finance* (January 2003): 44–49.

Similar to a continuous budget is a continuously updated budget. The objective of this budget is not to have 12 months of budgeted information at all times, but instead to update the master budget each month as new information becomes available. For example, every autumn, Chandler Engineering prepares a budget for the coming year. Then, at the end of each month of the year, the budget is transformed into a rolling forecast by recording year-to-date results and the forecast for the remainder of the year. In essence, the budget is continually updated throughout the year.

The first quarter of 2020 saw unprecedented demand for certain products and created a real strain on supply chains. **Kimberly-Clark Corp.**, maker of Huggies diapers, toilet paper, and other household goods experienced strong demand and created the need for more output of those staples. The company limited the number of products it makes to increase capacity for the basics. Companies have "to focus on the biggest, most important, most well-known brands," according to **Coca-Cola** CEO James Quincey. **Lockheed Martin** CEO Marillyn Hewson noted that disruptions caused by the coronavirus have lowered sales and production activity and caused it to advance more than $155 million to small and vulnerable suppliers—hoping to shore up its supply chain. As a result, companies have had to adjust budgets in real time to adapt to the new realities of business.[4]

Gathering Information for Budgeting

To begin the master budgeting process, the budget director alerts all segments of the company to begin gathering budget information. The data used to create the budget come from many sources. Historical data are one possibility. For example, last year's direct materials costs may give the production manager a good feel for potential materials costs for next year. Still, historical data alone cannot tell a company what to expect in the future.

Forecasting Sales The sales forecast is the basis for the sales budget, which, in turn, is the basis for all of the other operating budgets and most of the financial budgets. Accordingly, the accuracy of the sales forecast strongly affects the soundness of the entire master budget.

Creating the sales forecast is usually the responsibility of the Marketing Department. One approach is for the chief sales executive to have individual salespeople submit sales predictions, which are aggregated to form a total sales forecast. The accuracy of this sales forecast may be improved by considering other factors such as the general economic climate, competition, advertising, pricing policies, and so on. Some companies supplement the Marketing Department forecast with more formal approaches, such as time-series analysis, correlation analysis, econometric modeling, and industry analysis.

To illustrate an actual sales forecasting approach, consider the practices of a company that manufactures oil field equipment on a job-order basis. Each month, the Finance and Sales departments' heads meet to construct a sales forecast based on bookings. A booking is a probable sales order submitted by sales personnel in the field; it is meant to alert the Engineering and Manufacturing departments to a potential job. Past experience has shown that bookings are generally followed by sales or shipments within 30 to 45 days. Exhibit 8.3 shows the short-term bookings forecast for the company. Notice that the dollar amount of each booking is multiplied by its probability of occurrence to obtain a weighted dollar amount. The sum of weighted amounts is the forecast for sales for the month. The probability estimate is determined jointly by the salesperson and the controller. Each probability is initially set at 50 percent. Then, it is adjusted upward or downward based on any additional information

4 Nina Trentmann, "Fewer Products, Localized Production—Companies Seek Supply-Chain Solutions," *The Wall Street Journal* (April 29, 2020), https://www.wsj.com/articles/inventory-buildup-helps-hurts-paints-and-coatings-maker-ppg-industries-11588194117, accessed May 23, 2020.

Exhibit 8.3

Short-Term Bookings Forecast for Oil Field Equipment Company

Quote #	Region/Country	Customer	Product	Dollar Amount	Probability	Weighted Month Total
March 20x1						
1194-17	Spain	Valencia	Repair 3224	$ 37,500	100%	$ 37,500
1294-03	Bulgaria	Luecim	1256, 7188	74,145	80	59,316
0195-55	USA	Exxon	4498	25,000	95	23,750
0295-19	USA	BP/TX	6766, 1267	150,442	100	150,442
0295-23	China	China Res	7541, 8875	55,900	75	41,925
0295-45	China	China Res	8879, 0944	34,500	80	27,600
0395-36	Abu Dhabi	ADES	7400, 6751, 5669 & spares	30,000	50	15,000
March Total						$355,533
April 20x1						
1294-14	China	Jiang Han	6524, 5523, 0412, 4578, 3340	$234,000	80%	$187,200
0295-43	Russia	Geoserv	3356	76,800	60	46,080
0295-10	Venezuela	Petrolina	4450, 6713, 7122	112,500	90	101,250
0395-37	Indonesia	Chevron	8890, 0933	98,000	65	63,700
0395-71	Italy	CV International	7815	16,000	70	11,200
April Total						$409,430
May 20x1						
0295-21	Mexico	Instituto Mexicana	8900 & spares	$ 34,000	40%	$ 13,600
0395-29	Venezuela	Petrolina	8416, 8832	165,000	50	82,500
0495-11	USA	Branchwater, Inc.	9043, 8891	335,000	60	201,000
0495-68	Saudi Arabia	Aramco	0453	3,500	50	1,750
May Total						$298,850

about the sale. The probability is really a prediction of a compound event, the prediction of both getting the order and determining the month in which it will happen. The Sales Department tends toward overconfidence—both in terms of getting the order and in landing it sooner rather than later. As a result, the controller takes a more pessimistic view and modifies the forecast. The end result is the form shown in Exhibit 8.3.

Forecasting Other Variables Like sales, costs and cash-related items are critical in budgeting. Many of the same factors considered in sales forecasting apply to cost forecasting. Here, historical amounts can be of real value. Managers can adjust past figures based on their knowledge of coming events. For example, a three-year union contract takes much of the uncertainty out of wage prediction. (Of course, if the contract is expiring, the uncertainty returns.) Alert purchasing agents will have an idea of changing materials prices. In fact, large companies such as **Nestlé** and **The Coca-Cola Company** have entire departments devoted to forecasting commodity prices and supplies. They invest in commodity futures to smooth out price fluctuations, an action that facilitates budgeting. Overhead is broken down into its component costs; these can be predicted using past data and relevant inflation figures.

The cash budget is a critically important part of the master budget, and some of its components, especially payment of accounts receivable, also require forecasting. This is discussed in more detail in the section on cash budgeting.

PREPARING THE OPERATING BUDGET

OBJECTIVE 2

Prepare the operating budget, identify its major components, and explain the interrelationships of the various components.

The first section of the master budget is the operating budget. It consists of a series of schedules for all phases of operations, culminating in a budgeted income statement. The following are the components of the operating budget.

1. Sales budget
2. Production budget
3. Direct materials purchases budget
4. Direct labor budget
5. Overhead budget
6. Ending finished goods inventory budget
7. Cost of goods sold budget
8. Marketing expense budget
9. Research and development expense budget
10. Administrative expense budget
11. Budgeted income statement

You may want to refer back to Exhibit 8.2 to see how these components of the operating budget fit into the master budget.

The example used to illustrate the components of the operating budget is based on ABT, Inc., a manufacturer of concrete block and pipe for the construction industry. For simplicity, we will prepare the operating budget for ABT's concrete block line. (The budget for the pipe product line is prepared in the same way and merged into the overall company budget.)

Sales Budget

The **sales budget** is the projection approved by the budget committee that describes expected sales for each product in units and dollars. The sales budget must be constructed first, before other budgets can be constructed.

Example 8.1 illustrates the sales budget for ABT's concrete block line. The sales budget shows that ABT's sales fluctuate seasonally. Most sales (75 percent) take place in the spring and summer. Also, note that ABT expects price to increase from $0.70 to $0.80 in the summer quarter. Because the price changes within the year, an average price must be used for the column that describes the total year's sales ($0.75 = $12,000,000/16,000,000). If ABT had two types of concrete blocks, a separate sales budget would be prepared for each type, as shown in Requirement 2 of Example 8.1.

Production Budget

The **production budget** describes how many units must be produced in order to meet sales needs and satisfy ending inventory requirements. The production budget depends on the unit sales shown in the sales budget.

A separate production budget is constructed for each product manufactured (or service provided). Both unit sales and unit finished goods inventories desired are required for the production budget. The basic equation for the production budget is:

$$\text{Units to be produced} = \text{Unit sales} + \text{Desired units in ending inventory} - \text{Units in beginning inventory}$$

Of course, if there were no inventories, the number of units to be produced would equal the number of units to be sold. In service firms, units of service provided equal the units of service sold since services are not inventoried. Similarly, in the JIT firm, units sold equal units

EXAMPLE 8.1

The HOW and WHY of Constructing a Sales Budget

Information:

ABT, Inc., manufactures and sells concrete block for residential and commercial building. ABT expects to sell the following in 20x1:

	Quarter 1	Quarter 2	Quarter 3	Quarter 4
Units	2,000,000	6,000,000	6,000,000	2,000,000
Unit selling price	$0.70	$0.70	$0.80	$0.80

Why:
The sales budget is the foundation for the master budget; all other budgets are based in part on the units sold or revenue given in the sales budget.

Required:

1. Construct a sales budget for the ABT concrete block line for the coming year. Show total sales by quarter and in total for the year.

2. *What if* there were two types of concrete block (type 1 and type 2) and 60 percent of the sales in each quarter were for type 1? Assume the selling price for type 1 is $0.60 in the first quarter and $0.70 for the rest of the year. The selling price of type 2 is $0.80 in Quarters 1 and 2 and is $0.90 per unit for the rest of the year. Construct a sales budget for ABT showing sales for both types and in total.

Solution:

1.

Sales Budget
For the Year Ended December 31, 20x1

	Quarter 1	Quarter 2	Quarter 3	Quarter 4	Total
Units	2,000,000	6,000,000	6,000,000	2,000,000	16,000,000
Unit selling price	× $0.70	× $0.70	× $0.80	×$0.80	×$0.75
Sales	$1,400,000	$4,200,000	$4,800,000	$1,600,000	$12,000,000

2.

Sales Budget
For the Year Ended December 31, 20x1

	Quarter 1	Quarter 2	Quarter 3	Quarter 4	Total
Type 1 block[1]					
Units	1,200,000	3,600,000	3,600,000	1,200,000	9,600,000
Unit selling price	× $0.60	× $0.70	× $0.70	× $0.70	× $0.6875[2]
Sales	$ 720,000	$2,520,000	$2,520,000	$ 840,000	$ 6,600,000
Type 2 block[3]					
Units	800,000	2,400,000	2,400,000	800,000	6,400,000
Unit selling price	× $0.80	× $0.80	× $0.90	× $0.90	× $0.85[4]
Sales	$ 640,000	$1,920,000	$2,160,000	$ 720,000	$ 5,440,000
Total sales	$1,360,000	$4,440,000	$4,680,000	$1,560,000	$12,040,000

[1]Units in each quarter equal 60% of the unit sales in Requirement 1.
[2]Average price for the year = $6,600,000/9,600,000 = $0.6875
[3]Units in each quarter equal 40% of the unit sales in Requirement 1.
[4]Average price for the year = $5,440,000/6,400,000 = $0.85

produced, since a customer order triggers production. Usually, however, the production budget must consider the existence of beginning and ending inventories. Notice that the production budget is expressed in terms of units; we do not yet know how much they will cost. Example 8.2 shows how and why a production budget is constructed.

EXAMPLE 8.2

The HOW and WHY of Constructing a Production Budget

Information:
ABT expects the following unit sales and desired ending inventory in 20x1:

Quarter	Unit Sales	Ending Inventory
1	2,000,000	500,000
2	6,000,000	500,000
3	6,000,000	100,000
4	2,000,000	100,000

Inventory on both January 1, 20x1, and January 1, 20x2, is expected to be 100,000 blocks.

> **Why:**
> The production budget is needed to tell production how much to produce in the coming year. The number of units produced will be used to determine budgeted costs for direct materials, direct labor, and overhead.

Required:

1. Construct a production budget for the ABT concrete block line for the coming year. Show total units produced by quarter and in total for the year.

2. *What if* ABT did not provide the desired ending inventory in units, but instead relied on an inventory rule—that the desired ending inventory of blocks was equal to 5 percent of the next period's sales? Further, assume that the budgeted unit sales in Quarter 1, 20x2, equaled 2,500,000, and that the beginning inventory for Quarter 1, 20x1, met the inventory rule. Construct a production budget for ABT showing units produced by quarter and in total for the year.

Solution:

1.

Production Budget
For the Year Ended December 31, 20x1

	Quarter 1	Quarter 2	Quarter 3	Quarter 4	Total
Unit sales	2,000,000	6,000,000	6,000,000	2,000,000	16,000,000
Desired ending inventory	500,000	500,000	100,000	100,000	100,000
Total needed	2,500,000	6,500,000	6,100,000	2,100,000	16,100,000
Less: Beginning inventory*	100,000	500,000	500,000	100,000	100,000
Units produced	2,400,000	6,000,000	5,600,000	2,000,000	16,000,000

*Beginning inventory for Quarter 1 is given. Beginning inventory for the succeeding quarters is equal to the ending inventory of the previous quarter. That is, beginning inventory for Quarter 2 is equal to desired ending inventory for Quarter 1.

Notice that desired ending inventory for the year equals the desired ending inventory for Quarter 4. Beginning inventory for the year equals the beginning inventory for Quarter 1.

2. If desired ending inventory of blocks equals 5 percent of the next quarter's sales, then the desired ending inventory for each quarter is as follows:
Quarter 1 ending inventory = 0.05 × 6,000,000 = 300,000
Quarter 2 ending inventory = 0.05 × 6,000,000 = 300,000
Quarter 3 ending inventory = 0.05 × 2,000,000 = 100,000
Quarter 4 ending inventory = 0.05 × 2,500,000 = 125,000

Production Budget
For the Year Ended December 31, 20x1

	Quarter 1	Quarter 2	Quarter 3	Quarter 4	Total
Unit sales	2,000,000	6,000,000	6,000,000	2,000,000	16,000,000
Desired ending inventory	300,000	300,000	100,000	125,000	125,000
Total needed	2,300,000	6,300,000	6,100,000	2,125,000	16,125,000
Less: Beginning inventory*	100,000	300,000	300,000	100,000	100,000
Units produced	2,200,000	6,000,000	5,800,000	2,025,000	16,025,000

*Beginning inventory for Quarter 1 = ending inventory for Quarter 4 of 20x0
Desired ending inventory for Quarter 4, 20x0 = 0.05 × 2,000,000 = 100,000

Desired ending inventory for Quarter 4, 20x0 = 0.05 × 2,000,000 = 100,000

Notice that desired ending inventory for the year equals the desired ending inventory for Quarter 4. Beginning inventory for the year equals the beginning inventory for Quarter 1.

Direct Materials Purchases Budget

After the production budget is completed, budgets for direct materials, direct labor, and overhead can be prepared. The **direct materials purchases budget** is similar in format to the production budget; it is based on the amount of materials needed for production and the inventories of direct materials.

Expected direct materials usage is determined by the input-output relationship (the technical relationship existing between direct materials and output). This relationship is often determined by the Engineering Department or the industrial designer. For example, one lightweight concrete block requires approximately 26 pounds of materials (cement, sand, gravel, shale, pumice, and water). The relative mix of these ingredients is fixed for a specific kind of concrete block. Thus, it is fairly easy to determine expected usage for each material from the production budget by multiplying the amount of material needed per unit of output times the number of units of output.

Once expected usage is computed, the purchases (in units) are computed as follows:

Purchases = Expected usage + Desired ending inventory of direct materials
− Beginning inventory of direct materials

The quantity of direct materials in inventory is determined by the firm's inventory policy. Example 8.3 shows how and why to prepare the direct materials purchases budget. For simplicity, all materials are treated jointly (as if there were only one material input). In reality, a separate direct materials purchases budget would be needed for each kind of material.

Information:

ABT makes concrete blocks. Each block requires 26 pounds of raw materials (a mixture of cement, sand, gravel, shale, pumice, and water). ABT's raw materials inventory policy is to have 5 million pounds in ending inventory for the third and fourth quarters and 8 million pounds in ending inventory for the first and second quarters. Thus, desired direct materials inventory on both January 1, 20x1, and January 1, 20x2, is 5,000,000 pounds of materials. Each pound of raw materials costs $0.01.

Recall from Example 8.2 that ABT budgeted 2,400,000 units in Quarter 1, 6,000,000 units in Quarter 2, 5,600,000 units in Quarter 3, and 2,000,000 units in Quarter 4.

> **Why:**
> The direct materials purchases budget is constructed for each type of direct materials used in production. It tells managers the amount and cost of purchases to support the production budget for the coming year. Dollar purchases will be used later in disbursements under the cash budget.

Required:

1. Construct a direct materials purchases budget for the raw materials for the ABT concrete block line for the coming year. Show total amounts by quarter and in total for the year.

2. *What if* ABT did not provide the desired ending inventory in units, but instead relied on an inventory rule—that the desired ending inventory of raw materials was equal to 2 percent of the next period's production needs? Further, assume that the budgeted production for Quarter 1, 20x2, equaled 2,200,000 concrete blocks, and that the beginning inventory of materials for Quarter 1, 20x1, met the inventory rule. Construct a direct materials purchases budget showing pounds purchased and purchase cost by quarter and in total for the year.

Solution:

1.

Direct Materials Purchases Budget
For the Year Ended December 31, 20x1

	Quarter 1	Quarter 2	Quarter 3	Quarter 4	Total
Units produced	2,400,000	6,000,000	5,600,000	2,000,000	16,000,000
Direct materials per unit	× 26	× 26	× 26	× 26	× 26
Production needs (lbs.)	62,400,000	156,000,000	145,600,000	52,000,000	416,000,000
Desired ending inventory (lbs.)	8,000,000	8,000,000	5,000,000	5,000,000	5,000,000
Total needed	70,400,000	164,000,000	150,600,000	57,000,000	421,000,000
Less: Beginning inventory*	5,000,000	8,000,000	8,000,000	5,000,000	5,000,000
Units produced	65,400,000	156,000,000	142,600,000	52,000,000	416,000,000
Cost per pound	× $0.01	× $0.01	× $0.01	× $0.01	× $0.01
Total purchase cost	$ 654,000	$ 1,560,000	$ 1,426,000	$ 520,000	$ 4,160,000

*Beginning inventory for Quarter 1 is given. Beginning inventory for the succeeding quarters is equal to the ending inventory of the previous quarter. That is, beginning inventory for Quarter 2 is equal to desired ending inventory for Quarter 1.

EXAMPLE 8.3

The HOW and WHY of Constructing a Direct Materials Purchases Budget

EXAMPLE 8.3

(Continued)

Notice that desired ending inventory for the year equals the desired ending inventory for Quarter 4. Beginning inventory for the year equals the beginning inventory for Quarter 1.

2. If desired ending inventory of blocks equals 2 percent of the next quarter's production needs, then the desired ending inventory of raw materials for each quarter is as follows:

Quarter 1 ending inventory = 0.02 × (26 × 6,000,000) = 3,120,000
Quarter 2 ending inventory = 0.02 × (26 × 5,600,000) = 2,912,000
Quarter 3 ending inventory = 0.02 × (26 × 2,000,000) = 1,040,000
Quarter 4 ending inventory = 0.02 × (26 × 2,200,000) = 1,144,000

Direct Materials Purchases Budget
For the Year Ended December 31, 20x1

	Quarter 1	Quarter 2	Quarter 3	Quarter 4	Total
Units produced	2,400,000	6,000,000	5,600,000	2,000,000	16,000,000
Direct materials per unit	× 26	× 26	× 26	× 26	× 26
Production needs (lbs.)	62,400,000	156,000,000	145,600,000	52,000,000	416,000,000
Desired ending inventory (lbs.)	3,120,000	2,912,000	1,040,000	1,144,000	1,144,000
Total needed	65,520,000	158,912,000	146,640,000	53,144,000	417,144,000
Less: Beginning inventory*	1,248,000	3,120,000	2,912,000	1,040,000	1,248,000
Units produced	64,272,000	155,792,000	143,728,000	52,104,000	415,896,000
Cost per pound	× $0.01	× $0.01	× $0.01	× $0.01	× $0.01
Total purchase cost	$ 642,720	$ 1,557,920	$ 1,437,280	$ 521,040	$ 4,158,960

*Beginning inventory for Quarter 1 = 0.02 × (26 × 2,400,000) = 1,248,000. Beginning inventory for the succeeding quarters = the ending inventory of the previous quarter. That is, beginning inventory for Quarter 2 = desired ending inventory for Quarter 1.

Notice that desired ending inventory for the year equals the desired ending inventory for Quarter 4. Beginning inventory for the year equals the beginning inventory for Quarter 1.

Direct Labor Budget

The **direct labor budget** shows the total direct labor hours and direct labor cost needed for the number of units in the production budget. As with direct materials, the usage of direct labor is determined by the technological relationship between labor and output. For example, if a batch of 100 concrete blocks requires 1.5 direct labor hours, then the direct labor time per block is 0.015 hour (1.5/100). Assuming that direct labor is used efficiently, this rate is fixed for the existing technology. The relationship will change only if a new approach to manufacturing is introduced. **Example 8.4** shows how and why to prepare a direct labor budget.

EXAMPLE 8.4

The HOW and WHY of Constructing a Direct Labor Budget

Information:
ABT makes concrete blocks. Each block requires 0.015 direct labor hour; direct labor is paid $14 per direct labor hour.

Recall from Example 8.2 that ABT budgeted 2,400,000 units in Quarter 1, 6,000,000 units in Quarter 2, 5,600,000 units in Quarter 3, and 2,000,000 units in Quarter 4.

Why:
The direct labor budget is constructed for each type of direct labor used in production. It tells managers the amount and cost of direct labor needed to support the production budget for the coming year. Dollar direct labor costs will be used later in disbursements under the cash budget.

Required:

1. Construct a direct labor budget for the ABT concrete block line for the coming year. Show total amounts by quarter and in total for the year.

2. *What if* ABT required two types of direct labor—mixers and shapers. Each concrete block requires 0.005 hour of mixing time at $10 per direct labor hour. Each concrete block requires 0.01 hour of shaping time at $16 per direct labor hour. Prepare a direct labor budget for each type of labor. Show hours and cost for each quarter and in total for the year.

Solution:

1.

Direct Labor Budget
For the Year Ended December 31, 20x1

	Quarter 1	Quarter 2	Quarter 3	Quarter 4	Total
Units produced	2,400,000	6,000,000	5,600,000	2,000,000	16,000,000
Direct labor per unit	× 0.015	× 0.015	× 0.015	× 0.015	× 0.015
Direct labor hours needed	36,000	90,000	84,000	30,000	240,000
Cost per direct labor hour	× $14	× $14	× $14	× $14	× $14
Total direct labor cost	$ 504,000	$1,260,000	$1,176,000	$ 420,000	$ 3,360,000

2.

Direct Labor Budget
For the Year Ended December 31, 20x1

	Quarter 1	Quarter 2	Quarter 3	Quarter 4	Total
Type 1 labor					
Units produced	2,400,000	6,000,000	5,600,000	2,000,000	16,000,000
Mixing labor per unit	× 0.005	× 0.005	× 0.005	× 0.005	× 0.005
Mixing hours needed	12,000	30,000	28,000	10,000	80,000
Cost per mixing hour	× $10	× $10	× $10	× $10	× $10
Total mixing labor cost	$ 120,000	$ 300,000	$ 280,000	$ 100,000	$ 800,000
Type 2 labor					
Units produced	2,400,000	6,000,000	5,600,000	2,000,000	16,000,000
Shaping labor per unit	× 0.01	× 0.01	× 0.01	× 0.01	× 0.01
Shaping hours needed	24,000	60,000	56,000	20,000	160,000
Cost per shaping hour	× $16	× $16	× $16	× $16	× $16
Total shaping labor cost	$ 384,000	$ 960,000	$ 896,000	$ 320,000	$2,560,000
Total direct labor cost	$ 504,000	$1,260,000	$1,176,000	$ 420,000	$3,360,000

In the direct labor budget, the wage rate used is the *average* wage paid the direct laborers associated with production. Since it is an average, it allows for the possibility of differing wage rates paid to individual laborers. If there were different categories of workers, however, with differing skill levels and wage rates, separate direct labor budgets may be prepared for each category of worker.

Overhead Budget

The **overhead budget** shows the expected cost of all indirect manufacturing items. Unlike direct materials and direct labor, there is no readily identifiable input-output relationship for overhead items. Recall, however, that overhead consists of two types of costs: variable and fixed. Past experience can be used as a guide to determine how overhead varies with activity level. Items that vary with activity level are identified (e.g., supplies and utilities used for production machinery), and the amount that is expected to be spent for each item per unit of activity is estimated. Individual rates are then totaled to obtain a variable overhead rate. **Example 8.5** shows how and why to prepare an overhead budget.

Ending Finished Goods Inventory Budget

The **ending finished goods inventory budget** supplies information needed for the balance sheet and also serves as an important input for the preparation of the cost of goods sold budget. To prepare this budget, the unit cost of producing each concrete block must be calculated using

---

EXAMPLE 8.5

The HOW and WHY of Constructing an Overhead Budget

Information:
ABT makes concrete blocks. Each block requires 0.015 direct labor hour. Variable overhead is $8 per direct labor hour. Fixed overhead is budgeted at $320,000 per quarter ($100,000 for supervision, $200,000 for depreciation, and $20,000 for rent). Recall from Example 8.4 that ABT budgeted 36,000 direct labor hours in Quarter 1, 90,000 direct labor hours in Quarter 2, 84,000 direct labor hours in Quarter 3, and 30,000 direct labor hours in Quarter 4.

> **Why:**
> The overhead budget is prepared based on variable and fixed overhead used in production. It tells managers the cost of overhead needed to support the production budget for the coming year. Dollar overhead costs will be used later in disbursements under the cash budget.

Required:

1. Construct an overhead budget for the ABT concrete block line for the coming year. Show total amounts by quarter and in total for the year.

2. *What if* ABT's fixed overhead were $350,000 per quarter? How would that affect variable overhead? Fixed overhead? Total overhead?

EXAMPLE 8.5

(*Continued*)

Solution:

1.

Overhead Budget
For the Year Ended December 31, 20x1

	Quarter 1	Quarter 2	Quarter 3	Quarter 4	Total
Budgeted direct labor hours	36,000	90,000	84,000	30,000	240,000
Variable overhead rate	× $8	× $8	× $8	× $8	× $8
Budgeted variable overhead	$ 288,000	$ 720,000	$ 672,000	$ 240,000	$1,920,000
Budgeted fixed overhead	320,000	320,000	320,000	320,000	1,280,000
Total overhead cost	$ 608,000	$1,040,000	$ 992,000	$ 560,000	$3,200,000

2. If fixed overhead increased to $350,000 per quarter, variable overhead would be unaffected. However, the fixed overhead amounts would increase from $320,000 to $350,000 per quarter, and the total overhead would increase by $30,000 per quarter. The yearly overhead would increase by $120,000 (4 × $30,000).

information from Examples 8.2, 8.3, 8.4, and 8.5. **Example 8.6** shows how and why to prepare the ending finished goods inventory budget.

Information:
ABT makes concrete blocks. Example 8.3 shows that each unit (block) requires 26 pounds of raw materials costing $0.01 per pound. Therefore, each unit has budgeted direct materials cost of $0.26. Example 8.4 shows the budgeted direct labor hours per unit (0.015 hour) and wage rate ($14 per direct labor hour). Example 8.5 shows the budgeted variable overhead per unit ($8 × 0.015 direct labor hour) and total fixed overhead for the year ($1,280,000). Recall from Example 8.2 that 16,000,000 units were expected to be produced during the year and that 100,000 units were budgeted for ending finished goods inventory.

Why:
The finished goods inventory budget is needed in order to prepare the cost of goods sold budget. It relies on information from the production, direct materials purchases, direct labor, and overhead budgets.

Required:

1. Prepare an ending finished goods inventory budget for ABT for the year.

2. *What if* the ending inventory of blocks increased to 120,000? How would that affect the ending finished goods inventory budget?

EXAMPLE 8.6

(Continued)

Solution:

1.

Unit costs:	
Direct materials	$0.26
Direct labor (0.015 × $14)	0.21
Overhead:	
Budgeted variable overhead	0.12
Budgeted fixed overhead*	0.08
Total cost per unit	$0.67

*Fixed overhead per unit = $1,280,000/16,000,000 = $0.08

Total ending inventory cost = Units ending inventory × Unit cost

= 100,000 × $0.67 = $67,000

2. If the number of units in ending inventory increases, the cost of ending inventory will also increase. If there are 120,000 units in ending inventory, the cost of ending finished goods inventory will be $80,400 (120,000 × $0.67).

Cost of Goods Sold Budget

Once the ending finished goods inventory budget is finished, it is possible to construct a cost of goods sold budget. This budget will be used in preparing the budgeted income statement later on. **Example 8.7** shows how and why to prepare a cost of goods sold budget.

EXAMPLE 8.7

The HOW and WHY of Preparing the Cost of Goods Sold Budget

Information:
ABT makes concrete blocks. Example 8.3 shows the total budgeted direct materials cost ($4,160,000). Example 8.4 shows the budgeted total direct labor cost ($3,360,000). Example 8.5 shows the budgeted total overhead for the year ($3,200,000). Recall from Example 8.6 that the cost of ending finished goods inventory is budgeted at $67,000. ABT also provided the information that beginning finished goods inventory is $55,000.

> **Why:**
> The cost of goods sold budget shows the budgeted manufacturing costs used to make the units that are expected to be sold. The budgeted cost of goods sold will be used as an input to the budgeted income statement.

Required:

1. Prepare a cost of goods sold budget for ABT for the year.

2. *What if* the beginning inventory of finished goods was $60,000? How would that affect the cost of goods sold budget?

EXAMPLE 8.7

(Continued)

Solution:

1.

Direct materials	$ 4,160,000
Direct labor	3,360,000
Overhead	3,200,000
Total manufacturing cost	$10,720,000
Add: Beginning inventory, finished goods	55,000
Less: Ending inventory, finished goods	67,000
Cost of goods sold	$10,708,000

2. If the cost of beginning inventory of finished goods increases, the cost of goods sold will also increase. If the cost of beginning inventory of finished goods is $60,000, the cost of goods sold would increase to $10,713,000.

Marketing Expense Budget

The next budget to be prepared—the **marketing expense budget**—outlines planned expenditures for selling and distribution activities. As with overhead, marketing expenses can be broken into fixed and variable components. Such items as sales commissions, freight, and supplies vary with sales activity. Salaries of the marketing staff, depreciation on office equipment, and advertising are fixed expenses. The marketing expense budget is illustrated in **Example 8.8**.

EXAMPLE 8.8

The HOW and WHY of Constructing a Marketing Expense Budget

Information:
ABT's only variable marketing expense is a $0.05 commission per unit (block) sold. Fixed marketing expenses for each quarter include the following:

Salaries	$20,000
Depreciation	5,000
Travel	3,000

Advertising expense is $10,000 in Quarters 1, 3, and 4. However, at the beginning of the summer building season, ABT increases advertising; in Quarter 2, advertising expense is $15,000.

Why:
The marketing expense budget is prepared to help the sales and marketing managers understand the expected costs of selling and distribution for the coming year. The total marketing expense will be used later in preparing the budgeted income statement.

EXAMPLE 8.8

(Continued)

Required:

1. Construct a marketing expense budget for the ABT concrete block line for the coming year. Show total amounts by quarter and in total for the year.

2. *What if* ABT's variable marketing expense per unit increased to $0.06? How would that affect variable marketing expense? Fixed marketing expense? Total marketing expense?

Solution:

1.

Marketing Expense Budget
For the Year Ended December 31, 20x1

	Quarter 1	Quarter 2	Quarter 3	Quarter 4	Total
Budgeted unit sales	2,000,000	6,000,000	6,000,000	2,000,000	16,000,000
Unit variable marketing expense	× $0.05	× $0.05	× $0.05	× $0.05	× $0.05
Total variable marketing expense	$ 100,000	$ 300,000	$ 300,000	$ 100,000	$ 800,000
Fixed marketing expense:					
Salaries	$ 20,000	$ 20,000	$ 20,000	$ 20,000	$ 80,000
Depreciation	5,000	5,000	5,000	5,000	20,000
Travel	3,000	3,000	3,000	3,000	12,000
Advertising	10,000	15,000	10,000	10,000	45,000
Total fixed expense	$ 38,000	$ 43,000	$ 38,000	$ 38,000	$ 157,000
Total marketing expense	$ 138,000	$ 343,000	$ 338,000	$ 138,000	$ 957,000

2. If the sales commission rises to $0.06, total variable marketing expense for the year will increase to $960,000 ($0.06 × 16,000,000 units). Fixed marketing expense will be unaffected. Total marketing expense will increase to $1,117,000.

Administrative Expense Budget

The final budget to be developed for operations is the administrative expense budget. Like the research and development or marketing expense budgets, the **administrative expense budget** consists of estimated expenditures for the overall organization and operation of the company. Most administrative expenses are fixed with respect to sales. They include salaries, depreciation on the headquarters building and equipment, legal and auditing fees, and so on. Example 8.9 shows how and why to prepare the administrative expense budget.

Additional Operating Budgets

Companies may have other major departments that require a budget that is part of the master budget. One such budget is the **research and development expense budget**, which contains planned expenditures for a separate department devoted to new product research and development. If a company has such a department, the budgeted expenditures are presented in a format very similar to that of the administrative expense budget illustrated in **Example 8.9**.

Information:

ABT has no variable administrative expense. Fixed administrative expenses for each quarter include the following:

Salaries	$35,000
Insurance	4,000
Depreciation	12,000
Travel	2,000

Why:

The administrative expense budget is prepared to help managers understand the expected costs of running the company for the coming year. The total administrative expense will be used later in preparing the budgeted income statement.

Required:

1. Construct an administrative expense budget for the ABT concrete block line for the coming year. Show total amounts by quarter and in total for the year.

2. *What if* ABT sold equipment with quarterly depreciation of $1,000 (and did not replace it) at the beginning of Quarter 3? How would that affect quarterly administrative expense? Total administrative expense for the year?

Solution:

1.

Administrative Expense Budget
For the Year Ended December 31, 20x1

	Quarter 1	Quarter 2	Quarter 3	Quarter 4	Total
Salaries	$ 35,000	$ 35,000	$ 35,000	$ 35,000	$140,000
Insurance	4,000	4,000	4,000	4,000	16,000
Depreciation	12,000	12,000	12,000	12,000	48,000
Travel	2,000	2,000	2,000	2,000	8,000
Total administrative expense	$ 53,000	$ 53,000	$ 53,000	$ 53,000	$212,000

2. The sale of equipment at the beginning of Quarter 3 will reduce depreciation in Quarters 3 and 4 by $1,000. Thus, total administrative expense in those two quarters will decrease by $1,000. Total administrative expense for the year will decrease by $2,000.

There would probably be no variable expense for that budget as it is unlikely that it varies with sales or units produced. As a result, the expenses would be fixed, changing only with management discretion. Of course, companies without a research and development department will not have this budget. Our example company, ABT, Inc., does not have a research and development budget.

Budgeted Income Statement

With the completion of the administrative expense schedule, all the operating budgets needed to prepare an estimate of operating income have been completed. The budgeted income statement is shown in **Example 8.10**.

EXAMPLE 8.10

The HOW and WHY of Constructing a Budgeted Income Statement

Information:
Recall from Example 8.1 that ABT sales for the year total $12,000,000. Example 8.7 calculated cost of goods sold for the year at $10,708,000. Example 8.8 calculated total marketing expense of $957,000. Example 8.9 calculated total administrative expense of $212,000. Income taxes are paid at the rate of 30 percent of operating income.

> **Why:**
> The budgeted income statement pulls the results of all the operating budgets together and helps managers determine what the company's performance will be by the end of the year. If the net income does not meet management's objectives, they must go back and find ways to increase sales and/or decrease expenses.

Required:

1. Construct a budgeted income statement for ABT, Inc., for the coming year.

2. *What if* ABT's income tax rate increased to 40 percent? What effect would that have on operating income? On income before taxes? On net income?

Solution:

1.

ABT, Inc.,
Budgeted Income Statement
For the Year Ended December 31, 20x1

Sales		$12,000,000
Less: Cost of goods sold		10,708,000
Gross margin		$ 1,292,000
Less:		
Marketing expense	$957,000	
Administrative expense	212,000	1,169,000
Operating income		$ 123,000
Less: Interest expense (see Example 8.12)		81,000
Income before income taxes		$ 42,000
Less: Income taxes (0.30 × $42,000)		12,600
Net income		$ 29,400

2. If ABT's income tax rate rises to 40 percent, there would be no impact on operating income or income before taxes. However, income taxes would increase to $16,800, and net income would decrease to $25,200.

Operating income is *not* equivalent to the net income of a firm. To yield net income, interest expense and taxes must be subtracted from operating income. The interest expense paid is taken from the cash budget (shown later in Example 8.12). The taxes owed depend on the current tax laws.

Operating Budgets for Merchandising and Service Firms

While the budgets in the master budget described previously are widely used in manufacturing firms, the special needs of service and merchandising firms deserve mention.

In a merchandising firm, the production budget is replaced with a merchandise purchases budget. This budget identifies the quantity of each item that must be purchased for resale, the unit cost of the item, and the total purchase cost. The format is identical to that of the direct materials purchases budget in a manufacturing firm. The only other difference between the operating budgets of manufacturing and merchandising firms is the absence of direct materials purchases and direct labor budgets in a merchandising firm.

In a for-profit service firm, the sales budget is also the production budget. The sales budget identifies each service and the quantity of it that will be sold. Since there are no finished goods inventories, services produced will be identical to services sold.

Big Data Used for Budgeting in Large Retail Firms

Large retailers (and many small retailers) now have a point-of-sale (POS) system in which the cash registers are actually computers taking data on each sale and then directing it to large corporate databases. These systems have allowed large retailers such as **Macy's** and **Nordstrom** to integrate in-store and online sales. Not only does this result in more efficiency, such as being able to tell a customer just which models of a dress are in stock, but it also allows the company to reduce purchasing requirements.

When a company builds the purchases budget, it makes a separate budget for each type of item stocked in a retail store. In a company like Nordstrom, the various purchases budgets would be aggregated across the stores, so that the company would know, for example, that 10,000 parkas of a certain style and color would be bought overall as well as how those parkas would be distributed across the individual stores. Recall that the budget begins with sales and then adds desired ending inventory. But what is the desired ending inventory of parkas? Ideally, it is zero, because once winter is over, the store would like all parkas to be sold to make room for spring clothing. But the store may want to keep some safety stock on hand in case demand outstrips supply (think a colder than expected winter). Does each store need that safety stock? No, not with a sophisticated POS system. So, for example, if the Chicago store runs out of a size 10 **North Face** gray parka, the sales associate can check immediately to see whether or not that item is on hand in another store, then sell it and have it shipped to the customer. The end result is higher customer satisfaction, because stock-outs are rare, and lower overall inventory, requiring lower carrying costs for the company.

Data analytics can also be used to track sales over a period of time to predict which colors and sizes are most likely to sell in a particular geographic area. Thus, clothing colors offered for sale in Miami differ from those offered in New York City due to the differing consumer preference for particular colors. All of these data are then used as inputs in the sales and purchases budgets.

In a not-for-profit service firm, the sales budget is replaced by a budget that identifies the levels of the various services that will be offered for the coming year and the sources of funds to pay for producing those services. The source of the funds may be tax revenues, contributions, payments by users of the services, or some combination. Years of data on operating expenses and revenues from alternate sources allow charitable organizations to use data analytics to predict what the potential costs and revenues will be under various scenarios. For example, a local **United Way**'s board of directors will budget the campaign target (dollars of contributions) for the coming year and then distribute the total funds among the qualifying agencies according to three possible levels of contribution—pessimistic, expected, and optimistic.

Both for-profit and not-for-profit service organizations lack finished goods inventory budgets. All the remaining operating budgets found in a manufacturing organization, however, have counterparts in service organizations. A not-for-profit service organization's income statement is replaced by a statement of sources and uses of funds.

Once the operating budgets are complete, the firm can construct the financial budgets.

OBJECTIVE 3

Identify the components of the financial budget, and prepare a cash budget.

PREPARING THE FINANCIAL BUDGET

The remaining budgets found in the master budget are the financial budgets. Typical financial budgets include the budget for capital expenditures, the cash budget, the budgeted balance sheet, and the budgeted statement of cash flows.

While the master budget is a plan for one year, the **capital expenditures budget** is a financial plan outlining the expected acquisition of long-term assets and typically covers a number of years. Decision making in regard to capital expenditures is considered in Chapter 19. Details on the budgeted statement of cash flows are appropriately reserved for another course. Accordingly, only the cash budget and the budgeted balance sheet will be illustrated here.

The Cash Budget

Understanding cash flow is critical to managing a business. Often, a business can successfully produce and sell a product but fails because of timing problems associated with cash inflows and outflows. By knowing when cash deficiencies and surpluses are likely to occur, a manager can plan to borrow cash when needed and to repay the loans during periods of excess cash. Bank loan officers use a company's cash budget to document the need for cash, as well as the company's ability to repay. Because cash flow is the lifeblood of an organization, the cash budget is one of the most important budgets in the master budget.

Components of the Cash Budget   The **cash budget** is the detailed plan that shows all expected sources and uses of cash. The cash budget, illustrated in Exhibit 8.4, has the following five main sections:

1. Total cash available
2. Cash disbursements
3. Cash excess or deficiency
4. Financing
5. Cash balance

The *total cash available* section consists of the beginning cash balance and the expected cash receipts. Expected cash receipts include all sources of cash for the period being considered. One source of cash is cash sales. Often, however, a significant proportion of sales is on account; thus, a major task of an organization is to determine the pattern of collection for its accounts receivable.

Beginning cash balance
+ Cash receipts
Cash available
− Cash disbursements
− Minimum cash balance
Excess or deficiency of cash
− Repayments
+ Loans
+ Minimum cash balance
Ending cash balance

Exhibit 8.4

The Cash Budget

If a company has been in business for a while, it can use past experience to create an accounts receivable aging schedule. In other words, the company can determine, on average, what percentages of its accounts receivable are paid in the months following the sales. **Example 8.11** shows how and why to prepare a cash receipts budget, including an accounts receivable aging schedule.

EXAMPLE 8.11

The HOW and WHY of Constructing a Cash Receipts Budget with an Accounts Receivable Aging Schedule

Information:

Recall from Example 8.1 that in 20x1 ABT sales are Quarter 1, $1,400,000; Quarter 2, $4,200,000; Quarter 3, $4,800,000; and Quarter 4, $1,600,000. In ABT's experience, 50 percent of sales are paid in cash. Of the sales on account, 70 percent are collected in the quarter of sale; the remaining 30 percent are collected in the quarter following the sale. Total sales for the fourth quarter of 20x0 totaled $2,000,000.

> **Why:**
> The cash receipts budget shows sources of cash for the period. Some sales may be cash; some are on account and may be received later. The embedded accounts receivable aging schedule helps managers determine how much of a period's sales on account will actually be received in cash. Cash receipts are a critical part of the cash budget.

Required:

1. Calculate cash sales expected in each quarter of 20x1.

2. Construct a cash receipts budget including an accounts receivable aging schedule for ABT, Inc., for each quarter of the coming year.

3. *What if* ABT determined that the percentage received in the quarter after the quarter of sale was 25 percent and that the remaining 5 percent was never collected? How would that affect cash received in each quarter?

Solution:

1. Quarter 1, 20x1, Cash sales = 0.50 × $1,400,000 = $700,000

   Quarter 2, 20x1, Cash sales = 0.50 × $4,200,000 = $2,100,000

   Quarter 3, 20x1, Cash sales = 0.50 × $4,800,000 = $2,400,000

   Quarter 4, 20x1, Cash sales = 0.50 × $1,600,000 = $800,000

EXAMPLE 8.11

(Continued)

2.

	Quarter 1	Quarter 2	Quarter 3	Quarter 4
Cash sales	$ 700,000	$2,100,000	$2,400,000	$ 800,000
Received on account from:				
Quarter 4, 20x0[a]	300,000			
Quarter 1, 20x1[b]	490,000	210,000		
Quarter 2, 20x1[c]		1,470,000	630,000	
Quarter 3, 20x1[d]			1,680,000	720,000
Quarter 4, 20x1[e]				560,000
Total cash receipts	$1,490,000	$3,780,000	$4,710,000	$2,080,000

[a] $1,000,000 × 0.30 = $300,000

[b] $700,000 × 0.70 = $490,000; $700,000 × 0.30 = $210,000

[c] $2,100,000 × 0.70 = $1,470,000; $2,100,000 × 0.30 = $630,000

[d] $2,400,000 × 0.70 = $1,680,000; $2,400,000 × 0.30 = $720,000

[e] $800,000 × 0.70 = $560,000

3. The 5 percent of accounts receivable that ABT never collects is bad debts expense. It never appears on the cash budget since it is never collected in cash. The cash received in the quarter after the quarter of sale would be reduced and total cash would be reduced. The following is the cash receipts budget with the updated accounts receivable aging schedule using the new assumption.

	Quarter 1	Quarter 2	Quarter 3	Quarter 4
Cash sales	$ 700,000	$2,100,000	$2,400,000	$ 800,000
Received on account from:				
Quarter 4, 20x0	250,000			
Quarter 1, 20x1	490,000	175,000		
Quarter 2, 20x1		1,470,000	525,000	
Quarter 3, 20x1			1,680,000	600,000
Quarter 4, 20x1				560,000
Total cash receipts	$1,440,000	$3,745,000	$4,605,000	$1,960,000

The *cash disbursements* section lists all planned cash outlays for the period except for interest payments on short-term loans (these payments appear in the financing section). All expenses not resulting in a cash outlay are excluded from the list. (Depreciation, for example, is never included in the disbursements section.)

The *cash excess or deficiency* section compares the cash available with the cash needed. Cash needed includes the total cash disbursements plus the minimum cash balance required by company policy. The minimum cash balance is the lowest amount of cash on hand that the firm finds acceptable. Consider your own checking account. You probably try to keep at least some cash in the account, perhaps because a minimum balance avoids service charges or because it allows you to make an unplanned purchase. Similarly, companies also require minimum cash balances. The amount varies from firm to firm and is determined by each company's particular needs. If the total cash available is less than the cash needs, a deficiency exists. In such a case, a short-term loan will be needed. On the other hand, with a cash excess (cash available is greater than the firm's cash needs), the firm can repay loans and perhaps make some temporary investments.

The *financing* section of the cash budget consists of borrowings and repayments. If there is a deficiency, the financing section shows the necessary amount to be borrowed. When excess cash is available, the financing section shows planned repayments, including interest.

The final section of the cash budget is the planned ending cash balance. Remember that the minimum cash balance was subtracted to find the cash excess or deficiency. However, the minimum cash balance is not a disbursement, so it must be added back to yield the planned ending balance.

Once all sections of the cash budget are understood, it is time to construct one. **Example 8.12** shows how and why to prepare the cash budget.

EXAMPLE 8.12

The HOW and WHY of Constructing a Cash Budget

Information:

The information needed to prepare the cash budget comes from Examples 8.1 through 8.11 and from the following information.

a. ABT requires a $100,000 minimum cash balance for the end of each quarter. On December 31, 20x0, the cash balance was $120,000.

b. Money can be borrowed and repaid in multiples of $100,000. Interest is 12 percent per year. Interest payments are made only for the amount of the principal being repaid. All borrowing takes place at the beginning of a quarter, and all repayment takes place at the end of a quarter.

c. All materials are purchased on account; 80 percent of purchases are paid for in the quarter of purchase. The remaining 20 percent are paid in the following quarter. The purchases for the fourth quarter of 20x0 were $500,000.

d. Budgeted depreciation is $200,000 per quarter for overhead, $5,000 for marketing expense, and $12,000 for administrative expense. (Remember that depreciation is not a cash expense and must be deleted from total expenses before the cash budget is prepared.)

e. The capital budget for 20x1 revealed plans to purchase additional equipment for $600,000 in the first quarter. The acquisition will be financed with operating cash, supplementing it with short-term loans as necessary.

f. Corporate income taxes of $12,600 will be paid at the end of the fourth quarter.

> **Why:**
> The cash budget is critical to managers' planning. It shows how much cash will be available each time period. Companies without sufficient cash may go under even if their net income is positive.

Required:

1. Calculate cash payments for purchases expected in each quarter of 20x1. (Hint: Use Example 8.3.)

2. Prepare a cash budget for ABT, Inc., for each quarter of the coming year.

3. *What if* ABT did not have access to short-term financing? How would that affect the cash budget? ABT's ability to stay in business?

EXAMPLE 8.12

(Continued)

Solution:

1. Payments in current quarter = 0.8(current quarter purchases)
   + 0.2(prior quarter purchases)

   Payments Quarter 1 = 0.8($654,000) + 0.2($500,000) = $623,200
   Payments Quarter 2 = 0.8($1,560,000) + 0.2($654,000) = $1,378,800
   Payments Quarter 3 = 0.8($1,426,000) + 0.2($1,560,000) = $1,452,800
   Payments Quarter 4 = 0.8($520,000) + 0.2($1,426,000) = $701,200

2.

	Quarter 1	Quarter 2	Quarter 3	Quarter 4	Year
Beginning balance (a)*	$ 120,000	$ 100,800	$ 123,000	$ 166,200	$ 120,000
Collections (C8.11):					
Cash sales	700,000	2,100,000	2,400,000	800,000	6,000,000
Received on account:					
Current quarter sales	490,000	1,470,000	1,680,000	560,000	4,200,000
Prior quarter sales	300,000	210,000	630,000	720,000	1,860,000
Total cash available	$ 1,610,000	$ 3,880,800	$ 4,833,000	$ 2,246,200	$ 12,180,000
Disbursements:					
Payments for purchases:					
Current quarter purchases	$ 523,200	$ 1,248,000	$ 1,140,800	$ 416,000	$ 3,328,000
Prior quarter purchases	100,000	130,800	312,000	285,200	828,000
Direct labor (C8.4)	504,000	1,260,000	1,176,000	420,000	3,360,000
Overhead (C8.5, d)	408,000	840,000	792,000	360,000	2,400,000
Marketing expense (C8.8, d)	133,000	338,000	333,000	133,000	937,000
Administrative expense (C8.9, d)	41,000	41,000	41,000	41,000	164,000
Income tax (f)				12,600	12,600
Equipment (e)	600,000				600,000
Total disbursements	$ 2,309,200	$ 3,857,800	$ 3,794,800	$ 1,667,800	$ 11,629,600
Minimum cash balance (a)	100,000	100,000	100,000	100,000	100,000
Total cash needs	$ 2,409,200	$ 3,957,800	$ 3,894,800	$ 1,767,800	$ 11,729,600
Excess (deficiency)	$ (799,200)	$ (77,000)	$ 938,200	$ 478,400	$ 450,400
Financing (b):					
Borrowings	$ 800,000	$ 100,000			$ 900,000
Repayments			$ (800,000)	$ (100,000)	(900,000)
Interest			(72,000)	(9,000)	(81,000)
Total financing	$ 800,000	$ 100,000	$ (872,000)	$ (109,000)	$ (81,000)
Add: Minimum cash balance	100,000	100,000	100,000	100,000	100,000
Ending cash balance	$ 100,800	$ 123,000	$ 166,200	$ 469,400	$ 469,300

*Parenthetical references refer to Examples: for example, C8.11 is Example 8.11, or to the information stated above.

3. If ABT had no access to short-term financing, then the company would be in severe trouble by the end of Quarter 1. By the end of Quarter 1, ABT has a shortfall of nearly $800,000. It would not be able to make the cash payments it plans to make and would very possibly be forced out of business. The seasonal nature of ABT's sales makes it imperative for the company to use borrowed money early in the year and to make up for it later in the year.

The cash budget shown in Example 8.12 underscores the importance of breaking down the annual budget into smaller time periods. The cash budget for the year implies that there is enough cash from operations to buy the new equipment. Quarterly information, however, shows that short-term borrowing is needed to buy the new equipment earlier in the year rather than later. Breaking down the annual cash budget into smaller time periods conveys more information. Most firms prepare monthly cash budgets; some even prepare weekly and daily cash budgets.

ABT's cash budget shows another important piece of information. By the end of the fourth quarter, the firm holds a considerable amount of cash ($469,400). ABT should consider investing this cash in an interest-bearing account or short-term marketable securities rather than allow it to sit idly in a bank account. The management of ABT could also consider making additional long-term investments. Once plans are finalized for use of the excess cash, the cash budget should be revised to reflect those plans. Budgeting is a dynamic process. As the budget is developed, new information becomes available and better plans can be formulated.

Budgeted Balance Sheet

The budgeted balance sheet for the coming year depends on information contained in the balance sheet for the end of the current year and in the other budgets in the master budget. It represents the culmination of the financial events of the coming year and shows management where the company is expected to be at the end of the year. The balance sheet for the beginning of the year is given in Exhibit 8.5. This balance sheet is necessary in preparing the end-of-the-year budgeted balance sheet that is shown in Exhibit 8.6.

As we have described the individual budgets that make up the master budget, the interdependencies of the component budgets have become apparent. You may want to refer back to Exhibit 8.2 to review these interrelationships.

ABT, Inc. Balance Sheet December 31, 20x0 Assets		
Current assets:		
Cash	$ 120,000	
Accounts receivable	300,000	
Materials inventory	50,000	
Finished goods inventory	55,000	
Total current assets		$ 525,000
Property, plant, and equipment (PP&E):		
Land	$ 2,500,000	
Buildings and equipment	9,000,000	
Accumulated depreciation	(4,500,000)	
Total PP&E		7,000,000
Total assets		$7,525,000
Liabilities and Stockholders' Equity		
Current liabilities:		
Accounts payable		$ 100,000
Stockholders' equity:		
Common stock, no par	$ 600,000	
Retained earnings	6,825,000	
Total stockholders' equity		7,425,000
Total liabilities and stockholders' equity		$7,525,000

Exhibit 8.5

Balance Sheet for ABT, Inc.

Exhibit 8.6

Budgeted Balance Sheet for ABT, Inc.

ABT, Inc. **Budgeted Balance Sheet** **December 31, 20x1** Assets		
Current assets:		
Cash[a]	$ 469,400	
Accounts receivable[b]	240,000	
Materials inventory[c]	50,000	
Finished goods inventory[d]	67,000	
Total current assets		$ 826,400
Property, plant, and equipment (PP&E):		
Land[e]	$ 2,500,000	
Buildings and equipment[f]	9,600,000	
Accumulated depreciation[g]	(5,368,000)	
Total PP&E		6,732,000
Total assets		$7,558,400
Liabilities and Stockholders' Equity		
Current liabilities:		
Accounts payable[h]		$ 104,000
Stockholders' equity:		
Common stock, no par[i]	$ 600,000	
Retained earnings[j]	6,854,400	
Total stockholders' equity		7,454,400
Total liabilities and stockholders' equity		$7,558,400

[a] Ending cash balance for the year from Example 8.12.
[b] From Example 8.1 and Example 8.11, fourth quarter credit sales times 0.3 (percentage to be collected in the following quarter).
[c] From Example 8.3, fourth quarter desired ending inventory of 5,000,000 lbs. times $0.01 (cost per pound).
[d] From Example 8.6.
[e] From Exhibit 8.5, December 31, 20x0, balance sheet, Land account.
[f] From Exhibit 8.5, December 31, 20x0, balance sheet, Buildings and Equipment account plus $600,000 for new equipment purchase.
[g] From Exhibit 8.5, December 31, 20x0, balance sheet, accumulated depreciation balance, plus depreciation balances from Example 8.12 ($4,500,000 + $800,000 + $20,000 + $48,000).
[h] Equals 20 percent of fourth-quarter purchases of direct materials; see Examples 8.3 and 8.12.
[i] From Exhibit 8.5, December 31, 20x0, balance sheet, Common Stock account.
[j] From Exhibit 8.5, December 31, 20x0, balance sheet, retained earnings balance plus net income from Example 8.10.

Shortcomings of the Traditional Master Budget Process

Criticisms of the master budget can be classified into several categories. The traditional master budget is:

1.   department oriented and does not recognize the interdependencies among departments.

2.   static, not dynamic.

3.   results, not process, oriented.

   Let's look more closely at each of these.

Departmental Orientation   In traditional budgeting, each department develops its own budget. These budgets are then aggregated to form the overall company budget. The focus on departmental planning results in planning forward from resources to outputs. That is, a department may start by determining what resources (i.e., labor, supplies, etc.) it currently has and then adjust those levels for the potential level of output. An alternative approach starts by asking what level of output is desired and then works backward to see what resources are necessary to achieve that level of output. We might ask, what difference does it make? Couldn't you achieve the same effect whether you go backward or forward? The answer, rooted in human behavior, is no. By concentrating on last year's costs and going forward, a department locks in past ways of doing things.

As a result, traditional budgeting may have managers feeling embattled. There is a sense of "every department for itself." Managers feel encouraged to use every cent of budgeted resources, whether or not those resources are needed. Indeed, if the department did not use the full level of budgeted resources, it would have a hard time making a case for increased—or even the same level of—resources in the coming year.

Static Rather than Dynamic Budgets A **static budget** is one developed for a single level of activity. Recall that the master budget is based on budgeted sales for the coming year. Once that amount is determined, production, marketing, and administrative budgets are built around it. An adjunct to the static nature of the budget is the use of last year's budget to create this year's budget. Often, the current budget is based on last year's amounts as adjusted for inflation. This approach to budgeting, called the **incremental approach**, can incorporate last year's inefficiencies into the current budget. Under the incremental approach, heads of budgeting units often strive to spend all of the year's budget so that no surplus exists at the end of the year. (This is particularly true for government agencies.) This action is taken to maintain the current level of the budget and enable the head of the unit to request additional funds.

At an Air Force base, a bomber wing was faced with the possibility of a surplus at the end of the fiscal year. The base commander, however, found ways to spend the extra money before the year ended. Missile officers, who normally drove to the missile command site, were flown to the sites in helicopters; several bags of lawn fertilizer were given away to all personnel with houses on base; and new furniture was acquired for the bachelor officer quarters.

The waste and inefficiency portrayed in this example are often perpetuated and encouraged by incremental budgeting.

Zero-base budgeting is an alternative approach.[5] Unlike incremental budgeting, the prior year's budgeted level is not taken for granted. Existing operations are analyzed, and continuance of the activity or operation must be justified on the basis of its need or usefulness to the organization. The burden of proof is on each manager to justify why any money should be spent at all. Zero-base budgeting requires extensive, in-depth analysis. Although this approach has been used successfully in industry and government (e.g., **Texas Instruments** and the state of Georgia), it is time consuming and costly. Advocates of the incremental approach argue that incremental budgeting also uses extensive, in-depth reviews but not as frequently because they are not justified on a cost-benefit basis. A reasonable compromise may be to use zero-base budgeting every three to five years in order to weed out waste and inefficiency. Especially in a period of intense competition and reengineering, zero-base budgeting can force managers to "break set" and see their units in a different perspective.

5 Zero-base budgeting was developed by Peter Pyhrr of Texas Instruments. For a detailed discussion of the approach, see Peter Pyhrr, *Zero-Base Budgeting* (New York: Wiley, 1973).

The city of Prattville, Alabama, recently applied a blend of zero-base budgeting and activity-based budgeting to the city budget. The various departments of the city prepared budgets for "activity packages" that related various levels of service to the resources required to provide those services. Then, the mayor and city council were able to construct a budget that met the needs of the citizens while staying within the level of resources available to fund those services. Interestingly, preparing the budget was only one outcome of the budgeting exercise. Better control was also developed as departmental managers began to see that the budget was realistically related to the demands placed on their departments.[6]

Results Orientation Closely allied to the static nature of the master budget is a results orientation. By focusing on results instead of process, managers may disconnect the process from its output. When budgets are resource driven rather than output driven, then managers concentrate on resources and may fail to see the link between resources and output. Then, when the need for cost cutting arises, they make across-the-board cuts, slicing every department's budget by the same percentage. This has the superficial appearance of fairness—in that every department "shares the pain." Unfortunately, some departments have more fat than others, and some may be downright unneeded. Across-the-board cuts do not cut true waste and inefficiency.

Why, if it has all of these problems, has the traditional approach to budgeting been used for so long? It is important to realize that the master budget is not inherently flawed. In fact, it has been very useful over the decades and many managers strongly agree that "budgets are indispensable and companies couldn't manage without them."[7] However, the past 30 or so years have been characterized by rapid change. In a period of change, managers may not realize that previously acceptable ways of doing things no longer work. This is the case for the master budget. For example, consider its static nature. If sales are much the same from year to year, if the production process does not change, and if the firm's product mix is fairly simple and stable, then a static budget based in large part on last year's numbers makes sense. This is not, however, the situation for the vast majority of businesses today. Flexible budgets can give managers some feel for the impact of fixed and variable costs. Activity-based budgets go further, by recognizing the numerous drivers for variable costs and by starting with outputs and working backward to resources. In this way, budgets can go beyond the predictive use of data to the diagnostic and prescriptive uses as firms determine what went wrong and how best to fix it.

 OBJECTIVE 4
Define flexible budgeting, and discuss its role in planning, control, and decision making.

FLEXIBLE BUDGETS FOR PLANNING AND CONTROL

Budgets are useful control measures. To be used in performance evaluation, however, two major considerations must be addressed. The first is to determine how budgeted amounts should be compared with actual results. The second consideration involves the impact of budgets on human behavior.

---

6 Marco Lam, Mike Carver, and David Miller, "Implementing a Target Budget for Prattville, Alabama," *Strategic Finance* (October 2008): 38–43.

7 This quote is taken from an article discussing the results of a survey of IMA members on budgeting. Theresa Libby and R. Murray Lindsay, "Beyond Budgeting or Better Budgeting? IMA Members Express Their Views," *Strategic Finance* (August 2007): 46–51 (quote taken from pp. 48–49).

Static Budgets versus Flexible Budgets

Master budget amounts, while vital for planning, are less useful for control. The reason is that the anticipated level of activity rarely equals the actual level of activity. Therefore, comparing budgeted costs and revenues with actual costs and revenues can give a misleading picture.

Static Budgets Budgets that are developed around a single level of activity are static budgets. Master budgets are an example of a static budget since the budget is built around one level of activity—the expected sales for the year. Because the revenues and costs prepared for static budgets depend on a level of activity that rarely equals actual activity, they are not very useful when it comes to preparing performance reports.

To illustrate, let's return to the ABT, Inc., example used in developing the master budget. Suppose that ABT provides quarterly performance reports. Recall that ABT anticipated sales of 2 million units in the first quarter and had budgeted production of 2.4 million units to support that level of sales (Example 8.2). Suppose instead that sales activity was greater than expected in the first quarter; 2.6 million concrete blocks were sold instead of the 2 million originally budgeted. Because of increased sales, production was increased over the planned level from 2.4 million units to 3 million units. A performance report comparing the actual production costs for the first quarter with the original planned production costs is given in Exhibit 8.7.

According to the report, unfavorable variances occurred for direct materials, direct labor, supplies, indirect labor, and rent. However, something is fundamentally wrong with the report. Actual costs for production of *3 million concrete blocks* are being compared with planned costs for production of *2.4 million*. Because direct materials, direct labor, and variable overhead are variable costs, we expect them to be greater as more is produced. Thus, even if cost control were perfect for the production of 3 million units, unfavorable variances would be shown for all variable costs.

	Actual	Budgeted	Variance	
Units produced	3,000,000	2,400,000	600,000	F[a]
Direct materials cost	$ 927,300	$ 624,000[b]	$303,300	U[c]
Direct labor cost	630,000	504,000[d]	126,000	U
Overhead:[e]				
Variable:				
Supplies	80,000	72,000	8,000	U
Indirect labor	220,000	168,000	52,000	U
Power	40,000	48,000	(8,000)	F
Fixed:				
Supervision	90,000	100,000	(10,000)	F
Depreciation	200,000	200,000	0	
Rent	30,000	20,000	10,000	U
Total	$2,217,300	$1,736,000	$481,300	U

Exhibit 8.7

ABT Performance Report for Quarter 1: Comparison of Actual with Static (Master) Budget Amounts

[a] F means the variance is favorable.
[b] 2,400,000 units × $0.26 (Example 8.6 gives unit costs for direct materials and direct labor).
[c] U means the variance is unfavorable.
[d] 2,400,000 units × $0.21 (Example 8.6 gives unit costs for direct materials and direct labor).
[e] Variable overhead equals 2,400,000 units times: $0.03 for supplies; $0.07 for indirect labor; and $0.02 for power.
  Budgeted fixed overhead per quarter is given in Example 8.5.

To create a meaningful performance report, actual costs and expected costs must be compared at the *same* level of activity. Since actual output often differs from planned output, some method is needed to compute what the costs should have been for the actual output level.

Flexible Budgets   There are two types of flexible budgets. A **flexible budget** (1) provides expected costs for a variety of activity levels, or (2) provides budgeted costs for the actual level of activity. Flexible budgeting can be used in planning by showing what costs will be at various levels of activity. When used this way, managers can deal with uncertainty by examining the expected financial results for a number of plausible scenarios. Spreadsheets are particularly useful in developing this type of flexible budget.

The flexible budget can be used after the fact, for control, to compute what costs should have been for the actual level of activity. Once expected costs are known for the actual level of activity, a performance report that compares those expected costs to actual costs can be prepared. When used for control, flexible budgets help managers compare "apples to apples" in assessing performance. **Example 8.13** shows how and why to prepare a flexible budget for varying levels of activity.

EXAMPLE 8.13

The HOW and WHY of Constructing a Flexible Budget for Varying Levels of Activity

Information:
ABT, Inc., has the following budgeted variable costs per unit produced:

Direct materials	$0.26
Direct labor	0.21
Variable overhead:	
Supplies	0.03
Indirect labor	0.07
Power	0.02

Budgeted fixed overhead costs per quarter include supervision of $100,000, depreciation of $200,000, and rent of $20,000.

> **Why:**
> A flexible budget allows managers to see what impact changes in activity level will have on total costs. When the budget includes fixed costs, increases in activity level lead to increases in total cost, but less than proportionately.

Required:

1. Prepare a flexible budget for all costs of production for the following levels of production: 2,400,000 units, 3,000,000 units, and 3,600,000 units.

2. What is the per-unit total product cost for each of the production levels from Requirement 1?

3. *What if* ABT found that indirect labor was really fixed at $210,000 per quarter? How would that affect the unit product costs calculated in Requirement 2?

EXAMPLE 8.13

(*Continued*)

Solution:

1.

	Variable Cost per Unit	Range of Production in Units		
		2,400,000	3,000,000	3,600,000
Production costs:				
Variable:				
Direct materials	$0.26	$ 624,000	$ 780,000	$ 936,000
Direct labor	0.21	504,000	630,000	756,000
Variable overhead:				
Supplies	0.03	72,000	90,000	108,000
Indirect labor	0.07	168,000	210,000	252,000
Power	0.02	48,000	60,000	72,000
Total variable costs	$0.59	$1,416,000	$ 1,770,000	$ 2,124,000
Fixed overhead:				
Supervision		$ 100,000	$ 100,000	$ 100,000
Depreciation		200,000	200,000	200,000
Rent		20,000	20,000	20,000
Total fixed costs		$ 320,000	$ 320,000	$ 320,000
Total production costs		$1,736,000	$ 2,090,000	$ 2,444,000

2. Per-unit product cost @ 2,400,000 units = $1,736,000/2,400,000
   = $0.72 (rounded)

   Per-unit product cost @ 3,000,000 units = $2,090,000/3,000,000
   = $0.70 (rounded)

   Per-unit product cost @ 3,600,000 units = $2,444,000/3,600,000
   = $0.68 (rounded)

3. If indirect labor was fixed at $210,000 per quarter, there would be no difference in the total or per-unit cost for 3,000,000 units produced. However, at 2,400,000 units produced, the indirect labor cost would be higher than it currently is, and therefore the total product cost and per-unit cost would be higher. At 3,600,000 units produced, the indirect labor cost would be lower than it currently is, and therefore the total product cost and per-unit cost would be lower.

Notice in Example 8.13 that total budgeted production costs increase as output increases. Budgeted costs change because of variable costs. Because of this, a flexible budget is sometimes referred to as a **variable budget**. Example 8.13 reveals what the costs should have been for the actual level of activity (3 million blocks). A revised performance report that compares actual and budgeted costs for the actual level of activity is illustrated in **Example 8.14**.

The revised performance report in Example 8.14 paints a much different picture than the one in Exhibit 8.7. By comparing budgeted costs for the actual level of activity with actual costs for the same level, **flexible budget variances** are generated. Managers can locate possible problem areas by examining these variances. According to the ABT flexible budget variances, expenditures for direct materials are excessive. (The other unfavorable variances seem relatively small.) With this knowledge, management can search for the causes of the excess expenditures and prevent the same problems from occurring in the future.

EXAMPLE 8.14

The HOW and WHY of Constructing a Flexible Budget for the Actual Level of Activity

Information:

ABT, Inc., produced 3,000,000 units and has the following actual costs in the first quarter:

Direct materials	$927,300
Direct labor	630,000
Supplies	80,000
Indirect labor	220,000
Power	40,000
Supervision	90,000
Depreciation	200,000
Rent	30,000

Refer to Example 8.13 for budgeted overhead costs per quarter for production of 3,000,000 units.

> **Why:**
> A flexible budget allows managers to see what impact a change in activity level will have on total costs. When the flexible budget is used for control, budgeted costs for the actual activity experienced can be compared with actual costs to get a meaningful idea of whether or not costs were as expected.

Required:

1. Prepare a performance report for actual costs for the first quarter, comparing them with the flexible budget amounts for the actual level of production found in Example 8.13.

2. What is the actual per-unit cost? What is the flexible budgeted per-unit product cost?

3. *What if* ABT had the same actual costs but had only produced 2,900,000 units? Would the total variance be more or less unfavorable than it is in Requirement 1?

Solution:

1.

	Actual	Budgeted	Variance	
Units produced	3,000,000	3,000,000	0	
Direct materials cost	$ 927,300	$ 780,000	$147,300	U
Direct labor cost	630,000	630,000	0	
Overhead:				
Variable:				
Supplies	80,000	90,000	(10,000)	F
Indirect labor	220,000	210,000	10,000	U
Power	40,000	60,000	(20,000)	F
Fixed:				
Supervision	90,000	100,000	(10,000)	F
Depreciation	200,000	200,000	0	
Rent	30,000	20,000	10,000	U
Total	$2,217,300	$2,090,000	$127,300	U

EXAMPLE 8.14

(Continued)

2. Actual per-unit cost = \$2,217,300/3,000,000 = \$0.7391

    Budgeted per-unit cost = \$2,090,000/3,000,000 = \$0.6967

3. If only 2,900,000 units had been produced, the flexible budget amounts for variable overhead would have been smaller and every variable overhead variance would have been more unfavorable (or less favorable). The total variance would have been more unfavorable.

Budgets can be used to examine the efficiency and effectiveness of a company. **Efficiency** is achieved when the business process is performed in the best possible way, with little or no waste. The flexible budget provides an assessment of the efficiency of a manager. This is so because the flexible budget compares the actual costs for a given level of output with the budgeted costs for the same level. **Effectiveness** means that a manager achieves or exceeds the goals described by the static budget. Thus, efficiency examines how well the work is done, and effectiveness examines whether or not the right work is being accomplished. Any differences between the flexible budget and the static budget are attributable to differences in volume. They are called *volume variances*. A five-column performance report that reveals both the flexible budget variances and the volume variances can be used. Exhibit 8.8 provides an example of this report using the ABT data.

As the report in Exhibit 8.8 reveals, production volume was 600,000 units greater than the original budgeted amount. This volume variance is labeled *favorable* because actual output exceeds the original production goal. (Recall that the *reason* for the extra production was because the demand for the product was greater than expected. Thus, the increase in production over the original amount was truly favorable.) However, the budgeted variable costs are greater than expected because of the increased production. This difference is labeled unfavorable because the costs are greater than expected. Because the increase in costs is due to the increase in production, it is totally reasonable. For this particular example, the effectiveness of the manager is not in question; thus, the main issue is how well the manager controlled costs as revealed by the flexible budget variances.

Exhibit 8.8

Managerial Performance Report: Quarterly Production (in thousands)

	Actual Results (1)	Flexible Budget (2)	Flexible Budget Variances (3) = (1) − (2)		Static Budget (4)	Volume Variances (5) = (2) − (4)	
Units produced	3,000,000	3,000,000	0		2,400,000	600,000	F
Direct materials cost	\$ 927,300	\$ 780,000	\$ 147,300	U	\$ 624,000	\$156,000	U
Direct labor cost	630,000	630,000	0		504,000	126,000	U
Overhead:							
Variable:							
Supplies	80,000	90,000	(10,000)	F	72,000	18,000	U
Indirect labor	220,000	210,000	10,000	U	168,000	42,000	U
Power	40,000	60,000	(20,000)	F	48,000	12,000	U
Fixed:							
Supervision	90,000	100,000	(10,000)	F	100,000	0	
Depreciation	200,000	200,000	0		200,000	0	
Rent	30,000	20,000	10,000	U	20,000	0	
Total	\$ 2,217,300	\$2,090,000	\$ 127,300	U	\$1,736,000	\$354,000	U

Flexible budgeting may also be accomplished using data from an activity-based costing system. In this case, a variety of drivers would be used rather than the single unit-based driver in the previous example. We can think of flexible budgeting using ABC costs and drivers as a simplified sort of activity-based budgeting. The ABC flexible budget is a more accurate tool for planning and does give an indication of more costly versus less costly activities. Thus, an ABC flexible budget can support continuous improvement and process management.

Flexible budgeting is a powerful tool for planning and control. The ability to determine costs at varying levels of activity helps managers to overcome the drawback of the static nature of the master budget. Activity-based budgeting adds still more power to the manager's budgeting toolkit.

OBJECTIVE 5

Define activity-based budgeting, and discuss its role in planning, control, and decision making.

ACTIVITY-BASED BUDGETS

We just saw that flexible budgeting can solve some of the problems that arise from using static budgets for performance evaluation. Flexible budgeting allows the firm to create a budget for varying levels of activity. Just as the static master budget was useful for firms that faced relatively constant sales and production from year to year, however, the flexible budget is useful for a particular set of circumstances as well. The ABT situation is tailor made for flexible budgeting. The output is homogeneous, and the production process is fairly simple. Basing variable costs on a volume-based driver works well. Many firms, however, have found that product diversity requires a richer set of drivers to describe their cost structure. These firms will find that activity-based budgeting is more useful for their needs.[8]

The activity-based budget begins with output and then determines the resources necessary to create that output. Ideally, the organization translates its vision into a strategy with definable objectives in order to create value. Ways of creating value include growing market share, improving sales rates, reducing expenses, increasing profit margins, increasing productivity, and reducing the cost of capital. We can see how clearly activity-based budgeting (ABB) is related to performance evaluation and, in particular, to economic value added (as discussed in Chapter 10).

We can look at a department's budget from three perspectives: a traditional approach, a flexible budgeting approach, and an activity-based approach. Traditional budgeting relies on the use of line items, such as salaries, supplies, depreciation on equipment, and so on. The flexible budget uses knowledge of cost behavior to split the line items into fixed and variable components. The activity-based budget works backward from activities and their drivers to the underlying costs.

We can use the new Secure-Care Department of a large regional public accounting firm to illustrate the differences among traditional, flexible, and activity-based budgeting. First, let's review the history of the Secure-Care Department. A couple of years ago, Brad Covington, one of the firm's younger partners, persuaded his other partners to put an eldercare program into effect. Eldercare is a multifaceted program of personal financial and assurance services. Typical clients are the older parents of a grown child who lives outside the parents' city. The parents may need help paying monthly bills, balancing their checking account, and finding and paying for in-home health and personal care. Brad felt that there was a need for eldercare services in the metropolitan area and that his accounting firm was ideally suited to provide these services. Not only were the financial services a natural for a public accounting firm, but the high confidence the public placed in accountants made it likely that clients would feel comfortable relying on their expertise in finding appropriate caretakers. The main problem, in Brad's mind, was the term "eldercare." After some discussion among firm members, the name Secure-Care was settled on. The Secure-Care Department was established two years ago.

---

8 Much of this section relies on ideas expressed in James A. Brimson and John Antos, *Driving Value Using Activity-Based Budgeting* (New York, NY: John Wiley & Sons, 1999). This book is a thorough approach to the subject.

During the two-year period, Brad developed a client base of 60. A variety of services were offered. For all clients, all business mail was rerouted to the accounting firm. The clients' checking, savings, and money market accounts were kept up to date and reconciled each month by the firm. All bills were paid from the appropriate accounts. In addition, personal and household services were contracted out. The Secure-Care Department advertised for, interviewed, and investigated the backgrounds of all individuals hired to provide personal and household services to clients. Monthly personal visits were made to each client to ensure that their needs were being met. Finally, a monthly report on the financial and personal status of each client was prepared and delivered to the clients and any concerned adult children.

The Secure-Care Department consisted of a receptionist, two administrative assistants, and Brad—the managing partner for the department. Because there was insufficient room in the main offices of the accounting firm, Brad rented office space across the street. All investigative services (for background checks) were contracted out to a local private investigator with extensive experience in this area.

Exhibit 8.9 depicts the traditional budget for the coming year for the Secure-Care Department. Notice that the expense categories are listed along with a dollar amount for each one. How would a typical company using functional budgeting arrive at these figures? It would be a safe bet to assume that they would be based to a large extent on the level of those same expenses for the previous year. Maybe there would be some adjustment of certain figures (e.g., if salaries were expected to rise by 3 percent due to anticipated raises).

Suppose that Brad thinks the costs of the Secure-Care Department vary according to the number of clients. Cost behavior concepts can be used to break the expense categories into fixed and variable components. Assume that supplies are strictly variable, at $166.67 per client. Telephone is a mixed cost, with a fixed component of $1,200 and a variable rate of $60 per client. The remaining expenses appear to be predominantly fixed. Then, a flexible budget for the following year's 60 estimated clients would appear as the one shown in Exhibit 8.10. Notice that the total amount is still $273,800. The flexible budget shown here does not look like a great step forward. Its power lies in its ability to show changes in total cost as activity level changes. For example, the budget could be extended to show total costs at 50 and 70 clients as well. The key requirement is that the product is much the same from client to client. In the case of the Secure-Care Department, that would mean the needs of each client are very similar.

Brad was not satisfied with the results of the flexible budget. He knew that many of the expense categories were variable but that they did not necessarily vary with the number of clients. For example, one important and time-consuming activity was paying monthly bills, but the number of bills varied greatly from client to client. Similarly, some clients had just a couple of checking and savings accounts while others had five or six checking, money market, and

Expense Category		Budgeted Amounts
Salaries and benefits:		
Brad	$110,000	
Administrative assistants	70,000	
Receptionist	30,000	$210,000
Rent		36,000
Supplies		10,000
PCs and Internet		4,000
Travel		3,000
Investigative services		6,000
Telephone		4,800
Total		$273,800

Exhibit 8.9

Traditional Budget for the Secure-Care Department

Exhibit 8.10

Flexible Budget for the Secure-Care Department

Expense Category		Budgeted Amounts for 60 Clients
Variable expenses:		
Supplies	$ 10,000	
Telephone	3,600	
Total variable expenses		$ 13,600
Fixed expenses:		
Salaries and benefits	$210,000	
Rent	36,000	
PCs and Internet	4,000	
Travel	3,000	
Investigative services	6,000	
Telephone	1,200	
Total fixed expenses		260,200
Total expenses		$273,800

savings accounts. Each of these had to be monitored and reconciled at the end of the month. In summary, there was considerable diversity among the clients. Therefore, Brad decided to build an activity-based budget.

To build an activity-based budget for the Secure-Care Department, four steps are needed: (1) the output of the department must be determined; (2) the activities needed to deliver the output, along with their related drivers, must be identified; (3) the demand for each activity must be estimated; and (4) the cost of resources required to produce the relevant activities must be determined. It is critically important to see that ABB is based on expected output. The traditional budget often plans forward from last year's experience, while the ABB plans backward from next year's output. The differences between the two approaches are more than semantic. While it may appear that the same results would hold in both cases, in practice, that is not so. In addition, the ABB approach, using resources and activities to create output, gives the manager much more information as well as ability to consider eliminating non-value-added activities.

The following information about the Secure-Care Department was developed:

- All clients received varying levels of the department's activities.
- The first activity is "processing mail." Brad decided that number of clients was a reasonable driver for this activity. All clients had mail, and the amount varied from week to week. The receptionist opened all the mail and sorted it into folders by client. It took approximately two hours a day to perform this task.
- The second activity is "paying bills." There were approximately 1,000 bills per month, or 12,000 per year. The number of bills varied widely from client to client. The administrative assistants performed this activity, using computer software to enter and pay bills. Based on the amount of time this took and the cost of supplies, software, and postage, the average cost of paying one bill was $1.75.
- The third activity is "reconciling accounts." The administrative assistants performed this activity, and it took about 30 minutes per account each month. There were 350 accounts. This averaged out to one administrative assistant working full time on reconciling accounts. Related supplies and the use of a computer and software added another $4,900 to the total.
- The firm advertised for and interviewed caregivers for their clients as needed. The driver for this activity is number of new hires. The yearly cost, including all forms of advertising

and the time of the administrative assistants, totaled $7,200 per year. On average, there were estimated to be 60 new hires in a year.

- A private investigator was retained to perform thorough background checks of prospective caregivers. Each background check cost $25, and an average of four prospective caregivers was checked for every successful new hire.
- Every month, the administrative assistants made personal visits to each client. The number of clients was a good driver for this activity, and the total cost was about $650 per client, per year.
- Each month, Brad or one of the administrative assistants prepared a monthly report for every client. The report detailed the financial activity and included the notes taken from the home visits. Prospective issues and problems were raised. These reports were sent to the clients as well as to interested adult children. The cost of time, supplies, and postage averaged $175 per client, per year.
- The final activity is managing the department and signing up new clients. Brad is responsible for the bulk of this activity. The activity does not have a driver, but instead consists of the remaining costs of the department.

The Secure-Care Department's activity-based budget is shown in Exhibit 8.11. Notice that the department has identified eight activities and four drivers. This level of detail is much richer than that for the flexible budget presented in Exhibit 8.10, where there was only one driver, the number of clients. With an activity-based budget, we get a feel for the diversity among the clients. Some have more accounts, and some more bills to pay. In other words, "clients" are not all the same. There is considerable product diversity, and this diversity is not captured in either the traditional or the simple flexible budget.

The traditional, flexible, and activity-based budgets for the Secure-Care Department all total $273,800. But notice the richness of detail in the activity-based budget. Here we can see the relationship between output and resource usage. The manager's attention is also focused on the most costly activities: paying bills, reconciling accounts, and visiting homes. Brad may want to use this information in pricing the various parts of the secure-care service.

Earlier, we noted that both the traditional and flexible budgeting approaches worked well for particular sets of circumstances. Recall that a key feature is that the environment of the company remains stable. When that is the case, one year is much like the next. The technology is the same, and there is little product diversity. A single volume-based driver works well to account for any changes. However, many companies now face an environment that is changing rapidly in many ways. These companies are ill served by budgets that are founded on the notion that everything remains the same. Companies in a changing environment, whether it relates to changing technology, competition, or customer base, need a much more flexible technique for planning and control. The activity-based budget can be extended to include feature costing. This provides an even more powerful tool for planning and control.

Activity Description	Activity Driver	Cost per Unit of Driver	Amount of Driver	Activity Cost
Processing mail	Number of clients	$125.00	60	$ 7,500
Paying bills	Number of bills	1.75	12,000	21,000
Reconciling accounts	Number of accounts	114.00	350	39,900
Advertising/interviewing	Number of new hires	120.00	60	7,200
Investigating	Number of new hires	100.00	60	6,000
Visiting homes	Number of clients	650.00	60	39,000
Writing reports	Number of clients	175.00	60	10,500
Managing department				142,700
Total				$273,800

Exhibit 8.11

Activity-Based Budget for the Secure-Care Department

Feature costing assigns costs to activities and products or services based on the product's or service's features.[9] In the Secure-Care Department, we could see that one client was not necessarily the same as another. In other words, different clients had different features that required the department to use different sets of activities to handle them. A client with only one checking account and a few repetitive bills took little time. Other clients had numerous accounts and bills. Some clients may be difficult to get along with, leading to rapid turnover of their caregivers and necessitating additional interviewing and background investigation. If the company wanted to extend the ABB process, it could add feature costing. That is, it could determine what features of clients differentiate them into groups that require different sets of activities. We can easily imagine that the company might delve further into the various features, asking what leads to the different features (root cause analysis) and what could be done to modify the more costly features. For example, perhaps the monthly reports could be posted, using appropriate security, on the Internet. The reports could be updated relatively easily, and postage and printing costs could be minimized.

OBJECTIVE 6

Identify and discuss the key features that a budgetary system should have to encourage managers to engage in goal-congruent behavior.

THE BEHAVIORAL DIMENSION OF BUDGETING

Budgets are often used to judge the actual performance of managers. Bonuses, salary increases, and promotions are all affected by a manager's ability to achieve or beat budgeted goals. Since a manager's financial status and career can be affected, budgets can have a significant behavioral effect. Whether that effect is positive or negative depends to a large extent on how budgets are used.

Positive behavior occurs when the goals of individual managers are aligned with the goals of the organization and the manager has the drive to achieve them. The alignment of managerial and organizational goals is often referred to as **goal congruence**. In addition to goal congruence, however, a manager must also exert effort to achieve the goals of the organization.

If the budget is improperly administered, the reaction of subordinate managers may be negative. This negative behavior can be manifested in numerous ways, but the overall effect is subversion of the organization's goals. **Dysfunctional behavior** involves individual behavior that is in basic conflict with the goals of the organization.

ETHICS   A theme underlying the behavioral dimension of budgeting is ethics. The importance of budgets in performance evaluation and managers' pay raises and promotions leads to the possibility of unethical action. All of the dysfunctional actions regarding budgets that a manager may choose to take can have an unethical aspect. For example, a manager who deliberately underestimates sales and overestimates costs for the purpose of making the budget easier to achieve is engaging in unethical behavior. It is the responsibility of the company to create budgetary incentives that do not encourage unethical behavior. It is the responsibility of the manager to avoid engaging in such behavior. •

Characteristics of a Good Budgetary System

An ideal budgetary system is one that achieves complete goal congruence and simultaneously creates a drive in managers to achieve the organization's goals in an ethical manner. While an ideal budgetary system probably does not exist, research and practice have identified some key features that promote a reasonable degree of positive behavior. These features include frequent feedback on performance, monetary and nonmonetary incentives, participation, realistic standards, controllability of costs, and multiple measures of performance.

---

9   J. A. Brimson, "Feature Costing: Beyond ABC," *Journal of Cost Management* (January/February 1998): 6–12.

Frequent Feedback on Performance   Managers need to know how they are doing as the year unfolds. Providing them with frequent, timely performance reports allows them to know how successful their efforts have been and gives managers time to take corrective actions and change plans as necessary. Frequent performance reports can reinforce positive behavior and give managers the time and opportunity to adapt to changing conditions.

The use of flexible budgets allows management to see if actual costs and revenues are in accord with budgeted amounts. Selective investigation of significant variances allows managers to focus only on areas that need attention. This process is called *management by exception.*

Monetary and Nonmonetary Incentives   A sound budgetary system encourages goal-congruent behavior. **Incentives** are the means that are used to encourage managers to work toward achieving the organization's goals. Incentives can be either negative or positive. Negative incentives use fear of punishment to motivate; positive incentives use rewards. What incentives should be tied to an organization's budgetary system?

The most successful companies view people as their most important asset. Their budgets reflect their underlying philosophy by including significant expenditures on recruiting and career development in good times. Even in difficult economic times, employees are protected to the extent possible.

For example, in 2008–2009, **FedEx** worked to keep costs under control and help save jobs. Pay was cut 5 percent across the board, and the CEO took a 20 percent pay cut. Similarly, **General Electric** CEO Jeff Immelt took a 28 percent pay cut and asked for no bonus for 2008.[10]

In 2020, many CEOs in the airline, hospitality, health care, and other industries took pay cuts both to help conserve cash and send a message of shared sacrifice to their workforce. **Delta** CEO Ed Bastian cut his salary by 100 percent for six months, and their Board of Directors gave up their compensation. **Marriott's** CEO gave up his entire salary for the remainder of 2020 and cut his executive team's pay by 50 percent. GE's CEO decided to forego his full salary.[11]

Of course, negative incentives can be used as well. The most serious negative incentive is the threat of dismissal. Other negative incentives include loss of bonuses, promotions, or raises.

Participative Budgeting   Rather than imposing budgets on subordinate managers, **participative budgeting** allows subordinate managers considerable say in how the budgets are established. Typically, overall objectives are communicated to the manager, who helps develop a budget that will accomplish these objectives. In participative budgeting, the emphasis is on the accomplishment of the broad objectives, not on individual budget items.

The budget process described earlier for ABT uses participative budgeting. The company provides the sales forecast to its profit centers and requests a budget that shows planned expenditures and expected profits given that specific level of sales. The managers of the profit centers are fully responsible for preparing the budgets by which they will later be evaluated. Although the budgets must be approved by the president, disapproval is uncommon; the budgets are usually in line with the sales forecast and last year's operating results adjusted for expected changes in revenues and costs.

---

10 "World's Most Admired Companies 2009," *Fortune* (March 16, 2009), http://money.cnn.com/magazines/fortune /mostadmired/2009/snapshots/170.html

11 Ethan Wolff-Mann, "Here's a List of CEOs Taking Pay Cuts Amid the Coronavirus Crisis," *Yahoo Finance* (March 30, 2020), https://finance.yahoo.com/news/heres-a-list-of-ce-os-taking-pay-cuts-amidst-the-coronavirus-crisis-171206258 .html

Participative budgeting communicates a sense of responsibility to subordinate managers and fosters creativity. Since the subordinate manager creates the budget, it is more likely that the budget's goals will become the manager's personal goals, resulting in greater goal congruence. Advocates of participative budgeting claim that the increased responsibility and challenge inherent in the process provide nonmonetary incentives that lead to a higher level of performance. They argue that individuals involved in setting their own standards will work harder to achieve them. In addition to the behavioral benefits, participative budgeting has the advantage of involving individuals whose knowledge of local conditions may enhance the entire planning process.

Participative budgeting has three potential problems that should be mentioned:

1. Setting standards that are either too high or too low
2. Building slack into the budget (often referred to as *padding the budget*)
3. Pseudoparticipation

Some managers may tend to set either too loose or too tight a budget. Since budgeted goals tend to become the manager's goals when participation is allowed, making this mistake in setting the budget can result in decreased performance levels. If goals are too easily achieved, a manager may lose interest, and performance may actually drop. Challenge is important to aggressive and creative individuals. Similarly, setting the budget too tight ensures failure to achieve the standards and frustrates the manager. This frustration, too, can lead to poor performance. The trick is to get managers in a participative organization to set high but achievable goals.

The second problem with participative budgeting is the opportunity for managers to build slack into the budget. **Budgetary slack** exists when a manager deliberately underestimates revenues or overestimates costs. Either approach increases the likelihood that the manager will achieve the budget and consequently reduces the risk that the manager faces. Padding the budget also unnecessarily ties up resources that might be used more productively elsewhere.

Slack in budgets can be virtually eliminated if top management dictates lower expense budgets. The benefits to be gained from participation, however, may far exceed the costs associated with padding the budget. Even so, top management should carefully review budgets proposed by subordinate managers and provide input, where needed, in order to decrease the effects of building slack into the budget.

The third problem with participation occurs when top management assumes total control of the budgeting process, seeking only superficial participation from lower-level managers. This practice is termed **pseudoparticipation**. Top management is simply obtaining formal acceptance of the budget from subordinate managers, not seeking real input. Accordingly, none of the behavioral benefits of participation will be realized.

Realistic Standards Budgeted objectives are used to gauge performance; accordingly, they should be based on realistic conditions and expectations. Budgets should reflect operating realities such as actual levels of activity, seasonal variations, efficiencies, and general economic trends. Flexible budgets, for example, are used to ensure that the budgeted costs provide standards that are compatible with the actual activity level. Another factor to consider is that of seasonality. Some businesses receive revenues and incur costs uniformly throughout the year; thus, spreading the annual revenues and costs evenly over quarters and months is reasonable for interim performance reports. However, for businesses with seasonal variations, this practice would result in distorted performance reports.

Factors such as efficiency and general economic conditions are also important. Occasionally, top management makes arbitrary cuts in prior-year budgets with the belief that the cuts will reduce fat or inefficiencies that allegedly exist. In reality, some units may be operating efficiently and others inefficiently. An across-the-board cut without any formal evaluation may impair the ability of some units to carry out their missions. General economic conditions also need to be considered. Budgeting for a significant increase in sales when a recession is projected is not only foolish but also potentially harmful.

Sustainability Budgeting at 3M

The lessons of budgeting are particularly relevant to sustainability issues. Forward-thinking companies set goals, operationalize them, and then measure progress toward those goals. Some of the measures may be financial measures, either in terms of increased revenues or decreased costs, whereas some are quantitative measures that logically should result in decreased costs down the road. For example, decreased emissions should lead to lower rates of illness and decreased sick leave payments, which are not detailed on the financial statements. **3M Corporation** is a good example of a company that sets sustainability goals, tracks them, and reports results in an annual sustainability report.

3M's 2015 sustainability goals[12] included the following:

- Reduce volatile air emissions 15 percent by 2015 from 2010 base year, indexed to net sales
- Reduce waste 10 percent by 2015 from 2010 base year, indexed to net sales
- Improve energy efficiency 25 percent by 2015 from 2005 base year, indexed to net sales
- Reduce greenhouse gas emissions 5 percent by 2011 from 2006 base year, indexed to net sales (this goal was set in 2007)
- Develop water conservation plans in 3M locations where water is categorized as scarce or in a stressed area

By the end of 2015, results showed achievement in all areas. Volatile air emissions were reduced by 15 percent, waste was reduced by 10 percent, energy efficiency was improved by 25 percent, greenhouse gas emissions decreased by 5 percent, and water conservation plans were developed in 3M locations where water was categorized as scarce or in a stressed area. Notice that the goals provide a road map—or budget— for the coming year(s).

In a move congruent with continuous budgeting, now that 2015 goals are being met, 3M has developed further goals extending to 2025 that involve the following categories: raw materials, water, energy and climate, education and development, and health and safety. Each category has measureable goals and can be monitored by 3M corporate officials.

Controllability of Costs Conventional thought maintains that managers should be held accountable only for costs over which they have control. **Controllable costs** are costs whose level a manager can influence. In this view, a manager who has no responsibility for a cost should not be held accountable for it. For example, divisional managers have no power to authorize such corporate-level costs as research and development and salaries of top managers. Therefore, they should not be held accountable for the incurrence of those costs.

Many firms, however, do put noncontrollable costs in the budgets of subordinate managers. Making managers aware of the need to cover all costs is one rationale for this practice. If noncontrollable costs are included in a budget, they should be separated from controllable costs and labeled as *noncontrollable*.

12 Taken from 3M's 2016 Sustainability Report, http://www.3m.com/3M/en_US/sustainability-report/goals-and-results/.

For example, **JEA**, a utility system in Jacksonville, Florida, recently renovated its ABC system. While previously, the ABC reporting system emphasized cost reports for process owners rather than internal customers, the newer reports showed internal customers how their actions led to increased costs. Each ABC analysis is coded in green (costs that are "variable or mixed and can be reduced directly by director-level decisions"), yellow (costs that are "discretionary fixed and can be reduced by vice president–level decisions"), and red (costs that are "essentially fixed and can be reduced only by higher management"). The CIO found that internal customers willingly reduced printing costs by changing to automatic duplex (double-sided) printing. A green cost, this was one cost-saving measure that could be easily implemented.[13]

Multiple Measures of Performance   Often, organizations make the mistake of using budgets as their only measure of managerial performance. Overemphasis on this measure can lead to a form of dysfunctional behavior called *milking the firm* or *myopia*. **Myopic behavior** occurs when a manager takes actions that improve budgetary performance in the short run but bring long-run harm to the firm.

There are numerous examples of myopic behavior. To meet budgeted cost objectives or profits, managers can reduce expenditures for preventive maintenance, advertising, and new product development. Managers can also fail to promote deserving employees to keep the cost of labor low and can choose to use lower-quality materials to reduce the cost of materials. In the short run, these actions will lead to improved budgetary performance, but in the long run, productivity will fall, market share will decline, and capable employees will leave for more attractive opportunities.

Managers who engage in this kind of behavior often have a short tenure. In these cases, managers spend three to five years before being promoted or moving to a new area of responsibility. Their successors are the ones who pay the price for their myopic behavior. The best way to prevent myopic behavior is to measure the performance of managers on several dimensions, including some long-run attributes. Productivity, quality, and personnel development are examples of other areas of performance that could be evaluated. Financial measures of performance are important, but overemphasis on them can be counterproductive.

SUMMARY OF LEARNING OBJECTIVES

LO1. Define budgeting, and discuss its role in planning, controlling, and decision making.
- A budget is a financial plan for the future.
- Budgeting is important for planning, control, and decision making.
- The master budget is the comprehensive plan for the coming year. It consists of:
    - The operating budget
    - The financial budget

LO2. Prepare the operating budget, identify its major components, and explain the interrelationships of the various components.
- The sales budget shows the expected sales quantity and price of each product or service.
- The production budget shows the budgeted units to be produced in each period to meet sales and desired ending inventory needs. It includes:
    - The direct materials purchases budget
    - The direct labor budget
    - The overhead budget

- Ending finished goods inventory and cost of goods sold budgets are used in the budgeted income statement.
- Operating expense budgets include:
  - The marketing expense budget
  - The administrative expense budget
  - Any other needed budgets for operating departments (e.g., Research and Development)
- The budgeted income statement is the culmination of the operating budget.

LO3. Identify the components of the financial budget, and prepare a cash budget.
- The cash budget shows the sources and disbursements of cash by period for the coming year.
  - Only cash items are shown in the cash budget.
  - The accounts receivable aging schedule helps companies determine the timing of cash receipts.
- The cash budget is critically important to the ability of a company to meet its obligations.
- The budgeted balance sheet shows the expected assets, liabilities, and owners' equity for the end of the coming year.

LO4. Define flexible budgeting, and discuss its role in planning, control, and decision making.
- A flexible budget shows costs for varying levels of activity.
  - Useful for planning
  - Useful for sensitivity analysis
- A flexible budget can be constructed for the actual level of activity.
  - Useful for control
  - Compares actual costs to budgeted amounts for actual level of activity

LO5. Define activity-based budgeting, and discuss its role in planning, control, and decision making.
- Activity-based budgeting recognizes interdependencies among departments.
- It also focuses on business processes.

LO6. Identify and discuss the key features that a budgetary system should have to encourage managers to engage in goal-congruent behavior.
- Dysfunctional behavior can occur when budgets are overemphasized as a control mechanism.
- Budgets are better performance measures when used with:
  - Participative budgeting
  - Other nonmonetary incentives
  - Frequent feedback on performance
  - Ensuring that the budgetary objectives reflect reality
  - Holding managers accountable for only controllable costs

EXAMPLE 8.1   The HOW and WHY of Constructing a Sales Budget, page 380

EXAMPLE 8.2   The HOW and WHY of Constructing a Production Budget, page 381

EXAMPLE 8.3   The HOW and WHY of Constructing a Direct Materials Purchases Budget, page 383

EXAMPLE 8.4   The HOW and WHY of Constructing a Direct Labor Budget, page 385

EXAMPLE 8.5   The HOW and WHY of Constructing an Overhead Budget, page 386

EXAMPLE 8.6   The HOW and WHY of Preparing the Ending Finished Goods Inventory Budget, page 387

EXAMPLE 8.7   The HOW and WHY of Preparing the Cost of Goods Sold Budget, page 388

EXAMPLE 8.8   The HOW and WHY of Constructing a Marketing Expense Budget, page 389

EXAMPLE 8.9   The HOW and WHY of Constructing an Administrative Expense Budget, page 391

EXAMPLE 8.10   The HOW and WHY of Constructing a Budgeted Income Statement, page 392

EXAMPLE 8.11   The HOW and WHY of Constructing a Cash Receipts Budget with an Accounts Receivable Aging Schedule, page 395

EXAMPLE 8.12   The HOW and WHY of Constructing a Cash Budget, page 397

EXAMPLE 8.13   The HOW and WHY of Constructing a Flexible Budget for Varying Levels of Activity, page 404

EXAMPLE 8.14   The HOW and WHY of Constructing a Flexible Budget for the Actual Level of Activity, page 406

KEY TERMS

Administrative expense budget, 390

Budget committee, 375

Budget director, 375

Budgetary slack, 414

Budgets, 374

Capital expenditures budget, 394

Cash budget, 394

Continuous budget, 375

Control, 374

Controllable costs, 415

Direct labor budget, 384

Direct materials purchases budget, 382

Dysfunctional behavior, 412

Effectiveness, 407

Efficiency, 407

Ending finished goods inventory budget, 386

Feature costing, 412

Financial budgets, 375

Flexible budget, 404

Flexible budget variances, 405

Goal congruence, 412

Incentives, 413

Incremental approach, 401

Marketing expense budget, 389

Master budget, 375

Myopic behavior, 416

Operating budgets, 375

Overhead budget, 386

Participative budgeting, 413

Production budget, 379

Pseudoparticipation, 414

Research and development expense budget, 390

Rolling budget, 375

Sales budget, 379

Static budget, 401

Variable budget, 405

Zero-base budgeting, 401

BRIEF EXERCISES

Brief Exercise 8-1 Sales Budget

OBJECTIVE ▶ 2
Example 8.1

Smart Strike Company manufactures and sells soccer balls for teams of children in elementary and high school. Smart Strike's best-selling lines are the practice ball line (durable soccer balls for training and practice) and the match ball line (high-performance soccer balls used in games). In the first four months of next year, Smart Strike expects to sell the following:

	Practice Balls		Match Balls	
	Units	Selling Price	Units	Selling Price
January	50,000	$12	7,000	$25
February	58,000	$12	7,500	$25
March	80,000	$12	13,000	$25
April	100,000	$12	18,000	$25

Required:

1. Construct a sales budget for Smart Strike for the first three months of the coming year. Show total sales for each product line by month and in total for the first quarter.
2. *What if* Smart Strike added a third line—tournament quality soccer balls that were expected to take 40 percent of the units sold of the match balls and would have a selling price of $45 each in January and February, and $48 each in March? Prepare a sales budget for Smart Strike for the first three months of the coming year. Show total sales for each product line by month and in total for the first quarter.

Brief Exercise 8-2 Production Budget

OBJECTIVE ▶ 2
Example 8.2

Refer to **Brief Exercise 8-1**, through Requirement 1. Smart Strike requires ending inventory of product to equal 25 percent of the next month's unit sales. Beginning inventory in January was 2,400 practice soccer balls and 400 match soccer balls.

Required:

1. Construct a production budget for each of the two product lines for Smart Strike Company for the first three months of the coming year.
2. *What if* Smart Strike wanted a production budget for the two product lines for the month of April? What additional information would you need to prepare this budget?

Brief Exercise 8-3 Direct Materials Purchases Budget

OBJECTIVE ▶ 2
Example 8.3

Refer to **Brief Exercise 8-2** for the production budgets for practice balls and match balls. Every practice ball requires 0.7 square yard of polyvinyl chloride panels, one bladder with valve (to fill with air), and 3 ounces of glue. Smart Strike's policy is that 10 percent of the following month's production needs for raw materials be in ending inventory. Beginning inventory in January for all raw materials met this requirement.

Required:

1. Construct a direct materials purchases budget for each type of raw materials for the practice ball line for January and February of the coming year.
2. *What if* Smart Strike increased the ending inventory percentage to 15 percent of the next month's production needs? What impact would that have on the direct materials purchases budgets prepared in Requirement 1?

OBJECTIVE ▶2▶

Example 8.4

Brief Exercise 8-4   Direct Labor Budget for Service

The School of Accounting (SOA) at State University is planning its annual fundraising campaign for accounting alumni. This year, the SOA is planning a call-a-thon and will ask Beta Alpha Psi members to volunteer to make phone calls to a list of 5,000 alumni. The Dean's office has agreed to let Beta Alpha Psi use their offices from 6 p.m. to 9 p.m. each weekday so that they will have access to phones. Each volunteer will be provided with a phone and a script with an introduction and suggested responses to various questions that had been asked in the past. Monique Johnson, Beta Alpha Psi faculty advisor, estimates the following:

1. Of the 5,000 phone numbers, roughly 10 percent will be wrong numbers (because alumni change addresses and phone numbers without updating State University). In that case, the student is instructed to apologize to the answering party, hang up, and move on to the next phone number. Each of these calls takes about three minutes.

2. Another 15 percent will be correct numbers, but no one answers and it goes to voicemail. In that case, the student is instructed to simply hang up and move on to the next phone number. Each of these calls takes about two minutes.

3. Each time an alumnus answers the phone, the student is instructed to introduce him or herself and read the scripted introduction. The student is encouraged to engage the alumnus in conversation and reminiscences about State U and bring the alum up to date on the wonderful things that are happening in the SOA. Some calls are longer, some shorter, but the average call length is 10 minutes.

Required:

1. Prepare a direct labor budget, in hours, for the fundraising call-a-thon. If 15 students volunteer, how many evenings will the phone-a-thon take? (Round to two significant digits.)

2. ***What if*** the phone-a-thon can be moved to the State University Foundation phone bank? That facility has an automated calling system that will automatically dial the phone numbers and route all answered calls directly to students. As a result, no time is spent dialing and listening to answering machines. The time savings due to having the numbers automatically dialed and routed mean that the average length of a wrong number call drops to one minute and the average length of an alumni call drops to eight minutes. Prepare a direct labor budget, in hours, for the fundraising call-a-thon at the State University Foundation. If 15 students volunteer, how many evenings will the phone-a-thon take? (Round to two significant digits.)

OBJECTIVE ▶2▶

Example 8.5

Brief Exercise 8-5   Overhead Budget

Johnston Company cleans and applies powder coat paint to metal items on a job-order basis. Johnston has budgeted the following amounts for various overhead categories in the coming year.

Supplies	$216,000
Gas	50,000
Indirect labor	176,000
Supervision	73,500
Depreciation on equipment	47,000
Depreciation on the building	40,000
Rental of special equipment	11,000
Electricity (for lighting, heating, and air conditioning)	28,900
Telephone	4,300
Landscaping service	1,200
Other overhead	50,000

In the coming year, Johnston expects to powder coat 120,000 units. Each unit takes 1.3 direct labor hours. Johnston has found that supplies and gas (used to run the drying ovens—all units pass through the drying ovens after powder coat paint is applied) tend to vary with the number of units produced. All other overhead categories are considered to be fixed. (Round all overhead rates to the nearest cent.)

Required:

1. Calculate the number of direct labor hours Johnston must budget for the coming year. Calculate the variable overhead rate. Calculate the total fixed overhead for the coming year.
2. Prepare an overhead budget for Johnston for the coming year. Show the total variable overhead, total fixed overhead, and total overhead. Calculate the fixed overhead rate and the total overhead rate (rounded to the nearest cent).
3. *What if* Johnston had expected to make 118,000 units next year? Assume that the variable overhead per unit does not change and the total fixed overhead amounts do not change. Calculate the new budgeted direct labor hours and prepare a new overhead budget. Calculate the fixed overhead rate and the total overhead rate (rounded to the nearest cent).

Brief Exercise 8-6 Ending Finished Goods Inventory Budget

OBJECTIVE ◀ 2
Example 8.6

Play-Disc makes Frisbee-type plastic discs. Each 12-inch diameter plastic disc has the following manufacturing costs:

Direct materials	$1.67
Direct labor	0.56
Variable overhead	0.72
Fixed overhead	1.80
Total unit cost	$4.75

For the coming year, Play-Disc expects to make 300,000 plastic discs, and to sell 285,000 of them. Budgeted beginning inventory in units is 16,000 with unit cost of $4.75. (There are no beginning or ending inventories of work in process.)

Required:

1. Prepare an ending finished goods inventory budget for Play-Disc for the coming year.
2. *What if* sales increased to 290,000 discs? How would that affect the ending finished goods inventory budget? Calculate the value of budgeted ending finished goods inventory.

Brief Exercise 8-7 Cost of Goods Sold Budget

OBJECTIVE ◀ 2
Example 8.7

Refer to **Brief Exercise 8-6**.

Required:

1. Calculate the total budgeted cost of units produced for Play-Disc for the coming year. Show the cost of direct materials, direct labor, and overhead.
2. Prepare a cost of goods sold budget for Play-Disc for the year.
3. *What if* the beginning inventory of finished goods was $75,200 (for 16,000 units)? How would that affect the cost of goods sold budget? (Assume Play-Disc uses the FIFO method.)

Brief Exercise 8-8 Marketing Expense Budget

OBJECTIVE ◀ 2
Example 8.8

Timothy Donaghy has developed a unique formula for growing hair. His proprietary lotion, used regularly for 45 days, will grow hair in bald spots (with varying degrees of success). Timothy calls his lotion Hair-Again and is selling it via the telephone and Internet. His major form of marketing is through 15-minute infomercials and Internet advertising. Timothy sells each 16-ounce bottle of Hair-Again for $15 and pays a commission of 3 percent of sales to telephone operators who field the 1-800 phone calls from potential customers. Fixed marketing expenses for each quarter of the coming year include:

Internet banner ads	$7,600
Telephone operator time	4,000
Travel	3,000

In addition, early next year Timothy intends to film and show infomercials on television. He expects the cost to be $10,000 in quarters 1 and 2, and that the cost will rise to $25,000 in each of quarters 3 and 4. Timothy expects the following unit sales of Hair-Again:

Quarter 1	5,000
Quarter 2	15,000
Quarter 3	40,000
Quarter 4	35,000

Required:

1. Construct a marketing expense budget for Hair-Again for the coming year. Show total amounts by quarter and in total for the year.
2. *What if* the cost of Internet ads rises to $15,000 in Quarters 2 through 4? How would that affect variable marketing expense? Fixed marketing expense? Total marketing expense?

OBJECTIVE 2
Example 8.9

Brief Exercise 8-9 Administrative Expense Budget

Green Earth Landscaping Company provides monthly and weekly landscaping and maintenance services to residential customers in the tri-city area. Green Earth has no variable administrative expense. Fixed administrative expenses for June, July, and August include:

Salaries	$9,600
Insurance	2,500
Depreciation	3,700
Accounting services	500

Required:

1. Construct an administrative expense budget for Green Earth Landscaping Company for the three summer months. Show total amounts by month and in total for the three-month period.
2. *What if* Green Earth Landscaping Company's insurance rates increased at the beginning of July to $2,600 per month? How would that affect monthly administrative expense?

OBJECTIVE 2
Example 8.10

Brief Exercise 8-10 Budgeted Income Statement

Coral Seas Jewelry Company makes and sells costume jewelry. For the coming year, Coral Seas expects sales of $15.9 million and cost of goods sold of $8.75 million. Advertising is a key part of Coral Seas' business strategy, and total marketing expense for the year is budgeted at $2.8 million. Total administrative expenses are expected to be $675,000. Coral Seas has no interest expense. Income taxes are paid at the rate of 40 percent of operating income.

Required:

1. Construct a budgeted income statement for Coral Seas Jewelry Company for the coming year.
2. *What if* Coral Seas had interest payments of $500,000 during the year? What effect would that have on operating income? On income before taxes? On net income?

Brief Exercise 8-11 Cash Receipts Budget and Accounts Receivable Aging Schedule

OBJECTIVE ◀ 3
Example 8.11

Shalimar Company manufactures and sells industrial products. For next year, Shalimar has budgeted the follow sales:

Quarter 1	$4,600,000
Quarter 2	5,100,000
Quarter 3	5,000,000
Quarter 4	7,600,000

In Shalimar's experience, 10 percent of sales are paid in cash. Of the sales on account, 65 percent are collected in the quarter of sale, 25 percent are collected in the quarter following the sale, and 7 percent are collected in the second quarter after the sale. The remaining 3 percent are never collected. Total sales for the third quarter of the current year are $4,900,000 and for the fourth quarter of the current year are $6,850,000.

Required:

1. Calculate cash sales and credit sales expected in the last two quarters of the current year, and in each quarter of next year.
2. Construct a cash receipts budget for Shalimar Company for each quarter of the next year, showing the cash sales and the cash collections from credit sales.
3. *What if* the recession led Shalimar's top management to assume that in the next year 10 percent of credit sales would never be collected? The expected payment percentages in the quarter of sale and the quarter after sale are assumed to be the same. How would that affect cash received in each quarter? Construct a revised cash budget using the new assumption.

Brief Exercise 8-12 Cash Budget

OBJECTIVE ◀ 3
Example 8.12

Khloe Company imports gift items from overseas and sells them to gift shops and department stores throughout the United States. Khloe Company provided the following information:

a. The October 31 balance in the cash account is $53,817.
b. All sales are on account. Sales in September were $950,000 and in October were $1,240,000.
c. November sales are expected to be $2,145,000.
d. In Khloe's experience, 70 percent of sales are collected in the month of sale and 28 percent are collected in the month following sale. The remaining credit sales are uncollectible.
e. Khloe purchases all merchandise on account. Purchases in September were $750,000 and in October were $980,000. November purchases are expected to be $2,000,000 as Khloe prepares for the Christmas buying season. Fifteen percent of purchases are paid in the month of purchase, while the remainder is paid in the month following the purchase month.
f. Khloe Company has nine employees who are paid a total of $48,000 per month. Due to timing issues, about 90 percent of total wages are paid in the month earned and the remaining 10 percent are paid in the following month.
g. Rent for office and warehouse space is $12,300 paid monthly in cash.
h. Utilities average $6,100 per month and are paid in cash.
i. In November, Khloe expects to pay employment taxes of $6,625.
j. Since Khloe imports product from overseas, customs duty and shipping to the central location of 30 percent of current monthly purchase cost must be paid in the month of purchase.
k. Other cash expenses for November are expected to be $41,500.

Required:

1. Prepare a cash budget for Khloe Company for the month of November.
2. *What if* Khloe faced a customs duty and shipping percentage of 35 percent? How would that affect the November cash budget?

OBJECTIVE ▶4

Example 8.13

Brief Exercise 8-13 Flexible Budget for Varying Levels of Activity

Nashler Company has the following budgeted variable costs per unit produced:

Direct materials	$7.20
Direct labor	1.54
Variable overhead:	
Supplies	0.23
Maintenance	0.19
Power	0.18

Budgeted fixed overhead costs per month include supervision of $98,000, depreciation of $76,000, and other overhead of $245,000.

Required:

1. Prepare a flexible budget for all costs of production for the following levels of production: 160,000 units, 170,000 units, and 175,000 units.
2. What is the per-unit total product cost for each of the production levels from Requirement 1? (Round each unit cost to the nearest cent.)
3. *What if* Nashler Company's cost of maintenance rose to $0.22 per unit? How would that affect the unit product costs calculated in Requirement 2?

OBJECTIVE 4▶

Example 8.14

Brief Exercise 8-14 Flexible Budget for Varying Levels of Activity

Refer to **Brief Exercise 8-13**. In March, Nashler Company produced 163,200 units and had the following actual costs:

Direct materials	$1,170,000
Direct labor	258,000
Supplies	38,100
Maintenance	30,960
Power	29,300
Supervision	99,450
Depreciation	76,000
Other overhead	244,300

Required:

1. Prepare a performance report for Nashler Company comparing actual costs with the flexible budget for actual units produced.
2. *What if* Nashler Company's actual direct materials cost were $1,175,040? How would that affect the variance for direct materials? The total cost variance?

EXERCISES

OBJECTIVE 2▶

Exercise 8-15 Production Budget

Palmgren Company produces consumer products. The sales budget for four months of the year is presented below.

	Unit Sales	Dollar Sales
July	32,500	$ 975,000
August	33,700	1,061,550
September	38,000	1,197,000
October	36,000	1,141,200

Company policy requires that ending inventories for each month be 25 percent of next month's sales. At the beginning of July, the beginning inventory of consumer products met that policy.

Required:

Prepare a production budget for the third quarter of the year. Show the number of units that should be produced each month as well as for the quarter in total.

Exercise 8-16 Sales and Production Budgets

OBJECTIVE ▶ 2

EXCEL   SHOW ME HOW

Archer Company produces two products: the custom and the basic. The custom sells for $30, and the basic sells for $8. Projected sales of the two models for the coming four quarters are given below.

	Custom	Basic
First quarter	9,000	90,000
Second quarter	12,000	88,400
Third quarter	16,000	92,000
Fourth quarter	20,000	91,600

The president of the company believes that the projected sales are realistic and can be achieved by the company. In the factory, the production supervisor has received the projected sales figures and gathered information needed to compile production budgets. He found that 800 customs and 1,140 basics were in inventory on January 1. Company policy dictates that ending inventory should equal 20 percent of the next quarter's sales for customs and 10 percent of next quarter's sales for basics.

Required:

1. Prepare a sales budget for each quarter and for the year in total. Show sales by product and in total for each time period.
2. What factors might Archer Company have considered in preparing the sales budget?
3. Prepare a separate production budget for each product for each of the first three quarters of the year.

Exercise 8-17 Direct Materials Purchases Budget: Direct Labor Budget

OBJECTIVE ▶ 2

EXCEL   SHOW ME HOW

Macchu Company produces stuffed toy animals; one of these is "Andie the Llama." Each Andie takes 0.30 yard of fabric and eight ounces of polyfiberfill. Fabric costs $3.50 per yard and polyfiberfill is $0.05 per ounce. Macchu has budgeted production of Andies for the next four months as follows:

	Units
October	42,000
November	90,000
December	50,000
January	40,000

Inventory policy requires that sufficient fabric be in ending monthly inventory to satisfy 10 percent of the following month's production needs and sufficient polyfiberfill be in inventory to satisfy 15 percent of the following month's production needs. Inventory of fabric and polyfiberfill at the beginning of October equals exactly the amount needed to satisfy the inventory policy.

Each Andie produced requires (on average) 0.25 direct labor hour. The average cost of direct labor is $14 per hour.

Required:

1. Prepare a direct materials purchases budget of fabric for the last quarter of the year showing purchases in units and in dollars for each month and for the quarter in total.
2. Prepare a direct materials purchases budget of polyfiberfill for the last quarter of the year showing purchases in units and in dollars for each month and for the quarter in total.
3. Prepare a direct labor budget for the last quarter of the year showing the hours needed and the direct labor cost for each month and for the quarter in total.

OBJECTIVE  **2**

SHOW ME HOW

Exercise 8-18 Sales Forecast and Budget

Video-Forward, Inc., designs and manufactures wearable video cameras. Models A-1, A-2, and A-3 are lightweight video cameras that can be used on arms and headbands. Models A-4 and A-5 have larger memory, better resolution, and more Wi-Fi-related features. It is now early January and Video-Forward's budgeting team is finalizing the sales budget for this year. Sales in units and in dollars for last year were as follows:

Model	Number Sold	Price	Revenue
A-1	20,000	$ 50	$1,000,000
A-2	30,000	75	2,250,000
A-3	50,000	90	4,500,000
A-4	15,000	120	1,800,000
A-5	2,000	200	400,000
			$9,950,000

In looking over last year's sales figures, Video-Forward's sales budgeting team recalled the following:

a. Model A-1 costs were rising faster than the price could rise. Preparatory to phasing out this model, Video-Forward, Inc., planned to slash advertising for this model and raise its price by 30 percent. The number of units of Model A-1 to be sold was forecast to be 50 percent of last year's units.

b. Model A-5 was introduced on November 1 of last year. It contains a built-in 20 GB hard drive and can be synchronized with several popular music software programs. Video-Forward brought out this model to match competitors' video cameras, but the price is so much higher than other Video-Forward products, that sales have been disappointing. The company plans to discontinue this model on June 30 of this year, and thinks that monthly sales will remain at last year's level if the sales price remains unchanged.

c. Video-Forward plans to introduce Model A-6 on July 1 of this year. It will be a high-end player that will be lighter and more versatile than Model A-5 (which it will replace). The target price for this model is $180; unit sales are estimated to equal 2,500 per month.

d. A competitor has announced plans to introduce an improved version of Model A-3. Video-Forward believes that the Model A-3 price must be cut 20 percent to maintain unit sales at last year's level.

e. It was assumed that unit sales of all other models would increase by 10 percent, prices remaining constant.

Required:

Prepare a sales forecast by product and in total for Video-Forward, Inc., for this year.

Exercise 8-19 Purchases Budget

OBJECTIVE ◄ 2

SHOW ME
HOW

Tiger Drug Store carries a variety of health and beauty aids, including 500-count bottles of vitamins. The sales budget for vitamins for the first six months of the year is presented below.

	Unit Sales	Dollar Sales
January	170	$1,530
February	160	1,440
March	180	1,620
April	190	1,710
May	210	1,890
June	200	1,800

The owner of Tiger Drug believes that ending inventories should be sufficient to cover 10 percent of the next month's projected sales. On January 1, 23 bottles of vitamins were in inventory.

Required:

1. Prepare a merchandise purchases budget in bottles of vitamins for as many months as you can.
2. If vitamins are priced at cost plus 80 percent, what is the dollar cost of purchases for each month of your purchases budget?

Exercise 8-20 Schedule of Cash Receipts

OBJECTIVE ◄ 3

SHOW ME
HOW

Rosita Flores owns Rosita's Mexican Restaurant in Tempe, Arizona. Rosita's is an affordable restaurant near campus and several hotels. Rosita accepts cash and checks. Checks are deposited immediately. The bank charges $0.50 per check; the amount per check averages $75. "Bad" checks that Rosita cannot collect make up 3 percent of check revenue.

During a typical month, Rosita's has sales of $45,000. About 80 percent are cash sales. Estimated sales for the next three months are as follows:

April	$32,000
May	45,000
June	56,000

Required:

Prepare a schedule of cash receipts for May and June. (Round all amounts to the nearest dollar.)

Exercise 8-21 Schedule of Cash Receipts

OBJECTIVE ◄ 3

SHOW ME
HOW

Refer to **Exercise 8-20**. Rosita thinks that it may be time to refuse to accept checks and to start accepting credit cards. She is negotiating with VISA/MasterCard and American Express, and she would start the new policy on April 1. Rosita estimates that with the drop in sales from the "no checks" policy and the increase in sales from the acceptance of credit cards, the net increase in sales will be 30 percent. The credit cards do involve added costs as follows:

VISA/MasterCard: Rosita will accumulate these credit card receipts throughout the month and submit them in one bundle for payment on the last day of the month. The money will be credited to her account by the fifth day of the following month. A fee of 3.5 percent is charged by the credit card company.

American Express: Rosita will accumulate these receipts throughout the month and send them to American Express for payment on the last day of the month. American Express will credit her account by the sixth day of the following month. A fee of 5.5 percent is charged by American Express.

Rosita estimates the following breakdown of revenues among the various payment methods.

Cash	10%
VISA/Mastercard	75
American Express	15

Required:

Prepare a schedule of cash receipts for May and June that incorporates the changes in policy. (Round all amounts to the nearest dollar.)

OBJECTIVE 3

SHOW ME
HOW   EXCEL

Exercise 8-22 Cash Budget

LeeAnn Ortiz owns a retail store that sells new and used sporting equipment. LeeAnn has requested a cash budget for October. After examining the records of the company, you find the following:

a. Cash balance on October 1 is $980.

b. Actual sales for August and September are as follows:

	August	September
Cash sales	$ 6,000	$ 4,800
Credit sales	60,000	62,000
Total sales	$66,000	$66,800

c. Credit sales are collected over a three-month period: 45 percent in the month of sale, 36 percent in the next month, and 16 percent in the second month after the sale. The remaining sales are uncollectible.

d. Inventory purchases average 70 percent of a month's total sales. Of those purchases, 40 percent are paid for in the month of purchase. The remaining 60 percent are paid for in the following month.

e. Salaries and wages total $4,000 per month.

f. Rent is $3,150 per month.

g. Taxes to be paid in October are $1,635.

h. LeeAnn usually withdraws $3,500 each month as her salary.

i. Advertising is $1,500 per month.

j. Other operating expenses total $3,700 per month.

k. Internet and telephone fees are $320 per month.

LeeAnn tells you that she expects cash sales of $5,200 and credit sales of $63,000 for October. She likes to have $3,000 on hand at the end of the month and is concerned about the potential October ending balance.

Required:

1. Prepare a cash budget for October. Include supporting schedules for cash collections and cash payments. (Round all amounts to the nearest dollar.)
2. Did the business meet LeeAnn's desired ending cash balance for October? Assuming that the owner has no hope of establishing a line of credit for the business, what recommendations would you give the owner for meeting the desired cash balance?
3. Explain how each of the four data analytic types—descriptive, diagnostic, predictive, or prescriptive—can be used in LeeAnn's budgeting process. (See Exhibits 2.5 and 2.6, pp. 37, 40, for a review of data analytic types.)

DATA
ANALYTICS

Exercise 8-23 Budgeted Cash Collections

OBJECTIVE ▸ 3

CMA

SHOW ME
HOW

Historically, Ragman Company has had no significant bad debt experience with its customers. Cash sales have accounted for 20 percent of total sales, and payments for credit sales have been received as follows:

40 percent of credit sales in the month of the sale

35 percent of credit sales in the first subsequent month

20 percent of credit sales in the second subsequent month

5 percent of credit sales in the third subsequent month

The forecast for both cash and credit sales is as follows.

January	$185,000
February	182,000
March	192,000
April	196,000
May	210,000

Required:

1. What is the forecasted cash inflow for Ragman Company for May?
2. Due to deteriorating economic conditions, Ragman Company has now decided that its cash forecast should include a bad debt adjustment of 2 percent of credit sales, beginning with sales for the month of April. Because of this policy change, what will happen to the total expected cash inflow related to sales made in April? *(CMA adapted)*

Exercise 8-24 Schedule of Cash Receipts

OBJECTIVE ▸ 3

EXCEL   SHOW ME
HOW

Del Spencer is the owner and founder of Del Spencer's Men's Clothing Store. Del Spencer's has its own house charge accounts and has found from past experience that 10 percent of its sales are for cash. The remaining 90 percent are on credit. An aging schedule for accounts receivable reveals the following pattern:

15 percent of credit sales are paid in the month of sale.

65 percent of credit sales are paid in the first month following the sale.

14 percent of credit sales are paid in the second month following the sale.

6 percent of credit sales are never collected.

Credit sales that have not been paid until the second month following the sale are considered overdue and are subject to a 3 percent late charge.

Del Spencer's has developed the following sales forecast:

May	$60,000
June	55,000
July	45,000
August	56,000
September	83,000

Required:

Prepare a schedule of cash receipts for August and September.

Exercise 8-25 Cash Disbursements Schedule

OBJECTIVE ▸ 3

SHOW ME
HOW

Refer to **Exercise 8-24**. Del Spencer's purchases clothing evenly throughout the month. All purchases are on account. On the first of every month, Jana Spencer, Del's wife, pays for all of the previous month's purchases. Terms are 2/10, n/30 (i.e., a 2 percent discount can be taken if the bill is paid within 10 days; otherwise, the entire amount is due within 30 days).

The forecast purchases for the months of May through September are as follows:

May	$30,000
June	27,500
July	22,500
August	28,000
September	41,500

Required:

1. Prepare a cash disbursements schedule for the months of August and September. (Round all cash amounts to the nearest dollar.)
2. Now, suppose that Del wants to see what difference it would make to have someone pay for any purchases that have been made three times per month, on the 1st, the 11th, and the 21st. Prepare a cash disbursements schedule for the months of July and August assuming this new payment schedule. (Round all cash amounts to the nearest dollar.)
3. Suppose that Jana (who works full-time as a school teacher and is the mother of two small children) does not have time to make payments on two extra days per month and that a temporary employee is hired on the 11th and 21st at $20 per hour, for four hours each of those two days. Is this a good decision? Explain.

OBJECTIVE **2**

**SHOW ME
HOW**

Exercise 8-26 Production, Purchases, and Direct Labor Budgets

Ingles Corporation is a manufacturer of tables sold to schools, restaurants, hotels, and other institutions. The table tops are manufactured by Ingles, but the table legs are purchased from an outside supplier. The Assembly Department takes a manufactured table top and attaches the four purchased table legs. It takes 16 minutes of labor to assemble a table. The company follows a policy of producing enough tables to ensure that 40 percent of next month's sales are in the finished goods inventory. Ingles also purchases sufficient materials to ensure that materials inventory is 60 percent of the following month's scheduled production. Ingles's sales budget in units for the next quarter is as follows:

July	2,450
August	2,900
September	2,100

Ingles's ending inventories in units for July 31 are as follows:

Finished goods	1,900
Materials (legs)	4,000

Required:

1. Calculate the number of tables to be produced during August.
2. Disregarding your response to Requirement 1, assume the required production units for August and September are 2,100 and 1,900, respectively, and the July 31 materials inventory is 4,000 units. Compute the number of table legs to be purchased in August.
3. Assume that Ingles Corporation will produce 2,340 units in September. How many employees will be required for the Assembly Department in September? (Fractional employees are acceptable since employees can be hired on a part-time basis. Assume a 40-hour week and a 4-week month.) *(CMA adapted)*

Exercise 8-27 Flexible Budget

In an attempt to improve budgeting, the controller for Engersol, Inc., has developed a flexible budget for overhead costs. Engersol, Inc., makes two types of products, commercial floor cleaners and household floor cleaners. The company expects to produce 300,000 units of the commercial cleaner and 120,000 units of the household cleaner during the coming year. The commercial cleaner requires 0.04 direct labor hour per unit, and the household cleaner requires 0.06. The controller has developed the following cost formulas for each of the four overhead items:

	Cost Formula
Maintenance	$30,000 + $1.25 DLH
Power	$0.50 DLH
Indirect labor	$65,000 + $2.30 DLH
Rent	$28,000

Required:

1. Prepare an overhead budget for the expected activity level for the coming year.
2. Prepare an overhead budget that reflects production that is 10 percent higher than expected (for both products) and a budget for production that is 20 percent lower than expected.
3. Which of the four data analytic types—descriptive, diagnostic, predictive, or prescriptive—is being used in creating the three flexible budgets? (See Exhibits 2.5 and 2.6, pp. 37, 40, for a review of data analytic types.)

Exercise 8-28 Flexible Budget

Refer to **Exercise 8-27**. At the end of the year, Engersol, Inc., actually produced 305,000 units of the commercial cleaner and 120,000 of the deluxe model. The actual overhead costs incurred were:

Maintenance	$ 56,900
Power	10,000
Indirect labor	108,700
Rent	28,000

Required:

Prepare a performance report for the period.

Exercise 8-29 Sales Forecast and Flexible Budget

Olympus, Inc., manufactures three models of mattresses: the Sleepeze, the Plushette, and the Ultima. Forecast sales for next year are 15,000 for the Sleepeze, 12,000 for the Plushette, and 5,000 for the Ultima. Gene Dixon, vice president of sales, has provided the following information:

a. Salaries for his office (including himself at $65,000, a marketing research assistant at $40,000, and an administrative assistant at $25,000) are budgeted for $130,000 next year.

b. Depreciation on the offices and equipment is $20,000 per year.

c. Office supplies and other expenses total $21,000 per year.

d. Advertising has been steady at $20,000 per year. However, the Ultima is a new product and will require extensive advertising to educate consumers on the unique features of this high-end mattress. Gene believes the company should spend 15 percent of first-year Ultima sales for a print and television campaign.

e. Commissions on the Sleepeze and Plushette lines are 5 percent of sales. These commissions are paid to independent jobbers who sell the mattresses to retail stores.

f. Last year, shipping for the Sleepeze and Plushette lines averaged $50 per unit sold. Gene expects the Ultima line to ship for $75 per unit sold since this model features a larger mattress.

Required:

1. Suppose that Gene is considering three sales scenarios as follows:

	Pessimistic		Expected		Optimistic	
	Price	Quantity	Price	Quantity	Price	Quantity
Sleepeze	$180	12,500	$ 200	15,000	$ 200	18,000
Plushette	300	10,000	350	12,000	360	14,000
Ultima	900	2,000	1,000	5,000	1,200	5,000

Prepare a revenue budget for the Sales Division for the coming year for each scenario.

2. Prepare a flexible expense budget for the Sales Division for the three scenarios above.

OBJECTIVE 5

SHOW ME HOW

Exercise 8-30 Activity-Based Budget

Refer to **Exercise 8-29**. Suppose Gene determines that next year's Sales Division activities include the following:

Research—researching current and future conditions in the industry
Shipping—arranging for shipping of mattresses and handling calls from purchasing agents at retail stores to trace shipments and correct errors
Jobbers—coordinating the efforts of the independent jobbers who sell the mattresses
Basic ads—placing print and television ads for the Sleepeze and Plushette lines
Ultima ads—choosing and working with the advertising agency on the Ultima account
Office management—operating the Sales Division office

The percentage of time spent by each employee of the Sales Division on each of the above activities is given in the following table:

	Gene	Research Assistant	Administrative Assistant
Research	—	75%	—
Shipping	30%	—	20%
Jobbers	15	10	20
Basic ads	—	15	40
Ultima ads	30	—	5
Office management	25	—	15

Additional information is as follows:

a. Depreciation on the office equipment belongs to the office management activity.

b. Of the $21,000 for office supplies and other expenses, $5,000 can be assigned to telephone costs which can be split evenly between the shipping and jobbers' activities. An additional $2,400 per year is attributable to Internet connections and fees, and the bulk of these costs (80 percent) are assignable to research. The remainder is a cost of office management. All other office supplies and costs are assigned to the office management activity.

Required:

1. Prepare an activity-based budget for next year by activity. Use the expected level of sales activity.
2. On the basis of the budget prepared in Requirement 1, advise Gene regarding actions that might be taken to reduce expenses.

PROBLEMS

Problem 8-31 Operating Budget, Comprehensive Analysis

OBJECTIVE ◄ 2 3

Ponderosa, Inc., produces wiring harness assemblies used in the production of semi-trailer trucks. The wiring harness assemblies are sold to various truck manufacturers around the world. Projected sales in units for the coming five months are given below.

January	10,000
February	10,500
March	13,000
April	16,000
May	18,500

The following data pertain to production policies and manufacturing specifications followed by Ponderosa:

a. Finished goods inventory on January 1 is 900 units. The desired ending inventory for each month is 20 percent of the next month's sales.

b. The data on materials used are as follows:

Direct Material	Per-Unit Usage	Unit Cost
Part #K298	2	$4
Part #C30	3	7

Inventory policy dictates that sufficient materials be on hand at the beginning of the month to satisfy 30 percent of the next month's production needs. This is exactly the amount of material on hand on January 1.

c. The direct labor used per unit of output is one and one-half hours. The average direct labor cost per hour is $20.

d. Overhead each month is estimated using a flexible budget formula. (Activity is measured in direct labor hours.)

	Fixed Cost Component	Variable Cost Component
Supplies	$ —	$1.00
Power	—	0.20
Maintenance	12,500	1.10
Supervision	14,000	—
Depreciation	45,000	—
Taxes	4,300	—
Other	86,000	1.60

e. Monthly selling and administrative expenses are also estimated using a flexible budgeting formula. (Activity is measured in units sold.)

	Fixed Costs	Variable Costs
Salaries	$ 88,500	—
Commissions	—	$1.40
Depreciation	25,000	—
Shipping	—	3.60
Other	137,000	1.60

f. The unit selling price of the wiring harness assembly is $110.

g. In February, the company plans to purchase land for future expansion. The land costs $68,000.

h. All sales and purchases are for cash. The cash balance on January 1 equals $62,900. The firm wants to have an ending cash balance of at least $25,000. If a cash shortage develops, sufficient cash is borrowed to cover the shortage and provide the desired ending balance. Any cash borrowed must be borrowed in $1,000 increments and is repaid the following month, as is the interest due. The interest rate is 12 percent per annum.

Required:

Prepare a monthly operating budget for the first quarter with the following schedules:
1. Sales budget
2. Production budget
3. Direct materials purchases budget
4. Direct labor budget
5. Overhead budget
6. Selling and administrative expense budget
7. Ending finished goods inventory budget
8. Cost of goods sold budget
9. Budgeted income statement (ignore income taxes)
10. Cash budget

OBJECTIVE **3**

DATA ANALYTICS

Problem 8-32 Cash Budget, Pro Forma Balance Sheet

Bernard Creighton is the controller for Creighton Hardware Store. In putting together the cash budget for the fourth quarter of the year, he has assembled the following data.

a. Sales

July (actual)	$100,000
August (actual)	120,000
September (estimated)	90,000
October (estimated)	100,000
November (estimated)	135,000
December (estimated)	150,000

b. Each month, 20 percent of sales are for cash, and 80 percent are on credit. The collection pattern for credit sales is 20 percent in the month of sale, 50 percent in the following month, and 30 percent in the second month following the sale.

c. Each month, the ending inventory exactly equals 40 percent of the cost of next month's sales. The markup on goods is 33.33 percent of cost.

d. Inventory purchases are paid for in the month following purchase.

e. Recurring monthly expenses are as follows:

Salaries and wages	$10,000
Depreciation on plant and equipment	4,000
Utilities	1,000
Other	1,700

f. Property taxes of $15,000 are due and payable on September 15.

g. Advertising fees of $6,000 must be paid on October 20.

h. A lease on a new storage facility is scheduled to begin on November 2. Monthly payments are $5,000.

i. The company has a policy to maintain a minimum cash balance of $10,000. If necessary, it will borrow to meet its short-term needs. All borrowing is done at the beginning of the month. All payments on principal and interest are made at the end of the month. The annual interest rate is 9 percent. The company must borrow in multiples of $1,000.

j. A partially completed balance sheet as of August 31 is given below. (Accounts payable is for inventory purchases only.)

	Assets	Liabilities & Owners' Equity
Cash	$?	
Accounts receivable	?	
Inventory	?	
Plant and equipment	431,750	
Accounts payable		$?
Common stock		220,000
Retained earnings		268,750
Totals	$?	$?

Required:

1. Complete the balance sheet given in part (j).
2. Bernard wants to see how the company is doing prior to starting the month of December. Prepare a cash budget for the months of September, October, and November and for the three-month period in total (the period begins on September 1). Provide a supporting schedule of cash collections.
3. Prepare a pro forma balance sheet as of November 30.
4. Bernard prepared cash budgets for three months of the year as well as for the overall three-month period. How does the additional data give him additional information? (See Exhibits 2.5 and 2.6, pp. 37, 40, for a review of data analytic types).

Problem 8-33 Production, Direct Labor, Direct Materials, Sales Budgets, Budgeted Contribution Margin

OBJECTIVE ▶ 2

Laghari Company makes and sells high-quality glare filters for microcomputer monitors. John Tanaka, controller, is responsible for preparing Laghari's master budget and has assembled the following data for the coming year. The direct labor rate includes wages, all employee-related benefits, and the employer's share of FICA. Labor saving machinery will be fully operational by March. Also, as of March 1, the company's union contract calls for an increase in direct labor wages that is included in the direct labor rate. Laghari expects to have 5,600 glare filters in inventory on December 31 of the current year, and has a policy of carrying 35 percent of the following month's projected sales in inventory. Information on the first four months of the coming year is as follows:

	January	February	March	April
Estimated unit sales	36,000	34,500	39,000	38,600
Sales price per unit	$80	$80	$75	$75
Direct labor hours per unit	3.0	3.0	2.5	2.5
Direct labor hourly rate	$18	$18	$20	$20
Direct materials cost per unit	$9	$9	$9	$9

Required:

1. Prepare the following monthly budgets for Laghari Company for the first quarter of the coming year. Be sure to show supporting calculations.

   a. Production budget in units

   b. Direct labor budget in hours

   c. Direct materials cost budget

   d. Sales budget

2. Calculate the total budgeted contribution margin for Laghari Company by month and in total for the first quarter of the coming year. Be sure to show supporting calculations. *(CMA adapted)*

OBJECTIVE 3

CMA

Problem 8-34 Cash Budget

Friendly Freddie's is an independently owned major appliance and electronics discount chain with seven stores located in a Midwestern metropolitan area. Rapid expansion has created the need for careful planning of cash requirements to ensure that the chain is able to replenish stock adequately and meet payment schedules to creditors. Fred Ferguson, founder of the chain, has established a banking relationship that provides a $200,000 line of credit to Friendly Freddie's. The bank requires that a minimum balance of $8,200 be kept in the chain's checking account at the end of each month. When the balance goes below $8,200, the bank automatically extends the line of credit in multiples of $1,000 so that the checking account balance is at least $8,200 at month-end.

Friendly Freddie's attempts to borrow as little as possible and repays the loans quickly in multiples of $1,000 plus 2 percent monthly interest on the entire loan balance. Interest payments and any principal payments are paid at the end of the month following the loan. The chain currently has no outstanding loans.

The following cash receipts and disbursements data apply to the fourth quarter of the current calendar year.

Estimated beginning cash balance	$ 8,800
Estimated cash sales:	
October	14,000
November	29,000
December	44,000
Sales on account:	
July (actual)	130,000
August (actual)	104,000
September (actual)	128,000
October (estimated)	135,000
November (estimated)	142,000
December (estimated)	188,000

Projected cash collection of sales on account is estimated to be 70 percent in the month following the sale, 20 percent in the second month following the sale, and 6 percent in the third month following the sale. The 4 percent beyond the third month following the sale is determined to be uncollectible. In addition, the chain is scheduled to receive $13,000 cash on a note receivable in October.

All inventory purchases are made on account as the chain has excellent credit with all vendors because of a strong payment history. The following information regarding inventory purchases is available.

Inventory Purchases	
September (actual)	$120,000
October (estimated)	112,000
November (estimated)	128,000
December (estimated)	95,000

Cash disbursements for inventory are made in the month following purchase using an average cash discount of 3 percent for timely payment. Monthly cash disbursements for operating expenses during October, November, and December are estimated to be $38,000, $41,000, and $46,000, respectively.

Required:

Prepare Friendly Freddie's cash budget for the months of October, November, and December showing all receipts, disbursements, and credit line activity, where applicable. (*CMA adapted*)

Problem 8-35 Flexible Budget

OBJECTIVE ◀ 4

The controller for Muir Company's Salem plant is analyzing overhead in order to determine appropriate drivers for use in flexible budgeting. She decided to concentrate on the past 12 months since that time period was one in which there was little important change in technology, product lines, and so on. Data on overhead costs, number of machine hours, number of setups, and number of purchase orders are in the following table.

Month	Overhead Costs	Machine Hours	Number of Setups	Number of Purchase Orders
January	$ 32,296	1,000	20	216
February	31,550	930	18	250
March	36,280	1,100	21	300
April	36,867	1,050	23	270
May	36,790	1,170	22	285
June	37,800	1,200	25	240
July	40,024	1,235	27	237
August	39,256	1,190	24	303
September	33,800	1,070	20	255
October	33,779	1,210	22	195
November	37,225	1,207	23	270
December	27,500	1,084	15	150
Totals	$423,167	13,446	260	2,971

Required:

1. Calculate an overhead rate based on machine hours using the total overhead cost and total machine hours. (Round the overhead rate to the nearest cent and predicted overhead to the nearest dollar.) Use this rate to predict overhead for each of the 12 months.
2. The controller decided to use data analytics for forecasting by running a regression equation using only machine hours as the independent variable. Prepare a flexible budget for overhead for the 12 months using the results of this regression equation. (Round the intercept and x-coefficient to the nearest cent and predicted overhead to the nearest dollar.) Is this flexible budget better than the budget in Requirement 1? Why or why not?

DATA ANALYTICS

Problem 8-36 Flexible Budget, Multiple Regression

Refer to **Problem 8-35** for data.

DATA ANALYTICS

Required:

1. Run a multiple regression equation using machine hours, number of setups, and number of purchase orders as independent variables. Prepare a flexible budget for overhead for the 12 months using the results of this regression equation. (Round the regression coefficients to the nearest cent and predicted overhead to the nearest dollar.) Which flexible budget is better—the one based on simple regression (with machine hours as the only independent variable) or the one based on multiple regression? Why?

2. Now, suppose that the controller remembers that the factory throws two big parties each year, one for the 4th of July and the other for Christmas. Rerun the multiple regression with machine hours, number of setups, and number of purchase orders, and add a dummy variable called "Party." (This variable takes the value one for months with a factory-sponsored party, and zero otherwise.) Prepare a flexible budget for the 12 months using the results of this regression. Discuss the implications of using this new regression for decision making.

CMA

Problem 8-37 Participative versus Imposed Budgeting

An effective budget converts the goals and objectives of an organization into data. The budget serves as a blueprint for management's plans. The budget is also the basis for control. Management performance can be evaluated by comparing actual results with the budget.

Thus, creating the budget is essential for the successful operation of an organization. Finding the resources to implement the budget—that is, moving from a starting point to the ultimate goal—requires the extensive use of human resources. How managers perceive their roles in the process of budgeting is important to the successful use of the budget as an effective tool for planning, communicating, and controlling.

Required:

1. Discuss the behavioral implications of planning and control when a company's management employs: (a) an imposed budgetary approach, and (b) a participative budgetary approach.

2. Communications plays an important role in the budgetary process whether a participative or an imposed budgetary approach is used.

   a. Discuss the differences between communication flows in these two budgetary approaches.

   b. Discuss the behavioral implications associated with the communication process for each of the budgetary approaches. *(CMA adapted)*

CMA

Problem 8-38 Information for Budgeting, Ethics

Norton Company, a manufacturer of infant furniture and carriages, is in the initial stages of preparing the annual budget for the coming year. Scott Ford has recently joined Norton's accounting staff and is interested in learning as much as possible about the company's budgeting process. During a recent lunch with Marge Atkins, sales manager, and Pete Granger, production manager, Ford initiated the following conversation.

FORD: "Since I'm new around here and am going to be involved with the preparation of the annual budget, I'd be interested in learning how the two of you estimate sales and production numbers."

ATKINS: "We start out very methodically by looking at recent history, discussing what we know about current accounts, potential customers, and the general state of consumer spending. Then, we add that usual dose of intuition to come up with the best forecast we can."

GRANGER: "I usually take the sales projections as the basis for my projections. Of course, we have to make an estimate of what this year's closing inventories will be, which is sometimes difficult."

FORD: "Why does that present a problem? There must have been an estimate of closing inventories in the budget for the current year."

GRANGER: "Those numbers aren't always reliable since Marge makes some adjustments to the sales numbers before passing them on to me."

FORD: "What kind of adjustments?"

ATKINS: "Well, we don't want to fall short of the sales projections so we generally give ourselves a little breathing room by lowering the initial sales projection anywhere from 5 to 10 percent."

GRANGER: "So, you can see why this year's budget is not a very reliable starting point. We always have to adjust the projected production rates as the year progresses, and of course, this changes the ending inventory estimates. By the way, we make similar adjustments to expenses by adding at least 10 percent to the estimates; I think everyone around here does the same thing."

Required:

1. Marge Atkins and Pete Granger have described the use of budgetary slack.
   a. Explain why Atkins and Granger behave in this manner, and describe the benefits they expect to realize from the use of budgetary slack.
   b. Explain how the use of budgetary slack can adversely affect Atkins and Granger.
2. As a management accountant, Rose Amin believes that the behavior described by Marge Atkins and Pete Granger may be unethical and that she may have an obligation not to support this behavior. By citing the specific standards of competence, confidentiality, integrity, and/or credibility from the "Statement of Ethical Professional Practice" (in Chapter 1), explain why the use of budgetary slack may be unethical. *(CMA adapted)*

The items that appear within this chapter that are from the CMA are Exercises 8-23, 8-26, Problems 8-33, 8-34, 8-37, and 8-38. Source: Materials from the Certified Management Accountant Examination, Copyright 1981, 1982, 1983, 1984, 1985, 1989, 1990, 1991, 1992, 1995, 1996 by the Institute of Certified Management Accountants are reprinted and/or adapted with permission.

9

Standard Costing: A Functional-Based Control Approach

After studying this chapter, you should be able to:

1 ▶ Describe how unit input standards are developed, and explain why standard costing systems are adopted.

2 ▶ Explain the purpose of a standard cost sheet.

3 ▶ Compute and journalize the direct materials and direct labor variances, and explain how they are used for control.

4 ▶ Compute overhead variances three different ways, and explain overhead accounting.

5 ▶ Calculate mix and yield variances for direct materials and direct labor.

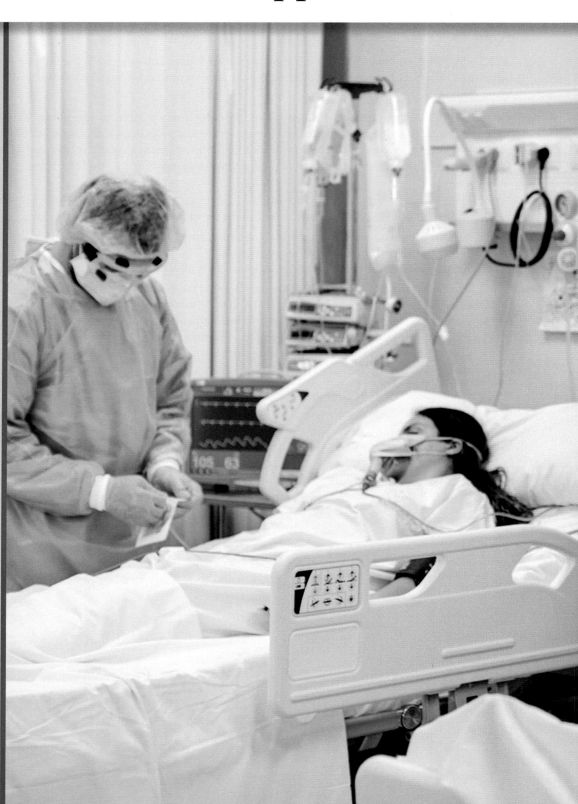

iStockphoto/Morsa Images

STANDARD COSTING AND VARIANCES

at Advocate Aurora Health

The explosion of coronavirus cases in the United States in March 2020 led to significant changes in the way hospitals were able to do business. All elective medical procedures were put on hold, while resources were poured into the emergency rooms and intensive care units. While doctors, nurses, and respiratory therapists scrambled to care for an influx of patients, hospital accountants worked hard to understand how costs and revenues were changing and how best to adapt to them.

Advocate Aurora Health, serving eastern Wisconsin, saw revenues declining $168 million in March. In April, "estimated revenues were down approximately 51 percent, almost a $524 million unfavorable variance from budget," they reported.[1]

The sophisticated budgeting and standard costing techniques used by modern health centers allowed them to get early warning of looming financial problems. In April, the Illinois Health and Hospital Association estimated that the state's more than 200 hospitals were losing a total of $1.4 billion a month amid COVID-19, with outpatient revenues down 50 to 70 percent. As a result, organizations like Advocate Aurora Health, Loyola Medicine, and the University of Chicago Medical Center have had to cut costs. Many have sharply cut CEO and senior administrators' pay, eliminated bonuses, and furloughed workers. Some hospitals have postponed capital improvement projects.

By May 2020, with state restrictions loosening, hospitals and ambulatory surgical centers began to perform inpatient and outpatient procedures. However, it was not back to business as usual. Medical facilities had to use more personal protective equipment (PPE), such as masks and surgical gowns. Patients had to be tested for COVID-19 within 72 hours of scheduled procedures and so on. As a result, the cost of the procedures increased, contributing to increased losses.

Standard costing and variance analysis are helping medical facilities to keep a handle on the costs of materials, labor and overhead.[2] As you read this chapter, you will notice that there are a number of ways actual materials used, for example, may differ from what is expected. In this case, unit prices are rising, unit quantities used are rising (nurses and doctors need much more PPE), and the mix of materials is tending toward the more expensive—as face shields and N95 masks must replace simple surgical masks. Their accountants are busy revising standard costs to reflect changes in the environment. For example, PPE is in high demand, and prices of masks, gowns, and gloves have risen precipitously. Budgets for the rest of the year are being revised, and top administration is tasked with the necessity of finding new sources of revenue as well as areas for cost reduction.

---

1 Stephanie Goldberg, "Hospital CEOs Take Pay Cuts amid COVID-19," Modern Healthcare, May 11, 2020, https://www.modernhealthcare.com/finance/hospital-ceos-take-pay-cuts-amid-covid-19, accessed August 31, 2020.

2 Sales, revenue, and profit variances are covered in Chapter 18.

Budgets help managers in planning and setting standards that are used to control and evaluate managerial performance. In Chapter 8, we saw that budgets can be classified as static or flexible. Static budgets are not very useful for assessing efficiency; their main value is assessing whether or not the targeted level of activity is achieved and, thus, provide some insight concerning managerial effectiveness. Flexible budgets evaluate efficiency by comparing the actual costs and actual revenues with the corresponding budgeted amounts for the *same* level of activity. These flexible budget variances generate important feedback for managers but fail to reveal whether the sources of the variances are attributable to input prices, input quantities, or both.

DEVELOPING UNIT INPUT STANDARDS

Although flexible budget variances provide significant information for control, developing standards for input prices and input quantities allows a more detailed understanding of the sources of these variances. **Price standards** specify how much should be paid for the quantity of the input to be used. **Quantity standards** specify how much of the input should be used per unit of output. The **unit standard cost** is defined as the product of these two standards: Standard price × Standard quantity or ($SP \times SQ$).

For example, Helado Company, a manufacturer of specialty ice creams and frozen yogurts, may decide that 25 ounces of yogurt should be used for every quart of frozen yogurt produced (the quantity standard) and that the price to be paid for the yogurt should be $0.04 per ounce (the price standard). The standard cost of the yogurt per quart of frozen yogurt is then $1.00 ($0.04 × 25). The standard cost of yogurt per quart can be used to predict what the total cost of yogurt should be as the activity level varies; it thus becomes a flexible budget formula. If 20,000 quarts of frozen yogurt are produced, the total expected cost of yogurt is $20,000 ($1.00 × 20,000); if 30,000 quarts are produced, the total expected cost of yogurt is $30,000 ($1.00 × 30,000). Standard costs, therefore, facilitate budgeting, but the input price and quantity standards will also allow us to obtain a more detailed analysis of the flexible budget variance.

Establishing Standards

Developing standards requires significant input from a variety of sources. Historical experience, engineering studies, and input from operating personnel are three potential sources of quantitative standards. Historical experience should be used with caution because relying on input-output relationships from the past may perpetuate operating inefficiencies. Engineers and operating personnel can provide valuable insights concerning efficient levels of input quantities. Similar comments can be made about input price standards. Price standards are the joint responsibility of operations, purchasing, personnel, and accounting. Operations determine the quality of the inputs required; personnel and purchasing are responsible for acquiring the input quality requested at the lowest price. Market forces, trade unions, and other external forces limit the range of choices for price standards. In setting price standards, purchasing must consider discounts, freight, and quality; personnel must consider payroll taxes, fringe benefits, and qualifications. Accounting is responsible for recording price standards and for preparing reports that compare actual performance to the standard.

Standards are often classified as either *ideal* or *currently attainable*. **Ideal standards** demand maximum efficiency and can be achieved only if everything operates perfectly. No machine breakdowns, slack, or lack of skill (even momentarily) are allowed. **Currently attainable standards** can be achieved under efficient operating conditions. Allowance is made for normal breakdowns, interruptions, less than perfect skill, and so on. These standards are demanding but achievable. One cautionary observation about standards should be made. If standards are too tight and never achievable, workers become frustrated, and performance levels decline. However, challenging but achievable standards can lead to higher performance levels—particularly when the individuals subject to the standards have participated in their creation.

Kaizen Standards

Another type of standard, a *kaizen* standard, is also possible. **Kaizen standards** are continuous improvement standards. They reflect planned improvement and are a type of currently attainable standard. Kaizen standards have a cost reduction focus and, because of their emphasis on continuous improvement, are constantly changing. Kaizen standards are discussed in detail in Chapter 12. This chapter focuses on the more traditional standard cost system.

Standards and Activity-Based Costing Standards also play an important role in activity-based systems. An activity's cost is determined by the amount of resources consumed by each activity. Standard consumption patterns are identified based on historical experience. The purpose of standards in this case is to facilitate cost assignments; standards used in this sense were discussed in Chapter 4. Activity-based systems also use standards for control, where control is specifically defined as cost reduction. Activities are classified as either value-added or non-value-added. This activity-based approach to control is described in Chapter 12.

Usage of Standard Costing Systems

Standard costing systems are widely used. For example, according to one survey, 74 percent of the respondents were using a standard costing system, with the usage emphasis being placed on planning and control.[3] Several reasons for adopting a standard costing system include managing costs, improving planning and control, facilitating decision making, and facilitating product costing.

Cost Management Standard costing allows managers to manage costs by establishing standards that reflect efficient operating conditions. Standards also help managers understand what needs to be done to improve current and future performance. Furthermore, for firms concerned with continuous improvement, kaizen standards are useful aids in achieving significant cost reductions.

Planning and Control Standard costing systems enhance planning and control and improve performance measurement. Unit standards are a fundamental requirement for a flexible budgeting system, which is a key feature of a meaningful planning and control system. Budgetary control systems compare actual costs with budgeted costs by computing variances, the difference between the actual and planned costs for the actual level of activity. By developing unit price and quantity standards, an overall variance can be decomposed into a *price variance* and a *usage* or *efficiency variance*. By performing this decomposition, a manager has more information. For example, a manager can tell whether the variance is due to differences between planned prices and actual prices, to differences between planned usage and actual usage, or to both. The use of efficiency variances enhances operational control. Additionally, by breaking out the price variance, over which managers have little control, the system provides an improved measure of managerial efficiency.

Decision Making and Product Costing Standard costing systems are useful for decision making and product costing. For example, standard costing systems provide readily available unit cost information that can be used for pricing decisions. This is particularly useful for companies that engage in extensive bidding and for companies that are paid on a cost-plus basis. Standard product costs are determined using quantity and price standards for direct materials, direct labor, and overhead. In contrast, a normal costing system predetermines overhead costs for the purpose of product costing but assigns direct materials and direct labor to products by

Exhibit 9.1   Cost Assignment Approaches

	Manufacturing Costs		
	Direct Materials	**Direct Labor**	**Overhead**
Actual costing system	Actual	Actual	Actual
Normal costing system	Actual	Actual	Budgeted
Standard costing system	Standard	Standard	Standard

using actual costs. An actual costing system assigns the actual costs of all three manufacturing inputs to products. Exhibit 9.1 summarizes these three cost assignment approaches.

Standard costing also simplifies product costing for firms in process industries. For example, if a process-costing system uses standard costing to assign product costs, there is no need to compute a unit cost for each equivalent unit-cost category. A standard unit cost would exist for direct materials, transferred-in materials, and conversion costs categories.[4] Usually, a standard process-costing system will follow the equivalent-unit calculation of the FIFO approach. That is, *current* equivalent units of work are calculated. By calculating current equivalent units of work, current actual production costs can be compared with standard costs (costs allowed for current production) for control purposes.

Sustainability in the Restaurant Industry

Setting standard quantities and costs is important for the restaurant industry. Head chefs and owners need to know about what it costs to cook and serve a meal. Unfortunately, one important component of that cost is food waste. All food cost goes into the expected quantities, even if some of the purchases go bad or are uneaten by customers. A 2013 study found that there is nearly a 16 percent food loss across the industry. This is even more significant given the relatively thin margins generated by restaurants. A reduction in food waste not only reduces waste in landfills, but is also a non-value-added cost whose reduction goes directly to the bottom line. So how do restaurants attempt to reduce food waste? There are two areas of focus: back of the house and front of the house.[5]

Back of the house refers to the kitchen and areas other than the dining area. The head chef creates menus that use foods on hand, develops specials that use up any leftovers from the night before, and recycles waste that cannot be used. Any fine dining restaurant worth its salt has a stockpot going at all times on a back burner. Peelings and leftover bits of onions, carrots, and other vegetables go into the stockpot to make stock that can be used in gravies, sauces, and soups. Even better, any leftover stock can be frozen for later use. Fast food restaurants, such as **Darden Restaurants** (Red Lobster, Olive Garden, etc.), recycle used cooking oil and sell it for reuse in bio-fuel production.[6] Careful attention to these details reduces waste considerably and reduces overall food costs.

The front of the house is the dining room. Waste here is a result of uneaten food on diners' plates. How can that be addressed? One way is to ensure that adequately sized take-home boxes are available and encouraged. Additionally, if portions are too large, waste can be reduced by downsizing them or offering half plates.

Taken together, these measures reduce waste and lead to tighter food standards that help the restaurant in budgeting and profit analysis.

---

4 If you have not read the chapter on process costing (Chapter 6), the discussion on the merits of standard costing will not be as meaningful. However, the point being made is still relevant. Standard costing can produce useful computational savings.

5 Jan Lee, "It's Time to Rethink Restaurant Food Waste," *Triple Pundit*, November 5, 2015, http://www.triplepundit .com/special/food-waste/its-time-to-rethink-food-waste-in-restaurants/#

6 Mary Mazzoni, "Red Lobster, Olive Garden Recycle Cooking Oil," *Earth 911*, December 4, 2012, http://earthnew .wpengine.com/food/red-lobster-olive-garden-recycle-fryer-oil/. Darden Waste Reduction, https://www.darden.com /citizenship/planet/waste-reduction, accessed June 14, 2020.

STANDARD COST SHEETS

OBJECTIVE 2
Explain the purpose of a standard cost sheet.

Standard costing systems can be used in both manufacturing and service organizations. Both products and services use inputs such as direct materials, direct labor, and overhead. Standard costing simply establishes price and quantity standards for these inputs regardless of whether the inputs are associated with tangible or intangible products. To illustrate standard costing for a service setting, consider a hospital. Hospital costing systems often use a homogeneous work unit called a relative value unit (*RVU*). An *RVU* measures the relative amount of time required to perform a procedure. For example, a test with an *RVU* of three will take three times as long to perform as a test with an *RVU* of one. Historical standards can be computed by dividing the variable direct labor costs of a hospital department by the number of *RVU*s performed by that department. This standard direct labor cost per *RVU* can then be multiplied by the *RVU*s of a given procedure to obtain the standard direct labor cost for that procedure.[7]

Standard costs are developed for direct materials, direct labor, and overhead used in producing a product or service. The total of these standard costs yields the **standard cost per unit**. The **standard cost sheet** provides the detail underlying the standard unit cost. To illustrate, let us develop a standard cost sheet for a quart of deluxe strawberry frozen yogurt, produced by Helado Company. The production of the strawberry frozen yogurt begins by creating two different mixtures. The first mixture consists of milk and gelatin. These two ingredients are mixed, heated, and then cooled. The second mixture consists of yogurt, cream, and crushed strawberries. The two mixtures are blended and mixed well. This final mixture is then poured into a one-quart container and frozen. The process is automated. Direct labor is used to operate the equipment and inspect the product for consistency and flavor. The standard cost sheet is given in Exhibit 9.2.

Five materials are used to produce the deluxe strawberry frozen yogurt: yogurt, strawberries, milk, cream, and gelatin. The container in which the yogurt is placed is also classified as a direct material. Direct labor consists of machine operators (who also inspect). Variable overhead,

Description	Standard Price		Standard Usage		Standard Cost	Subtotal
Direct materials:						
Yogurt	$ 0.04	×	25 oz.	=	$1.00	
Strawberries	0.02	×	10 oz.	=	0.20	
Milk	0.03	×	8 oz.	=	0.24	
Cream	0.05	×	4 oz.	=	0.20	
Gelatin	0.02	×	1 oz.	=	0.02	
Container	0.06	×	1	=	0.06	
Total direct materials						$1.72
Direct labor:						
Machine operators	16.00	×	0.01 hr.	=	$0.16	
Total direct labor						0.16
Overhead:						
Variable overhead	12.00	×	0.01 hr.	=	$0.12	
Fixed overhead	40.00	×	0.01 hr.	=	0.40	
Total overhead						0.52
Total standard unit cost						$2.40

Exhibit 9.2 Standard Cost Sheet for Deluxe Strawberry Frozen Yogurt

---

7 For an interesting description of how historical labor standards can be developed in a hospital setting, see Richard D. McDermott, Kevin D. Stocks, and Joan Ogden, *Code Blue* (Syracuse, Utah: Traemus Books, 2000): 212–221.

applied using direct labor hours, is made up of three costs: gas (used in cooking), electricity (used to operate the equipment), and water (used for cleaning). Fixed overhead, also applied using direct labor hours, consists of salaries, depreciation, taxes, and insurance. Notice that 37 ounces of liquids (yogurt, milk, and cream) are used to produce a quart of frozen yogurt. This extra input is needed for two reasons. First, some liquid is lost through evaporation. Second, Helado wants slightly more than 32 ounces of frozen yogurt placed in each container to ensure customer satisfaction and to meet the requirements for each state's office of weights and measures.

Exhibit 9.2 reveals other important insights. The standard usage for variable and fixed overhead is tied to the direct labor standards. For variable overhead, the rate is $12.00 per direct labor hour. Since one quart of frozen yogurt uses 0.01 direct labor hour, the variable overhead cost assigned to a quart is $0.12 ($12.00 × 0.01). For fixed overhead, the rate is $40 per direct labor hour, making the fixed overhead cost per quart $0.40 ($40 × 0.01). Using direct labor hours as the only driver to assign overhead reveals that Helado uses a traditional, volume-based cost accounting system.

The standard cost sheet reveals the quantity of each input that should be used to produce one unit of output. The unit quantity standards can be used to compute the total amount of inputs allowed for the actual output. This computation is an essential component in computing efficiency variances. A manager should be able to compute the **standard quantity of materials allowed** (*SQ*) and the **standard hours allowed** (*SH*) for the actual output. This computation must be done for every class of direct material and for every class of direct labor. **Example 9.1** shows how and why the standard amounts for actual production are computed.

EXAMPLE 9.1

The HOW and WHY of Computing Standard Quantities Allowed (*SQ* and *SH*)

Information:

During the first week of April, Helado Company produced 20,000 quarts of deluxe strawberry frozen yogurt. Exhibit 9.2 shows that the unit quantity standard is 25 ounces of yogurt per quart and that the unit standard is 0.01 direct labor hour per quart.

> **Why:**
> Unit standards must be converted to the standard quantities of inputs allowed for actual production in order to determine how much of each resource is expected to be used. Managers can use the standard quantities allowed in planning (to estimate how much will be required for planned production) or in control (to compare with the actual quantities used).

Required:

1. Calculate the ounces of yogurt that should have been used (*SQ*) for the production of 20,000 quarts of frozen yogurt.

2. Calculate the hours of direct labor that should have been used (*SH*) for the production of 20,000 quarts of frozen yogurt.

3. *What if* 22,000 quarts of frozen yogurt had actually been produced in the first week of April? Would the standard quantities of yogurt (in ounces) and of direct labor hours be higher or lower than the amounts calculated in Requirements 1 and 2? What would the new standard quantities be?

Solution:

1. Yogurt allowed:

    SQ = Unit quantity standard $\times$ Actual output

    = 25 $\times$ 20,000

    = 500,000 ounces

2. Operator hours allowed:

    SH = Unit labor standard $\times$ Actual output

    = 0.01 $\times$ 20,000

    = 200 direct labor hours

3. If 22,000 quarts were produced instead of 20,000, the standard quantities allowed would be higher, since the production of more frozen yogurt takes more yogurt and more direct labor hours. The SQ for yogurt would be 550,000 ounces (25 $\times$ 22,000), and the SH for direct labor hours would be 220 hours (0.01 $\times$ 22,000).

VARIANCE ANALYSIS AND ACCOUNTING: DIRECT MATERIALS AND DIRECT LABOR

OBJECTIVE ◀ 3

Compute and journalize the direct materials and direct labor variances, and explain how they are used for control.

A flexible budget can be used to identify the direct material or direct labor input costs that should have been incurred for the actual level of activity. This planned cost is obtained by multiplying the amount of input allowed for the actual output by the standard unit price. Letting SP be the standard unit price of an input and SQ the standard quantity of inputs allowed for the actual output, the planned or budgeted input cost is $SP \times SQ$. The actual input cost is $AP \times AQ$, where AP is the actual price per unit of the input, and AQ is the actual quantity of input used. The **total budget variance** is the difference between the actual cost of the input and its standard cost:

$$\text{Total budget variance} = (AP \times AQ) - (SP \times SQ)$$

The total budget variance measures the difference between the actual cost of direct materials and direct labor and their budgeted costs for the actual level of activity. While it is interesting to know whether or not the actual costs were as planned, the detail of the standard cost card allows managers to determine what aspects of total cost were different than planned. The next sections discuss the way that the total variances can be decomposed into the price and usage variances for direct materials and the rate and efficiency variances for direct labor.

Calculating the Direct Materials Price Variance and Direct Materials Usage Variance

The total budget variance can be broken down into price and usage variances. **Price (rate) variance** is the difference between the actual and standard unit prices of an input multiplied by the actual quantity of input. **Usage (efficiency) variance** is the difference between the actual and standard quantity of input multiplied by the standard unit price of the input. An **unfavorable (U) variance** occurs whenever actual prices or usage of inputs are greater than standard prices or usage. When the opposite occurs, a **favorable (F) variance** is obtained. Every nonzero variance must be tagged as favorable or unfavorable. This lets the manager know the direction of the deviation from standard.

The price and usage variances can be computed using formulas or a graphical, three-pronged approach. The choice is up to the individual; some people find the formulas more meaningful, others appreciate the graphical approach. Both approaches will be illustrated in the Example features of this chapter. First, we will set up the formulas for the direct materials price and usage variances.

Let:

AP = Actual price per unit

SP = Standard price per unit

AQ = Actual quantity of direct material used in production

SQ = Standard quantity of input for actual quantity of output

MPV = Materials price variance

MPV = Materials usage variance

The **direct materials price variance (MPV)** is the difference between what was actually paid for direct materials and what would have been paid for the actual quantity bought if it had been bought at the standard price. Thus, the materials price variance is:

$$MPV = (AP \times AQ) - (SP \times AQ)$$

or, factoring, we have:

$$MPV = (AP - SP)AQ$$

The MPV is calculated as the difference between actual and standard prices multiplied by the actual quantity. If the actual price is greater than standard, the MPV is U (unfavorable). If the actual price is less than the standard price, the MPV is F (favorable).

The **direct materials usage variance (MUV)** is the difference between the amount of materials actually used and what should have been used for the actual quantity of units produced multiplied by the standard price. Thus, the materials usage variance is:

$$MUV = (SP \times AQ) - (SP \times SQ)$$

or, factoring, we have:

$$MUV = (AQ - SQ)SP$$

The MUV is quickly calculated as the difference between actual and standard amounts of direct materials multiplied by the standard price. If the actual quantity is greater than the standard quantity, the MUV is U (unfavorable). If the actual quantity is less than standard, the MUV is F (favorable). **Example 9.2** shows the how and why of calculating the direct materials price and usage variances.

EXAMPLE 9.2

The HOW and WHY of Computing the Direct Materials Price Variance (MPV) and Direct Materials Usage Variance (MUV)

Information:
Helado Company provided the following information for the production of deluxe strawberry frozen yogurt during the month of April:

Actual production: 30,000 quarts

Actual yogurt usage: 745,000 ounces (no beginning or ending yogurt inventory)

Actual price paid per ounce of yogurt: $0.05

EXAMPLE 9.2

(Continued)

Recall from Exhibit 9.2 that the unit quantity standard is 25 ounces of yogurt per quart, the standard price of yogurt is $0.04 per ounce, and the direct labor standard is 0.01 direct labor hour per quart.

Why:

The total direct materials variance can be due to a difference between actual and planned prices for the materials, between actual quantity used versus the standard quantity, or a combination of both. Computing the direct materials price variance (*MPV*) and the direct materials usage variance (*MUV*) tells managers whether the difference is due to price, usage, or both. Any variance can be investigated further to see if there is a problem.

Required:

1. Calculate the ounces of yogurt that should have been used (*SQ*) for the actual production of frozen yogurt for the month of April.

2. Calculate the direct materials price variance (*MPV*) and the direct materials usage variance (*MUV*) for April using the formula approach.

3. Calculate the direct materials price variance (*MPV*) and the direct materials usage variance (*MUV*) for April using the graphical approach.

4. Calculate the total direct materials variance for yogurt for April.

5. ***What if*** the actual price paid in April was $0.04 per ounce of yogurt? What impact would that have had on the materials price variance (*MPV*)? On the materials usage variance (*MUV*)?

Solution:

1. Yogurt allowed:

   SQ = Unit quantity standard $\times$ Actual output

       = 25 $\times$ 30,000

       = 750,000 ounces

2. Formulas (recommended approach for materials variances because materials purchases may differ from materials used in production):

   Materials price variance $(MPV) = (AP - SP)AQ = (\$0.05 - \$0.04)745,000$

                                    = $\$0.01 \times 745,000 = \$7,450$ U

   Materials usage variance $(MUV) = (AQ - SQ)SP = (745,000 - 750,000)\$0.04$

                                    = $(5,000 \times \$0.04) = \$200$ F

EXAMPLE 9.2

(Continued)

3.

4. Total direct materials variance $= (AP \times AQ) - (SP \times SQ) = MPV + MUV$

$$= (\$0.05 \times 745{,}000) - (\$0.04 \times 750{,}000)$$

$$= \$37{,}250 - \$30{,}000$$

$$= \$7{,}250 \text{ U}$$

Notice that $7,250 U is also equal to the sum of the *MPV* and *MUV*.

$(MPV + MUV) = \$7{,}450 \text{ U} + \$200 \text{ F}$

$\qquad\qquad\qquad = \$7{,}250 \text{ U}$

5. If the actual price was $0.04 per ounce, it would be exactly equal to the standard price and the materials price variance would be zero. There would be no impact on the materials usage variance because the actual price is not used in that computation.

Example 9.2 calculated only the *MPV* and *MUV* for one input, yogurt, in order to simplify the example. In actuality, Helado would calculate these two variances for each type of direct material used.

Timing of the Price Variance Computation   The direct materials price variance can be computed at one of two points: (1) when the direct materials are issued for use in production or (2) when they are purchased. Computing the price variance at the point of purchase is preferable. It is better to have information on variances earlier rather than later. The more timely the information, the more likely proper managerial action can be taken. Old information is often useless information. Direct materials may sit in inventory for weeks or months before they are needed in production. By the time the direct materials price variance is computed, signaling a problem, it may be too late to take corrective action. Or, even if corrective action is still possible, the delay may cost the company thousands of dollars.

If the direct materials price variance is computed at the point of purchase, then *AQ* needs to be redefined as the actual quantity of direct materials *purchased*, rather than actual direct materials used. Since the direct materials purchased may differ from the direct materials used, the overall direct materials budget variance is not necessarily the sum of the direct materials price variance and the direct materials usage variance. When the direct materials purchased are all used in production for the period in which the variances are calculated, the two variances will equal the total budget variance. If this is not the case, then the only way to compute each direct materials variance is by using the formula approach. The three-pronged approach will not work.

The direct materials price variance can give managers an early warning of price increases that will impact the production and sale of product. For example, a close watch on the price of hops (responsible for the characteristic bitterness and aroma of beer) allowed beer makers to anticipate the impact of escalating prices on the sale of the product. Some brewers used the information to find substitute hops varieties. Others investigated long-term contracts to lock in a stable price. Still others began instituting gradual price increases of the final product.[8]

Timing of the Direct Materials Usage Variance Computation The direct materials usage variance should be computed as direct materials are issued for production. To facilitate this process, many companies use three forms: a standard bill of materials, color-coded excessive usage forms, and color-coded returned-materials forms. The **standard bill of materials** identifies the quantity of direct materials that should be used to produce a predetermined quantity of output. A standard bill of materials for Helado Company is illustrated in Exhibit 9.3.

The standard bill of materials acts as a materials requisition form. The production manager presents this form to the materials manager and receives the standard quantity allowed for the indicated output. If the production manager has to requisition more direct materials later,

Product: Quarts of Deluxe Strawberry Frozen Yogurt		Output: 30,000 Quarts
Direct Material	**Unit Standard**	**Total Requirements**
Yogurt	25 oz.	750,000 oz.
Strawberries	10 oz.	300,000 oz.
Milk	8 oz.	240,000 oz.
Cream	4 oz.	120,000 oz.
Gelatin	1 oz.	30,000 oz.
Container	1 container	30,000 containers

Exhibit 9.3 Standard Bill of Materials

8 David Kesmodel and Janet Adamy, "Why Price Increases Are Brewing for Craft Beers," *The Wall Street Journal* (October 5, 2007): B1.

the excessive usage form is used. This form, different in color from the standard bill of materials, provides immediate feedback to the production manager that excess direct materials are being used. If, on the other hand, fewer direct materials are used than the standard requires, the production manager can return the leftover direct materials, along with the returned-materials form. This form also provides immediate feedback.

Accounting for Direct Materials Price and Usage Variances

As a general rule, in a *standard costing system, all inventories are carried at standard*. Actual costs are never entered into an inventory account. Following this general rule means that the direct materials price variance is computed at the point of purchase. In recording variances, unfavorable variances are always debits, and favorable variances are always credits. The general form of the journal entry associated with the purchase of direct materials for a standard costing system follows. This entry assumes an unfavorable *MPV* and that *AQ* is defined as direct materials purchased.

Materials	$SP \times AQ$	
Direct Materials Price Variance	$(AP - SP)AQ$	
Accounts Payable		$AP \times AQ$

For the Helado Company example, the entry pertaining to the acquisition of yogurt would be:

Materials	29,800	
Direct Materials Price Variance	7,450	
Accounts Payable		37,250

The direct materials usage variance is recognized when direct materials are issued. The standard cost of the direct materials issued is assigned to Work in Process. The general form for the entry to record the issuance and usage of direct materials, assuming an unfavorable *MUV*, is as follows:

Work in Process	$SQ \times SP$	
Direct Materials Usage Variance	$(AQ - SQ)SP$	
Materials		$AQ \times SP$

The entry to record Helado's usage of yogurt during the first week of May is as follows:

Work in Process	30,000	
Direct Materials Usage Variance		200
Materials		29,800

Calculating Direct Labor Variances   The rate (price) and efficiency (usage) variances for direct labor can be calculated using either the graphical, three-pronged approach or a formula approach. We will present the formulas for the direct labor rate variance and the direct labor efficiency variance. **Example 9.3** shows the how and why of calculating these variances using the formula and graphical approaches.

Information:

Helado Company provided the following information for the production of deluxe strawberry frozen yogurt during the month of April:

Actual production: 30,000 quarts

Actual direct labor hours worked: 325 hours

Actual rate paid per hour to direct labor: $15.90

Recall from Exhibit 9.2 that the unit quantity standard is 0.01 hour of direct labor per quart and that the standard wage rate is $16 per direct labor hour.

> **Why:**
> The total direct labor variance can be due to a difference between actual and planned wage rates for direct labor, between actual hours worked versus the standard hours allowed for actual production, or a combination of both. Computing the direct labor rate variance (*LRV*) and the direct labor efficiency variance (*LEV*) tells managers whether the difference is due to wage rates, hours worked, or both. Any variance can be investigated further to see if there is a problem.

Required:

1. Calculate the direct labor hours that should have been worked (*SH*) for the actual production of frozen yogurt for the month of April.

2. Calculate the direct labor rate variance (*LRV*) and the direct labor efficiency variance (*LEV*) for April using the formula approach.

3. Calculate the direct labor rate variance (*LRV*) and the direct labor efficiency variance (*LEV*) for April using the graphical approach.

4. Calculate the total direct labor variance for yogurt for April.

5. *What if* only 295 hours were actually worked in April? What impact would that have had on the direct labor rate variance (*LRV*)? On the direct labor efficiency variance (*LEV*)?

Solution:

1. Direct labor hours at standard for actual production:

   SH = Unit quantity standard $\times$ Actual output

        = 0.01 $\times$ 30,000

        = 300 hours

2. Formulas:

   $$\text{Labor rate variance } (LRV) = (AR - SR)AH = (\$15.90 - \$16.00)325$$

   $$= \$0.10 \times 325 = \$32.50 \text{ F}$$

   $$\text{Labor efficiency variance } (LEV) = (AH - SH)SR = (325 - 300)\$16.00$$

   $$= (25 \times \$16.00) = \$400 \text{ U}$$

EXAMPLE 9.3

(Continued)

3.

4.   Total direct labor variance $= (AR \times AH) - (SR \times SH) = LRV + LEV$

$= (\$15.90 \times 325) - (\$16.00 \times 300)$

$= \$5,167.50 - \$4,800$

$= \$367.50$ U

Notice that $\$367.50$ U is also equal to the sum of the *LRV* and *LEV*.

$(LRV + LEV) = \$32.50$ F $+ \$400$ U

$= \$367.50$ U

5.   If 295 hours had been worked in April, the direct labor rate variance would decrease to $\$29.50$ F (295 actual hours $\times \$0.10$). The direct labor efficiency variance would be favorable since 295 hours is less than the standard direct labor hours allowed for actual production. The *LEV* in that case would be $\$80$ F [(295 − 300) $\$16.00$].

Direct Labor Rate and Efficiency Variances: Formula Approach   The **direct labor rate variance** (**LRV**) computes the difference between what was paid to direct laborers and what should have been paid:

$$LRV = (AR \times AH) - (SR \times AH)$$

Or, factoring, we have:

$$LRV = (AR - SR)AH$$

where

$AR =$ Actual hourly wage rate

$SR =$ Standard hourly wage rate

$AH =$ Actual direct labor hours used

The **direct labor efficiency variance (*LEV*)** measures the difference between the direct labor hours that were actually used and the direct labor hours that should have been used:

$$LEV = (AH \times SR) - (SH \times SR)$$

Or, factoring, we have:

$$LEV = (AH - SH)SR$$

where

AH = Actual direct labor hours used

SH = Standard direct labor hours that should have been used

SR = Standard hourly wage rate

Accounting for the Direct Labor Rate and Efficiency Variances The journal entry to record the direct labor rate and efficiency variance is made simultaneously. The general form of this journal entry follows. (It assumes a favorable direct labor rate variance and an unfavorable direct labor efficiency variance.)

Work in Process	$SH \times SR$	
Direct Labor Efficiency Variance	$(AH - SH)SR$	
Direct Labor Rate Variance		$(AR - SR)AH$
Wages Payable		$AH \times AR$

Notice that only standard hours and standard rates are used to assign direct labor costs to Work in Process. Actual prices and quantities are not used. This emphasizes the principle that all inventories are carried at standard.

The journal entry for Helado's use of direct labor during the first week of May follows. The direct labor efficiency variance is unfavorable, so it is debited. The direct labor rate variance is favorable so it is credited.

Work in Process	4,800.00	
Direct Labor Efficiency Variance	400.00	
Direct Labor Rate Variance		32.50
Wages Payable		5,167.50

Investigating Direct Materials and Labor Variances

Rarely will actual performance exactly meet the established standards, nor does management expect it to do so. Random variations around the standard are expected. Because of this, management should have in mind an acceptable range of performance. When variances are within this range, they are assumed to be caused by random factors. When a variance falls outside this range, the deviation is likely to be caused by nonrandom factors, either factors that managers can control or factors they cannot control. In the noncontrollable case, managers need to revise the standard. For the controllable case, an investigation should be undertaken only if the expected benefits of investigating and correcting the problem are greater than the expected costs. In making this assessment, a manager must consider whether a variance will recur. If so, the process may be permanently out of control, meaning that periodic savings may be achieved if corrective action is taken. For example, consider Helado's unfavorable materials price variance. Assume that investigation reveals that the unfavorable direct materials price variance was the result of purchasing higher quality strawberries than needed. In this case, a new purchasing agent mistakenly bought large, perfectly shaped strawberries suitable for decoration, rather than smaller strawberries suitable for crushing and mixing into the frozen yogurt mix. The agent was trained in the difference between grades of strawberries, and no further problems were noticed.

Because it is difficult to assess the costs and benefits of variance analysis on a case-by-case basis, many firms adopt the general guideline of investigating variances only if they fall outside an acceptable range. The acceptable range is the standard, plus or minus an allowable deviation. The top and bottom measures of the allowable range are called the **control limits**. The *upper control limit* is the standard plus the allowable deviation, and the *lower control limit* is the standard minus the allowable deviation. Current practice sets the control limits subjectively: based on past experience, intuition, and judgment, management determines the allowable deviation from standard.[9]

The control limits are usually expressed both as a percentage of the standard and as an absolute dollar amount. For example, the allowable deviation may be expressed as the lesser of 10 percent of the standard amount or $10,000. In other words, management will not accept a deviation of more than $10,000 even if that deviation is less than 10 percent of the standard. Alternatively, even if the dollar amount is less than $10,000, an investigation is required if the deviation is more than 10 percent of the standard amount. Formal statistical procedures can also be used to set the control limits. In this way, less subjectivity is involved and a manager can assess the likelihood of the variance being caused by random factors. The use of such formal procedures has gained little acceptance. **Example 9.4** shows how and why control limits can be used to guide variance investigation decisions.

EXAMPLE 9.4

The HOW and WHY of Using Control Limits to Determine When to Investigate a Variance

Information:

Standard cost: $100,000; allowable deviation is ± $10,000. Actual costs for the past six months are as follows:

June	$ 97,500	September	$102,500
July	105,000	October	107,500
August	95,000	November	112,500

> **Why:**
> Because actual costs rarely are exactly equal to standard, variances occur frequently. Investigating variances is costly. Therefore, it is useful for managers to have a rule that tells them when variances should be investigated, and when they are likely of little consequence.

Required:

1. Calculate the variance from standard for each month. Which months should be investigated?

2. *What if* the company uses a two-part rule for investigating variances? The allowable deviation is the lesser of 5 percent of the standard amount or $10,000. Now which months should be investigated?

Solution:

1. Variance for June = $100,000 − $97,500 = $2,500 F

    Variance for July = $100,000 − $105,000 = $5,000 U

---

9 Bruce R. Gaumnitz and Felix P. Kollaritsch, "Manufacturing Variances: Current Practices and Trends," *Journal of Cost Management* (Spring 1991): 58–64. In this article, the authors report that about 45–47 percent of firms use dollar or percentage control limits. Most of the remaining firms use judgment rather than any formal identification of limits.

EXAMPLE 9.4

(*Continued*)

Variance for August = $100,000 − $95,000 = $5,000 F

Variance for September = $100,000 − $102,500 = $2,500 U

Variance for October = $100,000 − $107,500 = $7,500 U

Variance for November = $100,000 − $112,500 = $12,500 U

Only November should be investigated, as its variance is greater than $10,000 from standard.

2. 5% of standard cost = 0.05 × $100,000 = $5,000

As before, November is investigated because its variance is greater than $10,000. However, now July, August, and October will also be investigated since their variances are greater than 5 percent of standard.

An example from the pharmaceutical industry may drive home the importance of variance investigation.[10] Drugs must contain a certain amount of the active ingredient, plus or minus a small percent (e.g., aspirin claiming to have five grains per tablet must really have somewhere between 90 and 110 percent of the specified amount). The **Food and Drug Administration (FDA)** is responsible for ensuring the safety and efficacy of drugs manufactured at home and abroad. An anonymous letter alerted the FDA to manufacturing problems with an antibiotic produced by a Canadian firm, **Novopharm Ltd**. Basically, the drug was too strong and could potentially destroy beneficial bacteria along with the harmful bacteria. Upon investigation, the FDA found the blending process to be "out of control." The result was that the firm stopped shipping that drug until the process could be corrected. Another FDA investigation centered on **Haimen Pharmaceutical Factory** in China. There, the FDA found the samples of an antileukemia drug to be too weak. Again, large variances from the standard triggered an investigation. Interestingly, the question of what to do about the company and the drug was not clear-cut. In this case, the FDA did not withdraw its approval because the drug was in short supply.

REAL-WORLD EXAMPLE

Responsibility for the Direct Materials Variances The responsibility for controlling the direct materials price variance is usually the purchasing agent's. Admittedly, the price of direct materials is largely beyond his or her control; however, the price variance can be influenced by such factors as quality, quantity discounts, distance of the source from the plant, and so on. These factors are often under the control of the agent. The production manager is generally responsible for direct materials usage. Minimizing scrap, waste, and rework are all ways in which the manager can ensure that the standard is met. However, at times, the cause of the variance is attributable to others outside the production area. For example, the purchase of lower quality direct materials may produce bad output. In this case, responsibility would be assigned to purchasing rather than production. Notice that data analytics are used diagnostically here, to determine why things are going in an unexpected direction.

Using the price variance to evaluate the performance of purchasing has some limitations. Emphasis on meeting or beating the standard can produce some undesirable outcomes. For example, if the purchasing agent feels pressured to produce favorable variances, he or she may purchase lower quality direct materials or acquire too much inventory in order to take advantage of quantity discounts. As with the price variance, applying the usage variance to evaluate performance can lead to undesirable behavior. For example, a production manager who feels pressure to produce a favorable variance might allow a defective unit to be transferred to

---

10 The examples given here are taken from an article by Christopher Drew, "Medicines from Afar Raise Safety Concerns," *The New York Times* (October 29, 1995): A1, A16.

finished goods. While this avoids the problem of wasted direct materials, it may create customer relations problems once a customer gets stuck with the bad product.

Responsibility for the Direct Labor Variances   Direct labor rates are largely determined by such external forces as labor markets and union contracts. When direct labor rate variances occur, they often do so because an average wage rate is used for the rate standard or because more skilled and more highly paid laborers are used for less skilled tasks. Wage rates for a particular direct labor activity often differ among workers because of differing levels of seniority. Rather than selecting direct labor rate standards reflecting those different levels, an average wage rate is often used. As the seniority mix changes, the average rate changes, giving rise to a direct labor rate variance. This calls for a new standard to reflect the new seniority mix. Controllability is not assignable for this cause of a direct labor rate variance.

The *use* of direct labor, however, is controllable by the production manager. The use of more skilled workers to perform less skilled tasks (or vice versa) is a decision that a production manager consciously makes. For this reason, responsibility for the direct labor rate variance is generally assigned to the individuals who decide how direct labor will be used. The same is true of the direct labor efficiency variance. As is true of all variances, however, once the cause is discovered, responsibility may be assigned elsewhere. For example, frequent breakdowns of machinery may cause interruptions and nonproductive use of direct labor. But the responsibility for these breakdowns may be faulty maintenance. If so, the maintenance manager should be charged with the unfavorable direct labor efficiency variance.

Production managers may be tempted to engage in dysfunctional behavior if too much emphasis is placed on the direct labor variances. For example, to avoid losing hours and using additional hours because of possible rework, a production manager could deliberately transfer defective units to finished goods.

REAL-WORLD EXAMPLE

Developing Big Data in the Restaurant Industry

The overriding importance of food costs and waste generation in the restaurant industry has led the **National Restaurant Association** to endorse an automated food waste monitoring system called Lean Path 360.[11] The system allows individual restaurants to record what is thrown away when it is being discarded. Staff members record the food being thrown away, the reason for discard, and the related station (e.g., kitchen, storage areas, dining room). The data are uploaded to a dashboard that can be used by chefs and owners to analyze the data, see trends and patterns, and determine where opportunities for waste reduction exist. Chefs can adjust purchasing, production, and staff training depending on the types and value of food discarded. Food cost savings of 6 percent have been recorded.

Disposition of Direct Materials and Direct Labor Variances

Most companies dispose of variances at the end of the year by either closing them to Cost of Goods Sold or prorating them among Work in Process, Cost of Goods Sold, and Finished Goods. If the variances are immaterial, then the most expedient disposition is simply to assign them to Cost of Goods Sold. In that case, a debit balance in a variance account (indicating an overall unfavorable variance) would require an equal amount credited to that account (to bring its ending balance to zero) and an offsetting debit to Cost of Goods Sold. This debit to Cost of Goods Sold will increase the total cost, which makes sense since originally Cost of Goods Sold is carried at standard cost, but an unfavorable variance means that actual cost is greater than standard. Therefore, Cost of Goods Sold must be increased at the end of the year to reflect the

---

11   The National Restaurant Association's Conserve Program, http://conserve.restaurant.org/solutions/Leanpath

higher actual cost. Of course, favorable variances would be credited to Cost of Goods Sold to bring the standard cost down to the lower actual cost.

If the variances are considered material, then the proration option is usually exercised. This option is driven by GAAP requirements that inventories and Cost of Goods Sold be reported at actual costs. Yet, if variances are measures of inefficiency, it seems difficult to justify carrying costs of inefficiency as assets. It seems more logical to write off the costs of inefficiency as a cost of the period. When proration is done, the direct materials and direct labor variances can be assigned in proportion to the total prime costs in each of the three inventory accounts. **Example 9.5** shows how to close out the variance accounts at the end of the year and explains why this is done.

Other proration variations are possible. For example, direct materials variances could be assigned in proportion to the total direct materials cost in each account, and the direct labor variances could be assigned in proportion to the total direct labor costs. Some even argue that finer assignments of the variances may be needed. The direct materials price variance, for example, could be assigned to the *MUV*, materials inventory, work-in-process, finished goods, and cost of goods sold accounts (with the other variances assigned only to the usual three inventory accounts).

EXAMPLE 9.5

The HOW and WHY of Closing the Balances in the Variance Accounts at the End of the Year

Information:
Helado Company has the following balances in its direct materials and direct labor variance accounts at year-end:

	Debit	Credit
Direct Materials Price Variance	$45,600	
Direct Materials Usage Variance	5,800	
Direct Labor Rate Variance	4,350	
Direct Labor Efficiency Variance		$61,250

Unadjusted Cost of Goods Sold equals $982,140, unadjusted Work in Process equals $205,700, and unadjusted Finished Goods equals $143,000.

> **Why:**
> Companies may carry costs at standard throughout the year, but must restate costs and inventories at the end of the year to actual cost. Therefore, variance accounts must be closed out and their balances applied to Cost of Goods Sold (if immaterial) or prorated among Cost of Goods Sold, Work in Process, and Finished Goods.

Required:

1.   Assume that the ending balances in the variance accounts are immaterial and prepare the journal entries to close them to Cost of Goods Sold. What is the adjusted balance in Cost of Goods Sold after closing out the variances?

2.   *What if* the ending balances in the variance accounts are considered material? The prime cost in Cost of Goods Sold is $767,520, the prime cost in Work in Process is $161,200, and the prime cost in Finished Goods is $111,280. Prorate the variances among the three accounts and prepare the journal entry to close them out. What are the adjusted balances in Work in Process, Finished Goods, and Cost of Goods Sold after closing out the variances?

EXAMPLE 9.5

(Continued)

Solution:

1.

Direct Labor Efficiency Variance	61,250	
Cost of Goods Sold		61,250
Cost of Goods Sold	55,750	
Direct Materials Price Variance		45,600
Direct Materials Usage Variance		5,800
Direct Labor Rate Variance		4,350

Adjusted Cost of Goods Sold = $982,140 + $45,600 + $5,800
$$+ \$4,350 - \$61,250 = \$976,640$$

2.

	Prime Costs	Percentage of Total
Work in Process	$ 161,200	15.5%
Finished Goods	111,280	10.7
Cost of Goods Sold	767,520	73.8
Total	$1,040,000	100.0%

Total variance = $45,600 + $5,800 + $4,350 − $61,250 = $5,500 F

Direct Labor Efficiency Variance	61,250.00	
Work in Process (0.155 × $61,250)		9,493.75
Finished Goods (0.107 × $61,250)		6,553.75
Cost of Goods Sold (0.738 × $61,250)		45,202.50
Work in Process (0.155 × $55,750)	8,641.25	
Finished Goods (0.107 × $55,750)	5,965.25	
Cost of Goods Sold (0.738 × $55,750)	41,143.50	
Direct Materials Price Variance		45,600.00
Direct Materials Usage Variance		5,800.00
Direct Labor Rate Variance		4,350.00

Work in Process = $205,700 − (0.155 × $5,500) = $205,700 − $852.50
$$= \$204,847.50$$

Finished Goods = $143,000 − (0.107 × $5,500) = $143,000 − $588.50
$$= \$142,411.50$$

Cost of Goods Sold = $982,140 − (0.738 × $5,500) = $982,140 − $4,059
$$= \$978,081$$

OBJECTIVE 4

Compute overhead variances three different ways, and explain overhead accounting.

VARIANCE ANALYSIS: OVERHEAD COSTS

For direct materials and direct labor, total variances are broken down into price and efficiency variances. The total overhead variance—the difference between applied and actual overhead—is also broken down into component variances. The number of component variances computed depends on the method of variance analysis used. Common methods are the two-, three-, and four-variance methods. The four-variance method provides the most detail, and its component variances can be combined to form the variances for the two- and three-variance methods which are described later.

In analyzing overhead variances, a traditional approach is assumed. Standard overhead rates are computed in basically the same way that was described in Chapter 4. Traditional overhead rate computations rely on unit-level drivers such as direct labor hours and machine hours. The overhead analysis in this chapter assumes that direct labor hours is the only driver used to assign overhead costs to products. Thus, when we speak of variable and fixed overhead, we are assuming that it is fixed or variable with respect to direct labor hours, a unit-level driver. In Chapter 12, variance analysis is extended to a more general setting where both unit-level and non-unit-level drivers are allowed.

Four-Variance Method for Calculating Overhead Variances

The four-variance method calculates two variances for variable overhead and two variances for fixed overhead. We first divide overhead into categories: variable and fixed. Next, we look at component variances for each category. The total variable overhead variance is divided into two components: the variable overhead spending variance and the variable overhead efficiency variance. Similarly, the total fixed overhead variance is divided into two components: the fixed overhead spending variance and the fixed overhead volume variance.

Example 9.6 shows the how and why of calculating the total variable overhead variance. To illustrate the variable overhead variances, we will continue to use the Helado Company example. Variances will be constructed for the month of May.

EXAMPLE 9.6

The HOW and WHY of Calculating the Total Variable Overhead Variance

Information:

Helado Company provided the following information for the month of May:

Variable overhead rate (standard)	$12.00 per direct labor hour[a]
Actual variable overhead costs	$16,120
Actual hours worked	1,300
Quarts of deluxe strawberry frozen yogurt produced	120,000
Hours allowed for actual production	1,200[b]
Applied variable overhead	$14,400[c]

[a]See Exhibit 9.2 for the standard cost card.
[b]0.01 direct labor hour at standard × 120,000 actual quarts produced (see Exhibit 9.2 for unit standards and prices).
[c]$12.00 × 1,200 (overhead is applied using standard hours allowed).

> **Why:**
> The total variable overhead variance shows the difference between actual overhead and the amount expected given the actual level of production. Managers can see whether there is a difference and begin to understand reasons for it.

Required:

1. Calculate the total variable overhead variance.

2. *What if* actual production had been 110,000 quarts? How would that affect the total variable overhead variance?

EXAMPLE 9.6

(Continued)

Solution:

1. Total variable overhead variance

    = Actual variable overhead − (Variable overhead rate
       × Standard hours for actual production)

    = $16,120 − ($12 × 1,200) = $16,120 − $14,400

    = $1,720 U

2. If production had been only 110,000 quarts, fewer hours would have been allowed at standard and the flexible budget amount for variable overhead would be smaller. Thus, the total variable overhead variance would be a larger unfavorable variance.

As we see in Example 9.6, Helado Company has a $1,720 U total variable overhead variance. In other words, the actual spending on variable overhead is $1,720 more than the amount of variable overhead assigned to production at standard. Why did this occur? We gain more insight into this question by dividing the total variable overhead variance into the variable overhead spending variance and the variable overhead efficiency variance.

Calculating the Variable Overhead Spending Variance and Variable Overhead Efficiency Variance

The **variable overhead spending variance** measures the aggregate effect of differences in the actual variable overhead rate ($AVOR$) and the standard variable overhead rate ($SVOR$). The actual variable overhead rate is simply actual variable overhead divided by actual hours. For example, if actual variable overhead is $3,640 and actual hours worked are 1,400, this rate is $2.60 ($3,640/1,400 direct labor hours). The formula for computing the variable overhead spending variance is as follows:

$$\text{Variable overhead spending variance} = (AVOR \times AH) - (SVOR \times AH)$$
$$= (AVOR - SVOR)AH$$

Variable overhead is assumed to vary as the production volume changes. Thus, variable overhead changes in proportion to changes in the direct labor hours used. The **variable overhead efficiency variance** measures the change in variable overhead consumption that occurs because of efficient (or inefficient) use of direct labor. The efficiency variance is computed using the following formula:

$$\text{Variable overhead efficiency variance} = (SVOR \times AH) - (SVOR \times SH)$$
$$= (AH - SH)SVOR$$

Example 9.7 shows the how and why of calculating the variable overhead spending and efficiency variances. It uses both the formula approach explained above as well as the three-pronged graphical approach.

Information:

Helado Company provided the following information for the month of May:

Variable overhead rate (standard)	$12.00 per direct labor hour[a]
Actual variable overhead costs	$16,120
Actual hours worked	1,300
Quarts of deluxe strawberry frozen yogurt produced	120,000
Hours allowed for actual production	1,200[b]
Applied variable overhead	$14,400[c]

[a]See Exhibit 9.2 for the standard cost card.
[b]0.01 direct labor hour at standard × 120,000 actual quarts produced (see Exhibit 9.2 for unit standards and prices).
[c]$12.00 × 1,200 (overhead is applied using standard hours allowed).

> **Why:**
>
> The total variable overhead variance is broken into the variable overhead spending and efficiency variances. The spending variance shows the difference between the actual variable overhead rate and the standard variable overhead rate. The variable overhead efficiency variance shows the impact of a difference between actual hours worked and the standard hours that should have been worked on the variable overhead. These variances indicate where managers could begin to investigate overhead variances.

Required:

1. Calculate the variable overhead spending variance using the formula approach.

2. Calculate the variable overhead efficiency variance using the formula approach.

3. Calculate the variable overhead spending variance and variable overhead efficiency variance using the three-pronged graphical approach.

4. *What if* only 1,190 direct labor hours were actually worked in May? What impact would that have had on the variable overhead spending variance? On the variable overhead efficiency variance?

Solution:

1. Variable overhead spending variance $= (AVOR - SVOR)AH$

$$= [(\$16,120/1,300) - \$12.00]1,300$$

$$= (\$12.40 - \$12.00) \times 1,300 = \$520 \text{ U}$$

2. Variable overhead efficiency variance $= (AH - SH)SVOR$

$$= (1,300 - 1,200)\$12 = \$1,200 \text{ U}$$

EXAMPLE 9.7

(Continued)

3.

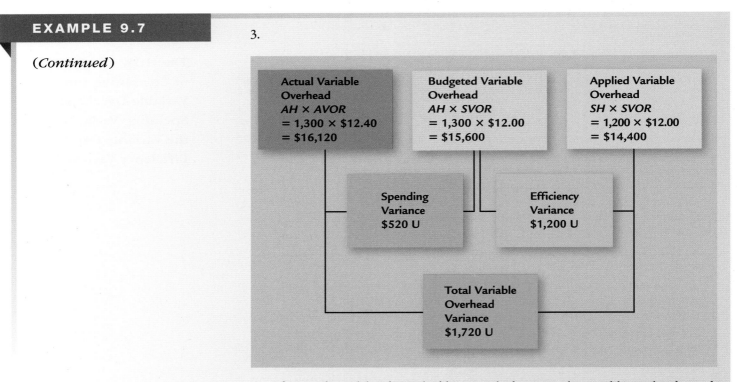

4. If 1,190 direct labor hours had been worked in May, the variable overhead spending variance would be larger (more unfavorable). However, the variable overhead efficiency variance would be favorable since 1,190 hours is less than the standard direct labor hours allowed for actual production.

Interpreting the Variable Overhead Variances

The variable overhead spending variance and the variable overhead efficiency variance give managers information they can use in controlling costs.

Interpreting the Variable Overhead Spending Variance The variable overhead spending variance is similar to the price variances of direct materials and direct labor, although there are some conceptual differences. Variable overhead is not a homogeneous input—it is made up of a large number of individual items such as indirect materials, indirect labor, electricity, maintenance, and so on. The standard variable overhead rate represents the weighted cost per direct labor hour that should be incurred for all variable overhead items. The difference between what should have been spent per hour and what actually was spent per hour is a type of price variance.

A variable overhead spending variance can arise because prices for individual variable overhead items have increased or decreased. Assume, for the moment, that the price changes of individual overhead items are the only cause of the spending variance. If the spending variance is unfavorable, then price increases for individual variable overhead items are the cause; if the spending variance is favorable, then price decreases dominate.

If the only source of the variable overhead spending variance were price changes, then it would be completely analogous to the price variances of direct materials and direct labor. Unfortunately, the spending variance also is affected by how efficiently overhead is used. Waste or inefficiency in the use of variable overhead increases the actual variable overhead cost. This increased cost, in turn, is reflected in an increased actual variable overhead rate. Thus, even if the actual prices of the individual overhead items were equal to the budgeted or standard prices, an unfavorable variable overhead spending variance could still take place. Similarly, efficiency can decrease the actual variable overhead cost and decrease the actual variable overhead rate. Efficient use of variable overhead items contributes to a favorable spending variance. If the waste effect dominates, then the net contribution will be unfavorable; if efficiency dominates, then the net contribution is favorable. Thus, the variable overhead spending variance is the result of both price and efficiency.

Many variable overhead items are affected by several responsibility centers. For example, utilities are a joint cost. Assigning the cost to a specific area of responsibility requires that cost be traced—not allocated—to the area. To the extent that consumption of variable overhead can be traced to a responsibility center, responsibility can be assigned. Consumption of indirect materials is an example of a traceable variable overhead cost.

Controllability is a prerequisite for assigning responsibility. Price changes of variable overhead items are essentially beyond the control of supervisors. If price changes are small (as they often are), the spending variance is primarily a matter of the efficient use of overhead in production, which is controllable by production supervisors. Accordingly, responsibility for the variable overhead spending variance is generally assigned to production departments.

The $520 unfavorable spending variance simply reveals that, in the aggregate, Helado Company spent more on variable overhead than expected. Even if the variance was insignificant, it reveals nothing about how well costs of individual variable overhead items were controlled. Control of variable overhead requires line-by-line analysis for each individual item. Exhibit 9.4 presents a performance report that supplies the line-by-line information essential for proper control of variable overhead. Assuming that Helado investigates any item that deviates more than 10 percent from budget, the cost of electricity and gas would be investigated. The investigation reveals that the utility companies increased the rates for electricity and water. The increase is expected to be permanent. In this case, the cause of the unfavorable variances is beyond the control of the company. The correct response is to revise the budget formula to reflect the increased cost of electricity and water.

Interpreting the Variable Overhead Efficiency Variance The variable overhead efficiency variance is directly related to the direct labor efficiency or usage variance. If variable overhead is truly driven by direct labor hours, then like the direct labor usage variance, the variable overhead efficiency variance is caused by efficient or inefficient use of direct labor. If more (or fewer) direct labor hours are used than the standard calls for, then the total variable overhead cost will increase (or decrease). The validity of the measure depends on the validity of the relationship between variable overhead costs and direct labor hours. In other words, do variable overhead costs *really* change in proportion to changes in direct labor hours? If so, responsibility for the variable overhead efficiency variance should be assigned to the individual who has responsibility for the use of direct labor: the production manager.

	Cost Formula[a]	Actual Costs	Budget[b]	Spending Variance
Helado Company Performance Report For the Month Ended May 31, 2013				
Natural gas	$ 7.60	$ 9,640	$ 9,880	$240 F
Electricity	4.00	5,850	5,200	650 U
Water	0.40	630	520	110 U
Total	$12.00	$16,120	$15,600	$520 U

[a]Per direct labor hour.
[b]The budget allowance is computed using the cost formula and 1,300 actual direct labor hours.

Exhibit 9.4

Variable Overhead Spending Variance by Item

The reasons for the unfavorable variable overhead efficiency variance are generally the same as those offered for the unfavorable labor usage variance. For example, some of the variance can be explained by the fact that overtime hours were used during the first week to make up for a bad batch of yogurt. The remaining deficiency was caused by the use of new employees who took longer to carry out tasks because of their lack of experience.

More information concerning the effect of direct labor usage on variable overhead is available in a line-by-line analysis of individual variable overhead items. This can be accomplished by comparing the budget allowance for the actual hours used with the budget allowance for the standard hours allowed for each item. A performance report that makes this comparison for all variable overhead costs is shown in Exhibit 9.5. From Exhibit 9.5, we can see that the cost of natural gas is affected most by inefficient use of direct labor. For example, inexperienced laborers may heat the mix of gelatin and milk longer than is really needed, thus using more gas.

The column labeled *Budget for Standard Hours* gives the amount that should have been spent on variable overhead for the actual output. The total of all items in this column is the applied variable overhead, the amount assigned to production in a standard costing system. Note that in a standard costing system, variable overhead is applied using the hours allowed for the actual output (*SH*), while in normal costing, variable overhead is applied using actual hours. Although not shown in Exhibit 9.5, the difference between actual costs and this column is the total variable overhead variance (underapplied by $340). Thus, the underapplied variable overhead variance is the sum of the spending and efficiency variances.

Four-Variance Analysis: The Two Fixed Overhead Variances

The total fixed overhead variance is the difference between the actual fixed overhead and the applied fixed overhead. To help managers understand why fixed overhead may differ from applied fixed overhead, the total variance can be broken down into two variances: the fixed overhead spending variance and the fixed overhead volume variance.

Calculating the Fixed Overhead Spending Variance and Fixed Overhead Volume Variance

The **fixed overhead spending variance** is defined as the difference between the actual fixed overhead and the budgeted fixed overhead. If less is spent on fixed overhead items than was budgeted, the spending variance is favorable, and vice versa. The formula for computing the fixed overhead variance follows (*AFOH* = Actual fixed overhead and *BFOH* = Budgeted fixed overhead):

$$\text{Fixed overhead spending variance} = AFOH - BFOH$$

Exhibit 9.5 Variable Overhead Spending and Efficiency Variances by Item

	Cost Formula[a]	Actual Costs	Budget[b]	Spending Variance	Budget for Standard Hours[c]	Efficiency Variance
		Helado Company **Performance Report** **For the Month Ended May 31, 2013**				
Natural gas	$ 7.60	$ 9,640	$ 9,880	$240 F	$ 9,120	$ 760 U
Electricity	4.00	5,850	5,200	650 U	4,800	400 U
Water	0.40	630	520	110 U	480	40 U
Total	$12.00	$16,120	$15,600	$520 U	$14,400	$1,200 U

[a]Per direct labor hour.
[b]The budget allowance is computed using the cost formula and 1,300 actual direct labor hours.
[c]Standard hours for actual production equal 1,200 (0.01 hours × 120,000 quarts).

Any difference between actual fixed overhead and budgeted fixed overhead must be due to a change in the amount of fixed overhead—some item has increased or decreased vis-à-vis what was expected. This difference is called a spending variance.

The **fixed overhead volume variance** is the difference between budgeted fixed overhead and applied fixed overhead.

Volume variance = Budgeted fixed overhead − Applied fixed overhead

Keep in mind that the budgeted fixed overhead was determined in advance of the year, and that the fixed overhead rate, used to apply fixed overhead to production, was calculated then as well. Thus, the fixed overhead rate is the rate that it would take to apply fixed overhead to production *assuming that the actual production equals the budgeted production.* For example, if 2,000 units are budgeted, each unit taking three direct labor hours, then 6,000 direct labor hours are budgeted. If the budgeted fixed overhead is $24,000, then the fixed overhead rate would be $4. If 2,000 units are actually produced, then $24,000 will be applied to production ($4 × 2,000 units × 3 direct labor hours). There is no volume variance. Suppose instead that 2,100 units are actually produced. Then $25,200 ($4 × 2,100 units × 3 direct labor hours) is applied, an amount that is $1,200 higher than the budgeted fixed overhead. This difference is solely due to the increased production. We refer to this variance as "favorable" and a variance in which the actual production is less than budgeted as "unfavorable." As a rule, if actual production is less than budgeted production, the volume variance will be unfavorable; if actual production is more than budgeted production, the volume variance will be favorable.

Example 9.8 shows the how and why of calculating the fixed overhead spending and volume variances.

EXAMPLE 9.8

The HOW and WHY of Computing the Fixed Overhead Spending Variance and the Fixed Overhead Volume Variance

Information:
Helado Company provided the following information for the month of May:

Budgeted/planned items for May:	
Budgeted fixed overhead	$40,000
Expected production in quarts of frozen yogurt	100,000
Expected activity in direct labor hours (0.01 × 100,000)	1,000 direct labor hours
Standard fixed overhead rate ($40,000/1,000)	$40 per direct labor hour
Actual results for May:	
Actual production of yogurt in quarts	120,000
Actual fixed overhead cost	$40,500
Standard hours allowed for actual production (0.01 × 120,000)	1,200 direct labor hours

Why:
The total fixed overhead variance is broken into the fixed overhead spending and volume variances. The spending variance shows the difference between the actual fixed overhead and the budgeted fixed overhead. The volume variance shows the impact of a difference between actual units produced and the budgeted units. These variances indicate where managers could begin to investigate overhead variances.

EXAMPLE 9.8

(Continued)

Required:

1. Calculate the fixed overhead spending variance using the formula approach.

2. Calculate the volume variance using the formula approach.

3. Calculate the fixed overhead spending variance and volume variance using the three-pronged graphical approach.

4. ***What if*** only 95,000 quarts of frozen yogurt had actually been produced in May? What impact would that have had on the fixed overhead spending variance? On the volume variance?

Solution:

1. Fixed overhead spending variance = Actual fixed overhead

$$- \text{ Budgeted fixed overhead}$$
$$= \$40,500 - \$40,000$$
$$= \$500 \text{ U}$$

2. Volume variance = Budgeted fixed overhead $-$ Applied fixed overhead

$$= \text{Budgeted fixed overhead} - (\text{Fixed overhead rate} \times SH)$$
$$= \$40,000 - (\$40 \times 1,200) = \$8,000 \text{ F}$$

3.

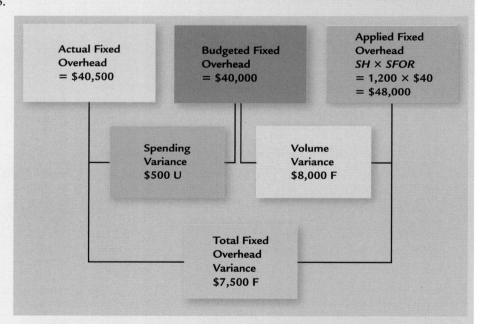

4. If 95,000 units had been produced in May, there would have been no impact on the fixed overhead spending variance (assuming that actual fixed overhead stayed the same). However, there would have been an unfavorable volume variance. That volume variance would have been $2,000 U [$40,000 − ($40 × 950)].

Interpreting the Fixed Overhead Variances

As was the case with the variable overhead variances, managers can gain useful information from the fixed overhead variances. Due to the fixed nature of the costs involved, however, managers find that it is useful to spend time looking at fixed overhead on an item-by-item basis. If this is done, then the data analytics are used descriptively, to describe what is actually happening. Then further investigation can be used diagnostically or prescriptively to correct any out-of-control processes.

Interpreting the Fixed Overhead Spending Variance Fixed overhead is made up of a number of individual items such as salaries, depreciation, taxes, and insurance. Many fixed overhead items—long-run investments, for instance—are not subject to change in the short run; consequently, fixed overhead costs are often beyond the immediate control of management. Since many fixed overhead costs are affected primarily by long-run decisions, not by changes in production levels, the budget variance is usually small. For example, depreciation, salaries, taxes, and insurance costs are not likely to be much different than planned.

Because fixed overhead is made up of many individual items, a line-by-line comparison of budgeted costs with actual costs provides more information concerning the causes of the spending variance. Exhibit 9.6 provides such a report. The report reveals that the fixed overhead spending variance is essentially in line with expectations. The fixed overhead spending variances, both on a line-item basis and in the aggregate, are relatively small (all less than 10 percent of the budgeted costs).

Interpreting the Fixed Overhead Volume Variance The volume variance occurs because the actual output differs from the budgeted output or volume. At the beginning of the month, if management had expected 120,000 quarts with 1,200 standard hours, the volume variance would not have existed. In this view, the volume variance is seen as prediction error—a measure of the inability of management to select the correct volume over which to spread fixed overhead.

If, however, the budgeted volume represented the amount that management believed *could* be produced and sold, the volume variance conveys more significant information. If the actual volume is more than the budgeted volume, the volume variance signals that a gain has occurred (relative to expectations). That gain is not equivalent, however, to the dollar value of the volume variance. The gain is equal to the increase in contribution margin on the extra units produced and sold. The volume variance, however, is positively correlated with the gain. Suppose that the contribution margin per standard direct labor hour is $100. By producing 120,000 quarts of frozen yogurt instead of 100,000 quarts, the company gained sales of 20,000 quarts. This is equivalent to 200 hours (0.01 × 20,000). At $100 per hour, the gain is $20,000 ($100 × 200). The favorable volume variance of $4,000 signals this gain but understates it. In this sense, the volume variance is a measure of this year's *planned* utilization of capacity.

Helado Company Performance Report For the Month Ended May 31, 2013			
	Actual Costs	**Budgeted Cost**	**Spending Variance**
Depreciation	$10,000	$10,000	$ 0
Salaries	26,300	25,800	500 U
Taxes	2,200	1,200	1,000 U
Insurance	2,000	3,000	1,000 F
Total	$40,500	$40,000	$ 500 U

Exhibit 9.6

Fixed Overhead Spending Variance by Item

On the other hand, if *practical capacity* is used as the budgeted volume, then the volume variance is a direct measure of capacity utilization. Practical capacity measures the most that can be produced under efficient operating conditions (and, thus, represents the productive capacity the firm has acquired). The difference between available hours of production and actual hours is a measure of underutilization, and when multiplied by the standard fixed overhead rate, the volume variance becomes a measure of the cost of underutilization of capacity. This is similar in concept to the activity capacity utilization measure described in Chapter 3. The principal difference is that the fixed overhead rate used to measure the cost of unused capacity contains more than the cost of acquiring the productive capacity. Fixed overhead is made up of many costs incurred for reasons other than obtaining productive capacity (e.g., the salaries of the plant supervisor, janitors, and industrial engineers).

Assuming that volume variance measures capacity utilization implies that the general responsibility for this variance should be assigned to the production department. At times, however, investigation into the reasons for a significant volume variance may reveal the cause to be factors beyond the control of production. Then, specific responsibility may be assigned elsewhere. For example, if purchasing acquires direct materials of lower quality than usual, significant rework time may result, causing lower production and an unfavorable volume variance. In this case, responsibility for the variance rests with purchasing, not production.

Accounting for Overhead Variances

Overhead is applied to production by debiting Work in Process and crediting variable and fixed overhead control accounts. The amount assigned is simply the respective overhead rates multiplied by the standard hours allowed for actual production. The actual overhead is accumulated on the debit side of the overhead control accounts. Periodically (e.g., monthly), overhead variance reports are prepared. At the end of the year, the applied variable and fixed overhead costs and the actual fixed overhead costs are closed out and the variances isolated. The overhead variances are then disposed of by closing them to Cost of Goods Sold if they are not material or by prorating them among Work in Process, Finished Goods, and Cost of Goods Sold if they are material. We will use the May transactions for Helado Company to illustrate the process that would occur at the end of the year. Essentially, we are assuming that the May transactions reflect an entire year for illustrative purposes.

To assign overhead to production, we have the following entry:

Work in Process	62,400	
Variable Overhead Control		14,400
Fixed Overhead Control		48,000

To recognize the incurrence of actual overhead, the following entry is needed:

Variable Overhead Control	16,120	
Fixed Overhead Control	40,500	
Various Accounts		56,620

To recognize the variances, the following entry is needed:

Fixed Overhead Control	7,500	
Variable Overhead Spending Variance	520	
Variable Overhead Efficiency Variance	1,200	
Fixed Overhead Spending Variance	500	
Variable Overhead Control		1,720
Fixed Overhead Volume Variance		8,000

Finally, to close out the variances to Cost of Goods Sold, we would have the following entries. (Entries assume that variances are immaterial.)

Fixed Overhead Volume Variance	8,000	
Cost of Goods Sold		8,000
Cost of Goods Sold	2,220	
Variable Overhead Spending Variance		520
Variable Overhead Efficiency Variance		1,200
Fixed Overhead Spending Variance		500

Two- and Three-Variance Analysis Methods

One drawback of the four-variance method is that it requires a company to identify the actual variable and fixed costs as well as budgeted rates and costs. For companies that wish to avoid the need to track actual variable and fixed costs, the two- and three-variance methods can be used.

The two- and three-variance analyses do not require knowledge of actual variable and actual fixed overhead. These methods provide less detail and, thus, less information. We will simply present the method of computation for the two forms of analysis. The four-variance method is recommended over these two approaches. The May data for Helado Company will be used to illustrate the two methods with the assumption that only the total actual overhead is known: $56,620.

Two-Variance Analysis The two-variance analysis is shown in Exhibit 9.7. (*SVOR* designates the standard variable overhead rate.) Several points should be made relative to the four-variance analysis shown in Examples 9.7 and 9.8. First, the total variance is the sum of the total fixed and variable overhead variances. Second, the volume variance is the same as that of the four-variance method. Notice that in the computation of the volume variance, the applied variable overhead term, $SVOR \times SH$, is common to the middle and right prongs of the diagram. Thus, when the right number is subtracted from the left number, we are left with budgeted fixed overhead minus applied fixed overhead, which is the fixed overhead volume variance. Third, the budget variance is the sum of the spending and efficiency variances of the four-variance method ($520 U + $500 U + $1,200 U = $2,220 U). As indicated, the two-variance method sacrifices a lot of information.

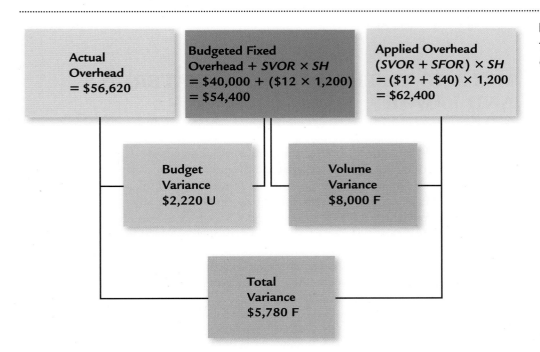

Exhibit 9.7

Two-Variance Analysis: Helado Company

Exhibit 9.8   Three-Variance Analysis: Helado Company

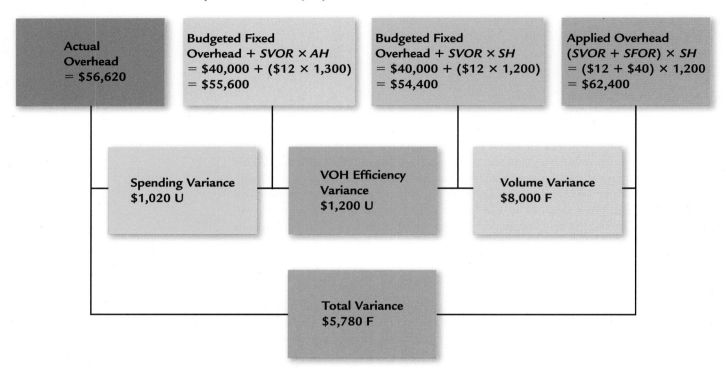

Three-Variance Analysis   The three-variance analysis is shown in Exhibit 9.8. Again, some observations can be made about this method relative to the four-variance method. First, the total variance is again the sum of the total variable and fixed overhead variances. Second, the spending variance is the sum of the variable and fixed overhead spending variances. The variable overhead efficiency and the fixed overhead volume variances are the same. The three-variance method also illustrates that the budget variance of the two-variance method breaks down into spending and efficiency variances.

OBJECTIVE 5

Calculate mix and yield variances for direct materials and direct labor.

MIX AND YIELD VARIANCES: MATERIALS AND LABOR

For some production processes, it may be possible to substitute one direct material input for another or one type of direct labor for another. Usually, a standard mix specification identifies the proportion of each direct material and the proportion of each type of direct labor that should be used for producing the product. For example, in producing an orange-pineapple fruit drink, the standard direct materials mix may call for 30 percent pineapple and 70 percent orange, and the standard direct labor mix may call for 33 percent of fruit preparation labor and 67 percent of fruit-processing labor. Clearly, within reason, it is possible to make input substitutions. Substituting direct materials or direct labor, however, may produce *mix* and *yield* variances. A **mix variance** is created whenever the actual mix of inputs differs from the standard mix. A **yield variance** occurs whenever the actual yield (output) differs from the standard yield. For example, a basic recipe for chocolate chip cookies says it will make three dozen two-inch cookies. But many of us who have baked these cookies know that you never get three dozen two-inch cookies because some of the cookie dough "disappears" before it ever gets to the baking sheet. This difference between the number of cookies you should get and the number you actually do get is the yield variance. For direct materials, the sum of the mix and yield variances equals the direct materials usage variance; for direct labor, the sum is the direct labor efficiency variance.

Direct Materials Mix Variance The mix variance is the difference in the standard cost of the actual mix of inputs used and the standard cost of the mix of inputs that should have been used. Let SM be the quantity of each input that should have been used given the total actual input quantity. This quantity is computed as follows for each direct material input:

$$SM = \text{Standard mix proportion} \times \text{Total actual input quantity}$$

The standard mix quantity is computed for each input.[12] The total actual input quantity is the sum of the quantities of all inputs put into production.

Given SM, the mix variance is computed as follows:

$$\text{Mix variance} = \Sigma (AQ_i - SM_i)SP_i \tag{9.1}$$

Basically, the mix variance is the sum of the differences between the actual amount of each input and its standard mix amount, multiplied by the standard price. If relatively more of a more expensive input is used, the mix variance will be unfavorable. If relatively more of a less expensive input is used, the mix variance will be favorable. **Example 9.9** shows the how and why of calculating the mix variance.

EXAMPLE 9.9

The HOW and WHY of Computing the Mix Variance

Information:

Malcom Nut Company produces mixed nuts using peanuts and almonds. Malcom developed the following standard mix for producing 120 pounds of mixed nuts. (Almonds and peanuts are purchased in the shell and processed.)

Direct Material	Mix	Mix Proportion	SP	Standard Cost
Peanuts	128 lbs.	0.80	$0.50	$64
Almonds	32	0.20	1.00	32
Total	160 lbs.			$96

Malcom put a batch of 1,600 pounds of nuts into process. Of the total, 1,120 pounds were peanuts, and the remaining 480 pounds were almonds. The actual yield was 1,300 pounds.

> **Why:**
> The materials usage variance tells managers whether total materials are in accordance with standards. The mix variance gives further information about materials usage since different materials have different standard prices.

Required:

1. Calculate the standard mix (SM) in pounds for peanuts and for almonds.

2. Calculate the mix variance.

---

12 The standard mix amounts are not the standard quantities allowed for actual output. The total standard quantity allowed is computed by dividing the actual yield by the standard yield ratio. The total standard input allowed is then multiplied by the standard mix ratios to compute the quantity of each direct material input that should have been used for the actual output. Alternatively, the unit direct material standards can be developed by dividing the standard input mix quantity by the standard yield. Multiplying the unit standards by the actual yield will also produce SQ for each input.

EXAMPLE 9.9

(Continued)

3. Calculate the actual proportion used of peanuts and almonds. Use these results to explain why the mix variance is unfavorable.

4. *What if* of the total 1,600 pounds of nuts put into process, 1,360 pounds were peanuts and 240 pounds were almonds? How would that affect the mix variance?

Solution:

1. SM = Standard mix proportion × Total actual input quantity

   SM peanuts = $0.80 \times 1,600 = 1,280$ pounds

   SM almonds = $0.20 \times 1,600 = 320$ pounds

2. The formula can be applied most easily using the following approach:

Direct Material	AQ	SM	$AQ - SM$	SP	$(AQ - SM)\,SP$
Peanuts	1,120	1,280	(160)	$0.50	$ (80)
Almonds	480	320	160	1.00	160
Mix variance					$ 80 U

3. Actual mix proportion peanuts = $1,120/1,600 = 0.70$, or 70%

   Actual mix proportion almonds = $480/1,600 = 0.30$, or 30%

   The mix variance is unfavorable because a larger percentage of the relatively more expensive input, almonds, was used.

4. Since peanuts now account for 85 percent ($1,360/1,600$) of the total, almonds account for only 15 percent. The mix variance will be favorable since relatively more peanuts, the cheaper input, are used.

Notice in Example 9.9 that the mix variance is unfavorable. This occurs because more almonds are used than are called for in the standard mix, and almonds are a more expensive input. If the mix variance is material, then an investigation should be undertaken to determine the cause of the variance so that corrective action can be taken.

Note that Example 9.9 can also be used to calculate the mix variance for inputs other than direct materials. For example, there may be different types of direct labor needed to make a product. It is possible to substitute relatively more of a more or less expensive type of direct labor and obtain a direct labor mix variance.

Direct Materials Yield Variance   The direct materials yield variance is designed to show the extent to which the amount of input resulted in the expected amount of output. Using the standard mix information and the actual results, the yield variance is computed by the following formula:

$$\text{Yield variance} = (\text{Standard yield} - \text{Actual yield})SP_y \qquad (9.2)$$

where

Standard yield = Yield ratio × Total actual inputs

Yield ratio = Total output/Total input

SP_y = Standard cost of the yield (equal to total cost of a standard batch divided by the amount of the yield)

Example 9.10 shows the how and why of calculating the yield variance.

Direct Labor Yield Variance Using the standard mix information and the actual results, the direct labor yield variance is computed as follows:

$$
\begin{aligned}
\text{Direct labor yield variance} &= (\text{Standard yield} - \text{Actual yield})SPy \\
&= [(24 \times 50) - 1{,}300]\$0.45 \\
&= (1{,}200 - 1{,}300)\$0.45 \\
&= \$45 \text{ F}
\end{aligned}
$$

The direct labor yield variance is favorable because the actual yield is greater than the standard yield.

SUMMARY OF LEARNING OBJECTIVES

LO1. Describe how unit input standards are developed, and explain why standard costing systems are adopted.
- A standard costing system budgets quantities and costs on a unit basis for direct labor, direct materials, and overhead.
- Standard costs are the amount that should be expended to produce a product or service. They are set using:
  - Historical experience
  - Engineering studies
  - Input from operating personnel, marketing, and accounting
- Currently attainable standards are those that can be achieved under efficient operating conditions.
- Ideal standards are those achievable under maximum efficiency or ideal operating conditions.
- Standard costing systems are used for:
  - Planning
  - Operating
  - Control
  - Decision making

LO2. Explain the purpose of a standard cost sheet.
- The standard cost sheet shows the amount and cost of direct materials, direct labor, and overhead needed to make one unit of output.
- Using these unit quantity standards, the standard quantity of direct materials allowed and the standard hours allowed can be computed for the actual output.
- These computations play an important role in variance analysis.

LO3. Compute and journalize the direct materials and direct labor variances, and explain how they are used for control.
- The direct materials price variance compares the actual price of materials with the standard price. This difference is multiplied by the actual amount purchased.
- The direct materials usage variance compares the actual amount of materials used with the standard amount of materials for actual production. This difference is multiplied by the standard price.
- The direct labor rate variance is the difference between actual wage and standard wage multiplied by the actual number of direct labor hours.
- The direct labor efficiency variance is the difference between the actual hours worked and the standard hours for actual production multiplied by the standard wage.
- All variances are closed out at the end of the year.
  - Immaterial variances are closed to Cost of Goods Sold.
  - Materials variances are prorated among Work in Process, Finished Goods, and Cost of Goods Sold.

LO4. Compute overhead variances three different ways, and explain overhead accounting.
- The four-variance method is the most detailed. It includes the following variances:
  - Variable overhead spending variance
  - Variable overhead efficiency variance
  - Fixed overhead spending variance
  - Volume variance
- The three-variance method does not require dividing costs into fixed and variable amounts. It includes the following variances:
  - Spending variance
  - Efficiency variance
  - Volume variance
- The two-variance method does not require dividing costs into fixed and variable amounts. It includes the following variances:
  - Budget variance
  - Volume variance

LO5. Calculate mix and yield variances for direct materials and direct labor.
- The mix variance shows the impact of different input proportions on the cost of the output.
- The yield variance shows the difference between the amount of output that was produced versus the expected output for a given amount of input.

EXAMPLE 9.1	The HOW and WHY of Computing Standard Quantities Allowed (*SQ* and *SH*), page 446
EXAMPLE 9.2	The HOW and WHY of Computing the Direct Materials Price Variance (*MPV*) and Direct Materials Usage Variance (*MUV*), page 448
EXAMPLE 9.3	The HOW and WHY of Computing the Direct Labor Rate Variance (*LRV*) and Direct Labor Efficiency Variance (*LEV*), page 453
EXAMPLE 9.4	The HOW and WHY of Using Control Limits to Determine When to Investigate a Variance, page 456
EXAMPLE 9.5	The HOW and WHY of Closing the Balances in the Variance Accounts at the End of the Year, page 459
EXAMPLE 9.6	The HOW and WHY of Calculating the Total Variable Overhead Variance, page 461
EXAMPLE 9.7	The HOW and WHY of Computing the Variable Overhead Spending Variance and the Variable Overhead Efficiency Variance, page 463
EXAMPLE 9.8	The HOW and WHY of Computing the Fixed Overhead Spending Variance and the Fixed Overhead Volume Variance, page 467
EXAMPLE 9.9	The HOW and WHY of Computing the Mix Variance, page 473
EXAMPLE 9.10	The HOW and WHY of Computing the Yield Variance, page 475

KEY TERMS

Control limits, 456

Currently attainable standards, 442

Direct labor efficiency variance (*LEV*), 455

Direct labor rate variance (*LRV*), 454

Direct materials price variance (*MPV*), 448

Direct materials usage variance (*MUV*), 448

Favorable (F) variance, 447

Fixed overhead spending variance, 466

Fixed overhead volume variance, 467

Ideal standards, 442

Kaizen standards, 443

Mix variance, 472

Price (rate) variance, 447

Price standards, 442

Quantity standards, 442

Standard bill of materials, 451

Standard cost per unit, 445

Standard cost sheet, 445

Standard hours allowed, 446

Standard quantity of materials allowed, 446

Total budget variance, 447

Unfavorable (U) variance, 447

Unit standard cost, 442

Usage (efficiency) variance, 447

Variable overhead efficiency variance, 462

Variable overhead spending variance, 462

Yield variance, 472

BRIEF EXERCISES

Brief Exercise 9-1 Calculating Standard Quantities for Actual Production

OBJECTIVE ▸ 1
Example 9.1

Guillermo's Oil and Lube Company is a service company that offers oil changes and lubrication for automobiles and light trucks. On average, Guillermo has found that a typical oil change takes 24 minutes and 6.2 quarts of oil are used. In June, Guillermo's Oil and Lube had 980 oil changes.

Required:

1. Calculate the number of quarts of oil that should have been used (*SQ*) for 980 oil changes.
2. Calculate the hours of direct labor that should have been used (*SH*) for 980 oil changes.
3. *What if* there had been 970 oil changes in June? Would the standard quantities of oil (in quarts) and of direct labor hours be higher or lower than the amounts calculated in Requirements 1 and 2? What would the new standard quantities be?

Brief Exercise 9-2 Calculating the Direct Materials Price Variance and the Direct Materials Usage Variance

OBJECTIVE ▸ 3
Example 9.2

Refer to **Brief Exercise 9-1**. Guillermo's Oil and Lube Company provided the following information for the production of oil changes during the month of June:

Actual number of oil changes performed: 980
Actual number of quarts of oil used: 6,020 quarts
Actual price paid per quart of oil: $5.10
Standard price per quart of oil: $5.05

Required:

1. Calculate the direct materials price variance (*MPV*) and the direct materials usage variance (*MUV*) for June using the formula approach.
2. Calculate the direct materials price variance (*MPV*) and the direct materials usage variance (*MUV*) for June using the graphical approach.
3. Calculate the total direct materials variance for oil for June.
4. *What if* the actual number of quarts of oil purchased in June had been 6,100 quarts, and the materials price variance was calculated at the time of purchase? What would be the materials price variance (*MPV*)? The materials usage variance (*MUV*)?

OBJECTIVE 3
Example 9.3

Brief Exercise 9-3 Calculating the Direct Labor Rate Variance and the Direct Labor Efficiency Variance

Refer to **Brief Exercise 9-1**. Guillermo's Oil and Lube Company provided the following information for the production of oil changes during the month of June:

Actual number of oil changes performed: 980
Actual number of direct labor hours worked: 386 hours
Actual rate paid per direct labor hour: $14.50
Standard rate per direct labor hour: $14.00

Required:

1. Calculate the direct labor rate variance (*LRV*) and the direct labor efficiency variance (*LEV*) for June using the formula approach.
2. Calculate the direct labor rate variance (*LRV*) and the direct labor efficiency variance (*LEV*) for June using the graphical approach.
3. Calculate the total direct labor variance for oil changes for June.
4. *What if* the actual wage rate paid in June was $12.40? What impact would that have had on the direct labor rate variance (*LRV*)? On the direct labor efficiency variance (*LEV*)?

OBJECTIVE 3
Example 9.4

Brief Exercise 9-4 Using Control Limits to Determine When to Investigate a Variance

Kavallia Company set a standard cost for one item at $328,000; allowable deviation is ± $14,500. Actual costs for the past six months are as follows:

June	$330,500	September	$314,000
July	343,000	October	332,000
August	346,800	November	323,000

Required:

DATA ANALYTICS

1. Calculate the variance from standard for each month. Which months should be investigated?
2. *What if* the company uses a two-part rule for investigating variances? The allowable deviation is the lesser of 4 percent of the standard amount or $14,500. Now which months should be investigated?

OBJECTIVE 3
Example 9.5

Brief Exercise 9-5 Closing the Balances in the Variance Accounts at the End of the Year

Yohan Company has the following balances in its direct materials and direct labor variance accounts at year-end:

	Debit	Credit
Direct Materials Price Variance	$13,450	
Direct Materials Usage Variance		$1,100
Direct Labor Rate Variance		870
Direct Labor Efficiency Variance	$12,340	

Unadjusted Cost of Goods Sold equals $1,500,000, unadjusted Work in Process equals $236,000, and unadjusted Finished Goods equals $180,000.

Required:

1. Assume that the ending balances in the variance accounts are immaterial and prepare the journal entries to close them to Cost of Goods Sold. What is the adjusted balance in Cost of Goods Sold after closing out the variances?
2. *What if* any ending balance in a variance account that exceeds $10,000 is considered material? Close the immaterial variance accounts to Cost of Goods Sold and prorate the material variances among Cost of Goods Sold, Work in Process, and Finished Goods on the basis of prime costs in these accounts. The prime cost in Cost of Goods Sold is $1,050,000, the prime cost in Work in Process is $165,200, and the prime cost in Finished Goods is $126,000. What are the adjusted balances in Work in Process, Finished Goods, and Cost of Goods Sold after closing out all variances? (Round ratios to four significant digits. Round journal entries to the nearest dollar.)

Brief Exercise 9-6 Calculating the Total Overhead Variance

OBJECTIVE ◀ 4

Example 9.6

Standish Company manufactures consumer products and provided the following information for the month of February:

Units produced	131,000
Standard direct labor hours per unit	0.20
Standard variable overhead rate (per direct labor hour)	$3.40
Actual variable overhead costs	$88,670
Actual hours worked	26,350

Required:

1. Calculate the total variable overhead variance.
2. *What if* actual production had been 129,600 units? How would that affect the total variable overhead variance?

Brief Exercise 9-7 Calculating the Variable Overhead Spending and Efficiency Variances

OBJECTIVE ◀ 4

Example 9.7

Refer to **Brief Exercise 9-6**.

Required:

1. Calculate the variable overhead spending variance using the formula approach. (If you compute the actual variable overhead rate, carry your computations out to five significant digits and round the variance to the nearest dollar.)
2. Calculate the variable overhead efficiency variance using the formula approach.
3. Calculate the variable overhead spending variance and variable overhead efficiency variance using the three-pronged graphical approach.
4. *What if* 26,100 direct labor hours were actually worked in February? What impact would that have had on the variable overhead spending variance? On the variable overhead efficiency variance?

OBJECTIVE ▶4
Example 9.8

Brief Exercise 9-8 Calculating the Fixed Overhead Spending and Volume Variances

Standish Company manufactures consumer products and provided the following information for the month of February:

Units produced	131,000
Standard direct labor hours per unit	0.20
Standard fixed overhead rate (per direct labor hour)	$2.50
Budgeted fixed overhead	$65,000
Actual fixed overhead costs	$68,300
Actual hours worked	26,350

Required:

1. Calculate the fixed overhead spending variance using the formula approach.
2. Calculate the volume variance using the formula approach.
3. Calculate the fixed overhead spending variance and volume variance using the three-pronged graphical approach.
4. *What if* 129,600 units had actually been produced in February? What impact would that have had on the fixed overhead spending variance? On the volume variance?

OBJECTIVE ▶5
Example 9.9

Brief Exercise 9-9 Calculating the Direct Materials Mix Variance

Mangia Pizza Company makes frozen pizzas that are sold through grocery stores. Mangia developed the following standard mix for spreading on premade pizza shells to produce 16 giant-size sausage pizzas.

Direct Material	Mix	Mix Proportion	SP	Standard Cost
Tomato sauce	13 lbs.	0.325	$1.40	$18.20
Cheese	15	0.375	2.80	42.00
Sausage	12	0.300	2.10	25.20
Total	40 lbs.			$85.40

Mangia put a batch of 2,000 pounds of direct materials (enough for 800 frozen sausage pizzas) into process. Of the total, 700 pounds were tomato sauce, 840 pounds were cheese, and the remaining 460 pounds were sausage. The actual yield was 780 pizzas.

Required:

1. Calculate the standard mix (*SM*) in pounds for tomato sauce, for cheese, and for sausage.
2. Calculate the mix variance.
3. Calculate the actual proportion used of tomato sauce, cheese, and sausage. Use these results to explain the direction (favorable or unfavorable) of the mix variance.
4. *What if* of the total 2,000 pounds of ingredients put into process, 700 pounds were tomato sauce, 700 pounds were cheese, and 600 pounds were sausage? How would that affect the mix variance?

OBJECTIVE ▶5
Example 9.9

Brief Exercise 9-10 Calculating the Direct Labor Mix Variance

Mangia Pizza Company makes frozen pizzas that are sold through grocery stores. Mangia uses two types of direct labor: machine operators and packers. Mangia developed the following standard mix for spreading on premade pizza shells to produce 16 giant-size sausage pizzas.

Direct Material	Mix	Mix Proportion	SP	Standard Cost
Machine operators	0.5 hr.	0.50	$16	$ 8
Packers	0.5	0.50	12	6
Total	1.0 hr.			$14

Mangia's recent batch (designed to produce 400 pizzas) used 400 direct labor hours. Of the total, 160 were for machine operators, and the remaining 240 hours were for packers. The actual yield was 780 pizzas.

Required:

1. Calculate the standard mix (*SM*) in hours for machine operators and for packers.
2. Calculate the mix variance.
3. Calculate the actual proportion of hours worked by machine operators and by packers. Use these results to explain the direction (favorable or unfavorable) of the mix variance.
4. *What if* of the total 400 direct labor hours worked, 200 were worked by each type of direct labor? How would that affect the mix variance?

Brief Exercise 9-11 Calculating the Yield Variance

Refer to **Brief Exercise 9-9**.

OBJECTIVE ◀ 5
Example 9.10

Required:

1. Calculate the yield ratio based on the standard amounts given.
2. Calculate the standard cost per pound of the yield (rounded to the nearest cent).
3. Calculate the standard yield for actual input of 2,000 pounds of direct materials.
4. Calculate the yield variance.
5. *What if* the total 2,000 pounds of direct materials put into process resulted in a yield of 825 pizzas? How would that affect the yield variance?

EXERCISES

Exercise 9-12 Setting Standards, Ethical Behavior

Quincy Farms is a producer of items made from farm products that are distributed to super-markets. For many years, Quincy's products have had strong regional sales on the basis of brand recognition. However, other companies have been marketing similar products in the area, and price competition has become increasingly important. Doug Gilbert, the company's controller, is planning to implement a standard costing system for Quincy and has gathered considerable information from his coworkers on production and direct materials requirements for Quincy's products. Doug believes that the use of standard costing will allow Quincy to improve cost control and make better operating decisions.

OBJECTIVE ◀ 1 2

SHOW ME
HOW

Quincy's most popular product is strawberry jam. The jam is produced in 10-gallon batches, and each batch requires six quarts of good strawberries. The fresh strawberries are sorted by hand before entering the production process. Because of imperfections in the straw-berries and spoilage, one quart of strawberries is discarded for every four quarts of acceptable berries. Three minutes is the standard direct labor time required for sorting strawberries in order to obtain one quart of strawberries. The acceptable strawberries are then processed with the other ingredients: processing requires 12 minutes of direct labor time per batch. After pro-cessing, the jam is packaged in quart containers. Doug has gathered the following information from Joe Adams, Quincy's cost accountant, relative to processing the strawberry jam.

a. Quincy purchases strawberries at a cost of $0.80 per quart. All other ingredients cost a total of $0.45 per gallon.
b. Direct labor is paid at the rate of $9.00 per hour.
c. The total cost of direct material and direct labor required to package the jam is $0.38 per quart.

Joe has a friend who owns a strawberry farm that has been losing money in recent years. Because of good crops, there has been an oversupply of strawberries, and prices have dropped to

$0.50 per quart. Joe has arranged for Quincy to purchase strawberries from his friend's farm in hopes that the $0.80 per quart will put his friend's farm in the black.

Required:

1. Discuss which coworkers Doug probably consulted to set standards. What factors should Doug consider in establishing the standards for direct materials and direct labor?
2. Develop the standard cost sheet for the prime costs of a 10-gallon batch of strawberry jam.
3. Citing the specific standards of the IMA Statement of Ethical Professional Practice described in Chapter 1, explain why Joe's behavior regarding the cost information provided to Doug is unethical. *(CMA adapted)*

OBJECTIVE    **Exercise 9-13 Computation of Inputs Allowed, Direct Materials and Direct Labor**

During the year, Vandy Company produced 280,000 components for industrial metal working machinery. Vandy's direct materials and direct labor standards per unit are as follows:

Direct materials (3.70 lbs. @ $6)	$22.20
Direct labor (1.80 hr. @ $15)	28.80

Required:

1. Compute the standard pounds of direct materials allowed for the production of 240,000 units.
2. Compute the standard direct labor hours allowed for the production of 240,000 units.

OBJECTIVE   **Exercise 9-14 Direct Materials and Direct Labor Variances**

SHOW ME HOW   EXCEL

Berner Company produces a dark chocolate candy bar. Recently, the company adopted the following standards for one bar of the candy:

Direct materials (8.2 oz. @ $0.09)	$0.738
Direct labor (0.07 hr. @ $18.00)	1.26
Standard prime cost	$1.998

During the first week of operation, the company experienced the following actual results:
a. Bars produced: 78,000.
b. Ounces of direct materials purchased: 640,000 ounces at $0.084 per ounce.
c. There are no beginning or ending inventories of direct materials.
d. Direct labor: 5,510 hours at $18.

Required:

1. Compute price and usage variances for direct materials.
2. Compute the rate variance and the efficiency variance for direct labor.
3. Prepare the journal entries associated with direct materials and direct labor.

OBJECTIVE   **Exercise 9-15 Overhead Variances, Four-Variance Analysis**

SHOW ME HOW   EXCEL

Oerstman, Inc., uses a standard costing system and develops its overhead rates from the current annual budget. The budget is based on an expected annual output of 120,000 units requiring 480,000 direct labor hours. (Practical capacity is 500,000 hours.) Annual budgeted overhead costs total $787,200, of which $556,800 is fixed overhead. A total of 119,400 units using 478,000 direct labor hours were produced during the year. Actual variable overhead costs for the year were $230,600, and actual fixed overhead costs were $556,250.

Required:

1. Compute the fixed overhead spending and volume variances. How would you interpret the spending variance? Discuss the possible interpretations of the volume variance. Which is most appropriate for this example?
2. Compute the variable overhead spending and efficiency variances. How is the variable overhead spending variance like the price variances of direct labor and direct materials? How is it different? How is the variable overhead efficiency variance related to the direct labor efficiency variance?

Exercise 9-16 Overhead Variances, Two- And Three-Variance Analyses

Refer to the data in **Exercise 9-15**.

OBJECTIVE ◀ 4

SHOW ME
HOW

Required:

1. Compute overhead variances using a two-variance analysis.
2. Compute overhead variances using a three-variance analysis.
3. Illustrate how the two- and three-variance analyses are related to the four-variance analysis.

Exercise 9-17 Direct Materials Mix and Yield Variances

Chypre, Inc., produces a cologne mist using a solvent mix (water and pure alcohol) and aromatic compounds (the scent base) that it sells to other companies for bottling and sale to consumers. Chypre developed the following standard cost sheet:

OBJECTIVE ◀ 5

SHOW ME
HOW

Direct Material	Mix	Mix Proportion	SP	Standard Cost
Solvent mix	760 gallons	0.95	$ 5.27	$ 4,005.20
Aromatic compounds	40	0.05	8,000.00	320,000.00
Total	800 gallons			$324,005.20
Yield	720 gallons			

On May 2, Chypre produced a batch of 1,000 gallons with the following actual results:

Direct Material	Actual Mix
Solvent mix	945 gallons
Aromatic compounds	55
Total	1,000 gallons
Yield	880 gallons

Required:

1. Calculate the yield ratio.
2. Calculate the standard cost per unit of the yield. (Round to the nearest cent.)
3. Calculate the direct materials yield variance. (Round to the nearest cent.)
4. Calculate the direct materials mix variance. (Round to the nearest cent.)

Exercise 9-18 Direct Materials Variances: Journal Entries

Refer to **Exercise 9-17**. Chypre, Inc., purchased the amount used of each direct material input on May 2 for the following actual prices: solvent mix for $5.20 per gallon, and aromatic compound for $8,010 per gallon.

OBJECTIVE ◀ 3 5

SHOW ME
HOW

Required:

1. Compute and journalize the direct materials price variances.
2. Compute and journalize the direct materials usage variances.
3. Offer some possible reasons for why the variances occurred.

OBJECTIVE 5

SHOW ME
HOW

EXCEL

Exercise 9-19 Direct Labor Mix and Yield Variances

Redfield Company uses two types of direct labor for the manufacturing of its products: fabricating and assembly. Redfield has developed the following standard mix for direct labor, where output is measured in units.

Direct Labor Type	Mix	SP	Standard Cost
Fabricating	3 hrs.	$20	$60
Assembly	2	15	30
Total	5 hrs.		$90
Yield	25 units		

During the second week in April, Redfield produced the following results:

Direct Labor	Type Actual Mix
Fabricating	20,000 hrs.
Assembly	45,000
Total	65,000 hrs.
Yield	320,000 units

Required:

1. Calculate the yield ratio.
2. Calculate the standard cost per unit of the yield.
3. Calculate the direct labor yield variance.
4. Calculate the direct labor mix variance.

OBJECTIVE 3

Exercise 9-20 Direct Labor and Direct Materials Variances, Journal Entries

Samson Company produces paper towels. The company has established the following direct materials and direct labor standards for one case of paper towels:

Paper pulp (4 lbs. @ $0.30)	$ 1.20
Labor (1.8 hrs. @ $18)	32.40
Total prime cost	$33.60

During the first quarter of the year, Samson produced 40,000 cases of paper towels. The company purchased and used 160,300 pounds of paper pulp at $0.27 per pound. Actual direct labor used was 80,000 hours at $18.20 per hour.

Required:

1. Calculate the direct materials price and usage variances.
2. Calculate the direct labor rate and efficiency variances.
3. Prepare the journal entries for the direct materials and direct labor variances.
4. Describe how flexible budgeting variances relate to the direct materials and direct labor variances computed in Requirements 1 and 2.

OBJECTIVE 3

Exercise 9-21 Investigation of Variances

Madison Company uses the following rule to determine whether direct labor efficiency variances ought to be investigated. A direct labor efficiency variance will be investigated anytime the amount exceeds the lesser of $12,000 or 10 percent of the standard labor cost. Reports for the past five weeks provided the following information:

Week	LEV	Standard Labor Cost
1	$ 14,000 F	$160,000
2	15,600 U	175,000
3	12,000 F	160,000
4	10,000 U	170,000
5	11,500 U	110,000

Required:

1. Using the rule provided, identify the cases that will be investigated.
2. Suppose that investigation reveals that the cause of an unfavorable direct labor efficiency variance is the use of lower quality direct materials than are usually used. Who is responsible? What corrective action would likely be taken?
3. Suppose that investigation reveals that the cause of a significant favorable direct labor efficiency variance is attributable to a new approach to manufacturing that takes less labor time but causes more direct materials waste. Upon examining the direct materials usage variance, it is discovered to be unfavorable, and it is larger than the favorable direct labor efficiency variance. Who is responsible? What action should be taken? How would your answer change if the unfavorable variance were smaller than the favorable?

DATA
ANALYTICS

Exercise 9-22 Overhead Variances, Four-Variance Analysis, Journal Entries

OBJECTIVE ◀ **4**

Janson, Inc., uses a standard costing system. The predetermined overhead rates are calculated using practical capacity. Practical capacity for a year is defined as 100,000 units requiring 20,000 standard direct labor hours. Budgeted overhead for the year is $76,000, of which $30,000 is fixed overhead. During the year, 96,000 units were produced using 19,000 direct labor hours. Actual annual overhead costs totaled $80,000, of which $29,600 is fixed overhead.

SHOW ME
HOW

Required:

1. Calculate the fixed overhead spending and volume variances. Explain the meaning of the volume variance to the manager of Jason.
2. Calculate the variable overhead spending and efficiency variances. Is the spending variance the same as the direct materials price variance? If not, explain how it differs.
3. Prepare the journal entries that reflect the following:
   a. Assignment of overhead to production
   b. Recognition of the incurrence of actual overhead
   c. Recognition of overhead variances
   d. Closing out overhead variances, assuming they are not material

PROBLEMS

Problem 9-23 Standard Costs, Decomposition of Budget Variances, Direct Materials and Direct Labor

OBJECTIVE ◀ **2** **3**

EZ Tees Corporation produces T-shirts. The company uses a standard costing system and has set the following standards for direct materials and direct labor (for one shirt):

Fabric (0.8 yds. @ $1.60)	$ 1.28
Direct labor (0.1 hr. @ $15)	1.50
Total prime cost	$ 2.78

During the year, EZ Tees produced 124,000 T-shirts. The actual fabric purchased was 99,000 yards at $1.55 per yard. There were no beginning or ending inventories of fabric. Actual direct labor was 12,500 hours at $14.80 per hour.

Required:

1. Compute the costs of fabric and direct labor that should have been incurred for the production of 124,000 T-shirts.
2. Compute the total budget variances for direct materials and direct labor.
3. Break down the total budget variance for direct materials into a price variance and a usage variance. Prepare the journal entries associated with these variances.
4. Break down the total budget variance for direct labor into a rate variance and an efficiency variance. Prepare the journal entries associated with these variances.

OBJECTIVE 4

EXCEL

Problem 9-24 Overhead Application, Overhead Variances, Journal Entries

Plimpton Company produces countertop ovens. Plimpton uses a standard costing system. The standard costing system relies on direct labor hours to assign overhead costs to production. The direct labor standard indicates that two direct labor hours should be used for every oven produced. The normal production volume is 100,000 units. The budgeted overhead for the coming year is as follows:

Fixed overhead	$770,000
Variable overhead	444,000*

*At normal volume.

Plimpton applies overhead on the basis of direct labor hours.

During the year, Plimpton produced 97,000 units, worked 196,000 direct labor hours, and incurred actual fixed overhead costs of $780,000 and actual variable overhead costs of $435,600.

Required:

1. Calculate the standard fixed overhead rate and the standard variable overhead rate.
2. Compute the applied fixed overhead and the applied variable overhead. What is the total fixed overhead variance? Total variable overhead variance?
3. Break down the total fixed overhead variance into a spending variance and a volume variance. Discuss the significance of each.
4. Compute the variable overhead spending and efficiency variances. Discuss the significance of each.
5. Now assume that Plimpton's cost accounting system reveals only the total actual overhead. In this case, a three-variance analysis can be performed. Using the relationships between a three- and four-variance analysis, indicate the values for the three overhead variances.
6. Prepare the journal entries that would be related to fixed and variable overhead during the year and at the end of the year. Assume variances are closed to Cost of Goods Sold.

OBJECTIVE 3 4

Problem 9-25 Direct Materials, Direct Labor, and Overhead Variances, Journal Entries

Rand Company produces dry fertilizer. At the beginning of the year, Rand had the following standard cost sheet:

Direct materials (8 lbs. @ $1.30)	$10.40
Direct labor (0.2 hr. @ $18.00)	3.60
Fixed overhead (0.2 hr. @ $3.00)	0.60
Variable overhead (0.20 hr. @ $1.70)	0.34
Standard cost per unit	$14.94

Overhead rates are computed using practical volume, which is 50,000 units. The actual results for the year are as follows:

a. Units produced: 51,000
b. Direct materials purchased: 408,000 pounds @ $1.32 per pound
c. Direct materials used: 406,800 pounds
d. Direct labor: 10,500 hours at $17.95 per hour
e. Fixed overhead: $30,680
f. Variable overhead: $18,000

Required:

1. Compute price and usage variances for direct materials.
2. Compute the direct labor rate and labor efficiency variances.
3. Compute the fixed overhead spending and volume variances. Interpret the volume variance.
4. Compute the variable overhead spending and efficiency variances.

5. Prepare journal entries for the following:
   a. The purchase of direct materials
   b. The issuance of direct materials to production (Work in Process)
   c. The addition of direct labor to Work in Process
   d. The addition of overhead to Work in Process
   e. The incurrence of actual overhead costs
   f. Closing out of variances to Cost of Goods Sold

Problem 9-26 Solving for Unknowns

OBJECTIVE

Misterio Company uses a standard costing system. During the past quarter, the following variances were computed:

Variable overhead efficiency variance	$ 24,000 U
Direct labor efficiency variance	120,000 U
Direct labor rate variance	10,400 U

Misterio applies variable overhead using a standard rate of $2 per direct labor hour allowed. Two direct labor hours are allowed per unit produced. (Only one type of product is manufactured.) During the quarter, Misterio used 30 percent more direct labor hours than should have been used.

Required:

1. What were the actual direct labor hours worked? The total hours allowed?
2. What is the standard hourly rate for direct labor? The actual hourly rate?
3. How many actual units were produced?

Problem 9-27 Basic Variance Analysis, Revision of Standards, Journal Entries

OBJECTIVE

Petrillo Company produces engine parts for large motors. The company uses a standard cost system for production costing and control. The standard cost sheet for one of its higher volume products (a valve) is as follows:

Direct materials (7 lbs. @ $5.40)	$37.80
Direct labor (1.75 hrs. @ $18)	31.50
Variable overhead (1.75 hrs. @ $4.00)	7.00
Fixed overhead (1.75 hrs. @ $3.00)	5.25
Standard unit cost	$81.55

During the year, Petrillo had the following activity related to valve production:

a. Production of valves totaled 20,600 units.
b. A total of 135,400 pounds of direct materials was purchased at $5.36 per pound.
c. There were 10,000 pounds of direct materials in beginning inventory (carried at $5.40 per pound). There was no ending inventory.
d. The company used 36,500 direct labor hours at a total cost of $656,270.
e. Actual fixed overhead totaled $110,000.
f. Actual variable overhead totaled $168,000.

Petrillo produces all of its valves in a single plant. Normal activity is 20,000 units per year. Standard overhead rates are computed based on normal activity measured in standard direct labor hours.

Required:

1. Compute the direct materials price and usage variances.
2. Compute the direct labor rate and efficiency variances.
3. Compute overhead variances using a two-variance analysis.

4. Compute overhead variances using a four-variance analysis.
5. Assume that the purchasing agent for the valve plant purchased a lower-quality direct material from a new supplier. Would you recommend that the company continue to use this cheaper direct material? If so, what standards would likely need revision to reflect this decision? Assume that the end product's quality is not significantly affected.
6. Prepare all possible journal entries (assuming a four-variance analysis of overhead variances).

OBJECTIVE 1 2 3 4

Problem 9-28 Unit Costs, Multiple Products, Variance Analysis, Journal Entries

Business Specialty, Inc., manufactures two staplers: small and regular. The standard quantities of direct labor and direct materials per unit for the year are as follows:

	Small	Regular
Direct materials (oz.)	6.0	10.00
Direct labor (hrs.)	0.1	0.15

The standard price paid per pound of direct materials is $1.60. The standard rate for labor is $8.00. Overhead is applied on the basis of direct labor hours. A plantwide rate is used. Budgeted overhead for the year is as follows:

Budgeted fixed overhead	$360,000
Budgeted variable overhead	480,000

The company expects to work 12,000 direct labor hours during the year; standard overhead rates are computed using this activity level. For every small stapler produced, the company produces two regular staplers.

Actual operating data for the year are as follows:

a. Units produced: small staplers, 35,000; regular staplers, 70,000.
b. Direct materials purchased and used: 56,000 pounds at $1.55—13,000 for the small stapler and 43,000 for the regular stapler. There were no beginning or ending direct materials inventories.
c. Direct labor: 14,800 hours—3,600 hours for the small stapler and 11,200 hours for the regular stapler. Total cost of direct labor: $114,700.
d. Variable overhead: $607,500.
e. Fixed overhead: $350,000.

Required:

1. Prepare a standard cost sheet showing the unit cost for each product.
2. Compute the direct materials price and usage variances for each product. Prepare journal entries to record direct materials activity.
3. Compute the direct labor rate and efficiency variances for each product. Prepare journal entries to record direct labor activity.
4. Compute the variances for fixed and variable overhead. Prepare journal entries to record overhead activity. All variances are closed to Cost of Goods Sold.
5. Assume that you know only the total direct materials used for both products and the total direct labor hours used for both products. Can you compute the total direct materials and direct labor usage variances? Explain.

OBJECTIVE 3 5

Problem 9-29 Direct Materials Usage Variance, Direct Materials Mix and Yield Variances

Vet-Pro, Inc., produces a veterinary grade anti-anxiety mixture for pets with behavioral problems. Two chemical solutions, Aranol and Lendyl, are mixed and heated to produce a chemical that is sold to companies that produce the anti-anxiety pills. The mixture is produced in batches and has the following standards:

Direct Material	Standard Mix	Standard Unit Price	Standard Cost
Aranol	3,000 gallons	$4.00 per gallon	$ 12,000
Lendyl	17,000	6.00	102,000
Total	20,000 gallons		$114,000
Yield	16,000 gallons		

During March, the following actual production information was provided:

Direct Material	Actual Mix
Aranol	60,000 gallons
Lendyl	140,000
Total	200,000 gallons
Yield	166,000 gallons

Required:

1. Compute the direct materials mix and yield variances.
2. Compute the total direct materials usage variance for Aranol and Lendyl. Show that the total direct materials usage variance is equal to the sum of the direct materials mix and yield variances.

Problem 9-30 Direct Labor Efficiency Variance, Direct Labor Mix and Yield Variances

OBJECTIVE ◄ 3 5

Refer to the data in **Problem 9-29**. Vet-Pro, Inc., also uses two different types of direct labor in producing the anti-anxiety mixture: mixing and drum-filling labor (the completed product is placed into 50-gallon drums). For each batch of 20,000 gallons of direct materials input, the following standards have been developed for direct labor:

Direct Labor Type	Mix	SP	Standard Cost
Mixing	2,000 hrs.	$14.00	$28,000
Drum filling	1,200	9.50	11,400
Total	3,200 hrs.		$39,400
Yield	16,000 gallons		

The actual direct labor hours used for the output produced in March are also provided:

Direct Labor	Type Mix
Mixing	18,000 hrs.
Drum filling	12,000
Total	30,000 hrs.
Yield	158,400 gallons

Required:

1. Compute the direct labor mix and yield variances. (Round standard price of yield to four significant digits.)
2. Compute the total direct labor efficiency variance. Show that the total direct labor efficiency variance is equal to the sum of the direct labor mix and yield variances.

OBJECTIVE 3 5

Problem 9-31 Direct Materials Usage Variances: Direct Materials Mix and Yield Variances

Energy Products Company produces a gasoline additive, Gas Gain. This product increases engine efficiency and improves gasoline mileage by creating a more complete burn in the combustion process.

   Careful controls are required during the production process to ensure that the proper mix of input chemicals is achieved and that evaporation is controlled. If the controls are not effective, there can be a loss of output and efficiency.

   The standard cost of producing a 500-liter batch of Gas Gain is $135. The standard direct materials mix and related standard cost of each chemical used in a 500-liter batch are as follows:

Chemical	Mix	SP	Standard Cost
Echol	200 liters	$0.200	$ 40.00
Protex	100	0.425	42.50
Benz	250	0.150	37.50
CT-40	50	0.300	15.00
Total	600 liters		$135.00

   The quantities of chemicals purchased and used during the current production period are shown in the following schedule. A total of 140 batches of Gas Gain were manufactured during the current production period. Energy Products determines its cost and chemical usage variations at the end of each production period.

Chemical	Quantity Used
Echol	26,600 liters
Protex	12,880
Benz	37,800
CT-40	7,140
Total	84,420 liters

Required:

Compute the total direct materials usage variance, and then break down this variance into its mix and yield components. *(CMA adapted)*

OBJECTIVE 3 4

Problem 9-32 Solving for Unknowns, Overhead Analysis

Nuevo Company produces a single product. Nuevo employs a standard cost system and uses a flexible budget to predict overhead costs at various levels of activity. For the most recent year, Nuevo used a standard overhead rate equal to $6.25 per direct labor hour. The rate was computed using expected activity. Budgeted overhead costs are $80,000 for 10,000 direct labor hours and $120,000 for 20,000 direct labor hours. During the past year, Nuevo generated the following data:

   a. Actual production: 4,000 units
   b. Fixed overhead volume variance: $1,750 U
   c. Variable overhead efficiency variance: $3,200 F
   d. Actual fixed overhead costs: $41,335
   e. Actual variable overhead costs: $70,000

Required:

   1. Determine the fixed overhead spending variance.
   2. Determine the variable overhead spending variance.
   3. Determine the standard hours allowed per unit of product.
   4. Assuming the standard labor rate is $9.50 per hour, compute the direct labor efficiency variance.

Problem 9-33 Flexible Budget, Standard Cost Variances, T-Accounts

OBJECTIVE ◀ 1 3 4

Ingles Company manufactures external hard drives. At the beginning of the period, the following plans for production and costs were revealed:

Units to be produced and sold	25,000
Standard cost per unit:	
Direct materials	$ 10
Direct labor	8
Variable overhead	4
Fixed overhead	3
Total unit cost	$ 25

During the year, 24,800 units were produced and sold. The following actual costs were incurred:

Direct materials	$264,368
Direct labor	204,352
Variable overhead	107,310
Fixed overhead	73,904

There were no beginning or ending inventories of direct materials. The direct materials price variance was $10,168 unfavorable. In producing the 24,800 units, a total of 12,772 hours were worked, 3 percent more hours than the standard allowed for the actual output. Overhead costs are applied to production using direct labor hours.

Required:

1. Prepare a performance report comparing expected costs to actual costs.
2. Determine the following:
   a. Direct materials usage variance
   b. Direct labor rate variance
   c. Direct labor usage variance
   d. Fixed overhead spending and volume variances
   e. Variable overhead spending and efficiency variances
3. Use T-accounts to show the flow of costs through the system. In showing the flow, you do not need to show detailed overhead variances. Show only the over- and underapplied variances for fixed and variable overhead.

Problem 9-34 Standard Costing: Planned Variances

OBJECTIVE ◀ 2 3

CMA

As part of its cost control program, Tracer Company uses a standard costing system for all manufactured items. The standard cost for each item is established at the beginning of the fiscal year, and the standards are not revised until the beginning of the next fiscal year. Changes in costs, caused during the year by changes in direct materials or direct labor inputs or by changes in the manufacturing process, are recognized as they occur by the inclusion of planned variances in Tracer's monthly operating budgets.

The following direct labor standard was established for one of Tracer's products, effective June 1, 2012, the beginning of the fiscal year:

Assembler A labor (5 hrs. @ $10)	$ 50
Assembler B labor (3 hrs. @ $11)	33
Machinist labor (2 hrs. @ $15)	30
Standard cost per 100 units	$113

The standard was based on the direct labor being performed by a team consisting of five persons with Assembler A skills, three persons with Assembler B skills, and two persons with machinist skills; this team represents the most efficient use of the company's skilled employees.

The standard also assumed that the quality of direct materials that had been used in prior years would be available for the coming year.

For the first seven months of the fiscal year, actual manufacturing costs at Tracer have been within the standards established. However, the company has received a significant increase in orders, and there is an insufficient number of skilled workers to meet the increased production. Therefore, beginning in January, the production teams will consist of eight persons with Assembler A skills, one person with Assembler B skills, and one person with machinist skills. The reorganized teams will work more slowly than the normal teams, and as a result, only 80 units will be produced in the same time period in which 100 units would normally be produced. Faulty work has never been a cause for units to be rejected in the final inspection process, and it is not expected to be a cause for rejection with the reorganized teams.

Furthermore, Tracer has been notified by its direct materials supplier that lower-quality direct materials will be supplied beginning January 1. Normally, one unit of direct materials is required for each good unit produced, and no units are lost due to defective direct materials. Tracer estimates that 6 percent of the units manufactured after January 1 will be rejected in the final inspection process due to defective direct materials.

Required:

DATA ANALYTICS

1. Determine the number of units of lower quality direct materials that Tracer Company must enter into production in order to produce 47,000 good finished units.
2. How many hours of each class of direct labor must be used to manufacture 47,000 good finished units?
3. Using data analytics for predictive purposes, determine the amount that should be included in Tracer's January operating budget for the planned direct labor variance caused by the reorganization of the direct labor teams and the lower quality direct materials. *(CMA adapted)*

OBJECTIVE 2 3

Problem 9-35 Variance Analysis in a Process-Costing Setting (Chapter 6 Required), Service Firm

Aspen Medical Laboratory performs comprehensive blood tests for physicians and clinics throughout the Southwest. Aspen uses a standard process-costing system for its comprehensive blood work. Skilled technicians perform the blood tests. Because Aspen uses a standard costing system, equivalent units are calculated using the FIFO method. The standard cost sheet for the blood test follows (these standards were used throughout the calendar year):

Direct materials (4 oz. @ $4.50)	$18
Direct labor (2 hrs. @ $18.00)	36
Variable overhead (2 hrs. @ $5.00)	10
Fixed overhead (2 hrs. @ $10.00)	20
Standard cost per test	$84

For the month of November, Aspen reported the following actual results:
a. Beginning work in process: 1,250 tests, 60 percent complete
b. Tests started: 25,000
c. Ending work in process: 2,500 tests, 40 percent complete
d. Direct labor: 47,000 hours at $19 per hour
e. Direct materials purchased and used: 102,000 at $4.25 per ounce
f. Variable overhead: $144,000
g. Fixed overhead: $300,000
h. Direct materials are added at the beginning of the process.

Required:

1. Explain why the FIFO method is used for process costing when a standard costing system has been adopted.
2. Calculate the cost of goods transferred out (tests completed and transferred out) for the month of November. Does standard costing simplify process costing? Explain.
3. Calculate price and quantity variances for direct materials and direct labor.

Problem 9-36 Setting Standards, Calculating and Using Variances

OBJECTIVE ◀ 1 3

CMA

Leather Works is a family-owned maker of leather travel bags and briefcases located in the northeastern part of the United States. Foreign competition has forced its owner, Heather Gray, to explore new ways to meet the competition. One of her cousins, Wallace Hayes, who recently graduated from college with a major in accounting, told her about the use of cost variance analysis to learn about efficiencies of production.

In May of last year, Heather asked Matt Nunez, chief accountant, and Lucy Wu, production manager, to implement a standard costing system. Matt and Lucy, in turn, retained Shannon Leikam, an accounting professor at Harding's College, to set up a standard costing system by using information supplied to her by Matt's and Lucy's staff. To verify that the information was accurate, Shannon visited the plant and measured workers' output using time and motion studies. During those visits, she was not accompanied by either Matt or Lucy, and the workers knew about Shannon's schedule in advance. The cost system was implemented in June of last year.

Recently, the following dialogue took place among Heather, Matt, and Lucy:

HEATHER: How is the business performing?

LUCY: You know, we are producing a lot more than we used to, thanks to the contract that you helped obtain from Lean, Inc., for laptop covers. (Lean is a national supplier of computer accessories.)

MATT: Thank goodness for that new product. It has kept us from sinking even more due to the inroads into our business made by those foreign suppliers of leather goods.

HEATHER: What about the standard costing system?

MATT: The variances are mostly favorable, except for the first few months when the supplier of leather started charging more.

HEATHER: How did the union members take to the standards?

LUCY: Not bad. They grumbled a bit at first, but they have taken it in stride. We've consistently shown favorable direct labor efficiency variances and direct materials usage variances. The direct labor rate variance has been flat.

MATT: It should be since direct labor rates are negotiated by the union representative at the start of the year and remain the same for the entire year.

HEATHER: Matt, would you send me the variance report for laptop covers immediately?

The following chart summarizes the direct materials and direct labor variances from November of last year through April of this year (extracted from the report provided by Matt). Standards for each laptop cover are as follows:

a. Three feet of direct materials at $7.50 per foot
b. Forty-five minutes of direct labor at $14 per hour

Month	Actual Cost (Direct Materials + Direct Labor)	Direct Materials Price Variance	Direct Materials Efficiency Variance	Direct Labor Rate Variance	Direct Labor Efficiency Variance
November	$150,000	$10,000 U	$5,000 F	$100 U	$5,000 F
December	155,000	11,000 U	5,200 F	110 U	6,500 F
January	152,000	10,100 U	4,900 F	105 U	7,750 F
February	151,000	9,900 U	4,500 F	95 U	6,950 F
March	125,000	9,000 U	3,000 F	90 U	8,200 F
April	115,000	8,000 U	2,000 F	90 U	8,500 F

In addition, the data for May of this year, but not the variances for the month, are as follows:

Laptop covers made in May	2,900 units
Total actual direct materials costs incurred	$ 68,850
Actual quantity of direct materials purchased and used	8,500 feet
Total actual direct labor cost incurred	$ 25,910
Total actual direct labor hours	1,837.6 hours

Actual direct labor cost per hour exceeded the budgeted rate by $0.10 per hour.

Required:

DATA ANALYTICS

1. For May of this year, calculate the price and quantity variances for direct labor and direct materials.
2. Discuss the trend of the direct materials and labor variances.
3. What type of actions must the workers have taken during the period they were being observed for the setting of standards?
4. What can be done to ensure that the standards are set correctly? *(CMA adapted)*

The items that appear within this chapter that are from the CMA are Problems 9-31, 9-34, and 9-36. Source: Materials from the Certified Management Accountant Examination, Copyright 1981, 1982, 1983, 1984, 1985, 1989, 1990, 1991, 1992, 1995, 1996 by the Institute of Certified Management Accountants are reprinted and/or adapted with permission.

10

Decentralization: Responsibility Accounting, Performance Evaluation, and Transfer Pricing

After studying this chapter, you should be able to:

1 Define responsibility accounting, and describe the four types of responsibility centers.

2 Explain why firms choose to decentralize.

3 Compute and explain return on investment (ROI), residual income (RI), and economic value added (EVA).

4 Discuss methods of evaluating and rewarding managerial performance.

5 Explain the role of transfer pricing in a decentralized firm.

6 Discuss the methods of setting transfer prices.

RETURN ON INVESTMENT

at Nike

At the Chicago Marathon in October 2019, Brigid Kosgei smashed the women's marathon record. Her time of 2:14:04 was almost 1.5 minutes faster than ever before. That same month, Eliud Kipchoge recorded a time of 1:59:40 at an unofficial marathon event in Vienna, breaking the two-hour barrier. Both were wearing **Nike**'s colorful Next% shoes, the Vaporfly. Neon bright, weighing less than a half pound per shoe, and composed of revolutionary materials—a carbon-fiber plate under the sole and a new kind of foam layer—the shoe is said to be around 87 percent efficient in energy return. The upshot is that runners feel that their shoes spring them up and forward, protecting their legs from the impact of striking the ground.[1]

Bryce Dyer, a sports technologist at Bournemouth University, United Kingdom, described the soles, featuring a patented "rubber known as Pebax, … and … carbon fiber plates that work together to absorb and then return a percentage of the energy that the runner puts into them." Runners say that "it leaves legs less sore because it's absorbing the energy. It's not hammering the legs—because running is a very, very impact-related sport. So it's not just about allowing the runner to move faster when they're actually racing, but it's also actually allowing them possibly to stitch together more workouts with less fatigue in the longer run as well."[2]

Nike holds the patent on both the Pebax and the carbon-fiber plates, meaning that other shoe companies cannot use them in their designs. Nike's extensive research and development (R&D) and design efforts keep the company at the forefront of running shoe technology and help explain why the company is one of the most popular shoe manufacturers in the world. These efforts are expensive, and Nike invests considerable funding to create new designs and technology. Nike's emphasis on profit and return on investment (ROI) ensure that these expenditures for R&D are matched by significant income. A quick look at the past few years' data shows healthy income, ROI, and growth.[3]

12 months ended:	May 31, 2019	May 31, 2018	May 31, 2017	May 31, 2016	May 31, 2015
Net income	4,029	1,933	4,240	3,760	3,273
ROI	25.42%	11.72%	23.84%	23.44%	21.44%

The Vaporfly shoes are not without controversy. They have been described as technological doping, giving some athletes an unfair advantage. The World Athletics organization had to weigh in to authorize their use, subject to

1 Aylin Woodward, "Nike's Controversial Vaporfly Shoes Powered the World's 2 Fastest Marathoners to Victory," *Business Insider* (January 30, 2020), https://www.businessinsider.com/what-nike-vaporfly-shoes-are-like-to-wear-2020-1, accessed Oct. 26, 2020.

2 Michel Martin, host, "Nike Vaporfly Shoes Controversy," NPR, *All Things Considered*, (February 23, 2020), https://www.npr.org/2020/02/23/808681604/nike-vaporfly-shoes-controversy, accessed Oct. 26, 2020.

3 https://www.stock-analysis-on.net/NYSE/Company/Nike-Inc/Financial-Statement/Income-Statement, accessed Oct. 26, 2020.

certain controls, for example, that athletes cannot wear prototypes that have not been available to the general public for at least four months. Meanwhile, the general public can buy and wear these shoes and have all the shoe advantages of elite runners. The price, however, is definitely a sticking point—at $250+ they can make the weekend warrior stop and think. Besides, the physical advantages of elite athletes are not for sale!

As a firm grows, duties are divided, creating spheres of responsibility that become centers of responsibility. Closely allied to the subject of responsibility is decision making. Most companies decentralize decision-making authority. Issues related to decentralization include performance evaluation, management compensation, and transfer pricing.

OBJECTIVE
Define responsibility accounting, and describe the four types of responsibility centers.

RESPONSIBILITY ACCOUNTING

In general, companies are organized along lines of responsibility. The traditional pyramid-shaped organizational chart illustrates the lines of responsibility, which flow from the CEO through the vice presidents to middle and lower-level managers. As organizations grow larger, these lines of responsibility become longer and more numerous. There is a strong link between an organization's structure and its responsibility accounting system. Ideally, the responsibility accounting system mirrors and supports the structure of an organization.

Types of Responsibility Centers

As the firm grows, top management typically creates areas of responsibility known as responsibility centers and assigns subordinate managers to those areas. A **responsibility center** is a part of the business whose manager is accountable for specified activities. **Responsibility accounting** is a system that measures the results of each responsibility center and compares those results with expected or budgeted outcomes. The four major types of responsibility centers are as follows:

1. **Cost center:** a responsibility center in which a manager is responsible only for costs
2. **Revenue center:** a responsibility center in which a manager is responsible only for revenues
3. **Profit center:** a responsibility center in which a manager is responsible for both revenues and costs
4. **Investment center:** a responsibility center in which a manager is responsible for revenues, costs, and investments

A production department within the factory, such as Assembly or Finishing, is an example of a cost center. The supervisor of a production department does not set prices or make marketing decisions, but can control manufacturing costs. Therefore, the production department supervisor is evaluated on the basis of how well costs are controlled.

The Marketing Department manager sets prices and projected sales. Therefore, the Marketing Department may be evaluated as a revenue center. Direct costs of the Marketing Department and overall sales are the responsibilities of the sales manager.

In some companies, plant managers are responsible for pricing and selling products they manufacture. These plant managers control both costs and revenues, putting them in control of a profit center. Operating income is an important performance measure for profit center managers.

Finally, divisions are often cited as examples of investment centers. In addition to having control over cost and pricing decisions, divisional managers can make investment decisions, such as plant closings and openings, and decisions to keep or drop a product line. As a result, both operating income and some type of ROI are important performance measures for investment center managers.

It is important to realize that while the responsibility center manager has responsibility for only the activities of that center, decisions made by that manager can affect other responsibility centers. For example, the sales force at a floor care products firm routinely offers customers price discounts at the end of the month. Sales increase dramatically, but the factory is forced to incur extra costs by putting in overtime shifts.

The Role of Information and Accountability

Information is the key to appropriately holding managers responsible for outcomes. For example, a production department manager is responsible for departmental costs but not for sales. This is because the production department manager not only controls some of these costs but also is best informed regarding them. Any deviation between actual and expected costs can best be explained at this level. Sales are the responsibility of the sales manager, because this manager understands and can explain price and quantity sold.

The management accountant has an expanded role in the development of a responsibility accounting system in the global business environment. Business looks to the accountant for financial and business expertise. The accountant's job is not cut and dried. Knowledge, creativity, and flexibility are needed to help managers make decisions. Good training, education, and staying up to date with one's field are important to any accountant. However, the job of the accountant in the international firm is made more challenging by the ambiguous and ever-changing nature of global business. Since much of the accountant's job is to provide relevant information to management, staying up to date requires reading in a variety of business areas, including information systems, marketing, management, politics, and economics. In addition, the accountant must be familiar with the financial accounting rules of the countries in which the firm operates.

An example of the modern accountant is Nick, one of the authors' students who graduated from Oklahoma State University in the 1990s. Nick spent three years with a Big-6 (at the time) firm in Tulsa. He was drawn by opportunities in the international arena and joined PricewaterhouseCoopers' office in Vladivostok. Nick's focus in Russia was on business development and consulting. In essence, he was a management accountant working for a public accounting firm. Nick faced hurdles including language (he had to get up to speed on Russian quickly), legal differences (often, bodyguards armed with uzis accompanied him on trips to client firms), tax differences (Russia's ever-changing, and frequently retroactive, tax laws drove a number of foreign firms out of the country), and cultural differences.

Responsibility also entails accountability. Accountability implies performance measurement, which means that actual outcomes are compared with expected or budgeted outcomes. This system of responsibility, accountability, and performance evaluation is often referred to as *responsibility accounting* because of the key role that accounting measures and reports play in the process.

DECENTRALIZATION

OBJECTIVE 2
Explain why firms choose to decentralize.

Firms with multiple responsibility centers choose one of two approaches to manage their diverse and complex activities: centralized decision making or decentralized decision making. In **centralized decision making**, decisions are made at the very top level, and lower-level managers are charged with implementing these decisions. On the other hand, **decentralized decision making** allows managers at lower levels to make and implement key decisions pertaining to their areas of responsibility. **Decentralization** is the practice of delegating decision-making authority to the lower levels.

Organizations range from highly centralized to strongly decentralized. Although some firms lie at either end of the continuum, most fall somewhere between the two extremes, with the majority of these tending toward a decentralized approach. A special case of the decentralized firm is the **multinational corporation (MNC)**. The MNC is a corporation that "does business in more than one country in such a volume that its well-being and growth rest in more than one country."[4]

---

4 Yair Aharoni, "On the Definition of a Multinational Corporation," in A. Kapoor and Phillip D. Grub, eds., *The Multinational Enterprise in Transition* (Princeton, NJ: Darwin Press, 1972): 4.

Reasons for Decentralization

Seven reasons why firms may prefer the decentralized approach include better access to local information, cognitive limitations, more timely response, focusing of central management, training and evaluation of segment managers, motivation of segment managers, and enhanced competition. Let's look at these in more detail.

Better Access to Local Information   Decision quality is affected by the quality of information available. Lower-level managers who are in contact with immediate operating conditions (e.g., the strength and nature of local competition, the nature of the local labor force, and so on) have better access to local information. As a result, local managers are often in a position to make better decisions. This advantage of decentralization is particularly applicable to multinational corporations, where far-flung divisions may be operating in a number of different countries, subject to various legal systems and customs.

For example, Henkel Corporation, maker of adhesives and cleaning products, among other things, has local managers run their own divisions. In particular, marketing and pricing are under local administration. Language is not a problem as local managers are in control. Similarly, local managers are conversant with their own laws and customs.

Cognitive Limitations   Even if central management had good local information, those managers would face another problem. In a large, complex organization operating in diverse markets with hundreds or thousands of different products, no one person has the expertise and training needed to process and use all of the information. Cognitive limitation means that individuals with specialized skills would still be needed. Rather than having different individuals at headquarters for every specialized area, why not let these individuals have direct responsibility in the field? In this way, the firm can avoid the cost and bother of collecting and transmitting local information to headquarters. The structure of American business is changing. No longer are middle managers individuals with "people skills" and organization skills only. They must have specific fields of expertise in addition to managerial talent. For example, a middle manager in a bank may refer to herself as a financial specialist even though she manages 20 people. The capability to add skilled expertise is seen as crucial in today's downsized environment.

More Timely Response   In a centralized setting, it takes time to transmit local information to headquarters and then transmit the decision back to the local unit. These two transmissions cause delay and increase the potential for miscommunication. Under decentralization, where the local manager both makes and implements the decision, this problem does not arise.

Local managers in the MNC can respond quickly to customer discount demands, local government demands, and changes in the political climate. The different languages native to managers of divisions in the MNC make miscommunication an even greater problem. MNCs address this problem in two ways. First, a decentralized structure pushes decision making down to the local manager level, eliminating the need to interpret instructions from above. Second, MNCs are learning to incorporate technology that overrides the language barrier and eases cross-border data transfer. Technology is of great help in smoothing communication difficulties between parent and subsidiary and between one subsidiary and another.

Henkel's Loctite plant in Ireland uses computerized labeling on adhesives bound for Britain or Israel. Bar code technology "reads" the labels, eliminating the need for foreign language translation.

Focusing of Central Management   Managers at higher levels of the chain of command have broader responsibilities and powers. By decentralizing the operating decisions, top management is free to focus on strategic planning and decision making. Top management can concentrate on the long-run survival of the organization rather than day-to-day operations.

Training and Evaluation of Segment Managers   An organization always needs well-trained managers to replace higher-level managers who retire or move on to other opportunities. By decentralizing, lower-level managers have the opportunity to make and implement decisions. What better way to prepare a future generation of higher-level managers than by giving them the chance to make significant decisions? This also enables top managers to evaluate the local manager's capabilities, so that those who make the best decisions can be promoted to central management.

An additional advantage of decentralization is that home country managers gain broader experience by interacting with managers of foreign divisions. The chance to learn from each other is much greater in a decentralized MNC. Off and on throughout the past 50 years, a tour of duty at a foreign subsidiary has been a part of the manager's climb to the top. Now, foreign subsidiary managers may expect to spend some time at headquarters in the home office, as well.

At **General Electric**, for example, senior executives are sent on four-week tours of foreign markets and return to brief top management. Other senior executives are posted to Asian and Indian divisions. Similarly, foreign executives receive GE management training.

Motivation of Segment Managers   By giving local managers freedom to make decisions, some of their higher-level needs (self-esteem and self-actualization) are being met. Greater responsibility can produce more job satisfaction and motivate the local manager to work harder. Initiative and creativity are encouraged. Of course, the extent to which the motivational benefits can be realized depends to a large degree on how managers are evaluated and rewarded for their performance.

Enhanced Competition   In a highly centralized company, large overall profit margins can mask inefficiencies within the various subdivisions. A decentralized approach allows the company to determine each division's contribution to profit and to expose each division to market forces.

The Units of Decentralization

Decentralization is usually achieved by segmenting the company into *divisions*. One way in which divisions are differentiated is by the types of goods or services produced.

PepsiCo divisions include the **PepsiCo Americas Beverages** (including **Gatorade**, **Tropicana**, **Lipton**, **Ocean Spray**, and **Aquafina Water**, as well as its flagship soft drink division), **PepsiCo Americas Foods** (including **Frito-Lay**, **Quaker Foods & Snacks**, **Sabritas**, and **Gamesa and Latin America Foods**), and **PepsiCo International**. Some divisions depend on other divisions. For example, PepsiCo spun off **KFC**, **Taco Bell**, and **Pizza Hut** into **Yum! Brands**. In these restaurants, the cola you purchase will be Pepsi—not Coke.

In a decentralized setting, some interdependencies usually exist; otherwise, a company would merely be a collection of totally separate entities. The presence of these interdependencies creates the need for transfer pricing, which is discussed later in this chapter.

Similarly, companies create divisions according to the type of customer served.

Wal-Mart has five retail divisions. The Wal-Mart stores division targets discount store customers. The supercenter division targets customers of Wal-Mart's supercenter stores, which sell a variety of food, drug, and household items. **Sam's Club** focuses on buyers for small business. **Wal-Mart Neighborhood Markets** offer smaller convenience stores.

Organizing divisions as responsibility centers differentiates them on the degree of decentralization and creates the opportunities to control them through responsibility accounting. Control of cost centers is achieved by evaluating the efficiency and the effectiveness of divisional managers. **Efficiency** means how well activities are performed; it might be measured by the number of units produced per hour or by the cost of those units. **Effectiveness** can be defined as whether the manager has performed the right activities. Measures of effectiveness might focus on value-added versus non-value-added activities.

Profit centers are evaluated by the unit's profit contribution, measured on income statements. Since performance reports and contribution income statements have been discussed previously, this chapter will focus on the evaluation of investment centers.

Sustainability at Procter & Gamble

Increased interest in sustainability has led many companies to create sustainability goals and provide annual sustainability reports. Goals and objectives are detailed, and the annual progress toward those goals is reported. A company using this approach is **Procter & Gamble** (P&G), a global consumer products company that has been providing sustainability reports for 20 years.

P&G's 2018 report[5] details three major areas of emphasis: climate, water, and waste. The 2020 goals include the following:

- Reducing energy in P&G plants by 20 percent and ensuring that 30 percent of energy is from renewable sources
- Using 100 percent renewable or recycle materials for all products and packaging
- Having zero consumer and manufacturing waste go to landfills
- Reducing water use in manufacturing facilities by 20 percent

By identifying measurable objectives, actual performance can be compared with the plan.

To reduce plastics going into the ocean, nearly 100 percent of packaging in Charmin, Puffs, and Bounty is recyclable.

To increase the use of renewable or recycled materials and reduce waste going to landfills, manufacturing facilities are encouraged to "think of waste as worth." So suds that do not meet P&G standards are sold to car washes. Scraps from some femcare products become cat litter.

The existence of the annual sustainability performance report leads companies to formulate measurable, achievable goals and to hold their executives accountable.

MEASURING THE PERFORMANCE OF INVESTMENT CENTERS

OBJECTIVE ▸ **3**

Compute and explain return on investment (ROI), residual income (RI), and economic value added (EVA).

Companies maintain control of responsibility centers by developing performance measures for each center and basing rewards on a manager's ability to control the responsibility center.

Performance measures provide direction for managers of decentralized units and are used to evaluate their performance. The development of performance measures and the specification of a reward structure are major issues for a decentralized organization. Because performance measures can affect the behavior of managers, the measures chosen should encourage goal congruence. **Goal congruence** means that the goals of the manager are closely aligned with the goals of the firm. Well-chosen performance measures influence managers to pursue the company's objectives. Three performance evaluation measures for investment centers are ROI, residual income, and economic value added.

Return on Investment

While divisional income could be used to rank the divisions of a company, it may provide misleading information about segment performance. For example, suppose that two divisions report profits of $100,000 and $200,000, respectively. Is the second division performing better than the first? What if the first division used an investment of $500,000 to produce the contribution of $100,000, while the second used an investment of $2 million to produce the $200,000 contribution? Clearly, relating the reported operating profits to the assets used to produce them is a more meaningful measure of performance.

One way to relate operating profits to assets employed is to compute the profit earned per dollar of investment. For example, the first division earned $0.20 per dollar invested ($100,000/$500,000); the second division earned only $0.10 per dollar invested ($200,000/$2,000,000). In percentage terms, the first division provides a 20 percent rate of return and the second division, 10 percent. This method of computing the relative profitability of investments is known as the ROI.

5 Taken from Procter & Gamble's 2018 Citizenship Report, "Environmental Sustainability," https://www.pg.com /citizenship2018/index.html#/Environmental-Sustainability

Return on investment (ROI) is the most common measure of performance for an investment center. It is useful both externally and internally. Externally, ROI is used by stockholders to indicate the health of a company. Internally, ROI is used to measure the relative performance of divisions.

ROI can be defined in the following three ways:

$$\text{ROI} = \text{Operating income/Average operating assets}$$
$$= (\text{Operating income/Sales}) \times (\text{Sales/Average operating assets})$$
$$= \text{Operating income margin} \times \text{Operating asset turnover}$$

Operating income refers to earnings before interest and income taxes and is typically used for divisions. Net income is used in the calculation of ROI for the company as a whole. **Operating assets** include all assets used to generate operating income. They usually include cash, receivables, inventories, land, buildings, and equipment. Average operating assets is computed as follows:

$$\text{Average operating assets} = (\text{Beginning net book value} + \text{Ending net book value})/2$$

Opinions vary regarding how long-term assets (plant and equipment) should be valued (e.g., gross book value versus net book value or historical cost versus current cost). Most firms use historical cost net book value.[6] **Example 10.1** shows the how and why of calculating average operating assets, margin, turnover, and ROI.

EXAMPLE 10.1

The HOW and WHY of Calculating Average Operating Assets, Margin, Turnover, and Return on Investment (ROI)

Information:

Multidiv, Inc., provided the following information for two of its divisions for last year:

	Snack Foods Division	Appliance Division
Sales	$30,000,000	$117,000,000
Operating income	1,800,000	3,510,000
Operating assets, January 1	9,600,000	17,500,000
Operating assets, December 31	10,400,000	21,500,000

Why:
ROI is a key measure of performance. It relates the income earned to the investment needed to produce that income. It is appropriate for companies and for investment centers.

Required:

1. For the Snack Foods Division, calculate:
    a. Average operating assets
    b. Margin
    c. Turnover
    d. ROI

2. For the Appliance Division, calculate:
    a. Average operating assets
    b. Margin
    c. Turnover
    d. ROI

---

6 For a discussion of the relative merits of gross book value, see James S. Reese and William R. Cool, "Measuring Investment Center Performance," *Harvard Business Review* (May–June 1978): 28–46, 174–176.

EXAMPLE 10.1

(Continued)

3. **What if** ending assets for the Snack Foods Division were $14,400,000? How would that affect average operating assets? Margin? Turnover? ROI?

Solution:

1. a. Average operating assets = (Beginning assets + Ending assets)/2
    = ($9,600,000 + $10,400,000)/2
    = $10,000,000

    b. Margin = Operating income/Sales
    = $1,800,000/$30,000,000
    = 0.06, or 6%

    c. Turnover = Sales/Average operating assets
    = $30,000,000/$10,000,000
    = 3.0

    d. ROI = Margin × Turnover
    = 0.06 × 3.0
    = 0.18, or 18%

    OR

    ROI = Operating income/Average operating assets
    = $1,800,000/$10,000,000
    = 0.18, or 18%

2. a. Average operating assets = (Beginning assets + Ending assets)/2
    = ($17,500,000 + $21,500,000)/2
    = $19,500,000

    b. Margin = Operating income/Sales
    = $3,510,000/$117,000,000
    = 0.03, or 3%

    c. Turnover = Sales/Average operating assets
    = $117,000,000/$19,500,000
    = 6.0

    d. ROI = Margin × Turnover
    = 0.03 × 6.0
    = 0.18, or 18%

    OR

    ROI = Operating income/Average operating assets
    = $3,510,000/$19,500,000
    = 0.18, or 18%

3. If ending operating assets for the Snack Foods Division were $14,400,000, then the average operating assets would be higher. Higher average operating assets leads to lower turnover and lower ROI. Margin would not be affected. New amounts would be:

    Average operating assets = ($9,600,000 + $14,400,000)/2 = $12,000,000
    Turnover = $30,000,000/$12,000,000 = 2.5
    ROI = 0.06 × 2.5 = 0.15, or 15%

Margin and Turnover   The ROI formula is broken into two component ratios: *margin* and *turnover*. **Margin** is the ratio of operating income to sales. It shows the portion of sales that is available for interest, income taxes, and profit. **Turnover** is found by dividing sales by average operating assets. The result shows how productively assets are being used to generate sales.

Both measures can affect ROI. Let's examine the relationship of margin, turnover, and ROI more closely by considering Example 10.1. Both divisions have the same ROI, 18 percent. The Snack Foods Division, however, has a margin of 6 percent versus the Appliance Division margin of 3 percent. This tells us that the Snack Foods Division earns twice as much per dollar of sales than the Appliance Division. However, the Appliance Division has higher turnover, indicating that it is using its operating assets more effectively than the Snack Foods Division. That is, it takes fewer dollars of assets to support every dollar of income earned.

Consider a second year of data for each of the two divisions:

	Snack Foods Division	Appliance Division
	Year 2	**Year 2**
Sales	$40,000,000	$117,000,000
Operating income	$ 2,000,000	$ 2,925,000
Average operating assets	$10,000,000	$ 19,500,000
Margin	5%	2.5%
Turnover	4.0	6.0
ROI	20%	15%

The Snack Foods Division improved its ROI from 18 percent to 20 percent from Year 1 to Year 2, while the Appliance Division's ROI dropped from 18 percent to 15 percent. Notice that the margins for both divisions dropped from Year 1 to Year 2. A declining margin could be explained by increasing expenses, competitive pressures (forcing a decrease in selling prices), or both.

Despite the declining margin, the Snack Foods Division increased its rate of return. This increase resulted from an increase in the turnover rate that more than compensated for the decline in margin. The increase in turnover could be explained by a deliberate policy to reduce inventories (the average assets remained the same for the Snack Foods Division even though sales increased by $10 million).

**DATA
ANALYTICS**

The Appliance Division, on the other hand, had lower ROI because margin declined and the turnover rate stayed constant. Although more information is needed before any definitive conclusion is reached, their different responses to similar difficulties may say something about the relative skills of the two managers. Data analytics are used descriptively to give managers a better understanding of why profitability has changed. Managers can use it diagnostically to determine what is wrong with the declining margin and correct it if possible.

Advantages of the ROI Measure   When ROI is used to evaluate performance, division managers naturally try to increase it. This can be accomplished by increasing sales, decreasing costs, and/or decreasing investment. Three advantages of using ROI are as follows:

1. It encourages investment center managers to pay careful attention to the relationships among sales, expenses, and investment.
2. It encourages cost efficiency.
3. It discourages excessive investment in operating assets.

Each of these three advantages is discussed in turn.

The first advantage is that ROI encourages managers to consider the interrelationship of income and investment. Suppose that the marketing vice president suggests that a division manager increase her advertising budget by $100,000, arguing that this will boost sales by $200,000 and raise the contribution margin by $110,000. If the division were evaluated on the basis of operating income, this information is enough. However, if ROI is used, the manager will want to know how much additional investment is required to support the increased production and sales. Suppose that an additional $50,000 of operating assets will be needed.

Currently, the division has sales of $2 million, operating income of $150,000, and operating assets of $1 million. Current ROI is 15 percent ($150,000/$1,000,000).

If advertising increased by $100,000 and the contribution margin by $110,000, operating income would increase by $10,000 ($110,000 − $100,000). Investment in operating assets must also increase by $50,000. With the additional advertising, the ROI is 15.24 percent ($160,000/$1,050,000). Since the ROI is increased by the proposal, the divisional manager should increase advertising.

The second advantage is that ROI encourages cost efficiency. The manager of an investment center always has control over costs. Therefore, increasing efficiency through judicious cost reduction is a common method of increasing ROI. For example, decreasing non-value-added activities is a good way to decrease cost without decreasing production, sales, or quality. (Chapter 12 explains this in more detail.) There are ways to decrease costs in the short run that have a harmful effect on the business. This possibility is discussed in the section on disadvantages of ROI.

The third advantage is that ROI encourages efficient investment. Divisions that have cut costs to the extent possible must focus on investment reduction. For example, operating assets can be trimmed through the reduction of materials inventory and work-in-process inventory, perhaps by installing just-in-time purchasing and manufacturing systems. New, more productive machinery can be installed, inefficient plants can be closed, and so on. Companies are taking a hard look at their level of investment and acting to reduce it. This is a positive result of ROI-based evaluation.

Disadvantages of the ROI Measure   The use of ROI to evaluate performance also has disadvantages. Two negative aspects associated with ROI are frequently mentioned.

1. It discourages managers from investing in projects that would decrease the divisional ROI but would increase the profitability of the company as a whole. (Generally, projects with an ROI less than a division's current ROI would be rejected.)
2. It can encourage myopic behavior, in that managers may focus on the short run at the expense of the long run.

The first disadvantage can be illustrated by an example. Suppose that the Snack Foods Division has the opportunity to invest in two projects for the coming year. The first project is a new cheese-coated corn chip that requires additional factory space and special coating machinery. The second project is star-shaped corn chips. That project will require special extruding machinery to create the desired shapes. The outlay required for each investment, the dollar returns, and the ROI are as follows:

	Project I	Project II
Investment	$10,000,000	$4,000,000
Operating income	$ 1,500,000	$ 760,000
ROI	15%	19%

The division is currently earning an ROI of 18 percent, using operating assets of $10 million to generate operating income of $1.8 million. Corporate headquarters will approve up to $15 million in new investment capital and requires that all investments earn at least 12 percent. Any capital not used by a division is invested by headquarters so that it earns exactly 12 percent.

The divisional manager has four alternatives: (a) add Project I, (b) add Project II, (c) add both Projects I and II, and (d) maintain the status quo (invest in neither project). The divisional ROI was computed for each alternative.

	Add Project I	Add Project II	Add Both Projects	Maintain Status Quo
Operating income	$ 3,300,000	$ 2,560,000	$ 4,060,000	$ 1,800,000
Operating assets	$20,000,000	$14,000,000	$24,000,000	$10,000,000
ROI	16.50%	18.29%	16.92%	18.00%

The divisional manager chose to invest only in Project II, since it would have a favorable effect on the division's ROI (18.29 percent is greater than 18.00 percent).

Assuming that any capital not used by the division is invested at 12 percent, the manager's choice produced a lower profit for the company than could have been realized. If Project I had been selected, the company would have earned $1.5 million. By not selecting Project I, the $10 million in capital is invested at 12 percent, earning only $1.2 million (0.12 × $10,000,000). By maximizing the division's ROI, then, the divisional manager cost the company $300,000 in profits ($1,500,000 − $1,200,000).

The second disadvantage of using ROI to evaluate performance is that it can encourage myopic behavior. However, while some cost reduction can result in more efficiency in the short run, it can result in lower efficiency in the long run. The emphasis on short-run results at the expense of the long run is **myopic behavior**. Examples are laying off more highly paid employees, cutting the advertising budget, delaying promotions and employee training, reducing preventive maintenance, and using cheaper materials.

Each of these steps reduces expenses, increases income, and raises ROI in the short run, but may have some long-run negative consequences. Laying off more highly paid salespeople may hurt the division's future sales. For example, it has been estimated that the average monthly cost of replacing a sales representative with five to eight years' experience with a representative with less than one year of experience was $36,000 of lost sales. Low employee turnover has been linked to high customer satisfaction.[7] Future sales could also be harmed by cutting back on advertising and using cheaper materials. By delaying promotions, employee morale would be affected, which could, in turn, lower productivity and future sales. Finally, reducing preventive maintenance will likely cut into the productive capability of the division by increasing downtime and decreasing the life of the productive equipment. While these actions raise current ROI, they lead to lower future ROI.

Residual Income

To avoid managers using ROI to turn down investments that are profitable for the company but that lower a division's ROI, some companies have adopted an alternative performance measure known as *residual income*. **Residual income** is the difference between operating income and the minimum dollar return required on a company's operating assets:

Residual income = Operating income − (Minimum rate of return × Operating assets)

Example 10.2 shows the how and why of calculating residual income.

EXAMPLE 10.2		
The HOW and WHY of Calculating Residual Income		

Information:

Multidiv, Inc., provided the following information for two of its divisions for last year:

	Snack Foods Division	Appliance Division
Sales	$30,000,000	$117,000,000
Operating income	1,800,000	3,510,000
Average operating assets	10,000,000	19,500,000

Multidiv, Inc., requires a 12 percent minimum rate of return.

---

7   James L. Heskett, Thomas O. Jones, Gary W. Loveman, W. Earl Sasser Jr., and Leonard A. Schlesinger, "Putting the Service-Profit Chain to Work," *Harvard Business Review* Vol. 74, No. 2 (March/April 1994): 164–174.

EXAMPLE 10.2

(Continued)

Why:
Residual income is measured in dollar amounts rather than percentages. It relates the income earned to the minimum required ROI and overcomes the tendency for managers to turn down profitable projects that might lower divisional ROI.

Required:

1. Calculate residual income for the Snack Foods Division.

2. Calculate residual income for the Appliance Division.

3. *What if* the minimum required rate of return was 16 percent? How would that affect the residual income of the two divisions?

Solution:

1. Residual income = Operating income − (Minimum rate of return × Operating assets)
   = $1,800,000 − (0.12 × $10,000,000)
   = $600,000

2. Residual income = Operating income − (Minimum rate of return ×
   Operating assets)
   = $3,510,000 − (0.12 × $19,500,000)
   = $1,170,000

3. If the minimum rate of return was 16 percent, the residual income of both divisions would be lower.
   Snack Foods residual income = $1,800,000 − (0.16 × $10,000,000) = $200,000

   Appliance residual income = $3,510,000 − (0.16 × $19,500,000) = $390,000

Example 10.2 shows that the residual incomes of the two divisions are different, even though their ROIs are the same. Clearly, Multidiv earns more from the larger Appliance Division than it does from the Snack Foods Division.

Advantages of Residual Income Residual income is a dollar measure of performance. While the percentage rate of return is familiar to managers, and takes away the impact of size from the measure, at the end of the day, the dollar income does count. A manager can become so focused on the ROI, that profitable projects that return more than their cost of capital may be rejected. Residual income refocuses the manager on dollar profit.

To illustrate the use of residual income, consider the Snack Foods Division example again. Recall that the division manager rejected Project I because it would have reduced divisional ROI, which cost the company $300,000 in profits. The use of residual income as the performance measure would have prevented this loss. The residual income for each project is computed as follows.

Project I:

Residual income = Operating income − (Minimum rate of return × Operating assets)
= $1,500,000 − (0.12 × $10,000,000)
= $300,000

Project II:

Residual income = Operating income − (Minimum rate of return × Operating assets)
= $760,000 − (0.12 × $4,000,000)
= $280,000

Notice that both projects increase residual income; in fact, Project I increases the division's residual income more than Project II does. Thus, both would be selected by the divisional manager. For comparative purposes, the divisional residual income for each of the four alternatives identified earlier follows:

	Add Project I	Add Project II	Add Both Projects	Maintain Status Quo
Operating assets	$20,000,000	$14,000,000	$24,000,000	$10,000,000
Operating income	$ 3,300,000	$ 2,560,000	$ 4,060,000	$ 1,800,000
Minimum return[a]	2,400,000	1,680,000	2,880,000	1,200,000
Residual income	$ 900,000	$ 880,000	$ 1,180,000	$ 600,000

[a]Minimum return = 0.12 × Operating assets.

When residual income is used as the performance measure, both projects are clearly profitable and would be chosen. Managers are encouraged to move beyond a focus on the percentage ROI to look at the absolute dollar value of the additional profit.

Disadvantages of Residual Income   Two disadvantages of residual income are that it is an absolute measure of return and that it does not discourage myopic behavior. Absolute measures of return make it difficult to directly compare the performance of divisions. For example, consider the residual income computations for Division A and Division B, where the minimum required rate of return is 8 percent.

	Division A	Division B
Average operating assets	$15,000,000	$2,500,000
Operating income	$ 1,500,000	$ 300,000
Minimum return[a]	1,200,000	200,000
Residual income	$ 300,000	$ 100,000
Residual return[b]	2%	4%

[a]0.08 × Operating assets.
[b]Residual income divided by operating assets.

It is tempting to claim that Division A outperforms Division B, since its residual income is three times higher. Notice, however, that Division A used six times as many assets to produce this difference. If anything, Division B is more efficient.

One possible way to correct this disadvantage is to compute a residual ROI by dividing residual income by average operating assets. This measure indicates that Division B earned 4 percent while Division A earned only 2 percent. Another possibility is to compute both ROI and residual income and use both measures for performance evaluation. ROI could then be used for interdivisional comparisons.[8] Descriptive analysis of these data showed the importance of determining residual income and the residual rate of return. They can be used prescriptively to encourage a closer link between income and assets used to achieve income.

DATA ANALYTICS

The second disadvantage of residual income is that it can encourage a short-run orientation. Just as a manager can choose to cut maintenance, training, and sales force expenses when being evaluated under ROI, the manager being evaluated on the basis of residual income can take the same actions. The problem of myopic behavior is not solved by switching to this measure. A preferable method of reducing the myopic behavior problem of residual income is the economic value added method, discussed next.

---

8   In their study, Reese and Cool found that only 2 percent of the companies surveyed used residual income by itself, whereas 28 percent used both residual income and ROI. See Reese and Cool, "Measuring Investment Center Performance."

Economic Value Added

Another measure of profitability for performance evaluation of investment centers is *economic value added.*[9] **Economic value added (EVA)** is after-tax operating income minus the total annual cost of capital. If EVA is positive, the company is creating wealth. If it is negative, then the company is destroying wealth. Over the long term, only those companies creating capital, or wealth, can survive. Over the past two decades, many companies have used EVA to adjust management compensation; EVA encourages managers to use existing and new capital for maximum gain, including **The Coca-Cola Company, General Electric, Intel,** and **Merck.** Currently, **Ball Corp., Nike,** and **Whole Foods** are using EVA.[10]

EVA is a dollar figure, not a percentage rate of return. However, it does bear a resemblance to rates of return such as ROI because it links net income (return) to capital employed. The key feature of EVA is its emphasis on *after-tax* operating income and the *actual* cost of capital. Other return measures may use accounting book value numbers that may or may not represent the true cost of capital. Residual income, for example, typically uses a minimum expected rate of return. Investors like EVA because it relates profit to the amount of resources needed to achieve it.

Calculating EVA EVA is after-tax operating income minus the dollar cost of capital employed. The equation for EVA is expressed as follows:

$$\text{EVA} = \text{After-tax operating income} - (\text{Weighted average cost of capital} \times \text{Total capital employed})$$

The difficulty faced by most companies is computing the cost of capital employed. Two steps are involved: (1) determine the **weighted average cost of capital** (a percentage figure), and (2) determine the total dollar amount of capital employed.

To calculate the weighted average cost of capital, the company must identify all sources of invested funds. Typical sources are borrowing and equity (stock issued). Typically, borrowed money has an interest rate attached, and that rate is adjusted for its tax deductibility. For example, if a company issued 10-year bonds at an annual interest rate of 8 percent and the tax rate is 40 percent, then the after-tax cost of the bonds is 4.8 percent $[0.08 - (0.4 \times 0.08)]$. Equity is handled differently. The cost of equity financing is the opportunity cost to investors. Over time, stockholders have received an average return that is six percentage points higher than the return on long-term government bonds. If these bond rates are about 4 percent, then the average cost of equity is 10 percent $(4\% + 6\%)$. Riskier stocks command a higher return; more stable and less risky stocks offer a somewhat lower return. Finally, the proportionate share of each method of financing is multiplied by its percentage cost and summed to yield the total dollar amount of capital employed.

Suppose that a company has two sources of financing: $2 million of long-term bonds paying 9 percent interest and $6 million of common stock, which is considered to be of average risk (with a 6 percent premium). If the company's tax rate is 35 percent and the rate of interest on long-term government bonds is 3 percent, the company's weighted average cost of capital is computed as follows:

	Amount	Percent	$\times$	After-Tax Cost	$=$	Weighted Cost
Bonds	$2,000,000	0.25		$0.09(1 - 0.35) = 0.0585$		0.0146
Equity	6,000,000	0.75		$0.06 + 0.03 = 0.090$		0.0675
Total	$8,000,000					0.0821

Thus, the company's weighted average cost of capital is 8.21 percent.

---

9 EVA° is a registered trademark of Stern Stewart & Co.

10 Geoff Colvin, "A New Financial Checkup," *CNN Money* (January 11, 2010), http://money.cnn.com/2010/01/08 /news/ economy/eva_momentum.fortune/index.htm. Also, Whole Foods website, http://www.wholefoodsmarket .com/company/eva.php. Ball Corporation, "EVA Measuring Our Long Term Success," March 12, 2019, https:// ballcorp.gcs-web.com/static-files/d392ff04-d61d-45ff-9463-414886185ede. Asit Sharma, "Understanding Whole Foods Market's Approach to Competition," The Motley Fool (September 15, 2015), https://www.fool.com/investing /general/2015/09/15/understanding-whole-foods-market-incs-approach-to.aspx. https://www.stock-analysis-on.net /NYSE/Company/Nike-Inc/Performance-Measure/Economic-Value-Added.

Next we need to know the amount of capital employed. Clearly, the amount paid for buildings, land, and machinery must be included. Other expenditures meant to have a long-term payoff, however, such as R&D employee training, and so on, should also be included. Despite the fact that the latter are classified by GAAP as expenses, EVA is an internal management accounting measure, and therefore these expenses can be thought of as the investments that they truly are. **Example 10.3** shows the how and why of calculating the weighted average cost of capital, the total dollar amount of capital employed, and EVA.

EXAMPLE 10.3

The HOW and WHY of Calculating the Weighted Average Cost of Capital and EVA

Information:
Furman, Inc., had after-tax operating income last year of $1,583,000. Three sources of financing were used by the company: $2 million of mortgage bonds paying 8 percent interest, $3 million of unsecured bonds paying 10 percent interest, and $10 million in common stock, which was considered to be no more or less risky than other stocks. (Over time, stockholders have received an average return that is six percentage points higher than the return on long-term government bonds.) The rate of return on long-term U.S. Treasury bonds is 6 percent. Furman, Inc., pays a marginal tax rate of 40 percent.

> **Why:**
> Economic value added adjusts earnings by the true cost of capital employed. As a result, it is a measure of wealth created or destroyed by a company.

Required:

1. Calculate the after-tax cost of each method of financing.

2. Calculate the weighted average cost of capital for Furman, Inc. Calculate the total dollar amount of capital employed for Furman, Inc.

3. Calculate economic value added (EVA) for Furman, Inc., for last year. Is Furman, Inc., creating or destroying wealth?

4. *What if* Furman, Inc., had $15 million in common stock and no mortgage bonds or unsecured bonds? How would that affect the weighted average cost of capital? How would it affect EVA?

Solution:

1. After-tax cost of mortgage bonds = Interest rate − (Tax rate × Interest rate)
   $$= [0.08 − (0.4 × 0.08)] = 0.048$$
   After-tax cost of unsecured bonds = Interest rate − (Tax rate × Interest rate)
   $$= [0.10 − (0.4 × 0.10)] = 0.06$$
   Cost of common stock = Return on long-term Treasury bonds
   $$+ \text{ Average premium}$$
   $$= 0.06 + 0.06 = 0.12$$

2.

	Amount	Percent	×	After-Tax Cost	=	Weighted Cost
Mortgage bonds	$ 2,000,000	0.1333		0.048		0.0064
Unsecured bonds	3,000,000	0.2000		0.060		0.0120
Common stock	10,000,000	0.6667		0.120		0.0800
Total	$15,000,000					0.0984

Weighted average percentage cost of capital = 0.0984, or 9.84%
Total dollar amount of capital employed = 0.0984 × $15,000,000 = $1,476,000

EXAMPLE 10.3

(Continued)

3.

After-tax operating income	$1,583,000
Less: Total dollar amount of capital employed	1,476,000
EVA	$ 107,000

Furman, Inc., is creating capital because EVA is positive (the after-tax earnings are greater than the after-tax cost of capital).

4. If all $15 million of financing were in common stock, the weighted average percentage cost of capital would be 12 percent and the total dollar amount of capital employed would be $1,800,000 (0.12 × $15,000,000). EVA would be negative, and Furman, Inc., would be destroying wealth, not creating it.

$$EVA = \$1,583,000 - \$1,800,000 = \$(217,000)$$

Behavioral Aspects of EVA Some companies have found that EVA encourages the right kind of behavior from their divisions in a way that emphasis on operating income alone cannot. The underlying reason is EVA's reliance on the true cost of capital. In many companies, the responsibility for investment decisions rests with corporate management. As a result, the cost of capital is considered a corporate expense. If a division builds inventories and investment, the cost of financing that investment is passed on to the overall income statement, and does not reduce the division's operating income. Investment seems free to the divisions, and of course, they want more. As a result, EVA should be measured for subsets of the company.

Suppose that Supertech, Inc., has two divisions, the Hardware Division and the Software Division. Operating income statements for the divisions are as follows:

	Hardware Division	Software Division
Sales	$5,000,000	$2,000,000
Cost of goods sold	2,000,000	1,100,000
Gross profit	$3,000,000	$ 900,000
Divisional selling and administrative expenses	2,000,000	400,000
Operating income	$1,000,000	$ 500,000

It looks as if both divisions are doing a good job. Now, consider each division's use of capital. Suppose that Supertech's weighted average cost of capital is 11 percent. Hardware, by increasing inventories of components and finished goods, use of warehouses, and so on, uses capital amounting to $10 million, so its dollar cost of capital is $1,100,000 (0.11 × $10,000,000). Software does not need large materials inventories, but it does invest heavily in training and research and development. Its capital usage is $2 million, and its total dollar cost of capital is $220,000 (0.11 × $2,000,000). The EVA for each division can be calculated as follows:

	Hardware Division	Software Division
Operating income	$1,000,000	$500,000
Less: Cost of capital	1,100,000	220,000
EVA	$ (100,000)	$280,000

Now, it is clear that the Hardware Division is actually losing wealth by using too much capital. The Software Division, on the other hand, has created wealth for Supertech. By using EVA, the Hardware Division's manager will no longer consider inventories and warehouses to be "free" goods. Instead, the manager will strive to reduce capital usage and increase EVA. Reducing capital to $8 million, for example, would boost EVA to $120,000 [$1,000,000 − (0.11 × $8,000,000)].

REAL-WORLD EXAMPLE

Quaker Oats faced a similar situation. Prior to 1991, Quaker Oats evaluated its business segments on the basis of quarterly profits. To keep quarterly earnings on an upward march, segment managers sharply discounted prices at the end of each quarter. This resulted in huge orders from retailers and surges in production at Quaker's plants at the end of each three-month period. This practice is called trade loading because it "loads up the trade" (retail stores) with product. However, trade loading is expensive because it requires massive amounts of capital (e.g., working capital, inventories, and warehouses to store the quarterly spikes in output). Quaker's plant in Danville, Illinois, produces snack foods and breakfast cereals. Before EVA, the Danville plant ran well below capacity early in the quarter. Purchasing, however, bought huge quantities of boxes, plastic wrappers, granola, and chocolate chips, in anticipation of the production surge of the last six weeks of the quarter. As the products were finished, Quaker packed 15 warehouses with finished goods. Because all costs associated with inventories were absorbed by corporate headquarters, they appeared to be free to the plant managers, who built ever higher inventories. The advent of EVA and the cancellation of trade loading led to a smoothing of production throughout the quarter, higher overall production (and sales), and lower inventories. Quaker's Danville plant reduced inventories from $15 million to $9 million. Quaker has closed one-third of its 15 warehouses, saving $6 million annually in salaries and capital costs.[11]

Multiple Measures of Performance

ROI, residual income, and EVA are important measures of managerial performance. However, they are financial measures, and may tempt managers to focus only on dollar figures. This focus may not tell the whole story for the company. In addition, lower-level managers and employees may feel unable to affect net income or investment. To counter this, nonfinancial operating measures have been developed. For example, top management could look at such factors as market share, customer complaints, personnel turnover ratios, and personnel development. By letting lower-level managers know that attention to long-run factors is also vital, the tendency to over-emphasize financial measures is reduced.

Modern managers are especially likely to use multiple measures of performance and to include nonfinancial as well as financial measures. For example, Sam's Club and **CVS** send emails to a sample of customers immediately after a visit to measure customer satisfaction. Others, such as **USAA**, ask customers to stay on the line after phoning customer service to check on the experience. The Balanced Scorecard (discussed in Chapter 13) was developed to measure a firm's performance in multiple areas.

REAL-WORLD EXAMPLE

Using Big Data in Professional Golf

PGA golf pros are basically small businessmen. They earn money from tour winnings and endorsements. However, they have substantial expenses, including travel, personnel (caddies, coaches, business manager, etc.), and equipment. Competition in each tour event is intense, and the margin of victory in a tournament can be just one or two strokes over a 72-hole series (three- to four-day period). In the past, golfers relied on training, expert help from caddies and coaches, and instinct to guide them in making shots. However, since 2003, the PGA Tour's ShotLink system has recorded the location of every shot hit at a tour event. Analytics firms have analyzed the massive amount of raw data to guide golfers.[12]

11 G. Bennett Stewart III, "EVA Works—but Not If You Make These Common Mistakes," *Fortune* (May 1, 1995): 117–118.
12 Brian Costa "Golfers Join Rest of World, Use Data," *The Wall Street Journal* (May 17, 2016): D6.

For example, 2016 PGA Master's winner Danny Willett used analysis from London firm **15th Club** to determine some of his playing strategies. The firm advised him that players who lay up before a water hazard on Augusta's par-5 holes do better than those who go for the green. This was one aspect of his tournament-winning play.

The PGA Tour is now publishing the "strokes gained putting" and "strokes gained tee to green" statistics. Players use these statistics to evaluate which parts of their game need improvement. Some go further. The caddie and swing coach of golfer Jason Day, number 1 in the world, shares data on how past tournaments have been won and uses those reports to set goals for every hole. These goals can affect whether Day attacks a hole aggressively or more conservatively. Brandt Snedeker, number 16 in the world rankings, uses the data to determine which courses best utilize his strengths. He avoids some courses he loves to play in order to concentrate on the ones that suit his short game.

Even a small edge can affect world rankings and money earnings. Top golfers cannot afford to ignore big data.

MEASURING AND REWARDING THE PERFORMANCE OF MANAGERS

OBJECTIVE ◀ **4**

Discuss methods of evaluating and rewarding managerial performance.

While some companies consider the performance of the division to be equivalent to the performance of the manager, there is a compelling reason to separate the two. Often, the performance of the division is subject to factors beyond the manager's control. It is particularly important, then, to take a responsibility accounting approach and evaluate managers on the basis of factors under their control. A serious concern is the creation of a compensation plan that is closely tied to the performance of the division.

Incentive Pay for Managers—Encouraging Goal Congruence

Managerial evaluation and incentive pay would be of little concern if all managers were equally likely to perform up to the best of their abilities, and if those abilities were known in advance. In the case of a small company, owned and managed by the same person, there is no problem. The owner puts in as much effort as they wish and receives all of the income as a reward for performance. In most companies, however, the owner hires managers to operate the company on a day-to-day basis and delegates decision-making authority to them. The stockholders of a company hire the CEO through the board of directors, and division managers are hired by the CEO to operate their divisions on behalf of the owners. Then, the owners must ensure that the managers are providing good service.

Why wouldn't managers provide good service? There are three reasons: (1) they may be unable to perform the job, (2) they may prefer not to work hard, and (3) they may prefer to spend company resources on perquisites. The first reason requires owners to discover information about the manager before hiring them. Recall that one reason for decentralization was to provide training for future managers. The training process provides signals about the managerial ability of division managers. The second and third reasons require the owner to monitor the manager or to arrange an incentive scheme that will more closely ally the manager's goals with those of the owner. Some managers may not want to do hard or routine work. Some may be risk-averse and not take actions which expose them, and the company, to risky situations. Thus, it is necessary to compensate them for undertaking risk and hard work. Closely related to the desire of some managers to shirk responsibility is the tendency of managers to overuse perquisites. **Perquisites** are a type of fringe benefit received over and above salary. Some examples are a nice office, use of a company car or jet, expense accounts, and company-paid country club memberships. While some perquisites are legitimate uses of company resources, they can be abused. A well-structured incentive pay plan can help to encourage goal congruence between managers and owners.

Managerial Rewards

Managerial rewards frequently include incentives tied to performance. The objective is to encourage goal congruence, so that managers will act in the best interests of the firm. Arranging managerial compensation to encourage managers to adopt the same goals as the overall firm is an important issue. Managerial rewards include salary increases, bonuses based on reported income, stock options, and noncash compensation.

Cash Compensation   Cash compensation includes salaries and bonuses. Raises are one way for a company to reward good managerial performance. However, once the raise takes effect, it is usually permanent. Bonuses give a company more flexibility. Many companies use a combination of salary and bonus to reward performance by keeping salaries fairly level and allowing bonuses to fluctuate with reported income. Managers may find their bonuses tied to divisional net income or to targeted increases in net income. For example, a division manager may receive an annual salary of $75,000 and a yearly bonus of 5 percent of the increase in reported net income. If net income does not rise, the manager's bonus is zero. This incentive pay scheme makes increasing net income, an objective of the owner, important to the manager as well.

Income-based compensation can encourage dysfunctional behavior. The manager may engage in unethical practices, such as postponing needed maintenance. If the bonus is capped at a certain amount (say, the bonus is equal to 1 percent of net income but cannot exceed $50,000), managers may postpone revenue recognition from the end of the year in which the maximum bonus has already been achieved to the next year. Those who structure the reward systems need to understand both the positive incentives built into the system as well as the potential for negative behavior.

Profit-sharing plans make employees partial owners in the sense that they receive a share of the profits. They are not owners in the sense of decision making or downside risk sharing. This is a form of risk sharing, in particular, sharing of upside risk. Typically, employees are paid a flat rate, and then, any profits to be shared are over and above wages. The objective is to provide an incentive for employees to work harder and smarter.

Stock-Based Compensation   Stock is a share in the company, and theoretically, it should increase in value as the company does well and decrease in value as the company does poorly. Thus, the issue of stock to managers makes them part owners of the company and should encourage goal congruence. Many companies encourage employees to purchase shares of stock, or they grant shares as a bonus. A disadvantage of stock as compensation is that share price can fall for reasons beyond the control of managers.

Companies frequently offer stock options to managers. A **stock option** is the right to buy a certain number of shares of the company's stock, at a particular price and after a set length of time. The objective of awarding stock options is to encourage managers to focus on the longer term. The price of the option shares is usually set at market price at the time of issue. Then, if the stock price rises in the future, the manager may exercise the option, thus purchasing stock at a below-market price and realizing an immediate gain.

For example, Lois Canfield, head of the Toiletries Division of Palgate, Inc., was granted an option to purchase 100,000 shares of Palgate stock at the current market price of $20 per share. The option was granted in August 20x0 and could be exercised after two years. If, by August 20x2, Palgate stock has risen to $23 per share, Lois can purchase all 100,000 shares for $2,000,000 (100,000 × $20 option price) and immediately sell them for $2,300,000 (100,000 × $23). She will realize a profit of $300,000. Of course, if Palgate stock drops below $20, Lois will not exercise the option. Typically, however, stock prices rise along with the market, and Lois can safely bet on a future profit as long as Palgate does not perform worse than the market.

Companies are becoming more aware of the impact on options of the overall movement of the stock market. If the market moves strongly higher, there is the potential for windfall profits. That is, any profit realized from selling stock based on low-cost options may be more closely related to the overall rise in the stock market and less related to outstanding performance by top management. In addition, top executives with a number of options may focus on the short-term movements of the stock price rather than on the long-term indicators of company performance. In essence, they may trade long-term returns for short-term returns.

Typically, there are constraints on the exercise of the options. For example, the stock purchased with options may not be sold for a certain period of time. A disadvantage of stock options is that the price of the stock is based on many factors and is not completely within the manager's control.

Issues to Consider in Structuring Income-Based Compensation The underlying objective of a company that uses income-based compensation is goal congruence between owner and manager. To the extent that the owners of the company want net income and stock price to rise, basing management compensation on such increases encourages managerial efforts in that direction. Single measures of performance, however, which are often the basis of bonuses, are subject to gaming behavior in that managers may increase short-term measures at the expense of long-term measures. For example, a manager may keep net income high by refusing to invest in more modern and efficient equipment. Depreciation expense remains low, but so do productivity and quality. Clearly, the manager has an incentive to understand the computation of the accounting numbers used in performance evaluation. An accounting change from FIFO to LIFO or in the method of depreciation, for example, will change net income even though sales and costs remain unchanged. Frequently, we see that a new CEO of a troubled corporation will take a number of losses (e.g., inventory write-downs) all at once. This is referred to as the "big bath" and usually results in very low (or negative) net income in that year. Then, the books are cleared for a good increase in net income, and a correspondingly large bonus, for the next year.

Both cash bonuses and stock options can encourage a short-term orientation. To encourage a longer-term orientation, some companies require top executives to purchase and hold a certain amount of company stock to retain employment.

Another issue to be considered in structuring management compensation plans is that owners and managers may be affected differently by risk. Managers with much of their own capital—both financial and human—invested in the company may be less apt to take risks. Owners, because of their ability to diversify away some of the risk, may prefer a more risk-taking attitude. As a result, managers must be somewhat insulated from catastrophic downside risk in order to encourage them to make entrepreneurial decisions.

Noncash Compensation Noncash compensation is an important part of the management reward structure. Autonomy in the conduct of their daily business is an important type of noncash compensation. At Hewlett-Packard, cross-functional teams "own" their business and have the authority to reinvest earnings to react quickly to changing markets.

Perquisites are also important. We often see managers who trade off increased salary for improvements in title, office location and trappings, use of expense accounts, and so on. Perquisites can be well used to make the manager more efficient. For example, a busy manager may be able to effectively employ several assistants and may find that use of a corporate jet allows them to more efficiently schedule travel in overseeing far-flung divisions. However, perquisites may be abused as well. For instance, one wonders how the shareholders of Tyco benefitted from their 50 percent share of the $2 million party that former Tyco chief Dennis Kozlowski threw for his wife's birthday, or from Kozlowski's $6,000 shower curtain.[13]

---

13 John Bringardner, "Tyco Trial Shows Benefits, and Limits, of Technology," *Law Technology News*, Law.com (September 27, 2005), http://securities.stanford.edu/news-archive/2005/20050927_Headline100900_News.html, and Andrew Ross Sorkin and Roben Farzad, "At Tyco Trial No. 2, Similarities to No. 1," *The New York Times* (June 20, 2005), http://www.nytimes.com/2005/06/20/business/20jury.html

OBJECTIVE

Explain the role of transfer pricing in a decentralized firm.

TRANSFER PRICING

Often, the output of one division can be used as input for another division. For example, integrated circuits produced by one division can be used by a second division to make video recorders. **Transfer prices** are the prices charged for goods produced by one division and transferred to another. The price charged affects the revenues of the transferring division and the costs of the receiving division. As a result, the profitability, ROI, and managerial performance evaluation of both divisions are affected.

The Impact of Transfer Pricing on Income

Exhibit 10.1 illustrates the effect of the transfer price on two divisions of ABC, Inc. Division A produces a component and sells it to another division of the same company, Division C. The $30 transfer price is revenue to Division A and increases division income; clearly, Division A wants the price to be as high as possible. Conversely, the $30 transfer price is cost to Division C and decreases division income, just like the cost of any materials. Division C prefers a lower transfer price. For the company as a whole, A's revenue minus C's cost equals zero.

While the actual transfer price nets out for the company as a whole, transfer pricing can affect the level of profits earned by the company as a whole if it affects divisional behavior. Divisions may set transfer prices that maximize divisional profits but lower firmwide profits. For example, suppose that Division A in Exhibit 10.1 sets a transfer price of $30 for a component that costs $24 to produce. If Division C can obtain the component from an outside supplier for $28, it will refuse to buy from Division A. Division C will realize a savings of $2 per component ($30 internal transfer price − $28 external price). If Division A, however, cannot replace the internal sales with external sales, the company as a whole will be worse off by $4 per component ($28 external cost − $24 internal cost). This outcome would increase the total cost to the firm as a whole. Thus, how transfer prices are set can be critical for profits of the business as a whole.

OBJECTIVE

Discuss the methods of setting transfer prices.

SETTING TRANSFER PRICES

A transfer pricing system should satisfy three objectives: accurate performance evaluation, goal congruence, and preservation of divisional autonomy.[14] Accurate performance evaluation means that no one divisional manager should benefit at the expense of another (in the sense that one division is made better off while the other is made worse off). Goal congruence means that divisional managers select actions that maximize firm-wide profits. Autonomy means that

Exhibit 10.1

Impact of Transfer Price on Transferring Divisions and the Company as a Whole

ABC, Inc.	
Division A	**Division C**
Produces component and transfers it to C for transfer price of $30 per unit	Purchases component from A at transfer price of $30 per unit and uses it in production of final product
Transfer price = $30 per unit	Transfer price = $30 per unit
Revenue to A	Cost to C
Increases net income	Decreases net income
Increases ROI	Decreases ROI
Transfer price revenue = Transfer price cost	
Zero impact on ABC, Inc.	

---

14 Joshua Ronen and George McKinney, "Transfer Pricing for Divisional Autonomy," *Journal of Accounting Research* (Spring 1970): 1002101.

central management should not interfere with the decision-making freedom of divisional managers. The **transfer pricing problem** concerns finding a system that simultaneously satisfies all three objectives.

We can evaluate the degree to which a transfer price satisfies the objectives of a transfer pricing system by considering the opportunity cost of the goods transferred.

The *opportunity cost approach* can be used to describe a wide variety of transfer pricing practices. Under certain conditions, this approach is compatible with the objectives of performance evaluation, goal congruence, and autonomy.

The **opportunity cost approach** identifies the minimum price that a selling division would be willing to accept and the maximum price that the buying division would be willing to pay. These minimum and maximum prices correspond to the opportunity costs of transferring internally and they define a *bargaining range*. They are defined for each division as follows:

1. The **minimum transfer price**, or floor, is the transfer price that would leave the selling division no worse off if the good is sold to an internal division. Note that the selling division would prefer a higher price; however, the minimum transfer price is the absolute lowest that could be accepted.

2. The **maximum transfer price**, or ceiling, is the transfer price that would leave the buying division no worse off if an input is purchased from an internal division. Note that the buying division would prefer a lower price; however, the maximum transfer price is the absolute highest that could be accepted.

The opportunity cost approach tells us that a good should be transferred internally whenever the opportunity cost (minimum price) of the selling division is less than the opportunity cost (maximum price) of the buying division. By definition, this approach ensures that neither divisional manager is made worse off by transferring internally. This means that total divisional profits are not decreased by the internal transfer.

Central management rarely sets specific transfer prices. Instead, most companies develop some general policies that divisions must follow. Three commonly used policies are market-based transfer pricing, negotiated transfer pricing, and cost-based transfer pricing. Each of these can be evaluated according to the opportunity cost approach.

Market Price

If there is an outside market for the good to be transferred and that outside market is perfectly competitive, the correct transfer price is the market price.[15] In such a case, divisional managers' actions will simultaneously optimize divisional profits and firm-wide profits. No division can benefit at the expense of another division and central management will not be tempted to intervene.

The opportunity cost approach also signals that the correct transfer price is the market price. Since the selling division can sell all that it produces at the market price, transferring internally at a lower price would make that division worse off. Similarly, the buying division can always acquire the intermediate good at the market price, so it would be unwilling to pay more for an internally transferred good. Since the minimum transfer price for the selling division is the market price and since the maximum price for the buying division is also the market price, the only possible transfer price is the market price.

In fact, moving away from the market price will decrease the overall profitability of the firm. This principle can be used to resolve divisional conflicts that may occur, as the following example illustrates.

---

15 A perfectly competitive market for the intermediate product requires four conditions: (1) the division producing the intermediate product is small relative to the market as a whole and cannot influence the price of the product; (2) the intermediate product is indistinguishable from the same product of other sellers; (3) firms can easily enter and exit the market; and (4) consumers, producers, and resource owners have perfect knowledge of the market.

Yarrow Company is a decentralized manufacturer of small appliances. The Parts Division, which is at capacity, produces parts that are used by the Motor Division. The parts can also be sold to other manufacturers and to wholesalers at a market price of $8. For all practical purposes, the market for the parts is perfectly competitive.

Suppose that the Motor Division, operating at 70 percent capacity, receives a special order for 100,000 motors at a price of $30. Full manufacturing cost of the motors is $31, broken down as follows:

Direct materials	$10
Transferred-in part	8
Direct labor	2
Variable overhead	1
Fixed overhead	10
Total cost	$31

Notice that the motor includes a part transferred in from the Parts Division at a market-based transfer price of $8. Should the Parts Division lower the transfer price to allow the Motor Division to accept the special order? The opportunity cost approach helps us to answer this question.

Since the Parts Division can sell all that it produces, the minimum transfer price is the market price of $8. Any lower price would make the Parts Division worse off. For the Motor Division, identifying the maximum transfer price that can be paid so that it is no worse off is a bit more complex.

Since the Motor Division is under capacity, the fixed overhead portion of the motor's cost is not relevant. The relevant costs are those additional costs that will be incurred if the order is accepted. These costs, excluding for the moment the cost of the transferred-in component, equal $13 ($10 + $2 + $1). Thus, the contribution to profits before considering the cost of the transferred-in component is $17 ($30 − $13). The division could pay as much as $17 for the component and still break even on the special order. However, since the component can always be purchased from an outside supplier for $8, the maximum price that the division should pay internally is $8. Thus, the market price is the best transfer price.

Negotiated Transfer Prices

Perfectly competitive markets rarely exist. In most cases, producers *can* influence price (e.g., by being large enough to influence demand by dropping the price of the product or by selling closely related but differentiated products). When imperfections exist in the market for the intermediate product, market price may no longer be suitable. In this case, negotiated transfer prices may be a practical alternative. Opportunity costs help define the boundaries of the negotiation set.

Example 1: Avoidable Distribution Costs   Assume that a division produces a circuit board. Currently, the division sells 1,000 units per day, with variable manufacturing costs of $12 per unit. The division can sell all that it produces to the outside market at $22. Any outside sales incur a distribution cost of $2 per unit. Alternatively, the board can be sold internally to the company's recently acquired Electronic Games Division. There is no distribution cost if the board is sold internally.

The Electronic Games Division, also at capacity, produces and sells 350 games per day. These games sell for $45 per unit and have variable manufacturing costs of $32 per unit. Variable selling expenses of $3 per unit are also incurred. Sales and production data for each division are summarized in Exhibit 10.2.

How could the Games Division and the Circuit Board Division set a transfer price? If the Games Division currently pays $22 per circuit board, it would refuse to pay more than $22; thus, the maximum transfer price is $22. The minimum transfer price is set by the Circuit

	Circuit Board Division	Games Division
Units sold:		
Per day	1,000	350
Per year*	260,000	91,000
Unit data:		
Selling price	$22	$45
Variable costs:		
Manufacturing	$12	$32
Selling	$2	$3
Annual fixed costs	$1,480,000	$610,000

Exhibit 10.2

Summary of Sales and Production Data

*There are 260 selling days in a year.

Board Division. While this division prices its circuit boards at $22, it will avoid $2 of distribution cost if it sells internally. Therefore, the minimum transfer price is $20 ($22 − $2). The bargaining range for the transfer price is between $20 and $22.

Suppose that the Games Division manager offered a transfer price of $20. That division would be better off by $2 per circuit board, since it had previously paid $22 per board. Its profits would increase by $700 per day ($2 × 350 units per day). The Circuit Board Division, on the other hand, would be no better, or worse, off than before and would earn no additional profit. While a transfer price of $20 per circuit board is possible, it is unlikely that the Circuit Board manager would agree to it.

Now suppose that the Circuit Board Division counters with an offer of $21.10 per board. That transfer price allows the Circuit Board Division to increase its profits by $385 per day [($21.10 − $20) × 350 units]. The Games Division would increase its profits by $315 per day [($22 − $21.10) × 350 units].

While we cannot tell exactly where the Circuit Board Division and the Games Division would set a transfer price, we can see that it will be somewhere within the bargaining range. (The minimum transfer price [$20] and the maximum transfer price [$22] set the limits of the bargaining range.) Exhibit 10.3 provides income statements for each division before and after the agreement. Notice how the total profits of the firm increase by $182,000 as claimed; notice, too, how that profit increase is split between the two divisions.

Before Negotiation: All Sales External			
	Circuit Board Division	Games Division	Total
Sales	$ 5,720,000	$4,095,000	$9,815,000
Less variable expenses:			
Cost of goods sold	(3,120,000)	(2,912,000)	(6,032,000)
Variable selling	(520,000)	(273,000)	(793,000)
Contribution margin	$ 2,080,000	$ 910,000	$2,990,000
Less: Fixed expenses	1,480,000	610,000	2,090,000
Operating income	$ 600,000	$ 300,000	$ 900,000
After Negotiation: Internal Transfers @ $21.10			
	Circuit Board Division	Games Division	Total
Sales	$5,638,100	$4,095,000	$9,733,100
Less variable expenses:			
Cost of goods sold	(3,120,000)	(2,830,100)	(5,950,100)
Variable selling	(338,000)	(273,000)	(611,000)
Contribution margin	$2,180,100	$ 991,900	$3,172,000
Less: Fixed expenses	1,480,000	610,000	2,090,000
Operating income	$ 700,100	$ 381,900	$1,082,000
Change in operating income	$ 100,100	$ 81,900	$ 182,000

Exhibit 10.3

Comparative Income Statements

Example 2: Excess Capacity   In perfectly competitive markets, the selling division can sell all that it wishes at the prevailing market price and would produce at capacity. In a less ideal setting, a selling division may be unable to sell all that it produces; accordingly, the division may have excess capacity.[16]

To illustrate the role of transfer pricing and negotiation in this setting, consider the dialogue between Sharena Casper, manager of a Plastics Division, and Manny Rogers, manager of a Pharmaceutical Division:

MANNY: Sharena, my division has shown a loss for the past three years. When I took over the division at the beginning of the year, I set a goal with headquarters to break even. At this point, projections show a loss of $5,000—but I think I have a way to reach my goal, if I can get your cooperation.

SHARENA: If I can help, I will. What do you have in mind?

MANNY: I need a special deal on your plastic bottle Model 3. A large West Coast retail chain wants to buy 250,000 bottles. But we have to give them a real break on price. They have offered $0.85 per unit. My variable cost per unit is $0.60, not including the cost of the plastic bottle. I normally pay $0.40 for your bottle, but if I do that, the order will lose me $37,500. I can't afford that kind of loss. I know that you have excess capacity. If you can make 250,000 bottles, I'll pay your variable cost per unit, provided it is no more than $0.25. Are you interested? Can you handle that size order?

SHARENA: I have enough excess capacity to handle the order easily and my variable cost is $0.15. However, I want part of the profit. I'll let you have the order for $0.20. That way, we both make $0.05 per bottle, for a total contribution of $12,500. That'll put you in the black and help me get closer to my budgeted profit goal.

MANNY: Great! Thanks so much. If this West Coast chain provides more orders in the future—as I expect it will—and at better prices, I'll make sure you get our business.

Notice the role that opportunity costs play in the negotiation. In this case, the minimum transfer price is the Plastic Division's variable cost ($0.15), representing the incremental outlay if the order is accepted. Since the division has excess capacity, only variable costs are relevant to the decision. By covering the variable costs, the order does not affect the division's total profits. For the buying division, the maximum transfer price is the purchase price that would allow the division to cover its incremental costs on the special order ($0.25). Adding the $0.25 to the other costs of processing ($0.60), the total incremental costs incurred are $0.85 per unit. Since the selling price is also $0.85 per unit, the division is made no worse off. Both divisions, however, can be better off if the transfer price is between the minimum price of $0.15 and the maximum price of $0.25.

Comparative statements showing the contribution margin earned by each division and the firm as a whole are shown in Exhibit 10.4 for each of the four transfer prices discussed. These statements show that the firm earns the same profit for all four transfer prices; however, different prices do affect the individual divisions' profits differently. Because of the autonomy of each division, there is no guarantee that the firm will earn the maximum profit. For example, if Sharena had insisted on maintaining the price of $0.40, no transfer would have taken place, and the overall $25,000 increase in profits would have been lost.

Disadvantages of Negotiated Transfer Prices   Negotiated transfer prices have three disadvantages that are commonly mentioned.

1. One divisional manager with private information may take advantage of another divisional manager.
2. Performance measures may be distorted by the negotiating skills of managers.
3. Negotiation can consume considerable time and resources.

---

16   Output can be increased by decreasing selling price. Of course, decreasing selling price to increase sales volume may not increase profits—in fact, profits could easily decline. We assume in this example that the divisional manager has chosen the most advantageous selling price and that the division is still left with excess capacity.

ETHICS It is interesting that Manny, the manager of the Pharmaceutical Division, did not know the variable cost of producing the plastic bottle. Yet, that cost was a key to the negotiation. Clearly, he had not done his homework before starting the negotiation. This lack of knowledge gave Sharena, the other divisional manager, the opportunity to exploit the situation. For example, she could have claimed that the variable cost was $0.27 and offered to sell for $0.25 per unit as a favor to Manny, saying that she would absorb a $5,000 loss in exchange for a promise of future business. In this case, she would capture the full $25,000 benefit of the transfer. Alternatively, she could have misrepresented the figure and used it to turn down the request, thus preventing Manny from achieving his budgetary goal; after all, she may be competing with Manny for promotions, bonuses, salary increases, and so on.

Fortunately, Sharena displayed sound judgment and acted with integrity.[17] For negotiation to work, managers must be willing to share relevant information. How can this requirement be satisfied? Perhaps the best course of action is to hire managers with integrity—managers who have a commitment to ethical behavior. Additionally, top management can take other actions to discourage the use of private information for exploitive purposes. For example, corporate headquarters could base some part of the management reward structure on overall profitability to encourage actions that are in the best interests of the company as a whole. •

The second disadvantage of negotiated transfer prices is that the practice distorts the measurement of managerial performance. According to this view, divisional profitability may be affected too strongly by the negotiating skills of managers, masking the actual management of resources entrusted to each manager. Although this argument may have some merit, it ignores the fact that negotiating is a desirable skill. Perhaps divisional profitability should reflect differences in negotiating skills.

	Transfer Price of $0.40			**Exhibit 10.4**
	Pharmaceutical	**Plastics**	**Total**	Comparative Statements
Sales	$212,500	$100,000	$312,500	
Less: Variable expenses	250,000	37,500	287,500	
Contribution margin	$ (37,500)	$ 62,500	$ 25,000	
	Transfer Price of $0.25			
Sales	$212,500	$ 62,500	$275,000	
Less: Variable expenses	212,500	37,500	250,000	
Contribution margin	$ 0	$ 25,000	$ 25,000	
	Transfer Price of $0.20			
Sales	$212,500	$ 50,000	$262,500	
Less: Variable expenses	200,000	37,500	237,500	
Contribution margin	$ 12,500	$ 12,500	$ 25,000	
	Transfer Price of $0.15			
Sales	$212,500	$ 37,500	$250,000	
Less: Variable expenses	187,500	37,500	225,000	
Contribution margin	$ 25,000	$ 0	$ 25,000	

---

17 Because of the excess capacity, her agreement to work with Manny was beneficial for both of their divisions. Note that if she had not had excess capacity, it would have been better for her division and for the company as a whole to refuse the special offer to Manny's division and to sell for full price to outsiders.

The third criticism of this technique is that negotiating is time consuming. The time spent in negotiation could be spent managing other activities necessary to the success of the division. Sometimes, negotiations reach an impasse, forcing top management to spend time mediating the process.[18] Although negotiating takes time, a mutually satisfactory outcome can increase profits for the divisions and the firm. Furthermore, negotiation does not have to be repeated each time for similar transactions.

Advantages of Negotiated Transfer Prices Although time consuming, negotiated transfer prices offer some hope of complying with the three criteria of goal congruence, autonomy, and accurate performance evaluation. Just as important, however, is the process of making sure that actions of the different divisions mesh together so that the company's overall goals are attained. If negotiation helps ensure goal congruence, there is no need for central management to intervene. Finally, if negotiating skills of divisional managers are comparable or if the firm views these skills as an important managerial skill, concerns about motivation and accurate performance measures are avoided. **Example 10.4** shows the how and why of calculating market-based and negotiated transfer prices.

EXAMPLE 10.4

The HOW and WHY of Calculating Market-Based and Negotiated Transfer Prices

Information:

Omni, Inc., has a number of divisions, including Alpha Division, a producer of circuit boards, and Delta Division, a heating and air conditioning manufacturer.

Alpha Division produces the cb-117 model that can be used by Delta Division to produce thermostats that regulate the heating and air conditioning systems. The market price of the cb-117 is $14. Cost information for the cb-117 model is:

Variable product cost	$2.50
Fixed cost	6.50
Total product cost	$9.00

Delta needs 30,000 units of model cb-117 per year. Alpha Division is at full capacity (100,000 units of cb-117).

> **Why:**
> Market-based transfer prices, when available, are best because they help maximize overall company profitability.

Required:

1. If Omni, Inc., has a transfer pricing policy that requires transfer at market price, what would the transfer price be? Do you suppose that Alpha and Delta divisions would choose to transfer at that price?

2. Now suppose that Omni, Inc., allows negotiated transfer pricing and that Alpha Division can avoid $3 of selling and distribution expense by selling to Delta Division. Which division sets the minimum transfer price? What is it? Which division sets the maximum transfer price? What is it? Do you think that Alpha and Delta divisions would choose to transfer somewhere in the bargaining range?

---

18 The involvement of top management may be very cursory, however. In the case of a very large oil company that negotiates virtually all transfer prices, two divisional managers could not come to an agreement after several weeks of effort and appealed to their superior. His response: "Either come to an agreement within 24 hours, or you are both fired." Needless to say, an agreement was reached within the allotted time.

3. *What if* Alpha Division can produce and sell only 65,000 units of cb-117 next year (excess capacity exists)? Which division sets the minimum transfer price? What is it? Which division sets the maximum transfer price? What is it? Do you think that Alpha and Delta divisions would choose to transfer somewhere in the bargaining range?

EXAMPLE 10.4

(Continued)

Solution:

1. The market price is $14. Both Delta and Alpha divisions would be willing to transfer at that price (since neither division would be worse off than if it bought or sold in the outside market).

2. Minimum transfer price = $14 − $3 = $11. It is set by Alpha, the selling division. Maximum transfer price = $14. It is the market price and is set by Delta, the buying division.

   Yes, both divisions would be willing to accept a transfer price within the bargaining range. The actual transfer price set depends on the negotiating skills of the Alpha and Delta division managers.

3. Minimum transfer price = $2.50 (the variable cost of production). This price is set by Alpha, the selling division. Maximum transfer price = $14. This is the market price and is set by Delta, the buying division.

   Both divisions would be willing to accept a transfer price within the bargaining range. The actual transfer price depends on the negotiating skills of the Alpha and Delta division managers. (Notice that the fixed product costs are not included in the minimum transfer price because Alpha will have to pay total fixed cost no matter how many units are produced.)

Cost-Based Transfer Prices

Three forms of cost-based transfer pricing will be considered: full cost, full cost plus markup, and variable cost plus fixed fee. In all cases, standard costs should be used to avoid passing on the inefficiencies of one division to another. A more important issue, however, is the propriety of cost-based transfer prices. Under what circumstances, if any, should they be used?

Full-Cost Transfer Pricing Perhaps the least desirable type of transfer pricing approach is full cost. Its only real virtue is simplicity. Full-cost transfer pricing can provide perverse incentives and distort performance measures. As we have seen, the opportunity costs of both the buying and selling divisions are essential for determining the propriety of internal transfers. At the same time, they provide useful reference points for determining a mutually satisfactory transfer price. Only rarely will full cost provide accurate information about opportunity costs.

A full-cost transfer price would have shut down the negotiations described earlier. In the first example, the manager would never have considered transferring internally if the price had to be full cost. Yet, by transferring at selling price less some distribution expenses, both divisions—and the firm as a whole—were better off. In the second example, the manager of the Pharmaceutical Division could never have accepted the special order with the West Coast chain. Both divisions and the company would have been worse off.

Full Cost Plus Markup Full cost plus markup suffers from virtually the same problems as full cost. It is somewhat less perverse, however, if the markup can be negotiated. For example, a full-cost-plus-markup formula could have been used to represent the negotiated transfer price of the first example. In some cases, a full-cost-plus-markup formula may be the outcome of negotiation; if so, it is simply another example of negotiated transfer pricing. In these cases, the use of this method is fully justified. Using full cost plus markup to represent all negotiated prices, however, is not possible (e.g., it could not be used to represent the negotiated price of the second example). The superior approach is negotiation, since more cases can be represented, and full consideration of opportunity costs is possible.

Variable Cost Plus Fixed Fee   Like full cost plus markup, variable cost plus fixed fee can be a useful transfer pricing approach provided that the fixed fee is negotiable. This method has one advantage over full cost plus markup: if the selling division is operating below capacity, variable cost is its opportunity cost. Assuming that the fixed fee is negotiable, the variable cost approach can be equivalent to negotiated transfer pricing. Negotiation with full consideration of opportunity costs is preferred.

Propriety of Use   Despite the disadvantages of cost-based transfer prices, many companies use these methods, especially full cost and full cost plus markup. These methods are simple and objective. Often transfers between divisions have a small impact on the profitability of either division. Thus, it may be cost effective to use an easy-to-identify, cost-based formula rather than spending valuable time and resources on negotiation.

In other cases, the use of full cost plus markup may simply be the formula agreed upon in negotiations. That is, the full-cost-plus-markup formula is the outcome of negotiation, but the transfer pricing method being used is reported as full cost plus markup. Once established, this formula could be used until the original conditions change to the point where renegotiation is necessary. In this way, the time and resources of negotiation can be minimized. For example, the goods transferred may be custom-made, and the managers may have little ability to identify an outside market price. In this case, reimbursement of full costs plus a reasonable rate of return may be a good surrogate for the transferring division's opportunity costs. **Example 10.5** shows how and why cost-based transfer prices are calculated.

EXAMPLE 10.5

The HOW and WHY of Calculating Cost-Based Transfer Prices

Information:
Omni, Inc., has a number of divisions, including Alpha Division, producer of circuit boards, and Delta Division, a heating and air conditioning manufacturer.

Alpha Division produces the cb-117 model that can be used by Delta Division in the production of thermostats that regulate the heating and air conditioning systems. The market price of the cb-117 is $14. Cost information for the cb-117 model is:

Variable product cost	$2.50
Fixed cost	6.50
Total product cost	$9.00

Delta needs 30,000 units of model cb-117 per year. Alpha Division is at full capacity (100,000 units of cb-117).

> **Why:**
> Cost-based transfer prices are used most frequently by companies because they are easy to apply, and can be used when there is no market price for the product.

Required:

1.   If Omni, Inc., has a transfer pricing policy that requires transfer at full product cost, what would the transfer price be? Do you suppose that Alpha and Delta divisions would choose to transfer at that price?

2.   If Omni, Inc., has a transfer pricing policy that requires transfer at full cost plus 25 percent, what would the transfer price be? Do you suppose that Alpha and Delta divisions would choose to transfer at that price?

EXAMPLE 10.5

(Continued)

3. If Omni, Inc., has a transfer pricing policy that requires transfer at variable product cost plus a fixed fee of $12.00 per unit, what would the transfer price be? Do you suppose that Alpha and Delta divisions would choose to transfer at that price?

4. **What if** Alpha Division plans to produce and sell only 65,000 units of cb-117 next year? The Omni, Inc., policy is that all transfers be at full cost. Which division sets the minimum transfer price, and what is it? Which division sets the maximum transfer price, and what is it? Do you suppose that Alpha and Delta divisions would choose to transfer?

Solution:

1. The full cost transfer price is $9.00. Delta Division would be delighted with that price, but Alpha Division would refuse to transfer since $14 could be earned in the outside market.

2. The cost-plus transfer price is $11.25 ($9.00 + $2.25). Again, Delta Division would be delighted with that price, but Alpha Division would refuse to transfer since $14 could be earned in the outside market.

3. The variable product cost plus fixed fee is $14.50 ($2.50 + $12). In this case, Alpha would be delighted, but Delta would refuse, since it can buy all it needs on the outside market for $14.

4. Minimum transfer price = $9.00 (the full cost of production). This price is set by Alpha, the selling division. Maximum transfer price = $14. This is the market price and is set by Delta, the buying division.

   Yes, both divisions would be willing to accept the transfer price of $9.00 per unit.

SUMMARY OF LEARNING OBJECTIVES

LO1. Define responsibility accounting, and describe the four types of responsibility centers.
- Responsibility accounting is a system that measures the results of each responsibility center and compares those results with some expected or budgeted outcome.
- In a decentralized organization, lower-level managers make and implement decisions; in a centralized organization, lower-level managers are responsible only for implementing decisions.
- Four types of responsibility centers are:
  - Cost centers—manager is responsible for costs.
  - Revenue centers—manager is responsible for price and quantity sold.
  - Profit centers—manager is responsible for costs and revenues.
  - Investment centers—manager is responsible for costs, revenues, and investment.

LO2. Explain why firms choose to decentralize.
- Local managers can make better decisions using local information.
- Local managers can also provide a more timely response to changing conditions.
- Cognitive limitations make it difficult for any one central manager to be fully knowledgeable about all products and markets.
- Decentralization permits training and motivating local managers.
- Top management is free to spend time on longer-range activities, such as strategic planning.
- Decentralization enhances competition among the divisions.

LO3. Compute and explain return on investment (ROI), residual income (RI), and economic value added (EVA).
- ROI is the ratio of operating income to average operating assets.
- Margin is operating income divided by sales *or* margin times turnover.
- Turnover is sales divided by average operating assets.
- Advantage: ROI encourages managers to focus on improving sales, controlling costs, and using assets efficiently.
- Disadvantage: ROI can encourage managers to sacrifice long-run benefits for the short run.
- Residual income (RI) is operating income minus a minimum percentage cost of capital times capital employed.
  - If RI > 0, then the division is earning more than the minimum cost of capital.
  - If RI < 0, then the division is earning less than the minimum cost of capital.
  - If RI = 0, then the division is earning just the minimum cost of capital.
- Economic value added is *after-tax* operating profit minus the *actual* total annual cost of capital.
  - If EVA > 0, then the company is creating wealth.
  - If EVA < 0, then the company is destroying capital.

LO4. Discuss methods of evaluating and rewarding managerial performance.
- Goal congruence means that the goals of the manager are aligned with the goals of the company.
- Firms encourage goal congruence by constructing management compensation programs that reward managers for taking actions which benefit the firm. These programs can include:
  - Salary
  - Bonuses
  - Stock options
  - Noncash benefits (perquisites)

LO5. Explain the role of transfer pricing in a decentralized firm.
- When one division of a company produces a product that can be used in production by another division, transfer pricing exists.
- A transfer price is the price charged by one division of a company to another division of the same company.
- The transfer price is revenue to the selling division and cost to the buying division.

LO6. Discuss the methods of setting transfer prices.
- Three methods are commonly used to set transfer prices:
  - Market-based price
  - Cost-based price
  - Negotiated price
- The buying division sets the maximum transfer price.
- The selling division sets the minimum transfer price.

EXAMPLE 10.1   The HOW and WHY of Calculating Average Operating Assets, Margin, Turnover, and Return on Investment (ROI), page 506

EXAMPLE 10.2   The HOW and WHY of Calculating Residual Income, page 510

EXAMPLE 10.3   The HOW and WHY of Calculating the Weighted Average Cost of Capital and EVA, page 514

EXAMPLE 10.4   The HOW and WHY of Calculating Market-Based and Negotiated Transfer Prices, page 526

EXAMPLE 10.5   The HOW and WHY of Calculating Cost-Based Transfer Prices, page 528

KEY TERMS

Centralized decision making, 501

Cost center, 500

Decentralization, 501

Decentralized decision making, 501

Economic value added (EVA), 513

Effectiveness, 504

Efficiency, 504

Goal congruence, 505

Investment center, 500

Margin, 508

Maximum transfer price, 521

Minimum transfer price, 521

Multinational corporation (MNC), 501

Myopic behavior, 510

Operating assets, 506

Operating income, 506

Opportunity cost approach, 521

Perquisites, 517

Profit center, 500

Residual income, 510

Responsibility accounting, 500

Responsibility center, 500

Return on investment (ROI), 506

Revenue center, 500

Stock option, 518

Transfer prices, 520

Transfer pricing problem, 521

Turnover, 508

Weighted average cost of capital, 513

BRIEF EXERCISES

OBJECTIVE 3
Example 10.1

Brief Exercise 10-1 Calculating Average Operating Assets, Margin, Turnover, Return on Investment (ROI)

Forchen, Inc., provided the following information for two of its divisions for last year:

	Small Appliances Division	Cleaning Products Division
Sales	$34,670,000	$31,320,000
Operating income	2,773,600	1,252,800
Operating assets, January 1	6,394,000	5,600,000
Operating assets, December 31	7,474,000	6,000,000

Required:

1. For the Small Appliances Division, calculate:
   a. Average operating assets
   b. Margin
   c. Turnover
   d. ROI

2. For the Cleaning Products Division, calculate:
   a. Average operating assets
   b. Margin
   c. Turnover
   d. ROI

3. *What if* operating income for the Small Appliances Division was $2,000,000? How would that affect average operating assets? Margin? Turnover? ROI? Calculate any changed ratios (round to four significant digits).

OBJECTIVE 3
EXAMPLE 10.2

Brief Exercise 10-2 Calculating Residual Income

Refer to **Brief Exercise 10-1**. Forchen, Inc., requires an 8 percent minimum rate of return.

Required:

1. Calculate residual income for the Small Appliances Division.
2. Calculate residual income for the Cleaning Products Division.
3. *What if* the minimum required rate of return was 9 percent? How would that affect the residual income of the two divisions?

OBJECTIVE 3
EXAMPLE 10.3

Brief Exercise 10-3 Calculating Weighted Average Cost of Capital and Economic Value Added (EVA)

Ignacio, Inc., had after-tax operating income last year of $1,196,500. Three sources of financing were used by the company: $2 million of mortgage bonds paying 4 percent interest, $4 million of unsecured bonds paying 6 percent interest, and $9 million in common stock, which was considered to be relatively risky (with a risk premium of 8 percent). The rate on long-term treasuries is 4 percent. Ignacio, Inc., pays a marginal tax rate of 30 percent. (Round all ratios to four significant digits.)

Required:

1. Calculate the after-tax cost of each method of financing.
2. Calculate the weighted average cost of capital for Ignacio, Inc. Calculate the total dollar amount of capital employed for Ignacio, Inc.
3. Calculate economic value added (EVA) for Ignacio, Inc., for last year. Is the company creating or destroying wealth?
4. *What if* Ignacio, Inc., had common stock which was less risky than other stocks and commanded a risk premium of 5 percent? How would that affect the weighted average cost of capital? How would it affect EVA?

OBJECTIVE 6
EXAMPLE 10.4

Brief Exercise 10-4 Determining Market-Based and Negotiated Transfer Prices

Carreker, Inc., has a number of divisions, including the Alamosa Division, producer of surgical blades, and the Tavaris Division, a manufacturer of medical instruments.

Alamosa Division produces a 2.6 cm steel blade that can be used by Tavaris Division in the production of scalpels. The market price of the blade is $21. Cost information for the blade is:

Variable product cost	$ 9.70
Fixed cost	5.50
Total product cost	$15.20

Tavaris needs 15,000 units of the 2.6 cm blade per year. Alamosa Division is at full capacity (90,000 units of the blade).

Required:

1. If Carreker, Inc., has a transfer pricing policy that requires transfer at market price, what would the transfer price be? Do you suppose that Alamosa and Tavaris divisions would choose to transfer at that price?
2. Now suppose that Carreker, Inc., allows negotiated transfer pricing and that Alamosa Division can avoid $1.75 of selling and distribution expense by selling to Tavaris Division. Which division sets the minimum transfer price, and what is it? Which division sets the maximum transfer price, and what is it? Do you suppose that Alamosa and Tavaris divisions would choose to transfer somewhere in the bargaining range?
3. *What if* Alamosa Division plans to produce and sell only 65,000 units of the 2.6 cm blade next year? Which division sets the minimum transfer price, and what is it? Which division sets the maximum transfer price, and what is it? Do you suppose that Alamosa and Tavaris divisions would choose to transfer somewhere in the bargaining range?

Brief Exercise 10-5 Determining Market-Based and Negotiated Transfer Prices

Refer to **Brief Exercise 10-4**.

OBJECTIVE ◄ **6**

Example 10.5

Required:

1. If Carreker, Inc., has a transfer pricing policy that requires transfer at full product cost, what would the transfer price be? Do you suppose that Alamosa and Tavaris divisions would choose to transfer at that price?

2. If Carreker, Inc., has a transfer pricing policy that requires transfer at full cost plus 25 percent, what would the transfer price be? Do you suppose that Alamosa and Tavaris divisions would choose to transfer at that price?

3. If Carreker, Inc., has a transfer pricing policy that requires transfer at variable product cost plus a fixed fee of $2.00 per unit, what would the transfer price be? Do you suppose that Alamosa and Tavaris divisions would choose to transfer at that price?

4. *What if* Alamosa Division plans to produce and sell only 65,000 units of the 2.6 cm blade next year? The Carreker, Inc., policy is that all transfers be at full cost. Which division sets the minimum transfer price, and what is it? Which division sets the maximum transfer price, and what is it? Do you suppose that Alamosa and Tavaris divisions would choose to transfer?

EXERCISES

Exercise 10-6 ROI and Margin

OBJECTIVE ◄ **3**

Arbus Company provided the following information:

Turnover	1.4
Operating assets	$120,000
Operating income	6,720

Required:

1. What is ROI?
2. What is margin?

Exercise 10-7 ROI, Margin, Turnover

OBJECTIVE ◄ **3**

Allard, Inc., presented two years of data for its Frozen Foods Division and its Canned Foods Division.

EXCEL   **SHOW ME HOW**

Frozen Foods Division:

	Year 1	Year 2
Sales	$6,000,000	$6,200,000
Operating income	420,000	434,000
Average operating assets	4,000,000	4,000,000

Canned Foods Division:

	Year 1	Year 2
Sales	$2,400,000	$2,600,000
Operating income	120,000	117,000
Average operating assets	1,000,000	1,000,000

Required:

1. Compute the ROI and the margin and turnover ratios for each year for the Frozen Foods Division. (Round your answers to four significant digits.)

**DATA
ANALYTICS**

2. Compute the ROI and the margin and turnover ratios for each year for the Canned Foods Division. (Round your answers to four significant digits.)
3. Explain the change in ROI from Year 1 to Year 2 for each division.
4. Which of the data analytic types—descriptive, diagnostic, predictive or prescriptive—is Allard using in comparing Year 1 to Year 2 for the ratios? Explain. (See Exhibits 2.5 and 2.6, pp. 37, 40, for a review of data analytic types.)

OBJECTIVE 3

**SHOW ME
HOW** **EXCEL**

Exercise 10-8 ROI and Investment Decisions

Refer to **Exercise 10-7** for data. At the end of Year 2, the manager of the Canned Foods Division is concerned about the division's performance. As a result, he is considering the opportunity to invest in two independent projects. The first is juice boxes for elementary school children. The second is fruit and veggie pouches for kids on the go. Without the investments, the division expects that Year 2 data will remain unchanged. The expected operating incomes and the outlay required for each investment are as follows:

	Juice Box	Fruit Pouch
Operating income	$ 6,250	$ 3,800
Outlay	50,000	40,000

Allard's corporate headquarters has made available up to $100,000 of capital for this division. Any funds not invested by the division will be retained by headquarters and invested to earn the company's minimum required rate of return, 9 percent.

Required:

1. Compute the ROI for each investment.
2. Compute the divisional ROI (rounded to four significant digits) for each of the following four alternatives:
   a. The juice box is added.
   b. The fruit pouch is added.
   c. Both investments are added.
   d. Neither investment is made; the status quo is maintained.
   Assuming that divisional managers are evaluated and rewarded on the basis of ROI performance, which alternative do you think the divisional manager will choose?
3. Which of the data analytic types—descriptive, diagnostic, predictive or prescriptive—is used in determining which, if any, new investment to make? Explain. (See Exhibits 2.5 and 2.6, pp. 37, 40, for a review of data analytic types.)

**DATA
ANALYTICS**

OBJECTIVE 3

**SHOW ME
HOW** **EXCEL**

Exercise 10-9 Residual Income and Investment Decisions

Refer to the data given in **Exercise 10-8**.

Required:

1. Compute the residual income for each of the opportunities. (Round to the nearest dollar.)
2. Compute the divisional residual income (rounded to the nearest dollar) for each of the following four alternatives:
   a. The juice box is added.
   b. The fruit pouch is added.
   c. Both investments are added.
   d. Neither investment is made; the status quo is maintained.
   Assuming that divisional managers are evaluated and rewarded on the basis of residual income, which alternative do you think the divisional manager will choose?
3. Based on your answer in Requirement 2, compute the profit or loss from the divisional manager's investment decision. Was the correct decision made?

Exercise 10-10 Calculating EVA

Brewster Company manufactures elderberry wine. Last year, Brewster earned operating income of $192,000 after income taxes. Capital employed equaled $2.3 million. Brewster is 45 percent equity and 55 percent 10-year bonds paying 6 percent interest. Brewster's marginal tax rate is 40 percent. The company is considered a fairly risky investment and probably commands a 12-point premium above the 4 percent rate on long-term Treasury bonds.

OBJECTIVE 3

EXCEL SHOW ME
HOW

Jonathan Brewster's aunts, Abby and Martha, have just retired, and Brewster is the new CEO of Brewster Company. He would like to improve EVA for the company. Compute EVA under each of the following independent scenarios that Brewster is considering. (Use a spreadsheet to perform your calculations and round all percentage figures to four significant digits.)

Required:

1. No changes are made; calculate EVA using the original data.
2. Sugar will be used to replace another natural ingredient (atomic number 33) in the elderberry wine. This should not affect costs but will begin to affect the market assessment of Brewster Company, bringing the premium above long-term Treasury bills to 10 percent the first year and 7 percent the second year. Calculate revised EVA for both years.
3. Brewster is considering expanding but needs additional capital. The company could borrow money, but it is considering selling more common stock, which would increase equity to 80 percent of total financing. Total capital employed would be $3,000,000. The new after-tax operating income would be $375,000. Using the original data, calculate EVA. Then, recalculate EVA assuming the materials substitution described in Requirement 2. New after-tax income will be $375,000, and in Year 1, the premium will be 10 percent above the long-term Treasury rate. In Year 2, it will be 7 percent above the long-term Treasury rate. (*Hint:* You will calculate three EVAs for this requirement.)

Exercise 10-11 Operating Income for Segments

Xenold, Inc., manufactures and sells cooktops and ovens through three divisions: Home, Restaurant, and Specialty. Each division is evaluated as a profit center. Data for each division for last year are as follows (numbers in thousands):

OBJECTIVE 3

EXCEL SHOW ME
HOW

	Home	Restaurant	Specialty
Sales	$4,140	$3,600	$2,520
Cost of goods sold	2,900	2,640	1,700
Selling and administrative expenses	950	410	320

The income tax rate for Xenold, Inc., is 40 percent. Xenold, Inc., has two sources of financing: bonds paying 5 percent interest, which account for 25 percent of total investment, and equity accounting for the remaining 75 percent of total investment. Xenold, Inc., has been in business for over 15 years and is considered a relatively stable stock, despite its link to the cyclical construction industry. As a result, Xenold stock has an opportunity cost of 5 percent over the 4 percent long-term government bond rate. Xenold's total capital employed is $5.04 million ($2,600,000 for the Home Division, $1,700,000 for the Restaurant Division, and the remainder for the Specialty Division).

Required:

1. Prepare a segmented income statement for Xenold, Inc., for last year.
2. Calculate Xenold's weighted average cost of capital. (Round to four significant digits.)
3. Calculate EVA for each division and for Xenold, Inc.
4. Comment on the performance of each of the divisions.

OBJECTIVE ▸ 5 6

SHOW ME
HOW

Exercise 10-12 Transfer Pricing, Idle Capacity

Asgard Farms, Inc., has a number of divisions that produce jams and jellies, condiments, and glassware. The Glassware Division manufactures a variety of bottles that can be sold externally (to soft-drink and juice bottlers) or internally to Asgard Farm's Jams Division. Sales and cost data on a case of 24 basic 12-ounce bottles are as follows:

Unit selling price	$2.30
Unit variable cost	$0.90
Unit product fixed cost*	$0.70
Practical capacity in cases	500,000

*$350,000/500,000

During the coming year, the Glassware Division expects to sell 390,000 cases of this bottle. The Jams and Jellies Division currently plans to buy 100,000 cases on the outside market for $2.30 each. Bella Howard, manager of the Glassware Division, approached Paul Vining, manager of the Jams and Jellies Division, and offered to sell the 100,000 cases for $2.24 each. Bella explained to Paul that she can avoid selling costs of $0.12 per case by selling internally and that she would split the savings by offering a $0.06 discount on the usual price.

Required:

1. What is the minimum transfer price that the Glassware Division would be willing to accept? What is the maximum transfer price that the Jams and Jellies Division would be willing to pay? Should an internal transfer take place? What would be the benefit (or loss) to the firm as a whole if the internal transfer takes place?
2. Suppose Paul knows that the Glassware Division has idle capacity. Do you think that he would agree to the transfer price of $2.24? Suppose he counters with an offer to pay $1.60. If you were Ellyn, would you be interested in this price? Explain with supporting computations.
3. Suppose that Asgard Farm's policy is that all internal transfers take place at full manufacturing cost. What would the transfer price be? Would the transfer take place?

OBJECTIVE ▸ 3

SHOW ME
HOW

Exercise 10-13 ROI and Residual Income

A multinational corporation has a number of divisions, two of which are the North American Division and the Pacific Rim Division. Data on the two divisions are as follows:

	North American	Pacific Rim
Average operating assets	$15,000,000	$6,700,000
Operating income	1,250,000	610,000
Minimum required return	7%	7%

Round all rates of return to four significant digits.

Required:

1. Compute residual income for each division. By comparing residual income, is it possible to make a useful comparison of divisional performance? Explain.
2. Compute the residual rate of return by dividing the residual income by the average operating assets. Is it possible now to say that one division outperformed the other? Explain.
3. Compute the ROI for each division. Can we make meaningful comparisons of divisional performance? Explain.
4. Add the residual rate of return computed in Requirement 2 to the required rate of return. Compare these rates with the ROI computed in Requirement 3. Will this relationship always be the same?

Exercise 10-14 Margin, Turnover, ROI

OBJECTIVE ◀3

Consider the data for each of the following four independent companies:

SHOW ME
HOW

	A	B	C	D
Revenue	$10,000	$48,000	$96,000	?
Expenses	$ 8,000	?	$90,000	?
Operating income	$ 2,000	$12,000	?	?
Assets	$40,000	?	$48,000	$9,600
Margin	?	25%	?	6.25%
Turnover	?	0.50	?	2.00
ROI	?	?	?	?

Required:

1. Calculate the missing values in the above table. (Round rates to four significant digits.)
2. Assume that the cost of capital is 9 percent for each of the four firms. Compute the residual income for each of the four firms.

Exercise 10-15 ROI, Residual Income

OBJECTIVE ◀3

The following selected data pertain to the Argent Division for last year:

SHOW ME
HOW

Sales	$1,000,000
Variable costs	$ 624,000
Traceable fixed costs	$ 100,000
Average invested capital	$1,500,000
Imputed interest rate	15%

Required:

1. How much is the residual income?
2. How much is the ROI? (Rounded to four significant digits.)

Exercise 10-16 Stock Options

OBJECTIVE ◀3

Fermat, Inc., has acquired two new companies, one in consumer products and the other in financial services. Fermat's top management believes that the executives of the two newly acquired companies can be most quickly assimilated into the parent company if they own shares of Fermat stock. Accordingly, on April 1, Fermat approved a stock option plan whereby each of the top four executives of the new companies could purchase up to 20,000 shares of Fermat stock at $15 per share. The option will expire in five years.

Required:

1. If Fermat stock rises to $26.50 per share by December 1, what is the value of the option to each executive?
2. Discuss some of the advantages and disadvantages of the Fermat stock option plan.

PROBLEMS

Problem 10-17 Margin, Turnover, ROI

For each of the following scenarios, determine whether the specified variable would increase, decrease, or remain the same. Explain your choice.

1. If sales and average operating assets for Kayman Company for Year 2 are identical to their values in Year 1, yet operating income is higher, ROI for Year 2 will _____.

2. Amy Company budgeted sales of $450,000, operating expenses of $310,000, and average operating assets of $1,000,000. At the end of the year, operating expenses had risen, while sales and average operating assets remained the same. What happened at the end of the year to margin, turnover, and ROI? (Did each increase, decrease, or remain the same?)

3. If margin increased over the course of the year and average operating assets decreased, what happened to turnover? ROI?

4. If sales, operating expenses, and average operating assets all stayed constant from Year 1 to Year 2, and minimum required rate of return increased, what happened for Year 2 to margin, turnover, ROI, and residual income? (Did each increase, decrease, or remain the same?)

OBJECTIVE 5 6

CMA

Problem 10-18 Transfer Pricing

Reddy Industries is a vertically integrated firm with several divisions that operate as decentralized profit centers. Reddy's Systems Division manufactures scientific instruments and uses the products of two of Reddy's other divisions. The Board Division manufactures printed circuit boards (PCBs). One PCB model is made exclusively for the Systems Division using proprietary designs, while less complex models are sold in outside markets. The products of the Transistor Division are sold in a well-developed competitive market; however, one transistor model is also used by the Systems Division. The costs per unit of the products used by the Systems Division are as follows:

	PCB	Transistor
Direct materials	$1.85	$0.40
Direct labor	4.20	0.90
Variable overhead	2.40	0.70
Fixed overhead	0.85	0.75
Total cost	$9.30	$2.75

The Board Division sells its commercial product at full cost plus a 30 percent markup and believes the proprietary board made for the Systems Division would sell for $12 per unit on the open market. The market price of the transistor used by the Systems Division is $3.45 per unit.

Required:

1. What is the minimum transfer price for the Transistor Division? What is the maximum transfer price of the transistor for the Systems Division?

2. Assume the Systems Division is able to purchase a large quantity of transistors from an outside source at $2.75 per unit. Further assume that the Transistor Division has excess capacity. Can the Transistor Division meet this price?

3. The Board and Systems divisions have negotiated a transfer price of $11 per printed circuit board. Discuss the impact this transfer price will have on each division. *(CMA adapted)*

DATA ANALYTICS

OBJECTIVE 1 3 4

CMA

Problem 10-19 ROI, Residual Income

Garcia Industries produces tool and die machinery for manufacturers. The company expanded vertically in 20x1 by acquiring one of its suppliers of alloy steel plates, Keimer Steel Company. To manage the two separate businesses, the operations of Keimer are reported separately as an investment center.

Garcia monitors its divisions on the basis of both unit contribution and return on average investment (ROI), with investment defined as average operating assets employed. Management bonuses are determined on ROI. All investments in operating assets are expected to earn a minimum return of 13 percent before income taxes.

Keimer's cost of goods sold is considered to be entirely variable, while the division's administrative expenses are not dependent on volume. Selling expenses are a mixed cost with 40 percent attributed to sales volume. Keimer contemplated a capital acquisition with an estimated ROI of 14.5 percent; however, division management decided against the investment because it believed that the investment would decrease Keimer's overall ROI.

The 20x2 operating statement for Keimer follows. The division's operating assets employed were $12,600,000 at November 30, 20x2, a 5 percent increase over the 20x1 year-end balance.

Keimer Steel Company
Operating Statement
For the Year Ended November 30, 20x2

Sales revenue		$25,000,000
Less expenses:		
Cost of goods sold	$16,500,000	
Administrative expenses	3,955,000	
Selling expenses	2,700,000	23,155,000
Operating income before income taxes		$ 1,845,000

Required:

1. Calculate the unit contribution (rounded to the nearest cent) for Keimer Steel Company if 1,187,000 units were produced and sold during the year ended November 30, 20x2.
2. Calculate the following performance measures for 20x2 for Keimer Steel Company:
   a. Pretax return on average investment in operating assets employed (ROI)
   b. Residual income calculated on the basis of average operating assets employed
3. Explain why the management of Keimer Steel Company would have been more likely to accept the contemplated capital acquisition if residual income rather than ROI were used as a performance measure.
4. Keimer Steel Company is a separate investment center within Garcia Industries. Identify several items that Keimer should control if it is to be evaluated fairly by either the ROI or residual income performance measures. *(CMA adapted)*

Problem 10-20 Bonuses and Stock Options

OBJECTIVE ▶ **4**

Lawanna Davis graduated from State U with a major in accounting five years ago. She obtained a position with a well-known professional services firm upon graduation and has become one of their outstanding performers. In the course of her work, she has developed numerous contacts with business firms in the area. One of them, Shasta, Inc., recently offered her a position as head of their Financial Services Division. The offer includes a salary of $50,000 per year, annual bonuses of 1 percent of divisional operating income, and a stock option for 10,000 shares of Shasta stock to be exercised at $15 per share in two years. Last year, the Financial Services Division earned $1,110,000. This year, it is budgeted to earn $1,600,000. Shasta stock has increased in value at the rate of 16 percent per year over the past five years. Lawanna currently earns $65,000.

Required:

Advise Lawanna on the relative merits of the Shasta offer.

Problem 10-21 Setting Transfer Prices—Market Price versus Full Cost

OBJECTIVE ▶ **5** **6**

Ardmore, Inc., manufactures heating and air conditioning units in its six divisions. One division, the Components Division, produces electronic components that can be used by the other five. All the components produced by this division can be sold to outside customers; however, from the beginning, about 70 percent of its output has been used internally. The current policy requires that all internal transfers of components be transferred at full cost.

Recently, Cynthia Busby, the new chief executive officer of Ardmore, decided to investigate the transfer pricing policy. She was concerned that the current method of pricing internal transfers might force decisions by divisional managers that would be suboptimal for the firm. As part of her inquiry, she gathered some information concerning Part 4CM, used by the Small AC Division in its production of a window air conditioner, Model 7AC.

The Small AC Division sells 10,000 units of Model 7AC each year at a unit price of $58. Given current market conditions, this is the maximum price that the division can charge for Model 7AC. The cost of manufacturing the air conditioner is computed as follows:

Part 4CM	$ 6.45
Direct materials	23.00
Direct labor	15.00
Variable overhead	3.50
Fixed overhead	6.50
Total unit cost	$54.45

The window unit is produced efficiently, and no further reduction in manufacturing costs is possible.

The manager of the Components Division indicated that he could sell 10,000 units (the division's capacity for this part) of Part 4CM to outside buyers at $12 per unit. The Small AC Division could also buy the part for $12 from external suppliers. The following detail on the manufacturing cost of the component was provided:

Direct materials	$2.75
Direct labor	0.80
Variable overhead	1.10
Fixed overhead	1.80
Total unit cost	$6.45

Required:

1. Compute the firmwide contribution margin associated with Part 4CM and Model 7AC. Also, compute the contribution margin earned by each division.
2. Suppose that Cynthia Busby abolishes the current transfer pricing policy and gives divisions autonomy in setting transfer prices. Can you predict what transfer price the manager of the Components Division will set? What should be the minimum transfer price for this part? The maximum transfer price?
3. Given the new transfer pricing policy, predict how this will affect the production decision for Model 7AC of the manager of the Small AC Division. How many units of Part 4CM will the manager of the Small AC Division purchase, either internally or externally?
4. Given the new transfer price set by the Components Division and your answer to Requirement 3, how many units of 4CM will be sold externally?

OBJECTIVE 3 5 6 ▶ **Problem 10-22 Transfer Pricing with Idle Capacity**

Oriole, Inc., owns a number of food service companies. Two divisions are the Coffee Division and the Donut Shop Division. The Coffee Division purchases and roasts coffee beans for sale to supermarkets and specialty shops. The Donut Shop Division operates a chain of donut shops where the donuts are made on the premises. Coffee is an important item for sale along with the donuts and, to date, has been purchased from the Coffee Division. Company policy permits each manager the freedom to decide whether or not to buy or sell internally. Each divisional manager is evaluated on the basis of ROI and residual income.

Recently, an outside supplier has offered to sell coffee beans, roasted and ground, to the Donut Shop Division for $4.30 per pound. Since the current price paid to the Coffee Division is $4.75 per pound, Ashleigh Tremont, the manager of the Donut Shop Division, was interested in the offer. However, before making the decision to switch to the outside supplier, she decided to approach Santigui Melendez, manager of the Coffee Division, to see if he wanted to offer an even better price. If not, then Ashleigh would buy from the outside supplier.

Upon receiving the information from Ashleigh about the outside offer, Santigui gathered the following information about the coffee:

Direct materials	$0.95
Direct labor	0.45
Variable overhead	0.72
Fixed overhead*	1.53
Total unit cost	$3.65

*Fixed overhead is based on $1,530,000/1,000,000 pounds.

Selling price per pound	$4.75
Production capacity	1,000,000 pounds
Internal sales	100,000 pounds

Required:

1. Suppose that the Coffee Division is producing at capacity and can sell all that it produces to outside customers. How should Santigui respond to Ashleigh's request for a lower transfer price? What will be the effect on firmwide profits? Compute the effect of this response on each division's profits.

2. Now, assume that the Coffee Division is currently selling 950,000 pounds. If no units are sold internally, total coffee sales will drop to 850,000 pounds. Suppose that Santigui refuses to lower the transfer price from $4.75 and the Donut Division purchases from the external supplier. Compute the effect on each division's profits and on the profits of the firm as a whole.

3. Refer to Requirement 2. What are the minimum and maximum transfer prices? Suppose that the transfer price is set at the maximum price less $1. Will the two divisions accept this transfer price? Compute the effect on the firm's profits and on each division's profits.

4. Suppose that the Coffee Division has operating assets of $2,000,000. Assume that the Coffee Division sells 850,000 pounds to outsiders and 100,000 pounds to the Donut Division at a price of $4.75 per pound. What is divisional ROI (rounded to four significant digits) based on this situation? Now, refer to Requirement 3. What will divisional ROI (rounded to four significant digits) be if the transfer price of the maximum price less $1 is implemented? How will the change in ROI affect Santigui? What information has he gained as a result of the transfer pricing negotiations?

Problem 10-23   Transfer Pricing: Various Computations

OBJECTIVE ◀ 5 6

Corning Company has a decentralized organization with a divisional structure. Two of these divisions are the Appliance Division and the Manufactured Housing Division. Each divisional manager is evaluated on the basis of ROI.

The Appliance Division produces a small automatic dishwasher that the Manufactured Housing Division can use in one of its models. Appliance can produce up to 20,000 of these dishwashers per year. The variable costs of manufacturing the dishwashers are $98. The Manufactured Housing Division inserts the dishwasher into the model house and then sells the manufactured house to outside customers for $73,000 each. The division's capacity is 4,000 units. The variable costs of the manufactured house (in addition to the cost of the dishwasher itself) are $42,600.

Required:

Assume each part is independent, unless otherwise indicated.

1. Assume that all of the dishwashers produced can be sold to external customers for $320 each. The Manufactured Housing Division wants to buy 4,000 dishwashers per year. What should the transfer price be?

2. Refer to Requirement 1. Assume $24 of avoidable distribution costs. Identify the maximum and minimum transfer prices. Identify the actual transfer price, assuming that negotiation splits the difference.

3. Assume that the Appliance Division is operating at 75 percent capacity. The Manufactured Housing Division is currently buying 4,000 dishwashers from an outside supplier for $290 each. Assume that any joint benefit will be split evenly between the two divisions. What is the expected transfer price? How much will the profits of the firm increase under this arrangement? How much will the profits of the Appliance Division increase, assuming that it sells the extra 4,000 dishwashers internally?

OBJECTIVE 1 2 3

Problem 10-24 Managerial Performance Evaluation

Greg Peterson has recently been appointed vice president of operations for Webster Corporation. Greg has a manufacturing background and previously served as operations manager of Webster's Tractor Division. The business segments of Webster include the manufacture of heavy equipment, food processing, and financial services.

In a recent conversation with Carol Andrews, Webster's chief financial officer, Greg suggested that segment managers be evaluated on the basis of the segment data appearing in Webster's annual financial report. This report presents revenues, earnings, identifiable assets, and depreciation for each segment for a five-year period. Greg believes that evaluating segment managers by criteria similar to that used in evaluating the company's top management would be appropriate. Carol has expressed her reservations about using segment information from the annual financial report for this purpose and has suggested that Greg consider other ways to evaluate the performance of segment managers.

Required:

1. Explain why the segment information prepared for public reporting purposes may not be appropriate for the evaluation of segment management performance.
2. Describe the possible behavioral impact of Webster Corporation's segment managers if their performance is evaluated on the basis of the information in the annual financial report.
3. Identify and describe several types of financial information that would be more appropriate for Greg to review when evaluating the performance of segment managers. (*CMA adapted*)

OBJECTIVE 4

Problem 10-25 Management Compensation

Renslen, Inc., a truck manufacturing conglomerate, has recently purchased two divisions: Meyers Service Company and Wellington Products, Inc. Meyers provides maintenance service on large truck cabs for 10-wheeler trucks, and Wellington produces air brakes for the 10-wheeler trucks.

The employees at Meyers take pride in their work, as Meyers is proclaimed to offer the best maintenance service in the trucking industry. The management of Meyers, as a group, has received additional compensation from a 10 percent bonus pool based on income before income taxes and bonus. Renslen plans to continue to compensate the Meyers management team on this basis as it is the same incentive plan used for all other Renslen divisions, except for the Wellington division.

Wellington offers a high-quality product to the trucking industry and is the premium choice even when compared to foreign competition. The management team at Wellington strives for zero defects and minimal scrap costs; current scrap levels are at 2 percent. The incentive compensation plan for Wellington management has been a 1 percent bonus based on gross margin. Renslen plans to continue to compensate the Wellington management team on this basis.

The following condensed income statements are for both divisions for the fiscal year ended May 31, 20x1:

Renslen, Inc.
Divisional Income Statements
For the Year Ended May 31, 20x1

	Meyers Service Company	Wellington Products, Inc.
Revenues	$4,000,000	$10,000,000
Cost of product	$ 75,000	$ 4,950,000
Salaries*	2,200,000	2,150,000
Fixed selling expenses	1,000,000	2,500,000
Interest expense	30,000	65,000
Other operating expenses	278,000	134,000
Total expenses	$3,583,000	$ 9,799,000
Income before income taxes and bonus	$ 417,000	$ 201,000

*Each division has $1,000,000 of management salary expense that is eligible for the bonus pool.

Renslen has invited the management teams of all its divisions to an off-site management workshop in July where the bonus checks will be presented. Renslen is concerned that the different bonus plans at the two divisions may cause some heated discussion.

Required:

1. Determine the 20x1 bonus pool available for the management team at:
   a.   Meyers Service Company
   b.   Wellington Products, Inc.
2. Identify at least two advantages and disadvantages to Renslen, Inc., of the bonus pool incentive plan at:
   a.   Meyers Service Company
   b.   Wellington Products, Inc.
3. Having two different types of incentive plans for two operating divisions of the same corporation can create problems.
   a.   Discuss the behavioral problems that could arise within management for Meyers Service Company and Wellington Products, Inc., by having different types of incentive plans.
   b.   Present arguments that Renslen, Inc., can give to the management teams of both Meyers and Wellington to justify having two different incentive plans.

Problem 10-26 ROI, Residual Income, Behavioral Issues

OBJECTIVE ▶ 3

CMA

Jump Start Company (JSC), a subsidiary of Mason Industries, manufactures go-carts and other recreational vehicles. Family recreational centers that feature go-cart tracks along with miniature golf, batting cages, and arcade games have increased in popularity. As a result, JSC has been pressured by Mason management to diversify into some of these other recreational areas. Recreational Leasing, Inc. (RLI), one of the largest firms leasing arcade games to these family recreational centers, is looking for a friendly buyer. Mason's top management believes that RLI's assets could be acquired for an investment of $3.2 million and has strongly urged Bill Grieco, division manager of JSC, to consider acquiring RLI.

Bill has reviewed RLI's financial statements with his controller, Marie Donnelly, and they believe that the acquisition may not be in the best interest of JSC.

"If we decide not to do this, the Mason people are not going to be happy," said Bill. "If we could convince them to base our bonuses on something other than return on investment, maybe this acquisition would look more attractive. How would we do if the bonuses were based on residual income using the company's 15 percent cost of capital?"

Mason has traditionally evaluated all of its divisions on the basis of ROI, which is defined as the ratio of operating income to total assets. The desired rate of return for each division is 20 percent. The management team of any division reporting an annual increase in the ROI is automatically eligible for a bonus. The management of divisions reporting a decline in the ROI must provide convincing explanations for the decline to be eligible for a bonus, and this bonus is limited to 50 percent of the bonus paid to divisions reporting an increase.

The following condensed financial statements are for both JSC and RLI for the fiscal year ended May 31:

	JSC	RLI
Sales revenue	$10,500,000	
Leasing revenue		$2,800,000
Variable expenses	(7,000,000)	(1,000,000)
Fixed expenses	(1,500,000)	(1,200,000)
Operating income	$ 2,000,000	$ 600,000
Current assets	$ 2,300,000	$1,900,000
Long-term assets	5,700,000	1,100,000
Total assets	$ 8,000,000	$3,000,000
Current liabilities	$ 1,400,000	$ 850,000
Long-term liabilities	3,800,000	1,200,000
Stockholders' equity	2,800,000	950,000
Total liabilities and stockholders' equity	$ 8,000,000	$3,000,000

Required:

1. If Mason Industries continues to use ROI as the sole measure of division performance, explain why JSC would be reluctant to acquire RLI. Be sure to support your answer with appropriate calculations.
2. If Mason Industries could be persuaded to use residual income to measure the performance of JSC, explain why JSC would be more willing to acquire RLI. Be sure to support your answer with appropriate calculations.
3. Discuss how the behavior of division managers is likely to be affected by the use of:
   a. ROI as a performance measure
   b. Residual income as a performance measure (*CMA adapted*)
4. How is Bill using data analytic types—descriptive, diagnostic, predictive or prescriptive—to determine whether or not residual income should be used to affect manager behavior? Explain. (See Exhibits 2.5 and 2.6, pp. 37, 40, for a review of data analytic types.)

DATA ANALYTICS

OBJECTIVE **3**

Problem 10-27 Case on ROI and Residual Income: Ethical Considerations

Grate Care Company specializes in producing products for personal grooming. The company operates six divisions, including the Hair Products Division. Each division is treated as an investment center. Managers are evaluated and rewarded on the basis of ROI performance. Only those managers who produce the best ROIs are selected to receive bonuses and to fill higher-level managerial positions. Fred Olsen, manager of the Hair Products Division, has always been one of the top performers. For the past two years, Fred's division has produced the largest ROI; last year, the division earned an operating income of $2.56 million and employed average operating assets valued at $16 million. Fred is pleased with his division's performance and has been told that if the division does well this year, he will be in line for a headquarters position.

For the coming year, Fred's division has been promised new capital totaling $1.5 million. Any of the capital not invested by the division will be invested to earn the company's required rate of return (9 percent). After some careful investigation, the marketing and engineering staff recommended that the division invest in equipment that could be used to produce a crimping and waving iron, a product currently not produced by the division. The cost of the equipment was estimated at $1.2 million. The division's marketing manager estimated operating earnings from the new line to be $156,000 per year.

After receiving the proposal and reviewing the potential effects, Fred turned it down. He then wrote a memo to corporate headquarters, indicating that his division would not be able to employ the capital in any new projects within the next eight to 10 months. He did note, however, that he was confident that his marketing and engineering staff would have a project ready by the end of the year. At that time, he would like to have access to the capital.

Required:

1. Explain why Fred Olsen turned down the proposal to add the capability of producing a crimping and waving iron. Provide computations to support your reasoning.
2. Compute the effect that the new product line would have on the profitability of the firm as a whole. Should the division have produced the crimping and waving iron?
3. Suppose that the firm used residual income as a measure of divisional performance. Do you think Fred's decision might have been different? Why?
4. Explain why a firm like Grate Care might decide to use both residual income and ROI as measures of performance.
5. Did Fred display ethical behavior when he turned down the investment? In discussing this issue, consider why he refused to allow the investment.

Making the Connection

DATA ANALYTICS

Beauville Furniture Corporation produces sofas, recliners, and lounge chairs. Beauville is located in a medium-sized community in the southeastern part of the United States. It is a major employer in the community. In fact, the economic well-being of the community is tied very strongly to Beauville. Beauville operates a sawmill, a fabric plant, and a furniture plant in the same community.

The sawmill buys logs from independent producers. The sawmill then processes the logs into four grades of lumber: firsts and seconds, No. 1 common, No. 2 common, and No. 3 common. All costs incurred in the mill are common to the four grades of lumber. All four grades of lumber are used by the furniture plant. The mill transfers everything it produces to the furniture plant, and the grades are transferred at cost. Trucks are used to move the lumber from the mill to the furniture plant. Although no outside sales exist, the mill could sell to external customers, and the selling prices of the four grades are known.

The fabric plant is responsible for producing the fabric that is used by the furniture plant. To produce three totally different fabrics (identified by fabric ID codes FB60, FB70, and FB80, respectively), the plant has three separate production operations—one for each fabric. Thus, production of all three fabrics occurs at the same time in different locations in the plant. Each fabric's production operation has two processes: the weaving and pattern process and the coloring and bolting process. In the weaving and pattern process, yarn is used to create yards of fabric with different designs. In the next process, the fabric is dyed, cut into 25-yard sections, and wrapped around cardboard rods to form 25-yard bolts. The bolts are transported by forklift to the furniture plant's Receiving Department. All of the output of the fabric plant is used by the furniture plant (to produce the sofas and chairs). For accounting purposes, the fabric is transferred at cost to the furniture plant.

The furniture plant produces orders for customers on a special-order basis. The customers specify the quantity, style, fabric, lumber grade, and pattern. Typically, jobs are large (involving at least 500 units). The plant has two production departments: Cutting and Assembly. In the Cutting Department, the fabric and wooden frame components are sized and cut. Other components are purchased from external suppliers and are removed from stores as needed for assembly. After the fabric and wooden components are finished for the entire job, they are moved to the Assembly Department. The Assembly Department takes the individual components and assembles the sofas (or chairs).

Beauville Furniture has been in business for over two decades and has a good reputation. However, during the past five years, Beauville experienced eroding profits and declining sales. Bids were increasingly lost (even aggressive bids) on the more popular models. Yet, the company was winning bids on some of the more-difficult-to-produce items. Lance Hays, the owner and manager, was frustrated. He simply couldn't understand how some of his competitors could sell for such low prices. On a common sofa job involving 500 units, Beauville's bids were running $25 per unit, or $12,500 per job more than the winning bids (on average). Yet, on the more difficult items, Beauville's bids were running about $60 per unit less than the next closest bid. Gisela Berling, vice president of finance, was assigned the task of preparing a cost analysis of the company's product lines. Lance wanted to know if the company's costs were excessive. Perhaps the company was being wasteful, and it was simply costing more to produce furniture than it was costing its competitors.

Gisela prepared herself by reading recent literature on cost management and product costing and attending several conferences that explored the same issues. She then reviewed the costing procedures of the company's mill and two plants and did a preliminary assessment of their soundness. The production costs of the mill were common to all lumber grades and were assigned using the physical units method. Since the output and production costs were fairly uniform throughout the year, the mill used an actual costing system. Although Gisela had no difficulty with actual costing, she decided to explore the effects of using the sales-value-at-split-off method. Thus, cost and production data for the mill were gathered so that an analysis could be conducted. The two plants used normal costing systems. The fabric plant used process costing, and the furniture plant used job-order costing. Both plants used plantwide overhead rates based on direct labor hours. Based on her initial reviews, she concluded that the costing procedures for the fabric plant were satisfactory. Essentially, there was no evidence of product diversity. A statistical analysis revealed that about 90 percent of the variability in the plant's overhead cost could be explained by direct labor hours. Thus, the use of a plantwide overhead rate based on direct labor hours seemed justified. What did concern her, though, was the material waste that she observed in the plant. Maybe a standard cost system would be useful for increasing the overall cost efficiency of the plant. Consequently, as part of her report to Lance, she decided to include a description of the fabric plant's costing procedures—at least for one of the fabric types. She also decided to develop a standard cost sheet for the chosen fabric. The furniture plant, however, was a more difficult matter. Product diversity was present and could be causing some distortions in product costs. Furthermore, statistical analysis revealed that only about 40 percent of the variability in overhead cost was explained by the direct labor hours. She decided that additional analysis was needed so that a sound product costing method could be recommended. One possibility would be to increase the number of overhead rates. Thus, she decided to include departmental data so that the effect of moving to departmental rates could be assessed. Finally, she also wanted to explore the possibility of converting the sawmill and fabric plant into profit centers and changing the existing transfer pricing policy.

With the cooperation of the cost accounting manager for the mill and each plant's controller, she gathered the following data for last year:

Sawmill:

Joint manufacturing costs: $900,000

Grade	Quantity Produced (board feet)	Price at Split-Off (per 1,000 board foot)
Firsts and seconds	1,500,000	$300
No. 1 common	3,000,000	225
No. 2 common	1,875,000	140
No. 3 common	1,125,000	100
Total	7,500,000	

Fabric Plant:

Budgeted overhead: $1,200,000 (50% fixed)
Practical volume (direct labor hours): 120,000 hours
Actual overhead: $1,150,000 (50% fixed)
Actual hours worked:

	Weaving and Pattern	Coloring and Bolting	Total
Fabric FB60	20,000	12,000	32,000
Fabric FB70	28,000	14,000	42,000
Fabric FB80	26,000	18,000	44,000
Total	74,000	44,000	118,000

Departmental data on Fabric FB70 (actual costs and actual outcomes):

	Weaving and Pattern	**Coloring and Bolting**
Beginning inventories:		
Units*	20,000	400
Costs:		
Transferred in	$0	$100,000
Materials	$80,000	$8,000
Labor	$18,000	$6,600
Overhead	$22,000	$9,000
Current production:		
Units started	80,000	?
Units transferred out	80,000	3,200
Costs:		
Transferred in	$0	?
Materials	$320,000	$82,000
Labor	$208,000	$99,400
Overhead	?	?
Percentage completion:		
Beginning inventory	30%	40%
Ending inventory	40%	50%

*Units are measured in yards for the Weaving and Pattern Department and in bolts for the Coloring and Bolting Department. *Note*: With the exception of the cardboard bolt rods, materials are added at the beginning of each process. The cost of the rods is relatively insignificant and is included in overhead.

Proposed standard cost sheet for Fabric FB70 (for the Coloring and Bolting Department only):

Transferred-in materials (25 yards @ $10)	$250.00
Other materials (100 ounces @ $0.20)	20.00
Labor (3.1 hours @ $8)	24.80
Fixed overhead (3.1 hours @ $5)	15.50
Variable overhead (3.1 hours @ $5)	15.50
Standard cost per unit	$325.80

Furniture Plant:

Departmental data (budgeted):

	Service Departments				**Producing Departments**	
	Receiving	**Power**	**Maintenance**	**General Factory**	**Cutting**	**Assembly**
Overhead	$450,000	$600,000	$300,000	$525,000	$750,000	$375,000
Machine hours	—	—	—	—	60,000	15,000
Receiving orders	—	—	—	—	13,500	9,000
Square feet	1,000	5,000	4,000	—	15,000	10,000
Direct labor hours	—	—	—	—	50,000	200,000

After some discussion with the furniture plant controller, Gisela decided to use machine hours to calculate the overhead rate for the Cutting Department and direct labor hours for the Assembly Department rate (the Cutting Department was more automated than the Assembly Department). As part of her report, she wanted to compare the effects of plantwide rates and departmental rates on the cost of jobs. She wanted to know if overhead costing could be the source of the pricing problems the company was experiencing.

To assess the effect of the different overhead assignment procedures, Gisela decided to examine two prospective jobs. One job, Job A500, could produce 500 sofas, using a frequently requested style and Fabric FB70. Bids on this type of job were being lost more frequently to competitors. The second job, Job B75, would produce 75 specially designed recliners. This job involved a new design and was more difficult for the workers to build. It involved some special cutting requirements and an unfamiliar assembly. Recently, the company seemed to be winning more bids on jobs of this type. To compute the costs of the two jobs, Gisela assembled the following information on the two jobs:

Job A500:

Direct materials:	
Fabric FB70	180 bolts @ $350
Lumber (No. 1 common)	20,000 board feet @ $0.12
Other components	$26,600
Direct labor:	
Cutting Department	400 hours @ $10
Assembly Department	1,600 hours @ $8.75
Machine time:	
Cutting Department	350 machine hours
Assembly Department	50 machine hours

Job B75:

Direct materials:	
Fabric FB70	26 yards @ $350
Lumber (first and seconds)	2,200 board feet @ $0.12
Other components	$3,236
Direct labor:	
Cutting Department	70 hours @ $10
Assembly Department	240 hours @ $8.75
Machine time:	
Cutting Department	90 machine hours
Assembly Department	15 machine hours

Required:

1.

a. Complete the following table by calculating the sawmill's cost per board foot for each grade using both the physical units method and the sales-value-at-split-off method (round to three decimal places):

	Sawmill Cost and Production Data	
Grade	**Physical Units Method: Cost per Board Foot**	**Sales-Value-at-Split-Off Method: Cost per Board Foot**
Firsts and seconds		
No. 1 common		
No. 2 common		
No. 3 common		

b. Given that the sawmill provides lumber at cost to the furniture plant, using the sales-value-at-split-off method (**select**: increases, decreases) the cost of Job A500 by $_____ and (**select**: increases, decreases) the cost of Job B75 by $_____.

c. The *physical units method*, often used in the lumber industry, essentially assumes that it costs (**select**: the same, more) to produce each board foot (**select**: regardless of, depending on) the grade. Thus, (**select**: the same, a higher) cost of lumber would be assigned to a sofa or chair (**select**: regardless of, depending on) which grade is used. This approach has some drawbacks. Intuitively, the higher grades should cost (**select**: the same, more). Certainly, if the company was buying this input from suppliers, there would be (**select**: a cost difference, no cost difference) for sofas and chairs (**select**: regardless of, depending on) the grade of lumber purchased, because the higher grades have a (**select**: higher, lower) selling price.

The *relative sales value method* assigns (**select**: the same, a higher) cost to grades that have a (**select**: lower, higher) market value. Thus, the cost assigned to sofas and chairs (**select**: would differ, be the same) (**select**: according to, regardless of) the grade of lumber used.

d. Review the data analytic concepts and metrics found in Exhibits 2.5 and 2.6, pp. 37, 40. What are the data analytic models being considered for the Sawmill? Which of the data analytic types is being used in Part a of Requirement 1? And for Part b? Part c? Note: More than one data analytic type may apply. Which of the data analytic models in play would you recommend for assigning the joint manufacturing sawmill costs? Explain.

2. Calculate the following for the fabric plant:

   a. The plantwide overhead rate
   b. The amount of under- or overapplied overhead

3.

   a. Using the weighted average method, complete the following information regarding the Weaving and Pattern production process:
      i. Physical flow schedule (measured in yards)
      ii. Equivalent units schedule (measured in yards)
      iii. Unit cost
      iv. Cost of goods transferred out
   b. To convert the output of the Weaving and Pattern Department to the output of the Coloring and Bolting Department, yards transferred is (**select**: multiplied, divided) by

   _____.
   c. Using the weighted average method, complete the following for the Coloring and Bolting Department:
      i. Physical flow schedule (measured in bolts)
      ii. Equivalent units schedule (measured in bolts)
      iii. Unit cost

4. Currently, the three types of fabrics are produced simultaneously in different locations of the fabric plant using similar processes. Process costing methods are used to determine the unit cost of each fabric. Historically, the plant has never fully utilized any of the three processes. The maximum historical utilization of the capacity has been about 50 percent. Juana Sandoval, the fabric plant manager, is confident that the three operations can be consolidated in a way that there would be sufficient capacity to produce all three fabrics while capturing significant savings by reducing labor and overhead costs. In fact, total direct labor and variable overhead costs would be reduced by 25 percent and fixed overhead costs by 50 percent. Production of the three fabrics can be managed by using a batch production approach; however, one problem is that the yarn used for each fabric differs significantly in cost. Conversion activity is the same for each fabric regardless of the type of yarn. The cost accounting manager has assembled the following budgeted annual data for each process that reflects the expected reductions:

	Weaving and Pattern	Coloring and Bolting
Conversion cost	$900,000	$570,000
Expected activity (direct labor hours)	60,000	30,000

   a. Calculate the conversion rate for each process using direct labor hours (round to whole dollars):
   Weaving and Pattern Process: $_____ per hour
   Coloring and Bolting Process: $_____ per hour
   b. Assume a batch of 400 bolts of FB70 is produced. The cost of yarn requisitioned for the batch is $40,000. The batch used 2,550 direct labor hours in Weaving and Pattern and 1,200 hours in Coloring and Bolting. In Coloring and Bolting, another $10,000 of materials (dyes) were requisitioned for the batch. Calculate the cost per bolt for the production run of 400 bolts (round to the nearest cent).

5. In the Coloring and Bolting Department, 400,000 ounces of other materials were purchased and used to produce Fabric FB70's output of the period.
   a. Using the proposed standard cost sheet for Fabric FB70, calculate the following variances for the Coloring and Bolting Department (round actual unit costs and prices to three decimal places; round variances to the nearest dollar):
      i. Materials price variance (for other materials only)
      ii. Materials usage variance (for other materials only)
      iii. Labor rate variance
      iv. Labor efficiency variance
   In calculating the variances, which method did you use to compute the actual output of the period—FIFO or weighted average? Explain.
   b. Prepare the journal entries for materials and labor:
      i. Purchase of 400,000 ounces of other materials
      ii. Usage of 400,000 ounces of other materials
      iii. Assignment of direct labor costs
   c. Assume that the standard hours allowed for the actual total output of the *fabric* plant are 115,000. Calculate the following variances (round to whole dollar):
      i. Fixed overhead spending variance
      ii. Fixed overhead volume variance
      iii. Variable overhead spending variance
      iv. Variable overhead efficiency variance

6. Suppose that the fabric plant has 500 bolts of FB70 in beginning finished goods inventory. The current-year plan is to have 1,000 bolts of FB70 in finished goods inventory at the end of the year. This fabric has an external market price of $400 per bolt. If the fabric plant is set up as a profit center, it could sell 3,000 bolts per year to outside customers and supply 2,000 bolts per year internally to Beauville's furniture plant. If the fabric plant were designated as a profit center, the plant would transfer all goods internally at market price. Using the proposed standard cost sheet (as needed) and any other relevant data, prepare the following for Fabric FB70:
   a. Sales budget
   b. Production budget
   c. Direct labor budget
   d. Cost of goods sold budget

7. Calculate the following overhead rates for the furniture plant: (1) plantwide rate and (2) departmental rates. Use the direct method for assigning service costs to producing departments.

8. For each of the overhead rates computed in Requirement 7, calculate unit bid prices for Jobs A500 and B75. Assume that the company's aggressive bidding policy is unit cost plus 50 percent. Did departmental overhead rates have any effect on Beauville's winning or losing bids? What recommendation would you make? Explain. Now, adjust the costs and bids for departmental rate bids using the proposed standard costs for the Coloring and Bolting Department. Did this make a difference? What does this tell you?

9. Suppose that the fabric plant is set up as a profit center. Bolts of Fabric FB70 sell for $400 (or can be bought for $400 from outside suppliers). The fabric plant and the furniture plant both have excess capacity. Assume that Job A500 is a special order. The fabric and furniture plants have sufficient excess capacity to satisfy the demands of Job A500. What is the minimum transfer price for a bolt of FB70? If the maximum transfer price is $400, by how much do the fabric plant's profits increase if the two profit centers negotiate a transfer price that splits the joint benefit?

11 Strategic Cost Management

After studying this chapter, you should be able to:

1 Explain what strategic cost management is and how it can be used to help a firm create a competitive advantage.

2 Explain enterprise risk management and its importance for achieving strategy.

3 Discuss value-chain analysis and the strategic role of activity-based customer and supplier costing.

4 Tell what life-cycle cost management is and how it can be used to maximize profits over a product's life cycle.

5 Identify the basic features of JIT purchasing and manufacturing.

6 Describe the effect JIT has on cost traceability and product costing.

USING ENTERPRISE RISK MANAGEMENT TO IMPLEMENT STRATEGY

at Cardinal Health

Cardinal Health is an Ohio-based Fortune 25 company that distributes a vast array of medical and pharmaceutical products to businesses and individual consumers. Its range of medical products includes molecular diagnostic laboratory equipment, influenza test kits (e.g., for rapid diagnosis and point-of-care treatment), anesthesia masks and intubating stylets, vascular and wound closure devices, patient-monitoring tools, smart compression stockings, and clinical chemistry accessories. Its pharmaceutical products include radiopharmaceuticals (for molecular imaging—Cardinal Health operates a network of 130 nuclear pharmacies across 45 states), single photon emission computed tomography (SPECT) imaging, and biosimilars (e.g., a fast-growing class of therapeutic products that are highly similar to existing FDA-approved branded biologics). Like nearly all companies, Cardinal Health must carefully identify and effectively implement appropriate strategies to guide its decision making across the organization. One of the company's key strategies is to establish the reputation for and capability of being "a one stop shop for insights, information, products, research, and all manner of health-care related functions."[1]

Cardinal Health is a large organization—both in terms of sales revenue and number of employees—with sophisticated products and services that operates in a complex and highly regulated industry. As a result, it faces many important enterprise-wide (i.e., across the value chain) risks that, if not properly managed, could prevent the company from achieving its strategies as quickly or as effectively as possible, and in an extreme case, even drive it out of business. Therefore, Cardinal Health invests heavily in its enterprise risk management (ERM) program in an attempt to effectively manage top risks and exploit key opportunities in a way that helps the company achieve its strategies and increase organizational value. Cardinal discussed the program at its annual shareholder meeting noting that management has "developed and administers an enterprise risk management program…[through which management] identifies and prioritizes enterprise risks and develops systems to assess, monitor, and mitigate those risks. Management reviews and discusses with the Board significant risks identified through this program."[2]

As one specific example of risk and subsequent risk management efforts, Cardinal Health's radiopharmaceutical products present significant risk given their potential danger (i.e., they are radioactive), fragility (e.g., they must be maintained under particular conditions and transported using certain procedures), and extremely short-lived shelf life (i.e., they become worthless

1 "How Cardinal Health Is Creating a Holistic Content Strategy," MedForce, 2020, https://medforceeu.wbresearch.com/blog/heres-how-cardinal-health-is-creating-a-holistic-content-strategy, accessed August 25, 2020.

2 "2019 Proxy Statement—Notice of Annual Meeting of Shareholders," Cardinal Health, https://s1.q4cdn.com/238390398/files/doc_financials/2019/ar/359886(1)_1_Cardinal-Health-Proxy_PR_LR.pdf, accessed August 25, 2020.

if not administered within only a few hours). As a result, the company provides a range of services to support these products, including nuclear pharmacists who are available 24/7 and a fleet of specially certified drivers who optimize delivery of nuclear medicine. These risk management actions are based in part on a sophisticated analysis, including key cost management inputs, of the most financially effective techniques for ensuring that the resulting residual risks fall within the company's established risk appetite level. In addition to having individuals or teams responsible for ERM efforts, many large companies also form a Risk Committee to help implement and oversee management of the company's most important risks, including their escalation to the appropriate areas across the company. These formal ERM efforts provide considerable assistance in executing strategy and delivering value for the company's shareholders and other key stakeholders.

Why is one brand of ice cream viewed as better than another brand? It may reflect a deliberate decision by an ice cream producer to design and make an ice cream product that uses special ingredients and flavors rather than simply the ordinary. It is a means of differentiating the product and making it unlike those of competitors. It also may mean a conscious decision has been made to target certain types of consumers—consumers who are willing to pay for a higher-quality, specialized ice cream. Whether this is a good strategy or not depends on its profitability. Cost management plays a vital role in strategic decision making. Cost information is critical in formulating and choosing strategies as well as in evaluating the continued viability of existing strategic positions.

In Chapter 4, the basic concepts of activity-based costing were introduced. These concepts were illustrated using the traditional product cost definition. Activity-based product costing can significantly improve the accuracy of traditional product costs. Thus, inventory valuation is improved, and managers (and other information users) have better information concerning the costs of products leading to more informed decision making. Yet, the value of the traditional product cost definition is limited and may not be very useful in certain decision contexts. For example, corporations engage in decision making that affects their long-run competitive position and profitability. Strategic planning and decision making require a much broader set of cost information than that provided by product costs. Cost information about customers, suppliers, and different product designs is also needed to support strategic management objectives.

This broader set of information should satisfy two requirements. First, it should include information about the firm's environment and internal workings. Second, it must be prospective and thus should provide insight about future periods and activities. A value-chain framework with cost data to support a value-chain analysis satisfies the first requirement. Cost information to support product life-cycle analysis is needed to satisfy the second requirement. Value-chain analysis can produce organizational changes that fundamentally alter the nature and demand for cost information. Just-in-time (JIT) manufacturing is an example of a strategic approach that alters the nature of the cost accounting information system. In this chapter, we introduce strategic cost management, life-cycle cost management, and JIT manufacturing. The JIT approach is used to illustrate the value-chain concepts. However, given the breadth of its application and its effect on cost accounting, enterprise risk management, JIT is a topic that by itself merits study. Furthermore, JIT's linkages to strategic cost management justify this topic's inclusion in the same chapter with strategic cost management.

OBJECTIVE

Explain what strategic cost management is and how it can be used to help a firm create a competitive advantage.

STRATEGIC COST MANAGEMENT: BASIC CONCEPTS

Decision making that affects the long-term competitive position of a firm must explicitly consider the strategic elements of a decision. The most important strategic elements for a firm are its long-term growth and survival. Thus, **strategic decision making** is choosing among alternative strategies with the goal of selecting a strategy, or strategies, that provides a company with reasonable assurance of long-term growth and survival. The key to achieving this goal is to gain a *competitive advantage*. **Strategic cost management** is the use of cost data to develop and identify superior strategies that will produce a sustainable competitive advantage. For example, this proactive usage of strategic cost management, increasingly augmented with digital technology (e.g., using cloud computing instead of a large, expensive IT department), helps management more quickly identify and pursue value adding opportunities for the organization.[3]

Strategic Positioning: The Key to Creating and Sustaining a Competitive Advantage

Competitive advantage is creating better customer value for the same or lower cost than offered by competitors or creating equivalent value for lower cost than offered by competitors. **Customer value** is the difference between what a customer receives (customer realization) and what the customer gives up (customer sacrifice). What a customer receives is more than simply the basic level of performance provided by a product.[4] What is received is called the *total product*. The **total product** is the complete range of tangible and intangible benefits that a customer receives from a purchased product. Thus, customer realization includes basic and special product features, service, quality, instructions for use, reputation, brand name, and any other factors deemed important by customers. Customer sacrifice includes the cost of purchasing the product, the time and effort spent acquiring and learning to use the product, and **post-purchase costs**, which are the costs of using, maintaining, and disposing of the product.

Increasing customer value to achieve a competitive advantage is tied closely to judicious strategy selection. Three general strategies have been identified: *cost leadership*, *product differentiation*, and *focusing*.[5]

Cost Leadership The objective of a **cost leadership strategy** is to provide the same or better value to customers at a *lower cost* than offered by competitors. Essentially, if customer value is defined as the difference between realization and sacrifice, a low-cost strategy increases customer value by minimizing customer sacrifice. In this case, cost leadership is the goal of the organization. For example, a company might redesign a product so that fewer parts are needed, lowering production costs and the costs of maintaining the product after purchase.

Differentiation A **differentiation strategy**, on the other hand, strives to increase customer value by increasing what the customer receives (customer realization). A competitive advantage is created by providing something to customers that is not provided by competitors. Therefore, product characteristics must be created that set the product apart from its competitors. This differentiation can occur by adjusting the product so that it is different from the norm or by promoting some of the product's tangible or intangible attributes. Differences can be functional, aesthetic, or stylistic. For example, a retailer of computers might offer on-site repair service, a feature not offered by other rivals in the local market. Or a producer of crackers may offer animal-shaped crackers, as Nabisco did with Teddy Grahams®, to differentiate its product from other brands with more conventional shapes. To be of value, however, customers must see the variations as important. Furthermore, the value added to the customer by differentiation must exceed the firm's costs of providing the differentiation. If customers see the variations as important and if the value added to the customer exceeds the cost of providing the differentiation, then a competitive advantage has been established.

---

3 "How Digital Technology Is Transforming Cost Management," Wharton School, University of Pennsylvania (March 29, 2019), https://knowledge.wharton.upenn.edu/article/cost-management-in-the-digital-age/, accessed August 25, 2020.

4 Keep in mind that our definition of *product* includes services. Services are intangible products.

5 See M. E. Porter, *Competitive Advantage: Creating and Sustaining Superior Performance* (New York: Free Press, 1985), for a more complete discussion of the three strategic positions.

Focusing   A **focusing strategy** is selecting or emphasizing a market or customer segment in which to compete. One possibility is to select the markets and customers that appear attractive and then develop the capabilities to serve these targeted segments. Another possibility is to select specific segments where the firm's core competencies in the segments are superior to those of competitors. A focusing strategy recognizes that not all segments (e.g., customers and geographic regions) are the same. Given the capabilities and potential capabilities of the organization, some segments are more attractive than others.

Strategic Positioning   In reality, many firms will choose not just one general strategy, but a combination of the three general strategies. **Strategic positioning** is the process of selecting the optimal mix of these three general strategic approaches. The mix is selected with the objective of creating a sustainable competitive advantage. A **strategy**, reflecting combinations of the three general strategies, can be defined as:

> *... choosing the market and customer segments the business unit intends to serve, identifying the critical internal business processes that the unit must excel at to deliver the value propositions to customers in the targeted market segments, and selecting the individual and organizational capabilities required for the internal, customer, and financial objectives.*[6]

As used in the definition, "choosing the market and customer segments" is actually focusing; and "deliver[ing] the value propositions" is choosing to increase customer realization and/or decrease sacrifice and, therefore, entails cost leadership and/or differentiation strategies. Developing the necessary capabilities to serve the segments is related to all three general strategies.

What is the role of cost management in strategic positioning? The *objective* of strategic cost management is to *reduce* costs while simultaneously *strengthening* the chosen strategic position. Remember that a competitive advantage is tied to costs. For example, suppose that an organization is providing the same customer value at a higher cost than its competitors. By increasing customer value for specific customer segments (e.g., differentiation and focusing are used to strengthen the strategic position) and, at the same time, *decreasing* costs, the organization might reach a state where it is providing greater value at the same or less cost than its competitors, thus creating a competitive advantage.

Value-Chain Framework, Linkages, and Activities

Choosing an optimal (or most advantageous) strategic position requires managers to understand the activities that contribute to its achievement. Successful pursuit of a sound strategic position mandates an understanding of the *industrial value chain*. The **industrial value chain** is the linked set of value-creating activities from basic raw materials to the disposal of the finished product by end-use customers. Exhibit 11.1 illustrates a possible industrial value chain for the petroleum industry. A given firm operating in the oil industry may not—and likely will not—span the entire value chain. The exhibit illustrates that different firms participate in different portions of the value chain. Most large oil firms such as **ExxonMobil** and **ConocoPhillips** are involved in the value chain from exploration to service stations (like Firm A in Exhibit 11.1). Yet, even these oil giants purchase oil from other producers and also supply gasoline to service station outlets that are owned by others. Furthermore, there are many oil firms that engage exclusively in smaller segments of the chain such as exploration and production or refining and distribution (like Firms B and C in Exhibit 11.1). Regardless of its position in the value chain, to create and sustain a competitive advantage, a firm must understand the entire value chain and not just the portion in which it operates.

Thus, breaking down the value chain into its strategically relevant activities is basic to successful implementation of cost leadership and differentiation strategies. A value-chain framework is a compelling approach to understanding a firm's strategically important activities. Fundamental to a value-chain framework is the recognition that there exist complex linkages

6   Robert S. Kaplan and David P. Norton, *The Balanced Scorecard* (Boston: Harvard Business School Press, 1996): 37.

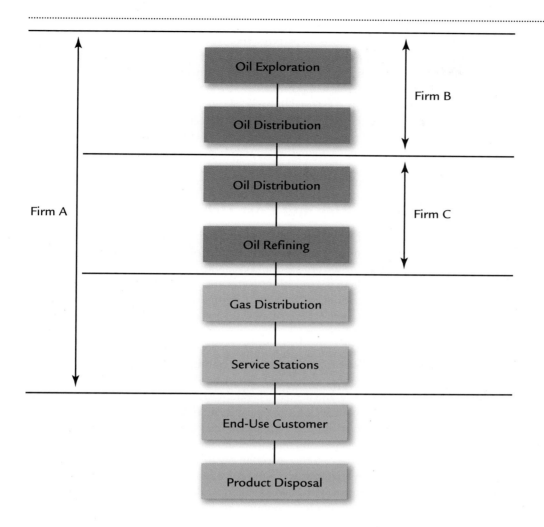

Exhibit 11.1

Value Chain for the Petroleum Industry

and interrelationships among activities both within and beyond the firm. Two types of linkages must be analyzed and understood: *internal linkages* and *external linkages*. **Internal linkages** are relationships among activities that are performed within a firm's portion of the value chain. **External linkages**, on the other hand, describe the relationship of a firm's value-chain activities that are performed with its suppliers and customers. External linkages, therefore, are of two types: *supplier linkages* and *customer linkages*.

External linkages emphasize the fact that a company must understand the entire value chain and not just the portion of the chain in which it participates. An *external* focus is needed for effective strategic cost management. A company cannot ignore supplier and customer linkages and expect to establish a sustainable competitive advantage. A company needs to understand its relative position in the industrial value chain. An assessment of the economic strength and relationships of each stage in the entire value-chain system can provide a company with several significant strategic insights. For example, knowing the revenues and costs of the different stages may reveal the need to forward or backward integrate to increase overall economic performance. Alternatively, it may reveal that divestiture and a narrowing of participation in the industrial value chain comprise a good strategy. Finally, knowing the supplier power and buyer power can have a significant effect on how external linkages are exploited. Supplier and buyer power can be assessed for a company by comparing the percentage of profits earned in the industrial value chain with the percentages earned by suppliers and by customers. For example, suppose that the profit earned per gallon of gasoline by an independent refiner and producer is $0.15 and the profit earned by a network of service stations that buy the gasoline (not owned by the independent) is $0.05 per gallon. The percentage of profit earned in this segment of the value chain by the downstream stage is 25 percent ($0.05/$0.20), while the independent earns 75 percent of the profit. Buyer power is weak relative to the refiner and producer. If, in addition, the return on assets being earned by the service station segment is high, this may reveal that integrating forward is both desirable and possible.

To exploit a firm's internal and external linkages, we must identify the firm's activities and select those that can be used to produce (or sustain) a competitive advantage. This selection process requires knowledge of the cost and value of each activity. For strategic analysis, activities are classified as *organizational activities* and *operational activities*; the costs of these activities, in turn, are determined by *organizational* and *operational cost drivers*.

Organizational Activities and Cost Drivers

Organizational activities are of two types: *structural* and *executional*. **Structural activities** are activities that determine the underlying economic structure of the organization. **Executional activities** are activities that define the processes and capabilities of an organization and thus are directly related to the ability of an organization to execute successfully. **Organizational cost drivers** are structural and executional factors that determine the long-term cost structure of an organization. Thus, there are two types of organizational drivers: *structural cost drivers* and *executional cost drivers*. Possible structural and executional activities with their cost drivers are listed by category in Exhibit 11.2.

As the exhibit shows, it is possible (and perhaps common) that a given organizational activity can be driven by more than one driver. For example, the cost of building plants is affected by number of plants, scale, and degree of centralization. Firms that have a commitment to a high degree of centralization may build larger plants so that there can be more geographic concentration and greater control. Similarly, complexity may be driven by number of different products, number of unique processes, and number of unique parts.

Organizational drivers are factors that affect an organization's long-term cost structure. This relationship is readily understood by simply considering the various drivers shown in Exhibit 11.2. Among the structural drivers are the familiar drivers of scale, scope, experience, technology, and complexity. For example, economies and diseconomies of scale are well-known economic phenomena, and the learning curve effect (experience) is also well documented. An interesting property of structural cost drivers is that more is not always better. Moreover, the efficiency level of a structural driver can change. For example, changes in technology can affect the scale driver by changing the optimal size of a plant. In the steel industry, minimill

---

Exhibit 11.2

Organizational Activities and Drivers

Structural Activities	Structural Cost Drivers
Building plants	Number of plants, scale, degree of centralization
Management structuring	Management style and philosophy
Grouping employees	Number and type of work units
Complexity	Number of product lines, number of unique processes, number of unique parts, degree of complexity
Vertically integrating	Scope, buying power, selling power
Selecting and using process technologies	Types of process technologies, experience

Executional Activities	Executional Cost Drivers
Using employees	Degree of involvement
Providing quality	Quality management approach
Providing plant layout	Plant layout efficiency
Designing and producing products	Product configuration
Providing capacity	Capacity utilization

technology has eliminated scale economies (in the form of megamills) as a competitive advantage. Plants of much smaller scale can now achieve the same level of efficiency once produced only by larger steel plants.

Of more recent interest and emphasis are executional drivers. Considerable managerial effort is being expended to improve how things are done in an organization. Continuous improvement and its many faces (employee empowerment, total quality management, process value analysis, life-cycle assessment, etc.) are what executional efficiency is all about. Consider employee involvement and empowerment. The cost of using employees decreases as the degree of involvement increases. Employee or worker involvement refers to the culture, degree of participation, and commitment to the objective of continuous improvement.

Operational Activities and Drivers

Operational activities are day-to-day activities performed as a result of the structure and processes selected by the organization. Examples include receiving and inspecting incoming parts, moving materials, shipping products, testing new products, servicing products, and setting up equipment. **Operational cost drivers** (activity drivers) are those factors that drive the cost of operational activities. They include such factors as number of parts, number of moves, number of products, number of customer orders, and number of returned products. As should be evident, operational activities and drivers are the focus of activity-based costing. Possible operational activities and their drivers are listed in Exhibit 11.3.

The structural and executional activities define the number and nature of the day-to-day activities performed within the organization. For example, if an organization decides to produce more than one product at a facility, then this structural choice produces a need for scheduling, a product-level activity. Similarly, providing a plant layout defines the nature and extent of the materials handling activity (usually a batch-level activity). Furthermore, although organizational activities define operational activities, analysis of operational activities and drivers can be used to suggest strategic choices of organizational activities and drivers. For example, knowing that the number of moves is a measure of consumption of the materials handling activity by individual products may suggest that resource spending can be reduced if the plant layout is redesigned to reduce the number of moves needed. Operational and organizational activities and their associated drivers are strongly interrelated. Exhibit 11.4 illustrates the circular nature of these relationships.

Unit-Level Activities	Unit-Level Drivers
Grinding parts	Grinding machine hours
Assembling parts	Assembly labor hours
Drilling holes	Drilling machine hours
Using materials	Pounds of material
Using power	Number of kilowatt-hours
Batch-Level Activities	**Batch-Level Drivers**
Setting up equipment	Number of setups
Moving batches	Number of moves
Inspecting batches	Inspection hours
Reworking products	Number of defective units
Product-Level Activities	**Product-Level Drivers**
Redesigning products	Number of change orders
Expediting	Number of late orders
Scheduling	Number of different products
Testing products	Number of procedures

Exhibit 11.3

Operational Activities and Drivers

Exhibit 11.4

Organizational and Operational Activity Relationships

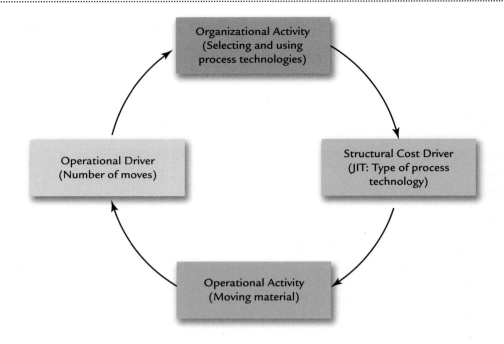

OBJECTIVE 2

Explain enterprise risk management and its importance for achieving strategy.

ENTERPRISE RISK MANAGEMENT

As discussed in the previous section, choosing the most appropriate strategy, or strategies, presents an important, yet challenging endeavor for most companies. However, effectively implementing the chosen strategy can be even more challenging as many obstacles, or risks, often hinder such strategy implementation efforts. Examples of risks that can affect strategy implementation include overregulation, trade conflicts, uncertain economic growth, cyber threats, availability of key employee skills, geopolitical uncertainty, speed of technological change, and changing consumer behavior.[7] **Enterprise risk management (ERM)** is the formal process of aligning an organization's overall desired level of risk taking with its strategy and then managing its top risks in a manner that maintains this alignment. The goal of ERM is to optimize, rather than minimize, the risks and opportunities facing the company. Therefore, companies such as **Cardinal Health** (see the opening scenario) increasingly utilize an ERM program to more effectively and efficiently implement their chosen strategy through improved decision making that considers key risks and enhanced compliance with laws and regulations. Approximately 99 percent of large companies (i.e., revenues in excess of $1 billion) and 75 percent of all companies (i.e., including public and private, for-profit and not-for-profit, and large and small) have at least some degree of an ERM process in place, although the level of ERM maturity varies widely across companies.[8] Companies spend considerable resources on ERM programs. For example, approximately 50 percent of companies spend more than $1 million on their annual ERM operating costs, whereas some companies spend in excess of $10 million.[9]

---

7 PricewaterhouseCoopers, "23rd Annual Global CEO Survey: Navigating the Rising Tide of Uncertainty," 2020, https://www.pwc.com/gx/en/ceo-survey/2020/reports/pwc-23rd-global-ceo-survey.pdf, accessed August 25, 2020.

8 M. Beasley, B. Branson, and B. Hancock, *The State of Risk Oversight: An Overview of Enterprise Risk Management Practices*, 11e, North Carolina State University, Poole College of Management. Enterprise Risk Management Initiative, 2020, https://erm.ncsu.edu/library/article/2020-the-state-of-risk-oversight-an-overview-of-erm-practices, accessed August 25, 2020.

9 K. Park, D. Griffiths, M. Bethell, and S. Sen, "All Together Now: Third-Party Governance and Risk Management," Deloitte Global, 2019, https://www2.deloitte.com/content/dam/Deloitte/ch/Documents/risk/deloitte-ch-extended-enterprise-risk-management-global-survey-2019.pdf, accessed August 25, 2020.

Companies appear likely to continue investing in ERM programs as an astonishing gap exists between the data that CEOs want for making risk-informed decisions versus the risk-related data they currently receive. For example, whereas 87 percent of CEOs report that receiving data about the key business risks they face is critically important, only 22 percent report that they receive comprehensive data about such key business risks.[10] Furthermore, surveys of executives—over half of which are the chief financial officer, chief risk officer, or controller for their company—report that the volume and complexity of risks is increasing extensively and that key stakeholders expect companies to have strong risk management practices in place.[11] Adding to this realization that ERM presents valuable opportunities to accountants, the Institute of Management Accountants (IMA) describes understanding ERM as a core competency for managerial accountants. Specifically, the IMA details that accountants should be able to provide inputs, including strategic cost information, that help companies identify, assess, and manage risks.[12] For example, a cost management perspective is helpful for estimating the cost impact (or magnitude) of potential risks, such as the expected increase in warranty repairs or lost future sales (e.g., an opportunity cost) that would result should the risk of quality defects materialize. Additionally, this perspective can be helpful for estimating the incremental cost of particular risk response activities, such as those involved in implementing additional quality improvements to help reduce the risk of quality defects. This section focuses primarily on the value that a cost management perspective can provide to the various steps within the ERM process, which are listed in Exhibit 11.5.

Determining Risk Appetite

An organization's overall desired level of risk taking is referred to as its **risk appetite**. Geronimo Company offers preparatory services for graduate entrance exams, such as the MCAT, LSAT, and GMAT. Panel A of Exhibit 11.6 shows Geronimo's risk appetite as the green line that connects the horizontal axis (i.e., likelihood) and the vertical axis (i.e., impact). The company's risk appetite can be considered moderate in nature because it is neither very near nor very far from the origin but rather connects the midpoints of the likelihood and impact axes.

Identifying Top Risks

After determining its risk appetite, a company next identifies its most important risks. Some managers or board of director members refer to these most important risks as a Top Ten list or, more casually, as the risks that "keep them up at night." Risk identification requires input from a cross functional team to capture all of the perspectives of the organization to understand the risks (or threats), as well as the opportunities, facing the organization. Most companies separate identified risks into various categories, such as strategic risk, operational risk, compliance risk, financial reporting risk, and so on, that can be further tailored to the specifics of a particular company or industry. Each top risk is assigned a "risk owner" (as noted in the later Bayer

- **Risk Appetite Determination**: Determine the organization's desired overall level of risk taking that should be pursued to generate the financial returns expected by shareholders.
- **Risk Identification**: Identify top risks.
- **Risk Assessment**: Assess top risks at the inherent level.
- **Risk Response**: Identify, evaluate, and implement the best response alternatives for inherent risks that bring the portfolio of residual risks into alignment with risk appetite.
- **Risk Monitoring**: Continually search for new emerging risks, reevaluate accuracy of risk assessments, and consider more effective risk response alternatives.

Exhibit 11.5

Key Steps within the ERM Process

10 PricewaterhouseCoopers, "22nd Annual Global CEO Survey," https://www.pwc.com/mu/pwc-22nd-annual-global-ceo-survey-mu.pdf, accessed August 25, 2020.

11 Beasley, Branson, and Hancock, *The State of Risk Oversight*.

12 Institute of Management Accounting, *IMA Management Accounting Competency Framework*, 2019, https://www.imanet.org/-/media/590889ef44ad401bb94d83cd43e584b8.ashx?la=en, accessed August 25, 2020.

example) who has responsibility for overseeing the successful management of that risk throughout the ERM process.

Assessing Inherent Risks

After being identified, management must assess top risks at the inherent level. An **inherent risk** is the risk that exists absent of any risk management action to reduce or avoid the risk. Most ERM programs assess, or estimate, two aspects of uncertainty for inherent risks—(1) the *likelihood*, or probability P, of an event occurring and (2) the *impact*, or magnitude, on the company should an event actually occur. Probability P is measured as falling between 0 (no chance of occurring) and 1 (will occur for sure)—(i.e., $0 \leq P \leq 1$). Impact can be measured in qualitative terms (e.g., company reputation), in nonfinancial quantitative terms (e.g., percentage of quality defects), or financial quantitative terms (e.g., additional costs incurred or revenues lost). Both probability and impact are difficult to quantify. Managers increasingly rely on the measurement expertise of management accountants to estimate these amounts, especially cost and other financially oriented impact measures. Panel B of Exhibit 11.6 plots Geronimo Company's eight most important inherent risks (IR) shown as IR_1 through IR_8.

REAL-WORLD EXAMPLE

ERM analyses often contain confidential internal information, and as a result, companies typically have not shared such information publicly. However, companies are beginning to realize the value of properly disclosing effective ERM practices via corporate sustainability reports, integrated reports, and annual reports. For example, Bayer's annual report provides insights into how this large (approximately €47 billion in annual sales) pharmaceutical and agricultural company uses ERM to achieve its goal of "health for all, hunger for none" by considering the impact and likelihood of its most critical risks.[13]

The Bayer Group is a German company founded in 1863 and consists of approximately 400 consolidated companies in over 80 countries with over 100,000 employees across the globe. It owns a range of highly recognizable products including Bayer Aspirin, Claritin, and Xarelto. Exhibit 11.7 displays Bayer's ERM risk chart, which it includes within its annual report. Bayer's chart should be interpreted in the same manner as the risk charts depicted in Exhibit 11.6—the further from the origin, the greater the risk as measured by likelihood of occurrence and the potential impact should the risk occur. First, Bayer estimates the *quantitative* impact using the potential effect on future cash flows. It estimates the *qualitative* impact using the potential effect on strategy, reputation, loss of stakeholder confidence, and incomplete compliance with sustainability principles (e.g., involving safety, environmental protection, or human rights). The higher the combined quantitative and qualitative assessment, the higher the resulting impact measure for placement on the risk chart. Second, Bayer estimates the likelihood of occurrence using the expected probability of the risk event transpiring over a maximum period of 10 years. It further estimates the likelihood by considering the speed at which the impact is expected to be realized should the risk occur.

In addition, Bayer attempts to take into consideration the interrelationships between risks—also known as risk correlation—when placing key risks on the chart. For example, changes in Bayer's socially oriented risks might affect the assessed likelihood or impact of Bayer's regulatory-, legal-, and/or product safety–oriented risks. A cost management perspective, combined with data analytic tools, can help provide valuable insights into how such risk correlations might affect both impact and likelihood risk measures for assessing key risks. After assessing its key risks at an inherent level, Bayer's ERM team assigns a risk owner to each key risk who decides on the most appropriate risk response, or treatment, to the given risk based on a cost-benefit analysis of the possible response options, including risk avoidance, risk reduction, risk transfer, and risk acceptance.

---

13 From Bayer's 2019 Annual Report, page 91, http://release.ace.bayer.com/sites/default/files/bayer-ag-annual -report-2019_9.pdf, accessed October 19, 2020.

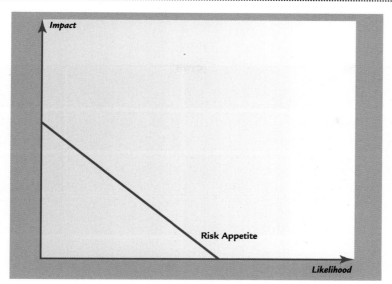

Panel A: Risk Appetite

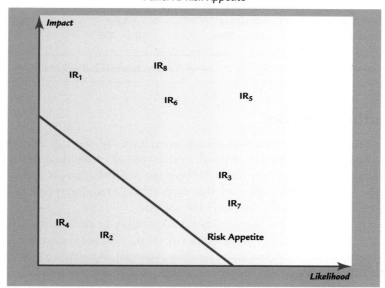

Panel B: Inherent Risks

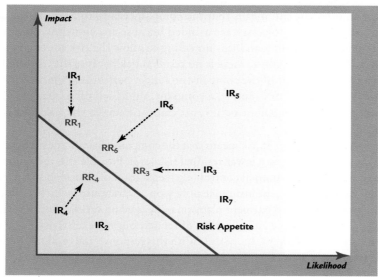

Panel C: Residual Risks

Exhibit 11.6

Key Elements of a Portfolio Risk Management Perspective

Exhibit 11.7   Enterprise Risk Management at Bayer

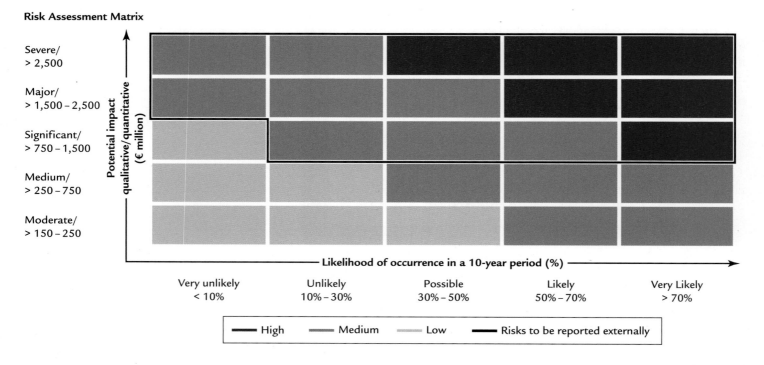

Risk Assessment Matrix

Responding to Risks

Once management assesses its top risks at an inherent level, the next step in the ERM process is to decide how best to manage, or respond, to each top risk. A **residual risk** is the risk that remains after any risk management action has been taken. ERM attempts to manage the company's most important inherent risks such that the portfolio, or aggregate collection, of residual risks that remains aligns with the company's risk appetite.

Generally, there are three alternatives for responding to an inherent risk: (1) *accept*, (2) *avoid*, or (3) *reduce*. To *accept* an inherent risk means that the company does nothing in response—it simply continues conducting business as normal. Many risks are managed this way simply because companies do not have enough money and personnel resources to reduce all of their top risks. With this response, the residual risk is the same as the inherent risk because no response action is taken.

To *avoid* an inherent risk means that the company ceases to perform the activity that gave rise to the risk. Some top risks are avoided because the company cannot reduce the risk in a cost-beneficial manner and it is unwilling to allow the risk to remain at its current inherent level. With this response, there is no residual risk because the risk itself is removed from the company as a result of the company no longer performing the activity that caused the inherent risk to exist. For example, a company might sell off a business unit or product or service line if management believes it cannot manage the associated risk(s) in a cost-beneficial manner.

Finally, to *reduce* an inherent risk means that the company enacts some particular procedure to decrease the inherent risk to a lower residual risk level. Possible risk reduction procedures include a specific activity or internal control (e.g., separation of duties), insurance policy (e.g., a fire or other catastrophic event insurance policy on a warehouse facility), strategic alliance (e.g., a new digital **Mastercard** payment platform to be used on various **Apple** devices), or even an entire business process (i.e., a collection of related business activities, such as customer experience for the **Walt Disney Company**). With this response, the residual risk will be lower than the inherent risk as a result of the chosen risk reduction alternative.

Net Benefit of Risk Response

Each risk response alternative produces a benefit. **Risk response benefit** can be defined as the difference between the inherent risk and the residual risk produced by the particular risk response. Inherent risk is the probability (or likelihood) of a risk occurring multiplied by the impact should it actually occur, which in essence is an expected value calculation. Residual risk is calculated in the same manner, except that the equation uses the probability and the impact that are expected to exist *after* the risk response in question has been implemented (i.e., the residual amounts).

Risk Response Benefit = Inherent Risk − Residual Risk

Most risk responses also incur a cost in order to be implemented. **Risk response cost** can be defined as the incremental cost incurred by the company to implement the given risk response. This incremental cost (see Chapter 17 for a discussion of incremental, or relevant, costs) can include both direct and indirect costs (see Chapter 2 for a discussion of direct and indirect costs) and often is quite challenging to estimate accurately.[14] Accountants using a cost management perspective can add tremendous value to organizations by accurately estimating the incremental costs of each risk response alternative under consideration.

Effective ERM requires that management evaluate and implement the most appropriate risk response to each top risk—in other words, the response that generates the greatest positive net benefit. **Risk response net benefit** is measured as the benefit of risk response minus the cost of risk response.

Risk Response Net Benefit = Response Benefit − Response Cost

Only after risk response costs have been accurately estimated and subtracted from the response benefit can management estimate the net benefit of each risk response alternative and select the best course of action (i.e., the alternative with the greatest positive net benefit).

Returning to Geronimo Company, Panel C of Exhibit 11.6 plots Geronimo's residual risks (RR) shown in red as RR_1, RR_3, RR_4, and RR_6. Assume that IR_1 represents the inherent risk of the exam tutoring facility being damaged or destroyed by a natural disaster (e.g., flood, tornado, or fire). Panel C shows that Geronimo management chose to *reduce* IR_1 down to the lower RR_1 level to be in alignment with the company's risk appetite. Note that the response to IR_1 was to lessen the impact with no change to the likelihood (i.e., the downward arrow connecting IR_1 to RR_1 is vertical only). This particular type of risk reduction is typical when companies utilize an insurance policy to manage risk. Assume that IR_3 represents the risk of insufficient topical knowledge being possessed by the employees who serve customers as exam tutors. Panel C shows that management also chose to reduce IR_3 down to the lower RR_3 level. However, in this case, note that the response to IR_3 was to lessen the likelihood with no change to the impact (i.e., the leftward arrow connecting IR_3 to RR_3 is horizontal only). Furthermore, management also decided to reduce IR_6 as evidenced by RR_6 being located closer to the risk appetite (i.e., the downward and leftward arrow connecting IR_6 to RR_6 is both partly vertical and partly horizontal). Notice that IR_4 is considerably below the risk appetite and, as a result, likely not generating sufficiently high returns (or other important performance measures) to please investors and other key stakeholders. Therefore, management elected to respond to IR_4 by taking on *more* risk as depicted by RR_4 being much closer to the risk appetite. For example, management might decide to take on more risk (e.g., that student exam performance decreases) by replacing one-on-one tutoring sessions with small-group tutoring sessions in order to generate higher returns. The ability to take on more risk in such a targeted manner—in order to generate higher returns—represents one of the key benefits of an effective ERM system. Risk taking usually proves more effective when management understands that the majority of its other key residual risks align with the company's risk appetite.

---

14 B. Ballou, D. Heitger, and T. Schultz, "Measuring the Costs of Responding to Business Risk," *Management Accounting Quarterly*, Vol. 10, No. 2 (2009): 1–11.

Changing to a different risk response option, management chose to *avoid* IR$_8$, as evidenced by the absence of either an IR$_8$ or a RR$_8$ from Panel C. In other words, IR$_8$ was deemed too significant simply to accept (i.e., do nothing), and yet also was too costly to reduce to a point where its residual risk aligned with the company's overall risk appetite. Changing to yet another risk response option, management chose to *accept* IR$_2$, IR$_7$, and IR$_5$. When considered in isolation, IR$_7$ is too risky (i.e., it exceeds the risk appetite) and IR$_2$ is not risky enough (i.e., it falls below the risk appetite—similar to IR$_4$, investors will demand a higher return than what will be generated by this overly conservative position). However, IR$_7$ exceeds the risk appetite line by approximately the same amount that IR$_2$ falls short of the risk appetite line. When considered from a portfolio perspective, IR$_7$ and IR$_2$ offset each other and, thus, together align with Geronimo's risk appetite. Finally, management chose to accept IR$_5$ even though there is no offsetting risk equally below the risk appetite. This type of accept response decision can be made when the company has no choice but to continue with the underlying business activity that gives rise to the risk (i.e., the company cannot choose to avoid the risk) and management has no way to reduce the risk in a cost-effective manner. For example, SpaceX had no choice but to accept certain key risks when it successfully partnered with NASA to launch human astronauts into space aboard its new Dragon spaceship. In conclusion, Geronimo's collective set of residual risks are, in essence, in alignment with its risk appetite, thereby demonstrating the concept of portfolio risk management.

Management must understand how to evaluate multiple risk response alternatives and select the one that best manages the given risk in a cost-effective manner. **Example 11.1** illustrates how net benefit can be used to evaluate and select between risk response alternatives.

EXAMPLE 11.1

The HOW and WHY of Using Net Benefit to Evaluate Risk Response Alternatives

Information:

Fast Water Rafting Company provides thrilling adventures along the Snake River outside of Jackson, Wyoming. One of its most popular adventures is a guided two-hour raft tour through Class III rapids. Fast Water's management is concerned about the additional costs the company would incur from potential fines paid to state regulators and payments made to customers resulting from injuries they sustain from falling out of the raft. The chart below contains a description of this top risk, an inherent risk assessment, three risk response alternatives (A through C), and a residual risk assessment for each response alternative.

Risk	Inherent Risk		Risk Response Alternatives	Residual Risk	
	Likelihood	*Impact (Operating Costs)*	*Risk Response Alternatives*	*Likelihood*	*Impact (Operating Costs)*
Customers fall out of the raft and sustain injuries (strike submerged rocks, become submerged underwater or trapped under the raft, strain muscles trying to swim back to the raft or to shore, etc.) that lead to regulatory fines and compensatory payments to customers.	10%	$2,500,000	**A**—Develop an extensive new safety video and require customers to watch it and pass a skills test prior to rafting.	6%	$1,000,000
			B—Develop and install more effective safety mechanisms for ensuring customers stay within the raft (stronger footholds, better fitting sandals, etc.).	7%	$2,000,000
			C—Take no action in response to possible new lawsuits or fines.	10%	$2,500,000

EXAMPLE 11.1

(*Continued*)

Fast Water's management accountants estimate that the incremental cost of implementing risk response A is $140,000 and the incremental cost of implementing risk response B is $35,000.

> **Why:**
> Focusing on net benefit helps ensure that the chosen risk response alternative has a benefit that outweighs its cost and produces the greatest positive net benefit from the possible set of risk response alternatives.

Required:

1. Calculate the inherent risk for Fast Water.

2. Calculate the residual risk for Fast Water associated with each of the three risk response alternatives A, B, and C.

3. Calculate the benefit for Fast Water associated with each of the three risk response alternatives A, B, and C.

4. Calculate the net benefit for Fast Water associated with each of the three risk response alternatives A, B, and C.

5. Using net benefit as the criterion, which risk response should Fast Water choose to implement?

Solution:

1. The *inherent risk* for this risk equals the likelihood of the risk occurring multiplied by the impact that is expected should the risk actually occur.

   Therefore, the *inherent risk* (IR) is:
   = 0.10 (likelihood) × $2,500,000 (impact) = $250,000

2. The *residual risk* associated with a particular risk response alternative equals the likelihood that remains after the alternative is implemented multiplied by the impact that remains after the alternative is implemented.

   Therefore, *residual risk* (RR) for response *alternative A* is:
   = 0.06 (likelihood) × $1,000,000 (impact) = $60,000

   Therefore, *residual risk* (RR) for response *alternative B* is:
   = 0.07 (likelihood) × $2,000,000 (impact) = $140,000

   Therefore, *residual risk* (RR) for response *alternative C* is:
   = 0.10 (likelihood) × $2,500,000 (impact) = $250,000

3. The *benefit* associated with a particular risk response alternative equals the inherent risk (IR) minus the residual risk (RR).

   Therefore, the *benefit* for risk response *alternative A* is:
   = $250,000 (IR) − $60,000 (RR) = $190,000

   Therefore, the *benefit* for risk response *alternative B* is:
   = $250,000 (IR) − $140,000 (RR) = $110,000

   Therefore, the *benefit* for risk response *alternative C* is:
   = $250,000 (IR) − $250,000 (RR) = $0

EXAMPLE 11.1

(Continued)

4. The *net benefit* associated with a particular risk response alternative equals the benefit minus the cost.

    Therefore, the *net benefit* for risk response *alternative A* is:

    = \$190,000 (benefit) − \$140,000 (cost) = \$50,000

    Therefore, the *net benefit* for risk response *alternative B* is:

    = \$110,000 (benefit) − \$35,000 (cost) = \$75,000

    Therefore, the *net benefit* for risk response *alternative C* is:

    = \$0 (benefit) − \$0 (cost) = \$0

5. As calculated in requirement 3, alternative A has a larger benefit (\$190,000) than alternative B (\$110,000). However, alternative A also has a substantially greater incremental cost to implement than does alternative B. Therefore, using net benefit as the criterion, Fast Water should select and implement risk response alternative B because this option has the greatest positive net benefit (\$75,000) as compared to alternative A (\$50,000) or alternative C (\$0).

Monitoring the ERM Process

Finally, risk monitoring means that management proceeds through the ERM process in an iterative fashion, continually looking for ways to improve any and all steps along the way. One common mistake made by management in implementing ERM is treating it as a checklist that simply requires one-time consideration. Instead, management should initially proceed through the complete ERM process and then return each year to begin the process again.

Well-run companies continuously look for ways to improve their ERM process and turn to management accountants to play an important role in providing key cost-related inputs throughout the ERM process. For example, management accountants can help continually reevaluate key inputs, such as identifying emerging—yet previously ignored—risks and reassessing the stated risk appetite to verify that it aligns with the company's strategy and expectations from key stakeholders. Finally, from a measurement perspective, management accountants should play an important role in more creatively and accurately estimating inherent risks, the incremental cost of specific risk response alternatives, the residual risk that is expected to be achieved from the selected risk response plan, and the residual risk that actually is achieved after the selected risk response plan has been implemented.

 OBJECTIVE 3

Discuss value-chain analysis and the strategic role of activity-based customer and supplier costing.

VALUE-CHAIN ANALYSIS

Value-chain analysis is identifying and exploiting internal and external linkages with the objective of strengthening a firm's strategic position. The exploitation of linkages relies on analyzing how costs and other nonfinancial factors vary as different bundles of activities are considered. For example, organizations change their structure and processes as needed to meet new challenges and take advantage of new opportunities. This may include new approaches to differentiation. Additionally, managing organizational and operational cost drivers to create long-term cost reduction outcomes is an important input in value-chain analysis when cost leadership is emphasized. The objective, of course, is to control cost drivers better than competitors can (thus creating a competitive advantage).

Exploiting Internal Linkages

Sound strategic cost management mandates the consideration of that portion of the value chain in which a firm participates (called the *internal value chain*). Exhibit 11.8 reviews the internal value-chain activities for an organization. Activities before and after production must be identified and their linkages recognized and exploited. Exploiting internal linkages means that relationships between activities are assessed and used to reduce costs and increase value. For example, product design and development activities occur before production and are linked to production activities. The way the product is designed affects the costs of production. How production costs are affected requires a knowledge of cost drivers. Thus, knowing the cost drivers of activities is crucial for understanding and exploiting linkages. If design engineers know that the number of parts is a cost driver for various production activities (material usage, direct labor usage, assembly, inspection, materials handling, and purchasing are examples of activities where costs could be affected by number of parts), then redesigning the product so that it has standard parts, multiple sources, short lead times, and high quality can significantly reduce the overall cost of the product. **Example 11.2** illustrates how internal linkages can be exploited to reduce costs in the internal value chain.

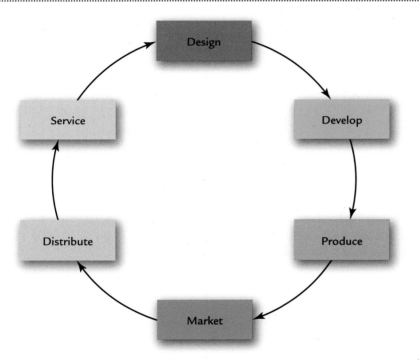

Exhibit 11.8

Internal Value Chain

Information:
A firm currently produces a high-tech medical product with 20 parts. Design engineering has produced a new configuration for the product that requires only eight parts. Current activity capacity and demand (20-part configuration) and expected activity demand (8-part configuration) are provided.

EXAMPLE 11.2

The HOW and WHY of Exploiting Internal Linkages to Reduce Costs and Increase Value

EXAMPLE 11.2

(Continued)

Activities	Activity Driver	Activity Capacity	Current Activity Demand	Expected Activity Demand
Material usage	Number of parts	200,000	200,000	80,000
Assembling parts	Direct labor hours	10,000	10,000	5,000
Purchasing parts	Number of orders	15,000	12,500	6,500

Additionally, the following activity cost data are provided:

Material usage: $3 per part used; no fixed activity cost.

Assembling parts: $12 per direct labor hour; no fixed activity cost.

Purchasing parts: Three salaried clerks, each earning a $30,000 annual salary; each clerk is capable of processing 5,000 purchase orders. Variable activity costs: $0.50 per purchase order processed for forms, postage, etc.

> **Why:**
> Exploiting internal linkages means that relationships between activities in the internal value chain are assessed and used to reduce costs and increase value.

Required:

1. Calculate the cost reduction produced by the new design.

2. Suppose that 10,000 units are being produced and sold for $400 per unit and that the price per unit will be reduced by the per-unit savings. What is the new price for the eight-part configured product?

3. *What if* the expected activity demand for purchase orders was 4,500? How would this affect the answers to Requirements 1 and 2?

Solution:

1.

Material usage cost reduction [(200,000 − 80,000)$3]	$360,000
Labor usage cost reduction [(10,000 − 5,000)$12]	60,000
Purchasing cost reduction* [$30,000 + $0.50(12,500 − 6,500)]	33,000
Total savings	$453,000

*Based on the new demand, the number of purchasing agents can be reduced by one, saving $30,000.

2. New price = $400 − ($453,000/10,000) = $354.70.

3. Since each purchasing agent can process only 5,000 orders, one agent is needed, saving an additional $30,000 of salary costs. Variable purchasing costs would also drop by an additional $1,000 [$0.50 × (6,500 − 4,500)]. Thus, total savings would increase by $31,000, and the new price would decrease by an additional $3.10 ($31,000/10,000) to $351.60 ($354.70 − $3.10).

Example 11.2 underscores the importance of individual activities for assessing the impact of the new design. Knowing the cost of different design strategies is made possible by assessing the linkages of activities and the effects of changes in demand for the activities. Notice the key role that the resource usage model plays in this analysis.[15] The purchasing activity currently supplies 15,000 units of activity capacity, acquired in steps of 5,000 units. (Capacity is measured in the

---

15 The resource usage model was introduced in Chapter 3.

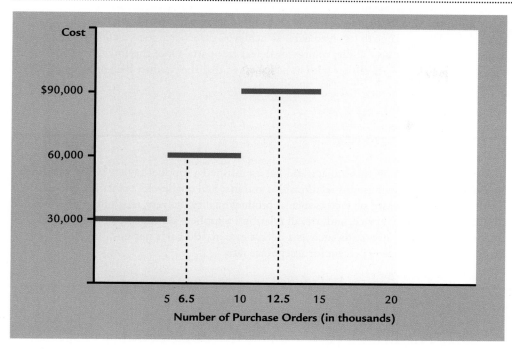

Exhibit 11.9

Step-Cost Behavior: Purchasing Activity

Note: The bold numbers represent the demand before and after product reconfiguration (12.5 before and 6.5 after).

number of purchase orders—see Exhibit 11.9 for a graphical illustration of the activity's step-cost behavior.) Unused activity for the current product configuration is 2,500 units (15,000 − 12,500). Reconfiguring the product reduces the demand from 12,500 orders to 6,500 orders. This increases the unused activity capacity to 8,500 units (15,000 − 6,500). At this point, management has the capability of reducing resource spending on the resources acquired in advance of usage. Since activity capacity is acquired in chunks of 5,000 units, resource spending can be reduced by $30,000 (the price of one purchasing clerk). Furthermore, since demand decreases, resource spending for the resources acquired as needed is also reduced $3,000 by the variable component ($0.50 × 6,000). The activity-based costing model and knowledge of activity cost behavior are powerful and integral components of strategic cost management.

In Example 11.2, the analysis implicitly assumed that resource spending on the engineering design activity would remain unchanged. Therefore, there was no cost to exploiting the linkage. Suppose, however, that an increase in resource spending of $50,000 is needed to exploit the linkages between engineering design and activities downstream in the firm's value chain. Spending $50,000 to save $453,000 is certainly sound. Spending on one activity to save on the cost of other activities is a fundamental principle of strategic cost analysis.

Exploiting Supplier Linkages

Although each firm has its own value chain, as was shown in Exhibit 11.1 on page 557, each firm also belongs to a broader value chain—the *industrial value chain*. The value-chain system also includes value-chain activities that are performed by suppliers and buyers. A firm cannot ignore the interaction between its own value-chain activities and those of its suppliers and buyers. Linkages with activities external to the firm can also be exploited. Exploiting external linkages means managing these linkages so that both the company and the external parties receive an increase in benefits.

Suppliers provide inputs and, as a consequence, can have a significant effect on a user's strategic positioning. For example, assume that a company adopts a *total quality control* approach to differentiate and reduce overall quality costs. **Total quality control** is an approach to managing quality that demands the production of defect-free products. Reducing defects, in turn, reduces the total costs spent on quality activities. Yet, if the components are delivered late and are of low quality, then there is no way the buying company can produce high-quality products and deliver them on time to its customers. To achieve a defect-free state, a company is strongly dependent on its suppliers' ability to provide defect-free parts. Once this linkage is understood, then a company can work closely with its suppliers so that the product being purchased meets its needs.

REAL-WORLD EXAMPLE

Honeywell understands this linkage and has established a supplier review board with the objective of improving business relationships and material quality. Its evaluation and selection of suppliers are based on factors such as product quality, delivery, reliability, continuous improvement, product price, and overall relations. Suppliers are expected to meet certain quality and delivery standards such as a defect rate of 500 parts per million, 99 percent on-time delivery, and a 99 percent lot acceptance rate.

Managing Procurement Costs Using Activity-Based Costing   Clearly, to avoid weakening its strategic position, a firm must carefully choose its suppliers. To encourage purchasing managers to choose suppliers whose quality, reliability, and delivery performance are acceptable, two essential requirements have been identified.[16] First, a broader view of component costs is needed. Unit-based costing systems typically reward purchasing managers solely on purchase price (e.g., materials price variances). A broader view means that the costs associated with quality, reliability, and late deliveries are added to the purchase costs. Purchasing managers are then required to evaluate suppliers based on total cost, not just purchase price. Second, supplier costs are assigned to products using causal relationships.

Activity-based costing is the key to satisfying both requirements. To satisfy the first requirement, suppliers are defined as a cost object and costs relating to purchase, quality, reliability, and delivery performance are traced to suppliers. In the second case, products are the cost objects, and supplier costs are traced to specific products. By tracing supplier costs to products—rather than averaging them over all products as unit-based costing does—managers can see the effect of large numbers of unique components requiring specialty suppliers versus products with only standard components. Knowing the costs of more complex products helps product designers better evaluate the trade-offs between functionality and cost as they design new products. Additional functions should provide more benefits (by an increased selling price) than costs. By accurately tracing supplier costs to products, a better understanding of product profitability is produced, and product designers are more capable of choosing among competing product designs. **Example 11.3** illustrates the concepts and calculations associated with activity-based supplier costing.

The results of Example 11.3 show that the "low-cost" supplier actually costs more when the linkages with the internal activities of reworking and expediting are considered. If the purchasing manager is provided all costs, then the choice becomes clear: Oro Limited is the better supplier. It provides a higher-quality product on a timely basis and at a lower overall cost per unit.

---

16 These requirements are discussed in Robin Cooper and Regine Slagmulder, "The Scope of Strategic Cost Management," *Management Accounting* (February 1998): 16–18. Much of the discussion in this section is based on this article.

EXAMPLE 11.3

The HOW and WHY of Activity-Based Supplier Costing

Information:

A purchasing manager uses two suppliers for the source of two electronic components, X1Z and Y2Z. Data associated with these two components are supplied below.

I. Activity Costs (component failure and late delivery are attributable to suppliers; process failure is caused by internal processes):

Activity	Component Failure/ Late Delivery	Process Failure
Reworking products	$200,000	$40,000
Expediting products	50,000	10,000

II. Supplier Data

	Fielding Electronics		Oro Limited	
	X1Z	Y2Z	X1Z	Y2Z
Unit purchase price	$10	$26	$12	$28
Units purchased	40,000	20,000	5,000	5,000
Failed units	800	190	5	5
Late shipments	30	20	0	0

> **Why:**
> Activity-based supplier costing uses drivers to trace costs associated with quality, reliability, and late deliveries to individual suppliers and adds these costs to the direct purchase costs. This enables managers to improve their evaluation and selection of suppliers, with the objective of reducing total supplier costs.

Required:

1. Calculate the activity rates for assigning costs to suppliers.

2. Calculate the total unit purchasing cost for each component for each supplier.

3. *What if* the quantity of X1Z that can be purchased is limited to 50,000 units from Fielding and 30,000 units from Oro Limited? There is no limit from either source for Y2Z. Based on cost, what purchasing mix should be chosen?

Solution:

1. Reworking rate = $200,000/1,000* = $200 per failed component

   *(800 + 190 + 5 + 5)

   Expediting rate = $50,000/50* = $1,000 per late delivery

   *(30 + 20)

2.

	Fielding Electronics		Oro Limited	
	X1Z	Y2Z	X1Z	Y2Z
Reworking products:				
$200 × 800	$160,000			
$200 × 190		$38,000		
$200 × 5			$1,000	
$200 × 5				$1,000

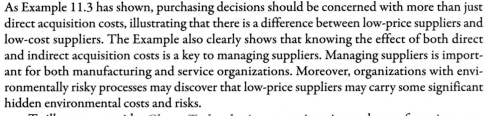

	Fielding Electronics		Oro Limited	
	X1Z	Y2Z	X1Z	Y2Z
Expediting products:				
$1,000 × 30	30,000			
$1,000 × 20		20,000		
Total costs	$ 190,000	$ 58,000	$ 1,000	$ 1,000
Units	÷ 40,000	÷ 20,000	÷ 5,000	÷ 5,000
Unit cost	$ 4.75	$ 2.90	$ 0.20	$ 0.20
Unit purchase cost	10.00	26.00	12.00	28.00
Total unit supplier cost	$ 14.75	$ 28.90	$ 12.20	$ 28.20

EXAMPLE 11.3

(Continued)

3. Based on lowest cost: X1Z: 15,000 units from Fielding and 30,000 units from Oro; Y2Z: 0 from Fielding and 25,000 from Oro.

Sustainability

As Example 11.3 has shown, purchasing decisions should be concerned with more than just direct acquisition costs, illustrating that there is a difference between low-price suppliers and low-cost suppliers. The Example also clearly shows that knowing the effect of both direct and indirect acquisition costs is a key to managing suppliers. Managing suppliers is important for both manufacturing and service organizations. Moreover, organizations with environmentally risky processes may discover that low-price suppliers may carry some significant hidden environmental costs and risks.

To illustrate, consider Clarus Technologies, an engineering and manufacturing company that makes innovative products for reprocessing fluids. Its customers view Clarus as a high-price supplier because its prices are typically much higher than its competitors. For example, one of its products, the Tornado, cleans tanks containing such fluids as heating oil, JP-8, or turbine oil. The Tornado inserts a suction and discharge hose into the tank and cleans the tank and the fuel, with little loss of fuel. Lower-priced competitive systems require that all the fuel be removed and replaced, use more personnel to clean the tank, have higher insurance rates because personnel must enter the tank to clean it, and must dispose of the removed contaminated fuel as a hazardous waste. Once the savings from these additional activities are considered, the Tornado easily becomes the low-cost product. One customer, a military base, reported savings of at least $200,000 relative to competitors' systems.[17]

Exploiting Customer Linkages

Customers can also have a significant influence on a firm's strategic position. Choosing marketing segments, of course, is one of the principal elements that define strategic position. For example, selling a medium-level quality product to low-end dealers for a special, low price because of idle capacity could threaten the main channels of distribution for the product. This is true even if the dealers apply their own private labels to the product. Why? Because selling the product to low-end dealers creates a direct competitor for its regular, medium-level dealers. Potential customers of the regular retail outlets could switch to the lower-end outlets because they can buy the same quality for a lower price. And what if the regular outlets deduce what has happened? What effect would this have on the company's medium-level differentiation strategy? The long-term damage to the company's profitability may be much greater than any short-run benefit from selling the special order.

17   Julie Lockhart, Audrey Taylor, Karl Thomas, Brenda Levetsovitis, and Jason Wise, "When a Higher Price Pays Off," *Strategic Finance* (January 2011): 29–35.

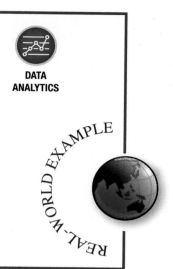

DATA
ANALYTICS

Big Data

The **IBM Institute for Business Value** and the **Saïd Business School** at the University of Oxford conducted a survey of 1,144 businesses and information technology (IT) professionals about their use of big data. They found that about two-thirds of the respondents believed that the use of big data and analytics was creating a competitive advantage for their organizations. Interestingly, about half of the respondents identified customer-centric outcomes as the top functional objective for big data. As another example, **Kraft** used data analytics to yield the counter-intuitive realization that the best way to foster sales growth in its Velveeta cheese product line was to promote it even more heavily to Velveeta's most passionate existing consumers. This group, deemed "super consumers", was found to have the most upside potential for increasing Velveeta sales—accounting for three times as much growth as other consumers—because they possessed the greatest passion for and innovation in use of the Velveeta product line.[18]

Managing Customer Costs A key objective for strategic costing is the identification of a firm's sources of profitability. In a unit-based costing system, selling and general and administrative costs are usually treated as period costs and, if assigned to customers, are typically assigned in proportion to the revenues generated. Thus, the message of unit-based costing is that either servicing customers costs nothing or they all appear to cost the same percentage of their sales revenue. If customer-servicing costs are significant, then failure to assign them at all or to assign them accurately will prevent sales representatives from managing the customer mix effectively. Why? Because sales representatives will not be able to distinguish between customers who place significant demands on servicing resources and those who place virtually no demand on these resources. This lack of knowledge can lead to actions that will weaken a firm's strategic position. To avoid this outcome and encourage actions that strengthen strategic position, customer-related costs should be assigned to customers using activity-based costing. Accurate assignment of customer-related costs allows the firm to classify customers as profitable or unprofitable. For example, using activity-based customer costing, a small Polish company found that only 400 out of almost 1,400 customers were profitable. Some of the most regular customers were actually in the unprofitable category. Analysis revealed that the most profitable customers were those who placed large orders, paid on time, received moderate volume discounts, ordered standard products, and required standard delivery conditions. Analysis of customer profitability also revealed that the most significant problem causing unprofitability was small orders.

Once customers are identified as profitable or unprofitable, actions can be taken to strengthen the strategic position of the firm. For profitable customers, an organization can undertake efforts to increase satisfaction by offering higher levels of service, lower prices, new services, or some combination of the three. For unprofitable customers, an organization can attempt to deliver the customer services more efficiently (thus, decreasing service costs), increase prices to reflect the cost of the resources being consumed, encourage unprofitable customers to leave (by reducing selling efforts to this segment), or some combination of the three actions. **Example 11.4** illustrates the power and utility of activity-based customer costing.

---

18 Eddie Yoon, Steve Carlotti, and Dennis Moore, "Make Your Best Customers Even Better." *Harvard Business Review*. 2014 (March).

EXAMPLE 11.4

The HOW and WHY of Activity-Based Customer Costing

Information:

Thompson Company produces precision parts for 11 major buyers. Of the 11 customers, one accounts for 50 percent of sales and the other 10 account for the remainder of sales, who purchase parts in roughly equal quantities. Orders are priced by adding manufacturing cost to ordering costs and then adding a 20 percent markup. Under this pricing structure, the large customer approaches Thompson and reveals a bid from a Thompson competitor that is $0.50 per part less than Thompson charges and threatens to take its business elsewhere without a price concession.

	One Large Customer	Ten Smaller Customers
Units purchased	500,000	500,000
Orders placed	2	200
Manufacturing cost	$3,000,000	$3,000,000
Order-filling cost allocated*	$ 303,000	$ 303,000
Order cost per unit	$ 0.606	$ 0.606

*Order-filling capacity is purchased in blocks (steps) of 45, each step costing $40,400; variable order-filling activity costs are $2,000 per order. The activity capacity is 225 orders; thus, the total order-filling cost is $606,000 [(5 × $40,400) + ($2,000 × 202)]. Current practice allocates ordering cost in proportion to the units purchased; therefore, the large customer receives half the total ordering cost.

> **Why:**
> Activity-based customer costing assigns the costs of customer-caused activities to individual customers or customer types. Customers can then be classified as profitable or unprofitable (or as causing or not causing inefficiencies), and actions can be taken to improve efficiency and profitability.

Required:

1. Calculate the unit price offered to Thompson's customers using the current order-filling cost allocation.

2. Assume that a newly implemented ABC system concludes that the number of orders placed is the best cost driver for the order-filling activity. Assign order-filling costs using this driver to each customer type and then calculate the new unit price for each customer type. Can Thompson beat the bid of its competitor?

3. *What if* Thompson offers a discount for orders of 10,000 units or more to the smaller customers? Assume that all the small customers can and do take advantage of this offer at the minimum level possible. Can Thompson offer the original price of $7.93 (from Requirement 1) to the small customers and not decrease its profitability?

Solution:

1. Unit price for each customer type = [($3,000,000 + $303,000) × 1.20]/500,000 = $7.93 per unit (rounded to the nearest cent).

2. Order-filling rate = $606,000/202 = $3,000 per order. Large customer ordering cost = $3,000 × 2 = $6,000; small customer ordering cost = $3,000 × 200 = $600,000. Large customer unit price = [($3,000,000 + $6,000) × 1.20]/500,000 = $7.21 (rounded to the nearest cent); small customer unit price = [($3,000,000 + $600,000) × 1.20]/500,000 = $8.64. The new large customer price is $0.72 ($7.93 − $7.21) less and easily beats the competitor's price.

> **EXAMPLE 11.4**
>
> *(Continued)*
>
> 3. The number of orders for the 10 smaller customers would decrease to 50 (500,000/10,000). This means that the total order-filling cost will decrease to $184,800 [(2 × $40,400) + ($2,000 × 52)]. Thus, the new order-filling rate is $184,800/52 = $3,554 (rounded to the nearest dollar); therefore, the new small customer ordering cost = $3,554 × 50 = $177,700. Finally, the new small customer unit price = [($3,000,000 + $177,700) × 1.20]/500,000 = $7.63 (rounded to the nearest dollar). This price is less than the original price.

Example 11.4 reveals some interesting insights concerning the benefits of activity-based customer costing. First, some customers may benefit by price corrections. The large customer, for example, could be granted an immediate price decrease. This price decrease also benefits Thompson, because the price correction is needed to maintain half of its current business. A company such as Thompson, however, may also face the difficult task of announcing a price increase for some of its customers (such was the prospect regarding the 10 smaller customers). Activity-based customer analysis, however, should go much deeper than accurate cost assignment and fair pricing. For Thompson, identifying the right cost driver (number of orders processed) revealed a linkage between the order-filling activity and customer behavior. Smaller, frequent orders were imposing costs on Thompson, which were then passed on to all customers through the use of the sales volume allocation. Since the total cost is marked up 20 percent, the price charged was even higher. Furthermore, decreasing the number of orders can decrease order-filling costs. Knowing this insight, Thompson could offer price discounts for larger orders. For example, providing an incentive (quantity discounts) to increase the size of the orders of the small customers can create sufficient savings to make it unnecessary to increase the selling price to the smaller customers. But there are other possible linkages as well. Larger and less frequent orders will also decrease the demand on other internal activities, such as setting up equipment and materials handling. Reduction in other activity demands could produce further cost reductions and additional price cuts, making companies like Thompson more competitive. Ultimately, exploiting customer linkages can make both the seller and the buyer better off.

LIFE-CYCLE COST MANAGEMENT

> **OBJECTIVE ◄ 4**
>
> Tell what life-cycle cost management is and how it can be used to maximize profits over a product's life cycle.

Strategic cost management emphasizes the importance of an external focus and the need to recognize and exploit both internal and external linkages. Life-cycle cost management is a related approach that builds a conceptual framework that facilitates management's ability to exploit internal and external linkages. To understand what is meant by life-cycle cost management, we first need to understand basic product life-cycle concepts.

Product Life-Cycle Viewpoints

Product life cycle is simply the time a product exists—from conception to abandonment. Usually, product life cycle refers to a product class as a whole—such as automobiles— but it can also refer to specific forms (such as sports utility vehicles) and to specific brands or models (such as a Toyota Sequoia). Also, by replacing "conception" with "purchase," we obtain a customer-oriented definition of product life cycle. The producer-oriented definition refers to the life of classes, forms, or brands, whereas the customer-oriented definition refers to the life of a specific unit of product. These producer and customer orientations can be refined by looking at the concepts of revenue-producing life and consumable life. **Revenue-producing life** is the time a product generates revenue for a company. A product begins its revenue-producing life with the sale of the first product. **Consumable life**, on the other hand, is the length of time that

Exhibit 11.10

Product Sales Revenue Life Cycle: Marketing Viewpoint

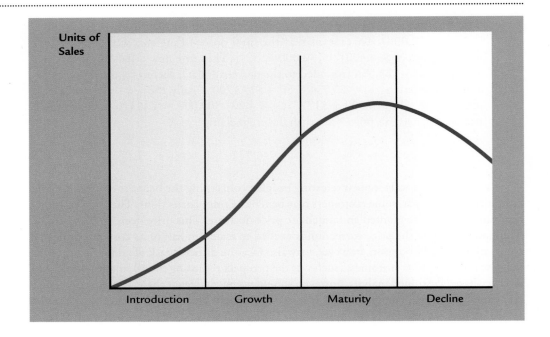

a product serves the needs of a customer. Revenue-producing life is clearly of most interest to the producer, while consumable life is of most interest to the customer. Consumable life, however, is also of interest to the producer because it can be used as a competitive tool.

Marketing Viewpoint The producer of goods or services has two viewpoints concerning product life cycle: the marketing viewpoint and the production viewpoint. The marketing viewpoint describes the general sales pattern of a product as it passes through distinct life-cycle stages. Exhibit 11.10 illustrates the general pattern of the marketing view of product sales revenue life cycle. The distinct stages identified by the exhibit are introduction, growth, maturity, and decline. The **introduction stage** is characterized by preproduction and startup activities, where the focus is on obtaining a foothold in the market. As the graph indicates, there are no sales for a period of time (the preproduction period) and then slow sales growth as the product is introduced. The **growth stage** is a period of time when sales increase more quickly. The **maturity stage** is a period of time when sales increase more slowly. Eventually, the slope (of the sales curve) in the maturity stage becomes neutral and then turns negative. This **decline stage** is when the product loses market acceptance and sales begin to decrease.

Production Viewpoint The production viewpoint of the product life cycle defines stages of the life cycle by changes in the type of activities performed: research and development activities, production activities, and logistical activities. The production viewpoint emphasizes life-cycle costs, whereas the market viewpoint emphasizes sales revenue behavior. **Life-cycle costs** are all costs associated with the product for its entire life cycle. These costs include research (product conception), development (planning, design, and testing), production (conversion activities), and logistics support (advertising, distribution, warranty, customer service, product servicing, and so on). The product cost life cycle and the associated cost commitment curve are illustrated in Exhibit 11.11. Notice that 90 percent or more of the costs (shown on the green curve) associated with a product are *committed* prior to its entering production (i.e., are used for activities involving research, planning, design, and testing) of the product's life cycle. Committed means that most of the costs that will be incurred are predetermined—set by the nature of the product design and the processes needed to produce the design.

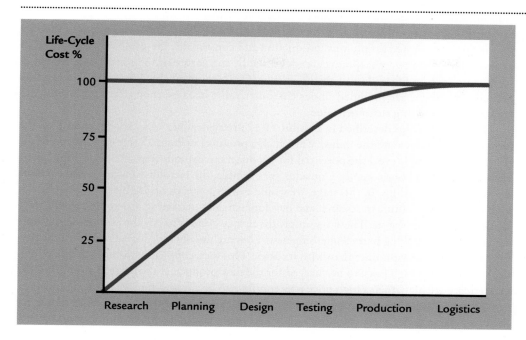

Exhibit 11.11

Product Cost Life Cycle: Production Viewpoint

Consumable Life-Cycle Viewpoint Like the production life cycle, the consumption life cycle's stages are related to activities. These activities define four stages: purchasing, operating, maintaining, and disposal. The consumable life-cycle viewpoint emphasizes product performance for a given price. Price refers to the costs of ownership, which include the following elements: purchase cost, operating costs, maintenance costs, and disposal costs. Thus, total customer satisfaction is affected by both the purchase price and post-purchase costs. Because customer satisfaction is affected by post-purchase costs, producers also have a vital interest in managing the level of these costs. How producers can exploit the linkage of post-purchase activities with producer activities is a key element of product life-cycle cost management.

Interactive Viewpoint

All three life-cycle viewpoints offer insights that can be useful to producers of goods and services. In fact, producers cannot afford to ignore any of the three. A comprehensive life-cycle cost management program must pay attention to the variety of viewpoints that exist. This observation produces an integrated, comprehensive definition of life-cycle cost management. **Life-cycle cost management** consists of actions taken that cause a product to be designed, developed, produced, marketed, distributed, operated, maintained, serviced, and disposed of so that life-cycle profits are maximized. Maximizing life-cycle profits means producers must understand and capitalize on the relationships that exist among the three life-cycle viewpoints. Once these relationships are understood, then actions can be implemented that take advantage of revenue enhancement and cost reduction opportunities.

Relationships among Life-Cycle Viewpoints The marketing viewpoint is concerned with the nature of the sales pattern over the life cycle of the product; it is a *revenue-oriented viewpoint*. The production viewpoint, however, emphasizes the internal activities needed to develop, produce, market, and service products. The production stages exist to support the sales objectives of the marketing stages. This sales support requires resource expenditure; thus, the production life cycle can be described as a *cost-oriented viewpoint*. The consumption life cycle is concerned with product performance and price (including post-purchase costs). The ability to generate revenues and the level of resource expenditure are both related to product performance and price. The producer must be concerned with what the customer receives and what the customer gives up. Thus, the consumption life cycle can be described as a *customer value–oriented viewpoint*. Exhibit 11.12 illustrates the relationships among the stages of the three viewpoints. The stages of marketing viewpoint are listed as columns; production and consumable life-cycle viewpoints appear as rows. These last two viewpoints are identified by the nature of their attributes: expenses for the production life cycle and customer value for the consumable life cycle. Competition and customer type are included under customer value because they affect the producer's approach to providing customer value.

The relationships described in Exhibit 11.12 are typical but can vary depending on the nature of the product and the industry in which a producer operates. Some explanation of the relationships should reveal the potential for producers to exploit them. Relationships can be viewed vertically or horizontally. Consider, for example, the introduction stage, and examine the vertical relationships. In this stage, we would expect losses or negligible profits because of high levels of expenditure in research and development and marketing. Customers at this stage are described as innovators. These are simply the first customers to buy the product. Innovators are venturesome, willing to try something new. They are usually more concerned with the performance of the new product than with its price. This fact, coupled with the lack of competitors, may allow a high price to be charged for the new product. If the barriers to entry in the marketplace are high, then a high price may continue to be charged for some time. If, however, competition grows as indicated by the horizontal dimension of the table, and if price sensitivity increases, then the producer will need to rely on further research and development and differentiation to maintain a competitive advantage.

Exhibit 11.12

Typical Relationships of Product Life-Cycle Viewpoints

Marketing Product Life Cycle:

Attributes	Introduction	Growth	Maturity	Decline
Sales	Low	Rapid growth	Slow growth, peak sales	Declining

Production Life Cycle:

Attributes	Introduction	Growth	Maturity	Decline
Expenses:				
Product R&D	High	Moderate	Moderate	Low
Product R&D	Moderate	High	Moderate	Low
Plant & equipment	Low to moderate	High	Moderate	Low
Advertising	Moderate to high	High	Moderate	Low
Service	Low	Moderate	High	Low

Consumable Life Cycle:

Attributes	Introduction	Growth	Maturity	Decline
Customer value:				
Customer type	Innovators	Mass market	Mass market, differentiated	Laggards
Performance sensitivity	High	High	High	Moderate
Price sensitivity	Low	Moderate	High	Moderate
Competition	None	Growing	High	Low

Attributes	Introduction	Growth	Maturity	Decline
Profits	Negligible to loss	Peak levels	Moderate to high	Low

Revenue Enhancement Revenue-generating approaches depend on marketing life-cycle stages and on customer value effect. Pricing strategy, for example, varies with stages. In the introductory stage, as mentioned earlier, higher prices can be charged because customers are less price sensitive and more interested in performance.

In the maturity stage, customers are highly sensitive to both price and performance. This suggests that adding features, increasing durability, improving maintainability, and offering customized products may all be good strategies to follow. In this stage, differentiation is important. For revenue enhancement to be viable, however, the customer must be willing to pay a premium for any improvement in product performance. Furthermore, this premium must exceed the cost the producer incurs in providing the new product attribute. In the decline stage, revenues may be enhanced by finding new uses and new customers for the product. A good example is the use of **Arm & Hammer's**® of Church and Dwight baking soda to absorb refrigerator odors in addition to its normal role in baking goods.

Cost Reduction Cost reduction, not cost control, is the emphasis of life-cycle cost management. Cost reduction strategies should explicitly recognize that actions taken in the early stages of the production life cycle can lower costs for later production and consumption stages. Since 90 percent or more of a product's life-cycle costs are determined during the development stage, it makes sense to emphasize management of activities during this phase of a product's existence. Studies have shown that every dollar spent on preproduction activities saves $8–10 on production and post-production activities, including customer maintenance, repair, and disposal costs.[19] Apparently, many opportunities for cost reduction occur before production begins. Managers need to invest more in preproduction assets and dedicate more resources to activities in the early phases of the product life cycle to reduce production, marketing, and post-purchase costs.

Product design and process design afford multiple opportunities for cost reduction by designing to reduce (1) manufacturing costs, (2) logistical support costs, and (3) post-purchase costs, which include customer time involved in maintenance, repair, and disposal. For these approaches to be successful, managers of producing companies must have a good understanding of activities and cost drivers and know how the activities interact. Manufacturing, logistical, and post-purchase activities are not independent. Some designs may reduce post-purchase costs and increase manufacturing costs. Others may simultaneously reduce production, logistical, and post-purchase costs.

A unit-based costing system usually will not supply the information needed to support life-cycle cost management. Unit-based costing systems emphasize the use of unit-based cost drivers to describe cost behavior, focus on production activities, ignore logistical and post-purchase activities, and expense research and development and other nonmanufacturing costs as they are incurred. Unit-based costing systems rarely, if ever, collect a complete history of a product's costs over its life cycle. An activity-based costing system, however, produces information about activities, including both preproduction and postproduction activities, and cost drivers. Activity-based costing information is critical for life-cycle cost reduction decisions as is shown by **Example 11.5**.

EXAMPLE 11.5

The HOW and WHY of Activity-Based Life-Cycle Cost Reduction

Information:

Design engineers are considering two new product designs that reduce direct materials and direct labor content. Data for both unit-based and ABC systems are provided below.

Unit-based system:

Variable conversion activity rate: $40 per direct labor hour

Material usage rate: $8 per part

ABC system:

Labor usage: $10 per direct labor hour

---

19 Mark D. Shields and S. Mark Young, "Managing Product Life Cycle Costs: An Organizational Model," and R. L. Eng-wall, "Cost Management for Defense Contractors," *Cost Accounting for the 90's: Responding to Technological Change* (Montvale, NJ: National Association of Accountants, 1988).

EXAMPLE 11.5

(Continued)

Material usage (direct materials): $8 per part

Machining: $28 per machine hour

Purchasing activity: $60 per purchase order

Setup activity: $1,000 per setup hour

Warranty activity: $200 per returned unit (usually requires extensive rework)

Customer repair cost: $10 per repair hour

Activity and Resource Information (annual estimates)

	Design A	Design B
Units produced	10,000	10,000
Direct material usage	100,000 parts	60,000 parts
Labor usage	50,000 hours	80,000 hours
Machine hours	25,000	20,000
Purchase orders	300	200
Setup hours	200	100
Returned units	400	75
Repair time (customer)	800	150

> **Why:**
> ABC produces better and more detailed information for cost reduction decisions concerning process and product designs by recognizing that manufacturing, logistical, and post-purchase activities are not independent.

Required:

1. Select the lower-cost design using unit-based costing. Are logistical and post-purchase activities considered in this analysis?

2. Select the lower-cost design using ABC analysis. Explain why the analysis differs from the unit-based analysis.

3. *What if* the customer repair costs were $10 *per unit* for Design A and $50 per unit for Design B? Assume that every unit must face repair by the consumer during the consumable life cycle. Now which is the better design?

Solution:

1.

	Design A	Design B
Direct materials[a]	$ 800,000	$ 480,000
Conversion cost[b]	2,000,000	3,200,000
Total manufacturing costs	$2,800,000	$3,680,000
Units produced	÷ 10,000	÷ 10,000
Unit cost	$ 280	$ 368

[a]$8 × 100,000; $8 × 60,000
[b]$40 × 50,000; $40 × 80,000

Logistical and post-purchase costs are not considered.

2.

	Design A	Design B
Direct materials	$ 800,000	$ 480,000
Direct labor[a]	500,000	800,000
Machining[a]	700,000	560,000
Purchasing[b]	18,000	12,000
Setups[b]	200,000	100,000
Warranty[b]	80,000	15,000
Total product costs	$2,298,000	$1,967,000
Units produced	÷ 10,000	÷ 10,000
Unit cost	$ 230*	$ 197*
Post-purchase costs[c]	$ 8,000	$ 1,500

[a]$10 × 50,000; $10 × 80,000; $28 × 25,000; $28 × 20,000
[b]$60 × 300; $60 × 200; $1,000 × 200; $1,000 × 100; $200 × 400; $200 × 75
[c]$10 × 800; $10 × 150
*Rounded to the nearest dollar.

ABC assigns manufacturing costs using both unit and non-unit drivers. It also considers the effects of manufacturing, logistical, and post-purchase activities (unit-based uses only manufacturing activities).

3. The post-purchase costs for Design A would be $240 ($230 + $10) and for Design B would be $247 ($197 + $50). Design A is the cheaper of the two designs when post-purchase costs are considered.

Role of Target Costing

Life-cycle cost management emphasizes cost reduction, not cost control. Target costing becomes a particularly useful tool for establishing cost reduction goals during the design stage. A **target cost** is the difference between the sales price needed to capture a predetermined market share and the desired per-unit profit. The sales price reflects the product specifications or functions valued by the customer (referred to as *product functionality*). If the target cost is less than what is currently achievable, then management must find cost reductions that move the actual cost toward the target cost. Finding those cost reductions is the principal challenge of target costing.

Three cost reduction methods are typically used: (1) reverse engineering, (2) value analysis, and (3) process improvement. In reverse engineering, the competitors' products are closely analyzed (a "tear-down" analysis) in an attempt to discover more design features that create cost reductions. Value analysis attempts to assess the value placed on various product functions by customers. If the price customers are willing to pay for a particular function is less than its cost, the function is a candidate for elimination. Another possibility is to find ways to reduce the cost of providing the function (e.g., using common components). Both reverse engineering and value analysis focus on product design to achieve cost reductions. The processes used to produce and market the product are also sources of potential cost reductions. Thus, redesigning processes to improve their efficiency can also contribute to achieving the needed cost reductions. The target-costing model is summarized in Exhibit 11.13.

A simple example can be used to illustrate the concepts described by Exhibit 11.13. Assume that a company is considering the production of a new trencher. Current product specifications and the targeted market share call for a sales price of $250,000. The required profit is $50,000 per unit. The target cost is computed as follows:

$$\text{Target cost} = \$250,000 - \$50,000$$
$$= \$200,000$$

Exhibit 11.13

Target-Costing Model

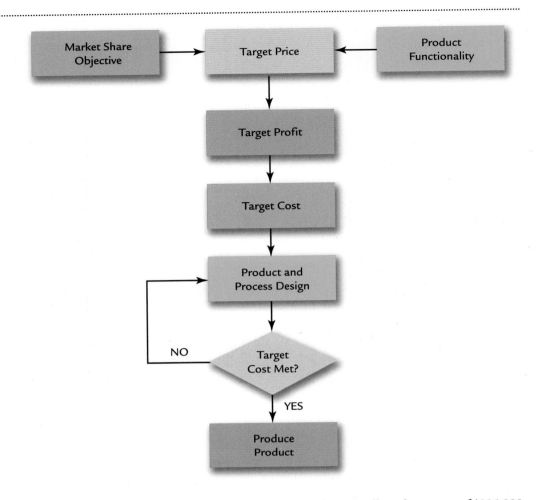

It is estimated that the current product and process designs will produce a cost of $225,000 per unit. Thus, the cost reduction needed to achieve the target cost and desired profit is $25,000 ($225,000 − $200,000). A tear-down analysis of a competitor's trencher revealed a design improvement that promised to save $5,000 per unit. When compared with the $25,000 reduction needed, additional effort was still necessary. A marketing study of customer reactions to product functions revealed that the extra trenching speed in the new design was relatively unimportant. Changing the design to reflect a lower trenching speed saved $10,000. The company's supplier also proposed the use of a standardized component, reducing costs by another $5,000. Finally, the design team was able to change the process design and reduce the test time by 50 percent. This saved $6,000 per unit. The last change reached the threshold value, and production for the new model was approved.

Target costs are a type of currently attainable standard. But they are conceptually different from traditional standards. What sets them apart is the motivating force. Traditional standards are internally motivated and set, based on concepts of efficiency developed by industrial engineers and production managers. Target costs, on the other hand, are externally driven, generated by an analysis of markets and competitors. Chapter 18 provides additional discussion of target costing as it pertains to pricing decisions.

Supplier and Firm Interaction The example just given indicated that one source of cost reduction came from a supplier suggestion. During the design stage, target costing requires a close interaction between the firm and its suppliers. This interaction should produce lower cost solutions than would be possible if the design teams acted in isolation.[20] Joint design efforts

---

20 Robin Cooper and Regine Slagmulder, "Cost Management beyond the Boundaries of the Firm," *Management Accounting* (March 1998): 18–20.

require cooperative relationships. Incentives for such relationships come from a willingness to search for mutually beneficial solutions.

Short Life Cycles Although life-cycle cost management is important for all manufacturing firms, it is particularly important for firms that have products with short life cycles. Products must recover all life-cycle costs and provide an acceptable profit. If a firm's products have long life cycles, profit performance can be increased by such actions as redesigning, changing prices, reducing costs, and altering the product mix. In contrast, firms that have products with short life cycles usually do not have time to react in this way so their approach must be proactive. Thus, for short life cycles, good life-cycle planning is critical, and prices must be set properly to recover all the life-cycle costs and provide a good return. Activity-based costing can be used to encourage good life-cycle planning. By careful selection of cost drivers, design engineers can be motivated to choose cost-minimizing designs.

JUST-IN-TIME (JIT) MANUFACTURING AND PURCHASING

OBJECTIVE ◀ 5

Identify the basic features of JIT purchasing and manufacturing.

JIT manufacturing and purchasing systems offer a prominent example of how managers can use the strategic concepts discussed earlier in the chapter to bring about significant changes within an organization. Firms that implement JIT are pursuing a cost reduction strategy by redefining the structural and procedural activities performed within an organization. Cost reduction is supportive of either a cost leadership or differentiation strategy. Cost reduction is directly related to cost leadership. Successful differentiation depends on offering greater value; yet, this value added must be more than the cost of providing it. JIT can help add value by reducing waste. Successful implementation of JIT has brought about significant improvements, such as better quality, increased productivity, reduced lead times, major reductions in inventories, reduced setup times, lower manufacturing costs, and increased production rates. For example, **Oregon Cutting Systems**, a manufacturer of cutting chain (for chain saws), timber-harvesting equipment, and sporting equipment—within a period of three to five years—reduced defects by 80 percent, waste by 50 percent, setup times from hours to minutes (one punch press had setup time reduced from three hours to 4.5 minutes), lead times from 21 days to three days, and manufacturing costs by 35 percent.[21] JIT techniques have also been implemented by the following companies with similar results:

AT&T	Harley-Davidson	Toys "R" Us
Black & Decker	Hewlett-Packard	Wal-Mart
BorgWarner	Intel	Westinghouse
Chrysler	John Deere	Xerox
Ford	Mercury Marine	
General Electric	Motorola	

Adopting a JIT manufacturing system has a significant effect on the nature of the cost management accounting system. Installing a JIT system affects the traceability of costs, enhances product costing accuracy, diminishes the need for allocation of service-center costs, changes the behavior and relative importance of direct labor costs, impacts job-order and process-costing systems, decreases the reliance on standards and variance analysis, and decreases the importance of inventory tracking systems. To understand and appreciate these effects, we need a fundamental understanding of what JIT manufacturing is and how it differs from traditional manufacturing.

JIT manufacturing is a demand-pull system. The objective of **JIT manufacturing** is to eliminate waste by producing a product only when it is needed and only in the quantities demanded by customers. Demand pulls products through the manufacturing process. Each operation produces only what is necessary to satisfy the demand of the succeeding operation.

---

21 Jack C. Bailes and Ilene K. Kleinsorge, "Cutting Waste with JIT," *Management Accounting* (May 1992): 28–32.

No production takes place until a signal from a succeeding process indicates a need to produce. Parts and materials arrive just in time to be used in production. JIT assumes that all costs other than direct materials are driven by time and space drivers. JIT then focuses on eliminating waste by compressing time and space.

JIT systems also must consider the potential likelihood and impact of key risks (see the earlier discussion of ERM in Objective 2). For example, the extremely abrupt and worldwide in scale economic shutdown brought about by the unexpected COVID-19 global pandemic caught many companies by surprise. Companies with small inventory levels, such as with JIT systems, faced significant supply chain interruptions. Well-established companies in nearly every industry were forced to cope with inventory stockouts and other inventory management challenges as a result of the pandemic.[22]

Inventory Effects

Usually, the push-through system produces significantly higher levels of finished goods inventory than does a JIT system. JIT manufacturing relies on the exploitation of a customer linkage. Specifically, production is tied to customer demand. This linkage extends back through the value chain and also affects how a manufacturer deals with suppliers. **JIT purchasing** requires suppliers to deliver parts and materials just in time to be used in production. Thus, supplier linkages are also vital. Supply of parts must be linked to production, which is linked to demand. One effect of successful exploitation of these linkages is to reduce all inventories to much lower levels. From 1980 to just after the beginning of the century, inventories in the United States have fallen from 26 to 15 percent of the gross domestic product.[23]

Traditionally, inventories of raw materials and parts are carried so that a firm can take advantage of quantity discounts and hedge against future price increases of the items purchased. The objective is to lower the cost of inventory. JIT achieves the same objective without carrying inventories. The JIT solution is to exploit supplier linkages by negotiating long-term contracts with a few chosen suppliers located as close to the production facility as possible and by establishing more extensive supplier involvement. Suppliers are not selected on the basis of price alone.

Performance—the quality of the component and the ability to deliver as needed—and commitment to JIT purchasing are vital considerations. Every effort is made to establish a partners-in-profits relationship with suppliers. Suppliers need to be convinced that their well-being is intimately tied to the well-being of the buyer.

To help reduce the uncertainty in demand for the supplier and establish the mutual confidence and trust needed in such a relationship, JIT manufacturers emphasize long-term contracts. Other benefits of long-term contracts exist. They stipulate prices and acceptable quality levels. Long-term contracts also reduce dramatically the number of orders placed, which helps to drive down the ordering and receiving costs. Another effect of long-term contracting is a reduction in the cost of parts and materials—usually in the range of 5–20 percent less than what was paid in a traditional setting. The need to develop close supplier relationships often drives the supplier base down dramatically.

REAL-WORLD EXAMPLE

For example, Mercedes-Benz U.S. International's factory in Vance, Alabama, saved time and money by streamlining its supplier list from 1,000 to 100 primary suppliers. In exchange for annual 5 percent price cuts, the chosen suppliers have multiyear contracts (as opposed to the yearly bidding process practiced at other Mercedes' plants) and can adapt off-the-shelf parts to Mercedes' needs. The end result is lower costs for both Mercedes and its suppliers.[24]

22 G. Bora, "Covid-19 Has Upended A Key Management Principle—Or Has It?" *The Economic Times* (June 20, 2020), https://economictimes.indiatimes.com/small-biz/sme-sector/covid-19-has-upended-a-key-management-principle-just-in-time-jit-inventory/articleshow/76477328.cms?from=mdr

23 Art Raymond, "Is JIT Dead?" *FDM* (January 2002): 30–32.

24 David Woodruff and Karen Lowry Miller, "Mercedes' Maverick in Alabama," *BusinessWeek* (September 11, 1995): 64–65.

Suppliers also benefit. The long-term contract ensures a reasonably stable demand for their products. A smaller supplier base typically means increased sales for the selected suppliers. Thus, both buyers and suppliers benefit—a common outcome when external linkages are recognized and exploited.

By reducing the number of suppliers and working closely with those that remain, the quality of the incoming materials can be improved significantly—a crucial outcome for the success of JIT. As the quality of incoming materials increases, some quality-related costs can be avoided or reduced. For example, the need to inspect incoming materials disappears, and rework requirements decline.

Plant Layout

The type and efficiency of plant layout are another executional cost drivers that are managed differently under JIT manufacturing. (See Exhibit 11.2 on page 558 for a review of executional cost drivers.) In traditional job and batch manufacturing, products are moved from one group of identical machines to another. Typically, machines with identical functions are located together in an area referred to as a *department* or *process*. Workers who specialize in the operation of a specific machine are located in each department. Thus, the executional cost driver for a traditional setting is departmental structure. JIT replaces this traditional plant layout with a pattern of manufacturing cells. The executional cost driver for a JIT setting is cell structure. Cell structure is chosen over departmental structure because it increases the ability of the organization to "execute" successfully. Some of the efficiencies cited earlier for Oregon Cutting Systems (OCS), such as reduced lead times and lower manufacturing costs, are a direct result of the cellular structure. The cellular manufacturing design can also affect structural activities, such as plant size and number of plants, because it typically requires less space. OCS, for example, cut its space requirement by 40 percent. Space savings like this can reduce the demand to build new plants and will affect the size of new plants when they are needed.

Manufacturing cells contain machines that are grouped in families, usually in a semi-circle. The machines are arranged so that they can be used to perform a variety of operations in sequence. Each cell is set up to produce a particular product or product family. Products move from one machine to another from start to finish. Workers are assigned to cells and are trained to operate all machines within the cell. In other words, labor in a JIT environment is multiskilled, not specialized. Each manufacturing cell is essentially a mini-factory; in fact, cells are often referred to as a *factory within a factory*. A comparison of the JIT's plant layout with the traditional pattern is shown in Exhibit 11.14.

Grouping of Employees

Another major structural difference between JIT and traditional organizations relates to how employees are grouped. As just indicated, each cell is viewed as a mini-factory; thus, each cell requires easy and quick access to support services, which means that centralized service departments must be scaled down and their personnel reassigned to work directly with manufacturing cells. For example, with respect to raw materials, JIT calls for multiple stock points, each one located near where the material will be used. There is no need for a central store location—in fact, such an arrangement actually hinders efficient production. A purchasing agent can be assigned to each cell to handle material requirements. Similarly, other service personnel, such as manufacturing and quality engineers, can be assigned to cells.

Other support services may be relocated to the cell by training cell workers to perform the services. For example, in addition to direct production work, cell workers may perform setup duties, move partially completed goods from station to station within the cell, perform preventive

Exhibit 11.14   Plant Layout Pattern: Traditional versus JIT

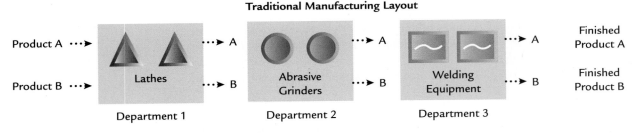

Traditional Manufacturing Layout

Each product passes through departments that specialize in one process. Departments process multiple products.

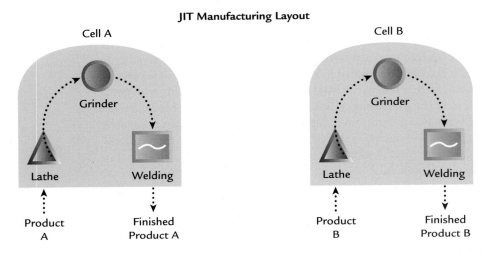

JIT Manufacturing Layout

Notice that each product passes through its own cell. All machines necessary to process each product are placed within the cell. Each cell is dedicated to the production of one product or one subassembly.

maintenance and minor repairs, conduct quality inspections, and perform janitorial tasks. This multiple task capability is directly related to the pull-through production approach. Producing on demand means that production workers (formerly direct laborers) may often have "free" time. This nonproduction time can be used to perform some of the other support activities.

Employee Empowerment

A major procedural difference between traditional and JIT environments is the degree of participation allowed workers in the management of the organization. According to the JIT view, increasing the degree of participation (the executional cost driver) increases productivity and overall cost efficiency. Workers are allowed a say in how the plant operates. For example, workers are allowed to shut down production to identify and correct problems. Managers seek workers' input and use their suggestions to improve production processes. Workers are often involved in interviewing and hiring other employees, sometimes even prospective bosses. The reason? If the "chemistry is right," then the workforce will be more efficient, and they will work together better.

Employee empowerment, a procedural activity, also affects other structural and procedural activities. The management structure must change in response to greater employee involvement. Because workers assume greater responsibilities, fewer managers are needed, and the organizational structure becomes flatter. Flatter structures speed up and increase the quality of information exchange. The style of management needed in the JIT firm also changes. Managers

JIT	Traditional
1. Pull-through system	1. Push-through system
2. Insignificant inventories	2. Significant inventories
3. Small supplier base	3. Large supplier base
4. Long-term supplier contracts	4. Short-term supplier contracts
5. Cellular structure	5. Departmental structure
6. Multiskilled labor	6. Specialized labor
7. Decentralized services	7. Centralized services
8. High employee involvement	8. Low employee involvement
9. Facilitating management style	9. Supervisory management style
10. Total quality control	10. Acceptable quality level
11. Buyers' market	11. Sellers' market
12. Value-chain focus	12. Value-added focus

Exhibit 11.5

Comparison of JIT Approaches with Traditional Manufacturing and Purchasing

in the JIT environment need to act as facilitators more than as supervisors. Their role is to develop people and their skills so that they can make value-adding contributions.

Total Quality Control

JIT necessarily carries with it a much stronger emphasis on managing quality. A defective part brings production to a grinding halt. Poor quality simply cannot be tolerated in a manufacturing environment that operates without inventories. Simply put, JIT cannot be implemented without a commitment to total quality control (TQC). TQC is essentially a never-ending quest for perfect quality: the striving for a defect-free product design and manufacturing process. This approach to managing quality is diametrically opposed to the traditional doctrine, called **acceptable quality level (AQL)**. AQL permits or allows defects to occur provided they do not exceed a predetermined level.

The major differences between JIT manufacturing and traditional manufacturing are summarized in Exhibit 11.15. These differences will be referred to and discussed in greater detail as the implications of JIT manufacturing for cost management are examined.

JIT AND ITS EFFECT ON THE COST MANAGEMENT SYSTEM

OBJECTIVE ◀ 6

Describe the effect JIT has on cost traceability and product costing.

The numerous changes in structural and procedural activities that we have described for a JIT system also change traditional cost management practices. Both the cost accounting and operational control systems are affected. In general, the organizational changes simplify the cost management accounting system and simultaneously increase the accuracy of the cost information being produced.

Traceability of Overhead Costs

Costing systems use three methods to assign costs to individual products: direct tracing, driver tracing, and allocation. Of the three methods, the most accurate is direct tracing; for this reason, it is preferred over the other two methods. In a JIT environment, many overhead costs assigned to products using either driver tracing or allocation are now directly traceable to products. Cellular manufacturing, multiskilled labor, and decentralized service activities are the major features of JIT responsible for this change in traceability.

In a departmental structure, many different products may be subjected to a process located in a single department (e.g., Grinding). After completion of the process, the products are then transferred to other processes located in different departments (e.g., Assembly, Painting, and so on). Although a different set of processes is usually required for each product, most processes are applicable to more than one product. For example, 30 different products may need grinding. Because more than one product is processed in a department, the costs of that department are common to all products passing through it, and therefore the costs must be assigned to products using activity drivers or allocation. In a manufacturing-cell structure, however, all processes necessary for the production of each product or major subassembly are collected in one area called a cell. Thus, the costs of operating that cell can be assigned to the cell's product or subassembly using direct tracing. (If a family of products uses a cell, however, then we must resort to drivers and allocation to assign costs.)

Equipment formerly located in other departments, for example, is now reassigned to cells, where it may be dedicated to the production of a single product or subassembly. In this case, depreciation is now a directly attributable product cost. Multiskilled workers and decentralized services add to the effect. Workers in the cell are trained to set up the equipment in the cell, maintain it, and operate it. Additionally, cell workers may also be used to move a partially finished part from one machine to the next or to perform maintenance, setups, and materials handling. These support functions were previously done by a different set of laborers for all product lines. Additionally, people with specialized skills (e.g., industrial engineers and production schedulers) are assigned directly to manufacturing cells. Because of multitask assignments and redeployment of other support personnel, many support costs can now be assigned to a product using direct tracing. Exhibit 11.16 compares the traceability of some selected costs in a traditional manufacturing environment with their traceability in the JIT environment (assuming single-product cells). Comparisons are based on the three cost assignment methods.

Product Costing

One consequence of increasing directly attributable costs is to increase the accuracy of product costing. Directly traceable costs are associated (usually by physical observation) with the product and can safely be said to belong to it. Other costs, however, are common to several products and must be assigned to these products using activity drivers and allocation. Because of cost and convenience, activity drivers that are less than perfectly correlated with the consumption of overhead activities may be chosen. JIT manufacturing reduces the need for this difficult assessment by converting many common costs to directly attributable costs. Note, however, that the driving force behind these changes is not the cost management system itself but the changes in the structural and procedural activities brought about by implementing a JIT system. While

---

Exhibit 11.16

Product Cost Assignment:
Traditional versus JIT Manufacturing

Manufacturing Cost	Traditional Environment	JIT Environment
Direct labor	Direct tracing	Direct tracing
Direct materials	Direct tracing	Direct tracing
Materials handling	Direct tracing	Direct tracing
Repairs and maintenance	Direct tracing	Direct tracing
Energy	Direct tracing	Direct tracing
Operating supplies	Direct tracing	Direct tracing
Supervision (department)	Allocation	Direct tracing
Insurance and taxes	Allocation	Allocation
Plant depreciation	Allocation	Allocation
Equipment depreciation	Driver tracing	Direct tracing
Custodial services	Allocation	Direct tracing
Cafeteria services	Driver tracing	Direct tracing

activity-based costing offers significant improvement in product costing accuracy, focusing offers even more potential improvement.

Exhibit 11.16 illustrates that JIT does not convert all costs into directly traceable costs. Even with JIT in place, some overhead activities remain common to the manufacturing cells. These remaining support activities are mostly facility-level activities. In a JIT system, the batch size is one unit of product. Thus, all batch-level activities convert into unit-level activities. Additionally, many of the batch-level activities are reduced or eliminated. For example, materials handling may be significantly reduced because of the reorganization from a departmental structure to a cellular structure. Similarly, for single-product cells, there is no setup activity. Even for cells that produce a family of products, setup times would be minimal. Furthermore, it is likely that the need to use activity drivers for the cost of product-level activities is significantly diminished because of decentralizing these support activities to the cell level. Is there, then, a role for activity-based costing (ABC) in a JIT firm?

Although JIT diminishes the value of ABC for tracing manufacturing costs to individual products, an activity-based costing system has much broader application than just tracing manufacturing costs to products. For many strategic and tactical decisions, the product cost definition needs to include nonmanufacturing costs. For example, value-line and operational product costing is an invaluable tool for strategic costing analysis and for life-cycle cost management. Also, including post-purchase costs as part of the product cost definition provides valuable insights. Thus, knowing and understanding general and administrative, research, development, marketing, customer service, and post-purchase activities and their cost drivers are essential for sound cost analysis. Furthermore, as we have already seen, using ABC to assign costs accurately to suppliers and customers is an essential part of strategic cost management.

JIT's Effect on Job-Order and Process-Costing Systems

In implementing JIT in a job-order setting, the firm should first separate its repetitive business from its unique orders. Manufacturing cells can then be established to deal with the repetitive business. For those products where demand is insufficient to justify its own manufacturing cell, groups of dissimilar machines can be set up in a cell to make families of products or parts that require the same manufacturing sequence.

With this reorganization of the manufacturing layout, job orders are no longer needed to accumulate product costs. Instead, costs can be accumulated at the cellular level. Additionally, because lot sizes are now too small (as a result of reducing work-in-process and finished goods inventories), it is impractical to have job orders for each job. Add to this the short lead time of products occurring because of the time and space compression features of JIT (virtually no setup time and cellular structures), and it becomes difficult to track each piece moving through the cell. In effect, the job environment has taken on the nature of a process-costing system.

JIT simplifies process costing. A key feature of JIT is lower inventories. Assuming that JIT is successful in reducing work in process (Oregon Cutting Systems, for example, reduced work in process by 85 percent), the need to compute equivalent units vanishes. Calculating product costs follows the simple pattern of collecting costs for a cell for a period of time and dividing the costs by the units produced for that period.

Backflush Costing

The JIT system also offers the opportunity to simplify the accounting for manufacturing cost flows. Given low inventories, it may not be desirable to spend resources tracking the cost flows through all the inventory accounts. In a traditional system, there was a work-in-process account for each department so that manufacturing costs could be traced as work proceeded through the factory. Under JIT, there are no departments, a 14-day lead time (for example) has been decreased to four hours, and it would be absurd to trace costs from station to station within a cell. After all, if production cycle time is in minutes or hours, and goods are shipped immediately upon completion, then all of each day's manufacturing costs flow to Cost of Goods

Sold. Recognizing this outcome leads to a simplified approach of accounting for manufacturing cost flows. This simplified approach, called **backflush costing**, uses trigger points to determine when manufacturing costs are assigned to key inventory and temporary accounts.

Varying the number and location of trigger points creates several types of backflush costing. Trigger points are simply events that prompt ("trigger") the accounting recognition of certain manufacturing costs. There are four variations, depending on the definition of the trigger points (which, in turn, depends on how fully the firm has implemented JIT):

1.   The purchase of raw materials (trigger point 1) and the completion of goods (trigger point 2)
2.   The purchase of raw materials (trigger point 1) and the sale of goods (trigger point 2)
3.   The completion of goods (only trigger point)
4.   The sale of goods (only trigger point)

Variations 1 and 2   For Variations 1 and 2, the first trigger point is the purchase of raw materials. When materials are purchased in a JIT system, they are immediately placed into process. Raw Materials and In Process Inventory (RIP) is debited, and Accounts Payable is credited. The RIP inventory account is used only for tracking the cost of raw materials. There is no separate materials inventory account and no work-in-process inventory account. Combining direct labor and overhead into one category is a second feature of backflush costing. As firms implement JIT and become automated, the traditional direct labor cost category disappears. Multiskilled workers perform setup activities, machine-loading activities, maintenance, materials handling, etc. As labor becomes multifunctional, the ability to track and report direct labor separately becomes impossible. Consequently, backflush costing usually combines direct labor costs with overhead costs in a temporary account called *Conversion Cost Control*. This account accumulates the *actual* conversion costs on the debit side and the applied conversion costs on the credit side. Any difference between the actual conversion costs and the applied conversion costs is closed to Cost of Goods Sold.

In the first variant of backflush costing, the completion of goods triggers the recognition of the manufacturing costs used to produce the goods (the second trigger point). At this point, conversion cost application is recognized by debiting Finished Goods Inventory and crediting Conversion Cost Control; the cost of direct materials is recognized by debiting Finished Goods Inventory and crediting the RIP inventory account. Therefore, the costs of manufacturing are "flushed" out of the system after the goods are completed.

In the second variant of backflush costing, the second trigger point is defined by the point when goods are sold rather than when they are completed. For this variant, the costs of manufacturing are flushed out of the system *after* the goods are sold. Thus, the application of conversion cost and the transfer of direct materials cost are accomplished by debiting Cost of Goods Sold and crediting Conversion Cost Control and RIP Inventory, respectively. Other entries are the same as Variation 1.

Variations 3 and 4   Under Variations 3 and 4, there is only one trigger point. Both variations recognize actual conversion costs by debiting Conversion Cost Control and crediting various accounts (such as Accumulated Depreciation). Neither variation makes any entry for the purchase of raw materials. For Variation 3, when the goods are completed, all costs, including direct materials cost, are flushed out of the system. This is done by debiting Finished Goods Inventory for the cost of all manufacturing inputs and crediting Accounts Payable for the cost of direct materials and Conversion Cost Control for the application of conversion costs. For Variation 4, the costs are flushed out of the system when the goods are sold. Thus, Cost of Goods Sold is debited, and Accounts Payable and Conversion Cost Control are credited. Of the four variations, only Variation 4 avoids all inventory accounts and, thus, would be the approach used for a pure JIT firm. **Example 11.6** illustrates backflush costing.

Information:

A JIT company had the following transactions during June:

1. Purchased raw materials on account for $160,000.

2. Placed all materials received into production.

3. Incurred actual direct labor costs of $25,000.

4. Incurred actual overhead costs of $225,000.

5. Applied conversion costs of $235,000 ($25,000 of direct labor + $210,000 of applied overhead).

6. Completed all work for the month.

7. Sold all completed work.

8. Computed the difference between actual and applied costs.

EXAMPLE 11.6

The HOW and WHY of Backflush Costing

Why:
Reduced cycle time and immediate shipping of goods simplify accounting for manufacturing cost flows. How simplified depends on the completeness of the JIT system (measured by "trigger points").

Required:

1. Prepare the journal entries for traditional and backflush costing. For backflush costing, assume there are two trigger points: (1) the purchase of raw materials, and (2) the completion of the goods.

2. Assume the second trigger point in Requirement 1 is the sale of goods. What would change for the backflush-costing journal entries?

3. *What if* there is only one trigger point and it is (a) completion of the goods, or (b) sale of goods? How would the backflush-costing journal entries differ from Requirement 1 for (a) and (b)?

Solution:

1.

Transaction	Traditional Journal Entries		Backflush Journal Entries: Variation 1	
1. Purchase of raw materials	Materials Inventory 160,000		Raw Materials and In	
	Accounts Payable	160,000	Process Inventory 160,000	
			Accounts Payable	160,000
2. Materials issued to production	Work-in-Process		No entry	
	Inventory 160,000			
	Materials			
	Inventory	160,000		
3. Direct labor cost incurred	Work-in-Process		Combined with overhead:	
	Inventory 25,000		see next entry.	
	Wages Payable	25,000		
4. Overhead cost incurred	Overhead Control 225,000		Conversion Cost Control 250,000	
	Accounts Payable	225,000	Wages Payable	25,000
			Accounts Payable	225,000
5. Application of overhead	Work-in-Process		No entry	
	Inventory 210,000			
	Overhead Control	210,000		

EXAMPLE 11.6

(Continued)

6. Completion of goods	Finished Goods Inventory	395,000		Finished Goods Inventory	395,000	
	Work-in-Process Inventory		395,000	Raw Materials and In Process Inventory		160,000
				Conversion Cost Control		235,000
7. Goods are sold	Cost of Goods Sold	395,000		Cost of Goods Sold	395,000	
	Finished Goods Inventory		395,000	Finished Goods Inventory		395,000
8. Variance is recognized	Cost of Goods Sold	15,000		Cost of Goods Sold	15,000	
	Overhead Control		15,000	Conversion Cost Control		15,000

2. The entries for Transactions 6 and 7 in Requirement 1 are replaced with the following entry:

Cost of Goods Sold	395,000	
Raw Materials and In Process Inventory		160,000
Conversion Cost Control		235,000

All other entries follow those in Requirement 1.

3. (a) There is no entry for Transaction 1. Transaction 6 is replaced with the following entry:

Finished Goods Inventory	395,000	
Accounts Payable		160,000
Conversion Cost Control		235,000

(b) There is no entry for Transaction 1. Transactions 6 and 7 are replaced with the following entry:

Cost of Goods Sold	395,000	
Accounts Payable		160,000
Conversion Cost Control		235,000

SUMMARY OF IMPORTANT EQUATIONS

1. Risk Response Benefit = Inherent Risk − Residual Risk
2. Risk Response Net Benefit = Response Benefit − Response Cost

SUMMARY OF LEARNING OBJECTIVES

LO1. Explain what strategic cost management is and how it can be used to help a firm create a competitive advantage.
- Obtaining a competitive advantage so that long-term survival is ensured is the goal of strategic cost management.

- Different strategies create different bundles of activities. By assigning costs to activities, the costs of different strategies can be assessed.
- There are three generic or general strategies: cost leadership, differentiation, and focusing. The particular mix and relative emphasis of these three strategies define a firm's strategic position.
- The objective of strategic cost management is to reduce costs while simultaneously strengthening a firm's strategic position.

LO2. Explain enterprise risk management and its importance for achieving strategy.

- The most important reason for using ERM is to help the organization achieve its strategy through identifying, measuring, and managing its most important risks and opportunities.
- Determining an organization's desired level of risk taking, or risk appetite, is necessary to ensure that the organization can best manage its portfolio of residual risks and opportunities.
- After determining risk appetite, ERM involves identifying the top risks, assessing risks at the inherent level, and managing (or responding to) risks such that the remaining residual risks align with the organization's risk appetite as expected by its shareholders and other key stakeholders.
- Risk monitoring is the final step in the iterative ERM process, whereby management continually searches for emerging risks, reevaluates the accuracy of its risk assessments, and considers more effective risk response alternatives.

LO3. Discuss value-chain analysis and the strategic role of activity-based customer and supplier costing.

- Knowledge of organizational and operational activities and their associated cost drivers is fundamental to strategic cost analysis. Knowledge of the firm's value chain and the industrial value chain is also critical.
- Value-chain analysis relies on identifying and exploiting internal and external linkages.
- Good cost management of supplier and customer linkages requires an understanding of what suppliers cost and how much it costs to service customers.
- Activity-based assignments to suppliers and customers provide the accurate cost information needed.

LO4. Tell what life-cycle cost management is and how it can be used to maximize profits over a product's life cycle.

- Life-cycle cost management is related to strategic cost analysis and, in fact, could be called a type of strategic cost analysis.
- Life-cycle cost management requires an understanding of the three types of life-cycle viewpoints: the marketing viewpoint, the production viewpoint, and the consumable life viewpoint.
- Target costing plays an essential role in life-cycle cost management by providing a methodology for reducing costs in the design stage by considering and exploiting both customer and supplier linkages.

LO5. Identify the basic features of JIT purchasing and manufacturing.

- JIT purchasing and manufacturing offer a totally different set of structural and procedural activities from those of the traditional organization.
- In JIT purchasing, parts and materials arrive just in time to be used in production. JIT assumes that all costs other than direct materials are driven by time and space drivers.
- Understanding supplier and customer linkages is vital for a successful JIT system.

LO6. Describe the effect JIT has on cost traceability and product costing.

- In a JIT environment, many overhead costs assigned to products using either driver tracing or allocation are now directly traceable to products.
- A vastly simplified process-costing system is the usual structure for a JIT environment.
- Product costing is more accurate because of increased traceability of costs.
- Accounting for the cost accounting cycle is simplified using backflush costing.

EXAMPLE 11.1   The HOW and WHY of Using Net Benefit to Evaluate Risk Response Alternatives, page 566

EXAMPLE 11.2   The HOW and WHY of Exploiting Internal Linkages to Reduce Costs and Increase Value, page 569

EXAMPLE 11.3   The HOW and WHY of Activity-Based Supplier Costing, page 573

EXAMPLE 11.4   The HOW and WHY of Activity-Based Customer Costing, page 576

EXAMPLE 11.5   The HOW and WHY of Activity-Based Life-Cycle Cost Reduction, page 581

EXAMPLE 11.6   The HOW and WHY of Backflush Costing, page 593

KEY TERMS

Acceptable quality level (AQL), 589

Backflush costing, 592

Competitive advantage, 555

Consumable life, 577

Cost leadership strategy, 555

Customer value, 555

Decline stage, 578

Differentiation strategy, 555

Enterprise risk management (ERM), 560

Executional activities, 558

External linkages, 557

Focusing strategy, 556

Growth stage, 578

Industrial value chain, 556

Inherent risk, 562

Internal linkages, 557

Introduction stage, 578

JIT manufacturing, 585

JIT purchasing, 586

Life-cycle cost management, 579

Life-cycle costs, 578

Manufacturing cells, 587

Maturity stage, 578

Operational activities, 559

Operational cost drivers, 559

Organizational cost drivers, 558

Post-purchase costs, 555

Product life cycle, 577

Residual risk, 564

Revenue-producing life, 577

Risk appetite, 561

Risk response benefit, 565

Risk response cost, 565

Risk response net benefit, 565

Strategic cost management, 555

Strategic decision making, 554

Strategic positioning, 556

Strategy, 556

Structural activities, 558

Target cost, 583

Total product, 555

Total quality control, 571

Value-chain analysis, 568

BRIEF EXERCISES

Brief Exercise 11-1 Using Net Benefit to Evaluate Risk Response Alternatives

OBJECTIVE ▸ 2
Example 11.1

Alejandro's Moab Grill features authentic Mexican dishes delivered in a relaxing Western motif. Given the short summer tourist season, Alejandro (the owner) decided to identify his top risk. Alejandro is most concerned that his restaurant will go relatively unnoticed by tourists as the number of other local competing restaurants continues to increase. As a result, he worries about the risk that the restaurant attracts fewer diners, thereby causing a decrease in sales revenue. The chart below contains a description of this top risk, an inherent risk assessment, three risk response alternatives (A through C), and a residual risk assessment for each response alternative.

Risk	Inherent Risk		Risk Response Alternatives	Residual Risk	
	Likelihood	Impact (On Lost Revenues)		Likelihood	Impact (On Lost Revenues)
Fewer tourists choose to dine at Alejandro's, thereby causing the restaurant to lose considerable sales revenue.	60%	$3,000,000	A—Switch the advertising campaign to more directly target tourists.	40%	$2,000,000
			B—Redesign the restaurant's exterior appearance to increase its curb appeal to tourists.	30%	$1,000,000
			C—Take no action in response to possibility of insufficient tourist diners.	60%	$3,000,000

Finally, Alejandro estimates that the cost of implementing risk response A is $100,000 and the cost of implementing risk response B is $1,000,000.

Required:

1. Calculate the inherent risk for Alejandro.
2. Calculate the residual risk for Alejandro associated with each of the three risk response alternatives A, B, and C.
3. Calculate the benefit for Alejandro associated with each of the three risk response alternatives A, B, and C.
4. Calculate the net benefit Alejandro associated with each of the three risk response alternatives A, B, and C.
5. Using net benefit as the criterion, which risk response should Alejandro choose to implement?

Brief Exercise 11-2 Exploiting Internal Linkages

OBJECTIVE ▸ 3
Example 11.2

Woodruff Company is currently producing a snowmobile that uses five specialized parts. Engineering has proposed replacing these specialized parts with commodity parts, which will cost less and can be purchased in larger order quantities. Current activity capacity and demand (with specialized parts required) and expected activity demand (with only commodity parts required) are provided.

Activities	Activity Driver	Activity Capacity	Current Activity Demand	Expected Activity Demand
Material usage	Number of parts	192,000	192,000	192,000
Installing parts	Direct labor hours	90,000	90,000	72,000
Purchasing parts	Number of orders	20,000	17,100	10,500

Additionally, the following activity cost data are provided:

Material usage: $20 per specialized part used; $16 per commodity part; no fixed activity cost.
Installing parts: $14 per direct labor hour; no fixed activity cost.
Purchasing parts: Four salaried clerks, each earning a $45,000 annual salary; each clerk is capable of processing 5,000 purchase orders. Variable activity costs: $0.80 per purchase order processed for forms, postage, etc.

Required:

1. Calculate the cost reduction produced by using commodity parts instead of specialized parts.
2. Suppose that 50,000 units are being produced and sold for $8,800 per unit and that the price per unit will be reduced by the per-unit savings. What is the new price for the configured product?
3. *What if* the expected activity demand for purchase orders was 8,500? How would this affect the answers to Requirements 1 and 2?

OBJECTIVE 3
Example 11.3

Brief Exercise 11-3 Activity-Based Supplier Costing

Tulsa Company is a car brake repair and replacement company operating in the after-sales market. Tulsa's purchasing manager uses two suppliers (Stridulo and Fallimento) for the source of its passenger car brakes. Data relating to brake discs (Discs) and brake pads (Pads) are given on the next page.

I. Activity Costs

Activity	
Adverse buying*	$800,000
Supplier returns**	100,000

*Extra cost of purchasing from local car dealer because of insufficient delivery of supplier.
**Brakes returned because they were not ordered or because they were defective.

II. Supplier Data

	Stridulo Brakes		Fallimento Brakes	
	Discs	**Pads**	**Discs**	**Pads**
Unit purchase price	$ 53.75	$148.75	$ 46.50	$146.50
Units purchased	10,000	10,000	15,000	15,000
Insufficient units	2,000	2,000	6,000	6,000
Returned units	500	500	1,500	1,500

Required:

1. Calculate the activity rates for assigning costs to suppliers.
2. Calculate the total unit purchasing cost for each component for each supplier.
3. *What if* the quantity of brake pads that can be purchased is limited to 20,000 units from Stridulo and 25,000 units from Fallimento? There is no limit from either source for brake discs. Based on cost, what purchasing mix should be chosen? What problem does this create? What else might you suggest if you were the manager of Tulsa?

OBJECTIVE 3
Example 11.4

Brief Exercise 11-4 Activity-Based Customer Costing

Deeds Company sells custom-made machine parts to industrial equipment manufacturers by bidding cost plus 40 percent, where cost is defined as manufacturing cost plus order processing cost. There are two types of customers: those who place small, frequent orders and those who place larger, less frequent orders. Cost and sales information by customer category is provided below.

	Frequently Ordering Customers	Less Frequently Ordering Customers
Sales orders	35,000	3,500
Order size	10	100
Average unit manufacturing cost	$ 50	$ 50
Order-processing activity costs:		
Processing sales orders		$2,365,000

Order-filling capacity is purchased in steps (order-processing clerks) of 1,000, each step costing $40,000; variable order-filling activity costs are $30 per order. The activity capacity is 39,000 orders; thus, the total order-filling cost is $2,715,000 [(39 steps × $40,000) + ($30 × 38,500)]. Current practice allocates ordering cost in proportion to the units purchased.

Deeds recently lost a bid for 100 units. (The per-unit bid price was $2 per unit more than the winning bid.) The manager of Deeds was worried that this was a recurring trend for the larger orders. (Other large orders had been lost with similar margins of loss.) No such problem was taking place for the smaller orders; the company rarely lost bids on smaller orders.

Required:

1. Calculate the unit bid price offered to Deeds's customers assuming that order-filling cost is allocated to each customer category in proportion to units sold.
2. Assume that a newly implemented ABC system concludes that the number of orders placed is the best cost driver for the order-filling activity. Assign order-filling costs using this driver to each customer type and then calculate the new unit bid price for each customer type. Using this new price, would Deeds have won the bid for the 100 units recently lost?
3. *What if* Deeds offers a discount for orders of 35 units or more to the frequently ordering customers? Assume that all the frequently ordering customers can and do take advantage of this offer at the minimum level possible. Can Deeds offer the original price from Requirement 1 to the frequently ordering customers and not decrease its profitability?

Brief Exercise 11-5 Activity-Based Life-Cycle Costing

OBJECTIVE ◀ 3
Example 11.5

Kagle design engineers are in the process of developing a new "green" product, one that will significantly reduce impact on the environment and yet still provide the desired customer functionality. Currently, two designs are being considered. The manager of Kagle has told the engineers that the cost for the new product cannot exceed $550 per unit (target cost). In the past, the Cost Accounting Department has given estimated costs using a unit-based system. At the request of the Engineering Department, Cost Accounting is providing both unit- and activity-based accounting information (made possible by a recent pilot study producing the activity-based data).

Unit-based system:

Variable conversion activity rate: $100 per direct labor hour
Material usage rate: $20 per part

ABC system:

Labor usage: $15 per direct labor hour
Material usage (direct materials): $20 per part
Machining: $75 per machine hour
Purchasing activity: $150 per purchase order
Setup activity: $3,000 per setup hour
Warranty activity: $500 per returned unit (usually requires extensive rework)
Customer repair cost: $25 per repair hour (average)

Activity and Resource Information (annual estimates)

	Design A	Design B
Units produced	25,000	25,000
Direct material usage	300,000 parts	275,000 parts
Labor usage	50,000 hours	120,000 hours
Machine hours	50,000	60,000
Purchase orders	2,000	1,500
Setup hours	600	200
Returned units	1,000	250
Repair time (customer)	2,000	500

Required:

1. Select the lower-cost design using unit-based costing. Are logistical and post-purchase activities considered in this analysis?
2. Select the lower-cost design using ABC analysis. Explain why the analysis differs from the unit-based analysis.
3. *What if* the post-purchase cost was an environmental contaminant and amounted to $10 *per unit* for Design A and $40 per unit for Design B? Assume that the environmental cost is borne by society. Now which is the better design?

OBJECTIVE 6

Example 11.6

Brief Exercise 11-6 Backflush Costing

Hepworth Company has implemented a JIT system and is considering the use of backflush costing. Hepworth had the following transactions for the current fiscal year:

1. Purchased raw materials on account for $600,000.
2. Placed all materials received into production.
3. Incurred actual direct labor costs of $90,000.
4. Incurred actual overhead costs of $625,000.
5. Applied conversion costs of $675,000.
6. Completed all work for the month.
7. Sold all completed work.
8. Computed the difference between actual and applied costs.

Required:

1. Prepare the journal entries for traditional and backflush costing. For backflush costing, assume there are two trigger points: (1) the purchase of raw materials, and (2) the completion of the goods.
2. Assume the second trigger point in Requirement 1 is the sale of goods. What would change for the backflush-costing journal entries?
3. *What if* there is only one trigger point and it is (a) completion of the goods or (b) sale of the goods? How would the backflush-costing journal entries differ from Requirement 1 for (a) and (b)?

EXERCISES

OBJECTIVE 1

Exercise 11-7 Competitive Advantage: Basic Concepts

Keith Golding has decided to purchase a personal computer. He has narrowed his choices to two: Brand A and Brand B. Both brands have the same processing speed, hard disk capacity, RAM, graphics card memory, and basic software support package. Both come from companies with good reputations. The selling price for each is identical. After some review, Keith discovers that the cost of operating and maintaining Brand A over a three-year period is estimated to be

$200. For Brand B, the operating and maintenance cost is $600. The sales agent for Brand A emphasized the lower operating and maintenance cost. She claimed that it was lower than any other PC brand. The sales agent for Brand B, however, emphasized the service reputation of the product. She provided Keith with a copy of an article appearing in a PC magazine that rated service performance of various PC brands. Brand B was rated number one. Based on all the information, Keith decided to buy Brand B.

Required:

1. What is the total product purchased by Keith?
2. Is the Brand A company pursuing a cost leadership or differentiation strategy? The Brand B company? Explain.
3. When asked why he purchased Brand B, Keith replied, "I think Brand B offered more value than Brand A." What are the possible sources of this greater value? If Keith's reaction represents the majority opinion, what suggestions could you offer to help improve the strategic position of Brand A?

Exercise 11-8 Strategic Positioning

OBJECTIVE ◄ 1

DATA
ANALYTICS

San Jose Goodwill Bank has been experiencing significant competition from nonbanking financial service providers such as mutual funds. As a result, interest rates were lower, and the bank found it more difficult to maintain or increase deposits. Profits had declined for the past two years. Concerned about the situation, the bank's executive managers commissioned a consulting group to assess the profitability of the bank's products and customers. The consulting group implemented an ABC system that traced costs to both products and customers. An ABC customer profitability analysis rated the customers on a scale of one to five, with one being the most lucrative. Customers in the number one category earned an average profit of $1,500 per year for the bank, while customers in the fifth category were costing the bank an average of $500 per year. The consulting group also conducted a marketing survey and discovered that the higher-end customers were leaving for banks that offered a broader range of financial products. Armed with the financial and marketing information provided by the consulting group, the banking executives decided to implement the following:

1. Broaden the markets to include investment and insurance products. The goal was to become a complete financial services provider to stop the loss of the higher-end customers. The broadening would also reduce the dependence of the bank on interest-based revenue. (Investment and insurance products produce fee-based revenues.)
2. Alter the customer mix by targeting only the upper three customer segments.
3. Set the bank apart from competitors by offering special, high-quality services to targeted customers:
   a. The upper segment of customers will be classified as "Premier One" and will be issued a gold card. When presenting the card to a concierge at the door, the customer will be taken to a special teller window with no line, or to the desk of a specially trained bank officer.
   b. For the highest-end customers, no-questions-asked refunds on fees that they think they shouldn't pay (categories one and two). Middle-end customers can negotiate. Low-end customers must pay the fees (categories four and five).
   c. Provide secret, toll-free "VIP" numbers to customers in the Premier One category. In this way, they will have immediate access to a bank official for any inquiry they may have.
   d. Impose a $4 teller fee for lower-end customers (categories four and five).
4. Improve operating efficiency by increasing productivity and eliminating costs that produce no revenues.

Required:

1. Describe the strategic positioning of San Jose Goodwill Bank in terms of the three general strategies: cost leadership, differentiation, and focusing. Of the three, which one(s) are apparently receiving the most emphasis?

2. Describe the role of cost management in defining the strategic position of the bank. What role do you think cost management will play as the bank attempts to establish and enhance its strategic position?

3. Briefly explain the role that the Bank's strategy should play within its data analytics endeavors (refer to Exhibit 2.5 "The Role of Data Analytics in Cost Management" for a review of the core issues within data analytics).

OBJECTIVE `1`   ### Exercise 11-9 Driver Classification

Classify the following cost drivers as structural, executional, or operational.

a. Number of plants
b. Number of moves
c. Degree of employee involvement
d. Capacity utilization
e. Number of product lines
f. Number of distribution channels
g. Engineering hours
h. Direct labor hours
i. Scope
j. Product configuration
k. Quality management approach
l. Number of receiving orders
m. Number of defective units
n. Employee experience
o. Types of process technologies
p. Number of purchase orders
q. Type and efficiency of layout
r. Scale
s. Number of functional departments
t. Number of planning meetings

OBJECTIVE `1`   ### Exercise 11-10 Operational and Organizational Activities

McConkie Company has decided to pursue a cost leadership strategy. This decision is prompted, in part, by increased competition from foreign firms. McConkie's management is confident that costs can be reduced by more efficient management of the firm's operational activities. Improving operational activity efficiency, however, often requires some strategic changes in organizational activities. McConkie currently uses a very traditional manufacturing approach. Plants are organized along departmental lines. Management follows a typical pyramid structure. Labor is specialized and located in departments. Quality management follows a conventional acceptable quality level approach. (Batches of products are accepted if the number of defective units is below some predetermined level.) Materials are purchased from a large number of suppliers, and sizable inventories of materials, work in process, and finished goods are maintained. The company produces many different products that use a variety of different parts, many of which are purchased from suppliers.

Required:

Given this brief description of the firm and its setting, for each of the following operational activities and their associated drivers, suggest some strategic changes in organizational activities (and drivers) that might reduce the cost of performing the indicated operational activity. Explain your reasoning.

Operational Activity	Operational Cost Driver
Inspecting products	Number of inspection hours
Moving materials	Distance moved
Reworking products	Number of defective units
Setting up equipment	Setup time
Purchasing parts	Number of different parts
Storing goods and materials	Days in inventory
Expediting orders	Number of late orders
Warranty work	Number of bad units sold

Exercise 11-11 Managing Risks Using a Portfolio Perspective

OBJECTIVE ◀ 2

Grand Teton Inc. provides numerous back country tours to adventure-seeking outdoor enthusiasts. Grand Teton's enterprise risk management team has chosen its particular risk response to each of its top eight inherent risks. The risk graph below shows Grand Teton's risks *after* all of the team's risk responses have been enacted.

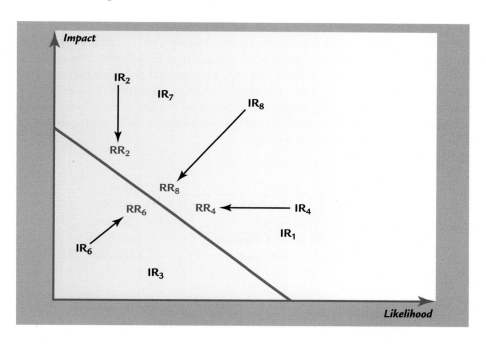

Required:

Refer to Grand Teton's risk graph. Determine the particular risk response decision from the following list of six lettered possibilities A through F (a letter can be used more than once) that the team chose to implement for each of the company's eight inherent risks 1 (IR_1) through 8 (IR_8).

A) Reduce the given risk by implementing a new training quality control activity that decreases the likelihood of the risk.

B) Take on more of the given risk by relaxing an existing internal control procedure.

C) Avoid the given risk by no longer performing the underlying activity that gave rise to the risk.

D) Reduce the given risk by taking out a traditional insurance policy.

E) Accept the given risk.

F) Reduce the given risk by entering into a new strategic alliance that decreases both the impact and the likelihood of the risk.

1. $IR_1 =$ _____
2. $IR_2 =$ _____
3. $IR_3 =$ _____
4. $IR_4 =$ _____
5. $IR_5 =$ _____
6. $IR_6 =$ _____
7. $IR_7 =$ _____
8. $IR_8 =$ _____

OBJECTIVE 3

SHOW ME HOW   **DATA ANALYTICS**   **EXCEL**

Exercise 11-12 External Linkages, Activity-Based Supplier Costing

Jackson, Inc., manufactures motorcycles. Jackson produces all the components necessary for the production of the cycles except for one (a carburetor). This component is purchased from two local suppliers: Harvey Parts and Curtis, Inc. Harvey sells the component for $64 per unit, while Curtis sells the same component for $57. Because of the lower price, Jackson purchases 75 percent of its components from Curtis. Jackson purchases the remaining 25 percent from Harvey to ensure an alternative source. The total annual demand is 160,000 carburetors.

Harvey's sales manager is pushing Jackson to purchase more of its units, arguing that its component is of much higher quality and so should prove to be less costly than Curtis's lower-quality component. Harvey has sufficient capacity to supply all the carburetors needed and is asking for a long-term contract. With a five-year contract for 120,000 or more units, Harvey will sell the component for $60 per unit with a contractual provision for an annual product-specific inflationary adjustment. Jackson's purchasing manager is intrigued by the offer and wonders if the higher-quality carburetor actually does cost less than the lower-quality Curtis carburetor. To help assess the cost effect of the two products, the following data were collected for quality-related activities and suppliers:

I. Activity data:

Activity	Cost
Inspecting components (sampling only)	$ 180,000
Expediting work (due to late delivery)	144,000
Reworking products (due to failed component)	1,026,000
Warranty work (due to failed component)	1,800,000

II. Supplier data:

	Harvey	Curtis
Unit purchase price	$ 64	$ 57
Units purchased	40,000	120,000
Expediting orders	30	270
Sampling hours*	90	4,410
Rework hours	270	4,230
Warranty hours	300	5,700

*The Quality Control Department indicates that sampling inspection for the Harvey component has been reduced because the reject rate is so low.

Required:

1. Calculate the cost per component for each supplier, taking into consideration the costs of the quality-related activities and using the current prices and sales volume. Given this information, what do you think the purchasing manager ought to do? Explain.
2. Suppose the Quality Control Department estimates that the company loses $3,300,000 in sales per year because of the reputation effect of defective units attributable to failed components. What information would you like to have to assign this cost to each supplier? Suppose that you had to assign the cost of lost sales to each supplier using one of the

drivers already listed. Which would you choose? Using this driver, calculate the change in the cost of the Curtis carburetor attributable to lost sales.

3. Briefly explain the type or types (i.e., Descriptive, Diagnostic, Predictive, and Prescriptive) of data analytics that you conducted in responding to requirements 1 and 2. (See Exhibits 2.5 and 2.6, pp. 37, 40, for a review of data analytics types.)

Exercise 11-13 External Linkages, Customer Costing, Customer Profitability

Huang Company sells small machine parts to heavy equipment manufacturers for an average price of $1.05 per part. There are two types of customers: those who place small, frequent orders and those who place larger, less frequent orders. Each time an order is placed and processed, a setup is required. Scheduling is also needed to coordinate the many different orders that come in and place demands on the plant's manufacturing resources. Huang also inspects a sample of the products each time a batch is produced to ensure that the customer's specifications have been met. Inspection takes essentially the same time regardless of the type of part being produced. Huang's Cost Accounting Department has provided the following budgeted data for customer-related activities and costs (the amounts expected for the coming year):

	Frequently Ordering Customers	Less Frequently Ordering Customers
Sales orders	21,000	2,100
Average order size	2,100	21,000
Number of setups	26,250	5,250
Scheduling hours	36,750	5,250
Inspections	26,250	5,250
Average unit cost*	$ 0.56	$ 0.56

*This cost does not include the cost of the following "customer-related" activities:

Customer-related activity costs:	
Processing sales orders	$ 2,310,000
Scheduling production	1,260,000
Setting up equipment	3,780,000
Inspecting batches	5,040,000
Total	$12,390,000

Required:

1. Assign the customer-related activity costs to each category of customers in proportion to the sales revenue earned by each customer type. Calculate the profitability of each customer type. Discuss the problems with this measure of customer profitability.
2. Assign the customer-related activity costs to each customer type using activity rates. Now calculate the profitability of each customer category. As a manager, how would you use this information?

Exercise 11-14 Product Life Cycle

The following series of statements or phrases are associated with product life-cycle viewpoints. Identify whether each one is associated with the marketing, production, or customer viewpoint. Where possible, identify the particular characteristic being described. If the statement or phrase fits more than one viewpoint, label it as interactive. Explain the interaction.

1. a. Sales are increasing at an increasing rate.
   b. The cost of maintaining the product after it is purchased.
   c. The product is losing market acceptance and sales are beginning to decrease.
   d. A design is chosen to minimize post-purchase costs.
   e. Ninety percent or more of the costs are committed during the development stage.

f. The length of time that the product serves the needs of a customer.
g. All the costs associated with a product for its entire life cycle.
h. The time in which a product generates revenue for a company.
i. Profits tend to reach peak levels during this stage.
j. Customers have the lowest price sensitivity during this stage.
k. Describes the general sales pattern of a product as it passes through distinct life-cycle stages.
l. The concern is with product performance and price.
m. Actions taken so that life-cycle profits are maximized.
n. Emphasizes internal activities that are needed to develop, produce, market, and service products.

2. Briefly explain the types (i.e., Descriptive, Diagnostic, Predictive, and Prescriptive) of data analytics that might be useful for informing product life cycle decisions. Include within your explanation the specific reasoning for why you selected those particular types. (See Exhibits 2.5 and 2.6, pp. 37, 40, for a review of data analytics types.)

OBJECTIVE   **Exercise 11-15 JIT and Traceability of Costs**

Assume that a company has recently switched to JIT manufacturing. Each manufacturing cell produces a single product or major subassembly. Cell workers have been trained to perform a variety of tasks. Additionally, many services have been decentralized. Costs are assigned to products using direct tracing, driver tracing, and allocation. For each cost listed, indicate the most likely product cost assignment method used *before* JIT and *after* JIT. Set up a table with three columns: Cost Item, Before JIT, and After JIT. You may assume that direct tracing is used whenever possible, followed by driver tracing, with allocation being the method of last resort.

a. Inspection costs
b. Power to heat, light, and cool plant
c. Minor repairs on production equipment
d. Salary of production supervisor (department/cell)
e. Oil to lubricate machinery
f. Salary of plant supervisor
g. Costs to set up machinery
h. Salaries of janitors
i. Power to operate production equipment
j. Taxes on plant and equipment
k. Depreciation on production equipment
l. Raw materials
m. Salary of industrial engineer
n. Parts for machinery
o. Pencils and paper clips for production supervisor (department/cell)
p. Insurance on plant and equipment
q. Overtime wages for cell workers
r. Plant depreciation
s. Materials handling
t. Preventive maintenance

OBJECTIVE   **Exercise 11-16 JIT Features and Product Costing Accuracy**

Prior to installing a JIT system, Buckner Company, a producer of automobile parts, used maintenance hours to assign maintenance costs to its three products (wheels, rims, and ball bearings). The maintenance costs totaled $12,000,000 per year. The maintenance hours used by each product and the quantity of each product produced are as follows:

	Maintenance Hours	Quantity Produced
Wheels	150,000	187,500
Rims	300,000	281,250
Bearings	350,000	350,000

After installing JIT, three manufacturing cells were created, and cell workers were trained to perform preventive maintenance and minor repairs. A full-time maintenance person was also assigned to each cell. Maintenance costs for the three cells still totaled $12,000,000; however, these costs are now traceable to each cell as follows:

Cell, wheels	$2,640,000
Cell, rims	4,560,000
Cell, bearings	5,600,000

Required:

1. Compute the pre-JIT maintenance cost per unit for each product (round answers to two decimal places).
2. Compute the maintenance cost per unit for each product after installing JIT (round answers to two decimal places).
3. Explain why the JIT maintenance cost per unit is more accurate than the pre-JIT cost.

Exercise 11-17 Backflush versus Traditional Costing: Variation 1

OBJECTIVE 6

EXCEL **SHOW ME HOW**

Potter Company has installed a JIT purchasing and manufacturing system and is using backflush accounting for its cost flows. It currently uses a two-trigger approach with the purchase of materials as the first trigger point and the completion of goods as the second trigger point. During the month of June, Potter had the following transactions:

Raw materials purchased	$243,000
Direct labor cost	40,500
Overhead cost	202,500
Conversion cost applied	263,250*

*$40,500 labor plus $222,750 overhead.

There were no beginning or ending inventories. All goods produced were sold with a 60 percent markup. Any variance is closed to Cost of Goods Sold. (Variances are recognized monthly.)

Required:

1. Prepare the journal entries that would have been made using a traditional accounting approach for cost flows.
2. Prepare the journal entries for the month using backflush costing.

Exercise 11-18 Backflush Costing: Variation 2

OBJECTIVE 6

SHOW ME HOW

Refer to Exercise 11-17.

Required:

Prepare the journal entries for the month of June using backflush costing, assuming that Potter uses the sale of goods as the second trigger point instead of the completion of goods.

Exercise 11-19 Backflush versus Traditional Costing: Variations 3 and 4

OBJECTIVE 6

SHOW ME HOW

Refer to Exercise 11-17.

Required:

1. Prepare the journal entries for the month of May using backflush costing, assuming that Potter uses the completion of goods as the only trigger point.
2. Prepare the journal entries for the month of May using backflush costing, assuming that Potter uses the sale of goods as the only trigger point.

OBJECTIVE 5 6

SHOW ME
HOW

Exercise 11-20 Cost Assignment and JIT

Rodriguez Company produces two types of glucose monitors (basic and advanced). Both pass through two producing departments: Fabrication and Assembly. Rodriguez also has an Inspection Department that is responsible for testing monitors to ensure that they perform within prespecified tolerance ranges (a sampling procedure is used). Budgeted data for the three departments are as follows:

	Inspection	Fabrication	Assembly
Overhead	$480,000	$720,000	$204,000
Number of tests	—	30,000	90,000
Direct labor hours	—	72,000	36,000

In the Fabrication Department, the basic model requires 0.5 hour of direct labor and the advanced model requires 1.0 hour. In the Assembly Department, the basic model requires 0.7 hour of direct labor and the advanced model requires 1.25 hours. There are 45,000 basic units produced and 24,000 advanced units.

Immediately after preparing the budgeted data, a consultant suggests that two manufacturing cells be created: one for the manufacture of the basic model and the other for the manufacture of the advanced model. Raw materials would be delivered to each cell, and goods would be shipped immediately to customers upon completion. Workers within each cell would also be trained to perform monitor testing. The total direct overhead costs estimated for each cell would be $228,000 for the basic cell and $720,000 for the advanced cell.

Required:

1. Allocate the inspection costs to each department, and compute the overhead cost per unit for each monitor. (Overhead rates use direct labor hours.)
2. Compute the overhead cost per unit if manufacturing cells are created. Which unit overhead cost do you think is more accurate—the one computed with a departmental structure, or the one computed using a cell structure? Explain.
3. Note that the total overhead costs for the cell structure are lower. Explain why.

PROBLEMS

OBJECTIVE 2

DATA
ANALYTICS

Problem 11-21 Evaluating Risk Response Alternatives

Phil DaStands is the athletic director at Rarelly Wynn University. The university experienced a decline in athletic event attendance over the past several years, resulting in decreasing Athletic Department revenues from ticket, concession, and merchandise sales. In an attempt to better understand the situation, Phil met with the university's enterprise risk management committee, as well as key stakeholders such as season ticketholders. Based on what he learned, Phil believes that the Athletic Department's most critical risk for the upcoming academic year is a continuing decline in the department's total revenues.

Phil visited peer universities in an attempt to understand the root cause of his department's risk and help identify possible response alternatives. The visits convinced Phil that his department's large, but relatively inexperienced, staff is not adequately trained to understand how to provide Rarelly Wynn fans with the outstanding and unique type of customer service experiences that are necessary to increase fan spending to the level desired by the university. To address the risk of declining fan spending, Phil is considering implementing one of the following four separate risk response alternatives. The following chart contains a description of the Athletic Department's top risk, an inherent risk assessment, four risk response alternatives (A through D), and a residual risk assessment for each response alternative.

Risk	Inherent Risk		Risk Response Alternatives	Residual Risk	
	Likelihood	Impact (On Lost Revenues)		Likelihood	Impact (On Lost Revenues)
Athletic Department sales revenue declines significantly for the following academic year.	80%	$75,000,000	**A**—Embark on a widespread marketing campaign touting the historical success of particular university sports programs and the fun of attending current sporting events.	50%	$40,000,000
			B—Create a new credit card rebate program co-branded with a large regional bank in which fans receive a cash rebate on all university sports-related purchases using the card.	60%	$50,000,000
			C—Offer unique sports-related prizes (special dinners with coaches and players, signed authentic memorabilia, free trips to end-of-season tournaments, etc.) to winners of raffles and other new programs open only to fans who purchase tickets to university sporting events.	40%	$60,000,000
			D—Take no action in response to possible new regulation.	80%	$75,000,000

Additionally, Phil asked Rarelly Wynn University's chief financial officer, Bee Wildered, to help estimate the incremental cost of implementing each of the possible risk response alternatives:

Response A involves the Athletic Department embarking on a widespread marketing campaign in which Athletic Department staff would reach out via phone, email, and face-to-face visits with current and prospective fans. During these interactions, the staff would tout the historical success of particular university sports programs (league championships, national tournament victories, bowl game appearances, etc.) and the fun of attending current sporting events (offering complimentary courtside or side line tickets, watching exciting half-time shows, etc.). The Athletic Department could utilize its existing staff to handle all of the fan interactions for this response. However, by utilizing the staff's time for such new interactions, the department would have to discontinue its summertime alumni event on campus that raises an average of $25 million of revenue annually for the Athletic Department.

Response B involves a new co-branded credit card program that provides fans with a cash rebate on all purchases of university items, including tickets. The program is structured with the regional bank such that the Athletic Department pays the bank 10 percent of the total annual sales generated by the program. Phil estimates that the program will generate total annual sales of $85 million for the following academic year. In addition, the university would have to hire a new director with a $200,000 annual salary to oversee the program. However, the new director would spend only half of the year overseeing the credit card program, while the other half would be spent performing miscellaneous tasks that would allow the Athletic Department to avoid $100,000 of existing annual expenses that it would have to spend if the program were not adopted. Finally, the program agreement with the regional bank also requires the university to pay the bank a fixed $400,000 annual fee.

Finally, response C involves the Athletic Department creating unique university-related sports experiences exclusively for its fans who purchase tickets to university sporting events. The experiences would serve as prizes given away via raffles and other interactive engagements that encourage fans to purchase athletic tickets. Each of 20 staff members would spend $80,000 annually traveling to the university's most famous sports alumni (many of whom reside internationally) to have them sign various university memorabilia as prize giveaways. The Athletic Department also would spend $24 million on special dinners and other events for prize winners. Finally, Phil believes a number of the sports alumni who normally attend one on-campus fundraising event each year will no longer do so as a result of spending time with the Athletic Department staff who travel to them to obtain their memorabilia signatures. Phil estimates that the Athletic Department would forfeit $1 million in total from these alumni no longer attending the on-campus fundraising events if response C is implemented.

Required:

1. Calculate the net benefit for each of Phil's four risk response alternatives (A, B, C, and D) under consideration.
2. Based on the net benefit calculated in requirement 1, which risk response alternative should Phil select? Explain your reasoning.
3. Beyond net benefit, identify and briefly explain additional criteria that might be helpful in evaluating and selecting the most appropriate risk response alternative.
4. By what amount would the incremental cost of alternative A need to decrease in order for alternative A to be preferred to alternative B (assume that everything else remains unchanged)?
5. Risk correlation is an ERM phrase that generally includes any situation in which the implementation of a particular risk response also brings about consequences in other areas of the business. Briefly explain how the $1 million forfeited fundraising amount in risk response alternative C represents an example of risk correlation.
6. Identify and briefly explain which of the seven core Data Analytic issues (What, Why, etc. detailed in Exhibit 2.5, pg. 37 "The Role of Data Analytics in Cost Management") are most likely to pertain to Phil's attempt to effectively identify and respond to the Athletic Department's top risk.

OBJECTIVE **3**

Problem 11-22 Internal Linkages, Cost Management, and Strategic Decision Making

Evans, Inc., has a unit-based costing system. Evans's Miami plant produces 10 different electronic products. The demand for each product is about the same. Although they differ in complexity, each product uses about the same labor time and materials.

The plant has used direct labor hours for years to assign overhead to products. To help design engineers understand the assumed cost relationships, the Cost Accounting Department developed the following cost equation. (The equation describes the relationship between total manufacturing costs and direct labor hours; the equation is supported by a coefficient of determination of 60 percent.)

$$Y = \$5,000,000 + \$30X, \text{ where } X = \text{direct labor hours}$$

The variable rate of $30 is broken down as follows:

Direct labor	$ 9
Variable overhead	5
Direct materials	16

Because of competitive pressures, product engineering was given the charge to redesign products to reduce the total cost of manufacturing. Using the above cost relationships, product engineering adopted the strategy of redesigning to reduce direct labor content. As each design was completed, an engineering change order was cut, triggering a series of events such as design approval, vendor selection, bill of materials update, redrawing of schematic, test runs, changes in setup procedures, development of new inspection procedures, and so on.

After one year of design changes, the normal volume of direct labor was reduced from 250,000 hours to 200,000 hours, with the same number of products being produced. Although each product differs in its labor content, the redesign efforts reduced the labor content for all products. On average, the labor content per unit of product dropped from 1.25 hours per unit to one hour per unit. Fixed overhead, however, increased from $5,000,000 to $6,600,000 per year.

Suppose that a consultant was hired to explain the increase in fixed overhead costs. The consultant's study revealed that the $30 per hour rate captured the unit-level variable costs; however, the cost behavior of other activities was quite different. For example, setting up equipment is a step-fixed cost, where each step is 2,000 setup hours, costing $90,000. The study also revealed that the cost of receiving goods is a function of the number of different components. This activity has a variable cost of $2,000 per component type and a fixed cost that follows a step-cost pattern. The step is defined by 20 components with a cost of $50,000 per step. Assume also that the consultant indicated that the design adopted by the engineers increased the demand for setups from 20,000 setup hours to 40,000 setup hours and the number of different components from 100 to 250. The demand for other non-unit-level activities remained unchanged. The consultant also recommended that management take a look at a rejected design for its products. This rejected design increased direct labor content from 250,000 hours to 260,000 hours, decreased the demand for setups from 20,000 hours to 10,000 hours, and decreased the demand for purchasing from 100 component types to 75 component types, while the demand for all other activities remained unchanged.

Required:

1. Using normal volume, compute the manufacturing cost per labor hour before the year of design changes. What is the cost per unit of an "average" product?
2. Using normal volume after the one year of design changes, compute the manufacturing cost per hour. What is the cost per unit of an "average" product?
3. Before considering the consultant's study, what do you think is the most likely explanation for the failure of the design changes to reduce manufacturing costs? Now use the information from the consultant's study to explain the increase in the average cost per unit of product. What changes would you suggest to improve Evans's efforts to reduce costs?
4. Explain why the consultant recommended a second look at a rejected design. Provide computational support. What does this tell you about the strategic importance of cost management?

Problem 11-23 External Linkages, Activity-Based Supplier Costing

OBJECTIVE ◄ 3

Cortalo, Inc., manufactures riding lawn mowers. Cortalo uses JIT manufacturing and carries insignificant levels of inventory. Cortalo manufactures everything needed for the riding lawn mowers except for the engines. Several sizes of mowers are produced. The most popular line is the small mower line. The engines for the small mower line are purchased from two sources: Verity Engines and Villa Machining. The Verity engine is the more expensive of the two sources and has a price of $330. The Villa engine is $297 per unit. Cortalo produces and sells 13,200 units of the small mower. Of the 13,200 engines purchased, 2,400 are purchased from Verity Engines, and 10,800 are purchased from Villa Machining. Although Linda Vasquez, production manager, prefers the Verity engine, Mark Shorts, purchasing manager, maintains that the price difference is too great to buy more than the 2,400 units currently purchased. Mark, however, does want to maintain a significant connection with Verity just in case the less expensive source cannot supply the needed quantities. Even though Linda understands the price argument, she has argued in many meetings that the quality of the Verity engine is worth the price difference. Mark remains unconvinced.

Li Sun, controller, has recently overseen the implementation of an activity-based costing system. He has indicated that an ABC analysis would shed some light on the conflict between production and purchasing. To support this position, the following data have been collected:

I. Activity cost data:

Testing engines[a]	$264,000
Reworking products[b]	440,000
Expediting orders[c]	330,000
Repairing engines[d]	594,000

[a] All units are tested after assembly, and a certain percentage are rejected because of engine failure.
[b] Defective engines are removed, replaced (supplier will replace any failed engine), and retested before being sold to customers. Engine failure often causes collateral damage, and other parts need to be remanufactured and replaced before the unit is again functional.
[c] Due to late or failed delivery of engines.
[d] Repair work is for units under warranty and almost invariably is due to engine failure. Repair usually means replacing the engine. This cost plus labor, transportation, and other costs make warranty work very expensive.

II. Supplier data:

	Villa	Verity
Engines replaced by source	1,089	11
Rework hours	5,390	110
Late or failed shipments	108	2
Warranty repairs (by source)	1,342	33

Upon hearing of the proposed ABC analysis, Linda and Mark were both supportive. Mark, however, noted that even if the analysis revealed that the Verity engine was actually less expensive, it would be unwise to completely abandon Villa. He argued that Verity may be hard pressed to meet the entire demand. Its productive capacity was not sufficient to handle the kind of increased demand that would be imposed. Additionally, having only one supplier was simply too risky.

Required:

1. Calculate the total supplier cost (acquisition cost plus supplier-related activity costs). Convert this to a per-engine cost to find out how much the company is paying for the engines. Which of the two suppliers is the low-cost supplier? Explain why this is a better measure of engine cost than the usual purchase costs assigned to the engines.
2. Consider the supplier cost information obtained in Requirement 1. Suppose further that Verity can supply only a total of 6,000 units. What actions would you advise Cortalo to undertake with its suppliers? Comment on the strategic value of activity-based supplier costing.

Problem 11-24 External Linkages, Activity-Based Customer Costing, and Strategic Decision Making

Moss Manufacturing produces several types of bolts. The products are produced in batches according to customer order. Although there are a variety of bolts, they can be grouped into three product families. The number of units sold is the same for each family. The selling prices for the three families range from $0.50 to $0.80 per unit. Because the product families are used in different kinds of products, customers also can be grouped into three categories, corresponding to the product family they purchase. Historically, the costs of order entry, processing, and handling were expensed and not traced to individual products. These costs are not trivial and totaled $6,300,000 for the most recent year. Furthermore, these costs had been increasing over time. Recently, the company had begun to emphasize a cost reduction strategy; however, any cost reduction decisions had to contribute to the creation of a competitive advantage.

Because of the magnitude and growth of order-filling costs, management decided to explore the causes of these costs. They discovered that order-filling costs were driven by the number of customer orders processed. Further investigation revealed the following cost behavior:

Step-fixed cost component: $70,000 per step; 2,000 orders define a step*
Variable cost component: $28 per order

*Moss currently has sufficient steps to process 100,000 orders.

The expected customer orders for the year total 140,000. The expected usage of the order-filling activity and the average size of an order by product family are as follows:

	Family A	Family B	Family C
Number of orders	70,000	42,000	28,000
Average order size	600	1,000	1,500

As a result of the cost behavior analysis, the marketing manager recommended the imposition of a charge per customer order. The president of the company concurred. The charge was implemented by adding the cost per order to the price of each order (computed using the projected ordering costs and expected orders). This ordering cost was then reduced as the size of the order increased and eliminated as the order size reached 2,000 units. (The marketing manager indicated that any penalties imposed for orders greater than this size would lose sales from some of the smaller customers.) Within a short period of communicating this new price information to customers, the average order size for all three product families increased to 2,000 units.

Required:

1. Moss traditionally has expensed order-filling costs (following GAAP guidelines). Under this approach, how much cost is assigned to customers? Do you agree with this practice? Explain.

2. Consider the following claim: by expensing the order-filling costs, all products were undercosted; furthermore, products ordered in small batches are significantly undercosted. Explain, with supporting computations where possible. Explain how this analysis also reveals the costs of various customer categories.

3. Calculate the reduction in order-filling costs produced by the change in pricing strategy. (Assume that resource spending is reduced as much as possible and that the total units sold remain unchanged.) Explain how exploiting customer linkages produced this cost reduction. Moss also noticed that other activity costs, such as those for setups, scheduling, and materials handling costs, were reduced significantly as a result of this new policy. Explain this outcome, and discuss its implications.

4. Suppose that one of the customers complains about the new pricing policy. This buyer is a lean, JIT firm that relies on small, frequent orders. In fact, this customer accounted for 30 percent of the Family A orders. How should Moss deal with this customer?

5. One of Moss's goals is to reduce costs so that a competitive advantage might be created. Describe how the management of Moss might use this outcome to help create a competitive advantage.

Problem 11-25 Internal and External Linkages, Strategic Cost Management

OBJECTIVE ◀ 3

Maxwell Company produces a variety of kitchen appliances, including cooking ranges and dishwashers. Over the past several years, competition has intensified. In order to maintain—and perhaps increase—its market share, Maxwell's management decided that the overall quality of its products had to be increased. Furthermore, costs needed to be reduced so that the selling prices of its products could be reduced. After some investigation, Maxwell concluded that many of its problems could be traced to the unreliability of the parts that were purchased from outside suppliers. Many of these components failed to work as intended, causing performance problems. Over the years, the company had increased its inspection activity of the final products. If a problem could be detected internally, then it was usually possible to rework the appliance so that the desired performance was achieved. Management also had increased its warranty coverage; warranty work had been increasing over the years.

David Haight, president of Maxwell Company, called a meeting with his executive committee. Lee Linsenmeyer, chief engineer; Kit Applegate, controller; and Jeannie Mitchell, purchasing manager, were all in attendance. How to improve the company's competitive position was the meeting's topic. The conversation of the meeting was recorded as seen on the following page:

DAVID: We need to find a way to improve the quality of our products and at the same time reduce costs. Lee, you said that you have done some research in this area. Would you share your findings?

LEE: As you know, a major source of our quality problems relates to the poor quality of the parts we acquire from the outside. We have a lot of different parts, and this adds to the complexity of the problem. What I thought would be helpful would be to redesign our products so that they can use as many interchangeable parts as possible. This will cut down the number of different parts, make it easier to inspect, and cheaper to repair when it comes to warranty work. My engineering staff has already come up with some new designs that will do this for us.

JEANNIE: I like this idea. It will simplify the purchasing activity significantly. With fewer parts, I can envision some significant savings for my area. Lee has shown me the designs so I know exactly what parts would be needed. I also have a suggestion. We need to embark on a supplier evaluation program. We have too many suppliers. By reducing the number of different parts, we will need fewer suppliers. And we really don't need to use all the suppliers that produce the parts demanded by the new designs. We should pick suppliers that will work with us and provide the quality of parts that we need. I have done some preliminary research and have identified five suppliers that seem willing to work with us and assure us of the quality we need. Lee may need to send some of his engineers into their plants to make sure that they can do what they are claiming.

DAVID: This sounds promising. Kit, can you look over the proposals and their estimates and give us some idea if this approach will save us any money? And if so, how much can we expect to save?

KIT: Actually, I am ahead of the game here. Lee and Jeannie have both been in contact with me and have provided me with some estimates on how these actions would affect different activities. I have prepared a handout that includes an activity table revealing what I think are the key activities affected. I have also assembled some tentative information about activity costs. The table gives the current demand and the expected demand after the changes are implemented. With this information, we should be able to assess the expected cost savings.

Handout

Activities	Activity Driver	Capacity	Current Demand	Expected Demand
Purchasing parts	Number of different parts	2,000	2,000	500
Inspecting products	Inspection hours	50,000	50,000	25,000
Reworking products	Number reworked	As needed	62,500	25,000
Warranty repair	Number of defective products	10,000	9,000	3,500

Additionally, the following activity cost data are provided:

Purchasing parts: Variable activity cost: $30 per part number; 20 salaried clerks, each earning a $45,000 annual salary. Each clerk is capable of processing orders associated with 100 part numbers.

Inspecting parts: Twenty-five inspectors, each earning a salary of $40,000 per year. Each inspector is capable of 2,000 hours of inspection.

Reworking products: Variable activity cost: $25 per unit reworked (labor and parts).

Warranty: Twenty repair agents, each paid a salary of $35,000 per year. Each repair agent is capable of repairing 500 units per year. Variable activity costs: $15 per product repaired.

Required:

1. Compute the total savings possible as reflected by Kit's handout. Assume that resource spending is reduced where possible.
2. Explain how redesign and supplier evaluation are linked to the savings computed in Requirement 1. Discuss the importance of recognizing and exploiting internal and external linkages.
3. Identify the organizational and operational activities involved in the strategy being considered by Maxwell Company. What is the relationship between organizational and operational activities?

Problem 11-26 External Linkages and Strategic Cost Management

Pawnee Works makes machine parts for manufacturers of industrial equipment. Over the years, Pawnee has been a steady and reliable supplier of quality parts to medium- and small-machine manufacturers. Michael Murray, owner of Pawnee Works, once again was disappointed in the year-end income statement. Profits had again failed to meet expectations. The performance was particularly puzzling given that the shop was operating at 100 percent capacity and had been for two years—ever since it had landed a *Fortune 500* firm as a regular customer. This firm currently supplies 40 percent of the business—a figure that had grown over the two years. Convinced that something was wrong, Michael called Brooke Harker, a partner in a large regional CPA firm. Brooke agreed to look into the matter.

A short time later, Brooke made an appointment to meet with Michael. Their conversation was recorded as follows:

BROOKE: Michael, I think I have pinpointed your problem. I think your main difficulty is poor pricing—you're undercharging your major customer. The firm is getting high-precision machined parts for much less than the cost to you. And I bet that you have been losing some of your smaller customers. You may want to rethink your strategic position. You are a small player in the industrial machine industry. This *Fortune 500* customer has 40 percent of the industrial machine market. Over the years, you have carved out a good reputation among small- and medium-size manufacturers. Right?

MICHAEL: Well, you're right. Over the years, our customers have not been giants. But we saw this business with the *Fortune 500* company as an opportunity to play in the big leagues. We thought it might mean the opportunity to expand the size of our operation. And we have expanded—at least we have added employees and some specialized engineering equipment. My engineering and programming costs have skyrocketed—resource increases we needed, though, to meet the specs of this larger customer. Profits have increased slightly, but nothing like I expected. You're also right about losing some of our smaller customers. Many have complained that the price of their jobs has increased. They have all indicated that they like the work we do and that we are conveniently located, but they argue that they simply cannot afford to keep paying the price we require. The small customers we have kept are also complaining and threatening to go elsewhere. I doubt we'll be able to hold onto their business for much longer—unless a change is made. So far, though, the business we have lost has been replaced with more orders from our large customer. I expect we could do even more business for the large customer. But how can the large buyer be getting the great deal you've described? It has the same markup as our regular jobs—full manufacturing cost plus 25 percent.

BROOKE: I have prepared a report illustrating the total overhead costs for a typical quarter. This report details your major activities and their associated costs. It also provides a comparison of a typical job for your small customers and the typical job for your large customer. Part of the problem is that your accounting system does not react to certain external events. It fails to show the effect of the large customer's activities on your activities and those that relate to your other customers. Given that you assign overhead costs using machine hours, I think you'll find it quite revealing.

MICHAEL: I'll have my controller examine the report for me. You know, if you are right about underpricing the large customer, I have a big problem. I'm not sure that I can increase the price of the parts without losing this big guy's business. After all, it can go to a dozen machine shops like mine and get the work done. A price increase may not work. Then I'd be faced with the loss of 40 percent of my jobs. I suppose, though, that I might be able to regain most of the business with the small customers. In fact, I am positive that we could get most of that business back. I wonder if that's what I ought to do.

Report Regional CPA Firm

I. Major Activities and Their Costs

Activity	Total Activity Costs	Cost Behavior*
Setups	$209,000	Variable
Engineering	151,200	Step-fixed, step = 105 hours
NC programming	130,400	Variable
Machining	100,000	Variable
Rework	101,400	Variable
Inspecting	23,000	Step-fixed, step = 230 hours
Sales support	80,000	Step-fixed, step = 23 orders
Total	$795,000	

*Behavior is defined with respect to individual cost drivers. The costs given are total costs for the quarter's activities. Thus, for step-fixed costs, the reported activity cost is for all steps being used by the activity; the cost per step is the total cost divided by the number of steps being used.

II. Job Profiles

Resources Used	Small Customer Job	Fortune 500 Job
Setup hours	3	10
Engineering hours	2	6
Programming hours	1	8
Defective units	20	10
Inspection hours	2	2
Machine hours	2,000	200
Prime costs	$14,000	$1,600
Other data:		
Job size	1,000 parts	100 parts
Quarterly jobs (orders)	15	100
Overhead rate	$14.30 per machine hour	$14.30 per machine hour

Note: All activities are being fully utilized each quarter. (There is no unused activity capacity.)

Required:

1. Without any calculation, explain why the machining company is losing money. Discuss the strategic insights provided by knowledge of activities, their costs, and customer linkages. Comment on the observation made by Brooke that the current accounting system fails to reflect external events. What changes would be needed to correct this deficiency (if true)?

2. Compute the unit price currently being charged each customer type (using machine hours to assign overhead costs).

3. Compute the unit price that would be charged each customer assuming that overhead is assigned using an ABC approach. Was the CPA right? Is the large customer paying less than the cost of producing the unit? How is this conclusion affected if the sales support activity is traced to jobs? (Use orders—jobs—as the cost driver.)

4. Compute the quarterly profit that is currently being earned and the amount that would be earned if Pawnee Works sold only to small customers (a small customer strategy). For the second income statement, use ABC for cost assignments. For the second income statement, the large customer is replaced with 10 smaller customers with the same characteristics as the 15 currently buying parts from Pawnee. Assume that any opportunities to reduce resource spending and usage will be reflected in the profit associated with a small customer strategy. Also, only the cost of activity usage is assigned to jobs. Any cost of unused activity is reported as a separate item on the income statement. Report sales support as a period expense.

5. What change in strategy would you recommend? In making this recommendation, consider the firm's value-chain framework.

Problem 11-27 Life-Cycle Cost Management and Target Costing

Nico Parts, Inc., produces electronic products with short life cycles (of less than two years). Development has to be rapid, and the profitability of the products is tied strongly to the ability to find designs that will keep production and logistics costs low. Recently, management has also decided that post-purchase costs are important in design decisions. Last month, a proposal for a new product was presented to management. The total market was projected at 200,000 units (for the two-year period). The proposed selling price was $130 per unit. At this price, market share was expected to be 25 percent. The manufacturing and logistics costs were estimated to be $120 per unit.

Upon reviewing the projected figures, Terrell Smith, president of Nico, called in his chief design engineer, Mark Williams, and his marketing manager, Cathy McCourt. The following conversation was recorded:

TERRELL: Mark, as you know, we agreed that a profit of $15 per unit is needed for this new product. Also, as I look at the projected market share, 25 percent isn't acceptable. Total profits need to be increased. Cathy, what suggestions do you have?

CATHY: Simple. Decrease the selling price to $125 and we expand our market share to 35 percent. To increase total profits, however, we need some cost reductions as well.

TERRELL: You're right. However, keep in mind that I do not want to earn a profit that is less than $15 per unit.

MARK: Does that $15 per unit factor in preproduction costs? You know we have already spent $100,000 on developing this product. To lower costs will require more expenditure on development.

TERRELL: Good point. No, the projected cost of $120 does not include the $100,000 we have already spent. I do want a design that will provide a $15-per-unit profit, including consideration of preproduction costs.

CATHY: I might mention that post-purchase costs are important as well. The current design will impose about $10 per unit for using, maintaining, and disposing our product. That's about the same as our competitors. If we can reduce that cost to about $5 per unit by designing a better product, we could probably capture about 50 percent of the market. I have just completed a marketing survey at Mark's request and have found out that the current design has two features not valued by potential customers. These two features have a projected cost of $6 per unit. However, the price consumers are willing to pay for the product is the same with or without the features.

Required:

1. Calculate the target cost associated with the initial 25 percent market share. Does the initial design meet this target? Now calculate the *total* life-cycle profit that the current (initial) design offers (including preproduction costs).
2. Assume that the two features that are apparently not valued by consumers will be eliminated. Also assume that the selling price is lowered to $125.
   a. Calculate the target cost for the $125 price and 35 percent market share.
   b. How much more cost reduction is needed?
   c. What are the total life-cycle profits now projected for the new product?
   d. Describe the three general approaches that Nico can take to reduce the projected cost to this new target. Of the three approaches, which is likely to produce the most reduction?
3. Suppose that the Engineering Department has two new designs: Design A and Design B. Both designs eliminate the two nonvalued features. Both designs also reduce production and logistics costs by an *additional* $8 per unit. Design A, however, leaves post-purchase costs at $10 per unit, while Design B reduces post-purchase costs to $4 per unit. Developing and testing Design A costs an additional $150,000, while Design B costs an additional $300,000. Assuming a price of $125, calculate the total life-cycle profits under each design.

Which would you choose? Explain. What if the design you chose cost an additional $500,000 instead of $150,000 or $300,000? Would this have changed your decision?

4. Refer to Requirement 3. For every extra dollar spent on preproduction activities, how much benefit was generated? What does this say about the importance of knowing the linkages between preproduction activities and later activities?

OBJECTIVE ▶ 4   **Problem 11-28 Life-Cycle Cost Management**

Jolene Askew, manager of Feagan Company, has committed her company to a strategically sound cost reduction program. Emphasizing life-cycle cost management is a major part of this effort. Jolene is convinced that production costs can be reduced by paying more attention to the relationships between design and manufacturing. Design engineers need to know what causes manufacturing costs. She instructed her controller to develop a manufacturing cost formula for a newly proposed product. Marketing had already projected sales of 25,000 units for the new product. (The life cycle was estimated to be 18 months. The company expected to have 50 percent of the market and priced its product to achieve this goal.) The projected selling price was $20 per unit. The following cost formula was developed:

$$Y = \$200,000 + \$10X_1$$

where

$$X_1 = \text{Machine hours (The product is expected to use one}$$
$$\text{machine hour for every unit produced.)}$$

Upon seeing the cost formula, Jolene quickly calculated the projected gross profit to be $50,000. This produced a gross profit of $2 per unit, well below the targeted gross profit of $4 per unit. Jolene then sent a memo to the Engineering Department, instructing them to search for a new design that would lower the costs of production by at least $50,000 so that the target profit could be met.

Within two days, the Engineering Department proposed a new design that would reduce unit-variable cost from $10 per machine hour to $8 per machine hour (Design Z). The chief engineer, upon reviewing the design, questioned the validity of the controller's cost formula. He suggested a more careful assessment of the proposed design's effect on activities other than machining. Based on this suggestion, the following revised cost formula was developed. This cost formula reflected the cost relationships of the most recent design (Design Z).

$$Y = \$140,000 + \$8X_1 + \$5,000X_2 + \$2,000X_3$$

where

$$X_1 = \text{Machine hours}$$
$$X_2 = \text{Number of batches}$$
$$X_3 = \text{Number of engineering change orders}$$

Based on scheduling and inventory considerations, the product would be produced in batches of 1,000; thus, 25 batches would be needed over the product's life cycle. Furthermore, based on past experience, the product would likely generate about 20 engineering change orders.

This new insight into the linkage of the product with its underlying activities led to a different design (Design W). This second design also lowered the unit-level cost by $2 per unit but decreased the number of design support requirements from 20 orders to 10 orders. Attention was also given to the setup activity, and the design engineer assigned to the product created a design that reduced setup time and lowered variable setup costs from $5,000 to $3,000 per setup. Furthermore, Design W also creates excess activity capacity for the setup activity, and resource spending for setup activity capacity can be decreased by $40,000, reducing the fixed cost component in the equation by this amount.

Design W was recommended and accepted. As prototypes of the design were tested, an additional benefit emerged. Based on test results, the post-purchase costs dropped from an estimated $0.70 per unit sold to $0.40 per unit sold. Using this information, the Marketing Department revised the projected market share upward from 50 percent to 60 percent (with no price decrease).

Required:

1. Calculate the expected gross profit per unit for Design Z using the controller's original cost formula. According to this outcome, does Design Z reach the targeted unit profit? Repeat, using the engineer's revised cost formula. Explain why Design Z failed to meet the targeted profit. What does this say about the use of unit-based costing for life-cycle cost management?

2. Calculate the expected profit per unit using Design W. Comment on the value of activity information for life-cycle cost management.

3. The benefit of the post-purchase cost reduction of Design W was discovered in testing. What direct benefit did it create for Feagan Company (in dollars)? Reducing post-purchase costs was not a specific design objective. Should it have been? Are there any other design objectives that should have been considered?

Problem 11-29 JIT, Traceability of Costs, Product Costing Accuracy, JIT Effects on Cost Accounting Systems

OBJECTIVE ◀ 5 6

Homer Manufacturing produces different models of 22-calibre rifles. The manufacturing costs assigned to its economy model rifle before and after installing JIT are given in the following table. Cell workers do all maintenance and are also responsible for moving materials, cell janitorial work, and inspecting products. Janitorial work outside the cells is still handled by the Janitorial Department.

In both the pre- and post-JIT setting, 10,000 units of the economy model are manufactured. In the JIT setting, manufacturing cells are used to produce each product. The management of Homer Manufacturing reported a significant decrease in manufacturing costs for all of its rifles after JIT was installed. It also reported less inventory-related costs and a significant decrease in lead times. Accounting costs also decreased because Homer switched from a job-order costing system to a process-costing system.

	Before	After
Direct materials	$ 60,000	$ 55,000
Direct labor	40,000	50,000
Maintenance	50,000	30,000
Inspection	30,000	10,000
Rework	60,000	9,000
Power	10,000	6,000
Depreciation	12,500	10,000
Materials handling	8,000	2,000
Engineering	80,000	50,000*
Setups	15,000	0
Janitorial	40,000	20,000
Building and grounds	11,800	12,400
Supplies	4,000	3,000
Supervision (plant)	10,000	8,000
Cell supervision	—	35,000
Cost accounting	40,000	25,000
Departmental supervision	18,000	—
Total	$489,300	$325,400

*Salary of engineer assigned to the cell.

Required:

1. Compute the unit cost of the product before and after JIT.
2. Explain why the JIT unit cost is more accurate. Also explain what JIT features may have produced a decrease in production costs. Use as many specific cost items as possible to illustrate your explanation.
3. Explain why Homer Manufacturing switched from a job-order costing system to a process-costing system after JIT was implemented.
4. Classify the costs in the JIT environment according to how they are assigned to the cell: direct tracing, driver tracing, or allocation. Which cost assignment method is most common? What does this imply regarding product-costing accuracy?

OBJECTIVE 5 6

EXCEL

Problem 11-30 JIT and Product Costing

Mott Company recently implemented a JIT manufacturing system. After one year of operation, Heidi Burrows, president of the company, wanted to compare product cost under the JIT system with product cost under the old system. Mott's two products are weed eaters and lawn edgers. The unit prime costs under the old system are as follows:

	Eaters	Edgers
Direct materials	$12	$45
Direct labor	4	30

Under the old manufacturing system, the company operated three service centers and two production departments. Overhead was applied using departmental overhead rates. The direct overhead costs associated with each department for the year preceding the installation of JIT are as follows:

Maintenance	$110,000
Materials handling	90,000
Building and grounds	150,000
Machining	280,000
Assembly	175,000
Total	$805,000

Under the old system, the overhead costs of the service departments were allocated directly to the producing departments and then to the products passing through them. (Both products passed through each producing department.) The overhead rate for the Machining Department was based on machine hours, and the overhead rate for assembly was based on direct labor hours. During the last year of operations for the old system, the Machining Department used 80,000 machine hours, and the Assembly Department used 20,000 direct labor hours. Each weed eater required 1.0 machine hour in Machining and 0.25 direct labor hour in Assembly. Each lawn edger required 2.0 machine hours in Machining and 0.5 hour in Assembly. Bases for allocation of the service costs are as follows:

	Machine Hours	Number of Material Moves	Square Feet of Space
Machining	80,000	90,000	80,000
Assembly	20,000	60,000	40,000
Total	100,000	150,000	120,000

Upon implementing JIT, a manufacturing cell for each product was created to replace the departmental structure. Each cell occupied 40,000 square feet. Maintenance and materials handling were both decentralized to the cell level. Essentially, cell workers were trained to operate the machines in each cell, assemble the components, maintain the machines, and move the partially completed units from one point to the next within the cell. During the first year of the JIT system, the company produced and sold 20,000 weed eaters and 30,000 lawn edgers. This output was identical to that for the last year of operations under the old system. The following costs have been assigned to the manufacturing cells:

	Eater Cell	Edger Cell
Direct materials	$185,000	$1,140,000
Direct labor	66,000	660,000
Direct overhead	99,000	350,500
Allocated overhead*	75,000	75,000
Total	$425,000	$2,225,500

*Building and grounds are allocated on the basis of square footage.

Required:

1. Compute the unit cost for each product under the old manufacturing system.
2. Compute the unit cost for each product under the JIT system.
3. Which of the unit costs is more accurate? Explain. Include in your explanation a discussion of how the computational approaches differ.
4. Calculate the decrease in overhead costs under JIT, and provide some possible reasons that explain the decrease.

Problem 11-31 Backflush Costing, Conversion Rate

OBJECTIVE ◀ 5 6

Southward Company has implemented a JIT flexible manufacturing system. Nia Johnson, controller of the company, has decided to reduce the accounting requirements given the expectation of lower inventories. For one thing, she has decided to treat direct labor cost as a part of overhead and to discontinue the detailed direct labor accounting of the past. The company has created two manufacturing cells, each capable of producing a family of products: the radiator cell and the water pump cell. The output of both cells is sold to a sister division and to customers who use the radiators and water pumps for repair activity. Product-level overhead costs outside the cells are assigned to each cell using appropriate drivers. Facility-level costs are allocated to each cell on the basis of square footage. The budgeted direct labor and overhead costs are as follows:

	Radiator Cell	Water Pump Cell
Direct labor costs	$ 180,000	$ 90,000
Direct overhead	720,000	360,000
Product sustaining	270,000	108,000
Facility level	180,000	90,000
Total conversion cost	$1,350,000	$648,000

The predetermined conversion cost rate is based on available production hours in each cell. The radiator cell has 45,000 hours available for production, and the water pump cell has 27,000 hours. Conversion costs are applied to the units produced by multiplying the conversion rate by the actual time required to produce the units. The radiator cell produced 81,000 units, taking 0.5 hour to produce one unit of product (on average). The water pump cell produced 90,000 units, taking 0.25 hour to produce one unit of product (on average).

Other actual results for the year are as follows:

Direct materials purchased and issued	$1,530,000
Direct labor costs	2,700,000
Overhead	1,890,000

All units produced were sold. Any conversion cost variance is closed to Cost of Goods Sold.

Required:

1. Calculate the predetermined conversion cost rates for each cell.
2. Prepare journal entries using backflush accounting. Assume two trigger points, with completion of goods as the second trigger point.
3. Repeat Requirement 2, assuming that the second trigger point is the sale of the goods.
4. Explain why there is no need to have a work-in-process inventory account.
5. Two variants of backflush costing were presented in which each used two trigger points, with the second trigger point differing. Suppose that the only trigger point for recognizing manufacturing costs occurs when the goods are sold. How would the entries be listed here? When would this backflush variant be considered appropriate?

OBJECTIVE 5 6

Problem 11-32 JIT, Creation of Manufacturing Cells, Behavioral Considerations, Impact on Costing Practices

Reddy Heaters, Inc., produces insert heaters that can be used for various applications, ranging from coffeepots to submarines. Because of the wide variety of insert heaters produced, Reddy uses a job-order costing system. Product lines are differentiated by the size of the heater. In the early stages of the company's history, sales were strong and profits steadily increased. In recent years, however, profits have been declining, and the company has been losing market share. Alarmed by the deteriorating financial position of the company, President Doug Young requested a special study to identify the problems. Sheri Butler, the head of the Internal Audit Department, was put in charge of the study. After two months of investigation, Sheri was ready to report her findings.

SHERI: Doug, I think we have some real concerns that need to be addressed. Production is down, employee morale is low, and the number of defective units that we have to scrap is way up. In fact, over the past several years, our scrap rate has increased from 9 percent to 15 percent of total production. And scrap is expensive. We don't detect defective units until the end of the process. By that time, we lose everything. The nature of the product simply doesn't permit rework.

DOUG: I have a feeling that the increased scrap rate is related to the morale problem you've encountered. Do you have any feel for why morale is low?

SHERI: I get the feeling that boredom is a factor. Many employees don't feel challenged by their work. Also, with the decline in performance, they are receiving more pressure from their supervisors, which simply aggravates the problem.

DOUG: What other problems have you detected?

SHERI: Well, much of our market share has been lost to foreign competitors. The time it takes us to process an order, from time of receipt to delivery, has increased from 20 to 30 days. Some of the customers we have lost have switched to Japanese suppliers, from whom they receive heaters in less than 15 days. Added to this delay in our delivery is an increase in the number of complaints about poorly performing heaters. Our quality has definitely taken a nosedive over the past several years.

DOUG: It's amazing that it has taken us this long to spot these problems. It's incredible to me that the Japanese can deliver a part faster than we can, even in our more efficient days. I wonder what their secret is.

SHERI: I investigated that very issue. It appears that they can produce and deliver their heaters rapidly because they use a JIT purchasing and manufacturing system.

DOUG: Can we use this system to increase our competitive ability?

SHERI: I think so, but we'll need to hire a consultant to tell us how to do it. Also, it might be a good idea to try it out on only one of our major product lines. I suggest the small heater line.

It is having the most problems and has been showing a loss for the past two years. If JIT can restore this line to a competitive mode, then it'll work for the other lines as well.

Within a week, Reddy Heaters hired the services of a large CPA firm. The firm sent Kim Burnham, one of its managers, to do the initial background work. After spending some time at the plant, Kim wrote up the following description of the small heater production process:

The various departments are scattered throughout the factory. Labor is specialized and trained to operate the machines in the respective departments. Additionally, the company has a centralized stores area that provides the raw materials for production, a centralized Maintenance Department that has responsibility for maintaining all production equipment, and a group of laborers responsible for moving the partially completed units from department to department.

Under the current method of production, small heaters pass through several departments, where each department has a collection of similar machines. The first department cuts a metal pipe into one of three lengths: three, four, or five inches long. The cut pipe is then taken to the Laser Department, where the part number is printed on the pipe. In a second department, ceramic cylinders—cut to smaller lengths than the pipe—are wrapped with a fine wire (using a wrapping machine). The pipe and the wrapped ceramic cylinders are then taken to the Welding Department, where the wrapped ceramic cylinders are placed inside the pipe, centered, and filled with a substance that prevents electricity from reaching the metal pipe. Finally, the ends of the pipe are welded shut with two wire leads protruding from one end. This completed heater is then transferred to the Testing Department, which uses special equipment to see if the heater functions properly.

The small heaters are produced in batches of 300. It takes 50 hours to cut 300 metal pipes and prepare 300 ceramic cylinders (1/6 hour per unit, both processes occurring at the same time). After 50 hours of production time, the 300 metal pipes are transported to the Laser Department (20 minutes transport time), and the 300 ceramic cylinders are transported to the Welding Department (20 minutes transport time). In the Laser Department, it takes 50 hours to imprint the part number (1/6 hour per pipe). The 300 metal pipes are then transported to the Welding Department. In the Welding Department, the ceramic and metal pipes are joined and welded. The welding process takes 50 hours (1/6 hour per pipe). Finally, the 300 units are transported (20 minutes) to the Testing Department. Each unit requires 1/6 hour for testing, or a total of 50 hours for the 300 units. From start to finish, the total production time for the 300 units is as follows:

Cutting and ceramic	50 hours
Laser	50
Welding	50
Testing	50
Moving	1
Total time	201 hours

Notice that Laser must wait 50 hours before it can begin imprinting. Similarly, Welding must wait 100 hours before it can begin working on the batch, and finally, Testing must wait 150 hours before it can begin working on the batch.

Based on the information gathered, Kim estimated that the production time for 300 units could be cut from 201 hours to about 50 hours by creating a small heater manufacturing cell.

Required:

1. One of the first actions taken by Reddy Heaters was to organize a manufacturing cell for the small heater line. Describe how you would organize the manufacturing cell. How does it differ from the traditional arrangement? Will any training costs be associated with the transition to JIT? Explain.

2. Explain, with computational support, how the production time for 300 units can be reduced to about 50 hours. If this is a true reduction in production time, what implications does it have for Reddy's competitive position?

3. Describe the organizational and operational activities that must be managed to bring about the reduction in production time. What are the cost drivers associated with these activities? For operational drivers, indicate the expected effect on activity costs.

4. Initially, the employees resented the change to JIT. After a small period of time, however, morale improved significantly. Explain why the change to JIT increased employee morale.

5. Within a few months, Reddy was able to offer a lower price for its small heaters. Additionally, the number of complaints about the performance of the small heaters declined sharply. By the end of the second year, the product line was reporting profits greater than had ever been achieved. Discuss the JIT features that may have made the lower price and higher profits possible.

6. Within a year of the JIT installation, Reddy's controller remarked, "We have a much better idea than ever before of what it is costing us to produce these small insert heaters." Offer some justification for the controller's statement.

7. Discuss the impact that JIT has on other management accounting practices.

12 Activity-Based Management

After studying this chapter, you should be able to:

1 ▸ Describe how activity-based management and activity-based costing differ.

2 ▸ Define process value analysis.

3 ▸ Describe activity-based financial performance measurement.

4 ▸ Discuss the implementation issues associated with an activity-based management system.

5 ▸ Explain how activity-based management is a form of responsibility accounting, and tell how it differs from financial-based responsibility accounting.

USING ACTIVITY MANAGEMENT

at Ipsen Pharma Biotech

Ipsen is a global pharmaceutical group that produces innovative medicines in oncology, neuroscience, and rare diseases. In 2019, Ipsen Group reported over €2.5 billion in revenues and expects to have group sales greater than €2.8 billion in 2022. Ipsen sells more than 22 drugs in over 115 countries.[1] Ipsen Pharma Biotech, located in Signes, France, manufactures drug products and is one of Ipsen's most strategic sites. **Ipsen Pharma Biotech** (Ipsen Signes) produces more than 3.5 million boxes of sterile drug products per year, has about 300 employees, and manufactures two of Ipsen Group's flagship products.[2]

Ipsen Signes began its journey for operational excellence in 2005. In 2020, Ipsen Signes received the Shingo Prize, an award that recognizes organizations that have achieved an exceptional culture, one that excels in fostering continuous improvement. Continuous improvement is a paradigm that requires an organization to constantly search for ways to eliminate non-value-adding activities and improve value-adding activities. The results for Ipsen Signes were increased efficiency, better quality, and less waste. These efforts over a five-year period produced some remarkable results. For example, the cost per unit was reduced by 55 percent, productivity increased by 14 percent, and products produced correctly the first time increased from 72 percent to 97 percent. During this same five-year period, Ipsen Signes has experienced growth of about 45 percent and received about €20 million per year in investment from Ipsen Group to support this growth.[3]

The key to Ipsen Signes' achieving operational excellence was improving its processes, in effect, managing how it performs all the activities found within the organization. However, activities are carried out by people, and so Ipsen Signes had to engage its employees. Employees had to be committed and trained to identify opportunities for improving how activities were being performed. A culture of continuous improvement had to be established. Kaizen is one of the tools used by Ipsen Signes to involve all its employees. Each quarter the company recognizes the best ideal behaviors and kaizen initiatives of its employees. Employee contributions from kaizen, ideas, and projects have produced €10 million in savings over a five-year period.[4] In reality, the culture of continuous improvement achieved by Ipsen Signes touches many areas: employee morale and capabilities, safety, health, environment, quality, productivity, cost, delivery performance, and customer satisfaction.

---

1   Ipsen Press Release, "Ipsen Presents Its 2019 Results, Provides 2020 Guidance and Updates 2022 Financial Outlook," February 13, 2020, https://www.ipsen.com/websites/Ipsen_Online/wp-content/uploads/2020/02/12213006/Ipsen-Full-Year-2019-English-Finale-clear2.pdf, accessed June 9, 2020.
2   https://shingo.org/awards, accessed company profile at https://usu.app.box.com/s/1gdtvopuacjgy7t6bhqk3ysw5ffzigk6 on June 9, 2020.
3   Ibid.
4   Ibid.

Many firms operate in rapidly changing environments. Typically, these firms, like Ipsen, face stiff national and international competition. This stringent competitive environment demands that firms offer customized products and services to diverse customer segments. This, in turn, means that firms must find cost-efficient ways of producing their products. To find ways to improve performance, firms operating in this kind of environment not only must know what it currently *costs* to do things, but, like Ipsen Signes, they must also evaluate *why* and *how* they do things. As the Ipsen Signes experience shows, improving performance translates into constantly searching for ways to eliminate waste—a process known as **continuous improvement**. Activity-based costing and activity-based management are important tools in this ongoing improvement effort.

OBJECTIVE ▶ **1**

Describe how activity-based management and activity-based costing differ.

THE RELATIONSHIP OF ACTIVITY-BASED COSTING AND ACTIVITY-BASED MANAGEMENT

Activity accounting is an essential factor for operationalizing continuous improvement. Processes are the source of many of the improvement opportunities that exist within an organization. Processes are made up of activities that are linked to perform a specific objective. Improving processes means improving the way activities are performed. Thus, management of activities, not costs, is the key to successful control for firms operating in continuous improvement environments. The realization that activities are crucial to both improved product costing and effective control has led to a new view of business processes called activity-based management.

Activity-based management (ABM) is a systemwide, integrated approach that focuses management's attention on activities with the objectives of improving customer value and the profit achieved by providing this value. Activity-based costing (ABC) is the major source of information for activity-based management. Thus, the activity-based management model has two dimensions: a cost dimension and a process dimension. This two-dimensional model is presented in Exhibit 12.1. The cost dimension provides cost information about resources,

Exhibit 12.1

The Two-Dimensional Activity-Based Management Model

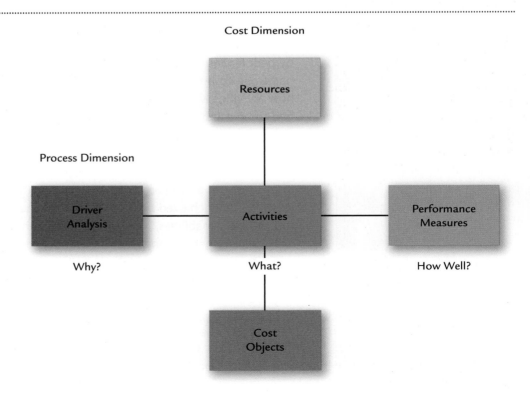

activities, and cost objects of interest such as products, customers, suppliers, and distribution channels. The objective of the cost dimension is improving the accuracy of cost assignments. As the model suggests, the cost of resources is traced to activities, and then the cost of activities is assigned to cost objects. This activity-based costing dimension is useful for product costing, strategic cost management, and tactical analysis. The second dimension, the process dimension, provides information about what activities are performed, why they are performed, and how well they are performed. This dimension's objective is cost reduction. It is this dimension that provides the ability to engage in and measure continuous improvement. To understand how the process view connects with continuous improvement, a more explicit understanding of process value analysis is needed.

PROCESS VALUE ANALYSIS

OBJECTIVE ◀ 2

Define process value analysis.

Process value analysis (PVA) is fundamental to activity-based responsibility accounting, focuses on accountability for activities rather than costs, and emphasizes the maximization of systemwide performance instead of individual performance. It is a powerful data analytic model that focuses on identifying and evaluating activities (descriptive and diagnostic), assessing why they are performed (diagnostic), and measuring how well they are performed (descriptive and prescriptive). Process value analysis moves activity management from a conceptual basis to an operational basis. As the model in Exhibit 12.1 illustrates, process value analysis is concerned with (1) *driver analysis*, (2) *activity analysis*, and (3) *performance measurement*.

Driver Analysis: Defining Root Causes

Managing activities requires an understanding of what factors cause activities to be performed and what causes activity costs to change. Activities consume inputs (resources) and produce outputs. For example, if the activity is maintaining the payroll master file, the resources used would be such things as a payroll clerk, a computer, a printer, computer paper, and disks. The output would be an updated employee file. An **activity output measure** is the number of times the activity is performed. It is the quantifiable measure of the output. For example, the number of employee files maintained is a possible output measure for maintaining the payroll master file.

The output measure calculates the demands placed on an activity and is an *activity driver*. As the demands for an activity change, the cost of the activity can change. For example, as the number of employee files maintained increases, the activity of maintaining the master payroll may need to consume more inputs (labor, disks, paper, and so on). However, output measures (activity drivers), such as the number of files maintained, may not and usually do not correspond to the *root causes* of activity costs; rather, they are the consequences of the activity being performed. The purpose of *driver analysis* is to reveal the root causes. It is diagnostic in nature. Thus, **driver analysis** is the effort expended to identify those factors that are the root causes of activity costs. For example, an analysis may reveal that the root cause of treating and disposing of toxic waste is product design. Once the root cause is known, then action can be taken to improve the activity. Specifically, creating a new product design may reduce or eliminate the cost of treating and disposing of toxic waste.

Often, several activities may have the same root cause. For example, the costs of inspecting incoming components (output measure number of inspection hours) and reordering (output measure number of reorders) may both be caused by poor quality of purchased components. By working with carefully selected suppliers to help them improve their product quality, both activities may be improved. Typically, root causes are identified by asking one or more "why" questions. Example: Why are we inspecting incoming components? Answer: Because some may be defective. Question: Why are we reordering components? Answer: Because some components are judged to be defective by the inspection. Question: Why are some purchased components defective? Answer: Because our suppliers are not providing reliable components.

Once the answers to the why questions are obtained, then the answers to "how" questions are possible. Example: How do we improve the quality of incoming components? Answer: By selecting (or developing) suppliers that provide higher-quality components. The why questions identify the root causes, and the how questions enable management to identify ways to improve.

Activity Analysis: Identifying and Assessing Value Content

The heart of process value analysis is *activity analysis*. **Activity analysis** is the process of identifying, describing, and evaluating the activities an organization performs. Activity analysis should produce four outcomes: (1) what activities are performed, (2) how many people perform the activities, (3) the time and resources required to perform the activities, and (4) an assessment of the value of the activities to the organization, including a recommendation to select and keep only those that add value. Steps 1–3 have been described in Chapter 4. Those steps were critical for assigning costs. Step 4, determining the value-added content of activities, is concerned with cost reduction rather than cost assignment. Thus, this may be considered the most important part of activity analysis. Activities can be classified as *value-added* or *non-value-added*.

Value-Added Activities **Value-added activities** are those activities necessary to remain in business. Value-added activities contribute to customer value and/or help meet an organization's needs. Activities that comply with legal mandates are value-added because they exist to meet organizational needs. Moreover, they add to customer value by allowing the business to continue operating so that the products and services desired by the customer can be obtained. Even though mandated activities are necessary, customers should insist that they be performed as efficiently as possible to reduce the cost impact on goods and services. Examples of mandated activities include those needed to comply with the reporting requirements of the SEC and the filing requirements of the IRS. The remaining activities in the firm are *discretionary*. Classifying discretionary activities as value-added is more of an art than a science and depends heavily on subjective judgment. It is possible, however, to identify three conditions that, if simultaneously met, are sufficient to classify a discretionary activity as value-added. These conditions are as follows: (1) the activity produces a change of state, (2) the change of state was not achievable by preceding activities, and (3) the activity enables other activities to be performed.

For example, consider the production of metal components used in medical equipment. The first activity, gating, creates a wax mold replica of the final product. The next activity, shelling, creates a ceramic shell around the wax mold. After removing the wax, molten metal is poured into the resulting cavity. The shell is then broken to reveal the desired metal component. The gating activity is value-added because (1) it causes a change of state—unformed wax is transformed into a wax mold; (2) no prior activity was supposed to create this change of state; and (3) it enables the shelling activity to be performed. Similar comments hold for the shelling and pouring activities. The value-added properties are easy to see for operational activities like gating and shelling, but what about a more general activity like supervising production workers? A managerial activity is specifically designed to manage other value-added activities—to ensure that they are performed in an efficient and timely manner. Supervision certainly satisfies the enabling condition. Is there a change in state? There are two ways of answering in the affirmative. First, supervising can be viewed as an enabling resource that is consumed by the operational activities that do produce a change of state. Thus, supervising is a secondary activity that serves as an input needed to help bring about the change of state expected for value-added primary activities. Second, it could be argued that the supervision brings order by changing the state from uncoordinated activities to coordinated activities.

Once value-added activities are identified, we can define value-added costs. **Value-added costs** are the costs to perform value-added activities with perfect efficiency. Implicit in this definition is the notion that value-added activities may contain nonessential actions that create unnecessary cost.

Non-Value-Added Activities **Non-value-added activities** are unnecessary and are not valued by internal or external customers. Non-value-added activities often are those that fail to produce a change in state or those that replicate work because it wasn't done correctly the first time. Inspecting wax molds, for example, is a non-value-added activity. Inspection is a *state-detection activity*, not a state-changing activity. (It tells us the state of the mold—whether or not it is of the right shape.) As a general rule, state-detection activities are not value-added. Now, consider the activity of recasting molds that fail inspection. This recasting is designed to bring the mold from a nonconforming state to a conforming state. Thus, a change of state occurs. Yet, the activity is non-value-added because it *repeats* work; it is doing something that should have been done by preceding activities, the first time the wax mold was cast. Thus, it is a *state-correction activity*.

Non-value-added costs are costs that are caused either by non-value-added activities or the inefficient performance of value-added activities. Because of increased competition, many firms are attempting to eliminate non-value-added activities and nonessential portions of value-added activities as they add unnecessary cost and impede performance. Therefore, activity analysis attempts to identify and eventually eliminate all unnecessary activities and, simultaneously, increase the efficiency of necessary activities.

Assessing the value content of activities enables managers to eliminate waste. As waste is eliminated, costs are reduced. Cost reduction *follows* the elimination of waste. Note the value of managing the *causes* of the costs rather than the costs themselves. Increasing the efficiency of a non-value-added activity is not a good long-term strategy. For example, training inspectors in sampling procedures may increase the efficiency of the activity of inspecting incoming components, but it is better to implement a supplier evaluation program that leads to suppliers that provide defect-free components, thus eliminating the need for inspection.

The **University of Minnesota Medical Center, Fairview**, undertook process improvement efforts within its in-patient pharmacy with the objectives of enhancing work-flow, eliminating non-value-added activities, reducing errors and waste, and creating significant savings. The greatest opportunities for improvement were identified in the sterile products and inventory areas. For the sterile products area, data were collected for waste, missing dose, and production errors, while unnecessary moving activities were also identified. Production errors often required rework such as the return of numerous intravenous doses because of outdating or change in dose. Understanding the root causes allowed some activities to be redesigned or improved, while others were eliminated. For the inventory area, installing a double-bin system substantially reduced the time required for the picking activity and also improved the efficiency of the reordering activity. Using first-in, first-out (FIFO) as the inventory flow method for removal and restocking made it easier to reduce waste by avoiding outdated products. The net effect was to produce an estimated annual cost saving of $289,256.[5]

Examples of Non-Value-Added Activities Reordering parts, expediting production, and rework due to defective parts are examples of non-value-added activities. Other examples include warranty work, handling customer complaints, and reporting defects. Non-value-added activities can exist anywhere in the organization. In the manufacturing operation, five major activities are often cited as wasteful and unnecessary, as shown below.

1. *Scheduling.* An activity that uses time and resources to determine when different products have access to processes (or when and how many setups must be done) and how much will be produced.

---

5 Barbara L. Hintzen, Scott J. Knoer, Christie J. Van Dyke, and Brian S. Milavitz, "Effect of Lean Improvement Process Techniques on a University Hospital Inpatient Pharmacy," *American Journal of Health System Pharmacy* (November 15, 2009): 2042–2047.

2. *Moving.* An activity that uses time and resources to move materials, work in process, and finished goods from one department to another.

3. *Waiting.* An activity in which materials or work in process use time and resources by waiting on the next process.

4. *Inspecting.* An activity in which time and resources are spent ensuring that the product meets specifications.

5. *Storing.* An activity that uses time and resources while a good or material is held in inventory.

None of these activities adds any value for the customer. Scheduling, for example, is not necessary if the company has learned how to produce on demand. Similarly, inspecting would not be necessary if the product is produced correctly the first time. The challenge of activity analysis is to find ways to produce the good without using any of these activities.

Cost Reduction through Activity Management   Competitive conditions dictate that companies must deliver products the customers want, on time, and at the lowest possible cost. This means that an organization must continually strive for cost improvement. **Kaizen costing** is characterized by constant, incremental improvements to existing processes and products. Activity management is a fundamental part of kaizen costing. Activity management can reduce costs in four ways:[6]

1. Activity elimination
2. Activity selection
3. Activity reduction
4. Activity sharing

Activity elimination focuses on eliminating non-value-added activities. For example, the activity of expediting production seems necessary at times to ensure that customers' needs are met. Yet, this activity is necessary only because of the company's failure to produce efficiently. By improving cycle time, a company may eventually eliminate the need for expediting. Cost reduction then follows.

Activity selection involves choosing among various sets of activities that are caused by competing strategies. Different strategies cause different activities. Different product design strategies, for example, can require significantly different activities. Activities, in turn, cause costs. Each product design strategy has its own set of activities and associated costs. All other things being equal, the lowest cost design strategy should be chosen. In a kaizen cost framework, *redesign* of existing products and processes can lead to a different, lower cost set of activities. Thus, activity selection can have a significant effect on cost reduction.

Activity reduction decreases the time and resources required by an activity. This approach to cost reduction should be aimed primarily at improving the efficiency of necessary activities or act as a short-term strategy for moving non-value-added activities toward the point of elimination. For example, by improving product quality, customer complaints should decrease and, consequently, the demand for handling customer complaints should decrease.

Activity sharing increases the efficiency of necessary activities by using economies of scale. Specifically, the quantity of the cost driver is increased without increasing the total cost of the activity itself. This lowers the per-unit cost of the cost driver and the amount of cost traceable to the products that consume the activity. For example, a new product can be designed to use components already being used by other products. By using existing components, the activities associated with these components already occur, and the company avoids the creation of a whole new set of activities.

---

6   Peter B. B. Turney, "How Activity-Based Costing Helps Reduce Cost," *Journal of Cost Management* (Winter 1991): 29–35.

Sustainability

Activity selection can reduce costs by selecting from different sets of activities caused by competing strategies. Activity selection can not only reduce the costs of the activities but also reduce the environmental impacts. For example, Dow Chemical Company has a major chemical processing company in the Netherlands in the city of Terneuzen. For Dow Terneuzen, fresh water is an important manufacturing input. Although Terneuzen is surrounded on three sides by water, fresh water is scarce because the local aquifers are brackish as a result of their tendency to be shallow and contaminated by sea water. Thus, fresh water has to be imported to meet the needs for potable water as well as industrial use. Initially, Dow Terneuzen operated a plant to desalinate the brackish water, but this approach was costly both economically and environmentally.

In 2007, Dow partnered with the municipal water board and Evides, a local water company, to implement a new integrated water management system. Dow now takes the city's treated waste water (which previously was discharged into a river) and uses it twice. First, water is used as steam for its production plants, and second, the water is used again in cooling towers, where it is released into the atmosphere as a vapor. Compared with the desalinization approach, this integrated system has reduced Dow's energy usage by 95 percent and reduced carbon dioxide emissions by about 60,000 tons per year.[7]

REAL-WORLD EXAMPLE

Assessing Activity Performance

Activity performance measurement is designed to assess how well an activity was performed and the results achieved. Measures of activity performance are both financial and nonfinancial and center on three major dimensions: (1) efficiency, (2) quality, and (3) time. *Efficiency* is concerned with the relationship of activity outputs to activity inputs. For example, activity efficiency is improved by producing the same activity output with fewer inputs. Costs trending downward is evidence that activity efficiency is improving. *Quality* is concerned with doing the activity right the first time it is performed. If the activity output is defective, then the activity may need to be repeated, causing unnecessary cost and reduction in efficiency. The *time* required to perform an activity is also critical. Longer times usually mean more resource consumption and less ability to respond to customer demands. Time measures of performance tend to be non-financial, whereas efficiency and quality measures are both financial and nonfinancial.

FINANCIAL MEASURES OF ACTIVITY EFFICIENCY

OBJECTIVE **3**

Describe activity-based financial performance measurement.

Assessing activity performance should reveal the current level of efficiency and the potential for increased efficiency. Both financial and nonfinancial measures are used to reveal past performance and signal future potential gains in efficiency. Financial measures of activity performance are emphasized in this chapter, and nonfinancial measures are discussed in Chapter 13. **Financial measures** of performance should provide specific information about the dollar effects of activity performance changes. Thus, financial measures should indicate both potential and actual savings. Financial measures of activity efficiency include (1) value-added and non-value-added activity costs, (2) trends in activity costs, (3) kaizen standard setting, (4) benchmarking, (5) activity flexible budgeting, and (6) activity capacity management.

---

7 Cornelis Groot, "Fresh Thinking to Improve Business and Sustainability," *World Water*, May–June 2013, http://www .dow.com/scripts/litorder.asp?filepath=liquidseps/pdfs/noreg/609-50111.pdf&pdf=true

Reporting Value- and Non-Value-Added Costs

Reducing non-value-added costs is one way to increase activity efficiency. A company's accounting system should distinguish between value-added costs and non-value-added costs because improving activity performance requires eliminating non-value-added activities and optimizing value-added activities. A firm should identify and formally report the value- and non-value-added costs of each activity. Highlighting non-value-added costs reveals the magnitude of the waste the company is currently experiencing, thus providing some information about the potential for improvement. This encourages managers to place more emphasis on controlling non-value-added activities. Progress can then be assessed by preparing trend and cost reduction reports. Tracking these costs over time permits managers to assess the effectiveness of their activity management programs.

Knowing the amount of costs saved is important for strategic purposes. For example, if an activity is eliminated, then the costs saved should be traceable to individual products. These savings can produce price reductions for customers, making the firm more competitive. Changing the pricing strategy, however, requires knowledge of the cost reductions realized by activity analysis. A cost-reporting system, therefore, is an important ingredient in an activity-based responsibility accounting system.

Value-added costs are the only costs that an organization should incur. The *value-added standard* calls for the complete elimination of non-value-added activities; for these activities, the optimal output is zero, with zero cost. The value-added standard also calls for the complete elimination of the inefficiency of activities that are necessary but inefficiently carried out. Hence, value-added activities also have an optimal output level. A **value-added standard**, therefore, identifies the optimal activity output. Identifying the optimal activity output requires activity output measurement.

Setting value-added standards does not mean that they will be (or should be) achieved immediately. The idea of continuous improvement is to move toward the ideal. Workers (teams) can be rewarded for improvement. Moreover, nonfinancial activity performance measures can be used to supplement and support the goal of eliminating non-value-added costs (these are discussed later in the chapter). Finally, measuring the efficiency of individual workers and supervisors is not the way to eliminate non-value-added activities. Remember, activities cut across departmental boundaries and are part of processes. Focusing on activities and providing incentives to improve processes is a more productive approach. Improving the process should lead to improved results.

By comparing actual activity costs with value-added activity costs, management can assess the level of activity inefficiency and the potential for improvement. To identify and calculate value- and non-value-added costs, output measures for each activity must be defined. Once output measures are defined, then value-added standard quantities (SQ) for each activity can be defined. Value-added costs can be computed by multiplying the value-added standard quantities by the price standard (SP). Non-value-added costs can be calculated as the difference between the actual level of the activity's output (AQ) and the value-added level (SQ), multiplied by the standard price. These formulas are presented in Exhibit 12.2. Some further explanation is needed.

For flexible resources (resources acquired as needed), AQ is the actual quantity of activity used. For committed resources (resources acquired in advance of usage), AQ represents the actual quantity of activity capacity acquired, as measured by the activity's practical capacity. This definition of AQ allows the computation of non-value-added costs for both variable and fixed activity costs. For fixed activity costs, SP is the budgeted activity costs divided by AQ, where AQ is practical activity capacity. **Example 12.1** illustrates the power of these concepts.

Notice from the information in Example 12.1 that the value-added standards (SQ) for inspection and grinding call for their elimination. Ideally, there should be no defective molds; by improving quality, changing production processes, and so on, inspection and grinding can eventually be eliminated. The cost report of Example 12.1 allows managers to see the non-value-added costs; as a consequence, it emphasizes the opportunity for improvement. By redesigning the products and reducing the number of parts required, purchase time can be reduced. By improving the molding process and labor skill, management can reduce the demands for molding time, inspection, and grinding. Thus, reporting value- and non-value-added costs at a point in time may trigger actions to manage activities more effectively. Once

$$\text{Value-added costs} = SQ \times SP$$

$$\text{Non-value-added costs} = (AQ - SQ)SP$$

where

SQ = The value-added output level for an activity

SP = The standard price per unit of activity output measure

AQ = The actual quantity used of flexible resources or the practical
activity capacity acquired for committed resources

Exhibit 12.2

Formulas for Value- and Non-Value-Added Costs

EXAMPLE 12.1

The HOW and WHY of Value- and Non-Value-Added Cost Reporting

Information:

A manufacturing firm has four activities: purchasing materials, molding, inspecting molds, and grinding imperfect molds. Purchasing and molding are necessary activities; inspection and grinding are unnecessary. The following data pertain to the four activities for the year ending 20x1 (actual price per unit of the activity driver is assumed to be equal to the standard price):

Activity	Activity Driver	SQ	AQ	SP
Purchasing	Purchasing hours	20,000	24,000	$20
Molding	Molding hours	30,000	34,000	12
Inspecting	Inspection hours	0	6,000	15
Grinding	Number of units	0	5,000	6

> **Why:**
> A cost report that shows value and non-value-added costs allows managers to see the amount of waste, assess its materiality, and identify opportunities for improvement.

Required:

1. Prepare a cost report for the year ending 20x1 that shows value-added costs, non-value-added costs, and total costs for each activity.

2. Explain why inspection and grinding are non-value-added activities.

3. *What if* purchasing cost is a step-fixed cost with each step being 2,000 hours, whereas molding cost is a variable cost? What is the implication for reducing the cost of waste for each activity?

Solution:

1.

Value- and Non-Value-Added Cost Report for the Year Ended 20x1

Activity	Value-Added Costs	Non-Value-Added Costs	Total Costs
Purchasing	$400,000	$ 80,000	$ 480,000
Molding	360,000	48,000	408,000
Inspecting	0	90,000	90,000
Grinding	0	30,000	30,000
Total	$760,000	$248,000	$1,008,000

EXAMPLE 12.1

(Continued)

2. Inspection is a state-detection activity, and grinding is a state-correction activity.

3. For purchasing, cost reduction occurs only when the actual demand for purchasing hours is reduced by each block of 2,000 hours. For molding, each hour saved produces a savings of $12. Accordingly, cost savings will likely materialize more quickly for molding than for purchasing.

they see the amount of waste, managers may be induced to search for ways to improve activities and bring about cost reductions. Reporting these costs may also help managers improve planning, budgeting, and pricing decisions. For example, a manager might consider it possible to lower a selling price to meet a competitor's price if that manager can see the potential for reducing non-value-added costs to absorb the effect of the price reduction.

Trend Reporting of Non-Value-Added Costs

As managers take actions to improve activities, do the cost reductions follow as expected? One way to answer this question is to compare the costs for each activity over time. The goal is activity improvement as measured by cost reduction. We should see a decline in non-value-added costs from one period to the next—provided the activity improvement initiatives are effective. The trend report will also reveal the amount of cost reduction still available. Cost reduction for value-added activities focuses on increasing the efficiency of these activities, while the cost reduction goal for non-value-added activities is their eventual elimination. **Example 12.2** provides an illustration of trend reporting of non-value-added costs.

EXAMPLE 12.2

The HOW and WHY of Non-Value-Added Cost Trend Reporting

Information:
See the information for Example 12.1. Assume that at the beginning of 20x2, the molding process was redesigned and the employees in Molding were trained in a new work technique. By reducing the number of bad molds, the firm hoped to significantly reduce waste for all four activities. Purchasing and Inspecting resources are purchased in steps of 2,000 hours. The other two activities are acquired as used and needed. At the end of 20x2, the following results were reported for the four activities:

Activity	Activity Driver	SQ	AQ	SP
Purchasing	Purchasing hours	20,000	22,000	$20
Molding	Molding hours	30,000	32,000	12
Inspecting	Inspection hours	0	2,000	15
Grinding	Number of units	0	2,500	6

Why:
Comparing changes in non-value-added costs over time reveals where cost reductions have been achieved, allows managers to assess the effectiveness of improvement measures undertaken, and shows how much improvement potential still remains.

Required:

1. Prepare a trend report that shows the non-value-added costs for each activity for 20x1 and 20x2 and the change in costs for the two periods. Discuss the report's implications.

2. Explain the role of activity reduction for both value-added activities and non-value-added activities.

EXAMPLE 12.2

(Continued)

3. ***What if*** at the end of 20x2, the selling price of a competing product is reduced by $10 per unit? Assume that the firm produces and sells 10,000 units of its product and that its product is associated only with the four activities being considered. By virtue of the waste-reduction savings, can the competitor's price reduction be matched without reducing the unit profit margin of the product that prevailed at the beginning of the year?

Solution:

1.

Trend Report: Non-Value-Added Costs

Activity	20x1	20x2*	Change
Purchasing	$ 80,000	$ 40,000	$ 40,000
Molding	48,000	24,000	24,000
Inspecting	90,000	30,000	60,000
Grinding	30,000	15,000	15,000
Total	$248,000	$109,000	$139,000

*Since the reductions for the purchasing and inspection were in multiples of 2,000, the cost savings is simply *SP* multiplied by the reduction in *AQ*.

The trend report shows a significant reduction in non-value-added costs, validating the improvement actions taken.

2. For value-added activities, the non-value-added component is usually the result of using more of the activity than should be used; thus, activity reduction is the objective for improving activity efficiency. For non-value-added activities, activity reduction is an intermediate step that ultimately will lead to activity elimination. Depending on the nature of the resources consumed by the activity, activity reduction can also lead to cost reductions.

3. From Requirement 1, the savings per unit of product are $13.90 ($139,000/10,000), indicating that the competitor's price reduction can be matched (or beat) without changing the unit profit margin that existed at the beginning of the year.

The trend report in Example 12.2 reveals that more than half of the non-value-added costs have been eliminated. It also reveals that there is still ample room for improvement, but activity improvement so far has been successful. Reporting non-value-added costs, however, not only reveals cost reduction but also indicates where the reduction occurred. It provides managers with information on how much potential for cost reduction remains, assuming that the value-added standards remain the same. Value-added standards, however, like other standards, are not cast in stone. New technology, new designs, and other innovations can change the nature of activities performed. As new ways for improvement surface, value-added standards can change. Managers should not become content but should continually seek higher levels of efficiency.

Drivers and Behavioral Effects

Activity output measures are needed to compute and track non-value-added costs. Reducing a non-value-added activity should produce a reduction in the demand for the activity and, therefore, a reduction in the activity output measures. If a team's performance is affected by its ability to reduce non-value-added costs, then the selection of activity drivers (as output measures) and the way the drivers are used can affect behavior. For example, if the output measure for setup costs is chosen as setup time, an incentive is created for workers to reduce setup time. Since the value-added standard for setup costs calls for their complete elimination, then the incentive to drive setup time to zero is compatible with the company's objectives, and the induced behavior is beneficial.

Suppose, however, that the objective is to reduce the number of unique parts a company processes, thus reducing the demand for activities such as purchasing and incoming inspection. If the costs of these activities are assigned to products based on the number of parts, the incentive created is to reduce the number of parts in a product. Yet, if too many parts are eliminated, the functionality of the product may be reduced to a point where its marketability is adversely affected. Identifying the value-added standard number of parts for each product through the use of functional analysis can discourage this type of behavior.[8] Designers can then be encouraged to reduce the non-value-added costs by designing to reach the value-added standard number of parts. The standard has provided a concrete objective and defined the kind of behavior that the incentive allows.

The Role of Kaizen Standards

Kaizen costing is concerned with reducing costs by identifying small, continuous improvements for *existing* products and processes. In operational terms, this translates into reducing non-value-added costs. Controlling this cost reduction process is accomplished through the repetitive use of two major subcycles: (1) the kaizen or continuous improvement cycle, and (2) the maintenance cycle. The kaizen subcycle is defined by a Plan-Do-Check-Act sequence. If a company is emphasizing the reduction of non-value-added costs, the amount of improvement planned for the coming period (month, quarter, etc.) is set (the *Plan* step). A **kaizen standard** reflects the planned improvement for the upcoming period. The planned improvement is assumed to be attainable, and kaizen standards are a type of currently attainable standard. Actions are taken to implement the planned improvements (the *Do* step). Next, actual results (e.g., costs) are compared with the kaizen standard to provide a measure of the level of improvement attained (the *Check* step). Setting this new level as a minimum standard for future performance locks in the realized improvements and simultaneously initiates the maintenance cycle and a search for additional improvement opportunities (the *Act* step). The maintenance cycle follows a traditional Establish-Do-Check-Act sequence. A standard is set based on prior improvements (locking in these improvements). Next, actions are taken (the *Do* step) and the results checked to ensure that performance conforms to this new level (the *Check* step). If not, then corrective actions are taken to restore performance (the *Act* step). The kaizen cost reduction process is summarized in Exhibit 12.3. **Example 12.3** demonstrates an application of kaizen costing.

An important tool in the process of using kaizen for workplace organization and improvement is referred to as a kaizen 5S analysis. "5S" stands for sort, set in order, sweep, standardize, and sustain. Sorting means eliminating all unnecessary activities and resources. The sorting step is the source of planned improvements. Setting in order means that resources needed for carrying out the planned work activities are located so that they are easily accessible and avoid unnecessary movement. The governing principle is "a place for everything and everything in its place." Sweep (or straighten) means to keep the work area clean and organized. Standardizing is the "locking-in" of the best practices. Sustaining simply means that the new way of operating must be maintained, avoiding any regression to old practices. Clearly, locking in new practices requires that they be sustainable. Canon, for example, uses both kaizen and kaizen 5S. Other companies that use kaizen include Toyota, Nestlé, and Lockheed Martin.[9]

---

8 Functional analysis compares the price customers are willing to pay for a particular product function with the cost of providing that function.

9 Keith Breen, "East Meets West: What Can Western Managers Learn from Their Japanese Colleagues?" *Forbes*, January 30, 2018, https://www.forbes.com/sites/mitsubishiheavyindustries/2018/01/30/east-meets-west-what-can-western-managers-learn-from-their-japanese-colleagues/?utm_source=FBPAGE&utm_medium=social&utm_content=1364351233&utm_campaign=sprinklrForbesMainFB#31c476de5407, accessed June 10, 2020.

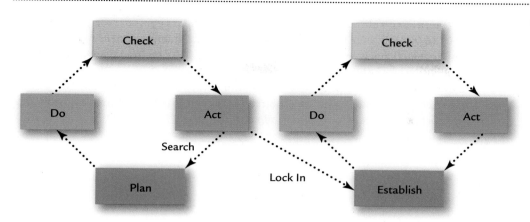

Exhibit 12.3

Kaizen Cost Reduction Process

EXAMPLE 12.3

The HOW and WHY of Kaizen Costing

Information:

An automotive parts division has a grinding activity for the subassemblies that it produces. Activity output is measured using grinding hours. The value-added standard (SQ) for this activity is zero grinding hours. On January 1, at the beginning of the fiscal year, eight grinding hours were allowed per batch (which almost always corresponded to the actual grinding hours used). The standard wage rate is $18 per grinding hour. During January, a new procedure for production of the subassemblies was developed with the expectation that the demand for grinding would be reduced by 25 percent. The new procedure was implemented in February and expectations concerning the effect on the grinding activity were met.

Why:

Kaizen costing has the objective of continuously improving the efficiency of activities and processes. It can be characterized as a *dynamic* standard costing system. Maintenance standards are revised based on achieved, sustainable improvements produced by the kaizen subcycle.

Required:

1. What is the maintenance standard for grinding hours and the associated expected cost at the beginning of February? The kaizen standard and expected associated cost?

2. What is the maintenance standard for grinding hours and the associated cost at the end of February? Explain. What is the next step in the kaizen cost reduction process?

3. *What if* the new procedure implemented in February produced a 20 percent reduction instead of a 25 percent reduction? What would the new maintenance standard and cost be?

Solution:

1. Maintenance standard: 8 hours per batch; expected cost per batch: $144 (8 × $18); kaizen standard: 6 hours per batch (0.75 × 8); and expected cost per batch: $108 (6 × $18).

EXAMPLE 12.3

(Continued)

2. Maintenance standard: 6 hours per batch; and expected cost per batch: $108 (6 × $18). After determining that the suggested improvement works and is sustainable, the new level of performance is locked in by revising the maintenance standard from eight hours to six hours. The next step is to search for another improvement opportunity that will then produce a new kaizen standard and expected batch cost. The ultimate objective is to eliminate all the non-value-added cost through a series of kaizen improvements.

3. You lock in the level actually achieved by the suggested improvement approach. In this case, the maintenance standard would be 6.4 hours (0.80 × 8) and the standard batch cost $115.20 (6.4 × $18).

Big Data

Kaizen costing is characterized by identifying small, continuous improvements for products or processes. Big data sets and advanced analytics can significantly enhance kaizen efforts. This may involve, for example, the setup of special data-optimization labs or cells within the operating units. This entails creating small teams of employees skilled in operations research and statistical methods and, of course, access to big data.

For example, statisticians in a steel company analyzed historical data of an important process and were able to recognize that the process suffered from multiple bottlenecks, which changed according to differing conditions. They discovered that although one part of the process caused problems 60 percent of the time, there were two other parts that could also adversely affect output. Armed with this information, they made some changes that improved the availability of three key pieces of equipment, resulting in a 20 percent increase in throughput and a savings of more than $50 million.[10]

Benchmarking

Benchmarking is complementary to kaizen costing and activity-based management, and it can be used as a search mechanism to identify opportunities for improvement. **Benchmarking** uses best practices found within and outside the organization as the standard for evaluating and improving activity performance. The objective of benchmarking is to become the best at performing activities and processes (thus, benchmarking represents an important activity management methodology). The approach certainly seems to have considerable merit. For example, an APQC study revealed that benchmarking returns ranged from $1.5 million to $189.4 million.[11] Interestingly, there was a direct correlation between the level of return and the degree of senior management support.

Internal Benchmarking   Benchmarking against internal operations is called *internal benchmarking.* Within an organization, different units (e.g., different plant sites) that perform the same activities are compared. The unit with the best performance for a given activity sets the standard. Other units then have a target to meet or exceed. Furthermore, the best practices unit can share information with other units on how it has achieved its superior results. Internal

10   Rajat Dhawan, Kunwar Singh, and Ashish Tuteja, "When Big Data Goes Lean," *McKinsey Quarterly*, February 2014, http://www.mckinsey.com/business-functions/operations/our-insights/when-big-data-goes-lean, accessed May 23, 2016.

11   Kate Vitasek and Karl Mandrodt, *Benchmarking: Prerequisite for Best-In-Class Supply Chains*, an APQC white paper (see knowledge base section) (February 5, 2007), http://www.apqc.org/portal/apqc/ksn?paf_gear _id=contentgearhome&paf_dm=full&pageselect=detail&docid=129520, accessed May 27, 2009.

benchmarking has several advantages. First, a significant amount of information is often readily available that can be shared throughout the organization. Second, immediate cost reductions are often realized. Third, the best internal standards that spread throughout the organization become the benchmark for comparison against external benchmarking partners. This last advantage also suggests the major disadvantage of internal benchmarking. Specifically, the best internal performance may fall short of what others are doing, particularly direct competitors.

There are numerous examples of the benefits of internal benchmarking.[12] Thomson Corporation collected and broadcast best practices through internal benchmarking throughout the company and saved $200 million in one year. Chevron saved $150 million by transferring energy use management techniques throughout the company. Public Service Enterprise Group used internal benchmarking to improve the process for ripping up a street, repairing a line, backfilling the hole, and repaving the area. The improvement dropped costs from an average of $2,200 to just $200 per incident.

External Benchmarking Benchmarking that involves comparison with others outside the organization is called *external benchmarking*. The three types of external benchmarking are competitive benchmarking, functional benchmarking, and generic benchmarking. Competitive benchmarking is a comparison of activity performance with direct competitors. The main problem with competitive benchmarking is that it is very difficult to obtain information beyond that found in the public domain. At times, however, it is possible. The Ritz-Carlton, for example, dramatically improved its housekeeping process by studying the best practices of a competitor.[13] Functional benchmarking is a comparison with firms that are in the same industry but do not compete in the same markets. For example, a Japanese communications firm might be able to compare its customer service process with that of AT&T. Generic benchmarking studies the best practices of noncompetitors outside a firm's industry. Certain activities and processes are common to all organizations. If superior external best practices can be identified, then they can be used as standards to motivate internal improvements. For example, Verizon improved its field service process by studying the field service process of an elevator company.[14]

Activity Flexible Budgeting

The ability to identify changes in activity costs as activity output changes allows managers to more carefully plan and monitor activity improvements. **Activity flexible budgeting** is the prediction of what activity costs will be as activity output changes. Variance analysis within an activity framework makes it possible to improve traditional budgetary performance reporting. It also enhances the ability to manage activities.

In a unit-based approach, budgeted costs for the actual level of activity are obtained by assuming that a single unit-based driver (units of product or direct labor hours) drives all costs. A cost formula is developed for each cost item as a function of units produced or direct labor hours. Exhibit 12.4 presents a unit-based flexible budget based on direct labor hours. If, however, costs vary with respect to more than one driver and the drivers are not highly correlated with direct labor hours, then the predicted costs can be misleading.

The solution, of course, is to build flexible budget formulas for more than one driver. Cost estimation procedures (high-low method, the method of least squares, and so on) can be used to estimate and validate the cost formulas for each activity. This multiple cost-formula approach allows managers to predict more accurately what costs should be for different levels of activity usage, as measured by the activity output measure. These costs can then be compared with the actual costs to help assess budgetary performance. Exhibit 12.5 provides an example of an activity flexible budget. Notice that the budgeted amounts for direct materials and direct

---

12 Frank Jossi, "Take a Peek Inside," *HRMagazine* (June 2002): 46–52.
13 Robert C. Camp, *Business Process Benchmarking* (Milwaukee, WI: ASQC Quality Press, 1995): 273.
14 Ibid.

Exhibit 12.4

Flexible Budget: Direct Labor Hours

	Cost Formula		Direct Labor Hours	
	Fixed	**Variable**	**10,000**	**20,000**
Direct materials	—	$10	$100,000	$200,000
Direct labor	—	8	80,000	160,000
Maintenance	$ 20,000	3	50,000	80,000
Machining	15,000	1	25,000	35,000
Inspections	120,000	—	120,000	120,000
Setups	50,000	—	50,000	50,000
Purchasing	220,000	—	220,000	220,000
Total	$425,000	$22	$645,000	$865,000

Exhibit 12.5

Activity Flexible Budget

DRIVER: DIRECT LABOR HOURS

	Formula		Level of Activity	
	Fixed	**Variable**	**10,000**	**20,000**
Direct materials	—	$10	$100,000	$200,000
Direct labor	—	8	80,000	160,000
Subtotal	—	$18	$180,000	$360,000

DRIVER: MACHINE HOURS

	Fixed	**Variable**	**8,000**	**16,000**
Maintenance	$20,000	$5.50	$64,000	$108,000
Machining	15,000	2.00	31,000	47,000
Subtotal	$35,000	$7.50	$95,000	$155,000

DRIVER: NUMBER OF SETUPS

	Fixed	**Variable**	**25**	**30**
Inspections	$80,000	$2,100	$132,500	$143,000
Setups	—	1,800	45,000	54,000
Subtotal	$80,000	$3,900	$177,500	$197,000

DRIVER: NUMBER OF ORDERS

	Fixed	**Variable**	**15,000**	**25,000**
Purchasing	$211,000	$1	$226,000	$236,000
Total			$678,500	$948,000

labor are the same as those reported in Exhibit 12.4; they use the same activity output measure. The budgeted amounts for the other items differ significantly from the traditional amounts because the activity output measures differ.

Assume that the first activity level for each driver in Exhibit 12.5 corresponds to the actual activity usage levels. Exhibit 12.6 compares the budgeted costs for the actual activity usage levels with the actual costs. One item is on target, and the other six items are mixed. The net outcome is a favorable variance of $21,500.

The performance report in Exhibit 12.6 compares total budgeted costs for the actual level of activity with the total actual costs for each activity. It is also possible to compare the actual fixed activity costs with the budgeted fixed activity costs, and the actual variable activity costs with the budgeted variable costs. Moreover, Exhibit 12.5 presents the budget formulas for each

	Actual Costs	Budgeted Costs	Budget Variance
Direct materials	$101,000	$100,000	$ 1,000 U
Direct labor	80,000	80,000	—
Maintenance	55,000	64,000	9,000 F
Machining	29,000	31,000	2,000 F
Inspections	125,500	132,500	7,000 F
Setups	46,500	45,000	1,500 U
Purchasing	220,000	226,000	6,000 F
Total	$657,000	$678,500	$21,500 F

Exhibit 12.6

Activity-Based Performance Report*

* Activity levels of drivers: 10,000 direct labor hours, 8,000 machine hours, 25 setups, and 15,000 orders.

activity without any indication of how these formulas can be derived. **Example 12.4** demonstrates how an activity-based flexible budget formula can be derived and then used for performance reporting with a detailed breakdown of fixed and variable activity costs.

EXAMPLE 12.4

The HOW and WHY of Activity-Based Flexible Budgeting

Information:

Thomas Company has a "maintaining equipment" activity and wants to develop a flexible budget formula for the activity. The following resources are used by the activity:

- Three portable diagnostic units, with a lease cost of $8,000 per year per unit
- Three maintenance personnel each paid a salary of $45,000 per year (A total of 6,000 maintenance hours are supplied by the three workers.)
- Parts and supplies: $100 per diagnosis
- Maintenance hours: Four hours used per diagnosis

During the year, the activity operated at 80 percent of capacity and incurred the following actual activity and resource costs:

- Lease cost: $24,000
- Salaries: $145,000
- Parts and supplies: $135,000

Why:

The variable cost component for each activity corresponds to resources acquired as needed (flexible resources), and the fixed cost component corresponds to resources acquired in advance of usage (committed resources). Performance reporting compares the actual activity costs with the costs budgeted for the actual activity level (for a given time period).

Required:

1. Prepare a flexible budget formula for the maintenance activity using maintenance hours as the driver.

2. Prepare a performance report for the maintenance activity.

3. *What if* maintenance workers were hired through outsourcing and paid $20 per hour (the diagnostic units are still leased by Thomas)? Repeat Requirement 1 for the outsourcing case.

EXAMPLE 12.4

(Continued)

Solution:

1. Acquired in advance of usage:

Diagnostic equipment	$ 24,000 (3 × $8,000)
Maintenance workers	135,000 (3 × $45,000)
Total fixed costs	$159,000

Acquired as needed:

Parts and supplies: $100/4 = $25 per maintenance hour (X)

Formula: Maintenance cost = $159,000 + $25X$

2.

Activity-Based Performance Report

Activity	Actual Cost	Budgeted Cost (80% level)*	Budget Variance
Maintenance:			
Fixed cost	$169,000	$159,000	$10,000 U
Variable cost	135,000	120,000	15,000 U

* $159,000 (fixed); $25 × 0.80 × 6,000 (variable)

3. Maintenance cost = $24,000 + $45X$ (The cost of diagnostic equipment is fixed; the variable cost is the $20 per hour of contract labor plus the $25 per hour for parts and supplies.)

As Example 12.4 shows, breaking each variance into fixed and variable components provides more insight into the source of the variation in planned and actual expenditures. Activity budgets also provide valuable information about capacity usage.

Activity Capacity Management

Activity capacity is the number of times an activity can be performed. Activity drivers measure activity capacity. For example, consider inspecting finished goods as the activity. A sample from each batch is taken to determine the batch's overall quality. The demand for the inspection activity determines the amount of activity capacity that is required. For instance, suppose that the number of batches inspected measures activity output. Now, suppose that 60 batches are scheduled to be produced. Then, the required capacity is 60 batches. Finally, assume that a single inspector can inspect 20 batches per year. Thus, three inspectors must be hired to provide the necessary capacity. If each inspector is paid a salary of $40,000, the budgeted cost of the activity capacity is $120,000. This is the cost of the resources (labor) acquired in advance of usage. The budgeted activity rate is $2,000 per batch ($120,000/60).

Several questions relate to activity capacity and its cost. First, what *should* the activity capacity be? The answer to this question provides the ability to measure the amount of improvement possible. Second, how much of the capacity acquired was actually used? The answer to this question signals a nonproductive cost and, at the same time, an opportunity for capacity reduction and cost savings.

Capacity Variances   To determine the potential for improvement and the progress made in the objective of eliminating waste, two capacity variances are defined and calculated: the *activity volume variance* and the *unused capacity variance*. The **activity volume variance** is the difference between the actual activity level acquired (practical capacity, AQ) and the value-added standard quantity of activity that should be used (SQ), multiplied by the budgeted activity rate (SP):

$$\text{Activity volume variance} = (AQ - SQ)\,SP$$

The volume variance in this framework has a useful economic interpretation: it is the non-value-added cost of the inspection activity. It measures the amount of improvement that is possible through analysis and management of activities. Since the supply of the activity must be acquired in advance of usage (usually in blocks or steps, for example, one inspector at a time), however, it is also important to measure the current demand for the activity (actual usage). If AQ is more than SQ ($AQ > SQ$), then the variance is unfavorable (indicating that non-value-added cost is present).

When supply exceeds demand by a large enough quantity, management can take action to reduce the quantity of the activity provided. Thus, the **unused capacity variance** is defined as the difference between activity availability (AQ) and activity usage (AU), multiplied by the budgeted activity rate (SP):

$$\text{Unused capacity variance} = (AU - AQ)\,SP$$

The unused capacity variance is important information that should be provided to management. The goal is to reduce the demand for the activity until such time as the unused capacity variance equals the volume variance. Why? Because the volume variance is a non-value-added cost and the unused activity variance measures the progress made in reducing this non-value-added cost. Thus, the variance is labeled as favorable. **Example 12.5** shows the calculation and usage of the two capacity variances.

EXAMPLE 12.5

The HOW and WHY of Activity Capacity Management

Information:

Inspecting finished goods is the activity. Activity output is measured by inspection hours. The following data pertain to the activity for the most recent year:

Activity supply: 6,000 hours (three inspectors @ 2,000 hours per year)

Inspector cost (salary): $40,000 per year

Actual usage: 4,500 inspection hours

> **Why:**
> The volume variance measures the non-value-added cost of the activity, and the unused capacity variance measures the progress toward reducing the activity waste. Knowing these two variances is valuable information for managing activity capacity.

Required:

1. Calculate the volume variance and explain its significance.

2. Calculate the unused capacity variance and explain its use.

3. *What if* the actual usage is 3,500 hours? What effect will this have on capacity management?

Solution:

1. Inspection generally is classified as a non-value-added activity. Thus,

    $$\begin{aligned} \text{Volume variance} &= (AQ - SQ)\,SP \\ &= (6,000 - 0)\,\$20^* \\ &= \$120,000\ \text{U} \end{aligned}$$

    *Activity rate = ($40,000 × 3)/6,000

    The volume variance is a measure of the non-value-added cost. In this case, the entire cost of the activity is non-value-added. Management should strive to find ways to reduce and eventually eliminate the activity.

EXAMPLE 12.5

(Continued)

2. Unused capacity variance $= (AU - AQ)\,SP$
    $= (4{,}500 - 6{,}000)\,\$20$
    $= \$30{,}000\ F$

The demand for the activity has been reduced; however, the reduction is not sufficient to produce a reduction in activity spending.

3. Recalculating the unused capacity variance:
    Unused capacity variance $= (AU - AQ)\,SP$
    $= (3{,}500 - 6{,}000)\,\$20$
    $= \$50{,}000\ F$

At this level of demand, only two inspectors are needed to meet the demand; thus, resource spending can be reduced by $40,000.

In Example 12.5, we know that the supply of inspection resources is greater than its usage. Assume that this unused capacity exists because management has been engaged in a quality-improvement program that has reduced the need to inspect certain batches of products. When the cost of unused capacity reaches $40,000, this difference between the supply of the inspection resources and their usage should impact future spending plans. Furthermore, because of the quality-improvement program, we can expect this difference to persist and even become greater (with the ultimate goal of reducing the cost of inspection activity to zero). Management now must be willing to exploit the unused capacity it has created. Essentially, when the savings reach the price of one inspector, activity availability can be reduced; thus, the spending on inspection can be decreased. A manager can use several options to achieve this outcome. When the inspection demand has been reduced to at most 4,000 hours, the company needs only two full-time inspectors. The extra inspector could be permanently reassigned to an activity where resources are in short supply. If reassignment is not feasible, the company should lay off the extra inspector.

This example illustrates an important feature of activity capacity management. Activity improvement can create unused capacity, but managers must be willing and able to make the tough decisions to reduce resource spending on the redundant resources to gain the potential profit increase. Profits can be increased by reducing resource spending or by transferring the resources to other activities that will generate more revenues.

OBJECTIVE **4**

Discuss the implementation issues associated with an activity-based management system.

IMPLEMENTING ACTIVITY-BASED MANAGEMENT

Activity-based management (ABM) is a more comprehensive system than an ABC system. ABM adds a process view to the cost view of ABC. ABM encompasses ABC and uses it as a major source of information. ABM can be viewed as an information system that has the broad objectives of (1) improving decision making by providing accurate cost information, and (2) reducing costs by encouraging and supporting continuous improvement efforts. The first objective is the domain of ABC, while the second objective belongs to process value analysis. The second objective requires more detailed data than ABC's objective of improving the accuracy of costing assignments. If a company intends to use both ABC and PVA, then its approach to implementation must be carefully conceived. For example, if ABC creates aggregate cost pools based on homogeneity, much of the detailed activity information may not be needed. Yet, for PVA, this detail must be retained. Clearly, how to implement an ABM system is a major consideration. Exhibit 12.7 provides a representation of an ABM implementation model.

Discussion of the ABM Implementation Model

The model in Exhibit 12.7 shows that the overall objective of ABM is to improve a firm's profitability, an objective achieved by identifying and selecting opportunities for improvement and using more accurate information to make better decisions. Root cause analysis, for example, reveals opportunities for improvement. By identifying non-value-added costs, priorities can be established based on the initiatives that offer the most cost reduction. Furthermore, the potential cost reduction itself is measured by ABC calculations.

Exhibit 12.7 also reveals that 10 steps define an ABM implementation: two common steps and four that are associated with either ABC or PVA. The PVA steps have been discussed extensively in this chapter, whereas the ABC steps were discussed in Chapter 4. The two common steps are (1) systems planning, and (2) activity identification, definition, and classification.

Exhibit 12.7 ABM Implementation Model

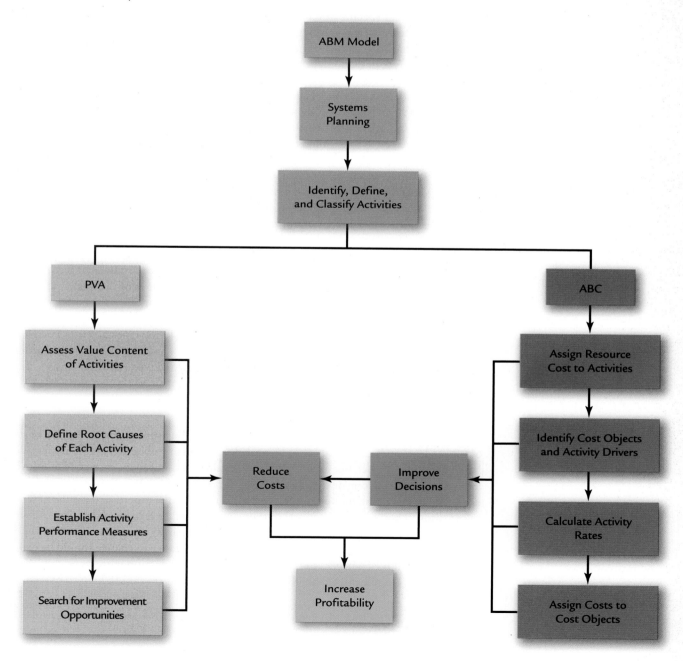

Systems Planning   Systems planning provides the justification for implementing ABM and addresses the following issues:

1.   The purpose and objectives of the ABM system
2.   The organization's current and desired competitive position
3.   The organization's business processes and product mix
4.   The timeline, assigned responsibilities, and resources required for implementation
5.   The ability of the organization to implement, learn, and use new information

To obtain buy-in by operating personnel, the objectives of an ABM system must be carefully identified and related to the firm's desired competitive position, business processes, and product mix. The broad objectives have already been mentioned (improving accuracy and continuous improvement); however, it is also necessary to develop specific desired outcomes associated with each of these two objectives. For example, one specific outcome is that of changing the product mix based on more accurate costs (with the expectation that profits will increase). Another specific outcome is that of improving the firm's competitive position by increasing process efficiency through elimination of non-value-added activities. Planning also entails establishing a timeline for the implementation project, assigning specific responsibilities to individuals or teams, and developing a detailed budget. Although all five issues listed are important, the information usage issue deserves special attention. Successful implementation is strongly dependent on the organization's ability to learn how to use the new information provided by ABM. Users must be convinced that this new information can solve specific problems. They also need to be trained to use activity-based costing information to produce better decisions, and they need to understand how ABM drives and supports continuous improvement.

Activity Identification, Definition, and Classification   Identifying, defining, and classifying activities require more attention for ABM than for ABC. The activity dictionary should include a detailed listing of the tasks that define each activity. Knowing the tasks that define an activity can be very helpful for improving the efficiency of value-added activities. Classification of activities also allows ABM to connect with other continuous improvement initiatives such as Just in Time (JIT), total quality management, and total environmental quality cost management. For example, identifying quality-related and environmental activities enables management to focus attention on the non-value-added activities of the quality and environmental categories. ABC also provides a more complete understanding of the effect that quality and environmental costs have on products, processes, and customers. It is important to realize that successful implementation requires time and patience. This is especially true when it comes to using the new information provided by an ABM system. Ford and Coca Cola are prominent examples of companies that have successfully implemented and used ABM systems.[15]

Why ABM Implementations Fail

ABM can fail as a system for a variety of reasons. One of the major reasons is the lack of support of higher-level management. Not only must this support be obtained before undertaking an implementation project, but it must also be maintained. Loss of support can occur if the implementation takes too long or the expected results do not materialize. Results may not occur as expected because operating and sales managers do not have the expertise to use the new activity information. Thus, significant efforts to train and educate need to be undertaken. Advantages of the new data need to be spelled out carefully, and managers must be taught how these data can be used to increase efficiency and productivity. Resistance to change should be expected; it is not unusual for managers to receive the new cost information with skepticism. Showing how this information can enable them to be better managers should help to overcome this

---

15   Danielle Smith, "What Types of Businesses Do Activity Costing," Bizfluent, November 5, 2019, htps://bizfluent.com /info-12105073-types-businesses-activitybased-costing.html, accessed June 10, 2020.

resistance. Involving nonfinancial managers in the planning and implementation stages may also reduce resistance and secure the required support.

Failure to integrate the new system is another major reason for an ABM system breakdown. The probability of success is increased if the ABM system is not in competition with other improvement programs or the official accounting system. It is important to communicate the concept that ABM complements and enhances other improvement programs. Moreover, it is important that ABM be integrated to the point that activity costing outcomes are not in direct competition with the traditional accounting numbers. Managers may be tempted to continue using the traditional accounting numbers in lieu of the new data.

Although there are firms who adopt ABC and then abandon the new system, the rate of failure is not high. There is apparently not widespread dissatisfaction with ABC and its promised benefits. In a recent survey, only 2.8 percent of firms surveyed previously used ABC but no longer use it. Moreover, about 87 percent of the organizational respondents indicated that an ideal cost allocation system would include some form of ABC (although only 50 percent are using ABC currently), indicating significant potential for future adoption of ABC.[16]

FINANCIAL-BASED VERSUS ACTIVITY-BASED RESPONSIBILITY ACCOUNTING

OBJECTIVE **5**

Explain how activity-based management is a form of responsibility accounting, and tell how it differs from financial-based responsibility accounting.

Responsibility accounting is a fundamental tool of managerial control and is defined by four essential elements: (1) assigning responsibility, (2) establishing performance measures or benchmarks, (3) evaluating performance, and (4) assigning rewards. The objective of responsibility accounting is to influence behavior in such a way that individual and organizational initiatives are aligned to achieve a common goal or goals. Exhibit 12.8 illustrates the responsibility accounting model.

A particular responsibility accounting system is defined by how the four elements in Exhibit 12.8 are defined. Three types of responsibility accounting systems have evolved over time: *financial-based*, *activity-based*, and *strategic-based*. All three are found in practice today. Essentially, firms choose the responsibility accounting system that is compatible with the requirements and economics of their particular operating environment. Firms that operate in a stable environment with standardized products and processes and low competitive pressures will likely find the less complex, financial-based responsibility accounting systems to be quite adequate. As organizational complexity increases and the competitive environment becomes much more dynamic, activity-based and strategic-based systems are likely to be more suitable. Strategic-based responsibility accounting systems are discussed in Chapter 13.

The responsibility accounting system for a stable environment is referred to as *financial-based responsibility accounting*. A **financial-based responsibility accounting system** assigns responsibility to organizational units and expresses performance measures in financial terms. It emphasizes a financial perspective. *Activity-based responsibility accounting*, on the other hand, is the responsibility accounting system developed for those firms operating in continuous improvement environments. **Activity-based responsibility accounting** assigns responsibility to processes and uses both financial and nonfinancial measures of performance, thus emphasizing both financial and process perspectives. A comparison of each of the four elements of the responsibility accounting model for each responsibility system reveals the key differences between the two approaches.

---

16 William Stratton, Dennis Desroches, Raef A. Lawson, and Toby Hatch, "Activity-Based Costing: Is It Still Relevant?" *Management Accounting Quarterly* (Spring 2009): 31–40.

Exhibit 12.8

The Responsibility Accounting Model

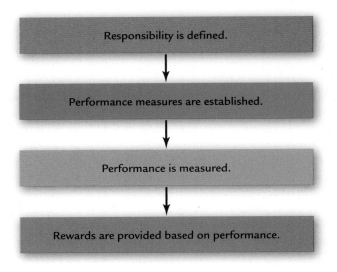

Assigning Responsibility

Exhibit 12.9 lists the differences in responsibility assignments between the two systems. Financial-based responsibility accounting focuses on *functional* organizational units and individuals. First, a responsibility center is identified. This center is typically an organizational unit such as a plant, department, or production line. Whatever the functional unit is, responsibility is assigned to the individual in charge. Responsibility is defined in financial terms (e.g., costs). Emphasis is on achieving optimal financial results at the local level (i.e., organizational unit level). Exhibit 12.9 reveals that in an activity- or process-based responsibility system, the focal point changes from units and individuals to processes and teams. Systemwide optimization is the emphasis. Also, financial responsibility continues to be vital. The reasons for the change in focus are simple. In a continuous improvement environment, the financial perspective translates into continuously *enhancing revenues, reducing costs*, and *improving asset utilization*. Creating this continuous growth and improvement requires an organization to constantly improve its capabilities of delivering value to customers and shareholders. A process perspective is chosen instead of an organizational-unit perspective because processes are the *sources* of value for customers and shareholders and because they are the key to achieving an organization's financial objectives. The customer can be internal or external to the organization. Procurement, new product development, manufacturing, and customer service are examples of processes.

Since processes are the way things are done, changing the way things are done means changing processes. Three methods can change the way things are done: *process improvement*, *process innovation*, and *process creation*. **Process improvement** refers to incremental and constant increases in the efficiency of an existing process. For example, **Merit Medical Systems, Inc.**, a manufacturer of medical devices used for interventional, diagnostic, and therapeutic procedures, improved its processes by creating a culture of daily improvement using kaizen and employee engagement. Over a four-year period, the company reduced waste and improved the average unit cost of its products by 24.9 percent, with a range of 10 percent to 60 percent.[17] Activity-based management is particularly useful for bringing about process improvements. Processes are made up of activities that are linked by a common objective. Listing these activities and classifying them as value-added or non-value-added immediately suggest a way to make the process better: eliminate the non-value-added activities.

---

17 Merit Medical Systems Company Profile, 2019, https://shingo.org/awards/; accessed company profile at https://usu .app.box.com/s/zkosmzbv1ke4eu6fsngbt2yk9pg916y9 on June 12, 2020.

Financial-Based Responsibility	**Activity-Based Responsibility**
1. Organizational units	1. Processes
2. Local operating efficiency	2. Systemwide efficiency
3. Individual accountability	3. Team accountability
4. Financial outcomes	4. Financial outcomes

Exhibit 12.9

Responsibility Assignments Compared

Process innovation (business reengineering) refers to the performance of a process in a radically new way with the objective of achieving dramatic improvements in response time, quality, and efficiency. **IBM Credit**, for example, radically redesigned its credit approval process and reduced its time for preparing a quote from seven days to one; similarly, **Federal-Mogul**, a parts manufacturer, used process innovation to reduce development time for part prototypes from 20 weeks to 20 days.[18] **Process creation** refers to the installation of an entirely new process with the objective of meeting customer and financial objectives. **Chemical Bank**, for example, identified three *new* internal processes: understanding customer segments, developing new products, and cross-selling the product line.[19] These new internal processes were viewed as critical by the bank's management for improving the customer and profit mix and creating an enabled organization. It should be mentioned that process creation does not mean that the process has to be *original* to the organization. It means that it is *new* to the organization. For example, developing new products is a process common to many organizations but evidently was new to Chemical Bank.

Many processes cut across functional boundaries. This facilitates an integrated approach that emphasizes the firm's value-chain activities. It also means that cross-functional skills are needed for effective process management. Teams are the natural outcome of this process management requirement. Teams also improve the quality of work life by fostering friendships and a sense of belonging. Process improvement, innovation, and creation require significant group activity (and support) and cannot be carried out effectively by individuals. **General Electric**, **Xerox**, **Martin Marietta Materials**, and **Aetna** have all begun to use teams as their basic work unit.[20]

Establishing Performance Measures

Once responsibility is defined, performance measures must be identified and standards set to serve as benchmarks for performance measurement. Exhibit 12.10 provides a comparison of the two systems' approaches to the task of defining performance measures. According to Exhibit 12.10, budgeting and standard costing are the Examples of the benchmark activity for a financial-based system. This, of course, implies that performance measures are objective and financial in nature. Furthermore, they tend to support the status quo and are relatively stable over time. Exhibit 12.10 reveals some striking differences for firms operating in a continuous improvement environment. First, performance measures are process-oriented and, thus, must be concerned with process attributes such as process time, quality, and efficiency. Second, performance measurement standards are structured to support change. Therefore, standards are dynamic in nature. They change to reflect new conditions and new goals and to help maintain any progress that has been realized. For example, standards can be set that reflect some desired level of improvement for a process. Once the desired level is achieved, the standard is changed to encourage an additional increment of improvement. In an environment where constant improvement is sought, standards cannot be static. Third, optimal standards assume a vital role. They set the ultimate achievement target and, thus, identify the potential for improvement. Finally, standards should reflect the value added by individual activities and processes. Identifying a value-added standard for each activity is much more ambitious than the traditional financial responsibility system. It expands control to include the entire organization.

---

18 Thomas H. Davenport, *Process Innovation* (Boston: Harvard Business School Press, 1993): 2.

19 Norman Klein and Robert Kaplan, *Chemical Bank: Implementing the Balanced Scorecard*, Case 125–210 (Boston: Harvard Business School Press, 1995): 5–6.

20 Davenport, *Process Innovation*, 97.

Exhibit 12.10

Performance Measures Compared

Financial-Based Measures	Activity-Based Measures
1. Organizational unit budgets	1. Process-oriented standards
2. Standard costing	2. Value-added standards
3. Static standards	3. Dynamic standards
4. Currently attainable standards	4. Optimal standards

Evaluating Performance

Exhibit 12.11 compares performance evaluation under financial- and activity-based responsibility accounting systems. In a financial-based framework, performance is measured by comparing actual outcomes with budgeted outcomes. In principle, individuals are held accountable only for those items over which they have control. Financial performance, as measured by the ability to meet or beat a stable financial standard, is strongly emphasized. In the activity-based framework, performance is concerned with more than just the financial perspective. The process perspective adds time, quality, and efficiency as critical dimensions of performance. Decreasing the time a process takes to deliver its output to customers is viewed as a vital objective. Thus, nonfinancial, process-oriented measures such as cycle-time and on-time deliveries become important. Performance is evaluated by gauging whether these measures are improving over time. The same is true for measures relating to quality and efficiency. Improving a process should translate into better financial results. Hence, measures of cost reductions achieved, trends in cost, and cost per unit of output are all useful indicators of whether a process has improved. Progress toward achieving optimal standards and interim standards needs to be measured. The objective is to provide low-cost, high-quality products, delivered on a timely basis.

Assigning Rewards

In both systems, individuals are rewarded or penalized according to the policies and discretion of higher management. As Exhibit 12.12 shows, many of the same financial instruments (e.g., salary increases, bonuses, profit sharing, and promotions) are used to provide rewards for good performance. Of course, the nature of the incentive structure differs in each system. For example, the reward system in a financial-based responsibility accounting system is designed to encourage individuals to achieve or beat budgetary standards. Furthermore, for the activity-based responsibility system, rewarding individuals is more complicated than it is in a unit-based setting. Individuals simultaneously have accountability for team and individual performance. Since process-related improvements are mostly achieved through team efforts, group-based rewards are more suitable than individual rewards. In one company (a producer of electronic components), for example, optimal standards have been set for unit costs, on-time delivery, quality, inventory turns, scrap, and cycle time.[21] Bonuses are awarded to the team whenever performance is maintained on all measures and improves on at least one measure. Notice the multidimensional nature of this measurement and reward system. Another

Exhibit 12.11

Performance Evaluation Compared

Financial-Based Performance Evaluation	Activity-Based Performance Evaluation
1. Financial efficiency	1. Time reductions
2. Controllable costs	2. Quality improvements
3. Actual versus standard	3. Cost reductions
4. Financial measures	4. Trend measurement

---

21 C. J. McNair, "Responsibility Accounting and Controllability Networks," *Handbook of Cost Management* (Boston: Warren Gorham Lamont, 1993): E41–E43.

Financial-Based Rewards	**Activity-Based Rewards**
1. Financial performance basis	1. Multidimensional performance basis
2. Individual rewards	2. Group rewards
3. Salary increases	3. Salary increases
4. Promotions	4. Promotions
5. Bonuses and profit sharing	5. Bonuses, profit sharing, and gainsharing

Exhibit 12.12

Rewards Compared

difference concerns the notion of gainsharing versus profit sharing. Profit sharing is a global incentive designed to encourage employees to contribute to the overall financial well-being of the organization. Gainsharing is more specific. Employees are allowed to share in gains related to specific improvement projects. Gainsharing helps obtain the necessary buy-in for specific improvement projects inherent to activity-based management.

SUMMARY OF LEARNING OBJECTIVES

LO1. Describe how activity-based management and activity-based costing differ.
- Activity-based management encompasses both activity-based costing and process value analysis.
- Activity-based costing is concerned with accurate assignment of costs to cost objects and is an important source of information for managing activities. ABC, however, is not concerned with the issue or presence of waste in activities.
- Identifying waste and its causes and eliminating it fall within the domain of process value analysis.

LO2. Define process value analysis.
- Process value analysis emphasizes activity management with the intent of maximizing systemwide performance. It consists of three elements: driver analysis, activity analysis, and performance measurement.
- Driver analysis is also referred to as root cause analysis. It seeks to identify why activities are performed.
- Activity analysis identifies all activities and the resources they consume and classifies activities as value-added or non-value-added.
- Performance measurement is concerned with how well activities are performed.

LO3. Describe activity-based financial performance measurement.
- Reporting value- and non-value-added costs is an integral part of a sound activity-based management system. Tracking trends in these costs over time is an effective control measure.
- Once management determines the source of non-value-added costs, a focused program of continuous improvement can be implemented.
- Kaizen costing is a well-accepted approach for reducing costs by eliminating waste.
- Activity flexible budgeting and activity capacity management offer additional control capabilities.
- Activity flexible budgeting differs from the traditional approach by using more than unit-level drivers to predict what costs will be at different levels of activity output.
- Activity capacity management involves identification of the volume variance (non-value-added cost) and the unused capacity variance (progress toward reducing non-value-added cost).

LO4. Discuss the implementation issues associated with an activity-based management system.
- Implementing an activity-based management system requires careful planning and execution.
- The objectives of the system must be identified and explained.
- The benefits of the system and the anticipated effects should also be noted.
- A key issue is assessing and managing the ability of the organization to implement, learn, and use the new activity information. Strong support from higher management is critical for this process.

LO5. Explain how activity-based management is a form of responsibility accounting, and tell how it differs from financial-based responsibility accounting.
- A firm can adopt one of three responsibility accounting systems.
- Two are discussed in this chapter: financial-based responsibility accounting and activity-based responsibility accounting.
- Financial-based responsibility accounting focuses on organizational units such as departments and plants; uses financial outcome measures, static standards, and benchmarks to evaluate performance; and emphasizes status quo and organizational stability.
- Activity-based responsibility accounting focuses on processes, uses both operational and financial measures, employs dynamic standards, and emphasizes and supports continuous improvement.

EXAMPLE 12.1   The HOW and WHY of Value- and Non-Value-Added Cost Reporting, page 635

EXAMPLE 12.2   The HOW and WHY of Non-Value-Added Cost Trend Reporting, page 636

EXAMPLE 12.3   The HOW and WHY of Kaizen Costing, page 639

EXAMPLE 12.4   The HOW and WHY of Activity-Based Flexible Budgeting, page 643

EXAMPLE 12.5   The HOW and WHY of Activity Capacity Management, page 645

KEY TERMS

Activity analysis, 630

Activity capacity, 644

Activity elimination, 632

Activity flexible budgeting, 641

Activity output measure, 629

Activity reduction, 632

Activity selection, 632

Activity sharing, 632

Activity volume variance, 644

Activity-based management (ABM), 628

Activity-based responsibility accounting, 649

Benchmarking, 640

Continuous improvement, 628

Driver analysis, 629

Financial measures, 633

Financial-based responsibility accounting system, 649

Kaizen costing, 632

Kaizen standard, 638

Non-value-added activities, 631

Non-value-added costs, 631

Process creation, 651

Process improvement, 650

Process innovation (business
reengineering), 651

Process value analysis (PVA), 629

Responsibility accounting, 649

Unused capacity variance, 645

Value-added activities, 630

Value-added costs, 630

Value-added standard, 634

BRIEF EXERCISES

Brief Exercise 12-1 Value- and Non-Value-Added Cost Reporting

OBJECTIVE ◄ 3

Example 12.1

Cicleta Manufacturing has four activities: receiving materials, assembly, expediting products, and storing goods. Receiving and assembly are necessary activities; expediting and storing goods are unnecessary. The following data pertain to the four activities for the year ending 20x1 (actual price per unit of the activity driver is assumed to be equal to the standard price):

Activity	Activity Driver	SQ	AQ	SP
Receiving	Receiving orders	12,000	18,000	$21
Assembly	Labor hours	75,000	90,000	15
Expediting	Orders expedited	0	6,000	50
Storing	Number of units	0	12,000	7

Required:

1. Prepare a cost report for the year ending 20x1 that shows value-added costs, non-value-added costs, and total costs for each activity.
2. Explain why expediting products and storing goods are non-value-added activities.
3. *What if* receiving cost is a step-fixed cost with each step being 1,500 orders whereas assembly cost is a variable cost? What is the implication for reducing the cost of waste for each activity?

Brief Exercise 12-2 Trend Reporting for Non-Value-Added Costs

OBJECTIVE ◄ 3

Example 12.2

Refer to **Brief Exercise 12-1**. Assume that at the beginning of 20x2, Cicleta trained the assembly workers in a new approach that had the objective of increasing the efficiency of the assembly process. Cicleta also began moving toward a JIT purchasing and manufacturing system. When JIT is fully implemented, the demand for expediting is expected to be virtually eliminated. It is expected to take two to three years for full implementation. Assume that receiving cost is a step-fixed cost with steps of 1,500 orders. The other three activities employ resources that are acquired as used and needed. At the end of 20x2, the following results were reported for the four activities:

Activity	Activity Driver	SQ	AQ	SP
Receiving	Receiving orders	12,000	12,000	$21
Assembly	Labor hours	75,000	78,000	15
Expediting	Orders expedited	0	3,000	50
Storing	Number of units	0	6,000	7

Required:

1. Prepare a trend report that shows the non-value-added costs for each activity for 20x1 and 20x2 and the change in costs for the two periods. Discuss the report's implications.
2. Explain the role of activity reduction for receiving and for expediting. What is the expected value of *SQ* for each activity after JIT is fully implemented?

3. ***What if*** at the end of 20x2, the selling price of a competing product is reduced by $27 per unit? Assume that the firm produces and sells 20,000 units of its product and that its product is associated only with the four activities being considered. By virtue of the waste-reduction savings, can the competitor's price reduction be matched without reducing the unit profit margin of the product that prevailed at the beginning of the year? If not, how much more waste reduction is needed to achieve this outcome? In this case, what price decision would you recommend?

OBJECTIVE 3
Example 12.3

Brief Exercise 12-3 Kaizen Costing

Gordon Company produces custom-made machine parts. A setup activity is required for the batches of parts that it produces. Activity output is measured using setup hours. The value-added standard (SQ) for this activity is zero. On July 1, at the beginning of the fiscal year, 10 setup hours were allowed and used per batch. The standard wage rate for setup labor is $20 per setup hour. During the first quarter of the new fiscal year, the company is planning to implement a new setup method developed by Gordon's industrial engineers that is expected to reduce setup time by 40 percent. The new procedure was implemented during the first quarter and the improvement expected was realized.

Required:

1. What is the setup standard for setup hours and the associated expected cost at the beginning of the first quarter? The kaizen standard and expected associated cost?
2. What is the setup standard for setup hours and the associated cost at the end of the first quarter? Explain. What is the next step in the kaizen cost reduction process?
3. ***What if*** the new procedure implemented in the first quarter only produced a 30 percent reduction in setup time instead of the expected 40 percent reduction? What would the new maintenance standard and cost be? What criteria would you logically expect to be met before maintenance standards and costs are modified?

OBJECTIVE 3
Example 12.4

Brief Exercise 12-4 Activity-Based Flexible Budgeting

Wade Paving Company has a sealcoating activity and wants to develop a flexible budget formula for the activity. The following resources are used by the activity:

- Five truck-mounted sealing units, with a lease cost of $15,000 per year per unit
- Ten sealcoating employees each paid a salary of $40,000 per year (A total of 20,000 sealcoating hours are supplied by the 10 workers.)
- Sealcoating materials: $1,000 per job
- Sealcoating hours: Four hours used per job

During the year, the activity operated at 90 percent of capacity and incurred the following actual activity and resource costs:
- Lease cost: $75,000
- Salaries: $420,000
- Sealcoating materials: $4,400,000

Required:

1. Prepare a flexible budget formula for the sealcoating activity using sealcoating hours as the driver.
2. Prepare a performance report for the welding activity.
3. ***What if*** sealcoating employees were hired through outsourcing and paid $18 per hour (the sealcoating equipment is provided by Wade)? Repeat Requirement 1 for the outsourcing case.

Brief Exercise 12-5 Activity Capacity Management

Uchdorf Manufacturing just completed a study of its purchasing activity with the objective of improving its efficiency. The driver for the activity is number of purchase orders. The following data pertain to the activity for the most recent year:

Activity supply: five purchasing agents capable of processing 2,400 orders per year (12,000 orders)
Purchasing agent cost (salary): $45,600 per year
Actual usage: 10,600 orders per year
Value-added quantity: 7,000 orders per year

Required:

1. Calculate the volume variance and explain its significance.
2. Calculate the unused capacity variance and explain its use.
3. *What if* the actual usage drops to 9,000 orders? What effect will this have on capacity management? What will be the level of spending reduction if the value-added standard is met?

EXERCISES

Exercise 12-6 ABC Versus ABM

DATA ANALYTICS   SHOW ME HOW

Whitaker Company produces two models of blenders for restaurants: the "Super Model" (priced at $1,600) and the "Special Model" (priced at $800). Recently, Whitaker has been losing market share with its Special Model because of competitors offering blenders with the same quality and features but at a lower price. A careful market study revealed that if Whitaker could reduce the price of its Special Model to $750, it would regain its former share of the market. Management, however, is convinced that any price reduction must be accompanied by a cost reduction of the same amount so that per-unit profitability is not affected. James Davis, company controller, has indicated that poor overhead costing assignments may be distorting management's view of each product's cost and, therefore, the ability to know how to set selling prices. James has identified the following overhead activities: machining, inspection, and rework. The three activities, their costs, and practical capacities are as follows:

Activity	Cost	Practical Capacity
Machining	$21,600,000	360,000 machine hours
Inspection	14,400,000	180,000 inspection hours
Rework	7,200,000	180,000 rework hours

The consumption patterns of the two products are as follows:

	Special	Super
Units	200,000	60,000
Machine hours	200,000	160,000
Inspection hours	40,000	140,000
Rework hours	30,000	150,500

Whitaker assigns overhead costs to the two products using a plantwide rate based on machine hours.

Required:

1. Calculate the unit overhead cost of the Special Model using machine hours to assign overhead costs. Now, repeat the calculation using ABC to assign overhead costs. Did improving the accuracy of cost assignments solve Whitaker's competitive problem? What did it reveal?

2. Now, assume that *in addition* to improving the accuracy of cost assignments, James observes that defective supplier components are the root cause of both the inspection and rework activities. Suppose further that Whitaker has found a new supplier that provides higher-quality components such that inspection and rework costs are reduced by 60 percent. Now, calculate the cost of the Special Model (assuming that inspection and rework times are also reduced by 60 percent) using ABC. The relative consumption patterns also remain the same. Comment on the difference between ABC and ABM.

3. In Requirements 1 and 2, identify which of the data analytic types apply (descriptive, diagnostic, predictive, and prescriptive). See Exhibits 2.5 and 2.6, pp. 37, 40, for a brief review of data analytic types.

OBJECTIVE `2`

Exercise 12-7 Root Cause (Driver Analysis)

For the following two activities, ask a series of "why" questions (with your answers) that reveal the root cause. Once the root cause is identified, use a "how" question to reveal how the activity can be improved (with your answer).

Activity 1: Daily cleaning of a puddle of oil near production machinery.
Activity 2: Providing customers with sales allowances.

OBJECTIVE `2`

**SHOW ME
HOW**

Exercise 12-8 Non-Value-Added Activities: Non-Value-Added Cost

Thayne Company has 30 clerks that work in its Accounts Payable Department. A study revealed the following activities and the relative time demanded by each activity:

Activities	Percentage of Clerical Time
Comparing purchase orders and receiving orders and invoices	12%
Resolving discrepancies among the three documents	73
Preparing checks for suppliers	10
Making journal entries and mailing checks	5
The average salary of a clerk is $40,000	

Required:

Classify the four activities as value-added or non-value-added, and calculate the clerical cost of each activity. For non-value-added activities, indicate why they are non-value-added.

OBJECTIVE `2`

Exercise 12-9 Root Cause (Driver Analysis)

Refer to **Exercise 12-8**.

Required:

Suppose that clerical error—either Thayne's or the supplier's—is the common root cause of the non-value-added activities. For each non-value-added activity, ask a series of "why" questions that identify clerical error as the activity's root cause.

OBJECTIVE `2` `5`

Exercise 12-10 Process Improvement and Innovation

Refer to **Exercise 12-8**. Suppose that clerical error is the common root cause of the non-value-added activities. Paying bills is a subprocess that belongs to the procurement process. The procurement process is made up of three subprocesses: purchasing, receiving, and paying bills.

Required:

1. What is the definition of a process? Identify the common objective for the procurement process. Repeat for each subprocess.
2. Now, suppose that Thayne decides to attack the root cause of the non-value-added activities of the bill-paying process by improving the skills of its purchasing and receiving clerks.

As a result, the number of discrepancies found drops by 30 percent. Discuss the potential effect this initiative might have on the bill-paying process. Does this initiative represent process improvement or process innovation? Explain.

Exercise 12-11 Process Improvement and Innovation

OBJECTIVE ◀ 2 5

Refer to **Exercise 12-10**. Suppose that Thayne attacks the root cause of the non-value-added activities by establishing a totally different approach to procurement called electronic data interchange (EDI). EDI gives suppliers access to Thayne's online database that reveals Thayne's production schedule. By knowing Thayne's production schedule, suppliers can deliver the parts and supplies needed just in time for their use. When the parts are shipped, an electronic message is sent from the supplier to Thayne that the shipment is en route. When the order arrives, a bar code is scanned with an electronic wand initiating payment for the goods. EDI involves no paper, no purchase orders, no receiving orders—and no invoices.

Required:

Discuss the potential effects of this solution on Thayne's bill-paying process. Is this process innovation or process improvement? Explain.

Exercise 12-12 Value-Added and Non-Value-Added Costs, Unused Capacity

OBJECTIVE ◀ 2 3

For Situations 1 through 6, provide the following information:
a. An estimate of the non-value-added cost caused by each activity
b. The root causes of the activity cost (such as plant layout, process design, and product design)
c. The appropriate cost reduction measure: activity elimination, activity reduction, activity sharing, or activity selection

1. It takes 45 minutes and six pounds of material to produce a product using a traditional manufacturing process. A process reengineering study provided a new manufacturing process design (using existing technology) that would take 15 minutes and four pounds of material. The cost per labor hour is $12, and the cost per pound of material is $8.
2. With its original design, a product requires 15 hours of setup time. Redesigning the product could reduce the setup time to an absolute minimum of 30 minutes. The cost per hour of setup time is $200.
3. A product currently requires eight moves. By redesigning the manufacturing layout, the number of moves can be reduced from eight to zero. The cost per move is $10.
4. Inspection time for a plant is 8,000 hours per year. The cost of inspection consists of salaries of four inspectors, totaling $120,000. Inspection also uses supplies costing $2 per inspection hour. A supplier evaluation program, product redesign, and process redesign reduced the need for inspection by creating a zero-defect environment.
5. Each unit of a product requires five components. The average number of components is 5.3 due to component failure, requiring rework and extra components. By developing relations with the right suppliers and increasing the quality of the purchased component, the average number of components can be reduced to five components per unit. The cost per component is $600.
6. A plant produces 100 different electronic products. Each product requires an average of eight components that are purchased externally. The components are different for each part. By redesigning the products, it is possible to produce the 100 products so that they all have four components in common. This will reduce the demand for purchasing, receiving, and paying bills. Estimated savings from the reduced demand are $900,000 per year.

OBJECTIVE **2** **3** **4**

SHOW ME HOW   **DATA ANALYTICS**   **EXCEL**

Exercise 12-13 Calculation of Value-Added and Non-Value-Added Costs, Activity Volume and Unused Capacity Variances

Rico Company produces custom-made machine parts. Rico recently has implemented an activity-based management (ABM) system with the objective of reducing costs. Rico has begun analyzing each activity to determine ways to increase its efficiency. Setting up equipment was among the first group of activities to be carefully studied. The study revealed that setup hours was a good driver for the activity. During the last year, the company incurred fixed setup costs of $840,000 (salaries of 20 employees). The fixed costs provide a capacity of 40,000 hours (2,000 per employee at practical capacity). The setup activity was viewed as necessary, and the value-added standard was set at 4,000 hours. Actual setup hours used in the most recent period were 38,200.

Required:

1. Calculate the volume and unused capacity variances for the setup activity. Explain what each variance means.
2. Prepare a report that presents value-added, non-value-added, and actual costs for setup. Explain why highlighting the non-value-added costs is important.
3. Management predicts that, during the coming year, they will be able to reduce the demand for the setup activity so that the actual hours needed drop from 26,200 to 4,000. If they achieve this reduction, what will be the unused capacity variance? Given this reduction, what actions should now be taken regarding activity capacity management?
4. Another activity studied was inspection of supplier materials and components. Explain why inspecting incoming goods should be viewed as a non-value-added activity. In providing your explanation, consider the following counterargument: "Inspecting incoming goods adds value because it reduces the demand for other unnecessary activities such as rework, reordering, and warranty work."
5. For Requirements 1 and 3, identify which of the data analytic types apply (descriptive, diagnostic, predictive, and prescriptive). Explain your reasoning for the choices. Exhibits 2.5 and 2.6, pp. 37, 40, provide a brief review of data analytic types.

OBJECTIVE **2** **3**

SHOW ME HOW   **EXCEL**

Exercise 12-14 Cost Report, Value-Added and Non-Value-Added Costs

Sanford, Inc., has developed value-added standards for four activities: purchasing parts, receiving parts, moving parts, and setting up equipment. The activities, the activity drivers, the standard and actual quantities, and the price standards for 20x1 are as follows:

Activities	Activity Driver	SQ	AQ	SP
Purchasing parts	Purchase orders	2,600	3,640	$300
Receiving parts	Receiving orders	5,200	7,800	195
Moving parts	Number of moves	0	2,600	390
Setting up equipment	Setup hours	0	10,400	117

The actual prices paid per unit of each activity driver were equal to the standard prices.

Required:

1. Prepare a cost report that lists the value-added, non-value-added, and actual costs for each activity.
2. Which activities are non-value-added? Explain why. Also, explain why value-added activities can have non-value-added costs.

OBJECTIVE **2** **3**

SHOW ME HOW

Exercise 12-15 Trend Report, Non-Value-Added Costs

Refer to **Exercise 12-14**. Suppose that for 20x2, Sanford, Inc., has chosen suppliers that provide higher-quality parts and redesigned its plant layout to reduce material movement. Additionally, Sanford implemented a new setup procedure and provided training for its purchasing agents. As a consequence, less setup time is required and fewer purchasing mistakes are made. At the end of 20x2, the following information is provided:

Activities	Activity Driver	SQ	AQ	SP
Purchasing parts	Purchase orders	2,600	3,120	$300
Receiving parts	Receiving orders	5,200	6,500	195
Moving parts	Number of moves	0	840	395
Setting up equipment	Setup hours	0	2,600	117

Required:

1. Prepare a report that compares the non-value-added costs for 20x2 with those of 20x1.
2. What is the role of activity reduction for non-value-added activities? For value-added activities?
3. Comment on the value of a trend report.

Exercise 12-16 Implementation of Activity-Based Management

OBJECTIVE ◀ 4

Jane Erickson, manager of an electronics division, was not pleased with the results that had recently been reported concerning the division's activity-based management implementation project. For one thing, the project had taken eight months longer than projected and had exceeded the budget by nearly 35 percent. But even more vexatious was the fact that after all was said and done, about three-fourths of the plants were reporting that the activity-based product costs were not much different for most of the products than those of the old costing system. Plant managers were indicating that they were continuing to use the old costs as they were easier to compute and understand. Yet, at the same time, they were complaining that they were having a hard time meeting the bids of competitors. Reliable sources were also revealing that the division's product costs were higher than many competitors'. This outcome perplexed plant managers because their control system still continued to report favorable materials and labor efficiency variances. They complained that ABM had failed to produce any significant improvement in cost performance.

Jane decided to tour several of the plants and talk with the plant managers. After the tour, she realized that her managers did not understand the concept of non-value-added costs nor did they have a good grasp of the concept of kaizen costing. No efforts were being made to carefully consider the activity information that had been produced. One typical plant manager threw up his hands and said: "This is too much data. Why should I care about all this detail? I do not see how this can help me improve my plant's performance. They tell me that inspection is not a necessary activity and does not add value. I simply can't believe that inspecting isn't value-added and necessary. If we did not inspect, we would be making and sending more bad products to customers."

Required:

Explain why Jane's division is having problems with its ABM implementation.

Exercise 12-17 Financial-Based versus Activity-Based Responsibility Accounting

OBJECTIVE ◀ 5

For each of the following situations, two scenarios are described, labeled A and B. Choose which scenario is descriptive of a setting corresponding to activity-based responsibility accounting and which is descriptive of financial-based responsibility accounting. Provide a brief commentary on the differences between the two systems for each situation, addressing the possible advantages of the activity-based view over the financial-based view.

Situation 1

A: The purchasing manager, receiving manager, and accounts payable manager are given joint responsibility for procurement. The charges given to the group of managers are to reduce costs of acquiring materials, decrease the time required to obtain materials from outside suppliers, and reduce the number of purchasing mistakes (e.g., wrong type of materials or the wrong quantities ordered).

B: The plant manager commended the manager of the Grinding Department for increasing her department's machine utilization rates—and doing so without exceeding the department's budget. The plant manager then asked other department managers to make an effort to obtain similar efficiency improvements.

Situation 2

A: Delivery mistakes had been reduced by 70 percent, saving over $40,000 per year. Furthermore, delivery time to customers had been cut by two days. According to company policy, the team responsible for the savings was given a bonus equal to 25 percent of the savings attributable to improving delivery quality. Company policy also provided a salary increase of 1 percent for every day saved in delivery time.

B: Bill Johnson, manager of the Product Development Department, was pleased with his department's performance on the last quarter's projects. They had managed to complete all projects under budget, virtually assuring Bill of a fat bonus, just in time to help with this year's holiday purchases.

Situation 3

A: "Harvey, don't worry about the fact that your department is producing at only 70 percent capacity. Increasing your output would simply pile up inventory in front of the next production department. That would be costly for the organization as a whole. Sometimes, one department must reduce its performance so that the performance of the entire organization can improve."

B: "Gina, I am concerned about the fact that your department's performance measures have really dropped over the past quarter. Labor usage variances are unfavorable, and I also see that your machine utilization rates are down. Now, I know you are not a bottleneck department, but I get a lot of flack when my managers' efficiency ratings drop."

Situation 4

A: Colby was muttering to himself. He had just received last quarter's budgetary performance report. Once again, he had managed to spend more than budgeted for both materials and labor. The real question now was how to improve his performance for the next quarter.

B: Great! Cycle time had been reduced and, at the same time, the number of defective products had been cut by 35 percent. Cutting the number of defects reduced production costs by more than planned. Trends were favorable for all three performance measures.

Situation 5

A: Cambry was furious. An across-the-board budget cut! "How can they expect me to provide the computer services required on less money? Management is convinced that costs are out of control, but I would like to know where—at least in my department!"

B: After a careful study of the Accounts Payable Department, it was discovered that 80 percent of an accounts payable clerk's time was spent resolving discrepancies between the purchase order, receiving document, and the supplier's invoice. Other activities such as recording and preparing checks consumed only 20 percent of a clerk's time. A redesign of the procurement process eliminated virtually all discrepancies and produced significant cost savings.

Situation 6

A: Five years ago, the management of Breeann Products commissioned an outside engineering consulting firm to conduct a time-and-motion study so that labor efficiency standards could be developed and used in production. These labor efficiency standards are still in use today and are viewed by management as an important indicator of productive efficiency.

B: Janet was quite satisfied with this quarter's labor performance. When compared with the same quarter of last year, labor productivity had increased by 23 percent. Most of the increase was due to a new assembly approach suggested by production line workers. She was also pleased to see that materials productivity had increased. The increase in materials productivity was attributed to reducing scrap because of improved quality.

Situation 7

A: "The system converts materials into products, not people at work stations. Therefore, process efficiency is more important than labor efficiency—but we also must pay particular attention to those who use the products we produce, whether inside or outside the firm."

B: "I was quite happy to see a revenue increase of 15 percent over last year, especially when the budget called for a 10 percent increase. However, after reading the recent copy of our trade journal, I now wonder whether we are doing so well. I found out that the market expanded by 30 percent, and our leading competitor increased its sales by 40 percent."

PROBLEMS

Problem 12-18 ABM Implementation, Activity Analysis, Activity Drivers, Driver Analysis, Behavioral Effects

OBJECTIVE ◀ 1 2 4

Joseph Fox, controller of Thorpe Company, has been in charge of a project to install an activity-based cost management system. This new system is designed to support the company's efforts to become more competitive. For the past six weeks, he and the project committee members have been identifying and defining activities, associating workers with activities, and assessing the time and resources consumed by individual activities. Now, he and the project committee are focusing on three additional implementation issues: (1) identifying activity drivers, (2) assessing value content, and (3) identifying cost drivers (root causes). Joseph has assigned a committee member the responsibilities of assessing the value content of five activities, choosing a suitable activity driver for each activity, and identifying the possible root causes of the activities. Following are the five activities with possible activity drivers:

Activity	Possible Activity Drivers
Setting up equipment	Setup time, number of setups
Performing warranty work	Warranty hours, number of defective units
Welding subassemblies	Welding hours, subassemblies welded
Moving materials	Number of moves, distance moved
Inspecting components	Hours of inspection, number of defective components

The committee member ran a regression analysis for each potential activity driver, using the method of least squares to estimate the variable and fixed cost components. In all five cases, costs were highly correlated with the potential drivers. Thus, all drivers appeared to be good candidates for assigning costs to products. The company plans to reward production managers for reducing product costs.

Required:

1. What is the difference between an activity driver and a cost driver? In answering the question, describe the purpose of each type of driver.
2. For each activity, assess the value content and classify each activity as value-added or non-value-added (justify the classification). Identify some possible root causes of each activity, and describe how this knowledge can be used to improve activity performance. For purposes of discussion, assume that the value-added activities are not performed with perfect efficiency.
3. Describe the behavior that each activity driver will encourage, and evaluate the suitability of that behavior for the company's objective of becoming more competitive.

OBJECTIVE 2 3 5

**DATA
ANALYTICS**

Problem 12-19 ABM, Kaizen Costing

Volante, Inc., supplies wheels for a large bicycle manufacturing company. The bicycle company has recently requested that Volante decrease its delivery time. Volante made a commitment to reduce the lead time for delivery from seven days to one day. To help achieve this goal, engineering and production workers had made the commitment to reduce time for the setup activity (other activities such as moving materials and rework were also being examined simultaneously). Current setup times were 10 hours. Setup cost was $800 per setup hour. For the first quarter, engineering developed a new process design that it believed would reduce the setup time from 10 hours to eight hours. After implementing the design, the actual setup time dropped from 10 hours to six hours. Engineering believed the actual reduction was sustainable. In the second quarter, production workers suggested a new setup procedure. Engineering gave the suggestion a positive evaluation, and they projected that the new approach would save an additional four hours of setup time. Setup labor was trained to perform the new setup procedures. The actual reduction in setup time based on the suggested changes was two hours.

Required:

1. What kaizen setup standard would be used at the beginning of each quarter?
2. Describe the kaizen subcycle using the two quarters of data provided by Volante.
3. Describe the maintenance subcycle for setups using the two quarters of data provided by Volante.
4. How much non-value-added cost was eliminated by the end of two quarters? Discuss the role of kaizen costing in activity-based management. Now explain why kaizen costing is compatible with activity-based responsibility accounting while standard costing is compatible with financial-based responsibility accounting.
5. For each of the following activities, identify which of the data analytic types (descriptive, diagnostic, predictive, and prescriptive) apply. (See Exhibits 2.5 and 2.6, pp. 37, 40, for a review of data analytic types.)
   a. Setting the kaizen setup standard at the beginning of each quarter.
   b. Locking in or establishing a new standard for the maintenance subcycle.
   c. Calculating the non-value-added cost that was eliminated at the end of two quarters.
   d. In the maintenance subcycle, finding out why a new setup time deteriorates so that corrective action can be taken.

OBJECTIVE 3

Problem 12-20 Activity Flexible Budgeting, Performance Report, Volume Variance

Novo, Inc., wants to develop an activity flexible budget for the activity of moving materials. Novo uses eight forklifts to move materials from receiving to stores. The forklifts are also used to move materials from stores to the production area. The forklifts are obtained through an operating lease that costs $18,000 per year per forklift. Novo employs 25 forklift operators who receive an average salary of $50,000 per year, including benefits. Each move requires the use of a crate. The crates are used to store the parts and are emptied only when used in production. Crates are disposed of after one cycle (two moves), where a cycle is defined as a move from receiving to stores to production. Each crate costs $1.80. Fuel for a forklift costs $3.60 per gallon. A gallon of gas is used every 20 moves. Forklifts can make three moves per hour and are available for 280 days per year, 24 hours per day (the remaining time is downtime for various reasons). Each operator works 40 hours per week and 50 weeks per year.

Required:

1. Prepare a flexible budget for the activity of moving materials, using the number of cycles as the activity driver.

2. Calculate the activity capacity for moving materials. Suppose Novo works at 80 percent of activity capacity and incurs the following costs:

Salaries	$1,290,000
Leases	144,000
Crates	118,000
Fuel	24,000

Prepare the budget for the 80 percent level and then prepare a performance report for the moving materials activity.

3. Calculate and interpret the volume variance for moving materials.

4. Suppose that a redesign of the plant layout reduces the demand for moving materials to one-third of the original capacity. What would be the budget formula for this new activity level? What is the budgeted cost for this new activity level? Has activity performance improved? How does this activity performance evaluation differ from that described in Requirement 2? Explain.

Problem 12-21 Activity-Based Management, Non-Value-Added Costs, Target Costs, Kaizen Costing

OBJECTIVE ◀ 2 3

Joseph Hansen, president of Electronica, Inc., was concerned about the end-of-the-year marketing report that he had just received. According to Asha Kumar, marketing manager, a price decrease for the coming year was again needed to maintain the company's annual sales volume of integrated circuit boards (CBs). This would make a bad situation worse. The current selling price of $27 per unit was producing a $3-per-unit profit—half the customary $6-per-unit profit. Foreign competitors keep reducing their prices. To match the latest reduction would reduce the price from $27 to $21. This would put the price below the cost to produce and sell it. How could the foreign firms sell for such a low price? Determined to find out if there were problems with the company's operations, Joseph decided to hire Ahmed Kumar, a well-known consultant and brother of Asha, who specializes in methods of continuous improvement. Ahmed indicated that he felt that an activity-based management system needed to be implemented. After three weeks, Ahmed had identified the following activities and costs:

Batch-level activities:	
Setting up equipment	$ 187,500
Materials handling	270,000
Inspecting products	183,000
Product-sustaining activities:	
Engineering support	180,000
Handling customer complaints	150,000
Filling warranties	255,000
Storing goods	120,000
Expediting goods	112,500
Unit-level activities:	
Using materials	750,000
Using power	72,000
Manual insertion labor[a]	375,000
Other direct labor	225,000
Total costs	$2,880,000[b]

[a]Diodes, resistors, and integrated circuits are inserted manually into the circuit board.
[b]This total cost produces a unit cost of $24 for last year's sales volume.

Ahmed indicated that some preliminary activity analysis shows that per-unit costs can be reduced by at least $10.50. Since Asha had indicated that the market share (sales volume) for the boards could be increased by 50 percent if the price could be reduced to $18, Joseph became quite excited.

Required:

1. What is activity-based management? What connection does it have to continuous improvement?

2. Identify as many non-value-added costs as possible. Compute the cost savings per unit that would be realized if these costs were eliminated. Was Ahmed correct in his preliminary cost reduction assessment? Discuss actions that the company can take to reduce or eliminate the non-value-added activities.

3. Compute the target cost required to maintain current market share, while earning a profit of $6 per unit. Now, compute the target cost required to expand sales by 50 percent. How much cost reduction would be required to achieve each target?

4. Assume that Ahmed suggested that kaizen costing be used to help reduce costs. The first suggested kaizen initiative is described by the following: switching to automated insertion would save $90,000 of engineering support and $135,000 of direct labor. Now, what is the total potential cost reduction per unit available? With these additional reductions, can Electronica achieve the target cost to maintain current sales? To increase it by 50 percent? What form of activity analysis is this kaizen initiative: reduction, sharing, elimination, or selection?

5. Calculate income based on current sales, prices, and costs. Now, calculate the income using a $21 price and an $18 price, assuming that the maximum cost reduction possible is achieved (including Requirement 4's kaizen reduction). What price should be selected?

OBJECTIVE 3

EXCEL

Problem 12-22 Value-Added and Kaizen Standards, Non-Value-Added Costs, Volume Variance, Unused Capacity

Angie Ramirez, vice president of Dunn Company (a producer of plastic products), has been supervising the implementation of an activity-based cost management system. One of Angie's objectives is to improve process efficiency by improving the activities that define the processes. To illustrate the potential of the new system to the president, Angie has decided to focus on two processes: production and customer service.

Within each process, one activity will be selected for improvement: molding for production and sustaining engineering for customer service. (Sustaining engineers are responsible for redesigning products based on customer needs and feedback.) Value-added standards are identified for each activity. For molding, the value-added standard calls for nine pounds per mold. (Although the products differ in shape and function, their size, as measured by weight, is uniform.) The value-added standard is based on the elimination of all waste due to defective molds (materials is by far the major cost for the molding activity). The standard price for molding is $15 per pound. For sustaining engineering, the standard is 60 percent of current practical activity capacity. This standard is based on the fact that about 40 percent of the complaints have to do with design features that could have been avoided or anticipated by the company.

Current practical capacity (the first year) is defined by the following requirements: 18,000 engineering hours for each product group that has been on the market or in development for five years or less, and 7,200 hours per product group of more than five years. Four product groups have less than five years' experience, and 10 product groups have more. There are 72 engineers, each paid a salary of $70,000. Each engineer can provide 2,000 hours of service per year. There are no other significant costs for the engineering activity.

For the first year, actual pounds used for molding were 25 percent above the level called for by the value-added standard; engineering usage was 138,000 hours. There were 240,000 units of output produced. Angie and the operational managers have selected some improvement measures that promise to reduce non-value-added activity usage by 30 percent in the second year. Selected actual results achieved for the second year are as follows:

Units produced	240,000
Pounds of material	2,600,000
Engineering hours	120,000

The actual prices paid per pound and per engineering hour are identical to the standard or budgeted prices.

Required:

1. For the first year, calculate the non-value-added usage and costs for molding and sustaining engineering. Also, calculate the cost of unused capacity for the engineering activity.
2. Using the targeted reduction, establish kaizen standards for molding and engineering (for the second year).
3. Using the kaizen standards prepared in Requirement 2, compute the second-year usage variances, expressed in both physical and financial measures, for molding and engineering. (For engineering, explain why it is necessary to compare actual resource usage with the kaizen standard.) Comment on the company's ability to achieve its targeted reductions. In particular, discuss what measures the company must take to capture any realized reductions in resource usage.

Problem 12-23 Benchmarking and Non-Value-Added Costs, Target Costing

OBJECTIVE ▶ **2** **3**

EXCEL   **DATA ANALYTICS**

Tidwell, Inc., has two plants that manufacture a line of wheelchairs. One is located in Dallas, and the other in Oklahoma City. Each plant is set up as a profit center. During the past year, both plants sold their tilt wheelchair model for $1,782. Sales volume averages 20,000 units per year in each plant. Recently, the Dallas plant reduced the price of the tilt model to $1,584. Discussion with the Dallas manager revealed that the price reduction was possible because the plant had reduced its manufacturing and selling costs by reducing what was called "non-value-added costs." The Dallas manufacturing and selling costs for the tilt model were $1,386 per unit. The Dallas manager offered to loan the Oklahoma City plant his cost accounting manager to help it achieve similar results. The Oklahoma City plant manager readily agreed, knowing that his plant must keep pace—not only with the Dallas plant but also with competitors. A local competitor had also reduced its price on a similar model, and Oklahoma City's marketing manager had indicated that the price must be matched or sales would drop dramatically. In fact, the marketing manager suggested that if the price were dropped to $1,550 by the end of the year, the plant could expand its share of the market by 20 percent. The plant manager agreed but insisted that the current profit per unit must be maintained. He also wants to know if the plant can at least match the $1,386 per-unit cost of the Dallas plant and if the plant can achieve the cost reduction using the approach of the Dallas plant.

The plant controller and the Dallas cost accounting manager have assembled the following data for the most recent year. The actual cost of inputs, their value-added (ideal) quantity levels, and the actual quantity levels are provided (for production of 20,000 units). Assume there is no difference between actual prices of activity units and standard prices.

	SQ	AQ	Actual Cost
Materials (lbs.)	940,500	990,000	$20,790,000
Labor (hrs.)	225,720	237,600	2,970,000
Setups (hrs.)	—	15,840	1,188,000
Materials handling (moves)	—	39,600	2,772,000
Warranties (no. repaired)	—	39,600	3,960,000
Total			$31,680,000

Required:

1. Calculate the target cost for expanding the Oklahoma City plant's market share by 20 percent, assuming that the per-unit profitability is maintained as requested by the plant manager.
2. Calculate the non-value-added cost per unit. Assuming that non-value-added costs can be reduced to zero, can the Oklahoma City plant match the Dallas per-unit cost? Can the target cost for expanding market share be achieved? What actions would you take if you were the plant manager?

3. Describe the role that benchmarking played in the effort of the Oklahoma City plant to protect and improve its competitive position.

4. There are four data analytic types: (1) descriptive, (2) diagnostic, (3) predictive, and (4) prescriptive. (See Exhibits 2.5 and 2.6, pp. 37, 40, for a brief review.) Choose which data analytic type(s) apply for each of the following (justify your selection):

   a. The target cost calculated in Requirement 1.
   b. The calculation of the non-value-added cost in Requirement 2.
   c. The assessment of whether the target cost can be achieved (Requirement 2).
   d. The actions recommended (Requirement 2).

OBJECTIVE 2 3 5 ▶ **Problem 12-24 Financial versus Activity Flexible Budgeting**

Kelly Gray, production manager, was upset with the latest performance report, which indicated that she was $100,000 over budget. Given the efforts that she and her workers had made, she was confident that they had met or beat the budget. Now, she was not only upset but also genuinely puzzled over the results. Three items—direct labor, power, and setups—were over budget. The actual costs for these three items follow:

	Actual Costs
Direct labor	$210,000
Power	135,000
Setups	140,000
Total	$485,000

Kelly knew that her operation had produced more units than originally had been budgeted, so more power and labor had naturally been used. She also knew that the uncertainty in scheduling had led to more setups than planned. When she pointed this out to John Huang, the controller, he assured her that the budgeted costs had been adjusted for the increase in productive activity. Curious, Kelly questioned John about the methods used to make the adjustment.

JOHN: If the actual level of activity differs from the original planned level, we adjust the budget by using budget formulas—formulas that allow us to predict what the costs will be for different levels of activity.

KELLY: The approach sounds reasonable. However, I'm sure something is wrong here. Tell me exactly how you adjusted the costs of labor, power, and setups.

JOHN: First, we obtain formulas for the individual items in the budget by using the method of least squares. We assume that cost variations can be explained by variations in productive activity where activity is measured by direct labor hours. Here is a list of the cost formulas for the three items you mentioned. The variable X is the number of direct labor hours:

Labor cost = $10X$
Power cost = $5,000 + $4X$
Setup cost = $100,000

KELLY: I think I see the problem. Power costs don't have a lot to do with direct labor hours. They have more to do with machine hours. As production increases, machine hours increase more rapidly than direct labor hours. Also, ...

JOHN: You know, you have a point. The coefficient of determination for power cost is only about 50 percent. That leaves a lot of unexplained cost variation. The coefficient for labor, however, is much better—it explains about 96 percent of the cost variation. Setup costs, of course, are fixed.

KELLY: Well, as I was about to say, setup costs also have very little to do with direct labor hours. And I might add that they certainly are not fixed—at least not all of them. We had to do more setups than our original plan called for because of the scheduling changes. And we have to pay our people when they work extra hours. It seems as if we are always paying overtime. I wonder if we simply do not have enough people for the setup activity. Supplies are used for each setup, and these are not cheap. Did you build these extra costs of increased setup activity into your budget?

JOHN: No, we assumed that setup costs were fixed. I see now that some of them could vary as the number of setups increases. Kelly, let me see if I can develop some cost formulas based on better explanatory variables. I'll get back with you in a few days.

Assume that after a few days' work, John developed the following cost formulas, all with a coefficient of determination greater than 90 percent:

Labor cost = $10X$; where X = Direct labor hours
Power cost = $68,000 + 0.9Y$; where Y = Machine hours
Setup cost = $98,000 + $400Z$; where Z = Number of setups

The actual measures of each of the activity drivers are as follows:

Direct labor hours	20,000
Machine hours	90,000
Number of setups	110

Required:

1. Prepare a performance report for direct labor, power, and setups using the direct-labor-based formulas.
2. Prepare a performance report for direct labor, power, and setups using the multiple cost driver formulas that John developed.
3. Of the two approaches, which provides the most accurate picture of Kelly's performance? Why?
4. After reviewing the approach to performance measurement, a consultant remarked that non-value-added cost trend reports would be a much better performance measurement approach than comparing actual costs with budgeted costs—even if activity flexible budgets were used. Do you agree or disagree? Explain.

Problem 12-25 Activity Flexible Budgeting, Non-Value-Added Costs   OBJECTIVE ◄ 2 3 5

Douglas Davis, controller for Marston, Inc., prepared the following budget for manufacturing costs at two different levels of activity for 20X1:

	Level of Activity	
Driver: Direct Labor Hours	*50,000*	*100,000*
Direct materials	$ 300,000	$ 600,000
Direct labor	200,000	400,000
Depreciation (plant)	100,000	100,000
Subtotal	$ 600,000	$1,100,000
Driver: Machine Hours	*200,000*	*300,000*
Maintaining equipment	$ 360,000	$ 510,000
Machining	112,000	162,000
Subtotal	$ 472,000	$ 672,000
Driver: Material Moves	*20,000*	*40,000*
Moving materials	$ 165,000	$ 290,000
Driver: Number of Batches Inspected	*100*	*200*
Inspecting products	$ 125,000	$ 225,000
Total	$1,362,000	$2,287,000

During 20X1, Marston worked a total of 80,000 direct labor hours, used 250,000 machine hours, made 32,000 moves, and performed 120 batch inspections. The following actual costs were incurred:

Direct materials	$440,000
Direct labor	355,000
Depreciation	100,000
Maintaining equipment	425,000
Machining	142,000
Moving materials	232,500
Inspecting products	160,000

Marston applies overhead using rates based on direct labor hours, machine hours, number of moves, and number of batches. The second level of activity (the right column in the preceding table) is the practical level of activity (the available activity for resources acquired in advance of usage) and is used to compute predetermined overhead pool rates.

Required:

1. Prepare a performance report for Marston's manufacturing costs in the current year.
2. Assume that one of the products produced by Marston is budgeted to use 10,000 direct labor hours, 15,000 machine hours, and 500 moves and will be produced in five batches. A total of 10,000 units will be produced during the year. Calculate the budgeted unit manufacturing cost.
3. One of Marston's managers said the following: "Budgeting at the activity level makes a lot of sense. It really helps us manage costs better. But the previous budget really needs to provide more detailed information. For example, I know that the moving materials activity involves the use of forklifts and operators, and this information is lost when only the total cost of the activity for various levels of output is reported. We have four forklifts, each capable of providing 10,000 moves per year. We lease these forklifts for five years, at $10,000 per year. Furthermore, for our two shifts, we need up to eight operators if we run all four forklifts. Each operator is paid a salary of $30,000 per year. Also, I know that fuel costs about $0.25 per move."

   Assuming that these are the only three items, expand the detail of the flexible budget for moving materials to reveal the cost of these three resource items for 20,000 moves and 40,000 moves, respectively. Based on these comments, explain how this additional information can help Marston better manage its costs. (Especially consider how activity-based budgeting may provide useful information for non-value-added activities.)

13 Strategic-Based Control Systems and the Balanced Scorecard

After studying this chapter, you should be able to:

1. ▶ Explain the need for and elements of a strategic-based control system.

2. ▶ Discuss the basic features of the Balanced Scorecard.

3. ▶ Explain how the Balanced Scorecard links measures to strategy.

4. ▶ Describe how an organization can achieve strategic alignment.

STRATEGIC-BASED CONTROL SYSTEM CHALLENGES

at Wells Fargo

Wells Fargo has perhaps the most storied and well-known history of any bank in the United States. Founded in 1852 by Henry Wells and William Fargo as a financial services company, Wells Fargo started by helping pioneer miners, merchants, and ranchers in the West by delivering gold, silver, and other financial packages by the fastest means possible—stagecoach, steamship, railroad, and the Pony Express. By 1858, Wells Fargo was able to deliver packages, letters, and passengers by stagecoach from St. Louis to San Francisco in the record time of 24 hours by traveling both day and night!

Over 160 years later, Wells Fargo dominated the news for the fallout resulting from its deeply flawed strategic-based control system (SBCS)—the connection between a company's strategy, performance measures, and employee incentive compensation programs. Specifically, in a desire to drastically increase the sales revenue generated from customer service fees, the CEO (John Stumpf) created and internally pushed a sales slogan of "Eight Is Great!" The slogan meant that each Wells Fargo employee was expected to sell an average of eight different financial products (checking account, savings account, credit card, automobile loan, online bill payment services, etc.) to each customer. Employees who failed to meet this performance target were humiliated by their bosses by performing in programs such as "Running the Gauntlet" and "Dialing for Dollars" that inflicted a level of constant pressure that some employees described as crippling and unbearable.[1] Therefore, although admittedly a catchy rhyme, the target in "Eight Is Great!" was nearly unattainable, as evidenced by the fact that even under such extreme pressures to perform, Wells Fargo employees averaged only 6.15 financial products sold per customer household, which was nearly four times the industry average. Although bonuses or the option to go home early were provided to employees who met the sales target, the negative incentives for failing to meet the target appeared to far outweigh any positive incentive. This system led Wells Fargo employees to open millions of fake bank accounts without customer knowledge or consent, which prompted a high-level and very public federal investigation of the bank and its activities.

In the end, this dysfunctional SBCS culminated in significant negative outcomes for the bank and its key stakeholders. For example, Wells Fargo fired 5,300 of its employees as a result of the scandal. In addition, U.S. federal regulators slapped the bank with billions of dollars in fines.[2] Furthermore, in an unprecedented maneuver, federal regulators also placed a cap on Wells Fargo's growth. Finally, the bank suffered negative stock performance

1   B. Levin, "Six Ways Wells Fargo Made Its Employees' Lives a Living Hell," *VanityFair.com* (April 10, 2017), https://www.vanityfair.com/news/2017/04/wells-fargo-john-stumpf-carrie-tolstedt, accessed August 31, 2020.

2   J. Kelly, "Wells Fargo Forced to Pay $3 Billion for the Bank's Fake Account Scandal," *Forbes.com* (February 24, 2020), https://www.forbes.com/sites/jackkelly/2020/02/24/wells-fargo-forced-to-pay-3-billion-for-the-banks-fake-account-scandal/, accessed August 31, 2020.

consequences (relative to industry competitors) and considerable reputational damage. In a rare public admission of corporate guilt, Wells Fargo released a widespread advertising campaign several years after the scandal broke in which the company admitted that it lost the public's trust and was committed to reestablishing itself to winning back such trust and its own positive reputation. This Wells Fargo saga serves as a strong example of the power of incentives and the utmost importance that companies should place on developing an effective SBCS in order to be successful.

We learned in Chapter 12 that activity-based management describes the fundamental economics that drive a company and, thus, helps managers to better understand the causes of cost. In turn, understanding these root causes enables managers to more effectively improve performance by continuously improving processes, which is particularly important in dynamic, rapidly changing business environments. However, activity-based management does not specifically link directly to company strategy and, as a result, is not sufficient on its own for successfully guiding high-level strategic decisions. For example, continuous improvement initiatives, along with other activity-based efforts, can come across as fragmented in nature and ultimately fail if they lack connection to the company's overall mission and strategy. Such failures highlight the importance and challenge of considering company strategy in high-level decision making. The opening scenario featuring Wells Fargo's widespread struggle to appropriately balance strategy, performance measures, and incentive programs further illustrates the extent of this challenge. Therefore, this chapter examines SBCS and their importance to long-term company success.

 OBJECTIVE 1

Explain the need for and elements of a strategic-based control system.

STRATEGIC-BASED CONTROL SYSTEMS

Successfully starting a new or maintaining an existing company presents an extremely difficult challenge. For example, of the 500 companies that appeared on the first Fortune 500 list of the world's biggest companies (as measured by sales revenue) in 1955, only 10 percent (52 out of the original 500) remain on the annual list, including General Motors, Coca-Cola, Eli Lily, Hershey, IBM, Kellogg, and General Electric.[3] In other words, 90 percent of the original Fortune 500 companies have failed to manage themselves in a successful enough manner to remain in business! Many factors explain this challenge, including increasing operational complexity, intensifying global competition, incessantly unpredictable regulatory scrutiny, and constantly changing stakeholder preferences from customers, employees, and the general public.

Regardless of the nature of the challenge, companies must find a way to incentivize employees to engage in behaviors that are in the company's best interest. However, as demonstrated so bluntly

---

3   Mark Perry, "Only 52 US Companies Have Been on the Fortune 500 since 1955," American Enterprise Institute (May 22, 2019), https://www.aei.org/carpe-diem/only-52-us-companies-have-been-on-the-fortune-500-since-1955 -thanks-to-the-creative-destruction-that-fuels-economic-prosperity/

by the 10 percent survival statistic for Fortune 500 companies, very few companies are able to accomplish this critical task. In essence, in order to be successful, or business sustainable (i.e., create and sustain organizational value over the long term), companies must possess an effective SBCS. A **strategic-based control system** translates a company's strategy into operational objectives whose performance is measured and linked to employee compensation.

As displayed in Exhibit 13.1, an SBCS contains three elements: strategy, performance measures, and incentive programs. In order for an SBCS to be effective, all three elements need to complement one other to motivate employees to consistently behave in the company's best interest. For example, Walmart's website clearly communicates its strategy as, "Every Day Low Price is the cornerstone of our strategy, and our price focus has never been stronger."[4] Indeed, Walmart's prices, on average, are consistently below that of its competitors. How has Walmart repeatedly achieved this impressive feat for over a half-century? Such success can be attributed in large part to its SBCS that motivates management's "laser ... and long-standing focus on keeping costs low."[5] Walmart has created an internal culture of promoting and rewarding cost management and resulting profit improvements by communicating to employees the expense and profit measure results of the areas they manage, as well utilizing a system of performance-linked employee compensation based partly on company profits.[6] In addition, Walmart management continually chooses to invest in large cost-cutting initiatives, These initiatives have produced a 15 percent reduction in the costs of employee uniform vests by making them out of recyclable materials, a \$100 million reduction in annual energy costs by centralizing how store equipment is maintained, a \$200 million reduction in annual energy costs by replacing all store fluorescent light fixtures with LEDs, and a \$60 million reduction in annual costs by changing the company's process for buying shopping bags.[7] Finally, Walmart utilizes major strategic cost management initiatives, such as zero-based budgeting. Although Walmart's decision making process incorporates additional factors beyond costs, its SBCS would not work as effectively to increase long-term value if the majority of its performance measures and associated incentive programs focused more on these additional factors, such as innovation (which typically is relatively expensive) rather than on cost control. In summary, these measures and incentive programs are consistent with Walmart's low-price strategy and collectively represent an effective SBCS.

Further observations are warranted concerning the considerable influence of SBCS on employee behavior. Specifically, performance measures and incentive programs undeniably impact employee behavior and actions in powerful ways, thereby ultimately affecting company performance. Not surprisingly, given this reality, the SBCS largely determines the company's culture. The term *culture* can be perceived as vague in nature. However, as discussed within the context of an SBCS, culture represents a very concrete and powerful force. In particular, executives rarely manage items that are not measured and employees rarely care about items that do not affect their compensation. Thus, the *failure* of an SBCS to include strategically *important* performance measures, as well as associated incentive rewards based on those important measures, usually causes employees to pay inadequate attention to (or even ignore) performance measures that are important to the company's overall success. For example, failing to measure and reward product quality, customer loyalty, or employee satisfaction often leads to subsequent problems with the company regarding poor product quality, expensive new customer acquisition efforts, and costly employee turnover.

- **Company Strategy** that is consistent (or in alignment) with key performance measures
- **Performance Measures** that are balanced across important characteristics.
- **Incentive Programs** that link key performance measures to employee compensation.

Exhibit 13.1

The Three Elements of a Strategic-Based Control System

---

4 S. John, "How Walmart Keeps Its Prices So Low," *Business Insider* (April 8, 2019), https://www.businessinsider.com /walmart-low-price-strategy-tips-2019-4

5 L. Rothman, "Walmart's Low-Cost Approach Wins Again," *The Motley Fool* (May 30, 2020), https://www.fool.com /investing/2020/05/30/walmarts-low-cost-approach-wins-again.aspx

6 C. Keller, "What Is Walmart's Secret to Success," *Profitworks.ca*. https://profitworks.ca/small-business-sales-and -marketing-resources/blog/marketing-strategy/579-sam-walton-wal-mart-what-is-wal-mart-s-secret-to-success.html

7 L. Thomas, "Walmart Changed the Way It Buys Shopping Bags and Saved \$60 Million—and That's Just One Way It Cut Costs," *CNBC.com* (February 18, 2020), https://www.cnbc.com/2020/02/18/walmart-saves-millions-of-dollars-each -year-by-making-these-small-changes.html

At the other extreme, the *inclusion* within an SBCS of strategically *unimportant* performance measures, as well as associated incentive rewards based on those unimportant measures, usually causes employees to pay considerable attention (or even fixate on) performance measures that are unimportant—and sometimes even detrimental—to the company's overall success. For example, consider the monumental failure of Wells Fargo's SBCS featured in the chapter's opening scenario. The chief executive officer's "Eight Is Great" mantra led the company to fixate almost solely on one performance measure (number of financial products sold per customer) and a dysfunctional compensation system that ultimately resulted in the company's multiyear, multibillion-dollar disaster.[8]

An SBCS can assume different forms, with one of the most common being that of the Balanced Scorecard. The **Balanced Scorecard** is an SBCS that typically identifies objectives and measures for four different perspectives: the financial perspective, the customer perspective, the process perspective, and the learning and growth perspective. The Balanced Scorecard converts a company's strategy into executable actions that are deployed throughout the organization. The Balanced Scorecard approach has spread rapidly in the United States and throughout the world. A **Bain & Company** survey of a broad range of international executives revealed that a majority of the companies surveyed were using (or planning to use) the Balanced Scorecard. Because of its widespread use and popularity, we focus our discussion of performance management on the Balanced Scorecard. A general overview of the Balanced Scorecard will first be provided by comparing the specific responsibility elements of an SBCS with those of the Balanced Scorecard. In the remainder of the chapter, more specific details of the Balanced Scorecard are provided.

Company Strategy

Chapter 11 discusses strategy selection in detail, including the use of strategic positioning to help create competitive advantage for the company. In addition, Chapter 11 examines the use of enterprise risk management (ERM) as a program that helps the company implement its existing strategy by managing the top risks and opportunities that might affect the achievement of its strategy. By comparison, this chapter examines SBCSs, which sit atop programs such as ERM and guide management to make any alterations to the company's strategy, performance measures, or compensation system that are necessary to increase long-term value. Therefore, the company's SBCS (which helps evaluate and alter strategy) and ERM program (which helps implement strategy) optimally should complement one another by improving the company's business sustainability over the long term.

As noted earlier, the Balanced Scorecard contains four perspectives—financial, customer, process, and learning and growth. Although more perspectives could be added or exchanged, these four are essential for creating a competitive advantage and allowing managers to articulate and communicate the company's mission and strategy. Only perspectives that serve as a potential source for a competitive advantage should be included (e.g., an environmental perspective). Regardless of the number or types of scorecard perspectives, all employees should understand the company's strategy and know how their specific responsibilities support achieving the strategy. Proper selection and definition of performance measures and associated incentive programs are key to this employee understanding.

Performance Measures

In an SBCS, performance measures must be integrated so that they are mutually consistent and reinforcing. In effect, performance measures should be designed so that they are derived from and communicate an organization's strategy and objectives. By translating the organization's strategy into objectives and measures that can be understood, communicated, and acted upon, it is possible to more completely align individual and organizational goals and initiatives. Thus, the measures must be balanced and linked to the organization's strategy.

For a firm to have balanced measures, it means that the measures selected are balanced between *lag measures* and *lead measures*, between *objective measures* and *subjective measures*, between *financial measures* and *nonfinancial measures*, between *external measures* and *internal measures* and between *mandatory measures* and *optional measures*. **Lag measures** are outcome

8   J. Kelly, "Wells Fargo Forces to Pay $3 Billion for the Bank's Fake Account Scandal," *Forbes.com* (February 24, 2020), https://www .forbes.com/sites/jackkelly/2020/02/24/wells-fargo-forced-to-pay-3-billion-for-the-banks-fake-account-scandal/#3b70292b42d2

measures—measures of results from past efforts (e.g., customer profitability). **Lead measures (performance drivers)** are factors that drive future performance (e.g., hours of employee training). **Objective measures** are those that can be readily quantified and verified (e.g., market share), whereas **subjective measures** are less quantifiable and more judgmental in nature (e.g., employee capabilities). **Financial measures** are those expressed in monetary terms (e.g., cost per unit), whereas **nonfinancial measures** use nonmonetary units (e.g., number of dissatisfied customers). **External measures** are those that relate to *customers* versus *shareholders* (e.g., customer satisfaction and return on investment). **Internal measures** are those measures that relate to the *processes* and *capabilities* that create value for customers and shareholders (e.g., process efficiency and employee satisfaction). Finally, management should consider the mix of optional and mandatory performance measures. **Mandatory measures** are required by regulators (e.g., concise and logical disclosure of significant risk factors) and thus, companies must collect (and sometimes publicly disclose) such measures to comply with rules and regulations. For example, certain stock markets and regulatory bodies around the globe increasingly are requiring companies to measure and disclose various environment performance measures, such as greenhouse gas emissions. **Optional measures**, on the other hand, are voluntary rather than required. Thus, companies that choose to collect measures voluntarily do so because they believe that such measures provide useful insights into important decisions. For example, some companies like **The Kroger Co.** choose to spend resources measuring the value of customer loyalty because management believes that customer loyalty creates direct and measurable financial benefits. Exhibit 13.2 summarizes these important characteristics to consider when creating a balanced set of performance measures.

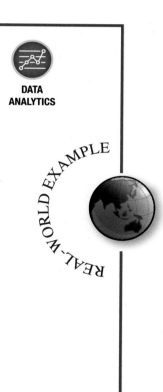

Big Data

DATA ANALYTICS

REAL-WORLD EXAMPLE

Companies continue to develop and utilize more balanced and sophisticated performance measures that emphasize important measurement characteristics. Measures that are leading, subjective, optional, or nonfinancial in nature represent examples of these emerging performance measurement characteristics. As performance measures become more sophisticated, so too do the data analytic techniques that accountants use in order to extract useful insights. Accountants must continually improve their ability to appropriately match data analytic techniques to the types of performance measures being used to understand internally and communicate externally the intricacies of company performance. In other words, data analytics can help accountants understand and tell "the story" of how the company has performed in the past and is expected to perform in the future. For example, many companies use sentiment analysis to help them better understand the underlying causal drivers of their performance. Sentiment analysis refers generally to "the process of evaluating pieces of text to determine their emotional tone."[9] Using this algorithmic technique to scan customer emails or social postings, for instance, can help accountants infer whether the customer's writing had a positive, negative, or neutral attitude toward the given topic, such as employee helpfulness or product feature quality. Such insights can provide companies with insights regarding leading indicators of future customer behavior, such as product purchases, or company actions, such as product warranty replacements. **Sentieo**, a financial and corporate research platform used by investors, utilizes various data analytic tools to review the content conveyed in quarterly earnings call transcripts for public companies like **UPS**.[10] Such analyses help investors make more informed decisions about their stock portfolios.

An SBCS uses many different kinds of measures because of the need to build an effective link to strategy. In the traditional, financial-based responsibility model, performance measures are almost always financial and, therefore, almost always lag measures. While important, financial and lag measures alone are not sufficient to link effectively with strategy. Many strategic objectives are

---

9 "What Could Sentiment Analysis Offer Accountancy?" *ICAEW.com* (February 7, 2020), https://www.icaew.com/insights/features/2020/feb-2020/what-could-sentiment-analysis-offer-accountancy

10 N. Mazing, "UPS: Negative NLP Sentiment," *Sentio.com* (April 19, 2020), https://sentieo.com/ups-transcript-smart-summary-highlights-from-may-28/?utm_content=bufferfea18&utm_medium=social&utm_source=facebook.com&utm_campaign=buffer

Exhibit 13.2

Balancing Performance Measure
Characteristics

Lead (performance drivers)	vs.	Lag (outcome results)
Subjective (judgment based)	vs.	**Objective** (readily quantified and verified)
Nonfinancial (nonmonetary units)	vs.	**Financial** (monetary units)
Internal (processes and capabilities)	vs.	**External** (customers and shareholders)
Optional (discretion of management)	vs.	**Mandatory** (required by regulator)

nonfinancial in nature and require the inclusion of nonfinancial measures to promote and measure progress. For example, as noted earlier, Kroger and other companies realize that increasing customer loyalty may be a key strategic objective that will lead to increased revenues and profits. Yet, how is customer loyalty measured? The number of repeat orders is a good possible measure, and it is a nonfinancial measure. Similarly, what factors might represent drivers of customer loyalty? Increasing product quality? Increasing on-time deliveries? Additionally, how are these critical success factors measured? Percentage of defective units and percentage of on-time deliveries are good possibilities. Clearly, to express the desired linkages among strategic objectives, nonfinancial measures are needed.

The concept of lead measures also is critical. A lead measure, by definition, is one that has a causal linkage with the strategy. For example, if the number of defective units decreases, will customer loyalty actually increase? If the number of repeat orders increases, will revenues and profits actually increase? Assuming a causal relationship exists, when in reality it does not, can be quite costly. For example, **Xerox** assumed that increasing customer satisfaction would lead to increased financial performance. It then spent millions of dollars surveying and measuring customer satisfaction only to discover that increasing customer satisfaction did not increase financial performance. As it turned out, a customer loyalty measure was the correct lead measure for improving financial performance.[11]

Finally, it should be noted that to communicate an organization's strategy through the language of measurement requires both scope and flexibility. Scope implies that both internal and external measures are needed. Flexibility requires subjective and objective measurement as well as nonfinancial measures. In effect, a Balanced Scorecard expresses the complete story of a company's strategy through an integrated set of financial and nonfinancial measures that are both predictive and historical, measured subjectively or objectively, and focused on critical internal and external issues.

Incentive Programs

The previous section examined how companies increasingly are expanding the breadth and depth—or balance—of the performance factors they measure. We now move on to the third and final element of an SBCS—incentive programs. In order to ensure that employees sufficiently consider important performance measures as they make various decisions, most companies include at least a subset of such measures within employees' performance evaluation and resulting compensation calculations.

In addition to linking to compensation, performance evaluation in a Balanced Scorecard framework should also consider the effectiveness and viability of the company's strategy. This emphasis is communicated by establishing *stretch* targets for the individual performance measures of the various perspectives. **Stretch targets** are targets that are set at levels that, if achieved, will transform the organization within a period of three to five years. Performance for a given period is evaluated by comparing the actual values of the various measures with the targeted values. Two key features make stretch targets feasible: (1) the measures are linked

---

11 Christopher Ittner and David Larcker, "Coming Up Short on Nonfinancial Performance Measurement," *Harvard Business Review* (November 2003): 88–95.

by causal relationships, and (2) because of the linkages, the targets are not set in isolation but rather through a consensus of all those in the organization.

Management Control System at Royal Dutch Shell

Shell spends considerable effort measuring and rewarding employee performance in a manner that helps the company achieve its strategy (and other related business objectives). These three elements—performance measures, compensation, and strategy—represent the three key elements of the company's strategic-based control system (SBCS). As discussed later in the chapter, Shell specifically utilizes the Balanced Scorecard technique to implement and communicate these important SBCS elements to all employees. The following chart from Shell's annual report displays its Balanced Scorecard, including: (1) the financial, operational excellence, and sustainable development performance measures, (2) the bonus weighting for each performance measure (30 percent, 50 percent, and 20 percent), and (3) the link to strategy for each performance measure.

Performance measure	Weighting
Financial	30%
Operational excellence	50%
Sustainable development	20%

	Link to strategy
Financial ▪ Cashflow from operating activities	Aligned with our financial priorities, reflecting our ability to generate cash to service and reduce debt, pay the dividend and fund capital investment.
Operational excellence ▪ Production ▪ LNG liquefaction volumes ▪ Refinery and chemical plant availability ▪ Project delivery	Representative performance metrics from our main business lines to drive focus on the operational delivery critical to our success and inspire a shared culture and alignment with our purpose, strategy and values. These metrics measure the effectiveness with which we operate our assets and portfolio base. This operational performance underpins the successful delivery of our financial framework and ambitions to progress in the energy transition. Shell's longer-term strategic ambitions are measured in the LTIP metrics.
Sustainable development ▪ Safety ▪ Environmental performance	We must maintain focus on safety and environmental performance, as this provides assurance to shareholders, employees and society of our commitment to safety and progress in the energy transition.

REAL-WORLD EXAMPLE

* Graphic from *Annual Report and Accounts: Energy for a Better Future*, Royal Dutch Shell PLC, 2019, https://reports. shell.com/annual-report/2019/servicepages/downloads/files/shell_annual_report_2019.pdf, accessed August 31, 2020.

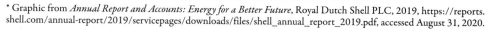

More specifically, Shell calculates an employee's annual bonus as such: base salary $\times$ target bonus percentage $\times$ scorecard result (which ranges from 0 to 2). The maximum bonus for top executives, such as the chief executive officer and chief financial officer, maxes out at approximately 250 percent of their base salary. In other words, bonuses appear to be large enough in amount so as to affect employee behavior. Shell's decision to incorporate employee performance along key measures into their compensation system strongly signals internally to employees that achieving strategy is important to the company and that they play critical roles in this process. The decision to publicly disclose such SBCS specifics signals externally how the company plans to achieve its strategy. The value of such disclosures appears significant, especially given that, as Shell acknowledges, scorecard targets include "commercially sensitive" information content. Such actions speak louder than words to many key stakeholders as not all companies can "walk the talk" of effectively setting strategy and consistently measuring and rewarding appropriate employee behavior to the extent reflected in Shell's SBCS.

For any SBCS to be successful, the reward system must be linked to the performance measures. A Balanced Scorecard approach can be very useful for driving organizational change through its structured presentation of key performance measures, especially when such measures are linked clearly and consistently to employee rewards (e.g., compensation). It is very unlikely that an organization can secure the needed support for a Balanced Scorecard of measures unless compensation is tied to the scorecard measures. Equally important, the SBCS must be carefully designed so as not to link employee compensation to the wrong performance measures. Such mistakes usually lead employees to pursue actions that do not result in optimal outcomes for the company (i.e., because employees "chase after the wrong things"). The chapter's opening feature on Wells Fargo represents a stark example of such a mistake that cost the company billions of dollars in fines and penalties.

OBJECTIVE ▶2

Discuss the basic features of the Balanced Scorecard.

BASIC CONCEPTS OF THE BALANCED SCORECARD

The Balanced Scorecard permits an organization to create a strategic focus by *translating* an organization's strategy into operational objectives and performance measures for four different perspectives: the financial perspective, the customer perspective, the internal business process perspective, and the learning and growth (infrastructure) perspective. The Balanced Scorecard is an effective way of implementing and managing a company's strategy. A number of companies attribute their recent financial success to this SBCS.

Strategy Translation

Strategy, according to the creators of the Balanced Scorecard framework, is defined as:[12]

> *choosing the market and customer segments the business unit intends to serve, identifying the critical internal and business processes that the unit must excel at to deliver the value propositions to customers in the targeted market segments, and selecting the individual and organizational capabilities required for the internal, customer, and financial objectives.*

Strategy, then, is identifying and defining management's desired relationships among the four perspectives. *Strategy translation*, on the other hand, means specifying objectives, measures, targets, and initiatives for each perspective. The strategy translation process is illustrated in Exhibit 13.3. Consider, for example, a company that wishes to pursue a revenue growth strategy. For the financial perspective, the company may specify an *objective* of growing revenues by introducing new products. The *performance measure* may be the percentage of revenues from the sale of new products. The *target* or *standard* for the coming year for the measure may be 20 percent. (That is, 20 percent of the total revenues for the coming year must be from the sale of new products.) The *initiative* describes *how* this is to be accomplished. The "how," of course, involves the other three perspectives. The customer segments, internal processes, and individual and organizational capabilities that will permit the realization of the revenue growth objective must now be identified. This illustrates the fact that the financial objectives serve as the focus for the objectives, measures, and initiatives of the other three perspectives. It also illustrates the need to carefully define the relationships among the four perspectives so that strategy becomes visible and operational. Before examining how these causal relationships define and operationalize the strategy, however, we first need a better understanding of the four perspectives, their objectives, and their measures.

---

12   Robert S. Kaplan and David P. Norton, *The Balanced Scorecard* (Boston: Harvard Business School Press, 1996).

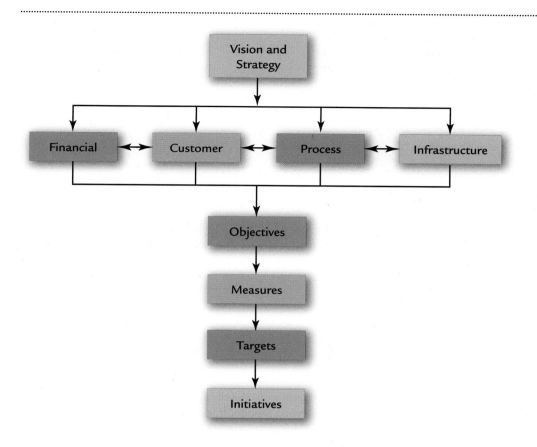

Exhibit 13.3
Strategy Translation Process

The Financial Perspective, Objectives, and Measures

The **financial perspective** establishes the long- and short-term financial performance objectives expected from the organization's strategy and simultaneously describes the economic consequences of actions taken in the other three perspectives. This implies that the objectives and measures of the other perspectives should be chosen so that they cause or bring about the desired financial outcomes. The financial perspective has three strategic themes: revenue growth, cost reduction, and asset utilization. These themes serve as the building blocks for the development of specific operational objectives and measures. Of course, the three themes are constrained by the need for managers to manage risk.

Revenue Growth Increasing revenues can be achieved in a variety of ways, and the potential strategic objectives reflect these possibilities. Among these possibilities are the following objectives: increase the number of new products, create new applications for existing products, develop new customers and markets, and adopt a new pricing strategy. Once operational objectives are known, performance measures can be designed. Possible measures for the preceding list of objectives (in the order given) are percentage of revenue from new products, percentage of revenue from new applications, percentage of revenue from new customers and market segments, and profitability by product or customer.

Cost Reduction Reducing the cost per unit of product, per customer, or per distribution channel are examples of cost reduction objectives. The appropriate measures are obvious: the cost per unit of the particular cost object. Trends in these measures will tell whether or not the costs are being reduced. For these objectives, the accuracy of cost assignments is especially important. Activity-based costing can play an essential measurement role, especially for selling and administrative costs—costs not usually assigned to cost objects like customers and distribution channels.

Exhibit 13.4

Summary of Objectives and Measures: Financial Perspective

Objectives	Measures
Revenue Growth:	
Increase the number of new products	Percentage of revenues from new products
Create new applications	Percentage of revenues from new applications
Develop new customers and markets	Percentage of revenues from new sources
Adopt a new pricing strategy	Product and customer profitability
Cost Reduction:	
Reduce unit product cost	Unit product cost
Reduce unit customer cost	Unit customer cost
Reduce distribution channel cost	Cost per distribution channel
Asset Utilization:	
Improve asset utilization	Return on investment
	Economic value added

Asset Utilization Improving asset utilization is the principal objective. Financial measures such as return on investment and economic value added are used. Since return on investment and economic value-added measures were discussed in detail in Chapter 10, they will not be discussed here. The objectives and measures for the financial perspective are summarized in Exhibit 13.4.

Risk Management Managing the risk associated with the adopted strategy is another critical strategic theme—one that is common to the three strategic financial themes already discussed. Diversification of customer types, product lines, and suppliers are common means of lowering risk. Sourcing materials from only one supplier may lower costs, but it may also jeopardize the firm's throughput if something happens to the supplier (e.g., a labor strike). Similarly, revenues may be increased by relying on one very large customer—but what happens if the customer decides to buy elsewhere? Thus, any strategic initiative must be balanced with careful consideration of the risk involved (see Chapter 11 for a more thorough discussion of enterprise risk management).

Customer Perspective, Objectives, and Measures

The **customer perspective** defines the customer and market segments in which the business unit will compete and describes the way that value is created for customers. The customer perspective is the source of the revenue component for the financial objectives. Failure to deliver the right kinds of products and services to the targeted customers means revenue will not be generated.

Core Objectives and Measures

Once the customers and segments are defined, then *core objectives* and *measures* are developed. **Core objectives and measures** are those that are common across all organizations. There are five key core objectives: increase market share, increase customer retention, increase customer acquisition, increase customer satisfaction, and increase customer profitability. Possible core measures for these objectives, respectively, are market share (percentage of the market), percentage growth of business from existing customers and percentage of repeating customers, number of new customers, ratings from customer satisfaction surveys, and individual and segment profitability. Activity-based costing is a key tool in assessing customer profitability (see Chapter 11). Notice that customer profitability is the only financial measure among the core measures. This measure, however, is critical because it emphasizes the importance of the *right* kind of customers. What good is it to have customers if they are not profitable? The obvious answer spells out the difference between being customer focused and customer obsessed.

Customer Value

In addition to the core measures and objectives, measures are needed that drive the creation of *customer value* and, thus, drive the core outcomes. For example, increasing customer value builds customer loyalty (increases retention) and increases customer satisfaction. **Customer value** is the difference between realization and sacrifice, where realization is what the customer receives and sacrifice is what is given up. Realization includes such attributes as product functionality (features), product quality, reliability of delivery, delivery response time, image, and reputation. Sacrifice includes attributes such as product price, time required to learn to use the product, operating cost, maintenance cost, and disposal cost. The costs incurred by the customer *after* purchase are called **post-purchase costs**.

The attributes associated with realization and sacrifice provide the basis for the objectives and measures that will lead to improving the core outcomes. The objectives for the sacrifice side of the value equation are the simplest: decrease price and decrease post-purchase costs. Selling price and post-purchase costs are important measures of value creation. Decreasing these costs decreases customer sacrifice, and, thus, increases customer value. Increasing customer value should impact favorably on most of the core objectives. Similar favorable effects can be obtained by increasing realization. Realization objectives, for example, would include the following: improve product functionality, improve product quality, increase delivery reliability, and improve product image and reputation. Possible measures for these objectives include, respectively, feature satisfaction ratings, percentage of returns, on-time delivery percentage, and product recognition rating. Of these objectives and measures, delivery reliability will be used to illustrate how measures can affect managerial behavior, indicating the need to be careful in the choice and use of performance measures.

Delivery reliability means that output is delivered on time. On-time delivery is a commonly used operational measure of reliability. To measure on-time delivery, a firm sets delivery dates and then finds on-time delivery performance by dividing the orders delivered on time by the total number of orders delivered. The goal, of course, is to achieve a ratio of 100 percent. This measure used by itself, however, may produce undesirable behavioral consequences.[13] Specifically, plant managers were giving priority to filling orders not yet late over orders that were already late. The performance measure was encouraging managers to have one very late shipment rather than several moderately late shipments! A chart measuring the age of late deliveries could help mitigate this problem. Exhibit 13.5 summarizes the objectives and measures for the customer perspective.

Objectives	Measures
Core:	
Increase market share	Market share (percentage of market)
Increase customer retention	Percentage growth, existing customers
	Percentage of repeating customers
Increase customer acquisition	Number of new customers
Increase customer satisfaction	Ratings from customer surveys
Increase customer profitability	Customer profitability
Performance Value:	
Decrease price	Price
Decrease post-purchase costs	Post-purchase costs
Improve product functionality	Ratings from customer surveys
Improve product quality	Percentage of returns
Increase delivery reliability	On-time delivery percentage
	Aging schedule
Improve product image and reputation	Ratings from customer surveys

Exhibit 13.5

Summary of Objectives and Measures: Customer Perspective

---

13 Joseph Fisher, "Nonfinancial Performance Measures," *Journal of Cost Management* (Spring 1992): 31–38.

Process Perspective, Objectives, and Measures

The **internal business process perspective** describes the internal processes needed to provide value for customers and owners. Processes are the means by which strategies are executed. Thus, the process perspective entails the identification of the critical processes needed that affect customer and shareholder satisfaction. To provide the framework needed for this perspective, a *process value chain* is defined. The **process value chain** is made up of three processes: the *innovation process*, the *operations process*, and the *post-sales service process*.[14] The **innovation process** anticipates the emerging and potential needs of customers and creates new products and services to satisfy those needs. It represents what is called the *long wave* of value creation. The **operations process** produces and delivers *existing* products and services to customers. It begins with a customer order and ends with the delivery of the product or service. It is the *short wave* of value creation. The **post-sales service process** provides critical and responsive services to customers after the product or service has been delivered.

Innovation Process: Objectives and Measures

Objectives for the innovation process include the following: increase the number of new products, increase percentage of revenue from proprietary products, and decrease the time to develop new products. Associated measures are actual new products developed versus planned products, percentage of total revenues from new products, percentage of revenues from proprietary products, and development cycle time (time to market).

Operations Process: Objectives and Measures

Three operations process objectives are almost always mentioned and emphasized: increase process quality, increase process efficiency, and decrease process time. Examples of process quality measures are quality costs, output yields (good output/good input), and percentage of defective units (good output/total output). Quality costing and control are discussed extensively in Chapter 14. Measures of process efficiency are concerned mainly with process cost and process productivity. Measuring and tracking process costs are facilitated by activity-based costing and process value analysis. These issues were explored in depth in the activity-based management chapter (Chapter 12). Productivity measurement is explored in Chapter 15. Common process time measures are cycle time, velocity, and manufacturing cycle efficiency (MCE).

Cycle Time and Velocity

The time it takes a company to respond to a customer order is referred to as *responsiveness*. *Cycle time* and *velocity* are two operational measures of responsiveness. **Cycle time (manufacturing)** is the length of time it takes to produce a unit of output from the time materials are received (starting point of the cycle) until the good is delivered to finished goods inventory (finishing point of the cycle).[15] Thus, cycle time is the time required to produce a product (time/units produced). **Velocity** is the number of units of output that can be produced in a given period of time (units produced/time). Although cycle time has been defined for the operations process, it is defined in a similar way for innovation and post-sales service processes. For example, how long does it take to create a new product and introduce it to the market? Or, how long does it take to resolve a customer complaint (from start to finish)?

Incentives can be used to encourage operational managers to reduce manufacturing cycle time or to increase velocity, thus improving delivery performance. A natural way to accomplish

---

14   Kaplan and Norton, *The Balanced Scorecard*, 96.

15   Other definitions of cycles are possible (e.g., a cycle's starting point could begin when the customer order is received and the finishing point when the goods are delivered to the customer). For a JIT firm, delivery to the customer is a reasonable finishing point. Another possibility for the finishing point is when the customer receives the goods. Cycle time measures the time elapsed from start to finish, regardless of how the starting and finishing points are defined.

this objective is to tie product costs to cycle time and reward operational managers for reducing product costs. For example, in a Just-in-Time (JIT) firm, cell conversion costs can be assigned to products on the basis of the time that it takes a product to move through the cell. Using the theoretical productive time available for a period (in minutes), a value-added standard cost per minute can be computed.

> Standard cost per minute = Cell conversion costs /Minutes available

To obtain the conversion cost per unit, this standard cost per minute is multiplied by the actual cycle time used to produce the units during the period. By comparing the unit cost computed using the actual cycle time with the unit cost possible using the theoretical or optimal cycle time, a manager can assess the potential for improvement. Note that the more time it takes a product to move through the cell, the greater the unit product cost. With incentives to reduce product cost, this approach to product costing encourages operational managers and cell workers to find ways to decrease cycle time or increase velocity. **Example 13.1** illustrates the concepts of cycle time and velocity.

EXAMPLE 13.1

The HOW and WHY of Calculating Cycle Time and Velocity

Information:
Assume that a company has the following data for one of its manufacturing cells:

> Theoretical velocity: 40 units per hour
> Productive minutes available (per year): 1,200,000
> Annual conversion costs: $4,800,000
> Actual velocity: 30 units per hour

> **Why:**
> Cycle time (time/units produced) and velocity (units produced/time) measure the time it takes for a firm to respond to such things as customer orders, customer complaints, and the development of new products.

Required:

1. Calculate the actual conversion cost per unit using actual cycle time and the standard cost per minute.

2. Calculate the ideal conversion cost per unit using theoretical cycle time and the standard cost per minute. What incentive exists for managers when cycle time costing is used?

3. *What if* the actual velocity is 36 units per hour? What is the conversion cost per unit? What effect will this improvement have on delivery performance?

Solution:

1. Actual cycle time = 60 minutes/30 units = 2 minutes per unit
   (Notice that cycle time is the reciprocal of velocity.)
   Standard cost per minute = $4,800,000/1,200,000 = $4 per minute
   Conversion cost per unit = $4 × 2 = $8 per unit

2. Theoretical cycle time = 60 minutes/40 units = 1.5 minutes per unit
   Conversion cost per unit = $4 × 1.5 = $6 per unit
   The incentive is to reduce cycle time because it reduces the cost per unit.

3. Actual cycle time = 60 minutes/36 units = 1.67 minutes
   Conversion cost per unit = $4 × 1.67 = $6.68 per unit
   The company should be able to deliver orders more quickly and performance should improve.

Manufacturing Cycle Efficiency (MCE)

Another time-based operational measure calculates manufacturing cycle efficiency (MCE) as follows:

MCE = Processing time /(Processing time + Move time + Inspection time + Waiting time + Other non-value-added time)

where processing time is the efficient or ideal time it takes to convert materials into a finished good. The other activities and their times are viewed as wasteful, and the goal is to reduce those times to zero. If this is accomplished, the value of MCE would be 1.0. Many manufacturing companies have MCEs less than 0.05.[16] As MCE improves (moves toward 1.0), cycle time decreases. Furthermore, since the only way MCE can improve is by decreasing waste, cost reduction must also follow. **Example 13.2** provides a detailed illustration of MCE.

EXAMPLE 13.2

The HOW and WHY of Calculating Manufacturing Cycle Efficiency (MCE)

Information:
A company has provided the following information for one of its products for each hour of production:

       Actual velocity: 100 units (per hour)

       Move time: 20 minutes

       Inspection time: 15 minutes

       Rework time: 10 minutes

> **Why:**
> MCE measures the proportion of manufacturing cycle time attributable to value-added processing. Without waste, the ratio should be equal to 1.0.

Required:

1. Calculate MCE. Comment on its significance.

2. What is the theoretical cycle time? Calculate MCE using actual and theoretical cycle times.

3. *What if* waste is reduced by one-third? What is the new MCE? New cycle time?

Solution:

1. Process time = 60 minutes − 20 minutes − 15 minutes − 10 minutes

          = 15 minutes

    MCE = Process time/ (Process time + Move time + Inspection time + Rework time)

        = 15/ (15 + 20 + 15 + 10)

        = 0.25

    A value of 0.25 indicates that 75 percent of the manufacturing cycle is attributable to waste.

2. Theoretical cycle time = 15 minutes/100 units = 0.15 minute

    Actual cycle time = 60 minutes/100 units = 0.60 (includes theoretical cycle time plus the waste)

    MCE = Theoretical cycle time/Actual cycle time

        = 0.15/0.60 = 0.25

---

16 Kaplan and Norton, *The Balanced Scorecard*, 117.

EXAMPLE 13.2

(*Continued*)

3.   New waste = $(2/3) (20 \text{ minutes} + 15 \text{ minutes} + 10 \text{ minutes})$

$= 30 \text{ minutes}$

MCE $= 15/(15 + 30) = 0.33$

(It now takes 45 minutes to produce units.)

Post-Sales Service Process: Objectives and Measures

Increasing quality, increasing efficiency, and decreasing process time are also objectives that apply to the post-sales service process. Service quality, for example, can be measured by first-pass yields where first-pass yields are defined as the percentage of customer requests resolved with a single service call. Efficiency can be measured by cost trends and productivity measures. Process time can be measured by cycle time where the starting point of the cycle is defined as the receipt of a customer request and the finishing point is when the customer's problem is solved. The objectives and measures for the process perspective are summarized in Exhibit 13.6.

Learning and Growth Perspective

The **learning and growth (infrastructure) perspective** defines the capabilities that an organization needs to create long-term growth and improvement. This last perspective is concerned with three major *enabling factors*: employee capabilities, information systems capabilities, and employee attitudes. Employee capabilities are concerned with skills, talent, and knowledge. Information system capabilities are concerned with databases, networks, and technology infrastructure and the provision of accurate and timely information. Employee attitudes have to do with motivation, empowerment, and alignment (teamwork). These factors enable processes to be executed efficiently. The learning and growth perspective is the source of the capabilities that enable the accomplishment of the other three perspectives' objectives. This perspective has

Objectives	Measures
Innovation:	
Increase the number of new products	Number of new products/total products; R&D expenses
Increase proprietary products	Percentage revenue from proprietary products Number of patents pending
Decrease product development cycle time	Time to market (from start to finish)
Operations:	
Increase process quality	Quality costs Output yields Percentage of defective units
Increase process efficiency	Unit cost trends Output/input(s)
Decrease process time	Cycle time and velocity MCE
Post-Sales Service:	
Increase service quality	First-pass yields
Increase service efficiency	Cost trends Output/input(s)
Decrease service time	Cycle time

Exhibit 13.6

Summary of Objectives and Measures: Process Perspective

three major objectives: increase employee capabilities; increase motivation, empowerment, and alignment; and increase information systems capabilities.

Employee Capabilities   Three core *outcome* measurements for employee capabilities are employee satisfaction ratings, employee turnover percentages, and employee productivity (e.g., revenue per employee). Examples of lead measures or performance drivers for employee capabilities include hours of training and strategic job coverage ratios (percentage of critical job requirements filled). As new processes are created, new skills are often demanded. Training and hiring are sources of these new skills. Furthermore, the percentage of the employees needed in certain key areas with the requisite skills signals the capability of the organization to meet the objectives of the other three perspectives.

Mackay Memorial Hospital in Taiwan, for example, had a specific learning and growth objective of promoting employees' ability of performing research, teaching, and innovation. Two specific performance measures for this objective were the *number of science citation index (SCI) papers* and *the number of research projects*. Thus, the more specific objectives were to increase the number of SCI papers and the number of research projects. Over a three-year time period, the number of SCI papers increased from 132 to 1,945, and the number of research projects increased from 46 to 61.[17]

Motivation, Empowerment, and Alignment   Employees must not only have the necessary skills, but they must also have the freedom, motivation, and initiative to use those skills effectively. The number of suggestions per employee and the number of suggestions implemented per employee are possible measures of motivation and empowerment. Suggestions per employee provide a measure of the degree of employee involvement, whereas suggestions implemented per employee signal the quality of the employee participation. The second measure also signals to employees whether or not their suggestions are being taken seriously.

Information Systems Capabilities   Increasing information system capabilities means providing more accurate and timely information to employees so that they can improve processes and effectively execute new processes. Measures should be concerned with the *strategic information availability*. For example, possible measures include percentage of processes with real-time feedback capabilities and percentage of customer-facing employees with online access to customer and product information. Exhibit 13.7 summarizes the objectives and measures for the learning and growth perspective.

OBJECTIVE 3
Explain how the Balanced Scorecard links measures to strategy.

LINKING MEASURES TO STRATEGY

The Balanced Scorecard is a collection of critical performance measures that have some special properties. First, the performance measures are derived from a company's vision, strategy, and objectives. To link measures to a strategy, they must be derived from strategy. Second, performance measures should be chosen so that they are *balanced* between outcome and lead measures. Outcome measures such as profitability, return on investment, and market share tend to be generic and, therefore, common to most strategies and organizations. Performance drivers make

---

17   Wen-Cheng Chang, Yu-Chi Tung, Chun-Hsiung Huang, and Ming-Chin Yang, "Performance Improvement after Implementing the Balanced Scorecard: A Large Hospital's Experience in Taiwan," *Total Quality Management* 19, no. 11 (November 2008): 1143–1154.

Objectives	Measures
Increase employee capabilities	Employee satisfaction ratings
	Employee turnover percentages
	Employee productivity (revenue/employee)
	Hours of training
	Strategic job coverage ratio (percentage of critical job requirements filled)
Increase motivation and alignment	Suggestions per employee
	Suggestions implemented per employee
Increase information systems capabilities	Percentage of processes with real-time feedback capabilities
	Percentage of customer-facing employees with online access to customer and product information

Exhibit 13.7

Summary of Objectives and Measures: Learning and Growth Perspective

things happen; consequently, lead measures are indicators of how the outcomes are going to be realized. Lead measures usually distinguish one strategy from another. Thus, lead measures are often unique to a strategy and because of this uniqueness support the objective of linking measures to strategy. Third, all scorecard measures should be linked by cause-and-effect relationships.

The Concept of a Testable Strategy with Strategic Feedback

This last requirement—that of linking through the use of cause-and-effect relationships—is the most important requirement. Cause-and-effect relationships are the means by which lead and lag measures are integrated and simultaneously serve as the mechanism for expressing and revealing the firm's strategy. Outcome measures are important because they reveal whether the strategy is being implemented successfully with the desired economic consequences. Lead measures supposedly cause the outcome. For example, if the number of defective products is decreased (a lead measure), does this result in a greater market share (an outcome or lag measure)? Does a greater market share (acting now as a lead measure), in turn, result in more revenues and profits (lag measures)? These questions reveal the vital role of cause-and-effect relationships in expressing an operational model of a strategy—a strategy that can be expressed in a testable format. In fact, a **testable strategy** can be defined as a set of linked objectives aimed at an overall goal. The testability of the strategy is achieved by restating the strategy into a set of cause-and-effect hypotheses that are expressed by a sequence of if-then statements.[18]

Perhaps the most important message associated with the cause-and-effect structure is that the viability of the strategy is testable. Strategic feedback is available that allows managers to test the reasonableness of the strategy. For example, if the number of defective products decreases, we would expect to see an increase in market share. If not, it could be due to one of two causes: (1) implementation problems, or (2) an invalid strategy. First, it is possible that a *key performance indicator* such as the number of defective units did not achieve its targeted level (that is, the reduction in the number of defective units was less than planned). In this case, the failure to produce the expected *outcomes* for other objectives (e.g., market share and revenue) could be merely an implementation problem. On the other hand, if the targeted levels of performance drivers were achieved and the expected outcomes did not materialize, then the problem could very well lie with the strategy itself. This is an example of *double-loop feedback*. **Double-loop feedback** occurs whenever managers receive information about both the *effectiveness* of strategy implementation as well as the *validity* of the assumptions underlying the strategy. In a traditional performance management system, typically, only *single-loop feedback* is provided. **Single-loop feedback** emphasizes

---

18 Kaplan and Norton, *The Balanced Scorecard*, 149. (Kaplan and Norton describe the sequence of if-then statements only as a strategy. Calling it a testable strategy distinguishes it from the earlier, more general definition offered.)

only the effectiveness of implementation. In single-loop feedback, actual results deviating from planned results are a signal to take corrective action so that the plan (strategy) can be executed as intended. The validity of the assumptions underlying the plan is usually not questioned.

Double-loop feedback is the foundation for strategic learning. In the Balanced Scorecard framework, strategic planning is dynamic—not static. Hypothesis testing makes it possible to change and adapt once it becomes clear that some parts of the strategy may not be viable. For example, it may be that improving quality by reducing the number of defects may not increase market share. If all other competitors are also improving quality, then the correct view may be that improving quality is needed to *maintain* market share. Increasing market share may require the company to search for some other value proposition that will be unique and innovative (e.g., offering a new product).

The **strategy map** is a useful tool that graphically illustrates the cause-and-effect relationships and connects the Balanced Scorecard strategy with an organization's operating activities. The strategy map provides a concise and pictorial representation of the firm's strategy. The linkages portrayed are for each of the firm's objectives and show how these objectives are linked for each of the four perspectives. **Example 13.3** illustrates strategy mapping.

The strategy map of Exhibit 13.8 illustrates the value-growth strategy described in Example 13.3. This exhibit reveals at least four interesting features. First, each of the four perspectives is represented by strategic objectives linked through the cause-and-effect relationships hypothesized. Second, notice that process improvement and employee skills are jointly hypothesized to cause an improvement in process cycle time. This emphasizes the fact that an outcome can be caused by more than one performance driver. Third, it is also possible that a lead indicator can cause more than one outcome. Notice that decreasing cycle time causes both an improvement in delivery reliability (affecting the customer perspective) and a decrease in process costs (affecting the financial perspective). Fourth, as indicated in Example 13.3, a performance measure can serve as both a lag indicator and a lead indicator. For example, under the influence of employee skills and process redesign, cycle time serves as a lag indicator. But changes in cycle time affect process costs and delivery performance, thus serving as a lead indicator.

EXAMPLE 13.3

The HOW and WHY of Strategy Mapping

Information:

Consider the following value-growth strategy expressed as a sequence of if-then statements:

- If employee skills are upgraded and if the manufacturing process is redesigned, then manufacturing cycle time will be decreased.
- If cycle time decreases, then delivery reliability will improve and process costs will decrease.
- If delivery reliability improves, then customer retention will increase.
- If customer retention increases, then market share will increase.
- If market share increases, then sales will increase.
- If sales increase and costs decrease, then profits will increase.
- If profits increase, then shareholder value will increase.

> **Why:**
> A strategy map links the cause-and-effect relationships for the objectives of each of the four perspectives. It is a concise graphical representation of a testable Balanced Scorecard strategy. Failure to achieve the expected outcomes for each hypothesis is due to either bad implementation or an invalid strategy.

Required:

1. Prepare a strategy map for value-growth strategy as described by the series of cause-and-effect relationships.

2. Explain how a performance measure can act as both a lag variable and a lead indicator.

EXAMPLE 13.3

(*Continued*)

3. ***What if*** shareholder value did not increase to the targeted level? Explain how this result could be attributable to either an implementation problem or an invalid strategy. What actions would likely be taken for each case?

Solution:

1. See Exhibit 13.8.

2. Consider the objective of increasing cycle time. Cycle time is an outcome (lag) measure for the objectives of increasing employee skills and redesigning the manufacturing process. However, it also acts as a performance driver (lead variable) for the objectives of improving delivery reliability and decreasing process costs.

3. Assuming that the value-growth strategy is valid, increasing the targeted shareholder value is dependent on achieving the targeted values of all the preceding lead variables. If, for example, the manufacturing process was not redesigned, then the targeted improvement in cycle time may not occur. This, in turn, would ripple through the series and may explain why the targeted shareholder value was not achieved. In this case, ensuring that the planned actions are actually implemented is the solution. If, on the other hand, the process was redesigned and employees' skills were upgraded at the targeted levels but the targeted shareholder value is not achieved, then there is a problem with the strategy. Assume, for example, that the first two hypotheses are valid, but that the third does not hold. In this case, the premise that increasing customer retention will increase market share apparently is not valid. Reexamination of the hypothesis may lead to the conclusion that quality is also needed as a performance driver to increase market share.

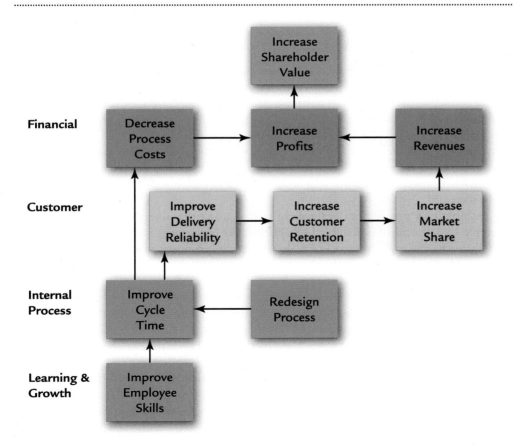

Exhibit 13.8
Strategy Map for Example 13.3

OBJECTIVE 4

Describe how an organization can achieve strategic alignment.

STRATEGIC ALIGNMENT

Creating a strategy is one thing. Implementing the strategy successfully is another. For the Balanced Scorecard to be successful, the entire organization must be committed to its achievement. The Balanced Scorecard is designed to bring about organizational change. For this change to take place, employees must be fully informed of the strategy; they must share ownership for the objectives, measures, targets, and initiatives; incentives must be structured to support the strategy; and resources must be allocated to support the strategy.

Communicating the Strategy

The scorecard objectives and measures, once developed, become the means for articulating and communicating the strategy of the organization to its employees and managers. The objectives and measures also serve the purpose of aligning individual objectives and actions with organizational objectives and initiatives. Videos, newsletters, brochures, and the company's computer network (e.g., internal email or intranet systems, social media apps or platforms) are examples of media that can be used to inform employees of the strategy, objectives, and measures associated with the Balanced Scorecard. How much specific detail to communicate is certainly a relevant question. Communicating too much detail may create a potential problem with competitors. The Balanced Scorecard is a very explicit representation of the company's targeted markets and the means required for obtaining gains in these markets. This representation can contain very sensitive information; the more employees who are aware of it, the more likely it may end up in the hands of competitors. Yet, it is important that employees have a sufficient understanding of what is happening so that they will accept and agree to the strategic efforts of the organization. Articulation of the Balanced Scorecard should be clear enough that individuals can see the linkage between what they do and the organization's long-term objectives. Seeing this linkage increases the likelihood that personal goals and actions are congruent with organizational goals.

Targets and Incentives

Once objectives and measures have been defined and communicated, performance expectations must be established. Performance expectations are communicated by setting targeted values for the measures associated with each objective. Managers are held accountable for the assigned responsibility by comparing the actual values of the measures with the targeted values. Finally, compensation is linked to achievement of the scorecard objectives. It is vital that the reward system be tied to all the scorecard objectives and not just to traditional financial measures. Failure to change the compensation system will encourage managers to continue their focus on short-term financial performance with little reason to pay attention to the strategic objectives of the scorecard.

Exhibit 13.9 provides an example of targets using the objectives and measures for Example 13.3 illustrated in Exhibit 13.8. The relative importance management has assigned to each perspective and objective is revealed by weights expressed as percentages. Targets are set for both the long term and the short term (e.g., a three- to five-year horizon and a one-year horizon) and should be backed up with initiatives that can be undertaken to achieve them. For example, is it really possible to increase share prices by 50 percent over a three-year span? And how much increase will be targeted for the coming year? The increase is dependent on increasing revenues by 30 percent and decreasing costs by 20 percent. These changes are, in turn, dependent on other events in other perspectives. Can cycle time be reduced to two days (say, from a current level of five days)?

How to structure incentive compensation with multiple dimensions is a challenging task. Typically, weights that reflect the relative importance of the perspectives are used to determine the percentage of the bonus pool that will be assigned to each perspective. Thus, from Exhibit 13.9, we see that for this example each perspective would be assigned

Exhibit 13.9   Targets and Weighting Scheme Illustrated

Perspectives	Objectives	Measures	Targets
Financial (25%)	Increase shareholder value (25%)	Share price	50% increase
	Increase profits (25%)	Profits	100%
	Increase revenues (25%)	Revenues	30% increase
	Decrease process costs (25%)	Costs	20% decrease
Customer (25%)	Increase market share (20%)	Market share	25%
	Increase customer retention (30%)	Repeat orders	70%
	Improve delivery reliability (50%)	On-time percentage	100%
Internal Process (25%)	Improve cycle time (60%)	Cycle time	2 days
	Redesign process (40%)	Yes or No	Yes
Learning & Growth (25%)	Improve employee skills (100%)	Hours of training	30 hours per employee

25 percent of the total bonus pool. But within each category, there are usually multiple objectives and multiple measures. For example, within the customer category, there are three performance measures. How much of the 25 percent bonus pool should be assigned to each measure? Again, weights that reflect the relative importance of each objective within its category are used to make this determination. Exhibit 13.9, for example, reveals that management has decided to assign 50 percent of the customer category bonus to the on-time delivery objective, 30 percent to the customer retention objective, and 20 percent to the market share objective. Thus, of the original bonus pool, 12.5 percent is assigned to the delivery objective (0.50 × 0.25).

Distributing potential bonus money to the various perspectives and measures is one thing, but payment of incentive compensation is dependent on *performance*. The actual values of the measures are compared to the targeted values for a given time period. Compensation is then paid, based on the percentage achievement of each objective. However, there is one major qualification for the Balanced Scorecard framework. To ensure that proper (balanced) attention is given to all measures, no incentive compensation is paid unless each strategic measure exceeds a prespecified minimum threshold value.[19]

Firms adopting the Balanced Scorecard seem to realize the necessity of connecting their reward system to the objectives and measures of the new performance management system. In fact, a survey found that after two years of having a Balanced Scorecard in place, about 81 percent had linked compensation to the scorecard.[20] The Gold Coin Group, an Asian animal and fish food provider and wheat distributor, provides a specific example. Group directors receive 50 percent of their pay in fixed compensation and 50 percent in variable compensation. The company decided to give high priority to the customer perspective, by allocating 45 percent of the variable pay to the customer perspective, while assigning 20 percent to the financial perspective, 20 percent to the process perspective, and 15 percent to learning and growth. The outcomes seemed to support the decision. After two years, customer retention improved by 30 percent, customer acquisition improved by 30 percent, customer complaints dropped by 40 percent, and delivery lead times fell by 50 percent. Of course, profits increased because of the improvements in these customer-related performance measures.[21]

---

19   Ibid., 219–220

20   Laura Downing, "Progress Report on the Balanced Scorecard: A Global Users' Survey," *Balanced Scorecard Report* (November 15, 2000)

21   James Creelman, "Aligning Compensation with the Balanced Scorecard," http://www.EPMReview.com/Resources /case-studies/aligning-compensation.html, accessed September 17, 2011.

REAL-WORLD EXAMPLE

Sustainability

As discussed earlier, **Shell** uses Balanced Scorecards extensively throughout the company to measure, motivate, and compensate employee performance to help achieve its strategic objectives. The Balanced Scorecard is easily adapted to include a business sustainability component. One way to do so is to create a fifth perspective that focuses on the business sustainability issues of greatest strategic importance to the company. For example, given that safety represents an important value driver for Shell (i.e., "safety ... is fundamental to our business approach"), safety performance is included in the annual bonus scorecard for all Shell employees.[22] As disclosed in its Annual Report, Shell's performance on its "Health, Safety, and Security" measure equals 0.9, indicating that company employees experienced 0.9 recordable case frequencies (injuries) per million working hours. The inclusion of safety measures, including employee compensation calculations, within scorecards helps the company continuously improve its safety performance. For example, Shell notes that it relentlessly pursues a goal frequency of zero-safety incidents. This pursuit is reflected in the company's increasing investments in accident-prevention procedures, as well as training to help employees better respond to the safety-related aspects of uncertainties that inevitably arise when working in the energy industry. Not surprisingly, Shell also similarly measures, rewards, and discloses considerable information concerning its environmental performance as well.

Resource Allocation

Achieving strategic targets such as those envisioned in Exhibit 13.9 requires that resources be allocated to the corresponding strategic initiatives. This successful allocation requires two major changes. First, an organization must decide how much of the strategic targets will be achieved for the coming year. Second, the operational budgetary process must be structured to provide the resources necessary for achievement of these short-time advances along the strategic path. If these changes are not incorporated, then it is difficult to imagine that the strategy will truly become actionable.

SUMMARY OF LEARNING OBJECTIVES

LO1. Explain the need for and elements of an SBCS.
- SBCSs consist of three elements—company strategy, performance measures, and incentive programs.
- These three SBCS elements should complement, as opposed to contradict, one another to help the company sustain and succeed over the long term.

LO2. Discuss the basic features of the Balanced Scorecard.
- The Balanced Scorecard is an SBCS that translates the vision and strategy of an organization into operational objectives and measures.
- Objectives and measures are developed for each of four perspectives: the financial perspective, the customer perspective, the process perspective, and the learning and growth perspective.

LO3. Explain how the Balanced Scorecard links measures to strategy.
- Performance measures are derived from a company's vision, strategy, and objectives.
- Performance measures are balanced between outcome and lead measures.
- All scorecard measures are linked by cause-and-effect relationships.
- The cause-and-effect relationships produce a set of testable hypotheses expressed by a sequence of if-then statements.

---

22 See https://reports.shell.com/annual-report/2019/servicepages/downloads/files/shell_annual_report_2019.pdf

LO4. Describe how an organization can achieve strategic alignment.
- The entire organization must be committed to the Balanced Scorecard.
- Employees must be fully informed of the strategy and share ownership for the objectives, measures, targets, and initiatives.
- Incentives (e.g., compensation) must be structured to support the strategy, and resources must be allocated to support the strategy.
- Thus, alignment with the strategy expressed by the Balanced Scorecard is achieved by communication, incentives, and allocation of resources to support the strategic initiatives.

EXAMPLE 13.1 The HOW and WHY of Calculating Cycle Time and Velocity, page 685

EXAMPLE 13.2 The HOW and WHY of Calculating Manufacturing Cycle Efficiency (MCE), page 686

EXAMPLE 13.3 The HOW and WHY of Strategy Mapping, page 690

KEY TERMS

Balanced Scorecard, 676

Core objectives and measures, 682

Customer perspective, 682

Customer value, 683

Cycle time (manufacturing), 684

Double-loop feedback, 689

External measures, 677

Financial measures, 677

Financial perspective, 681

Innovation process, 684

Internal business process perspective, 684

Internal measures, 677

Lag measures, 676

Lead measures (performance drivers), 677

Learning and growth (infrastructure) perspective, 687

Mandatory measures, 677

Nonfinancial measures, 677

Objective measures, 677

Operations process, 684

Optional measures, 677

Post-purchase costs, 683

Post-sales service process, 684

Process value chain, 684

Single-loop feedback, 689

Strategic-based control system (SBCS), 675

Strategy, 680

Strategy map, 690

Stretch targets, 678

Subjective measures, 677

Testable strategy, 689

Velocity, 684

BRIEF EXERCISES

OBJECTIVE ▶2
Example 13.1

Brief Exercise 13-1 Cycle Time and Velocity

Bemidii Company has the following data for one of its production departments:

> Theoretical velocity: 400 units per hour
> Productive minutes available per year: 5,000,000
> Annual conversion costs: $120,000,000
> Actual velocity: 240 units per hour

Required:

1. Calculate the actual conversion cost per unit using actual cycle time and the standard cost per minute.
2. Calculate the ideal conversion cost per unit using theoretical cycle time and the standard cost per minute. What incentive exists for managers when cycle time costing is used?
3. *What if* the actual velocity is 300 units per hour? What is the conversion cost per unit? What effect will this improvement have on delivery performance?

OBJECTIVE ▶2
Example 13.2

Brief Exercise 13-2 MCE

Fontane, Inc., has provided the following information for one of its products for each hour of production:

> Actual velocity: 400 units (per hour)
> Move time: 25 minutes
> Inspection time: 5 minutes
> Rework time: 10 minutes

Required:

1. Calculate MCE. Comment on its significance. Round answers to two decimal points.
2. What is the theoretical cycle time? Calculate MCE using actual and theoretical cycle times. Round answers to two decimal points.
3. *What if* waste is reduced by 20 percent? What is the new MCE? New cycle time? Round answers to two decimal points.

OBJECTIVE ▶3
Example 13.3

Brief Exercise 13-3 Strategy Map

Harmon Community Hospital developed the following series of if-then statements for its Balanced Scorecard strategy:

- If employee turnover rate decreases and employee satisfaction increases, then the quality of health care service will improve.
- If the quality of health care service improves, then operating efficiency will increase and patient satisfaction will increase.
- If operating efficiency increases, then operating costs will decrease.
- If patient satisfaction increases, then market share will increase.
- If market share increases, then revenues will increase.
- If revenues increase and costs decrease, then profits will increase.

Required:

1. Prepare a strategy map for Harmon's strategy as described by the series of cause-and-effect relationships.
2. Explain how a performance measure can act as both a lag variable and a lead indicator.
3. *What if* profits did not increase to the targeted level? Explain how this result could be attributable to either an implementation problem or an invalid strategy. What actions would likely be taken for each case?

EXERCISES

Exercise 13-4 Performance Measure Characteristics

DATA ANALYTICS

Required:

1. For each numbered (1–10) performance measure characteristic, select the appropriate lettered (A–J) descriptor that best explains the characteristic.

1. Financial	_____	A. Readily quantified
2. Internal	_____	B. Monetary units
3. Mandatory	_____	C. Processes and capabilities
4. Lead	_____	D. Performance drivers
5. Objective	_____	E. Required by regulator
6. Nonfinancial	_____	F. Discretion of management
7. Subjective	_____	G. Nonmonetary units
8. External	_____	H. Customers and shareholders
9. Lag	_____	I. Judgment based
10. Optional	_____	J. Outcome results

2. Briefly explain how a performance measure's particular characteristic (Lead, Subjective, etc.) might affect its use in a data analytics context (see Exhibits 2.5 and 2.6, pp. 37, 40 for a review of data analytic types). For example, how might a *leading* performance measure be used differently than a *lagged* performance measure within data analytics?

Exercise 13-5 Strategic-Based Control Systems

"A Balanced Scorecard expresses the complete story of a company's strategy through an integrated set of financial and nonfinancial measures that are both predictive and historical and that may be measured subjectively or objectively."

Required:

1. Using the above statement about scorecard measures, explain how scorecard measurement differs from that of an activity-based management system.
2. Explain what is meant by historical and predictive measures. Why are both types important for describing a company's strategy?

Exercise 13-6 Strategic-Based Control Systems

DATA ANALYTICS

Iron Mountain Outdoor Adventures is considering implementing the Balanced Scorecard to drive change within the company Iron Mountain management believes that performance evaluation is an integral part of this effort. More specifically, performance evaluation within the Balanced Scorecard framework also is concerned with the effectiveness and viability of the organization's strategy.

Required:

1. Describe how the Balanced Scorecard might be used to drive organizational change within Iron Mountain Outdoor Adventures.
2. Explain how performance evaluation might be used to assess the effectiveness and viability of Iron Mountain's strategy.
3. Assume that Iron Mountain Outdoors Adventures recently received permission from its customers to access their texts, emails, and social media postings that pertain to their Iron Mountain shopping experiences. Briefly explain how Iron Mountain's accountants might utilize data analytics to decipher this newly accessed customer data to improve company decisions (see Exhibits 2.5 and 2.6, pp. 37, 40 for a review of data analytic types).

OBJECTIVE

Exercise 13-7 Balanced Scorecard, Perspectives, Classification of Performance Measures

Consider the following list of scorecard measures:

a. Product profitability
b. Ratings from customer surveys
c. Number of patents pending
d. Strategic job coverage ratio
e. Revenue per employee
f. Quality costs
g. Percentage of market
h. Employee turnover percentages
i. First-pass yields
j. On-time delivery percentage
k. Percentage of revenues from new sources
l. Economic value added

Required:

Classify each measure according to the following: perspective, financial or nonfinancial, subjective or objective, and external or internal. When the perspective is process, identify which type of process: innovation, operations, or post-sales service.

OBJECTIVE

SHOW ME HOW   DATA ANALYTICS

Exercise 13-8 Cycle Time and Conversion Cost per Unit

Hatch Manufacturing produces multiple machine parts. The theoretical cycle time for one of its products is 65 minutes per unit. The budgeted conversion costs for the manufacturing cell dedicated to the product are $12,960,000 per year. The total labor minutes available are 1,440,000. During the year, the cell was able to produce 0.6 units of the product per hour. Suppose also that production incentives exist to minimize unit product costs.

Required:

1. Compute the theoretical conversion cost per unit.
2. Compute the applied conversion cost per minute (the amount of conversion cost actually assigned to the product).
3. Discuss how this approach to assigning conversion cost can improve delivery time performance. Explain how conversion cost acts as a performance driver for on-time deliveries.
4. Briefly explain how Hatch Manufacturing might further benefit from its accountants utilizing prescriptive data analytics (see Exhibit 2.6, pp. 40 for a review of data analytic types).

OBJECTIVE

SHOW ME HOW   EXCEL

Exercise 13-9 Cycle Time and Velocity, MCE

Computador has a manufacturing plant in Des Moines that has the theoretical capability to produce 243,000 laptops per quarter but currently produces 91,125 units. The conversion cost per quarter is $7,290,000. There are 60,750 production hours available within the plant per quarter. In addition to the processing minutes per unit used, the production of the laptops uses 10 minutes of move time, 20 minutes of wait time, and 5 minutes of rework time. (All work is done by cell workers.)

Required:

1. Compute the theoretical and actual velocities (per hour) and the theoretical and actual cycle times (minutes per unit produced).
2. Compute the ideal and actual amounts of conversion cost assigned per laptop.
3. Calculate MCE. How does MCE relate to the conversion cost per laptop?

Exercise 13-10 Cycle Time and Velocity, MCE

Refer to **Exercise 13-9**. Assume that the company identifies poor plant layout as the root cause of wait time and move time.

OBJECTIVE 2 3

SHOW ME HOW

Required:

1. Express an improvement strategy as a series of if-then statements that will reduce the conversion cost per laptop.
2. Assume that you set an MCE target of 75 percent, based on the improvement strategy described in Requirement 1. What is the expected conversion cost per unit? Explain how you can use these targets to test the viability of your quality improvement strategy.

Exercise 13-11 Balanced Scorecard, Lead and Lag Variables, Double-Loop Feedback

The following if-then statements were taken from a Balanced Scorecard:

OBJECTIVE 1 2 3

DATA ANALYTICS

a. If employee capabilities increase, then process time decreases.
b. If process time decreases, then customer retention will increase.
c. If customer retention increases, then market share will increase.
d. If market share increases, then revenues will increase.

Required:

1. Identify the lead and lag variables, and explain your reasoning.
2. Discuss the implications of Requirement 1 for the financial and learning and growth perspectives.
3. Using the first if-then statement, explain the concept of double-loop feedback.
4. Identify and briefly explain the data analytic category type (Descriptive, Diagnostic, Predictive, or Prescriptive) to which the lead-lag variables most likely belong (see Exhibit 2.6, pp. 40, for a review of data analytic types).

Exercise 13-12 Testable Strategy, Strategy Map

OBJECTIVE 3

Consider the following quality improvement strategy as expressed by a series of if-then statements:

- If real-time feedback information capabilities improve, then post-sales service time will improve.
- If post-sales service time improves, then post-sales service quality will increase.
- If post-sales service quality increases, then customer satisfaction will increase.
- If customer satisfaction increases, then market share will increase.
- If market share increases, then sales will increase.
- If sales increase, then profits will increase.

Required:

1. Prepare a strategy map that shows the cause-and-effect relationships of the quality improvement strategy (see Exhibit 13.8 for an illustrative example).
2. Explain how the quality improvement strategy can be tested.

Exercise 13-13 Balanced Scorecard, Strategy Translation, Strategy Map, Double-Loop Feedback

OBJECTIVE 2 3

Bannister Company, an electronics firm, buys circuit boards and manually inserts various electronic devices into the printed circuit board. Bannister sells its products to original equipment manufacturers. Profits for the last two years have been less than expected. Mandy Confer, owner of Bannister, was convinced that her firm needed to adopt a revenue growth and cost reduction strategy to increase overall profits.

After a careful review of her firm's condition, Mandy realized that the main obstacle for increasing revenues and reducing costs was the high defect rate of her products (a 6 percent reject rate). She was certain that revenues would grow if the defect rate was reduced dramatically. Costs would also decline as there would be fewer rejects and less rework. By decreasing the defect rate, customer satisfaction would increase, causing, in turn, an increase in market share. Mandy also felt that the following actions were needed to help ensure the success of the revenue growth and cost reduction strategy:

a. Improve the soldering capabilities by sending employees to an outside course.
b. Redesign the insertion process to eliminate some of the common mistakes.
c. Improve the procurement process by selecting suppliers that provide higher-quality circuit boards.

Required:

1. State the revenue growth and cost reduction strategy using a series of cause-and-effect relationships expressed as if-then statements.
2. Illustrate the strategy using a strategy map.
3. Explain how the revenue growth strategy can be tested. In your explanation, discuss the role of lead and lag measures, targets, and double-loop feedback.

OBJECTIVE 4 ▶ **Exercise 13-14 Balanced Scorecard, Strategic Alignment**

Refer to **Exercise 13-13**. Suppose that Mandy communicates the following weights to her CEO:

Perspective: Financial, 40%; Customer, 20%; Process, 20%; Learning & growth, 20%
Financial objectives: Profits, 50%; Revenues, 25%; Costs, 25%
Customer objectives: Customer satisfaction, 60%; Market share, 40%
Process objectives: Defects decrease, 40%; Supplier selection, 30%; Redesign process, 30%
Learning & growth objective: Training, 100%

Mandy next sets up a bonus pool of $100,000 and indicates that the weighting scheme just described will be used to determine the amount of potential bonus for each perspective and each objective.

Required:

1. Calculate the potential bonus for each perspective and objective.
2. Describe how Mandy might award actual bonuses so that her managers will be encouraged to implement the Balanced Scorecard.
3. What are some other ways that Mandy can encourage alignment with the company's strategic objectives (other than incentive compensation)?

PROBLEMS

OBJECTIVE 1 ▶ **Problem 13-15 Activity-Based Responsibility Accounting versus Strategic-Based Control Systems**

Carson Wellington, president of Mallory Plastics, was considering a report sent to him by Emily Sorensen, vice president of operations. The report was a summary of the progress made by an activity-based management system that was implemented three years ago. Significant progress had indeed been realized. At the conclusion of the report, Emily urged Carson to consider the adoption of the Balanced Scorecard as a logical next step in the company's efforts to establish itself as a leader in its industry. Emily clearly was impressed by the Balanced Scorecard and intrigued by the possibility that the change would enhance the overall competitiveness of

Mallory. She requested a meeting of the executive committee to explain the similarities and differences between the two approaches. Carson agreed to schedule the meeting but asked Emily to prepare a memo in advance, listing the most important similarities and differences between the two approaches to managerial accounting.

Required:

Prepare the memo requested by Carson.

Problem 13-16 Scorecard Measures, Strategy Translation

EXCEL

At the end of 20x1, Mejorar Company implemented a low-cost strategy to improve its competitive position. Its objective was to become the low-cost producer in its industry. A Balanced Scorecard was developed to guide the company toward this objective. To lower costs, Mejorar undertook a number of improvement activities such as JIT production, total quality management, and activity-based management. Now, after two years of operation, the president of Mejorar wants some assessment of the achievements. To help provide this assessment, the following information on one product has been gathered:

	20x 1	20x3
Theoretical annual capacity*	249,600	249,600
Actual production**	208,000	234,000
Market size (in units sold)	1,300,000	1,300,000
Production hours available (40 workers)	104,000	104,000
Very satisfied customers	83,200	140,400
Actual cost per unit	$325	$260
Days of inventory	15.6	7.8
Number of defective units	13,000	5,200
Total worker suggestions	104	312
Hours of training	260	1,040
Selling price per unit	$195	$195
Number of new customers	5,200	26,000

*Amount that could be produced given the available production hours; everything produced is sold.
**Amount that was produced given the available production hours.

Required:

1. Compute the following measures for 20x1 and 20x3:
   a. Actual velocity and cycle time
   b. Percentage of total revenue from new customers (assume one unit per customer)
   c. Percentage of very satisfied customers (assume each customer purchases one unit)
   d. Market share
   e. Percentage change in actual product cost (for 20x3 only)
   f. Percentage change in days of inventory (for 20x3 only)
   g. Defective units as a percentage of total units produced
   h. Total hours of training
   i. Suggestions per production worker
   j. Total revenue
   k. Number of new customers

2. For the measures listed in Requirement 1, list likely strategic objectives, classified according to the four Balance Scorecard perspectives. Assume there is one measure per objective.

OBJECTIVE 2 3

Problem 13-17 If-Then Statements, Strategy Map

Refer to the data in **Problem 13-16.**

1. Express Mejorar's strategy as a series of if-then statements. What does this tell you about Balanced Scorecard measures?
2. Prepare a strategy map that illustrates the relationships among the likely strategic objectives.

OBJECTIVE 2 3

Problem 13-18 Strategic Objectives, Scorecard Measures, Strategy Map

The following strategic objectives have been derived from a strategy that seeks to improve asset utilization by more careful development and use of its human assets and internal processes:

a. Increase revenue from new products.
b. Increase implementation of employee suggestions.
c. Decrease operating expenses.
d. Decrease cycle time for the development of new products.
e. Decrease rework.
f. Increase employee morale.
g. Increase customer satisfaction.
h. Increase access of key employees to customer and product information.
i. Increase customer acquisition.
j. Increase return on investment (ROI).
k. Increase employee productivity.
l. Decrease the collection period for accounts receivable.
m. Increase employee skills.

The heart of the strategy is developing the company's human resources. Management is convinced that empowering employees will lead to an increase in economic returns. Studies have shown that there is a positive relationship between employee morale and customer satisfaction. Furthermore, the more satisfied customers pay their bills more quickly. It was hypothesized that as employees became more involved and more productive, their morale would improve. Thus, the strategy incorporated key objectives that would lead to an increase in productivity and involvement.

Required:

1. Classify the objectives by perspective, and suggest a measure for each objective.
2. Prepare a strategy map that illustrates the likely causal relationships among the strategic objectives.

OBJECTIVE 2

Problem 13-19 Cycle Time, Conversion Cost per Unit, MCE

EXCEL

Lander Parts, Inc., produces various automobile parts. In one plant, Lander has a manufacturing cell with the theoretical capability to produce 450,000 fuel pumps per quarter. The conversion cost per quarter is $9,000,000. There are 150,000 production hours available within the cell per quarter.

Required:

1. Compute the theoretical velocity (per hour) and the theoretical cycle time (minutes per unit produced).
2. Compute the ideal amount of conversion cost that will be assigned per subassembly.
3. Suppose the actual time required to produce a fuel pump is 40 minutes. Compute the amount of conversion cost actually assigned to each unit produced. What happens to product cost if the time to produce a unit is decreased to 25 minutes? How can a firm encourage managers to reduce cycle time? Finally, discuss how this approach to assigning conversion cost can improve delivery time.
4. Assuming the actual time to produce one fuel pump is 40 minutes, calculate MCE. How much non-value-added time is being used? How much is it costing per unit?
5. Cycle time, velocity, MCE, conversion cost per unit (theoretical conversion rate × actual conversion time), and non-value-added costs are all measures of performance for the cell process. Discuss the incentives provided by these measures.

Problem 13-20 MCE, Testable Strategy, Strategy Map

Auflegger, Inc., manufactures a product that experiences the following activities (and times):

	Hours
Processing (two departments)	42.0
Inspecting	2.8
Rework	7.0
Moving (three moves)	11.2
Waiting (for the second process)	33.6
Storage (before delivery to customer)	43.4

Required:

1. Compute the MCE for this product.
2. A study lists the following root causes of the inefficiencies: poor quality components from suppliers, lack of skilled workers, and plant layout. Suggest a possible cost reduction strategy, expressed as a series of if-then statements that will reduce MCE and lower costs. Finally, prepare a strategy map that illustrates the causal paths. In preparing the map, use only three perspectives: learning and growth, process, and financial.
3. Is MCE a lag or a lead measure? If and when MCE acts as a lag measure, what lead measures would affect it?

Problem 13-21 Cycle Time, Velocity, Product Costing

Mulhall, Inc., has a JIT system in place. Each manufacturing cell is dedicated to the production of a single product or major subassembly. One cell, dedicated to the production of mopeds, has four operations: machining, finishing, assembly, and qualifying (testing). The machining process is automated, using computers. In this process, the model's frame and engine are constructed. In finishing, the frame is sandblasted, buffed, and painted. In assembly, the frame and engine are assembled. Finally, each model is tested to ensure operational capability.

For the coming year, the moped cell has the following budgeted costs and cell time (both at theoretical capacity):

Budgeted conversion costs	$ 6,696,000
Budgeted materials	$18,600,000
Cell time	37,200
Theoretical output	27,900 models

During the year, the following actual results were obtained:

Actual conversion costs	$6,696,000
Actual materials	$4,030,000
Actual cell time	37,200 hours
Actual output	23,250 models

Required:

1. Compute the velocity (number of models per hour) that the cell can theoretically achieve. Now, compute the theoretical cycle time (number of hours or minutes per model) that it takes to produce one model.
2. Compute the actual velocity and the actual cycle time.
3. Compute MCE. Comment on the efficiency of the operation.
4. Compute the budgeted conversion cost per minute. Using this rate, compute the conversion cost per model if theoretical output is achieved. Using this measure, compute the conversion cost per model for actual output. Does this product costing approach provide an incentive for the cell manager to reduce cycle time? Explain.

OBJECTIVE  **1** **2** **3** **4**

Problem 13-22 Balanced Scorecard, Non-Value-Added Activities, Strategy Translation, Kaizen Costing

At the beginning of the last quarter of 20x1, Youngston, Inc., a consumer products firm, hired Maria Carrillo to take over one of its divisions. The division manufactured small home appliances and was struggling to survive in a very competitive market. Maria immediately requested a projected income statement for 20x1. In response, the controller provided the following statement:

Sales	$25,000,000
Variable expenses	20,000,000
Contribution margin	$ 5,000,000
Fixed expenses	6,000,000
Projected loss	$ (1,000,000)

After some investigation, Maria soon realized that the products being produced had a serious problem with quality. She once again requested a special study by the controller's office to supply a report on the level of quality costs. By the middle of November, Maria received the following report from the controller:

Inspection costs, finished product	$ 400,000
Rework costs	2,000,000
Scrapped units	600,000
Warranty costs	3,000,000
Sales returns (quality-related)	1,000,000
Customer complaint department	500,000
Total estimated quality costs	$7,500,000

Maria was surprised at the level of quality costs. They represented 30 percent of sales, which was certainly excessive. She knew that the division had to produce high-quality products to survive. The number of defective units produced needed to be reduced dramatically. Thus, Maria decided to pursue a quality-driven turnaround strategy. Revenue growth and cost reduction could both be achieved if quality could be improved. By growing revenues and decreasing costs, profitability could be increased.

After meeting with the managers of production, marketing, purchasing, and human resources, Maria made the following decisions, effective immediately (end of November 20x1):

a. More will be invested in employee training. Workers will be trained to detect quality problems and empowered to make improvements. Workers will be allowed a bonus of 10 percent of any cost savings produced by their suggested improvements.

b. Two design engineers will be hired immediately, with expectations of hiring one or two more within a year. These engineers will be in charge of redesigning processes and products with the objective of improving quality. They will also be given the responsibility of working with selected suppliers to help improve the quality of their products and processes. Design engineers were considered a strategic necessity.

c. Implement a new process: evaluation and selection of suppliers. This new process has the objective of selecting a group of suppliers that are willing and capable of providing nondefective components.

d. Effective immediately, the division will begin inspecting purchased components. According to production, many of the quality problems are caused by defective components purchased from outside suppliers. Incoming inspection is viewed as a transitional activity. Once the division has developed a group of suppliers capable of delivering nondefective components, this activity will be eliminated.

e. Within three years, the goal is to produce products with a defect rate less than 0.10 percent. By reducing the defect rate to this level, marketing is confident that market share will increase by at least 50 percent (as a consequence of increased customer satisfaction). Products with better quality will help establish an improved product image and reputation, allowing the division to capture new customers and increase market share.

f. Accounting will be given the charge to install a quality information reporting system. Daily reports on operational quality data (e.g., percentage of defective units), weekly updates of trend graphs (posted throughout the division), and quarterly cost reports are the types of information required.

g. To help direct the improvements in quality activities, kaizen costing is to be implemented. For example, for the year 20x1, a kaizen standard of 6 percent of the selling price per unit was set for rework costs, a 25 percent reduction from the current actual cost.

To ensure that the quality improvements were directed and translated into concrete financial outcomes, Maria also began to implement a Balanced Scorecard for the division. By the end of 20x2, progress was being made. Sales had increased to $26,000,000, and the kaizen improvements were meeting or beating expectations. For example, rework costs had dropped to $1,500,000.

At the end of 20x3, two years after the turnaround quality strategy was implemented, Maria received the following quality cost report:

Quality training	$ 500,000
Supplier evaluation	230,000
Incoming inspection costs	400,000
Inspection costs, finished product	300,000
Rework costs	1,000,000
Scrapped units	200,000
Warranty costs	750,000
Sales returns (quality-related)	435,000
Customer complaint department	325,000
Total estimated quality costs	$4,140,000

Maria also received an income statement for 20x3:

Sales	$30,000,000
Variable expenses	22,000,000
Contribution margin	$ 8,000,000
Fixed expenses	5,800,000
Income from operations	$ 2,200,000

Maria was pleased with the outcomes. Revenues had grown, and costs had been reduced by at least as much as she had projected for the two-year period. Growth next year should be even greater as she was beginning to observe a favorable effect from the higher-quality products. Also, further quality cost reductions should materialize as incoming inspections were showing much higher-quality purchased components.

Required:

1. Identify the strategic objectives, classified by the Balanced Scorecard perspective. Next, suggest measures for each objective.
2. Using the results from Requirement 1, describe Maria's strategy using a series of if-then statements. Next, prepare a strategy map.
3. Explain how you would evaluate the success of the quality-driven turnaround strategy. What additional information would you like to have for this evaluation?
4. Explain why Maria felt that the Balanced Scorecard would increase the likelihood that the turnaround strategy would actually produce good financial outcomes.
5. Advise Maria on how to encourage her employees to align their actions and behavior with the turnaround strategy.

14 Quality and Environmental Cost Management

After studying this chapter, you should be able to:

1 ▸ Describe how quality costs are defined, classified, and measured.

2 ▸ Explain how a quality cost report is prepared and used.

3 ▸ Explain why quality cost information is needed and how it is used.

4 ▸ Prepare three different types of quality performance reports.

5 ▸ Discuss how environmental costs can be measured, reported, and reduced.

6 ▸ Show how environmental costs can be assigned to products and processes.

QUALITY AND ENVIRONMENTAL INFORMATION

at Baxter International

Baxter International is a Fortune 500 company headquartered in Deerfield, Illinois. Baxter produces products, technologies, and therapies for critical care, nutrition, renal treatment, hospital care, and surgical care. Baxter's products are available in over 100 countries, and the company has manufacturing facilities in over 20 countries, with more than 50,000 employees worldwide. Baxter has R&D centers in Belgium, Germany, China, Sweden, India, Italy, and the United States. Its revenues exceed $11 billion.[1]

Two important areas of emphasis for Baxter are product quality and environmental quality. Baxter set specific five-year improvement goals for both areas. Reducing the number of external failure incidents for its products was a high priority. For example, three years into its improvement program, Baxter reports on its progress for four specific external failure categories: (1) complaint incidents (number of alleged product defects globally), (2) medical device reports (number of reports submitted to the U.S. Food and Drug Administration [FDA] for certain medical device malfunctions), (3) field alert reports (reports submitted to the FDA for a specific drug application and category), and (4) field actions (recalled products and nonrecall actions taken on products globally). Compared to the base year, Baxter had reduced complaint incidents by 19 percent, medical device reports by 73 percent, field alert reports by 63 percent, and field actions by 42 percent.[2] In the third year alone, Baxter reported more than 100 improvements to its products, resulting in enhanced patient safety and quality, better product performance, and increased customer satisfaction, all of which likely improved Baxter's overall financial performance.[3]

Improving environmental quality by reducing negative environmental impacts is another area of emphasis for Baxter. Adopting ISO 14001, the international standard for environmental management systems, is strong evidence of Baxter's commitment to environmental quality. Baxter reported that 59 locations, including 43 of its manufacturing sites, met the requirements of ISO 14001.[4] During the first three years of its five-year improvement program, Baxter has also been successful in reducing negative environmental impacts. For example, their five-year goal was to reduce energy use, water use, and waste generation by 15 percent. By the end of the third year, energy use had been reduced by 7 percent, water consumption by 7 percent, and total waste generation by 10 percent.[5] Interestingly, in the third year of the improvement program, Baxter managed to recycle 80 percent of its nonhazardous waste and 51 percent

---

1 Baxter 2018 Corporate Responsibility Report, https://www.baxter.com/sites/g/files/ebysai746/files/2019 -06/Baxter_2018_Corporate_Responsibility_Report.pdf, accessed June 20, 2020.
2 Ibid., p. 11.
3 Ibid., p. 12.
4 Ibid., p. 23
5 Ibid.

of regulated waste, generating a net recycling income of $5 million.[6] Moreover, through a process of product innovation, over a two-year period, Baxter eliminated 1,593 metric tons of packaging material from products shipped to customers.[7] Clearly, improving both environmental and quality performance also improves Baxter's economic performance, underscoring the importance of studying quality and environmental cost management.

**DATA
ANALYTICS**

As Baxter International so vividly illustrates, there are numerous quality- and environmental-related activities, all of which consume resources that determine the level of quality and environmental costs incurred by a firm. Inspecting or testing parts, for example, is a quality appraisal activity that has the objective of detecting bad products, whereas contamination tests are designed to measure the level of pollution. Detecting bad products and correcting them before they are sent to customers are usually less expensive than letting them be acquired by customers. Similarly, preventing contamination and waste from entering the environment is also usually less expensive. The objective of quality and environmental cost management is to find ways to minimize total quality and environmental costs. Interestingly, there are remarkable similarities between the two approaches. Furthermore, both approaches rely strongly on data analytics to assess and measure progress. Data visualization is important to describe and assess quality and environmental costs and to see the effects of planned improvements. Quality cost management will first be explored, followed by environmental cost management.

Competitive forces are requiring firms to pay increasing attention to quality. Customers are demanding higher-quality products and services. Improving quality may actually be the key to survival for many firms. Improving process quality and the quality of products and services is a fundamental strategic objective that is part of any well-designed Balanced Scorecard. If quality is improved, then customer satisfaction increases; if customer satisfaction increases, then market share will increase; and if market share increases, then revenues will increase; moreover, if quality improves, then operating costs will also decrease. Thus, improving quality can increase market share and sales, while simultaneously decreasing costs. The overall effect enhances a firm's financial and competitive position.

One indication of the importance of quality in the United States is the creation of the Malcolm Baldrige National Quality Award (Public Law 100-107) in 1987. The Baldrige Award was created to recognize U.S. companies that excel in quality management and achievement. There are six eligibility award categories: manufacturing, small business, service, education, health care, and nonprofit. Since no more than 18 awards are given across the six categories, it is difficult to win and highly sought after. The first awards were given in 1988. In 2019, there were six winners of the Baldrige award:

> Howard Community College (education)
> Adventist Health White Memorial (health care)
> Mary Greeley Medical Center (health care)
> Center for Organ Recovery and education (nonprofit)
> City of Germantown, Tennessee (nonprofit)
> Illinois Municipal Retirement Fund (nonprofit)[8]

Improving quality can increase firm value because it increases a firm's profitability. Improving quality can increase profitability in at least two ways: (1) by increasing customer demand and (2) by decreasing the costs of providing goods and services.

---

6 Ibid., p. 26.
7 Ibid., p. 8.
8 National Institute of Standards and Technology, "Six Health Care, Nonprofit and Educational Organizations Win Baldridge Awards for Performance Excellence," November 14, 2019, https://www.nist.gov/news-events/news/2019/11/six-health-care-nonprofit-and-education-organizations-win-baldrige-awards, accessed June 19, 2020.

COSTS OF QUALITY

Over the past 20 to 30 years, American industry has made significant strides in improving quality. Even so, much remains to be done. The costs of quality can be substantial and a source of significant savings. According to some experts, most companies, if they properly evaluate their costs of quality, will find that they are between 15 and 25 percent of sales.[9] According to the six sigma model, if the average quality performance of a company is three sigma (a defect rate of about 6.7 percent), then quality costs would range between 25 and 40 percent of sales.[10] Yet, quality experts indicate that the optimal quality level should be about 2 to 4 percent of sales (at six sigma levels [a defect rate of 0.00034 percent], the costs of quality would be less than 1 percent). This difference between actual and optimal figures represents a veritable gold mine of opportunity. Improving quality can produce significant improvements in profitability.

In 2010 **MEDRAD**, a producer of devices for diagnosing and treating diseases, won a Malcolm Baldrige Quality Award for the second time in 10 years (the first award was given to them in 2003). Quality improvements helped MEDRAD increase its revenues from $120 million in 1997 to $625 million in 2009. Its customer loyalty, satisfaction, and service levels exceeded best-in-class benchmarks. Its employee value improvement program (which measures, tracks, and recognizes employee improvement ideas) went from 50 employees participating in 1999 to more than 600 participating in 2009. Moreover, the value provided by this program went from $23,000 per employee in 2005 to $45,000 per employee in 2009. MEDRAD also managed to improve its environmental performance. For example, it reduced its hydrochlorofluorcarbon and ethylene emissions from 55,000 pounds in 2007 to about 27,000 pounds in 2009.[11]

REAL-WORLD EXAMPLE

As companies implement quality improvement programs, a need arises to monitor and report on the progress of these programs. Managers need to know what quality costs are and how they are changing over time. Reporting and measuring quality performance is absolutely essential to the success of an ongoing quality improvement program. A fundamental prerequisite for this reporting is measuring the costs of quality. But to measure those costs, an operational definition of quality is needed.

Quality Defined

Operationally, a **quality product or service** is one that meets or exceeds customer expectations. In effect, quality is customer satisfaction. But what is meant by "customer expectations"? Customers can be concerned with such product attributes as reliability, durability, fitness for use, and conformance to specifications. Although many important attributes can affect customer satisfaction, the quality attributes that are measurable tend to receive more emphasis. Conformance, in particular, is strongly emphasized. In fact, many quality experts believe that **"quality of conformance"** is the best operational definition. There is some logic to this position. Product specifications should explicitly consider such things as reliability, durability, and fitness for use. Implicitly, a conforming product is reliable, durable, and fit for use, and it performs well.

9 M. J. Harry and R. Schroeder, *Six Sigma: The Breakthrough Management Strategy Revolutionizing the World's Top Corporations* (New York: Doubleday, Random House, 2000); see also https://asq.org/quality-resources/cost-of-quality, accessed June 16, 2020.

10 Arne Buthman, "Cost of Quality: Not Only Failure Costs," *iSixSigma: Quality Resources for Achieving Six Sigma Results*, https://www.isixsigma.com/implementation/financial-analysis/cost-quality-not-only-failure-costs/, accessed June 19, 2020

11 National Institute of Standards and Technology, "MEDRAD," http://www.nist.gov/baldridge/award_recipients /medrad_profile.cfm, accessed September 21, 2011.

The product should be produced as the design specifies it; specifications should be met. Conformance is the basis for defining what is meant by a nonconforming, or *defective*, product.

A **defective product** is one that does not conform to specifications. **Zero defects** means that all products conform to specifications. But what is meant by "conforming to specifications"? Traditional conformance defines an acceptable range of values for each specification or quality characteristic. A target value is defined, and upper and lower limits are set that describe acceptable product variation for a given quality characteristic. Any unit that falls within the limits is deemed nondefective. For example, the targeted specification for a machined part may be a drilled hole that is two inches in diameter, and any part that is within 1/32 inch of the target is acceptable. On the other hand, the *robust quality view* of conformance emphasizes exactness of conformance. **Robustness** means exact conformance to the target value (no tolerance allowed). There is no range in which variation is acceptable. A nondefective machine part in the robust setting would be one that has a drilled hole that measures exactly two inches. Since evidence exists that product variation can be costly, the robust quality definition of conformance is superior to the traditional definition.

Costs of Quality Defined

Quality-linked activities are those activities performed because poor quality may or does exist. The costs of performing these activities are referred to as costs of quality. Thus, **costs of quality** are the costs that exist because poor quality may or does exist. This definition implies that quality costs are associated with two subcategories of quality-related activities: *control activities* and *failure activities*. **Control activities** are performed by an organization to prevent or detect poor quality (because poor quality may exist). Thus, control activities are made up of prevention and appraisal activities. **Control costs** are the costs of performing control activities. **Failure activities** are performed by an organization or its customers in response to poor quality (poor quality does exist). If the response to poor quality occurs before delivery of a bad (nonconforming, unreliable, not durable, and so on) product to a customer, the activities are classified as internal failure activities; otherwise, they are classified as external failure activities. **Failure costs** are the costs incurred by an organization because failure activities are performed. Some call failure costs as the costs of poor quality and control costs as the costs of good quality. Notice that the definitions of failure activities and failure costs imply that customer response to poor quality can impose costs on an organization. The definitions of quality-related activities also imply four categories of quality costs: (1) prevention costs, (2) appraisal costs, (3) internal failure costs, and (4) external failure costs.

Prevention costs are incurred to prevent poor quality in the products or services being produced. As prevention costs increase, we would expect the costs of failure to decrease. Examples of prevention costs are quality engineering, quality training programs, quality planning, quality reporting, supplier evaluation and selection, quality audits, quality circles, field trials, and design reviews.

Appraisal costs are incurred to determine whether products and services are conforming to their requirements or customer needs. Examples include inspecting and testing materials, packaging inspection, supervising appraisal activities, product acceptance, process acceptance, measurement (inspection and test) equipment, and outside endorsements. Two of these terms require further explanation.

Product acceptance involves sampling from batches of finished goods to determine whether they meet an acceptable quality level; if so, the goods are accepted. *Process acceptance* involves sampling goods while in process to see if the process is in control and producing nondefective goods; if not, the process is shut down until corrective action can be taken. The main objective of the appraisal function is to prevent nonconforming goods from being shipped to customers.

Internal failure costs are incurred because products and services do not conform to specifications or customer needs. This nonconformance is detected prior to the product being shipped or the service being delivered to outside parties. These are the failures detected by appraisal activities. Examples of internal failure costs are scrap, rework, downtime (due to defects), reinspection, retesting, and design changes. These costs disappear if no defects exist.

External failure costs are incurred because products and services fail to conform to requirements or satisfy customer needs after being delivered to customers. Of all the costs of quality, this category can be the most devastating. Costs of recalls, for example, can run into the hundreds of millions. Other examples include lost sales because of poor product performance, returns and allowances because of poor quality, warranties, repair, product liability, customer dissatisfaction, lost market share, and complaint adjustment. External failure costs, like internal failure costs, disappear if no defects exist.

Exhibit 14.1 summarizes the four quality cost categories and lists specific examples of costs. Each of the costs could have been expressed as the cost of quality-related activities such as the cost of certifying vendors, inspecting incoming materials, adjusting complaints, etc.

Quality Cost Measurement

Quality costs can also be classified as *observable* or *hidden*. **Observable quality costs** are those that are available from an organization's accounting records. **Hidden quality costs** are opportunity costs resulting from poor quality. (Opportunity costs are not usually recognized in accounting records.) Consider, for example, all the examples of quality costs listed in Exhibit 14.1. With the exception of lost sales, customer dissatisfaction, and lost market share, all the quality costs are observable and should be available from the accounting records. Note also that the hidden costs are all in the external failure category. These hidden quality costs can be significant and should be estimated. Although estimating hidden quality costs is not easy, three methods have been suggested: (1) the multiplier method, (2) the market research method, and (3) the Taguchi quality loss function.

The Multiplier Method   The multiplier method assumes that the total failure cost is simply some multiple of measured failure costs:

$$\text{Total external failure cost} = k(\text{Measured external failure costs})$$

where k is the multiplier effect. The value of k is based on experience. For example, Westinghouse Electric reports a value of k between 3 and 4.[12] Thus, if the measured external failure costs are \$3 million, the actual external failure costs are between \$9 million and \$12 million. Sampling and surveying are common methods used by companies to determine the

Prevention Costs	Appraisal (Detection) Costs
Quality engineering	Inspection of materials
Quality training	Packaging inspection
Recruiting	Product acceptance
Quality audits	Process acceptance
Design reviews	Field testing
Quality circles	Continuing supplier verification
Marketing research	
Prototype inspection	
Vendor certification	

Internal Failure Costs	External Failure Costs
Scrap	Lost sales (performance-related)
Rework	Returns/allowances
Downtime (defect-related)	Warranties
Reinspection	Discounts due to defects
Retesting	Product liability
Design changes	Complaint adjustment
Repairs	Recalls
	Ill will

Exhibit 14.1

Examples of Quality Costs by Category

12   T. L. Albright and P. R. Roth, "The Measurement of Quality Costs: An Alternative Paradigm," *Accounting Horizons* (June 1992): 15–27.

value of the multiplier.[13] Including hidden costs in assessing the amount of external failure costs allows management to more accurately determine the level of resource spending for prevention and appraisal activities. Specifically, with an increase in failure costs, we would expect management to increase its investment in control costs.

The Market Research Method   Formal market research methods are used to assess the effect of poor quality on sales and market share. Customer surveys and interviews with members of a company's sales force can provide significant insights into the magnitude of a company's hidden costs. Market research results can be used to project future profit losses attributable to poor quality.

The Taguchi Quality Loss Function   The traditional zero defects definition assumes that hidden quality costs exist only for units that fall outside the upper and lower specification limits. The **Taguchi loss function** assumes that any variation from the target value of a quality characteristic causes hidden quality costs. Furthermore, the hidden quality costs increase quadratically as the actual value deviates from the target value. The Taguchi quality loss function, illustrated in Exhibit 14.2, can be described by the following equation:

$$L(y) = k(y - T)^2$$

where

k = A proportionality constant dependent upon the organization's external failure cost structure
y = Actual value of quality characteristic
T = Target value of quality characteristic
L = Quality loss

Exhibit 14.2

The Taguchi Quality Loss Function

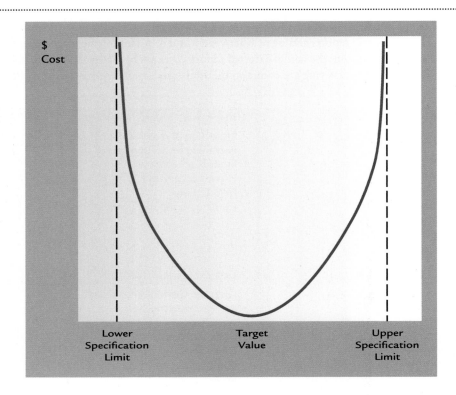

$ Cost

Lower Specification Limit   Target Value   Upper Specification Limit

---

13 V. Sower, "Estimating External Failure Costs: A Key Difficulty in COQ Systems," *Quality Congress. ASQ's Annual Quality Congress Proceedings,* 58 (2004): 547–552.

Unit No.	Time Gained (Lost) (y)	y − T	(y − T)²	k(y − T)²
1	−1	−1	1	$ 2.00
2	2	2	4	8.00
3	4	4	16	32.00
4	−3	−3	9	18.00
			30	$60.00
Units			÷4	÷4
Average			7.5	$15.00

Exhibit 14.3

Quality Loss Computation Illustrated

Exhibit 14.2 demonstrates that the quality cost is zero at the target value and increases symmetrically, at an increasing rate, as the actual value varies from the target value. Assume, for example, that a company produces watches and the quality characteristic is accuracy (as measured by how much time is gained or lost in three months). Assume $k = \$2$ and $T = 0$ minutes. Exhibit 14.3 illustrates the computation of the quality loss for four units. Notice that the cost quadruples when the deviation from target doubles (Units 2 and 3). Notice also that the average deviation squared and the average loss per unit can be computed. These averages can be used to compute the total expected hidden quality costs for a product. If, for example, the total units produced are 5,000 and the average squared deviation is 7.5, then the expected cost per unit is $15 (7.5 × $2) and the total expected loss for the 5,000 units would be $75,000 ($15 × 5,000).

To apply the Taguchi loss function, k must be estimated. The value for k is computed by dividing the estimated cost at one of the specification limits by the squared deviation of the limit from the target value:

$$k = c/d^2$$

where
  c = Loss at the lower or upper specification limit
  d = Distance of limit from target value

This means that we still must estimate the loss for a given deviation from the target value. The first two methods, the multiplier method or the market research method, may be used to help in this estimation (a one-time assessment need). Once k is known, the hidden quality costs can be estimated for any level of variation from the target value.

REPORTING QUALITY COSTS

OBJECTIVE 2

Explain how a quality cost report is prepared and used.

A quality cost reporting system is essential to an organization serious about improving and controlling quality costs. The first and simplest step in creating such a system is assessing current actual quality costs. A detailed listing of actual quality costs by category can provide two important insights. First, it reveals the magnitude of the quality costs in each category, allowing managers to assess their financial impact. Second, it shows the distribution of quality costs by category, allowing managers to assess the relative importance of each category. **Example 14.1** illustrates a quality cost report for Chesser Company.

EXAMPLE 14.1

The HOW and WHY of Preparing a Quality Cost Report

Information:

Chesser Company had total sales of $5,000,000 for fiscal year ended March 31, 20x1. Chesser's costs of quality-related activities are as follows:

Warranty	$250,000
Scrap	150,000
Reliability engineering	65,000
Rework	100,000
Quality training	10,000
Process acceptance	70,000
Materials inspection	30,000
Customer complaints	325,000

Why:

A quality cost report reveals the magnitude of the quality costs by category, and it also shows the relative distribution of these costs. The relative distribution allows the manager to assess the importance of the various categories and to determine where quality improvement emphasis is needed.

Required:

1. Prepare a quality cost report, classifying costs by category and expressing each category as a percentage of sales. What message does the cost report provide?

2. Prepare a bar graph and pie chart that illustrates each category's contribution to total quality costs. Comment on the significance of the distribution.

3. *What if* five years from now, quality costs are 2.5 percent of sales, with control costs being 80 percent of the total quality costs? What would your conclusion be?

Solution:

1.

Quality Cost Report Chesser Company
For the Year Ended March 31, 20x1

	Quality Costs		Percentage of Sales[a]
Prevention costs:			
Quality training	$ 10,000		
Reliability engineering	65,000	$ 75,000	1.50%
Appraisal costs:			
Materials inspection	$ 30,000		
Process acceptance	70,000	100,000	2.00
Internal failure costs:			
Scrap	$150,000		
Rework	100,000	250,000	5.00
External failure costs:			
Warranty	$250,000		
Customer complaints	325,000	575,000	11.50
Total quality costs		$1,000,000	20.00%[b]

[a]Actual sales of $5,000,000.
[b]$1,000,000/$5,000,000 = 20 percent.

EXAMPLE 14.1

(*Continued*)

The report clearly indicates that quality costs are too high as 20 percent of sales is much greater than the desired 2 to 4 percent of sales that prevails for companies with good quality performance.

2. See Exhibit 14.4. The graphs reveal that failure costs are approximately 82 percent of the total quality costs, suggesting that Chesser needs to invest more in control activities to drive down failure costs.

3. First, assuming that the reduction in quality costs is due to quality improvements, the 2.5 percent level reveals that the company is producing at a very high quality level. In practical terms, if quality costs are in the 2 to 4 percent range with virtually no failure costs (0.5 percent of sales in this case), then the company has effectively and practically achieved a zero-defects state.

The financial significance of quality costs can be assessed more easily by expressing these costs as a percentage of actual sales. The quality cost report in Example 14.1, for example, reports Chesser Company's quality costs as representing 20 percent of sales for fiscal 20x1. Given the rule of thumb that quality costs should be no more than about 2.5 percent, Chesser Company has ample opportunity to improve profits by decreasing quality costs by improving quality.

Example 14.1 suggests that Chesser Company needs to embark on a serious quality improvement program to reduce its quality costs. But by how much should quality cost be reduced? Is there an optimal level of costs that a manager should be striving to achieve?

Optimal Distribution of Quality Costs: Zero-Defects with Robust Quality View

The original or traditional zero-defects model makes the claim that it is cost beneficial to reduce *nonconforming units* to zero. In the mid-1980s, the zero-defects model was taken one step further by the robust quality model, which made the definition of a defective or nonconforming unit much tighter. According to the robust view, a loss is experienced from producing products that vary from a target value; the greater the distance from the target value, the greater the loss. In other words, variation from the ideal is costly, and specification limits serve no useful purpose and, in fact, may be deceptive.

Exhibit 14.4 Quality Cost Categories: Relative Contribution Graphs

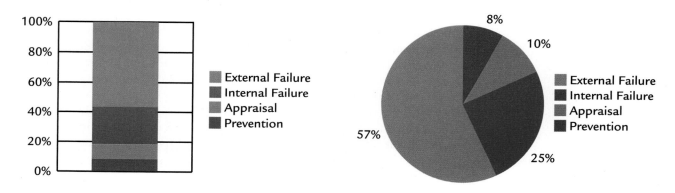

Exhibit 14.5

Robust Quality and the Zero-Defects Quality Graph

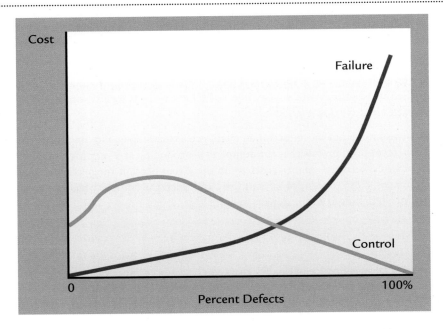

The zero-defects model understates the quality costs and, thus, the potential for savings from even greater efforts to improve quality (remember the multiplication factor of **Westinghouse Electric**). Therefore, the robust quality model tightened the definition of a defective unit, refined our view of quality costs, and intensified the quality race.

For firms operating in an intensely competitive environment, improving quality is a competitive necessity. If the robust quality view is correct, then firms can capitalize on it, decreasing the number of defective units (robustly defined as zero tolerance) while simultaneously decreasing their total quality costs. Exhibit 14.5 shows a quality cost function consistent with the robust quality view of zero defects. Essentially, as firms increase their prevention and appraisal costs and reduce their failure costs, they discover that they can then cut back on their prevention and appraisal costs. Notice that failure costs can be reduced to zero according to this model and that control costs are finite at the zero-defect point.

This graphical representation in Exhibit 14.5 is consistent with the strategy to reduce quality costs recommended by the American Society for Quality Control:[14]

> *The strategy for reducing quality costs is quite simple: (1) take direct attack on failure costs in an attempt to drive them to zero; (2) invest in the "right" prevention activities to bring about improvement; (3) reduce appraisal costs according to results achieved; and, (4) continuously evaluate and redirect prevention efforts to gain further improvement. This strategy is based on the premise that:*

- *For each failure there is a root cause.*
- *Causes are preventable.*
- *Prevention is always cheaper.*

This ability to reduce total quality costs dramatically in all categories is borne out by real-world experiences. **Tennant Company**, for example, over an eight-year period, reduced its costs of quality from 17 percent of sales, with failure costs accounting for 50 percent of the total costs of quality (8.5 percent of sales), to 2.5 percent of sales, with failure costs accounting for only 15 percent of the total costs of quality (0.375 percent of sales). Further support for the total quality control model is provided by Westinghouse Electric. Similar to Tennant's experience, Westinghouse Electric found that its profits continued to improve until its control costs accounted for about 70 to 80 percent of total quality costs.[15] Based on these two companies'

---

14   Jack Campanella, ed., *Principles of Quality Costs* (Milwaukee: ASQC Quality Press, 1990): 12.

15   These factual observations are based on those reported by Lawrence Carr and Thomas Tyson, "Planning Quality Cost Expenditures," *Management Accounting* (August 1995).

experiences, we know that it is possible to reduce total quality costs significantly—in all categories—and that the process radically alters the relative distribution of the quality cost categories.

The Role of Activity-Based Cost Management

Activity-based costing (ABC) can be used to calculate the quality costs per unit of a firm's products. Once an ABC system is in place, the only requirement is to identify those activities that are quality related, such as inspection, rework, and warranty work. Assume, for example, that the cost of the rework activity is $250,000. Now, assume that a company produces 10,000 units each of two products: a regular model and a deluxe model. The number of units reworked is 1,000 for the regular model and 4,000 for the deluxe model (units reworked is the activity driver). The activity rate is $50 per reworked unit ($250,000/5,000), and the rework costs (an internal failure cost) assigned to each product are $50,000 and $200,000 for the regular model and the deluxe model, respectively. This provides a signal that the deluxe model is of lower quality than the regular model. Thus, ABC can be used as a means to identify cost objects with quality problems, such as low-quality products, low-quality processes, and low-quality suppliers. This can then allow more focused management of quality costs.

Activity-based management (ABM) is also useful. ABM classifies activities as value-added and non-value-added and keeps only those that add value. This principle can be applied to quality-related activities. Appraisal and failure activities and their associated costs are non-value-added and should be eliminated (eventually). Prevention activities— performed efficiently—can be classified as value-added and should be retained. **Grede Foundries, Inc.**, of Milwaukee, one of the world's largest foundry companies, has been tracking all four categories of quality costs for more than 15 years. However, it does not report prevention costs as part of its final cost-of-quality figures because it does not want its managers to reduce quality costs by cutting prevention activities. It feels strongly that spending money on prevention activities pays off. For example, it has found that a 1 percent reduction in scrap reduces external defects by about 5 percent.[16]

Root causes (cost drivers) can also be identified, especially for failure activities, and used to help managers understand what is causing the costs of the activities. This information can then be used to select ways of reducing quality costs to the level demonstrated in Exhibit 14.5. In effect, activity-based management supports the robust zero-defect view of quality costs. There is no optimal trade-off between control and failure costs; the latter are non-value-added costs and should be reduced to zero. Some control activities are non-value-added and should be eliminated. Other control activities are value-added but may be performed inefficiently, and the costs caused by the inefficiency are non-value-added. Thus, costs for these categories may also be reduced to lower levels.

QUALITY COST INFORMATION AND DECISION MAKING

OBJECTIVE 3

Explain why quality cost information is needed and how it is used.

Reporting quality costs can improve managerial planning, control, and decision making. For example, if a company wants to implement a process reengineering program to improve the quality of its products, it will need to assess the following: current quality costs by item and by category, the additional costs associated with the program, and the projected savings by item and by category. *When* the costs and savings will occur must also be projected. Then, a capital budgeting analysis can be produced to determine the merits of the proposed program. If the outcome is favorable and the program is initiated, then it becomes important to monitor the program through performance reporting.

---

16 Nancy Chase, "Accounting for Quality: Counting Costs, Reaping Returns," *Quality,* Vol. 37, No. 10 (October 1998): 38–42.

Using quality cost information to implement and monitor the effectiveness of quality programs is only one use of a quality cost system. Other important uses can also be identified. Quality cost information is an important input to management decision making. It is also important to outside parties as they assess the quality of the company, through programs such as ISO 9000.

Decision-Making Contexts

Managers need quality cost information in a number of decision-making contexts. Two of these contexts are strategic pricing and cost-volume-profit analysis.

Strategic Pricing   Consider AMD, Inc., which produces electronic measurement devices. Market share for the company's low-level electronic measurement instruments had been steadily dropping. Linda Werther, marketing manager, identified price as the major problem. She knew that Japanese firms produced and sold the low-level instruments for less than AMD could. If AMD reduced its price to that of the competition, the new price would be below cost. Yet, if something were not done, the Japanese firms would continue to expand their market share. One possibility was simply to drop the low-level line and concentrate on instruments in the medium- and high-level categories. Linda knew, however, that this was a short-term solution, since soon the same Japanese firms would be competing at the higher levels. A brief income statement for the low-level instruments is as follows:

Revenues (1,000,000 @ $20)	$ 20,000,000
Cost of goods sold	(15,000,000)
Operating expenses	(3,000,000)
Product-line income	$ 2,000,000

Linda strongly believed that a 15 percent price decrease would restore the instrument line's market share and profitability to its former levels. One possibility was the implementation of total quality management. Her first action was to request information on the quality costs for the lower-level instruments. AMD's controller, Eugene Sadler, admitted that the costs were not tracked separately. For example, the cost of scrap was buried in the work-in-process inventory account. He did promise, however, to estimate some of the costs. Data from his report for the low-level instruments are as follows:

Quality costs (estimated):	
Inspection of materials	$ 200,000
Scrap	800,000
Rejects	500,000
Rework	400,000
Product inspection	300,000
Warranty work	1,000,000
Total estimate	$3,200,000

Upon receiving the report, Linda, Eugene, and Art Smith, manager of the Quality Control Department, met to determine possible ways of reducing quality costs for the low-level line. Art was confident that the quality costs could be reduced by 50 percent within 18 months. He had already begun planning the implementation of a new quality program. Linda calculated that a 50 percent reduction in the quality costs associated with the low-level instruments would reduce costs by about $1.60 per unit ($1,600,000/1,000,000)—which would make up slightly more than half of the $3 reduction in selling price that would be needed (the reduction is 15 percent of $20). Based on this outcome, Linda decided to implement the price reduction in three phases: a $1 reduction immediately, a $1 reduction in six months, and the final reduction of $1 in 12 months. This phased reduction would likely prevent any further erosion of market share and would start increasing market share sometime in the second phase. By phasing in the price reductions, the Quality Control Department would have time to reduce costs so that any big losses could be avoided.

The AMD, Inc., example illustrates that both quality cost information and the implementation of a total quality control program contributed to a significant strategic decision. It also illustrates that improving quality was not a panacea. The reductions were not as large as needed to bear the full price reduction. Other productivity gains will be needed to ensure the long-range viability of the product line. Implementing Just-in-Time (JIT) manufacturing, for example, might reduce inventories and decrease costs of materials handling and maintenance.

Cost-Volume-Profit Analysis and Strategic Design Decisions Traditionally, cost-volume-profit analysis relies on the analysis of fixed and variable costs in conjunction with cost. Terry Foster, the marketing manager, and Sarah Fox, the design engineer, discovered shortcomings in the traditional analysis when they proposed a new product. They had been certain that a proposal for the new product was going to be approved. Instead, they received the following report from the controller's office:

Report: New Product Analysis, Project 675

Projected sales potential: 44,000 units
Production capacity: 45,000 units
Unit selling price: $60
Unit variable costs: $40
Fixed costs:

Product development	$ 500,000
Manufacturing	200,000
Selling	300,000
Total	$1,000,000

Projected break-even: 50,000 units
Decision: Reject
Reason(s): The break-even point is greater than the
production capacity as well as the projected sales volume

In an effort to discover just why the cost figures came out so poorly for a project that both individuals felt strongly would be profitable, the two met with Bob Brown, the assistant controller. The following conversation took place:

SARAH: Bob, I would like to know why there is a $3-per-unit scrap cost. Can you explain it?

BOB: Sure. It's based on the scrap cost that we track for existing, similar products.

SARAH: Well, I think you have overlooked the new design features of this new product. Its design virtually eliminates any waste—especially when you consider that the product will be made on a numerically controlled machine.

TERRY: Also, this $2-per-unit charge for repair work should be eliminated. The new design that Sarah is proposing solves the failure problems we have had with related products. It also means that the $100,000 of fixed costs associated with the Repair Center can be eliminated.

BOB: Sarah, how certain are you that this new design will eliminate some of these quality problems?

SARAH: I'm absolutely positive. The early prototypes did exactly as we expected. The results of those tests are included in the proposal.

BOB: Right. Reducing the variable cost by $5 per unit and the fixed costs by $100,000 produces a break-even point of 36,000 units. These changes alone make the project viable. I'll change the report to reflect a positive recommendation.

The above scenario illustrates the importance of further classifying quality costs by behavior. Although only unit-based behavior is assumed, activity-based classification is also possible and could enhance the decision usefulness of quality costs. The scenario also reinforces the importance of identifying and reporting quality costs separately. The new product was designed to reduce its quality costs, and only by knowing the quality costs assigned could Sarah and Terry have discovered the error in the break-even analysis. Finally, notice the effect total quality management has on design decisions. By being aware of the quality costs and their causes, the new product's design was structured to avoid many of the existing quality problems.

Certifying Quality Through ISO 9000

Just as a company assesses the quality of its suppliers, that same company may supply other companies that require vendor certification of quality. ISO (pronounced ICE-OH) 9000 is a family of international quality standards developed by the International Organization for Standardization in Geneva, Switzerland, that address quality management. These standards center on the concept of documentation and control of nonconformance and change. ISO 9000 has been a success in Europe, and U.S. companies doing business in Europe were the first to board the ISO 9000 bandwagon, simply because it is a requirement of doing business. A program called ISO 9001:2015 is the latest edition that outlines the standardized set of procedures required for quality verification. In effect, ISO 9001:2015 is an internationally defined standard that outlines the requirements for a quality management system.

Companies that attain ISO 9000 certification have been audited by an independent test company, which certifies that the company meets certain quality standards. The standards on which certification is currently based are ISO 9001:2015 standards. The ISO 9001:2015 standards deal with quality systems and specifically with quality assurance models relating to quality systems that are concerned with such things as design/development, production, installation, final inspection, and testing. It is important to understand that these standards do not apply to the production of a particular product or service. Instead, they apply to the way in which an organization ensures quality, for example, by organizing and improving processes, focusing on customers, engaging and empowering employees, testing products, keeping records, and fixing defects.

The ISO 9001:2015 standard encourages organizations to use the Plan-Do-Check-Act methodology to manage their processes and to establish a culture of continuous improvement. The standard also encourages the use of a risk-based approach to identify and manage the possible opportunities and losses associated with change. Many companies have found that the process of applying for ISO 9001 certification, while lengthy and expensive, yields important benefits such as greater efficiency, greater quality, and improved financial performance. At the end of 2018, 21,848 ISO 9001 valid certificates had been awarded in the United States; worldwide, ISO 9002 valid certificates totaled 878,664.[17]

OBJECTIVE 4
Prepare three different types of quality performance reports.

CONTROLLING QUALITY COSTS

Good quality cost management requires that quality costs be reported and controlled (control having a cost reduction emphasis). Control enables managers to compare actual outcomes with standard outcomes to gauge performance and take any necessary corrective actions. Quality cost performance reports have two essential elements: actual outcomes and standard or expected outcomes. Deviations of actual outcomes from the expected outcomes are used to evaluate managerial performance and provide signals concerning possible problems.

Performance reports are essential to quality improvement programs. A report like the one shown in Example 14.1 (see page 714) forces managers to identify the various costs that should

---

17   See https://www.iso.org/the-iso-survey.html, accessed June 18, 2020.

appear in a performance report, to identify the current quality performance level of the organization, and to begin thinking about the level of quality performance that should be achieved. Identifying the quality standard is a key element in a quality performance report. The standard should emphasize cost reduction opportunities.

Choosing the Quality Standard

The Total Quality Approach The total quality management standard that will be used is referred to as the *robust zero-defects standard*. This standard calls for products and services to be produced and delivered that meet the targeted value. The need for total quality control is inherent in JIT and lean manufacturing approaches. JIT or lean manufacturing, however, is not a prerequisite for moving toward total quality control. This approach can stand by itself.

Admittedly, the total quality standard is one that may not be completely attainable; however, evidence exists that it can be closely approximated. Defects are caused either by lack of knowledge or by lack of attention. Lack of knowledge can be corrected by proper training, and lack of attention by effective leadership. Note also that total quality control implies the ultimate elimination of failure costs. Those who believe that no defects should be permitted will continue to search for new ways to improve quality costs.

Consider the following case. A firm engaged in a significant volume of business through mailings. On average, 15 percent of the mailings were sent to the wrong address. Returned merchandise, late payments, and lost sales all resulted from this error rate. In one case, a tax payment was sent to the wrong address. By the time the payment arrived, it was late, causing a penalty of $300,000. Why not spend the resources (surely less than $300,000) to get the mailing list right and have no errors: Is a mailing list that is 100 percent accurate really impossible to achieve? Why not do it right the first time around?

Quantifying the Quality Standard Quality can be measured by its costs; as the costs of quality decrease, higher quality results—at least up to a point. Even if the standard of zero defects is achieved, a company must still have prevention and appraisal costs. A company with a well-run quality management program can get by with quality costs of about 2.5 percent of sales. (If zero defects are achieved, this cost is for prevention and appraisal.) This 2.5 percent standard is accepted by many quality control experts and many firms that are adopting aggressive quality improvement programs.

The 2.5 percent standard is for total costs of quality. Costs of individual quality factors, such as quality training or materials inspection, will be less. Each organization must determine the appropriate standard for each individual factor. Budgets can be used to set spending for each standard so that the total budgeted cost meets the 2.5 percent goal.

Physical Standards For line managers and operating personnel, physical measures of quality—such as number of defects per unit, the percentage of external failures, billing errors, contract errors, and other physical measures—may be more meaningful. For physical measures, the quality standard is zero defects or errors. The objective is to get everyone to do it right the first time.

Use of Interim Standards For most firms, the standard of zero defects is a long-range goal. The ability to achieve this standard is strongly tied to supplier quality. For most companies, materials and services purchased from outside parties make up a significant part of a product's cost. For example, more than 65 percent of the product cost for Tennant Company was from materials and parts purchased from more than 500 different suppliers. To achieve the desired quality level, Tennant had to launch a major campaign to involve its suppliers in similar quality improvement programs. Developing the relationships and securing the needed cooperation from suppliers takes time—in fact, it takes years. Similarly, getting people within the company itself to understand the need for quality improvement and to have confidence in the program can take several years.

Because improving quality to the zero-defects level can take years, yearly quality improvement standards should be developed so that managers can use performance reports to assess the progress made on an interim basis. These **interim quality standards** express quality goals for the year. Progress should be reported to managers and employees in order to gain the confidence needed to achieve the ultimate standard of zero defects. Even though reaching the zero-defects level is a long-range project, management should expect significant progress on a yearly basis. For example, Tennant cut its quality costs from 17 percent of sales to 8 percent of sales over a period of six years—an average reduction of more than 1 percent per year. Furthermore, once the 2.5 percent goal is reached, efforts must be expended continuously to maintain it. Performance reports, at this stage, assume a strict control role.

Types of Quality Performance Reports

Quality performance reports measure the progress realized by an organization's quality improvement program. Three types of progress can be measured and reported:

1. Progress with respect to a current-period standard or goal (an interim standard report)
2. The progress trend since the inception of the quality improvement program (a multiple-period trend report)
3. Progress with respect to the long-range standard or goal (a long-range report)

Interim Standard Report The organization must establish an interim quality standard each year and make plans to achieve this targeted level. Since quality costs are a measure of quality, the targeted level can be expressed in dollars budgeted for each category of quality costs and for each cost item within the category. Often, the interim quality standard is simply the quality costs incurred in the previous year, adjusted for management's desired reduction. At the end of the period, the **interim quality performance report** compares the actual quality costs for the period with the budgeted costs. This report measures the progress achieved within the period relative to the planned level of progress for that period. **Example 14.2** illustrates such a report.

EXAMPLE 14.2

The HOW and WHY of Preparing Interim Quality Performance Reports

Information:
The actual quality costs of AMD, Inc., for years ended June 30, 20x4 and 20x5, are provided:

	20x4	20x5
Prevention costs:		
Quality training	$ 64,000	$ 80,000
Reliability engineering	128,000	160,000
Appraisal costs:		
Materials inspection	$ 66,400	$ 84,000
Process acceptance	76,000	96,000
Internal failure costs:		
Scrap	$ 55,000	$ 50,000
Rework	120,625	100,000
External failure costs:		
Customer complaints	$ 81,250	$ 65,000
Warranty	184,375	165,000

At the end of 20x4, management decided to increase its investment in control costs by 25 percent for each category's items with the expectation that failure costs would decrease by 20 percent for each item of the failure categories. Sales were $8,000,000 for both 20x4 and 20x5.

EXAMPLE 14.2

(Continued)

> **Why:**
> The quality standard expressed in dollars for a given year represents the budgeted costs for that year. Budgeted costs are a reduction in the prior year's quality costs resulting from planned quality improvements. An interim quality performance report compares actual quality costs with budgeted quality costs.

Required:

1. Calculate the budgeted costs for 20x5, and prepare an interim quality performance report.

2. Comment on the significance of the report. How much progress has AMD made?

3. *What if* sales were $8,000,000 for 20x4 and $10,000,000 for 20x5? What adjustment to budgeted scrap costs would be made? Budgeted quality training? Assuming the actual costs for 20x5 do not change, what does this adjustment say about AMD's performance?

Solution:

1.

AMD, Inc.
Interim Standard Performance Report: Quality Costs
For the Year Ended June 30, 20x5

	Actual Costs	Budgeted Costs	Variance
Prevention costs:			
Quality training	$ 80,000	$ 80,000[a]	$ 0
Reliability engineering	160,000	160,000[a]	0
Total prevention costs	$240,000	$240,000	$ 0
Appraisal costs:			
Materials inspection	$ 84,000	$ 83,000[a]	$ 1,000 U
Process acceptance	96,000	95,000[a]	1,000 U
Total appraisal costs	$180,000	$178,000	$ 2,000 U
Internal failure costs:			
Scrap	$ 50,000	$ 44,000[b]	$ 6,000 U
Rework	100,000	96,500[b]	3,500 U
Total internal failure costs	$150,000	$140,500	$ 9,500 U
External failure costs:			
Customer complaints	$ 65,000	$ 65,000[b]	$ 0
Warranty	165,000	147,500[b]	17,500 U
Total external failure costs	$230,000	$212,500	$17,500 U
Total quality costs	$800,000	$771,000	$29,000 U
Percentage of sales	10.0%	9.64%	0.36% U

[a]2012 actual control cost × 1.25 (e.g., quality training = $64,000 × 1.25 = $80,000).
[b]2012 actual failure cost × 0.80 (e.g., scrap = $55,000 × 0.80 = $44,000).

2. AMD has come very close to meeting the planned outcomes (only 0.36 percent short overall). Thus, management's belief that investing an additional 25 percent in control costs would produce a 20 percent reduction in failure costs seems to be validated.

3. Scrap would be expected to vary with sales. Thus, a 20 percent increase in sales would cause a 20 percent increase in budgeted scrap costs: $44,000 × 1.20 = $52,800. This would create a favorable scrap variance of $2,800 ($50,000 − $52,800). All variable costs would have increased budgets, and the budgeted variance would be more favorable than initially calculated. Quality training is likely a discretionary fixed cost and so its budget would not be affected by changes in sales revenue.

Multiple-Period Trend Report The interim quality report provides management with information concerning the within-period progress measured relative to specific goals. Also useful is a picture of how the quality improvement program has been doing since its inception. Is the multiple-period trend—the overall change in quality costs—moving in the right direction? Are significant quality gains being made each period? Answers to these questions can be given by providing a chart or graph that tracks the change in quality from the beginning of the program to the present. Such a graph is called a **multiple-period quality trend report**. By plotting quality costs as a percentage of sales against time, the overall trend in the quality program can be assessed. The first year plotted is the year prior to the implementation of the quality improvement program. **Example 14.3** provides a detailed example of multiple-period trend reporting.

EXAMPLE 14.3

The HOW and WHY of Multiple-Period Quality Trend Reporting

Information:

Assume that AMD, Inc., has experienced the following:

	Quality Costs	Actual Sales	Costs as a Percentage of Sales
20x1	$1,000,000	$5,000,000	20.0%
20x2	990,000	5,500,000	18.0
20x3	900,000	6,000,000	15.0
20x4	868,000	6,200,000	14.0
20x5	800,000	8,000,000	10.0

By cost category as a percentage of sales for the same period of time:

	Prevention	Appraisal	Internal Failure	External Failure
20x1	2.0%	2.0%	6.0%	10.0%
20x2	3.0	2.4	4.0	8.6
20x3	3.0	3.0	3.0	6.0
20x4	4.0	3.0	2.5	4.5
20x5	4.1	2.4	2.0	1.5

> **Why:**
> Trend in quality costs as a percentage of sales reveals the effects of quality improvement initiatives over time. Expressing these trends by quality cost category provides insight concerning the effect of quality improvement initiatives on the relative distribution of quality costs.

Required:

1. Prepare a bar graph that reveals the trend in quality cost as a percentage of cost (time on the horizontal axis and percentages on the vertical). Comment on the message of the graph.

2. Prepare a bar graph for each cost category as a percentage of sales. What does this graph tell you?

3. *What if* management would like to have the trend in *relative* distribution of quality costs? Express this as a bar graph and comment on its significance.

Solution:

EXAMPLE 14.3

(Continued)

1. See Exhibit 14.6. From Exhibit 14.6, it is clear that there has been a steady downward trend in quality costs as a percentage of sales (dropping from 20 percent to 10 percent). The graph also reveals that there is still ample room for improvement.

2. See Exhibit 14.7. From Exhibit 14.7, we can see that AMD has had dramatic success in reducing internal and external failure costs. More money is being spent on prevention (the percentage has doubled). Also, appraisal costs have increased and then decreased, suggesting that AMD is becoming more confident in its prevention initiatives.

3. See Exhibit 14.8. This graph reveals that failure costs have gone from 80 percent of the total quality costs (16%/20%) to 35 percent (3.5%/10%), whereas control costs have gone from 20 percent to 65 percent. It appears that increasing prevention costs (value-added) has caused the failure costs (non-value-added) to decrease.

Long-Range Report At the end of each period, a report that compares the period's actual quality costs with the costs that the firm eventually hopes to achieve should be prepared. This report forces management to keep the ultimate quality goal in mind, reveals the room left for improvement, and facilitates planning for the coming period. Under a zero-defects philosophy, the costs of failure should be virtually nonexistent. (They are non-value-added costs.) Reducing the costs of failure increases a firm's competitive ability. Tennant Company, for example, was able to offer warranties that lasted two to four times longer than those of its competitors because of improved quality resulting in lower external failure rates.

Remember that achieving higher quality will not totally eliminate prevention and appraisal costs. (In fact, increased emphasis on zero defects may actually increase the cost of prevention, depending on the type and level of prevention activities initially present.) Generally, we would expect appraisal costs to decrease significantly. Product acceptance, for example, may be phased out entirely as product quality increases; however, increased emphasis on process acceptance is likely. The firm must have assurance that the process is operating in a zero-defects mode. A **long-range quality performance report** compares the current actual costs with the costs that would be allowed if the zero-defects standard were being met (assuming a sales level equal to that of the current period). The target costs are, if chosen properly, value-added costs. The variances are non-value-added costs. Thus, the long-range performance report is simply a variation of the value- and non-value-added cost report. **Example 14.4** illustrates this long-range report.

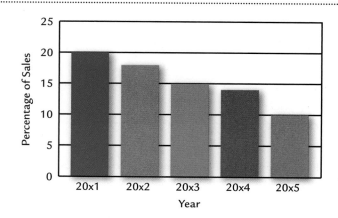

Exhibit 14.6

Multiple-Period Trend Graph: Total Quality Costs

Exhibit 14.7

Multiple-Period Trend Graph: Individual Quality Cost Categories

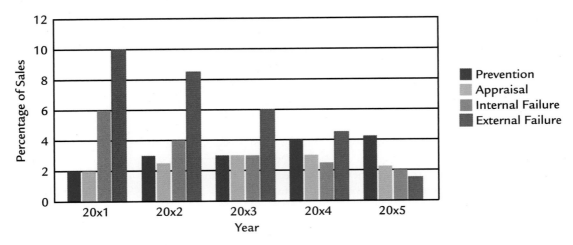

Incentives for Quality Improvement Most organizations provide both monetary and nonmonetary recognition for significant contributions to quality improvement. Of the two types of incentives, many quality experts believe that the nonmonetary are more useful.

Nonmonetary Incentives As with budgets, participation helps employees internalize quality improvement goals as their own. One approach used by many companies in their efforts to involve employees is the use of error cause identification forms. **Error cause identification** is a program in which employees describe problems that interfere with their ability to do the job right the first time. The error-cause-removal approach is one of the 14 steps in Philip Crosby's quality improvement program.[18] To ensure the success of the program, each employee submitting an entry should receive a note of appreciation from management. Additional recognition should be given to those who submit particularly beneficial information.

Other nonfinancial awards can also be given to recognize employees for their efforts. One restaurant, for example, gives monthly awards to food servers who have made no errors when punching diners' orders into the kitchen printout computer. Servers who make the most errors

Exhibit 14.8

Multiple-Period Trend Graph: Relative Quality Costs

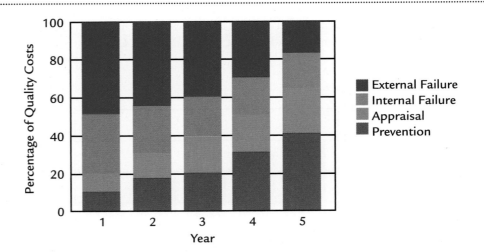

18 Philip Crosby, *Quality Is Free* (New York: New American Library, 1980).

see their names posted on an error list (no punishment, just names). The error rate plummeted, saving the restaurant thousands of dollars a month in wasted food.[19] The important thing is not the award itself but public recognition that leads to improved performance. By publicly recognizing significant quality contributions, management underscores its commitment to quality improvement. Also, the individuals and groups so recognized feel the benefits of that recognition, which include pride, job satisfaction, and a further commitment to quality.

<table>
<tr><td colspan="2">**Information:**</td></tr>
</table>

The actual quality costs for the year ended June 30, 20x5, for AMD, Inc., are given below:

Prevention costs:	
Quality training	$ 80,000
Reliability engineering	160,000
Total prevention costs	$240,000
Appraisal costs:	
Materials inspection	$ 84,000
Process acceptance	96,000
Total appraisal costs	$180,000
Internal failure costs:	
Scrap	$ 50,000
Rework	100,000
Total internal failure costs	$150,000
External failure costs:	
Customer complaints	$ 65,000
Warranty	165,000
Total external failure costs	$230,000
Total quality costs	$800,000

EXAMPLE 14.4

The HOW and WHY of Long-Range Quality Performance Reporting

At the zero-defect state, AMD expects to spend $50,000 on quality training, $100,000 on reliability engineering, and $25,000 on process acceptance. Assume sales of $8,000,000.

Why:
The long-range performance report compares the current actual costs with the costs that would be present if no poor quality existed. It is, in effect, a listing of the non-value-added costs and reflects the potential for further savings by improving quality.

Required:

1. Prepare a long-range performance report for 20x5. What does this report tell the management of AMD?

2. Explain why quality costs still are present for the zero-defect state.

3. *What if* AMD achieves the zero-defect state reflected in the report? What are some of the implications of this achievement?

19   Leonard L. Berry and A. Parasuramna, *Marketing Services: Competing Through Quality* (New York: The Free Press, Macmillan, 1991).

EXAMPLE 14.4

(Continued)

Solution:

1.

AMD, Inc.
Long-Range Performance Report
For the Year Ended June 30, 20x5

	Actual Costs	Target Costs	Variance
Prevention costs:			
Quality training	$ 80,000	$ 50,000	$ 30,000 U
Reliability engineering	160,000	100,000	60,000 U
Total prevention costs	$240,000	$150,000	$ 90,000 U
Appraisal costs:			
Materials inspection	$ 84,000	$ 0	$ 84,000 U
Process acceptance	96,000	25,000	71,000 U
Total appraisal costs	$180,000	$ 25,000	$155,000 U
Internal failure costs:			
Scrap	$ 50,000	$ 0	$ 50,000 U
Rework	100,000	0	100,000 U
Total internal failure costs	$150,000	$ 0	$150,000 U
External failure costs:			
Customer complaints	$ 65,000	$ 0	$ 65,000 U
Warranty	165,000	0	165,000 U
Total external failure costs	$230,000	$ 0	$230,000 U
Total quality costs	$800,000	$175,000	$625,000 U
Percentage of sales	10.0%	2.2%	7.8% U

AMD is spending too much money on failure activities. More effort at improving quality is still needed.

2. Prevention costs are value-added costs and would be necessary to maintain the quality gains. The presence of appraisal costs may not be necessary in a strictly theoretical sense (if there are no defective units, then there is no need to engage in detection activities).

3. By spending less money on defects, AMD can use the savings to expand and to employ additional people to support this expansion. Improved quality may naturally cause expansion by enhancing its competitive position. Thus, although improved quality may mean fewer jobs in some areas (such as inspection and warranty service), it also means that additional jobs will be created through expanded business activity.

Monetary Incentives **Gainsharing** provides cash incentives for a company's entire work-force that are keyed to quality or productivity gains. For example, suppose a company has a target of reducing the number of defective units by 10 percent during the next quarter for a particular plant. If the goal is achieved, the company estimates that $1,000,000 will be saved (through avoiding such things as reworks and warranty repairs). Gainsharing provides an incentive by offering a bonus to the employees equal to a percentage of the cost savings. At Tennant Company, for example, employees who submitted adopted proposals for quality changes received 20 percent of the first year's savings realized from these submissions.

Big Data

LNS Research marketing analyst, Mike Roberts, has identified five ways big data impacts quality management. First, using big data, performance metrics can be correlated across multiple plants. Using intelligence derived from big data, universal best practices can be applied, resulting in a better alignment of processes and, thus, an improvement in quality performance. Second, predictive modeling of large sets of manufacturing data will often find hidden or unexpected meaning such as identifying a spike in failure rates when a certain machine is activated. Third, analyzing supplier data and manufacturing data can provide significant insights about the actual cost of supplier nonconformance and, thus, motivate better long-term continuous improvement. Fourth, faster customer service and support will result from the impact of both the internet of things (i.e., the physical devices that collect and exchange data) and large data sets. Fifth, big data software algorithms are being developed that will allow "the right information to get to the right user at the right time."[20]

REAL-WORLD EXAMPLE

DEFINING, MEASURING, AND CONTROLLING ENVIRONMENTAL COSTS

OBJECTIVE 5

Discuss how environmental costs can be measured, reported, and reduced.

Historically, firms have often released contaminants into the atmosphere and water without bearing the full cost of such activities. Many people believe that polluters should bear the full cost of any environmental damage caused by production of goods and services (the polluter pays principle). By bearing the full cost (it is argued), firms may then seek more *ecoefficient* production methods. Interestingly, some initial experiences suggest that it may be possible to improve environmental quality without reducing useful goods and services while simultaneously increasing profits. If true, then a more proactive approach is both needed and appropriate. Moreover, proactive environmental decisions require information about environmental costs and benefits—information that has not existed as a separate and well-defined category. According to a concept known as *ecoefficiency*, meeting sound business objectives and resolving environmental concerns are not mutually exclusive.

The Ecoefficiency Paradigm

Ecoefficiency is defined as the ability to produce competitively priced goods and services that satisfy customer needs while *simultaneously* reducing negative environmental impacts, resource consumption, and costs. Ecoefficiency means producing more goods and services using less materials, energy, water, and land, while at the same time minimizing air emissions, water discharges, waste disposal, and the dispersion of toxic substances. However, perhaps the most important claim of the ecoefficiency paradigm is that preventing pollution and avoiding waste is economically beneficial—that it is possible to do more with less. Moreover, it is complementary to and supportive of *sustainable development*. **Sustainable development** is defined as development that meets the needs of the present without compromising the ability of future generations to meet their own needs. Although absolute sustainability may not be attainable, progress toward its achievement certainly seems to have some merit.

---

20 Mike Thomas, "5 Ways Big Data Will Impact Quality Management," http://www.hertzler.com/2014/06/5-ways-big-data-will-impact-quality-management/, accessed June 21, 2016.

Exhibit 14.9   Ecoefficiency Relationships

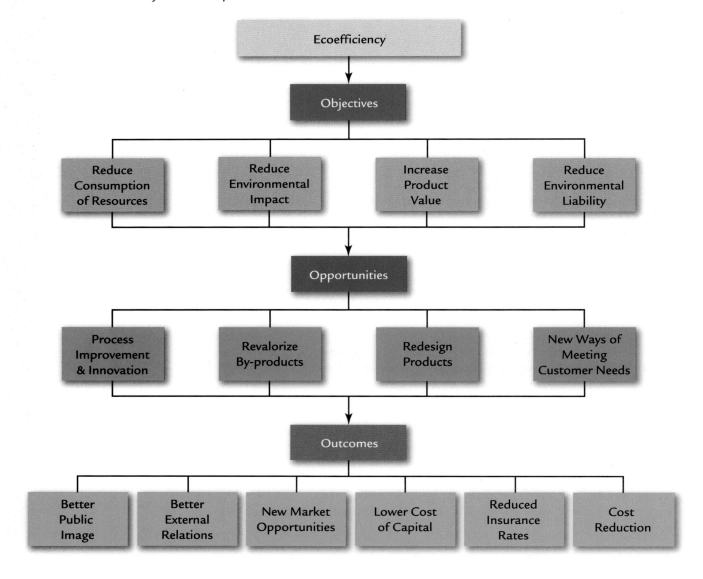

Ecoefficiency implies a positive relationship between environmental and economic performance. Exhibit 14.9 illustrates the objectives, opportunities, and outcomes that define the relationships envisioned by ecoefficiency.[21] Four broad objectives are revealed: (1) reduce the consumption of resources, (2) reduce the environmental impact, (3) increase product value, and (4) reduce environmental liability. Reducing the consumption of resources entails such things as reducing the use of energy, materials, water, and land. It also includes increasing product durability and enhancing product recyclability. Reducing environmental impact is primarily concerned with minimizing releases of pollutants into the environment and encouraging the sustainable use of renewable resources. Increasing product value means that products are produced that provide the functionality that customers need but with fewer materials and less resources. It also means that products are produced without degrading the environment, and

---

21   The objectives and opportunities are those identified by the World Business Council for Sustainable Development (WBCSD). See WBCSD, "Eco-efficiency: Creating More Value with Less Impact," October 1, 2000, http://www .wbcsd.org/web/publications/eco_efficiency_creating_more_value.pdf.

their use and disposal are environmentally friendly. The fourth objective, reducing environmental liability, requires that a company identify and efficiently manage the risks and opportunities relating to the environment. Achievement of the objectives requires a firm to seek opportunities to improve ecoefficiency, which brings us to the second level of Exhibit 14.9.

Process improvement and innovation are familiar methods for increasing efficiency. In this case, however, the objective is to increase ecoefficiency, which means that process changes must focus simultaneously on reducing costs and improving environmental performance. Process improvement is most useful for improving relative environmental performance, but process reengineering is probably more suitable for major advances in ecoefficiency. "Revalorizing by-products" describes the search for ways to convert waste materials into useful products or useful inputs for other companies' products. **LURA Group**, for example, converted the sludge from its wastewater treatment facility into commercial compost.[22] Product redesign is another key method for improving ecoefficiency. Products can be redesigned so that they use fewer materials, a smaller variety of materials, and less toxic materials and are easier to take apart for recycling while simultaneously providing a high degree of functionality for users. Finally, ecoefficiency can be improved by finding different and better ways of satisfying customer needs. This may entail redefining markets and reshaping supply and demand. For example, providing a service instead of selling a product has the potential of creating higher resource efficiency and less pollution. Car sharing is an example of this last approach.

Mobility, a carsharing company in Switzerland, provides a service to people who want to use a car without buying their own. These cars are parked at convenient locations such as railway stations. Clients arrange to use the cars for a prearranged period of time. Interestingly, this service has changed travel behavior. Carsharing clients increase their use of public transportation and, thus, reduce the need for cars and fuel.[23]

The third and final level of Exhibit 14.9 illustrates the payoffs of ecoefficiency. Pursuing the opportunities just discussed can produce a number of beneficial outcomes. Reduced environmental impacts can create social benefits like a better public image and better relations in the community and with regulators. This, in turn, improves the company's image and enhances its ability to sell products and services. Efforts to improve ecoefficiency also may increase revenues by creating new markets (e.g., creating outputs that were formerly classified as useless residues). Ecoefficient firms tend to reduce their environmental risks and, consequently, capture external benefits such as a lower cost of capital and lower insurance rates. Finally, cost reductions follow improvements in environmental performance.

The cost reduction outcome is particularly important. Environmental costs can be a significant percentage of total operating costs; many of these costs can be reduced or eliminated through effective management. For example, knowledge of environmental costs and their causes may lead to redesign of a process that, as a consequence, reduces the materials used and the pollutants emitted to the environment (an interaction between the innovation and cost reduction incentives). Thus, current and future environmental costs are reduced, and the firm becomes more competitive. To provide this financial information, it is necessary to define, measure, classify, and assign environmental costs to processes, products, and other cost objects of interest.

---

22 WBCSD, "Eco-efficiency: Creating More Value with Less Impact," http://www.wbcsd.org/web/publications/eco _efficiency_creating_more_value.pdf.

23 Ibid.

Environmental Costs Defined

Before environmental cost information can be provided to management, environmental costs must be defined. Various possibilities exist; however, an appealing approach is to adopt a definition consistent with a total environmental quality model. In the total environmental quality model, the ideal state is that of zero damage to the environment (analogous to the zero-defects state of total quality management). *Damage* is defined as either direct degradation of the environment such as the emission of solid, liquid, or gaseous residues into the environment (e.g., water contamination and air pollution) or indirect degradation such as *unnecessary* usage of materials and energy. Accordingly, environmental costs can be referred to as *environmental quality costs*. In a similar sense to quality costs, **environmental costs** are costs that are incurred because poor environmental quality exists or *may* exist. Thus, environmental costs are associated with the creation, detection, remediation, and prevention of environmental degradation. With this definition, environmental costs can be classified into four categories:

1. **Environmental prevention costs** are the costs of activities carried out to prevent the production of contaminants and/or waste that could cause damage to the environment.

2. **Environmental detection costs** are the costs of activities executed to determine if products, processes, and other activities within the firm are in compliance with appropriate environmental standards. The environmental standards and procedures that a firm seeks to follow are defined in three ways: (1) regulatory laws of governments, (2) voluntary standards (ISO 14000) developed by the International Standards Organization, and (3) environmental policies developed by management.

3. **Environmental internal failure costs** are costs of activities performed because contaminants and waste have been produced but not discharged into the environment. Thus, internal failure costs are incurred to eliminate and manage contaminants or waste once produced. Internal failure activities have one of two goals: (1) to ensure that the contaminants and waste produced are not released to the environment, or (2) to reduce the level of contaminants released to an amount that complies with environmental standards.

4. **Environmental external failure costs** are the costs of activities performed *after* discharging contaminants and waste into the environment. **Realized external failure costs** are those incurred and paid for by the firm. **Unrealized external failure (societal) costs** are caused by the firm but are incurred and paid for by parties outside the firm. Societal costs can be further classified as (1) those resulting from environmental degradation and (2) those associated with an adverse impact on the property or welfare of individuals. In either case, the costs are borne by others and not by the firm even though the firm causes them.

Exhibit 14.10 summarizes the four environmental cost categories and lists specific activities for each category. Within the external failure cost category, societal costs are labeled with an "S." The costs for which the firm is financially responsible are called **private costs**. All costs without the S label are private costs. Of the four categories of environmental activities, the external failure cost category is the one that causes the most economic hardship for an organization.

Environmental Cost Report

Environmental cost reporting is essential if an organization is serious about improving its environmental performance and controlling environmental costs. Reporting environmental costs by category reveals two important outcomes: (1) the impact of environmental costs on firm profitability and (2) the relative amounts expended in each category. **Example 14.5** provides an example of a simple environmental cost report.

Prevention Activities	**Internal Failure Activities**
Evaluating and selecting suppliers	Operating pollution control equipment
Evaluating and selecting pollution control equipment	Treating and disposing of toxic waste
Designing processes	Maintaining pollution equipment
Designing products	Licensing facilities for producing contaminants
Carrying out environmental studies	Recycling scrap
Auditing environmental risks	
Developing environmental management systems	
Recycling products	
Obtaining ISO 14001 certification	

Detection Activities	**External Failure Activities**
Auditing environmental activities	Cleaning up a polluted lake
Inspecting products and processes	Cleaning up oil spills
Developing environmental performance measures	Cleaning up contaminated soil
Testing for contamination	Settling personal injury claims (environmentally related)
Verifying supplier environmental performance	Restoring land to natural state
Measuring contamination levels	Losing sales due to poor environmental reputation
	Using materials and energy inefficiently
	Receiving medical care due to polluted air (S)
	Losing employment because of contamination (S)
	Losing a lake for recreational use (S)
	Damaging ecosystems from solid waste disposal (S)

(S) = societal costs.

Exhibit 14.10

Classification of Environmental Costs by Activity Type

EXAMPLE 14.5

The HOW and WHY of an Environmental Cost Report

Information:

Operating costs for Verde Corporation as of December 31, 20x5, are $30,000,000. Environmental costs are as follows:

Maintaining pollution equipment	$ 400,000
Developing measures	240,000
Operating pollution equipment	1,200,000
Designing products	600,000
Training employees	240,000
Restoring land	2,100,000
Inspecting processes	720,000
Cleaning up lake	3,300,000

Required:

1. Prepare an environmental cost report, classifying costs by quality category and expressing each as a percentage of total operating costs. What is the message of this report?

2. Prepare a pie chart that shows the relative distribution of environmental costs by category. What does this report tell you?

3. *What if* Verde deliberately did not include the cost of polluting a lake in the report? Offer possible reasons for this decision.

EXAMPLE 14.5

(Continued)

Solution:

1.

Verde Corporation
Environmental Cost Report
For the Year Ended December 31, 20x5

	Environmental Costs		Percentage of Operating Costs[a]
Prevention costs:			
Training employees	$ 240,000		
Designing products	600,000	$ 840,000	2.80%
Detection costs:			
Inspecting processes	$ 720,000		
Developing measures	240,000	960,000	3.20
Internal failure costs:			
Operating pollution equipment	$1,200,000		
Maintaining pollution equipment	400,000	1,600,000	5.33
External failure costs:			
Cleaning up lake	$3,300,000		
Restoring land	2,100,000	5,400,000	18.00
Total quality costs		$8,800,000	29.33%[b]

[a]Actual opening costs of $30,000,000.
[b]$8,800,000/$30,000,000 = 29.33%.

Environmental costs are 29.33 percent of total operating costs, seemingly a significant amount. Reducing environmental costs by improving environmental performance can significantly increase a firm's profitability.

2. See Exhibit 14.11. Of the total environmental costs, only 21 percent are from the prevention and detection categories, and 79 percent of the environmental costs are failure costs. Thus, increasing prevention activities should drive down the costs of failure activities in a way that is cost beneficial.

3. The most likely reason is that the cost is a social cost and not paid for by the company and thus not of direct interest to Verde. In fact, such formal recognition may create a potential liability for the company. (Could this be an ethical issue?)

Exhibit 14.11

Relative Distribution: Environmental Costs

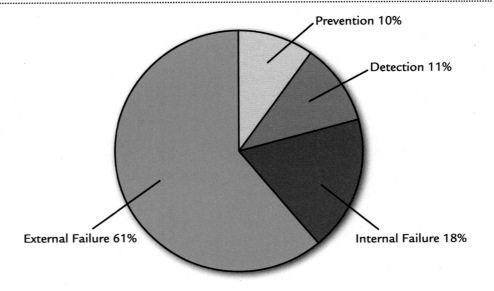

Prevention 10%

Detection 11%

Internal Failure 18%

External Failure 61%

Environmental Cost Reduction

Investing more in prevention and detection activities can bring about a significant reduction in environmental failure costs. Environmental costs appear to behave in much the same way as quality costs. The lowest environmental costs are attainable at the *zero-damage point* much like the zero-defects point of the total quality cost model. Thus, an ecoefficient solution would focus on prevention with the usual justification that *prevention is cheaper than the cure*. Analogous to the total quality management model, zero damage is the lowest cost point for environmental costs.

An Environmental Financial Report

Ecoefficiency suggests a possible modification to environmental cost reporting. Specifically, in addition to reporting environmental costs, why not report *environmental benefits*? In a given period, there are three types of benefits:

1. Additional revenues

2. Current savings

3. Cost avoidance (ongoing savings)

    Additional revenues are revenues that flow into the organization due to environmental actions such as recycling paper, finding new applications for nonhazardous waste (e.g., using wood scraps to make wood chess pieces and boards), and increasing sales due to an enhanced environmental image. Cost avoidance refers to ongoing savings of costs that had been paid in prior years. Current savings refer to reductions in environmental costs achieved in the current year. By comparing benefits produced with environmental costs incurred in a given period, a type of environmental financial statement is produced. Managers can use this statement to assess progress (benefits produced) and potential for progress (environmental costs). The environmental financial statement could also form part of an environmental progress report that is provided to shareholders on an annual basis. Exhibit 14.12

Verde Corporation
Environmental Financial Statement
For the Year Ended December 31, 20x5

Environmental benefits:	
Income sources:	
Recycling income..	$ 600,000
Revenues from waste-derived products...	150,000
Ongoing savings:	
Cost reductions, contaminants..	900,000
Cost reductions, hazardous waste disposal...................................	1,200,000
Current savings:	
Energy conservation cost savings..	300,000
Packaging cost reductions...	450,000
Total environmental benefits..	$3,600,000
Environmental costs:	
Prevention costs:	
Designing processes for the environment.......................................	$ 640,000
Supplier evaluation and selection..	200,000
Detection costs:	
Testing for contamination..	560,000
Measuring contamination levels...	400,000

Exhibit 14.12

Environmental Financial Statement

Exhibit 14.12
(continued)

Internal failure costs:	
Waste treatment, transport, and disposal.......................................	1,500,000
Operating pollution control equipment..	300,000
External failure costs:	
Inefficient materials usage...	1,400,000
Cleaning up soil...	4,000,000
Total environmental costs...	$9,000,000

provides an example of an environmental financial statement. The benefits reported reveal good progress, but the costs are still two and one-half times the benefits, indicating that more improvements are clearly needed.

OBJECTIVE 6

Show how environmental costs can be assigned to products and processes.

ENVIRONMENTAL COSTING

Both products and processes are sources of environmental costs. Processes that *produce* products can create solid, liquid, and gaseous residues that are subsequently introduced into the environment. These residues have the potential of degrading the environment. Residues, then, are the causes of both internal and external environmental failure costs (e.g., investing in equipment to prevent the introduction of the residues into the environment and cleaning up residues after they are allowed into the environment). Production processes are not the only source of environmental costs. Packaging is also a source.

Products themselves can be the source of environmental costs. After selling a product, its use and disposal by the customer can produce environmental degradation. These are examples of *environmental post-purchase costs.* Most of the time, environmental post-purchase costs are borne by society and not by the company and, thus, are societal costs. On occasion, however, environmental post-purchase costs are converted into realized external costs.

Environmental Product Costs

The environmental costs of processes that produce, market, and deliver products and the environmental post-purchase costs caused by the use and disposal of the products are examples of *environmental product costs.* **Full environmental costing** is the assignment of all environmental costs, both private and societal, to products. **Full private costing** is the assignment of only private costs to individual products. Private costing, then, would assign the environmental costs to products caused by the internal processes of the organization. Private costing is probably a good starting point for many firms. Private costs can be assigned using data created *inside* the firm. Full costs require gathering of data that are produced outside the firm from third parties.

Assigning environmental costs to products can produce valuable managerial information. For example, it may reveal that a particular product is responsible for much more toxic waste than other products. This information may lead to an alternative design for the product or its associated processes that is more efficient and environmentally friendly. It could also reveal that with the environmental costs correctly assigned, the product is not profitable. This could mean something as simple as dropping the product to achieve significant improvement in environmental performance and economic efficiency. Many opportunities for improvement may exist, but knowledge of the environmental product costs is the key. Moreover, environmental costs must be assigned accurately.

Activity-Based Environmental Cost Assignments

Activity-based costing facilitates environmental costing. Tracing the environmental costs to the products responsible for those costs is a fundamental requirement of a sound environmental accounting system. Each environmental activity is assigned costs, activity rates are computed, and the rates are then used to assign environmental costs to products based on usage of the activity. **Example 14.6** shows how to assign environmental costs to two different types of industrial cleaners.

The cost assignments shown in Example 14.6 allow managers to see the relative environmental economic impact of the two products, and to the extent that environmental costs reflect environmental damage, the unit environmental cost can also act as an index or measure of product cleanliness. The "dirtier" products can then be the focus of efforts to improve environmental performance and economic efficiency. Example 14.6 reveals, for example, that Cleanser B has more environmental problems than Cleanser A. Cleanser B's environmental costs total $370,000 ($3.70 × 100,000) and are 18.5 percent of the total manufacturing costs. Furthermore, its environmental failure costs (maintenance plus toxic waste) are $310,000, representing 83.8 percent of the total environmental costs. Cleanser A portrays a much better picture. Its environmental costs total $80,000, which is 8.0 percent of the total manufacturing costs, and the failure costs are 18.75 percent of the total environmental costs. It is evident that Cleanser B offers the most environmental and economic potential for improvement.

EXAMPLE 14.6

The HOW and WHY of Activity-Based Environmental Cost Assignments

Information:

Pearson Company reported the following:

1. Environmental activity costs

Activity	Costs
Design processes (to reduce pollution)	$ 45,000
Inspect processes (for pollution problems)	80,000
Maintain environmental equipment	125,000
Toxic waste disposal	200,000

2. Driver data

	Cleanser A	Cleanser B
Design hours	2,000	1,000
Inspection hours	1,750	2,250
Maintenance hours	200	4,800
Pounds of waste	1,000	19,000

3. Other production data

	Cleanser A	Cleanser B
Nonenvironmental production costs	$920,000	$1,630,000
Units produced	100,000	100,000

EXAMPLE 14.6

(Continued)

> **Why:**
> Activity-based assignments of environmental costs can provide managers the ability to assess the relative environmental impact of various products. Knowing this allows them to devise ways to improve the environmental impact of their products.

Required:

1. Calculate the activity rates that will be used to assign environmental costs to products.

2. Determine the unit environmental and unit costs of each product using ABC.

3. *What if* the design costs increased to $80,000 and the cost of toxic waste decreased to $100,000? Assume that Product B uses 2,000 out of 4,000 design hours. Also assume that toxic waste is cut in half and that Cleanser B uses 9,000 of 10,000 pounds of toxic waste. What is the new environmental cost for Cleanser B?

Solution:

1. Rates:

   Design process: $45,000/3,000 = $15 per design hour
   Inspection: $80,000/4,000 = $20 per inspection hour
   Maintaining equipment: $125,000/5,000 = $25 per maintenance hour
   Waste disposal: $200,000/20,000 = $10 per pound

2. Product costs:

Activities	Cleanser A	Cleanser B
Design processes ($15 × 2,000; $15 × 1,000)	$ 30,000	$ 15,000
Inspect processes ($20 × 1,750; $20 × 2,250)	35,000	45,000
Maintain equipment ($25 × 200; $25 × 4,800)	5,000	120,000
Toxic waste disposal ($10 × 1,000; $10 × 19,000)	10,000	190,000
Total environmental cost	$ 80,000	$ 370,000
Other manufacturing costs (nonenvironmental)	920,000	1,630,000
Total cost (environmental + other)	$1,000,000	$2,000,000
Unit environmental cost*	$0.80	$3.70
Unit cost (environmental + other)*	$10.00	$20.00

*Cost divided by 100,000 units.

3. Using the associated activity rates of $20 per design hour ($80,000/4,000) and $10 per pound of waste ($100,000/10,000), the design cost assigned to B increases by $25,000 (from $15,000 to $40,000), and the toxic waste cost assigned to B decreases by $100,000 (from $190,000 to $90,000). The net decrease is $75,000 ($100,000 − $25,000), and the total environmental cost for B decreases to $295,000 ($370,000 − $75,000); thus, the unit environmental cost for Cleanser B is now $2.95 ($295,000/100,000).

SUMMARY OF LEARNING OBJECTIVES

LO1. Describe how quality costs are defined, classified, and measured.
- Quality costs are those costs that are incurred because products may fail or actually fail to meet design specifications.
- Prevention costs are those costs incurred to prevent poor quality.
- Appraisal costs are incurred to detect poor quality.
- Internal failure costs are incurred because products fail to conform to specifications and are discovered before an external sale takes place.
- External failure costs are incurred because products fail to conform to expectations after being sold.

LO2. Explain how a quality cost report is prepared and used.
- A quality cost report is prepared by listing costs for each item within each of the four major quality cost categories.
- Knowing the magnitude of quality costs allows managers to assess their financial impact.
- Knowing the distribution of quality costs by category allows managers to assess the relative importance of each category.

LO3. Explain why quality cost information is needed and how it is used.
- Quality cost information is needed to help managers control quality performance and to serve as input for decision making.
- Quality cost information also is used to evaluate the overall performance of quality improvement programs.
- Quality cost information is fundamental in a company's pursuit of continual improvement.

LO4. Prepare three different types of quality performance reports.
- The interim report is used to evaluate the firm's ability to meet its budgeted quality costs. Managers use the report to compare the actual quality costs with those that were targeted for the period.
- The multiple-period trend report is a trend graph for several years. The graph allows managers to assess the direction and magnitude of change since the inception of a total quality program.
- The long-range report compares actual costs with ideal or zero-defect level.

LO5. Discuss how environmental costs can be measured, reported, and reduced.
- Environmental costs are those costs incurred because poor environmental quality exists or may exist.
- There are four categories of environmental costs: prevention, detection, internal failure, and external failure.
- The external failure category is divided into realized and unrealized costs. Realized costs are those external costs the firm has to pay; unrealized or societal costs are those costs caused by the firm but paid for by society.
- An environmental cost report is prepared by listing costs for each item within the four environmental cost categories.

LO6. Show how environmental costs can be assigned to products and processes.
- Managers must decide whether they will assign only private costs or whether they want all costs to be assigned (full costing).
- ABC assigns costs to environmental activities and then calculates activity rates.
- ABC rates are then used to assign environmental costs to products.
- By assigning environmental cost to products, management can classify products according to their degree of "dirtiness."

EXAMPLE 14.1   The HOW and WHY of Preparing a Quality Cost Report, page 714

EXAMPLE 14.2   The HOW and WHY of Preparing Interim Quality Performance Reports, page 722

EXAMPLE 14.3   The HOW and WHY of Multiple-Period Quality Trend Reporting, page 724

EXAMPLE 14.4   The HOW and WHY of Long-Range Quality Performance Reporting, page 727

EXAMPLE 14.5   The HOW and WHY of an Environmental Cost Report, page 733

EXAMPLE 14.6   The HOW and WHY of Activity-Based Environmental Cost Assignments, page 737

KEY TERMS

Appraisal costs, 710

Control activities, 710

Control costs, 710

Costs of quality, 710

Defective product, 710

Ecoefficiency, 729

Environmental costs, 732

Environmental detection costs, 732

Environmental external failure costs, 732

Environmental internal failure costs, 732

Environmental prevention costs, 732

Error cause identification, 726

External failure costs, 711

Failure activities, 710

Failure costs, 710

Full environmental costing, 736

Full private costing, 736

Gainsharing, 728

Hidden quality costs, 711

Interim quality performance report, 722

Interim quality standards, 722

Internal failure costs, 710

Long-range quality performance report, 725

Multiple-period quality trend report, 724

Observable quality costs, 711

Prevention costs, 710

Private costs, 732

"Quality of conformance," 709

Quality product or service, 709

Realized external failure costs, 732

Robustness, 710

Sustainable development, 729

Taguchi loss function, 712

Unrealized external failure (societal) costs, 732

Zero defects, 710

BRIEF EXERCISES

OBJECTIVE 1
Example 14.1

Brief Exercise 14-1 Quality Cost Report

Evans Company had total sales of $3,000,000 for fiscal 20x5. The costs of quality-related activities are given below.

Returns/allowances	$150,000
Design changes	180,000
Prototype inspection	39,000
Downtime	120,000
Quality circles	6,000
Packaging inspection	42,000
Field testing	18,000
Complaint adjustment	195,000

Required:

1. Prepare a quality cost report, classifying costs by category and expressing each category as a percentage of sales. What message does the cost report provide?

2. Prepare a bar graph and pie chart that illustrate each category's contribution to total quality costs. Comment on the significance of the distribution.

3. *What if*, five years from now, quality costs are 7.5 percent of sales, with control costs being 65 percent of the total quality costs? What would your conclusion be?

Brief Exercise 14-2 Interim Quality Performance Report

OBJECTIVE ▶ 3
Example 14.2

Davis, Inc., had the following quality costs for the years ended December 31, 20x4 and 20x5:

	20x4	20x5
Prevention costs:		
Quality audits	$ 60,000	$ 90,000
Vendor certification	120,000	180,000
Appraisal costs:		
Product acceptance	$ 90,000	$135,000
Process acceptance	75,000	109,500
Internal failure costs:		
Retesting	$102,000	$ 90,000
Rework	216,000	180,000
External failure costs:		
Recalls	$150,000	$120,000
Warranty	330,000	300,000

At the end of 20x4, management decided to increase its investment in control costs by 50 percent for each category's items with the expectation that failure costs would decrease by 20 percent for each item of the failure categories. Sales were $12,000,000 for both 20x4 and 20x5.

Required:

1. Calculate the budgeted costs for 20x5, and prepare an interim quality performance report.

2. Comment on the significance of the report. How much progress has Davis made?

3. *What if* sales were $12,000,000 for 20x4 and $15,000,000 for 20x5? What adjustment to budgeted rework costs would be made? Budgeted quality audits? Assuming the actual costs for 20x5 do not change, what does this adjustment say about Davis's performance?

Brief Exercise 14-3 Quality Trend Report Objective

OBJECTIVE ▶ 3
Example 14.3

Kanumba Company implemented a quality improvement program and tracked the following for the five years:

	Quality Costs	Actual Sales	Costs as a Percentage of Sales
20x1	$500,000	$2,000,000	25.00%
20x2	495,000	2,200,000	22.50
20x3	450,000	2,400,000	18.75
20x4	434,000	2,480,000	17.50
20x5	400,000	3,200,000	12.50

By cost category as a percentage of sales for the same period of time:

	Prevention	Appraisal	Internal Failure	External Failure
20x1	2.50%	2.50%	7.50%	12.50%
20x2	3.75	3.00	5.00	10.75
20x3	3.75	3.75	3.75	7.50
20x4	5.00	3.75	3.12	5.63
20x5	6.00	3.00	1.50	2.00

Required:

1. Prepare a bar graph that reveals the trend in quality cost as a percentage of sales (time on the horizontal axis and percentages on the vertical). Comment on the message of the graph.
2. Prepare a bar graph for each cost category as a percentage of sales. What does this graph tell you?
3. *What if* management would like to have the trend in *relative* distribution of quality costs? Express this as a bar graph and comment on its significance.

OBJECTIVE 3
Example 14.4

Brief Exercise 14-4 Long-Term Performance Report

Nabors Company had actual quality costs for the year ended June 30, 20x5, as given below.

Prevention costs:	
Prototype inspection	$ 300,000
Vendor certification	600,000
Total prevention costs	$ 900,000
Appraisal costs:	
Process acceptance	315,000
Test labor	360,000
Total appraisal costs	$ 675,000
Internal failure costs:	
Retesting	$ 187,500
Rework	375,000
Total internal failure costs	$ 562,500
External failure costs:	
Recalls	$ 243,750
Product liability	618,750
Total external failure costs	$ 862,500
Total quality costs	$3,000,000

At the zero-defect state, Nabors expects to spend $375,000 on prototype inspection, $75,000 on vendor certification, and $50,000 on process acceptance. Assume sales to be $25,000,000.

Required:

1. Prepare a long-range performance report for 20x5. What does this report tell the management of Nabors?
2. Explain why quality costs still are present for the zero-defect state.
3. *What if* Nabors achieves the zero-defect state reflected in the report? What are some of the implications of this achievement?

Brief Exercise 14-5 Environmental Cost Report

OBJECTIVE ◀ 5

Example 14.5

Verde Company reported operating costs of $50,000,000 as of December 31, 20x5, with the following environmental costs:

Testing for contamination	$ 700,000
Inspecting products	420,000
Treating toxic waste	2,100,000
Obtaining ISO 14001 certification	1,050,000
Designing processes	420,000
Cleaning up oil spills	3,675,000
Maintaining pollution equipment	1,250,000
Cleaning up contaminated soil	5,775,000

Required:

1. Prepare an environmental cost report, classifying costs by quality category and expressing each as a percentage of total operating costs. What is the message of this report?
2. Prepare a pie chart that shows the relative distribution of environmental costs by category. What does this report tell you?
3. *What if* Verde deliberately did not include the cost of damaging the ecosystem because of solid waste disposal in its environmental cost report? Offer possible reasons for this decision. If consciously avoided, is this decision unethical?

Brief Exercise 14-6 Activity-Based Environmental Cost Assignments

OBJECTIVE ◀ 5

Example 14.6

Shultz Company had the following environmental activities and product information:
1.   Environmental activity costs

Activity	Costs
Design products (to reduce pollution)	$ 405,000
Test for contamination	720,000
Treat toxic waste	2,250,000
Operate pollution control equipment	1,800,000

2.   Driver data

	Cleanser X	Cleanser Y
Design hours	9,000	4,500
Testing hours	15,750	20,250
Pounds of waste	1,800	43,200
Machine hours	9,000	171,000

3.   Other production data

	Cleanser X	Cleanser Y
Nonenvironmental production costs	$7,560,000	$14,670,000
Units produced	900,000	900,000

Required:

1. Calculate the activity rates that will be used to assign environmental costs to products.
2. Determine the unit environmental and unit costs of each product using ABC.
3. *What if* the design costs increased to $540,000 and the cost of toxic waste decreased to $1,125,000? Assume that Cleanser Y uses 9,000 out of 18,000 design hours. Also assume that waste is cut by 50 percent and that Cleanser Y is responsible for 21,375 of 22,500 pounds of toxic waste. What is the new environmental cost for Cleanser Y?

EXERCISES

OBJECTIVE ▶ 1

Exercise 14-7 Quality Definition and Quality Costs

Rachel Boyce, president of a company that manufactures electronic components, has a number of questions concerning quality and quality costs. She has heard a few things about quality and has asked you to respond to the following questions.

Required:

1. What does it mean to have a quality product or service? Explain how product quality and conformance are related.
2. Yesterday, my quality manager told me that we need to redefine what we mean by a defective product. He said that conforming to specifications ignores the cost of product variability and that further reduction of product variability is a veritable gold mine—just waiting to be mined. What did he mean?

OBJECTIVE ▶ 1

Exercise 14-8 Quality Definition and Quality Costs

Quality attributes such as performance and aesthetics are important to customers. Performance refers to how consistently and how well a product functions. Aesthetics is concerned with the appearance of tangible products as well as the appearance of the facilities, equipment, personnel, and communication materials associated with services.

Required:

1. Do you agree that aesthetics is an important quality dimension for services? Use dental services as the framework for providing your response.
2. For services, performance can be more carefully defined by expanding its definition to include responsiveness, assurance, and empathy. Describe what you think is meant by these three characteristics as applied to service quality.

OBJECTIVE ▶ 1

Exercise 14-9 Taguchi Loss Function

Lanman, Inc., estimates its hidden external failure costs using the Taguchi loss function. Lanman produces plastic sheets that vary in thickness and grade. For one of its large-volume products, it was determined that $k = \$40,000$ and $T = 0.31$ inches in diameter. A sample of four units produced the following values:

Unit No.	Actual Diameter (y)
1	0.33
2	0.30
3	0.29
4	0.32

Required:

1. Calculate the average loss per unit.
2. Assuming that 100,000 units were produced, what is the total hidden cost?
3. Assume that the multiplier for Lanman's hidden external failure costs is six. What are the measured external costs? Explain the difference between measured costs and hidden costs.

OBJECTIVE ▶ 1

Exercise 14-10 Quality Cost Classification

Classify the following quality costs as prevention costs, appraisal costs, internal failure costs, or external failure costs:

1. Inspection of reworked units
2. Inspecting and testing a newly developed product (not yet being sold)

EXCEL

3. Retesting a reworked product
4. Repairing a computer still under warranty
5. Discount allowed to customers because products failed to meet customer specifications
6. Goods returned because they failed to meet specifications
7. The cost of evaluating and certifying suppliers
8. Stopping work to correct process malfunction (discovered using statistical process control procedures)
9. Testing products in the field
10. Discarding products that cannot be reworked
11. Lost sales because of recalled products
12. Inspection of incoming materials
13. Redesigning a product to eliminate the need to use an outside component with a high defect rate
14. Purchase order changes
15. Replacing a defective product
16. Inspecting and testing prototypes
17. Repairing products in the field
18. Correcting a design error discovered during product development
19. Engineering resources used to help selected suppliers improve their product quality
20. Packaging inspection
21. Processing and responding to consumer complaints
22. Training production line workers in new quality procedures
23. Sampling a batch of goods to determine if the batch has an acceptable defect rate

Exercise 14-11 Activity-Based Quality Costing

OBJECTIVE ▶ 1 2

SHOW ME
HOW

Ivanov, Inc., produces two different generators and is concerned about their quality. The company has identified the following quality activities and costs associated with the two products:

	Generator A	Generator B
Units produced	170,000	340,000
Warranty work (units)	1,700	850
Scrapped units (number)	3,400	850
Inspection (hours)	3,400	1,700
Quality training (hours)	85	85
Activities:		
Performing warranty work	$816,000	
Scrapping units	612,000	
Inspecting	306,000	
Quality training	85,000	

Required:

1. Calculate the quality cost per unit for each product, and break this unit cost into quality cost categories. Which of the two seems to have the lowest quality?
2. How might a manager use the unit quality cost information?

Exercise 14-12 Quality Cost Report

OBJECTIVE ◀ 2

SHOW ME
HOW

Kang Company reported sales of $3,240,000 in 20x5. At the end of the calendar year, the following quality costs were reported:

Design review	$162,000
Recalls	54,000
Reinspection	27,000

Materials inspection	21,600
Quality training	54,000
Process acceptance	27,000
Scrap	18,900
Lost sales	108,000
Product inspection	16,200
Returned goods	51,300

Required:

1. Prepare a quality cost report.
2. Prepare a graph (pie chart or bar graph) that shows the relative distribution of quality costs, and comment on the distribution.

OBJECTIVE **2 3**

SHOW ME
HOW

Exercise 14-13 Quality Improvement and Profitability Objective

Ming Company reported the following sales and quality costs for the past four years. Assume that all quality costs are variable and that all changes in the quality cost ratios are due to a quality improvement program.

Year	Sales Revenues	Quality Costs as a Percent of Revenues
1	$40,000,000	25%
2	44,000,000	22
3	44,000,000	18
4	48,000,000	14

Required:

1. Compute the quality costs for all four years. By how much did net income increase from Year 1 to Year 2 because of quality improvements? From Year 2 to Year 3? From Year 3 to Year 4?
2. The management of Ming Company believes it is possible to reduce quality costs to 2.5 percent of sales. Assuming sales will continue at the Year 4 level, calculate the additional profit potential facing Ming. Is the expectation of improving quality and reducing costs to 2.5 percent of sales realistic? Explain.
3. Assume that Ming produces one type of product, which is sold on a bid basis. In Years 1 and 2, the average bid was $400. In Year 1, total variable costs were $250 per unit. In Year 3, competition forced the bid to drop to $320. Compute the total contribution margin in Year 3 assuming the same percentage of quality costs as in Year 1. Now, compute the total contribution margin in Year 3 using the actual quality costs for Year 3. What is the increase in profitability resulting from the quality improvements made from Year 1 to Year 3?

OBJECTIVE  **2 3 4**

Exercise 14-14 Quality Costs: Profit Improvement and Distribution Across Categories, Gainsharing

Muskogee Company had sales of $60,000,000 in 20x1. In 20x5, sales had increased to $75,000,000. A quality improvement program was implemented at the beginning of 20x1. Overall conformance quality was targeted for improvement. The quality costs for 20x1 and 20x5 follow. Assume any changes in quality costs are attributable to improvements in quality.

	20x1	20x5
Internal failure costs	$ 4,500,000	$ 225,000
External failure costs	6,000,000	150,000
Appraisal costs	2,700,000	562,500
Prevention costs	1,800,000	937,500
Total quality costs	$15,000,000	$1,875,000

Required:

1. Compute the quality cost-to-sales ratio for each year. Is this type of improvement possible?
2. Calculate the relative distribution of costs by category for 20x1. What do you think of the way costs are distributed? (A pie chart or bar graph may be of some help.) How do you think they will be distributed as the company approaches a zero-defects state?
3. Calculate the relative distribution of costs by category for 20x5. What do you think of the level and distribution of quality costs? (A pie chart or bar graph may be of some help.) Do you think further reductions are possible?
4. The quality manager for Muskogee indicated that the external failure costs reported are only the measured costs. He argued that the 20x5 external costs were much higher than those reported and that additional investment ought to be made in control costs. Discuss the validity of his viewpoint.
5. Suppose that the manager of Muskogee received a bonus equal to 10 percent of the quality cost savings each year. Do you think that gainsharing is a good or a bad idea? Discuss the risks of gainsharing.

Exercise 14-15 Trade-Offs Among Quality Cost Categories, Total Quality Control, Gainsharing

 OBJECTIVE ◀ **2** **3**

DATA ANALYTICS

Oaks Company has sales of $12 million and quality costs of $2,400,000. The company is embarking on a major quality improvement program. During the next three years, Oaks intends to attack failure costs by increasing its appraisal and prevention costs. The "right" prevention activities will be selected, and appraisal costs will be reduced according to the results achieved. For the coming year, management is considering six specific activities: quality training, process control, product inspection, supplier evaluation, prototype testing, and redesign of two major products. To encourage managers to focus on reducing non-value-added quality costs and select the right activities, a bonus pool is established relating to reduction of quality costs. The bonus pool is equal to 10 percent of the total reduction in quality costs.

Current quality costs and the costs of these six activities are given in the following table. Each activity is added sequentially so that its effect on the cost categories can be assessed. For example, after quality training is added, the control costs increase to $480,000, and the failure costs drop to $1,560,000. Even though the activities are presented sequentially, they are totally independent of each other. Thus, only beneficial activities need be selected.

	Control Costs	Failure Costs
Current quality costs	$ 240,000	$2,160,000
Quality training	480,000	1,560,000
Process control	780,000	1,080,000
Product inspection	900,000	984,000
Supplier evaluation	1,080,000	300,000
Prototype testing	1,440,000	180,000
Engineering redesign	1,500,000	60,000

Required:

1. Identify the control activities that should be implemented, and calculate the total quality costs associated with this selection. Assume that an activity is selected only if it increases the bonus pool.

2. Given the activities selected in Requirement 1, calculate the following:

    a. The expected reduction in total quality costs
    b. The expected percentage distribution for control and failure costs
    c. The expected amount for this year's bonus pool

3. Suppose that a quality engineer complained about the gainsharing incentive system. Basically, he argued that the bonus should be based only on reductions of failure and appraisal costs. In this way, investment in prevention activities would be encouraged, and eventually, failure and appraisal costs would be eliminated. After eliminating the non-value-added costs, focus could then be placed on the level of prevention costs. If this approach were adopted, what activities would be selected? What would be the bonus pool? Do you agree or disagree with this approach? Explain.

4. Explain why the following statements would be true:

    a. The principal data analytic type for the analysis in Requirement 1 is prescriptive.
    b. The principal data analytic type for Requirement 2 is predictive.
    c. Requirement 3 uses prescriptive, predictive, and diagnostic data analytic types.

OBJECTIVE **4**

EXCEL

Exercise 14-16 Trend, Long-Range Performance Report

In 20x4, Tru-Delite Frozen Desserts, Inc., instituted a quality improvement program. At the end of 20x5, the management of the corporation requested a report to show the amount saved by the measures taken during the year. The actual sales and quality costs for 20x4 and 20x5 are as follows:

	20x4	20x5
Sales	$600,000	$600,000
Scrap	15,000	15,000
Rework	20,000	10,000
Training program	5,000	6,000
Consumer complaints	10,000	5,000
Lost sales, incorrect labeling	8,000	—
Test labor	12,000	8,000
Inspection labor	25,000	24,000
Supplier evaluation	15,000	13,000

Tru-Delite's management believes that quality costs can be reduced to 2.5 percent of sales within the next five years. At the end of 20x9, Tru-Delite's sales are projected to grow to $750,000. The projected relative distribution of quality costs at the end of 20x9 is as follows:

Scrap	15%
Training program	20
Supplier evaluation	25
Test labor	25
Inspection labor	15
Total quality costs	100%

Required:

1. Profits increased by what amount due to quality improvements made in 20x5?
2. Prepare a long-range performance report that compares the quality costs incurred at the end of 20x5 with the quality cost structure expected at the end of 20x9.
3. Are the targeted costs in the year 20x9 all value-added costs? How would you interpret the variances if the targeted costs are value-added costs?
4. What would be the profit increase in 20x9 if the 2.5 percent performance standard is met in that year?

Exercise 14-17 Multiple-Year Trend Reports; Benefits of Data Visualization

OBJECTIVE ◀ 4

**DATA
ANALYTICS**

The controller of Willson Company has computed quality costs as a percentage of sales for the past five years (20x1 was the first year the company implemented a quality improvement program). This information is as follows:

	Prevention	Appraisal	Internal Failure	External Failure	Total
20x1	2%	3%	8.0%	12%	25.0%
20x2	3	4	7.0	10	24.0
20x3	4	5	5.5	6	20.5
20x4	5	4	3.0	5	17.0
20x5	6	3	1.0	2	12.0

Required:

1. Prepare a trend graph for total quality costs. Comment on what the graph has to say about the success of the quality improvement program.
2. Prepare a graph that shows the trend for each quality cost category. What does the graph have to say about the success of the quality improvement program? Does this graph supply more insight than the total cost trend graph does?
3. Prepare a graph that compares the trend in relative quality costs. What does this graph tell you?
4. Data visualization is an important tool of data analytics. Discuss the role the above graphs in Requirements 1 through 3 might have for each of the four different analytic types: descriptive, diagnostic, predictive, and prescriptive (see Exhibits 2.5 and 2.6, pp. 37, 40, for a brief review of data analytic types).

Exercise 14-18 Ecoefficiency

OBJECTIVE ◀ 5

For years, companies dealt with pollution problems through compliance management (ensuring that a company follows environmental laws and regulations as cheaply as possible). No effort was made to improve environmental performance beyond the minimal performance that satisfied environmental regulations (improving environmental performance and increasing economic efficiency were viewed as incompatible objectives). Recently, two alternative views of managing environmental cost have been proposed: (1) ecoefficiency and (2) guided ecoefficiency.

Required:

1. Explain why ecoefficiency may be a better view of the world than that espoused by compliance management. Discuss factors that may support this view.
2. Some believe that even if the ecoefficient view is true, regulatory intervention still may be needed. The type of intervention, however, must be carefully designed. Explain what is meant by properly designed regulation, and identify the key assumptions that must hold for the guided ecoefficiency view to be valid.

OBJECTIVE `5`   **Exercise 14-19 Ecoefficiency and Sustainable Development**

Achieving sustainable development will likely require the cooperation of communities, governments, and businesses. The World Business Council for Sustainable Development (WBCSD) claims that ecoefficiency is "the business contribution to sustainable development."

Required:

1. What is sustainable development?
2. Explain why the WBCSD's claim about ecoefficiency may be true.
3. WBCSD has noted (**http://www.wbcsd.org**): "the good news is that ecoefficiency is working in the companies that try it. The troubling news is that it is not being tried on a large enough scale, even though it makes good business sense." Why do you think the ecoefficiency paradigm is not as widely accepted as it perhaps ought to be? What would you suggest to increase the number of companies involved in ecoefficient projects?

OBJECTIVE `5`   **Exercise 14-20 Classification of Environmental Costs**

Classify the following environmental activities as prevention costs, detection costs, internal failure costs, or external failure costs. For external failure costs, classify the costs as societal or private. Also, label those activities that are compatible with sustainable development (SD).

1. A company takes actions to reduce the amount of material in its packages.
2. After the activated carbon's useful life, a soft-drink producer returns this material used for purifying water for its beverages to the supplier. The supplier reactivates the carbon for a second use in nonfood applications. As a consequence, many tons of material are prevented from entering landfills.
3. An evaporator system is installed to treat wastewater and collect usable solids for other uses.
4. The inks used to print snack packages (for chips) contain heavy metals.
5. Processes are inspected to ensure compliance with environmental standards.
6. Delivery boxes are used five times and then recycled. This prevents 112 million pounds of cardboard from entering landfills and saves 2 million trees per year.
7. Scrubber equipment is installed to ensure that air emissions are less than the level permitted by law.
8. Local residents are incurring medical costs from illnesses caused by air pollution from automobile exhaust pollution.
9. As part of implementing an environmental perspective for the Balanced Scorecard, environmental performance measures are developed.
10. Because of liquid and solid residues being discharged into a local lake, the lake is no longer fit for swimming, fishing, and other recreational activities.
11. To reduce energy consumption, magnetic ballasts are replaced with electronic ballasts, and more efficient light bulbs and lighting sensors are installed. As a result, 2.3 million kilowatt-hours of electricity are saved per year.
12. Due to a legal settlement, a chemicals company must spend $20,000,000 to clean up contaminated soil.
13. A soft-drink company uses the following practice: In all bottling plants, packages damaged during filling are collected and recycled (glass, plastic, and aluminum).
14. Products are inspected to ensure that the gaseous emissions produced during operation follow legal and company guidelines.
15. Operating pollution control equipment incurs costs.
16. An internal audit is conducted to verify that environmental policies are being followed.

Exercise 14-21 Environmental Cost Report

OBJECTIVE ◀ 5

SHOW ME
HOW

At the end of 20x5, Bing Pharmaceuticals began to implement an environmental quality management program. As a first step, it identified the following costs in its accounting records as environmentally related for the calendar year just ended:

	20x5
Settling personal injury claims	$ 3,000,000
Treating and disposing of toxic waste	12,000,000
Cleanup of chemically contaminated soil	4,500,000
Inspecting products and processes	1,500,000
Operating pollution control equipment	2,100,000
Licensing facilities for producing contaminants	900,000
Evaluating and selecting suppliers	300,000
Developing performance measures	150,000
Recycling products	187,500

Required:

1. Prepare an environmental cost report by category. Assume that total operating costs are $150,000,000.
2. Use a pie chart to illustrate the relative distribution percentages for each environmental cost category. Comment on what this distribution communicates to a manager.

Exercise 14-22 Reporting Social Costs

OBJECTIVE ◀ 5

Refer to **Exercise 14-21**. Suppose that the newly hired environmental manager examines the report and makes the following comment: "This report understates the total environmental costs. It fails to consider the costs we are imposing on the local community. For example, we have polluted the river and lake so much that swimming and fishing are no longer possible. I have heard rumblings from the local citizens, and I'll bet that we will be facing a big cleanup bill in a few years."

Subsequent to the comment, environmental engineering estimated that cleanup costs for the river and lake will cost $7,500,000, assuming the cleanup efforts are required within five years. To pay for the cleanup, annual contributions of $1,312,500 will be invested with the expectation that the fund will grow to $7,500,000 by the end of the fifth year. Assume also that the loss of recreational opportunities is costing the local community $3,000,000 per year.

Required:

1. How would this information alter the report in **Exercise 14-21**?
2. Current financial reporting standards require that contingent liabilities be disclosed if certain conditions are met. Thus, it is possible that Bing may need to disclose the $7,500,000 cleanup liability. Yet, the opportunity cost for the recreational opportunities need not be disclosed to outside parties. Should Bing voluntarily disclose this cost? Is it likely that it would?

Exercise 14-23 Environmental Cost Assignment

OBJECTIVE ◀ 5

Waurika Pharmaceuticals produces two organic chemicals (Org AB and Org XY) used in the production of two of its most wide-selling anti-cancer drugs. The controller and environmental manager have identified the following environmental activities and costs associated with the two products:

	Org AB	Org XY
Pounds produced	7,500,000	17,250,000
Packaging materials (pounds)	4,470,000	2,280,000
Energy usage (kilowatt-hours)	1,500,000	750,000
Toxin releases (pounds into air)	3,750,000	750,000
Pollution control (machine hours)	600,000	150,000
Costs of activities:		
Using packaging materials	$6,750,000	
Using energy	1,800,000	
Releasing toxins (fines)	900,000	
Operating pollution control equipment	2,100,000	

Required:

1. Calculate the environmental cost per pound for each product. Which of the two products appears to cause the most degradation to the environment?
2. In which environmental category would you classify excessive use of materials and energy?
3. Suppose that the toxin releases cause health problems for those who live near the chemical plant. The costs, due to missed work and medical treatments, are estimated at $4,050,000 per year. How would assignment of these costs change the unit cost? Should they be assigned?

OBJECTIVE **5**

**SHOW ME
HOW**

Exercise 14-24 Environmental Costing, Ecoefficiency, and Competitive Advantage

Refer to the data in **Exercise 14-23**. Suppose that Waurika's manager decides to launch an environmental performance improvement program. First, efforts were made to reduce the amount of packaging. The demand for packaging materials was reduced by 10 percent. Second, a way was found to reuse the packaging materials. Usage of packaging materials changed from one time to two times. Both changes together saved $3,712,500 in packaging costs. Third, the manufacturing processes were redesigned to produce a reduced environmental load. The new processes were able to reduce emissions by 50 percent and private emission costs by 75 percent. The new processes also reduced the demand for energy by one-third. Energy costs were also reduced by the same amount. There was no change in the demand or cost of operating pollution control equipment.

The cost of implementing the changes was $1,507,500 (salaries of $900,000 for hiring six environmental engineers and $607,500 for treating the packaging materials so they can be reused). Engineering hours used for each process are 11,250 for the Org AB process and 3,750 for the Org XY process.

Required:

1. Calculate the new cost per pound for each product. Assume that the environmental reductions for each product are in the same proportions as the total reductions.
2. Calculate the net savings produced by the environmental changes for each product, in total, and on a per-unit basis. Does this support the concept of ecoefficiency?
3. Classify the activities as prevention, detection, internal failure, or external failure.
4. Describe how the environmental improvements can contribute to improving the firm's competitive position.

PROBLEMS

Problem 14-25 Quality Cost Report, Taguchi Loss Function

OBJECTIVE ▶ 1 ◀ 2

DATA
ANALYTICS

Gabrielle Alvarez, president of Oliver Company, was concerned with the trend in sales and profitability. The company had been losing customers at an alarming rate. Furthermore, the company was barely breaking even. Investigation revealed that poor quality was at the root of the problem. At the end of 20x5, Gabrielle decided to begin a quality improvement program. As a first step, she identified the following costs in the accounting records as quality related:

	20x5
Sales (600,000 units @ $100)	$60,000,000
Retesting	1,800,000
Rework	2,400,000
Vendor certification	720,000
Consumer complaints	1,200,000
Warranty	2,400,000
Test labor	1,800,000
Inspection labor	1,500,000
Design reviews	180,000

Required:

1. Prepare a quality cost report by quality cost category. Now calculate the relative distribution percentages for each quality cost category.
2. The preparation of the quality cost report and the calculation of the relative distribution percentages are examples of descriptive analytics. They describe what is happening. To illustrate the other three data analytic types, do the following:

   a. Offer some likely explanations for why the costs are reported and distributed as shown (diagnostic analytics).
   b. Indicate what Oliver should do (or needs to do) to achieve the optimal level of quality performance (prescriptive analytics).
   c. Assuming that sales remain the same, predict what the increase in income will likely be if Oliver reduces its quality costs to the ideal level (predictive analytics).

3. Using the Taguchi loss function, an average loss per unit is computed to be $15 per unit. What are the hidden costs of external failure? How does this affect the relative distribution?
4. Alvarez's quality manager decided not to bother with the hidden costs. He argued that any efforts to reduce measured external failure costs will also reduce the hidden costs. Do you agree or disagree? Explain.

Problem 14-26 Taguchi Loss Function

OBJECTIVE ▶ 2

Panguitch Company manufactures a component for tablet computers. Weight and durability of the component are the two most important quality characteristics for the tablet manufacturers. With respect to the weight dimension, the component has a target value of 100 grams. Specification limits are 100 grams, plus or minus five grams. Products produced at the lower specification limit of 95 grams lose $20. A sample of five units produced the following weight measures:

Unit No.	Measured Weight
1	100
2	105
3	110
4	90
5	85

During the first quarter, 100,000 units were produced.

Required:

1. Calculate the loss for each unit. Calculate the average loss for the sample of five.

2. Using the average loss, calculate the hidden quality costs for the first quarter.

3. Durability is another important quality characteristic. The target value is 20,000 hours of operation before failure. The lower specification limit set by engineering and marketing is 19,000 hours. They agreed that there should be no upper specification limit. They also noted that there is a $750 loss at the lower specification limit. Explain why there would be no upper specification limit. Use the lower limit and the *left half* of the Taguchi quadratic loss function to estimate the loss for components with the following lives: 6,500 hours, 11,000 hours, and 15,500 hours. What does this reveal about the importance of durability?

OBJECTIVE `3`   **Problem 14-27   Quality Costs, Pricing Decisions, Market Share**

Gaston Company manufactures furniture. One of its product lines is an economy-line kitchen table. During the last year, Gaston produced and sold 100,000 units for $100 per unit. Sales of the table are on a bid basis, but Gaston has always been able to win sufficient bids using the $100 price. This year, however, Gaston was losing more than its share of bids. Concerned, Terrell Franklin, owner and president of the company, called a meeting of his executive committee (Megan Johnson, marketing manager; Li Chen, quality manager; Kevin Jones, production manager; and Helen Jackson, controller).

TERRELL: I don't understand why we're losing bids. Megan, do you have an explanation?

MEGAN: Yes, as a matter of fact. Two competitors have lowered their price to $92 per unit. That's too big a difference for most of our buyers to ignore. If we want to keep selling our 100,000 units per year, we will need to lower our price to $92. Otherwise, our sales will drop to about 20,000 to 25,000 per year.

HELEN: The unit contribution margin on the table is $10. Lowering the price to $92 will cost us $8 per unit. Based on a sales volume of 100,000, we'd make $200,000 in contribution margin. If we keep the price at $100, our contribution margin would be $200,000 to $250,000. If we have to lose, let's just take the lower market share. It's better than lowering our prices.

MEGAN: Perhaps. But the same thing could happen to some of our other product lines. My sources tell me that these two companies are on the tail end of a major quality improvement program—one that allows them significant savings. We need to rethink our whole competitive strategy—at least if we want to stay in business. Ideally, we should match the price reduction and work to reduce the costs to recapture the lost contribution margin.

LI: I think I have something to offer. We are about to embark on a new quality improvement program of our own. I have brought the following estimates of the current quality costs for this economy line. As you can see, these costs run about 16 percent of current sales. That's excessive, and we believe that they can be reduced to about 4 percent of sales over time.

Scrap	$ 700,000
Rework	300,000
Rejects (sold as seconds to discount houses)	250,000
Returns (due to poor workmanship)	350,000
	$1,600,000

TERRELL: This sounds good. Li, how long will it take for you to achieve this reduction?

LI: All these costs vary with sales level, so I'll express their reduction rate in those terms. Our best guess is that we can reduce these costs by about 1 percent of sales per quarter. So it should take about 12 quarters, or three years, to achieve the full benefit. Keep in mind that this is with an improvement in quality.

MEGAN: This offers us some hope. If we meet the price immediately, we can maintain our market share. Furthermore, if we can ever reach the point of reducing the price below the $92 level, then we can increase our market share. I estimate that we can increase sales by about 10,000 units for every $1 of price reduction beyond the $92 level. Kevin, how much extra capacity for this line do we have?

KEVIN: We can handle an extra 30,000 or 40,000 tables per year.

Required:

1. Assume that Gaston immediately reduces the bid price to $92. How long will it be before the unit contribution margin is restored to $10, assuming that quality costs are reduced as expected and that sales are maintained at 100,000 units per year (25,000 per quarter)?
2. Assume that Gaston holds the price at $92 until the 4 percent target is achieved. At this new level of quality costs, should the price be reduced? If so, by how much should the price be reduced, and what is the increase in contribution margin? Assume that price can be reduced only in $1 increments.
3. Assume that Gaston immediately reduces the price to $92 and begins the quality improvement program. Now, suppose that Gaston does not wait until the end of the three-year period before reducing prices. Instead, prices will be reduced when profitable to do so. Assume that prices can be reduced only by $1 increments. Identify when the first future price change should occur (if any).
4. Discuss the differences in viewpoints concerning the decision to decrease prices and the short-run contribution margin analysis done by Helen, the controller. Did quality cost information play an important role in the strategic decision making illustrated by the problem?

Problem 14-28 Classification of Quality Costs

OBJECTIVE ◄ 1

Classify the following quality costs as prevention, appraisal, internal failure, or external failure. Also, label each cost as variable or fixed with respect to sales volume.

1. Quality engineering
2. Scrap
3. Product recalls
4. Returns and allowances because of quality problems
5. Sales data re-entered because of keying errors
6. Supervision of in-process inspection
7. Quality circles
8. Component inspection and testing
9. Quality training
10. Reinspection of reworked product
11. Product liability
12. Internal audit assessing the effectiveness of quality system
13. Disposal of defective product
14. Downtime attributable to quality problems
15. Quality reporting
16. Proofreading
17. Correction of typing errors
18. In-process inspection
19. Process controls
20. Pilot studies

OBJECTIVE 2

EXCEL

Problem 14-29 Quality Cost Summary

Wayne Johnson, president of Banshee Company, recently returned from a conference on quality and productivity. At the conference, he was told that many American firms have quality costs totaling 20 to 30 percent of sales. He, however, was skeptical about this statistic. But even if the quality gurus were right, he was sure that his company's quality costs were much lower—probably less than 5 percent. On the other hand, if he was wrong, he would be passing up an opportunity to improve profits significantly and simultaneously strengthen his competitive position. The possibility was at least worth exploring. He knew that his company produced most of the information needed for quality cost reporting—but there never was a need to bother with any formal quality data gathering and analysis.

This conference, however, had convinced him that a firm's profitability can increase significantly by improving quality—provided the potential for improvement exists. Thus, before committing the company to a quality improvement program, Wayne requested a preliminary estimate of the total quality costs currently being incurred. He also indicated that the costs should be classified into four categories: prevention, appraisal, internal failure, or external failure. He has asked you to prepare a summary of quality costs and to compare the total costs to sales and profits. To assist you in this task, the following information has been prepared from the past year, 20x5:

  a. Sales revenue, $15,000,000; net income, $1,500,000.

  b. During the year, customers returned 90,000 units needing repair. Repair cost averages $1 per unit.

  c. Four inspectors are employed, each earning an annual salary of $60,000. These four inspectors are involved only with final inspection (product acceptance).

  d. Total scrap is 150,000 units. Of this total, 60 percent is quality related. The cost of scrap is about $5 per unit.

  e. Each year, approximately 450,000 units are rejected in final inspection. Of these units, 80 percent can be recovered through rework. The cost of rework is $0.75 per unit.

  f. A customer cancelled an order that would have increased profits by $150,000. The customer's reason for cancellation was poor product performance.

  g. The company employs three full-time employees in its complaint department. Each earns $40,500 a year.

  h. The company gave sales allowances totaling $45,000 due to substandard products being sent to the customer.

  i. The company requires all new employees to take its three-hour quality training program. The estimated annual cost of the program is $30,000.

Required:

1. Prepare a simple quality cost report classifying costs by category.
2. Compute the quality cost-to-sales ratio. Also, compare the total quality costs with total profits. Should Wayne be concerned with the level of quality costs?
3. Prepare a pie chart for the quality costs. Discuss the distribution of quality costs among the four categories. Are they properly distributed? Explain.
4. Discuss how the company can improve its overall quality and at the same time reduce total quality costs.
5. By how much will profits increase if quality costs are reduced to 2.5 percent of sales?

OBJECTIVE 1 ▶ 2 ▶ 4

EXCEL

Problem 14-30 Quality Cost Report, Interim Performance Report

Recently, Ulrich Company received a report from an external consulting group on its quality costs. The consultants reported that the company's quality costs total about 21 percent of its sales revenues. Somewhat shocked by the magnitude of the costs, Rob Rustin, president of Ulrich Company, decided to launch a major quality improvement program. For the coming year, management decided to reduce quality costs to 17 percent of sales revenues. Although the amount of reduction was ambitious, most company officials believed that the goal could be realized. To improve the monitoring of the quality improvement program, Rob directed

Pamela Golding, the controller, to prepare monthly performance reports comparing budgeted and actual quality costs. Budgeted costs and sales for the first two months of the year are as follows:

	January	February
Sales	$500,000	$600,000
Quality costs:		
Warranty	$ 15,000	$ 18,000
Scrap	10,000	12,000
Incoming materials inspection	2,500	2,500
Product acceptance	13,000	15,000
Quality planning	2,000	2,000
Field inspection	12,000	14,000
Retesting	6,000	7,200
Allowances	7,500	9,000
New product review	500	500
Rework	9,000	10,800
Complaint adjustment	2,500	2,500
Downtime (defective parts)	5,000	6,000
Quality training	1,000	1,000
Total budgeted costs	$ 86,000	$100,500
Quality cost-to-sales ratio	17.2%	16.75%

The following actual sales and actual quality costs were reported for January:

Sales	$550,000
Quality costs:	
Warranty	17,500
Scrap	12,500
Incoming materials inspection	2,500
Product acceptance	14,000
Quality planning	2,500
Field inspection	14,000
Retesting	7,000
Allowances	8,500
New product review	700
Rework	11,000
Complaint adjustment	2,500
Downtime (defective parts)	5,500
Quality training	1,000

Required:

1. Reorganize the monthly budgets so that quality costs are grouped in one of four categories: appraisal, prevention, internal failure, or external failure. (Essentially, prepare a budgeted cost of quality report.) Also, identify each cost as variable (V) or fixed (F). (Assume that no costs are mixed.)
2. Prepare a performance report for January that compares actual costs with budgeted costs. Comment on the company's progress in improving quality and reducing its quality costs.

Problem 14-31 Quality Cost Performance Reporting: One-Year Trend, Long-Range Analysis

OBJECTIVE ◀ 4

In 20x5, Major Company initiated a full-scale, quality improvement program. At the end of the year, Amelia Hoxha, the president, noted with some satisfaction that the defects per unit of product had dropped significantly compared to the prior year. She was also pleased that relationships with suppliers had improved and defective materials had declined. The new quality training program was also well accepted by employees. Of most interest to the president, however, was the impact of the quality improvements on profitability. To help assess the dollar impact of the quality improvements, the actual sales and the actual quality costs for 20x4 and 20x5 are as follows by quality category:

	20x4	20x5
Sales	$8,000,000	$10,000,000
Appraisal costs:		
Packaging inspection	320,000	300,000
Product acceptance	40,000	28,000
Prevention costs:		
Quality circles	4,000	40,000
Design reviews	2,000	20,000
Quality improvement projects	2,000	100,000
Internal failure costs:		
Scrap	280,000	240,000
Rework	360,000	320,000
Yield losses	160,000	100,000
Retesting	200,000	160,000
External failure costs:		
Returned materials	160,000	160,000
Allowances	120,000	140,000
Warranty	400,000	440,000

All prevention costs are fixed (by discretion). Assume all other quality costs are unit-level variable.

Required:

1. Compute the relative distribution of quality costs for each year and prepare a pie chart. Do you believe that the company is moving in the right direction in terms of the balance among the quality cost categories? Explain.
2. Prepare a one-year trend performance report for 20x5 (compare the actual costs of 20x5 with those of 20x4, adjusted for differences in sales volume). How much have profits increased because of the quality improvements made by Major Company?
3. Estimate the additional improvement in profits if Major Company ultimately reduces its quality costs to 2.5 percent of sales revenues (assume sales of $10 million).

OBJECTIVE 4

Problem 14-32 Distribution of Quality Costs

Paper Products Division produces paper diapers, napkins, and paper towels. The divisional manager has decided that quality costs can be minimized by distributing quality costs evenly among the four quality categories and reducing them to no more than 5 percent of sales. He has just received the following quality cost report:

Paper Products Division
Quality Cost Report
For the Year Ended December 31, 20x5

	Diapers	Napkins	Paper Towels	Total
Prevention costs:				
Quality training	$ 3,000	$ 2,500	$ 2,000	$ 7,500
Quality engineering	3,500	1,000	2,500	7,000
Quality audits	—	500	1,000	1,500
Quality reporting	2,500	2,000	1,000	5,500
Total prevention costs	$ 9,000	$ 6,000	$ 6,500	$ 21,500

Appraisal costs:

Inspection, materials	$ 2,000	$ 3,000	$ 3,000	$ 8,000
Process acceptance	4,000	2,800	1,200	8,000
Product acceptance	2,000	1,200	2,300	5,500
Total appraisal costs	$ 8,000	$ 7,000	$ 6,500	$ 21,500

Internal failure costs:

Scrap	$10,000	$ 3,000	$ 2,500	$ 15,500
Disposal costs	7,000	2,000	1,500	10,500
Downtime	1,000	1,500	2,500	5,000
Total internal failure costs	$18,000	$ 6,500	$ 6,500	$ 31,000

External failure costs:

Allowances	$10,000	$ 3,000	$ 2,750	$ 15,750
Customer complaints	4,000	1,500	3,750	9,250
Product liability	1,000	—	—	1,000
Total external failure costs	$15,000	$ 4,500	$ 6,500	$ 26,000
Total quality costs	$50,000	$24,000	$26,000	$100,000

Assume that all prevention costs are fixed and that the remaining quality costs are variable (unit-level).

Required:

1. Assume that the sales revenue for the year totaled $2 million, with sales for each product as follows: diapers, $1 million; napkins, $600,000; and paper towels, $400,000. Evaluate the distribution of costs for the division as a whole and for each product line. What recommendations do you have for the divisional manager?

2. Now, assume that total sales are $1 million and have this breakdown: diapers, $500,000; napkins, $300,000; and paper towels, $200,000. Evaluate the distribution of costs for the division as a whole and for each product line in this case. Do you think it is possible to reduce the quality costs to 5 percent of sales for each product line and for the division as a whole and, simultaneously, achieve an equal distribution of the quality costs? What recommendations do you have?

3. Assume total sales of $1 million with this breakdown: diapers, $500,000; napkins, $180,000; and paper towels, $320,000. Evaluate the distribution of quality costs. What recommendations do you have for the divisional manager?

4. Discuss the value of having quality costs reported by segment.

Problem 14-33 Trend Analysis, Quality Costs, Data Visualization

In 20x1, Antonio Flores, president of Carbondale Electronics, received a report indicating that quality costs were 31 percent of sales. Faced with increasing pressures from imported goods, Antonio resolved to take measures to improve the overall quality of the company's products. After hiring a consultant in 20x0, the company began an aggressive program of total quality control. At the end of 20x5, Antonio requested an analysis of the progress the company had made in reducing and controlling quality costs. The Accounting Department assembled the following data:

DATA
ANALYTICS

	Sales	Prevention	Appraisal	Internal Failure	External Failure
20x1	$5,000,000	$ 50,000	$100,000	$800,000	$600,000
20x2	6,000,000	250,000	150,000	600,000	500,000
20x3	7,000,000	350,000	300,000	350,000	250,000
20x4	6,000,000	400,000	150,000	250,000	200,000
20x5	8,000,000	800,000	80,000	192,000	128,000

Required:

1. Compute the quality costs as a percentage of sales by category and in total for each year.
2. Prepare a multiple-year trend graph for quality costs, both by total costs and by category. Using the graph, assess the progress made in reducing and controlling quality costs. Does the graph provide evidence that quality has improved? Explain.
3. Using the 20x1 quality cost relationships (assume all costs are variable), calculate the quality costs that would have prevailed in 20x4. By how much did profits increase in 20x4 because of the quality improvement program? Repeat for 20x5.
4. Identify which data analytic type(s) (descriptive, diagnostic, predictive, and analytic) apply for Requirements 1, 2, and 3. In Requirement 2, discuss the value of data visualization in applying the data analytic type. *Note:* More than one type might apply (see Exhibits 2.5 and 2.6, pp. 37, 40, for a brief review of data analytic types).

OBJECTIVE ▶ 4

Problem 14-34 Case on Quality Cost Performance Reports

Iona Company, a large printing company, is in its fourth year of a five-year, quality improvement program. The program began in 20x0 with an internal study that revealed the quality costs being incurred. In that year, a five-year plan was developed to lower quality costs to 10 percent of sales by the end of 20x5. Sales and quality costs for each year are as follows:

	Sales Revenues	Quality Costs
20x1	$10,000,000	$2,000,000
20x2	10,000,000	1,800,000
20x3	11,000,000	1,815,000
20x4	12,000,000	1,680,000
20x5*	12,000,000	1,320,000

* Budgeted figures.

Quality costs by category are expressed as a percentage of sales as follows:

	Prevention	Appraisal	Internal Failure	External Failure
20x1	1.0%	3.0%	7.0%	9.0%
20x2	2.0	4.0	6.0	6.0
20x3	2.5	4.0	5.0	5.0
20x4	3.0	3.5	4.5	3.0
20x5	3.5	3.5	2.0	2.0

The detail of the 20x5 budget for quality costs is also provided.

Prevention costs:	
Quality planning	$ 150,000
Quality training	20,000
Quality improvement (special project)	80,000
Quality reporting	10,000
Appraisal costs:	
Proofreading	500,000
Other inspection	50,000
Failure costs:	
Correction of typos	150,000
Rework (because of customer complaints)	75,000
Plate revisions	55,000
Press downtime	100,000
Waste (because of poor work)	130,000
Total quality costs	$1,320,000

All prevention costs are fixed; all other quality costs are variable.

During 20x5, the company had $12 million in sales. Actual quality costs for 20x4 and 20x5 are as follows:

	20x5	20x4
Quality planning	$150,000	$140,000
Quality training	20,000	20,000
Quality improvement	100,000	120,000
Quality reporting	12,000	12,000
Proofreading	520,000	580,000
Other inspection	60,000	80,000
Correction of typos	165,000	200,000
Rework	76,000	131,000
Plate revisions	58,000	83,000
Press downtime	102,000	123,000
Waste	136,000	191,000

Required:

1. Prepare an interim quality cost performance report for 20x5 that compares actual quality costs with budgeted quality costs. Comment on the firm's ability to achieve its quality goals for the year.
2. Prepare a one-period quality performance report for 20x5 that compares the actual quality costs of 20x4 with the actual costs of 20x5. How much did profits change because of improved quality?
3. Prepare a graph that shows the trend in total quality costs as a percentage of sales since the inception of the quality improvement program.
4. Prepare a graph that shows the trend for all four quality cost categories for 20x1 through 20x5. How does this graph help management know that the reduction in total quality costs is attributable to quality improvements?
5. Assume that the company is preparing a second five-year plan to reduce quality costs to 2.5 percent of sales. Prepare a long-range quality cost performance report assuming sales of $15 million at the end of five years. Assume that the final planned relative distribution of quality costs is as follows: proofreading, 50 percent; other inspection, 13 percent; quality training, 30 percent; and quality reporting, 7 percent.

Problem 14-35 Environmental Responsibility Accounting, Cost Trends

OBJECTIVE ◀ 5

At the beginning of 20x2, Heber Company, an international telecommunications company, embarked on an environmental improvement program. The company set a goal to have all its facilities ISO 14001 registered by 20x5. (There are 60 facilities worldwide.) To communicate the environmental progress made, management decided to issue, on a voluntary basis, an annual environmental progress report. Internally, the Accounting Department issued monthly progress reports and developed a number of measures that could be reported even more frequently to assess progress. Heber also asked an international CPA firm to prepare an auditor's report that would comment on the reasonableness and fairness of Heber's approach to assessing and measuring environmental performance.

At the end of 20x5, the controller had gathered data that would be used in preparing the environmental progress report. A sample of the data collected is as follows:

Year	Number of ISO 14001 Registrations	Energy Consumption (BTUs)[a]	Greenhouse Gases[b]
20x2	6	6,000	80,000
20x3	18	5,850	78,000
20x4	30	5,800	76,000
20x5	48	5,700	72,000

[a]In billions (measures electricity, natural gas, and heating oil usage).
[b]In tons.

As part of its environmental cost reporting system, Heber tracks its total environmental costs. Consider the following cost and sales data:

Year	Total Environmental Costs	Sales Revenue
20x2	$60,000,000	$500,000,000
20x3	50,000,000	500,000,000
20x4	44,000,000	550,000,000
20x5	38,500,000	550,000,000

Required:

1. Using the data, prepare a bar graph for each of the three environmental variables provided (registrations, energy, and greenhouse gases). Comment on the progress made on these three dimensions.
2. Prepare a bar graph for environmental costs expressed as a percentage of sales. Explain why environmental costs have decreased.
3. Normalize energy consumption by expressing it as a multiple of sales (BTUs/Sales). Now, prepare a bar graph for energy. Comment on the progress made in reducing energy consumption. How does this compare with the conclusion that would be reached using a non-normalized measure of progress? Which is the best approach? Explain.

OBJECTIVE 5   6

Problem 14-36 Cost Classification, Ecoefficiency, Strategic Environmental Objectives

The following items are listed in an environmental financial statement (issued as part of an environmental progress report):

Environmental benefits (savings, income, and cost avoidance):

- Ozone-depleting substances cost reductions
- Hazardous waste disposal cost reductions
- Hazardous waste material cost reductions
- Nonhazardous waste disposal cost reductions
- Nonhazardous waste material cost reductions
- Recycling income
- Energy conservation cost savings
- Packaging cost reductions

Environmental costs:

- Corporate-level administrative costs
- Auditor fees
- Environmental engineering
- Facility professionals and programs
- Packaging professionals and programs for packaging reductions
- Pollution controls: Operations and maintenance
- Pollution controls: Depreciation
- Attorney fees for cleanup claims, and notices of violations (NOVs)
- Settlements of government claims
- Waste disposal
- Environmental taxes for packaging
- Remediation/cleanup: On-site
- Remediation/cleanup: Off-site

Required:

1. Classify each item in the statement as prevention, detection, internal failure, or external failure. In classifying the items listed in the environmental benefits category, first classify the underlying cost item (e.g., the cost of hazardous waste disposal). Next, think of how you would classify the cost of the activities that led to the cost reduction. That is, how would you classify the macro activity: *reducing hazardous waste cost disposal?*
2. Assuming ecoefficiency, what relationship over time would you expect to observe between the environmental benefits category and the environmental costs category?

Problem 14-37 Environmental Financial Reporting, Ecoefficiency, Improving Environmental Performance

OBJECTIVE ◄ 5 ◄ 6

Refer to **Problem 14-36**. In the environmental benefits section of the report, three types of benefits are listed: income, savings, and cost avoidance. Now, consider the following data for selected items for a four-year period:

Year	Engineering Design Costs	Cost of Ozone-Depleting Substances
20x2	$ 180,000	$3,240,000
20x3	1,440,000	2,160,000
20x4	720,000	1,440,000
20x5	90,000	360,000

The engineering design costs were incurred to redesign the production processes and products. Redesign of the product allowed the substitution of a material that produced less ozone-depleting substances. Modifications in the design of the processes also accomplished the same objective. Because of the improvements, the company was able to reduce the demand for pollution control equipment (with its attendant depreciation and operating costs) and avoid fines and litigation costs. All of the savings generated in a given year represent costs avoided for future years. The engineering costs are investments in design projects. Once the results of the project are realized, design costs can be reduced to lower levels. However, since some ongoing design activity is required for maintaining the system and improving it as needed, the environmental engineering cost will not be reduced lower than the $90,000 reported in 20x5.

Required:

1. Prepare a partial environmental financial statement, divided into benefit and cost sections for 20x3, 20x4, and 20x5.
2. Evaluate and explain the outcomes. Does this result support or challenge ecoefficiency? Explain.

Problem 14-38 Environmental Financial Report

OBJECTIVE 5 ▶

The following environmental cost reports for 20x3, 20x4, and 20x5 (year end December 31) are for the Communications Products Division of Kartel, a telecommunications company. At the end of 20x2, Kartel committed itself to a continuous environmental improvement program, which was implemented throughout the company.

Environmental Activity	20x3	20x4	20x5
Disposing hazardous waste	$200,000	$150,000	$ 50,000
Measuring contaminant releases	10,000	100,000	70,000
Releasing air contaminants	500,000	400,000	250,000
Producing scrap (nonhazardous)	175,000	150,000	125,000
Operating pollution equipment	260,000	200,000	130,000
Designing processes and products	50,000	300,000	100,000

Environmental Activity	20x3	20x4	20x5
Using energy	180,000	162,000	144,000
Training employees (environmental)	10,000	20,000	40,000
Remediation (cleanup)	400,000	300,000	190,000
Inspecting processes	0	100,000	80,000

At the beginning of 20x5, Kartel began a new program of recycling nonhazardous scrap. The effort produced recycling income totaling $25,000. The marketing vice president and the environmental manager estimated that sales revenue had increased by $200,000 per year since 20x3 because of an improved public image relative to environmental performance. The company's Finance Department also estimated that Kartel saved $80,000 in 20x5 because of reduced finance and insurance costs, all attributable to improved environmental performance. All reductions in environmental costs from 20x3 to 20x5 are attributable to improvement efforts. Furthermore, any reductions represent ongoing savings.

Required:

1. Prepare an environmental financial statement for 20x5 (for the Products Division). In the cost section, classify environmental costs by category (prevention, detection, etc.).
2. Evaluate the changes in environmental performance.

OBJECTIVE 6

Problem 14-39 Assignment of Environmental Costs

Refer to **Problem 14-38**. In 20x3, Jack Carter, president of Kartel, requested that environmental costs be assigned to the two major products produced by the company. He felt that knowledge of the environmental product costs would help guide the design decisions that would be necessary to improve environmental performance. The products represent two different models of a cellular phone (Model XA2 and Model KZ3). The models use different processes and materials. To assign the costs, the following data were gathered for 20x3:

Activity	Model XA2	Model KZ3
Disposing hazardous waste (tons)	20	180
Measuring contaminant releases (transactions)	1,000	4,000
Releasing air contaminants (tons)	25	225
Producing scrap (pounds of scrap)	25,000	25,000
Operating pollution equipment (hours)	120,000	400,000
Designing processes and products (hours)	1,500	500
Using energy (BTUs)	600,000	1,200,000
Training employees (hours)	50	50
Remediation (labor hours)	5,000	15,000

During 20x3, Kartel's division produced 200,000 units of Model XA2 and 300,000 units of Model KZ3.

Required:

1. Using the activity data, calculate the environmental cost per unit for each model. How will this information be useful?
2. Upon examining the cost data produced in Requirement 1, an environmental engineer made the following suggestions: (1) substitute a new plastic for a material that appeared to be the source of much of the hazardous waste (the new material actually cost less than the contaminating material it would replace), and (2) redesign the processes to reduce the amount of air contaminants produced.

As a result of the first suggestion, by 20x5, the amount of hazardous waste produced had diminished to 50 tons, 10 tons for Model XA2 and 40 tons for Model KZ3. The second suggestion reduced the contaminants released by 50 percent by 20x5 (15 tons for Model XA2 and 110 tons for Model KZ3). The need for pollution equipment also diminished, and the hours required for operating this equipment for Model XA2 and Model KZ3 were reduced to 60,000 and 200,000, respectively. Calculate the unit cost reductions for the two models associated with the actions and outcomes described (assume the same production as in 20x3). Do you think the efforts to reduce the environmental cost per unit were economically justified? Explain.

15

Lean Accounting and Productivity Measurement

After studying this chapter, you should be able to:

1 ▸ Describe the basic features of lean manufacturing.

2 ▸ Describe lean accounting.

3 ▸ Define productive efficiency and partial productivity measurement.

4 ▸ Explain what total productivity measurement is, and describe its advantages.

LEAN ACCOUNTING

at Nestlé

By now, you should realize that the way products and services are manufactured affects the nature of how we measure, assign, and manage costs. For example, consider the differences in the accounting approaches for process manufacturing and job manufacturing. Did you know that **Ford** and **Toyota** each had a remarkable impact on current manufacturing practices? Henry Ford successfully developed and used a moving assembly line to mass-produce the Model T. He is often credited as the "father of mass production," but whether or not that is true, he has to be credited with being among the very first to find a way to reduce the time and cost of producing an automobile. His production techniques were widely successful. At Toyota Motor Company, Taiichi Ohno and Shigeo Shingo took the Ford production techniques and improved and changed them to develop what became known as the Toyota Production System. This new system emphasized such things as employee involvement, total quality management, cellular manufacturing, dramatic reductions in setup times (allowing product variety with an almost continuous flow like the Ford system), kaizen, and just-in-time purchasing and production. Over time, the strategic elements of the Toyota Production System have spread and have become incorporated into the production systems of diverse industries. This set of manufacturing practices is now widely called *lean manufacturing*. *Lean accounting* has the purpose of supporting lean manufacturing. **Nestlé Global** is an example of a large nonautomotive company involved in implementing lean manufacturing.

Nestlé Global is headquartered in Vaud, Switzerland. Nestlé Group is one of the world's largest nutrition, health, and wellness companies, with such familiar brands as Gerber, KitKat, Cheerios, Hot Pockets, and Lean Cuisine. In 2019, Nestlé had sales of 92.6 billion Swiss Francs (CHF).[1] Nestlé has the objectives of becoming a simpler, more efficient organization while simultaneously assuming a leadership role in sustainability.[2] Nestlé Waters UK (NWUK) provides a prominent example of how these objectives are being operationalized. Because of increased demand attributable to the success of its two local brands, Buxton Natural Mineral Water and Nestlé Pure Life spring water, NWUK needed to expand its production; however, the bottling plant had no space to meet the increased demand. Accordingly, a new site was selected, and a new state-of-the-art plant was constructed.[3]

The building of a new plant afforded NWUK a timely opportunity to implement lean production, which at Nestlé is called Nestlé Continuous Excellence. Using lean production tools such as kaizen and value stream mapping, NWUK studied the old plant and its processes to determine how

1 "Nestlé Global Annual Report," https://www.nestle.com/investors/annual-report, accessed July 1, 2020.
2 Ibid.
3 Business Case Studies, "Achieving Sustainability through Lean Production," Edition 8, October 29, 2019, https://businesscasestudies.co.uk/achieving-sustainability-through-lean-production/, accessed July 1, 2020.

the new facility could be designed to eliminate waste, improve efficiency, and enhance environmental performance. For example, unnecessary transport and wait time were reduced by relocation of pallet storage and recycling, which reduced travel time between operations. Just in time reduced the wait time for raw materials and enabled the delivery of goods as they are finished. Storage costs, transport costs, and the cost of waiting have all diminished. Lean thinking also improved environmental performance and reduced costs. For example, a heat recovery system transfers heat from the production lines to offices and to the warehouse, reducing the total energy being consumed.[4]

Lean manufacturing has the objective of minimizing waste and maximizing efficiency. In this chapter, you will learn the basics of lean manufacturing and the role of lean accounting. Lean accounting must be simple, accurate, and support and encourage continuous improvement. It must be able to measure and value changes in productivity. In its operational control role, it uses a mixture of financial and nonfinancial measures. Enjoy the journey! It will be interesting.

Consider a hypothetical company, Garn Autoparts, Inc., that produces four major product lines: shock absorbers, aluminum alloy and steel wheels, brake systems, and aluminum radiators. Garn is contemplating expansion into new international markets and is facing such competitors as **DENSO** (Japanese), **Bosch** (German), and **Maxion** (Brazilian). To achieve success in this endeavor, Garn needs to be more efficient by streamlining operating processes, eliminating waste, and improving quality and delivery performance. Clearly, an organization must be as good as or better than its competitors at taking materials, labor, machines, power, and other inputs and turning out high-quality goods and services. A company can create a competitive advantage by using fewer inputs to produce a given output or by producing more output for a given set of inputs. Management needs to assess the potential and actual effectiveness of decisions that are geared to improve efficiency. Management also needs to monitor and control efficiency changes. Measures of productive efficiency satisfy these performance and control objectives.

Lean manufacturing is concerned with eliminating waste in manufacturing processes. Promised benefits included such outcomes as reduced lead times, improved quality, improved on-time deliveries, less inventory, less space, less human effort, lower costs, and increased profitability. *Lean accounting* is a simplified approach to costing that supports lean manufacturing with both financial and nonfinancial measures. One key area that supports efficiency improvement is *productivity measurement*, which is concerned with the relationship between outputs and inputs. As waste decreases through lean manufacturing practices, productive efficiency should increase.

OBJECTIVE ▶ **1**

Describe the basic features of lean manufacturing.

LEAN MANUFACTURING

Garn Autoparts is typical of many companies that operate in an environment where change is rapid. Products and processes are constantly being redesigned and improved, and stiff national and international competitors are always present. The competitive environment demands that firms offer customized products and services to diverse customer segments. This, in turn, means that firms must find cost-efficient ways of producing high-variety, low-volume product and pay more attention to linkages between the firm and its suppliers and customers. Furthermore, for many industries, product life cycles are shrinking, placing greater demands on the need for innovation. Thus, organizations operating in a dynamic, rapidly changing environment are finding that adaptation and change are essential to survival. To find ways to improve performance, firms operating in this kind of environment are forced to reevaluate how they

---

4   Ibid.

do things. Improving performance translates into constantly searching for ways to eliminate waste and to undertake only those actions that bring value to the customer. This philosophical approach to manufacturing is often referred to as *lean manufacturing*. **Lean manufacturing** is thus an approach designed to eliminate waste and maximize customer value. It is characterized by delivering the right product, in the right quantity, with the right quality (zero-defect), at the exact time the customer needs it and at the lowest possible cost.

Lean manufacturing systems allow managers to eliminate waste, reduce costs, and become more efficient. Firms that implement lean manufacturing are pursuing a cost reduction strategy by redefining the activities performed within an organization. Cost reduction is directly related to cost leadership. Lean manufacturing adds value by reducing waste. Successful implementation of lean manufacturing has brought about significant improvements, such as better quality, increased productivity, reduced lead times, major reductions in inventories, reduced setup times, lower manufacturing costs, and increased production rates.

EGR, Inc., is based in Ontario, California, and manufactures automotive accessories including bonnet protectors, weather shields, and fender flares. EGR, Inc., implemented lean manufacturing. Within 18 months, EGR, Inc., had increased revenues by 45 percent using the same space, equipment, and overhead resources. Moreover, the company reduced finished goods inventories by 38 percent, work-in-process by 58 percent, increased labor productivity by 21 percent, and reduced lead times from a range of 7 to 21 days to 4 days.[5]

Lean manufacturing systems have also been implemented by the following companies with similar results:[6]

Ipsen Pharma Biotech, Signes, France

Abbott Nutrition Supply Chain, One China Enterprise

Abbott Nutrition Supply Chain, Sturgis

Boston Scientific, Coyol

Merit Medical Systems Inc.

In substance, lean manufacturing is the same as the *Toyota Production System* developed by Shigeo Shingo, Taiichi Ohno, and Eiji Toyoda. *World-class manufacturing* and *just-in-time (JIT) manufacturing and purchasing* are terms that encompass many of the same methods. Lean manufacturing is also similar in concept to Ford's lean enterprise system. The contributions of Shingo, Ohno, and Toyoda, however, overcame some of the major shortcomings and flaws of the Ford system. Specifically, the Ford system did not properly value employees and also was not structured to deal with product variety. High-variety, low-volume products were not compatible with the Ford production system. Employee empowerment, team structures, cellular manufacturing, reduced setup times, and small batches all came into being in the Toyota Production System and are integral parts of a lean manufacturing system.

What is it that allows companies to achieve the results like those described for US Synthetic? Becoming lean requires lean thinking. Lean manufacturing is distinguished by the following five principles of lean thinking:[7]

---

5 TXM Lean Solutions, "TXM Lean Case Study—EGR North America," https://txm.com/txm-lean-case-study-egr
   -north-america/, accessed June 30, 2020.

6 All of these companies are winners of the Shingo Prize, which recognizes successful lean manufacturing outcomes. See
   http://www.shingoprize.org/awards for information about each company's successful lean manufacturing efforts. The
   list is but a small percentage of companies that are implementing lean manufacturing systems.

7 James Womack and Daniel Jones, *Lean Thinking* (New York: Free Press, 2003).

- Precisely specify value by each particular product.
- Identify the "value stream" for each.
- Make value flow without interruption.
- Let the customer pull value from the producer.
- Pursue perfection.

Value by Product

Value is determined by the customer—at the very least, it is an item or feature for which the customer is willing to pay. Customer value is the difference between realization and sacrifice. Realization is what a customer receives. Sacrifice is what a customer gives up, including what they are willing to pay for the basic and special product features, quality, brand name, and reputation. Value thus relates to a specific product and to specific features of the product. Adding features and functions that are not wanted by the customers is a waste of time and resources. Furthermore, attempting to market features and products that customers don't want is a waste of time and resources. Assessing value is externally oriented and not internally generated. Only value-added features should be produced; non-value-added activities should be eliminated.

Value Stream

The **value stream** is made up of all activities, both value-added and non-value-added, required to bring a product group or service from its starting point (e.g., customer order or concept for a new product) to a finished product in the hands of the customer. There are several types of value streams, the most common being the *order fulfillment value stream*. The order fulfillment value stream focuses on providing current products to current customers. A second type of value stream is the *new product value stream*, which focuses on developing new products for new customers. A value stream reflects all that is done—both good and bad—to bring the product to a customer. Thus, analyzing the value stream allows management to identify waste. Activities within the value stream are value-added or non-value-added. Non-value-added activities are the source of waste. They are of two types: (1) activities avoidable in the short run and (2) activities unavoidable in the short run due to current technology or production methods. The first type is most quickly eliminated, while the second type requires more time and effort. Exhibit 15.1 visually portrays an order fulfillment value stream for one of Garn

---

Exhibit 15.1   Order Fulfillment Value Stream

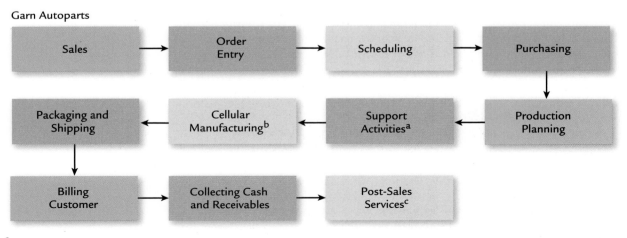

Garn Autoparts

[a]Moving materials, quality management, engineering, setting up equipment, maintenance, etc.
[b]Cutting, drilling and insertion, assembly, and finishing.
[c]Customer complaints, field repairs, warranty services, etc.

Exhibit 15.2   Matrix Approach to Identifying Value Streams

Wheel Model	Production Activities: Order Fulfillment Value Stream							
	Order Entry	Production Planning	Purchasing	Aluminum Cell[a]	Steel Cell[b]	Stress Testing[c]	Packaging & Shipping	Invoicing
A	X	X	X	X			X	X
B	X	X	X	X			X	X
C	X	X	X	X	X	X	X	X
D	X	X	X	X	X	X	X	X

[a]Casting, machining, painting, and finishing.
[b]Stamping, welding, and cladding (attaching stainless steel or painted plastic components to approximate the look of chromed aluminum).
[c]To ensure that the steel wheels have the same fatigue strength as aluminum, they go through a stress test.

Models A and B would be placed in one value stream.
Models C and D would define a second value stream.

Autoparts' family of aluminum wheels. This particular value stream only has one manufacturing cell; other value streams may have several cells.

A value stream may be created for every product; however, it is more common to group products that use common processes into the same value stream. One way to identify the value streams is to use a simple two-dimensional matrix, where the activities/processes are listed on one dimension and the products on a second dimension. Exhibit 15.2 provides a simple matrix for the four wheel models: aluminum Model A, aluminum Model B, steel Model C, and steel Model D. In this case, two value streams are indicated, where each is made up of two product models (notice that the steel models have two major processes different from the aluminum models and thus the need for two value streams).

Once value streams are identified, then the next step is to assign people and resources to the value streams. As a rule of thumb, each value stream should have between 25 and 150 people. As much as possible, the people, the machines, the manufacturing processes, and the support activities need to be dedicated to the value streams. This allows a sense of ownership and provides a means of direct accountability. It also simplifies and facilitates product costing. In a sense, the value stream is its own independent company, and the value-stream team is responsible for its improvement, growth, and profitability.

Value Flow

In a traditional manufacturing setup, production is organized by function into departments, and products are produced in large batches, moving from department to department. This approach requires significant move time and wait time as each batch *moves* from one department to another and *waits* for its turn if there is a batch in process in front of it. Often, lengthy changeovers are needed to prepare the equipment to produce the next batch of goods that may have some very different characteristics. Traditional batch production is not equipped to deal with product variety; furthermore, move and wait times are sources of waste. Batches must wait for a preceding batch and a subsequent setup *before* beginning a process. Once a batch starts a process, units are processed sequentially; as units are finished, they must wait for other units in the batch to be finished before the entire batch moves to the next process. For example, if a department can process one unit every five minutes, then the first unit of a batch of 10 will be completed after five minutes but must then wait an additional 45 minutes for the remaining units to be completed before moving to the next process. Thus, there is pre-process waiting and post-process waiting. Exhibit 15.3 illustrates Garn's current department layout for production of Model A aluminum wheels. The exhibit illustrates the presence of both wait and move times.

Exhibit 15.3

Garn's Current Departmental
Layout: Model A Aluminum Wheel
Production

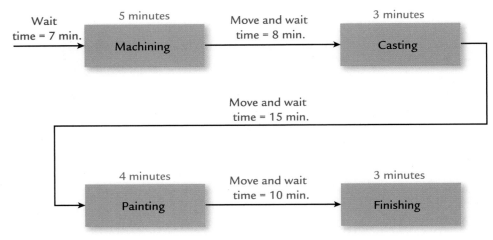

Color Code:
Blue = Value-added process time
Red = Non-value-added move and pre-process wait time

Reduced Setup/Changeover Times With large batches, setups are infrequent, and the fixed cost of a setup is spread out over many units. Typical results produce complexity in scheduling and large work-in-process and finished goods inventories. Lean manufacturing reduces wait and move times dramatically and allows the production of small batches (low volume) of differing products (high variety). The key factors in achieving these outcomes are lower setup times and cellular manufacturing. Reducing the time to configure equipment to produce a different type of product enables *smaller batches in greater variety* to be produced. It also decreases the time it takes to produce a unit of output, thus increasing the ability to respond to customer demand. Customers do not value changeover, and therefore it represents waste. While reducing setup times is important, even more critical is the use of cellular or continuous flow manufacturing.

Cellular Manufacturing Lean manufacturing uses a series of cells to produce families of similar products. A lean manufacturing system replaces the traditional plant layout with a pattern of manufacturing cells. Cell structure is chosen over departmental structure because it reduces lead time, decreases product cost, improves quality, and increases on-time delivery. **Manufacturing cells** contain all the operations in close proximity that are needed to produce a family of products. The machines used are typically grouped in a semicircle. The reason for locating processes close to one another is to minimize move time and to keep a continuous flow between operations while maintaining zero inventory between any two operations. The cell is usually dedicated to producing products that require similar operations. Exhibit 15.4 shows a proposed cellular manufacturing structure for Model A aluminum wheels. Notice that by grouping processes closely together and dedicating the cell to a family of products, the move and wait times are essentially eliminated. **Example 15.1** illustrates the value of cellular manufacturing relative to the traditional departmental approach.

Exhibit 15.4

Garn's Proposed Manufacturing
Cell (Model A)

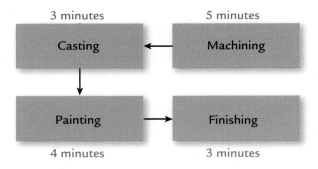

Blue = Value-added process time

EXAMPLE 15.1

The HOW and WHY of Cellular Manufacturing

Information:
See Exhibits 15.3 and 15.4.

> **Why:**
> Cellular manufacturing groups process closely together, and this act effectively eliminates wait and move times. For a given batch of units, total production time is reduced with subsequent decreases in lead time and cost and improved on-time delivery.

Required:

1. Calculate the total time it takes to produce a batch of 10 units using Garn's traditional departmental structure.

2. Using cellular manufacturing, how much time is saved producing the same batch of 10 units? Assuming the cell operates continuously, what is the production rate? Which process controls this production rate?

3. *What if* the processing time of machining is reduced from five to four minutes? What is the production rate now, and how long will it take to produce a batch of 10 units?

Solution:

1. Total lead time for a batch of 10 units:

Processing time	
Machining	50 minutes
Casting	30 minutes
Painting	40 minutes
Finishing	30 minutes
Total processing	150 minutes
Move and wait times	40 minutes
Total batch time	190 minutes

2.

Processing time (10 units):	Elapsed time
First unit	15 minutes
Second unit	20 minutes (processing begins five minutes after the first)
Tenth unit	60 minutes (total processing time)

Time saved over traditional manufacturing: 190 minutes − 60 minutes = 130 minutes

If the cell is processing continuously, then a unit is produced every five minutes after the start-up unit. Thus, the production rate is 12 units per hour (60/5). The *bottleneck* process (the one with the longest per-unit processing time) controls the production rate.

3. Four minutes is now the longest per-unit processing time, and so the production rate is 60/4 = 15 units per hour. Producing 10 units will take 40 minutes [(10/15) × 60].

Pull Value

Many firms produce for inventory and then try to sell the excess goods they have produced. Efforts are made to create demand for the excess goods—goods that customers probably do not even want. Lean manufacturing uses a *demand-pull* system. The objective of lean manufacturing is to eliminate waste by producing a product only when it is needed and only in the quantities demanded by customers. Demand pulls products through the manufacturing process. Each operation produces only what is necessary to satisfy the demand of the succeeding operation. No production takes place until a signal from a succeeding process indicates a need to produce. Parts and materials arrive just in time to be used in production. Low setup times and cellular manufacturing are the major enabling factors for producing on demand. The Kanban system described in Chapter 20 is one way to ensure that materials and products flow according to demand.

Customer demand extends back through the value chain and affects how a manufacturer deals with suppliers. Materials inventories also represent waste. Thus, managing supplier linkages is also vital to lean manufacturing. **JIT purchasing** requires suppliers to deliver parts and materials just in time to be used in production. Supply of parts must be linked to production, which is linked to demand. One effect of successful management of customer and supplier linkages is to reduce all inventories to much lower levels.

Traditionally, inventories of raw materials and parts are carried so that a firm can take advantage of quantity discounts and hedge against future price increases of the items purchased. The objective is to lower the cost of inventory. JIT purchasing achieves the same objective without carrying inventories. The JIT solution is to exploit supplier linkages by negotiating long-term contracts with a few chosen suppliers located as close to the production facility as possible and by establishing more extensive supplier involvement. Suppliers are not selected on the basis of price alone. Performance— the quality of the component and the ability to deliver as needed—and commitment to JIT purchasing are vital considerations. Every effort is made to establish a partners-in-profits relationship with suppliers. Suppliers need to be convinced that their well-being is intimately tied to the well-being of the buyer.

To help reduce the uncertainty in demand for the supplier and establish the mutual confidence and trust needed in such a relationship, lean manufacturers emphasize long-term contracts that stipulate prices and acceptable quality levels. Long-term contracts also reduce dramatically the number of orders placed, which helps to drive down the ordering and receiving costs. Another effect of long-term contracting is a reduction in the cost of parts and materials— usually in the range of 5 percent to 20 percent less than what was paid in a traditional setting. The need to develop close supplier relationships often drives the supplier base down dramatically. Suppliers also benefit, as the long-term contract ensures a reasonably stable demand for their products. A smaller supplier base typically means increased sales for the selected suppliers. Thus, both buyers and suppliers benefit, a common outcome when customer and supplier linkages are recognized and managed well. By reducing the number of suppliers and working closely with those that remain, the quality of the incoming materials can be improved significantly—a crucial outcome for the success of lean manufacturing. As the quality of incoming materials increases, some quality-related costs can be avoided or reduced. For example, the need to inspect incoming materials disappears, and rework requirements decline.

Pursue Perfection

Zero setup times, zero defects, zero inventories, zero waste, producing on demand, increasing a cell's production rates, minimizing cost, and maximizing customer value represent ideal outcomes that a lean manufacturer seeks. As the process of becoming lean begins to unfold and improvements are realized, the possibility of achieving perfection becomes more believable. The relentless and continuous pursuit of these ideals is fundamental to lean manufacturing. As the flow increases and processes begin to improve, more hidden waste tends to be exposed. The objective is to produce the highest-quality, lowest-cost products in the least amount of time. To achieve this objective, a lean manufacturer must identify and eliminate the various forms of waste.

Sources of Waste **Waste** consumes resources without adding value. Waste is anything customers do not value. Elimination of waste requires that its various forms be identified. The eight major sources of waste are listed next. Notice that the acronym DOWNTIME can be used to help remember the eight sources of waste.

- **D**efective Products (fail to meet specification)
- **O**verproduction (producing more than demanded)
- **W**aiting (waiting for the previous step in process to be completed)
- **N**on-utilized talent (not engaging employees)
- **T**ransportation (unnecessary or excessive)
- **I**nventory (waiting for processing or consumption)
- **M**otion (unnecessary movement of people or equipment)
- **E**xcess Processing (not necessary for product or service)

Employee Empowerment Employee involvement is vital for identifying and eliminating all forms of waste. A major procedural difference between traditional and lean environments is the degree of participation allowed workers in the management of the organization. In a lean environment, increasing the degree of participation increases productivity and overall cost efficiency. Managers seek workers' input and use their suggestions to improve production processes. The management structure must change in response to greater employee involvement. Because workers assume greater responsibilities, fewer managers are needed, and the organizational structure becomes flatter. Flatter structures speed up and increase the quality of information exchange. The style of management needed in a lean firm also changes. Managers in a lean environment act as facilitators more than as supervisors. Their role is to develop people and their skills so that they can make value-adding contributions.

Total Quality Control Lean manufacturing necessarily carries with it a much stronger emphasis on managing quality. A defective part brings production to a grinding halt. Poor quality simply cannot be tolerated in a manufacturing environment that operates without inventories. Simply put, lean manufacturing cannot be implemented without a commitment to total quality control (TQC). TQC is essentially a never-ending quest for perfect quality: the striving for a defect-free product design and manufacturing process. Quality cost management is discussed extensively in Chapter 14.

Inventories Overproduction of goods is controlled by letting customers pull goods through the system. Inventories are lowered by cellular manufacturing, low setup times, JIT purchasing, and a demand-pull system. Inventory management is of such importance that its treatment is covered in a separate chapter, Chapter 20.

Activity-Based Management Process value analysis is the methodology for identifying and eliminating non-value-added activities. Non-value-added activities are unnecessary activities, including waiting, and thus much of the waste in a lean system is attacked using process value analysis. Process value analysis searches for the root causes of the wasteful activities and then, over time, eliminates these activities. See Chapter 12 for a detailed discussion of process value analysis.

LEAN ACCOUNTING

OBJECTIVE ◄ **2**

Describe lean accounting.

The numerous changes in structural and procedural activities that we have described for a lean firm also change traditional cost management practices. The traditional cost management system may not work well in the lean environment. In fact, the traditional costing and operational control approaches may actually work against lean manufacturing. Standard costing variances and departmental budgetary variances will likely encourage overproduction and work against the demand-pull system needed in lean manufacturing. For example, emphasis on labor efficiency by comparing actual hours used with hours allowed for production encourages production to keep labor occupied and productive. Similarly, emphasis on departmental efficiency (e.g., machine utilization rates) will cause non-bottleneck departments to overproduce and build work-in-process inventory. Furthermore, we already know from our study of activity-based costing (ABC) that in a multiple-product plant, the use of a plantwide overhead rate can produce distorted product costs relative to focused manufacturing assignments or activity-based assignments. Distorted product costs can signal failure for lean manufacturing even when significant improvements may be occurring. To avoid obstacles and false signals, changes in both product-costing and operational control approaches are needed when moving to a value-stream-based lean manufacturing system.

Focused Value Streams and Traceability of Overhead Costs

Costing systems use three methods to assign costs to individual products: direct tracing, driver tracing, and allocation. Of the three methods, the most accurate is direct tracing; thus, it is preferred over the other two methods. Assume initially that a value stream is created for each product within a plant. In a lean environment, many overhead costs assigned to products using either driver tracing or allocation are now directly traceable to products. Equipment formerly located in other departments, for example, is now reassigned to value streams, and, under the single-product value-stream structure, is dedicated to the production of a single product. In this case, depreciation is now a directly traceable product cost. Multiskilled workers and decentralized services add to the effect. Workers are assigned to the value stream and are trained to set up the equipment in the cells within the stream, maintain them, and operate them. These support functions were previously handled by a different set of laborers for all product lines. Additionally, people with specialized skills (e.g., industrial engineers and production schedulers) are assigned directly to value streams. The labor cost of these employees is now directly assigned to each value stream. Typically, implementing the value-stream structure does not require an increase in the number of people needed. Lean manufacturing eliminates wasteful activities, reducing the demand for people. For example, when production planning is reduced

Exhibit 15.5

Value-Stream Costs

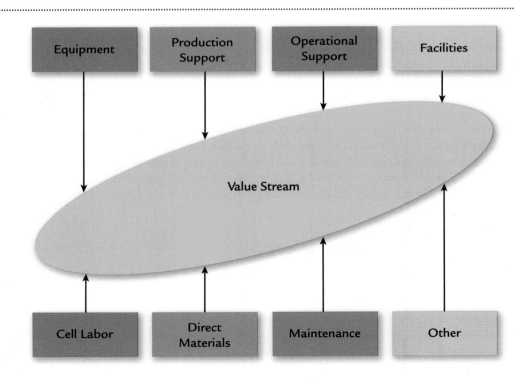

significantly because of an efficiently functioning demand-pull system, some of those working in production planning can be cross-trained to perform value-added activities within the value stream such as purchasing and quality control.

Exhibit 15.5 is a visual summary of value-stream cost assignments. Most costs are assigned directly to the value stream; however, some costs such as facility costs are assigned to each value stream using cost drivers. Facility costs are assigned using a cost per square foot (total cost/total square feet). If a value stream uses less square feet, it receives less cost. Thus, the purpose of this assignment is to motivate value-stream managers to find ways to occupy less space. As space is made available, it can be used for new product lines or to accommodate increased sales. For example, suppose that the facility costs are $200,000 per year for a plant occupying 20,000 square feet. The cost per square foot is $10. If a value stream occupies 5,000 square feet, it is assigned a cost of $50,000. Should the value stream figure out how to do the same tasks with 4,000 square feet, the cost would be reduced to $40,000. Any unabsorbed facility cost would be deducted from revenue as a separate item.

Limitations and Problems Initially, it may not be possible to assign all the people needed exclusively to a value stream. There may be some individuals working in more than one value stream. The cost of these shared workers can be assigned to individual value streams in proportion to the time spent in each stream. It is also true that even in the most ideal of circumstances, there will be some individuals who will remain outside any particular value stream (the plant manager, for example). With multiple value streams, however, the unassigned costs are likely to be a very small percentage of the total costs. Finally, in reality, having a value stream for every product is not practical. The usual practice is to organize value streams around a family of products.

Value-Stream Costing

Product Costing: Single-Product (Focused) Value Stream In a focused value stream, all value-stream costs belong exclusively to the product that the stream produces and, therefore, are assigned to a product using direct tracing. Value streams increase the number of directly traceable costs and therefore increase the accuracy of product costing. Focused value streams provide simple and accurate product costing. Typically, unit costs are calculated weekly and are based on actual costs, using the following formula:

Value-stream product cost = Total actual value-stream costs/Units shipped

Using units shipped in the unit cost calculation instead of units produced motivates managers to reduce inventories. If more units are shipped than produced, then the weekly unit cost will decrease and inventories will reduce. If more is produced than shipped, then the unit cost will increase (because the production costs of the units produced and not shipped are added to the numerator), creating a disincentive to produce for inventory.

Product Costing: Multiple-Product Value Stream Many value streams are formed around products with common processes. Manufacturing cells within a value stream are thus structured to make a family of products or parts that require the same manufacturing sequence. Since materials usage can differ, the weekly unit cost is the sum of each materials cost and the average conversion cost:

Value-stream product cost = Unit materials cost + Average conversion cost

where:

Unit materials cost (for each product) = Actual materials cost/Units shipped

Average conversion cost = Total actual conversion costs/Units shipped

The materials costs are assigned accurately as they are directly traced to each product. However, all products in the value stream receive the same average conversion cost per unit. The accuracy of the resulting average conversion cost depends on how homogeneous the products are. If they are very similar, then using the average conversion cost will approximate quite closely the individual product cost. Using the average conversion cost is useful, provided the products are similar and consume resources in approximately the same proportions. If products are quite similar, the resulting product cost will approximate the individual product costs. Furthermore, if the product mix is stable, then the trend in the average product cost over time is a reasonable measure of changes in economic efficiency. If, however, the products are heterogeneous or reflect a great deal of variety through custom designing, then using average conversion cost is not a good measure for tracking changes in value-stream efficiency, nor is there a clear indication of what the cost of individual products is. In this case, other product cost calculation approaches are needed—approaches that provide a much better level of accuracy.

Features and Characteristics Costing   An approach called *features and characteristics costing* is recommended (albeit reluctantly) by those advocating the simple average costing approach. This approach recognizes that some product components take more effort (time) to make than others and thus cost more. Differences in features and characteristics cause cost differences. An adjustment is made to the average product cost that reflects this complexity difference. Value streams with heterogeneous products find themselves in the same cost-distortion dilemma as plants with multiple products and plant-wide overhead rates. ABC solves the distortion problem using causal tracing. ABC could, of course, be used within a value stream; however, the argument is that ABC is too complex and too data intensive for a lean setting. Yet, there is no compelling evidence that features and characteristics costing provides simplicity with accuracy. A relatively new costing approach, called Duration-Based Costing (DBC), seems to offer both simplicity and accuracy and, thus, may be well suited for multiple-product value streams.

Duration-Based Costing   DBC uses a single rate to assign conversion costs and approximates a comprehensive ABC system based in duration drivers. To apply DBC to a value stream, first calculate a weekly value-stream conversion cost rate as follows:

$$\text{Conversion cost rate} = \text{Total actual conversion costs}/\text{Total net production hours}$$

The net total production hours are the *total hours available* for work whether the work is value- or non-value-added. Net hours mean that such things as break times and expected stoppages are excluded and thus correspond to practical capacity. Net hours for a value stream can be derived by multiplying the cycle time for a product by the units produced at practical capacity and then summing this over all products in the value stream. Another approach is to take the total productive labor hours in the value stream and multiply this by 85 percent (a typical percentage that is used for measuring hours at practical capacity). Once the rate is calculated, the unit conversion cost is calculated by multiplying the rate by the cycle time for each product:

$$\text{Conversion cost per unit} = \text{Conversion cost rate} \times \text{Cycle time}$$

Cycle time is the time that a unit of product spends in the value stream, from start to finish. It is not the same as the production rate.

The actual costs and production hours for the steel wheel value stream in Garn Auto Parts are shown in Exhibit 15.6 for the week ending April 6. Using this information, **Example 15.2** illustrates product costing for single-product and multiple-product value streams.

Garn Autoparts
This Week, April 6

	Net Hours	Materials	Salaries/ Wages	Machining	Other	Total Cost
Order processing	400		$ 12,000			$ 12,000
Production planning	25		24,000			24,000
Purchasing	200		18,000			18,000
Stamping	500	$250,000	25,000	$24,000	$12,000	311,000
Welding	600	100,000	28,000	28,000	8,000	164,000
Cladding	125	50,000				50,000
Testing	150		7,000			7,000
Packaging and shipping	150		6,000			6,000
Invoicing	350		8,000			8,000
Totals	2,500	$400,000	$128,000	$52,000	$20,000	$600,000

Exhibit 15.6

Steel Wheel Value-Stream Costs and Production Hours

EXAMPLE 15.2

The HOW and WHY of Value-Stream Product Costing

Information:

See Exhibit 15.6. During the week of April 6, Garn Autoparts produced and shipped 1,000 units of Model C and 4,000 units of Model D, for a total of 5,000 units. Model C has a cycle time of 1.1 hours, and Model D has a cycle time of 0.35 hours.

Why:

The unit cost of product(s) in a value stream is the *actual* value-stream costs divided by the *number of units shipped* for a given time period (usually a week). If materials costs are significantly different for multiple products, the unit cost is the average conversion cost plus the unit materials cost. If the products are not very homogeneous, DBC is recommended for value-stream costing.

Required:

1. Assume that the value-stream costs and total units shipped apply only to one model (a single-product value stream). Calculate the unit cost, and comment on its accuracy.

2. Assume that Model C is responsible for 50 percent of the materials cost. Using the average conversion cost approach, calculate the unit cost for Models C and D, and comment on its accuracy. Explain the rationale for using units shipped instead of units produced in the calculation.

3. *What if* Models C and D are not homogeneous products? Assume the same materials usage as in Requirement 2. Calculate the unit cost for the two models using DBC. Explain when and why this cost is more accurate than the unit cost calculated in Requirement 2. Is DBC a good method for value-stream costing? Explain.

Solution:

1. Unit cost = $600,000/5,000 = $120 per unit. The cost is very accurate as the value stream is dedicated to one product and its costs all belong to that product.

EXAMPLE 15.2

(*Continued*)

2. First, the unit materials cost is calculated separately:

Model C: $200,000/1,000 = $200
Model D: $200,000/4,000 = $50

*50% × $400,000

Next, the average unit conversion cost is calculated: $200,000/5,000 = $40.

Finally, the unit cost is computed (sum of materials and average conversion cost):

Model C: $200 + $40 = $240
Model D: $50 + $40 = $90

Since the materials usage differs significantly, separating this cost improves accuracy. The accuracy of the average conversion cost depends on how homogeneous the two products are. Using units shipped for the unit calculation motivates managers to reduce inventories.

3. First, calculate the conversion cost rate:

Conversion cost rate = Conversion cost/Total net production hours
= $200,000/2,500
= $80 per hour

Next, calculate the unit conversion cost for each product:

Conversion cost per unit = Conversion rate × Cycle time
Model C: $80 × 1.1 = $88
Model D: $80 × 0.35 = $28

Finally, add the unit materials cost:

Model C = $88 + $200 = $288
Model C = $28 + $90 = $118

DBC should be used if the products are not homogeneous products. It is more accurate as it approximates ABC assignments. DBC requires cycle time and net work hours, metrics readily available in lean manufacturing. DBC is an accurate, quick, and simple method, making it very appealing as a value-stream costing method.

Value-Stream Reporting

Costs are collected and reported by value stream. Consider a plant of Garn Autoparts that produces only four products. Within this plant are two value streams: (1) aluminum wheels (Models A and B) and (2) steel wheels (Models C and D). Exhibit 15.7 shows a profit and loss statement for the plant, for the week ending April 14. (The plant had significantly increased its sales of steel wheels to auto manufacturers that were replacing low-end aluminum wheels with steel units on new models.) Costs outside the value stream (sustaining costs) are reported in a separate column. The revenues and costs reported are the actual revenues and costs for the week. To avoid distorting the current week's performance, inventory reductions are reported separately form the value-stream contributions. Adding the inventory changes also allows the income to be stated correctly for external reporting.

	Aluminum Stream	Steel Stream	Sustaining Costs	Plant Totals
Week Ending April 14				
Revenues	$ 700,000	$1,500,000		$2,200,000
Material costs	(280,000)	(410,000)		(690,000)
Conversion costs	(70,000)	(190,000)		(260,000)
Value-stream profit	$ 350,000	$ 900,000		$1,250,000
Value-stream ROS*	50%	60%		
Employee costs			$(40,000)	(40,000)
Other expenses			(30,000)	(30,000)
Change in inventory:				
Current less prior period				(500,000)
Plant gross profit				$ 680,000
Plant ROS				31%

Exhibit 15.7

Garn Autoparts Profit and Loss Statement

*ROS = Return on sales = Profit/Sales.

Decision Making

Using the average product cost for a value stream means that the individual product costs are not known. In reality, a fully specified and accurate product cost is not needed for many decisions. Waste can be eliminated at the activity and process levels without knowing product costs. We do not need detailed variances by product to signal sources of waste and potential for improvement. In fact, as already noted, standard costing variances may actually impede improvement decisions. For other decisions, the effect of the decision on the profitability of value stream may be the only information needed for certain decisions. For example, special order and make-or-buy decisions can be made at the value-stream level.

Consider a make-or-buy decision. Suppose that Garn Autoparts is currently purchasing a component used in making its wheel products and is considering making the component. The decision can be made by comparing the profitability of the value stream under the buy scenario with the profitability under the make scenario. A typical analysis would be as follows for Garn's ABS value stream:

	Buy	Make
Revenue	$1,500,000	$1,500,000
Material costs	(410,000)	(380,000)
Conversion costs	(190,000)	(200,000)
Value-stream profit	$ 900,000	$ 920,000

The profitability of the value stream increases under the make alternative, and so the decision would be to make the component rather than buy it.

While analysis of the effect on value-stream profitability has its merits, it also has its perils. Many of the decisions are short term in nature and do not reflect the long-term consequences. For example, acceptance of a special order below the full cost of a product (unknown with average cost) may increase value-stream profitability because of existing unused value-stream capacity, but continued acceptance of such orders may not earn the return necessary to replace capacity that is eventually exhausted through use. Thus, other very important decisions may need individual product cost information, and a lean accounting system must provide this information.

Performance Measurement

Abandoning a standard cost system also removes a major operational control system, and it must be replaced. The lean control system uses a Box Scorecard that compares operational, capacity, and financial metrics with prior week performances and with a future desired state. Trends over time and the expectation of achieving some desired state in the near future are the means used to motivate constant performance improvement. Thus, the lean control approach uses a mixture of financial and nonfinancial measures for the value stream. The future desired state reflects targets for the various measures. Operational, nonfinancial measures are also used at the cell level. A typical value-stream Box Scorecard is shown in Exhibit 15.8 (metrics and format can vary). Only a brief introduction to the Box Scorecard is made because the Balanced Scorecard is a more thorough and integrated approach that encompasses the concepts of a Box Scorecard.

For the operational measures, units sold per person is a partial labor productivity measure and is therefore a measure of labor *efficiency*. Productivity measures are discussed more completely later in this chapter. Dock-to-dock is the *time* it takes for a product to be manufactured from the moment the materials arrive at the receiving dock until the finished product is shipped from the shipping dock. Dock-to-dock is a cycle time measure, a concept that was studied in Chapter 13. First-time through is a measure of *quality* and is simply the percentage of product that made it through production without being defective and thus needing to be rejected or reworked. Capacity is labeled as *productive* (value-added), *nonproductive* (non-value-added—used but wasteful), and *available* (unused) capacity. The scorecard measures are expected to improve over time and to be helpful in managing and bringing about improvement. For example, from the Box Scorecard in Exhibit 15.8, we see that the nonproductive capacity is targeted to go from 46 percent (current state) to 30 percent (future state), with productive capacity increasing from 20 percent to 25 percent and available capacity increasing from 34 percent to 45 percent. As waste is eliminated, the nonproductive capacity converts into available capacity. The machines, people, and other resources used for wasteful activities are now available for more productive work. For financial performance to improve, some decisions must be made with respect to the increase in available capacity. The most sensible and practical approach is to commit to use the freed-up resources to expand the business. One possibility is to add new product lines. Another possibility is to transfer the resources to other value streams that are in a high-growth state with increasing resource demands. Another is to realize cost reductions by reducing head-count and eliminating resources. This latter approach is the least desirable. It makes it hard to gain the cooperation and involvement of employees with the transformation into a lean workforce if their suggestions and actions are going to lead to the loss of their jobs or the jobs of their friends and coworkers.

Exhibit 15.8

ABS Value-Stream Box Scorecard

	Last Week	This Week (4/6/x5)	Planned Future State (6/30/x5)
For 4/6/20x5			
Operational			
Units sold per person	250	270	280
On-time delivery	90%	92%	97%
Dock-to-dock days	18.5	18	16
First-time through	56%	58%	65%
Average product cost	$ 128	$ 120	$ 115
Accounts receivable days	31	30	28
Capacity			
Productive	21%	20%	25%
Nonproductive	45%	46%	30%
Available	34%	34%	45%
Financial			
Weekly sales	$1,800,000	$1,500,000	$2,000,000
Weekly material cost	$ 800,000	$ 600,000	$ 600,000
Weekly conversion cost	$ 400,000	$ 300,000	$ 400,000
Weekly value-stream profit	$ 600,000	$ 600,000	$1,000,000
ROS	33%	40%	50%

Big Data

Big data is playing a prominent role in Intel's smart factories. Intel uses real time and big data to improve factory capabilities and increase efficiency. Specifically, big data has led to better process control and ongoing analysis and decision making, which, in turn, has improved productivity and quality. Big data has played a key role in optimizing factory flow, predictive maintenance, and pervasive robotics and tool control.

The analysis of big data focuses on three key performance measures: efficiency, velocity, and quality. Efficiency is concerned with the relationship of important inputs and outputs (e.g., operational costs as inputs and revenues as output). Velocity has to do with how fast a product can be delivered to the market, and quality is concerned with providing a nondefective product with the desired features to customers.

The results have been impressive. Intel has shown consistent year-to-year gains in the reduction of quality costs and labor costs and has also improved yield and time to market. Proactive real-time data analysis has produced actions that have reduced waste and saved millions. Real-time monitoring has produced shorter cycle times, greater tool availability, and increased labor efficiency.[8]

PRODUCTIVE EFFICIENCY

OBJECTIVE 3

Discuss and define productive efficiency and partial productivity measurement.

A key objective of lean manufacturing and accounting is that of increasing overall productive efficiency. **Productivity** is concerned with producing output efficiently, and it specifically addresses the relationship of output and the inputs used to produce the output. Usually, different combinations or mixes of inputs can be used to produce a given level of output. **Total productive efficiency** is the point at which two conditions are satisfied: (1) for any mix of inputs that will produce a given output, no more of any one input is used than necessary to produce the output; and (2) given the mixes that satisfy the first condition, the least costly mix is chosen. The first condition is driven by technical relationships and, therefore, is referred to as **technical efficiency**. Technical improvements in productivity can be achieved by using fewer inputs to produce the same output, by producing more output using the same inputs, or by producing more output with relatively fewer inputs. The second condition is driven by relative input price relationships and, therefore, is referred to as **allocative efficiency**. Input prices determine the *relative proportions* of each input that should be used. Choosing the right combination of inputs can also produce significant improvements in economic efficiency. Exhibits 15.9 and 15.10 illustrate technical and allocative efficiency improvements. The output in the exhibits is vehicles, and the inputs are labor (number of workers) and capital (dollars invested in automated equipment).

Partial Productivity Measurement Defined

Productivity measurement is simply a quantitative assessment of productivity changes. The objective is to assess whether productive efficiency has increased or decreased. Productivity measurement can be actual or prospective. Actual productivity measurement allows managers to assess, monitor, and control changes. Prospective measurement is forward looking, and it serves as input for strategic decision making. Specifically, prospective measurement allows managers to compare relative benefits of different input combinations, choosing the inputs and input mix that provide the greatest benefit. Productivity measures can be developed for each

---

8 Steve Chadwick, Duncan Lee, Steven J. Meyer, and Joe Sartini, "Using Big Data in Manufacturing at Intel's Smart Factories," White Paper, April 2016, http://www.intel.com/content/dam/www/public/us/en/documents/best -practices/using-big-data-in-manufacturing-at-intels-smart-factories-paper.pdf, accessed June 28, 2016.

Exhibit 15.9

Improving Technical Efficiency

Current Productivity:
Inputs:
Labor:

Output:

Capital:

Same Output, Fewer Inputs:
Inputs:
Labor:

Output:

Capital:

More Output, Same Inputs:
Inputs:
Labor:

Output:

Capital:

More Output, Fewer Inputs:
Inputs:
Labor:

Output:

Capital:

---

input separately or for all inputs jointly. Measuring productivity for one input at a time is called **partial productivity measurement**.

Productivity of a single input is typically measured by calculating the ratio of the output to the input as follows:

$$\text{Productivity ratio} = \text{Output/Input}$$

Because the productivity of only one input is being measured, the measure is called a *partial productivity measure*. If both output and input are measured in physical quantities, then we have an **operational productivity measure**. If output or input is expressed in dollars, then we have a **financial productivity measure**. Example 15.3 illustrates partial productivity measurement.

Assume, for example, that in 20x1, Nevada Company produced 240,000 frames for snow-mobiles and used 60,000 hours of labor. The labor productivity ratio is four frames per hour (240,000/60,000). This is an operational measure, since the units are expressed in physical

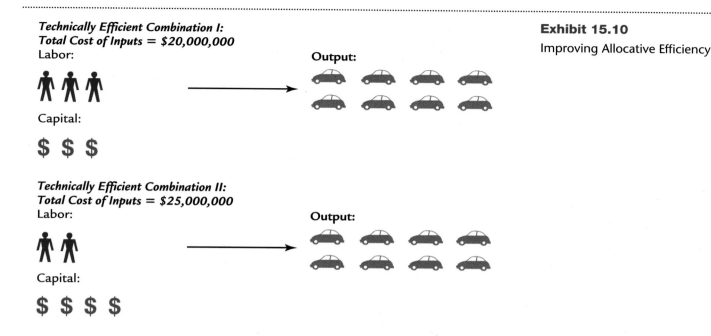

Technically Efficient Combination I:
Total Cost of Inputs = $20,000,000
Labor:

Capital:

Output:

Technically Efficient Combination II:
Total Cost of Inputs = $25,000,000
Labor:

Capital:

Output:

Exhibit 15.10

Improving Allocative Efficiency

terms. If the selling price of each frame is $30 and the cost of labor is $15 per hour, then output and input can be expressed in dollars. The labor productivity ratio, expressed in financial terms, is $8 of revenue per dollar of labor cost ($7,200,000/$900,000).

Partial Measures and Measuring Changes in Productive Efficiency

The labor productivity ratio of four frames per hour measures the 20x1 productivity experience of Nevada. By itself, the ratio conveys little information about productive efficiency or whether the company has improving or declining productivity. It is possible, however, to make a statement about increasing or decreasing productivity efficiency by measuring *changes* in productivity. To do so, the actual current productivity measure is compared with the productivity measure of a prior period. This prior period is referred to as the **base period** and serves to set the benchmark or standard for measuring changes in productive efficiency. The prior period can be any period desired. It could, for example, be the preceding year, the preceding week, or even the period during which the last batch of products was produced. For strategic evaluations, the base period is usually chosen as an earlier year. For operational control, the base period tends to be close to the current period—such as the preceding batch of products or the preceding week.

To illustrate, assume that 20x1 is the base period and that the labor productivity standard, therefore, is four frames per hour. Further assume that late in 20x1, Nevada decided to try a new procedure for producing and assembling the frames with the expectation that the new procedure would use less labor. In 20x2, 250,000 frames were produced, using 50,000 hours of labor. The labor productivity ratio for 20x2 is five frames per hour (250,000/50,000). The *change* in productivity is a one-unit-per-hour *increase* in productivity (from four units per hour in 20x1 to five units per hour in 20x2). The change is a significant improvement in labor productivity and provides evidence supporting the efficacy of the new process.

Advantages of Partial Measures

Partial measures allow managers to focus on the use of a particular input. Operating partial measures have the advantage of being easily interpreted by everyone within the organization. Consequently, partial operational measures are easy to use for assessing productivity performance of operating personnel. Laborers, for instance, can relate to units produced per hour or units produced per pound of material. Thus, partial operational measures provide feedback that operating personnel can relate to and understand—measures that deal with the specific inputs over which they have control. The ability of operating personnel to understand and relate to the measures increases the likelihood that the measures will be accepted. Furthermore, for operational control, the standards for performance are often very short run in nature. For example, standards can be the productivity ratios of prior batches of goods. Using this standard, productivity trends within the year itself can be tracked.

Disadvantages of Partial Measures

Partial measures, used in isolation, can be misleading. A decline in the productivity of one input may be necessary to increase the productivity of another. Such a trade-off is desirable if overall costs decline, but the effect would be missed by using either partial measure. For example, changing a process so that direct laborers take less time to assemble a product may increase scrap and waste while leaving total output unchanged. Labor productivity has increased, but productive use of materials has declined. If the increase in the cost of waste and scrap outweighs the savings of the decreased labor, then overall productivity has declined.

Two important conclusions can be drawn from this example. First, the possible existence of trade-offs mandates a total measure of productivity for assessing the merits of productivity decisions. Only by looking at the total productivity effect of all inputs can managers accurately draw any conclusions about overall productivity performance. Second, because of the possibility of trade-offs, a total measure of productivity must assess the aggregate financial consequences and, therefore, should be a financial measure.

<table>
<tr><td>

OBJECTIVE

Explain what total productivity measurement is, and describe its advantages.

</td><td>

TOTAL PRODUCTIVITY MEASUREMENT

Measuring productivity for all inputs at once is called **total productivity measurement**. In practice, it may not be necessary to measure the effect of all inputs. Many firms measure the productivity of only those factors that are thought to be relevant indicators of organizational performance and success. Thus, in practical terms, total productivity measurement can be defined as focusing on a limited number of inputs, which, in total, indicates organizational success. In either case, total productivity measurement requires the development of a multifactor measurement approach. A common multifactor approach suggested in the productivity literature (but rarely found in practice) is the use of aggregate productivity indexes. Aggregate indexes are complex and difficult to interpret and have not been generally accepted. Two approaches that have gained some acceptance are *profile measurement* and *profit-linked productivity measurement*.

</td></tr>
</table>

Profile Productivity Measurement

Producing a product involves numerous critical inputs such as labor, materials, capital, and energy. **Profile measurement** provides a series or vector of separate and distinct partial operational measures. Profiles (vectors or series of measures) can be compared over time to provide information about productivity changes. When the partial productivity ratios move in the same direction when compared with the base period ratios, some definitive statements about productivity changes can be made. However, if the ratios move in opposite directions, a trade-off exists and the comparison of profiles provides a mixed signal about productivity changes. Furthermore, while a profile analysis reveals if a trade-off exists, it does not reveal whether the trade-off is good or bad. If the economic effect of the productivity changes is positive, then the trade-off is good; otherwise, it must be viewed as bad. **Example 15.3** illustrates profile productivity measurement and reveals its limitations.

Information:

In 2015, Nevada Company implements a new production and assembly process affecting labor and materials with the following reported data:

	20x1	20x2
Number of frames produced	240,000	250,000
Labor hours used	60,000	50,000
Materials used (lbs.)	1,200,000	1,150,000

Why:

Profiles (vectors) of productivity measures can be compared over time to assess productivity changes. If the changes are in the same direction, then a definitive statement about productivity can be made; if a trade-off exists, valuing the individual input productivity changes is needed to assess the nature of the overall productivity change.

EXAMPLE 15.3

The HOW and WHY of Profile Productivity Measurement

Required:

1. Calculate the productivity profile for 20x1.

2. Calculate the productivity profile for 20x2, and comment on the effect of the new production and assembly process.

3. *What if* the materials used in 20x2 were 1,300,000 pounds? What does comparison of the 20x1 and 20x2 profiles now communicate?

Solution:

1. **Partial Operational**

Productivity Ratios	20x1 Profile*
Labor productivity ratio	4.000
Material productivity ratio	0.200

*Labor: 240,000/60,000; materials: 240,000/1,200,000

2. **Partial Operational**

Productivity Ratios	20x2 Profile*
Labor productivity ratio	5.000
Material productivity ratio	0.217

*Labor: 250,000/50,000; materials: 250,000/1,150,000

Comparing the 20x1 profile (4, 0.200) with the 20x2 profile (5, 0.217), productivity increased for each input; thus, the new process has improved overall productivity.

3. **Partial Operational**

Productivity Ratios	20x1 Profile[a]	20x2 Profile[b]
Labor productivity ratio	4.000	5.000
Material productivity ratio	0.200	0.192

[a]Labor: 240,000/60,000; materials: 240,000/1,200,000

[b]Labor: 250,000/50,000; materials: 250,000/1,300,000

Labor productivity has increased, and materials productivity has decreased. A trade-off between the two inputs exists and must be valued to assess the nature of the overall productivity change.

As Example 15.3 has just shown, profile analysis can provide managers with useful insights about changes in productivity. Comparing productivity profiles, however, will not always reveal the nature of the overall change in productive efficiency. Often, it may be necessary to *value* input productivity trade-offs to assess the nature of *overall* productivity change.

Profit-Linked Productivity Measurement

Assessing the effects of productivity changes on current profits is one way to value productivity changes. Profits change from the base period to the current period. Some of that profit change is attributable to productivity changes. Measuring the amount of profit change attributable to productivity change is defined as **profit-linked productivity measurement**.

Assessing the effect of productivity changes on current-period profits will help managers understand the economic importance of productivity changes. Linking productivity changes to profits is described by the following rule:

> **Profit-Linkage Rule.** *For the current period, calculate the cost of the inputs that would have been used in the absence of any productivity change and compare this cost with the cost of the inputs actually used. The difference in costs is the amount by which profits changed because of productivity changes.*

The formula corresponding to the linkage rule is given below.

$$\text{Profit-linked productivity change} = \Sigma PQ_i P_i - \Sigma AQ_i P_i$$

where

PQ_i = The amount of input i that would have been used for the current period in the absence of a productivity change

P_i = Current-period price of input i

AQ_i = Actual amount of input i used in the current period

To apply the linkage rule formula, the inputs that would have been used for the current period in the absence of a productivity change must be calculated. To determine PQ_i, divide the current-period output by the input's base-period productivity ratio:

$$PQ_i = \text{Current-period output/Base-period productivity ratio for input } i$$

The profit-linked measure computes the amount of profit change from the base period to the current period attributable to productivity changes. Generally, this will not be equal to the total profit change between the two periods. The difference between the total profit change and the profit-linked productivity change is called the **price-recovery component**. This component is the change in revenue less a change in the cost of inputs, *assuming no productivity changes*. It, therefore, measures the ability of revenue changes to cover changes in the cost of inputs, assuming no productivity change, and is calculated as follows:

$$\text{Price recovery} = \text{Total profit change} - \text{Profit-linked productivity change}$$

Example 15.4 illustrates the application of the profit-linked rule.

Example 15.4 reveals that the net effect of the process change implemented by Nevada was favorable, increasing profits by $12,500. Profit-linked productivity effects can be assigned to individual inputs. The increase in labor productivity creates a $187,500 increase in profits; however, the drop in materials productivity caused a $175,000 decrease in profits. Most of the profit decrease came from an increase in materials usage—apparently, waste, scrap, and spoiled units are much greater with the new process. Thus, the profit-linked measure provides partial measurement effects as well as a total measurement effect. The total profit-linked productivity measure is the sum of the individual partial measures. This property makes the profit-linked measure ideal for assessing trade-offs. A much clearer picture of the effects of the changes in productivity emerges. Unless waste and scrap can be brought under better control, the company ought to return to the old assembly process. Of course, it is possible that the learning effects of the new process are not yet fully captured and further improvements in labor productivity might be observed. As labor becomes more proficient at the new process, it is possible that the materials usage could also decrease.

Information:

In 2015, Nevada Company implements a new process affecting labor and materials. The following two years of expanded data are provided:

	20x1	20x2
Number of frames produced	240,000	250,000
Labor hours used	60,000	50,000
Materials used (lbs.)	1,200,000	1,300,000
Unit selling price (frames)	$30	$30
Wages per labor hour	$15	$15
Cost per pound of material	$3	$3.50

Why:

The productivity effect on current-period profit is the difference in the cost of the inputs that would have been used and the cost of the actual inputs used. Price recovery is the difference in the actual profit change and the profit-linked productivity change.

Required:

1. Calculate the cost of inputs in 20x2, assuming no productivity change from 20x1 to 20x2.

2. Calculate the actual cost of inputs for 20x2. What is the net value of the productivity changes? How much profit change is attributable to each input's productivity change?

3. *What if* a manager wants to know how much of the total profit change from 20x1 to 20x2 is attributable to price recovery? Calculate the price-recovery component and comment on its meaning.

Solution:

1. Base-period productivity ratios: 4 (labor) and 0.200 (materials). Thus, we have:

$$PQ\,(\text{labor}) = 250{,}000/4 = 62{,}500 \text{ hrs.}$$
$$PQ\,(\text{materials}) = 250{,}000/0.200 = 1{,}250{,}000 \text{ lbs.}$$

Cost of labor ($PQ \times P = 62{,}500 \times \$15$)	$ 937,500
Cost of materials ($PQ \times P = 1{,}250{,}000 \times \$3.50$)	4,375,000
Total PQ cost	$5,312,500

2.

Cost of labor ($AQ \times P = 50{,}000 \times \$15$)	$ 750,000
Cost of materials ($AQ \times P = 1{,}300{,}000 \times \$3.50$)	4,550,000
Total current cost	$5,300,000

EXAMPLE 15.4

(*Continued*)

Profit-linked productivity measure:

Input	(1) PQ	(2) PQ × P	(3) AQ	(4) AQ × P	(2) – (4) (PQ – AQ) × P
Labor	62,500	$ 937,500	50,000	$ 750,000	$ 187,500
Materials	1,250,000	4,375,000	1,300,000	4,550,000	(175,000)
		$5,312,500		$5,300,000	$ 12,500

Net productivity change = $12,500. Labor productivity change = $187,500. Materials productivity change = $(175,000).

3.

	20x1	20x2	20x2 – 20x1
Revenues	$ 7,200,000	$ 7,500,000	$ 300,000
Cost of inputs	(4,500,000)	(5,300,000)	(800,000)
Profit	$ 2,700,000	$ 2,200,000	$(500,000)

Price recovery = Total profit change − Profit-linked productivity change
= $(500,000) − $12,500
= $(512,500)

The increase in revenues would not have been sufficient to recover the increase in the cost of the inputs. The increase in productivity provided some relief for the price-recovery problem.

SUMMARY OF LEARNING OBJECTIVES

LO1. Describe the basic features of lean manufacturing.
- Lean manufacturing has two principal objectives: eliminating waste and creating value for the customer.
- It is characterized by lean thinking—focusing on customer value, value streams, production flow, demand-pull, and perfection.
- Value streams are made up of all activities, both value-added and non-value-added, required to bring a product group or service from its starting point (e.g., customer order or concept for a new product) to a finished product in the hands of the customer.
- Value-stream analysis allows waste to be identified and eliminated.

LO2. Describe lean accounting.
- Lean accounting is an approach designed to support and encourage lean manufacturing.
- Average costing, value-stream cost reporting, and the heavy use of nonfinancial measures for operational control are typical lean accounting approaches.
- The average product cost is the total value-stream cost of the period divided by the units shipped in the period.
- Value-stream costing reports the actual revenues and actual costs on a weekly basis (for each value stream).
- The lean control system uses a Box Scorecard that compares operational, capacity, and financial metrics with prior week performances and with a future desired state.
- Simplicity and compatibility are major characteristics of lean accounting.

LO3. Define productive efficiency and partial productivity measurement.
- Productivity deals with how efficiently inputs are used to produce the output.
- Technical efficiency is concerned with producing a given output using no more than necessary of any input.
- Allocative efficiency is concerned with choosing the least costly technically efficient combination of inputs.
- Partial measures of productivity evaluate the efficient use of single inputs.

LO4. Explain what total productivity measurement is, and describe its advantages.
- Total measures of productivity assess efficiency for all inputs.
- Profile measures are vectors of series of partial measures but provide mixed signals if the productivity changes for inputs are in opposite directions.
- Profit-linked measures value trade-offs in input productivity changes.

EXAMPLE 15.1	The HOW and WHY of Cellular Manufacturing, page 773
EXAMPLE 15.2	The HOW and WHY of Value-Stream Product Costing, page 779
EXAMPLE 15.3	The HOW and WHY of Profile Productivity Measurement, page 787
EXAMPLE 15.4	The HOW and WHY of Profit-Linked Productivity Measurement, page 789

KEY TERMS

Allocative efficiency, 783

Base period, 785

Cycle time, 778

Financial productivity measure, 784

JIT purchasing, 774

Lean manufacturing, 769

Manufacturing cells, 772

Operational productivity measure, 784

Partial productivity measurement, 784

Price-recovery component, 788

Productivity, 783

Productivity measurement, 783

Profile measurement, 786

Profit-Linkage Rule, 788

Profit-linked productivity measurement, 788

Technical efficiency, 783

Total productive efficiency, 783

Total productivity measurement, 786

Value stream, 770

Waste, 775

BRIEF EXERCISES

OBJECTIVE 1
Example 15.1

Brief Exercise 15-1 Continuous Flow versus Departmental Flow Manufacturing

Anderson Company has the following departmental manufacturing structure for one of its products:

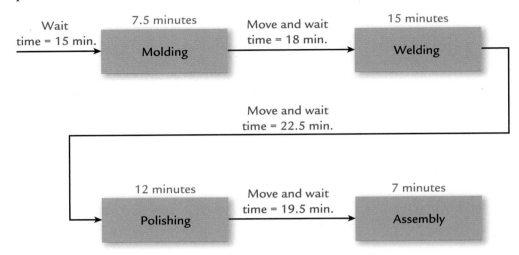

After some study, the production manager of Anderson recommended the following revised cellular manufacturing approach:

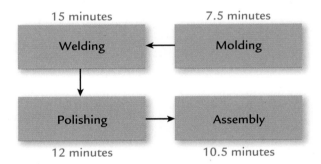

Required:

1. Calculate the total time it takes to produce a batch of 20 units using Anderson's traditional departmental structure.
2. Using cellular manufacturing, how much time is saved producing the same batch of 20 units? Assuming the cell operates continuously, what is the production rate? Which process controls this production rate?
3. *What if* the processing times of molding, welding, and assembly are all reduced to six minutes each? What is the production rate now, and how long will it take to produce a batch of 20 units?

OBJECTIVE 2
Example 15.2

Brief Exercise 15-2 Value-Stream Costing Objective

During the week of June 12, Harrison Manufacturing produced and shipped 25,000 units of its aluminum wheels: 5,000 units of Model A and 20,000 units of Model B. The cycle time for Model A is 0.80 hours and that of Model B is 0.55 hours. The total net work hours for the aluminum wheel value stream for the week were 15,000. The following costs were incurred:

	Materials	Salaries/ Wages	Machining	Other	Total Cost
Order processing		$ 36,000			$ 36,000
Production planning		72,000			72,000
Purchasing		54,000			54,000
Stamping	$ 750,000	75,000	$ 72,000	$ 36,000	933,000
Welding	300,000	84,000	84,000	24,000	592,000
Cladding	150,000				150,000
Testing		21,000			21,000
Packaging and shipping		18,000			18,000
Invoicing		24,000			24,000
Totals	$1,200,000	$384,000	$156,000	$60,000	$1,800,000

Required:

1. Assume initially that the value-stream costs and total units shipped apply only to one model (a single-product value stream). Calculate the unit cost, and comment on its accuracy.
2. Model A is responsible for 40 percent of the materials cost. Using the average conversion cost approach, calculate the unit cost for Models A and B, and comment on its accuracy. Explain the rationale for using units shipped instead of units produced in the calculation.
3. *What if* Model A and Model B are not homogeneous products? Assume the same materials usage as in Requirement 2. Use DBC to calculate the unit cost for the two products. Explain when and why this cost is more accurate than the unit cost calculated in Requirement 2. Explain why DBC is a good approach for value-stream costing.

Brief Exercise 15-3 Profile Productivity Measurement

In 20x2, Choctaw Company implements a new process affecting labor and materials. The following reported data are provided to evaluate the effect on the company's productivity:

OBJECTIVE ◀ 4
Example 15.3

	20x1	20x2
Number of units produced	540,000	450,000
Labor hours used	108,000	75,000
Materials used (lbs.)	2,160,000	1,500,000

Required:

1. Calculate the productivity profile for 20x1.
2. Calculate the productivity profile for 20x2, and comment on the effect of the new production and assembly process.
3. *What if* the labor hours used in 20x2 were 112,500? What does comparison of the 20x1 and 20x2 profiles now communicate?

Brief Exercise 15-4 Profit-Linked Productivity Measurement

Refer to **Brief Exercise 15-3.** Choctaw Company provides the following additional information so that total productivity can be valued:

OBJECTIVE ◀ 4
Example 15.4

	20x1	20x2
Number of units produced	540,000	450,000
Labor hours used	108,000	112,500
Materials used (lbs.)	2,160,000	1,500,000
Unit selling price	$20	$22
Wages per labor hour	$12	$ 14
Cost per pound of material	$3.40	$3.50

Required:

1. Calculate the cost of inputs in 20x2, assuming no productivity change from 20x1 to 20x2.
2. Calculate the actual cost of inputs for 20x2. What is the net value of the productivity changes? How much profit change is attributable to each input's productivity change?
3. *What if* a manager wants to know how much of the total profit change from 20x1 to 20x2 is attributable to price recovery? Calculate the price-recovery component, and comment on its meaning.

EXERCISES

OBJECTIVE ▶1▶   **Exercise 15-5 Value-Stream Identification**

Helix, Inc., formed the following matrix for its five products:

			Production Activities/Processes					
Product Model	Order Entry	Production Planning	Subassembly 47A Cell	Basic Cell	Assembly Cell	Inspecting	Packaging & Shipping	Warranty
A	×	×		×	×	×	×	×
B	×	×	×		×	×	×	
C	×	×		×			×	×
D	×	×		×	×	×	×	×
E	×	×	×		×	×	×	

Required:

Using the information in the matrix, identify the value streams.

OBJECTIVE ▶1▶   **Exercise 15-6 Continuous Flow versus Departmental Flow Manufacturing**

SHOW ME HOW

Bienestar Inc., has the following departmental structure for producing a well-known multivitamin:

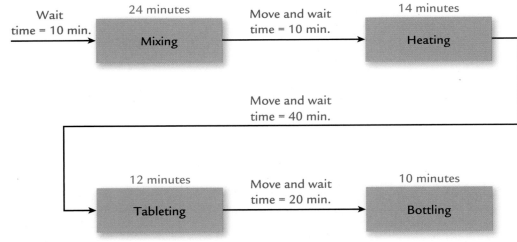

A consultant designed the following cellular manufacturing structure for the same product:

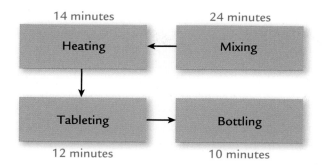

14 minutes   24 minutes

Heating ← Mixing

Tableting → Bottling

12 minutes   10 minutes

The times above the processes represent the time required to process one unit of product.

Required:

1. Calculate the time required to produce a batch of 15 bottles using a batch-processing departmental structure.
2. Calculate the time to process 15 units using cellular manufacturing.
3. How much manufacturing time will the cellular manufacturing structure save for a batch of 15 units?

Exercise 15-7 Bottleneck Operation: Improving Production Flow

Bienestar, Inc., implemented cellular manufacturing as recommended by a consultant. The production flow improved dramatically. However, the company was still faced with the competitive need to improve its cycle time so that the production rate is one bottle every four minutes (15 bottles per hour). The cell structure is shown below; the times above the process represent the time required to process one unit.

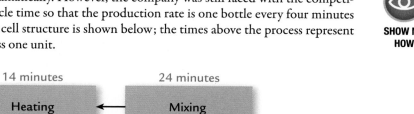

14 minutes   24 minutes

Heating ← Mixing

Tableting → Bottling

12 minutes   10 minutes

Required:

1. How many units can the cell produce per hour (on a continuous running basis)?
2. How long does it take the cell to produce one unit, assuming the cell is producing on a continuous basis?
3. What must happen so that the cell can produce one bottle every four minutes or 15 per hour, assuming the cell produces on a continuous basis?

Exercise 15-8 Value-Stream Costing

Henderson, Inc., has just created five order fulfillment value streams, two focused and three that produce multiple products. The size of the plant in which the value streams are located is 100,000 square feet. The facility costs total $1,000,000 per year. One of the focused value streams produces a basic MP3 product. The MP3 value stream occupies 20,000 square feet. Not counting facility costs, the MP3 value-stream costs total $1,800,000. There are 25,000

MP3 units produced annually. There were not sufficient quality personnel for each value stream; thus, the MP3 stream had to share a quality engineer who spends 40 percent of his time with the MP3 value stream and the other 60 percent with two other value streams. While 40 percent of the time is not sufficient time for the value streams, the contribution will be workable until other arrangements can be made. His salary is $75,000 per year. Vivian Olsen, an industrial engineer, is one of two employees assigned completely to the value stream from production planning. Vivian has not been with the company as long as the other production engineer. Because of the demand-pull nature of the new value stream, only one production planner is needed.

Required:

1. Explain how the value-stream costs of $1,800,000 were most likely assigned to the MP3 value stream. Explain how facility costs will be treated and why.
2. How many employees are likely to be located within the MP3 value stream?
3. Given that only one production planner is needed, what should the company do with its extra engineer (Vivian Olsen)?
4. Calculate the unit product cost for the MP3 value stream. Comment on the accuracy of this cost and its value for monitoring value-stream performance.

OBJECTIVE **2**

DATA ANALYTICS

Exercise 15-9 Value-Stream Average Costing, DBC, ABC Costs as Benchmarks

A value stream has three activities and two products. The units produced and shipped per week are 50 of the deluxe model (Model A) and 200 of the basic model (Model B). The cycle time for Model A is four hours and that of Model B is three hours. The resource consumption patterns are shown as follows:

	Model A	Model B	Costs of Value-Stream Activities
Cell manufacturing	2,400 min.	7,200 min.	$ 96,000
Engineering	60 hrs.	260 hrs.	40,000
Testing	100 hrs.	220 hrs.	30,000
Total			$166,000

Required:

1. Calculate the ABC product cost for Models A and B.
2. Calculate the value-stream average product cost. Assuming reasonable stability in the consumption patterns of the products and product mix, assess how well the products are grouped based on similarity.
3. Calculate the unit cost of each product using DBC. How does this compare with the ABC unit costs? Which of the three costing methods would you recommend, and why?
4. Identify and explain the data analytic types (descriptive, diagnostic, predictive, and prescriptive) that apply for each of the following:

   a. The calculation of the unit costs by each of the three analytic costing methods.
   b. Assessing how well the products are grouped based on similarity.
   c. Comparison of DBC unit costs with ABC unit costs.
   d. Recommending and explaining which costing method should be used.

   Note: See Exhibits 2.5 and 2.6, pp. 37, 40 for a review of data analytic types.

OBJECTIVE **2**

SHOW ME HOW

Exercise 15-10 Value-Stream Reporting with Inventory Decrease

Rivera Manufacturing, Inc., has implemented lean manufacturing in its Kansas City plant as a pilot program. One of its value streams produces a family of small electric tools. The value-stream team managers were quite excited about the results, as some of their efforts to eliminate waste were proving to be effective. During the most recent three weeks, the following data pertaining to the electric tool value stream were collected:

Week l:

Demand = 90 units @ $40
Beginning inventory = 10 units @ $20 ($5 materials and $15 conversion)
Production = 90 units using $450 of material and $1,350 of conversion cost

Week 2:

Demand = 100 units @ $40
Beginning inventory = 10 units @ $20 ($5 materials and $15 conversion)
Production = 90 units using $450 of material and $1,350 of conversion cost

Week 3:

Demand = 90 units @ $40
Beginning inventory = 0
Production = 100 units using $500 of material and $1,500 of conversion cost

Required:

1. Prepare a traditional income statement for each week.
2. Calculate the average value-stream product cost for each week. What does this cost signal, if anything?
3. Prepare a value-stream income statement for each week. Assume that any increase in inventory is valued at average cost. Comment on the financial performance of the value stream and its relationship to traditional income measurement.

Exercise 15-11 Box Scorecard

OBJECTIVE ◀ 2

The following Box Scorecard was prepared for a value stream:

	Last Week	This Week (6/30/20x2)	Planned Future State (12/31/20x2)
Operational			
Units sold per person	100	108	115
On-time delivery	85%	90%	95%
Dock-to-dock days	12	11	9
First-time through	60%	62%	70%
Average product cost	$75	$74	$70
Capacity			
Productive	25%	26%	27%
Nonproductive	65%	62%	40%
Available	10%	12%	33%
Financial			
Weekly sales	$800,000	$825,000	$1,000,000
Weekly material cost	$320,000	$330,000	$ 380,000
Weekly conversion cost	$280,000	$280,240	$ 320,000
Weekly value-stream profit	$200,000	$214,760	$ 300,000
ROS	25%	26%	30%

Required:

1. How many nonfinancial measures are used to evaluate performance? Why are nonfinancial measures used?
2. Classify the operational measures as time-based, quality-based, or efficiency-based. Discuss the significance of each category for lean manufacturing.

3. What is the role of the Planned Future State column?
4. Discuss the capacity category and explain the meaning of each measure and its significance.
5. Discuss the relationship between the financial measures and the measures in the operational and capacity categories.

OBJECTIVE **Exercise 15-12 Technical and Allocative Efficiency**

Listed below are several possible input combinations for producing 7,500 units of a pocket PC. Two of the input combinations are technically efficient.

	Materials	Labor	Energy
Unit input prices	$100	$ 60	$ 25
Input combinations:			
A	100	192	720
B	110	180	540
C	150	200	600
D	92	190	570

Required:

1. Identify the technically efficient input combinations. Explain your choices.
2. Which of the two technically efficient input combinations should be used? Explain.

OBJECTIVE **Exercise 15-13 Productivity Measurement, Technical and Allocative Efficiency, Partial Measures**

SHOW ME
HOW

DATA
ANALYTICS

Bellamy Company produces handcrafted pottery that uses two inputs: materials and labor. During the past quarter, 36,000 units were produced, requiring 144,000 pounds of materials and 72,000 hours of labor. An engineering efficiency study commissioned by the local university revealed that Bellamy can produce the same 36,000 units of output using either of the following two combinations of inputs:

	Combination F1	Combination F2
Inputs:		
Materials	108,000	118,800
Labor	54,000	50,400

The cost of materials is $12 per pound; the cost of labor is $18 per hour.

Required:

1. Compute the output-input ratio for each input of Combination F1. Does this represent a productivity improvement over the current use of inputs? What is the total dollar value of the improvement? Classify this as a technical or an allocative efficiency improvement. Finally, describe which data analytic types were used in addressing these issues (descriptive, diagnostic, predictive, and prescriptive; see Exhibits 2.5 and 2.6, pp. 37, 40 for a brief review).
2. Compute the output-input ratio for each input of Combination F2. Does this represent a productivity improvement over the current use of inputs? Now, compare these ratios to those of Combination F1. What has happened?
3. Compute the cost of producing 36,000 units of output using Combination F1. Compare this cost to the cost using Combination F2. Does moving from Combination F1 to Combination F2 represent a productivity improvement? Explain. What would be your recommendation to Bellamy?
4. Some would argue that the entire productivity analysis from start to finish is an example of a prescriptive data analytic model. What case would you make to support this position?

Exercise 15-14 Interperiod Measurement of Productivity Profiles

OBJECTIVE ◄ 4

Helena Company needs to increase its profits and so has embarked on a program to increase its overall productivity. After one year of operation, Kent Olson, manager of the Columbus plant, reported the following results for the base period and its most recent year of operations:

SHOW ME HOW

	20x1	20x2
Output	184,320	216,000
Power (quantity used)	23,040	10,800
Materials (quantity used)	46,080	48,600

Required:

Compute the productivity profiles for each year. Did productivity improve? Explain.

Exercise 15-15 Interperiod Measurement of Productivity, Profit-Linked Measurement

OBJECTIVE ◄ 4

Refer to **Exercise 15-14**. Suppose the following input prices are provided for each year:

SHOW ME HOW

	20x1	20x2
Unit price (power)	$ 2	$ 3
Unit price (materials)	16	15
Unit selling price	6	8

Required:

1. Compute the profit-linked productivity measure. By how much did profits increase due to productivity?
2. Calculate the price-recovery component for 20x2. Explain its meaning.

Exercise 15-16 Basics of Productivity Measurement

OBJECTIVE ◄ 4

Holbrook Company gathered the following data for the past two years:

EXCEL SHOW ME HOW

	Base Year	Current Year
Output	900,000	1,080,000
Output prices	$15	$15
Input quantities:		
Materials (lbs.)	1,200,000	1,080,000
Labor (hrs.)	300,000	540,000
Input prices:		
Materials	$5	$6
Labor	$8	$8

Required:

1. Prepare a productivity profile for each year.
2. Prepare partial income statements for each year. Calculate the total change in income.
3. Calculate the change in profits attributable to productivity changes.
4. Calculate the price-recovery component. Explain its meaning.

PROBLEMS

Problem 15-17 Focused Value Streams, Product Costing

OBJECTIVE ◄ 2

Sixty employees (all CPAs) of a local public accounting firm eat lunch at least twice weekly at a very popular pizza restaurant. The pizza restaurant recently began offering discounts for groups of 15 or more. Groups would be seated in a separate room, served individual bowls of salad costing $2 each, pitchers of root beer costing $3 each (each pitcher has a five-glass capacity), and medium, two-topping pizzas for $10 (10 slices each). The food would have to be ordered in advance.

Thirty of the CPAs commit to eating three slices of pizza, three glasses of root beer, and one bowl of salad [a consumption pattern of (3,3,1)]. The other 30 are more hearty eaters and commit to seven slices of pizza, two glasses of root beer, and one bowl of salad [a consumption pattern of (7,2,1)]. Each member of the group must pay an assessed amount for the lunch.

Required:

1. Determine the total number of pizzas, pitchers of root beer, and salads that must be ordered for the 60 employees.
2. One of the CPAs offered to determine the amount that each should pay. He suggested that the easiest way is to assign the average cost to each person eating in the group. Based on this suggestion, how much would each CPA pay for lunch?
3. One CPA objected to using average cost, noting that half of the CPAs are much lighter eaters than the other half. Based on the large differences in consumption behaviors, he suggested forming two groups: one for the light eaters and one for the heavier eaters. Calculate the lunch cost for each CPA for each group. Discuss the analogy to formation of focused value streams in a manufacturing environment. Calculate the cost that would be assigned using ABC. What does this tell you?

OBJECTIVE **3** **4**▶

Problem 15-18 Multiple-Product Value Streams, Product Costing, Creating Available Capacity

Refer to **Problem 15-17.**

After some detailed polling among the 60, four types of eaters were identified: two types of light eaters and two types of heavy eaters. The consumption patterns for each group are given (slices of pizza, glasses of root beer, and bowls of salad): Light Eaters (Group A): A1 = (2,2,1) and A2 = (3,3,1); Heavy Eaters (Group B): B1 = (6,3,1) and B2 = (7,2,1). There are an equal number of CPAs in each of the four groups.

Required:

1. Calculate the average lunch cost for each CPA in each of the two groups, A and B. Compare this to the ABC cost assignments. Discuss the merits of grouping based on similarity. Discuss the analogy to multiple-product value streams.
2. Suppose that members of the heavy-eating group (Group B) decided that they were eating more than necessary for their health and well-being and decided to reduce their total calories. They therefore agreed to reduce consumption of pizza by one slice and consumption of root beer by one glass for each member of the group. Relative to the original order, how much extra capacity exists? If the excess capacity is eliminated by reducing the order, what is the new average cost? Suppose that the decision is to use the extra capacity to invite four guests (two of Type B1 and two of Type B2) to lunch (at the cost of the CPAs). If the original order is used as the benchmark cost, what is the extra cost of the guest program? Comment on the conceptual significance of this for manufacturing firms.

OBJECTIVE **2**▶

DATA ANALYTICS

Problem 15-19 Multiple-Product Value Streams, Average Costing, ABC, DBC

Renlund Company is transitioning to a lean manufacturing system and has just finalized two order fulfillment value streams. One of the value streams has two products, and the other has four products. The two-product value stream produces precision machine parts, and the four-product value stream produces machine tools. Before moving to the value-stream structure, Renlund had a well-developed ABC system (one that used all duration drivers) and had experienced good success with the more accurate product costs. Management wanted to be sure that the average costing approach of value-stream costing did not produce distorted product costs. Accordingly, the most recent weekly activity data were provided for the two-product value stream to see how well average costing worked (see next); however, management did not want to continue using ABC because of its intense data demands and the cost of updating as changes unfolded due to lean practices. In the following table, the driver for each activity is a duration driver (time driven).

Machine Parts Value Stream
For the Coming Week

Activity	Conversion Cost	Part S55 (hours used)	Part K66 (hours used)	Total Activity Hours
Order Processing	$ 54,000	900	2,700	3,600
Purchasing	108,000	300	450	750
Lathe	162,000	720	480	1,200
Milling	300,000	1,200	1,800	3,000
Drilling	216,000	1,080	2,520	3,600
Assembly	105,000	1,800	1,200	3,000
Inspection	60,000	2,400	600	3,000
Shipping	27,000	900	300	1,200
Invoicing	48,000	1,050	1,200	2,250
Totals	$1,080,000	10,350	11,250	21,600

During the week, the machine parts value stream expects to produce and ship 15,000 units of S55 and 45,000 units of K66. Since materials cost is calculated separately, the main concern is with the unit conversion cost.

Required:

1. Calculate the average unit conversion cost for the two machine parts. Is this calculation using the value-stream average costing model an example of predictive or descriptive data analytic types? (See Exhibits 2.5 and 2.6, pp. 37, 40, for a brief review of data analytic types.)
2. Calculate the conversion cost per unit for each part, using ABC. Comparing ABC unit cost with the average cost, what would you recommend? Which data analytic type best fits the comparison of unit costs produced by the two different product costing models?
3. Calculate the conversion cost per unit using DBC (you will first need to calculate the cycle time for each product). Based on this outcome and the results of Requirements 1 and 2, what would you recommend to the management of Renlund Company? What data analytic types are being used in this analysis?
4. Intrigued by the DBC product costing model, the management of Renlund wants to know the effect on unit costs if the non-value-added activity of inspection is eliminated. Using DBC, provide the answer that Renlund's management is seeking. (Calculate cycle time to three decimal places.) Assume the same units produced and shipped for each product. Which data analytic type is being used?

Problem 15-20 Box Scorecard, Special Order Decision

OBJECTIVE ◀ 2

Bradford Company, a manufacturer of small tools, implemented lean manufacturing at the end of 20x1. The company's goal for the year was to increase the ROS to 40 percent of sales. A value-stream team was established and began to work on lean improvements. During the year, the team was able to achieve significant results on several fronts. The Box Scorecard below reflects the performance measures at the beginning of the year, midyear, and end of year. Although the team members were pleased with their progress, they were disappointed in the financial results. They were still far from the targeted ROS of 40 percent. They were also puzzled as to why the improvements made did not translate into significantly improved financial performance.

	January 1, 20x2	June 30, 20x2	December 31, 20x2
Operational			
Revenue per person	$15,000	$15,000	$15,000
On-time delivery	70%	90%	95%
Dock-to-dock days	15	6	5
First time through	60%	60%	90%
Average product cost	$60	$60	$59
Capacity			
Productive	40%	40%	40%
Nonproductive	50%	30%	10%
Available	10%	30%	50%
Financial			
Weekly sales	$800,000	$800,000	$800,000
Weekly material cost	$260,000	$260,000	$240,000
Weekly conversion cost	$300,000	$300,000	$300,000
Weekly value-stream profit	$240,000	$240,000	$260,000
ROS	30%	30%	32.5%

Required:

1. From the scorecard, what was the focus of the value-stream team for the first six months? The second six months? What are the implications of these changes?

2. Using information from the scorecard, offer an explanation for why the financial results were not as good as expected.

3. Suppose that on December 31, 20x2, a potential customer offered to purchase an order of goods that would increase weekly revenues in January by $100,000 and material cost by $30,000. Using the old standard cost system, the projected conversion cost of the order would be $60,000. Would you recommend that the order be accepted or rejected? Explain.

OBJECTIVE 1 2   **Problem 15-21 Lean versus Standard-Costing-Based Measures**

Continuous improvement is the governing principle of a lean accounting system. Following are several performance measures. Some of these measures would be associated with a traditional standard-costing accounting system, and some would be associated with a lean accounting system.

a. Materials price variances
b. Cycle time
c. Comparison of actual product costs with target costs
d. Materials quantity or efficiency variances
e. Comparison of actual product costs over time (trend reports)
f. Comparison of actual overhead costs, item by item, with the corresponding budgeted costs
g. Comparison of product costs with competitors' product costs
h. Percentage of on-time deliveries
i. First-time through
j. Reports of value- and non-value-added costs
k. Labor efficiency variances
l. Days of inventory
m. Downtime
n. Manufacturing cycle efficiency (MCE)
o. Unused (available) capacity variance
p. Labor rate variance
q. Using a sister plant's best practices as a performance standard

Required:

1. Classify each measure as lean or traditional (standard costing). If traditional, discuss the measure's limitations for a lean environment. If it is a lean measure, describe how the measure supports the objectives of lean manufacturing.
2. Classify the measures into operational (nonfinancial) and financial categories. Explain why operational measures are better for control at the shop level (production floor) than financial measures. Should any financial measures be used at the operational level?
3. Suggest some additional measures that you would like to see added to the list that would be supportive of lean objectives.

Problem 15-22 Productivity and Quality: Prospective Analysis

OBJECTIVE

DATA ANALYTICS

Richins Company is considering the acquisition of a computerized manufacturing system. The new system has a built-in quality function that increases the control over product specifications. An alarm sounds whenever the product falls outside the programmed specifications. An operator can then make some adjustments on the spot to restore the desired product quality. The system is expected to decrease the number of units scrapped because of poor quality. The system is also expected to decrease the amount of labor inputs needed. The production manager is pushing for the acquisition because he believes that productivity will be greatly enhanced—particularly when it comes to labor and material inputs. Output and input data follow. The data for the computerized system are projections.

	Current System	**Computerized System**
Output (units)	60,000	60,000
Output selling price	$80	$80
Input quantities:		
Materials	240,000	200,000
Labor	120,000	80,000
Capital (dollars)	$120,000	$600,000
Energy	60,000	150,000
Input prices:		
Materials	$8.00	$10.00
Labor	$18.00	$20.00
Capital (percent)	5.00%	5.00%
Energy	$4.00	$6.00

For each of the three following Requirements, identify the overall data analytic type that drives the analysis. Note that some of the subcomponents of the analysis may represent a particular data analytic type, but you should identify the type that drives the overall analysis. See Exhibits 2.5 and 2.6, pp. 37, 40, for a brief review of data analytic types.

Required:

1. Compute the partial operational ratios for materials and labor under each alternative. Is the production manager right in thinking that materials and labor productivity increase with the automated system?
2. Compute the productivity profiles for each system. Does the computerized system improve productivity?
3. Determine the amount by which profits will change if the computerized system is adopted. Are the trade-offs among the inputs favorable? Should the computerized system be adopted?

Problem 15-23 Productivity Measurement, Basics

OBJECTIVE 3 4

Khan Company produces handcrafted leather purses. Virtually all of the manufacturing cost consists of materials and labor. Over the past several years, profits have been declining because the cost of the two major inputs has been increasing. Lila Khan, the president of the company, has indicated that the price of the purses cannot be increased; thus, the only way to improve or at least stabilize profits is to increase overall productivity. At the beginning of 20x2, Lila implemented a new cutting and assembly process that promised less materials waste and a faster production time. At the end of 20x2, Lila wants to know how much profits have changed from the prior year because of the new process. In order to provide this information to Lila, the controller of the company gathered the following data:

	20x1	20x2
Unit selling price	$20	$20
Purses produced and sold	36,000	48,000
Materials used	72,000	80,000
Labor used	18,000	20,000
Unit price of materials	$4	$5
Unit price of labor	$9	$10

Required:

1. Compute the productivity profile for each year. Comment on the effectiveness of the new production process.
2. Compute the increase in profits attributable to increased productivity.
3. Calculate the price-recovery component, and comment on its meaning.

OBJECTIVE 3 4

Problem 15-24 Productivity Measurement, Technical and Price Efficiency

In 20x1, Fleming Chemicals used the following input combination to produce 55,000 gallons of an industrial solvent:

Materials	33,000 lbs.
Labor	66,000 hrs.

In 20x2, Fleming again planned to produce 55,000 gallons of solvent and was considering two different changes in process, both of which would be able to produce the desired output. The following input combinations are associated with each process change:

	Change I	**Change II**
Materials	38,500 lbs.	27,500 lbs.
Labor	44,000 hrs.	55,000 hrs.

The following combination is optimal for an output of 55,000 units. However, this optimal input combination is unknown to Fleming.

Materials	22,000 lbs.
Labor	44,000 hrs.

The cost of materials is $60 per pound, and the cost of labor is $15 per hour. These input prices hold for 20x1 and 20x2.

Required:

1. Compute the productivity profiles for each of the following:
   a. The actual inputs used in 20x1
   b. The inputs for each proposed 20x2 process change
   c. The optimal input combination. Will productivity increase in 20x2, regardless of which change is used? Which process change would you recommend based on the prospective productivity profiles?

2. Compute the cost of 20x1's productive inefficiency relative to the optimal input combination. Repeat for 20x2 proposed input changes. Will productivity improve from 20x1 to 20x2 for each process change? If so, by how much? Explain. Include in your explanation a discussion of changes in technical and allocative efficiency.

3. Since the optimal input combination is not known by Fleming, suggest a way to measure productivity improvement. Use this method to measure the productivity improvement achieved from 20x1 to 20x2. How does this measure compare with the productivity improvement measure computed using the optimal input combination?

DATA ANALYTICS

Jack Aerospace Technologies (JAT) researches, designs, manufactures, delivers, and services numerous product part components to the world's largest aircraft companies. JAT produces approximately 120 aircraft products using numerous processes and many employees. In recent years, JAT's profitability has suffered, which can be attributed to increased competition, customer dissatisfaction, and regulatory pressures. Noela, president of JAT, called a meeting to consider ways to improve profitability. She labeled the meeting a strategic planning session and invited the following officers: Katerina, environmental manager; Francisca, head of research and development; Misato, vice president of production and quality; Sakari, vice president of finance; and William, marketing vice president.

Noela: "You all have received the quarterly financial reports for the past two years. The trends are negative. We are losing market share, profits are decreasing, and our costs seem to be increasing. We need to take actions to increase sales, reduce costs, or both, and we need to do so as quickly as possible. Given our research strengths, it seems to me that our best bet is to grow revenues by introducing new products with proprietary rights. As far as costs are concerned, we need to improve our performance on that dimension as well. Lower per-unit costs for new and existing products are needed. Any suggestions?"

Francisca: "For our products, our ability to control costs resides in development—my area—rather than manufacturing. We probably need to pay more attention to product and process design issues if we are to successfully lower costs. Revenues also are affected in this stage. Once we patent a new part or component, the clock begins to tick, and we need to reduce time to market. Significantly, reducing time to market will allow us to generate revenues for a longer period of time than we currently are experiencing. For example, reducing the cycle time spent to convert new ideas into working engineering and other processes would help to improve time to market and also to increase revenues. Finally, we can grow revenues by increasing the volume of new products."

Misato: "While there is a lot of merit to the observation that the majority of our cost reduction opportunities reside in product development, significant cost reduction opportunities also involve manufacturing as well. For example, we might be able to reduce our manufacturing cycle time of converting raw materials into finished product. Furthermore, as you know, the Federal Aviation Administration (FAA) and other delegated authorities play a critical role in our business, as they must approve all our aircraft products. After more than a decade in our research lab, we recently received regulatory approval for a number of new state-of-the-art flight-critical engine parts, such as the bearing housings in the turbofan engine of maritime patrol aircrafts that navies use for patrol and search-and-rescue missions. This new manufacturing technology uses additive manufacturing, which often is referred to as 3D printing. Traditionally, many of these parts have been complicated to manufacture, which has made their replacement very costly for customer operators because of the low quantity of orders placed and the need for expensive molds for holding molten metal. However, with 3D printing, we can print such parts more quickly, in smaller quantities, and without the need for expensive tools as components are manufactured using layers of powdered metal fused together with a laser. Finally, for some parts, our new 3D manufacturing technology has drastically reduced our lead time from nearly two years to only two weeks."

Francisca: "Given that the FAA must approve all changes in our manufacturing process, we have been reluctant, historically, to engage in process improvement or reengineering. However, given our recent performance and regulatory success involving our new 3D printing manufacturing technologies, I wonder if we shouldn't reconsider this long-standing policy. We might be able to build on this success by expanding considerably on this line of product offerings. Some of the quality problems we have experienced could be corrected by changing some of our existing processes, and the costs saved might exceed any cost incurred from seeking FAA approval. I think our quality costs likely are significant and represent an opportunity for improvement."

Sakari: "Recent groundings of specific aircraft types for which we supply parts also has hurt our earnings. As a result, from a risk perspective, I wonder if broadening our customer base so that our parts and components are used on a greater number of different aircrafts might help reduce our concentration risk and help to limit the drop in sales revenues that usually accompanies specific aircraft groundings."

Katerina: "I agree that cost reduction—both in the product development stage and the manufacturing stage—should be a key strategic theme. The environmental area might offer some very good opportunities. A recent Pollution Prevention Act passed by the legislature requires that we monitor and report on the carbon emissions (across different Scope levels) of our products. We also have begun to calculate the costs of generating hazardous substances for each process. This Act was the push we needed to begin developing an environmental cost management system. The results so far indicate that environmental costs are much more than we realized. They are estimated to be in the range of 20 to 25 percent of total operating costs. Environmental costs can be reduced by such things as utilizing lighter yet stronger materials, eliminating the use of hazardous chemicals and other materials in production, advancing product designs that foster more efficient landings, reducing water usage throughout the value chain, and redesigning processes and products so that we can reduce both toxic residue release and carbon emissions. We might be able to have a really positive environmental impact while simultaneously reducing costs if more attention is paid to environmental issues during product development. However, I'm not sure if the financial numbers would support this assertion."

William: "I like what I am hearing because I think that it also affects our ability to increase market share and revenues. I know our incentive system focuses primarily on rewarding innovative new product designs with unique performance features. For example, environmental impact is one of our major concerns. Some aviation industry stakeholders increasingly pay particular attention to carbon footprints (and other environmental footprint impacts), and right now we are not competing well. Our environmental image is negative and needs to be improved. I am convinced that doing so will allow us to increase market share. Quality is another important matter. For example, many of our parts are considered "safety-critical" or "flight-critical" by the FAA, which means that they must function properly on every flight. Malfunction or failure of these parts poses major threats to safety and potentially could cause considerable aircraft damage. We have had to recall two batches of products during the past two years due to poor quality, which has hurt our image. Improving the processes to avoid these kinds of problems will save us a lot of grief. Product image and reputation are essential to increasing customer satisfaction and market share."

Noela: "Typically, we have tried to improve financial performance by investing more heavily in innovative research and development initiatives in an attempt to increase revenue. However, as mentioned earlier, perhaps it would be prudent to give more attention to cost management. So far, we have some very good suggestions to help achieve these two objectives, but I have some concerns. First, do we have the talent and capabilities to improve quality and environmental performance? Francisca, do your professionals really understand what they need to do to improve process and product designs so that we can see the desired quality and environmental improvements? Also, how can we reduce the cycle time for products and the time to market once patented?"

Francisca: "Let me answer those questions in order. First, we probably are lacking the understanding on the design issues. We will need to do some training to help our research scientists understand the consequences. We may need to hire additional specialty engineers who are equipped to help us ramp up our 3D design and manufacturing business lines if we decide to move in that direction. Second, we may need to make cost efficiencies, and other cost controls, significant performance measures and reward our people for actions that reduce those measures. Our employees need to align their interests with those of the company. If we can achieve these steps, we should see more profit produced per employee."

Noela: "Good. Now, Misato, tell us about production and quality. Do our manufacturing engineers and production workers need help with environmental and quality issues?"

Misato: "Well, I certainly consider our efforts around inspection to be quality related in nature. A less obvious but potentially important quality-related effort regards our waste production, which occurs both because of quality deficiencies in various facility areas and certain environmental challenges. Without question, training will be needed. Moreover, I really need to hire several quality engineers."

Katerina: "I also think that we need an environmental engineer with experience in aerospace manufacturing processes."

Noela: "Good. We certainly shouldn't ignore the necessary infrastructure to bring about the needed changes. Sakari, you have been relatively quiet; what do you think about all this? Do you have any suggestions?"

Sakari: "Infrastructure is important. If these changes are going to work, timely and accurate information will be needed. It is hard to design products and processes with cost being a significant issue without providing the right kind of cost information. We are in the process of revamping the cost management information system so that it is activity based and we can provide quality and environmental cost information. After listening to the comments made here, I might also suggest that we need to reevaluate our strategic-based control system that it can be used to align the interests of our employees with our strategy. People need to know what is important, that the most critical factors are being measured, and that they are going to be evaluated and rewarded based on those factors. Finally, I would encourage the use of target costing to help manage costs during product development. To help you all understand the importance of good information, I have assembled some activity data relating to two new products (FLI 4HY and FLI 2LW) currently under development. The data are organized into resource, activity, and cost object modules with an accompanying list of activity drivers to facilitate the use of an ABC software package recently acquired by JAT."

Risk Table

Risk	Risk Description	Likelihood of Risk Impact*	Risk Impact**
A	Poor media coverage creates negative public perception of JAT.	0.30	$25,000,000
B	Regulators ground aircraft as a result of poor JAT product performance.	0.10	$30,000,000
C	Full cost of new product designs causes JAT's prices to significantly exceed that of competitors.	0.70	$10,000,000
D	Global recession decreases demand for aircraft products.	0.25	$55,000,000
E	Internal product quality challenges consume excessive resources.	0.85	$70,000,000
F	Inability to attract and retain the best aerospace engineers and employees.	0.90	$50,000,000
G	Total time to develop, approve, and deliver new products to customers lags behind competitors.	0.45	$42,000,000
H	Environmental issues negatively impact JAT product design or manufacturing.	0.75	$75,000,000
I	Regulatory approval of new JAT products slows considerably.	0.50	$35,000,000
J	JAT's level of product feature innovation falls behind that of main competitors.	0.40	$60,000,000

*Measured as a probability (0% to 100%).
**Measured by a composite score that includes financial, regulatory, business interruption, time horizon, and reputational impact.

Resource Module (Projected General Ledger Costs of Manufacturing Process Associated with the Two Products)

Materials	$20,000,000
Salaries and wages	10,000,000
Energy	5,000,000
License fee (environmental)	2,000,000
Environmental fines	4,000,000
Depreciation; pollution control equipment	2,000,000
Total	$43,000,000

Activity Module

Resource Driver (Percentage Usage)

	Materials	Labor	Energy	Fees	Fines
Supervising process*	0%	20%	0%	0%	0%
Setting up	3	14	18	0	0
Blending chemicals	80	30	25	0	0
Producing waste	10	4	17	20	0
Disposing of hazardous waste	6	20	9	30	70
Inspecting products	0	8	6	0	0
Monitoring release of air contaminants (CO_2)	0	0	0	50	30
Operating pollution control equipment	1	4	25	0	0
	100%	100%	100%	100%	100%

*Secondary activity whose costs are assigned to primary activities in proportion to the labor time used.

List of Activity Drivers

Activity Drivers	Activity Capacity
Setup hours	30,000
Direct labor hours (blending)	60,000*
Pounds of wastes	15,000*
Pounds of hazardous waste	18,000
Hours of inspection	6,000
Tons of air contaminants	10*
Machine hours (pollution control)	5,000

*Capacity is flexible (i.e., acquired as needed, and always matches usage). Capacity for other activities is acquired in advance of usage. For example, setups are acquired in units (steps) of 950 hours. Projected usage for setups equals practical capacity.

Cost Object Module (Products and Projected Activity Usage)

Cost Objects	FLI 4HY	FLI 2LW
Expected output (pounds)	50,000	50,000
Setup hours	18,000	10,500
Direct labor hours (blending)	36,000	24,000
Pounds of waste	12,000	3,000
Pounds of hazardous waste	12,000	5,000
Hours of inspection	5,000	1,000
Tons of air contaminants	8	2
Machine hours (pollution control)	4,000	1,000

Required:

1. Use the comments from the executive meeting to evaluate the three elements of JAT's strategic-based control system, including any recommended changes that would improve the system.

2. Use the data in JAT's Risk Table to construct a risk plot of JAT's inherent risks. Based on this inherent risk plot, identify and briefly discuss JAT's three most important risks.

3. Based on your suggested improvements to JAT's strategic-based control system (Requirement 1) and the results of your risk plot (Requirement 2), identify strategic objectives and possible quantitative performance measures for each of five perspectives: financial, customer, environmental, process, and learning and growth. Would you recommend the Balanced Scorecard for JAT? Why?

4. Consider the cost of activities (round all answers to three decimal places):

   a. Determine the cost of the primary activities (e.g., setting up, blending chemicals, producing waste, disposing of hazardous waste, inspecting products, monitoring release of air contaminants, and operating pollution control equipment) for the proposed new activity-based cost management system. *(Note: These costs will be part of the numerator when calculating the activity rates in Requirement 6.)*
   b. Assign the cost of the secondary activity (supervising) to the primary activities. *(Note: These costs also will be part of the numerator when calculating the activity rates in Requirement 6.)*

5. Classify the primary activities into three categories: environmental, quality, and other (neither quality nor environmental). Did some activities end up in more than one category? Also, are there any notable similarities or differences between the classifications of these primary activities and the results of the inherent risk plot (from Requirement 2)? Briefly explain your responses.

6. Consider the unit costs (round all answers to two decimal places):

   a. Determine the cost per unit for the two proposed products (FLI 4HY and FLI 2LW) by calculating primary activity rates and applying costs accordingly.
   b. Calculate the *environmental* cost per unit and the *quality* cost per unit.
   c. What do these unit cost data tell you about the relative desirability of the two products?
   d. How do the financial insights provided by these activity-based costs relate to the risk insights provided by the inherent risk plot (in Requirement 2)?

7. Following Sakari's suggestion, Noela decided to use target costing to help improve new product profitability. Based on analyses by Noela and William, the target prices for 4HY and 2LW are $500 per pound and $350 per pound, respectively. Noela has indicated that any new product should earn a gross profit equal to 20 percent of sales. Based on this information, answer the following items (round all answers to two decimal places):

   a. What is the target cost for each product? Given this information, recommend the action that should be taken with respect to offering or not offering the two new products. Briefly explain your recommendation. Also, calculate the impact of your recommendation on JAT's total profits.
   b. Suppose William indicates that unit sales for each product can be increased by 50 percent if the selling price is lowered by 10 percent. Assuming the same target profit (Noela wants the original target profit dollar amount per pound maintained), calculate the new target cost for each product. Furthermore, assume that Katerina believes that all environmental and quality costs are non-value-added. If all non-value-added costs

were eliminated, could these new target costs be met? (Calculate the unit cost at the 50,000 unit level.) Also, calculate the effect on total profits under a scenario where all non-value-added costs are eliminated. (Include in this analysis any possible increase in sales volume.) Based on your scenario analysis, recommend whether JAT should or should not implement this new target cost and eliminate non-value-added costs. Briefly explain your recommendation.

c. After additional consultation with JAT's general counsel, Katerina now believes that the cost to monitor the release of air contaminants is a value-added cost because it is required by the new Pollution Prevention Act. Recalculate the effect on total profits if the cost to monitor the release of air contaminants is treated as a value-added cost (i.e., not eliminated). Briefly explain how this treatment affects your recommendation (in Requirement 7b).

8. Sakari has decided that utilizing data analytics in responding to the issues raised in the planning meeting would allow for an easier and a quicker response to any subsequent "what-if?" questions and scenarios that might arise from management (e.g., what if particular activity usage or cost inputs changed?). Therefore, to assist Sakari with this endeavor:

   a. Use Excel (or some other software tool) to create your inherent risk plot (from Requirement 2).

   b. Use Excel (or some other software tool) to create a comprehensive spreadsheet that incorporates the necessary formulas and other cell references to respond to the quantitative requirements (i.e., Requirements 4, 6, and 7).

After studying this chapter, you should be able to:

1. Determine the number of units and amount of sales revenue needed to break even and to earn a target profit.

2. Determine the number of units and sales revenue needed to earn an after-tax target profit.

3. Apply cost-volume-profit analysis in a multiple-product setting.

4. Prepare a profit-volume graph and a cost-volume-profit graph, and explain the meaning of each.

5. Explain the impact of risk, uncertainty, and changing variables on cost-volume-profit analysis.

6. Discuss the impact of non-unit cost drivers on cost-volume-profit analysis.

Solomon7/Shutterstock.com

BREAK-EVEN ANALYSIS

at Instagram, Twitter, Snapchat, and YouTube

How much time do you spend online each day? Overall, people spend about two and a half hours a day on social media.[1] Instagram, Snapchat, Facebook, YouTube, and Twitter are among the most popular social media sites in the world.

Used by over 1 billion people worldwide, with 133 million in the United States alone, Instagram is a highly popular photo and video-posting site that allows users to post and tag photos and share them with followers; for example, an artfully arranged plate of food captioned "Dinner!", or Chrissy Teigen's banana bread recipe, or an amazing island sunset. Whether it's smashed avocado on toast or smashed peas and carrots on a highchair tray, posting pictures on Instagram allows users to share their lives with friends, family, and the immediate world. Importantly, for Instagram's business model, brands find the site to be invaluable for reaching customers. Its youthful audience says it's the best way for brands to reach them with promotions. Plus, they actually want to see advertising and say they turn to Instagram to discover products as they click on links for more details on a product.[2] Among the most popular or most followed Instagram accounts are Lionel Messi, Selena Gomez, Kim Kardashian, and National Geographic.[3]

Twitter, launched in 2006, was meant to allow individuals to send short texts via computer or mobile phone. Twitter users post short (140-character) thoughts called tweets with or without attached photos. Companies including **Starbucks**, **Whole Foods**, and **Michael Kors** use Twitter to connect with followers. Universities use Twitter to alert students to breaking news, such as campus closures due to bad weather. Individuals tweet personal opinions and political commentary. Among the most popular or most followed Twitter accounts are Barack Obama, Ariana Grande, CNN Breaking News, Justin Bieber, and Donald J. Trump.[4]

Snapchat, with its familiar ghost icon, initially focused on private, temporary, person-to-person photo sharing. Now it is used for a range of different tasks, including sending short videos, live video chatting, messaging, creating caricature-like Bitmoji avatars, and creating a chronological "story" to be broadcasted to all your followers. Prior to Snapchat, social media was very desktop based and focused on accumulating data. However, through Snapchat, a mobile phone is the focus. Millennials are an important market for Snapchat.

These companies are wildly popular, but how do they make money? What is the meaning of breakeven for a digital content provider? Like many companies, social media companies first lose money before breaking even.

1 "Average Time Spent Daily on Social Media, Broadband Search," https://www.broadbandsearch.net/blog/average-daily-time-on-social-media, accessed July 30, 2020.
2 Ellen Simon, "How Instagram Makes Money," https://www.investopedia.com/articles/personal-finance/030915/how-instagram-makes-money.asp, updated May 29, 2020, accessed July 30, 2020.
3 Joshua Boyd, "The Top 20 Most Followed Instagram Accounts," July 15, 2020, https://www.brandwatch.com/blog/top-most-instagram-followers/, accessed July 30, 2020.
4 Joshua Boyd, "The Most Followed Accounts on Twitter," July 30, 2020, https://www.brandwatch.com/blog/most-twitter-followers/, accessed July 30, 2020.

For example, Twitter posted years of losses, including the year 2014 when it went public. By 2018, however, it earned enough revenue over expenses to break even and post a profit. Snapchat went public in 2017 posting losses and has yet to break even, although that is forecast for 2022.[5]

The business model most social media companies use relies on ad revenue, and that depends on "clicks." Whenever a user goes to a site promoted on an ad, that's a click. There may be a small fee paid by ad owners for each click on a site with the ad visible. A direct click on the ad itself will produce a higher fee. Take YouTube as an example. If you are looking for help on training your dog or puppy, chances are you've checked out Zak George. Each training video gives invaluable tips on training and includes numerous opportunities to click on Zak's website, buy his book, or buy his sponsors' products. The inclusion of these ads within the video leads to revenue for Zak; clicking on the ads leads to higher revenue. That's how he uses YouTube to make money. YouTube, of course, is also earning money when you click on the ads, and that helps to cover the costs they incur for providing the platform, storing videos and content, making the search function usable, and so on.

Instagram earns money from paid ads, just like Facebook, its parent company. Facebook did not break out Instagram's finances, but for 2019, it collected $69.7 billion in advertising fees, with much of this coming directly from Instagram. Facebook is working to further monetize Instagram by giving brands the ability to sell directly from Instagram.[6]

Bottom line, social media companies are earning ad revenue and finding ways to monetize their offerings. Although social media companies can start out losing money, and even go public without making a profit, eventually, they must break even.

Cost-volume-profit analysis (CVP analysis) is a powerful tool for planning and decision making. Because CVP analysis emphasizes the interrelationships of costs, quantity sold, and price, it brings together all of the financial information of the firm. CVP analysis can be a valuable tool in identifying the extent and magnitude of the economic trouble a company is facing and helping pinpoint the necessary solution. The severe recession beginning in 2008, and continued economic difficulties, led a number of companies to concentrate on breaking even.

REAL-WORLD EXAMPLE

For example, the Mayo Clinic announced that it had broken even for 2008 despite missing its revenue goal by $133 million.[7] In March 2020, however, Mayo Clinic stopped all nonessential medical care and saw revenues plummeting, while expenses for ICU beds, ventilators, and personal protective equipment soared. Breakeven is not in the cards for 2020. The airline industry uses cost-volume-profit analysis in decisions ranging from whether to add another flight to whether to even start a new airline. In 2020, load factors, the percentage of seats that must be filled on a flight to break even, ranged from 72.5 percent for the Southwest to 78.9 percent for America. Clearly the virtually empty planes in the second quarter of 2020 foretell a year of losses for airlines.[8]

5 "Analysts Expect Breakeven for Snap, Inc.," Simply Wall Street, February 7, 2020, https://finance.yahoo.com/news/analysts-expect-breakeven-snap-inc-184800772.html, accessed July 30, 2020.

6 Ashley Carman, "Instagram Brought in $20 Billion in Ad Revenue Last Year, More Than a Quarter of Facebook's Earnings," *The Verge* (February 4, 2020), https://www.theverge.com/2020/2/4/21122956/instagram-ad-revenue-earnings-amount-facebook, accessed July 30, 2020.

7 Sea Stachura, "Mayo Clinic Breaks Even in 2008," Minnesota Public Radio, March 12, 2009, http://minnesota.publicradio.org/display/web/2009/03/12/mayobudget/, accessed October 6, 2011.

8 James Asquith, "Analysis—How Much Money Do Empty Flights Really Cost Airlines," *Forbes,* March 31, 2020, https://www.forbes.com/sites/jamesasquith/2020/03/31/analysis-how-much-money-do-empty-flights-really-cost-airlines/#3d3571745854, accessed November 12, 2020.

CVP analysis can address many issues, such as the number of units that must be sold to break even, the impact a given reduction in fixed costs can have on the break-even point, and the impact an increase in price can have on profit. Additionally, CVP analysis allows managers to conduct sensitivity analyses by examining the impact of various price or cost levels on profit.

While this chapter deals with the mechanics and terminology of CVP analysis, your objective in studying CVP analysis is more than to learn the mechanics. CVP analysis is an integral part of financial planning and decision making. Every accountant and manager should thoroughly understand and be able to apply its concepts.

THE BREAK-EVEN POINT AND TARGET PROFIT IN UNITS AND SALES REVENUE

OBJECTIVE ◀ 1

Determine the number of units and amount of sales revenue needed to break even and to earn a target profit.

To find out how revenues, expenses, and profits behave as volume changes, it is natural to begin by finding the firm's break-even point in units sold and in sales revenue. Two frequently used approaches to finding the break-even point are the operating income approach and the contribution margin approach. We will discuss these two approaches to find the **break-even point** (the point of zero profit) and then see how each can determine the total sales revenue at break-even. The determination of units or revenue needed to achieve a target profit is a generalized case of the break-even formulas.

The first step in implementing a units-sold approach to CVP analysis is to determine just what a unit is. For manufacturing firms, the answer is obvious.

Procter & Gamble may define a unit as a bar of Ivory soap. Service firms face more varied choices. **JetBlue Airways** may define a unit as a passenger mile or a one-way trip. **SeaWorld** counts the number of visitor-days. The **Jacksonville Naval Supply Center**, which provides naval, industrial, and general supplies to U.S. Navy ships stationed in northeastern Florida and the Caribbean, defines "productive units" to measure the activities involved in delivering services. In this way, more complicated services are assigned more productive units than are less complicated services, thereby standardizing service efforts.[9]

REAL-WORLD EXAMPLE

The second step is to separate costs into fixed and variable components. CVP analysis focuses on the factors that change the components of profit. Because we are looking at CVP analysis in terms of units sold, we need to determine the fixed and variable components of cost and revenue with respect to units. (This assumption is relaxed when we incorporate activity-based costing into CVP analysis.) It is important to realize that CVP focuses on the firm as a whole. Therefore, *all* costs of the company—manufacturing, marketing, and administrative—are taken into account. Variable costs include *all costs* that increase as more units are sold, including direct materials, direct labor, variable overhead, and variable selling and administrative costs. Similarly, fixed costs are composed of all fixed overhead and fixed selling and administrative expenses.

---

9   David J. Harr, "How Activity Accounting Works in Government," *Management Accounting* (September 1990): 36–40.

Recycling at Best Buy

For years, Best Buy, Inc., ran an in-store recycling program where customers could turn in used computer monitors, TVs, batteries, ink cartridges, computers, and so on.[10] There was no cost to the customer for this service, and Best Buy was able to sell some of the component parts to cover the administrative and distribution center costs involved. The service proved to be popular with communities and customers.

Early in 2016, however, Best Buy announced a change in the program. Customers in most states would pay $25 for every TV and computer monitor turned in. (Customers in Illinois and Pennsylvania would not be able to recycle these items because their states prohibit the collection of recycling fees.) The reason for the change? Best Buy's objective was to run the service at break-even. Previously, the cost of the program was balanced by the amounts realized from selling recycled components, such as glass from TVs and computer monitors. However, the increasing volume of e-waste and falling commodity prices for recycled glass reduced the revenue gained from component sales and made the overall program more costly. The fee for recycling monitors and TVs is meant to bring the program back to the break-even point. Remaining items (ink cartridges, etc.) continue to be recycled at no charge.

Basic Concepts for CVP Analysis

The fundamental concept underlying CVP analysis is that the firm's costs can be broken down into variable and fixed costs. A useful tool for organizing the firm's costs into fixed and variable categories is the contribution-margin-based income statement. Recall that operating income is income *before* income taxes. Operating income includes only revenues and expenses from the firm's normal operations. The term **net income** is used to mean operating income minus income taxes. **Example 16.1** illustrates basic CVP terms and the preparation of the contribution-margin-based income statement.

EXAMPLE 16.1

The HOW and WHY of Basic Cost Calculations and the Contribution-Margin-Based Income Statement

Information:

Blazin-Boards Company plans to sell 10,000 snowboards at $400 each in the coming year. Product costs include:

Direct materials per snowboard	$80
Direct labor per snowboard	$125
Variable overhead per snowboard	$15
Total fixed factory overhead	$800,000

Variable selling expense is a commission of 5 percent of price; fixed selling and administrative expenses total $400,000.

> **Why:**
> Since variable *product* cost per unit consists of variable production or manufacturing costs, the plant manager would use this data. The plant manager is responsible for making a quality product as inexpensively and efficiently as possible. Knowing that variable product cost is $220 per unit provides a starting place for seeing what process improvements might do to the unit cost.

---

10 Laura Bishop, "Best Buy's Recycling Program Is Changing. Here's How and Why," February 1, 2016, https://corporate .bestbuy.com/10556-2/, accessed July 12, 2016. Matthew Smith, "After Collecting 2 Billion Pounds of E-waste, Best Buy Expands Recycling Program," Corporate Best Buy, June 19, 2020, https://corporate.bestbuy.com/after -collecting-2-billion-pounds-of-e-waste-best-buy-expands-recycling-program/

EXAMPLE 16.1

(Continued)

The sales manager would be interested in the total variable cost per unit. Since this cost includes the sales commission, it reflects all of the variable costs. Sales managers can see the impact of the commissions (for which they are responsible) and can also see what impact a one-time discount might have on overall profitability.

Top management would use the unit contribution margin for budgeting to see what impact an increase or a decrease in unit sales would have on operating income. Since fixed costs stay the same when units change, the contribution margin gives important information.

Required:

1. Calculate the:
   a. Variable product cost per unit
   b. Selling expense per unit
   c. Total variable cost per unit
   d. Contribution margin per unit
   e. Contribution margin ratio
   f. Total fixed expense for the year

2. Prepare a contribution-margin-based income statement for Blazin-Boards Company for the coming year.

3. ***What if*** 13,000 boards could be manufactured and sold next year; how would that affect operating income? By what percent?

Solution:

1. a. Variable product cost per unit = Direct materials + Direct labor
      + Variable overhead
      = $80 + $125 + $15 = $220

   b. Selling expense per unit = $400 × 0.05 = $20

   c. Variable cost per unit = Direct materials + Direct labor
      + Variable overhead + Variable selling expense
      = $80 + $125 + $15 + $20 = $240

   d. Contribution margin per unit = Price − Variable cost per unit
      = $400 − $240 = $160

   e. Contribution margin ratio = (Price − Variable cost per unit)/Price
      = ($400 − $240)/$400 = 0.40 = 40%

      OR

      = (Sales − Total variable cost)/Sales
      = ($4,000,000 − $2,400,000)/$4,000,000
      = 0.4 = 40%

   f. Total fixed expense = $800,000 + $400,000 = $1,200,000

EXAMPLE 16.1

(Continued)

2.

Blazin-Boards Company
Contribution-Margin-Based Operating Income Statement
For the Coming Year

	Total	Per Unit
Sales ($400 × 10,000 snowboards)	$4,000,000	$400
Total variable expense ($240 × 10,000)	2,400,000	240
Total contribution margin	$1,600,000	$160
Total fixed expense	1,200,000	
Operating income	$ 400,000	

3.

Increase in sales (3,000 boards × $400)	$1,200,000
Less:	
Increase in variable cost (3,000 boards × $240)	720,000
Increase in fixed cost	0
Increase in operating income	$ 480,000

Operating income will be $480,000 higher, or $880,000 in total. This is a 120 percent ($480,000/$400,000) increase in operating income, even though the number of units sold would increase by 30 percent. (Since fixed costs have already been covered, any increase in contribution margin goes directly to income.)

Example 16.1 shows that the contribution-margin-based operating income statement is a powerful tool for analyzing a company's projected performance. Notice that the existence of fixed costs means that sales above the estimated 10,000 units, say a 1,000-unit or 10 percent increase, would yield more than a 10 percent increase in operating income. Similarly, a 1,000-unit or 10 percent decrease would decrease operating income by more than 10 percent. This is why an understanding of fixed and variable costs is so important to managers as they examine the impact of changing sales on income.

The Equation Method for Break-Even and Target Income

Companies frequently want to know how many units must be produced and sold to break even or to earn a target income. In other words, how many units will yield the desired (at break-even, zero) profit? The basic break-even/target income equation can be easily derived from the contribution-margin-based operating income statement.

$$\text{Operating income} = \text{Sales revenues} - \text{Variable expenses} - \text{Fixed expenses}$$

This operating income equation can be expanded by expressing sales revenue and variable expenses in terms of unit dollar amounts and number of units. Thus, sales revenue equals the unit selling price times the number of units sold, and total variable costs equal the unit variable cost times the number of units sold. With these expressions, the operating income statement becomes:

$$\text{Operating income} = (\text{Price} \times \text{Number of units}) - (\text{Variable cost per unit} \times \text{Number of units}) - \text{Total fixed costs}$$

Finally, the equation for a target profit is put in terms of units:

$$\text{Units for a target profit} = (\text{Total fixed cost} + \text{Target income})/(\text{Price} - \text{Variable cost per unit})$$

For the special case when target income is zero, the break-even equation becomes:

$$\text{Break-even units} = (\text{Total fixed cost} + 0)/(\text{Price} - \text{Variable cost per unit})$$
$$= \text{Total fixed cost}/(\text{Price} - \text{Variable cost per unit})$$

An important advantage of the operating income statement is that all further CVP equations are derived from the contribution-margin-based income statement. As a result, any CVP problem can be solved by using this approach. **Example 16.2** shows how and why to calculate the units needed to break even and to achieve a target profit.

EXAMPLE 16.2

The HOW and WHY of Calculating the Units Needed to Break Even and to Achieve a Target Profit

Information:
Blazin-Boards Company plans to sell 10,000 snowboards at $400 each in the coming year. Product costs include:

Direct materials per snowboard	$80
Direct labor per snowboard	$125
Variable overhead per snowboard	$15
Total fixed factory overhead	$800,000

Variable selling expense is a commission of 5 percent of price; fixed selling and administrative expense totals $400,000.

> **Why:**
> At the break-even point, total revenue equals total cost. Once the break-even point is reached, all fixed costs are covered and additional units add only variable costs. Thus, contribution margin earned above break-even will go toward profit. The target operating income is treated as fixed cost for the purpose of figuring the number of units that must be produced and sold. Knowing the break-even units gives managers an easy way to tell just when during the year the firm moves out of the red and into the black.

Required:

1. Calculate the number of units Blazin-Boards must sell to break even. Prepare a contribution-margin-based income statement for the calculated units.

2. Calculate the number of units Blazin-Boards must sell to achieve target operating income (profit) of $240,000.

3. *What if* Blazin-Boards wanted to achieve a target operating income of $300,000? Would the number of snowboards be larger or smaller than the number calculated in Requirement 2? Why?

Solution:

1. Break-even units = Total fixed costs/(Price − Unit variable cost)
   $$= \$1,200,000/(\$400 - \$240)$$
   $$= 7,500$$

Sales (7,500 units @ $400)	$3,000,000
Less: Variable expenses	1,800,000
Contribution margin	$1,200,000
Less: Fixed expenses	1,200,000
Operating income	$ 0

Indeed, selling 7,500 units does yield a zero profit.

EXAMPLE 16.2

(Continued)

2. Units for $240,000 = (Total fixed costs + Target profit)/
   (Price − Unit variable cost)
   = ($1,200,000 + $240,000)/($400 − $240)
   = 9,000

3. For a target profit of $300,000, more than 9,000 units must be sold. In fact, 9,375 units will yield this profit.

   Units for $300,000 = ($1,200,000 + $300,000)/($400 − $240) = 9,375

Contribution Margin Approach

A refinement of the equation approach is the contribution margin approach. It simply recognizes that at break-even, the total contribution margin equals the fixed expenses. The **contribution margin** is sales revenue minus total variable costs. By substituting the unit contribution margin for price minus unit variable cost in the operating income equation, and solving for the number of units, the following break-even expression is obtained:

Number of units = Fixed costs/Unit contribution margin

Recall that Example 16.1, Requirement 2, shows the income statement for the budgeted sales for the coming year for Blazin-Boards Company. The contribution margin per unit can be computed in one of two ways. One way is to divide the total contribution margin by the units to be sold for a result of $160 per unit ($1,600,000/10,000). A second way is to compute price minus variable cost per unit. Doing so yields the same result, $160 per unit ($400 − $240). Now, we can use the contribution margin approach to calculate the break-even number of units.

Number of units = $1,200,000/$160 per unit
= 7,500 units

Of course, the answer is identical to the one computed previously using the equation approach.

Another way to check this number of units computed in Example 16.2 is to use the break-even point. As was shown in Example 16.1, Blazin-Boards must sell 10,000 snowboards, or 2,500 more than the break-even volume of 7,500 units, to earn a profit of $400,000. The contribution margin per snowboard is $160. Multiplying $160 by the 2,500 snowboards *above* break-even produces the profit of $400,000 ($160 × 2,500). This outcome demonstrates that contribution margin per unit for each unit above break-even is equivalent to profit per unit. Since the break-even point had already been computed, the number of snowboards to be sold to yield a $900,000 operating income could have been calculated by dividing the unit contribution margin into the target profit and adding the resulting amount to the break-even volume.

Suppose that Blazin-Boards sells 11,000 snowboards rather than the 10,000 budgeted. What will operating income be in that case? Since fixed costs have already been covered when 10,000 units are sold, the only costs that must be covered on the additional units are the variable costs of $240 per unit. A quicker, more direct way to calculate the new, higher operating income is to take the original operating income of $400,000 for 10,000 units sold and add the contribution margin on the additional 1,000 units, or $160,000 (1,000 × $160). Thus, the total operating income for 11,000 units sold is $560,000 ($400,000 + $160,000). The importance of this concept for leverage is discussed later in this chapter.

Break-Even Point and Target Income in Sales Revenue   Sometimes, managers prefer to use sales revenue as the measure of sales activity instead of units sold. A units-sold measure can be converted to a sales-revenue measure simply by multiplying the unit sales price by the units sold. For example, the break-even point for Blazin-Boards Company was 7,500 snowboards. At the selling price per snowboard of $400, the break-even sales revenue

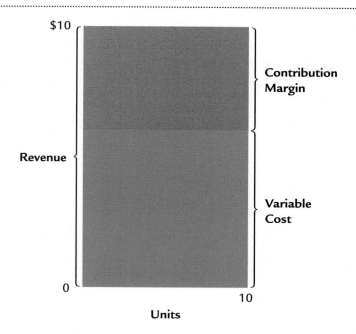

is $3,000,000 ($400 × 7,500). Any answer expressed in units sold can be easily converted to an answer expressed in terms of sales revenue, if the break-even units can be easily computed. This is seldom the case, however, in a multi-product firm. Fortunately, break-even revenue can be computed directly by developing a separate formula based on total fixed costs, target profit, and the contribution margin ratio. In this case, the important variable is sales revenue, so both the revenue and the variable costs must be expressed in dollars instead of units. Sales revenue is always expressed in dollars, so measuring that variable is no problem. Let's look more closely at variable costs and see how they can be expressed in terms of sales revenue.

To calculate the break-even point in sales revenue, variable costs are defined as a percentage of sales rather than as an amount per unit sold. Exhibit 16.1 illustrates the division of sales revenue into variable cost and contribution margin. In this exhibit, price is $10, and variable cost is $6. Of course, the remainder is contribution margin of $4 ($10 − $6). Focusing on 10 units sold, total variable costs are $60 ($6 × 10 units sold). Alternatively, since each unit sold earns $10 of revenue, we would say that for every $10 of revenue earned, $6 of variable costs are incurred, or, equivalently, that 60 percent of each dollar of revenue earned is attributable to variable cost ($6/$10). Thus, focusing on sales revenue, we would expect total variable costs of $60 for revenues of $100 (0.60 × $100).

To express variable cost in terms of sales revenue, we compute the **variable cost ratio**, which is the proportion of each sales dollar that must be used to cover variable costs. The variable cost ratio can be computed by using either total data or unit data. Of course, the percentage of sales revenue remaining after variable costs are covered is the contribution margin ratio. The **contribution margin ratio** is the proportion of each sales dollar available to cover fixed costs and provide for profit. In Exhibit 16.1, if the variable cost ratio is 60 percent of sales, then the contribution margin must be the remaining 40 percent of sales. It makes sense that the complement of the variable cost ratio is the contribution margin ratio. After all, the proportion of the sales revenue left after variable costs are covered should be the contribution margin component.

Just as the variable cost ratio can be computed using total or unit figures, the contribution margin ratio (40 percent in our exhibit) can also be computed in these two ways. That is, one can divide the total contribution margin by total sales ($40/$100), or one can use unit contribution margin divided by price ($4/$10). Naturally, if the variable cost ratio is known, it can be subtracted from 1 to yield the contribution margin ratio (1 − 0.60 = 0.40).

Where do fixed costs fit in? Since the contribution margin is revenue remaining after variable costs are covered, it must be the revenue available to cover fixed costs and contribute to profit. In other words, we compare total fixed costs to the total contribution margin. If total fixed costs equal the contribution margin, profit is zero. (The company is at break-even.) If total fixed costs are less than the contribution margin, the company earns a profit equal to the excess of contribution margin over fixed costs. Finally, if total fixed costs are greater than the contribution margin, the company faces an operating loss.

Now, let's consider the **sales-revenue approach** by looking at the basic income statement.

Operating income = Sales − Variable costs − Total fixed costs

Operating income = Sales − (Variable cost ratio × Sales) − Total fixed costs

Operating income = Sales (1 − Variable cost ratio) − Total fixed costs

Operating income = (Sales × Contribution margin ratio) − Total fixed costs

Sales = (Total fixed costs + Operating income)/Contribution margin ratio

At break-even, operating income equals zero, so the equation becomes:

Break-even sales = Total fixed costs/Contribution margin ratio

To earn a targeted operating income, sales equal the sum of the total fixed costs and target income divided by the contribution margin ratio.

What about the equation approach used in determining the break-even point in units? We can use that approach here as well. Recall that the formula for the break-even point in units is as follows:

Break-even point in units = Total fixed costs/(Price − Unit variable cost)

If we multiply both sides of the above equation by price, the left-hand side will equal sales revenue at break-even.

Break-even units × Price = Price[Total fixed costs/(Price − Unit variable cost)]

Break-even sales = Total fixed costs × [Price/(Price − Unit variable cost)]

Break-even sales = Total fixed costs × (Price/Contribution margin)

Break-even sales = Total fixed costs/Contribution margin ratio

Just as target income was added to total fixed costs in determining unit sales, target income is added to total fixed costs when calculating the sales revenue needed for a target income. **Example 16.3** illustrates the calculation of break-even sales revenue and sales revenue needed to achieve a target profit for Blazin-Boards Company.

In general, assuming that fixed costs remain unchanged, the contribution margin ratio can be used to find the profit impact of a change in sales revenue. To obtain the total change in profits from a change in revenue, simply multiply the contribution margin ratio by the change in sales. For example, if sales revenue is $4,000,000 instead of $4,600,000, how will the expected profits be affected? A decrease in sales revenue of $600,000 will cause a decrease in profits of $240,000 (0.40 × $600,000).

EXAMPLE 16.3

The HOW and WHY of Calculating Revenue for Break-Even and for a Target Profit

Information:
Blazin-Boards Company plans to sell 10,000 snowboards at $400 each in the coming year. Unit variable cost equals $240. Total fixed costs equal $1,200,000.

Why:
Companies frequently prefer to express the break-even point in sales revenue. To do that, we recognize that total sales revenue must cover both total fixed costs and desired operating income. That is, the proportion of revenue left after variable costs are covered is what is left to cover fixed costs and income.

EXAMPLE 16.3

(*Continued*)

Required:

1. What is the contribution margin per unit? What is the contribution margin ratio?

2. Calculate the sales revenue needed to break even.

3. Calculate the sales revenue needed to achieve a target profit of $240,000.

4. ***What if*** Blazin-Boards had target operating income (profit) of $350,000? Would sales revenue be larger or smaller than the one calculated in Requirement 3? Why? By how much?

Solution:

1. Contribution margin per unit = Price − Unit variable cost
$$= \$400 - \$240 = \$160$$
Contribution margin ratio = $160 / $400 = 0.40, or 40%

2. Break-even sales revenue = Total fixed cost/Contribution margin ratio
$$= \$1,200,000 / 0.40 = \$3,000,000$$

3. Target sales revenue = (Total fixed cost + Target profit)/
Contribution margin ratio
$$= (\$1,200,000 + \$240,000)/0.40 = \$3,600,000$$

4. Target profit of $350,000 is larger than $240,000, so the sales revenue needed would be larger by $275,000.

New target sales revenue = ($1,200,000 + $350,000)/0.40 = $3,875,000
Increase in sales revenue = $3,875,000 − $3,600,000 = $275,000

Targeted Income as a Percent of Sales Revenue Assume that Blazin-Boards Company wants to know the number of snowboards that must be sold in order to earn a profit equal to 15 percent of sales revenue. Sales revenue is selling price multiplied by the quantity sold. Thus, the targeted operating income is 15 percent of selling price times quantity. Using the operating income approach (which is simpler in this case), we obtain the following:

$$0.15(\$400)(\text{Units}) = (\$400)(\text{Units}) - (\$240)(\text{Units}) - \$1,200,000$$
$$(\$60)(\text{Units}) = (\$160)(\text{Units}) - \$1,200,000$$
$$\$100(\text{Units}) = \$1,200,000$$
$$\text{Units} = 12,000$$

Does a volume of 12,000 snowboards achieve a profit equal to 15 percent of sales revenue? For 12,000 snowboards, the total revenue is $4,800,000 ($400 × 12,000). The profit can be computed without preparing a formal income statement. Remember that above break-even, the contribution margin per unit is the profit per unit. The break-even volume is 7,500 snowboards. If 12,000 snowboards are sold, then 4,500 (12,000 − 7,500) snowboards above the break-even point are sold. The before-tax profit, therefore, is $720,000 ($160 × 4,500), which is 15 percent of sales ($720,000/$4,800,000).

Comparison of the Two Approaches

For a single-product setting, converting the break-even point in units answer to a sales-revenue answer is simply a matter of multiplying the unit sales price by the units sold. Then why bother with a separate formula for the sales-revenue approach? For a single-product setting, neither approach has any real advantage over the other. Both offer much the same level of conceptual and computational difficulty.

In a multiple-product setting, however, CVP analysis is more complex and the sales-revenue approach is significantly easier. This approach maintains essentially the same computational requirements found in the single-product setting, whereas the units-sold approach becomes more difficult. Even though the conceptual complexity of CVP analysis does increase with multiple products, the operation is reasonably straightforward.

OBJECTIVE ▶ **2**
Determine the number of units and sales revenue needed to earn an after-tax target profit.

AFTER-TAX PROFIT TARGETS

Income taxes are generally calculated as a percentage of income. When calculating the break-even point, income taxes play no role because the taxes paid on zero income are zero. When the company needs to know how many units to sell to earn a particular net income, however, some additional consideration is needed. Recall that net income is operating income minus income taxes and that our targeted income figure was expressed in before-tax terms. As a result, when the income target is expressed as net income, we must add back the income taxes to get operating income. Therefore, to use either the equation method or the contribution margin approach, the after-tax profit target must first be converted to a before-tax profit target.

In general, taxes are computed as a percentage of income. The after-tax profit, or net income, is computed by subtracting income taxes from the operating income (or before-tax profit).

$$\text{Net income} = \text{Operating income} - \text{Income taxes}$$
$$\text{Net income} = \text{Operating income} - (\text{Tax rate} \times \text{Operating income})$$
$$\text{Net income} = \text{Operating income}\,(1 - \text{Tax rate})$$

or

$$\text{Operating income} = \text{Net income}/(1 - \text{Tax rate})$$

Thus, to convert the after-tax profit to before-tax profit, simply divide the after-tax profit by the quantity $(1 - \text{Tax rate})$. **Example 16.4** shows how to calculate the number of units needed to achieve an after-tax profit target.

EXAMPLE 16.4

The HOW and WHY of Calculating the Number of Units to Generate an After-Tax Target Profit

Information:
Blazin-Boards Company wants to earn $390,000 in net (after-tax) income next year. Snowboards are priced at $400 each for the coming year. Product costs include:

Direct materials per snowboard	$80
Direct labor per snowboard	$125
Variable overhead per snowboard	$15
Total fixed factory overhead	$800,000

Variable selling expense is a commission of 5 percent of price; fixed selling and administrative expense totals $400,000. Blazin-Boards has a tax rate of 35 percent.

Why:
Top management may be interested in target net income, since income taxes are a legitimate expense of the business and owners are interested in after-tax income. The accountant must first convert net income into operating income since the tax rate is a variable that is not taken into account in the break-even equation. Once the conversion is made, the break-even equation can be applied.

EXAMPLE 16.4

(Continued)

Required:

1. Calculate the before-tax profit needed to achieve an after-tax target of $422,500.

2. Calculate the number of boards that will yield operating income calculated in Requirement 1 above.

3. Prepare an income statement for Blazin-Boards Company for the coming year based on the number of boards computed in Requirement 2.

4. ***What if*** Blazin-Boards had a 30 percent tax rate. Would the units sold to reach a $422,500 target net income be higher or lower than 11,563? Calculate the number of units needed.

Solution:

1. Before-tax income = After-tax income/(1 − Tax rate)
   = $422,500/(1 − 0.35)
   = $422,500/(0.65)
   = $650,000

2. Number of boards = (Total fixed cost + Target profit)/
   (Price − Variable cost per unit)
   = ($1,200,000 + $650,000)/($400 − $240)
   = 11,563 (rounded)

3.

Blazin-Boards Company
Income Statement
For the Coming Year

	Total	Per Unit
Sales ($400 × 11,563 snowboards)	$4,625,200	$400
Total variable expense ($240 × 11,563)	2,775,120	240
Total contribution margin	$1,850,080	$160
Total fixed expense	1,200,000	
Operating income	$ 650,080	
Less: Income taxes ($650,080 × 0.35)	227,528	
Net income*	$ 422,552	

*Note that net income is $52 higher than the target due to rounding the units up from 11,562.5 to 11,563.

4. The units would be lower than 11,523 since the lower tax rate means that a smaller operating income would be needed to yield the same target net income.

   Before-tax income = After-tax income/(1 − Tax rate)
   = $422,500/(1 − 0.30)
   = $603,571 (rounded)

   Number of boards = (Total fixed cost + Target profit)/
   (Price − Variable cost per unit)
   = ($1,200,000 + $603,571)/($400 − $240)
   = 11,272 (rounded)

Firms today are complex, offering many different products to diverse customer groups. The firms can use cost-volume-profit analysis to see what impact changes in any of these segments have on overall profit. For example, Mayo Clinic halted all nonemergency medical care at its clinics in March 2020 as they prepared for a surge of COVID-19 cases.[11] This meant that the product mix tilted toward largely away from the higher-profit surgeries and procedures and away from the higher-paying private insurance patients toward lower-profit Medicaid patients. Mayo had expected to earn $1 billion in net operating revenue but now expects to lose $900 million in 2020. This comes even after furloughing workers, cutting doctors' pay, and halting new construction projects. The change in product and patient mix resulted in a new business environment for Mayo.

OBJECTIVE

Apply cost-volume-profit analysis in a multiple-product setting.

MULTIPLE-PRODUCT ANALYSIS

Blazin-Boards Company has decided to offer two models of snowboards: a regular snowboard to sell for $400 and a deluxe snowboard, using graphite and designed for championship-caliber boarders, to sell for $600. The Marketing Department is convinced that 10,000 regular snowboards and 2,500 deluxe snowboards can be sold during the coming year. The controller has prepared the following projected income statement based on the sales forecast:

	Regular Snowboards	Deluxe Snowboards	Total
Sales	$4,000,000	$1,500,000	$5,500,000
Less: Variable expenses	2,400,000	750,000	3,150,000
Contribution margin	$1,600,000	$ 750,000	$2,350,000
Less: Direct fixed expenses	600,000	200,000	800,000
Product margin	$1,000,000	$ 550,000	$1,550,000
Less: Common fixed expenses			550,000
Operating income			$1,000,000

Note that the controller has separated direct fixed expenses from common fixed expenses. The **direct fixed expenses** are those fixed costs that can be traced to each segment and would be avoided if the segment did not exist. Examples of direct fixed expenses include salaries of the individual segment's supervisors, any equipment that must be leased or bought just for that segment, and so on. The **common fixed expenses** are the fixed costs that are not traceable to the segments and that would remain even if one of the segments was eliminated. Corporate headquarters costs are common fixed expenses, as are the costs of the factory manager and factory landscaping.

Break-Even Point in Units for the Multiple-Product Setting

The owner of Blazin-Boards is apprehensive about adding a new product line and wants to know how many of each model must be sold to break even. If you were given the responsibility to answer this question, how would you respond?

One possible response is to use the equation we developed earlier in which fixed costs were divided by the contribution margin. However, this equation was developed for a single-product analysis. For two products, there are two unit contribution margins. The regular snowboard

---

11   Sarah Kliff, "Hospitals Knew How to Make Money. Then Coronavirus Happened," *The New York Times* (May 15, 2020, updated May 20, 2020), https://www.nytimes.com/2020/05/15/us/hospitals-revenue-coronavirus.html, accessed November 12, 2020.

has a contribution margin per unit of $160 ($400 − $240), and the deluxe snowboard has one of $300 ($600 − $300). One possible solution is to apply the analysis separately to each product line. It is possible to obtain individual break-even points when income is defined as product margin. Break-even for the regular snowboard is as follows:

$$\text{Regular snowboard break-even units} = \text{Fixed costs}/(\text{Price} - \text{Unit variable cost})$$
$$= \$600{,}000/\$160$$
$$= 3{,}750 \text{ units}$$

Break-even for the deluxe snowboard can be computed as well.

$$\text{Deluxe snowboard break-even units} = \text{Fixed costs}/(\text{Price} - \text{Unit variable cost})$$
$$= \$200{,}000/\$300$$
$$= 667 \text{ units (rounded)}$$

Thus, 3,750 regular snowboards and 667 deluxe snowboards must be sold to achieve a break-even product margin. But a break-even product margin covers only direct fixed costs; the common fixed costs remain to be covered. Selling these numbers of snow-boards would result in a loss equal to the common fixed costs. No break-even point for the firm as a whole has yet been identified. Somehow, the common fixed costs must be factored into the analysis.

Allocating the common fixed costs to each product line before computing a break-even point may resolve this difficulty. However, any allocation of the common fixed costs is arbitrary. Thus, no meaningful break-even volume is readily apparent.

Another possible solution is to convert the multiple-product problem into a single-product problem. If this can be done, then all of the single-product CVP methodology can be applied directly. The key to this conversion is to identify the expected sales mix, in units, of the products being sold.

Sales Mix **Sales mix** is the relative combination of products being sold by a firm. Sales mix can be measured in units sold or in proportion of revenue. For example, if Blazin-Boards plans to sell 10,000 regular snowboards and 2,500 deluxe snowboards, then the sales mix in units is 10,000:2,500. Usually, the sales mix is reduced to the smallest possible whole numbers. Thus, the relative mix 10,000:2,500 can be reduced to 100:25 and further to 4:1. That is, for every four regular snowboards sold, one deluxe snowboard is sold.

Alternatively, the sales mix can be represented by the percent of total revenue contributed by each product. In that case, the regular snowboard revenue is $4,000,000 ($400 × 10,000), and the deluxe snowboard revenue is $1,500,000 ($600 × 2,500). The regular snowboard accounts for 70 percent of total revenue, and the deluxe snowboard accounts for the remaining 30 percent (where the percentages are rounded). It may seem as though the two sales mixes are different. The sales mix in units is 4:1; that is, of every five snowboards sold, 80 percent are regular snowboards and 20 percent are deluxe snowboards. However, the revenue-based sales mix is 70 percent for the regular snowboards. There is really no difference. The sales mix in revenue takes the sales mix in units and weights it by price. Therefore, even though the underlying proportion of snowboards sold remains 4:1, the lower priced regular snowboards are weighted less heavily when price is factored in. In the remaining discussion, we will use the sales mix expressed in units.

A number of different sales mixes can be used to define the break-even volume. For example, a sales mix of 5:1 will define a break-even point of 6,136 regular snowboards and 1,227 deluxe snowboards. The total contribution margin produced by this mix is $1,349,860 [($160 × 6,136) + ($300 × 1,227)]. Similarly, if 3,971 regular snowboards and 2,382 deluxe snowboards are sold (corresponding to a 5:3 sales mix), the total contribution margin is $1,349,960 [($160 × 3,971) + ($300 × 2,382)]. Since total fixed costs are $1,350,000, both sales mixes define break-even points. Fortunately, every sales mix need not be considered. Can Blazin-Boards really expect a sales mix of 5:1 or 5:3? For every two regular snowboards sold, does Blazin-Boards expect to sell a deluxe snowboard? Or for every regular snowboard, can Blazin-Boards really sell one deluxe snowboard?

According to Blazin-Boards's marketing study, a sales mix of 4:1 can be expected. This is the ratio that should be used; the others can be ignored. The sales mix that is expected to prevail should be used for CVP analysis.

Sales Mix and CVP Analysis Defining a particular sales mix allows us to convert a multiple-product problem to a single-product CVP format. Since Blazin-Boards expects to sell four regular snowboards for every deluxe snowboard, it can define the single product it sells as a package containing four regular snowboards and one deluxe snowboard. By defining the product as a package, the multiple-product problem is converted into a single-product one. **Example 16.5** illustrates the use of the package approach to calculating break-even units in the multiproduct firm.

EXAMPLE 16.5

The HOW and WHY of Calculating the Break-Even Number of Units in a Multiproduct Firm

Information:

Blazin-Boards Company plans to sell 10,000 regular snowboards and 2,500 deluxe snowboards in the coming year. Product price and cost information includes:

	Regular Snowboard	Deluxe Snowboard
Price	$ 400	$ 600
Unit variable cost	240	300
Direct fixed cost	600,000	200,000

Common fixed selling and administrative expense totals $550,000.

> **Why:**
> The break-even point in units gives managers a starting point for increasing profitability. If the company is making a loss, the break-even point tells management just what needs to be done to stop losing money. Once the break-even point is passed, the company will earn a profit. By looking at break-even points for each product, managers can see whether one product is being "carried" by other products.

Required:

1. What is the sales mix estimated for next year (calculated to the lowest whole number for each product)?

2. Using the sales mix from Requirement 1, form a package of regular and deluxe snowboards. Taking the package contribution margin to three decimal places, calculate the break-even number of regular snowboards and deluxe snowboards.

3. Prepare a contribution-margin-based income statement for Blazin-Boards Company based on the unit sales calculated in Requirement 2.

4. *What if* Blazin-Boards believed that 10,000 regular snowboards and 5,000 deluxe snowboards could be sold? What is the sales mix, and how many regular and deluxe snowboards must be produced and sold at break-even?

Solution:

1. Sales mix of regular to deluxe snowboards = 10,000:2,500 = 4:1

EXAMPLE 16.5

(*Continued*)

2.

Product	Price	Unit Variable Cost	Unit Contribution Margin	Sales Mix	Unit Contribution Margin × Sales Mix
Regular	$400	$240	$160	4	$640[a]
Deluxe	$600	$300	$300	1	300[b]
Package contribution margin					$940

[a]Found by multiplying the number of units in the package (4) by the unit contribution margin ($160).
[b]Found by multiplying the number of units in the package (1) by the unit contribution margin ($300).

Break-even packages = Total fixed cost/Package contribution margin
= ($600,000 + $200,000 + $550,000)/$940
= 1,436.170 packages

Break-even regular snowboards = (4 × 1,436.170) = 5,745
Break-even deluxe snowboards = (1 × 1,436.170) = 1,436

Note: Packages are not rounded off to a whole number because the number of packages is not an end in itself. The decimal amount may be important when multiplied by the sales mix. The number of snowboards is rounded to whole units, since no one will buy a fraction of a snowboard.

3.

Blazin-Boards
Income Statement
For the Coming Year

	Regular Snowboards	Deluxe Snowboards	Total
Sales	$2,298,000	$861,600	$3,159,600
Less: Variable expenses	1,378,800	430,800	1,809,600
Contribution margin	$ 919,200	$430,800	$1,350,000
Less: Direct fixed expenses	600,000	200,000	800,000
Product margin	$ 319,200	$230,800	$ 550,000
Less: Common fixed expenses			550,000
Operating income			$ 0

4. The sales mix is 10,000:5,000, or 2:1.

Product	Price	Unit Variable Cost	Unit Contribution Margin	Sales Mix	Unit Contribution Margin × Sales Mix
Regular	$400	$240	$160	2	$320[a]
Deluxe	$600	$300	$300	1	300[b]
Package contribution margin					$620

[a]Found by multiplying the number of units in the package (2) by the unit contribution margin ($160).
[b]Found by multiplying the number of units in the package (1) by the unit contribution margin ($300).

EXAMPLE 16.5

(Continued)

Break-even packages = Total fixed cost/Package contribution margin
= ($600,000 + $200,000 + $550,000)/$620
= 2,177.419 packages

Break-even regular snowboards = (2 × 2,177.419) = 4,355 (rounded)
Break-even deluxe snowboards = (1 × 2,177.419) = 2,177 (rounded)

**DATA
ANALYTICS**

For a given sales mix, CVP analysis can be used as if the firm were selling a single product. Actions that change the prices of individual products, however, can affect the sales mix because consumers may buy relatively more or less of the product. Accordingly, pricing decisions may involve a new sales mix and must reflect this possibility. Keep in mind that a new sales mix will affect the units of each product that need to be sold in order to achieve a desired profit target. If the sales mix for the coming period is uncertain, it may be necessary to look at several different mixes. This is sensitivity analysis, and it gives managers insight into the possible outcomes facing the firm.

The complexity of the break-even-point-in-units approach increases dramatically as the number of products increases. Imagine performing this analysis for a firm with several hundred products. This observation seems more overwhelming than it actually is. Data analytics using computers can easily handle a problem with so much data. Furthermore, many firms simplify the problem by analyzing product groups rather than individual products. Another way to handle the increased complexity is to switch from the units-sold to the sales-revenue approach. This approach can accomplish a multiple-product CVP analysis using only the summary data found in an organization's income statement. The computational requirements are much simpler.

Sales-Revenue Approach

To illustrate the break-even point in sales revenue, the same examples will be used. However, the only information needed is the projected income statement for Blazin-Boards Company as a whole.

	Total Snowboards
Sales	$5,500,000
Less: Variable expenses	3,150,000
Contribution margin	$2,350,000
Less: Total fixed expenses	1,350,000
Operating income	$1,000,000

Notice that this income statement corresponds to the total column of the more detailed income statement examined previously. The projected income statement rests on the assumption that 10,000 regular snowboards and 2,500 deluxe snowboards will be sold (a 4:1 sales mix). The break-even point in sales revenue also rests on the expected sales mix. (As with the units-sold approach, a different sales mix will produce different results.)

With the income statement, the usual CVP questions can be addressed. For example, how much sales revenue must be earned to break even? To answer this question, we divide the total fixed costs of $1,350,000 by the contribution margin ratio of 0.4273 ($2,350,000/$5,500,000).

Break-even sales = Fixed costs/Contribution margin ratio
= $1,350,000/0.4273
= $3,159,373

The break-even point in sales revenue implicitly uses the assumed sales mix but avoids the requirement of building a package contribution margin. No knowledge of individual product data is needed. The computational effort is similar to that used in the single-product setting. Moreover, the answer is still expressed in sales revenue. Unlike the break-even point in units, the answer to CVP questions using sales revenue is expressed in a single summary measure. The sales-revenue approach, however, does sacrifice information concerning individual product performance.

GRAPHICAL REPRESENTATION OF CVP RELATIONSHIPS

OBJECTIVE 4

Prepare a profit-volume graph and a cost-volume-profit graph, and explain the meaning of each.

DATA ANALYTICS

An important aspect of data analysis is to portray data visually since many managers are visually oriented. A graphical representation can help managers see the difference between variable cost and revenue and deepens their understanding of CVP relationships. It may also help managers understand quickly what impact an increase or decrease in sales will have on the break-even point. Two basic graphs, the profit-volume graph and the cost-volume-profit graph, are presented here.

The Profit-Volume Graph

A **profit-volume graph** portrays the relationship between profits and sales volume. The profit-volume graph is the graph of the operating income equation [Operating income = (Price × Units) − (Unit variable cost × Units) − Fixed costs]. In this graph, operating income (profit) is the dependent variable, and number of units is the independent variable. Usually, values of the independent variable are measured along the horizontal axis and values of the dependent variable along the vertical axis.

To make this discussion more concrete, a simple set of data will be used. Assume that Gordon Company produces a single product with the following cost and price data:

Total fixed costs	$100
Variable cost per unit	$ 5
Selling price per unit	$ 10

Using these data, operating income can be expressed as follows:

$$\text{Operating income} = (\$10 \times \text{Units}) - (\$5 \times \text{Units}) - \$100$$
$$= (\$5 \times \text{Units}) - \$100$$

This relationship is graphed by plotting units along the horizontal axis and operating income (or loss) along the vertical axis. Two points are needed to graph a linear equation. While any two points will do, the two points often chosen are those that correspond to zero sales volume and zero profits. When units sold are zero, Gordon has an operating loss of $100 (or a profit of −$100). The point corresponding to zero sales volume, therefore, is (0, −$100). In other words, when no sales take place, the company suffers a loss equal to its total fixed costs. When operating income is zero, the units sold are equal to 20. The point corresponding to zero profits (break-even) is (20, $0). These two points, plotted in Exhibit 16.2, define the profit graph shown in the same figure.

The graph in Exhibit 16.2 can be used to assess Gordon's profit (or loss) at any level of sales activity. For example, the profit associated with the sale of 40 units can be read from the graph by (1) drawing a vertical line from the horizontal axis to the profit line and (2) drawing a horizontal line from the profit line to the vertical axis. As we can see, the profit associated with sales of 40 units is $100. The profit-volume graph, while easy to interpret, fails to reveal how costs change as sales volume changes. A more comprehensive graph provides this detail.

Exhibit 16.2

Profit-Volume Graph

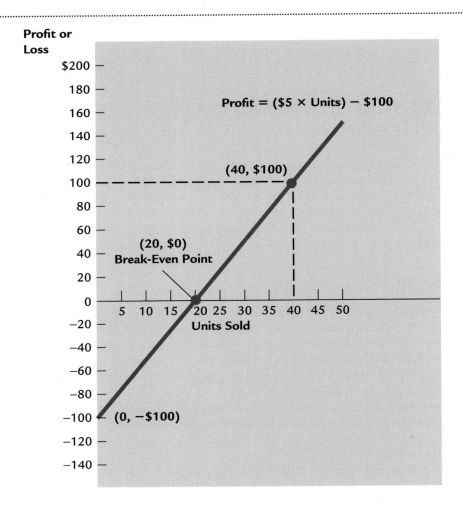

The Cost-Volume-Profit Graph

The **cost-volume-profit graph** depicts the relationships among cost, volume, and profits. To obtain the more detailed relationships, it is necessary to graph two separate lines: the total revenue line and the total cost line. These lines are represented, respectively, by the following two equations:

$$\text{Revenue} = \text{Price} \times \text{Units}$$
$$\text{Total cost} = (\text{Unit variable cost} \times \text{Units}) + \text{Fixed costs}$$

Using the Gordon Company example, the revenue and cost equations are as follows:

$$\text{Revenue} = \$10 \times \text{Units}$$
$$\text{Total cost} = (\$5 \times \text{Units}) + \$100$$

To portray both equations in the same graph, the vertical axis is measured in dollars and the horizontal axis in units sold.

Two points are needed to graph each equation. We will use the same x-coordinates used for the profit-volume graph. For the revenue equation, setting number of units equal to zero results in revenue of $0; setting number of units equal to 20 results in revenue of $200. Therefore, the two points for the revenue equation are (0, $0) and (20, $200). For the cost equation, units sold of zero and units sold equal to 20 produce the points (0, $100) and (20, $200). The graphs of both equations appear in Exhibit 16.3.

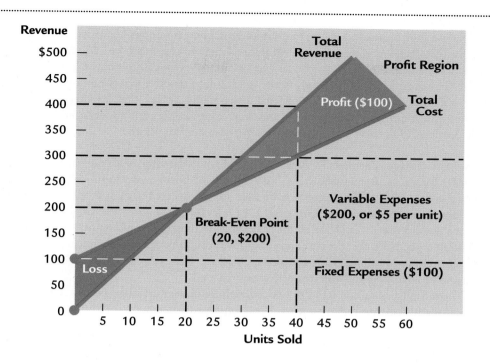

Exhibit 16.3

Cost-Volume-Profit Graph

Notice that the total revenue line begins at the origin and rises with a slope equal to the selling price per unit (a slope of 10). The total cost line intercepts the vertical axis at a point equal to total fixed costs and rises with a slope equal to the variable cost per unit (a slope of 5). When the total revenue line lies below the total cost line, a loss region is defined. Similarly, when the total revenue line lies above the total cost line, a profit region is defined. The point where the total revenue line and the total cost line intersect is the break-even point. To break even, Gordon Company must sell 20 units and thus receive $200 in total revenues.

Now, let's compare the information available from the CVP graph to that available from the profit-volume graph. To do so, consider the sale of 40 units. Recall that the profit-volume graph revealed that selling 40 units produced profit of $100. Examine Exhibit 16.3 again. The CVP graph also shows profits of $100, but it reveals more than that. The CVP graph discloses that total revenues of $400 and total costs of $300 are associated with the sale of 40 units. Furthermore, the total costs can be broken down into fixed costs of $100 and variable costs of $200. The CVP graph provides revenue and cost information not provided by the profit-volume graph. Unlike the profit-volume graph, some computation is needed to determine the profit associated with a given sales volume. Nonetheless, because of the greater information content, managers are likely to find the CVP graph a more useful tool.

Assumptions of Cost-Volume-Profit Analysis

The profit-volume and cost-volume-profit graphs just illustrated rely on some important assumptions. Some of these assumptions are as follows:

1. The analysis assumes a linear revenue function and a linear cost function.
2. The analysis assumes that price, total fixed costs, and unit variable costs can be accurately identified and remain constant over the relevant range.
3. The analysis assumes that what is produced is sold.
4. For multiple-product analysis, the sales mix is assumed to be known.
5. The selling prices and costs are assumed to be known with certainty.

The first assumption, linear cost and revenue functions, deserves additional consideration. Let's take a look at the underlying revenue and total cost functions identified in economics. Exhibit 16.4, Panel A, portrays the curvilinear revenue and cost functions. We see that as quantity sold increases, revenue also increases, but eventually revenue begins to rise less steeply than before. This is explained quite simply by the need to decrease price as many more units are sold. The total cost function is more complicated, rising steeply at first, then leveling off somewhat (as increasing returns to scale develop), and then rising steeply again (as decreasing returns to scale develop). How can we deal with these complicated relationships?

Relevant Range Fortunately, we do not need to consider all possible ranges of production and sales for a firm. Remember that CVP analysis is a short-run decision-making tool. (We know that it is short run in orientation because some costs are fixed.) It is only necessary for us to determine the current operating range, or relevant range, for which the linear cost and revenue relationships are valid. Exhibit 16.4, Panel B, illustrates a relevant range from 5,000 to 15,000 units. Note that the cost and revenue relationships are roughly linear in this range, allowing us to use our linear CVP equations. Of course, if the relevant range changes, different fixed and variable costs and different prices must be used.

The second assumption is linked to the definition of relevant range. Once a relevant range has been identified, then the cost and price relationships are assumed to be known and constant.

Production Equal to Sales The third assumption is that what is produced is sold. There is no change in inventory over the period. The fact that inventory has no impact on break-even analysis makes sense. Break-even analysis is a short-run decision-making technique, so we are looking to cover all costs of a particular period of time. Inventory embodies costs of a previous period and is not considered.

Constant Sales Mix The fourth assumption is a constant sales mix. In single-product analysis, the sales mix is obviously constant—100 percent of sales consists of the one product. Multiple-product break-even analysis requires a constant sales mix. However, it is virtually impossible to predict the sales mix with certainty. Typically, this constraint is handled in practice through sensitivity analysis. By using spreadsheet analysis, the sensitivity of variables to a variety of sales mixes can be readily assessed.

Exhibit 16.4   Cost and Revenue Relationships

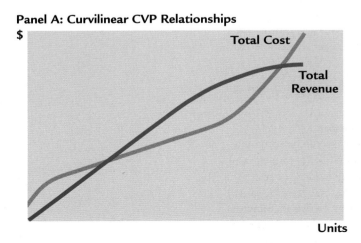

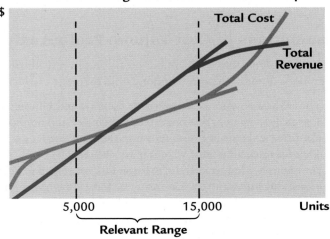

Prices and Costs Known with Certainty Finally, the fifth assumption is that prices and costs are known. Actually, firms seldom know variable costs and fixed costs with certainty. A change in one variable usually affects the value of others. Often, there is a probability distribution to consider. There are formal ways of explicitly building uncertainty into the CVP model. Exploration of these issues is introduced in the next section.

CHANGES IN THE CVP VARIABLES

OBJECTIVE 5

Explain the impact of risk, uncertainty, and changing variables on cost-volume-profit analysis.

DATA ANALYTICS

Because firms operate in a dynamic world, they must be aware of changes in prices, variable costs, and fixed costs. They must also account for the effects of risk and uncertainty. We can use data analytics to take a look at the effects on the break-even point of changes in price, unit variable cost, and fixed costs. We will also look at ways managers can handle risk and uncertainty within the CVP framework.

Let's return to the Blazin-Boards Company example before the deluxe snowboard was introduced (when only the regular snowboard is produced). Suppose that the Sales Department recently conducted a market study that revealed three different alternatives.

Alternative 1: If advertising expenditures increase by $16,500, sales will increase from 10,000 units to 10,100 units.

Alternative 2: A price decrease from $400 per snowboard to $375 per snowboard would increase sales from 10,000 units to 12,000 units.

Alternative 3: Decreasing prices to $375 and increasing advertising expenditures by $16,500 will increase sales from 10,000 units to 15,000 units.

Should Blazin-Boards maintain its current price and advertising policies, or should it select one of the three alternatives described by the marketing study?

Consider the first alternative. What is the effect on profits if advertising costs increase by $16,500 and sales increase by 100 units? This question can be answered just by using the contribution margin per unit. We know that the unit contribution margin is $160. Since units sold increase by 100, the incremental increase in total contribution margin is $16,000 ($160 × 100 units). However, since fixed costs increase by $16,500, profits will actually decrease by $500 ($16,500 − $16,000). Notice that we need to look only at the incremental increase in total contribution margin and fixed expenses to compute the increase in total profits. Exhibit 16.5 summarizes the effects of the first alternative.

For the second alternative, fixed expenses do not increase. Thus, it is possible to answer the question by looking only at the effect on total contribution margin. For the current price of $400, the contribution margin per unit is $160. If 10,000 units are sold, the total contribution margin is $1,600,000 ($160 × 10,000). If the price is dropped to $375, then the contribution margin drops to $135 per unit ($375 − $240). If 12,000 units are sold at the new price, then the new total contribution margin is $1,620,000 ($135 × 12,000). As shown in Exhibit 16.6, dropping the price results in a profit increase of $20,000 ($1,620,000 − $1,600,000).

The third alternative calls for a decrease in the unit selling price and an increase in advertising costs. Like the first alternative, the profit impact can be assessed by looking at the incremental effects on contribution margin and fixed expenses. The incremental profit change can be found by (1) computing the incremental change in total contribution margin, (2) computing the incremental change in fixed expenses, and (3) adding the two results.

The current total contribution margin for 10,000 units sold is $1,600,000. Since the new unit contribution margin is $135, and units sold increase to 12,000, the new total contribution margin is $1,620,000 ($135 × 12,000 units). Thus, the incremental increase in total contribution margin is $20,000 ($1,620,000 − $1,600,000). However, to achieve this incremental increase in contribution margin, an incremental increase of $16,500 in fixed costs is needed. The net effect is an incremental increase in profits of $3,500. The effects of the third alternative are summarized in Exhibit 16.7.

Exhibit 16.5

Summary of the Effects of
Alternative 1

	Before the Increased Advertising	With the Increased Advertising
Units sold	10,000	10,100
Unit contribution margin	× $160	× $160
Total contribution margin	$1,600,000	$1,616,000
Less: Fixed expenses	1,200,000	1,216,500
Profit	$ 400,000	$ 399,500

	Difference in Profit
Change in sales volume	100
Unit contribution margin	× $160
Change in contribution margin	$16,000
Less: Increase in fixed expenses	16,500
Decrease in profit	$ (500)

Exhibit 16.6

Summary of the Effects of
Alternative 2

New contribution margin ($135 × 12,000 units)	$1,620,000
Old contribution margin ($160 × 10,000 units)	1,600,000
Increased contribution margin	$ 20,000

Of the three alternatives identified by the marketing study, both the second and third alternatives promise a benefit. They increase total profits by $20,000 (alternative 2) and $3,500 (alternative 3). Clearly, alternative 2 has a higher profit potential.

These examples are all based on a units-sold approach. However, we could just as easily have applied a sales-revenue approach. The answers would be the same.

Introducing Risk and Uncertainty

An important assumption of CVP analysis is that prices and costs are known with certainty. This is seldom the case. Risk and uncertainty are a part of business decision making and must be considered. Formally, risk differs from uncertainty in that with risk, the probability distributions of the variables are known. With uncertainty, the probability distributions are not known. For our purposes, however, the terms will be used interchangeably.

Managers deal with risk and uncertainty in a variety of ways. First, of course, management must realize the uncertain nature of future prices, costs, and quantities. Next, managers move from consideration of a break-even point to what might be called a break-even band. In other words, given the uncertain nature of the data, perhaps a firm might break even when 1,800 to 2,000 units are sold—instead of the point estimate of 1,900 units. Further, managers may engage in sensitivity or what-if analyses. Here, a computer spreadsheet is helpful, as managers set up the break-even (or targeted profit) relationships and then check to see the impact that varying costs and prices have on quantity sold. Two concepts useful to management are *margin of safety* and *operating leverage*. Both of these may be considered measures of risk. Each requires knowledge of fixed and variable costs.

	Before Changes	With the Increased Advertising and Decreased Price
Units sold	10,000	12,000
Unit contribution margin	× $160	× $135
Total contribution margin	$1,600,000	$1,620,000
Less: Fixed expenses	1,200,000	1,216,500
Profit	$ 400,000	$ 403,500

Exhibit 16.7

Summary of the Effects of Alternative 3

	Difference in Profit
Decrease in contribution margin on 10,000 units	$(250,000)
Increase contribution margin on 2,000 units	270,000
Change in contribution margin	$ 20,000
Less: Increase in fixed expenses	16,500
Increase in profit	$ 3,500

Margin of Safety The **margin of safety** is the units sold or expected to be sold or the revenue earned or expected to be earned above the break-even volume. **Example 16.6** illustrates the margin of safety.

EXAMPLE 16.6

The HOW and WHY of Calculating Margin of Safety

Information:
Blazin-Boards Company plans to sell 10,000 snowboards at $400 each in the coming year. Product costs include:

Direct materials per snowboard	$80
Direct labor per snowboard	$125
Variable overhead per snowboard	$15
Total fixed factory overhead	$800,000

Variable selling expense is a commission of 5 percent of price; fixed selling and administrative expense totals $400,000.

> **Why:**
> Margin of safety is a crude measure of risk. The further above the break-even point, the larger the margin of safety and the further the company is away from break-even and a loss.

Required:

1. Calculate the margin of safety in units for the coming year. (Recall that the break-even point in units was calculated in Example 16.2.)

2. Calculate the break-even sales and the margin of safety in sales for the coming year.

3. *What if* Blazin-Boards Company actually sells 9,800 snowboards in the coming year? Calculate the margin of safety in units and sales revenue.

EXAMPLE 16.6

(Continued)

Solution:

1. Margin of safety = 10,000 units − 7,500 units = 2,500 units

2. Break-even sales = 7,500 units × $400 = $3,000,000
    Margin of safety = (10,000 units × $400) − $3,000,000 = $1,000,000

3. Margin of safety = 9,800 units − 7,500 units = 2,300 units
    Margin of safety = (9,800 units × $400) − $3,000,000 = $920,000

The margin of safety can be viewed as a crude measure of risk. There are always events, unknown when plans are made, that can lower sales below the original expected level. If a firm's margin of safety is large given the expected sales for the coming year, the risk of suffering losses should sales take a downward turn is less than if the margin of safety is small. Managers who face a low margin of safety may wish to consider actions to increase sales or decrease costs.

REAL-WORLD EXAMPLE

For example, **Walt Disney Company** faced lower theme park earnings in the last quarter of 2004 due to the unprecedented number of hurricanes that hit Florida during August. Disney's CFO explained that "near-term local attendance could be impacted as people put their lives together" after the disasters. He also noted that the company would focus on "increasing occupancy at theme park hotels, per capita spending by visitors to the theme parks, and managing costs." The objective is to reach an operating margin of at least 20 percent over the next three to four years.[12] A more robust operating margin at all theme parks would cushion Disney in the event of unforeseen events.

Operating Leverage   In physics, a lever is a simple machine used to multiply force. Basically, the lever magnifies the amount of effort applied to create a greater effect. The larger the load moved by a given amount of effort, the greater the mechanical advantage. In financial terms, operating leverage is concerned with the relative mix of fixed costs and variable costs in an organization. It is sometimes possible to trade off fixed costs for variable costs. As variable costs decrease, the unit contribution margin increases, making the contribution of each unit sold that much greater. In such a case, the effect of fluctuations in sales on profitability increases. Thus, firms that have lowered variable costs by increasing the proportion of fixed costs will benefit with greater increases in profits as sales increase than will firms with a lower proportion of fixed costs. Fixed costs are being used as leverage to increase profits. Unfortunately, it is also true that firms with a higher operating leverage will also experience greater reductions in profits as sales decrease. Therefore, **operating leverage** is the use of fixed costs to extract higher percentage changes in profits as sales activity changes.

The greater the degree of operating leverage, the more that changes in sales activity will affect profits. Because of this phenomenon, the mix of costs that an organization chooses can have a considerable influence on its operating risk and profit level.

The **degree of operating leverage** can be measured for a given level of sales by taking the ratio of total contribution margin to profit, as follows:

$$\text{Degree of operating leverage} = \text{Total contribution margin/Profit}$$

If fixed costs are used to lower variable costs such that contribution margin increases and profit decreases, then the degree of operating leverage increases—signaling an increase in risk. **Example 16.7** illustrates the degree of operating leverage, and the way it can be used to calculate the change in profit given a percentage change in sales.

---

12 Dwight Oestricher, "Disney CFO Staggs Sees Theme Park 1Q Hurt by Storms," *The Wall Street Journal* (September 30, 2004): B1 and B2.

Information:

Sharda Company is planning to add a new product line. To do so, the firm can choose to rely heavily on automation or on labor. Relevant data for a sales level of 10,000 units follow:

	Automated System	Manual System
Sales	$1,000,000	$1,000,000
Variable expenses	500,000	800,000
Contribution margin	$ 500,000	$ 200,000
Less total fixed expenses	375,000	100,000
Operating income	$ 125,000	$ 100,000
Unit selling price	$ 100	$ 100
Unit variable cost	50	80
Unit contribution margin	50	20

> ## EXAMPLE 16.7
>
> **The HOW and WHY of Calculating Degree of Operating Leverage and Percent Change in Profit**

Why:

The automated system has higher fixed costs, lower variable costs, and a higher contribution margin per unit. The higher fixed costs are used to extract more contribution margin from each unit sold, and this system will pay off nicely—if unit sales are high enough. The manual system will be less risky if unit sales are lower. The degree of operating leverage can help a firm determine how much riskier the automated system is.

Required:

1. Compute the degree of operating leverage for each system.

2. Suppose that sales are 40 percent higher than budgeted. By what percentage will operating income increase for each system? What will be the *increase* in operating income for each system?

3. *What if* unit sales are 30 percent lower than budgeted? By what percentage will operating income decrease for each system? What will be the *total operating income* for each system?

Solution:

1. Degree of operating leverage = Contribution margin/Profit
   Automated system degree of operating leverage = $500,000/$125,000 = 4.0
   Manual system degree of operating leverage = $200,000/$100,000 = 2.0

2. Automated system increase in profit percentage = 4.0 × 40% = 160%
   Manual system increase in profit percentage = 2.0 × 40% = 80%
   Automated system increase in profit = 1.6 × $125,000 = $200,000
   Manual system increase in profit = 0.8 × $100,000 = $80,000
   Automated system new profit = $125,000 + $200,000 = $325,000
   Manual system new profit = $100,000 + $80,000 = $180,000

3. Automated system decrease in profit percentage = 4.0 × 30% = 120%
   Manual system decrease in profit percentage = 2.0 × 30% = 60%
   Automated system decrease in profit = 1.2 × $125,000 = $150,000
   Manual system decrease in profit = 0.6 × $100,000 = $60,000
   Automated system new profit (loss) = $125,000 − $150,000 = $(25,000)
   Manual system new profit = $100,000 − $60,000 = $40,000

As Example 16.7 shows, the degree of operating leverage is a valuable piece of information. It can be used to quickly determine the impact of a percentage change in sales on operating income. We see that a 40 percent increase in sales can bring a significant benefit to the firm. The effect, however, is a two-edged sword. As sales decrease, the automated system will also show much higher percentage profit decreases. Moreover, the increased operating leverage is available under the automated system because of the presence of increased fixed costs. The break-even point for the automated system is 7,500 units ($375,000/$50), whereas the break-even point for the manual system is 5,000 units ($100,000/$20). Clearly, at a lower level of sales the manual system is better and at a higher level of sales the automated system is better. What is the sales level at which the manual and the automated systems are equally profitable? We can compute that by setting the operating income equations for each system equal to one another.

$$(\$100 \times \text{units}) - (\$50 \times \text{units}) - \$375,000 = (\$100 \times \text{units}) - (\$80 \times \text{units}) - \$100,000$$
$$(\$50 \times \text{units}) - \$375,000 = (\$20 \times \text{units}) - \$100,000$$
$$\text{Units} = 9,167 \text{ (rounded)}$$

In choosing between the automated and manual systems, the manager must assess the likelihood that sales will exceed 9,167 units. If, after careful study, there is a strong belief that sales will easily exceed this level, the choice is obvious: the automated system. On the other hand, if sales are unlikely to exceed 9,167 units, the manual system is preferable. Exhibit 16.8 summarizes the relative difference between the manual and automated systems in terms of some of the CVP concepts.

Sensitivity Analysis and CVP

The pervasiveness of personal computers and spreadsheets has made cost analysis within reach of most managers. An important tool is **sensitivity analysis**, a what-if technique that examines the impact of changes in underlying assumptions on an answer. It is relatively simple to input data on prices, variable costs, fixed costs, and sales mix and set up formulas to calculate break-even points and expected profits. Then, the data can be varied as desired to see what impact changes have on the expected profit.

In Example 16.7, a company analyzed the impact on profit of using an automated versus a manual system. The computations were essentially done by hand, and too much variation was cumbersome. Using the power of a computer, it would be an easy matter to change the sales price in $1 increments between $75 and $125, with related assumptions about quantity sold. At the same time, variable and fixed costs could be adjusted. For example, suppose that the automated system has fixed costs of $375,000, but that those costs could easily range up to twice as much in the first year and come back down in the second and third years as bugs are worked out of the system and workers learn to use it. Again, the spreadsheet can effortlessly handle the many computations.

Exhibit 16.8

Differences Between Manual and Automated Systems

	Manual System	Automated System
Price	Same	Same
Variable costs	Relatively higher	Relatively lower
Fixed costs	Relatively lower	Relatively higher
Contribution margin	Relatively lower	Relatively higher
Break-even point	Relatively lower	Relatively higher
Margin of safety	Relatively higher	Relatively lower
Degree of operating leverage	Relatively lower	Relatively higher
Downside risk	Relatively lower	Relatively higher
Upside potential	Relatively lower	Relatively higher

We must note that the spreadsheet, while wonderful for cranking out numerical answers, cannot do the most difficult job in CVP analysis. That job is determining the data to be entered in the first place. The accountant must be familiar with the cost and price distributions of the firm, as well as with the impact of changing economic conditions on these variables. The fact that variables are seldom known with certainty is no excuse for ignoring the impact of uncertainty on CVP analysis. Fortunately, sensitivity analysis can also give managers a feel for the degree to which a poorly forecast variable will affect an answer. That is also an advantage.

ETHICS Finally, it is important to note that the CVP results are only one input into business decisions. There are many other factors that may bear on decisions to choose one type of process over another, for example, or whether to delete certain costs. Businesses and nonprofit entities often face trade-offs involving safety. Ethical concerns also have an important place in CVP analysis. One possibility is that the cost of potential problems can be estimated and included in the CVP results. Often, however, the costs and probabilities are not known with sufficient certainty. In that case, these factors are included as qualitative factors in the ultimate decision-making process. Chapter 17, on short-run decision making, covers this topic in more detail. •

Using Big Data in Telecommunications

Traditional data warehouses are systems for gathering data and making them available for analyses that are generally produced internally and are well known and structured. Data are uploaded from internal systems like sales and production. They are arranged in formats usable by operations for well-specified reporting. For example, a manufacturing company may combine data on production and cost with sales data to determine budgeted amounts for the coming year.

Big data, on the other hand, includes data from both internal and external sources. For example, a telecommunications firm wanted to know the reasons for poor customer experience.[13] Using just internal databases, gathering and analyzing the information might have taken up to two years. The projects often had good returns on investment (ROI) and did break even by the end of the two-year period. However, two years is a long time to wait for results. Big data analytics helped the firm gather data from numerous internal and external sources and understand results in much less time, breaking even in three to four months. What is the difference between the two experiences? No doubt it is the use of external data, perhaps using social media to gather real-time information on customer experience from actual customers.

Telecom companies can use big data analytics in other ways to improve the customer experience.[14] Telecommunications companies can relate call center information, charging data records, and other customer relationship management (CRM) data to determine hot button issues, such as dropped calls and slow connections, to see which problems are most significant for customers. They can then prioritize those for further investment in infrastructure.

Big data analysis can also help reduce unnecessary in-person appointments and service calls. With data analytics, companies generate "what-if" scenarios and geographic maps of network traffic to see where issues may arise and allocate resources appropriately.

Telecoms can use data on high-definition television consumption and bandwidth usage to plan for more infrastructure. They search for peak usage times and dates and cluster those to identify usage patterns as they work to forecast future demand and need for investment.

The bottom line is that the use of big data by telecom companies is helping to improve the customer experience and network reliability.

 REAL-WORLD EXAMPLE

---

13 David Floyer, "Enterprise Big-Data," December 22, 2015, http://Wikibon.Org/Wiki/V/Enterprise_Big-Data, accessed July 12, 2016.

14 Vianney Martinez Alcantara, "Reader Forum: 3 Ways Telcos Use Big Data to Amplify Customer Experience," *Rcwireless.com* (February 22, 2016), http://www.rcrwireless.com/20160222/opinion/reader-forum-3-ways-telcos-use-big-data-to-amplify-customer-experience-tag10, accessed July 12, 2016.

OBJECTIVE

Discuss the impact of non-unit cost drivers on cost-volume-profit analysis.

CVP ANALYSIS AND NON-UNIT COST DRIVERS

Conventional CVP analysis assumes that all costs of the firm can be divided into two categories: those that vary with sales volume (variable costs) and those that do not (fixed costs). Furthermore, costs are assumed to be a linear function of sales volume. Frequently, however, there are costs that vary with non-unit cost drivers. An activity-based costing (ABC) system, in which costs are divided into unit- and non-unit-based categories, is a good example of this. Some costs, such as setting up production equipment, vary with the number of batches; other costs, such as purchasing and receiving costs, may vary with the number of different products. In conventional CVP, those non-unit variable costs are assumed to be fixed. However, CVP can be modified to take account of this richer set of variable costs. This type of modification can make CVP even more useful, since it provides more accurate insights concerning cost behavior. These insights produce better decisions.

To illustrate, assume that a company's costs can be explained by three variables: a unit-level cost driver, units sold; a batch-level cost driver, number of setups; and a product-level cost driver, engineering hours. The cost equation can then be expressed as follows:

$$\text{Total cost} = \text{Fixed costs} + (\text{Unit variable cost} \times \text{Number of units}) + (\text{Setup cost} \times \text{Number of setups}) + (\text{Engineering cost} \times \text{Number of engineering hours})$$

Operating income, as before, is total revenue minus total cost. This is expressed as follows:

$$\text{Operating income} = \text{Total revenue} - [\text{Fixed costs} + (\text{Unit variable cost} \times \text{Number of units}) + (\text{Setup cost} \times \text{Number of setups}) + (\text{Engineering cost} \times \text{Number of engineering hours})]$$

Let's use the contribution margin approach to calculate the break-even point in units. At break-even, operating income is zero, and the number of units that must be sold to achieve break-even is as follows:

$$\text{Break-even units} = [\text{Fixed costs} + (\text{Setup cost} \times \text{Number of setups}) + (\text{Engineering cost} \times \text{Number of engineering hours})]/(\text{Price} - \text{Unit variable cost})$$

A comparison of the ABC break-even point with the conventional break-even point reveals two significant differences. First, the fixed costs differ. Some costs previously identified as being fixed may actually vary with non-unit cost drivers, in this case setups and engineering hours. Second, the numerator of the ABC break-even equation has two non-unit-variable cost terms: one for batch-related activities and one for product-sustaining activities.

Example Comparing Conventional and ABC Analysis

To make the previous discussion more concrete, a comparison of conventional cost-volume-profit analysis with activity-based costing is useful. Let's assume that a company wants to compute the units that must be sold to earn a before-tax profit of $20,000. The analysis is based on the following data:

| | **Data About Variables** | |
Cost Driver	Unit Variable Cost	Level of Cost Driver
Units sold	$ 10	—
Setups	1,000	20
Engineering hours	30	1,000

Other data:

Total fixed costs (conventional)	$100,000
Total fixed costs (ABC)	50,000
Unit selling price	20

The units that must be sold to earn a before-tax profit of $20,000 are computed as follows:

Units = (Targeted income + Fixed costs)/(Price − Unit variable cost)
= ($20,000 + $100,000)/($20 − $10)
= $120,000/$10
= 12,000

Using the ABC equation, the units that must be sold to earn an operating income of $20,000 are computed as follows:

Units = [Targeted income + Fixed costs + (Setup cost × Setups)
+ (Engineering rate × Engineering hours)]/(Price − Unit variable cost)
= ($20,000 + $50,000 + $20,000 + $30,000)/($20 − $10)
= $120,000/$10
= 12,000

The number of units that must be sold is identical under both approaches. The reason is simple. The total fixed cost pool under conventional costing consists of non-unit-based variable costs plus costs that are fixed regardless of the cost driver. ABC breaks out the non-unit-based variable costs. These costs are associated with certain levels of each cost driver. For the batch-level cost driver, the level is 20 setups; for the product-level variable, the level is 1,000 engineering hours. As long as the levels of activity for the non-unit-based cost drivers remain the same, then the results for the conventional and ABC computations will also be the same. But these levels can change, and because of this, the information provided by the two approaches can be significantly different. The ABC equation for CVP analysis is a richer representation of the underlying cost behavior and can provide important strategic insights. To see this, let's use the same data provided previously and look at a different application.

Strategic Implications: Conventional CVP Analysis Versus ABC Analysis

Suppose that after the conventional CVP analysis, marketing indicates that only 10,000 units can be sold, not the 12,000 anticipated earlier. The president of the company directs the product design engineers to find a way to reduce the cost of making the product. The engineers also have been told that the conventional cost equation, with fixed costs of $100,000 and a unit variable cost of $10, holds. The variable cost of $10 per unit consists of the following: direct labor, $4; direct materials, $5; and variable overhead, $1. To comply with the request to reduce the break-even point, engineering produces a new design that requires less labor, thereby reducing the direct labor cost by $2 per unit. The design would not affect direct materials or variable overhead. The new variable cost is $8 per unit, and the break-even point is calculated as follows:

Units = Fixed costs/(Price − Unit variable cost)
= $100,000/($20 − $8)
= 8,333

The projected income if 10,000 units are sold is computed as follows:

Sales ($20 × 10,000)	$200,000
Less: Variable expenses ($8 × 10,000)	80,000
Contribution margin	$120,000
Less: Fixed expenses	100,000
Operating income	$ 20,000

Excited, the president approves the new design. A year later, the president discovers that the expected increase in income did not materialize. In fact, there was a loss. Why? The answer is provided by an ABC approach to CVP analysis.

The original ABC cost relationship for the example is as follows:

Total cost = $50,000 + ($10 × Units) + ($1,000 × Setups) + ($30 × Engineering hours)

Suppose that the new design requires a more complex setup, increasing the cost per setup from $1,000 to $1,600. Also, suppose that the new design, because of increased technical content, requires a 40 percent increase in engineering support (from 1,000 hours to 1,400 hours). The new cost equation, including the reduction in unit-level variable costs, is as follows:

Total cost = $50,000 + ($8 × Units) + ($1,600 × Setups) + ($30 × Engineering hours)

The break-even point, setting operating income equal to zero and using the ABC equation, is calculated as follows (assume that 20 setups are still performed):

$$\text{Units} = [\$50,000 + (\$1,600 \times 20) + (\$30 \times 1,400)]/(\$20 - \$8)$$
$$= \$124,000/\$12$$
$$= 10,333$$

And the income for 10,000 units is (recall that a maximum of 10,000 can be sold) as follows:

Sales ($20 × 10,000)		$200,000
Less: Unit-based variable expenses ($8 × 10,000)		80,000
Contribution margin		$120,000
Less non-unit-based variable expenses:		
Setups ($1,600 × 20)	$32,000	
Engineering support ($30 × 1,400)	42,000	74,000
Traceable margin		$ 46,000
Less: Fixed expenses		50,000
Operating income (loss)		$ (4,000)

How could the engineers have been off by so much? Didn't they know that the new design would increase setup cost and engineering support? Yes and no. They were probably aware of the increases in these two variables, but the conventional cost equation diverted attention from figuring just how much impact changes in those variables would have on units needed to break even. The information conveyed to the engineers by the conventional equation gave the impression that any reduction in labor cost—not affecting direct materials or variable overhead—would reduce total costs, since changes in the level of labor activity would not affect the fixed costs. The ABC equation, however, indicates that a reduction in labor input that adversely affects setup activity or engineering support might be undesirable. By providing more insight, better design decisions can be made. Providing ABC cost information to the design engineers would probably have led them down a different—and better—path for the company.

CVP Analysis and JIT

If a firm has adopted JIT, the variable cost per unit sold is reduced, and fixed costs are increased. Direct labor, for example, is now viewed as fixed instead of variable. Direct materials, on the other hand, is still a unit-based variable cost. In fact, the emphasis on total quality and long-term purchasing makes the assumption even more true that direct materials cost is strictly proportional to units produced (because waste, scrap, and quantity discounts are eliminated). Other unit-based variable costs such as power and sales commissions also persist. Additionally, the batch-level variable is gone (in JIT, the batch is one unit). Thus, the cost equation for JIT can be expressed as follows:

$$\text{Total cost} = \text{Fixed costs} + (\text{Unit variable cost} \times \text{Units})$$
$$+ (\text{Engineering cost} \times \text{Number of engineering hours})$$

Since its application is a special case of the ABC equation, no example will be given.

CVP Analysis, Multiple Drivers, and Nonprofit Entities

Clearly, cost-volume-profit analysis is helpful for manufacturing and service firms. It is also useful for not-for-profit entities. In the case of a nonprofit organization, there may be a variety of ways of gaining revenue and a variety of programs that generate costs. As a result, the straightforward application of cost-volume-profit equations may not be possible. Then, the managers will need to become aware of the different types of costs, the different drivers, and the underlying economic conditions that affect them.

For example, the **United States Postal Service (USPS)** is a semi-independent federal agency required by law to be "revenue neutral," that is, to break even. However, for the past few years, the USPS has been losing money. In an effort to raise additional revenue and to bring costs under control, the USPS has considered a number of actions, including selling some of its mail distribution centers, delivering mail five days per week rather than six, and closing up to 10 percent of its 32,000 post offices. Some of these actions relate to the reduction of fixed costs, such as the closing of numerous small post offices and selling up to 252 of its 487 mail distribution centers. Other actions aim to reduce variable costs, such as cutting back mail delivery from six to five days per week. Finally, the agency is looking for ways to increase revenue by encouraging more businesses to send bulk mailings. The difficulty with that is the complex mix of mail products and the virtual certainty that raising prices will result in decreased quantity.[15]

Knowing the cost structure makes it easier for the postal service to see just where cost cuts are possible and where revenue increases must be found. In complex cases like this, it might be best to use a spreadsheet to calculate costs and revenues under various scenarios.

SUMMARY OF LEARNING OBJECTIVES

LO1. Determine the number of units and amount of sales revenue needed to break even and to earn a target profit.
- At break-even, total costs (variable and fixed) equal total sales revenue.
- Break-even units equal total fixed costs divided by the contribution margin (price minus variable cost per unit).
- Break-even revenue equals total fixed costs divided by the contribution margin ratio.
- To earn a target (desired) profit, total costs (variable and fixed) plus the amount of target profit must equal total sales revenue.
- Units to earn target profit equal total fixed costs plus target profit divided by the contribution margin.
- Sales revenue to earn target profit equals total fixed costs plus target profit divided by the contribution margin ratio.

LO2. Determine the number of units and sales revenue needed to earn an after-tax target profit.
- Desired after-tax profit must be converted into before-tax profit to calculate units or revenue needed.
- To find the operating income implied by a certain after-tax profit, divide the after-tax profit by 1 minus the tax rate.
- Apply the break-even equations as before to the newly calculated before-tax profit target.

15 Jennifer Levitz, "Post Office's Rescue Plan: Junk Mail," *The Wall Street Journal* (October 6, 2011): A1 and A2.

LO3. Apply cost-volume-profit analysis in a multiple-product setting.
- Multiple-product analysis requires the expected sales mix.
- Break-even units for each product will change as the sales mix changes.
- Increased sales of high contribution margin products decrease the break-even point.
- Increased sales of low contribution margin products increase the break-even point.

LO4. Prepare a profit-volume graph and a cost-volume-profit graph, and explain the meaning of each.
- CVP assumes linear revenue and cost functions, no finished goods ending inventories, constant sales mix, and that selling prices and fixed and variable costs are known with certainty.
- Profit-volume graphs plot the relationship between profit (operating income) and units sold. Break-even units are shown where the profit line crosses the horizontal axis.
- CVP graphs plot a line for total costs and a line for total sales revenue. The intersection of these two lines is the break-even point in units.

LO5. Explain the impact of risk, uncertainty, and changing variables on cost-volume-profit analysis.
- Uncertainty regarding costs, prices, and sales mix affect the break-even point.
- Sensitivity analysis allows managers to vary costs, prices, and sales mix to show various possible break-even points.
- Margin of safety shows how far the company's actual sales and/or units are above or below the break-even point.
- Operating leverage is the use of fixed costs to increase the percentage changes in profits as sales activity changes.

LO6. Discuss the impact of non-unit cost drivers on cost-volume-profit analysis.
- Under ABC, cost drivers are separated into unit-based and non-unit-based drivers.
- Variable rates for the non-unit-based drivers are multiplied by the estimated level of the drivers and added to total fixed costs.
- The standard CVP models still hold under ABC.

SUMMARY OF IMPORTANT EQUATIONS

The subject of cost-volume-profit analysis naturally lends itself to the use of numerous equations. Some of the more common equations used in this chapter are summarized in Exhibit 16.9.

Exhibit 16.9

Summary of Important Equations

1. Sales revenue = Price × Units sold
2. Operating income = (Price × Units) − (Unit variable cost × Units) − Fixed cost
3. Break-even point in units = Fixed cost/(Price − Unit variable cost)
4. Contribution margin ratio = Contribution margin/Sales
   or   = (Price − Unit variable cost)/Price
5. Variable cost ratio = Total variable cost/Sales
   or   = Unit variable cost/Price
6. Break-even point in sales revenue = Fixed cost/Contribution margin ratio
   or   = Fixed cost/(1 − Variable cost ratio)
7. Margin of safety = Sales − Break-even sales
   or   = Units sold − Break-even units
8. Degree of operating leverage = Total contribution margin/Operating income
9. Percentage change in operating income = Degree of operating leverage × Percent change in sales

EXAMPLE 16.1	The HOW and WHY of Basic Cost Calculations and the Contribution-Margin-Based Income Statement, page 816
EXAMPLE 16.2	The HOW and WHY of Calculating the Units Needed to Break Even and to Achieve a Target Profit, page 819
EXAMPLE 16.3	The HOW and WHY of Calculating Revenue for Break-Even and for a Target Profit, page 822
EXAMPLE 16.4	The HOW and WHY of Calculating the Number of Units to Generate an After-Tax Target Profit, page 824
EXAMPLE 16.5	The HOW and WHY of Calculating the Break-Even Number of Units in a Multiproduct Firm, page 828
EXAMPLE 16.6	The HOW and WHY of Calculating Margin of Safety, page 837
EXAMPLE 16.7	The HOW and WHY of Calculating Degree of Operating Leverage and Percent Change in Profit, page 839

KEY TERMS

Break-even point, 815

Common fixed expenses, 826

Contribution margin, 820

Contribution margin ratio, 821

Cost-volume-profit graph, 832

Degree of operating leverage, 838

Direct fixed expenses, 826

Margin of safety, 837

Net income, 816

Operating leverage, 838

Profit-volume graph, 831

Sales mix, 827

Sales-revenue approach, 822

Sensitivity analysis, 840

Variable cost ratio, 821

BRIEF EXERCISES

Brief Exercise 16-1 Variable Costs, Contribution Margin, Contribution Margin Ratio

OBJECTIVE ◀ 1
Example 16.1

Super-Tees Company plans to sell 12,000 T-shirts at $16 each in the coming year. Product costs include:

Direct materials per T-shirt	$5.75
Direct labor per T-shirt	$1.25
Variable overhead per T-shirt	$0.60
Total fixed factory overhead	$43,000

Variable selling expense is the redemption of a coupon, which averages $0.80 per T-shirt; fixed selling and administrative expenses total $19,000.

Required:

1. Calculate the:
   a. Variable product cost per unit
   b. Total variable cost per unit
   c. Contribution margin per unit
   d. Contribution margin ratio (rounded to four significant digits)
   e. Total fixed expense for the year
2. Prepare a contribution-margin-based income statement for Super-Tees Company for the coming year.
3. *What if* the per unit selling expense increased from $0.80 to $1.75? Calculate the new values for the following:
   a. Variable product cost per unit
   b. Total variable cost per unit
   c. Contribution margin per unit
   d. Contribution margin ratio (rounded to four significant digits)
   e. Total fixed expense for the year

OBJECTIVE 1
Example 16.2

Brief Exercise 16-2 Break-Even Units: Units for Target Profit

Jay-Zee Company makes an in-car navigation system. Next year, Jay-Zee plans to sell 16,000 units at a price of $320 each. Product costs include:

Direct materials	$68
Direct labor	$40
Variable overhead	$12
Total fixed factory overhead	$500,000

Variable selling expense is a commission of 5 percent of price; fixed selling and administrative expenses total $116,400.

Required:

1. Calculate the sales commission per unit sold. Calculate the contribution margin per unit.
2. How many units must Jay-Zee Company sell to break even? Prepare an income statement for the calculated number of units.
3. Calculate the number of units Jay-Zee Company must sell to achieve target operating income (profit) of $333,408.
4. *What if* the Jay-Zee Company wanted to achieve a target operating income of $322,000? Would the number of units needed increase or decrease compared to your answer in Requirement 3? Compute the number of units needed for the new target operating income.

OBJECTIVE 1
Example 16.3

Brief Exercise 16-3 Break-Even Sales: Sales for Target Profit

Health-Temp Company is a placement agency for temporary nurses. It serves hospitals and clinics throughout the metropolitan area. Health-Temp Company believes it will place temporary nurses for a total of 23,500 hours next year. Health-Temp charges the hospitals and clinics $90 per hour and has variable costs of $75.60 per hour (this includes the payment to the nurse). Total fixed costs equal $321,000.

Required:

1. Calculate the contribution margin per unit and the contribution margin ratio.
2. Calculate the sales revenue needed to break even.
3. Calculate the sales revenue needed to achieve a target profit of $100,000.
4. *What if* Health-Temp had target operating income (profit) of $110,000? Would sales revenue be larger or smaller than the one calculated in Requirement 3? Why? By how much?

Brief Exercise 16-4 After-Tax Profit Targets

OBJECTIVE 2
Example 16.4

Olivian Company wants to earn $420,000 in net (after-tax) income next year. Its product is priced at $275 per unit. Product costs include:

Direct materials	$90
Direct labor	$65
Variable overhead	$16
Total fixed factory overhead	$440,000

Variable selling expense is $14 per unit; fixed selling and administrative expense totals $290,000. Olivian has a tax rate of 40 percent.

Required:

1. Calculate the before-tax profit needed to achieve an after-tax target of $420,000.
2. Calculate the number of units that will yield operating income calculated in Requirement 1 above. (Round to the nearest unit.)
3. Prepare an income statement for Olivian Company for the coming year based on the number of units computed in Requirement 2.
4. *What if* Olivian had a 35 percent tax rate? Would the units sold to reach a $420,000 target net income be higher or lower than the units calculated in Requirement 3? Calculate the number of units needed at the new tax rate. (Round dollar amounts to the nearest dollar and unit amounts to the nearest unit.)

Brief Exercise 16-5 Multiple-Product Break-Even and Target Profit

OBJECTIVE 1 3
Example 16.5

Vandenberg, Inc., produces and sells two products: a ceiling fan and a table fan. Vandenberg plans to sell 30,000 ceiling fans and 70,000 table fans in the coming year. Product price and cost information includes:

	Ceiling Fan	Table Fan
Price	$60	$15
Unit variable cost	$12	$7
Direct fixed cost	$23,600	$45,000

Common fixed selling and administrative expenses total $85,000.

Required:

1. What is the sales mix estimated for next year (calculated to the lowest whole number for each product)?
2. Using the sales mix from Requirement 1, form a package of ceiling fans and table fans. How many ceiling fans and table fans are sold at break-even?
3. Prepare a contribution-margin-based income statement for Vandenberg, Inc., based on the unit sales calculated in Requirement 2.
4. *What if* Vandenberg, Inc., wanted to earn operating income equal to $14,400? Calculate the number of ceiling fans and table fans that must be sold to earn this level of operating income. (*Hint:* Remember to form a package of ceiling fans and table fans based on the sales mix and to first calculate the number of packages to earn an operating income of $14,400.)

Brief Exercise 16-6 Break-Even Units and Sales Revenue: Margin of Safety

OBJECTIVE 1 5
Example 16.6

Dupli-Pro Copy Shop provides photocopying service. Next year, Dupli-Pro estimates it will copy 2,800,000 pages at a price of $0.08 each in the coming year. Product costs include:

Direct materials	$0.015
Direct labor	$0.004
Variable overhead	$0.001
Total fixed overhead	$80,000

There is no variable selling expense; fixed selling and administrative expenses total $46,000.

Required:

1. Calculate the break-even point in units.
2. Calculate the break-even point in sales revenue.
3. Calculate the margin of safety in units for the coming year.
4. Calculate the margin of safety in sales revenue for the coming year.
5. What if the total selling and administrative expenses are reduced to $38,800? Recalculate:
   a.   Break-even point in units
   b.   Break-even point in sales revenue
   c.   Margin of safety in units for the coming year
   d.   Margin of safety in sales revenue for the coming year

OBJECTIVE ▐1▐ ▐5▐
Example 16.7

Brief Exercise 16-7 Degree of Operating Leverage, Percent Change in Profit

Ringsmith Company is considering two different processes to make its product—process 1 and process 2. Process 1 requires Ringsmith to manufacture subcomponents of the product in-house. As a result, materials are less expensive, but fixed overhead is higher. Process 2 involves purchasing all subcomponents from outside suppliers. The direct materials costs are higher, but fixed factory overhead is considerably lower. Relevant data for a sales level of 30,000 units follow:

	Process 1	Process 2
Sales	$8,010,000	$8,010,000
Variable expenses	2,700,000	4,200,000
Contribution margin	$5,310,000	$3,810,000
Less total fixed expenses	3,650,625	1,428,750
Operating income	$1,659,375	$2,381,250
Unit selling price	$267	$267
Unit variable cost	$90	$140
Unit contribution margin	$177	$127

Required:

1. Compute the degree of operating leverage for each process.
2. Suppose that sales are 20 percent higher than budgeted. By what percentage will operating income increase for each process? What will be the *increase* in operating income for each system? What will be the *total operating income* for each process?
3. *What if* unit sales are 10 percent lower than budgeted? By what percentage will operating income decrease for each process? What will be the *total operating income* for each process?

EXERCISES

OBJECTIVE ▐1▐ ▐5▐

SHOW ME HOW   **EXCEL**

Exercise 16-8 Contribution Margin, Break-Even Units, Contribution Margin Income Statement, Margin of Safety

Cheetah Company manufactures custom-designed skins (covers) for iPods® and other portable electronic devices. Variable costs are $9.20 per custom skin, the price is $19, and fixed costs are $104,860.

Required:

1. What is the contribution margin for one custom skin?
2. How many custom skins must Cheetah Company sell to break even?
3. If Cheetah Company sells 13,000 custom skins, what is the operating income?
4. Calculate the margin of safety in units and in sales revenue if 13,000 custom skins are sold.

Exercise 16-9 Break-Even in Units

OBJECTIVE ◀ 1

SHOW ME
HOW

Gelbart Company manufactures gas grills. Fixed costs amount to $16,335,000 per year. Variable costs per gas grill are $225, and the average price per gas grill is $600.

Required:

1. How many gas grills must Gelbart Company sell to break even?
2. If Gelbart Company sells 46,775 gas grills in a year, what is the operating income?
3. If Gelbart Company's variable costs increase to $240 per grill while the price and fixed costs remain unchanged, what is the new break-even point?

Exercise 16-10 Contribution Margin Ratio, Break-Even Sales Revenue, Sales Revenue for Target Profit

OBJECTIVE ◀ 1

SHOW ME
HOW

Schylar Pharmaceuticals, Inc., plans to sell 130,000 units of antibiotic at an average price of $22 each in the coming year. Total variable costs equal $1,086,800. Total fixed costs equal $8,000,000. (Round all ratios to four significant digits, and round all dollar amounts to the nearest dollar.)

Required:

1. What is the contribution margin per unit? What is the contribution margin ratio?
2. Calculate the sales revenue needed to break even.
3. Calculate the sales revenue needed to achieve a target profit of $245,000.
4. *What if* the average price per unit increased to $23.50? Recalculate:
   a. Contribution margin per unit
   b. Contribution margin ratio (rounded to four decimal places)
   c. Sales revenue needed to break even
   d. Sales revenue needed to achieve a target profit of $245,000

Exercise 16-11 Break-Even in Units, Target Income, New Unit Variable Cost, Degree of Operating Leverage, Percent Change in Operating Income

OBJECTIVE ◀ 1 5

SHOW ME
HOW

Reagan, Inc., has developed a chew-proof dog bed—the Tuff-Pup. Fixed costs are $204,400 per year. The average price for the Tuff-Pup is $36, and the average variable cost is $22 per unit. Currently, Reagan produces and sells 20,000 Tuff-Pups annually.

Required:

1. How many Tuff-Pups must be sold to break even?
2. If Reagan wants to earn $95,900 in profit, how many Tuff-Pups must be sold? Prepare a variable-costing income statement to verify your answer.
3. Suppose that Reagan would like to lower the break-even units to 12,000. The company does not believe that the price or fixed cost can be changed. Calculate the new unit variable cost that would result in break-even units of 12,000. (Round to the nearest cent.)
4. What is Reagan's current contribution margin and operating income? Calculate the degree of operating leverage (round your answer to four decimal places). If sales increased by 10 percent next year, what would the percent change in operating income be? What would the new total operating income for next year be?
5. Reagan, Inc., has used data on the Tuff-Pup to answer a number of different questions. Identify the data analytic type (descriptive, diagnostic, predictive, or prescriptive) that Reagan used to answer these questions. (See Exhibits 2.5 and 2.6, pp. 37, 40, for a review of data analytic types. *Note:* More than one analytic type might apply.)

DATA
ANALYTICS

Exercise 16-12 Break-Even for a Service Firm

Jonah Graham owns and operates The Green Thumb Company (GTC), which provides live plants and flower arrangements to professional offices. Jonah has fixed costs of $3,240 per month for office/greenhouse rent, advertising, and a delivery van. Variable costs for the plants, fertilizer, pots, and other supplies average $24 per job. GTC charges $60 per month for the average job.

Required:

1. How many jobs must GTC average each month to break even?
2. What is the operating income for GTC in a month with 88 jobs? With 95 jobs?
3. Jonah faces a tax rate equal to 25 percent. How many jobs must Jonah have per month to earn an after-tax income of $1,200? (Round your answer to whole units.)
4. Suppose that Jonah's fixed costs increase to $3,400 per month and he decides to increase the price to $75 per job. What is the new break-even point in number of jobs per month? (Round your answer to the nearest whole number of jobs.)

Exercise 16-13 Break-Even in Sales Revenue

Big Red Motors, Inc., employs 15 sales personnel to market its line of luxury automobiles. The average car sells for $75,000, and a 6 percent commission is paid to the salesperson. Big Red Motors is considering a change to the commission arrangement where the company would pay each salesperson a salary of $1,600 per month plus a commission of 2 percent of the sales made by that salesperson. What is the amount of total monthly car sales at which Big Red Motors would be indifferent as to which plan to select? *(CMA adapted)*

Exercise 16-14 Break-Even in Sales Revenue, Margin of Safety

Sports-Reps, Inc., represents professional athletes and movie and television stars. The agency had revenue of $12,345,000 last year, with total variable costs of $5,678,700 and fixed costs of $2,192,400.

Required:

1. What is the contribution margin ratio for Sports-Reps based on last year's data? What is the break-even point in sales revenue?
2. What was the margin of safety for Sports-Reps last year?
3. One of Sports-Reps's agents proposed that the firm begin cultivating high school sports stars around the nation. This proposal is expected to increase revenue by $230,000 per year, with increased fixed costs of $122,500. Is this proposal a good idea? Explain.

Exercise 16-15 Break-Even in Units, After-Tax Target Income, CVP Assumptions

Campbell Company manufactures and sells adjustable canopies that attach to motor homes and trailers. The market covers both new unit purchases as well as replacement canopies. Campbell developed its business plan for the year based on the assumption that canopies would sell at a price of $400 each. The variable costs for each canopy were projected at $200, and the annual fixed costs were budgeted at $120,000. Campbell's after-tax profit objective was $225,000; the company's effective tax rate is 40 percent.

While Campbell's sales usually rise during the second quarter, the May financial statements reported that sales were not meeting expectations. For the first five months of the year, only 350 units had been sold at the established price, with variable costs as planned, and it was clear that the after-tax profit projection for the year would not be reached unless some actions were taken. Campbell's president assigned a management committee to analyze the situation and develop several alternative courses of action. The following mutually exclusive alternatives, labeled A, B, and C, were presented to the president:

A. Lower the variable costs per unit by $25 through the use of less expensive materials and slightly modified manufacturing techniques. The sales price will also be reduced by $30, and sales of 2,200 units for the remainder of the year are forecast.

B. Reduce the sales price by $40. The sales organization forecasts that with the significantly reduced sales price, 2,700 units can be sold during the remainder of the year. Total fixed and variable unit costs will stay as budgeted.

C. Cut fixed costs by $10,000, and lower the sales price by 5 percent. Variable costs per unit will be unchanged. Sales of 2,000 units are expected for the remainder of the year.

Required:

1. Determine the number of units that Campbell Company must sell in order to break even assuming no changes are made to the selling price and cost structure.
2. Determine the number of units that Campbell Company must sell in order to achieve its after-tax profit objective.
3. Determine which one of the alternatives Campbell Company should select to achieve its annual after-tax profit objective. Be sure to support your selection with appropriate calculations.
4. The precision and reliability of CVP analysis are limited by several underlying assumptions. Identify at least four of these assumptions. *(CMA adapted)*

Exercise 16-16 CVP: Before- and After-Tax Targeted Income

OBJECTIVE 1 2

SHOW ME
HOW

Helmet-Pro Company produces helmets for bicycle racing. Currently, Helmet-Pro charges a price of $240 per helmet. Variable costs are $96 per helmet, and fixed costs are $1,255,800. The tax rate is 25 percent. Last year, 14,000 helmets were sold.

Required:

1. What is Helmet-Pro's net income for last year?
2. What is Helmet-Pro's break-even revenue? (Round to the nearest dollar.)
3. Suppose Helmet-Pro wants to earn before-tax operating income of $850,000. How many units must be sold? (Round to the nearest unit.)
4. Suppose Helmet-Pro wants to earn after-tax net income of $625,000. How many units must be sold? (Round to the nearest unit.)
5. Suppose the income tax rate rises to 35 percent. How many units must be sold for Helmet-Pro to earn after-tax income of $625,000? (Round to the nearest unit.)

Exercise 16-17 CVP, Before- and After-Tax Targeted Income

OBJECTIVE   1 4

DATA
ANALYTICS

Sara Pacheco is a sophomore in college and earns a little extra money by making beaded key ring accessories. She sells them on Saturday mornings at the local flea market. Sara charges $5 per unit and has unit variable costs (beads, wire rings, etc.) of $2. Her fixed costs consist of small pliers, a glue gun, etc., which cost her $90.

Required:

1. Calculate Sara's break-even units.
2. Prepare a profit-volume graph for Sara.
3. Prepare a cost-volume-profit graph for Sara.

OBJECTIVE **2** **5**

CMA

SHOW ME
HOW

Exercise 16-18 Break-Even in Sales Revenue, Changes in Variables

Carmichael Corporation is in the process of preparing next year's budget. The pro forma income statement for the current year is as follows:

Sales		$1,800,000
Cost of sales:		
Direct materials	$250,000	
Direct labor	180,000	
Variable overhead	106,000	
Fixed overhead	100,000	636,000
Gross profit		$1,164,000
Selling and administrative expenses:		
Variable	$400,000	
Fixed	350,000	750,000
Operating income		$ 414,000

Required:

1. What is the break-even sales revenue (rounded to the nearest dollar) for Carmichael Corporation for the current year?
2. For the coming year, the management of Carmichael Corporation anticipates an 8 percent increase in variable costs and a $60,000 increase in fixed expenses. What is the break-even point in dollars for next year? *(CMA adapted)*

OBJECTIVE **1** **5**

Exercise 16-19 Assumptions and Use of Variables

Choose the *best* answer for each of the following multiple-choice questions.

1. Cost-volume-profit analysis includes some simplifying assumptions. Which of the following is **not** one of these assumptions?

    a. Cost and revenues are predictable.
    b. Cost and revenues are linear over the relevant range.
    c. Changes in beginning and ending inventory levels are insignificant in amount.
    d. Sales mix changes are irrelevant.

2. The term *relevant range*, as used in cost accounting, means the range

    a. over which costs may fluctuate
    b. over which cost relationships are valid
    c. of probable production
    d. over which production has occurred in the past 10 years

3. How would the following be used in calculating the number of units that must be sold to earn a targeted operating income?

	Price per Unit	Targeted Operating Income
a.	Denominator	Numerator
b.	Numerator	Numerator
c.	Not used	Denominator
d.	Numerator	Denominator

4. Information concerning Korian Corporation's product is as follows:

Sales	$300,000
Variable costs	240,000
Fixed costs	40,000

Assuming that Korian increased sales of the product by 20 percent, what should the operating income be?

a. $20,000

b. $24,000

c. $32,000

d. $80,000

5. The following data apply to McNally Company for last year:

Total variable costs per unit	$3.50
Contribution margin/Sales	30%
Break-even sales (present volume)	$1,000,000

McNally wants to sell an additional 50,000 units at the same selling price and contribution margin. By how much can fixed costs increase to generate additional profit equal to 10 percent of the sales value of the additional 50,000 units to be sold?

a. $50,000

b. $57,500

c. $67,500

d. $125,000

6. Bryan Company's break-even point is 8,500 units. Variable cost per unit is $140, and total fixed costs are $297,500 per year. What price does Bryan charge?

a. $140

b. $35

c. $175

d. Cannot be determined from the above data

Exercise 16-20 Contribution Margin, CVP, Net Income, Margin of Safety

OBJECTIVE ◄ 1 5

SHOW ME HOW

Nail Glow, Inc., produces novelty nail polishes. Each bottle sells for $5.90. Variable unit costs are as follows:

Acrylic base	$0.86	Bottle, packing material	$1.15
Pigments	0.57	Selling commission	0.14
Other ingredients	0.43		

Fixed overhead costs are $34,475 per year. Fixed selling and administrative costs are $6,720 per year. Nail Glow sold 35,000 bottles last year.

Required:

1. What is the contribution margin per unit for a bottle of nail polish? What is the contribution margin ratio? (Round to four significant digits.)
2. How many bottles must be sold to break even? What is the break-even sales revenue?
3. What was Nail Glow's operating income last year?
4. What was the margin of safety in revenue?
5. Suppose that Nail Glow, Inc., raises the price to $6.50 per bottle, but anticipated sales will drop to 28,750 bottles. What will the new break-even point in units be? Should Nail Glow raise the price? Explain.

OBJECTIVE 1 5

SHOW ME
HOW

Exercise 16-21 Operating Leverage

Income statements for two different companies in the same industry are as follows:

	Elgin, Inc.	Hobart, Inc.
Sales	$600,000	$600,000
Less: Variable costs	360,000	120,000
Contribution margin	$240,000	$480,000
Less: Fixed costs	120,000	360,000
Operating income	$120,000	$120,000

Required:

1. Compute the degree of operating leverage for each company.
2. Compute the break-even point for each company. Explain why the break-even point for Hobart, Inc., is higher.
3. Suppose that both companies experience a 30 percent increase in revenues. Compute the percentage change in profits for each company. Explain why the percentage increase in Hobart's profits is so much greater than that of Elgin.

OBJECTIVE 3

SHOW ME   EXCEL
HOW

Exercise 16-22 CVP Analysis of Multiple Products

Alo Company produces commercial printers. One is the regular model, a basic model that is designed to copy and print in black and white. Another model, the deluxe model, is a color printer-scanner-copier. For the coming year, Alo expects to sell 90,000 regular models and 36,000 deluxe models. A segmented income statement for the two products is as follows:

	Regular Model	Deluxe Model	Total
Sales	$13,500,000	$10,800,000	$24,300,000
Less: Variable costs	9,450,000	6,480,000	15,930,000
Contribution margin	$ 4,050,000	$ 4,320,000	$ 8,370,000
Less: Direct fixed costs	1,200,000	960,000	2,160,000
Segment margin	$ 2,850,000	$ 3,360,000	$ 6,210,000
Less: Common fixed costs			1,280,000
Operating income			$ 4,930,000

Required:

1. Compute the number of regular models and deluxe models that must be sold to break even.
2. Using information only from the total column of the income statement, compute the sales revenue that must be generated for the company to break even. (Round the contribution margin ratio to four significant digits and the sales revenue to the nearest dollar.)

OBJECTIVE 2 3 5

 CMA

SHOW ME
HOW

Exercise 16-23 After-Tax Target Income: Profit Analysis

X-Cee-Ski Company recently expanded its manufacturing capacity, which will allow it to produce up to 21,000 pairs of cross-country skis of the mountaineering model or the touring model. The Sales Department assures management that it can sell between 9,000 and 14,000 pairs of either product this year. Because the models are very similar, X-Cee-Ski will produce only one of the two models.

The following information was compiled by the Accounting Department:

	Per-Unit (Pair) Data	
	Mountaineering	Touring
Selling price	$180	$120
Variable costs	130	90

Fixed costs will total $320,000 if the mountaineering model is produced but will be only $220,000 if the touring model is produced. X-Cee-Ski is subject to a 40 percent income tax rate.

Required:

1. If X-Cee-Ski Company desires an after-tax net income of $48,000, how many pairs of touring model skis will the company have to sell?
2. Suppose that X-Cee-Ski Company decided to produce only one model of skis. What is the total sales revenue at which X-Cee-Ski Company would make the same profit or loss regardless of the ski model it decided to produce?
3. If the Sales Department could guarantee the annual sale of 12,000 pairs of either model, which model would the company produce, and why? *(CMA adapted)*

Exercise 16-24 CVP with Activity-Based Costing

Busy-Bee Baking Company produces a variety of breads. The average price of a loaf of bread is $1. Costs are as follows:

Cost Driver	Unit Variable Cost	Level of Cost Driver
Units sold	$0.65	—
Setups	$ 300	150
Maintenance hours	$15	2,500

Other data:

Total fixed costs (traditional)	$140,000
Total fixed costs (ABC)	57,500

Required:

1. Compute the break-even point in units using conventional analysis.
2. Compute the break-even point in units using activity-based analysis.
3. Suppose that Busy-Bee could reduce the setup cost by $100 per setup and could reduce the number of maintenance hours needed to 1,000. How many units must be sold to break even in this case? (Round answer *up* to whole units.)

Exercise 16-25 CVP with Activity-Based Costing and Multiple Products

Busy-Bee Baking Company produces a variety of breads. The plant manager would like to expand production into sweet rolls as well. The average price of a loaf of bread is $1. Anticipated price for a package of sweet rolls is $1.50. Costs for the new level of production are as follows:

Cost Driver	Unit Variable Cost	Level of Cost Driver
Loaf of bread	$0.65	—
Package of sweet rolls	$0.93	—
Setups	$300	250
Maintenance hours	$15	3,500

Other data:

Total fixed costs (traditional)	$185,000
Total fixed costs (ABC)	57,500

Busy-Bee believes it can sell 600,000 loaves of bread and 200,000 packages of sweet rolls in the coming year.

Required:

1. Prepare a contribution-margin-based income statement for next year. Be sure to show sales and variable costs by product and in total.
2. Compute the break-even sales for the company as a whole using conventional analysis.
3. Compute the break-even sales for the company as a whole using activity-based analysis.
4. Compute the break-even units of each product in units. Does it matter whether you use conventional analysis or activity-based analysis? Why or why not?
5. Suppose that Busy-Bee could reduce the setup cost by $100 per setup and could reduce the number of maintenance hours needed to 1,000. How many units of each product must be sold to break even in this case? (Round answers *up* to whole units.)

PROBLEMS

OBJECTIVE

Problem 16-26 Break-Even in Units

Aliyah Brown and two of her colleagues are considering opening a law office in a large metropolitan area that would make inexpensive legal services available to those who could not otherwise afford these services. The intent is to provide easy access for their clients by having the office open 360 days per year, 16 hours each day from 7:00 a.m. to 11:00 p.m. The office would be staffed by a lawyer, paralegal, legal secretary, and clerk-receptionist for each of the two 8-hour shifts.

In order to determine the feasibility of the project, Aliyah hired a marketing consultant to assist with market projections. The results of this study show that if the firm spends $500,000 on advertising the first year, the number of new clients expected each day would have the following probability distribution:

Number of New Clients per Day	Probability
20	0.10
30	0.30
55	0.40
85	0.20

Aliyah and her associates believe these numbers are reasonable and are prepared to spend the $500,000 on advertising. Other pertinent information about the operation of the office is as follows.

The only charge to each new client would be $30 for the initial consultation. All cases that warranted further legal work would be accepted on a contingency basis with the firm earning 30 percent of any favorable settlements or judgments. Aliyah estimates that 20 percent of new client consultations will result in favorable settlements or judgments averaging $2,000 each. Repeat clients are not expected during the first year of operations.

The hourly wages of the staff are projected to be $25 for the lawyer, $20 for the paralegal, $15 for the legal secretary, and $10 for the clerk-receptionist. Fringe benefit expenses will be 40 percent of the wages paid. A total of 400 hours of overtime is expected for the year; this will be divided equally between the legal secretary and the clerk-receptionist positions. Overtime will be paid at one and one-half times the regular wage, and the fringe benefit expense will apply to the full wages.

Aliyah has located 6,000 square feet of suitable office space, which rents for $28 per square foot annually. Associated expenses will be $22,000 for property insurance and $32,000 for utilities.

It will be necessary for the group to purchase malpractice insurance, which is expected to cost $180,000 annually. The initial investment in office equipment will be $60,000; this equipment has an estimated useful life of four years. The cost of office supplies has been estimated to be $4 per expected new client consultation.

Required:

1. Determine how many new clients must visit the law office being considered by Aliyah Brown and her colleagues in order for the venture to break even during its first year of operations.
2. Using the information provided by the marketing consultant, determine if it is feasible for the law office to achieve break-even operations. *(CMA adapted)*

Problem 16-27 Using a Computer Spreadsheet to Solve Multiple-Product Break-Even: Varying Sales Mix

OBJECTIVE 3

More-Power Company has projected sales of 75,000 regular sanders and 30,000 mini-sanders for next year. The projected income statement is as follows:

	Regular Sander	Mini-Sander	Total
Sales	$3,000,000	$1,800,000	$4,800,000
Less: Variable expenses	1,800,000	900,000	2,700,000
Contribution margin	$1,200,000	$ 900,000	$2,100,000
Less: Direct fixed expenses	250,000	450,000	700,000
Product margin	$ 950,000	$ 450,000	$1,400,000
Less: Common fixed expenses			600,000
Operating income			$ 800,000

Required:

1. Set up the given income statement on a spreadsheet (e.g., Excel®). Then, substitute the following sales mixes, and calculate operating income. Be sure to print the results for each sales mix (a through d).

DATA ANALYTICS

	Regular Sander	Mini-Sander
a.	75,000	37,500
b.	60,000	60,000
c.	30,000	90,000
d.	30,000	60,000

2. Calculate the break-even units for each product for each of the preceding sales mixes.

Problem 16-28 Contribution Margin: Unit Amounts

OBJECTIVE 1

Consider the following information on four independent companies.

	A	B	C	D
Sales	$10,000	$?	$?	$9,000
Less: Variable costs	8,000	11,700	9,750	?
Contribution margin	$ 2,000	$ 7,800	$?	$?
Less: Fixed costs	?	4,500	?	900
Operating income	$ 1,000	$?	$8,000	$2,850
Units sold	?	1,300	300	500
Price/Unit	$4	$?	$?	$?
Variable cost/Unit	$?	$9	$?	$?
Contribution margin/Unit	$?	$6	$?	$?
Contribution margin ratio	?	?	75%	?
Break-even in units	?	?	?	?

Required:

Calculate the correct amount for each question mark. Be sure to round any fractional break-even units *up* to the next whole number.

OBJECTIVE `1` `2` `5`   **Problem 16-29 Break-Even in Sales Revenue, Variable-Costing Ratio, Contribution Margin Ratio, Margin of Safety**

Nealon Company runs a driving range and golf shop. The budgeted income statement for the coming year is as follows.

Sales	$1,240,000
Less: Variable expenses	781,200
Contribution margin	$ 458,800
Less: Fixed expenses	425,500
Income before taxes	$ 33,300
Less: Income taxes	11,655
Net income	$ 21,645

Required:

1. What is Nealon's variable cost ratio? Its contribution margin ratio?
2. Suppose Nealon's actual revenues are $190,000 greater than budgeted. By how much will before-tax profits increase? Give the answer without preparing a new income statement.
3. How much sales revenue must Nealon earn in order to break even? What is the expected margin of safety? (Round your answers to the nearest dollar.)
4. How much sales revenue must Nealon generate to earn a before-tax profit of $50,000? An after-tax profit of $35,000? (Round your answers to the nearest dollar.) Prepare a contribution margin income statement to verify the accuracy of your last answer.

OBJECTIVE `1` `5`   **Problem 16-30 Changes in Break-Even Points with Changes in Unit Prices**

Cassius produces and sells novelty items for resort gift shops. Last year, Cassius sold 99,200 units. The income statement for Cassius, Inc., for last year is as follows:

Sales	$992,000
Less: Variable expenses	545,600
Contribution margin	$446,400
Less: Fixed expenses	180,000
Operating income	$266,400

Required:

1. Compute the break-even point in units and in revenues. Compute the margin of safety in sales revenue for last year.
2. Suppose that the selling price increases by 6 percent. Will the break-even point increase or decrease? Recompute the break-even point in units. (Round up to the nearest whole unit.)
3. Suppose that the variable cost per unit increases by $0.20. Will the break-even point increase or decrease? Recompute the break-even point in units. (Round up to the nearest whole unit.)
4. Can you predict whether the break-even point increases or decreases if both the selling price and the unit variable cost increase? Recompute the break-even point in units incorporating both of the changes in Requirements 2 and 3. (Round up to the nearest whole unit.)
5. Assume that total fixed costs decrease by $12,000. (Assume no other changes from the original data.) Will the break-even point increase or decrease? Recompute it. (Round up to the nearest whole unit.)

Problem 16-31 Break-Even, After-Tax Target Income, Margin of Safety, Operating Leverage

OBJECTIVE ◀ 1 2 5

Rahm Company produces a single product. The projected income statement for the coming year, based on sales of 160,000 units, is as follows:

Sales	$2,000,000
Less: Variable costs	1,400,000
Contribution margin	$ 600,000
Less: Fixed costs	450,000
Operating income	$ 150,000

Required:

1. Compute the unit contribution margin and the units that must be sold to break even. Suppose that 10,000 units are sold above the break-even point. What is the profit?
2. Compute the contribution margin ratio and the break-even point in dollars. Suppose that revenues are $87,500 greater than expected. What would the total profit be?
3. Compute the margin of safety in sales revenue.
4. Compute the operating leverage. Compute the new profit level if sales are 20 percent lower than expected.
5. How many units must be sold to earn a profit equal to 12 percent of sales?
6. Assume the income tax rate is 30 percent. How many units must be sold to earn an after-tax profit of $180,000?

Problem 16-32 Basic CVP Concepts

OBJECTIVE ◀ 1 2 5

Katayama Company produces a variety of products. One division makes neoprene wetsuits. The division's projected income statement for the coming year is as follows:

Sales (65,000 units)	$15,600,000
Less: Variable expenses	8,736,000
Contribution margin	$ 6,864,000
Less: Fixed expenses	4,012,000
Operating income	$ 2,852,000

Required:

1. Compute the contribution margin per unit, and calculate the break-even point in units. Repeat, using the contribution margin ratio.
2. The divisional manager has decided to increase the advertising budget by $140,000 and cut the average selling price to $200. These actions will increase sales revenues by $1 million. Will this improve the division's financial situation? Prepare a new income statement to support your answer.
3. Suppose sales revenues exceed the estimated amount on the income statement by $612,000. Without preparing a new income statement, determine by how much profits are underestimated.
4. How many units must be sold to earn an after-tax profit of $1.254 million? Assume a tax rate of 34 percent. (Round your answer up to the next whole unit.)
5. Compute the margin of safety in dollars based on the given income statement.
6. Compute the operating leverage based on the given income statement. (Round to three significant digits.) If sales revenues are 20 percent greater than expected, what is the percentage increase in profits?

OBJECTIVE 2 5

Problem 16-33 CVP Analysis: Sales-Revenue Approach, Pricing, After-Tax Target Income

Mahan Consulting is a service organization that specializes in the design, installation, and servicing of mechanical, hydraulic, and pneumatic systems. For example, some manufacturing firms, with machinery that cannot be turned off for servicing, need some type of system to lubricate the machinery during use. To deal with this type of problem for a client, Mahan designed a central lubricating system that pumps lubricants intermittently to bearings and other moving parts.

The operating results for the firm for the previous year are as follows:

Sales	$974,880
Less: Variable expenses	534,234
Contribution margin	$440,646
Less: Fixed expenses	264,300
Operating income	$176,346

In the coming year, Mahan expects variable costs to increase by 4 percent and fixed costs to increase by 3 percent.

Required:

1. What is the contribution margin ratio (rounded to three significant digits) for the previous year?
2. Compute Mahan's break-even point for the previous year in dollars.
3. Suppose that Mahan would like to see a 6 percent increase in operating income in the coming year. What percent (on average) must Mahan raise its bids to cover the expected cost increases and obtain the desired operating income? Assume that Mahan expects the same mix and volume of services in both years.
4. In the coming year, how much revenue must be earned for Mahan to earn an after-tax profit of $175,000? Assume a tax rate of 40 percent.

OBJECTIVE 3 5

Problem 16-34 Multiple Products, Break-Even Analysis, Operating Leverage, Segmented Income Statements

Ironjay, Inc., produces two types of weight-training equipment: the Jay-flex (a weight machine that allows the user to perform a number of different exercises) and a set of free weights. Ironjay sells the Jay-flex to sporting goods stores for $200. The free weights sell for $75 per set. The projected income statement for the coming year follows:

Sales	$600,000
Less: Variable expenses	390,000
Contribution margin	$210,000
Less: Fixed expenses	157,500
Operating income	$ 52,500

The owner of Ironjay estimates that 40 percent of the sales revenues will be produced by sales of the Jay-flex, with the remaining 60 percent by free weights. The Jay-flex is also responsible for 40 percent of the variable expenses. Of the fixed expenses, one-third are common to both products, and one-half are directly traceable to the Jay-flex line.

Required:

1. Compute the sales revenue that must be earned for Ironjay to break even.
2. Compute the number of Jay-flex machines and free weight sets that must be sold for Ironjay to break even.
3. Compute the degree of operating leverage for Ironjay. Now, assume that the actual revenues will be 40 percent higher than the projected revenues. By what percentage will profits increase with this change in sales volume?

4. Ironjay is considering adding a new product—the Jay-rider. The Jay-rider is a cross between a rowing machine and a stationary bicycle. For the first year, Ironjay estimates that the Jay-rider will cannibalize 600 units of sales from the Jay-flex. Sales of free weight sets will remain unchanged. The Jay-rider will sell for $180 and have variable costs of $140. The increase in fixed costs to support manufacture of this product is $5,700. Compute the number of Jay-flex machines, free weight sets, and Jay-riders that must be sold for Ironjay to break even. For the coming year, is the addition of the Jay-rider a good idea? Why or why not? Why might Ironjay choose to add the Jay-rider anyway?

Problem 16-35 Break-Even in Units and Sales Dollars, Margin of Safety

OBJECTIVE ◀ 1 5

Aubrey Company produces a single product. Last year's income statement is as follows:

Sales (12,000 units)	$1,218,000
Less: Variable costs	365,400
Contribution margin	$ 852,600
Less: Fixed costs	300,000
Operating income	$ 552,600

Required:

1. Compute the break-even point in units and sales revenue. (Round break-even units to the nearest unit and revenue to the nearest dollar.)
2. What was the margin of safety for the company last year?
3. Suppose that Aubrey Company is considering an investment in new technology that will increase fixed costs by $60,000 per year, but will lower variable costs to 28 percent of sales. Units sold will remain unchanged. Prepare a budgeted income statement assuming the company makes this investment. What is the new break-even point in units, assuming the investment is made?

Problem 16-36 CVP Analysis, Impact of Activity-Based Costing

OBJECTIVE ◀ 1 6

Salem Electronics currently produces two products: a programmable calculator and a tape recorder. A recent marketing study indicated that consumers would react favorably to a radio with the Salem brand name. Owner Kenneth Booth was interested in the possibility. Before any commitment was made, however, Kenneth wanted to know what the incremental fixed costs would be and how many radios must be sold to cover these costs.

In response, Betty Johnson, the marketing manager, gathered data for the current products to help in projecting overhead costs for the new product. The overhead costs based on 30,000 direct labor hours follow. (The high-low method using direct labor hours as the independent variable was used to determine the fixed and variable costs.)

	Fixed	Variable
Materials handling	$ —	$18,000
Power	—	22,000
Engineering	100,000	—
Machine costs	30,000*	80,000
Inspection	40,000	—
Setups	60,000	—

*All depreciation.

The following activity data were also gathered:

	Calculators	Recorders
Units produced	20,000	20,000
Direct labor hours	10,000	20,000
Machine hours	10,000	10,000
Material moves	120	120
Kilowatt-hours	1,000	1,000
Engineering hours	4,000	1,000
Hours of inspection	700	1,400
Number of setups	20	40

Betty was told that a plantwide overhead rate was used to assign overhead costs based on direct labor hours. She was also informed by engineering that if 20,000 radios were produced and sold (her projection based on her marketing study), they would have the same activity data as the recorders (use the same direct labor hours, machine hours, setups, and so on).

Engineering also provided the following additional estimates for the proposed product line:

Prime costs per unit	$ 18
Depreciation on new equipment	18,000

Upon receiving these estimates, Betty did some quick calculations and became quite excited. With a selling price of $26 and just $18,000 of additional fixed costs, only 4,500 units had to be sold to break even. Since Betty was confident that 20,000 units could be sold, she was prepared to strongly recommend the new product line.

Required:

1. Reproduce Betty's break-even calculation using conventional cost assignments. How much additional profit would be expected under this scenario, assuming that 20,000 radios are sold?
2. Use an activity-based costing approach, and calculate the break-even point and the incremental profit that would be earned on sales of 20,000 units.
3. Explain why the CVP analysis done in Requirement 2 is more accurate than the analysis done in Requirement 1. What recommendation would you make?

**DATA
ANALYTICS**

OBJECTIVE 3 6

Problem 16-37 ABC and CVP Analysis: Multiple Products

Good Scent, Inc., produces two colognes: Rose and Violet. Of the two, Rose is more popular. Data concerning the two products follow:

	Rose	Violet
Expected sales (in cases)	50,000	10,000
Selling price per case	$100	$80
Direct labor hours	36,000	6,000
Machine hours	10,000	3,000
Receiving orders	50	25
Packing orders	100	50
Material cost per case	$50	$43
Direct labor cost per case	$10	$7

The company uses a conventional costing system and assigns overhead costs to products using direct labor hours. Annual overhead costs follow. They are classified as fixed or variable with respect to direct labor hours.

	Fixed	Variable
Direct labor benefits	$ —	$200,000
Machine costs	200,000*	262,000
Receiving department	225,000	—
Packing department	125,000	—
Total costs	$550,000	$462,000

*All depreciation.

Required:

1. Using the conventional approach, compute the number of cases of Rose and the number of cases of Violet that must be sold for the company to break even.

2. Using an activity-based approach, compute the number of cases of each product that must be sold for the company to break even.

The items that appear within this chapter that are from the CMA are Exercise 16-13, 16-15, 16-18, 16-23, and Problem 16-31. Source: Materials from the Certified Management Accountant Examination, Copyright 1981, 1982, 1983, 1984, 1985, 1989, 1990, 1991, 1992, 1995, 1996 by the Institute of Certified Management Accountants are reprinted and/or adapted with permission.

17

Activity Resource Usage Model and Tactical Decision Making

After studying this chapter, you should be able to:

1 Describe the tactical decision-making model.

2 Define the concept of relevant costs and revenues.

3 Explain how the activity resource usage model is used in assessing relevancy.

4 Apply the tactical decision-making concepts in a variety of business situations.

SPECIAL ORDER DECISIONS

in the Airline Industry

Have you ever sat on an airplane with an empty seat next to you while anxiously awaiting the attendant to close the boarding door, thereby ensuring your ability to spread out comfortably during the ensuing flight? Although the empty seat might boost your enjoyment, it represents a missed opportunity for the airline to use the seat to increase profits from a paying customer. What if after you land and arrive at your hotel, the front-desk receptionist offers you a penthouse suite at a drastically discounted rate? Similar to the airplane offer, although the great deal on the penthouse suite likely would be an exciting upgrade for a first-time guest, it represents a missed opportunity for the hotel to use the available suite to increase profits from a regular guest who is accustomed to paying the much higher typical price for the luxury space.

Accountants commonly refer to these situations as special-order scenarios—an important tactical decision—that require them to determine how best to utilize unused capacity, such as empty plane seats or hotel rooms, at the end of the period (e.g., when the flight takes off or the hotel suite sits empty for the weekend). How do airlines set the price for these special-order decisions? **American Airlines'** managing director of revenue management explains that regular seat prices are set months before the given flight based largely on historical demand. However, the price decreases—sometimes dramatically and multiple times a day—as the flight date draws nearer in an attempt to fill empty seats.[1] From a tactical decision-making perspective, airlines must estimate the relevant (or incremental) costs incurred for a passenger to occupy a seat and then charge a price that exceeds this relevant cost so that the relevant profit from the special-order sale is positive. The packaged food and drink given to each passenger, hygiene kits (e.g., individually wrapped blanket, sleeping mask, and hand sanitizer) provided to each passenger, cleaning activities for each occupied seat (e.g., wiping down the seat after the flight), and baggage handling activities represent examples of relevant costs to include in a special-order airline analysis. Of course, many costs to operate a flight do not vary with the number of passengers, and thus, airlines must charge a high-enough price on its regular (i.e., non-special-order) seat tickets to cover these other costs if they wish to generate a positive profit.

Additionally, airlines must be prepared to manage special-order decisions during significant unexpected events, such as dramatic economic downturns, the September 11 terrorist event, the grounding of **Boeing**'s 737 Max aircrafts, and the COVID-19 global pandemic. The COVID-19 pandemic caused demand for passenger air travel to plummet more than 90 percent for a sustained time period, which created considerable excess

---

1 "The Man Who Set Prices for American Airlines Reveals How to Get the Cheapest Flights," *NextShark.com* (May 3, 2016), https://nextshark.com/tim-lyons-american-airlines-price-tickets/, accessed August 3, 2020.

capacity for airlines.[2] Interestingly, this crisis led passenger airlines to consider special-order offers to instead transport cargo, including delivering medical supplies and workers in the grocery and medical fields to areas in need of assistance.[3] Further complicating matters, in order to enable social distancing on its flights during the pandemic, **Delta** enacted self-imposed capacity constraints, such as capping seating at 50 percent in First Class and 60 percent in Main Cabin, as well as blocking (i.e., not selling) all middle seats unless adjacent to members of the same party.[4] These capacity-limiting actions force airlines to be even more careful in making effective special-order decisions because far fewer regular-priced tickets exist to cover other significant costs beyond the scope of the special-order scenario. Therefore, the next time you are fortunate enough to enjoy an empty adjacent seat, consider the special-order analysis that might have led to your good fortune.

This chapter focuses on one of the most widely applicable topics in cost management—tactical decision making. For example, companies use a tactical decision-making process like the one we examine here to analyze a wide range of important decisions, including which existing stores to close (or new ones to open), which current products or services to drop (or new ones to add), or which special offers from other companies to accept or reject. Such tactical decisions can be large or small in scale and often are observable in everyday life.

Tom and Ray Magliozzi (also known as Click and Clack, the Tappet Brothers) had a weekly radio show advising interested callers on their automotive problems. Frequently, Tom and Ray use tactical decision making to suggest possibilities. For example, one caller asked what to do about his wife's 13-year-old Ford Escort. The car needed its air filter replaced every six weeks due to oil buildup in the box that holds the filter. No mechanic had been able to solve the problem. Tom and Ray zoomed in the answer. The problem was due to "blowby"—a situation that occurs when combustion gases leak from inside the cylinders into the crankcase. Soon, the gas and pressure overwhelm the crankcase ventilation system and oil gets blown back into the air-filter housing, thus ruining the air filter. What to do? Tom and Ray suggest two solutions. First, replace the engine. This option will solve the underlying problem, but it will cost about $1,500. Second, just keep replacing the air filter every six weeks. They figured that, at $10 per time, the caller could do that every six weeks for the next 17 years. The point, of course, is that placing a new engine in an older car was almost surely a waste of money—the rest of the car would wear out long before the new engine wore out.

A major role of the cost management information system is supplying cost and revenue data that are useful in tactical decision making. This chapter focuses on the use of cost and revenue data in tactical decision making. To make sound decisions, the user of the cost information must be able to decide what information is relevant, as well as what information is irrelevant, to the decision.

OBJECTIVE

Describe the tactical decision-making model.

TACTICAL DECISION MAKING

Tactical decision making consists of choosing among alternatives with an immediate or limited end in view. As illustrated in the opening feature on the airline industry, accepting a special order for less than the normal selling price to use idle capacity and increase this year's profits is an example of tactical decision making. The immediate objective is to use idle productive capacity to

---

2   E. Dey, M. Schlangenstein, and Bloomberg, "Southwest Airlines CEO Predicts a 'Brutal Low-Fare Environment' to Lure Passengers," *Fortune.com* (May 30, 2020), https://fortune.com/2020/05/30/southwest-airlines-low-fare-price-competition-demand-coronavirus/, accessed August 3, 2020.

3   A. Curley, A. Dichter, V. Krishnan, R. Riedel, and S. Saxon, "Coronavirus: Airlines Brace for Severe Turbulence," McKinsey & Company, *McKinsey.com* (April 2020), https://www.mckinsey.com/industries/travel-logistics-and-transport-infrastructure/our-insights/coronavirus-airlines-brace-for-severe-turbulence, accessed August 3, 2020.

4   E. Wolf, "More Space through Summer: Delta Will Block Middle-Seat Selection, Cap Cabin Seating through September 30," *News.Delta.com* (June 26, 2020), https://news.delta.com/more-space-through-summer-delta-will-block-middle-seat-selection-cap-cabin-seating-through-sept-30, accessed August 3, 2020.

increase short-run profits. Thus, some tactical decisions tend to be *short run* in nature; however, it should be emphasized that short-run decisions often have long-run consequences. Consider a second example. Suppose that a company is considering producing a component instead of buying it from suppliers. The immediate objective may be to lower the cost of making the main product. Yet, this tactical decision may be a small part of the overall strategy of establishing a cost leadership position for the firm. Thus, tactical decisions often are *small-scale actions* that serve a larger purpose. Recall that the overall objective of strategic decision making is to establish a long-term competitive advantage. Tactical decision making should support this overall objective, even if the immediate objective is short run or small scale in nature. Thus, *sound* tactical decisions achieve not only the limited objective but also serve a larger purpose. In fact, all tactical decisions should serve the overall strategic goals of the company. As demonstrated throughout the chapter, tactical decisions create powerful impacts on financial performance and, thus, should be made wisely after utilizing an effective tactical decision-making process.

The Tactical Decision-Making Process

A general tactical decision-making model is outlined in the six-step process listed below.

1. Recognize and define the problem.
2. Identify alternatives as possible solutions to the problem, and eliminate any unfeasible alternatives.
3. Identify the costs and benefits associated with each feasible alternative. Eliminate the costs and benefits that are not relevant to the decision.
4. Compare the *relevant* costs and benefits for each alternative.
5. Assess qualitative factors.
6. Select the alternative with the greatest overall net benefit.

Step 1: Define the Problem To illustrate the steps of the process, consider an apple producer. Each year, 25 percent of the apples harvested are small and odd-shaped. These apples cannot be sold in the normal distribution channels and have simply been dumped in the orchards for fertilizer. The owner is not satisfied with this approach and wants to determine the best way to handle these apples.

Step 2: Identify Feasible Alternatives Several alternatives are being considered:

1. Sell the apples to pig farmers.
2. Bag the apples (five-pound bags) and sell them to local supermarkets as seconds.
3. Rent a local canning facility and convert the apples to applesauce.
4. Rent a local canning facility and convert the apples to pie filling.
5. Continue with the current dumping practice.

Of these alternatives, alternative 1 was eliminated because there were not enough local pig farmers interested in the apples; alternative 5, the status quo, was eliminated at the request of the owner. Alternative 4 was eliminated because the local canning facility did not have the equipment needed to produce pie filling. However, the local canning facility's equipment could be used to produce applesauce, making alternative 3 possible. Finally, since local supermarkets agreed to buy five-pound bags of irregular apples and bagging could be done at the warehouse, alternative 2 was also a possibility. Alternatives 2 and 3 were deemed feasible.

Step 3: Predict Costs and Benefits and Eliminate Irrelevant Costs Suppose that the apple producer predicts that labor and materials (bags and ties) for the bagging option would cost $0.05 per pound. The five-pound bags of apples could be sold for $1.30 per bag to the local supermarkets. Making applesauce would cost $0.40 per pound for facility rental, labor, apples, cans, and other materials. It takes six pounds of apples to produce five, 16-ounce cans of applesauce. Each 16-ounce can will sell for $0.78. The cost of growing and harvesting the apples is not relevant to choosing between the bagging alternative and the applesauce alternative.

Step 4: Compare Relevant Costs and Benefits   The bagging alternative costs $0.25 to produce a five-pound bag ($0.05 × 5 pounds), and the revenue is $1.30 per bag, or $0.26 per pound. Thus, the net benefit is $0.21 per pound ($0.26 − $0.05). For the applesauce alternative, six pounds of apples produce five 16-ounce cans of applesauce. The revenue for five cans is $3.90 (5 × $0.78), which converts to $0.65 per pound ($3.90/6). Thus, the net benefit is $0.25 per pound ($0.65 − $0.40). Of the two alternatives, the applesauce option offers $0.04 more per pound than the bagging option.

Step 5: Assess the Qualitative Factors   Qualitative factors are those items that are very difficult to translate into dollars. For the apple example, the producer currently is not involved in producing any apple consumer products and is reluctant to move into applesauce production. He has no experience in this part of the industrial value chain and knows little about the channels of distribution for applesauce. An outside expert would need to be hired. Additionally, the rental opportunity is a year-to-year issue. In the long term, a major capital commitment might be needed. Bagging the small apples, on the other hand, is a product differentiation strategy that allows the producer to operate within familiar territory.

Step 6: Select the Best Alternative   While the applesauce option is a bit more lucrative, the qualitative factors argue against it. Therefore, the bagging alternative should be chosen. This alternative maintains the current position in the industrial value chain and strengthens the producer's competitive position by following a differentiation strategy for the small, odd-shaped apples.

Summary of Decision-Making Process   The six steps define a simple decision model. A **decision model** is a set of procedures that, if followed, will lead to a decision. Exhibit 17.1 summarizes and illustrates the steps for the decision model for the apple producer. Steps 3 and 4 define *tactical cost analysis*. **Tactical cost analysis** is the use of relevant cost and revenue data to identify the alternative that provides the greatest net benefit to the organization. Thus, tactical analysis includes predicting, identifying, and comparing relevant costs and revenues. As we have seen, however, tactical cost and revenue analysis is only part of the overall decision process. Qualitative factors deserve more discussion.

Qualitative Factors

Step 5 of the decision-making model is critically important. While cost and revenue information is important, other information, often qualitative in nature, is needed to make an informed decision. For example, the relationship of the considered alternatives to the organization's strategic objectives is essentially a qualitative assessment.

How should qualitative factors be handled in the decision-making process? Firstly, they must be identified. Secondly, the decision maker should try to quantify them. Often, qualitative factors are simply more difficult to quantify, but not impossible. For example, possible unreliability of an outside supplier might be quantified as the probable number of days late multiplied by the labor cost of downtime in the plant. Furthermore, truly qualitative factors, such as the impact of late orders on customer relations, or the apple producer's discomfort with the canning option, must be taken into consideration in the final step of the decision-making model—the selection of the alternative with the greatest overall benefit. Finally, employee morale can be affected either negatively or positively by decisions to offshore or reshore product manufacturing or service delivery activities. The financial impact of such changes in employee morale should be quantified to the extent possible and factored into the associated make-or-buy decision.

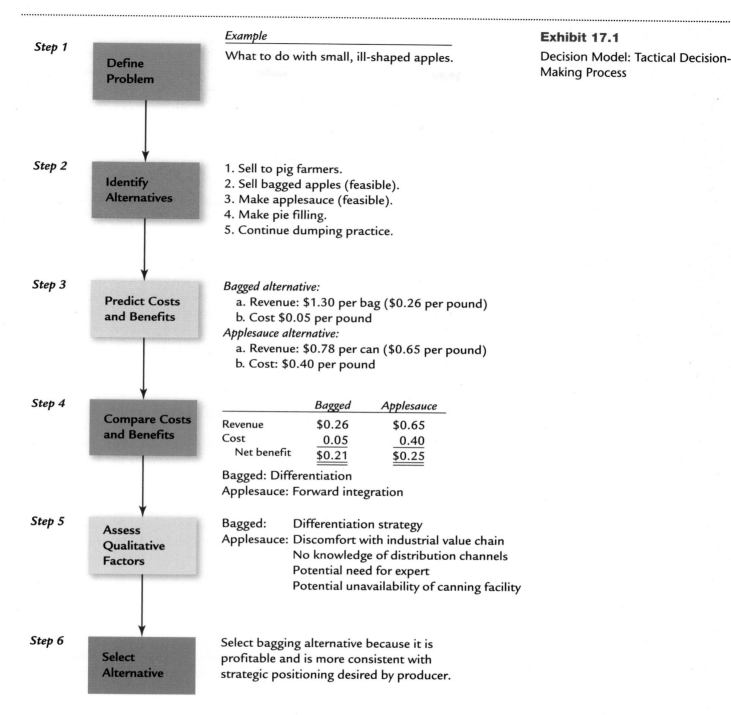

Exhibit 17.1

Decision Model: Tactical Decision-Making Process

Step 1 — Define Problem

Example

What to do with small, ill-shaped apples.

Step 2 — Identify Alternatives

1. Sell to pig farmers.
2. Sell bagged apples (feasible).
3. Make applesauce (feasible).
4. Make pie filling.
5. Continue dumping practice.

Step 3 — Predict Costs and Benefits

Bagged alternative:
  a. Revenue: $1.30 per bag ($0.26 per pound)
  b. Cost $0.05 per pound
Applesauce alternative:
  a. Revenue: $0.78 per can ($0.65 per pound)
  b. Cost: $0.40 per pound

Step 4 — Compare Costs and Benefits

	Bagged	*Applesauce*
Revenue	$0.26	$0.65
Cost	0.05	0.40
Net benefit	$0.21	$0.25

Bagged: Differentiation
Applesauce: Forward integration

Step 5 — Assess Qualitative Factors

Bagged: Differentiation strategy
Applesauce: Discomfort with industrial value chain
                  No knowledge of distribution channels
                  Potential need for expert
                  Potential unavailability of canning facility

Step 6 — Select Alternative

Select bagging alternative because it is profitable and is more consistent with strategic positioning desired by producer.

Sustainable Materials at Ford

An important sustainability objective for **Ford Motor Company** is to increase the use of recycled materials, renewable materials, and lightweight materials. Although the costs and benefits of changing to a different source of materials are considered, Ford also considers a wider range of costs and benefits. For example, using lightweight materials, such as aluminum and magnesium, and composite materials may or may not be less expensive than the heavier-weight materials they replace. However, lower-weight materials add significantly to the vehicle's fuel economy, as well as to improved acceleration and decreased stopping distance, which are all important quality improvements in their vehicles.

REAL-WORLD EXAMPLE

Interestingly, Ford uses life cycle assessment to consider materials and energy use over the entire life of a product. "We want to understand all the impacts our products and services have, so that we can manage them more effectively. To do this, we need to look at them holistically, over their entire life cycle. This wider view means we are better able to reduce our environmental footprint, through the materials and energy we use to make our vehicles, and the emissions generated by using them."[5] Engineers use life cycle assessment to help in choosing more environmentally friendly materials and designs. This assessment enables them to see the impact of different powertrains, electrified vehicles, and alternative fuels on cost and performance over the vehicle's life. This analysis helps customers choose the most appropriate sustainable vehicle for their needs.

Recycled materials are used to reduce waste as well as to reduce the depletion of natural resources. Upcycling recycles materials into uses with higher performance requirements than the original material. For example, upcycled postconsumer laundry detergent containers and milk bottles are incorporated into blow-molded automotive components. Polyurethane foam scrap is used to form new polyurethane foam components rather than being scrapped in landfills.

Renewable materials are often plant-based. For example, soy-based foam is used in seat cushions and backs, reducing petroleum usage by over 15 million pounds. Using the plant-based material also helps Ford avoid the volatility of petroleum prices. Natural fibers are used to reinforce plastics. A new composite plastic material, used in wiring harnesses, is reinforced with rice hulls. All in all, sustainability is an important input into all of Ford's vehicles.

OBJECTIVE ▶2

Define the concept of relevant costs and revenues.

RELEVANT COSTS AND REVENUES

In choosing between two alternatives, only the costs and revenues (or benefits) relevant to the decision should be considered. Identifying and comparing relevant costs and revenues are the heart of the tactical decision model illustrated in Exhibit 17.1. **Relevant costs (revenues)** are future costs (revenues) that differ across alternatives. Since relevant revenues are treated in the same way as relevant costs, we will simplify the discussion by concentrating on costs. All decisions relate to the future; accordingly, only future costs can be relevant. In addition, the cost also must differ from one alternative to another. If a future cost is the same for more than one alternative, it has no effect on the decision. Such a cost is an *irrelevant* cost. The ability to identify relevant and irrelevant costs is an important decision-making skill.

Relevant Costs Illustrated

To illustrate the concept of relevant costs, consider Avicom, Inc., a company that makes jet engines for commercial aircraft. A supplier has approached the company and offered to sell one component, nacelles (enclosures for jet engines), for what appears to be an attractive price. Avicom faces a make-or-buy decision. Assume that the cost of direct materials used to produce the nacelles is $270,000 per year (based on normal volume). Is this cost relevant? It is certainly a future cost. To produce the component for another year requires that materials be purchased. In addition, it differs across the two alternatives. If the component is purchased from an external supplier, no internal production is needed, and no direct materials need be purchased, reducing the materials cost to zero. Since the cost of direct materials differs across alternatives ($270,000 for the make alternative and $0 for the buy alternative), it is a relevant cost.

Notice that a past cost was used to estimate a future cost. For example, assume that the most recent cost of materials to produce the nacelles was $260,000. Adjusting this past cost for

5   Ford Motor Company. Sustainability Report. https://media.ford.com/content/dam/fordmedia/Europe/de/2018/06/Ford%20Sustainability%20Report%202017.pdf, accessed October 28, 2020.

anticipated price increases produced the projected cost of $270,000. Although past costs are never relevant, they are often used as the basis for predicting future costs.

Opportunity costs represent another example of relevant costs. An **opportunity cost** is the net benefit sacrificed or forgone when one alternative is chosen over another. Therefore, an opportunity cost is relevant because it is a future item that differs across alternatives. While opportunity costs can be difficult to identify and quantify, it is important to include them in the relevant analysis of tactical decisions. For instance, a summer spent studying abroad often represents one of the highlights of a student's collegiate career. If the student could earn $10,000 after expenses from a summer internship by staying home (i.e., not studying abroad), then the relevant analysis should include the forgone $10,000 internship earnings as an opportunity cost of choosing to study abroad.

Irrelevant Cost Illustrated

Avicom uses machinery to manufacture nacelles. This machinery was purchased five years ago and has an annual depreciation cost of $50,000. Is depreciation a future cost that differs across the two alternatives?

Past Costs A **sunk cost** is a past cost that has already occurred and cannot be changed by future actions. Therefore, sunk costs are irrelevant to tactical decisions. Depreciation represents an allocation of a cost already incurred, because no future decision can alter the original cost of the machinery; the original cost is the same for both alternatives. Therefore, depreciation is an example of a sunk cost. Although we allocate this sunk cost to future periods and call it *depreciation*, none of the original cost is avoidable. Thus, the acquisition cost of the machinery and its associated depreciation should not be a factor in the make-or-buy decision.

Sunk Costs and Concert Attendance

Many research studies illustrate that ignoring sunk costs when making tactical decisions often proves difficult. Many people feel a strong need to honor their sunk costs, which means that they choose to spend future money on projects simply because they have already spent past money on the same project. For example, assume that you purchase an advanced concert ticket, but when the date of the concert arrives, you feel like you are coming down with a cold and also need to study for an exam the following day and, therefore, would prefer to skip the concert and stay home to rest and study. However, if you instead choose to attend the concert rationalizing that "I have to go because I spent a lot of money on this ticket," then you are honoring your sunk cost and behaving irrationally (i.e., you will not get your ticket money back regardless of whether you stay or skip the concert). While you can take comfort that many other people in this scenario would behave in this same manner, it is important to realize that allowing sunk costs to affect such decisions should be avoided. Instead, you should choose to attend or skip the concert based on which option maximizes your future utility or happiness, just as a company should choose the option that maximizes its future profitability.

REAL-WORLD EXAMPLE

Future Costs Assume that the cost to heat and cool the plant—$40,000 per year—is allocated to different production departments, including the department that produces nacelles, which receives $4,000 of the cost. Is this $4,000 cost relevant to the make-or-buy decision facing Avicom?

The cost of providing plant utilities is a future cost, since it must be paid in future years. But does the cost differ across the make-and-buy alternatives? It is unlikely that the cost of heating and cooling the plant will change whether nacelles are produced or not. Thus, the cost is the same across both alternatives. The amount of the utility payment allocated to the remaining departments may change if production of nacelles is stopped, but the level of the total payment is unaffected by the decision. It is therefore an irrelevant cost.

OBJECTIVE ▶ **3**

Explain how the activity resource usage model is used in assessing relevancy.

RELEVANCY, COST BEHAVIOR, AND THE ACTIVITY RESOURCE USAGE MODEL

Understanding cost behavior is basic in determining relevancy. When costs were primarily unit-based, a simple distinction between fixed and variable costs could be made. Now, however, the ABC model has us focus on unit-level, batch-level, product-level, and facility-level costs. The first three are variable, but with respect to different types of activity drivers. The activity resource usage model can help us sort out the behavior of various activity costs and assess their relevance.

The **activity resource usage model** focuses on the use of resources and has two categories: (1) flexible resources and (2) committed resources. Recall from Chapter 3 that flexible resources are those that are acquired as used and needed. Committed resources are acquired in advance of usage. These categories and their usefulness in relevant costing are described in the following sections.

Flexible Resources

Resource spending is the cost of acquiring activity capacity. The amount paid for the supply of an activity is the activity cost. For flexible resources, the resources demanded (used) equal the resources supplied. Thus, for this category, *if the demand for an activity changes across alternatives*, then resource spending will change and the cost of the activity is relevant to the decision. For example, electricity supplied internally uses fuel for the generator. Fuel is a flexible resource. Consider the following two alternatives: (1) accept a special, one-time order, or (2) reject the special order. If accepting the order increases the demand for kilowatt-hours (power's activity driver), then the cost of power will differ across alternatives by the increase in fuel consumption. Thus, power cost is relevant to the decision.

Committed Resources

Committed resources are acquired in advance of usage through implicit contracting, and they are usually acquired in lumpy amounts. Consider an organization's employees. The implicit understanding may be that the organization will maintain employment levels even though there may be temporary downturns in the amount of an activity used, meaning that an activity may have unused capacity. Increased demand for an activity across alternatives may not mean increased cost—if there is sufficient unused capacity. For example, assume a company has five manufacturing engineers who can each work 2,000 hours and earn $50,000 per year; total engineering capacity is 10,000 (5 × 2,000 hours) engineering hours. Suppose that this year the company expects to use only 9,000 engineering hours for its normal business. This means that the engineering activity has 1,000 hours of unused capacity. If there is a special order that requires 500 engineering hours, the cost of engineering would be irrelevant. The order can be filled using unused engineering capacity, and the resource spending is the same for each alternative ($250,000 will be spent whether or not the order is accepted).

However, *if a change in demand for the activity requires a change in resource supply*, then the activity cost will be relevant to the decision. This change in cost can occur in one of two ways: (1) the demand for the resource exceeds the supply (increases resource spending), or (2) the demand for the resource drops permanently and supply exceeds demand enough so that activity capacity can be reduced (decreases resource spending).

To illustrate the first change, suppose that the special order requires 1,500 engineering hours. This exceeds the unused capacity of 1,000 hours. To meet the demand, the organization would need to hire a sixth engineer or perhaps use a consulting engineer. Either way, spending on engineering increases if the order is accepted; the cost of engineering is now a relevant cost.

To illustrate the second type of change, suppose that the company could purchase a component used for production instead of making it in house. Recall that 10,000 engineering hours are available and 9,000 are used. If the component is purchased, then the demand for engineering hours will drop from 9,000 to 7,000. This is a permanent reduction because engineering support will no longer be needed for manufacturing the component. Because unused capacity is now 3,000 hours, and engineering capacity is acquired in chunks of 2,000 hours, the company can reduce capacity and resource spending by laying off one engineer or reassigning the engineer to another plant where the services are in demand. Either way, the resource supply is reduced to 8,000 hours. Engineering cost would differ by $50,000 (the salary for one engineer) across the make-or-buy alternatives. This cost is then relevant to the decision.

Often, committed resources are acquired in advance for multiple periods—before resource demands are known. Leasing or buying a building is an example. Buying multiperiod activity capacity is often done by paying cash up front. In this case, an annual expense may be recognized, but no additional resource spending is needed. Up-front resource spending is a sunk cost and never relevant. Periodic resource spending, such as leasing, is essentially independent of resource usage. Even if a permanent reduction of activity usage is experienced, it is difficult to reduce resource spending because of formal contractual commitments.

For example, assume a company leases a plant for $100,000 per year for 10 years. The plant is capable of producing 20,000 units of a product—the level expected when the plant was leased. After five years, the demand for the product drops and the plant needs to produce only 15,000 units each year. The annual lease payment of $100,000 must still be paid even though units produced have decreased. Suppose instead that demand increases beyond the 20,000-unit capability. The company may consider buying or leasing an additional plant. Here, resource spending could change across alternatives. The decision, however, to acquire long-term activity capacity is not a short-term or small-scale decision. Decisions involving multiperiod capabilities are capital investment decisions and are covered in Chapter 19. Exhibit 17.2 summarizes the activity resource usage model's role in assessing relevancy.

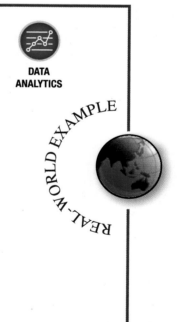

DATA ANALYTICS

Technology and Big Data Transform Bookstores

The corner bookstore has evolved throughout the years. Once a meeting place for book lovers, the bookstore kept a carefully curated list of titles on hand. If a customer wanted a book not in stock, the book store ordered it, and several days later, it was available. Of course, big-box stores and then Amazon.com nearly put an end to that model.

Technology has brought new life to the corner bookstore. The Espresso Book Machine prints books on demand. About the size of a large photocopier and connected to the Internet, the Espresso machine has access to about seven million titles. The resulting book is ready in about five minutes. Bookstores that own Espresso machines can succeed with a comparatively small footprint, perhaps just 2,000 square feet. The inventory of books on hand is much smaller, with only one or two copies of many books instead of 10 to 12. This also cuts back on overordering and then returning unsold books to the publisher. In essence, the machine allows the bookstores to offer books for the "long tail"—the relatively few readers who want the less popular or long out-of-copyright books, such as Nikolai Gogol's *Lost Souls* or Mark Twain's *Is Shakespeare Dead?*

A further advantage of printing on demand is the ability to self-publish books. Families can put together family albums and histories, printing off a limited number of copies economically. The result is that the corner bookstore remains a viable business model.[6]

---

6 Jeffrey A. Trachtenberg, "How Tech Is Bringing Readers Back into Bookstores," *The Wall Street Journal* (April 20, 2016): D1–D2.

Exhibit 17.2

Resource Demand and Supply

Category	Relationships	Relevancy
Flexible	Supply = Demand	
	a. Demand changes	a. Relevant
	b. Demand constant	b. Not relevant
Committed	Supply − Demand = Unused capacity	
	a. Demand increase < Unused capacity	a. Not relevant
	b. Demand increase > Unused capacity	b. Relevant
	c. Demand decrease (permanent)	
	1. Activity capacity reduced	1. Relevant
	2. Activity capacity unchanged	2. Not relevant

OBJECTIVE 4

Apply the tactical decision-making concepts in a variety of business situations.

ILLUSTRATIVE EXAMPLES OF TACTICAL DECISION MAKING

The activity resource usage model and the concept of relevancy are valuable tools in making tactical decisions. It is important to see how they are used to solve a variety of problems. Applications include decisions to make or buy a component, to keep or drop a segment or product line, to accept or reject a special order at less than the usual price, and to process a joint product further or sell it at the split-off point. Of course, this is not an exhaustive list. The same decision-making principles can be applied to other settings. Once you see how they are used, it is relatively easy to apply them in any appropriate setting. In illustrating the applications, we assume that the first two steps of the tactical decision-making model (see Exhibit 17.1) have already been performed. Thus, the emphasis is on tactical cost analysis.

Make-or-Buy Decisions

Organizations often face **make-or-buy decisions**—a decision of whether to make or to buy components or services used in making a product or providing a service. For example, a physician can buy laboratory tests from external suppliers (hospitals or for-profit laboratories), or these lab tests can be done internally. Similarly, a computer manufacturer can make its own disk drives, or they can be bought from external suppliers.

Outsourcing of technical and professional jobs has become an important make-or-buy issue. **Outsourcing** refers to the relocation of a business function to another company. When the other company is located outside of the country, the situation is referred to as **offshoring**. Over the past few decades, many companies have offshored key business functions in an attempt to cut costs. Interestingly, a large portion of such companies have subsequently chosen to reverse this decision through **reshoring**, which refers to the return of previously offshored business functions to the original country of origin.

REAL-WORLD EXAMPLE

While product outsourcing receives significant attention, some companies outsource services. In addition, many of these outsourced services are offshored to various countries around the world, such as India. For example, companies such as **Dell**, **Barclays**, **Oracle**, and **General Electric** have offshored their call center activities, including customer service and technical support, in an attempt to generate cost savings. However, as many companies have learned, offshoring opportunities should be studied carefully beforehand using a thorough relevant analysis to be sure that the major relevant costs have been identified and adequately quantified. Some companies have been unpleasantly surprised after moving forward with offshoring to learn that they had significantly overestimated the benefits and underestimated the costs of their offshoring endeavors.

Qualitative considerations are important in the outsourcing decision. Time is a valuable resource, and many companies have found that a global presence leads to time and quality enhancement. For example, software companies have found that call centers located in Ireland and the United States provide better customer service. At 8 a.m., a customer in New York who needs an answer to a question may not get help from a California-based call center, but will get help from a Dublin-based center. On the negative side, the political ramifications of outsourcing, with its overtones of "exporting jobs," have led companies to weigh the decision more carefully.

Remember that relevant analyses should include any associated opportunity costs. For example, assume that outsourcing the production of a particular part for a high-end coffee machine would free up plant capacity that could then be used to produce an upgrade feature (e.g., a more effective automatic bean grinder) that would increase the per-unit profit by $25. If the company decided not to outsource the part production (i.e., continue to produce the part in-house), then the $25 per-unit forgone profit would represent an opportunity cost for the decision to make the part and should be factored into the make-or-buy relevant analysis.

Make-or-buy decisions, while not short run in nature, fall into the small-scale tactical decision category. For example, the decision to make or buy may be motivated by cost leadership and/or differentiation strategies. Making instead of buying (or vice versa) may be one way to reduce the cost of producing the main product. Alternatively, choosing to make or buy may be a way of increasing the quality of the component and thus increasing the overall quality of the final product (differentiating on the basis of quality). **Example 17.1** shows the how and why of structuring the make-or-buy decision.

EXAMPLE 17.1

The HOW and WHY of Structuring a Make-or-Buy Decision

Information:

Talmadge Company produces 100,000 units of Part 34B, used in one of its snow-blower engines, each year. An outside supplier has offered to supply the part for $4.75. The unit cost is:

Direct materials	$0.50
Direct labor	2.40
Variable overhead (power)	0.90
Fixed overhead	1.05
Total unit cost	$4.85

Overhead is applied on the basis of machine hours; Part 34B requires 30,000 machine hours per year.

> **Why:**
> The make-or-buy situation requires the company to focus on relevant costs and benefits. The problem is set up with relevant costs and benefits organized under column headings for each alternative. The difference between the alternatives gives the quantitative advantage or disadvantage for each alternative.

Required:

1. What are the alternatives for Talmadge Company?

2. Assume that none of the fixed cost is avoidable. List the relevant cost(s) of internal production and of external purchase.

3. Which alternative is more cost effective and by how much?

4. *What if* $60,000 of fixed overhead is supervision for Part 34B that is avoided if the part is purchased? Which alternative is more cost effective and by how much?

EXAMPLE 17.1

(Continued)

Solution:

1. The alternatives are to make the part in house or buy the part externally.

2. The relevant costs of making the part are direct materials, direct labor, and variable factory overhead. The relevant cost of buying the part is the purchase price.

3.

	Make	Buy	Difference
Direct materials	$ 50,000	$ 0	$ 50,000
Direct labor	240,000	0	240,000
Variable overhead	90,000	0	90,000
Purchase price	0	475,000	(475,000)
Totals	$380,000	$475,000	$ (95,000)

Because the fixed overhead is not relevant, the analysis shows a $95,000 advantage in favor of making the part in house.

4.

	Make	Buy	Difference
Direct materials	$ 50,000	$ 0	$ 50,000
Direct labor	240,000	0	240,000
Variable overhead	90,000	0	90,000
Supervision	60,000	0	60,000
Purchase price	0	475,000	(475,000)
Totals	$440,000	$475,000	$ (35,000)

Now, supervision (part of fixed overhead) is relevant; the analysis shows a $35,000 advantage in favor of making the part in house.

Cost Analysis: Activity-Based Cost Management System The make-or-buy problem also can be illustrated in an activity-based costing format. The structure of the problem is the same as that shown in Example 17.1; however, typically the relevant costs are more extensive and care must be taken to determine which activities are relevant, and by how much. To illustrate the ABC analysis for Talmadge Company's Part 34B, we will use the data in Exhibit 17.3 along with the data from Example 17.1. All activity capacities are annual capacity measures. The cost of providing space includes annual plant depreciation, property taxes, and annual maintenance. This cost is allocated to the products based on the square feet of space occupied by the product's production equipment. The variable component of each activity represents the cost of flexible resources. The fixed cost component represents the cost of committed resources acquired in advance of usage. Units of purchase indicate how many units of the activity (as measured by its driver) must be acquired at a time. For example, if more capacity for moving materials is needed, it must be bought in lump sums of 25,000 moves at a time.

To determine whether Talmadge should continue to make Part 34B or buy it from an external supplier depends on how much *resource spending* can be reduced because of the ability to reduce resource usage (by buying instead of making). As is done in Example 17.1, the problem is structured as follows:

Activity Cost Formula:					
Activity		**Fixed Cost**	**Variable Rate**		**Amount of Driver**
Providing power	=	$0	+	$3	× Machine hours
Providing supervision	=	$0	+	$20,000	× Lines
Moving materials	=	$250,000	+	$0.60	× Number of moves
Inspecting product	=	$280,000	+	$1.50	× Inspection hours
Setting up equipment	=	$0	+	$10	× Setup hours
Providing space	=	$971,000			Square feet
Depreciation	=	$120,000			Units

Exhibit 17.3

Activity and Cost Information

Activity Driver	Total Capacity	Expected Usage	Part 34B Usage	Units of Purchase
Machine hours	As needed	750,000	30,000	1
Supervisory lines	15	15	3	3
Moves	250,000	240,000	40,000	25,000
Inspection hours	16,000	14,000	2,000	2,000
Setup hours	60,000	58,000	6,000	2,000
Providing space	971,000	971,000	5,000	50,000
Depreciation	620,000	100,000	100,000	15,000

	Make	Buy	Difference
Direct materials	$ 50,000	$ 0	$ 50,000
Direct labor	240,000	0	240,000
Providing power	90,000	0	90,000
Providing supervision	60,000	0	60,000
Moving materials	49,000	0	49,000
Inspecting product	38,000	0	38,000
Setting up equipment	60,000	0	60,000
Purchase price	0	475,000	(475,000)
Totals	$ 587,000	$475,000	$ 112,000

If Talmadge buys Part 34B instead of making it, *resource usage* decreases for each of the seven activities. Let's review them.

Direct materials, direct labor, and power are strictly variable and their amounts and costs are identical to those calculated in Example 17.1.

$$\text{Direct materials} = \$0.50 \times 100,000 \text{ units} = \$50,000$$
$$\text{Direct labor} = \$2.40 \times 100,000 \text{ units} = \$240,000$$
$$\text{Power} = \$0.90 \times 100,000 \text{ units} = \$90,000$$

Supervision is a lumpy resource and must be acquired in units of three lines. Since the making of Part 34B requires exactly three lines, the amount of supervision needed is $60,000 ($20,000 × 3 lines).

Moving materials and inspecting product are a bit more complicated since there is a variable and a fixed amount.

$$\text{Moving materials} = (\$250,000/250,000 \text{ total moves})(25,000)$$
$$+ (\$0.60 \times 40,000 \text{ moves})$$
$$= \$49,000$$

$$\text{Inspecting product} = (\$280{,}000/16{,}000 \text{ total inspection hours})(2{,}000)$$
$$+ (\$1.50 \times 2{,}000 \text{ inspection hours})$$
$$= \$38{,}000$$

Notice that the fixed amount associated with Part 34B is the amount by which fixed resource spending can be reduced, so it depends on the total capacity—250,000 moves for moving materials and 16,000 inspection hours for inspecting product. The fixed rate is multiplied by the lumpy amount or the units that must be purchased at once. The variable amount of resource spending associated with Part 34B is the amount of driver actually used in producing the part times the variable rate.

Setting up equipment is strictly variable with respect to the number of setup hours. Since Part 34B uses 6,000 setup hours, and the rate is $10 per setup hour, the production of the part requires $60,000.

Notice that providing space and equipment depreciation are ignored since they are irrelevant costs. They will remain the same in total no matter whether the part is made internally or purchased externally.

As we can see, the additional information provided by activity-based costing changed the analysis so that purchasing the part is better. The company will save $112,000 per year if the part is bought externally. Of course, this is just the quantitative analysis. There may be compelling qualitative factors that Talmadge should consider. For example, will the outside supplier maintain the quality needed by Talmadge? Will the supplier be able to meet delivery requirements? Only a full analysis that considers both quantitative and qualitative factors will give management the support to make a good decision.

DATA ANALYTICS

REAL-WORLD EXAMPLE

Make-or-Buy Analyses for Data Analytic Decisions

Many companies spend increasingly large amounts of resources for artificial intelligence (AI) systems. AI refers to any type of computer system that is capable of performing tasks that otherwise would require human intelligence, including learning, planning, and problem-solving.[7] As with other important endeavors, companies that wish to invest in AI must decide whether to build their own AI system (i.e., make it) or instead pay a specialist company to develop it for them (i.e., buy it). GLYNT.AI specializes in designing machine learning solutions that help companies retrieve unstructured data from various documents. GLYNT.AI recommends that companies conducting the make-or-buy tactical analysis for an AI system investment should consider the key factors that drive relevant costs and benefits. The first factor concerns the desired error rate (from AI-based predictions) that the company deems to be acceptable. Specifically, the company must determine the nature and extent of errors it finds acceptable as different types of errors, as well as error rates, can lead to very different costs. For example, a medical devices company likely is willing to incur greater cost to reduce device error rates than is an online clothing retailer focused on buyer sentiment.[8] The second factor concerns the extent and speed at which the company plans to roll out the AI insights across the company. The costs to roll out AI-powered analytic results include investments in various activities, such as data management, user interface, governance, software engineering, and security. These costs often increase dramatically as the breadth of rollout increases. Therefore, companies must consider the appropriate factors and their relevant costs in order to effectively analyze an AI make-or-buy decision.

---

7   R. Toews, "What Does 'Artificial Intelligence' Really Mean?" *Forbes.com* (February 17, 2020), https://www.forbes.com/sites/robtoews/2020/02/17/what-does-artificial-intelligence-really-mean/#23f4c5434c5f, accessed August 14, 2020.

8   S. Carrico, "To Make or Buy AI: Two Often Overlooked Factors," *Forbes.com* (January 30, 2019), https://www.forbes.com/sites/forbestechcouncil/2019/01/30/to-make-or-buy-ai-two-often-overlooked-factors/#d26bf366cae6, accessed August 14, 2020.

Keep-or-Drop Decisions

Often, a manager needs to determine whether a segment, such as a product or service line, should be kept or dropped. For example, automobile companies often make high-profile drop decisions, such as **General Motors**' decision to drop a number of car lines, including Oldsmobile, Hummer, Saab, and Buick. A **keep-or-drop decision** uses relevant cost analysis to determine whether a segment or line of business should be kept or dropped. In addition, the relevant (or incremental) analysis used to evaluate a keep-or-drop tactical decision can be applied to the evaluation of adding a segment or line of business. Returning to the automobile industry, Ford Motor Company decided to bring back (i.e., add) the Bronco product line after having dropped it several decades earlier.[9] This tactical decision can pose challenges, even for large, experienced companies. For example, from a service line perspective, Amazon realized in its first year of providing free one-day delivery (rather than its previous two-day delivery) that the relevant costs of this speedier service were significantly greater than it had estimated. Due in part to this cost underestimation, Amazon lowered its quarterly earnings expectation by approximately $1.6 billion as compared to the previous year.[10]

In a traditional cost management system, segmented income statements, using unit-based fixed or variable costs, improve the ability to make keep-or-drop decisions. **Example 17.2** shows the how and why of structuring the keep-or-drop decision analysis. Often the most difficult aspect of conducting an effective keep-or-drop relevant analysis is accurately estimating the costs that would go away, as opposed to remain, if the given segment or business line were dropped. The segmented income statement in Example 17.2 helps with these cost estimations by differentiating direct fixed costs (which affect product or segment margin) from common fixed costs. While exceptions exist, unless given information to the contrary, direct fixed costs typically are relevant and common fixed costs typically are irrelevant to tactical decision making. For example, workers across many different companies increasingly demonstrate an ability to work effectively from remote locations (e.g., a coffeehouse or even their home hundreds of miles away from the company office building). As a result, such companies are conducting keep-or-drop analyses with respect to their high-cost office facilities, which represents a direct fixed cost for certain product lines, service lines, or company divisions.[11]

As Example 17.2 shows, revenues and costs that are directly attributable to a segment must be identified. If the segment is dropped, then only the traceable revenues and costs should vanish. Furthermore, the traceable income (loss) determines whether a segment should be dropped or kept. *Product* (or segment) *margin* is equal to contribution margin (i.e., sales revenue minus variable cost) minus direct fixed costs. If the product margin is positive, then the segment is kept; if negative, then the segment may be dropped. Example 17.2 shows a traditional segmented income statement, where products are defined as segments. The statement indicates that both Runner's GPS and Chart Plotter models provide positive product margins and the Basic GPS model has a negative product margin. Thus, management likely would consider dropping the Basic GPS model. However, when the analysis considers potential complementary effects—the impact of the dropped product line on sales of the *other* two product lines—the decision likely would change. In the latter case, it is clear that customers prefer a full line of products, and that the Basic GPS somehow adds to the profitability of the other two GPS models.

A company can improve the differential analysis by looking beyond the traditional product costing model. That is, managers can consider more than the unit-based variable versus fixed cost categories by looking at the impact of non-unit costs.

9 S. Abuelsamid, "2021 Ford Bronco Aims for the Heart of Jeep," *Forbes.com* (July 13, 2020), https://www.forbes.com/sites/samabuelsamid/2020/07/13/2021-ford-bronco-aims-for-the-heart-of-jeep/#5e0c6b4e47a5, accessed August 14, 2020.

10 T. Soper, "Amazon's Big Bet on 1-Day Delivery Is Costing More Than Expected and Cutting into Profits," *GeekWire.com* (July 25, 2019), https://www.geekwire.com/2019/amazons-big-bet-1-day-delivery-costing-expected-cutting-profits/, accessed August 14, 2020.

11 A. Akala, "More Big Employers Are Talking about Permanent Work-From-Home Positions," *CNBC.com* (2020), https://www.cnbc.com/2020/05/01/major-companies-talking-about-permanent-work-from-home-positions.html, accessed August 14, 2020.

EXAMPLE 17.2

The HOW and WHY of Structuring a Keep-or-Drop Product Line Decision

Information:

Dexter Company makes three types of GPS devices. The Basic GPS model is an entry-level automotive GPS device; it is sold through discounters and Amazon.com. The Runner's GPS is a miniaturized model that allows the runner to track mileage, steps, and heart rate while running; it is sold through athletic stores and on sports gear websites. The Chart Plotter is a specialized GPS device for sailors; it can be customized with maps of the sea floor and specific geographic areas of coast line and deep water. It is sold via the Web on dedicated GPS sites. Dexter Company is considering dropping the Basic GPS line and keeping the Runner's GPS and Chart Plotter. The segmented income statement is presented below.

	Basic GPS	Runner's GPS	Chart Plotter	Total
Sales	$ 450,000	$ 980,000	$1,670,000	$ 3,100,000
Less variable costs	(324,000)	(372,000)	(601,600)	(1,297,600)
Contribution margin	$ 126,000	$ 608,000	$1,068,400	$ 1,802,400
Less direct fixed costs:				
Advertisings	(85,000)	(124,000)	(130,000)	(339,000)
Supervision	(60,000)	(115,000)	(135,000)	(310,000)
Product margin	$ (19,000)	$ 369,000	$ 803,400	$ 1,153,400
Less common fixed expenses				915,000
Operating income				$ 238,400

Why:

Companies need to consider whether a segment or product line should remain. This problem requires a look at the relevant costs and benefits of dropping the segment.

Required:

1. List the alternatives being considered.

2. List the relevant benefits and costs for each alternative.

3. Which alternative is more cost effective and by how much?

4. *What if* dropping the Basic GPS line would mean a 10 percent loss of volume for the Runner's GPS device and a 2 percent loss in volume for the Chart Plotter? Which alternative would be more cost effective and by how much?

Solution:

1. The two alternatives are to keep the Basic GPS line or to drop it.

2. The relevant benefits and costs of keeping the Basic GPS line include sales of $450,000, variable costs of $324,000, advertising cost of $85,000, and supervision cost of $60,000. All common fixed costs are irrelevant. None of the relevant benefits and costs of keeping the Basic GPS line would occur under the drop alternative.

3.

EXAMPLE 17.2

(*Continued*)

	Keep	Drop	Differential Amount to Keep
Sales	$450,000	$0	$ 450,000
Less variable costs	324,000	0	(324,000)
Contribution margin	$126,000	0	$ 126,000
Less direct fixed costs:			
Advertising	(85,000)	0	(85,000)
Supervision	(60,000)	0	(60,000)
Product margin	$(19,000)	0	$ (19,000)

There is a $19,000 loss if the Basic GPS line is kept.

4.

	Basic GPS	Runner's GPS	Chart Plotter	Total
Sales	$0	$ 882,000	$1,636,600	$2,518,600
Less variable costs	0	(334,800)	(589,568)	(924,368)
Contribution margin	$0	$ 547,200	$1,047,032	$1,594,232
Less direct fixed costs:				
Advertising	0	(124,000)	(130,000)	(254,000)
Supervision	0	(115,000)	(135,000)	(250,000)
Product margin	$0	$ 308,200	$ 782,032	$1,090,232
Less common fixed expenses				915,000
Operating income				$ 175,232

Difference in income = Income with all three lines − Income with only two lines

= $238,400 − $175,232 = $63,168

Because of the impact that dropping the Basic GPS line has on the sales of the other two lines, the analysis shows that dropping the line will actually decrease income by $63,168. Therefore, the Basic GPS line should be kept. However, it would be a good idea to consider ways to make production more efficient.

Let's continue the Dexter Company example using activity data. Suppose that Dexter Company finds that the common fixed expenses actually include some traceable fixed expenses that can be assigned to the product lines based on non-unit driver usage. In particular, included within Dexter's $915,000 of common fixed expenses are $140,000 for inspection, $150,000 for customer service, and $140,000 for material handling. The amount of these three expenses and their activity data are shown in the following table:

Activity	Driver	Total Capacity	Unused Capacity	Basic GPS Usage	Units of Purchase
Inspecting products	Number of batches	200	15	80	40
Customer service	Number of calls	30,000	900	12,000	1,000
Material handling	Number of moves	2,800	400	1,400	350

Now we can re-analyze the keep-or-drop decision with the additional activity information.

CVS Health enacted a highly visible and risky product-line keep-or-drop decision when it elected to discontinue selling all tobacco products in its approximately 7,600 stores. *Was this drop decision a big deal for CVS, its investors, and other key stakeholders?* The company estimated that its decision to drop tobacco products would cause it to forgo about *$2 billion* in annual sales revenue. Therefore, yes, most stakeholders, and investors in particular, likely considered the decision to be a big deal as it represented approximately 1.5 percent of the company's total sales! *Why did CVS make this particular drop decision?* CVS's CEO stated publicly that the sale of tobacco products simply was inconsistent with the company's purpose. Specifically, the dropping of tobacco products helped to more closely align the company's product mix offering with its continuing strategic shift toward being a health-oriented destination for customers. *What did the drop decision relevant analysis look like?* Presumably, the analysis forecasted a positive incremental profit resulting from this risky drop decision. However, it is unclear over what time horizon the profit from expected additional health-care-oriented product and service sales was expected to outweigh the lost profit from the forgone tobacco sales. Furthermore, the relevant analysis likely estimated the amount of collateral damage—lost sales of complementary products (food and beverages, lottery tickets, pharmacy products)—as some customers who used to buy CVS tobacco products might no longer make a special trip to CVS to buy these other products. Interestingly, a few years later, **Walgreens Boots Alliance**—one of CVS's fiercest competitors—joined CVS in banning the sale of e-cigarettes, as did **Rite Aid**, **Walmart**, and **Kroger**. However, Walgreens elected to keep its traditional tobacco (e.g., cigarette) product line. The stark difference in this product drop decision between two Fortune 25 competitors illustrates the complexity of evaluating and enacting effective product- and service-line drop decisions.

	Keep	Drop	Differential Amount to Keep
Sales	$ 450,000	$0	$ 450,000
Less variable costs	324,000	0	(324,000)
Contribution margin	$ 126,000	0	$ 126,000
Less direct fixed costs:			
Advertising	(85,000)	0	(85,000)
Supervision	(60,000)	0	(60,000)
Inspection[a]	(56,000)	0	(56,000)
Customer service[b]	(60,000)	0	(60,000)
Material handling[c]	(70,000)	0	(70,000)
Product margin	$(205,000)	0	$(205,000)

[a]Inspection rate = $140,000/200 = $700; $700 × 80 batches = $56,000
[b]Customer service rate = $150,000/30,000 = $5; $5 × 12,000 calls = $60,000
[c]Material handling rate = $140,000/2,800 = $50; $50 × 1,400 moves = $70,000

Notice that the amount of each traceable fixed activity used by the Basic GPS can be eliminated. There is a $205,000 loss if the Basic GPS line is kept. While the use of ABC does not change the structure or conceptual basis of the keep-or-drop decision, it does give managers a better idea of just which costs will be affected by the analysis.

As always, qualitative factors are considered in the keep-or-drop decision. If a line is being dropped, how will it affect customer loyalty? Will employees need to be laid off, or can the excess labor be absorbed into other lines? Some of these factors can be quantified, or probabilities can be assigned so that managers can use sensitivity analysis. Other factors are truly qualitative and must be considered subjectively.

Special-Order Decisions

In general, price discrimination laws require that firms engaged in interstate commerce sell identical products at the same price to competing customers in the same market. These restrictions do not apply to competitive bids or to noncompeting customers. Bid prices can vary to customers in the same market, and firms often have the opportunity to consider one-time special orders from potential customers in markets not ordinarily served. A **special-order decision** focuses on whether a specially priced order should be accepted or rejected. Special-order decisions are examples of tactical decisions with a short-term focus. Increasing short-term profits is the limited objective represented by this type of decision. Special-order decisions are financially attractive when the relevant revenues that would be earned from accepting the order are expected to exceed the relevant costs that would be incurred from accepting the order. Care should be taken to recognize when the acceptance of special orders might jeopardize normal distribution channels or adversely affect other strategic elements. Specifically, **cannibalization** occurs when a special-order sale takes away from (or eats into) the sale of a regular product or service. Cannibalization does not preclude the special order from being profitable for the company, but the financial impact of cannibalization should be factored into the special order's relevant analysis. Specifically, the amount of any lost profit that would result from turning away (e.g., cannibalizing) regular business so that the special-order can be fulfilled should be factored into the financial analysis as a relevant cost of accepting the special-order. Special orders often can be attractive, especially when the firm has unused (or excess) capacity (e.g,. excess machinery time, factory or warehousing space, hotel rooms, airplane seats, etc.). However, as an example of cannibalization, if the capacity required to fulfill the special order exceeds the amount of unused capacity, then the amount of any forgone profit from any lost regular sales should be factored into the analysis of whether to accept or reject the special order.

U.S. pharmaceutical giant **Pfizer**, in conjunction with German biotechnology company **BioNTech**, received an interesting special-order offer in late July from the U.S. government (Department of Health and Human Services) to develop and produce a COVID-19 vaccine by the end of the calendar year.[12] The United States' Warp Speed project hoped to drastically shorten the normal time it takes a company to design, test, approve, produce, and administer a vaccine. The special-order contract called for the U.S. government to pay Pfizer $1.95 billion for 100 million vaccine doses (about $20 per dose). However, the contract also stipulated that payment would occur *only if* Pfizer successfully proceeded through this vaccination value chain, including receiving approval from the Food and Drug Administration (FDA). Furthermore, the government would have the rights to acquire up to 500 million additional doses. This special-order offer presented Pfizer with considerable relevant revenue and relevant cost estimation challenges. For example, relevant revenue would be zero if Pfizer failed to successfully create an approved new vaccine. This financial outcome is daunting given that FDA approval typically is both uncertain and very time-consuming in most new drug scenarios. Also, Pfizer had to estimate all relevant costs of required activities involved with researching, testing, producing, and distributing its new vaccine. In addition to estimating the relevant profit for 100 million doses, Pfizer had to forecast the relevant profit for the additional 500 million vaccine doses to fully analyze the financial impact of accepting this unique special-order offer, which potentially might fall outside the relevant range associated with its current cost structure.

REAL-WORLD EXAMPLE

Special-order decisions have the potential to create long-term impacts. For example, during the COVID-19 global pandemic, Ford Motor Company decided to partner with 3M and GE Healthcare to make respirators and ventilators, which were in high demand and short supply in the U.S. medical field as important devices in treating intensive-care hospital patients struggling with serious virus reactions. Ford commented that the relevant analysis for this special order

---

12 N. Weiland, D. Grady, and D. Sanger, "Pfizer Gets $1.95 Billion to Produce Coronavirus Vaccine by Year's End," *NYTimes.com* (July 30, 2020), https://www.nytimes.com/2020/07/22/us/politics/pfizer-coronavirus-vaccine.html, accessed August 6, 2020.

involved estimating the relevant costs of "working on a new design leveraging parts from both companies (Ford and 3M)." Many of the parts that Ford anticipated using the special order were parts currently used in its best-selling F-150 pickup truck. The importance of considering the long-term impacts of such decisions is reflected in Ford Motor Company executive chairman Bill Ford's statement: "At Ford, we feel a deep obligation to step up and contribute in times of need, just as we always have through the 117-year history of our company."[13]

Suppose, for example, that Polarcreme, Inc., an ice-cream company, is operating at 80 percent of its productive capacity, 10 million one-quart units. An ice-cream distributor from a geographic region not normally served by the company has offered to buy 2 million units of premium ice cream at $1.75 per unit, provided its own label can be attached to the product. Normal selling price is $2.50 per unit. **Example 17.3** shows how and why the special-order decision should be structured.

EXAMPLE 17.3

The HOW and WHY of Structuring a Special-Order Decision

Information:

Polarcreme, Inc., an ice-cream company, is operating at 80 percent of its productive capacity, 10 million one-quart units. An ice-cream distributor from a different geographic region has offered to buy 2 million units of premium ice cream at $1.75 per unit, provided its own label can be attached to the product. Normal selling price is $2.50 per unit. Cost information for the premium ice cream follows:

	Total of 8,000,000 Units	Unit Cost
Variable costs:		
Direct materials	$ 7,600,000	$0.95
Direct labor	2,000,000	0.25
Packaging	1,600,000	0.20
Commissions	160,000	0.02
Distribution	240,000	0.03
Other variable costs	400,000	0.05
Non-unit-level costs:		
Purchasing ($8 × 40,000 purchase orders)	320,000	0.04
Receiving ($6 × 80,000 receiving orders)	480,000	0.06
Setting up ($8,000 × 50 setups)	400,000	0.05
Fixed costs	1,600,000	0.20
Total costs	$14,800,000	$1.85

The special order will not require commissions or distribution (the buyer will pick up the order at Polarcreme's factory). The order will require 10,000 purchase orders, 20,000 receiving orders, and 13 setups. In addition, a one-time cost for the special order's label template will be required at $24,500.

> **Why:**
> A special order is "special" because the price is lower than normal. Companies need to consider all relevant costs and benefits when considering a special order.

Required:

1. List the alternatives being considered.

2. List the relevant benefits and costs for each alternative.

---

13 P. Howard, "Ford Partners with 3M, GE Healthcare to Make Respirators, Ventilators to Fight Coronavirus," *Detroit Free Press* (March 24, 2020), https://www.freep.com/story/money/cars/2020/03/24/ford-ge-healthcare-3-m-coronavirus -covid-19-ventilators-respirators/2907167001/, accessed September 11, 2020.

EXAMPLE 17.3

(*Continued*)

3. Which alternative is more cost effective and by how much?

4. ***What if*** accepting the special order upset a regular customer who was considering expanding into the new geographical region and decided, then, to take their regular annual order of 2 million units of premium ice cream to another company? Which alternative would be better?

Solution:

1. The two alternatives are to accept or reject the special order.

2. The relevant benefits and costs of accepting the order include revenue, direct materials, direct labor, packaging, other variable costs, purchasing, receiving, setting up, and the cost of the label template. No fixed costs will be affected. If the order is rejected, the net benefit is zero.

3.

	Accept	Reject	Differential Amount to Accept
Sales	$ 3,500,000	$0	$ 3,500,000
Direct materials	(1,900,000)	0	(1,900,000)
Direct labor	(500,000)	0	(500,000)
Packaging	(400,000)	0	(400,000)
Other variable costs	(100,000)	0	(100,000)
Purchasing ($8 × 10,000 purchase orders)	(80,000)	0	(80,000)
Receiving ($6 × 20,000 receiving orders)	(120,000)	0	(120,000)
Setting up ($8,000 × 13 setups)	(104,000)		(104,000)
Label template	(24,500)	0	(24,500)
Net benefit	$ 271,500	0	$ 271,500

There is a $271,500 increase in operating income if the special order is accepted.

4. In this case, the regular order, at $2.50 per unit, would be better than the special order at $1.75 per unit and the company would be better off rejecting the special order. Even though the special order avoids the commission and distribution charge, those total only $0.05 per unit, and the company would be better off making the additional $0.75 in price with the regular customer, not to mention avoiding the $24,500 for the special label template.

Notice that the special order in Example 17.3 has a price of $1.75 per unit, well below the normal selling price of $2.50; in fact, it is even below the total unit cost. Even so, accepting the order was profitable for the company. The company has sufficient idle capacity, and the order will not displace (or cannibalize) regular units being produced to sell at the normal price. Additionally, some of the costs are not relevant, such as the commissions, distribution, and fixed cost. The added cost attributable to the special order is, of course, included in the analysis. Requirement 4 of Example 17.3 asks us to consider the potential impact of the special order on existing customers. In this case, it was easy to quantify the impact and see that the special order should be rejected. In other cases, managers may have to consider the impact on other customers as part of the qualitative factors impinging on the order.

Decisions to Sell or Process Further

As discussed in Chapter 7, joint products have common processes and costs of production up to a split-off point. At that point, they become distinguishable. For example, certain minerals such as copper and gold may both be found in a given ore. The ore must be mined, crushed, and treated before the copper and gold are separated. The point of separation is called the split-off point. The costs of mining, crushing, and treatment are common to both products.

Often, joint products are sold at the split-off point. But sometimes, it is more profitable to process a joint product further, beyond the split-off point, prior to selling it. Determining whether to **sell or process further** is an important decision that a manager must make. The key point in this decision is that all of the joint production costs are irrelevant to the sell or process further decision. By the time the split-off point is reached, all joint costs are sunk, and therefore, irrelevant.

To illustrate, consider Delrio Corporation. Delrio is an agricultural corporation that produces and sells fresh produce and canned food products. The San Juan Division of Delrio specializes in tomato products. San Juan has a large tomato farm that produces all the tomatoes used in its products. The farm is divided into plots that produce approximately 1,500 pounds of tomatoes; this defines a load. Each plot must be cultivated, fertilized, sprayed, watered, and harvested. When the tomatoes have ripened, they are harvested. The tomatoes are then transported to a warehouse, where they are washed and sorted. The approximate cost of all these activities is $200 per load.

Tomatoes are sorted into two grades (A and B). Grade A tomatoes are larger and better shaped than Grade B and are sold to large supermarkets. Grade B tomatoes are sent to the canning plant where they are processed into catsup, tomato sauce, and tomato paste. Each load produces about 1,000 pounds of Grade A tomatoes and 500 pounds of Grade B tomatoes. Recently, the manager of the canning plant requested that the Grade A tomatoes be used for a Delrio hot sauce. Studies have indicated that the Grade A tomatoes provided a better flavor and consistency for the sauce than did Grade B tomatoes. Furthermore, Grade B tomatoes are fully utilized for other products. **Example 17.4** shows the how and why of structuring a sell at split-off or process further decision.

EXAMPLE 17.4

The HOW and WHY of Structuring a Sell at Split-Off or Process Further Decision

Information:

Delrio Company grows and sells fresh and canned food products. The San Juan farm grows and harvests tomatoes. Each plot yields 1,500 pounds of tomatoes, referred to as a load; of the 1,500 pounds, 1,000 pounds are Grade A tomatoes and 500 are Grade B. The cost of growing and harvesting the tomatoes is $200 per load. Delrio can sell the 1,000 pounds of Grade A tomatoes in a load to grocers for $0.40 per pound. Alternatively, the tomatoes could be processed into hot sauce. Each bottle of hot sauce sells for $1.50 and requires one pound of tomatoes. The cost of additional processing averages $1 per bottle; this amount includes the remaining ingredients, bottles, labor, and needed processing activities.

> **Why:**
> Because joint costs are incurred prior to the split-off point, they are sunk costs in determining whether to sell a product at split-off or process it further. Only the sales value at split-off, the further processing costs, and the eventual sales value are relevant to this decision.

Required:

1. List the alternatives being considered.

2. List the relevant benefits and costs for each alternative.

3. Which alternative is more cost effective and by how much?

4. *What if* the best of the Grade A tomatoes, Premium A's, could be sold to grocers for $0.80 per pound? Of the 1,000 pounds of Grade A tomatoes in a load, about 30 percent are Premium A's. The grocers, however, will not buy the Premium A's unless they are also sold the regular Grade A tomatoes. (They will deal with another supplier instead.) It will cost an additional $50 per load to separate the Premium A's from the regular Grade A's. Which alternative would be better?

Solution:

EXAMPLE 17.4

(*Continued*)

1. The two alternatives are to sell the Grade A tomatoes at split-off or process them further.

2. The relevant benefits and costs of selling at split-off versus processing the tomatoes further include revenue from sale to grocers and revenue from selling the hot sauce less the additional (further) processing costs. The $200 per load cost of growing and harvesting the tomatoes is sunk and need not be considered.

3.

	Sell at Split-Off	Process Further	Differential Amount to Process Further
Sales	$400	$ 1,500	$ 1,100
Further processing cost	0	(1,000)	(1,000)
Total	$400	$ 500	$ 100

There is a $100 per load advantage to processing the Grade A tomatoes into hot sauce.

4. In this case, 300 of the Grade A tomatoes (Premium A's) are sold for $0.80 and the remaining 700 pounds are sold for $0.40. The total revenue at split-off would be $520 ($240 + $280). (You might think that the original alternative still exists—sell all of the Grade A tomatoes at split-off for $0.40 per pound. While that alternative does exist, it is so clearly dominated by the new alternative with the higher-priced Premium A's that it can be safely ignored. The firm will no longer consider it.)

	Sell at Split-Off	Process Further	Differential Amount to Process Further
Sales	$520	$ 1,500	$ 980
Further processing cost	(50)	(1,000)	(950)
Total	$470	$ 500	$ 30

There is a $30 per load advantage to processing the Grade A tomatoes into hot sauce.

Example 17.4 shows that the joint cost of production, the $200 per load to grow and harvest the tomatoes, is irrelevant and can be ignored. Recall that the allocation of joint cost to the various joint products is done solely for the purposes of costing product and valuing inventories. It is not a part of the "sell or process further" decision. There is one other situation in which the joint cost is considered, and that would be the management decision to engage in the joint production process at all. If the total revenues do not cover all costs (both joint and further processing), then the company may want to reconsider being in that line of business.

The Role of Differential Analysis in Forensic Accounting

As introduced in Chapter 1 (and exemplified in other chapters throughout the book), an understanding of cost management concepts is essential in common forensic accounting tasks, such as dispute resolution and litigation support. The forensic accountant helps the court understand the accounting issues in the case by providing analyses, evaluations, and opinions regarding the nature, amount, and impact of such issues. For example, most litigation cases require an estimate of damages incurred because of actions or lack of actions by some entity in the case. The process of determining damages often is very similar to the differential (or relevant) analysis performed in the tactical decisions studied in this chapter.

For example, assume that ABC Company has a patent on a unique technological device. Another company, the XYZ Company, manufactured and sold a similar product that clearly violated the patent rights held by ABC Company. By the time the ABC Company discovered the actions of XYZ Company, three years of "illegal" sales had occurred. The ABC Company (i.e., the plaintiff in the case) filed suit against the XYZ Company (i.e., the defendant in the case), claiming damages for the three years of patent infringement sales. Assume further that the issue of "liability" is established (i.e., XYZ's sales clearly violated the patent held by the ABC Company). The question before the court then becomes, "What is the amount of damages suffered by the ABC Company?" It is not a simple answer such as the dollar amount of sales made by the XYZ Company. Even if the ABC Company (rather than the XYZ Company) had made the additional sales, the amount of damages would not simply equal the amount of the sales because the company that actually makes the sales also would have incurred the various expenses associated with making, selling, distributing, and supporting the sold products.

Instead, the damage calculation would utilize the type of differential analysis used in making tactical decisions. In our forensic example, the analysis does not evaluate the difference between choices made by the ABC Company (such as whether the ABC Company should make or buy a product component), but rather it evaluates what the ABC Company would have expected the results to be absent the illegal acts of the XYZ Company selling products that were protected by the patent owned by the ABC Company.

Typically, a forensic accountant begins by estimating the lost profit the ABC Company experienced as a result of the illegal sales made by the XYZ Company. The following table illustrates the differential analysis for the ABC Company's forensic case:

Forensic Differential Analysis for the ABC Company

Item	Per Unit	Number of Units	Total
Sales	$150	75,000	$11,250,000
Variable manufacturing cost	$ 80	75,000	6,000,000
Variable selling commission	$ 15	75,000	1,125,000
Variable distribution costs	$ 6	75,000	450,000
= Total Damages from Lost Sales			$ 3,675,000

Assume that during the three-year period, the XYZ Company sold 75,000 units that were covered by the patent owned by ABC. Had the ABC Company made those sales, it would have generated $11,250,000 in sales (75,000 × $150 per units). During the period covered by the illegal sales, the ABC Company was operating at a level such that it would have been able to produce and sell the 75,000 units without any change in its production, sales, or distribution capacity. Therefore, the per-unit relevant expenses in the analysis would be $80 for variable manufacturing costs, $15 in sales commission costs, and $6 for distribution costs for a total of $101 per unit. Therefore, the damages from lost sales would be ($150 − $101) × 75,000 units or $3,675,000 (($150 − $80 − $15 − $6) × 75,000).

This relatively simple analysis makes sense given the description of the events and relevant factors involved. However, additional factors might potentially be argued before the court, thereby making the differential analysis more complex. For example, the ABC Company may argue that it lost sales (beyond those made by XYZ) or experienced other harm because of the illegal competition from the XYZ Company. Perhaps the ABC Company will argue that the reputation of its patented product was harmed by the inferior quality of the similar product sold by the XYZ Company. The financial impact of these additional factors would need to be estimated and included in the differential analysis.

It is common for each side in a litigation to hire a forensic accounting expert to present its opinion of the amount of damages (if any) claimed in the case. Often these forensic accounting experts do not make the business assumptions presented at trial but are expected to compute and defend the associated financial amounts that are claimed within the case. For example, the defendant's (XYZ Company) forensic accounting expert might suggest that the correct amount for product expense for the ABC Company's lost sales should include all costs of manufacturing, not just the variable manufacturing expenses, as this measure of cost would lead to a lower estimate of damages (i.e., a lower estimate of lost profits). The defendant's forensic accountant would be expected to present the reasoning underlying their estimate of damages, including why their chosen perspective is the correct way to view the case's financial issues.

Forensic accounting expert opinions play a crucial role in helping the court understand and correctly evaluate the accounting issues within a given case. Their role includes explaining in an articulate manner the rationale and reasons for their expert opinions. As such, in addition to understanding complex accounting computations and associated data analyses, forensic accountants must possess effective written and oral communication skills. As illustrated in this example, such communication often involves explaining *why* the use of differential analysis is the appropriate perspective to be taken, as well as *how* it should be applied to the given case.

Relevant Costing and Ethical Behavior

ETHICS Relevant costs are used in making tactical decisions—decisions that have an immediate view or limited objective in mind. In making these decisions, however, decision makers should always keep the decisions within an ethical framework. Reaching objectives is important, but how you get there is perhaps even more important. Unfortunately, some managers have the opposite view. Part of the reason for the problem is the extreme pressure to perform felt by many managers. Often, the individual who is not a top performer may be laid off or demoted. Under such conditions, the temptation is often great to engage in questionable behavior. •

Ethical considerations can occur in various tactical decisions. For example, the decision to offshore production activities can generate significant cost savings oftentimes pertaining to lower wage expenses. However, the underlying causes of such cost savings should be considered as they might involve ethical challenges, such as an unsafe work environment, inhumane working conditions, child labor, or detrimental environmental consequences. Relevant analyses can attempt to identify and quantify the impact of such ethical considerations on financial outcomes, as well as other important performance metrics, such as the company's reputation, ability to attract and retain talented workers, spurring potential future regulations and fines, and finally adherence to the company's corporate values. Fair trade initiatives represent another example of international companies, such as Patagonia, attempting to include ethical considerations into its material and labor sourcing decisions, both of which can factor into relevant analyses of tactical decisions. For example, Patagonia offers more Fair Trade Certified clothing styles than any other apparel brand.[14]

There can be endless debates about what is right and what is wrong. Chapter 1 discusses some ethical standards that have been developed to provide guidance for individuals. Additionally, some companies hire full-time ethics officers. Often, these officers set up hotlines or other digital platforms so that employees can register complaints or inquire about the propriety of certain actions. A more informal but perhaps just as useful ethics rule of thumb sometimes is expressed as *The Wall Street Journal* test, which cautions employees not to do or say anything that would make them uncomfortable if it were published on the front page of *The Wall Street Journal* or any other prominent news or social media site.

Relevant Cost Analysis in Personal Decision Making

Finally, it is useful to note that relevant costing analysis is important in personal decision making. Nearly any short-term decision can be improved by following the decision model outlined in this chapter.

---

14 See https://www.fairtradecertified.org/news/press-releases/campaigns-virtual-conference-2020, accessed September 11, 2020.

REAL-WORLD EXAMPLE

For many parents of young skiers, an important decision is whether to buy the child a new pair of skis or go with the seasonal rental approach. The problem, of course, is that children grow and a pair of skis that works this year may not be the right size next year. Children also change their minds. The child who can't wait to get onto the slopes may be sick and tired of the sport after an unsuccessful morning. Or the child may decide to switch to snowboarding. Further complicating the problem is that many alternatives are available—daily ski rental, seasonal ski rental, lease-to-own, purchasing new, or purchasing used. Interestingly, computer scientists have developed a ski-rental algorithm to help people decide when skis should be bought versus rented. In the final analysis, parents use a combination of their budgets, their assessment of the probabilities that their children will enjoy skiing and will go frequently, and the importance of the "coolness factor" of snazzy graphics applied to the new skis.

Throughout the years, many of our students have found it enlightening to use the model to consider their decisions to keep or buy a car, get a pet, choose a college, and so on. They could see that they had already implicitly used the decision-making model, and how explicit use could improve their decision making. They also could see how important qualitative factors were in those decisions, and in many cases they became more comfortable with the ultimate decision once they could see the legitimacy of relying on qualitative factors.

SUMMARY OF LEARNING OBJECTIVES

LO1. Describe the tactical decision-making model.
- Tactical decisions consist of choosing among alternatives with an immediate end in view.
  - These decisions are short term.
  - Larger strategic objectives are served.
- Six steps of the decision-making model are:
  - Recognize and define the problem.
  - Identify feasible alternatives.
  - Identify costs and benefits for each feasible alternative.
  - Compare total relevant costs and benefits for each alternative.
  - Assess qualitative factors.
  - Select best alternative.

LO2. Define the concept of relevant costs and revenues.
- Relevant costs are:
  - Future costs that differ across alternatives
  - Frequently variable costs—called flexible resources
- Past costs:
  - Are sunk and never relevant
  - May be used to predict future costs

LO3. Explain how the activity resource usage model is used in assessing relevancy.
- Resources can be classified as flexible resources and committed resources.
  - Flexible resources are acquired as needed.
  - Committed resources are acquired in advance of usage.
- The cost of flexible resources is relevant.
- The cost of committed resources is relevant if demand changes across alternatives lead to a change in capacity.
- Changes in activity capacity cause resource spending to change.

LO4. Apply the tactical decision-making concepts in a variety of business situations.
- Make-or-buy decision
- Keep-or-drop decision
- Special-order decision
- Further processing of joint products

EXAMPLE 17.1	The HOW and WHY of Structuring a Make-or-Buy Decision, page 877
EXAMPLE 17.2	The HOW and WHY of Structuring a Keep-or-Drop Product Line Decision, page 882
EXAMPLE 17.3	The HOW and WHY of Structuring a Special-Order Decision, page 886
EXAMPLE 17.4	The HOW and WHY of Structuring a Sell at Split-Off or Process Further Decision, page 888

KEY TERMS

Activity resource usage model, 874

Cannibalization, 885

Decision model, 870

Keep-or-drop decision, 881

Make-or-buy decision, 876

Offshoring, 876

Opportunity cost, 873

Outsourcing, 876

Relevant costs (revenues), 872

Reshoring, 876

Sell or process further, 888

Special-order decision, 885

Sunk cost, 873

Tactical cost analysis, 870

Tactical decision making, 868

BRIEF EXERCISES

Brief Exercise 17-1 Make-or-Buy Decision, Alternatives, Relevant Costs

Each year, Giada Company produces 25,000 units of a component part used in tablet computers. An outside supplier has offered to supply the part for $4.00. The unit cost is:

OBJECTIVE ◄ 2 4
Example 17.1

Direct materials	$1.60
Direct labor	1.25
Variable overhead	0.75
Fixed overhead	2.50
Total unit cost	$6.10

Required:

1. What are the alternatives for Giada Company?
2. Assume that none of the fixed cost is avoidable. List the relevant cost(s) of internal production and of external purchase.
3. Which alternative is more cost effective and by how much?
4. *What if* $25,000 of fixed overhead is rental of equipment used only in production of the component that can be avoided if the component is purchased? Which alternative is more cost effective and by how much?

Brief Exercise 17-2 Keep-Or-Drop Decision, Alternatives, Relevant Costs

Reshier Company makes three types of rug shampooers. Model 1 is the basic model rented through hardware stores and supermarkets. Model 2 is a more advanced model with both dry- and wet-vacuuming capabilities. Model 3 is the heavy-duty riding shampooer sold to hotels and convention centers. A segmented income statement is shown below.

	Model 1	Model 2	Model 3	Total
Sales	$246,000	$ 578,000	$ 634,600	$1,458,600
Less variable costs of goods sold	(93,500)	(164,160)	(348,000)	(605,660)
Less commissions	(5,000)	(28,000)	(21,750)	(54,750)
Contribution margin	$147,500	$ 385,840	$ 264,850	$ 798,190
Less common fixed expenses:				
Fixed factory overhead				(398,000)
Fixed selling and administrative				(290,000)
Operating income				$ 110,190

While all models have positive contribution margins, Reshier Company is concerned because operating income is less than 10 percent of sales and is low for this type of company. The company's controller gathered additional information on fixed costs to see why they were so high. The following information on activities and drivers was gathered:

			Driver Usage by Model		
Activity	Activity Cost	Activity Driver	Model 1	Model 2	Model 3
Engineering	$ 30,000	Engineering hours	800	75	125
Setting up	180,000	Setup hours	12,400	12,500	5,100
Customer service	110,000	Service calls	13,600	1,500	4,900

In addition, Model 1 requires the rental of specialized equipment costing $20,000 per year.

Required:

1. Reformulate the segmented income statement using the additional information on activities.
2. Using your answer to Requirement 1, assume that Reshier Company is considering dropping any model with a negative product margin. What are the alternatives? Which alternative is more cost effective and by how much? (Assume that any traceable fixed costs can be avoided.)
3. *What if* Reshier Company can only avoid 175 hours of engineering time and 5,000 hours of setup time that are attributable to Model 1? How does that affect the alternatives presented in Requirement 2? Which alternative is more cost effective and by how much?

Brief Exercise 17-3 Special-Order Decision, Alternatives, Relevant Costs

Redwood Elegance Company, manufactures wooden coffee tables for sale to specialty furniture stores. Currently, the company is operating at 85 percent of capacity. A chain of furniture outlet stores has offered to buy 5,000 units of Redwood's ornate rustic tables as long as the table can be customized with the outlet chain's logo. While the normal selling price is $125 per table, the chain has offered just $100 per table. Redwood can accommodate the special order without affecting current sales. Unit cost information is as follows:

Direct materials	$25
Direct labor	10
Variable overhead	30
Fixed overhead	15
Total cost per table	$80

Fixed overhead is $750,000 per year and will not be affected by the special order. Normally, there is a commission of 10 percent of price; this will not be paid on the special order since the outlet chain is dealing directly with the company. The special order will require additional fixed costs of $90,000 for the design and setup of the machinery to engrave the outlet chain's logo on each table.

Required:

1. List the alternatives being considered. List the relevant benefits and costs for each alternative.
2. Which alternative is more cost effective and by how much?
3. *What if* Redwood Elegance Company was operating at capacity and accepting the special order would require rejecting an equivalent number of tables sold to existing customers? Which alternative would be better?

Brief Exercise 17-4   Sell at Split-Off or Process Further Decision, Alternatives, Relevant Costs

OBJECTIVE ◀ 2 4
Example 17.4

Vihaan Chemicals Company processes a number of chemical compounds used in disinfecting health club fitness equipment. One compound is decomposed into two chemicals: flexalene and soreaphine. The cost of processing one batch of compound is $125,000, and the result is 5,000 gallons of flexalene and 10,000 gallons of soreaphine. Vihaan Chemicals can sell the flexalene at split-off for $7 per gallon and the soreaphine for $9 per gallon. Alternatively, the flexalene can be processed further at a cost of $10 per gallon (of flexalene) into lactine. It takes 5 gallons of flexalene for every gallon of lactine. A gallon of lactine sells for $95.

Required:

1. List the alternatives being considered.
2. List the relevant benefits and costs for each alternative.
3. Which alternative is more cost effective and by how much?
4. *What if* the production of flexalene into lactine required additional purchasing and quality inspection activity? Every 100 gallons of flexalene that undergo further processing require 25 more purchase orders at $5 each and 10 more quality inspection hours at $17 each. Which alternative would be better and by how much?

EXERCISES

Exercise 17-5   Determining Relevant Costs

OBJECTIVE ◀ 2

SHOW ME
HOW

Six months ago, Lee Anna Carver purchased a fire-engine red, used LeBaron convertible for $10,000. Lee Anna was looking forward to the feel of the sun on her shoulders and the wind whipping through her hair as she zipped along the highways of life. Unfortunately, the wind turned her hair into straw, and she didn't do much zipping along since the car spent so much of its time in the shop. So far, she has spent $1,200 on repairs, and she's afraid there is no end in sight. In fact, Lee Anna anticipates the following costs of restoration:

Rebuilt engine	$1,250
New paint job	560
Tires	460
New interior	500
Miscellaneous maintenance	340
Total	$3,110

On a visit to a used car dealer, Lee Anna found a five-year-old Honda CR-V in excellent condition for $9,100—Lee Anna thinks she might really be more the sport-utility type anyway. Lee Anna checked the Blue Book values and found that she can sell the LeBaron for only $3,600. If she buys the CR-V, she will pay cash but would need to sell the LeBaron.

Required:

1. In trying to decide whether to restore the LeBaron or buy the CR-V, Lee Anna is distressed because she has already spent $11,200 on the LeBaron. The investment seems too much to give up. How would you react to her concern?
2. List all costs that are relevant to Lee Anna's decision. What advice would you give her?

OBJECTIVE 2 3 4

**SHOW ME
HOW**

Exercise 17-6 Resource Supply and Usage, Special Order, Relevancy

Elliott, Inc., has four salaried clerks to process purchase orders. Each clerk is paid a salary of $25,750 and is capable of processing as many as 6,500 purchase orders per year. Each clerk uses a PC and laser printer in processing orders. Time available on each PC system is sufficient to process 6,500 orders per year. The cost of each PC system is $1,100 per year. In addition to the salaries, Elliott spends $27,560 for forms, postage, and other supplies (assuming 26,000 purchase orders are processed). During the year, 25,350 orders were processed.

Required:

1. Classify the resources associated with purchasing as (1) flexible or (2) committed.
2. Compute the total activity availability, and break this into activity usage and unused activity.
3. Calculate the total cost of resources supplied (activity cost), and break this into the cost of activity used and the cost of unused activity.
4. (a) Suppose that a large special order will cause an additional 500 purchase orders. What purchasing costs are relevant? By how much will purchasing costs increase if the order is accepted? (b) Suppose that the special order causes 700 additional purchase orders. How will your answer to (a) change?

OBJECTIVE 2 3 4

**SHOW ME
HOW**

Exercise 17-7 Resource Supply and Usage, Adding a Service Line, Relevancy

Roxanne Morton owns a beauty shop with eight hair and nail professionals. Her shop is relatively large and has four rooms at the back, three of which are currently empty (the fourth is used to store supplies). Roxanne's is popular and typically busy Monday through Friday all day and Saturday until noon. She has been thinking about adding a tanning salon in the back of the shop. She figures that she can buy two tanning beds for $10,000 each. The necessary supplies (cleaning materials, complimentary skin lotion in each room) will run about $450 per month. The extra electricity will cost about $100 per month. Currently, Roxanne pays part-time help to staff the front desk, make appointments, check clients in, and so on. For the hours that the beauty salon is open, the current staff can easily handle the additional tanning salon duties. However, Roxanne knows that she'll have to stay open an additional four hours each weeknight (from 5 p.m. until 9 p.m.) as well as six hours on both Saturday and Sunday afternoons. Hiring additional staff for the tanning salon during those hours will cost about $8 per hour.

Required:

1. Classify the resources associated with the tanning salon as (1) flexible or (2) committed.
2. (a) Suppose that the tanning salon does very well and Roxanne decides to add one more tanning bed, using the third room at the back of the shop. What additional costs are relevant? (b) Suppose that Roxanne decides to add two more tanning beds? How will your answer to (a) change?

Exercise 17-8 Special-Order Decision, Traditional Analysis, Qualitative Aspects

Feinan Sports, Inc., manufactures sporting equipment, including weight-lifting gloves. A national sporting goods chain recently submitted a special order for 4,600 pairs of weight-lifting gloves. Feinan Sports was not operating at capacity and could use the extra business. Unfortunately, the order's offering price of $12.80 per pair was below the cost to produce them. The controller was opposed to taking a loss on the deal. However, the personnel manager argued in favor of accepting the order even though a loss would be incurred; it would avoid the problem of layoffs and would help maintain the community image of the company. The full cost to produce a pair of weight-lifting gloves is presented below.

Direct materials	$ 7.50
Direct labor	3.90
Variable overhead	1.60
Fixed overhead	3.10
Total	$16.10

No variable selling or administrative expenses would be associated with the order. Non-unit-level activity costs are a small percentage of total costs and are therefore not considered.

Required:

1. Assume that the company would accept the order only if it increased total profits. Should the company accept or reject the order? Provide supporting computations.
2. Suppose that Feinan Sports has negotiated with the potential customer, and has determined that it can substitute cheaper materials, reducing direct materials cost by $0.95 per unit. In addition, the company's engineers have found a way to reduce direct labor cost by $0.50 per unit. Should the company accept or reject the order? Provide supporting computations.
3. Consider the personnel manager's concerns. Discuss the merits of accepting the order even if it decreases total profits.

Exercise 17-9 Make-or-Buy, Traditional Analysis

Wehner Company is currently manufacturing Part ABS-43, producing 55,000 units annually. The part is used in the production of several products made by Wehner. The cost per unit for ABS-43 is as follows:

Direct materials	$45.60
Direct labor	9.80
Variable overhead	2.75
Fixed overhead	3.90
Total	$62.05

Of the total fixed overhead assigned to ABS-43, $15,400 is direct fixed overhead (the annual lease cost of machinery used to manufacture Part ABS-43), and the remainder is common fixed overhead. An outside supplier has offered to sell the part to Wehner for $58. There is no alternative use for the facilities currently used to produce the part. No significant non-unit-based overhead costs are incurred.

Required:

1. Should Wehner Company make or buy Part ABS-43?
2. What is the maximum amount per unit that Wehner would be willing to pay to an outside supplier?

Exercise 17-10 Make-or-Buy, Traditional and ABC Analysis

Brees, Inc., a manufacturer of golf carts, has just received an offer from a supplier to provide 2,600 units of a component used in its main product. The component is a track assembly that is currently produced internally. The supplier has offered to sell the track assembly for $66 per unit. Brees is currently using a traditional, unit-based costing system that assigns overhead to jobs on the basis of direct labor hours. The estimated traditional full cost of producing the track assembly is as follows:

Direct materials	$40.00
Direct labor	16.50
Variable overhead	4.50
Fixed overhead	40.00

Prior to making a decision, the company's CEO commissioned a special study to see whether there would be any decrease in the fixed overhead costs. The results of the study revealed the following:

3 setups—$1,160 each (The setups would be avoided, and total spending could be reduced by $1,160 per setup.)

One half-time inspector is needed. The company already uses part-time inspectors hired through a temporary employment agency. The yearly cost of the part-time inspectors for the track assembly operation is $12,300 and could be totally avoided if the part were purchased.

Engineering work: 470 hours, $45/hour. (Although the work decreases by 470 hours, the engineer assigned to the track assembly line also spends time on other products, and there would be no reduction in his salary.)

75 fewer material moves at $30 per move.

Required:

1. Ignore the special study, and determine whether the track assembly should be produced internally or purchased from the supplier.
2. Now, using the special study data, repeat the analysis.
3. Discuss the qualitative factors that would affect the decision, including strategic implications.
4. After reviewing the special study, the controller made the following remark: "This study ignores the additional activity demands that purchasing would cause. For example, although the demand for inspecting the part on the production floor decreases, we may need to inspect the incoming parts in the receiving area. Will we actually save any inspection costs?" Is the controller right?
5. Briefly discuss how the use of various forms of graphical representation (i.e., data visualization) to communicate the results of the special study might impact how the CEO (or other interested parties within the company) use them in making the final make-or-buy decision.

Exercise 17-11 Resource Usage Model, Special Order

Ehrling, Inc., manufactures metal racks for hanging clothing in retail stores. Ehrling was approached by the CEO of Carly's Corner, a regional nonprofit food bank, with an offer to buy 350 heavy-duty metal racks for storing canned goods and dry food products. While racks normally sell for $245 each, Carly's Corner offered $75 per rack. The CEO explained that the number of families they served had grown significantly over the past two years, and that the charity needed additional storage for the donated food items. Since Ehrling is operating at 80 percent of capacity, and Ehrling employees have "adopted" Carly's Corner as their annual charity, the company wants to make the special order work. Ehrling's controller looked into the cost of the storage racks using the following information from the activity-based accounting system:

	Activity Driver	Unused Capacity	Quantity Demanded*	Activity Rate** Fixed	Variable
Direct materials	Number of racks	0	350	—	$82
Direct labor	Direct labor hours	0	525	—	15
Setups	Setup hours	60	1	$150	5
Inspection	Inspection hours	800	20	10	5
Machining	Machine hours	6,000	175	40	3

*This represents only the amount of resources demanded by the special order being considered.
**This is expected activity cost divided by activity capacity.

Expansion of activity capacity for setups, inspection, and machining must be done in steps. For setups, each step provides an additional 20 hours of setup activity and costs $3,000. For inspection, activity capacity is expanded by 2,000 hours per year, and the cost is $20,000 per year (the salary for an additional inspector). Machine capacity can be leased for a year at a rate of $40 per machine hour. Machine capacity must be acquired, however, in steps of 1,500 machine hours.

Required:

1. Compute the change in income for Ehrling, Inc., if the order is accepted.
2. Does the order require any change in capacity for setups, packing, or machining?
3. Suppose that the packing activity can be eliminated for this order since the customer is in town and does not need to have the racks boxed and shipped. Because of this, direct materials can be reduced by $13 per unit, and direct labor can be reduced by 0.5 hour per unit. How is the analysis affected?
4. Ehrling can find no other cost-saving measures for this special order. Why might the company decide to accept it even if it shows a loss?

Exercise 17-12 Keep-or-Drop: Traditional Versus Activity-Based Analysis

 OBJECTIVE

SHOW ME
HOW

Nutterco, Inc., produces two types of nut butter: peanut butter and cashew butter. Of the two, peanut butter is the more popular. Cashew butter is a specialty line using smaller jars and fewer jars per case. Data concerning the two products follow:

	Peanut Butter	Cashew Butter	Unused Capacity[a]	Units of Purchase[b]
Expected sales (in cases)	50,000	10,000	—	—
Selling price per case	$100	$80	—	—
Direct labor hours	40,000	10,000	—	As needed
Receiving orders	500	250	250	500
Packing orders	1,000	500	500	250
Material cost per case	$50	$48	—	—
Direct labor cost per case	$10	$8	—	—
Advertising costs	$200,000	$60,000	—	—

[a]Practical capacity less expected usage (all unused capacity is permanent).
[b]In some cases, activity capacity must be purchased in steps (whole units). These steps are provided as necessary. The cost per step is the fixed activity rate multiplied by the step units. The fixed activity rate is the expected fixed activity costs divided by practical activity capacity.

Annual overhead costs are listed below. These costs are classified as fixed or variable with respect to the appropriate activity driver.

Activity	Fixed[a]	Variable[b]
Direct labor benefits	$ 0	$200,000
Machine	200,000	250,000
Receiving	200,000	22,500
Packing	100,000	45,000
Total costs	$500,000	$517,500

[a]Costs associated with practical activity capacity. The machine fixed costs are all depreciation with direct labor hours as the driver.

[b]These costs are for the actual levels of the cost driver.

Required:

1. Prepare a traditional segmented income statement, using a unit-level overhead rate based on direct labor hours. Using this approach, determine whether the cashew butter product line should be kept or dropped.
2. Prepare an activity-based segmented income statement. Repeat the keep-or-drop analysis using an ABC approach.

 OBJECTIVE 2 4

SHOW ME
HOW

Exercise 17-13 Sell or Process Further, Basic Analysis

Carleigh, Inc., is a pork processor. Its plants, located in the Midwest, produce several products from a common process: sirloin roasts, chops, spare ribs, and the residual. The roasts, chops, and spare ribs are packaged, branded, and sold to supermarkets. The residual consists of organ meats and leftover pieces that are sold to sausage and hot dog processors. The joint costs for a typical week are as follows:

Direct materials	$84,500
Direct labor	29,000
Overhead	20,000

The revenues from each product are as follows: sirloin roasts, $68,000; chops, $71,000; spare ribs, $33,000; and residual, $9,800.

Carleigh's management has learned that certain organ meats are a prized delicacy in Asia. They are considering separating those from the residual and selling them abroad for $52,000. This would bring the value of the residual down to $2,650. In addition, the organ meats would need to be packaged and then air freighted to Asia. Further processing cost per week is estimated to be $27,500 (the cost of renting additional packaging equipment, purchasing materials, and hiring additional direct labor). Transportation cost would be $12,100 per week. Finally, resource spending would need to be expanded for other activities as well (purchasing, receiving, and internal shipping). The increase in resource spending for these activities is estimated to be $3,120 per week.

Required:

1. What is the gross profit earned by the original mix of products for one week?
2. Should the company separate the organ meats for shipment overseas or continue to sell them at split-off? What is the effect of the decision on weekly gross profit?

 OBJECTIVE 4

Exercise 17-14 Provide In-House or Outsource Decision, Services, Qualitative Aspects

Tony and Tina Roselli own and run TNT's Pizza Restaurant. Tony is responsible for managing the day-to-day aspects, hiring workers, and overseeing the kitchen, building, and grounds. He is the chief cook and handles all purchasing. Tina is the hostess and manages the front of the house (restaurant talk for the dining area). She schedules the wait staff, ensures that customers are well taken care of, and pitches in to bus tables and refill drinks as needed. Tina also handles the financial aspects of the business and is responsible for bookkeeping and tax compliance. Two years ago, Tony and Tina became parents of a baby boy, Joseph, nicknamed "LJ" for Little Joe. Tina brings LJ to work each day, and both Rosellis as well as the restaurant staff help out watching him. Recently, the restaurant has grown busier, so Tony and Tina expanded the hours of operation. As a result, the staff rarely has any free time and Tina feels she has too much to handle. Tony and Tina are considering outsourcing their bookkeeping and tax-filing needs to a local accountant.

Typically, Tina spends 15 hours per month on bookkeeping and taxes. This increases to 40 hours in April. She uses a room off the kitchen as her office (a room that is sorely needed for additional food storage given the expansion). If Tina continues to do the financial work, the restaurant will need to make up for 75 percent of her time by hiring additional help at $10 per hour (hourly wage plus the restaurant's cost of Social Security, Medicare, and unemployment insurance taxes). The local accountant will charge $25 per hour for bookkeeping services; he expects this service to average eight hours per month. Taxes are filed quarterly for labor as well as state and local income taxes. These tax forms should cost about $75 per quarter. The annual income tax filing is estimated to cost $350, payable at the time of filing in April.

Required:

1. Given the information, determine whether Tina should do the bookkeeping and tax work in house or outsource it to the accountant.
2. Discuss the qualitative factors that would affect the decision, including strategic implications.

Exercise 17-15 Special-Order Decision, Services, Qualitative Aspects

OBJECTIVE ◀ 4

SHOW ME
HOW

Jason Rogers works full-time for UPS and runs a lawn-mowing service part-time after work during the warm months of April through October. Jason has three men working with him, each of whom is paid $6 per lawn mowing. Jason has 30 residential customers who contract with him for once-weekly lawn mowing during the months of May through September, and twice-per-month mowings during April and October. On average, Jason charges $40 per lawn mowed. Recently, LStar Property Management Services asked Jason to mow the lawn at each of its 20 rental houses every two weeks during the months of May through September. LStar has offered to pay $20 per lawn mowing, and would forego the lawn edging that normally takes Jason's team about half of its regular mowing time. If Jason accepts the job, he can assign a two-man team to mow the rental house yards, and will have to buy an additional power lawn mower for about $350 used. Fuel to run the additional mower will be about $0.50 per yard.

Required:

1. If Jason accepts the special order, by how much will his income increase or decrease?
2. What are some of the qualitative reasons why Jason might want to accept or decline the special order?

Exercise 17-16 Keep-or-Drop, Services, Qualitative Aspects

OBJECTIVE ◀ 4

SHOW ME
HOW

Jem Hernandez owns Jem's Special Event Planning Service, a full-service event planner. Jem does much of the work herself and hires additional help as needed. She plans corporate events, weddings, and special occasion parties. Each of these is considered a separate line of business due to the specialized aspects of each type of event. Last year, Jem's accountant provided the following segmented income statement:

	Corporate	Wedding	Special Occasion	Total
Revenue	$ 55,300	$195,000	$168,000	$ 418,300
Less variable costs	(22,120)	(97,500)	(50,400)	(170,020)
Contribution margin	$ 33,180	$ 97,500	$117,600	$ 248,280
Less common fixed expenses:				
Fixed operating expense				(175,000)
Fixed selling				(55,000)
Operating income				$ 18,280

Jem was not pleased with last year's results; corporate events were down considerably from the previous few years. In addition, she thinks that dealing with the corporate party-throwers may be more work than it is worth. Two important aspects of event planning are negotiating with vendors (e.g., caterers, florists, bands and orchestras, and venues) on price and setting up for and being present at the event itself. The corporate negotiating seemed to consume extra time, and their restrictions on the price they would pay made the negotiations particularly difficult. She decided to gather some data on the negotiation and setting-up activities:

	Corporate	Wedding	Special Occasion
Negotiating hours	400	1,200	400
Setting-up hours	100	400	500
Total cost of negotiating	$40,000		
Total cost of setting up	$60,000		

Required:

1. Prepare a segmented income statement using the activity data for negotiating and setting up. The total cost of these two activities can be subtracted from the fixed operating expense. The remaining fixed operating expense will be the common fixed operating expense. What does this income statement suggest about the relative profitability of the three product lines?

2. Jem believes that next year will be even worse. Her hunch is that corporate business will be down and that these clients will be especially intent on saving money by reducing the rate paid to Jem. She believes total corporate revenue may decrease by 25 percent overall, while the variable costs associated with those events will only decrease by 20 percent. On the other hand, Jem expects weddings to increase. Her reputation is growing and she thinks she can raise her revenues in this area by 15 percent even if the number of weddings does not increase. As a result, she expects variable costs of weddings to remain static. The special occasions (wedding anniversary parties, bar and bat mitzvahs, and so on) line is also expected to increase—with revenue and variable costs expected to increase by 10 percent. Jem does not know quite what to expect with respect to the negotiating and setting-up activities, so she thinks she'll just keep those constant for planning purposes. Prepare a segmented income statement using the activity data and these assumptions. What does this income statement suggest about dropping the corporate segment?

OBJECTIVE 2 4

SHOW ME HOW

DATA ANALYTICS

Exercise 17-17 Relevant Analysis and Forensic Accounting

Petoskey Electronics Company manufactures specialized products for boats and recreational vehicles using its newly introduced patented engine analytics device. The first-year revenues and costs for the product device are as follows:

Selling price	$500 per unit
Direct materials	$175 per unit
Direct labor	$ 45 per unit
Variable manufacturing overhead	$ 40 per unit
Total fixed manufacturing overhead	$ 1,600,000
Variable selling and administrative	$ 30 per unit
Total fixed selling and administrative	$ 500,000
Sales and manufacturing volume	25,000 units

The second year the product device was available, Petoskey Company sold only 12,000 units of its device, because a competitor, Charlevoix Supply Company, produced and sold an identical device. Petoskey Company decided to file a lawsuit against the competitor for damages (in the form of lost profits) caused by the patent infringement.

Required:

1. Calculate Petoskey Company's profit on this product device during the first year it was sold.
2. Assume that Charlevoix Company is liable as alleged by Petoskey Company in the patent infringement lawsuit. Using a relevant analysis perspective, calculate the amount of damages that Petoskey Company experienced during the second year of the new product device as a result of Charlevoix's patent infringement.
3. Assume that Charlevoix Company is liable as alleged by Petoskey Company in the patent infringement lawsuit. Also, in an effort to mitigate the damages caused by Charlevoix's patent infringement, Petoskey created an advertising program that resulted in sales decreasing to only 17,000 units (rather than the 12,000 units stated above). The annual cost of the advertising program was $375,000. Using a relevant analysis perspective, calculate the amount of damages that Petoskey Electronic experienced during the second year of the new product device as a result of Charlevoix's patent infringement.
4. Briefly identify and explain any other relevant (or differential) items that might be included in estimating Petoskey Company's damages.
5. Briefly explain how the differential analysis conducted by the forensic accountant at either Petoskey Company or Charlevoix Company relates to one of the four data analytic types (see Exhibits 2.5 and 2.6, pp. 37, 40, for a review of data analytics types.)

PROBLEMS

Problem 17-18 Identifying Problems and Alternatives, Relevant Costs

OBJECTIVE ◄ 1 2

Norton Products, Inc., manufactures potentiometers. (A potentiometer is a device that adjusts electrical resistance.) Currently, all parts necessary for the assembly of products are produced internally. Norton has a single plant located in Wichita, Kansas. The facilities for the manufacture of potentiometers are leased, with five years remaining on the lease. All equipment is owned by the company. Because of increases in demand, production has been expanded significantly over the five years of operation, straining the capacity of the leased facilities. Currently, the company needs more warehousing and office space, as well as more space for the production of plastic moldings. The current output of these moldings, used to make potentiometers, needs to be expanded to accommodate the increased demand for the main product.

Leo Tidwell, owner and president of Norton Products, has asked his vice president of marketing, John Tidwell, and his vice president of finance, Lily Zhang, to meet and discuss the problem of limited capacity. This is the second meeting the three have had concerning the problem. In the first meeting, Leo rejected Lily's proposal to build the company's own plant. He believed it was too risky to invest the capital necessary to build a plant at this stage of the company's development. The combination of leasing a larger facility and subleasing the current plant was also considered but was rejected; subleasing would be difficult, if not impossible. At the end of the first meeting, Leo asked John to explore the possibility of leasing another facility comparable to the current one. He also assigned Lily the task of identifying other possible solutions. As the second meeting began, Leo asked John to give a report on the leasing alternative.

JOHN: "After some careful research, I'm afraid that the idea of leasing an additional plant is not a very good one. Although we have some space problems, our current level of production doesn't justify another plant. In fact, I expect it will be at least five years before we need to be concerned about expanding into another facility like the one we have now. My market studies reveal a modest growth in sales over the next five years. All this growth can be absorbed by our current production capacity. The large increases in demand that we experienced the past five years are not likely to be repeated. Leasing another plant would be an overkill solution."

LEO: "Even modest growth will aggravate our current space problems. As you both know, we are already operating three production shifts. But, John, you are right—except for plastic moldings, we could expand production, particularly during the graveyard shift. Lily, I hope that you have been successful in identifying some other possible solutions. Some fairly quick action is needed."

LILY: "Fortunately, I believe that I have two feasible alternatives. One is to rent an additional building to be used for warehousing. By transferring our warehousing needs to the new building, we will free up internal space for offices and for expanding the production of plastic moldings. I have located a building within two miles of our plant that we could use. It has the capacity to handle our current needs and the modest growth that John mentioned. The second alternative may be even more attractive. We currently produce all the parts that we use to manufacture potentiometers, including shafts and bushings. In the last several months, the market has been flooded with these two parts. Prices have tumbled as a result. It might be better to buy shafts and bushings instead of making them. If we stop internal production of shafts and bushings, this would free up the space we need. Well, Leo, what do you think? Are these alternatives feasible? Or should I continue my search for additional solutions?"

LEO: "I like both alternatives. In fact, they are exactly the types of solutions we need to consider. All we have to do now is choose the one best for our company."

Required:

1. Define the problem facing Norton Products.
2. Identify all the alternatives that were considered by Norton Products. Which ones were classified as not feasible? Why? Now identify the feasible alternatives.
3. For the feasible alternatives, what are some potential costs and benefits associated with each alternative? Of the costs that you have identified, which do you think are relevant to the decision?

OBJECTIVE 2 4

Problem 17-19 Keep-or-Drop for Service Firm, Complementary Effects, Traditional Analysis

Devern Assurance Company provides both property and automobile insurance. The projected income statements for the two products are as follows:

	Property Insurance	Automobile Insurance
Sales	$4,200,000	$12,000,000
Less variable expenses	3,830,000	9,600,000
Contribution margin	$ 370,000	$ 2,400,000
Less direct fixed expenses	400,000	500,000
Segment margin	$ (30,000)	$ 1,900,000
Less common fixed expenses (allocated)	100,000	200,000
Operating income (loss)	$ (130,000)	$ 1,700,000

The president of the company is considering dropping the property insurance. However, some policyholders prefer having their property and automobile insurance with the same company, so if property insurance is dropped, sales of automobile insurance will drop by 12 percent. No significant non-unit-level activity costs are incurred.

Required:

1. If Devern Assurance Company drops property insurance, by how much will income increase or decrease? Provide supporting computations.
2. Assume that dropping all advertising for the property insurance line and increasing the corporate advertising budget by $450,000 will increase sales of property insurance by 10 percent and automobile insurance by 8 percent. Prepare a segmented income statement that reflects the effect of increased advertising. Should advertising be increased?

Problem 17-20 Special Order, Traditional Analysis

Fiorello Company manufactures two types of cold-pressed olive oil, Refined Oil and Top Quality Oil, out of a joint process. The joint (common) costs incurred are $92,500 for a standard production run that generates 30,000 gallons of Refined Oil and 15,000 gallons of Top Quality Oil. Additional processing costs beyond the split-off point are $2.40 per gallon for Refined Oil and $1.95 per gallon for Top Quality Oil. Refined Oil sells for $4.25 per gallon, while Top Quality Oil sells for $8.30 per gallon.

MangiareBuono, a supermarket chain, has asked Fiorello to supply it with 30,000 gallons of Top Quality Oil at a price of $8 per gallon. MangiareBuono plans to have the oil bottled in 16-ounce bottles with its own MangiareBuono label.

If Fiorello accepts the order, it will save $0.23 per gallon in packaging of Top Quality Oil. There is sufficient excess capacity for the order. However, the market for Refined Oil is saturated, and any additional sales of Refined Oil would take place at a price of $3.10 per gallon. Assume that no significant non-unit-level activity costs are incurred.

Required:

1. What is the profit normally earned on one production run of Refined Oil and Top Quality Oil?
2. Should Fiorello accept the special order? Explain. *(CMA adapted)*
3. Briefly explain a specific example of how prescriptive analytics might help improve special-order decision making within Fiorello Company. (See Exhibits 2.5 and 2.6, pp. 37, 40, for a review of data analytic types.)

Problem 17-21 Keep-or-Drop-or-Add for Service Firm, Complementary Effects, Traditional

Two brothers, Enzo and Pietro, opened the Italian House Restaurant several years ago. The restaurant offers a variety of culinary dishes that are divided into two main product offerings: Primi (pasta first dishes) and Secondi (nonpasta meat and vegetarian second dishes). Although happy that the restaurant generates a positive profit, the brothers would like to increase its profitability and, thus, have developed two separate proposals to accomplish this goal. However, the two brothers differ strongly on which proposal should be pursued. Therefore, they have tasked the restaurant's accountant, Luigi, with analyzing the proposals to determine the most profitable course of action. The restaurant's segmented income statement for the most recent year, as well as details regarding the two proposals, are shown next.

Italian House Restaurant
Segmented Income Statement

	Primi	Secondi	TOTAL
Sales revenues	$900,000	$1,600,000	$2,500,000
Less variable costs	(600,000)	(1,000,000)	(1,600,000)
Contribution margin	$300,000	$ 600,000	$ 900,000
Less direct fixed costs			
Advertising	(150,000)	(25,000)	(175,000)
Supervision and equipment	(250,000)	(75,000)	(325,000)
Product margin	($100,000)	$ 500,000	$ 400,000
Less common fixed expenses			225,000
Operating income			$ 175,000

OBJECTIVE 2 4

 CMA

DATA
ANALYTICS

OBJECTIVE 2 4

DATA
ANALYTICS

Proposal 1: Drop the Primi Line

Enzo prefers Proposal 1 as he argues that the Primi line is losing money for the restaurant as evidenced by its negative product margin. He notes that he would be quite happy with earning an extra $50,000 in annual profit (i.e., his 50 percent share of the avoided product margin loss if Primi is dropped). After careful consideration, Luigi noted the following additional ramifications would result from dropping the Primi product line as part of Proposal 1:

- Twenty percent of Primi's supervision and equipment costs are tied to a regionally renowned kitchen specialist with a unique nontermination employment contract clause. As a result, this specialist would be retrained for other restaurant duties if the Primi line were dropped.
- Sales of the Secondi line would decrease by 15 percent if the Primi line were dropped because some Secondi customers would no longer patronize the restaurant as other members of their party demand pasta dishes.

Proposal 2: Add to the Primi Line (by Investing in It More Heavily)

On the other hand, Pietro prefers Proposal 2 as he argues that an Italian restaurant must sell pasta dishes. Furthermore, he believes that Primi's current negative product margin can be converted to a positive margin if Primi's unit sales volume can be increased significantly. After careful consideration, Luigi estimates that Primi's unit sales volume would double if the following steps were taken as part of Proposal 2:

- Decrease the price of all Primi dishes by 5 percent.
- Increase annual advertising spending by $55,000 for promotional items that solely feature the Primi line.
- Increase annual equipment lease cost by $35,000 to obtain additional pasta making and cooking machines (that would not be used by the Secondi line).
- Increase annual facilities rent cost (included in common fixed expenses) by $25,000 to obtain available space adjacent to the restaurant necessary to accommodate the additional customer volume. Furthermore, the majority of this additional space would be used to expand the size of the restaurant's bathrooms and waiting area, which would be enjoyed by all restaurant customers. The owners have wanted to make these expansions since opening but could not justify the expense without the increase in customer volume that would result from adding to the Primi line.

Required:

1. Perform a relevant analysis of Proposal 1. What is the new profit margin for each product line if Proposal 1 is implemented? By what amount does the restaurant's operating income change if Proposal 1 is implemented? Provide supporting computations.
2. Perform a relevant analysis of Proposal 2. What is the new profit margin for each product line if Proposal 1 is implemented? By what amount does the restaurant's operating income change if Proposal 2 is implemented? Provide supporting computations.
3. Based on the relevant analyses performed in requirements 1 and 2, should Enzo and Pietro choose to implement Proposal 1, Proposal 2, or remain with the status quo? Briefly explain your answer including specific references to your earlier computations.
4. How might an ABC perspective add additional insight into Luigi's Keep-or-Drop-or-Add relevant analysis and the resulting subsequent product-line decision?
5. Briefly explain how an accounting analysis from each of the four data analytic types could assist Luigi in his evaluation of Proposals 1 and 2. (See Exhibits 2.5 and 2.6, pp. 37, 40, for a review of data analytic types.)

Problem 17-22 Resource Usage, Special Order

St. John's Medical Center (SJMC) has five medical technicians who are responsible for conducting cardiac catheterization testing in SJMC's Cath Lab. Each technician is paid a salary of $36,000 and is capable of conducting 1,000 procedures per year. The cardiac catheterization equipment is one year old and was purchased for $250,000. It is expected to last five years. The equipment's capacity is 25,000 procedures over its life. Depreciation is computed on a straight-line basis, with no salvage value expected. The reading of the catheterization results is conducted by an outside physician whose fee is $120 per test. The technician's report with the outside physician's note of results is sent to the referring physician. In addition to the salaries and equipment, SJMC spends $50,000 for supplies and other costs needed to operate the equipment (assuming 5,000 procedures are conducted). When SJMC purchased the equipment, it fully expected to perform 5,000 procedures per year. In fact, during its first year of operation, 5,000 procedures were run. However, a larger hospital has established a clinic in the city and will siphon off some of SJMC's business. During the coming years, SJMC expects to run only 4,200 cath procedures yearly. SJMC has been charging $850 for the procedure—enough to cover the direct costs of the procedure plus an assignment of general overhead (e.g., depreciation on the hospital building, lighting and heating, and janitorial services).

At the beginning of the second year, an HMO from a neighboring community approached SJMC and offered to send its clients to SJMC for cardiac catheterization provided that the charge per procedure would be $550. The HMO estimates that it can provide about 500 patients per year. The HMO has indicated that the arrangement is temporary—for one year only. The HMO expects to have its own testing capabilities within one year.

Required:

1. Classify the resources associated with the cardiac catheterization activity into one of the following: (1) committed resources, or (2) flexible resources.
2. Calculate the activity rate for the cardiac catheterization activity. Break the activity rate into fixed and variable components. Now, classify each activity resource as relevant or irrelevant with respect to the following alternatives: (1) accept the HMO offer, or (2) reject the HMO offer. Explain your reasoning.
3. Assume that SJMC will accept the HMO offer if it reduces the hospital's operating costs. Should the HMO offer be accepted?
4. Jerold Bosserman, SJMC's hospital controller, argued against accepting the HMO's offer. Instead, he argued that the hospital should be increasing the charge per procedure rather than accepting business that doesn't even cover full costs. He also was concerned about local physician reaction if word got out that the HMO was receiving procedures for $550. Discuss the merits of Jerold's position. Include in your discussion an assessment of the price increase that would be needed if the objective is to maintain total revenues from cardiac catheterizations experienced in the first year of operation.
5. Chandra Denton, SJMC's administrator, has been informed that one of the Cath Lab technicians is leaving for an opportunity at a larger hospital. She met with the other technicians, and they agreed to increase their hours to pick up the slack so that SJMC won't need to hire another technician. By working a couple hours extra every week, each remaining technician can perform 1,050 procedures per year. They agreed to do this for an increase in salary of $2,000 per year. How does this outcome affect the analysis of the HMO offer?
6. Assuming that SJMC wants to bring in the same revenues earned in the cardiac catheterization activity's first year less the reduction in resource spending attributable to using only four technicians, how much must SJMC charge for a procedure?

OBJECTIVE

Problem 17-23 Activity-Based Resource Usage Model, Make-or-Buy

Brandy Dees recently bought Nievo Enterprises, a company that manufactures ice skates. Brandy decided to assume management responsibilities for the company and appointed herself president shortly after the purchase was completed. When she bought the company, Brandy's investigation revealed that with the exception of the blades, all parts of the skates are produced internally. The investigation also revealed that Nievo once produced the blades internally and still owned the equipment. The equipment was in good condition and was stored in a local warehouse. Nievo's former owner had decided three years earlier to purchase the blades from external suppliers.

Brandy Dees is seriously considering making the blades instead of buying them from external suppliers. The blades are purchased in sets of two and cost $8 per set. Currently, 100,000 sets of blades are purchased annually.

Skates are produced in batches, according to shoe size. Production equipment must be reconfigured for each batch. The blades could be produced using an available area within the plant. Prime costs will average $5.00 per set. There is enough equipment to set up three lines of production, each capable of producing 80,000 sets of blades. A supervisor would need to be hired for each line. Each supervisor would be paid a salary of $40,000. Additionally, it would cost $1.50 per machine hour for power, oil, and other operating expenses. Since three types of blades would be produced, additional demands would be made on the setup activity. Other overhead activities affected include purchasing, inspection, and materials handling. The company's ABC system provides the following information about the current status of the overhead activities that would be affected. (The lumpy quantity indicates how much capacity must be purchased should any expansion of activity supply be needed—the units of purchase. The purchase cost per unit is the fixed activity rate. The variable rate is the cost per unit of resources acquired as needed for each activity.)

Activity	Cost Driver	Current Activity Capacity	Activity Usage	Lumpy Quantity	Fixed Activity Rate	Variable Activity Rate
Setups	Number of setups	1,000	800	100	$200	$ 500
Purchasing	Number of orders	50,000	47,000	5,000	10	0.50
Inspecting	Inspection hours	20,000	18,000	2,000	15	None
Materials handling	Number of moves	9,000	8,700	500	30	1.50

The demands that the *production* of blades places on the overhead activities are as follows:

Activity	Resource Demands
Machining	50,000 machine hours
Setups	250 setups
Purchasing	4,000 purchase orders (associated with materials)
Inspection	1,500 inspection hours
Materials handling	650 moves

If the blades are made, the purchase of the blades from outside suppliers will cease. Therefore, purchase orders will decrease by 6,500 (the number associated with their purchase). Similarly, the moves for the handling of incoming blades will decrease by 400. Any unused activity capacity is viewed as permanent.

Required:

1. Should Nievo make or buy the blades?
2. Explain how the ABC resource usage model helped in the analysis. Also, comment on how a conventional approach would have differed.

Problem 17-24 Make-or-Buy, Traditional Analysis, Qualitative Considerations

OBJECTIVE 2 4

Apollonia Dental Services is part of an HMO that operates in a large metropolitan area. Currently, Apollonia has its own dental laboratory to produce two varieties of porcelain crowns—all porcelain and porcelain fused to metal. The unit costs to produce the crowns are as follows:

	All Porcelain	Porcelain Fused to Metal
Direct materials	$190	$ 80
Direct labor	50	20
Variable overhead	25	5
Fixed overhead	60	40
Total	$325	$145

Fixed overhead is detailed as follows:

Salary (supervisor)	$30,000
Depreciation	8,000
Rent (lab facility)	22,000

Overhead is applied on the basis of direct labor hours. The rates above were computed using 8,000 direct labor hours. No significant non-unit-level overhead costs are incurred.

A local dental laboratory has offered to supply Apollonia all the crowns it needs. Its price is $265 for all-porcelain crowns and $145 for porcelain-fused-to-metal crowns; however, the offer is conditional on supplying both types of crowns—it will not supply just one type for the price indicated. If the offer is accepted, the equipment used by Apollonia's laboratory would be scrapped (it is old and has no market value), and the lab facility would be closed. Apollonia uses 2,500 all-porcelain crowns and 1,000 porcelain-fused-to-metal crowns per year.

Required:

1. Should Apollonia continue to make its own crowns, or should they be purchased from the external supplier? What is the dollar effect of purchasing?
2. What qualitative factors should Apollonia consider in making this decision?
3. Suppose that the lab facility is owned rather than rented and that the $22,000 is depreciation rather than rent. What effect does this have on the analysis in Requirement 1?
4. Refer to the original data. Assume that the volume of crowns is 5,000 all porcelain and 2,000 porcelain fused to metal. Should Apollonia make or buy the crowns? Explain the outcome.

Problem 17-25 Sell or Process Further

OBJECTIVE 4

EXCEL

Pharmaco Corporation buys three chemicals that are processed to produce two popular ingredients for liquid pain relievers. The three chemicals are in liquid form. The purchased chemicals are blended for two to three hours and then heated for 15 minutes. The results of the process are two separate ingredients, PR1 and PR2. For every 4,300 gallons of chemicals used, 2,000 gallons of each pain reliever are produced. The pain relievers are sold to companies that process them into their final form. The selling prices are $34 per gallon for PR1 and $45 per gallon for PR2. The costs to produce one batch (containing 2,000 gallons of each chemical) are as follows:

Chemicals	$23,400
Direct labor	9,000
Catalyst	3,600
Overhead	8,000

The pain relievers are bottled in five-gallon plastic containers and shipped. The cost of each container is $2.10. The costs of shipping are $0.50 per container.

Pharmaco Corporation could process PR1 further by mixing it with inert powders and flavoring to form tablets. The tablets can be sold directly to retail drug stores as a generic brand. If this route is taken, the revenue received per case of tablets would be $13.50, with eight cases produced by every gallon of PR1. The costs of processing into tablets total $11.00 per gallon of PR1. Packaging costs $5.16 per case. Shipping costs are $1.68 per case.

Required:

1. Should Pharmaco sell PR1 at split-off, or should PR1 be processed and sold as tablets?
2. If Pharmaco normally sells 26,000 gallons of PR1 per year, what will be the difference in profits if PR1 is processed further?

Problem 17-26 Plant Shutdown or Continue Operations, Qualitative Considerations, Traditional Analysis

KarlAuto Corporation manufactures automobiles, vans, and trucks. Among the various Karl-Auto plants around the United States is the Bloomington plant, where vinyl covers and upholstery fabric are sewn. These are used to cover interior seating and other surfaces of KarlAuto products.

Pam Teegin is the plant manager for the Bloomington cover plant—the first KarlAuto plant in the region. As other area plants were opened, Teegin, in recognition of her management ability, was given the responsibility to manage them. Teegin functions as a regional manager, although the budget for her and her staff is charged to the Bloomington plant.

Teegin has just received a report indicating that KarlAuto could purchase the entire annual output of the Bloomington cover plant from outside suppliers for $32 million. Teegin was astonished at the low outside price, because the budget for the Bloomington plant's operating costs was set at $56.45 million. Teegin believes that the Bloomington plant will have to close down operations in order to realize the $24.45 million in annual cost savings.

The budget (in thousands) for the Bloomington plant's operating costs for the coming year follows:

Materials Labor:		$12,000
Direct	$13,800	
Supervision	3,750	
Indirect plant	4,300	21,850
Overhead:		
Depreciation—equipment	$ 5,000	
Depreciation—building	3,000	
Pension expense	5,600	
Plant manager and staff	3,000	
Corporate allocation	6,000	22,600
Total budgeted costs		$56,450

Additional facts regarding the plant's operations are as follows:

Due to the Bloomington plant's commitment to use high-quality fabrics in all of its products, the Purchasing Department was instructed to place blanket orders with major suppliers to ensure the receipt of sufficient materials for the coming year. If these orders are canceled as a consequence of the plant closing, termination charges would amount to 18 percent of the cost of direct materials.

Approximately 600 plant employees will lose their jobs if the plant is closed. This includes all direct laborers and supervisors as well as the plumbers, electricians, and other skilled workers classified as indirect plant workers. Some would be able to find new jobs, but many others would have difficulty. All employees would have difficulty matching the Bloomington plant's base pay of $29.40 per hour, the highest in the area. A clause in the Bloomington plant's contract with the union may help some employees; the company must provide employment assistance to its former employees for 12 months after a plant closing. The estimated cost to administer this service would be $1 million for the year.

Some employees would probably elect early retirement because the company has an excellent pension plan. In fact, $4.6 million of next year's pension expense would continue whether or not the plant is open.

Teegin and her staff would not be affected by the closing of the Bloomington plant. They would still be responsible for administering three other area plants.

Equipment depreciation for the plant is considered to be a variable cost and the units-of-production method is used to depreciate equipment; the Bloomington plant is the only KarlAuto plant to use this depreciation method. However, it uses the customary straight-line method to depreciate its building.

Required:

1. Prepare a quantitative analysis to help in deciding whether or not to close the Bloomington plant. Explain how you treated the nonrecurring relevant costs.
2. Consider the analysis in Requirement 1, and add to it the qualitative factors that you believe are important to the decision. What is your decision? Would you close the plant? Explain. *(CMA adapted)*

Problem 17-27 Make-or-Buy, Traditional Analysis

OBJECTIVE ▸ 1 2 4

Garcia Company produces two different types of gauges: a density gauge and a thickness gauge. The segmented income statement for a typical quarter follows.

	Density Gauge	Thickness Gauge	Total
Sales	$150,000	$80,000	$230,000
Less variable expenses	80,000	46,000	126,000
Contribution margin	$ 70,000	$34,000	$104,000
Less direct fixed expenses*	20,000	38,000	58,000
Segment margin	$ 50,000	$ (4,000)	$ 46,000
Less common fixed expenses			30,000
Operating income			$ 16,000

*Includes depreciation.

The density gauge uses a subassembly that is purchased from an external supplier for $25 per unit. Each quarter, 2,000 subassemblies are purchased. All units produced are sold, and there are no ending inventories of subassemblies. Garcia is considering making the subassembly rather than buying it. Unit-level variable manufacturing costs are as follows:

Direct materials	$2
Direct labor	3
Variable overhead	2

No significant non-unit-level costs are incurred.

Garcia is considering two alternatives to supply the productive capacity for the subassembly.
1. Lease the needed space and equipment at a cost of $27,000 per quarter for the space and $10,000 per quarter for a supervisor. There are no other fixed expenses.
2. Drop the thickness gauge. The equipment could be adapted with virtually no cost and the existing space utilized to produce the subassembly. The direct fixed expenses, including supervision, would be $38,000, $8,000 of which is depreciation on equipment. If the thickness gauge is dropped, sales of the density gauge will not be affected.

Required:

1. Should Garcia Company make or buy the subassembly? If it makes the subassembly, which alternative should be chosen? Explain and provide supporting computations.
2. Suppose that dropping the thickness gauge will decrease sales of the density gauge by 10 percent. What effect does this have on the decision?
3. Assume that dropping the thickness gauge decreases sales of the density gauge by 10 percent and that 2,800 subassemblies are required per quarter. As before, assume that there are no ending inventories of subassemblies and that all units produced are sold. Assume also that the per-unit sales price and variable costs are the same as in Requirement 1. Include the leasing alternative in your consideration. Now, what is the correct decision?

18 Pricing and Profitability Analysis

After studying this chapter, you should be able to:

1 Discuss basic pricing concepts.

2 Calculate a markup on cost and a target cost.

3 Discuss the impact of the legal system and ethics on pricing.

4 Explain why firms measure profit, and calculate measures of profit using absorption and variable costing.

5 Compute the sales price, sales volume, contribution margin, contribution margin volume, sales mix, market share, and market size variances.

6 Discuss the variations in price, cost, and profit over the product life cycle.

7 Describe some of the limitations of profit measurement.

EQRoy/Shutterstock

THE COMPLEXITY OF SETTING PRICES

in Big Pharma

Drug advertisements by large pharmaceutical companies (also known as "Big Pharma") appear to be everywhere. Watching television, walking or driving busy streets, or navigating popular websites often inundates us with enough advertising repetition that even casual observers, including children, likely can list multiple drugs, such as Humira, Trulicity, or Chantix, by their brand name. The largest Big Pharma companies, including **Johnson & Johnson**, **Roche**, **Pfizer**, **Bristol Myers Squibb**, **Novartis**, **Merck & Co.**, and **GlaxoSmithKline**, collectively generate hundreds of billions of dollars in annual sales.

Have you ever wondered how Big Pharma companies set drug prices for their life-changing and lifesaving drugs? The process of setting prices is complicated as displayed in the *Drug Discovery and Development: A Long, Risky Road* graphic. Big Pharma companies face *considerable costs* to research, develop, test, approve, manufacture, market, and distribute new drugs. For example, the full cost to develop a new drug from initial idea conception to final marketing approval is $2.6 billion![1] The average cost to navigate each new potential drug through the research and development process alone is $800 million to $1 billion.[2] Part of this staggering research and development cost includes high-tech facilities and highly skilled scientists and medical professionals. Pfizer's Pearl River innovation center in the photograph is located near midtown Manhattan and serves as the company's global Vaccine R&D headquarters for over 800 employees. Thus, prices must be set high enough to cover all these costs for the relatively few drugs that successfully make it all the way down the road of new drug discovery and development.

In addition to staggering costs, Big Pharma companies also face *high drug failure rates* due to the sizable uncertainty about whether any given new drug will work or instead fizzle out somewhere along the long road described earlier. For example, only 1 in 5,000 drugs that enter preclinical testing make it through the four stages of trial testing and eventually into the medicine cabinet. Furthermore, new drugs face a *long journey* as the average time period for drugs fortunate enough to make it through the entire process is 12 years![3] Competitors often further complicate matters as their similar and in-process drugs might make it to market first. Thus, prices also must be set high enough to cover all the costs associated with the 4,999 drugs (out of 5,000) that fail to successfully make it down the long road of new drug discovery and development.

1 "A Tough Road: Cost to Develop One New Drug Is $2.6 Billion," https://www.policymed.com/2014/12/a-tough-road-cost-to-develop-one-new-drug-is-26-billion-approval-rate-for-drugs-entering-clinical-de.html, accessed September 2, 2020.

2 http://www.jomoco-amr.com/about/, accessed September 2, 2020.

3 "Drug Approvals—From Invention to Market … A 12-Year Trip," https://www.medicinenet.com/script/main/art.asp?articlekey=9877, accessed September 2, 2020.

DRUG DISCOVERY AND DEVELOPMENT

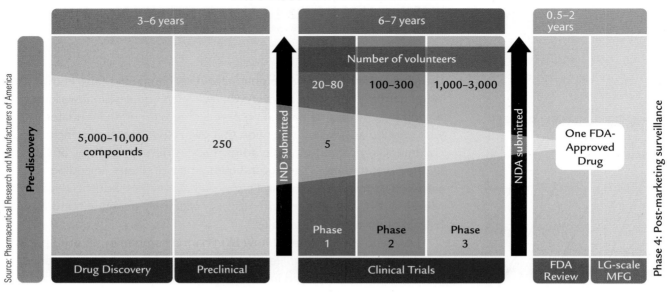

Source: Pharmaceutical Research and Manufacturers of America

Finally, while Big Pharma companies always have faced *considerable regulatory oversight*, their prices face *increasing public scrutiny* over various ethical and fairness concerns. For example, President Trump spent considerable effort negotiating with Big Pharma companies as he sought a Favored Nation status that would force Big Pharma companies to charge U.S. customers the same (usually much lower) price they charge consumers in other countries for the identical drug. Therefore, the next time you see a drug advertisement, remember the considerable cost, high drug failure rates, decade-long time frame, and increasing public and regulatory scrutiny surrounding the drug development process, and appreciate the complexity that goes into setting prices in the exciting world of Big Pharma.

Henry Ford said, "A business that does not make a profit for the buyer of a commodity, as well as for the seller, is not a good business. Buyer and seller must both be wealthier in some way as a result of a transaction, else the balance is broken."[4] Ford reminds us that the relationship between buyer and seller is an exchange relationship. Both expect to profit from it. Typically, we measure profit as the difference between revenues and costs. Price and revenue will be discussed first. Then, we will look at profit—the interplay of price and cost.

OBJECTIVE 1
Discuss basic pricing concepts.

BASIC PRICING CONCEPTS

One of the more difficult decisions facing a company is pricing. The accountant is the primary resource the firm turns to when financial data are needed, whether that information relates to cost or to price. Therefore, accountants must be familiar with sources of revenue data as well as the economic and marketing concepts needed to interpret those data.

Demand and Supply

Customers want high-quality goods and services at a low price. Although customer demand is studied in detail in marketing classes, accountants need to be aware of the way demand interacts with supply.

---

4   Henry Ford, *Today and Tomorrow* (Portland, OR: Productivity Press, 1926, reprinted in 1988).

With all else equal, customers will buy more at lower prices and less at higher prices. Producers, on the other hand, are able to supply more at higher prices than they can at lower prices. The market-clearing or equilibrium price is located at the intersection of the supply and demand curves. At this price, the amount that producers supply just equals the amount that consumers demand. If firms charge a price that is higher than the market-clearing price, demand falls short of supply. Producers see inventories pile up as consumers buy other goods. If the price is lower than the market-clearing price, everything that is produced is bought. Shortages and backlogs occur, signaling the need to increase production and/or to raise prices.

Factors other than price that influence demand include consumer income, quality of goods offered for sale, availability of substitutes, demand for complementary goods, whether the good is a necessity or a luxury, and so on. However, the basic demand-supply relationship remains, and producers know that raising prices nearly inevitably results in fewer units being sold. Price elasticity and market structure are two factors that influence companies' ability to adjust price.

Price Elasticity of Demand

Since price affects quantity sold, producers want to know just how much a price change will change quantity demanded. **Price elasticity of demand** is measured as the percentage change in quantity divided by the percentage change in price. If demand is relatively elastic, a small percent change in price will lead to a greater percent change in quantity demanded. The opposite is true for inelastic demand.

Goods that are price elastic tend to have many substitutes, are not necessities, and take a relatively large amount of consumer income. The demand for movie tickets, restaurant meals, and automobiles is relatively elastic.

Price-inelastic goods have few substitutes, are necessities, or constitute a relatively small percentage of consumer income. Prescription drugs, electricity, and foods like salt or chocolate are examples of price-inelastic goods. Price elasticity also applies to services. For example, certain medical services are price elastic, such as elective cosmetic surgery, while other medical services are price inelastic, such as emergency stroke care.

While price elasticity of demand is difficult to compute in real-world situations, it is possible to see its effects at work.

For example, Unilever, maker of Ben & Jerry's ice cream, Dove soap, Lipton teas, and Hellmann's mayonnaise, found its profit margins slipping after it raised prices on many products. Demand fell precipitously, leading to falling profit margins. The CEO quickly reversed that strategy, lowering prices and increasing quantity sold. Apparently, many of Unilever's products face elastic demand. The various ice creams, soaps, teas, and so on have numerous competitors. While a consumer may like Dove soap, for example, a price increase may send him or her to another brand.

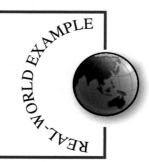

REAL-WORLD EXAMPLE

Other companies may have products with inelastic demand. For example, airlines define their core market as business travelers, who have inelastic demand for air travel. They need the flexibility to purchase tickets at the last minute, to change reservations, and to fly during the work week. Prices for tickets bought under these circumstances stay relatively high. Of course, elasticity of demand is just one factor that influences price. Another important determinant of price is market structure.

Using Data Analytics to Estimate Price Elasticity in the Medical Industry

The medical field presents many complex challenges that accountants must consider when conducting financial analyses to help inform medical provider business decisions. Many factors contribute to these challenges, including continually advancing technologically oriented treatment capabilities, an evolving insurance industry, omnipresent competition, impactful regulations, and an increasingly informed health-care customer (i.e., patient) population. As a result of these factors, customers increasingly are taking more control over the decisions that affect their consumption of particular health-care services, including whether, when, and from whom to obtain such services. Medical facilities must anticipate the future demand, including estimates of associated revenues and costs, for the various medical services they provide. Given the complexity and size of medical spending—estimated to be $4 trillion and nearly 20 percent of the U.S. gross domestic product[5]—accountants use data analytics to help estimate the price elasticity of demand for current and anticipated medical services. Results from descriptive and predictive analytic endeavors lead to the use of prescriptive analytics that recommend the most profitable medical services to offer in the future.[6] These recommendations require a solid understanding of customer demand for various medical services, including the price they would be willing to pay for such services, and the medical facility's cost to provide such services. For example, accounting data analytics were used in this manner to help inform the recent widespread trend away from building less profitable large hospital systems for overnight stays and toward building more profitable smaller facilities for outpatient medical services.

Market Structure and Price

Market structure affects price, as well as the costs necessary to support that price. In general, there are four types of market structure: perfect competition, monopolistic competition, oligopoly, and monopoly. These markets differ according to the number of buyers and sellers, the uniqueness of the product, and the relative ease of entry by firms into and out of the market (i.e., barriers to entry).

The **perfectly competitive market** has many buyers and sellers—no one of which is large enough to influence the market—a homogeneous product, and easy entry into and exit from the industry. Firms in a perfectly competitive market cannot charge a higher price than the market price because no one would buy their product, and they will not set a lower price because they can sell all they can produce at the market price.

At the opposite extreme is a monopoly. In a **monopoly**, barriers to entry are so high that there is only one firm in the market and the product is unique. The monopolistic firm is a price setter. While the monopolist sets the price, that does not mean it can force consumers to buy. It does mean that a somewhat higher price (with a lower quantity sold) can be set than would be set in a competitive market. Some monopolies have legally enforced barriers to entry (e.g., the **United States Postal Service**). Other firms are monopolies because of patent protection, specialized knowledge, or exceptionally high-cost production equipment. Pharmaceutical companies have a monopoly on new drugs due to patent protection. When the patent expires, generic drug companies can produce it, and the price of the drug plummets. As explored in the chapter opener on Pfizer, while Big Pharma companies possess considerable leeway in setting prices, they also must consider several important factors in pricing decisions.

---

5   "CMS: US Health Care Spending Will Reach $4T in 2020," Advisory Board, April 3, 2020, https://www.advisory.com /daily-briefing/2020/04/03/health-spending, accessed September 5, 2020.

6   "Healthcare Analytics Market—Global Opportunity Analysis and Industry Forecast," Meticulous Research, July 2020, https://www.meticulousresearch.com/product/healthcare-analytics-market/, accessed September 5, 2020.

Exhibit 18.1 Characteristics of the Four Basic Types of Market Structure

Market Structure Type	Number of Firms in Industry	Barriers to Entry	Uniqueness of Product	Expenses Related to Structure Type
Perfect competition	Many	Very low	Not unique	No special expenses
Monopolistic competition	Many	Low	Some unique features	Advertising, coupons, costs of differentiation
Oligopoly	Few	High	Fairly unique	Costs of differentiation, advertising, rebates, coupons
Monopoly	One	Very high	Very unique	Legal and lobbying expenditures

Monopolistic competition has characteristics of both monopoly and perfect competition, but it is much closer to the competitive situation. There are many sellers and buyers, but the products are differentiated on some basis. Restaurants are good examples of monopolistic competitors. Each restaurant serves food but attempts to differentiate itself in some way—ethnic style of food, closeness to work or schools, availability of a party room, gourmet versus casual atmosphere, and so on. The end result is to slightly raise prices above the perfectly competitive price, as customers agree to pay a little more for the unique feature that appeals to them.

An **oligopoly** is characterized by a few sellers. Typically, barriers to entry are high, and they are usually cost related. For example, the cereal industry is dominated by **Kellogg's**, **General Mills**, and **Quaker Oats**. The reason is not the high cost of manufacturing corn flakes. Instead, the huge selling expenditures (e.g., advertising and shelf space fees) of the big three effectively prevent smaller companies from entering the market.

The various types of market structure and their characteristics are summarized in Exhibit 18.1. Companies must be aware of the market structure in which they operate in order to understand their pricing options. Note that these market structures also have implications for the supply or cost side. The firm in the perfectly competitive industry has lower marketing costs (advertising, positioning, discounting, coupons) than the firm in the monopolistically competitive industry, which must constantly reinforce the consumer's perception of its product's uniqueness. The monopolist typically incurs expenses to protect its monopoly position, often through legal fees and lobbying (included in administrative expenses).

COST AND PRICING POLICIES

OBJECTIVE **2**

Calculate a markup on cost and a target cost.

Companies use various strategies to set price. Since cost is an important determinant of supply and is known to the producer, many companies base price on cost. Still other companies use a target-costing strategy, or strategies based on the initial conditions in the market.

Cost-Based Pricing

Demand is one side of the pricing equation; supply is the other side. Since revenue must cover cost for the firm to make a profit, many companies start with cost to determine price. Some studies suggest that approximately 80 percent of companies set prices by marking up costs. That is, they calculate product cost and add the desired profit. Therefore, **cost-based pricing** is the process by which particular costs are marked up by a chosen percentage to arrive at the price for a product or service. Companies that use cost-based pricing are referred to as price makers, whereas companies that have little or no control over prices are referred to as price takers. The mechanics of this approach are straightforward. Usually, there is some cost base and a markup. The **markup** is a percentage applied to base cost; it includes desired profit and any costs not included in the base cost. Companies that bid for jobs routinely base bid price on cost. **Example 18.1** shows the how and why of calculating a markup on cost.

EXAMPLE 18.1	

The HOW and WHY of Calculating a Markup on Cost

Information:

AudioPro Company, owned and operated by Chris McAnders, sells and installs audio equipment in homes and vehicles. Direct materials and direct labor costs are easy to trace to the jobs. Assemblers receive, on average, $12 per hour. AudioPro's income statement for last year is as follows.

Revenues		$350,350
Cost of goods sold:		
Direct materials	$122,500	
Direct labor	73,500	
Overhead	49,000	245,000
Gross profit		$105,350
Selling and administrative expenses		25,000
Operating income		$ 80,350

Chris wants to find a markup on cost of goods sold that will allow her to earn about the same amount of profit on each job as was earned last year.

Why:

Firms use a markup on cost as an easy way to price items so that, in general, all other costs and profit are included in the price. The cost is a known quantity and must be covered by price in order for the firm to earn a profit.

Required:

1. What is the markup on cost of goods sold (COGS) that will maintain the same profit as last year?

2. Suppose that Chris wants to expand her company's product line to include automobile alarm systems and electronic remote car door openers. She estimates the following costs for the sale and installation of one electronic remote car door opener.

Direct materials	$ 80.60
Direct labor (3 hours × $12)	36.00
Applied overhead	23.40
Total cost	$140.00

   What is the price Chris will use for this new product given the markup percentage calculated in Requirement 1?

3. *What if* Chris wants to calculate a markup on direct materials cost, since it is the largest cost of doing business? What is the markup on direct materials cost that will maintain the same profit as last year? What is the bid price Chris will use for the job given in Requirement 2 if the markup percentage is calculated on the basis of direct materials cost?

Solution:

EXAMPLE 18.1

(*Continued*)

1. The markup percentage must include all costs that are not a part of cost of goods sold plus desired profit.

    Markup on COGS = (Selling and administrative expenses
    + Operating income)/COGS
    = ($25,000 + $80,350)/$245,000
    = 0.43, or 43% of cost of goods sold

2. Price for new product = $140 + (0.43 × $140) = $140 + $60.20 = $200.20
    = $140 × 1.43 = $200.20

3. Mark up on direct materials = (Direct labor + Overhead + Selling and
    administrative expenses + Operating income)/
    Direct materials
    = ($73,500 + $49,000 + $25,000 + $80,350)/
    $122,500
    = 1.86, or 186% of direct materials cost

    Bid price = $80.60 + (1.86 × $80.60) = $80.60 + $149.92
    = $230.52 (rounded)

As can be seen in Example 18.1, the markup on cost of goods sold is 43 percent. Notice that the 43 percent markup covers both profit and selling and administrative expenses. The markup percentage of 186 percent of direct materials cost would yield the same amount of profit, assuming the level of operations and other expenses remained stable. The markup percentage on direct materials covers direct labor, overhead, selling and administrative expenses, and profit. The choice of base and markup percentage generally rests on convenience.

When the markup percentages calculated in Example 18.1 were used in determining bid price, they were initial prices. Chris can adjust the price based on her knowledge of competition for this type of job and other factors. The markup is a guideline, not an absolute rule. Considerable judgment exists in selecting both the costs to be marked up (i.e., the cost base) and the percentage by which to mark up costs (i.e., the markup). Mistakes in selecting either of these two critical cost-based pricing components can negatively affect the company's profitability.

If a company actually sets its prices based on markup percentages, is it guaranteed to make a profit? Not at all. If very few jobs are won, the entire markup will go toward selling and administrative expenses, the costs not explicitly included in the pricing calculations.

Markup pricing is often used by retail stores, and their typical markup is 100 percent of cost. If a sweater is purchased by Graham Department Store for $24, the retail price marked is $48 [$24 + (1.00 × $24)]. That 100 percent markup is meant to cover the salaries of the clerks, payment for space and equipment (cash registers, etc.), utilities, advertising, and so on, as well as profit. A major advantage of markup pricing is that standard markups are easy to apply. Consider the difficulty of setting a price for every piece of merchandise in a store. For example, **Pottery Barn** stocks a wide variety of goods, from glassware and pottery to furniture and textiles. Assessing the supply and demand characteristics of each item is time consuming. It is much simpler to apply a uniform markup to cost and then adjust prices as needed if less is demanded than anticipated.

Target Costing and Pricing

Most American companies, and nearly all European firms, set the price of a new product as the sum of the costs and the desired profit. The rationale is that the company must earn sufficient revenues to cover all costs and yield a profit. Peter Drucker in his classic quote notes that "this is true but irrelevant: Customers do not see it as their job to ensure manufacturers a profit. The only sound way to price is to start out with what the market is willing to pay."[7]

Target costing sets the cost of a product or service based on the price (target price) that customers are willing to pay. The Marketing Department determines what characteristics and price for a product are most acceptable to consumers. Then, it is the job of the company's engineers to design and develop, working with financial inputs from the accountants, the product such that cost and profit can be covered by that price. Target costing often becomes particularly important during periods of intense competition or challenging economic conditions. In these situations, increasing sales revenue is more difficult than usual, and therefore, increasing profit requires companies to decrease their costs. Accounting and other consulting firms provide clients with expertise in effectively executing target costing.[8]

Retail stores engage in a form of target costing when they look for goods which can be priced at a particular level to appeal to customers.

For example, many department stores work with clothing companies to develop house labels. The house label goods are typically good-quality items that cost less and are priced lower than comparable name brand items. The house label gives the store flexibility. The store is not in the business of manufacturing sweaters, for example, but can find a source that will deliver sweaters of particular quality for the cost that will allow the store to achieve a target price and profit. Caslon and 1901 are house brands of **Nordstrom Department Stores**. Kenmore and Craftsman are house brands of **Sears**.

Let's return to the AudioPro Company example in Example 18.1. Suppose Chris finds that other aftermarket audio installers price the remote car door opener at $155, while her initial price was $200.20. Should she drop her plans to expand into this product line? Not if she can tailor her price to the market price. Recall that the original price called for $80 of direct materials and $36 of direct labor. Perhaps Chris could offer one remote device instead of two, saving $15 in cost. In addition, she might be able to shave some time off the direct labor, once the workers are trained and able to work more efficiently. This would result in $16 of savings. Prime cost would be $85.60 ($80.60 − $15 + $36 − $16) instead of the original $116.60.

AudioPro Company applies overhead at the rate of 65 percent of direct labor cost. However, Chris must think carefully about this job. Perhaps somewhat less overhead will be incurred because purchasing is reduced. (Only one reliable supplier is needed, and the tools and facilities can be shared with the audio installation.) Perhaps overhead for this job will amount to $10 (50 percent of direct labor). That would make the cost of one job $105.60 ($65.60 + $30 + $10).

Now, if the standard markup of 43 percent is applied, the price would be $151, well within the other firms' price of $155. As you can see, target costing is an iterative process. Chris will go through the cycle until she either achieves the target cost or determines that she cannot. Note, however, that target costing has given Chris a chance to develop a profitable market, a chance she might not have had if the original cost-based price had been set.

Target costing involves much more upfront work than cost-based pricing. However, let's not forget the additional work that must be done if the cost-based price turns out to be higher than what customers will accept. Then, the arduous task of bringing costs into line to support a lower price, or the opportunity cost of missing the market altogether, begins.

7 W. Cohen, "Drucker's Five Deadly Sins in Business," July 3, 2012, https://www.processexcellencenetwork.com /lean-six-sigma-business-performance/columns/drucker-s-five-deadly-sins-in-business, accessed September 7, 2020.
8 "Target Costing in Disruptive Times," Deloitte, https://www2.deloitte.com/de/de/pages/operations/articles/target -costing-in-disruptive-times.html, accessed September 7, 2020.

Data Analytics Makes Finding the Best Customers Easier

In a world of global competition where customers can easily find the lowest price, companies look for ways to build loyalty and make their best customers happier. Loyalty programs appear more popular than ever as over 90 percent of companies have some sort of loyalty program. In the United States alone, there are over 3.3 billion loyalty memberships.[9] Doing this converts an important segment of their clientele as viewing the industry as one in which competition reigns—where hotel rooms, for example, are seen as fairly standard and customers focus only on price—to more of a monopolistic view in which the favored hotel (or airline, etc.) is distinguished from others on the basis of nonprice factors.

Large hotel brands such as **Marriott** and **Hyatt** have premium tiers in which customers who stay frequently enough may qualify for special privileges. For example, they may receive dedicated phone numbers and phone app access designed to provide them better service (such as rooms at a sold out hotel) or gifts such as spa treatments, luggage, or monogrammed bathrobes. Cruise lines like **Norwegian Cruise Lines** and **Royal Caribbean** have created ships within a ship where wealthier customers have 24-hour concierge and butler services. They also receive special disembarkation arrangements as well as private pools, sundecks, and restaurants.

But how do companies find those loyal customers and determine just which premium products and services will be most important to them? The answer is big data. Using the Internet and big data, companies can comb through financial and social media databases. They can figure out who spends more time at the concierge or goes skiing in February. Companies try to anticipate what these customers will want and when they will want it. Data analytics also help companies estimate how bad their service can be before customers will leave them for a competitor. For example, **Dialpad Inc.** analyzes call-center conversations in real time. The chief strategy officer notes that these analyses help client companies assess the tone of customer calls and can predict when an irritated customer is about to reach a sufficient threshold of discontent to leave for a competitor. With these crucial timing insights, the company can choose whether and how best to finally address the customer's concerns to prevent them from leaving.[10]

REAL-WORLD EXAMPLE

Other Pricing Policies

Target costing is also effectively used in conjunction with marketing decisions to engage in penetration pricing or price skimming. **Penetration pricing** is the pricing of a new product at a low initial price to build market share quickly. This approach is useful when the product or service is new and customers have great uncertainty as to its value. Similar to penetration pricing, **loss leader pricing** occurs when the price is set below cost (i.e., the product is sold or service is provided at a loss) to attract additional customers into the store who then also buy items with significantly positive profit margins. For example, **Costco** strategically sells nearly 90 million rotisserie chickens every year at a loss because its shoppers often buy higher-margin side dishes and beverages (including wine) along with their chicken. To help execute this profitable strategy, Costco displays its loss leader chickens near the back of stores so that customers need to push their large shopping carts past many high-margin products on their quest for chicken.[11] Penetration and loss leader pricing are not predatory

9   B. Morgan, "50 Stats That Show the Importance of Good Loyalty Programs, Even during a Crisis," *Forbes.com* (May 7, 2020), https://www.forbes.com/sites/blakemorgan/2020/05/07/50-stats-that-show-the-importance-of-good-loyalty-programs-even-during-a-crisis/#50daf5e22410, accessed September 7, 2020.

10 S. Terlep, "Everyone Hates Customer Service. This Is Why," *WSJOnline* (August 3, 2019), https://www.wsj.com/articles/everyone-hates-customer-service-this-is-why-11564804882, accessed September 7, 2020.

11 A. Gasparro, "Rotisserie Chickens: The '90s Gift to Supermarkets That Keeps on Giving," WSJ.com (January 4, 2020), https://www.wsj.com/articles/rotisserie-chickens-the-nineties-gift-to-supermarkets-that-keeps-on-giving-1515061801, accessed September 7, 2020.

pricing; the important difference is the intent. The penetration or loss leader price is not meant to destroy competition. Accountants, lawyers, and other professionals with new practices often use penetration pricing and loss leader pricing to establish a customer base.

Price skimming means that a higher price is charged when a product or service is first introduced. In essence, the company skims the cream off the market. It is used most effectively when the product is new, a small group of consumers values it, and the company enjoys a monopolistic advantage. Companies that engage in price skimming are hoping to recoup the expenses of research and development through high initial pricing. A cost consideration is that, in the start-up phase of production, economies of scale and learning effects have not occurred.

For example, in the late 1960s, Hewlett-Packard produced hand-held calculators. These were truly novel and very expensive. Priced at over $400, only scientists and engineers, who used the calculators in their work, felt the need for this product. As the market for hand-held calculators grew and technology improved, economies of scale kicked in, and the cost and price dropped dramatically. By the 1980s, tiny solar calculators were given away free as enticements to new subscribers of magazines.

Closely related to skimming is price gouging. **Price gouging** is said to occur when firms with market power price products "too high." How high is too high? Surely, cost is a consideration. Any time price just covers cost, gouging does not occur. This is why many firms go to considerable trouble to explain their cost structure and point out costs that consumers may not realize exist. Pharmaceutical companies, for example, emphasize the research and development costs associated with new drugs. When a high price is not clearly supported by cost, buyers take offense.

OBJECTIVE 3
Discuss the impact of the legal system and ethics on pricing.

THE LEGAL SYSTEM AND PRICING

Government also plays an important role in pricing. Over time, many laws have been passed regulating the way in which firms can set prices. The basic principle behind much pricing regulation is that competition is good and should be encouraged. Therefore, collusion by companies to set prices and the deliberate attempts to drive competitors out of business are prohibited.

Predatory Pricing

Predatory pricing is the practice of setting prices below cost for the purpose of injuring competitors and eliminating competition. It is important to note that pricing below cost is not necessarily predatory pricing. Companies frequently price an item below cost, by running weekly specials in a grocery store or practicing penetration pricing, for example. State laws on predatory pricing create a patchwork of legal definitions. About half the states have laws against predatory pricing, each differing somewhat in definition and rules.

For example, three Conway, Arkansas, drugstores filed suit against Wal-Mart.[12] The druggists contended that Wal-Mart engaged in predatory pricing by selling more than 100 products below cost. One difficulty is showing exactly what cost is. Wal-Mart has low overhead and phenomenal buying power. Suppliers are regularly required to shave prices to win Wal-Mart's business. Smaller concerns cannot win such price breaks. Thus, the fact that Wal-Mart prices products below competitors' costs does not necessarily mean that those products are priced below Wal-Mart's cost. (Although in this case, the CEO of Wal-Mart did concede that Wal-Mart on occasion prices products below its own cost.) More importantly, if predatory pricing is truly taking place, the below-cost price must be for the purpose of driving out competitors, a difficult point to prove. In general, states follow federal law in predatory pricing cases, and federal law makes it difficult to prove predatory pricing, since price competition is so highly valued.

Predatory pricing on the international market is called **dumping**, which occurs when companies sell below cost in other countries, and domestic industry is injured. The defense against a charge of dumping is demonstrating that the price is indeed above or equal to costs, or that domestic industry is unhurt.

Price Discrimination

The Robinson-Patman Act was passed in 1936 as a means of outlawing price discrimination. **Price discrimination** refers to the charging of different prices to different customers for essentially the same product. A key feature of the Robinson-Patman Act is that only manufacturers or suppliers are covered by the act; services and intangibles are not included.

Importantly, the Robinson-Patman Act does allow price discrimination under certain specified conditions: (1) if the competitive situation demands it and (2) if costs (including costs of manufacture, sale, or delivery) can justify the lower price. Clearly, this second condition is important for the accountant, as a lower price offered to one customer must be justified by identifiable cost savings. Additionally, the amount of the discount must be at least equaled by the amount of cost saved.

The burden of proof for firms accused of violating the Robinson-Patman Act is on the firms. The cost justification argument must be buttressed by substantial cost data. Proving a cost justification is an absolute defense; however, the expense of preparing evidence and the Federal Trade Commission's restrictive interpretations of the defense have made it a seldom used choice in the past. Now, the availability of large databases, the development of activity-based costing, and powerful computing make it a more palatable alternative. Still, problems remain. Cost allocations make such determinations particularly thorny. In justifying quantity discounts to larger companies, a company might keep track of sales calls, differences in time and labor required to make small and large deliveries, and so on.

In computing a cost differential, the company must create classes of customers based on the average costs of selling to those customers and then charge all customers in each group a cost-justifiable price. **Example 18.2** shows the how and why of calculating cost and profit by customer segment.

---

12 Wal-Mart lost the suit but won on appeal.

EXAMPLE 18.2

The HOW and WHY of Calculating Cost and Profit by Customer Class

Information:

Cobalt, Inc., manufactures vitamin supplements with an average manufacturing cost of $163 per case (a case contains 100 bottles of vitamins). Cobalt, Inc., sold 250,000 cases last year to the following three classes of customer.

Customer	Price per Case	Cases Sold
Large drugstore chain	$200	125,000
Small local pharmacies	232	100,000
Individual health clubs	250	25,000

The large drugstore chain special labeling costs $0.03 per bottle. The chain orders through electronic data interchange (EDI), which costs Cobalt about $50,000 annually in operating expenses and depreciation. Cobalt pays all shipping costs, which amounted to $1.5 million last year.

The small local pharmacies order in smaller lots that require special picking and packing in the factory; the special handling adds $20 to the cost of each case sold. Sales commissions to the independent jobbers who sell Cobalt products to the pharmacies average 10 percent of sales. Bad debts expense amounts to 1 percent of sales.

Individual health clubs purchase vitamins in even smaller lots; the special picking and packaging costs average $30 per case. There are no sales commissions for the health clubs. Instead, Cobalt advertises in health club management magazines, accepts orders by phone, and supplies point-of-sale posters and displays for the clubs. These marketing costs are $100,000 per year. Bad debts expense for this class of customer averages 10 percent.

Why:

Firms covered by price discrimination laws must be sure that price differentials are supported by cost differentials. On average, profit for each customer type is about the same.

Required:

1. Calculate the total cost per case for each of the three customer classes.

2. Using the costs from Requirement 1, calculate the profit per case per customer class. Does the cost analysis support the charging of different prices? Why or why not?

3. *What if* Cobalt charged the average price per case to all customer classes? How would that affect the profit percentages?

Solution:

1. Chain store:

Manufacturing cost per case	$163.00
Special labeling cost ($0.03 × 100)	3.00
EDI ($50,000/125,000 cases)	0.40
Shipping ($1,500,000/125,000 cases)	12.00
Total cost per case	$178.40

Small pharmacies:

Manufacturing cost per case	$163.00
Special handling per case	20.00
Sales commission ($232 × 0.10)	23.20
Bad debts expense ($232 × 0.01)	2.32
Total cost per case	$208.52

EXAMPLE 18.2

(Continued)

Health clubs:

Manufacturing cost per case	$163.00
Special handling per case	30.00
Selling expense ($100,000/25,000 cases)	4.00
Bad debts expense ($250 × 0.10)	25.00
Total cost per case	$222.00

2.

	Chain Store	Small Pharmacies	Health Clubs
Price per case	$ 200.00	$ 232.00	$ 250.00
Less: Cost per case	178.40	208.52	222.00
Profit per case	$ 21.60	$ 23.48	$ 28.00
Profit percent per case	10.80%	10.12%	11.20%

The profit percentages range from 10.12 percent to 11.20 percent. There appears to be cost justification for the price differentials among the three customer classes.

3. The average price per case is $227.33. If this price were charged to all three customers, the profit percentage for the chain store would increase and the profit percentages to the small pharmacies and health clubs would decrease. While Cobalt would earn the same overall profit percentage, this assumes that the chain store would continue to purchase the vitamin supplements from Cobalt at the new higher price. This assumption may be wrong. The chain store may well refuse to buy any product from Cobalt, leaving Cobalt with fewer units sold overall and a lower profit from the remaining customers.

Example 18.2 shows that price differences must be linked to cost differences. When this is done, the company's contention that higher prices are related to higher costs may shield it from charges of price discrimination and may also act as a behavioral prod to more expensive customers to change their way of doing business to qualify for price breaks.

ETHICS Just as a company can practice unethical behavior in applying costs, it can mislead in pricing. For example, Mylan, which makes EpiPens—a lifesaving auto-injector treatment for anaphylactic reactions to various allergens—faced considerable regulatory scrutiny and public ethical challenges over its EpiPen pricing decisions. Specifically, Mylan steadily raised the price of its patented EpiPen from $103 to $608, a roughly 500 percent increase, over a seven-year period. The CEO of Mylan argued that the prices of such drugs are driven largely by significant costs such as research and development. Additional drug costs also must be covered, such as manufacturing, drug distribution (including advertising), and patient assistance programs. However, the Department of Justice claimed that Mylan misclassified its patented EpiPen as a generic drug and, therefore, pursued legal action against the company, which Mylan ultimately settled for $465 million and a reclassification to a branded drug. Furthermore, Mylan's CEO appeared on numerous news outlets and testified before the House Committee on Oversight and Reform in attempts to defend her company's EpiPen drug pricing decisions. Therefore, as illustrated by this example, in addition to cost complexities, pricing decisions can involve serious ethical considerations. •

Explaining Costs and Benefits of Home Solar Systems

Pricing is difficult in selling sustainable technology, such as solar panels for houses. Homeowners can easily see that the upfront cost is high, perhaps $25,000 to $35,000 for a typical solar photovoltaic (PV) installation. Yet the prospective payoff occurs somewhere in the future. Sellers of solar technology must cobble together an assortment of costs and benefits for customers to convince them that the overall price is worth it.

Determining the actual cost of a home solar system is complex. Not only is there the cost of the equipment and installation, but there are also ongoing maintenance requirements and the yearly degradation of solar panels. (A system's electrical generating power decreases over the years.) On the plus side, there may be federal and state tax credits that must be figured in (and are of differing value to different taxpayers). Finally, owners of PV systems typically sell the electrical output generated back to the power companies, which then credit the PV owners' bills. In some cases, a system can pay for itself in as little as six years, whereas in other cases, it may never achieve payback.

The result of these factors is that customers find it difficult to directly compare prices and need significant help in determining not only the best system for their needs but also the entire cost of the system, taking all factors into account. Solar system installation specialists find that they must develop considerable cost accounting expertise in order to advise customers of the applicable cost and benefit scenarios.

The Role of Costs in Forensic Accounting Pricing Cases

As introduced in Chapter 1 (and exemplified in other chapters throughout the book), an understanding of cost management concepts is essential in common forensic accounting tasks, such as dispute resolution and litigation support. The forensic accountant helps the court understand the accounting issues in the case by providing analyses, evaluations, and opinions regarding the nature, amount, and impact of such issues. One common issue for forensic accountants to address involves the use of costs in cost-based pricing disputes. Specifically, forensic accountants ensure that the court reaches an appropriate decision in such disputes.

There are many situations in which one party in a contract enters into an agreement to provide services or products to another party based on some cost-based formula. Such contracts are logical and necessary in situations in which the service or product is not clearly defined, or at the time of the contract signing, some of the issues are unknown. In the government sector, in particular, many major contract issues for products or services are unique. For example, the development and production of military weapons or a vaccine during a pandemic contain unique and often unknown contract issues.

In these situations, some of the critically important accounting questions include exactly which costs should be included in the contract, how such costs should be measured, the correct timing of such costs, and the appropriate application of particular accounting concepts or rules under the contract. The greater the complexity of the contract deliverables, the greater the likelihood that there will be disagreement about the costs that were accumulated to arrive at the pricing amounts. Therefore, an understanding of cost-plus pricing is crucial to the logical and appropriate resolution of disputes involving cost-based pricing contract issues.

The Federal False Claims Act One particular area of cost-based pricing that is uniquely relevant to forensic accountants with cost management knowledge concerns the Federal False Claims Act (FFCA). A bit of history will help provide context for understanding the importance of the FFCA. The federal government, in particular, is a very large purchaser of products and services that often are priced using some form of cost-based pricing. Over the past two centuries, these cost-based contracts with the federal government have involved significant sums of money. Perhaps not surprisingly, there have been numerous contracts in which the opportunities to overcharge the government have been too large for some government suppliers to resist.

Even as long ago as the U.S. Civil War, some government suppliers carelessly, and sometimes intentionally, overcharged the government for contracted services or products. For example, during the Civil War, President Abraham Lincoln requested and Congress passed a law (the FFCA is also known as the "Lincoln Law"; March 2, 1863) that made it easier to find and prosecute such illegal behavior toward the federal government. The law provided a mechanism for individuals who were aware of such illegal overpricing behavior to file a "Qui Tam" suit against the alleged violator and to seek damages on behalf of the government. The Qui Tam suit filer can receive some percentage of the damages if the suit is successful. Remember that at the time the Qui Tam law was passed, there was no General Accounting Office (GAO), Army Audit Agency, or other government audit agency available to find (or whistleblow) such fraud.

The FFCA increases the ease and predictability of litigation that brings claims against contractors who overcharge the government for products or services. The use of Qui Tam suits still exists and many FFCA suits initially begin with a Qui Tam suit. When a Qui Tam suit is filed by a whistleblower on behalf of the federal government, it is sent to the U.S. Department of Justice, which reviews the case and decides whether or not it wants to take charge of the case and litigate the suit. If the Department of Justice decides not to take the case or chooses to litigate only selected parts of the case, then the whistleblower can elect to separately pursue any remaining parts of the case.

An interesting and important component of the FFCA is its operational definition of fraud. In criminal fraud cases, the prosecutor must prove both knowledge and intent on the part of the defendant, which can be challenging. However, because the FFCA imposes civil liability, the plaintiff has only to prove that the defendant acted with a "reckless disregard of the truth" in order to prove fraud. A reckless disregard for the truth might be exemplified by carelessly measuring costs or not keeping accurate accounting records even though doing so is required by the contract, either of which might suggest fraud under the FFCA. Accountants are uniquely able to identify, describe, and testify as to the nature and quality of the cost accounting measurements and the cost framework that is required for cost-based pricing contracts. Interestingly, FFCA cases commonly utilize forensic accounting experts on both sides (i.e., the plaintiff and the defendant).

Cost-based pricing contracts rely heavily on which costs should be included (e.g., direct material, direct labor, and variable manufacturing overhead only), how such costs should be measured (e.g., using a particular cost allocation technique or forecasting approach), and what issues should be considered in calculating costs under the contract (e.g., the specific omission of particular items, such as administrative costs, from the cost base). As a result, cost experts often should be utilized in writing and implementing such contracts. As with many areas of accounting, forensic accounting requires the use of sound judgment in conducting effective analyses and informing associated decisions.

MEASURING PROFIT

Profit is a measure of the difference between what a firm puts into making and selling a product or service and what it receives. There are a number of definitions of profit. Some are used for external reporting and some for internal reporting.

Reasons for Measuring Profit

Clearly, firms are interested in measuring profit. In fact, firms are classified according to whether or not profit is the primary objective—they are either for-profit or not-for-profit entities. Profits are measured for a number of reasons. These include determining the viability of the firm, measuring managerial performance, determining whether or not a firm adheres to government regulations, and signaling the market about the opportunities for others to earn a profit.

OBJECTIVE **4**

Explain why firms measure profit, and calculate measures of profit using absorption and variable costing.

Owners of a company want to know if the company is viable in both the short term and the long term. Work gives meaning to life. Staying in business is not only a means to an end but also an end in itself. *The Money Game*, by Adam Smith,[13] contains an interesting passage in which the author puzzles through John Maynard Keynes' reference to the stock market as a game. Smith writes:

> *Game? Game? Why did the Master say game? He could have said business, or profession, or occupation or what have you. What is a game? It is "sport, play, frolic or fun;" "a scheme or art employed in the pursuit of an object or purpose;" "a contest, conducted according to set rules, for amusement, recreation, or winning a stake." Does that sound like Owning a Share of American Industry? Participating in the Long-Term Growth of the American Economy? No, but it sounds like the stock market.*

That not only sounds like the stock market, but also sounds like many businesses. Steve Jobs started Apple Computer in a garage. Years later, a multimillionaire, he was eased out of Apple management—and immediately started NeXT. Later, he returned to Apple, became heavily involved in Pixar, and spearheaded the phenomenal success of the iPod, iPad, and iPhone until his death. Sam Walton stayed involved with Wal-Mart until his death, as did John D. Rockefeller with Standard Oil. Playing the game is important, and profit is a way of keeping score. Players must maintain positive profits to stay in the game. Enough losses and you're out.

Profit can be used to measure managerial performance. Assessing performance is complicated, but profit, because it is measured in dollars, simplifies scorekeeping. Top management is usually evaluated on the basis of profit and/or return on investment. Both measures require benefits to exceed costs.

Regulated firms must keep profits within certain limits. The profitability of a regulated monopoly is monitored to ensure that the public is served by this structure and that prices do not escalate to the level of an unregulated monopoly. Note that price alone is not set— instead, the price must be set to ensure a "reasonable rate of return," and it is tied to the costs incurred by the regulated firm. Examples of companies subject to regulation are utilities, local telephone companies, and cable television companies. These companies enjoy monopoly status, and they pay for the privilege through adherence to regulations.

Profit also signals others outside a company of potential opportunities. A highly profitable firm signals the market that others might also benefit from entry. Low profits do not entice competition. For this reason, companies may deliberately avoid high short-term profits.

Even though a not-for-profit entity has no profit, it still is engaged in an exchange relationship and must assess its performance and long-term viability. Donors want information on charities. Corporate donors, in particular, want better measures of how well a charity fulfills its mission, and how well it uses and accounts for resources. Supplies, postage, telephones, and office space all require money. Employee wages are not necessarily below the market wage; they simply have no claim to any residual. As a result, many of the concepts covered in this chapter have relevance to not-for-profit entities. The Girl Scouts of America, for example, expect to profit from cookie sales, although they may not refer to the money made above cost as profit. Not-for-profit firms are still interested in the relationship between revenues and expenses, or inflows and outflows.

Absorption-Costing Approach to Measuring Profit

Absorption costing, or full costing, is required for external financial reporting. According to GAAP, profit is a long-run concept and depends on the difference between revenues and expenses. Over the long run, of course, all costs are variable. Therefore, fixed costs are treated as if they were variable by assigning some to each unit of production. **Absorption costing** assigns

---

13 Actually, Adam Smith is a pseudonym for George J. W. Goodman. But you can probably find *The Money Game* (New York: Vintage Books, 1976) under Adam Smith. The book is a very readable exploration of investing and investors. The passage cited here can be found on page 16.

all manufacturing costs, direct materials, direct labor, variable overhead, and a share of fixed overhead, to each unit of product. In this way, each unit of product absorbs some of the fixed manufacturing overhead in addition to its variable manufacturing costs. When a unit of product is finished, it takes these costs into inventory with it. When it is sold, these manufacturing costs are shown on the income statement as cost of goods sold. It is absorption costing that is used to calculate three measures of profit: gross profit, operating income, and net income. **Example 18.3** shows the how and why of calculating the cost of inventory and preparing the income statement under absorption costing.

EXAMPLE 18.3

The HOW and WHY of Calculating Inventory Cost and Preparing the Income Statement Using Absorption Costing

Information:

Lasersave, Inc., a recycler of used toner cartridges for laser printers, began operations in August and manufactured 1,000 cartridges during the month with the following unit costs:

Direct materials	$ 5.00
Direct labor	15.00
Variable overhead	3.00
Fixed overhead*	20.00
Variable marketing cost	1.25

*Fixed overhead per unit = $20,000/1,000 units produced = $20.

Total fixed factory overhead is $20,000 per month. During August, 1,000 cartridges were sold at a price of $60, and fixed marketing and administrative expenses were $12,000.

> **Why:**
> Firms use absorption costing to value inventory and to calculate cost of goods sold for the income statement. This use is acceptable according to GAAP. It ensures that in the long run, all manufacturing costs are absorbed by the units produced.

Required:

1. Calculate the unit cost of each toner cartridge using absorption costing.

2. How many units remain in ending inventory? What is the cost of ending inventory using absorption costing?

3. Prepare an absorption-costing income statement for Lasersave, Inc., for the month of August.

4. *What if* September production was 1,250 units, costs were stable, and sales were 1,000 units? What is the cost of ending inventory? What is operating income for September?

Solution:

1. The unit product (manufacturing) cost under absorption costing is:

Direct materials	$ 5.00
Direct labor	15.00
Variable overhead	3.00
Fixed overhead	20.00
Total cost	$43.00

2. Units in ending inventory = Units, beginning inventory + Units produced
$$- \text{Units sold} = 0 + 1,000 - 1,000 = 0 \text{ units}$$
Cost of ending inventory = $0

EXAMPLE 18.3

(Continued)

3.

Lasersave, Inc.
Absorption-Costing Income Statement
For the Month of August

		Percent of Sales
Sales ($60 × 1,000)	$ 60,000	100.00%
Less: Cost of goods sold ($43 × 1,000)	43,000	71.67
Gross profit	$ 17,000	28.33%
Less:		
Variable marketing expenses ($1.25 × 1,000)	(1,250)	(2.08)
Fixed marketing and administrative expenses	(12,000)	(20.00)
Operating income	$ 3,750	6.25%

4. Units in ending inventory = Units, beginning inventory + Units produced
$\qquad$ − Units sold = 0 + 1,250 − 1,000 = 250 units

Cost of ending inventory = $39 × 250 = $9,750

The new operating income is $7,750, calculated as follows:

Sales ($60 × 1,000)	$ 60,000
Less: Cost of goods sold ($39* × 1,000)	39,000
Gross profit	$ 21,000
Less:	
Variable marketing expenses ($1.25 × 1,000)	(1,250)
Fixed marketing and administrative expenses	(12,000)
Operating income	$ 7,750

*Fixed manufacturing cost/Units manufactured = $20,000/1,250 = $16; therefore, unit product cost = $5 + $15 + $3 + $16 = $39.

The income statement shown in Example 18.3 is the familiar full-costing income statement used for external reporting. Recall that the difference between revenue and cost of goods sold is gross profit (or gross margin). This is not equal to operating income, because the marketing and administrative expenses remain to be covered. At one time, gross profit was a fairly useful measure of profitability. Marketing and administrative expenses were relatively stable and could be adjusted fairly easily. In today's economic environment, that is less true. Government regulations affect businesses in sometimes unforeseen ways. Environmental cleanup and modification of facilities to comply with the Americans with Disabilities Act are just two examples of regulations that increase nonmanufacturing expenses. Additionally, research and development, also an expense subtracted from gross profit to yield operating income, is increasingly important. Now, gross profit is less useful and cannot be used as a sole measure of the long-run health of the firm.

The income statement in Example 18.3 also shows the "Percent of Sales" column which is often associated with the absorption-costing income statement. Notice that Lasersave, Inc., earned a gross profit of just over 28 percent of sales, and that operating income was 6.25 percent of sales. Is this good or bad performance? It depends on the typical experience for the industry. If most firms in the industry earned a gross margin of 35 percent of sales, Lasersave would be considered below average, and it might look for opportunities to decrease cost of goods sold or to increase revenue.

What about absorption-costing operating income? Is it a reasonable measure of performance? Problems exist with this measure, too. First, managers can remove some current-period costs from the income statement by producing for inventory. Second, the absorption-costing format is not useful for decision making.

Disadvantages of Absorption Costing   In general, a company manufactures a product in order to sell it. In fact, that was the case for Lasersave for the month of August when every unit produced was sold. September is a different story. Lasersave produced 1,250 units but sold only 1,000. The price, variable cost per unit, and total fixed costs remain the same. Example 18.3 shows that even though September sales were the same as August sales, and costs remained stable, September operating income was higher than August operating income.

Operating income in September is $7,750 versus operating income for August of $3,750. The same number of units was sold, at the same price, and the same costs. What happened? The culprit is treating fixed manufacturing overhead as if it were variable. In August, 1,000 units were produced, and each one absorbed $20 ($20,000/1,000 units produced) of fixed overhead. In September, however, the same total fixed manufacturing overhead of $20,000 was spread out over 1,250 units, so each unit absorbed only $16 ($20,000/1,250). The 250 units that went into ending inventory took with them all of their variable costs of production of $5,750 ($23 × 250) plus $4,000 (250 × $16) of fixed manufacturing overhead from September. That $4,000 of inventoried fixed manufacturing overhead is precisely equal to the $4,000 difference in operating incomes.

Clearly, the absorption-costing income statement gives the wrong message in September. It seems to say that September performance was better than August performance, when the sales performance was identical and, arguably, production was off by 250 units. (Even if the company wanted to produce for inventory, it is misleading to increase income for the period as a result.)

Of course, the whole purpose of manipulating income by producing for inventory is to increase profit above what it would have been without the extra production. Managers who are evaluated on the basis of operating income know that they can temporarily improve profitability by increasing production. They may do this to ensure year-end bonuses or promotions. As a result, the usefulness of operating or net income as a measure of profitability is weakened. Companies that use absorption-costing income as a measure of profitability may institute rules regarding production. For example, a manufacturer of floor care products insists that the factory produce only the amounts called for in the master budget. While this will not erase the impact of changes in inventory on operating income, it does mean that the factory manager cannot deliberately manipulate production to increase income.

The second disadvantage of absorption costing is that it is not a useful format for decision making. Suppose that Lasersave was considering accepting a special order for 100 toner cartridges at $38. Should the company accept? If we focus on the absorption-costing income statement, who can tell? In August, the manufacturing cost per unit was $43. In September, it was $39. Neither figure included the marketing cost. The treatment of fixed overhead as a unit-level variable cost has made it difficult to see just what the incremental cost is.

Variable-Costing Approach to Measuring Profit

An approach to measuring profitability that avoids the problems inherent in making fixed overhead a variable cost is variable costing. **Variable costing** (sometimes called direct costing) assigns only unit-level variable manufacturing costs to the product; these costs include direct materials, direct labor, and variable overhead. Fixed overhead is treated as a period cost and is not inventoried with the other product costs. Instead, it is expensed in the period incurred.

The result of treating fixed manufacturing overhead as a period expense is to reduce the factory costs that are inventoriable. Under variable costing, only direct materials, direct labor, and variable overhead are inventoried. (Remember that marketing and administrative expenses are never inventoried—whether variable or fixed.) Therefore, the inventoriable variable product cost for Lasersave is $23 ($5 direct materials + $15 direct labor + $3 variable overhead).

The variable-costing income statement is set up a little differently from the absorption-costing income statement. **Example 18.4** shows the how and why of calculating the variable cost of inventory and preparing the variable-costing income statements for August and September.

EXAMPLE 18.4

The HOW and WHY of Calculating Inventory Cost and Preparing the Income Statement Using Variable Costing

Information:

Lasersave, Inc., a recycler of used toner cartridges for laser printers, began operations in August and manufactured 1,000 cartridges during the month with the following unit costs:

Direct materials	$ 5.00
Direct labor	15.00
Variable overhead	3.00
Fixed overhead*	20.00
Variable marketing cost	1.25

*Fixed overhead per unit = $20,000/1,000 units produced = $20.

Total fixed factory overhead is $20,000 per month. During August, 1,000 cartridges were sold at a price of $60, and fixed marketing and administrative expenses were $12,000.

> **Why:**
> Firms use variable costing to value inventory and to calculate cost of goods sold for the income statement for internal management decision making. Variable costing is not acceptable according to GAAP. However, it is a useful format for decision making and does not allow managers to manipulate income by producing for inventory.

Required:

1. Calculate the unit cost of each toner cartridge using variable costing.

2. How many units remain in ending inventory? What is the cost of ending inventory using variable costing?

3. Prepare a variable-costing income statement for Lasersave, Inc., for the month of August.

4. *What if* September production was 1,250 units, costs were stable, and sales were 1,000 units? What is the cost of ending inventory? What is operating income for September?

Solution:

1. The unit product (manufacturing) cost under variable costing is:

Direct materials	$ 5.00
Direct labor	15.00
Variable overhead	3.00
Total cost	$23.00

2. Units in ending inventory = Units, beginning inventory + Units produced
   − Units sold = 0 + 1,000 − 1,000 = 0 units
   Cost of ending inventory = $0

EXAMPLE 18.4

(*Continued*)

3.

Lasersave, Inc.
Variable-Costing Income Statement
For the Month of August

		Percent of Sales
Sales ($60 × 1,000)	$ 60,000	100.00%
Less:		
Variable cost of goods sold ($23 × 1,000)	(23,000)	(38.33)
Variable marketing expense ($1.25 × 1,000)	(1,250)	(2.08)
Contribution margin	$ 35,750	59.59%
Less:		
Fixed factory overhead	(20,000)	(33.33)
Fixed marketing and administrative expenses	(12,000)	(20.00)
Operating income	$ 3,750	6.25%*

*Percent totals may not equal due to rounding.

4. Units in ending inventory = Units, beginning inventory + Units produced
        − Units sold = 0 + 1,250 − 1,000 = 250 units
    Cost of ending inventory = $23 × 250 = $5,750

The new operating income is $3,750, calculated as follows:

Sales ($60 × 1,000)	$ 60,000
Less:	
Variable cost of goods sold ($23 × 1,000)	(23,000)
Variable marketing expense ($1.25 × 1,000)	(1,250)
Contribution margin	$ 35,750
Less:	
Fixed factory overhead	(20,000)
Fixed marketing and administrative expenses	(12,000)
Operating income	$ 3,750

As Example 18.4 shows, all unit-level variable costs (including variable manufacturing and variable marketing expenses) are summed and subtracted from sales to yield contribution margin. Then, all fixed expenses for the period, whether they are incurred by the factory or by marketing and administration, are subtracted to yield operating income.

Notice that the August and September variable-costing income statements for Lasersave are identical. This seems right. Each month had identical sales and costs. While September production was higher, those figures will show up as an increase in inventory on the balance sheet. As we can see, variable-costing operating income cannot be manipulated through overproduction, since fixed manufacturing overhead is not carried into inventory.

Let's take a closer look at each month. In August, production exactly equaled sales. In this case, none of the period's costs go into inventory, and absorption-costing operating income is equal to variable-costing income. In September, inventory increased, and absorption-costing operating income is higher than variable-costing operating income. The difference of $4,000 ($7,750 − $3,750) is just equal to the fixed overhead per unit multiplied by the increase in inventory ($16 × 250 units).

Exhibit 18.2

Changes in Inventory Under
Absorption and Variable Costing

If	Then
1. Production > Sales	Absorption-costing income > Variable-costing income
2. Production < Sales	Absorption-costing income < Variable-costing income
3. Production = Sales	Absorption-costing income = Variable-costing income

What happens when inventory decreases? Again, there is an effect on operating income under absorption costing but not under variable costing. Let's take Lasersave into the month of October, when production is 1,250 units (just like September), but 1,300 units are sold.

In this case, when inventory decreases (or production is less than sales), variable-costing operating income is greater than absorption-costing operating income. The difference of $800 ($14,475 − $13,675) is equal to the 50 units that, under absorption costing, came from inventory with $16 of the previous month's fixed manufacturing overhead attached. Exhibit 18.2 summarizes the impact of changes in inventory on operating income under absorption costing and variable costing.

To summarize, when inventories change from the beginning to the end of the period, the two costing approaches will give different operating incomes. The reason for this is that absorption costing assigns fixed manufacturing overhead to units produced. If those units are sold, the fixed overhead appears on the income statement under cost of goods sold. If the units are not sold, the fixed overhead goes into inventory. Under variable costing, however, all fixed overhead for the period is expensed. As a result, absorption costing allows managers to manipulate operating income by producing for inventory.

The variable-costing income statement has an advantage in addition to providing better signals regarding performance. It also provides more useful information for management decision making. For example, how much more will Lasersave earn if it sells one more unit? Example 18.3 indicates that $17 ($60 − $43) is the per-unit gross profit. However, that figure includes some fixed overhead, and fixed overhead will not change if another unit is produced and sold. The variable-costing income statement in Example 18.4 gives more useful information. Additional contribution margin of the extra unit is $35.75 ($60 − $23 − $1.25). The key insight of variable costing is that fixed expenses do not change as units produced and sold change. Therefore, while the variable-costing income statement cannot be used for external reporting, it is a valuable tool for some management decisions.

Profitability of Segments and Divisions

Companies often want to know the profitability of a segment of the business. That segment could be a product, division, sales territory, or customer group. Determining the profit attributable to subdivisions of the company is harder than determining overall profit because of the need to allocate expenses. Segmented income statements using variable, absorption, and activity-based costing have already been covered in previous chapters. For example, segmented income statements in the keep-or-drop decision are covered in Chapter 17. Activity-based segmented income statements by product line or customer class are covered in Chapters 4 and 12. As a result, we will not go into the computations in depth here. Instead, we will focus on the managerial use of variable-costing segmented income statements.

Profit by Product Line   It is easy to understand why a firm would like to know whether or not a particular product is profitable. A product that consistently loses money and has no potential to become profitable could be dropped. This would free up resources for a product with higher potential. On the other hand, a profitable product may merit additional time and attention.

Product line profitability would be easy to compute if all costs and revenues were easily traceable to each product. This is seldom the case. Therefore, companies must first determine how profit will be computed. Let's examine Alden Company, which manufactures two products: basic fax machines and multi-function fax machines. The basic fax machine has telephone and fax capability. This type of machine is less expensive and easier to produce. The multi-function fax machine is the high-end machine. It is a combination of two-line telephone, fax, computer printer, and copier. The multi-function fax machine uses more advanced technology and is more difficult to produce. Data on each product follow.

	Basic	Multi-Function
Number of units	20,000	10,000
Direct labor hours	40,000	15,000
Price	$ 200	$ 350
Prime cost per unit	$ 55	$ 95
Overhead per unit*	$ 30	$ 22.50

*Annual overhead is $825,000, and overhead is applied on the basis of direct labor hours.

Marketing expenses, all variable, amount to 10 percent of sales. Administrative expenses of $2 million, all fixed, are allocated to the products in accordance with revenue. Absorption-costing income by product line is shown in Exhibit 18.3.

Clearly, the multi-function fax machine is more profitable. But what does this tell us? Can we conclude that each basic fax machine sold adds $41.65 ($833,000/20,000 units) to profit? Does each multi-function fax machine sold add $104.20 ($1,042,000/10,000 units) to profit? No, Alden Company has intermingled variable and fixed costs and has allocated administrative expenses on the basis of revenue, when there is no reason to believe that revenue drives administrative expenses. Additionally, overhead has been assigned to the products on a per-unit basis, but we do not know just what it includes. Is $22.50 an accurate representation of the overhead resources required to produce one multi-function fax machine? A variable-costing segmented income statement will give better information.

Using Variable Costing to Measure Segment Profit Alden Company could use variable costing and segregate direct fixed and common fixed expenses as well. To apply variable costing to Alden Company, we need additional information on fixed and variable costs of overhead. Suppose that total variable overhead is $360,000 and total fixed overhead is $465,000. Since overhead is applied on the basis of direct labor hours, the variable overhead assigned to basic fax machines is $261,818 [$360,000 × (40,000/55,000)]. The variable overhead assigned to multi-function fax machines is $98,182 [$360,000 × (15,000/55,000)]. The variable-costing income statement is given in Exhibit 18.4. Notice that all fixed expenses that are not attributable to either of the product lines are subtracted from the total column.

	Basic	Multi-Function	Total
Sales	$ 4,000	$3,500	$ 7,500
Less: Cost of goods sold	1,700	1,175	2,875
Gross profit	$ 2,300	$2,325	$ 4,625
Less:			
Marketing expenses	(400)	(350)	(750)
Administrative expenses	(1,067)	(933)	(2,000)
Operating income	$ 833	$1,042	$ 1,875

Exhibit 18.3

Alden Company Absorption-Costing Income Statement (In thousands of dollars)

Exhibit 18.4

Alden Company Variable-Costing Income Statement (In thousands of dollars)

	Basic	Multi-Function	Total
Sales	$ 4,000	$ 3,500	$ 7,500
Less:			
Variable cost of goods sold	(1,362)	(1,048)	(2,410)
Sales commissions	(400)	(350)	(750)
Contribution margin	$ 2,238	$ 2,102	$ 4,340
Less:			
Fixed overhead			(465)
Administrative expenses			(2,000)
Operating income			$ 1,875

Divisional Profit Just as companies want to know the relative profitability of different products, they may want to assess the relative profitability of different divisions of the company. Divisional profit is often used in evaluating the performance of managers. Failure to earn a profit can lead to the division's closing. For example, General Motors decided to drop the Oldsmobile line due to its continued unprofitability.

Divisional profit may be calculated using any of three approaches described in the preceding section. Usually, the absorption-based approach is used, and a share of corporate expense is allocated to each division to remind them that all expenses of the company must be covered. Suppose that Polyglyph, Inc., is a conglomerate with four divisions: Alpha, Beta, Gamma, and Delta. Corporate expenses of $10 million are allocated to each division on the basis of sales. The divisional income statements are as follows:

	Alpha	Beta	Gamma	Delta	Total
Sales	$ 90	$ 60	$ 30	$120	$300
Less: Cost of goods sold	35	20	11	98	164
Gross profit	$ 55	$ 40	$ 19	$ 22	$136
Less:					
Division expenses	(20)	(10)	(15)	(20)	(65)
Corporate expenses	(3)	(2)	(1)	(4)	(10)
Operating income (loss)	$ 32	$ 28	$ 3	$ (2)	$ 61

How might Polyglyph view these results? Clearly, Delta has an operating loss. Corporate management would raise questions about Delta's continuing viability. However, notice that Delta's operating loss would be eliminated if allocated corporate expenses were not included. In fact, all divisions would look more profitable if corporate expenses were not allocated to the divisions. As a result, management might concentrate on Delta's potential for an improved profit picture. Delta's divisional expenses are relatively high. Perhaps this is due to an ambitious research and development program. If payoffs from this program can be anticipated, corporate management will be much less concerned than if the divisional expenses do not have potential. Corporate management will also be concerned with trends over time and the immediate and long-term prospects for each division. Even a seemingly profitable division, like Alpha, may need attention if it is in a declining industry or if it uses significantly more resources than indicated by the corporate expense allocation. Additional material on divisional profitability and responsibility accounting is covered in Chapter 10.

Overall Profit The computation of segmental profit is clearly useful in many management decisions. However, the allocation problems inherent in computing profit on divisions, segments, and product lines may mean that overall profit is most useful in some contexts. It is certainly easiest to compute, and it does have meaning. If the overall profit is consistently positive, the company remains in business, even if one or more segments is losing money.

For example, High Flight[14] is a company that engages in three services: flight training, short-haul flight services (basically a courier service for regional banks), and airplane leasing. High Flight had real difficulty determining the profitability of each service. The same planes were used for each, so the allocation of airplane depreciation to the three services would seem reasonable. But the owner of High Flight realized that such an allocation would divert attention from the underlying question: Should all three services be offered? Some costs were easily traceable to each segment (e.g., fuel costs and pilot services). Other costs were difficult to allocate; plane depreciation and hangar rent are examples. Ultimately, High Flight performed a modified profitability analysis of each service and determined that flight training was probably a money loser. What did management decide? They kept all three because they realized that pilots preferred to rent planes from the place where they received flight training. Thus, the linkage between flight training and airplane rental meant that the company had to retain both or neither.

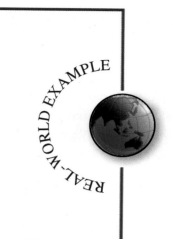

REAL-WORLD EXAMPLE

ANALYSIS OF PROFIT-RELATED VARIANCES

OBJECTIVE 5

Compute the sales price, sales volume, contribution margin, contribution margin volume, sales mix, market share, and market size variances.

Managers frequently want to compare actual profit earned with expected profit. This leads naturally to variance analysis, in which actual and budgeted amounts are compared. Profit variances center on the difference between budgeted and actual prices, volumes, and contribution margin.

Sales Price and Sales Volume Variances

Actual revenue may differ from expected revenue because actual price differs from expected price or because quantity sold differs from expected quantity sold, or both. The **sales price variance** is the difference between actual price and expected price multiplied by the actual quantity or volume sold. In equation form, it is the following:

Sales price variance = (Actual price − Expected price) × Quantity sold

The **sales volume variance** is the difference between actual volume sold and expected volume sold multiplied by the expected price. It can be expressed in the following equation:

Sales volume variance = (Actual volume − Expected volume) × Expected price

The overall sales variance is the sum of the sales price variance and the sales volume variance.

Overall sales variance = Sales price variance + Sales volume variance

As is the case with all variances, the sales price and sales volume variances are labeled favorable (F) if the variance increases profit above the amount expected. They are labeled unfavorable (U) if the variance decreases profit below the amount expected. **Example 18.5** shows the how and why of calculating the sales price, sales volume, and overall sales variance.

---

14 The High Flight example is real and is based on the author's conversations with High Flight's owner. However, the company's name has been changed for confidentiality reasons.

EXAMPLE 18.5

The HOW and WHY of Calculating the Sales Price Variance, the Sales Volume Variance, and the Overall Sales Variance

Information:

Armour Company distributes produce. In May, Armour Company expects to sell 20,000 pounds of produce at an average price of $0.20 per pound. Actual results are 23,000 pounds sold at an average price of $0.19 per pound.

> **Why:**
> The sales price variance tells managers what impact a difference between actual and expected sales price has on revenue. The sales volume variance tells managers what impact a difference between actual and expected units sold has on revenue.

Required:

1. Calculate the sales price variance for May.

2. Calculate the sales volume variance for May.

3. Calculate the overall sales variance for May. Explain why it is favorable or unfavorable.

4. *What if* May sales were actually 19,000 pounds? How would that affect the sales price variance? The sales volume variance? The overall sales variance?

Solution:

1. Sales price variance = (Actual price − Expected price) × Quantity sold
    $$= [(\$0.19 − \$0.20) × 23,000] = \$230 \text{ U}$$

2. Sales volume variance = (Actual volume − Expected volume) × Expected price
    $$= [(23,000 − 20,000) × \$0.20] = \$600 \text{ F}$$

3. Overall sales variance = Sales price variance + Sales volume variance
    $$= \$230 \text{ U} + \$600 \text{ F} = \$370 \text{ F}$$

    The overall sales variance is favorable because the favorable sales volume variance is larger than the unfavorable sales price variance. That is, the lower than expected sales price did reduce revenue; however, the greater than expected volume overcame that effect and raised revenue overall.

4. If May sales in pounds were 19,000, there would be a decrease in the sales price variance, since the actual number of pounds sold decreased. There would be an unfavorable sales volume variance, and the overall sales variance would be unfavorable because both the sales price variance and the sales volume variance are unfavorable.

As is shown in Example 18.5, the sum of the sales price and sales volume variances is the **total (overall) sales variance**. Of course, this is simply the difference between actual and expected revenue. Breaking the overall sales variance into price and volume components gives managers a better feel for why actual revenue may differ from budgeted revenue.

It is important to note that these variances just begin to alert managers to problems in pricing and sales. As is the case with all variances, significant variances are investigated to discover the underlying reasons for the difference between expected and actual results. In the case of an unfavorable sales price variance, the reason may be the giving of unanticipated price discounts, perhaps to meet competitors' prices. The sales price and sales volume variances interact. For example, an unfavorable sales price variance may be paired with a favorable sales volume variance because the lower price raised quantity sold.

Contribution Margin Variance

We have just looked at the price and sales variances. The cost variances were covered in Chapter 9. Now it is time to put sales and cost together and calculate any variances between actual and expected contribution margin. The **contribution margin variance** is the difference between actual and budgeted contribution margin.

Contribution margin variance = Actual contribution margin − Budgeted contribution margin

This variance is favorable if the actual contribution margin earned is higher than the budgeted amount. **Example 18.6** shows the how and why of calculating the contribution margin variance.

EXAMPLE 18.6

The HOW and WHY of Calculating the Contribution Margin Variance

Information:

Birdwell, Inc., produces and sells two types of bird feeders. The regular type is a simple plastic and wood model, which can be hung from a tree branch. The deluxe model is a larger, stand-alone model, which includes a post and a round squirrel shield to prevent squirrels from eating the bird seed. Budgeted and actual data for the two models are shown below.

Budgeted Amounts:

	Regular Model	Deluxe Model	Total
Sales:			
($10 × 1,500)	$15,000		
($50 × 500)		$25,000	$40,000
Variable expenses	9,000	17,500	26,500
Contribution margin	$ 6,000	$ 7,500	$13,500

Actual Amounts:

	Regular Model	Deluxe Model	Total
Sales:			
($10 × 1,250)	$12,500		
($50 × 625)		$31,250	$43,750
Variable expenses	7,500	21,875	29,375
Contribution margin	$ 5,000	$ 9,375	$14,375

Why:
The contribution margin variance tells managers the difference between actual and expected contribution margin. This is a starting point for analyzing the factors that led to any difference between actual and expected profit.

Required:

1. Calculate the contribution margin variance.

2. *What if* actual units sold of the deluxe bird feeder decreased? How would that affect the contribution margin variance? What if actual units sold of the deluxe bird feeder increased? How would that affect the contribution margin variance?

EXAMPLE 18.6

(Continued)

Solution:

1. Contribution margin variance = Actual contribution margin
    − Expected contribution margin
    = $14,375 − $13,500 = $875 F

2. If units sold of the deluxe bird feeder decrease while everything else stays the same, the contribution margin variance would decrease. Whether it turned unfavorable would depend on the amount of decrease in deluxe sales. On the other hand, if units sold of the deluxe bird feeder increase while everything else stays the same, the contribution margin variance would become larger and still be favorable.

The contribution margin variance is an overall variance. It can be broken into the contribution margin volume variance and the sales mix variance.

Contribution Margin Volume Variance   The **contribution margin volume variance** is the difference between the actual quantity sold and the budgeted quantity sold multiplied by the budgeted average unit contribution margin. Note the difference between the contribution margin volume variance and the sales volume variance. Both look at the difference between actual and budgeted volume sold. The sales volume variance multiplies that difference by sales price, however, while the contribution margin volume variance multiplies that difference by contribution margin. Therefore, the contribution margin volume variance gives management information about gained or lost profit due to changes in the quantity of sales.

Contribution margin volume variance = (Actual quantity sold − Budgeted quantity sold)
× Budgeted average unit contribution margin

The budgeted average unit contribution margin is the total budgeted contribution margin divided by the budgeted total number of units of all products to be sold. **Example 18.7** shows the how and why of calculating the contribution margin volume variance.

EXAMPLE 18.7

The HOW and WHY of Calculating the Contribution Margin Volume Variance

Information:
Recall from Example 18.6 that Birdwell, Inc., provided the following information:

	Budgeted	Actual
Sales in units, regular model	1,500	1,250
Sales in units, deluxe model	500	625
Total contribution margin	$13,500	$14,375

Why:
The contribution margin volume variance tells managers what impact a difference between actual and expected sales volume has on contribution margin. Unlike the sales volume variance, the contribution margin variance weights the difference between actual and expected volume by the contribution margin, which includes both price and variable cost. Thus, it is more closely related to profit.

EXAMPLE 18.7

(*Continued*)

Required:

1. Calculate the budgeted average unit contribution margin.

2. Calculate the contribution margin volume variance.

3. ***What if*** actual units sold of the deluxe bird feeder decreased? How would that affect the contribution margin volume variance? What if actual units sold of the deluxe bird feeder increased? How would that affect the contribution margin volume variance?

Solution:

1. Budgeted average unit contribution margin

   = Budgeted total contribution margin/Budgeted total units

   = $13,500/(1,500 + 500) = $6.75

2. Contribution margin volume variance

   = (Actual quantity sold − Budgeted quantity sold)

   × Budgeted average unit contribution margin

   = [(1,250 + 625) − (1,500 + 500)] × $6.75 = $843.75 U

3. If actual units sold of the deluxe bird feeder decrease while everything else stays the same, the contribution margin volume variance would decrease and become even more unfavorable. If actual units sold of the deluxe bird feeder increase while everything else stays the same, the contribution margin volume variance would increase and become less unfavorable. Whether it turned favorable would depend on the amount of the increase in deluxe bird feeder sales.

As Example 18.7 shows, the unfavorable contribution margin volume variance is the result of selling fewer units, in total, than budgeted. Still, we can see that Birdwell, Inc., actually had a higher contribution margin than expected. The shift in the sales mix explains why.

Sales Mix Variance   The sales mix represents the proportion of total sales yielded by each product. A company which produces only one product obviously has a sales mix of 100 percent for that product, and there is no effect of changing sales mix on profit. Multiproduct firms, however, do experience shifts in their sales mix. If relatively more of the high-profit product is sold, profit will be higher than expected. If the sales mix shifts toward the low-profit product, profit will be lower than expected. We can define the **sales mix variance** as the sum of the change in units for each product multiplied by the difference between the budgeted contribution margin and the budgeted average unit contribution margin.

Sales mix variance = [(Product 1 actual units − Product 1 budgeted units)
      × (Product 1 budgeted contribution margin
      − Budgeted average unit contribution margin)]
      + [(Product 2 actual units − Product 2 budgeted units)
      × (Product 2 budgeted contribution margin
      − Budgeted average unit contribution margin)]

The preceding sales mix variance equation, as detailed in **Example 18.8**, is for two products. If three products were produced, we would simply keep adding the change in units times the change in contribution margin for every additional product.

EXAMPLE 18.8

The HOW and WHY of Calculating the Sales Mix Variance

Information:

Recall from Example 18.6 that Birdwell, Inc., provided the following information:

	Budgeted	Actual
Sales in units, regular model	1,500	1,250
Sales in units, deluxe model	500	625
Unit contribution margin, regular model	$ 4.00	
Unit contribution margin, deluxe model	$ 15.00	
Total contribution margin	$13,500	$14,375

> **Why:**
> The sales mix variance tells managers what impact a difference between actual and expected percentages of products sold has on contribution margin. Only budgeted contribution margins are used to weight the differences in the sales mix.

Required:

1. Calculate the sales mix variance.

2. *What if* actual units sold of the deluxe bird feeder decreased? How would that affect the sales mix variance? What if actual units sold of the deluxe bird feeder increased? How would that affect the sales mix variance?

Solution:

1. Sales mix variance = [(Product 1 actual units − Product 1 budgeted units) × (Product 1 budgeted contribution margin − Budgeted average unit contribution margin)] + [(Product 2 actual units − Product 2 budgeted units) × (Product 2 budgeted contribution margin − Budgeted average unit contribution margin)]

   = [(1,250 − 1,500) × ($4.00 − $6.75)] + [(625 − 500) × ($15.00 − $6.75)]
   = $1,718.75 F

2. If actual units sold of the deluxe bird feeder (the high contribution margin product) decrease while everything else stays the same, the sales mix variance would decrease and become less favorable. Depending on the amount of decrease, the sales mix variance could become unfavorable. If, on the other hand, actual units sold of the deluxe bird feeder increase, then the sales mix variance would increase and become more favorable.

Now, we can see that the favorable sales mix variance of $1,718.75, combined with the unfavorable contribution margin volume variance of $843.75, explains the overall favorable contribution margin variance of $875.

Market Share and Market Size Variances

Managers not only want to look inward at contribution margin through the volume and sales mix variances, but also want to look outward to see how their company is doing compared with the rest of their industry. **Market share** gives the proportion of industry sales accounted for by a company. **Market size** is the total revenue for the industry. Clearly, both market share and market size have an impact on a company's profits.

The **market share variance** is the difference between the actual market share percentage and the budgeted market share percentage multiplied by actual industry sales in units times budgeted average unit contribution margin. The **market size variance** is the difference between actual and budgeted industry sales in units multiplied by the budgeted market share percentage times the budgeted average unit contribution margin.

Market share variance = [(Actual market share percentage − Budgeted market share percentage) × Actual industry sales in units] × Budgeted average unit contribution margin

Market size variance = [(Actual industry sales in units − Budgeted industry sales in units) × Budgeted market share percentage] × Budgeted average unit contribution margin

Example 18.9 shows the how and why of calculating the market share variance and the market size variance.

As Example 18.9 shows, the market share variance for Birdwell is $2,869 unfavorable. In other words, Birdwell's reduction in market share from 10 percent to 8.152 percent cost the company $2,869 in contribution margin.

EXAMPLE 18.9

The HOW and WHY of Calculating the Market Share Variance and the Market Size Variance

Information:
Budgeted unit sales for the entire bird feeder industry were 20,000 (of all model types), and actual unit sales for the industry were 23,000. Recall from Example 18.6 that Birdwell, Inc., provided the following information:

	Budgeted	Actual
Sales in units, regular model	1,500	1,250
Sales in units, deluxe model	500	625
Total contribution margin	$13,500	
Budgeted average unit contribution margin	$ 6.75	

Why:
The market share and market size variances allow firms to compare their performance with the market as a whole. This gives managers a chance to look outside their own companies and to see what the possibilities are in the market for their products.

Required:

1. Calculate the market share variance.

2. Calculate the market size variance.

3. *What if* Birdwell actually sold a total of 2,300 units (in total of the two models)? How would that affect the market share variance? The market size variance?

Solution:

1. Market share variance = [(Actual market share percentage − Budgeted market share percentage) × Actual industry sales in units] × Budgeted average unit contribution margin

   Actual market share percentage = 1,875/23,000 = 0.08152, or 8.152% (rounded)

   Budgeted market share percentage = 2,000/20,000 = 0.10, or 10%
   Market share variance = [(0.08152 − 0.10) × 23,000] × $6.75
   = $2,869 U (rounded to the nearest dollar)

   Note that the market share variance is unfavorable because Birdwell's actual share of the market is less than the budgeted share of the market.

EXAMPLE 18.9

(Continued)

2. Market size variance = [(Actual industry sales in units − Budgeted industry sales in units) × Budgeted market share percentage] × Budgeted average unit contribution margin
$$= [(23{,}000 - 20{,}000) \times 0.10] \times \$6.75$$
$$= \$2{,}025 \text{ F}$$

Note that the market size variance is favorable because the actual number of units sold in the market is larger than the number of units expected to be sold in the market.

3. If Birdwell actually sold a total of 2,300 units, then the actual market share percentage would be 10 percent, exactly equal to the budgeted market share percentage. The market share variance would be zero. There would be no impact on the market size percentage.

The impact of changing market size on Birdwell's profits can be assessed through the market size variance. It is $2,025 favorable. This means that the company's contribution margin would have increased by this amount had the actual market share percentage equaled the budgeted market share percentage. Unfortunately for Birdwell, the market share percentage slipped. Still, Birdwell is better off due to increasing market size, since a market share of 8.2 percent would yield even smaller profits from a smaller market.

While the contribution margin variances and the market share and market size variances yield important insights into profitability, companies may want to analyze profit further. The next section examines another dimension of profitability by looking at profit over the product life cycle.

OBJECTIVE ▸ **6**

Discuss the variations in price, cost, and profit over the product life cycle.

THE PRODUCT LIFE CYCLE

There are a number of views of the product life cycle. Chapter 11 introduced the marketing view, the production view, and the consumable view. We bring them together here to look at the impact of the product life cycle on profit. Many products have a predictable profit or product life cycle. Using the marketing viewpoint, the **product life cycle** describes the profit history of the product according to four stages: introduction, growth, maturity, and decline. In the introductory phase, profits are low for two reasons. First, revenues are low as the product gains market acceptance. Second, investment and learning may be high, leading to higher expenses. The growth stage is characterized by increasing market acceptance and sales, as well as economies of scale, which bring down expenses. The product breaks even, and profit rises. In the maturity phase, profits stabilize. The product has found its market, and revenues are relatively stable. Investment is down, and all learning effects in production are realized, leading to stable costs. Finally, in the decline phase, the product reaches the end of its cycle, and revenues and profits decline. Costs may still be low, but not enough to slip in below sales. Exhibit 18.5 illustrates the interaction of profit and the product life cycle with its four stages.

The product life cycle helps the firm understand the different competitive pressures on a product in each stage. Thus, it is important for planning purposes. The regularities in manufacturing, costs, and profit make the product life cycle just as important in cost management. Each stage of the product life cycle demonstrates a fairly predictable impact on various types of costs. Exhibit 18.6 summarizes these effects.

How long is the product life cycle? That depends on the product and the environment that the product faces. Television took years to reach maturity, partially due to its introduction during World War II, when necessary technical assets were diverted to the war effort. Video games typically reach maturity very quickly—in a matter of months. Fad products, such as Sourballs, may zip through the product life cycle in a matter of weeks.

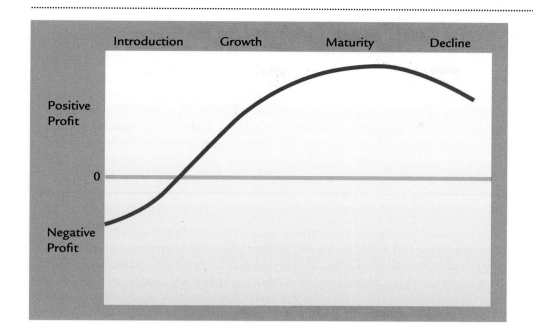

Exhibit 18.5

Product Life Cycle and Profitability

Exhibit 18.6 Impact of the Product Life Cycle on Cost Management

	Introduction	**Growth**	**Maturity**	**Decline**
Product	Basic design, few models	Some improvements, expanding product line	Proliferation of product lines, extensive differentiation	Minimal changes, reduced number of product lines
Learning effects	High costs, much learning, but little payoff	Still strong, learning begins to reduce costs	Stable production, little to no learning	No learning, labor as efficient as it can be
Setups	Few, but new and unfamiliar	More, as new models are introduced	Many, as product differentiation occurs	Fewer, as only best selling lines are produced
Purchasing	May be high as new materials and suppliers are sought	Lower, reliable suppliers found, few material changes	May be high depending on line changes	Fewer suppliers and orders as existing inventories are liquidated
Marketing expense	Low selling and distribution costs to small number of target markets	Increased advertising and distribution	Supportive advertising, increased trade discounts, high distribution cost	Minimal advertising, distribution, and promotion

Knowledge of the product life cycle is important for cost management. We can easily see the impact of the four stages on marketing and the growth and decline of sales. Less obvious is the impact on the cost side. Manufacturing must be aware of the impact of newness on costs. Any time a new product is introduced, there are learning effects. In other words, as a company makes more of the product, the employees become better at making it. Purchasing locates and becomes familiar with suppliers of the needed materials. Manufacturing learns to set up more quickly and efficiently the equipment for a new batch. The industrial engineers are able to "work the bugs out" of the process. The whole production process smoothes out and becomes faster and more efficient—and less expensive. However, that is not the whole story. As we can see in Exhibit 18.6, the maturity phase is marked by extensive product differentiation as line extensions proliferate.

Mattel's Barbie was first launched in 1959—but today we're not just talking basic Barbie anymore. Barbie has changed. Her arms and legs are bendable, and her hair is any number of lengths and colors. She has a dizzying array of outfits and accessories. More recently, Barbie's over 175 different lines include dolls that are bald, sport a prosthetic limb, or have other physical ailments such as vitiligo (a condition that causes patches of skin to lose melanin). Each version requires different materials and setups. In addition, Barbie has lots of friends—each with different production requirements. Barbie, her friends, and various vehicles, houses, and so on bring in nearly $1.2 billion in annual revenue for Mattel. With each decade's new cohort of little girls, Barbie and friends may be in the maturity phase for quite some time to come.[15]

The product life cycle has implications for activity-based costing (ABC). Recall that ABC categories are unit level, batch level, product level, and facility level. Unit-level costs are highest in the introduction phase, as new materials are sought in small order quantities. In addition, direct labor is higher per unit as labor learns how to manufacture the new item. Unit-level costs begin to fall in the growth phase as learning takes effect and quantity discounts on materials may occur. Similarly, the maturity phase should lead to stable unit-level costs. The decline phase, with fewer units produced, does not enjoy quantity discounts, but unit costs may remain low due to the liquidation of existing inventories and the avoidance of increasing prices.

Batch-level costs follow a similar pattern. Purchasing, receiving, setups, and inspection are high in the introductory phase due to unfamiliarity. In the growth phase, batch-level costs should decrease as the positive impact of learning occurs. Workers are better able to execute setups, for example. In the maturity phase, batch-level costs may increase as product differentiation occurs. Setup number and complexity increase, purchasing orders rise, and inspection costs may increase. Finally, in the decline stage, batch-level costs again fall as product lines are streamlined to just a few best-selling lines and batches decrease in number and complexity.

Product-level costs are highest in the introductory phase and generally fall throughout the rest of the life cycle—with possible spikes upward for new models in the maturity phase. An example is engineering change orders, which occur most frequently when the product is started into production. Facility-level costs may or may not be affected unless the product calls for a new facility or equipment—then they are highest in the introductory phase. Exhibit 18.7 depicts the general direction of costs in the ABC categories throughout the product life cycle.

Exhibit 18.7

Product Life-Cycle Costs in the ABC Categories

	Product Life-Cycle Phase			
ABC Category	**Introduction**	**Growth**	**Maturity**	**Decline**
Unit-level costs	High	Lower	Low to stable	Low
Batch-level costs	High	Lower	Higher	Low
Product-level costs	High	Lower	Low to stable	Low
Facility-level costs	High	Low	Low	Low

15 Maria Cramer, "After All These Years, Barbie Is Still Reinventing Herself," *NYTimes.com* (January 29, 2020), https://www.nytimes.com/2020/01/29/business/mattel-barbie-dolls-vitiligo.html, accessed September 7, 2020.

LIMITATIONS OF PROFIT MEASUREMENT

Profit measurement is important, and accountants can genuinely help a business by measuring profit levels. Still, there is more to life and business than monetary profit measurement. In this section, we look at the limitations of profit measurement.

One limitation to profitability analysis is its focus on past, not future, performance. The economic environment is unpredictable, and consistent profitability—brought about by great management, productive employees, and a high-quality product—does not guarantee success when economic conditions change. At that point, shifts in strategy may prove crucial. For example, the shift from payment for costs incurred to payment by diagnosis code has changed life considerably in the health-care industry. Previously, insurance companies and the federal government paid doctors and hospitals for all costs incurred. Clearly, cost cutting was not important. Now, the emphasis on efficiency and cost control has had a significant impact on all participants in the medical field.

Johnson & Johnson, for example, worked hard to change the rate of reimbursement for stents used in angioplasty. The J&J stent was technically superior to others on the market and cost more. However, Medicare paid hospitals the same amount no matter which stent was used. J&J was able to show, using data on 200,000 Medicare patients, that patients using the J&J stent were able to avoid a second and third angioplasty. Stent reimbursement increased.

REAL-WORLD EXAMPLE

The point is that companies must remain flexible and be aware of changing business conditions.

The savvy cost manager is aware of economic and environmental trends outside the company. These can determine the success of management plans. They also help provide a reference point for management in determining whether profits are good or bad. A small increase in profit during a recession may signal outstanding performance. The same increase during economic expansion raises doubts about management's ability.

Another limitation is profit's emphasis on quantifiable measures. Henry Ford said that both buyer and seller must be wealthier in some form as a result of a transaction. But must wealth always be measured in money? Some aspects of profit are, no doubt, qualitative. Start-up companies may be thrilled to have made it past the one-year mark. The confidence that comes with being able to successfully start and continue a business is part of their wealth. Many companies give back a portion of their profits to their communities; this, too, is a form of wealth.

Finally, we must remember that profit has a strong impact on people's behavior. Predictably, individuals prefer profit to loss. Their jobs, promotions, and bonuses may depend on the annual profit, and this dependence can affect their behavior in expected and unexpected ways. As accountants, it is important to realize that profit measurement can lead to different incentives for individuals to work harder and to act ethically.

ETHICS People's desire to avoid losses and their inclination to take a short-run perspective can affect the potential for unethical conduct. Unethical conduct can take any number of forms, but basically it comes down to lying. Companies may try to pass off inferior work or materials as high-quality work—worthy of a higher price. Companies may keep two sets of books—for the purpose of cheating on income and inventory taxes. They may overstate the value of inventory in order to understate the cost of goods sold and thereby overstate net income.

Companies that value numerical profit above all else should not be surprised if employees act accordingly and do what is in their power to increase the numbers. Not only does this overreliance on numerical profit lead to unethical behavior, but it also provides incentives to ignore the less measurable outcomes which might benefit the company. Workers basically look for companies to "put their money where their mouth is." If raises, promotions, and bonuses are awarded only on the basis of profit, employees will work to increase profits. Even if the company says other factors are important (e.g., good corporate citizenship, innovation, and high-quality products), this will be seen as mere lip service.

The ever-present salience of monthly, quarterly, and annual profit and loss statements may cause companies to emphasize short-run results. Too much emphasis on short-run optimization can lead to ethical problems. A solution is to focus on the long run. Companies that take a long-run orientation know that they cannot cheat customers and expect to retain their business. Eventually, shoddy materials and workmanship will be realized by the customer. The customer will go elsewhere, and regaining trust once lost is an agonizingly slow process. As a result, ethical people and companies often emphasize the long run as the best basis for behavior. •

SUMMARY OF LEARNING OBJECTIVES

LO1. Discuss basic pricing concepts.
- The basic economic interplay between demand and supply helps to set price.
  - Customers buy less at a high price than they do at a low price.
  - Producers (suppliers) are able to sell more at a high price than at a low price.
  - Equilibrium price is set where quantity demanded equals quantity supplied.
- Price elasticity of demand is the percent change in quantity demanded for a given percent change in price.
  - Products with elastic demand tend to:
    - Have many substitutes
    - Not be necessities
    - Take a relatively large amount of consumer income
  - Products with inelastic demand tend to:
    - Have few substitutes
    - Be necessities
    - Take a relatively small amount of consumer income
- Market structure affects the relationship between the company and other companies in its industry.
  - Perfectly competitive markets have many buyers and sellers. Price is set in the market.
  - Monopolistic competition is characterized by some ability to differentiate one's product from that of other firms.
  - Monopoly is characterized by one seller with the ability to increase price somewhat above that of a competitive market. There may be legal reasons for the monopoly.
  - Oligopoly is characterized by few sellers and many buyers. There are frequently high barriers to entry in this market.

LO2. Calculate a markup on cost and a target cost.
- Many firms use cost-based pricing; such firms are referred to as price makers.
  - Price is based on cost plus desired profit.
  - The markup is NOT pure profit—it also includes all costs not included in the base cost.
  - Strategy is supply based—it does not take demand into account until late in the process.
- Target cost-based pricing strategy begins with price and subtracts desired profit to determine allowable cost; such firms are referred to as price takers.

LO3. Discuss the impact of the legal system and ethics on pricing.
- The legal system supports competition and outlaws certain business practices.
  - Predatory pricing
  - Some forms of price discrimination
- Fairness and ethical conduct may prevent the exploitation of market power.
  - Price gouging
  - Dumping
- Forensic accounting includes pricing cases that rely on important cost management concepts.
  - Court cases involving pricing disputes often revolve around understanding, defining, analyzing, and communicating which costs should be included versus excluded from the cost base upon which prices are set.
  - The federal government is a large purchaser of products and services that are priced using some form of cost-based pricing.

LO4. Explain why firms measure profit, and calculate measures of profit using absorption and variable costing.
- Profit is measured to assess performance.
- Absorption-costing income measurement is required for external financial reporting.
  - All manufacturing costs are attached to units of product including:
    - Direct materials
    - Direct labor
    - Variable factory overhead
    - A portion of fixed factory overhead
  - Product costs for the period are assigned to units sold or units put into inventory.
- Variable costing is useful for management decision making.
  - All variable manufacturing costs are attached to units of product including:
    - Direct materials
    - Direct labor
    - Variable overhead
  - All fixed costs (including fixed factory overhead and fixed selling and administrative expense) are treated as period expenses on the income statement.
- Variable costing and ABC give better signals regarding performance and incremental costs.
- Profitability analysis can be accomplished for individual segments, including:
  - Product lines
  - Divisions
  - Customer groups

LO5. Compute the sales price, sales volume, contribution margin, contribution margin volume, sales mix, market share, and market size variances.
- Profit-related variances are used to analyze the changes in profit from one time period to another.
  - Sales price variance compares expected price with actual price and multiplies by actual volume.
  - Sales volume variance compares actual volume with expected volume and multiplies by expected price.
- Contribution margin variance considers interplay of price and variable cost.
  - Contribution margin volume variance shows the impact of a difference between expected and actual sales volume on contribution margin.
  - Sales mix variance shows the impact on contribution margin of changes in the actual versus expected sales mix.

- Market share and size variances allow a firm to compare its performance against competing firms.
  - Market share variance shows the impact of a difference between actual and expected percentage of market volume multiplied by budgeted average contribution margin.
  - Market size variance shows the impact on profit of a difference between actual volume sold in the market and expected volume.

LO6. Discuss the variations in price, cost, and profit over the product life cycle.
- The product life cycle has an important impact on price.
  - Introduction phase usually has negative profit.
  - Growth phase shows increasing profit.
  - Maturity phase is accompanied by a leveling off of profit.
  - Decline phase is the end of the product life cycle.
- Learning effects and increasing efficiency help costs decrease as the product life cycle changes from introduction through growth and maturity.

LO7. Describe some of the limitations of profit measurement.
- Limitations of profit include:
  - Focus on past performance
  - Uncertain economic conditions
  - Difficulty of capturing all important factors in financial measures
- Successful firms measure far more than accounting profit.
  - Impact on the community
  - Employees
- Ethical behavior is fostered by appropriate emphasis on profit.

EXAMPLE 18.1	The HOW and WHY of Calculating a Markup on Cost, page 918
EXAMPLE 18.2	The HOW and WHY of Calculating Cost and Profit by Customer Class, page 924
EXAMPLE 18.3	The HOW and WHY of Calculating Inventory Cost and Preparing the Income Statement Using Absorption Costing, page 929
EXAMPLE 18.4	The HOW and WHY of Calculating Inventory Cost and Preparing the Income Statement Using Variable Costing, page 932
EXAMPLE 18.5	The HOW and WHY of Calculating the Sales Price Variance, the Sales Volume Variance, and the Overall Sales Variance, page 938
EXAMPLE 18.6	The HOW and WHY of Calculating the Contribution Margin Variance, page 939
EXAMPLE 18.7	The HOW and WHY of Calculating the Contribution Margin Volume Variance, page 940
EXAMPLE 18.8	The HOW and WHY of Calculating the Sales Mix Variance, page 942
EXAMPLE 18.9	The HOW and WHY of Calculating the Market Share Variance and the Market Size Variance, page 943

KEY TERMS

Absorption costing, 928

Contribution margin variance, 939

Contribution margin volume variance, 940

Cost-based pricing, 917

Dumping, 923

Loss leader pricing, 921

Market share, 942

Market share variance, 942

Market size, 942

Market size variance, 942

Markup, 918

Monopolistic competition, 917

Monopoly, 916

Oligopoly, 917

Penetration pricing, 921

Perfectly competitive market, 916

Predatory pricing, 922

Price discrimination, 923

Price elasticity of demand, 915

Price gouging, 922

Price skimming, 922

Product life cycle, 944

Sales mix variance, 941

Sales price variance, 937

Sales volume variance, 937

Target costing, 920

Total (overall) sales variance, 938

Variable costing, 931

BRIEF EXERCISES

Brief Exercise 18-1 Markup on Cost, Job Pricing

OBJECTIVE ▸ 2
Example 18.1

Privacy Window and Wall Treatments Company provides draperies, shades, and various window treatments. Privacy works with the customer to design the appropriate window treatment, places the order, and installs the finished product. Direct materials and direct labor costs are easy to trace to the jobs. Privacy's income statement for last year is as follows:

Revenues		$1,000,000
Cost of goods sold:		
Direct materials	$350,000	
Direct labor	200,000	
Overhead	250,000	800,000
Gross profit		$ 200,000
Selling and administrative expenses		150,000
Operating income		$ 50,000

Privacy wants to find a markup on cost of goods sold that will allow them to earn about the same amount of profit on each job as was earned last year.

Required:

1. What is the markup on cost of goods sold (COGS) that will maintain the same profit as last year? (Round the percentage to two significant digits.)
2. A customer orders draperies and shades for a remodeling job. The job will have the following costs:

Direct materials	$ 7,000
Direct labor	2,000
Applied overhead	3,000
Total cost	$12,000

   What is the price that Privacy will quote given the markup percentage calculated in Requirement 1? (Round the price to the nearest dollar.)
3. **What if** Privacy wants to calculate a markup on direct materials cost, since it is the largest cost of doing business? What is the markup on direct materials cost that will maintain the same profit as last year? (Round the percentage to two significant digits.) What is the bid price Privacy will use for the job given in Requirement 2 if the markup percentage is calculated on the basis of direct materials cost? (Round to the nearest dollar.)

OBJECTIVE ▶ 3
Example 18.2

Brief Exercise 18-2 Costs of Different Customer Classes

Kaune Food Products Company manufactures canned mixed nuts with an average manufacturing cost of $52 per case (a case contains 24 cans of nuts). Kaune sold 150,000 cases last year to the following three classes of customer:

Customer	Price per Case	Cases Sold
Supermarkets	$58	80,000
Small grocers	93	40,000
Convenience stores	88	30,000

The supermarkets require special labeling on each can costing $0.04 per can. They order through electronic data interchange (EDI), which costs Kaune about $61,000 annually in operating expenses and depreciation. Kaune delivers the nuts to the stores and stocks them on the shelves. This distribution costs $45,000 per year.

The small grocers order in smaller lots that require special picking and packing in the factory; the special handling adds $25 to the cost of each case sold. Sales commissions to the independent jobbers who sell Kaune products to the grocers average 8 percent of sales. Bad debts expense amounts to 9 percent of sales.

Convenience stores also require special handling that costs $30 per case. In addition, Kaune is required to co-pay advertising costs with the convenience stores at a cost of $15,000 per year. Frequent stops are made to each convenience store by Kaune delivery trucks at a cost of $30,000 per year.

Required:

1. Calculate the total cost per case for each of the three customer classes. (Round unit costs to four significant digits.)
2. Using the costs from Requirement 1, calculate the profit per case per customer class. Does the cost analysis support the charging of different prices? Why or why not?
3. *What if* Kaune charged the average price per case to all customer classes? How would that affect the profit percentages?

OBJECTIVE ▶ 4
Example 18.3

Brief Exercise 18-3 Absorption Costing, Value of Ending Inventory, Operating Income

Pattison Products, Inc., began operations in October and manufactured 40,000 units during the month with the following unit costs:

Direct materials	$5.00
Direct labor	3.00
Variable overhead	1.50
Fixed overhead*	7.00
Variable marketing cost	1.20

*Fixed overhead per unit = $280,000/40,000 units produced = $7.

Total fixed factory overhead is $280,000 per month. During October, 38,400 units were sold at a price of $24, and fixed marketing and administrative expenses were $130,500.

Required:

1. Calculate the cost of each unit using absorption costing.
2. How many units remain in ending inventory? What is the cost of ending inventory using absorption costing?
3. Prepare an absorption-costing income statement for Pattison Products, Inc., for the month of October.
4. *What if* November production was 40,000 units, costs were stable, and sales were 41,000 units? What is the cost of ending inventory? What is operating income for November?

Brief Exercise 18-4 Variable Costing, Value of Ending Inventory, Operating Income

Refer to **Brief Exercise 18-3**.

Required:

1. Calculate the cost of each unit using variable costing.
2. How many units remain in ending inventory? What is the cost of ending inventory using variable costing?
3. Prepare a variable-costing income statement for Pattison Products, Inc., for the month of October.
4. *What if* November production was 40,000 units, costs were stable, and sales were 41,000 units? What is the cost of ending inventory? What is operating income for November?

Brief Exercise 18-5 Sales Price Variance, Sales Volume Variance, Overall Sales Variance

Holland Company is a garden products wholesale firm. In December, Holland Company expects to sell 84,000 bags of vegetable fertilizer at an average price of $8.75 per bag. Actual results are 85,000 bags sold at an average price of $8.50 per bag.

Required:

1. Calculate the sales price variance for December.
2. Calculate the sales volume variance for December.
3. Calculate the overall sales variance for December. Explain why it is favorable or unfavorable.
4. *What if* December sales were actually 83,500 bags? How would that affect the sales price variance? The sales volume variance? The overall sales variance?

Brief Exercise 18-6 Contribution Margin Variance

Ioannis Inc., produces and sells two types of countertop ovens—the toaster oven and the convection oven. Budgeted and actual data for the two models are shown below.

Budgeted Amounts:

	Toaster Oven	Convection Oven	Total
Sales:			
($1,000 × 25,000)	$25,000,000		
($500 × 15,000)		$7,500,000	$32,500,000
Variable expenses	6,250,000	1,500,000	7,750,000
Contribution margin	$18,750,000	$6,000,000	$24,750,000

Actual Amounts:

	Toaster Oven	Convection Oven	Total
Sales:			
($1,000 × 25,500)	$25,500,000		
($500 × 13,500)		$6,750,000	$32,250,000
Variable expenses	6,375,000	1,350,000	7,725,000
Contribution margin	$19,125,000	$5,400,000	$24,525,000

Required:

1. Calculate the contribution margin variance.
2. *What if* actual units sold of the convection oven decreased? How would that affect the contribution margin variance? What if actual units sold of the convection oven increased? How would that affect the contribution margin variance?

OBJECTIVE 5 ▶
Example 18.7

Brief Exercise 18-7 Contribution Margin Volume Variance

Refer to **Brief Exercise 18-6**.

Required:

1. Calculate the budgeted average unit contribution margin. (Round unit contribution margin to the nearest cent.)
2. Calculate the contribution margin volume variance. (Round each item to the nearest cent.)
3. *What if* actual units sold of the convection oven decreased? How would that affect the contribution margin volume variance? What if actual units sold of the convection oven increased? How would that affect the contribution margin volume variance?

OBJECTIVE 5 ▶
Example 18.8

Brief Exercise 18-8 Sales Mix Variance

Refer to **Brief Exercise 18-6**.

Required:

1. Calculate the sales mix variance.
2. *What if* actual units sold of the toaster oven increased? How would that affect the sales mix variance? What if actual units sold of the convection oven increased? How would that affect the sales mix variance?

OBJECTIVE 5 ▶
Example 18.9

Brief Exercise 18-9 Market Share Variance, Market Size Variance

Katie's Coffee Makers Inc. projected budgeted unit sales for the entire specialized coffee maker industry to be 2,500,000 (of all model types), and actual unit sales for the industry were 2,550,000.

	Budgeted	Actual
Sales in units, French Press	25,000	25,800
Sales in units, AeroPress	15,000	14,000
Total contribution margin	$3,250,000	
Budgeted average unit contribution margin	$ 81.25	

Required:

1. Calculate the market share variance (take percentages out to four significant digits).
2. Calculate the market size variance.
3. *What if* Katie actually sold a total of 41,000 units (in total of the two models)? How would that affect the market share variance? The market size variance?

EXERCISES

OBJECTIVE 1 ▶

Exercise 18-10 Elasticity of Demand and Market Structure

Janet Gordon and Phil Hopkins graduated several years ago with M.S. degrees in accounting and set up a full-service accounting firm. Janet and Phil have many small business clients and have noticed some pricing trends while compiling annual financial statements. The following data are for five of the pizza parlors that are Janet and Phil's clients.

	Quantity Sold	Average Price
Mamma Mia's	18,000	$10.00
Happy Time Pizza	21,000	7.90
Keg and Pie Pizza	22,000	8.00
Fast Freddy's Pizza	30,000	7.00
Pizza-pizza	24,000	7.50

Required:

1. Is the demand for pizza relatively more elastic or inelastic?
2. What type of market structure characterizes the pizza industry? How do you suppose that Mamma Mia's can charge so much more per pizza than Fast Freddy's does?

Exercise 18-11 Demand Curve and Characteristics of Market Structure

Amy Chang wants to start a business supplying florists with field-grown flowers. She has located an appropriate acreage and believes she can grow daisies, asters, chrysanthemums, carnations, and other assorted types during a nine-month growing period. By growing the flowers in a field as opposed to a greenhouse, Amy expects to save a considerable amount on herbicide and pesticide. She is considering passing the savings along to her customers by charging $1.25 per standard bunch versus the prevailing price of $1.50 per standard bunch.

Amy has turned to her neighbor, Bob Winters, for help. Bob is an accountant in town who is familiar with general business conditions. Bob gathered the following information for Amy:

a. There are 50 growers within a one-hour drive of Amy's acreage.
b. In general, there is little variability in price. Flowers are treated as commodities, and one aster is considered to be pretty much like any other aster.
c. There are numerous florists in the city, and the amount that Amy would supply could be easily absorbed by the florists at the prevailing price.

Required:

1. What type of market structure characterizes the flower-growing industry in Amy's region? Explain.
2. Given your answer to Requirement 1, what price should Amy charge per standard bunch? Why?

Exercise 18-12 Basics of Demand, Life-Cycle Pricing

Foster Hancock is an accountant who is planning to open an accounting firm in his hometown. He has heard that established accountants in town charge $65 per hour. That amount sounds good to Foster. In fact, he believes that he should be able to charge $75 an hour given his high GPA and the fact that he is up to date on current accounting issues.

Required:

1. Should Foster charge $75 per hour? What would you advise him to do?
2. Briefly explain why Foster might be wise to employ descriptive data analytics before moving forward with his pricing decision. Also, what, if any, data challenges might Foster encounter in performing descriptive data analytics? (See Exhibits 2.5 and 2.6, pp. 37, 40, for a review of data analytics types.)

Exercise 18-13 Markup on Cost, Cost-Based Pricing

Whang Construction Company is a general contractor that specializes in custom residential housing. Each job requires a bid that includes Whang's direct costs and subcontractor costs as well as an amount referred to as "overhead and profit." Whang's bidding policy is to estimate the costs of direct materials, direct labor, and subcontractors' costs. These are totaled, and a markup is applied to cover overhead and profit. In the coming year, the company believes it will be the successful bidder on 10 jobs with the following total revenues and costs:

Revenue		$4,900,000
Direct materials	$1,645,000	
Direct labor	1,480,000	
Subcontractors	1,250,000	4,375,000
Overhead and profit		$ 525,000

Required:

1. Given the preceding information, what is the markup percentage on total direct costs?
2. Suppose Whang is asked to bid on a job with estimated direct costs of $325,000. What is the bid? If the customer complains that the profit seems pretty high, how might Whang counter that accusation?
3. Briefly explain how Whang Construction's accountant might utilize data analytics to help decide on the markup percentage to use in setting prices. (see Exhibits 2.5 and 2.6, pp. 37, 40, for a review of data analytics types.)

OBJECTIVE 2   Exercise 18-14 Markup on Cost

Many different businesses employ markup on cost to arrive at a price. For each of the following situations, explain what the markup covers and why it is the amount that it is.

a. Department stores have a markup of 100 percent of purchase cost.
b. Jewelry stores charge anywhere from 100 percent to 300 percent of the cost of the jewelry. (The 300 percent markup is referred to as "keystone.")
c. Johnson Construction Company charges 12 percent on direct materials, direct labor, and subcontracting costs.
d. Hamilton Auto Repair charges customers for direct materials and direct labor. Customers are charged $45 per direct labor hour worked on their job; however, the employees actually cost Hamilton $15 per hour.

OBJECTIVE 2   Exercise 18-15 Cost-Based Pricing, Target Pricing

Carina Franks operates a catering company in Austin, Texas. Carina provides food and servers for parties. She also rents tables, chairs, dinnerware, glassware, and linens. Estefan and Maria Montero have contacted Carina about plans for their daughter's Quinceañera (a festive party thrown by Hispanic parents to celebrate their daughters' fifteenth birthdays). The Monteros would like a catered affair on the lawn of a rural church. They have requested an open bar, a sit-down dinner for 350 people, a large tent, and a dance floor. Of course, they expect Carina to supply serving staff, tables with linens, dinnerware, and glassware. They will handle the flowers, the decorations, and hiring the band on their own. Carina put together this bid:

Food (350 × $25)	$ 8,750
Beverages (350 × $15)	5,250
Servers (6 × 4 hours × $10)	240
Bartenders (2 × 4 hours × $10)	80
Clean-up staff (3 × 3 hours × $10)	90
Rental of:	
Dance floor	300
Linens	80
Tables	200
Dinnerware	120
Glassware	150
Total	$15,260

Required:

1. Explain where costs for Carina's services and profit are calculated in the preceding bid.
2. Suppose that the Monteros blanch when they see the preceding bid. One of them suggests that they had hoped to spend no more than $10,000 or so on the party. How could Carina work with the Monteros to achieve a target cost of that amount?
3. Estefan Montero protests the cost of dance floor rental. He said, "I've seen those for rent at U-Rent-It for $75." How would you respond to this remark if you were Carina? (*Hint:* You want this job and so telling him, "Go ahead and do it yourself, Cheapskate!" is not an option.)

Exercise 18-16 Cost-Based Pricing

OBJECTIVE ◀ 2

EXCEL   SHOW ME
HOW

CMA

Otero Fibers, Inc., specializes in the manufacture of synthetic fibers that the company uses in many products such as blankets, coats, and uniforms for police and firefighters. Otero has been in business since 1985 and has been profitable every year since 1993. The company uses a standard cost system and applies overhead on the basis of direct labor hours.

Otero has recently received a request to bid on the manufacture of 800,000 blankets scheduled for delivery to several military bases. The bid must be stated at full cost per unit plus a return on full cost of no more than 10 percent after income taxes. Full cost has been defined as including all variable costs of manufacturing the product, a reasonable amount of fixed overhead, and reasonable incremental administrative costs associated with the manufacture and sale of the product. The contractor has indicated that bids in excess of $30 per blanket are not likely to be considered.

In order to prepare the bid for the 800,000 blankets, Andrea Lightner, cost accountant, has gathered the following information about the costs associated with the production of the blankets.

Direct material	$1.70 per pound of fibers
Direct labor	$6.50 per hour
Direct machine costs*	$10.00 per blanket
Variable overhead	$3.00 per direct labor hour
Fixed overhead	$8.00 per direct labor hour
Incremental administrative costs	$2,450 per 1,000 blankets
Special fee**	$0.50 per blanket
Material usage	6 pounds per blanket
Production rate	4 blankets per direct labor hour
Effective tax rate	35%

*Direct machine costs consist of items such as special lubricants, replacement of needles used in stitching, and maintenance costs. These costs are not included in the normal overhead rates.

**Otero recently developed a new blanket fiber at a cost of $750,000. In an effort to recover this cost, Otero has instituted a policy of adding a $0.50 fee to the cost of each blanket using the new fiber. To date, the company has recovered $125,000. Lightner knows that this fee does not fit within the definition of full cost, as it is not a cost of manufacturing the product.

Required:

1. Calculate the minimum price per blanket that Otero Fibers could bid without reducing the company's operating income.
2. Using the full-cost criteria and the maximum allowable return specified, calculate Otero Fibers' bid price per blanket.
3. Without prejudice to your answer to Requirement 2, assume that the price per blanket that Otero Fibers calculated using the cost-plus criteria specified is greater than the maximum bid of $30 per blanket allowed. Discuss the factors that Otero Fibers should consider before deciding whether or not to submit a bid at the maximum acceptable price of $30 per blanket. (*CMA adapted*)

Exercise 18-17 Cost-Based Pricing and Forensic Accounting, Qualitative Aspects

OBJECTIVE ◀ 2 3

SHOW ME
HOW

Mayfair Electric Utility has excess electrical generating capacity. In order to utilize its excess capacity, Mayfair entered into a five-year contract with the U.S. government to sell Mayfair's generated excess power to the U.S. power grid. The contract called for Mayfair to sell its excess electrical power at its "lowest reasonable cost." During the five-year term of the contract, Mayfair charged the U.S. government a total of $80 million. Near the end of the contract term, Jeff, the chief accountant for Mayfair, informed the company's CEO that he believed the company had overcharged the government for the power it had purchased from Mayfair. The CEO disagreed with Jeff and decided to fire him. Jeff filed a Qui Tam suit against Mayfair alleging it had overcharged the government using six different overcharging methods. The U.S. Justice Department reviewed the Qui Tam suit and decided to litigate four of the alleged overcharging schemes. As the whistleblower, Jeff continued with the other two allegations in the case.

Required:

1. Briefly identify and describe the main issues that the plaintiff (i.e., the U.S. Justice Department and the whistleblower) will evaluate in trying to prove Mayfield has overcharged the government in this case.
2. Assume that Mayfield's general pricing objective is always to allocate some administrative overhead to all contracts. To accomplish this objective, Mayfield typically assigns 10 percent to each contract billing. Briefly explain whether or not this practice is allowed under Mayfield's contract with the U.S. government.
3. Assume that the court finds that Mayfair's billings to the government comprised 40 percent of Mayfair's fixed facility costs and 60 percent of Mayfair's variable costs (mostly fuel costs). Do these billing compositions appear to comply with the contract? Briefly explain your response.
4. If the U.S. government (plaintiff) hired you as a forensic accounting expert for the case, briefly explain the specific items you would want to examine and the issues you would most likely want to address as a forensic accounting expert.

OBJECTIVE 4

SHOW ME
HOW

Exercise 18-18 Absorption and Variable Costing with Over- and Underapplied Overhead

Flaherty, Inc., has just completed its first year of operations. The unit costs on a normal costing basis are as follows:

Manufacturing costs (per unit):	
Direct materials (4 lbs. @ $1.50)	$ 6.00
Direct labor (0.5 hr. @ $18)	9.00
Variable overhead (0.5 hr. @ $6)	3.00
Fixed overhead (0.5 hr. @ $9)	4.50
Total	$22.50
Selling and administrative costs:	
Variable	$2 per unit
Fixed	$238,000

During the year, the company had the following activity:

Units produced	24,000
Units sold	21,300
Unit selling price	$36
Direct labor hours worked	12,000

Actual fixed overhead was $12,000 less than budgeted fixed overhead. Budgeted variable overhead was $5,000 less than the actual variable overhead. The company used an expected actual activity level of 12,000 direct labor hours to compute the predetermined overhead rates. Any overhead variances are closed to Cost of Goods Sold.

Required:

1. Compute the unit cost using (a) absorption costing and (b) variable costing.
2. Prepare an absorption-costing income statement.
3. Prepare a variable-costing income statement.
4. Reconcile the difference between the two income statements.

Exercise 18-19 Variable Costing, Absorption Costing

During its first year of operations, Snobegon, Inc. (located in Lake Snobegon, Minnesota), produced 40,000 plastic snow scoops. Snow scoops are oversized shovel-type scoops that are used to push snow away. Unit sales were 38,200 scoops. Fixed overhead was applied at $0.75 per unit produced. Fixed overhead was underapplied by $2,900. This fixed overhead variance was closed to Cost of Goods Sold. There was no variable overhead variance. The results of the year's operations are as follows (on an absorption-costing basis):

Sales (38,200 units @ $20)	$764,000
Less: Cost of goods sold	546,260
Gross margin	$217,740
Less: Selling and administrative expenses (all fixed)	184,500
Operating income	$ 33,240

Required:

1. Calculate the cost of the firm's ending inventory under absorption costing. What is the cost of the ending inventory under variable costing? (Round unit costs to five significant digits.)
2. Prepare a variable-costing income statement. Reconcile the difference between the two income figures.

Exercise 18-20 Life-Cycle Pricing, Sales Price and Sales Volume Variances

Data for Torleson Company are as follows:

Budgeted price	$15.00
Actual price	$14.80
Budgeted quantity	1,450
Actual quantity sold	2,500

Required:

1. Calculate the sales price variance.
2. Calculate the sales volume variance.
3. Suppose that the product is in the introductory stage of the product life cycle. What information do these two variances provide to Torleson's managers?
4. Briefly explain how Torleson's management might benefit from the performance of diagnostic data analytics involving its sales quantities. (See Exhibits 2.5 and 2.6, pp. 37, 40, for a review of data analytics types.)

Exercise 18-21 Pricing Strategy, Sales Variances

Eastman, Inc., manufactures and sells three products: R, S, and T. In January, Eastman, Inc., budgeted sales of the following.

	Budgeted Volume	Budgeted Price
Product R	120,000	$26
Product S	150,000	22
Product T	20,000	20

At the end of the year, actual sales revenue for Product R and Product S was $3,075,000 and $3,254,000, respectively. The actual price charged for Product R was $25 and for Product S was $20. Only $10 was charged for Product T to encourage more consumers to buy it, and actual sales revenue equaled $540,000 for this product.

Required:

1. Calculate the sales price and sales volume variances for each of the three products based on the original budget.
2. Suppose that Product T is a new product just introduced during the year. What pricing strategy is Eastman, Inc., following for this product?

PROBLEMS

OBJECTIVE ▶2

**DATA
ANALYTICS**

Problem 18-22 Cost-Based Pricing and Loss Leaders

Quencher Beverage is a large regional retail establishment. Quencher recently decided to start selling one of its most popular products—Coca-Cola 10-packs—at a loss (i.e., a loss leader) in order to entice consumers to purchase *other* items in greater amounts than they would otherwise purchase. Quencher's loss leader pricing rule is to set unit price by marking up its unit variable product cost by 20 percent (as opposed to marking up full unit cost by a much larger percentage as it does for regular products). Quencher's accounting system reports a full unit cost for each 10-pack (considered as one unit) of $10.00. Quencher's full unit cost is based on an expected volume of 30,000 units and comprises its variable product costs, $2.00 per-unit for shipping, $50,000 of allocated fixed cost for R&D product packaging redesign, and $40,000 of allocated fixed cost for customer service-related activities (phone hotlines, website complaint monitoring, replacement of faulty or bad products, etc.). Quencher expects to sell 30,000 units (i.e., each participating customer will purchase one 10-pack).

Part 1 Requirements: Budgeted Results

1. Calculate Quencher's unit variable product cost.
2. Calculate Quencher's 10-pack loss leader unit selling price as well as expected total 10-pack revenues.
3. Quencher anticipates that the Coca-Cola loss leader strategy will bring in additional customer traffic that will result in incremental contribution margin of $100,000. Also, assume that the R&D costs and customer service-related costs are unaffected by Quencher's Coca-Cola loss leader decision. Estimate the expected total net financial impact from using the Coca-Cola 10-packs as a loss leader.

Part 2 Requirements: Actual Results

4. Unfortunately, upon reviewing the actual results, Quencher management was extremely disappointed with the performance of its Coca-Cola loss leader strategy. The perplexing part was that Quencher actually sold considerably more 10-packs than expected (10 times more to be exact), but the store's overall profit was down considerably. Upon conducting interviews with store employees, one cashier shared the following observation with Quencher management:

   > *I have observed many customers checking out through my lane. Do you know what I have learned fits perfectly inside a Quencher shopping cart?!* **Ten**, *10-packs of Coca-Cola with NO ROOM TO SPARE FOR ANYTHING ELSE!!*

   Finally, management now realizes that its regular contribution margin from non-loss leader products actually *decreased* by $200,000 as a result of loss leader customers filling their carts with excessive 10-packs and no longer buying as many regular products that they otherwise would have bought.
   Calculate the actual financial impact from Quencher's decision to pursue the Coca-Cola loss leader strategy.
5. What suggestions do you have for Quencher management when and if the company decides to continue its Coca-Cola loss leader strategy?

6. Briefly explain how Quencher's accountant might have utilized predictive data analytics to more effectively respond to requirement 3 (i.e., more accurately estimate the expected total net financial impact from the loss leader strategy). (See Exhibits 2.5 and 2.6, pp. 37, 40, for a review of data analytics types.)

Problem 18-23 Price Discrimination, Customer Costs

OBJECTIVE ▸ 3

Jorell, Inc., manufactures and distributes a variety of labelers. Annual production of labelers averages 340,000 units. A large chain store purchases about 30 percent of Jorell's production. Several thousand independent retail office supply stores purchase the other 70 percent. Jorell incurs the following costs of production per labeler:

Direct materials	$ 8.90
Direct labor	2.40
Overhead	3.20
Total	$14.50

Jorell has two salespeople assigned to the chain store account at a cost of $55,000 each per year. Delivery is made in 1,500 unit batches about three times a month at a delivery cost of $750 per batch. Eight salespeople service the remaining accounts. They call on the stores and incur salary and mileage expenses of approximately $41,000 each. Delivery costs vary from store to store, averaging $0.60 per unit.

Jorell charges the chain store $16.50 per labeler and the independent office supply stores $20 per labeler.

Required:

Is Jorell's pricing policy supported by cost differences in serving the two different classes of customer? Support your answer with relevant calculations. (Round unit costs to the nearest cent.)

Problem 18-24 Unit Costs, Inventory Valuation, Variable and Absorption Costing

OBJECTIVE ▸ 4

Snyder Company produced 90,000 units during its first year of operations and sold 87,000 at $21.80 per unit. The company chose practical activity—at 90,000 units—to compute its predetermined overhead rate. Manufacturing costs are as follows:

Direct materials	$540,000
Direct labor	99,000
Expected and actual variable overhead	369,000
Expected and actual fixed overhead	468,000

Required:

1. Calculate the unit cost and the cost of finished goods inventory under absorption costing.
2. Calculate the unit cost and the cost of finished goods inventory under variable costing.
3. What is the dollar amount that would be used to report the cost of finished goods inventory to external parties. Why?

Problem 18-25 Income Statements, Variable and Absorption Costing

OBJECTIVE ▸ 4

The following information pertains to Vladamir, Inc., for last year:

Beginning inventory, units	1,320
Units produced	100,000
Units sold	101,000
Variable costs per unit:	
Direct materials	$ 8.00
Direct labor	$ 9.50
Variable overhead	$ 1.25
Variable selling expenses	$ 2.00
Fixed costs per year:	
Fixed overhead	$234,000
Fixed selling and administrative expenses	$236,000

There are no work-in-process inventories. Normal activity is 100,000 units. Expected and actual overhead costs are the same. Costs have not changed from one year to the next.

Required:

1. How many units are in ending inventory?
2. Without preparing an income statement, indicate what the difference will be between variable-costing income and absorption-costing income.
3. Assume the selling price per unit is $29. Prepare an income statement using (a) variable costing and (b) absorption costing.

OBJECTIVE 4

Problem 18-26 Income Statements and Firm Performance: Variable and Absorption Costing

Jellison Company had the following operating data for its first two years of operations:

Variable costs per unit:		
Direct materials		4.00
Direct labor	$	2.90
Variable overhead		1.50
Fixed costs per year:		
Overhead		180,000
Selling and administrative		70,350

Jellison produced 90,000 units in the first year and sold 80,000. In the second year, it produced 80,000 units and sold 90,000. The selling price per unit each year was $12. Jellison uses an actual costing system for product costing.

Required:

1. Prepare income statements for both years using absorption costing. Has firm performance, as measured by income, improved or declined from Year 1 to Year 2?
2. Prepare income statements for both years using variable costing. Has firm performance, as measured by income, improved or declined from Year 1 to Year 2?
3. Which method do you think most accurately measures firm performance? Why?

OBJECTIVE 4

Problem 18-27 Absorption- and Variable-Costing Income Statements

San Mateo Optics, Inc., specializes in manufacturing lenses for large telescopes and cameras used in space exploration. As the specifications for the lenses are determined by the customer and vary considerably, the company uses a job-order costing system.

Manufacturing overhead is applied to jobs on the basis of direct labor hours, utilizing the absorption- or full-costing method. San Mateo's predetermined overhead rates for 20x1 and 20x2 were based on the following estimates.

	20x1	20x2
Direct labor hours	32,500	44,000
Direct labor cost	$325,000	$462,000
Fixed manufacturing overhead	$130,000	$176,000
Variable manufacturing overhead	$162,500	$198,000

Jim Cimino, San Mateo's controller, would like to use variable (direct) costing for internal reporting purposes as he believes statements prepared using variable costing are more appropriate for making product decisions. In order to explain the benefits of variable costing to the other members of San Mateo's management team, Cimino plans to convert the company's income statement from absorption costing to variable costing. He has gathered the following information for this purpose, along with a copy of San Mateo's 20x1 and 20x2 comparative income statement.

San Mateo Optics, Inc.
Comparative Income Statement
For the Years 20x1 and 20x2

	20x1	20x2
Net sales	$1,140,000	$1,520,000
Cost of goods sold:		
Finished goods at January 1	$ 16,000	$ 25,000
Cost of goods manufactured	720,000	976,000
Total available	$ 736,000	$1,001,000
Less: Finished goods at December 31	25,000	14,000
Unadjusted cost of goods sold	$ 711,000	$ 987,000
Overhead adjustment	12,000	7,000
Cost of goods sold	$ 723,000	$ 994,000
Gross profit	$ 417,000	$ 526,000
Selling expenses	(150,000)	(190,000)
Administrative expenses	(160,000)	(187,000)
Operating income	$ 107,000	$ 149,000

San Mateo's actual manufacturing data for the two years are as follows:

	20x1	20x2
Direct labor hours	30,000	42,000
Direct labor cost	$300,000	$435,000
Direct materials used	$140,000	$210,000
Manufacturing overhead	$132,000	$175,000

The company's actual inventory balances were as follows:

	December 31, 20x0	December 31, 20x1	December 31, 20x2
Direct materials	$32,000	$36,000	$18,000
Work in process:			
Costs	$44,000	$34,000	$60,000
Direct labor hours	1,800	1,400	2,500
Finished goods:			
Costs	$16,000	$25,000	$14,000
Direct labor hours	700	1,080	550

For both years, all administrative expenses were fixed, while a portion of the selling expenses resulting from an 8 percent commission on net sales was variable. San Mateo reports any over or underapplied overhead as an adjustment to the cost of goods sold.

Required:

1. For the year ended December 31, 20x2, prepare the revised income statement for San Mateo Optics, Inc., utilizing the variable-costing method. Be sure to include the contribution margin on the revised income statement.
2. Describe two advantages of using variable costing rather than absorption costing. *(CMA adapted)*

Problem 18-28 Contribution Margin Variance, Contribution Margin Volume Variance, Sales Mix Variance

 OBJECTIVE 5

 EXCEL

Haysbert Company provides management services for apartments and rental units. In general, Haysbert packages its services into two groups: basic and complete. The basic package includes advertising vacant units, showing potential renters through them, and collecting monthly rent and remitting it to the owner. The complete package adds maintenance of units and bookkeeping to the basic package. Packages are priced on a per-rental unit basis. Actual results from last year are as follows:

	Basic	Complete
Sales (rental units)	2,000	400
Selling price	$ 140	$300
Variable expenses	$ 85	$240

Haysbert had budgeted the following amounts:

	Basic	Complete
Sales (units)	1,950	460
Selling price	$ 145	$290
Variable expenses	$ 90	$242

Required:

1. Calculate the contribution margin variance (round answers to two decimal places).
2. Calculate the contribution margin volume variance (round answers to two decimal places).
3. Calculate the sales mix variance.

OBJECTIVE 5

Problem 18-29 Contribution Margin Variance, Contribution Margin Volume Variance, Market Share Variance, Market Size Variance

Sulert, Inc., produces and sells gel-filled ice packs. Sulert's performance report for April follows:

	Actual	Budgeted
Units sold	290,000	300,000
Sales	$1,450,000	$1,515,000
Variable costs	652,500	636,300
Contribution margin	$ 797,500	$ 878,700
Market size (in units)	1,250,000	1,200,000

Required:

1. Calculate the contribution margin variance and the contribution margin volume variance.
2. Calculate the market share variance and the market size variance. *(CMA adapted)*

OBJECTIVE 5

Problem 18-30 Contribution Margin Variance, Contribution Margin Volume Variance, Sales Mix Variance

Gasconia Company produces three models of a product. Actual results from last year are as follows:

	Model 1	Model 2	Model 3
Unit sales	2,725	1,310	965
Selling price	$ 52	$ 68	$ 34
Variable expenses	$ 18	$ 34	$ 14

Gasconia had budgeted the following amounts:

	Model 1	Model 2	Model 3
Unit sales	2,700	1,300	1,000
Selling price	$ 50	$ 70	$ 30
Variable expenses	$ 20	$ 30	$ 10

Required:

1. Calculate the contribution margin variance.
2. Calculate the contribution margin volume variance.
3. Calculate the sales mix variance.

Problem 18-31 Impact of Inventory Changes on Absorption-Costing Income: Divisional Profitability

OBJECTIVE ◀ 4

Dana Baird was manager of a new Medical Supplies Division. She had just finished her second year and had been visiting with the company's vice president of operations. In the first year, the operating income for the division had shown a substantial increase over the prior year. Her second year saw an even greater increase. The vice president was extremely pleased and promised Dana a $5,000 bonus if the division showed a similar increase in profits for the upcoming year. Dana was elated. She was completely confident that the goal could be met. Sales contracts were already well ahead of last year's performance, and she knew that there would be no increases in costs.

At the end of the third year, Dana received the following data regarding operations for the first three years:

	Year 1	Year 2	Year 3
Production	10,000	11,000	9,000
Sales (in units)	8,000	10,000	12,000
Unit selling price	$ 10	$ 10	$ 10
Unit costs:			
Fixed overhead*	$ 2.90	$ 3.00	$ 3.00
Variable overhead	$ 1.00	$ 1.00	$ 1.00
Direct materials	$ 1.90	$ 2.00	$ 2.00
Direct labor	$ 1.00	$ 1.00	$ 1.00
Variable selling	$ 0.40	$ 0.50	$ 0.50
Actual fixed overhead	$29,000	$30,000	$30,000
Other fixed costs	$ 9,000	$10,000	$10,000

*The predetermined fixed overhead rate is based on expected actual units of production and expected fixed overhead. Expected production each year was 10,000 units. Any under- or overapplied fixed overhead is closed to Cost of Goods Sold.

Yearly Income Statements

	Year 1	Year 2	Year 3
Sales revenue	$80,000	$100,000	$120,000
Less: Cost of goods sold*	54,400	67,000	86,600
Gross margin	$25,600	$ 33,000	$ 33,400
Less: Selling and administrative expenses	12,200	15,000	16,000
Operating income	$13,400	$ 18,000	$ 17,400

*Assumes a LIFO inventory flow.

Upon examining the operating data, Dana was pleased. Sales had increased by 20 percent over the previous year, and costs had remained stable. However, when she saw the yearly income statements, she was dismayed and perplexed. Instead of seeing a significant increase in income for the third year, she saw a small decrease. Surely, the Accounting Department had made an error.

Required:

1. Explain to Dana why she lost her $5,000 bonus.
2. Prepare variable-costing income statements for each of the three years. Reconcile the differences between the absorption-costing and variable-costing incomes.
3. If you were the vice president of Dana's company, which income statement (variable-costing or absorption-costing) would you prefer to use for evaluating Dana's performance? Why?

OBJECTIVE ▶ 3 4 7

Problem 18-32 Ethical Issues, Absorption Costing, Performance Measurement

Bill Fremont, division controller and CMA, was upset by a recent memo he received from the divisional manager, Steve Preston. Bill was scheduled to present the division's financial performance at headquarters in one week. In the memo, Steve had given Bill some instructions for this upcoming report. In particular, Bill had been told to emphasize the significant improvement in the division's profits over last year. Bill, however, didn't believe that there was any real underlying improvement in the division's performance and was reluctant to say otherwise. He knew that the increase in profits was because of Steve's conscious decision to produce more inventory.

In an earlier meeting, Steve had convinced his plant managers to produce more than they knew they could sell. He argued that by deferring some of this period's fixed costs, reported profits would jump. He pointed out two significant benefits. First, by increasing profits, the division could exceed the minimum level needed so that all the managers would qualify for the annual bonus. Second, by meeting the budgeted profit level, the division would be better able to compete for much-needed capital. Bill objected but had been overruled. The most persuasive counterargument was that the increase in inventory could be liquidated in the coming year as the economy improved. Bill, however, considered this event unlikely. From past experience, he knew that it would take at least two years of improved market demand before the productive capacity of the division was exceeded.

Required:

1. Discuss the behavior of Steve Preston, the divisional manager. Was the decision to produce for inventory an ethical one?
2. What should Bill Fremont do? Should he comply with the directive to emphasize the increase in profits? If not, what options does he have?
3. Chapter 1 listed ethical standards for management accountants. Identify any standards that apply in this situation.

OBJECTIVE ▶ 4

Problem 18-33 Segmented Income Statements, Adding and Dropping Product Lines

Dantrell Palmer has just been appointed manager of Kirchner Glass Products Division. He has two years to make the division profitable. If the division is still showing a loss after two years, it will be eliminated, and Dantrell will be reassigned as an assistant divisional manager in another division. The divisional income statement for the most recent year is as follows:

Sales	$4,590,000
Less: Variable expenses	3,953,450
Contribution margin	$ 636,550
Less: Direct fixed expenses	675,000
Divisional margin	$ (38,450)
Less: Common fixed expenses (allocated)	200,000
Divisional profit (loss)	$ (238,450)

Upon arriving at the division, Dantrell requested the following data on the division's three products:

	Product A	Product B	Product C
Sales (units)	12,000	14,500	10,000
Unit selling price	$ 150.00	$ 120.00	$ 70.00
Unit variable cost	$ 100.00	$ 83.00	$ 107.00
Direct fixed costs	$100,000	$425,000	$250,000

He also gathered data on a proposed new product (Product D). If this product is added, it would displace one of the current products; the quantity that could be produced and sold would equal the quantity sold of the product it displaces, although demand limits the maximum quantity that could be sold to 20,000 units. Because of specialized production equipment, it is not possible for the new product to displace part of the production of a second product. The information on Product D is as follows:

Unit selling price	$80
Unit variable cost	30
Direct fixed costs	240,000

Required:

1. Prepare segmented income statements for Products A, B, and C.
2. Determine the products that Dantrell should produce for the coming year. Prepare segmented income statements that prove your combination is the best for the division. By how much will profits improve given the combination that you selected? (*Hint:* Your combination may include one, two, or three products.)

Problem 18-34 Operating Income for Segments

OBJECTIVE 4

Alydar, Inc., manufactures and sells automotive tools through three divisions: Eastern, Southern, and International. Each division is evaluated as a profit center. Data for each division for last year are as follows:

	Eastern	Southern	International
Sales	$3,150,000	$987,000	$6,500,000
Cost of goods sold	1,580,000	680,000	4,100,000
Selling and administrative expenses	337,000	280,000	620,000

Alydar, Inc., had corporate administrative expenses equal to $585,000; these were not allocated to the divisions.

Required:

1. Prepare a segmented income statement for Alydar, Inc., for last year.
2. Comment on the performance of each of the divisions.

Problem 18-35 Product Profitability

OBJECTIVE  4 6

Porter Insurance Company has three lines of insurance: automobile, property, and life. The life insurance segment has been losing money for the past five quarters, and Leah Harper, Porter's controller, has done an analysis of that segment. She has discovered that the commission paid to the agent for the first year the policy is in place is 55 percent of the first-year premium. The second-year commission is 20 percent, and all succeeding years a commission equal to 5 percent of premiums is paid. No salaries are paid to agents; however, Porter does advertise on television and in magazines. Last year, the advertising expense was $500,000. The loss rate (payout on claims) averages 50 percent. Administrative expenses equal $450,000 per year. Revenue last year was $10,000,000 (premiums). The percentage of policies of various lengths is as follows:

First year in force	65%
Second year	25
More than two years in force	10

Experience has shown that if a policy remains in effect for more than two years, it is rarely cancelled.

Leah is considering two alternative plans to turn this segment around. Plan 1 requires spending $250,000 on improved customer claim service in hopes that the percentage of policies in effect will take on the following distribution:

First year in force	50%
Second year	15
More than two years in force	35

Total premiums would remain constant at $10,000,000, and there are no other changes in fixed or variable cost behavior.

Plan 2 involves dropping the independent agent and commission system and having potential policyholders phone in requests for coverage. Leah estimates that revenue would drop to $7,000,000. Commissions would be zero, but administrative expenses would rise by $1,200,000, and advertising (including direct mail solicitation) would increase by $1,000,000.

Required:

1. Prepare a variable-costing income statement for last year for the life insurance segment of Porter Insurance Company.
2. What impact would Plan 1 have on income?
3. What impact would Plan 2 have on income?

OBJECTIVE 4 6   **Problem 18-36 Customer Profitability, Life-Cycle Revenue**

Refer to the original data in **Problem 18-35**. Fred Morton has just purchased a life insurance policy from Porter with premiums equal to $1,500 per year.

Required:

1. Assume Fred holds the policy for one year and then drops it. What is his contribution to Porter's operating income?
2. Assuming Fred holds the policy for three years, what is his contribution to Porter's operating income in the second and third years? Over a three-year period? What implications does this hold for Porter's efforts to retain policyholders?

OBJECTIVE 4   **Problem 18-37 Customer Profitability**

Olin Company manufactures and distributes carpentry tools. Production of the tools is in the mature portion of the product life cycle. Olin has a sales force of 20. Salespeople are paid a commission of 7 percent of sales, plus expenses of $35 per day for days spent on the road away from home, plus $0.50 per mile. They deliver products in addition to making the sales, and each salesperson is required to own a truck suitable for making deliveries.

For the coming quarter, Olin estimates the following:

Sales	$1,300,000
Cost of goods sold	450,000

On average, a salesperson travels 6,000 miles per quarter and spends 38 days on the road. The fixed marketing and administrative expenses total $400,000 per quarter.

Required:

1. Prepare an income statement for Olin Company for the next quarter.
2. Suppose that a large hardware chain, MegaHardware, Inc., wants Olin Company to produce its new SuperTool line. This would require Olin Company to sell 80 percent of total output to the chain. The tools will be imprinted with the SuperTool brand, requiring Olin to purchase new equipment, use somewhat different materials, and reconfigure the production line. Olin's industrial engineers estimate that cost of goods sold for the SuperTool line would increase by 15 percent. No sales commission would be incurred, and MegaHardware would link Olin to its EDI system. This would require an annual cost of $100,000 on the part of Olin. MegaHardware would pay shipping. As a result, the sales force would shrink by 80 percent. Should Olin accept MegaHardware's offer? Support your answer with appropriate calculations.

Problem 18-38 Segmented Income Statements: Analysis of Proposals to Improve Profits

Shannon, Inc., has two divisions. One produces and sells paper party supplies (napkins, paper plates, invitations); the other produces and sells cookware. A segmented income statement for the most recent quarter is given below:

	Party Supplies Division	Cookware Division	Total
Sales	$500,000	$750,000	$1,250,000
Less: Variable expenses	425,000	460,000	885,000
Contribution margin	$ 75,000	$290,000	$ 365,000
Less: Direct fixed expenses	85,000	110,000	195,000
Segment margin	$(10,000)	$180,000	$ 170,000
Less: Common fixed expenses			130,000
Operating income			$ 40,000

On seeing the quarterly statement, Madge Shannon, president of Shannon, Inc., was distressed and discussed her disappointment with Bob Ferguson, the company's vice president of finance.

MADGE: "The Party Supplies Division is killing us. It's not even covering its own fixed costs. I'm beginning to believe that we should shut down that division. This is the seventh consecutive quarter it has failed to provide a positive segment margin. I was certain that Paula Kelly could turn it around. But this is her third quarter, and she hasn't done much better than the previous divisional manager."

BOB: "Well, before you get too excited about the situation, perhaps you should evaluate Paula's most recent proposals. She wants to spend $10,000 per quarter for the right to use familiar cartoon figures on a new series of invitations, plates, and napkins and at the same time increase the advertising budget by $25,000 per quarter to let the public know about them. According to her marketing people, sales should increase by 10 percent if the right advertising is done—and done quickly. In addition, Paula wants to lease some new production machinery that will increase the rate of production, lower labor costs, and result in less waste of materials. Paula claims that variable costs will be reduced by 30 percent. The cost of the lease is $95,000 per quarter."

Upon hearing this news, Madge calmed considerably and, in fact, was somewhat pleased. After all, she was the one who had selected Paula and had a great deal of confidence in Paula's judgment and abilities.

Required:

1. Assuming that Paula's proposals are sound, should Madge Shannon be pleased with the prospects for the Party Supplies Division? Prepare a segmented income statement for the next quarter that reflects the implementation of Paula's proposals. Assume that the Cookware Division's sales increase by 5 percent for the next quarter and that the same cost relationships hold.
2. Suppose that everything materializes as Paula projected except for the 10 percent increase in sales—no change in sales revenues takes place. Are the proposals still sound? What if the variable costs are reduced by 40 percent instead of 30 percent with no change in sales?

Problem 18-39 Segmented Reporting and Variances

Pittsburgh-Walsh Company (PWC) is a manufacturing company whose product line consists of lighting fixtures and electronic timing devices. The Lighting Fixtures Division assembles units for the upscale and mid-range markets. The Electronic Timing Devices Division manufactures instrument panels that allow electronic systems to be activated and deactivated at scheduled times for both efficiency and safety purposes. Both divisions operate out of the same manufacturing facilities and share production equipment.

PWC's budget for the year ending December 31, 20x1, follows and was prepared on a business segment basis under the following guidelines:

a. Variable expenses are directly assigned to the incurring division.
b. Fixed overhead expenses are directly assigned to the incurring division.
c. The production plan is for 8,000 upscale fixtures, 22,000 mid-range fixtures, and 20,000 electronic timing devices. Production equals sales.

PWC established a bonus plan for division management that required meeting the budget's planned operating income by product line, with a bonus increment if the division exceeds the planned product line operating income by 10 percent or more.

PWC Budget
For the Year Ending December 31, 20x1
(In Thousands of Dollars)

| | Lighting Fixtures | | Electronic Timing | |
	Upscale	Mid-Range	Devices	Total
Sales	$1,440	$ 770	$ 800	$ 3,010
Variable expenses:				
Cost of goods sold	(720)	(439)	(320)	(1,479)
Selling and administrative	(170)	(60)	(60)	(290)
Contribution margin	$ 550	$ 271	$ 420	$ 1,241
Fixed overhead expenses	140	80	80	300
Segment margin	$ 410	$ 191	$ 340	$ 941

Shortly before the year began, the CEO, Jack Parkow, suffered a heart attack and retired. After reviewing the 20x1 budget, the new CEO, Joe Kelly, decided to close the lighting fixtures mid-range product line by the end of the first quarter and use the available production capacity to grow the remaining two product lines. The marketing staff advised that electronic timing devices could grow by 40 percent with increased direct sales support. Increases above that level and increasing sales of upscale lighting fixtures would require expanded advertising expenditures to increase consumer awareness of PWC as an electronics and upscale lighting fixtures company. Kelly approved the increased sales support and advertising expenditures to achieve the revised plan. Kelly advised the divisions that for bonus purposes the original product-line operating income objectives must be met, but he did allow the Lighting Fixtures Division to combine the operating income objectives for both product lines for bonus purposes.

Prior to the close of the fiscal year, the division controllers were furnished with preliminary actual data for review and adjustment, as appropriate. These preliminary year-end data reflect the revised units of production amounting to 12,000 upscale fixtures, 4,000 mid-range fixtures, and 30,000 electronic timing devices and are presented as follows:

PWC Preliminary Actuals
For the Year Ending December 31, 20x1
(In Thousands of Dollars)

| | Lighting Fixtures | | Electronic Timing | |
	Upscale	Mid-Range	Devices	Total
Sales	$ 2,160	$140	$1,200	$ 3,500
Variable expenses:				
Cost of goods sold	(1,080)	(80)	(480)	(1,640)
Selling and administrative	(260)	(11)	(96)	(367)
Contribution margin	$ 820	$ 49	$ 624	$ 1,493
Fixed overhead expenses	140	14	80	234
Segment margin	$ 680	$ 35	$ 544	$ 1,259

The controller of the Lighting Fixtures Division, anticipating a similar bonus plan for 20x2, is contemplating deferring some revenues to the next year on the pretext that the sales are not yet final and accruing in the current year expenditures that will be applicable to the first quarter of 20x2. The corporation would meet its annual plan, and the division would exceed the 10 percent incremental bonus plateau in 20x1 despite the deferred revenues and accrued expenses contemplated.

Required:

1. Outline the benefits that an organization realizes from segment reporting. Evaluate segment reporting on a variable-costing basis versus an absorption-costing basis.
2. Calculate the contribution margin, contribution margin volume, and sales mix variances.
3. Explain why the variances occurred. *(CMA adapted)*

19 Capital Investment

After studying this chapter, you should be able to:

1 Describe the difference between independent and mutually exclusive capital investment decisions.

2 Explain the roles of the payback period and accounting rate of return in capital investment decisions.

3 Calculate the net present value (NPV) for independent projects.

4 Compute the internal rate of return (IRR) for independent projects.

5 Explain why NPV is better than IRR for choosing among mutually exclusive projects.

6 Convert gross cash flows to after-tax cash flows.

7 Describe capital investment for advanced technology and environmental impact settings.

Sundry Photography/Shutterstock.com

USING CAPITAL INVESTMENT DECISION MODELS

at Spacex

It is interesting and fascinating that capital investment decision making is playing a key role in the potential colonization of Mars. With the privatization of space exploration, there now exists a strong profit incentive for developing and investing in new and more efficient space exploration and transportation technologies. **Space Exploration Technologies Corporation** or **SpaceX** is a leading space transportation services company. SpaceX builds its own spacecraft and rockets and competes in the launch services market. In 2020, SpaceX's launch revenues are expected to be about $1.2 billion, which are about what the company has averaged over the prior six years. In 2014, the market value of SpaceX was $12 billion, yet, in 2020, the market value is $36 billion with about the same projected launch revenues as in 2014.[1] What is happening?

Clearly, the valuation of SpaceX is increasing more rapidly than its revenue. One driver of this increased value is the fact that SpaceX is offering launch services at a much lower price than competitors while still remaining profitable. This has allowed SpaceX to capture the largest market share in the commercial satellite launch industry.[2] One key to this success is investing in and developing many reusable components of the launch system. In fact, on May 30, 2020, SpaceX became the first private company to launch a human into orbit, using its Falcon 9 partially reusable rocket. As impressive as these accomplishments are, the increase in valuation is strongly connected to two major capital investments in process called Starlink and Starship.

Of the two projects, Starlink is probably having the greatest impact on firm value. Starlink is a network of low-orbit satellites that will provide low-latency, high-speed broadband internet access worldwide. SpaceX already has over 400 internet satellites in orbit and has approval from the Federal Communications Commission (FCC) for a total of 4,425.[3] Eventually, the company may have as many as 40,000 internet satellites in orbit. The objective is to provide internet access to all parts of the world, including remote and rural areas. Whereas the launch services market has a total of about $5 billion per year in revenues, the internet access market has a potential of about $1 trillion in revenues.[4] The prospect of SpaceX capturing a significant share of the internet market is the source of much

1 Forbes Interactive Dashboard for SpaceX, https://dashboards.trefis.com/no-login-required/yaQTBXoY/What-Is-Driving-SpaceX-s-Revenues-Valuation-?fromforbesandarticle=trefis200602, accessed July 10, 2020.

2 Trefis Team and Great Speculations, "Revisiting SpaceX's $36-Billion Valuation after Its First Manned Mission," *Forbes*, June 2, 2020, https://www.forbes.com/sites/greatspeculations/2020/06/02/revisiting-spacexs-36-billion-valuation-after-its-first-manned-mission/#7aeff82944fb, accessed July 10, 2020.

3 "FCC Authorizes SpaceX to Provide Broadband Satellite Services," https://www.fcc.gov/document/fcc-authorizes-spacex-provide-broadband-satellite-services, accessed July 10, 2020.

4 Mike Brown, "SpaceX: Why Starlink Depends on Starship to Fuel the Future of Humanity," *Inverse* (March 2, 2020), https://www.inverse.com/innovation/spacex-elon-musk-details-how-starlink-starship-are-inextricably-linked, accessed July 10, 2020.

of the increase in SpaceX's valuation. Moreover, the second project, Starship, is inextricably linked to Starlink.

The Starship rocket is SpaceX's next generation rocket. It will be fully reusable, similar to commercial aircraft. Moreover, it will be much bigger, capable of carrying payloads of up to 220,000 pounds (compared to the 50,000 pounds of the Falcon 9 rocket). The Starship rocket will be able to transport up to 100 persons and will be the means by which SpaceX will go to the moon and to Mars.[5] It clearly will be a much more cost-effective means of launching satellites into the orbit as it can carry many more satellites at a time than the Falcon 9 and, thus, will make the Starlink project even more profitable than it currently is forecast to be. Moreover, the profits from the Starlink system are expected to be a major source of the capital required to finance the colonization of Mars.

Organizations are often faced with the opportunity (or need) to invest in assets or projects that represent long-term commitments. New production systems, new plants, new equipment, and new product development are examples of assets and projects that fit this category. Usually, many alternatives are available. For example, FedEx has chosen to make a capital investment in airplanes, sorting equipment, and distribution facilities. The FedEx hub in Memphis represents a significant outlay of funds (capital outlay). Sound capital investment decision making of this type requires the estimation of a project's cash flows. How cash flows can be used to evaluate the merits of a proposed project is the focus of this chapter. You will be introduced to the basics of capital investment decision making. You will begin to understand the complexity and risks associated with investing in capital intensive projects. You will also learn about the data analytic models that help guide decision makers. Specifically, we will study four financial models that are useful in capital investment analysis: the payback period, the accounting rate of return, the net present value, and the internal rate of return.

OBJECTIVE

Describe the difference between independent and mutually exclusive capital investment decisions.

CAPITAL INVESTMENT DECISIONS

Capital investment decisions are concerned with the process of planning, setting goals and priorities, arranging financing, and using certain criteria to select long-term assets. Because capital investment decisions place large amounts of resources at risk for long periods of time and simultaneously affect the future development of the firm, they are among the most important decisions managers make. Every organization has limited resources, which should be used to maintain or enhance its long-run profitability. Poor capital investment decisions can be costly. Normally, the expectation is that capital investments will enhance profitability—not reduce it.

The process of making capital investment decisions is often referred to as **capital budgeting**. Two types of capital budgeting projects will be considered. **Independent projects** are projects that, if accepted or rejected, do not affect the cash flows of other projects. Suppose that the managers of the marketing and research and development departments jointly propose the addition of a new product line where each would entail significant outlays of working capital and equipment. Acceptance or rejection of one product line does not require the acceptance or rejection of the other product line. Thus, the investment decisions for the product lines are independent of each other.

The second type of capital budgeting project requires a firm to choose among competing alternatives that provide the same basic service. Acceptance of one option precludes the acceptance

---

5   Michael Sheetz, "Elon Musk Tells SpaceX Employees That Its Starship Rocket Is the Top Priority Now," CNBC, June 7, 2020, https://www.cnbc.com/2020/06/07/elon-musk-email-to-spacex-employees-starship-is-the-top-priority .html, accessed July 10, 2020.

of another. Thus, **mutually exclusive projects** are those projects that, if accepted, preclude the acceptance of all other competing projects. For example, a company may be faced with the choice of continuing with its existing manual production operation or replacing it with an automated system. Once one system is chosen, the other is excluded; they are mutually exclusive.

Capital investment decisions typically are concerned with investments in long-term capital assets. With the exception of land, these assets depreciate over their lives, and the original investment is used up as the assets are employed. In general terms, a sound capital investment will earn back its original capital outlay over its life and, at the same time, provide a reasonable return on the original investment. Thus, a manager should decide on the acceptability of independent projects and compare competing projects on the basis of their economic merits. But what is meant by reasonable return? It is generally agreed that any new project must cover the *opportunity cost* of the funds invested. For example, if a company takes money from a money market fund that is earning 6 percent and invests it in a new project, then the project must provide at least a 6 percent return (the return that could have been earned had the money been left in the money market fund). Of course, in reality, funds for investment often come from different sources— each representing a different opportunity cost. Thus, if a company uses two sources of funds, one with an opportunity cost of 4 percent and the other with an opportunity cost of 6 percent, then the return that must be earned is somewhere between 4 and 6 percent, depending on the relative amounts used from each source.

To make a capital investment decision, a manager must estimate the quantity and timing of cash flows, assess the risk of the investment, and consider the impact of the project on the firm's profits. One of the most difficult tasks is to estimate the cash flows. Projections must be made years into the future, and forecasting is far from a perfect science. Obviously, as the accuracy of cash flow forecasts increases, the reliability of the decision improves. In making projections, managers must identify and quantify the benefits associated with the proposed project(s). Although forecasting future cash flows is a critical part of the capital investment process, forecasting methods will not be considered here. Consequently, cash flows are assumed to be known; the focus will be on making capital investment decisions *given* these cash flows.

Managers must set goals and priorities for capital investments. They also must identify some basic criteria for the acceptance or rejection of proposed investments. In this chapter, we will study four data analytic models that are used to guide managers in accepting or rejecting potential investments. They can be applied to both independent and mutually exclusive projects. Two of the models use a nondiscounting approach, and two use a discounting approach. All four models transform future financial data (usually future cash flows) into a single value that can be used to assess the merits of proposed investment project(s). Thus, the models are inherently predictive in nature; however, when a benchmark is established that the value must meet or exceed to be acceptable, the models assume a prescriptive role. Using the predicted values to compare and analyze competing projects is an example of the diagnostic roles of the four models. Finally, if the models are used to calculate after-the-fact performance, they can assume both descriptive and diagnostic roles.

**DATA
ANALYTICS**

PAYBACK AND ACCOUNTING RATE OF RETURN: NONDISCOUNTING METHODS

OBJECTIVE 2

Explain the roles of the payback period and accounting rate of return in capital investment decisions.

Models used for making capital investment decisions fall into two major categories: *nondiscounting models* and *discounting models*. **Nondiscounting models** ignore the time value of money, whereas **discounting models** explicitly consider it. Although many accounting theorists disparage the nondiscounting models because they ignore the time value of money, many firms continue to use them in making capital investment decisions. However, the use of discounting models has increased over the years, and few firms use only one model—indeed, firms seem to use both types of models. This suggests that both categories supply useful information to managers as they struggle to make capital investment decisions.

Payback Period

One type of nondiscounting model is the *payback period*. The **payback period** is the time required for a firm to recover its original investment. When the cash flows of a project are assumed to be even, the following formula can be used to compute the project's payback period:

Payback period = Original investment/Annual cash flow

If, however, the cash flows are uneven, the payback period is computed by adding the annual cash flows until such time as the original investment is recovered. **Example 19.1** illustrates payback analysis for both even and uneven cash flows.

EXAMPLE 19.1

The HOW and WHY of Calculating the Payback Period

Information:
Suppose that a company is considering two different and mutually exclusive projects (A and B), where both have a five-year life and require an investment of $210,000. The cash flow patterns for each project are given below.

Project A: Even cash flows of $70,000 per year

Project B: $120,000, $100,000, $90,000, $50,000, and $30,000

> **Why:**
> The payback period is the time required to recover a project's initial investment. It may be useful to help assess such things as (1) the impact of an investment on liquidity, (2) financial risk, and (3) obsolescence risk.

Required:

1. Calculate the payback period for Project A (even cash flows).

2. Calculate the payback period for Project B (uneven cash flows). Which project should be accepted based on payback analysis? Explain.

3. *What if* a third mutually exclusive project, Project C, became available with the same investment and annual cash flows of $100,000? Now which project would be chosen?

Solution:

1. Even cash flows:

   Payback period = Original investment/Annual cash flow

   = $210,000/$70,000

   = 3.0 years

2. Uneven cash flows:

Year	Unrecovered Investment (Beginning of Year)	Annual Cash Flow	Time Needed for Payback
1	$210,000	$120,000	1.0 year
2	90,000	100,000	0.9 year*

*At the beginning of the year, an additional $90,000 is needed to recover the investment. Since a net cash flow of $100,000 is expected, only 0.9 year ($90,000/$100,000) is needed to recover the remaining $80,000, assuming a uniform cash flow throughout the year.

Project B has a shorter payback period and thus seems less risky and would have less impact on liquidity.

3. The payback for Project C is 2.1 years ($210,000/$100,000). Project B still has the better payback, but Project C promises more cash flow over its life and would have a more favorable impact on liquidity.

One approach is to set a maximum payback period for all projects and to reject any project that exceeds this level. Using the payback this way may provide a rough measure of risk, with the notion that the longer it takes for a project to pay for itself, the riskier it is. Also, firms with riskier cash flows could require a shorter payback period than normal. Additionally, firms with liquidity problems would be more interested in projects with quick paybacks. Another critical concern is obsolescence. In some industries, the risk of obsolescence is high; firms within these industries would be interested in recovering funds rapidly. Another reason for quick payback periods, less beneficial to the firms, is managerial self-interest. If a manager's performance is measured using such short-run criteria as annual operating income, he or she may choose projects with quick paybacks to show improved operating income as quickly as possible. This incentive can be mitigated by corporate budgeting policies and a budget review committee.

The payback period can be used to choose among competing alternatives. Under this approach, the investment with the shortest payback period is preferred over investments with longer payback periods. However, this use of the payback period is less defensible because this measure suffers from two major deficiencies: (1) it ignores the performance of the investments beyond the payback period, and (2) it ignores the time value of money.

These two significant deficiencies are easily illustrated. Assume that a tire manufacturing firm is considering two different types of automated conveyor systems—Autocon and Maticmuv. Each system requires an initial outlay of $600,000, has a five-year life, and displays the following annual cash flows:

Investment	Year 1	Year 2	Year 3	Year 4	Year 5
Autocon	$360,000	$240,000	$200,000	$200,000	$200,000
Maticmuv	160,000	440,000	100,000	100,000	100,000

Both investments have payback periods of two years. If a manager uses the payback period to choose among competing investments, then the two investments would be equally desirable. In reality, however, the Autocon system should be preferred over the Maticmuv system for two reasons. First, the Autocon system provides a much larger dollar return for the years beyond the payback period ($600,000 versus $300,000). Second, the Autocon system returns $360,000 in the first year, while Maticmuv returns only $160,000. The extra $200,000 that the Autocon system provides in the first year could be put to productive use, such as investing it in another project. It is better to have a dollar now than a dollar one year from now because the dollar on hand can be invested to provide a return one year from now.

In summary, the payback period provides managers with information that can be used as follows:

1. To help control the risks associated with the uncertainty of future cash flows
2. To help minimize the impact of an investment on a firm's liquidity problems
3. To help control the risk of obsolescence
4. To help control the effect of the investment on performance measures

However, the method suffers significant deficiencies: it ignores a project's total profitability and the time value of money. While the computation of the payback period may be useful to a manager, to rely on it solely for a capital investment decision would be foolish.

Accounting Rate of Return

The **accounting rate of return (ARR)** is the second commonly used nondiscounting model. The accounting rate of return measures the return on a project in terms of income, as opposed to using a project's cash flow. It is computed by the following formula:

Accounting rate of return = Average income/Original investment

Income is not equivalent to cash flows because of accruals and deferrals used in its computation. The average income of a project is obtained by adding the income for each year of the project and then dividing this total by the number of years. Average income is computed by summing annual income over the life of the project and then dividing by the number of years of the project. Annual income is approximated as annual cash flow less annual depreciation expense. Average income for a project also can be approximated by subtracting average depreciation from average cash flow. Assuming that all revenues earned in a period are collected and that depreciation is the only non-cash expense, the approximation is exact.

Unlike the payback period, the accounting rate of return does consider a project's profitability; like the payback period, it ignores the time value of money [as illustrated in **Example 19.2**, Question (3)]. Ignoring the time value of money is a critical deficiency and can lead a manager to choose investments that do not maximize profits. It is because the payback period and the accounting rate of return ignore the time value of money that they are referred to as *nondiscounting models*. Discounting models use **discounted cash flows**, which are future cash flows expressed in terms of their present value. The use of discounting models requires an understanding of the present value concepts. Present value concepts are reviewed in Appendix A at the end of this chapter. You should review these concepts and make sure that you understand them before studying capital investment discount models. Present value tables (Exhibits 19B.1 and 19B.2) are presented in Appendix B at the end of this chapter. These tables are referred to and used throughout the rest of the chapter.

EXAMPLE 19.2

The HOW and WHY of Calculating the Accounting Rate of Return

Information:

Assume that an investment requires an initial outlay of $300,000 with no salvage value. The life of the investment is five years with the following yearly cash flows (in chronological sequence): $90,000, $90,000, $120,000, $90,000, and $150,000.

> **Why:**
> The accounting rate of return for a project is average income for the project divided by the original investment. The accounting rate of return thus considers the profitability of an investment.

Required:

1. Calculate the annual net income for each of the five years.

2. Calculate the accounting rate of return.

3. *What if* a second competing project had the same initial outlay and salvage value but the following cash flows (in chronological sequence): $150,000, $120,000, $90,000, $90,000, and $90,000? Using the accounting rate of return metric, which project should be selected: the first or the second? Which project is really the better of the two?

Solution:

1. Yearly depreciation expense: ($300,000 – $0)/5 = $60,000
   Year 1 net income = $90,000 − $60,000 = $30,000
   Year 2 net income = $90,000 − $60,000 = $30,000
   Year 3 net income = $120,000 − $60,000 = $60,000
   Year 4 net income = $90,000 − $60,000 = $30,000
   Year 5 net income = $150,000 − $60,000 = $90,000

2. Total net income (five years) = $240,000
   Average net income = $240,000/5 = $48,000
   Accounting rate of return = $48,000/$300,000 = 0.16 (16%)

3. The second project has an identical accounting rate of return; thus, the metric would say there is no difference between the two projects. However, in reality, the second project would be preferred even though it provides the same total cash because it returns larger amounts of cash sooner than the first project.

THE NET PRESENT VALUE METHOD

OBJECTIVE ◀ **3**

Calculate the net present value (NPV) for independent projects.

Net present value (NPV) is one of two discounting models that explicitly considers the time value of money and, therefore, incorporates the concept of discounting cash inflows and outflows. The other discounting model is the *internal rate of return (IRR)*. The net present value method will be discussed first; the internal rate of return method is discussed in the following section.

Net present value (NPV) is the difference in the present value of the cash inflows and outflows associated with a project:

$$\text{NPV} = [\Sigma\, CF_t/(1 + i)^t - I]$$
$$= [\Sigma\,(CF_t)(df_t)] - I$$
$$= P - I \qquad\qquad\qquad (19\text{-}1)$$

where

I = The present value of the project's cost (usually the initial outlay)

CF_t = The cash inflow to be received in period t, with $t = 1, \ldots, n$

i = The required rate of return

n = The useful life of the project

t = The time period

P = The present value of the project's future cash inflows

$df_t = 1/(1 + i)^t$, the discount factor

Net present value measures the profitability of an investment. If the NPV is positive, it measures the increase in wealth. For a firm, this means that the size of a positive NPV measures the increase in the value of the firm resulting from an investment.

To use the NPV method, a required rate of return must be defined. The **required rate of return** is the minimum acceptable rate of return. It is also referred to as the *discount rate* or the *hurdle rate* and should correspond to the *cost of capital*. The **cost of capital** is a weighted average of the costs from various sources, where the weight is defined by the *relative amount* from each source. In theory, the cost of capital is the correct discount rate, although, in practice, some firms choose higher discount rates as a way to deal with the uncertain nature of future cash flows. Yet the cost of capital should already embed uncertainty in its value and so using higher discount rates may create an unhealthy bias. Thus, it will generally be assumed that the cost of capital is the required part of return.

If the net present value is positive, it signals that (1) the initial investment has been recovered, (2) the required rate of return has been recovered, and (3) a return in excess of (1) and (2) has been received. Thus, if NPV is greater than zero, then the investment is profitable and therefore acceptable. It also conveys the message that the value of the firm should increase because more than the cost of capital is being earned. If NPV equals zero, then the decision maker will find acceptance or rejection of the investment equal. Finally, if NPV is less than zero, then the investment should be rejected. In this case, it is earning less than the required rate of return. **Example 19.3** illustrates the use of NPV.

EXAMPLE 19.3

The HOW and WHY of Analyzing NPV

Information:

Polson Company is considering production of a new cell phone with the following associated data:

- Expected annual revenues: $750,000
- Projected product life cycle: five years
- Equipment: $800,000 with a salvage value of $100,000 after five years

EXAMPLE 19.3

(Continued)

- Expected increase in working capital: $100,000 (recoverable at the end of five years)
- Annual cash operating expenses: estimated at $450,000
- Required rate of return: 12 percent

> **Why:**
> NPV is the present value of future cash flows less the initial outlay. All projects with a positive (negative) NPV should be accepted (rejected). Present value of future cash flows is calculated using the required rate of return (usually the cost of capital).

Required:

1. Estimate the annual cash flows for the cell-phone project.

2. Using the estimated annual cash flows, calculate the NPV.

3. *What if* revenues were overestimated by $150,000? Redo the NPV analysis, correcting for this error. Assume the operating expenses remain the same.

Solution:

1.

Year	Item	Cash Flow
0	Equipment	$(800,000)
	Working capital	(100,000)
	Total	$(900,000)
1–4	Revenues	$ 750,000
	Operating expenses	(450,000)
	Total	$ 300,000
5	Revenues	$ 750,000
	Operating expenses	(450,000)
	Salvage	100,000
	Recovery of working capital	100,000
	Total	$ 500,000

2.

Year	Cash Flow	Discount Factor*	Present Value
0	$(900,000)	1.000	$(900,000)
1–4	300,000	3.037	911,100
5	500,000	0.567	283,500
Net present value			$ 294,600

*Years 1–4 from Exhibit 19B.2; Year 5 from Exhibit 19B.1.

3. Correcting for the overestimation error of $150,000 would cause the project to be rejected, as shown below.

Year	Cash Flow	Discount Factor*	Present Value
0	$(900,000)	1.000	$(900,000)
1–4	150,000	3.037	455,550
5	350,000	0.567	198,450
Net present value			$(246,000)

*Years 1–4 from Exhibit 19B.2; Year 5 from Exhibit 19B.1.

INTERNAL RATE OF RETURN

OBJECTIVE 4

Compute the internal rate of return (IRR) for independent projects.

The **internal rate of return (IRR)** is defined as the interest rate that sets the present value of a project's cash inflows equal to the present value of the project's cost. In other words, it is the interest rate that sets the project's NPV at zero. The following equation can be used to determine a project's IRR:

$$I = \Sigma \, CF_t/(1 + i)^t \tag{19.2}$$

where

$$t = 1, \ldots, n$$

The right-hand side of Equation 19.2 is the present value of future cash flows, and the left-hand side is the investment. I, CF_t, and t are known. Thus, the IRR (the interest rate, i, in the equation) can be found by setting $I = 0$ and solving Equation 19.2 for i. Once the IRR for a project is computed, it is compared with the firm's required rate of return. If the IRR is greater than the required rate, the project is deemed acceptable; if the IRR is equal to the required rate of return, acceptance or rejection of the investment is equal; and if the IRR is less than the required rate of return, the project is rejected.

Solving for I to determine the IRR is a straightforward process when the annual cash flows are uniform or even. Since the series of cash flows is uniform, a single discount factor from Exhibit 19B.2 can be used to compute the present value of the annuity. Letting df be this discount factor and CF be the annual cash flow, Equation 19.2 assumes the following form:

$$I = CF(df)$$

Solving for df, we obtain:

$$df = I/CF$$
$$= \text{Investment/Annual cash flow}$$

Once the discount factor is computed, go to Exhibit 19B.2, find the row corresponding to the life of the project, and move across that row until the computed discount factor is found. The interest rate corresponding to this discount factor is the IRR. Since Exhibit 19B.2 does not list all possible interest rates, it may be that a discount factor will fall in between two rates. In this case, it is possible to approximate the IRR by interpolation; however, for our purposes, we will simply identify the range for the IRR as indicated by the table values.

If the cash flows are not uniform, then Equation 19.2 must be solved by trial and error or by using a business calculator or a software package like Excel®. To solve by trial and error, start by selecting a possible value for i. Given this first guess, the present value of the future cash flows is computed and then compared to the initial investment. If the present value is greater than the initial investment, the interest rate is too low; if the present value is less than the initial investment, the interest rate is too high. The next guess is adjusted accordingly. **Example 19.4** illustrates how the IRR is calculated and used.

EXAMPLE 19.4

The HOW and WHY of Calculating the Internal Rate of Return

Information:
A firm with a cost of capital of 10 percent is considering two independent investments:

(1) A new computer-aided design system that costs $240,000 and will produce net cash inflows of $99,900 at the end of each year for the next three years

(2) An inventory management system that costs $50,000 and will produce labor savings of $30,000 and $36,000 at the end of the first year and second year, respectively.

EXAMPLE 19.4

(Continued)

> **Why:**
> The IRR is the interest rate where NPV = 0. The IRR is determined by solving Equation 19.2. Acceptable investments should have an IRR greater than the cost of capital (or required rate of return).

Required:

1. Calculate the IRR for the first investment and determine if it is acceptable or not.

2. Calculate the IRR of the second investment and comment on its acceptability. Use 18 percent as the first guess.

3. *What if* the cash flows for the first investment are $102,000 instead of $99,900?

Solution:

1. df = $240,000/$99,900 = 2.402. Since the life of the investment is three years, we must find the third row in Exhibit 19B.2 and move across this row until we encounter 2.402. The interest rate corresponding to 2.402 is 12 percent, which is the IRR. Since IRR > 0.10, the investment is acceptable.

2. To find the IRR, we must find i by trial and error such that $50,000 = $30,000/$(1 + i)$ + $36,000/$(1 + i)^2$. Using $i = 0.18$ as the first guess, Exhibit 19B.2 yields discount factors of 0.847 and 0.718 and thus the following present value for the two cash inflows:

$$P = (0.847 \times \$30,000) + (0.718 \times \$36,000)$$
$$= \$51,258$$

Since $P >$ $50,000, a higher interest rate is needed. Letting $i = 20$ percent, we obtain:

$$P = (0.833 \times \$30,000) + (0.694 \times \$36,000)$$
$$= \$49,974$$

Since this value is reasonably close to $50,000, we can say that IRR = 20 percent. Since IRR > 0.10, the investment is acceptable.

3. df = $240,000/$102,000 = 2.353. Using Exhibit 19B.2, this discount factor now lies between 12 and 14 percent, which means the IRR > 0.10.

The internal rate of return is the most widely used of the capital investment techniques. One reason for its popularity may be that it is a rate of return, a concept that managers are comfortable in using. Another possibility is that managers may believe (in most cases, incorrectly) that the IRR is the true or actual compounded rate of return being earned by the initial investment. Whatever the reasons for its popularity, a basic understanding of the IRR is necessary.

OBJECTIVE 5

Explain why NPV is better than IRR for choosing among mutually exclusive projects.

NPV VERSUS IRR: MUTUALLY EXCLUSIVE PROJECTS

Up to this point, we have focused on independent projects. Many capital investment decisions deal with mutually exclusive projects. How NPV analysis and IRR are used to choose among competing projects is an intriguing question. An even more interesting question to consider is whether NPV and IRR differ in their ability to help managers make wealth-maximizing decisions in the presence of competing alternatives. In reality, it can be shown that the NPV model is generally preferred to the IRR model when choosing among mutually exclusive alternatives.

NPV Compared with IRR

NPV and IRR both yield the same decision for independent projects. For example, if the NPV is greater than zero, then the IRR is also greater than the required rate of return; both models signal the correct decision. For competing projects, however, the two methods can produce different results. Intuitively, we believe that, for mutually exclusive projects, the project with the highest NPV or the highest IRR should be chosen. Since it is possible for the two methods to produce different rankings of mutually exclusive projects, the method that consistently reveals the wealth-maximizing project should be preferred. As will be shown, the NPV method is that model.

NPV differs from IRR in two major ways. First, NPV assumes that each cash inflow received is reinvested at the required rate of return, whereas the IRR method assumes that each cash inflow is reinvested at the computed IRR. Second, the NPV method measures profitability in absolute terms, whereas the IRR method measures it in relative terms. Because NPV is measured in absolute terms, it is affected by the size of the investment, whereas IRR is size independent. For example, an investment of $100,000 that produces a cash flow one year from now of $121,000 has the same IRR (21 percent) as an investment of $10,000 that produces a cash flow one year from now of $12,100. Note, however, that the NPV is $10,000 for the first investment and $1,000 for the second. Since absolute measures often produce different rankings than relative measures, it shouldn't be too surprising that NPV and IRR can, on occasion, produce different signals regarding the attractiveness of projects. When a conflict does occur between the two methods, NPV produces the correct signal, as can be shown by a simple example.

Assume that a manager is faced with the prospect of choosing between two mutually exclusive investments whose cash flows, timing, NPV, and IRR are given in Exhibit 19.1. (A required rate of return of 8 percent is assumed for NPV computation.) Both projects have the same life, require the same initial outlay, have positive NPVs, and have IRRs greater than the required rate of return. However, Project A has a higher NPV, whereas Project B has a higher IRR. The NPV and IRR give conflicting signals regarding which project should be chosen.

The preferred project can be identified by modifying the cash flows of one project so that the cash flows of both can be compared year by year. The modification, which appears in Exhibit 19.2, was achieved by carrying the Year 1 cash flow of Project B forward to Year 2. This can be done by assuming that the Year 1 cash flow of $686,342 is invested to earn the required rate of return. Under this assumption, the future value of $686,342 is equal to $741,249 (1.08 × $686,342). When $741,249 is added to the $686,342 received at the end of Year 2, the cash flow expected for Project B is $1,427,591.

As can be seen from Exhibit 19.2, Project A is preferable to Project B. It has the same outlay initially and a greater cash inflow in Year 2. (The difference is $12,409.) Since the NPV approach originally chose Project A over Project B, it provided the correct signal for wealth maximization.

Some may object to this analysis, arguing that Project B should be preferred, since it does provide a cash inflow of $686,342 at the end of Year 1, which can be reinvested at a much more attractive rate than the firm's required rate of return. The response is that if such an investment

Year	Project A	Project B
0	$(1,000,000)	$(1,000,000)
1	—	686,342
2	1,440,000	686,342
IRR	20%	24%
NPV	$ 234,080	$ 223,748

Exhibit 19.1

NPV and IRR: Conflicting Signals

Exhibit 19.2

Modified Comparison of Projects
A and B

	Projects	
Year	**A**	**Modified B**
0	$(1,000,000)	$(1,000,000)
1	—	—
2	1,440,000	1,427,591*

*(1.08 × $686,342) + $686,342

Exhibit 19.3

Modified Cash Flows with
Additional Opportunity

	Projects	
Year	**A**	**Modified B**
0	$(1,000,000)	$(1,000,000)
1	—	—
2	1,522,361[a]	1,509,952[b]

[a]$1,440,000 + [(1.20 × $686,342) − (1.08 × $686,342)]. This last term is what is needed to repay the capital and its cost at the end of Year 2.
[b]$686,342 + (1.20 × $686,342)

does exist, the firm should still invest in Project A, borrow $686,342 at the cost of capital, and invest that money in the attractive opportunity. Then, at the end of Year 2, the firm should repay the money borrowed plus the interest by using the combined proceeds of Project A and the other investment. For example, assume that the other investment promises a return of 20 percent. The modified cash inflows for Projects A and B are shown in Exhibit 19.3 (assuming that the additional investment at the end of Year 1 is made under either alternative). Notice that Project A is still preferable to Project B—and by the same $12,409.

NPV provides the correct signal for choosing among mutually exclusive investments. At the same time, it measures the impact that competing projects have on the value of the firm. Choosing the project with the largest NPV is consistent with maximizing the wealth of shareholders. On the other hand, IRR does not consistently result in choices that maximize wealth. IRR, as a *relative* measure of profitability, has the virtue of measuring accurately the rate of return of funds that remain internally invested. However, maximizing IRR will not necessarily maximize the wealth of firm owners because it cannot, by nature, consider the absolute dollar contributions of projects. In the final analysis, what counts are the total dollars earned—the absolute profits—not the relative profits. Accordingly, NPV, not IRR, should be used for choosing among competing, mutually exclusive projects, or competing projects when capital funds are limited.

An independent project is acceptable if its NPV is positive. For mutually exclusive projects, the project with the largest NPV is chosen. Selecting the best project from several competing projects involves three steps: (1) assessing the cash flow pattern for each project, (2) computing the NPV for each project, and (3) identifying the project with the greatest NPV. **Example 19.5** illustrates NPV and IRR analysis for mutually exclusive projects.

EXAMPLE 19.5

The HOW and WHY of Determining NPV and IRR for Mutually Exclusive Projects

Information:
Milagro Travel Agency is considering two different computer systems: the Standard T2 System and the Custom Travel System. The projected annual revenues, annual costs, capital outlays, and project life for each system (in after-tax cash flows) are as follows:

EXAMPLE 19.5

(*Continued*)

	Standard T2	Custom Travel
Annual revenues	$240,000	$300,000
Annual operating costs	120,000	160,000
System investment	360,000	420,000
Project life	5 years	5 years

Assume that the cost of capital for the company is 12 percent.

> **Why:**
> Choosing the project with the largest NPV is consistent with wealth maximization. Thus, NPV is recommended for choosing among competing projects.

Required:

1. Calculate the NPV for the Standard T2 System.

2. Calculate the NPV for the Custom Travel System. Which of the two computer systems should be chosen?

3. *What if* the owner of the Milagro Travel Agency wants to know why IRR is not being used for the investment analysis? Calculate the IRR for each project and explain why it is not suitable for choosing among mutually exclusive investments.

Solution:

1.

Standard T2 System: NPV Analysis

Year	Cash Flow	Discount Factor*	Present Value
0	$(360,000)	1.000	$(360,000)
1–5	120,000	3.605	432,600
Net present value			$ 72,600

*From Exhibit 19B.2.

2.

Custom Travel System: NPV Analysis

Year	Cash Flow	Discount Factor*	Present Value
0	$(420,000)	1.000	$(420,000)
1–5	140,000	3.605	504,700
Net present value			$ 84,700

*From Exhibit 19B.2.

The Custom Travel System has the larger NPV and so would be chosen.

3. IRR Analysis:

Standard T2: Discount factor = Initial investment/Annual cash flow
$$= \$360,000/\$120,000$$
$$= 3.0^*$$

Custom Travel: Discount factor = Initial investment/Annual cash flow
$$= \$420,000/\$140,000$$
$$= 3.0^*$$

*From Exhibit 19B.2; $df = 3.0$ implies that IRR ≈ 20 percent.

IRR is a relative measure of profits, and when comparing two competing projects it will not reveal the absolute dollar contributions of the projects and thus will not necessarily lead to choosing the project that maximizes wealth. The IRR is equal for the two computer systems, yet the Custom Travel System is clearly superior as it increases the value of the firm more than the other system.

COMPUTING AFTER-TAX CASH FLOWS

Determining the cash flow pattern for each project being considered is a critical step in capital investment analysis. In fact, the computation of cash flows may be the most critical step in the capital investment process. Erroneous estimates may result in erroneous decisions, regardless of the sophistication of the decision models being used. Two steps are needed to compute cash flows: (1) forecasting revenues, expenses, and capital outlays; and (2) adjusting these gross cash flows for inflation and tax effects. Of the two steps, the more challenging is the first. Forecasting cash flows is technically demanding, and its methodology is typically studied in management science and statistics courses. It is important to understand that estimating future cash flows involves considerable judgment on the part of managers. Once gross cash flows are estimated, they should be adjusted for significant inflationary effects. Finally, straightforward applications of tax law can then be used to compute the after-tax cash flows. At this level of study, we assume that gross cash forecasts are available and focus on adjusting forecasted cash flows to improve their accuracy and utility in capital expenditure analysis.

Conversion of Gross Cash Flows to After-Tax Cash Flows

Assuming that gross cash flows are predicted with the desired degree of accuracy, the analyst must adjust these cash flows for taxes. To analyze tax effects, cash flows are usually broken into three categories: (1) the initial cash outflows needed to acquire the assets of the project, (2) the cash flows produced over the life of the project (operating cash flows), and (3) the cash flows from the final disposal of the project. Cash outflows and cash inflows adjusted for tax effects are called *net* cash outflows and inflows. Net cash flows include provisions for revenues, operating expenses, depreciation, and relevant tax implications. They are the proper inputs for capital investment decisions.

After-Tax Cash Flows: Year 0 The net cash outflow in Year 0 (the initial out-of-pocket outlay) is simply the difference between the initial cost of the project and any cash inflows directly associated with it. The gross cost of the project includes such things as the cost of land, the cost of equipment (including transportation and installation), taxes on gains from the sale of assets, and increases in working capital. Cash inflows occurring at the time of acquisition include tax savings from the sale of assets, cash from the sale of assets, and other tax benefits such as tax credits.

Under current tax law, all costs relating to the acquisition of assets other than land must be capitalized and written off over the useful life of the assets. (The write-off is achieved through depreciation.) Depreciation is deducted from revenues in computing taxable income during each year of the asset's life; however, at the point of acquisition, no depreciation expense is computed. Thus, depreciation is not relevant at Year 0. The principal tax implications at the point of acquisition are related to recognition of gains and losses on the sale of existing assets and to the recognition of any investment tax credits.

Gains on the sale of assets produce additional taxes and, accordingly, reduce the cash proceeds received from the sale of old assets. Losses, on the other hand, are noncash expenses that reduce taxable income, producing tax savings. Consequently, the cash proceeds from the sale of an old asset are increased by the amount of the tax savings.

Adjusting cash inflows and outflows for tax effects requires knowledge of current corporate tax rates. Currently, most corporations face a federal tax rate of 21 percent. State corporate tax rates vary by state. For purposes of analysis, we will assume that 25 percent is the combined rate for state and federal taxes.[6]

Let us look at an example. Currently, Lewis Company uses two types of manufacturing equipment (M1 and M2) to produce one of its products. It is now possible to replace these two

---

6   The average combined state and federal rate is about 25.7 percent. See https://taxfoundation.org/us-corporate
   -income-tax-more-competitive/, accessed July 3, 2020.

machines with a flexible manufacturing system. Management wants to know the net investment needed to acquire the flexible system. If the system is acquired, the old equipment will be sold.

Disposition of Old Machines

	Book Value	Sale Price
M1	$ 600,000	$ 780,000
M2	1,500,000	1,200,000

Acquisition of Flexible System

Purchase cost	$7,500,000
Freight	60,000
Installation	600,000
Additional working capital	540,000
Total	$8,700,000

The net investment can be determined by computing the net proceeds from the sale of the old machines and subtracting those proceeds from the cost of the new system. The net proceeds are determined by computing the tax consequences of the sale and adjusting the gross receipts accordingly.

The tax consequences can be assessed by subtracting the book value from the selling price. If the difference is positive, the firm has experienced a gain and will owe taxes. Money received from the sale will be reduced by the amount of taxes owed. On the other hand, if the difference is negative, a loss is experienced—a noncash loss. However, this noncash loss does have cash implications. It can be deducted from revenues and, as a consequence, can shield revenues from being taxed; accordingly, taxes will be saved. Thus, a loss produces a cash inflow equal to the taxes saved.

To illustrate, consider the tax effects of selling M1 and M2 as illustrated in Exhibit 19.4.

By selling the two machines, the company receives the following net proceeds:

Sale price, M1	$ 780,000
Sale price, M2	1,200,000
Tax savings	48,000
Net proceeds	$2,028,000

Given these net proceeds, the net investment can be computed as follows:

Total cost of flexible system	$8,700,000
Less: Net proceeds of old machines	2,028,000
Net investment (cash outflow)	$6,672,000

Asset	Gain (Loss)
M1[a]	$ 180,000
M2[b]	(300,000)
Net gain (loss)	$ (120,000)
Tax rate	× 0.25
Tax savings	$ 30,000

Exhibit 19.4

Tax Effects of the Sale of M1 and M2

[a]Sale price minus book value is $780,000 − $600,000.
[b]Sale price minus book value is $1,200,000 − $1,500,000.

After-Tax Operating Cash Flows: Life of the Project In addition to determining the initial out-of-pocket outlay, managers must also estimate the annual after-tax operating cash flows expected over the life of the project. If the project generates revenue, the principal source of cash flows is from operations. Operating cash inflows can be assessed from the project's income statement. The annual after-tax cash flows are the sum of the project's after-tax profits and its noncash expenses. In terms of a simple formula, this computation can be represented as follows:

$$\text{After-tax cash flow} = \text{After-tax net income} + \text{Noncash expenses}$$
$$CF = NI + NC$$

The most prominent examples of noncash expenses are depreciation and losses. At first glance, it may seem odd that after-tax cash flows are computed using noncash expenses. Noncash expenses are not cash flows, but they do generate cash flows by reducing taxes.

The income approach to determine operating cash flows can be decomposed to assess the after-tax, cash flow effects of each individual item on the income statement. The decomposition approach calculates the operating cash flows by computing the after-tax cash flows for each item of the income statement as follows:

$$CF = [(1 - \text{Tax rate}) \times \text{Revenues}] - [(1 - \text{Tax rate}) \times \text{Cash expenses}]$$
$$+ (\text{Tax rate} \times \text{Noncash expenses})$$

The first term, $[(1 - \text{Tax rate}) \times \text{Revenues}]$, gives the after-tax cash inflows from cash revenues. The second term, $[(1 - \text{Tax rate}) \times \text{Cash expenses}]$, is the after-tax cash outflows from cash operating expenses. Because cash expenses can be deducted from revenues to arrive at taxable income, the effect is to shield revenues from taxation. The consequence of this shielding is to save taxes and to reduce the actual cash outflow associated with a given expenditure. The third term, $(\text{Tax rate} \times \text{Noncash expenses})$, is the cash inflow from the tax savings produced by the noncash expenses. Noncash expenses, such as depreciation, also shield revenues from taxation and thus create a *tax savings*. **Example 19.6** illustrates the use of the income and decomposition approaches for calculating after-tax cash flows.

EXAMPLE 19.6

The HOW and WHY of Calculating After-Tax Cash Flows

Information:
A company plans to make a new product that requires new equipment costing $1,600,000. Both the product and equipment have a life of four years. The equipment will be depreciated on a straight-line basis, with no expected salvage value. The annual income statement for the product is given below.

Revenues	$1,200,000
Less: Cash operating expenses	(500,000)
Depreciation	(400,000)
Income before income taxes	$ 300,000
Less: Income taxes (@ 25%)	75,000
Net income	$ 225,000

Why:
It is often convenient to calculate the after-tax cash flows for each item on the income statement. Adding the after-tax cash flows for each item yields the same results as the income approach.

EXAMPLE 19.6

(Continued)

Required:

1. Using the income approach, calculate the after-tax cash flows.

2. Using the decomposition approach, calculate the after-tax cash flows for each item of the income statement and show that the total is the same as the income approach.

3. *What if* it is desirable to express the decomposition approach in a spreadsheet format for the four years to facilitate the use of spreadsheet software packages? Express the decomposition approach in a spreadsheet format, with a column for each income item and a total column.

Solution:

1. $CF = NI + NC = \$225,000 + \$400,000 = \$625,000$

2.

$(1 - t) \times$ Revenue $= (1 - 0.25) \times \$1,200,000$	$\$900,000$	
$(1 - t) \times$ Cash expenses $= (1 - 0.25) \times \$(500,000)$	$(375,000)$	
$t \times$ Depreciation $= 0.25 \times \$400,000$	$\underline{100,000}$	
Operating cash flow	$\underline{\$625,000}$	

3.

Year	$(1-t)R^a$	$-(1-t)C^b$	tNC^c	CF
1	$\$900,000$	$\$(375,000)$	$\$100,000$	$\$625,000$
2	$900,000$	$(375,000)$	$100,000$	$625,000$
3	$900,000$	$(375,000)$	$100,000$	$625,000$
4	$900,000$	$(375,000)$	$100,000$	$625,000$

$^a R =$ Revenue.
$^b C =$ Cash operating expenses.
$^c NC =$ Noncash operating expenses.

MACRS Depreciation

For tax purposes, all depreciable business assets other than real estate are referred to as *personal property*, which is classified into one of six classes. Each class specifies the life of the assets that must be used for figuring depreciation. This life must be used even if the actual expected life is different from the class life; the class lives are set for purposes of recognizing depreciation and usually will be shorter than the actual life. Most equipment, machinery, and office furniture are classified as **seven-year assets**. Light trucks, automobiles, and computer equipment are classified as **five-year assets**. Most small tools are classified as **three-year assets**. Because the majority of personal property can be put into one of these categories, we will restrict our attention to them.

The taxpayer can use either the straight-line method or the **modified accelerated cost recovery system (MACRS)** to compute annual depreciation. Current law defines MACRS as the double-declining-balance method.[7] In computing depreciation, no consideration of salvage value is required. However, under either method, a **half-year convention** applies.[8] This convention assumes that a newly acquired asset is in service for one-half of its first taxable year of service, regardless of the date that use of the asset actually began. When the asset reaches the end of its life, the other half-year of depreciation can be claimed in the following year. If an asset is disposed of before the end of its class life, the half-year convention allows half the depreciation for that year.

---

7 The tax law also allows the 150-percent-declining-balance method; however, we will focus only on the straight-line method and the double-declining version of MACRS.

8 The tax law requires a mid-quarter convention if more than 40 percent of personal property is placed in service during the last three months of the year. We will not illustrate this scenario.

For example, assume that an automobile is purchased on March 1, 20x4. The automobile costs $30,000, and the firm elects the straight-line method. Automobiles are five-year assets (for tax purposes). The annual depreciation is $6,000 for a five-year period ($30,000/5). Using the half-year convention, however, the firm can deduct only $3,000 for 2014, half of the straight-line amount (0.5 × $6,000). The remaining half is deducted in the sixth year (or the year of disposal, if earlier). Deductions are as follows:

Year	Depreciation Deduction
20x4	$3,000 (half-year amount)
20x5	6,000
20x6	6,000
20x7	6,000
20x8	6,000
20x9	3,000 (half-year amount)

Assume that the asset is disposed of in April 20x6. In this case, only $3,000 of depreciation can be claimed for 20x6 (early disposal rule).

If the double-declining-balance method is selected, the amount of depreciation claimed in the first year is twice that of the straight-line method. Under this method, the amount of depreciation claimed becomes progressively smaller until eventually it is exceeded by that claimed under the straight-line method. When this happens, the straight-line method is used to finish depreciating the asset. Exhibit 19.5 provides a table of depreciation rates for the double-declining-balance method for assets belonging to the three-year, five-year, and seven-year classes. The rates shown in this table incorporate the half-year convention and therefore are the MACRS depreciation rates.

Both the straight-line and double-declining-balance methods yield the same total amount of depreciation over the life of the asset. Both methods also produce the same total tax savings (assuming the same tax rate over the life of the asset). Since the depreciation claimed in the early years of a project is greater using the double-declining-balance method, however, the tax savings are also greater during those years. Considering the time value of money, it is preferable to have the tax savings earlier rather than later. Thus, firms should prefer the MACRS method of depreciation to the straight-line method. This conclusion is illustrated by the following example.

A firm is considering the purchase of computer equipment for $60,000. The tax guidelines require that the cost of the equipment be depreciated over five years. However, tax guidelines also permit the depreciation to be computed using either the straight-line or double-declining-balance method. Of course, the firm should choose the double-declining-balance method because it brings the greater benefit.

From decomposition, we know that the cash inflows caused by shielding can be computed by multiplying the tax rate by the amount depreciated ($t \times NC$). The cash flows produced by each depreciation method and its present value, assuming a discount rate of 10 percent, are given in Exhibit 19.6. As you will see, the present value of the tax savings from using MACRS is greater than the present value realized using straight-line depreciation.

Exhibit 19.5

MACRS Depreciation Rates

Year	Three-Year Assets	Five-Year Assets	Seven-Year Assets
1	33.33%	20.00%	14.29%
2	44.45	32.00	24.49
3	14.81	19.20	17.49
4	7.41	11.52	12.49
5		11.52	8.93
6		5.76	8.92
7		—	8.93
8		—	4.46

Straight-Line Method

Year	Depreciation	Tax Rate	Tax Savings	Discount Factor	Present Value
1	$ 6,000	0.25	$1,500.00	0.909	$ 1,363.50
2	12,000	0.25	3,000.00	0.826	2,478.00
3	12,000	0.25	3,000.00	0.751	2,253.00
4	12,000	0.25	3,000.00	0.683	2,049.00
5	12,000	0.25	3,000.00	0.621	1,863.80
6	6,000	0.25	1,500.00	0.564	846
Net present value					$10,852.50

MACRS Method

Year	Depreciation*	Tax Rate	Tax Savings	Discount Factor	Present Value
1	$12,000	0.25	$3,000.00	0.909	$ 2,727.20
2	19,200	0.25	4,800.00	0.826	3,964.80
3	11,520	0.25	2,880.00	0.751	2,162.88
4	6,912	0.25	1,728.80	0.683	1,180.22
5	6,912	0.25	1,728.80	0.621	1,073.09
6	3,456	0.25	864.00	0.564	487.30
Net present value					$11,595.29

Exhibit 19.6

Value of Accelerated Methods Illustrated

*Computed by multiplying the five-year rates in Exhibit 19.5 by $60,000. For example, depreciation for Year 1 is 0.20 × $60,000.

After-Tax Cash Flows: Final Disposal At the end of the life of the project, there are two major sources of cash: (1) release of working capital, and (2) preparation, removal, and sale of the equipment (salvage value effects). Any working capital committed to a project is released at this point. The release of working capital is a cash inflow with no tax consequences. Thus, if $180,000 of additional working capital is needed at the beginning of a project, this $180,000 will be a cash inflow at the end of the project's life. Disposing of an asset associated with a project also has cash consequences. At times, an asset may have a market value at the end of its life. The selling price less the costs of removal and cleanup produces a gross cash inflow. For example, if an asset has a selling price of $120,000 and if its removal and cleanup costs are $30,000, then the gross cash inflow is $90,000. The tax effects of the transaction must also be assessed. If, for example, the book value of the asset is $15,000, then the firm must recognize a $75,000 gain on the sale of the asset ($90,000 – $15,000). If the tax rate is 0.25 percent, then the cash inflow from disposition is reduced by $18,750 ($75,000 × 0.25). Therefore, the expected cash inflow at the end of the project's life is $71,250 ($90,000 – 18,750).

CAPITAL INVESTMENT: ADVANCED TECHNOLOGY AND ENVIRONMENTAL CONSIDERATIONS

OBJECTIVE ◀ 7

Describe capital investment for advanced technology and environmental impact settings.

In today's manufacturing environment, long-term investments in advanced technology and in pollution prevention (P2) technology can be the sources of a significant competitive advantage. Investing in advanced manufacturing technology such as robotics and computer-integrated manufacturing can improve quality, increase flexibility and reliability, and decrease lead times.

As a consequence, customer satisfaction will likely increase, which will then produce an increase in market share. Likewise, P2 opportunities are now beginning to attract the attention of management. P2 takes a proactive approach that targets the causes of pollution rather than the consequences. It often calls for the redesign of complex products and processes and investment in new technologies. The potential for a competitive advantage stems from the possibility that a firm can eliminate the pollutants at their source and, thus, avoid the need for treating or disposing of these pollutants later on. This will then reduce environmental costs. The argument is that the reduction in environmental costs will produce positive net present values.

REAL-WORLD EXAMPLE

Vought Aircarft Industries, Inc., manufactures commercial and military components. The company uses autoclaves to cure composite aircraft components. High temperatures are needed, and city water is used to periodically cool the autoclaves. The cooling water was subsequently discharged to a stormwater outfall. Vought made the decision to invest in a new autoclave with a new cooling tower. The cooling tower allowed the water to be continually recycled. The new autoclave and new cooling tower produced $68,000 of annual savings in city water costs. Each autoclave now saves approximately 14 million gallons of water per year; moreover, the facility no longer discharges water to the stormwater outfall.[9]

Although discounted cash flow analysis (using net present value and internal rate of return) remains preeminent in capital investment decisions involving advanced technology or P2 opportunities, more attention must be paid to the inputs used in discounted cash flow models. How investment is defined, how operating cash flows are estimated, how salvage value is treated, and how the discount rate is chosen are all different in nature from the traditional approach.

How Investment Differs

Investment in automated manufacturing processes is much more complex than investment in the standard manufacturing equipment of the past. For standard equipment, the direct costs of acquisition represent virtually the entire investment. For automated manufacturing, the direct costs can represent as little as 50 or 60 percent of the total investment; software, engineering, training, and implementation are a significant percentage of the total costs. Thus, great care must be exercised to assess the actual cost of an automated system. It is easy to overlook the peripheral costs, which can be substantial. The reason is that there are often very large investments to be made in training. Until companies have experience with the technology, they are unable to adequately use its power and improve productivity. Similar comments can be made about P2 investments. P2 investments may involve radical new technology, and indirect costs can be substantial as well.

How Estimates of Operating Cash Flows Differ

Estimates of operating cash flows from investments in standard equipment have typically relied on directly identifiable tangible benefits, such as direct savings from labor, power, and scrap. Similarly, environmental investments in end-of-pipe emissions control have relied on the direct environmental cost savings (e.g., reductions in the costs of waste management and regulatory compliance). In reality, many environmental costs are hidden within other costs. Some are buried in overhead (e.g., the portion of maintenance cost attributable to maintaining equipment associated with end-of-pipe emissions control). Intangible benefits and indirect savings are ignored as they often are in traditional capital investment analyses; however, the intangible

---

9 Tennessee Pollution Prevention Partnership Success Story, "Installation of Cooling Towers for Autoclaves," (May 2010), http://tn.gov/environment/ea/tp3/documents/tp3_ss-vought-10lw.pdf, accessed December 21, 2011.

and indirect benefits can be material and critical to the viability of the project. Greater quality, more reliability, reduced lead time, improved customer satisfaction, and an enhanced ability to maintain market share are all important intangible benefits of an advanced manufacturing system. Reduction of labor in support areas such as production scheduling and stores are indirect benefits. More effort is needed to measure these intangible and indirect benefits in order to assess more accurately the potential value of investments. New automated systems, for example, may produce large savings in terms of reduced waste, lower inventories, increased quality, and reduced indirect labor. Direct labor savings alone may not be sufficient to justify the investment. These concerns illustrate the importance of a *postaudit*. A **postaudit** is a follow-up analysis of a capital project once it is implemented. It compares the actual benefits and costs with the estimated benefits and costs. Postaudits can reveal the importance of intangible and indirect benefits. In future investment decisions, these factors are more likely to be considered.

Big Data

According to a report by the McKinsey Global Institute, big data is becoming a major factor in competition and growth for business organizations and a potential source of increased efficiency for government organizations. However, to capture the value of big data, organizations must invest in new technologies such as storage, computing, and analytical software. Investing in big data promises multiple ways of creating value. Specifically, big data creates value by: (1) making information more transparent and usable; (2) providing more accurate and detailed performance information; (3) identifying more narrow segmentation of customers, thus allowing more precisely tailored products or services; (4) improving decision making by using sophisticated analytics; and (5) improving the development of new products and services.[10]

Clearly, because of value-creating steps 3 through 5, better capital investment decisions in advanced technologies, new products, and new services would be expected. Furthermore, value-creating steps 1 and 2 promise much more sophisticated postaudit capabilities for capital projects.

REAL-WORLD EXAMPLE

An Example: Investing in Advanced Technology

An example can be used to illustrate the importance of considering intangible and indirect benefits. Consider a company that is evaluating a potential investment in a flexible manufacturing system (FMS). The choice facing the company is to continue producing with its traditional equipment, expected to last 10 years, or to switch to the new system, which is also expected to have a useful life of 10 years. The company's discount rate is 12 percent. The data pertaining to the investment are presented in Exhibit 19.7. Using these data, the net present value of the proposed system can be computed as follows:

Present value ($4,000,000 × 5.65*)	$22,600,000
Less: Investment	18,000,000
Net present value	$ 4,600,000

*Discount factor for an interest rate of 12 percent and a life of 10 years (see Exhibit 19B.2).

---

10 James Manyika, Michael Chui, Brad Brown, Jacques Bughin, Richard Dobbs, Charles Roxburgh, and Angela Hung Byers, "Big Data: The Next Frontier for Innovation, Competition, and Productivity," Report, McKinsey Global Institute, May 2011, http://www.mckinsey.com/business-functions/business-technology/our-insights/big-data-the-next-frontier-for-innovation, accessed July 1, 2016.

Exhibit 19.7

Investment Data: Direct, Intangible, and Indirect Benefits

	FMS	Status Quo
Investment (current outlay):		
Direct costs	$10,000,000	$ 0
Software, engineering	8,000,000	—
Total current outlay	$18,000,000	$ 0
Net after-tax cash flow	$ 5,000,000	$1,000,000
Less: After-tax cash flow for status quo	1,000,000	n/a
Incremental benefit	$ 4,000,000	n/a
Incremental Benefit Explained		
Direct benefits:		
Direct labor	$1,500,000	
Scrap reduction	500,000	
Setups	200,000	$2,200,000
Intangible benefits: Quality savings		
Rework	$ 200,000	
Warranties	400,000	
Maintenance of competitive position	1,000,000	1,600,000
Indirect benefits:		
Production scheduling	$ 110,000	
Payroll	90,000	200,000
Total		$4,000,000

The net present value is positive and large in magnitude, and it clearly signals the acceptability of the FMS. This outcome is strongly dependent, however, on explicit recognition of both intangible and indirect benefits. If those benefits are eliminated, then the direct savings total $2.2 million, and the NPV is negative.

Present value ($2,200,000 × 5.65)	$12,430,000
Less: Investment	18,000,000
Net present value	$ (5,570,000)

The rise of activity-based costing has made identifying indirect benefits easier with the use of activity drivers. Once they are identified, they can be included in the analysis if they are material.

Examination of Exhibit 19.7 reveals the importance of intangible benefits. One of the most important intangible benefits is maintaining or improving a firm's competitive position. A key question that needs to be asked is what will happen to the cash flows of the firm if the investment is *not* made. That is, if the company chooses to forgo an investment in technologically advanced equipment, will it be able to continue to compete with other firms on the basis of quality, delivery, and cost? (The question becomes especially relevant if competitors choose to invest in advanced equipment.) If the competitive position deteriorates, the company's current cash flows will decrease.

If cash flows decrease if the investment is not made, this decrease should show up as an incremental benefit for the advanced technology. In Exhibit 19.7, the company estimates this competitive benefit as $1,000,000. Estimating this benefit requires some serious strategic planning and analysis, but its effect can be critical. If this benefit had been ignored or overlooked, then the net present value would have been negative, and the investment alternative rejected. This calculation is as follows:

Present value ($3,000,000 × 5.65)	$16,950,000
Less: Investment	18,000,000
Net present value	$ (1,050,000)

Salvage Value

Terminal or salvage value has often been ignored in investment decisions. The usual reason offered is the difficulty in estimating it. Because of this uncertainty, the effect of salvage value has often been ignored or heavily discounted. This approach may be unwise, however, because salvage value could make the difference between investing or not investing. Given the highly competitive environment, companies cannot afford to make incorrect decisions. A much better approach to deal with uncertainty is to use sensitivity analysis. **Sensitivity analysis** changes the assumptions on which the capital investment analysis relies and assesses the effect on the cash flow pattern. Sensitivity analysis is often referred to as **what-if analysis**. For example, this approach is used to address such questions as *what* is the effect on the decision to invest in a project *if* the cash receipts are 5 percent less than projected? 5 percent more? Although sensitivity analysis is computationally demanding if done manually, it can be done rapidly and easily using a software package such as Excel°. In fact, Excel and similar packages can be used to carry out the NPV and IRR computations that have been illustrated manually throughout the chapter. They have built-in NPV and IRR functions that greatly facilitate the computational requirements.

To illustrate the potential effect of terminal value, assume that the after-tax annual operating cash flow of the project shown in Exhibit 19.7 is $3.1 million instead of $4 million. The net present value without salvage value is as follows:

Present value ($3,100,000 × 5.65)	$17,515,000
Less: Investment	18,000,000
Net present value	$ (485,000)

Without the terminal value, the project would be rejected. The net present value with salvage value of $2 million, however, is a positive result, meaning that the investment should be made.

Present value ($3,100,000 × 5.65)	$17,515,000
Present value ($2,000,000 × 0.322*)	644,000
Less: Investment	(18,000,000)
Net present value	$ 159,000

*Discount factor for an interest rate of 12 percent and a life of 10 years (see Exhibit 19B.1).

But what if the salvage value is less than expected? Suppose that the worst possible outcome is a salvage value of $1,600,000? What is the effect on the decision? The NPV can be recomputed under this new scenario.

Present value ($3,100,000 × 5.65)	$17,515,000
Present value ($1,600,000 × 0.322)	515,200
Less: Investment	(18,000,000)
Net present value	$ 30,200

Thus, under a pessimistic scenario, the NPV is still positive. This illustrates how sensitivity analysis can be used to deal with the uncertainty surrounding salvage value. It can also be used for other cash flow variables.

Discount Rates

Being overly conservative with discount rates can prove even more damaging. In theory, if future cash flows are known with certainty, the correct discount rate is a firm's cost of capital. In practice, future cash flows are uncertain, and managers often choose a discount rate higher than the cost of capital to deal with that uncertainty. If the rate chosen is excessively high, it will bias the selection process toward short-term investments.

To illustrate the effect of an excessive discount rate, consider the project in Exhibit 19.7 once again. Assume that the correct discount rate is 12 percent but that the firm uses 18 percent. The net present value using an 18 percent discount rate is calculated as follows:

Present value ($4,000,000 × 4.494*)	$17,976,000
Less: Investment	18,000,000
Net present value	$ (24,000)

*Discount rate for an interest rate of 18 percent and a life of 10 years (see Exhibit 19B.2).

The project would be rejected. With a higher discount rate, the discount factor decreases in magnitude much more rapidly than the discount factor for a lower rate. (Compare the discount factor for 12 percent, 5.65, with the factor for 18 percent, 4.494.) The effect of a higher discount factor is to place more weight on earlier cash flows and less weight on later cash flows, which favors short-term over long-term investments. This outcome makes it more difficult for automated manufacturing systems to appear as viable projects, since the cash returns required to justify the investment are received over a longer period of time. The same problem exists with P2 projects.

SUMMARY OF LEARNING OBJECTIVES

LO1. Describe the difference between independent and mutually exclusive capital investment decisions.
- The two types of capital investment projects are independent and mutually exclusive.
- Independent projects are projects that, if accepted or rejected, do not affect the cash flows of other projects.
- Mutually exclusive projects are those projects that, if accepted, preclude the acceptance of all other competing projects.

LO2. Explain the roles of the payback period and accounting rate of return in capital investment decisions.
- Two nondiscounting models are the payback period and the accounting rate of return.
- The payback period is the time required for a firm to recover its initial investment.
- The payback period is useful in assessing and controlling risk, minimizing the impact of an investment on a firm's liquidity, and controlling the risk of obsolescence.
- The accounting rate of return is computed by dividing the average income expected from an investment by the original investment.
- The accounting rate of return does consider the profitability of a project; however, it ignores the time value of money.
- The accounting rate of return may be useful to managers to screen new investments to ensure that certain accounting ratios are not adversely affected.

LO3. Calculate the net present value (NPV) for independent projects.
- NPV is the difference between the present value of future cash flows and the initial investment outlay.
- To use the model, a required rate of return must be identified (usually, the cost of capital). The required rate of return is used to calculate the present value of future cash flows.
- If the NPV > 0, then the investment is acceptable.

LO4. Compute the internal rate of return (IRR) for independent projects.
- The IRR is computed by finding the interest rate that equates the present value of a project's cash inflows with the present value of its cash outflows.
- If IRR is greater than the cost of capital, then the investment is acceptable.

LO5. Explain why NPV is better than IRR for choosing among mutually exclusive projects.
- NPV measures the increase in a firm's wealth caused by a project. Thus, choosing the project that increases wealth the most makes sense.
- IRR sometimes will signal that one project is better than a second, even though the second increases wealth more.
- NPV consistently provides the correct signal when choosing among competing projects and is preferred to IRR.

LO6. Convert gross cash flows to after-tax cash flows.
- Accurate and reliable cash flow forecasts are absolutely critical for capital budgeting analyses.
- All cash flows in a capital investment analysis should be after-tax cash flows.
- There are two different, but equivalent, ways to compute after-tax cash flows: the income method and the decomposition method.
- Although depreciation is not a cash flow, it does have cash flow implications because tax laws allow depreciation to be deducted in computing taxable income.
- Accelerated methods of depreciation are preferred because of the tax benefits created.

LO7. Describe capital investment for advanced technology and environmental impact settings.
- Capital investment in advanced technology and P2 projects is affected by the way in which inputs are determined.
- Much greater attention must be paid to the investment outlays because peripheral items can require substantial resources.
- In assessing benefits, intangible items such as product quality, environmental quality, and maintaining competitive position can be deciding factors.
- Choice of the required rate of return is also critical. The tendency of firms to use hurdle rates that are much greater than the cost of capital should be discontinued.
- Since the salvage value of an automated system can be considerable, it should be estimated and included in the analysis.

EXAMPLE 19.1	The HOW and WHY of Calculating the Payback Period, page 976
EXAMPLE 19.2	The HOW and WHY of Calculating the Accounting Rate of Return, page 978
EXAMPLE 19.3	The HOW and WHY of Analyzing NPV, page 979
EXAMPLE 19.4	The HOW and WHY of Calculating the Internal Rate of Return, page 981
EXAMPLE 19.5	The HOW and WHY of Determining NPV and IRR for Mutually Exclusive Projects, page 984
EXAMPLE 19.6	The HOW and WHY of Calculating After-Tax Cash Flows, page 988

KEY TERMS

Accounting rate of return (ARR), 977

Annuity, 1000

Capital budgeting, 974

Capital investment decisions, 974

Compounding of interest, 998

Cost of capital, 979

Discount factor, 999

Discount rate, 999

Discounted cash flows, 978

Discounting, 999

Discounting models, 975

Five-year assets, 989

Future value, 998

Half-year convention, 989

Independent projects, 974

Internal rate of return (IRR), 981

Modified accelerated cost recovery system (MACRS), 989

Mutually exclusive projects, 975

Net present value (NPV), 979

Nondiscounting models, 975

Payback period, 976

Postaudit, 993

Present value, 998

Required rate of return, 979

Sensitivity analysis, 995

Seven-year assets, 989

Three-year assets, 989

What-if analysis, 995

APPENDIX A: PRESENT VALUE CONCEPTS

An important feature of money is that it can be invested and can earn interest. A dollar today is not the same as a dollar tomorrow. This fundamental principle is the backbone of discounting methods. Discounting methods rely on the relationships between current and future dollars. Thus, to use discounting methods, we must understand these relationships.

Future Value

Suppose a bank advertises a 4 percent annual interest rate. If a customer invests $100, he or she would receive, after one year, the original $100 plus $4 interest [$100 + (0.04 × $100) = (1 + 0.04) × $100 = 1.04 × $100 = $104]. This result can be expressed by the following equation, where F is the future amount, P is the initial or current outlay, and i is the interest rate:

$$F = P(1 + i) \qquad (19A.1)$$

For the example, $F = \$100 \times (1 + 0.04) = \$100 \times 1.04 = \$104$.

Now suppose that the same bank offers a 5 percent rate if the customer leaves the original deposit, plus any interest, on deposit for a total of two years. How much will the customer receive at the end of two years? Again, assume that a customer invests $100. Using Equation 19A.1, the customer will earn $105 at the end of Year 1 [$F = \$100 \times (1 + 0.05) = \$100 \times 1.05 = \$105$]. If this amount is left in the account for a second year, Equation 19A.1 is used again with P now assumed to be $105. At the end of the second year, then, the total is $110.25 [$F = \$105 \times (1 + 0.05) = \$105 \times 1.05 = \$110.25$]. In the second year, interest is earned on both the original deposit and the interest earned in the first year. The earning of interest on interest is referred to as **compounding of interest**. The value that will accumulate by the end of an investment's life, assuming a specified compound return, is the **future value**. The future value of the $100 deposit in the second example is $110.25.

A more direct way to compute the future value is possible. Since the first application of Equation 19A.1 can be expressed as $F = \$105 = \$100 \times 1.05$, the second application can be expressed as $F = \$105 \times 1.05 = \$100 \times 1.05 \times 1.05 = \$100(1.05)^2 = P(1 + i)^2$. This suggests the following formula for computing amounts for n periods into the future:

$$F = P(1 + i)^n \qquad (19A.2)$$

Present Value

Often, a manager needs to compute not the future value but the amount that must be invested *now* in order to earn some given future value. The amount that must be invested now to produce the future value is known as the **present value** of the future amount. For example, how much must be invested now in order to earn $363 two years from now, assuming that the interest rate is 10 percent? Or, put another way, what is the present value of $363 to be received two years from now?

Year	Cash Receipt	Discount Factor	Present Value*
1	$110.00	0.909	$100.00
2	121.00	0.826	100.00
3	133.10	0.751	100.00
			$300.00

Exhibit 19A.1

Present Value of an Uneven Series of Cash Flows

*Rounded.

In this example, the future value, the years, and the interest rate are all known; we want to know the current outlay that will produce that future amount. In Equation 19A.2, the variable representing the current outlay (the present value of F) is P. Thus, to compute the present value of a future outlay, all we need to do is solve Equation 19A.2 for P:

$$P = F/(1 + i)^t \qquad (19A.3)$$

Using Equation 19A.3, we can compute the present value of $363:

$$P = \$363/(1 + 0.1)^2$$
$$= \$363/1.21$$
$$= \$300$$

The present value, $300, is what the future amount of $363 is worth *today*. All other things being equal, having $300 today is the same as having $363 two years from now. Put another way, if a firm requires a 10 percent rate of return, the most the firm would be willing to pay today is $300 for any investment that yields $363 two years from now.

The process of computing the present value of future cash flows is often referred to as **discounting**; thus, we say that we have discounted the future value of $363 to its present value of $300. The interest rate used to discount the future cash flow is the **discount rate**.

The expression $1/(1 + i)^n$ in Equation 19A.3 is the **discount factor**. By letting the discount factor, called df, equal $1/(1 + i)^n$, Equation 19A.3 can be expressed as $P = F(df)$. To simplify the computation of present value, a table of discount factors is given for various combinations of i and n (see Exhibit 19B.1 in Appendix B). For example, the discount factor for $i = 10$ percent and $n = 2$ is 0.826. (Simply go to the 10 percent column of the table and move down to the second row.) With the discount factor, the present value of $363 is computed as follows:

$$P = F(df)$$
$$= \$363 \times 0.826$$
$$= \$300 \text{ (rounded)}$$

Year	Cash Receipt	Discount Factor	Present Value
1	$100	0.909	$ 90.90
2	100	0.826	82.60
3	100	0.751	75.10
		2.486	$248.60

Exhibit 19A.2

Present Value of a Uniform Series of Cash Flows

Note: The annual cash flow of $100 can be multiplied by the sum of the discount factors (2.486) to obtain the present value of the uniform series ($248.60).

Present Value of an Uneven Series of Cash Flows

Exhibit 19B.1 can be used to compute the present value of any future cash flow or series of future cash flows. A series of future cash flows is called an **annuity**. The present value of an annuity is found by computing the present value of each future cash flow and then summing these values. For example, suppose that an investment is expected to produce the following annual cash flows: $110, $121, and $133.10. Assuming a discount rate of 10 percent, the present value of this series of cash flows is computed in Exhibit 19A.1.

Present Value of a Uniform Series of Cash Flows

If the series of cash flows is even, the computation of the annuity's present value is simplified. Assume, for example, that an investment is expected to return $100 per year for three years. Using Exhibit 19B.1 and assuming a discount rate of 10 percent, the present value of the annuity is computed in Exhibit 19A.2.

As with the uneven series of cash flows, the present value in Exhibit 19A.2 was computed by calculating the present value of each cash flow separately and then summing them. However, in the case of an annuity displaying uniform cash flows, the computations can be reduced from three to one as described in the note to the exhibit. The sum of the individual discount factors can be thought of as a discount factor for an annuity of uniform cash flows. A table of discount factors that can be used for an annuity of uniform cash flows is available in Exhibit 19B.2 in Appendix B.

APPENDIX B: PRESENT VALUE TABLES

Exhibit 19B.1 Present Value of $1*

Periods	2%	4%	6%	8%	10%	12%	14%	16%	18%	20%	22%	24%	26%	28%	30%	32%	40%
1	0.980	0.962	0.943	0.926	0.909	0.893	0.877	0.862	0.847	0.833	0.820	0.806	0.794	0.781	0.769	0.758	0.714
2	0.961	0.925	0.890	0.857	0.826	0.797	0.769	0.743	0.718	0.694	0.672	0.650	0.630	0.610	0.592	0.574	0.510
3	0.942	0.889	0.840	0.794	0.751	0.712	0.675	0.641	0.609	0.579	0.551	0.524	0.500	0.477	0.455	0.435	0.364
4	0.924	0.855	0.792	0.735	0.683	0.636	0.592	0.552	0.516	0.482	0.451	0.423	0.397	0.373	0.350	0.329	0.260
5	0.906	0.822	0.747	0.681	0.621	0.567	0.519	0.476	0.437	0.402	0.370	0.341	0.315	0.291	0.269	0.250	0.186
6	0.888	0.790	0.705	0.636	0.564	0.507	0.456	0.410	0.370	0.335	0.303	0.275	0.250	0.227	0.207	0.189	0.133
7	0.871	0.760	0.665	0.583	0.513	0.452	0.400	0.354	0.314	0.279	0.249	0.222	0.198	0.178	0.159	0.143	0.095
8	0.853	0.731	0.627	0.540	0.467	0.404	0.351	0.305	0.266	0.233	0.204	0.179	0.157	0.139	0.123	0.108	0.068
9	0.837	0.703	0.592	0.500	0.424	0.361	0.308	0.263	0.225	0.194	0.167	0.144	0.125	0.108	0.094	0.082	0.048
10	0.820	0.676	0.558	0.463	0.386	0.322	0.270	0.227	0.191	0.162	0.137	0.116	0.099	0.085	0.073	0.062	0.035
11	0.804	0.650	0.527	0.429	0.350	0.287	0.237	0.195	0.162	0.135	0.112	0.094	0.079	0.066	0.056	0.046	0.025
12	0.788	0.625	0.497	0.397	0.319	0.257	0.208	0.168	0.137	0.112	0.092	0.076	0.062	0.052	0.043	0.036	0.018
13	0.773	0.601	0.469	0.368	0.290	0.229	0.182	0.145	0.116	0.093	0.075	0.061	0.050	0.040	0.033	0.027	0.013
14	0.758	0.577	0.442	0.340	0.263	0.205	0.160	0.125	0.099	0.078	0.062	0.049	0.039	0.032	0.025	0.021	0.009
15	0.743	0.555	0.417	0.315	0.239	0.183	0.140	0.108	0.084	0.065	0.051	0.040	0.031	0.025	0.020	0.016	0.006
16	0.728	0.534	0.394	0.292	0.218	0.163	0.123	0.093	0.071	0.054	0.042	0.032	0.025	0.019	0.015	0.012	0.005
17	0.714	0.513	0.371	0.270	0.198	0.146	0.108	0.080	0.060	0.045	0.034	0.026	0.020	0.015	0.012	0.009	0.003
18	0.700	0.494	0.350	0.250	0.180	0.130	0.095	0.069	0.051	0.038	0.028	0.021	0.016	0.012	0.009	0.007	0.002
19	0.686	0.475	0.331	0.232	0.164	0.116	0.083	0.060	0.043	0.031	0.023	0.017	0.012	0.009	0.007	0.005	0.002
20	0.673	0.456	0.312	0.215	0.149	0.104	0.073	0.051	0.037	0.026	0.019	0.014	0.010	0.007	0.005	0.004	0.001
21	0.660	0.439	0.294	0.199	0.135	0.093	0.064	0.044	0.031	0.022	0.015	0.011	0.008	0.006	0.004	0.003	0.001
22	0.647	0.422	0.278	0.184	0.123	0.083	0.056	0.038	0.026	0.018	0.013	0.009	0.006	0.004	0.003	0.002	0.001
23	0.634	0.406	0.262	0.170	0.112	0.074	0.049	0.033	0.022	0.015	0.010	0.007	0.005	0.003	0.002	0.002	0.000
24	0.622	0.390	0.247	0.158	0.102	0.066	0.043	0.028	0.019	0.013	0.008	0.006	0.004	0.003	0.002	0.002	0.000
25	0.610	0.375	0.233	0.146	0.092	0.059	0.038	0.024	0.016	0.010	0.007	0.005	0.003	0.002	0.001	0.001	0.000
26	0.598	0.361	0.220	0.135	0.084	0.053	0.033	0.021	0.014	0.009	0.006	0.004	0.002	0.002	0.001	0.001	0.000
27	0.586	0.347	0.207	0.125	0.076	0.047	0.029	0.018	0.011	0.007	0.005	0.003	0.002	0.001	0.001	0.001	0.000
28	0.574	0.333	0.196	0.116	0.069	0.042	0.026	0.016	0.010	0.006	0.004	0.002	0.002	0.001	0.001	0.000	0.000
29	0.563	0.321	0.185	0.107	0.063	0.037	0.022	0.014	0.008	0.005	0.003	0.002	0.001	0.001	0.000	0.000	0.000
30	0.552	0.308	0.174	0.099	0.057	0.033	0.020	0.012	0.007	0.004	0.003	0.002	0.001	0.001	0.000	0.000	0.000

*$P_n = A/(1 + i)^n$.

Exhibit 19B.2　Present Value of an Annuity of $1 in Arrears*

Periods	2%	4%	6%	8%	10%	12%	14%	16%	18%	20%	22%	24%	26%	28%	30%	32%	40%
1	0.980	0.962	0.943	0.926	0.909	0.893	0.877	0.862	0.847	0.833	0.820	0.806	0.794	0.781	0.769	0.758	0.714
2	1.942	1.866	1.833	1.783	1.736	1.690	1.647	1.605	1.566	1.528	1.492	1.457	1.424	1.392	1.361	1.331	1.224
3	2.884	2.775	2.673	2.577	2.487	2.402	2.322	2.246	2.174	2.106	2.042	1.981	1.923	1.868	1.816	1.766	1.589
4	3.808	3.630	3.465	3.312	3.170	3.037	2.914	2.798	2.690	2.589	2.494	2.404	2.320	2.241	2.166	2.096	1.849
5	4.713	4.452	4.212	3.993	3.791	3.605	3.433	3.274	3.127	2.991	2.864	2.745	2.635	2.532	2.436	2.345	2.035
6	5.601	5.242	4.917	4.623	4.355	4.111	3.889	3.685	3.498	3.326	3.167	3.020	2.885	2.759	2.643	2.534	2.168
7	6.472	6.002	5.582	5.206	4.868	4.564	4.288	4.039	3.812	3.605	3.416	3.242	3.083	2.937	2.802	2.677	2.263
8	7.325	6.733	6.210	5.747	5.335	4.968	4.639	4.344	4.078	3.837	3.619	3.421	3.241	3.076	2.925	2.786	2.331
9	8.162	7.435	6.802	6.247	5.759	5.328	4.946	4.607	4.303	4.031	3.786	3.566	3.366	3.184	3.019	2.868	2.379
10	8.983	8.111	7.360	6.710	6.145	5.650	5.216	4.833	4.494	4.192	3.923	3.682	3.465	3.269	3.092	2.930	2.414
11	9.787	8.760	7.887	7.139	6.495	5.938	5.453	5.029	4.656	4.327	4.035	3.776	3.543	3.335	3.147	2.978	2.438
12	10.575	9.385	8.384	7.536	6.814	6.194	5.660	5.197	4.793	4.439	4.127	3.851	3.606	3.387	3.190	3.013	2.456
13	11.348	9.986	8.853	7.904	7.103	6.424	5.842	5.342	4.910	4.533	4.203	3.912	3.656	3.427	3.223	3.040	2.469
14	12.106	10.563	9.295	8.244	7.367	6.628	6.002	5.468	5.008	4.611	4.265	3.962	3.695	3.459	3.249	3.061	2.478
15	12.849	11.118	9.712	8.559	7.606	6.811	6.142	5.575	5.092	4.675	4.315	4.001	3.726	3.483	3.268	3.076	2.484
16	13.578	11.652	10.106	8.851	7.824	6.974	6.265	5.668	5.162	4.730	4.357	4.033	3.751	3.503	3.283	3.088	2.489
17	14.292	12.166	10.477	9.122	8.022	7.120	6.373	5.749	5.222	4.775	4.391	4.059	3.771	3.518	3.295	3.097	2.492
18	14.992	12.659	10.828	9.372	8.201	7.250	6.467	5.818	5.273	4.812	4.419	4.080	3.786	3.529	3.304	3.104	2.494
19	15.678	13.134	11.158	9.604	8.365	7.366	6.550	5.877	5.316	4.843	4.442	4.097	3.799	3.539	3.311	3.109	2.496
20	16.351	13.590	11.470	9.818	8.514	7.469	6.623	5.929	5.353	4.870	4.460	4.110	3.808	3.546	3.316	3.113	2.497
21	17.011	14.029	11.764	10.017	8.649	7.562	6.687	5.973	5.384	4.891	4.476	4.121	3.816	3.551	3.320	3.116	2.498
22	17.658	14.451	12.042	10.201	8.772	7.645	6.743	6.011	5.410	4.909	4.488	4.130	3.822	3.556	3.323	3.118	2.498
23	18.292	14.857	12.303	10.371	8.883	7.718	6.792	6.044	5.432	4.925	4.499	4.137	3.827	3.559	3.325	3.120	2.499
24	18.914	15.247	12.550	10.529	8.985	7.784	6.835	6.073	5.451	4.937	4.507	4.143	3.831	3.562	3.327	3.121	2.499
25	19.523	15.622	12.783	10.675	9.077	7.843	6.873	6.097	5.467	4.948	4.514	4.147	3.834	3.564	3.329	3.122	2.499
26	20.121	15.983	13.003	10.810	9.161	7.896	6.906	6.118	5.480	4.956	4.520	4.151	3.837	3.566	3.330	3.123	2.500
27	20.707	16.330	13.211	10.935	9.237	7.943	6.935	6.136	5.492	4.964	4.524	4.154	3.839	3.567	3.331	3.123	2.500
28	21.281	16.663	13.406	11.051	9.307	7.984	6.961	6.152	5.502	4.970	4.528	4.157	3.840	3.568	3.331	3.124	2.500
29	21.844	16.984	13.591	11.158	9.370	8.022	6.983	6.166	5.510	4.975	4.531	4.159	3.841	3.569	3.332	3.124	2.500
30	22.396	17.292	13.765	11.258	9.427	8.055	7.003	6.177	5.517	4.979	4.534	4.160	3.842	3.569	3.332	3.124	2.500

*$P_n = (1/i) \times [1 - 1/(1 + i)^n]$.

BRIEF EXERCISES

Brief Exercise 19-1 Payback Period

OBJECTIVE ◂2
Example 19.1

Jan Booth is considering investing in either a storage facility or a car wash facility. Both projects have a five-year life and require an investment of $360,000. The cash flow patterns for each project are given below.

Storage facility: Even cash flows of $120,000 per year
Car wash: $112,500, $142,500, $60,000, $120,000, and $90,000

Required:

1. Calculate the payback period for the storage facility (even cash flows).
2. Calculate the payback period for the car wash facility (uneven cash flows). Which project should be accepted based on payback analysis? Explain.
3. *What if* a third mutually exclusive project, a laundry facility, became available with the same investment and annual cash flows of $150,000? Now which project would be chosen?

Brief Exercise 19-2 Accounting Rate of Return

OBJECTIVE ◂2
Example 19.2

WeCare Clinic is planning on investing in some new echocardiogram equipment that will require an initial outlay of $170,000. The system has an expected life of five years and no expected salvage value. The investment is expected to produce the following net cash flows over its life: $68,000, $68,000, $85,000, $85,000, and $102,000.

Required:

1. Calculate the annual net income for each of the five years.
2. Calculate the accounting rate of return.
3. *What if* a second competing revenue-producing investment has the same initial outlay and salvage value but the following cash flows (in chronological sequence): $102,000, $102,000, $102,000, $68,000, and $17,000? Using the accounting rate of return metric, which project should be selected: the first or the second? Which project is really the better of the two?

Brief Exercise 19-3 Net Present Value

OBJECTIVE ◂3
Example 19.3

Carsen Sorensen, controller of Thayn Company, just received the following data associated with production of a new product:

- Expected annual revenues: $750,000
- Projected product life cycle: five years
- Equipment: $800,000 with a salvage value of $100,000 after five years
- Expected increase in working capital: $100,000 (recoverable at the end of five years)
- Annual cash operating expenses: estimated at $450,000
- Required rate of return: 8 percent

Required:

1. Estimate the annual cash flows for the new product.
2. Using the estimated annual cash flows, calculate the NPV.
3. *What if* revenues were overestimated by $150,000? Redo the NPV analysis, correcting for this error. Assume the operating expenses remain the same.

OBJECTIVE 4
Example 19.4

Brief Exercise 19-4 Internal Rate of Return

Manzer Enterprises is considering two independent investments:

A new automated materials handling system that costs $900,000 and will produce net cash inflows of $300,000 at the end of each year for the next four years.
A computer-aided manufacturing system that costs $775,000 and will produce labor savings of $400,000 and $500,000 at the end of the first year and second year, respectively.

Manzer has a cost of capital of 8 percent.

Required:

1. Calculate the IRR for the first investment and determine if it is acceptable or not.
2. Calculate the IRR of the second investment and comment on its acceptability. Use 12 percent as the first guess.
3. *What if* the cash flows for the first investment are $250,000 instead of $300,000?

OBJECTIVE 5
Example 19.5

Brief Exercise 19-5 NPV Versus Internal Rate of Return

Nguyen Hospital is considering two different low-field MRI systems: the Clearlook System and the Goodview System. The projected annual revenues, annual costs, capital outlays, and project life for each system (in after-tax cash flows) are as follows:

	Clearlook	Goodview
Annual revenues	$720,000	$900,000
Annual operating costs	445,000	655,000
System investment	900,000	800,000
Project life	5 years	5 years

Assume that the cost of capital for the company is 8 percent.

Required:

1. Calculate the NPV for the Clearlook System.
2. Calculate the NPV for the Goodview System. Which MRI system would be chosen?
3. *What if* Nguyen Hospital wants to know why IRR is not being used for the investment analysis? Calculate the IRR for each project and explain why it is not suitable for choosing among mutually exclusive investments.

OBJECTIVE 6
Example 19.6

Brief Exercise 19-6 After-Tax Cash Flows

Warren Company plans to open a new repair service center for one of its electronic products. The center requires an investment in depreciable assets costing $480,000. The assets will be depreciated on a straight-line basis, over four years, and have no expected salvage value. The annual income statement for the center is given below.

Revenues	$ 360,000
Less: Cash operating expenses	(150,000)
Depreciation	(120,000)
Income before income taxes	$ 90,000
Less: Income taxes (@ 25%)	22,500
Net income	$ 67,500

Required:

1. Using the income approach, calculate the after-tax cash flows.
2. Using the decomposition approach, calculate the after-tax cash flows for each item of the income statement and show that the total is the same as the income approach.
3. *What if* it is desirable to express the decomposition approach in a spreadsheet format for the four years to facilitate the use of spreadsheet software packages? Express the decomposition approach in a spreadsheet format, with a column for each income item and a total column.

EXERCISES

Exercise 19-7 Payback and ARR

OBJECTIVE ◀ 2

SHOW ME HOW

Each of the following scenarios is independent. All cash flows are after-tax cash flows.

Required:

1. Michael Kimathi has purchased a tractor for $93,750. He expects to receive a net cash flow of $31,250 per year from the investment. What is the payback period for Michael?
2. Bertha Lafferty invested $360,000 in a laundromat. The facility has a 10-year life expectancy with no expected salvage value. The laundromat will produce a net cash flow of $108,000 per year. What is the accounting rate of return?
3. Melannie Bayless has purchased a business building for $336,000. She expects to receive the following cash flows over a 10-year period:

   Year 1: $42,000
   Year 2: $58,800
   Years 3–10: $84,000

   What is the payback period for Melannie? What is the accounting rate of return?

Exercise 19-8 (Appendix A) Future Value, Present Value

OBJECTIVE ◀ 3 4

SHOW ME HOW

The following cases are each independent of the others.

Required:

1. Sam Lilliam places $5,000 in a savings account that pays 3 percent. Suppose Sam leaves the original deposit plus any interest in the account for two years. How much will Sam have in savings after two years?
2. Suppose that the parents of a 12-year-old son want to have $80,000 in a fund six years from now to provide support for his college education. How much must they invest now to have the desired amount if the investment can earn 4 percent? 6 percent? 8 percent?
3. Killian Manufacturing is asking $500,000 for automated equipment, which is expected to last six years and will generate equal annual net cash inflows (because of reductions in labor costs, material waste, and so on). What is the minimum cash inflow that must be realized each year to justify the acquisition? The cost of capital is 8 percent.

Exercise 19-9 NPV and IRR

OBJECTIVE ◀ 3 4

DATA ANALYTICS   SHOW ME HOW

The first two scenarios are independent. All cash flows are after-tax cash flows.

Required:

1. Patz Corporation is considering the purchase of a computer-aided manufacturing system. The cash benefits will be $800,000 per year. The system costs $4,000,000 and will last eight years. Compute the NPV assuming a discount rate of 10 percent. Should the company buy the new system?
2. Amy Wetzel has just invested $270,000 in a restaurant specializing in German food. She expects to receive $43,470 per year for the next eight years. Her cost of capital is 5.5 percent. Compute the internal rate of return. Did Amy make a good decision?
3. For each of the previous two requirements, choose the data analytic type that applies and explain why (descriptive, diagnostic, predictive, or prescriptive). *Note:* More than one analytic type might apply. See Exhibits 2.5 and 2.6, pp. 37, 40, for a brief review of data analytics.

SHOW ME
HOW

Exercise 19-10 Basic Concepts

Sato Company is considering an investment in equipment that is capable of producing more efficiently than the current technology. The outlay required is $2,293,200. The equipment is expected to last five years and will have no salvage value. The expected cash flows associated with the project are as follows:

Year	Cash Revenues	Cash Expenses
1	$2,981,160	$2,293,200
2	2,981,160	2,293,200
3	2,981,160	2,293,200
4	2,981,160	2,293,200
5	2,981,160	2,293,200

Required:

1. Compute the project's payback period.
2. Compute the project's accounting rate of return.
3. Compute the project's net present value, assuming a required rate of return of 10 percent.
4. Compute the project's internal rate of return.

SHOW ME
HOW

Exercise 19-11 NPV

A clinic is considering the possibility of two new purchases: new MRI equipment and new biopsy equipment. Each project requires an investment of $425,000. The expected life for each is five years with no expected salvage value. The net cash inflows associated with the two independent projects are as follows:

Year	MRI Equipment	Biopsy Equipment
1	$200,000	$ 50,000
2	100,000	50,000
3	150,000	100,000
4	100,000	200,000
5	50,000	237,500

Required:

Compute the net present value of each project, assuming a required rate of 12 percent.

SHOW ME
HOW

Exercise 19-12 Payback, Accounting Rate of Return

Refer to Exercise **19-11**.
1. Compute the payback period for each project. Assume that the manager of the clinic accepts only projects with a payback period of three years or less. Offer some reasons why this may be a rational strategy even though the NPV computed in **Exercise 19-11** may indicate otherwise.
2. Compute the accounting rate of return for each project.

SHOW ME
HOW

Exercise 19-13 NPV: Basic Concepts

Buena Vision Clinic is considering an investment that requires an outlay of $600,000 and promises a net cash inflow one year from now of $810,000. Assume the cost of capital is 10 percent.

Required:

1. Break the $810,000 future cash inflow into three components:
   a. The return of the original investment
   b. The cost of capital
   c. The profit earned on the investment

2. Now, compute the present value of the profit earned on the investment.
3. Compute the NPV of the investment. Compare this with the present value of the profit computed in Requirement 2. What does this tell you about the meaning of NPV?

Exercise 19-14 Solving for Unknowns

OBJECTIVE ▶ 3 4

SHOW ME
HOW

Consider each of the following independent cases.

Required:

1. Hal's Stunt Company is investing $120,000 in a project that will yield a uniform series of cash inflows over the next four years. If the internal rate of return is 14 percent, how much cash inflow per year can be expected?
2. Warner Medical Clinic has decided to invest in some new blood diagnostic equipment. The equipment will have a three-year life and will produce a uniform series of cash savings. The net present value of the equipment is $1,750, using a discount rate of 8 percent. The internal rate of return is 12 percent. Determine the investment and the amount of cash savings realized each year.
3. A new lathe costing $60,096 will produce savings of $12,000 per year. How many years must the lathe last if an IRR of 18 percent is realized?
4. The NPV of a new product (a new brand of candy) is $6,075. The product has a life of four years and produces the following cash flows:

Year 1	$15,000
Year 2	20,000
Year 3	30,000
Year 4	?

The cost of the project is three times the cash flow produced in Year 4. The discount rate is 10 percent. Find the cost of the project and the cash flow for Year 4.

Exercise 19-15 Advanced Technology, Payback, NPV, IRR, Sensitivity Analysis

OBJECTIVE ▶ 2 3 4
5 7

EXCEL DATA SHOW ME
ANALYTICS HOW

Gina Ripley, president of Dearing Company, is considering the purchase of a computer-aided manufacturing system. The annual net cash benefits and savings associated with the system are described as follows:

Decreased waste	$300,000
Increased quality	400,000
Decrease in operating costs	600,000
Increase in on-time deliveries	200,000

The system will cost $9,000,000 and last 10 years. The company's cost of capital is 12 percent.

Required:

1. Calculate the payback period for the system. Assume that the company has a policy of only accepting projects with a payback of five years or less. Would the system be acquired?
2. Calculate the NPV and IRR for the project. Should the system be purchased—even if it does not meet the payback criterion?
3. The project manager reviewed the projected cash flows and pointed out that two items had been missed. First, the system would have a salvage value, net of any tax effects, of $1,000,000 at the end of 10 years. Second, the increased quality and delivery performance would allow the company to increase its market share by 20 percent. This would produce an additional annual net benefit of $300,000. Recalculate the payback period, NPV, and IRR given this new information. (For the IRR computation, initially ignore salvage value.) Does the decision change? Suppose that the salvage value is only half what is projected. Does this make a difference in the outcome? Does salvage value have any real bearing on the company's decision?

4. Select (and justify) the data analytic types used in Requirement 3. See Exhibits 2.5 and 2.6, pp. 37, 40, for a review of data analytic types.
5. Suppose that Dearing purchased the new system and that for the first years, the actual net cash flows were $2,000,000 per year. What was the actual payback period? What data analytic type was used in this case?

OBJECTIVE 5

SHOW ME HOW

Exercise 19-16 NPV Versus IRR

Covington Pharmacies has decided to automate its insurance claims process. Two networked computer systems are being considered. The systems have an expected life of two years. The net cash flows associated with the systems are as follows. The cash benefits represent the savings created by switching from a manual to an automated system.

Year	System I	System II
0	$(120,000)	$(120,000)
1	—	76,628
2	162,708	76,628

The company's cost of capital is 10 percent.

Required:

1. Compute the NPV and the IRR for each investment.
2. Show that the project with the larger NPV is the correct choice for the company.

OBJECTIVE 6

SHOW ME HOW

Exercise 19-17 Computation of After-Tax Cash Flows

Postman Company is considering two independent projects. One project involves a new product line, and the other involves the acquisition of forklifts for the Materials Handling Department. The projected annual operating revenues and expenses are as follows:

Project I (investment in a new product)	
Revenues	$ 270,000
Cash expenses	(135,000)
Depreciation	(45,000)
Income before income taxes	$ 90,000
Income taxes	(22,500)
Net income	$ 67,500

Project II (Acquisition of Two Forklifts)	
Cash expenses	$90,000
Depreciation	90,000

Required:

Compute the after-tax cash flows of each project. The tax rate is 25 percent and includes federal and state assessments.

OBJECTIVE 3 6

SHOW ME HOW   **EXCEL**

Exercise 19-18   MACRS, NPV

Lilly Company is planning to buy a set of special tools for its grinding operation. The cost of the tools is $18,000. The tools have a three-year life and qualify for the use of the three-year MACRS. The tax rate is 25 percent; the cost of capital is 12 percent.

Required:

1. Calculate the present value of the tax depreciation shield, assuming that straight-line depreciation with a half-year life is used.
2. Calculate the present value of the tax depreciation shield, assuming that MACRS is used.
3. What is the benefit to the company of using MACRS?

PROBLEMS

Problem 19-19 Pollution Prevention, P2 Investment

OBJECTIVE ◄ 2 3 4 5 6 7

Heaps Company produces jewelry that requires electroplating with gold, silver, and other valuable metals. Electroplating uses large amounts of water and chemicals, producing wastewater with a number of toxic residuals. Currently, Heaps uses settlement tanks to remove waste; unfortunately, the approach is inefficient, and much of the toxic residue is left in the water that is discharged into a local river. The amount of toxic discharge exceeds the legal, allowable amounts, and the company is faced with substantial, ongoing environmental fines. The environmental violations are also drawing unfavorable public reaction, and sales are being affected. A lawsuit is also impending, which could prove to be quite costly.

Management is now considering the installation of a zero-discharge, closed-loop system to treat the wastewater. The proposed closed-loop system would not only purify the wastewater, but also produce cleaner water than that currently being used, increasing plating quality. The closed-loop system would produce only four pounds of sludge, and the sludge would be virtually pure metal, with significant market value. The system requires an investment of $630,000 and will cost $45,000 in increased annual operation plus an annual purchase of $7,500 of filtration medium. However, management projects the following savings:

Water usage	$ 67,500
Chemical usage	42,000
Sludge disposal	90,000
Recovered metal sales	45,000
Sampling of discharge	120,000
Total	$364,500

The equipment qualifies as a seven-year MACRS asset. Management has decided to use straight-line depreciation for tax purposes, using the required half-year convention. The tax rate is 25 percent. The projected life of the system is 10 years. The hurdle rate is 12 percent for all capital budgeting projects, although the company's cost of capital is 8 percent.

Required:

1. Based on the financial data provided, prepare a schedule of expected cash flows.
2. What is the payback period?
3. Calculate the NPV of the closed-loop system. Should the company invest in the system?
4. The calculation in Requirement 3 ignored several factors that could affect the project's viability: savings from avoiding the annual fines, positive effect on sales due to favorable environmental publicity, increased plating quality from the new system, and the avoidance of the lawsuit. Can these factors be quantified? If so, should they have been included in the analysis? Suppose, for example, that the annual fines being incurred are $75,000, the sales effect is $60,000 per year, the quality effect is not estimable, and cancellation of the lawsuit because of the new system would avoid an expected settlement at the end of Year 3 (including legal fees) of $300,000. Assuming these are all after-tax amounts, what effect would their inclusion have on the payback period? On the NPV?

Problem 19-20 Discount Rates, Quality, Market Share, Contemporary Manufacturing Environment

OBJECTIVE ◄ 3 5 7

Sweeney Manufacturing has a plant where the equipment is essentially worn out. The equipment must be replaced, and Sweeney is considering two competing investment alternatives. The first alternative would replace the worn-out equipment with traditional production equipment; the second alternative uses contemporary technology and has computer-aided design and manufacturing capabilities. The investment and after-tax operating cash flows for each alternative are as follows:

Year	Traditional Equipment	Contemporary Technology
0	$(1,000,000)	$(4,000,000)
1	600,000	200,000
2	400,000	400,000
3	200,000	600,000
4	200,000	800,000
5	200,000	800,000
6	200,000	800,000
7	200,000	1,000,000
8	200,000	2,000,000
9	200,000	2,000,000
10	200,000	2,000,000

The company uses a discount rate of 18 percent for all of its investments. The company's cost of capital is 14 percent.

Required:

1. Calculate the net present value for each investment using a discount rate of 18 percent.
2. Calculate the net present value for each investment using a discount rate of 14 percent.
3. Which rate should the company use to compute the net present value? Explain.
4. Now, assume that if the traditional equipment is purchased, the competitive position of the firm will deteriorate because of lower quality (relative to competitors who did automate). Marketing estimates that the loss in market share will decrease the projected net cash inflows by 50 percent for Years 3–10. Recalculate the NPV of the traditional equipment given this outcome. What is the decision now? Discuss the importance of assessing the effect of intangible and indirect benefits.

OBJECTIVE `3` `6` `7`

DATA ANALYTICS   **EXCEL**

Problem 19-21 Competing P2 Investments

Ron Vargas, the CEO for Sunders Manufacturing, was wondering which of two pollution control systems he should choose. The firm's current production process produces a gaseous and a liquid residue. A recent state law mandated that emissions of these residues be reduced to levels considerably below current performance. Failure to reduce the emissions would invoke stiff fines and possible closure of the operating plant. Fortunately, the new law provided a transition period, and Ron had used the time wisely. His engineers had developed two separate proposals. The first proposal involved the acquisition of scrubbers for gaseous emissions and a treatment facility to remove the liquid residues. The second proposal was more radical. It entailed the redesign of the manufacturing process and the acquisition of new production equipment to support this new design. The new process would solve the environmental problem by avoiding the production of residues.

Although the equipment for each proposal normally would qualify as seven-year property, the state managed to obtain an agreement with the federal government to allow any pollution abatement equipment to qualify as five-year property. State tax law follows federal guidelines. Both proposals qualify for the five-year property benefit.

Ron's vice president of marketing has projected an increase in revenues because of favorable environmental performance publicity. This increase is the result of selling more of Sunders's products to environmentally conscious customers. However, because the second approach is "greener," the vice president believes that the revenue increase will be greater. Cost and other data relating to the two proposals are as follows:

	Scrubbers and Treatment	Process Redesign
Initial outlay	$50,000,000	$100,000,000
Incremental revenues	10,000,000	30,000,000
Incremental cash expenses	24,000,000	10,000,000

The expected life for each investment's equipment is six years. The expected salvage value is $2,000,000 for scrubbers and treatment equipment and $3,000,000 for process redesign equipment. The combined federal and state tax rate is 25 percent. The cost of capital is 10 percent.

Required:

1. Compute the NPV of each proposal and make a recommendation to Ron Vargas.
2. The environmental manager observes that the scrubbers and treatment facility enable the company to just meet state emission standards. She feels that the standards will likely increase within three years. If so, this would entail a modification at the end of three years costing an additional $8,000,000. Also, she is concerned that continued liquid residue releases—even those meeting state standards—could push a local lake into a hazardous state by the end of three years. If so, this could prompt political action requiring the company to clean up the lake. After-tax cleanup costs would range between $40,000,000 and $60,000,000. Analyze and discuss the effect this new information has on the two alternatives. If you have read the chapter on environmental cost management, describe how the concept of ecoefficiency applies to this setting.
3. Identify the data analytic type (descriptive, diagnostic, predictive, or prescriptive) used in Requirement 1 (see Exhibits 2.5 and 2.6, pp. 37, 40). *Note:* More than one analytic type may apply. Explain your choice. Does Requirement 2 affect your answer? Explain.

Problem 19-22 Payback, NPV, Managerial Incentives, Ethical Behavior

 OBJECTIVE ◀ 2 3

EXCEL

Kent Tessman, manager of a Dairy Products Division, was pleased with his division's performance over the past three years. Each year, divisional profits had increased, and he had earned a sizable bonus. (Bonuses are a linear function of the division's reported income.) He had also received considerable attention from higher management. A vice president had told him in confidence that if his performance over the next three years matched his first three, he would be promoted to higher management.

Determined to fulfill these expectations, Kent made sure that he personally reviewed every capital budget request. He wanted to be certain that any funds invested would provide good, solid returns. (The division's cost of capital is 10 percent.) At the moment, he is reviewing two independent requests. Proposal A involves automating a manufacturing operation that is currently labor intensive. Proposal B centers on developing and marketing a new ice cream product. Proposal A requires an initial outlay of $250,000, and Proposal B requires $312,500. Both projects could be funded, given the status of the division's capital budget. Both have an expected life of six years and have the following projected after-tax cash flows:

Year	Proposal A	Proposal B
1	$150,000	$ (37,500)
2	125,000	(25,000)
3	75,000	(12,500)
4	37,500	212,500
5	25,000	275,000
6	12,500	337,500

After careful consideration of each investment, Kent approved funding of Proposal A and rejected Proposal B.

Required:

1. Compute the NPV for each proposal.
2. Compute the payback period for each proposal.
3. According to your analysis, which proposal(s) should be accepted? Explain.
4. Explain why Kent accepted only Proposal A. Considering the possible reasons for rejection, would you judge his behavior to be ethical? Explain.

OBJECTIVE

**DATA
ANALYTICS**

Problem 19-23 Basic IRR Analysis

Friedman Company is considering installing a new IT system. The cost of the new system is estimated to be $2,250,000, but it would produce after-tax savings of $450,000 per year in labor costs. The estimated life of the new system is 10 years, with no salvage value expected. Intrigued by the possibility of saving $450,000 per year and having a more reliable information system, the president of Friedman has asked for an analysis of the project's economic viability. All capital projects are required to earn at least the firm's cost of capital, which is 12 percent.

Required:

1. Calculate the project's internal rate of return. Should the company acquire the new IT system?
2. Suppose that savings are less than claimed. Calculate the minimum annual cash savings that must be realized for the project to earn a rate equal to the firm's cost of capital. Comment on the safety margin that exists, if any.
3. Suppose that the life of the IT system is overestimated by two years. Repeat Requirements 1 and 2 under this assumption. Comment on the usefulness of this information.
4. Describe the data analytic type or types that apply to Requirement 1. Discuss the effect on your answer by the analyses that take place in Requirements 2 and 3. See Exhibits 2.5 and 2.6, pp. 37, 40, for a brief review of data analytics.

OBJECTIVE 3 5 6

Problem 19-24 Replacement Decision, Computing After-Tax Cash Flows, Basic NPV Analysis

Okmulgee Hospital (a large metropolitan for-profit hospital) is considering replacing its MRI equipment with a new model manufactured by a different company. The old MRI equipment was acquired three years ago, has a remaining life of five years, and will have a salvage value of $100,000. The book value is $2,000,000. Straight-line depreciation with a half-year convention is being used for tax purposes. The cash operating costs of the existing MRI equipment total $1,000,000 per year.

The new MRI equipment has an initial cost of $5,000,000 and will have cash operating costs of $500,000 per year. The new MRI will have a life of five years and a salvage value of $1,000,000 at the end of the fifth year. MACRS depreciation will be used for tax purposes. If the new MRI equipment is purchased, the old one will be sold for $500,000. The company needs to decide whether to keep the old MRI equipment or buy the new one. The cost of capital is 12 percent. The combined federal and state tax rate is 25 percent.

Required:

Compute the NPV of each alternative. Should the company keep the old MRI equipment or buy the new one?

OBJECTIVE 3 6 7

Problem 19-25 Capital Investment, Discount Rates, Intangible and Indirect Benefits, Time Horizon, Contemporary Manufacturing Environment

Mallette Manufacturing, Inc., produces washing machines, dryers, and dishwashers. Because of increasing competition, Mallette is considering investing in an automated manufacturing system. Since competition is most keen for dishwashers, the production process for this line has been selected for initial evaluation. The automated system for the dishwasher line would replace an existing system (purchased one year ago for $6 million). Although the existing system will be fully depreciated in nine years, it is expected to last another 10 years. The automated system would also have a useful life of 10 years.

The existing system is capable of producing 100,000 dishwashers per year. Sales and production data using the existing system are provided by the Accounting Department:

Sales per year (units)	100,000
Selling price	$300
Costs per unit:	
Direct materials	80
Direct labor	90
Volume-related overhead	20
Direct fixed overhead	40*

*All cash expenses with the exception of depreciation, which is $6 per unit.
The existing equipment is being depreciated using straight-line with no salvage
value considered.

The automated system will cost $34 million to purchase, plus an estimated $20 million in software and implementation. (Assume that all investment outlays occur at the beginning of the first year.) If the automated equipment is purchased, the old equipment can be sold for $3 million.

The automated system will require fewer parts for production and will produce with less waste. Because of this, the direct material cost per unit will be reduced by 25 percent. Automation will also require fewer support activities, and as a consequence, volume-related overhead will be reduced by $4 per unit and direct fixed overhead (other than depreciation) by $17 per unit. Direct labor is reduced by 60 percent. Assume, for simplicity, that the new investment will be depreciated on a pure straight-line basis for tax purposes with no salvage value. Ignore the half-life convention.

The firm's cost of capital is 12 percent, but management chooses to use 16 percent as the required rate of return for evaluation of investments. The combined federal and state tax rate is 25 percent.

Required:

1. Compute the net present value for the old system and the automated system. Which system would the company choose?
2. Repeat the net present value analysis of Requirement 1, using 12 percent as the discount rate.
3. Upon seeing the projected sales for the old system, the marketing manager commented: "Sales of 100,000 units per year cannot be maintained in the current competitive environment for more than one year unless we buy the automated system. The automated system will allow us to compete on the basis of quality and lead time. If we keep the old system, our sales will drop by 10,000 units per year." Repeat the net present value analysis, using this new information and a 12 percent discount rate.
4. An industrial engineer for Mallette noticed that salvage value for the automated equipment had not been included in the analysis. He estimated that the equipment could be sold for $4 million at the end of 10 years. He also estimated that the equipment of the old system would have no salvage value at the end of 10 years. Repeat the net present value analysis using this information, the information in Requirement 3, and a 12 percent discount rate.
5. Given the outcomes of the previous four requirements, comment on the importance of providing accurate inputs for assessing investments in automated manufacturing systems.

OBJECTIVE ▶ 3 6 ▶

CMA

Problem 19-26   NPV, Make or Buy, MACRS, Basic Analysis

Jonfran Company manufactures three different models of paper shredders including the waste container, which serves as the base. While the shredder heads are different for all three models, the waste container is the same. The number of waste containers that Jonfran will need during the following years is estimated as follows:

20x5	50,000
20x6	50,000
20x7	52,000
20x8	55,000
20x9	55,000

The equipment used to manufacture the waste container must be replaced because it is broken and cannot be repaired. The new equipment would have a purchase price of $945,000 with terms of 2/10, n/30; the company's policy is to take all purchase discounts. The freight on the equipment would be $11,000, and installation costs would total $22,900. The equipment would be purchased in December 20x4 and placed into service on January 1, 20x5. It would have a five-year economic life and would be treated as three-year property under MACRS. This equipment is expected to have a salvage value of $12,000 at the end of its economic life in 20x9. The new equipment would be more efficient than the old equipment, resulting in a 25 percent reduction in both direct materials and variable overhead. The savings in direct materials would result in an additional one-time decrease in working capital requirements of $2,500, resulting from a reduction in direct material inventories. This working capital reduction would be recognized at the time of equipment acquisition.

The old equipment is fully depreciated and is not included in the fixed overhead. The old equipment from the plant can be sold for a salvage amount of $1,500. Rather than replace the equipment, one of Jonfran's production managers has suggested that the waste containers be purchased. One supplier has quoted a price of $27 per container. This price is $8 less than Jonfran's current manufacturing cost, which is as follows:

Direct materials		$10
Direct labor		8
Variable overhead		6
Fixed overhead:		
Supervision	$2	
Facilities	5	
General	4	11
Total unit cost		$35

Jonfran uses a plantwide fixed overhead rate in its operations. If the waste containers are purchased outside, the salary and benefits of one supervisor, included in fixed overhead at $45,000, would be eliminated. There would be no other changes in the other cash and noncash items included in fixed overhead except depreciation on the new equipment.

Jonfran is subject to a 25 percent tax rate. Management assumes that all cash flows occur at the end of the year and uses a 12 percent after-tax discount rate.

Required:

1. Prepare a schedule of cash flows for the make alternative. Calculate the NPV of the make alternative.
2. Prepare a schedule of cash flows for the buy alternative. Calculate the NPV of the buy alternative.
3. Which should Jonfran do—make or buy the containers? What qualitative factors should be considered? *(CMA adapted)*

Problem 19-27 Structured Problem Solving, Cash Flows, NPV, Choice of Discount Rate, Advanced Manufacturing Environment

Ashley Thayn, president and owner of Orangeville Metal Works, has just returned from a trip to Europe. While there, she toured several plants that use robotic manufacturing. Seeing the efficiency and success of these companies, Ashley became convinced that robotic manufacturing is essential for Orangeville to maintain its competitive position.

Based on this conviction, Ashley requested an analysis detailing the costs and benefits of robotic manufacturing for the materials handling and merchandising equipment group. This group of products consists of such items as cooler shelving, stocking carts, and bakery racks. The products are sold directly to supermarkets.

A committee, consisting of the controller, the marketing manager, and the production manager, was given the responsibility to prepare the analysis. As a starting point, the controller provided the following information on expected revenues and expenses for the existing manual system:

		Percentage of Sales
Sales	$400,000	100%
Less: Variable cash expenses[a]	228,000	57
Contribution margin	$172,000	43
Less: Fixed expenses[b]	92,000	23
Income before income taxes	$ 80,000	20

[a]Variable cost detail (as a percentage of sales):

Direct materials	16%
Direct labor	25
Variable overhead	8
Variable selling	8

[b]$20,000 is depreciation; the rest is cash expenses.

Given the current competitive environment, the marketing manager thought that the preceding level of profitability would not likely change for the next decade.

After some investigation into various robotic equipment, the committee settled on an Aide 900 system, a robot that has the capability to weld stainless steel or aluminum. It is capable of being programmed to adjust the path, angle, and speed of the torch. The production manager was excited about the robotic system because it would eliminate the need to hire welders. This was an attractive possibility because the market for welders seemed perpetually tight. By reducing the dependence on welders, better production scheduling and fewer late deliveries would result. Moreover, the robot's production rate is four times that of a person.

It was also discovered that robotic welding is superior in quality to manual welding. As a consequence, some of the costs of poor quality could be reduced. By providing better-quality products and avoiding late deliveries, the marketing manager was convinced that the company would have such a competitive edge that it would increase sales by 50 percent for the affected product group by the end of the fourth year. The marketing manager provided the following projections for the next 10 years, the useful life of the robotic equipment:

	Year 1	Year 2	Year 3	Years 4–10
Sales	$400,000	$450,000	$500,000	$600,000

Currently, welding is the only variable direct labor cost. If the robot is acquired, it will need one operator, who will be paid a salary of $40,000 per year. Only one operator will be needed for the range of sales the company will experience. Because of improved quality, the robotic system will also reduce the cost of direct materials by 25 percent, the cost of variable overhead by 33.33 percent, and variable selling expenses by 10 percent. All of these reductions will take place immediately after the robotic system is in place and operating. Fixed costs will be increased by the depreciation associated with the robot. The robot will be depreciated using MACRS. (The manual system uses straight-line depreciation without a half-year convention and has a current book value of $200,000.) If the robotic system is acquired, the old system will be sold for $40,000.

The robotic system requires the following initial investment:

Purchase price	$380,000
Installation	70,000
Training	30,000
Engineering	40,000

At the end of 10 years, the robot will have a salvage value of $20,000. Assume that the company's cost of capital is 12 percent. The tax rate is 25 percent.

Required:

1. Prepare a schedule of after-tax cash flows for the manual and robotic systems.
2. Using the schedule of cash flows computed in Requirement 1, compute the NPV for each system. Should the company invest in the robotic system?
3. In practice, many financial officers tend to use a higher discount rate than is justified by the firm's cost of capital. For example, a firm may use a discount rate of 20 percent when its cost of capital is or could be 12 percent. Offer some reasons for this practice. Assume that the annual after-tax cash benefit of adopting the robotic system is $80,000 per year more than the manual system. The initial outlay for the robotic system is $340,000. Compute the NPV using 12 percent and 20 percent. Would the robotic system be acquired if 20 percent is used? Could this conservative approach have a negative impact on a firm's ability to stay competitive?

20

Inventory Management: Economic Order Quantity, JIT, and the Theory of Constraints

After studying this chapter, you should be able to:

1 Describe the just-in-case inventory management model.

2 Discuss just-in-time (JIT) inventory management.

3 Explain the basic concepts of constrained optimization.

4 Describe how the theory of constraints can be used to manage inventory.

THE THEORY OF CONSTRAINTS

at Dr. Reddy's Laboratories Limited

All of us have goals that are important to us. Sometimes our ability to obtain these goals is limited by constraints. Thus, to achieve an important goal, we often have to first eliminate or, at least, elevate the constraint that is impeding us. For example, we may wish to buy a car, but our income is insufficient to allow us to obtain a loan to do so. We are constrained by our lack of sufficient income. Thus, one way to achieve the goal is to obtain a job or a job that pays more—one that pays enough to qualify for an auto loan. We are learning to manage a critical constraint to improve our own well-being. Organizations are faced with the same problem. For example, the goal of a profit-making organization is to make money now and in the future. In a similar way, constraints often reduce or impede a company's ability to make money. The theory of constraints is a methodology that allows an organization to manage constraints to support the objective of continuous improvement. For the organization overall, the key to improving and making more profit is to identify the weakest link, the constraint that, if eliminated or elevated, will allow system performance to improve. Once that has been accomplished, another constraint becomes the weakest link, and the process is repeated. In this process, inventory plays an important buffering role in constraint management.

Since *The Goal* was written in 1984, thousands of firms throughout the world have implemented the theory of constraints.[1] Examples of firms using the theory of constraints include **Procter & Gamble**, **General Electric**, **Ford**, **Texas Instruments**, and **Dr. Reddy's**.[2] Dr. Reddy's Laboratories Limited is a multinational pharmaceutical company, founded in 1984, and headquartered in Hyderabad, Telangana, India. Dr. Reddy's revenues in FY 2020 were ₹174.6 billion (about $2.3 billion). Of that total revenue, ₹138.1 billion was earned by its global generic business segment, ₹25.7 billion from its active pharmaceutical ingredients (APIs) and services segment, and ₹11.7 billion from its proprietary products segment.[3] Clearly, the generic business segment is the major focus of Dr. Reddy's, and the company ranks among the top 10 producers globally.[4] However, Dr. Reddy's is also one of the world's leading producers of APIs.[5]

Dr. Reddy's discovered that to be competitive, new approaches were needed. The theory of constraints was one of the initiatives implemented to achieve this goal. The theory of constraints approach was applied to

1   E. M. Goldratt and J. Cox, *The Goal—A Process of Ongoing Improvement* (Croton-on-Hudson, NY: North River Press, 1984).
2   Theory of Constraints Institute, "Theory of Constraint Examples," https://www.tocinstitute.org/theory -of-constraints-examples.html, accessed July, 22, 2020.
3   Dr. Reddy's Laboratories Ltd., "Annual Report, 2019-20," https://www.drreddys.com/investors/reports-and -filings/annual-reports/, accessed July 23, 2020.
4   Tiash Saha, "The World's Biggest Generic Pharmaceutical Companies in 2018," *Pharmaceutical Technology* (April 3, 2019), https://www.pharmaceutical-technology.com/features/biggest-generic-pharmaceutical -companies-2018/, accessed July 23, 2020.
5   API Industry Guide, "Top API Manufacturers," http://www.mdtvalliance.org/top-api-manufacturers/, accessed July 23, 2020.

enhance supply chain effectiveness, manufacturing, and product development. Within five years of implementation, Dr. Reddy's tightened its supply chain, improved product quality, and improved its inventory management. In fact, the company won a best supplier in the United States.[6] With respect to new product development, Dr. Reddy's reduced development cycle time by 40 percent, had an 83 percent increase in the number of projects completed, and a 75 percent increase in the number of new product launches.[7]

This chapter not only introduces you to the theory of constraints but also explores other inventory management models. Based on Dr. Reddy's experience, you probably have realized that the theory of constraints is more than an inventory management model, although it certainly has inventory management as part of its focus. The same observation is made with respect to just in time. However, the just-in-case inventory management model that you will study is mostly concerned with inventory management. Still, as you will discover, each approach has a role, and all are used in real companies.

Excessive amounts of inventory can prove to be very costly. There are many ways to manage inventory costs, including the EOQ model, JIT, and the theory of constraints (TOC). All three methods offer ways of reducing inventory costs. The best approach usually depends on the nature of the organization as well as the nature of the inventory itself.

Inventory represents a significant investment of capital for most companies. Inventory ties up money that could be used more productively elsewhere. Thus, effective inventory management offers the potential for significant cost savings. Furthermore, quality, product engineering, prices, overtime, excess capacity, ability to respond to customers (due-date performance), lead times, and overall profitability are all affected by inventory levels.

Describing how inventory policy can be used to reduce costs and help organizations strengthen their competitive position is the main purpose of this chapter. First, we review **just-in-case inventory management**—a traditional inventory model based on anticipated demand. Learning the basics of this model and its underlying conceptual foundation will help us understand where it can still be appropriately applied. Understanding just-in-case inventory management also provides the necessary background for grasping the advantages of inventory management methods that are used in the contemporary manufacturing environment. These methods include JIT and the theory of constraints. To fully appreciate the theory of constraints, a brief introduction to constrained optimization (linear programming) is also needed. Although the focus of this chapter is inventory management, the theory of constraints is much more than an inventory management technique, and so we also explore what is called *constraint* or *throughput accounting*.

OBJECTIVE 1
Describe the just-in-case inventory management model.

JUST-IN-CASE INVENTORY MANAGEMENT

Inventory management is concerned with managing inventory costs. Three types of inventory costs can be readily identified with inventory: (1) the cost of acquiring inventory (other than the cost of the good itself), (2) the cost of holding inventory, and (3) the cost of not having inventory on hand when needed.

If the inventory is a material or good acquired from an outside source, then these inventory-acquisition costs are known as *ordering costs*. **Ordering costs** are the costs of placing

---

6 Priyanka Sangani, "Companies Resort to Theory of Constraints to Stay Ahead of the Game," *The Economic Times* (October 17, 2014), https://economictimes.indiatimes.com/companies-resort-to-theory-of-constraints-to-stay-ahead-in-the-game/articleshow/44835397.cms?from5mdr, accessed July 23, 2020.

7 Sanjeev Gupta, "Theory of Constraints Unleashes Product Development," *Industrial Management*, Vol. 59, No. 6 (November/December 2017): 12–17.

and receiving an order. Examples include the costs of processing an order (clerical costs and documents), insurance for shipment, and unloading costs. If the material or good is produced internally, then the acquisition costs are called *setup costs*. **Setup costs** are the costs of preparing equipment and facilities so they can be used to produce a particular product or component. Examples are wages of idled production workers, the cost of idled production facilities (lost income), and the costs of test runs (labor, materials, and overhead). Ordering costs and setup costs are similar in nature—both represent costs that must be incurred to acquire inventory. They differ only in the nature of the prerequisite activity (filling out and placing an order versus configuring equipment and facilities). Thus, in the discussion that follows, any reference to ordering costs can be viewed as a reference to setup costs.

Carrying costs are the costs of holding inventory. Examples include insurance, inventory taxes, obsolescence, the opportunity cost of funds tied up in inventory, handling costs, and storage space.

If demand is not known with certainty, a third category of inventory costs—called *stock-out costs*—exists. **Stock-out costs** are the costs of not having a product available when demanded by a customer. Examples are lost sales (both current and future), the costs of expediting (increased transportation charges, overtime, and so on), and the costs of interrupted production.

Justifying Inventory

Effective inventory management requires that inventory-related costs be minimized. Minimizing carrying costs favors ordering or producing in small lot sizes, whereas minimizing ordering costs favors large, infrequent orders (minimizing setup costs favors long, infrequent production runs). The need to balance these two sets of costs so that the *total* cost of carrying and ordering can be minimized is one reason organizations choose to carry inventory.

Demand uncertainty is a second major reason for holding inventory. If the demand for materials or products is greater than expected, inventory can serve as a buffer, giving organizations the ability to meet delivery dates (thus keeping customers satisfied). Although balancing conflicting costs and dealing with uncertainty are the two most frequently cited reasons for carrying inventories, other reasons exist.

Inventories of parts and materials are often viewed as necessary because of supply uncertainties. That is, inventory buffers of parts and materials are needed to keep production flowing in case of late deliveries or no deliveries. (Strikes, bad weather, and bankruptcy are examples of uncertain events that can cause an interruption in supply.) Unreliable production processes may also create a demand for producing extra inventory. For example, a company may decide to produce more units than needed to meet demand because the production process usually yields a large number of nonconforming units. Similarly, buffers of inventories may be required to continue supplying customers or processes with goods even if a process goes down because of a failed machine. Finally, organizations may acquire larger inventories than normal to take advantage of quantity discounts or to avoid anticipated price increases. Exhibit 20.1 summarizes the reasons typically offered for carrying

1. To balance ordering or setup costs and carrying costs
2. Demand uncertainty
3. Machine failure
4. Defective parts
5. Unavailable parts
6. Late delivery of parts
7. Unreliable production processes
8. To take advantage of discounts
9. To hedge against future price increases

Exhibit 20.1

Traditional Reasons for Carrying Inventory

inventory. It is important to realize that these reasons are given to *justify* carrying inventories. A host of other reasons can be offered that *encourage* the carrying of inventories. For example, performance measures such as measures of machine and labor efficiency may promote the buildup of inventories.

Economic Order Quantity: A Model for Balancing Acquisition and Carrying Costs

Of the nine reasons for holding inventory listed in Exhibit 20.1, the first reason is directly concerned with the trade-off between acquisition and carrying costs. Most of the other reasons are concerned directly or indirectly with stock-out costs, with the exception of the last two (which are concerned with managing the cost of the good itself). Initially, we will assume away the stock-out cost problem and focus only on the objective of balancing acquisition costs with carrying costs. To develop an inventory policy that deals with the trade-offs between these two costs, two basic questions given below must be addressed.

1. How much should be ordered (or produced) to minimize inventory costs?
2. When should the order be placed (or the setup done)?

The first question needs to be addressed before the second can be answered. Both these questions lead to the development of data analytic models that are useful for managing inventory.

Minimizing Total Ordering and Carrying Costs Assuming that demand is known, the total ordering (or setup) and carrying cost can be described by the following equation:

$$TC = PD/Q + CQ/2$$
$$= \text{Ordering (or setup) cost} + \text{Carrying cost} \qquad (20.1)$$

where

DATA ANALYTICS

TC = The total ordering (or setup) and carrying cost
 P = The cost of placing and receiving an order (or the cost of setting up a production run)
 Q = The number of units ordered each time an order is placed (or the lot size for production)
 D = The known annual demand
 C = The cost of carrying one unit of stock for one year

Using Equation 20.1, the cost of inventory can be computed for any organization that carries inventories, although the inventory cost model using setup costs and lot size as inputs pertains only to manufacturers. Ordering or setup cost is the number of orders (or setups), D/Q, multiplied by the ordering or setup cost. Carrying cost for the year is $CQ/2$, which is simply the average inventory on hand ($Q/2$) multiplied by the carrying cost (or setup cost) per unit (C). Assuming average inventory to be $Q/2$ is equivalent to assuming that inventory is consumed uniformly.

Equation 20.1 can be used to calculate the total inventory cost for any Q. However, the objective of inventory management is to identify the order quantity (or lot size) that minimizes this total cost (TC). Thus, the decision variable is the order quantity (or lot size). This quantity that minimizes the total cost is called the **economic order quantity (EOQ)** and is derived by taking the first derivative of Equation 20.1 with respect to Q and solving for Q:[8]

$$Q = EOQ = \sqrt{(2\,DP/C)} \qquad (20.2)$$

Example 20.1 illustrates both EOQ and the inventory cost equation.

---

8 $d(TC)/dQ = C/2 - DP/Q^2 = 0$; thus, $Q^2 = 2DP/C$ and $Q = \sqrt{2DP/C}$.

EXAMPLE 20.1

The HOW and WHY of Calculating the EOQ

Information:

Mantener Corporation does warranty work for a major producer of DVD players. The following values apply for a part used in the repair of the DVD players (the part is purchased from external suppliers):

$$D = 25,000 \text{ units}$$
$$Q = 500 \text{ units}$$
$$P = \$40 \text{ per order}$$
$$C = \$2 \text{ per unit}$$

> **Why:**
> Inventory cost is defined as the sum of ordering cost (or setup cost) plus carrying cost. The quantity ordered (or produced) determines the inventory cost. The quantity that minimizes total inventory cost is called the economic order quantity (EOQ).

Required:

1. For Mantener, calculate the ordering cost, the carrying cost, and the total cost associated with an order size of 500 units.

2. Calculate the EOQ and its associated ordering cost, carrying cost, and total cost. Compare and comment on the EOQ relative to the current order quantity.

3. *What if* Mantener enters into an exclusive supplier agreement with one supplier who will supply all of the demands with smaller more frequent orders? Under this arrangement, the ordering cost is reduced to $0.40 per order. Calculate the new EOQ and comment on the implications.

Solution:

1. Number of orders $= D/Q = 25,000/500 = 50$. Ordering cost $= P \times D/Q = 50 \times \$40 = \$2,000$. Carrying cost $= CQ/2 = (\$2 \times 500)/2 = \$500$. $TC = \$2,000 + \$500 = \$2,500$.

2. $EOQ = \sqrt{(2 \times 25,000 \times \$40)/\$2}$

   $= \sqrt{1,000,000}$

   $= 1,000$

   $TC =$ Ordering cost $+$ Carrying cost $= (\$40 \times 25,000/1,000)$
   $+ [(\$2 \times 1,000)/2]$
   $= \$1,000 + \$1,000 = \$2,000$

   Relative to the current order size, the economic order quantity is larger, with fewer orders placed; however, the total cost is $500 less. Notice that Carrying cost $=$ Ordering cost for EOQ.

3. $EOQ = \sqrt{(2 \times 25,000 \times \$0.40)/\$2}$

   $= \sqrt{10,000}$

   $= 100$

   $TC =$ Ordering cost $+$ Carrying cost $= (\$0.40 \times 25,000/100)$
   $+ [(\$2 \times 100)/2]$
   $= \$100 + \$100 = \$200$

   Smaller, more frequent orders can dramatically reduce the cost of inventory. This result foreshadows the power of just-in-time purchasing.

When to Order or Produce Not only must we know how much to order (or produce), but also we must know when to place an order (or to set up for production). Avoiding stock-out costs is a key element in determining when to place an order. The **reorder point** is the point in time when a new order should be placed (or setup started). It is a function of the EOQ, the lead time, and the rate at which inventory is depleted. It is expressed in level of inventory; that is, when the inventory of a part reaches a certain level, it triggers the placement of a new order. **Lead time** is the time required to receive the economic order quantity once an order is placed or a setup is initiated.

DATA ANALYTICS

To avoid stock-out costs and to minimize carrying costs, an order should be placed so that it arrives just as the last item in inventory is used. Knowing the rate of usage and lead time allows us to compute the reorder point that accomplishes these objectives:

$$\text{Reorder point} = \text{Rate of usage} \times \text{Lead time} \qquad (20.3)$$

If the demand for the part or product is not known with certainty, the possibility of stock-out exists. To avoid this problem, organizations often choose to carry safety stock. **Safety stock** is extra inventory carried to serve as insurance against fluctuations in demand. Safety stock is computed by multiplying the lead time by the difference between the maximum rate of usage and the average rate of usage. With the presence of safety stock, the reorder point is computed as follows:

$$\text{Reorder point} = (\text{Average rate of usage} \times \text{Lead time}) + \text{Safety stock} \qquad (20.4)$$

Example 20.2 illustrates reordering with both certainty and uncertainty.

EXAMPLE 20.2

The HOW and Why of Reordering

Information:
Mantener Corporation has an EOQ of 1,000 units. The company uses 100 units per day, and an order to replenish the part requires a lead time of four days.

> **Why:**
> The reorder point is a function of the EOQ, the lead time, and the rate at which inventory is depleted. If the amount of usage is uncertain, safety stock is used as a buffer for fluctuations in demand.

Required:

1. Calculate the reorder point, using Equation 20.3.

2. Graphically display the reorder point, where the vertical axis is inventory (units) and the horizontal axis is time (days). Show two replenishments, beginning at time zero with the economic order quantity in stock.

3. *What if* the *average* usage per day of the part is 100 units but a daily maximum usage of 120 units is possible? What is the reorder point when this demand uncertainty exists?

Solution:

1. Reorder point = Rate of usage × Lead time = 100 × 4 = 400 units. Thus, an order should be placed when the inventory level of the part drops to 400 units.

2. See Exhibit 20.2. Note that the inventory is depleted just as the order arrives and that the quantity on hand jumps back up to the EOQ level.

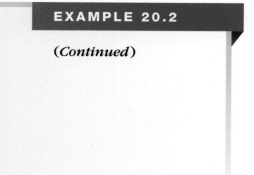

EXAMPLE 20.2

(Continued)

3.   With uncertainty, safety stock is needed. Safety stock is computed as follows:

Maximum usage	120
Average usage	(100)
Difference	20
Lead time	× 4
Safety stock	80

$$\text{Reorder point} = (\text{Average rate of usage} \times \text{Lead time}) + \text{Safety stock}$$
$$= (100 \times 4) + 80$$
$$= 480$$

Thus, an order is automatically placed whenever the inventory level drops to 480 units.

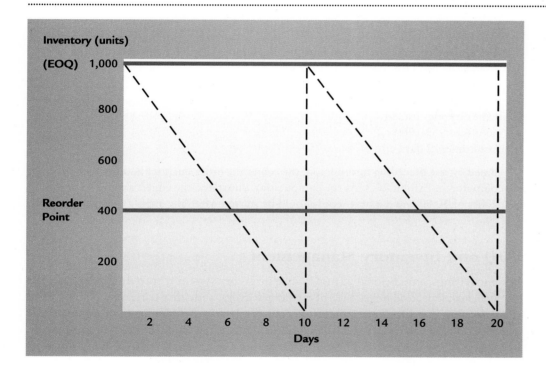

Exhibit 20.2

The Reorder Point

An Example Involving Setups

The same inventory management concepts apply to settings where inventory is manufactured. To illustrate, consider Expedition Company, a large manufacturer of garden and lawn equipment. One large plant in Kansas produces edgers. The manager of this plant is trying to determine the size of the production runs for the edgers. He is convinced that the current lot size is too large and wants to identify the quantity that should be produced to minimize the sum of the carrying and setup costs. He also wants to avoid stock-outs, since any stock-out would cause problems with the plant's network of retailers.

Exhibit 20.3

EOQ and Reorder Point Illustrated

$$EOQ = \sqrt{2DP/C}$$
$$= \sqrt{(2 \times 180{,}000 \times \$10{,}000)/\$4}$$
$$= \sqrt{900{,}000{,}000}$$
$$= 30{,}000 \text{ edgers}$$

Safety stock:	
Maximum usage	780
Average usage	(720)
Difference	60
Lead time	$\times 22$
Safety stock	1,320

Reorder point = (Average usage $\times$ Lead time) + Safety stock
$$= (720 \times 22) + 1{,}320$$
$$= 17{,}160 \text{ edgers}$$

To help him in his decision, the controller has supplied the following information:
Average demand for edgers: 720 per day
Maximum demand for edgers: 780 per day
Annual demand for edgers: 180,000
Unit carrying cost: $4
Setup cost: $10,000
Lead time: 22 days

Based on the preceding information, the economic order quantity and the reorder point are computed in Exhibit 20.3. As the computation illustrates, the edgers should be produced in batches of 30,000, and a new setup should be started when the supply of edgers drops to 17,160.

EOQ and Inventory Management

In some settings, a traditional or just-in-case inventory system is entirely appropriate. For example, hospitals need inventories of medicines, drugs, and other critical supplies on hand at all times so that life-threatening situations can be handled. Using an economic order quantity coupled with safety stock would seem eminently sensible in such an environment. Relying on a critical drug to arrive just in time to save a heart attack victim is simply not practical. Furthermore, many smaller retail stores, manufacturers, and services may not have the buying power to command alternative inventory management systems such as just-in-time purchasing.

As the edger example illustrates (Exhibit 20.3), the EOQ model is very useful in identifying the optimal trade-off between inventory carrying costs and setup costs. It also is useful in helping to deal with uncertainty by using safety stock. The historical importance of the EOQ model in many American industries can be better appreciated by understanding the nature of the traditional manufacturing environment. This environment has been characterized by the mass production of a few standardized products that typically have a very high setup cost. The production of the edgers fits this pattern. The high setup cost encouraged a large batch size: 30,000 units. The annual demand of 180,000 units can be satisfied using only six batches. Thus, production runs for these firms tended to be quite long. Furthermore, diversity was viewed as being costly and was avoided. Producing variations of the product can be quite expensive, especially since additional, special features would usually demand even more expensive and frequent setups—the reason for the standardized products.

Big Data and Inventory Management

Tesco, a British grocery and merchandiser retailer, has used big data analytics to improve its prediction of customer buying habits and its assessment of special sales offers. In particular, Tesco developed an analytic model that allows management to use weather patterns to properly stock store shelves. For example, warm weather following a cold spell means that the stores in the region should stock more barbeque meats and less cat litter. Using this type of predictive analytics, Tesco has reduced its out of stock for good weather products by a factor of four. Big data analytics have also allowed Tesco to better determine which special sales to run and to know how to alter stocking to accommodate increasing or decreasing demand for certain products. Tesco discovered, for example, that for nonperishable goods (such as cooking sauces), a "buy one, get one free" offer produces better sales than a 50 percent discount; the opposite is true for fruits and vegetables. This "big information" about customer buying habits and special sales has helped Tesco save about $24.5 million annually.[9]

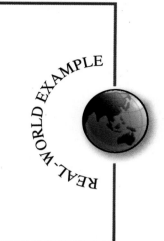

REAL-WORLD EXAMPLE

JIT INVENTORY MANAGEMENT

OBJECTIVE ▸ **2**

Discuss just-in-time (JIT) inventory management.

The manufacturing environment for many of these traditional, large-batch, high-setup-cost firms has changed dramatically in the past two or three decades. For one thing, the competitive markets are no longer defined by national boundaries. Advances in transportation and communication have contributed significantly to the creation of global competition. Advances in technology have contributed to shorter life cycles for products, and product diversity has increased. Foreign firms offering higher-quality, lower-cost products with *specialized features* have created tremendous pressures for our domestic large-batch, high-setup-cost firms to increase both quality and product diversity while simultaneously reducing total costs. These competitive pressures have led many firms to abandon the EOQ model in favor of a JIT approach. JIT has two strategic objectives: to increase profits and to improve a firm's competitive position. These two objectives are achieved by controlling costs (enabling better price competition and increased profits), improving delivery performance, and improving quality. JIT offers increased cost efficiency and simultaneously has the flexibility to respond to customer demands for better quality and more variety. Quality, flexibility, and cost efficiency are foundational principles for world-class competition.

Just-in-time inventory management represents the continual pursuit of productivity through the elimination of waste. JIT is an essential and integral part of lean manufacturing. Thus, when we speak of JIT practices, they are virtually identical to lean practices. Both have the objective of eliminating waste; lean manufacturing uses JIT concepts in its waste elimination approach. *Non-value-added* activities are a major source of waste. From Chapter 12, we know that non-value-added activities either are unnecessary or are necessary but inefficient and improvable. Necessary activities are essential to the business and/or are of value to customers. Eliminating non-value-added activities is a major thrust of JIT, but it is also a basic objective of any company following the path of continuous improvement—regardless of whether or not JIT is being used.

Clearly, JIT is much more than an inventory management system. Inventories, however, are particularly viewed as representing waste. They tie up resources such as cash, space, and labor. They also conceal inefficiencies in production and increase the complexity of a firm's information system. Thus, even though JIT focuses on more than inventory management,

---

9   Nancy Master, "Tesco Improves Supply Chain with Big Data, Automated Data Collection," April 17, 2013, http://www .rfgen.com/blog/bid/285148/Tesco-Improves-Supply-Chain-with-Big-Data-Automated-Data-Collection, accessed July 7, 2016.

control of inventory is an important ancillary benefit. In this chapter, the inventory dimension of JIT is emphasized. In Chapter 11, other benefits and features of JIT were described. Chapter 12, in particular, focused on non-value-added activity analysis.

A Pull System

JIT is a manufacturing approach that maintains that goods should be pulled through the system by present demand rather than pushed through the system on a fixed schedule based on anticipated demand. Many fast-food restaurants, like **Burger King**, use a pull system to control their finished goods inventory. When a customer orders a hamburger, it is taken from the rack. When the number of hamburgers gets too low, the cooks make new hamburgers. Customer demand pulls the materials through the system. This same principle is used in manufacturing settings. Each operation produces only what is necessary to satisfy the demand of the succeeding operation. The material or subassembly arrives just in time for production to occur so that demand can be met.

One effect of JIT is to reduce inventories to very low levels. The pursuit of insignificant levels of inventories is vital to the success of JIT. This idea of pursuing insignificant inventories, however, necessarily challenges the traditional reasons for holding inventories (see Exhibit 20.1). These reasons are no longer viewed as valid.

According to the traditional view, inventories solve some underlying problem related to each of the reasons listed in Exhibit 20.1. For example, the problem of resolving the conflict between ordering or setup costs and carrying costs is solved by selecting an inventory level that minimizes the sum of these costs. If demand is greater than expected or if production is reduced by breakdowns and production inefficiencies, then inventories serve as buffers, providing customers with products that otherwise might not have been available. Similarly, inventories can prevent stock-outs caused by late delivery of material, defective parts, and failures of machines used to produce subassemblies. Finally, inventories are often the solution to the problem of buying the best materials for the least cost through the use of quantity discounts.

JIT/lean practices refuse to use inventories as the solution to these problems. In fact, the JIT approach can be seen as substituting information for inventories. Companies must track materials and finished goods more carefully. JIT inventory management offers alternative solutions that do not require high inventories.

Setup and Carrying Costs: The JIT/Lean Approach

JIT takes a radically different approach to minimizing total carrying and setup costs. The traditional approach accepts the existence of setup costs and then finds the order quantity that best balances the two categories of costs. JIT, on the other hand, does not accept setup costs (or ordering costs) as a given; rather, JIT attempts to drive these costs to zero. If setup costs and ordering costs become insignificant, the only remaining cost to minimize is carrying cost, which is accomplished by reducing inventories to very low levels. This approach explains the push for zero inventories in a JIT system.

Long-Term Contracts, Continuous Replenishment, and Electronic Data Interchange
Ordering costs are reduced by developing close relationships with suppliers. Negotiating long-term contracts for the supply of outside materials will obviously reduce the number of orders and the associated ordering costs. Retailers have found a way to reduce ordering costs by adopting an arrangement known as *continuous replenishment*. **Continuous replenishment** means a manufacturer assumes the inventory management function for the retailer. The manufacturer tells the retailer when and how much stock to reorder. The retailer reviews the recommendation and approves the order if it makes sense.

Wal-Mart makes extensive use of Vendor Managed Inventory with its suppliers.[10] For example, Wal-Mart uses this arrangement with Procter & Gamble. The arrangement has reduced inventories for Wal-Mart and has also reduced stock-out problems. Additionally, Wal-Mart often sells Procter & Gamble's goods before it has to pay for them. Procter & Gamble, on the other hand, has become a preferred supplier, has more and better shelf space, and also has less demand uncertainty. The ability to project demand more accurately allows Procter & Gamble to produce and deliver continuously in smaller lots—a goal of JIT manufacturing. Moreover, as continuous replenishment increased as a percentage of the total orders for a customer, Procter & Gamble found that its production savings increased.

Similar arrangements can be made between manufacturers and suppliers.

The process of continuous replenishment is facilitated by *electronic data interchange*. **Electronic data interchange (EDI)** allows suppliers access to a buyer's online database. By knowing the buyer's production schedule (in the case of a manufacturer), the supplier can deliver the needed parts where they are needed just in time for their use. EDI involves no paper—no purchase orders or invoices. The supplier uses the production schedule, which is in the database, to determine its own production and delivery schedules. When the parts are shipped, an electronic message is sent from the supplier to the buyer that a shipment is en route. When the parts arrive, a bar code is scanned with an electronic wand, and this initiates payment for the goods. Clearly, EDI requires a close working arrangement between the supplier and the buyer—they almost operate as one company rather than two separate companies.

Reducing Setup Times Reducing setup times requires a company to search for new, more efficient ways to accomplish setup. Fortunately, experience has indicated that dramatic reductions in setup times can be achieved. A classic example is that of **Harley-Davidson**. Upon adopting a JIT system, Harley-Davidson reduced setup time by more than 75 percent on the machines evaluated.[11] In some cases, Harley-Davidson was able to reduce the setup times from hours to minutes. Other companies have experienced similar results.

Due-Date Performance: The JIT (Lean) Solution

Due-date performance is a measure of a firm's ability to respond to customer needs. In the past, finished goods inventories have been used to ensure that a firm is able to meet a requested delivery date. JIT solves the problem of due-date performance not by building inventory but by dramatically reducing lead times. Shorter lead times increase a firm's ability to meet requested delivery dates and to respond quickly to the demands of the market. Thus, the firm's competitiveness is improved. JIT cuts lead times by reducing setup times, improving quality, and using cellular manufacturing. Moreover, since the JIT approach is a fundamental part of lean manufacturing, JIT practices are essentially lean manufacturing practices. Thus, lean manufacturing is a logical extension and integration of JIT concepts.

Manufacturing cells reduce travel distance between machines and inventory; they can also have a dramatic effect on lead time, floor space required, productivity, cost, and quality.

10 Clara Lu, "Walmart's Successful Supply Chain Management," TradeGecko, October 4, 2018, https://www.tradegecko.com/blog/supply-chain-management/incredibly-successful-supply-chain-management-walmart, accessed July 13, 2020. Dan Gilmore, "Supply Chain Lessons from Proctor and Gamble," *Supply Chain Digest*, August 5, 2011, http://www.scdigest.com/assets/FirstThoughts/11-08-05.php?cid54822, accessed July 15, 2020.

11 Gene Schwind, "Man Arrives Just in Time to Save Harley-Davidson," *Material Handling Engineering* (August 1984): 28–35.

Smiths Medical produces medical procedural kits. For example, a sterile, sealed kit for an epidural procedure would contain the needed individual components such as tubing, needles, syringes, and medication. At Smiths' Keene, New Hampshire, location, the plant used two production lines to assemble kits for their Pain Management area. The two production lines were replaced with four work cells (with the same number of workers). Using the cellular approach, floor space was reduced from 4,700 square feet to 1,800 square feet; weekly output increased from 34,000 to 61,975 trays; units produced per labor hour increased from 7.2 to 14.4. Quality was maintained, costs were reduced, and productive efficiency increased.[12]

Avoidance of Shutdown and Process Reliability: The JIT/Lean Approach

Most shutdowns occur for one of three reasons: machine failure, defective material or subassembly, and unavailability of a material or subassembly. Holding inventories is one solution to all three problems.

Those espousing the JIT approach claim that inventories do not solve the problems but cover up or hide them. JIT proponents use the analogy of rocks in a lake. The rocks represent the three problems, and the water represents inventories. If the lake is deep (inventories are high), then the rocks are never exposed, and managers can pretend they do not exist. By reducing inventories to zero, the rocks are exposed and can no longer be ignored. JIT solves the three problems by emphasizing total preventive maintenance and total quality control in addition to building the right kind of relationship with suppliers.

Total Preventive Maintenance Zero machine failures is the goal of **total preventive maintenance**. By paying more attention to preventive maintenance, most machine breakdowns can be avoided. This objective is easier to attain in a JIT environment because of the interdisciplinary labor philosophy. It is fairly common for a cell worker to be trained in maintenance of the machines he or she operates. Because of the pull-through nature of JIT, cell workers may have idle manufacturing time. Some of this time, then, can be used productively by having the cell workers involved in preventive maintenance.

Total Quality Control The problem of defective parts is solved by striving for zero defects. Because JIT manufacturing does not rely on inventories to replace defective parts or materials, the emphasis on quality for both internally produced and externally purchased materials increases significantly. The outcome is impressive: the number of rejected parts tends to fall by 75–90 percent. Decreasing defective parts also diminishes the justification for inventories based on unreliable processes.

The Kanban System To ensure that parts or materials are available when needed, a system called the **Kanban system** is employed. This is an information system that controls production through the use of markers or cards. The Kanban system is responsible for ensuring that the necessary products (or parts) are produced (or acquired) in the necessary quantities at the necessary time. It is the heart of the JIT inventory management system.

A Kanban system uses cards or markers, which are plastic, cardboard, or metal plates measuring four inches by eight inches. The Kanban is usually placed in a vinyl sack and attached to the part or a container holding the needed parts.

---

12 Manufacturing Advancement Center, "Manufacturing Success Stories: Cellular Manufacturing a Real Shot in the Arm for Smiths Medical," http://www.massmac.org/newsline/0709/article05.htm, accessed September 15, 2020.

A basic Kanban system uses three cards: a *withdrawal Kanban*, a *production Kanban*, and a *vendor Kanban*. The first two control the movement of work among the manufacturing processes, while the third controls movement of parts between the processes and outside suppliers. A **withdrawal Kanban** specifies the quantity that a subsequent process should withdraw from the preceding process. A **production Kanban** specifies the quantity that the preceding process should produce. A **vendor Kanban** is used to notify suppliers to deliver more parts; it also specifies when the parts are needed. The three Kanbans are illustrated in Exhibits 20.4, 20.5, and 20.6, respectively.

How Kanban cards are used to control the work flow can be illustrated with a simple example. Assume that two processes are needed to manufacture a product. The first process (CB Assembly) builds and tests printed circuit boards (using a U-shaped manufacturing cell). The second process (Final Assembly) puts eight circuit boards into a subassembly purchased from an outside supplier. The final product is a personal computer.

Exhibit 20.7 provides the plant layout corresponding to the manufacture of the personal computers. Refer to the exhibit as the steps involved in using Kanbans are outlined.

Consider first the movement of work between the two processing areas. Assume that eight circuit boards are placed in a container and that one such container is located in the CB stores

Item No.	15670T07	Preceding Process	
Item Name	Circuit Board	CB Assembly	
Computer Type	TR6547 PC		
Box Capacity	8	Subsequent Process	
Box Type	C	Final Assembly	

Exhibit 20.4

Withdrawal Kanban

Item No.	15670T07	Preceding Process	
Item Name	Circuit Board	CB Assembly	
Computer Type	TR6547 PC		
Box Capacity	8		
Box Type	C		

Exhibit 20.5

Production Kanban

Item No.	15670T07	Name of Receiving Company	
Item Name	Computer Casting	Electro PC	
Box Capacity	8	Receiving Gate	
Box Type	A	75	
Time to Deliver	8:30 A.M., 12:30 P.M., 2:30 P.M.		
Name of Supplier	Gerry Supply		

Exhibit 20.6

Vendor Kanban

Exhibit 20.7

The Kanban Process

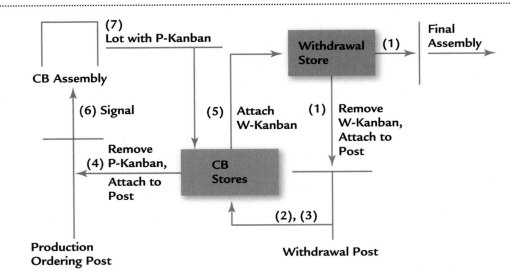

area. Attached to this container is a production Kanban (P-Kanban). A second container with eight circuit boards is located near the Final Assembly line (the withdrawal store) with a withdrawal Kanban (W-Kanban). Now assume that the production schedule calls for the immediate assembly of a computer.

The Kanban setups can be described as follows:

1. A worker from the Final Assembly line goes to the withdrawal store, removes the eight circuit boards, and places them into production. The worker also removes the withdrawal Kanban and places it on the withdrawal post.

2. The withdrawal Kanban on the post signals that the Final Assembly unit needs an additional eight circuit boards.

3. A worker from Final Assembly (or a material handler called a *carrier*) removes the withdrawal Kanban from the post and carries it to the CB stores area.

4. At the CB stores area, the carrier removes the production Kanban from the container of eight circuit boards and places it on the production ordering post.

5. The carrier next attaches the withdrawal Kanban to the container of parts and carries the container back to the Final Assembly area. Assembly of the next computer can begin.

6. The production Kanban on the production ordering post signals the workers of CB Assembly to begin producing another lot of circuit boards. The production Kanban is removed and accompanies the units as they are produced.

7. When the lot of eight circuit boards is completed, the units are placed in a container in the CB stores area with the production Kanban attached. The cycle is then repeated.

The use of Kanbans ensures that the subsequent process (Final Assembly) withdraws the circuit boards from the preceding process (CB Assembly) in the necessary quantity at the appropriate time. The Kanban system also controls the preceding process by allowing it to produce only the quantities withdrawn by the subsequent process. In this way, inventories are kept at a minimum, and the components arrive just in time to be used.

Essentially, the same steps are followed for a purchased subassembly. The only difference is the use of a vendor Kanban in place of a production Kanban. A vendor Kanban on a vendor post signals to the supplier that another order is needed. As with the circuit boards, the subassemblies must be delivered just in time for use. A JIT purchasing system requires the supplier to deliver small quantities on a frequent basis. These deliveries could be weekly, daily, or even several times a day. This calls for a close working relationship with suppliers. Long-term contractual agreements tend to ensure supply of materials.

Discounts and Price Increases: JIT Purchasing Versus Holding Inventories

Traditionally, inventories are carried so that a firm can take advantage of quantity discounts and hedge against future price increases of the items purchased. The objective is to lower the cost of inventory. JIT achieves the same objective without carrying inventories. The JIT solution is to negotiate long-term contracts with a few chosen suppliers located as close to the production facility as possible and to establish more extensive supplier involvement. Suppliers are not selected on the basis of price alone. Performance—the quality of the component and the ability to deliver as needed—and commitment to JIT purchasing are vital considerations. Other benefits of long-term contracts exist. They stipulate prices and acceptable quality levels. Long-term contracts also reduce dramatically the number of orders placed, which helps to drive down the ordering cost. Another effect of JIT purchasing is to lower the cost of purchased parts.

JIT's Limitations

JIT is not simply an approach that can be purchased and plugged in with immediate results. Its implementation should be more of an evolutionary process than a revolutionary process. Patience is needed. JIT is often referred to as a program of simplification—yet this does not imply that it is simple or easy to implement. Time is required, for example, to build sound relationships with suppliers. Insisting on immediate changes in delivery times and quality may not be realistic and may cause difficult confrontations between a company and its suppliers. Partnership, not coercion, should be the basis of supplier relationships. To achieve the benefits that are associated with JIT purchasing, a company may be tempted to redefine unilaterally its supplier relationships. Unilaterally redefining supplier relationships by extracting concessions and dictating terms may create supplier resentment and actually cause suppliers to retaliate. In the long run, suppliers may seek new markets, find ways to charge higher prices (than would exist with a preferred supplier arrangement), or seek regulatory relief. These actions may destroy many of the JIT benefits extracted by the impatient company.

Workers also may be affected by JIT. Studies have shown that sharp reductions in inventory buffers may cause a regimented work flow and high levels of stress among production workers. Some have suggested a deliberate pace of inventory reduction to allow workers to develop a sense of autonomy and to encourage their participation in broader improvement efforts. Forced and dramatic reductions in inventories may indeed reveal problems—but it may cause more problems: lost sales and stressed workers. If the workers perceive JIT as a way of simply squeezing more out of them, then JIT efforts may be doomed. Perhaps a better strategy for JIT implementation is one where inventory reductions follow the process improvements that JIT offers. Implementing JIT is not easy; it requires careful and thorough planning and preparation. Companies should expect some struggle and frustration.

The most glaring deficiency of JIT is the absence of inventory to buffer production interruptions. Current sales are constantly being threatened by an unexpected interruption in production. In fact, if a problem occurs, JIT's approach consists of trying to find and solve the problem before any further production activity occurs. Retailers who use JIT tactics also face the possibility of shortages. JIT retailers order what they need now—not what they expect to sell—because the idea is to flow goods through the channel as late as possible, hence keeping inventories low and decreasing the need for mark-downs. If demand increases well beyond the retailer's supply of inventory, the retailer may be unable to make order adjustments quickly enough to avoid irked customers and lost sales.

The COVID-19 pandemic is a striking example of JIT limitations. The pandemic produced shortages of various produces such as critical medical equipment and supplies, drugs, cleaning products, and toilet paper. When there is a surge in demand, JIT inventory management seems to lack the robustness and resilience needed for an effective response. In the coming years, many believe that companies will seek greater inventory, purchasing, and manufacturing flexibility. While JIT will likely survive, many companies will likely establish multiple sources for materials and manufacturing. They also may move to more regionalized supply and production, especially for those firms in critical industries.

Yet, in spite of the downside, many retailers and manufacturers seem to be strongly committed to JIT. Apparently, losing sales on occasion is less costly than carrying high levels of inventory.

Even so, we must recognize that a sale lost today is a sale lost forever. Installing a JIT system so that it operates with very little interruption is not a short-run project. Thus, losing sales is a real cost of installing a JIT system. An alternative, and perhaps complementary, approach is the theory of constraints (TOC). In principle, TOC can be used in conjunction with JIT manufacturing. After all, JIT manufacturing environments also have constraints. Furthermore, the TOC approach has the very appealing quality of protecting current sales while also striving to increase future sales by increasing quality, lowering response time, and decreasing operating costs. However, before we introduce and discuss the theory of constraints, we need to provide a brief introduction to constrained optimization theory.

OBJECTIVE 3

Explain the basic concepts of constrained optimization.

BASIC CONCEPTS OF CONSTRAINED OPTIMIZATION

Manufacturing and service organizations must choose the mix of products that they will produce and sell. Decisions about product mix can have a significant impact on an organization's profitability. Each mix represents an alternative that carries with it an associated profit level. A manager should choose the alternative that maximizes total profits. The usual approach is to assume that only unit-based variable costs are relevant to the product mix decision. Thus, assuming that non-unit-level costs are the same for different mixes of products, a manager needs to choose the mix alternative that maximizes total contribution margin.

If a firm possesses unlimited resources and the demand for each product being considered is unlimited, then the product mix decision is simple—produce an infinite number of each product. Unfortunately, every firm faces limited resources and limited demand for each product. These limitations are called **constraints**. **External constraints** are limiting factors imposed on the firm from external sources (such as market demand). **Internal constraints** are limiting factors found within the firm (such as machine or labor time availability). Although resources and demands may be limited, certain mixes may not meet all the demand or use all of the available resources. Constraints whose limited resources are not fully used by a product mix are **loose constraints**. If, on the other hand, a product mix uses all of the limited resources of a constraint, then the constraint is a **binding constraint**. **Constrained optimization** is choosing the optimal mix that maximizes the total contribution margin given the constraints faced by the firm. Some interesting insights are available when at most one internal constraint is allowed.

One Binding Internal Constraint

DATA ANALYTICS

Typically, the constrained optimization problem is modeled by (1) mathematically expressing the objective of maximizing total contribution margin and (2) mathematically expressing both the internal and external constraints. The function to be optimized (maximized in the case of contribution margin) is called the **objective function**. The objective function can be expressed mathematically by multiplying the unit contribution margin by the units to be produced for each product (which is expressed as an unknown variable) and then summing over all products. An internal constraint is expressed as an inequality, where the amount of scarce resource used per unit of product is multiplied by the units to be produced for each product and summed, to obtain the left-hand side of the inequality. The right-hand side of the inequality is simply the total amount of resource available to be used by the products. A similar approach is used for external constraints. **Example 20.3** illustrates constrained optimization with one internal constraint. In this simple data analytic model, the contribution margin per unit of scarce resource is the governing or deciding factor that is used to identify the optimal mix of products.

EXAMPLE 20.3

The HOW and WHY of Solving Constrained Optimization Problems with One Internal Constraint

Information:
Schaller Company produces two types of machine parts: X and Y, with unit contribution margins of $300 and $600, respectively. Assume initially that Schaller can sell all that is produced of either part. Part X requires one hour of drilling, and Part Y requires three hours of drilling. The firm owns three machines that together provide 120 drilling hours per week.

> **Why:**
> The objective is to produce the mix of parts that maximizes total contribution margin subject to the constraints faced by the firm. With one internal constraint, the maximum amount of the product with the *largest* contribution margin per unit of scarce resource should first be produced.

Required:

1.   Express the objective of maximizing total contribution margin subject to the drilling-hour constraint.

2.   Identify the optimal amount that should be produced of each machine part and the total contribution margin associated with this mix.

3.   *What if* market conditions are such that Schaller can sell at most 60 units of Part X and 100 units of Part Y? Express the objective function with its associated constraints for this case and identify the optimal mix and its associated total contribution margin.

Solution:

1.   Objective function: Max $Z = \$300X + \$600Y$

   Subject to: $X + 3Y \leq 120$ (drilling-hour constraint)

2.   Contribution margin (CM) per unit of scarce resource for Part X = $300 ($300 unit CM/1 drilling hour per unit) and for Part Y = $200 ($600 unit CM/3 drilling hours per unit). Thus, 120 units of Part X (120 hours/1 hour per unit) should be produced and sold for a total contribution margin of $36,000 ($300 × 120). None of Part Y should be produced.

3.   Max $Z = \$300X + \$600Y$

$$\text{subject to: } X + 3Y \leq 120 \text{ (drilling-hour constraint)}$$
$$X \leq 60 \text{ (demand constraint for Part } X)$$
$$Y \leq 100 \text{ (demand constraint for Part } Y)$$

The maximum amount of Part X should be produced: 60 units, using 60 drilling hours. This leaves 60 drilling hours so that 20 units of Part Y (60/3) can be produced. Total CM = ($300 × 60) + ($600 × 20) = $30,000.

Multiple Internal Binding Constraints

It is possible for an organization to have more than one binding constraint. All organizations face multiple constraints: limitations of materials, limitations of labor inputs, limited machine hours, and so on. The solution of the product mix problem in the presence of multiple internal binding constraints is considerably more complicated and requires the use of a specialized mathematical technique known as *linear programming*.

DATA ANALYTICS

Linear Programming A **linear programming model** expresses a constrained optimization problem as a linear objective function subject to a set of linear constraints. *Nonnegativity constraints* that simply reflect the reality that negative quantities of a product cannot be produced are usually included in the set of linear constraints. All constraints, taken together, are referred to as the **constraint set**. A **feasible solution** is a solution that satisfies the constraints in the linear programming model. The collection of all feasible solutions is called the **feasible set of solutions**. **Linear programming** is a method that searches among possible solutions until it finds the optimal solution. The theory of linear programming permits many solutions to be ignored. In fact, all but a finite number of solutions are eliminated by the theory, with the search then limited to the resulting finite set. Linear programming is a very powerful data analytic model.

When there are only two products, the optimal solution can be identified by graphing. It has been shown in the literature on linear programming that the optimal solution will always be one of the corner points. Thus, once the graph is drawn and the corner points are identified, finding the solution is simply a matter of computing the value of each corner point and selecting the one with the greatest value. Four steps are followed in solving the problem graphically.

1. Graph each constraint.
2. Identify the feasible set of solutions.
3. Identify all corner-point values in the feasible set.
4. Select the corner point that yields the largest value for the objective function.

Graphical solutions are not practical with more than two or three products. Fortunately, an algorithm called the **simplex method** can be used to solve larger linear programming problems. This algorithm has been coded and is available for use on computers to solve these larger problems.

Since solving a linear programming problem by graphing provides considerable insight into the way such problems are solved, it is illustrated in **Example 20.4** by expanding the Schaller Company problem. Exhibit 20.8 provides the detailed constraint data for this expanded problem.

Exhibit 20.8

Constraint Data: Schaller Company

Resource Name	Resource Available	Part X Resource Usage: Per Unit	Part Y Resource Usage: Per Unit
Grinding	80 grinding hours	One hour	One hour
Drilling	120 drilling hours	One hour	Three hours
Polishing	90 labor hours	Two hours	One hour
Market demand: Part X	60 units	One unit	Zero units
Market demand: Part Y	100 units	Zero units	One unit

EXAMPLE 20.4

The HOW and WHY of Solving Linear Programming Problems with Two Variables

Information:
Schaller Company produces two types of machine parts: X and Y, with unit contribution margins of $300 and $600, respectively. See also Exhibit 20.8.

> **Why:**
> Two-product linear programming problems can be solved graphically. Constraints are graphed, and the feasible corner point that yields the largest value (for maximization problems) is the optimal solution.

EXAMPLE 20.4

(Continued)

Required:

1. Express Schaller Company's constrained optimization problem as a linear programming model.

2. Using a graphical approach, solve the linear programming model expressed in Requirement 1. Which constraints are binding?

3. *What if* Schaller Company had five additional drilling hours with all other resources held constant? What is the new optimal mix and associated total contribution margin? What is the incremental benefit per drilling hour caused by the additional five hours, if any?

Solution:

1. Max $Z = \$300X + \$600Y$

   subject to

Internal constraints:	$X + Y \leq 80$ (grinding)
	$X + 3Y \leq 120$ (drilling)
	$2X + Y \leq 90$ (polishing)
External constraints:	$X \leq 60$
	$Y \leq 100$
Nonnegativity constraints:	$X \geq 0$
	$Y \geq 0$

2. See Exhibit 20.9 for the graph (to obtain the graph, identify two points for each constraint, plot, and connect). The coordinates of *A*, *B*, *C*, and *D* are obtained by solving the simultaneous equations of the associated intersecting constraints within the feasible set (Region *ABCD*, including the frontier).

Corner Point	X-Value	Y-Value	Z = \$300X + \$600Y
A	0	0	\$ 0
B	0	40	24,000
C	30	30	27,000*
D	45	0	13,500

   *Optimal solution.

   The binding constraints are drilling and polishing. Drilling: $30 + 3(30) = 120$; and polishing: $2(30) + 30 = 90$.

3. The only feasible corner point affected is *C*. Solving $X + 3Y = 125$ and $2X + Y = 90$, simultaneously, we obtain $X = 29$ and $Y = 32$, with $Z = \$27,900$. The incremental benefit is \$900 (\$27,900 – \$27,000), which is \$180 per drilling hour (total contribution margin increases by \$180 for each additional drilling hour).

As Example 20.4 shows, the linear programming model is an important tool for making product mix decisions. Requirement 3 of Example 20.4 illustrates that when the scarce resource is increased for drilling, a binding constraint, then total profitability can be increased. The example also produced the per-unit effect (\$180 per drilling hour for the Schaller example). This same per-unit information is produced as a by-product of the simplex method. The simplex method produces what are called *shadow prices*. **Shadow prices** indicate the amount by which contribution margin will increase for one additional unit of scarce resource. Thus, although the linear programming model produces an optimal product mix decision, its real managerial value may be more related to the kinds of inputs that must be generated for the model to be used and the way these inputs can be managed to create more favorable outcomes. For example,

Exhibit 20.9

Graphical Solution

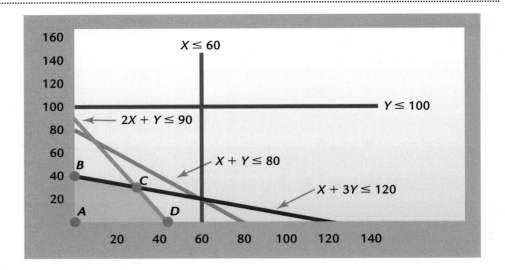

applying the model forces management to identify internal and external constraints. Internal constraints relate to how products consume resources; thus, resource usage relationships must be identified. Once the constrained relationships are known to management, they can be used by management to identify means of improving a firm's performance in a variety of ways, including inventory management.

OBJECTIVE 4

Describe how the theory of constraints can be used to manage inventory.

THEORY OF CONSTRAINTS

The goal of the **theory of constraints** is to make money now and in the future by managing constraints. The theory of constraints (TOC) recognizes that the performance of any organization (system) is limited by its constraints. In operational terms, every system has at least one constraint that limits its output. The theory of constraints develops a specific approach to manage constraints to support the objective of continuous improvement. TOC, however, focuses on the *system-level* effects of continuous improvement. Each company (i.e., system) is compared to a chain. Every chain has a weakest link that may limit the performance of the chain as a whole. The weakest link is the system's constraint and is the key to improving overall organizational performance. Why? Ignoring the weakest link and improving any other link cost money and will not improve system performance. On the other hand, by strengthening the weakest link, system performance can be improved. At some point, however, strengthening the weakest link shifts the focus to a different link that has now become the weakest. This next-weakest link is now the key system constraint, and it must be strengthened so that overall system performance can be improved. Thus, TOC can be thought of as a systems approach to continuous improvement.

Operational Measures

Given that the goal is to make money, TOC argues that the next crucial step is to identify operational measures that encourage achievement of the goal. TOC focuses on three operational measures of systems performance: *throughput*, *inventory*, and *operating expenses*. **Throughput** is the rate at which an organization generates money through sales. Operationally, throughput is the *rate* at which *contribution dollars* come into the organization. Thus, we have the following operational definition:

$$\text{Throughput} = (\text{Sales revenue} - \text{Unit-level variable expenses})/\text{Time} \tag{20.5}$$

Typically, the unit-level variable costs acknowledged are materials and power. Direct labor is viewed as a fixed unit-level expense and is not usually included in the definition. With this understanding, throughput corresponds to contribution margin. It is also important to note that it is a global measure and not a local measure. Finally, throughput is a rate. It is the contribution earned per unit of time (per day, per month, etc.).

Inventory is all the money the organization spends in turning materials into throughput. In operational terms, inventory is money invested in anything that it intends to sell and, thus, expands the traditional definition to include assets such as facilities, equipment (which are eventually sold at the end of their useful lives), fixtures, and computers. In the TOC world, inventory is the money spent on items that do not have to be immediately expensed. Thus, inventory represents the money tied up inside the organization.

Operating expenses are defined as all the money the organization spends in turning inventories into throughput and, therefore, represent all other money that an organization spends. This includes direct labor and all operating and maintenance expenses. Thus, throughput is a measure of money coming into an organization, inventory measures the money tied up within the system, and operating expenses represent money leaving the system. Based on these three measures, the objectives of management can be expressed as increasing throughput, minimizing inventory, and decreasing operating expenses.

By increasing these objectives, the following three traditional financial measures of performance will be affected favorably: net income and return on investment will increase and cash flow will improve. Of the three TOC factors, throughput is viewed as being the most important for improving financial performance, followed by inventory, and then by operating expenses. The rationale for this order is straightforward. Operating expenses and inventories can be reduced at most to zero (inventory, though, being the larger amount), while there is virtually no upper limit on throughput. Increasing throughput and decreasing operating expenses have always been emphasized as key elements in improving the three financial measures of performance; the role of minimizing inventory, however, in achieving these improvements has been traditionally regarded as less important than reducing operating expenses.

The theory of constraints, like JIT, assigns inventory management a much more prominent role than does the traditional just-in-case viewpoint. TOC recognizes that lowering inventory decreases carrying costs and, thus, decreases operating expenses and improves net income. TOC, however, argues that lowering inventory helps produce a competitive edge by having better products, lower prices, and faster response to customer needs.

Higher-Quality Products   Better products mean higher quality. It also means that the company is able to improve products and quickly provide these improved products to the market. The relationship between low inventories and quality has been described in the JIT section. Essentially, low inventories allow defects to be detected more quickly and the cause of the problem to be assessed.

Improving products is also a key competitive element. New or improved products need to reach the market quickly—before competitors can provide similar features. This goal is facilitated with low inventories. Low inventories allow new product changes to be introduced more quickly because the company has fewer old products (in stock or in process) that would need to be scrapped or sold before the new product is introduced.

Lower Prices   High inventories mean more productive capacity is needed, leading to a greater investment in equipment and space. Since lead time and high work-in-process inventories are usually correlated, high inventories may often be the cause of overtime. Overtime, of course, increases operating expenses and lowers profitability. Lower inventories reduce carrying costs, per-unit investment costs, and other operating expenses such as overtime and special shipping charges. By lowering investment and operating costs, the unit margin of each product is increased, providing more flexibility in pricing decisions.

Improved Delivery Performance   Delivering goods on time and producing goods with shorter lead times than the market dictates are important competitive tools. Delivering goods on time is related to a firm's ability to forecast the time required to produce and deliver goods. If a firm has higher inventories than its competitors, then the firm's production lead time is higher than the industry's forecast horizon. High inventories may obscure the actual time required to produce and fill an order. Lower inventories allow actual lead times to be more carefully observed, and more accurate delivery dates can be provided. Shortening lead times is also crucial. Shortening lead times is equivalent to lowering work-in-process inventories. A company carrying 10 days of work-in-process inventories has an average production lead time of 10 days. If the company can reduce lead time from 10 to five days, then the company should now be carrying only five days of work-in-process inventories. As lead times are reduced, it is also possible to reduce finished goods inventories. For example, if the lead time for a product is 10 days and the market requires delivery on demand, then the firms must carry, on average, 10 days of finished goods inventory (plus some safety stock to cover demand uncertainty). Suppose that the firm is able to reduce lead time to five days. In this case, finished goods inventory should also be reduced to five days. Thus, the level of inventories signals the organization's ability to respond. High levels relative to those of competitors translate into a competitive disadvantage. TOC, therefore, emphasizes reduction of inventories by reducing lead times.

Five-Step Method for Improving Performance

The theory of constraints uses five steps to achieve its goal of improving organizational performance:

1. Identify an organization's constraints.
2. Exploit the binding constraints.
3. Subordinate everything else to the decisions made in Step 2.
4. Elevate the organization's binding constraints.
5. Repeat the process as a new constraint emerges to limit output.

DATA ANALYTICS

Step 1: Identify an Organization's Constraints   Step 1 is identical in concept to the process described for linear programming. Internal and external constraints are identified. The optimal product mix is identified as the mix that maximizes throughput subject to all the organization's constraints. The optimal mix reveals how much of each constrained resource is used and which of the organization's constraints are binding.

Step 2: Exploit the Binding Constraints   One way to make the best use of any binding constraints is to ensure that the optimal product mix is produced. Making the best use of binding constraints, however, is more extensive than simply ensuring production of the optimal mix. This step is the heart of TOC's philosophy of short-run constraint management and is directly related to TOC's goal of reducing inventories and improving performance.

Most organizations have only a few binding resource constraints. The major binding constraint is defined as the **drummer**. Assume, for example, that there is only one internal binding constraint. By default, this constraint becomes the drummer. The drummer constraint's production rate sets the production rate for the entire plant. Downstream processes fed by the drummer constraint are naturally forced to follow its rate of production. Scheduling for downstream processes is easy. Once a part is finished at the drummer process, the next process begins its operation. Similarly, each subsequent operation begins when the prior operation is finished. Upstream processes that feed the drummer constraint are *scheduled* to produce at the same rate as the drummer constraint. Scheduling at the drummer rate prevents the production of excessive upstream work-in-process inventories.

For upstream scheduling, TOC uses two additional features in managing constraints to lower inventory levels and improving organizational performance: *buffers* and *ropes*. First, an inventory buffer is established in front of the major binding constraint. The inventory buffer is referred to as the *time buffer*. A **time buffer** is the inventory needed to keep the constrained resource busy for a specified time interval. The purpose of a time buffer is to protect the throughput of the organization from any disruption that can be overcome within the specified time interval. For example, if it takes one day to overcome most interruptions that occur upstream from the drummer constraint, then a two-day buffer should be sufficient to protect throughput from any interruptions. Thus, in scheduling, the operation immediately preceding the drummer constraint should produce the parts needed by the drummer resource two days in advance of their planned usage. Any other preceding operations are scheduled backwards in time to produce so that their parts arrive just in time for subsequent operations.

Ropes are actions taken to tie the rate at which material is released into the plant (at the first operation) to the production rate of the constrained resource. The objective of a rope is to ensure that the work-in-process inventory will not exceed the level needed for the time buffer. Thus, the drummer rate is used to limit the rate of material release and effectively controls the rate at which the first operation produces. The rate of the first operation then controls the rates of subsequent operations. The TOC inventory system is often called the **drum-buffer-rope (DBR) system**. Exhibit 20.10 illustrates the DBR structure for a general setting. **Example 20.5** illustrates the DBR structure for a specific example.

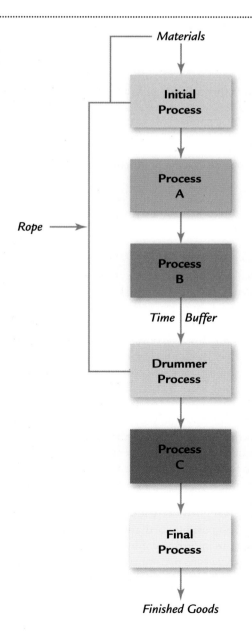

Exhibit 20.10

Drum-Buffer-Rope System: General Description

Step 3: Subordinate Everything Else to the Decisions Made in Step 2
Example 20.5 underscores the important TOC principle that the drummer constraint should set the capacity for the entire plant. All remaining departments should be subordinated to the needs of the drummer constraint. This principle requires many companies to change the way they view things. For example, the use of efficiency measures at the departmental level may no longer be appropriate. As Example 20.4 establishes, encouraging maximum productive efficiency for the Grinding Department would produce excess work-in-process inventories. The capacity of the Grinding Department is 80 units per week. Assuming the two-day buffer is in place, the Grinding Department would add 20 units per week to the buffer in front of the Drilling Department. Over a period of a year, the potential exists for building very large work-in-process inventories (1,000 units of the two parts would be added to the buffer over a 50-week period).

EXAMPLE 20.5

The HOW and WHY of a Drum-Buffer-Rope System

Information:
See Exhibit 20.8 and Example 20.4. Schaller Company has three *sequential* processes: grinding, drilling, and polishing. Optimal mix: Part X = 30 units per week; and Part Y = 30 units per week. The demand for each part is uniformly spread out over the five-day work week. Schaller requires a two-day buffer.

> **Why:**
> The major binding constraint sets the production rate (acts as the drummer). Buffers protect the company's throughput, and ropes ensure that work in process will not exceed the level of inventory required by the time buffer.

Required:

1.   Identify the drummer, the rate of production, the time buffer, and the rope.

2.   Illustrate the DBR structure of Schaller Company.

3.   ***What if*** the Grinding Department were allowed or encouraged to produce at capacity using the optimal mix ratio? What effect will this have on work-in-process inventories?

Solution:

1.   Binding constraints: drilling and polishing. Since the drilling process feeds the polishing process, the drilling constraint is the drummer for the plant. Production rate = six per day of each part (30/5). A two-day time buffer requires 12 units for Part X and 12 units for Part Y. To ensure that the time buffer does not increase at a rate greater than six per day for each part, materials should be released to the grinding process such that only six of each part can be produced each day.

2.   See Exhibit 20.11.

3.   The Grinding Department would produce 40 parts per week of each part, adding 20 units per week to the buffer in front of the drilling process. Thus, there would be a constant buildup of work-in-process inventory.

Step 4: Elevate the Organization's Binding Constraints   Once actions have been taken to make the best possible use of the existing constraints, the next step is to embark on a program of continuous improvement by reducing the limitations that the binding constraints have on the organization's performance. However, if there is more than one binding constraint, which one should be elevated? For example, in the Schaller Company setting, there are two binding constraints: the drilling constraint and the polishing constraint. In

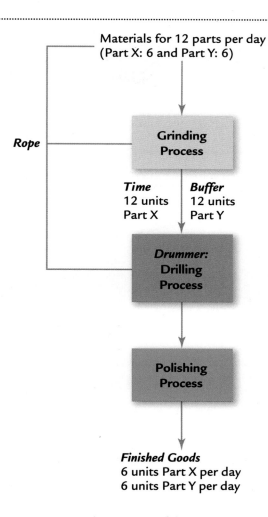

Exhibit 20.11

Drum-Buffer-Rope: Schaller Company

this case, the guideline is to increase the resource of the constraint that produces the greatest increase in throughput. Shadow prices can be useful guides for this decision. For the Schaller Company example, the shadow prices for the drilling and polishing resources are $180 and $60, respectively. Thus, Schaller should focus on busting the drilling constraint because it offers the most improvement.

Suppose, for example, that Schaller Company adds a half shift for the Drilling Department, increasing the drilling hours from 120 to 180 per week. Throughput will now be $37,800, an increase of $10,800 ($180 × 60 additional hours). Furthermore, as you can check, the optimal mix is now 18 units of Part X and 54 units of Part Y. Is the half shift worth it? This question is answered by comparing the cost of adding the half shift with the increased throughput. If the cost is labor—say overtime at $50 per hour (for all employees)—then the incremental cost is $3,000, and the decision to add the half shift is a good one.

Step 5: Repeat Process: Does a New Constraint Limit Throughput? Eventually, the drilling resource constraint will be elevated to a point where the constraint is no longer binding. Suppose, for example, that the company adds a full shift for the drilling operation, increasing the resource availability to 240 hours. The new constraint set is shown in Exhibit 20.12. Notice that the drilling constraint no longer affects the optimal mix decision. The grinding and polishing resource constraints are possible candidates for the new drummer constraint. Once the drummer constraint is identified, then the TOC process is repeated (Step 5). The objective is to continually improve performance by managing constraints. Do not allow inertia to cause a new constraint. Focus now on the next-weakest link.

Exhibit 20.12   New Constraint Set: Schaller Company

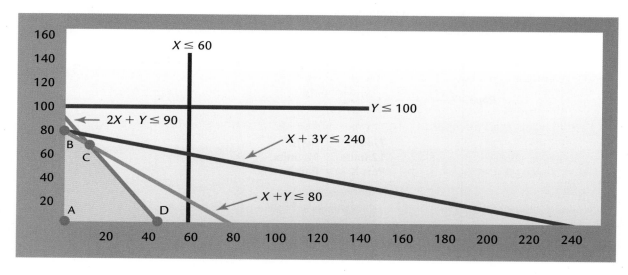

SUMMARY OF LEARNING OBJECTIVES

LO1. Describe the just-in-case inventory management model.
- The just-in-case approach uses inventories to manage the trade-offs between ordering (setup) costs and carrying costs.
- The traditional approach uses inventories to manage the trade-offs between ordering (setup) costs and carrying costs.
- Other reasons for inventories:
  - Due-date performance
  - Avoiding shutdowns (protecting throughput)
  - Hedging against future price increases
  - Taking advantage of discounts

LO2. Discuss just-in-time (JIT) inventory management.
- JIT argues that inventories are costly and are used to cover up fundamental problems that need to be corrected so that the organization can become more competitive.
- JIT uses long-term contracts, continuous replenishment, and EDI to reduce (eliminate) ordering costs. Engineering efforts are made to reduce setup times drastically.
- Once ordering costs and setup costs are reduced to minimal levels, then it is possible to reduce carrying costs by reducing inventory levels.
- JIT carries small buffers in front of each operation and uses a Kanban system to regulate production.

LO3. Explain the basic concepts of constrained optimization.
- Constrained optimization chooses the optimal mix given the constraints faced by the firm.
- Constraints are either internal or external.
- If a product mix uses up all of a given constrained resource, the constraint is binding.
- With only one binding internal constraint, the product with the largest contribution margin per unit of scarce resource will be produced to the maximum extent possible.
- With multiple binding internal constraints, either a graphical approach or the simplex method will be used to identify the optimal mix.

LO4. Describe how the theory of constraints can be used to manage inventory.
- TOC identifies an organization's constraints and exploits them so that throughput is maximized and inventories and operating costs are minimized.
- The major binding constraint is identified and is used to set the productive rate for the plant.
- Release of materials into the first process (operation) is regulated by the drummer constraint.
- A time buffer is located in front of critical constraints. This time buffer is sized so that it protects throughput from any interruptions.
- Performance is improved by exploiting the binding constraints and then taking efforts to elevate them.
- Because buffers are located only in front of critical constraints, TOC may actually produce smaller inventories than JIT.

EXAMPLE 20.1   The HOW and WHY of Calculating the EOQ, page 1023

EXAMPLE 20.2   The HOW and WHY of Reordering, page 1024

EXAMPLE 20.3   The HOW and WHY of Solving Constrained Optimization Problems with One Internal Constraint, page 1035

EXAMPLE 20.4   The HOW and WHY of Solving Linear Programming Problems with Two Variables, page 1036

EXAMPLE 20.5   The HOW and WHY of a Drum-Buffer-Rope System, page 1042

KEY TERMS

Binding constraint, 1034

Carrying costs, 1021

Constrained optimization, 1034

Constraint set, 1036

Constraints, 1034

Continuous replenishment, 1028

Drum-buffer-rope (DBR) system, 1041

Drummer, 1040

Economic order quantity (EOQ), 1022

Electronic data interchange (EDI), 1029

External constraints, 1034

Feasible set of solutions, 1036

Feasible solution, 1036

Internal constraints, 1034

Inventory, 1039

Just-in-case inventory management, 1020

Just-in-time inventory management, 1027

Kanban system, 1030

Lead time, 1024

Linear programming, 1036

Linear programming model, 1036

Loose constraints, 1034

Objective function, 1035

Operating expenses, 1039

Ordering costs, 1020

Production Kanban, 1031

Reorder point, 1024

Ropes, 1041

Safety stock, 1024

Setup costs, 1021

Shadow prices, 1037

Simplex method, 1036

Stock-out costs, 1021

Theory of constraints, 1038

Throughput, 1038

Time buffer, 1040

Total preventive maintenance, 1030

Vendor Kanban, 1031

Withdrawal Kanban, 1031

BRIEF EXERCISES

OBJECTIVE 1

EXAMPLE 20.1

Brief Exercise 20-1 EOQ

Thomas Corporation produces heating units. The following values apply for a part used in their production (purchased from external suppliers):

$$D = 12{,}500$$
$$Q = 250$$
$$P = \$45$$
$$C = \$4.50$$

Required:

1. For Thomas, calculate the ordering cost, the carrying cost, and the total cost associated with an order size of 250 units.
2. Calculate the EOQ and its associated ordering cost, carrying cost, and total cost. Compare and comment on the EOQ relative to the current order quantity.
3. *What if* Thomas enters into an exclusive supplier agreement with one supplier who will supply all of the demands with smaller, more frequent orders? Under this arrangement, the ordering cost is reduced to $0.45 per order. Calculate the new EOQ and comment on the implications.

OBJECTIVE 1

EXAMPLE 20.2

Brief Exercise 20-2 Reorder Point

Perez Corporation has an EOQ of 5,000 units. The company uses an average of 500 units per day. An order to replenish the part requires a lead time of five days.

Required:

1. Calculate the reorder point, using Equation 20.3.
2. Graphically display the reorder point, where the vertical axis is inventory (units) and the horizontal axis is time (days). Show two replenishments, beginning at time zero with the economic order quantity in inventory.
3. *What if* the *average* usage per day of the part is 500 units but a daily maximum usage of 575 units is possible? What is the reorder point when this demand uncertainty exists?

OBJECTIVE 3

EXAMPLE 20.3

Brief Exercise 20-3 Constrained Optimization: One Internal Binding Constraint

Wetzel Company produces two types of machine parts: Part A and Part B, with unit contribution margins of $450 and $840 respectively. Assume initially that Wetzel can sell all that is produced of either component. Part A requires three hours of assembly, and B requires six hours of assembly. The firm has 450 assembly hours per week.

Required:

1. Express the objective of maximizing the total contribution margin subject to the assembly-hour constraint.
2. Identify the optimal amount that should be produced of each machine part and the total contribution margin associated with this mix.

3. ***What if*** market conditions are such that Wetzel can sell at most 110 units of Part A and 90 units of Part B? Express the objective function with its associated constraints for this case and identify the optimal mix and its associated total contribution margin.

Brief Exercise 20-4 Constrained Optimization: Multiple Internal Constraints

OBJECTIVE ◀ 3
Example 20.4

Fisher Company produces two types of components for airplanes: A and B, with unit contribution margins of $400 and $600, respectively. The components pass through three sequential processes: cutting, welding, and assembly. Data pertaining to these processes and market demand are given below (weekly data).

Resource	Resource Available	Resource Usage (A)	Resource Usage (B)
Cutting	300 machine hours	Six hours	Ten hours
Welding	308 welding hours	Ten hours	Six hours
Assembly	400 labor hours	Four hours	Ten hours
Market demand (A)	50	One unit	Zero units
Market demand (B)	40	Zero units	One unit

Required:

1. Express Fisher Company's constrained optimization problem as a linear programming model.
2. Using a graphical approach, solve the linear programming model expressed in Requirement 1. Which constraints are binding?
3. ***What if*** Fisher Company had 10 additional machine hours (cutting) with all other resources held constant? What is the new optimal mix and associated total contribution margin? What is the incremental benefit per machine hour caused by the additional ten hours, if any?

Brief Exercise 20-5 Drum-Buffer-Rope

OBJECTIVE ◀ 4
Example 20.5

See **Brief Exercise 20-4**. Fisher Company has three *sequential* processes: cutting, welding, and assembly. Assume that the optimal mix is Component A = 0 units per week; and Component B = 30 units per week. Demand is uniformly spread out over the five-day work week. Fisher requires a 2.5-day buffer.

Required:

1. Identify the drummer, the rate of production, the time buffer, and the rope.
2. Illustrate the DBR structure of Fisher Company.
3. ***What if*** the Welding Department was allowed or encouraged to produce at capacity? What effect will this have on work-in-process inventories?

EXERCISES

Exercise 20-6 Ordering and Carrying Costs

OBJECTIVE ◀ 1

SHOW ME
HOW

Ottis, Inc., uses 640,000 plastic housing units each year in its production of paper shredders. The cost of placing an order is $30. The cost of holding one unit of inventory for one year is $15.00. Currently, Ottis places 160 orders of 4,000 plastic housing units per year.

Required:

1. Compute the annual ordering cost.
2. Compute the annual carrying cost.
3. Compute the cost of Ottis's current inventory policy. Is this the minimum cost? Why or why not?

OBJECTIVE ▶1

SHOW ME HOW　**EXCEL**

Exercise 20-7　Economic Order Quantity

Refer to the data in **Exercise 20-6**.

Required:

1. Compute the economic order quantity.
2. Compute the ordering, carrying, and total costs for the EOQ.
3. How much money does using the EOQ policy save the company over the policy of purchasing 4,000 plastic housing units per order?

OBJECTIVE 1

SHOW ME HOW

Exercise 20-8　Economic Order Quantity

Melchar Company uses 78,125 pounds of oats each year. The cost of placing an order is $18, and the carrying cost for one pound of oats is $0.45.

Required:

1. Compute the economic order quantity for oats.
2. Compute the carrying and ordering costs for the EOQ.

OBJECTIVE 1

SHOW ME HOW　**EXCEL**

Exercise 20-9　Reorder Point

Bautista Company manufactures backpacks. A heavy-duty strap is one part that the company orders from an outside supplier. Information pertaining to the strap is as follows:

Economic order quantity	6,300 units
Average daily usage	315 units
Maximum daily usage	375 units
Lead time	4 days

Required:

1. What is the reorder point assuming no safety stock is carried?
2. What is the reorder point assuming that safety stock is carried?

OBJECTIVE 1

SHOW ME HOW　**DATA ANALYTICS**

Exercise 20-10　EOQ with Setup Costs

Morrison Manufacturing produces casings for sewing machines: large and small. To produce the different casings, equipment must be set up. The setup cost per production run is $18,000 for either casing. The cost of carrying small casings in inventory is $6 per casing per year; the cost of large casings is $18 per unit per year. To satisfy demand, the company produces 2,400,000 small casings and 800,000 large casings.

Required:

1. Compute the number of small casings that should be produced per setup to minimize total setup and carrying costs.
2. Compute the setup, carrying, and total costs associated with the economic order quantity for the small casings.
3. What data analytic type was used in Requirement 1 (descriptive, diagnostic, predictive, or prescriptive)? Justify your selection. See Exhibits 2.5 and 2.6, pp. 37, 40, for a brief review of data analytics.
4. Suppose that Morrison's production engineer indicates that he has a method to reduce setup time; consequently, he predicts the setup cost will be reduced to $180. What will be the EOQ if this method works as predicted? Now indicate what data analytic type is being used.

OBJECTIVE 1

SHOW ME HOW

Exercise 20-11　EOQ with Setup Costs

Refer to **Exercise 20-10**.

Required:

1. Compute the number of large casings that should be produced per setup to minimize total setup and carrying costs for this product.
2. Compute the setup, carrying, and total costs associated with the economic order quantity for the large casings.

Exercise 20-12 Reorder Point

Refer to **Exercise 20-10**. Assume the economic lot size for small casings is 120,000 and that of the large casings is 40,000. Morrison Manufacturing sells an average of 9,600 small casings per workday and an average of 3,200 large casings per workday. It takes Morrison two days to set up the equipment for small or large casings. Once set up, it takes three workdays to produce a batch of small casings and five days for large casings. There are 250 workdays available per year.

Required:

1. What is the reorder point for small casings? Large casings?
2. Using the economic order batch size, is it possible for Morrison to produce the amount that can be sold of each casing? Does scheduling have a role here? Explain. Is this a push- or pull-through system approach to inventory management? Explain.

Exercise 20-13 Safety Stock

Eyring Manufacturing produces a component used in its production of washing machines. The time to set up and produce a batch of the components is two days. The average daily usage is 800 components, and the maximum daily usage is 875 components.

Required:

Compute the reorder point assuming that safety stock is carried by Eyring Manufacturing. How much safety stock is carried by Eyring?

Exercise 20-14 Kanban System, EDI

Hales Company produces a product that requires two processes. In the first process, a subassembly is produced (subassembly A). In the second process, this subassembly and a subassembly purchased from outside the company (subassembly B) are assembled to produce the final product. For simplicity, assume that the assembly of one final unit takes the same time as the production of subassembly A. Subassembly A is placed in a container and sent to an area called the subassembly stores (SB stores) area. A production Kanban is attached to this container. A second container, also with one subassembly, is located near the assembly line (called the withdrawal store). This container has attached to it a withdrawal Kanban.

Required:

1. Explain how withdrawal and production Kanban cards are used to control the work flow between the two processes. How does this approach minimize inventories?
2. Explain how vendor Kanban cards can be used to control the flow of the purchased subassembly. What implications does this have for supplier relationships? What role, if any, do continuous replenishment and EDI play in this process?

Exercise 20-15 JIT Limitations

Many companies have viewed JIT as a panacea—a knight in shining armor that promises rescue from sluggish profits, poor quality, and productive inefficiency. It is often lauded for its benefi-cial effects on employee morale and self-esteem. Yet, JIT may also cause a company to struggle and may produce a good deal of frustration. In some cases, JIT appears to deliver less than its reputation seems to call for.

Required:

Discuss some of the limitations and problems that companies may encounter when implementing a JIT system.

OBJECTIVE 3

SHOW ME HOW   DATA ANALYTICS   EXCEL

Exercise 20-16 Product Mix Decision, Single Constraint

Patz Company makes three types of stainless steel frying pans. Each of the three types of pans requires the use of a special machine that has total operating capacity of 273,000 hours per year. Information on each of the three products is as follows:

	Basic	Standard	Deluxe
Selling price	$18.00	$25.00	$48.00
Unit variable cost	$10.00	$16.00	$18.00
Machine hours required	0.10	0.20	0.50

The marketing manager has determined that the company can sell all that it can produce of each of the three products.

Required:

1. How many of each product should be sold to maximize the total contribution margin? What is the total contribution margin for this product mix?
2. Suppose that Patz can sell no more than 400,000 units of each type at the prices indicated. What product mix would you recommend, and what would be the total contribution margin?
3. What data analytic type(s) are being used in Requirements 1 and 2? Choose from the following types: descriptive, diagnostic, predictive, and prescriptive. Explain your choices. See Exhibits 2.5 and 2.6, pp. 37, 40, for a brief review of data analytics.

OBJECTIVE 4

Exercise 20-17 Drum-Buffer-Rope System

Duckstein, Inc., manufactures two types of aspirin: plain and buffered. It sells all it produces. Recently, Duckstein implemented a TOC approach for its Fort Smith plant. One binding constraint was identified, and the optimal product mix was determined. The following diagram reflects the TOC outcome:

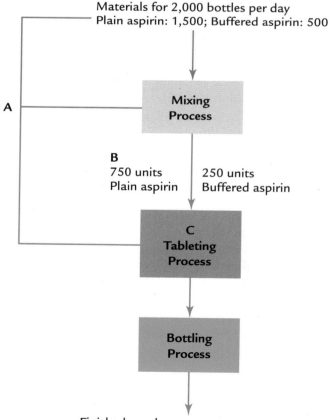

Required:

1. What is the daily production rate? Which process sets this rate?
2. How many days of buffer inventory is Duckstein carrying? How is this time buffer determined?
3. Explain what the letters A, B, and C in the exhibit represent. Discuss each of their roles in the TOC system.

PROBLEMS

Problem 20-18 EOQ, Safety Stock, Lead Time, Batch Size, and JIT

OBJECTIVE ◀ **1** **2**

Bateman Company produces helmets for drivers of motorcycles. Helmets are produced in batches according to model and size. Although the setup and production time vary for each model, the smallest lead time is six days. The most popular model, Model HA2, takes two days for setup, and the production rate is 750 units per day. The expected annual demand for the model is 36,000 units. Demand for the model, however, can reach 45,000 units. The cost of carrying one HA2 helmet is $3 per unit. The setup cost is $6,000. Bateman chooses its batch size based on the economic order quantity criterion. Expected annual demand is used to compute the EOQ.

Recently, Bateman has encountered some stiff competition—especially from foreign sources. Some of the foreign competitors have been able to produce and deliver the helmets to retailers in half the time it takes Bateman to produce. For example, a large retailer recently requested a delivery of 12,000 Model HA2 helmets with the stipulation that the helmets be delivered within seven working days. Bateman had 3,000 units of HA2 in stock. Bateman informed the potential customer that it could deliver 3,000 units immediately and the other 9,000 units in about 14 working days—with the possibility of interim partial orders being delivered. The customer declined the offer indicating that the total order had to be delivered within seven working days so that its stores could take advantage of some special local conditions. The customer expressed regret and indicated that it would accept the order from another competitor who could satisfy the time requirements.

Required:

1. Calculate the optimal batch size for Model HA2 using the EOQ model. Was Bateman's response to the customer right? Would it take the time indicated to produce the number of units wanted by the customer? Explain with supporting computations.
2. Upon learning of the lost order, the marketing manager grumbled about Bateman's inventory policy, "We lost the order because we didn't have sufficient inventory. We need to carry more units in inventory to deal with unexpected orders like these." Do you agree or disagree? How much additional inventory would have been needed to meet customer requirements? In the future, should Bateman carry more inventory? Can you think of other solutions?
3. Fenton Gray, the head of industrial engineering, reacted differently to the lost order: "Our problem is more complex than insufficient inventory. I know that our foreign competitors carry much less inventory than we do. What we need to do is decrease the lead time. I have been studying this problem, and my staff has found a way to reduce setup time for Model HA2 from two days to 1.5 hours. Using this new procedure, setup cost can be reduced to about $94. Also, by rearranging the plant layout for this product—creating what are called manufacturing cells—we can increase the production rate from 750 units per day to about 2,000 units per day. This is done simply by eliminating a lot of move time and waiting time—both non-value-added activities." Assume that the engineer's estimates are on target. Compute the new optimal batch size (using the EOQ formula). What is the new lead time? Given this new information, would Bateman have been able to meet the customer's time requirements? Assume that there are eight hours available in each workday.

4. Suppose that the setup time and cost are reduced to 0.5 hour and $10, respectively. What is the batch size now? As setup time approaches zero and the setup cost becomes negligible, what does this imply? Assume, for example, that it takes five minutes to set up, and costs are about $0.864 per setup.

OBJECTIVE

Problem 20-19 Product Mix Decisions, Multiple Constraints

Rahimi Company produces two types of gears: Model 12 and Model 15. Market conditions limit the number of each gear that can be sold. For Model 12 no more than 15,000 units can be sold, and for Model 15 no more than 40,000 units. Each gear must be notched by a special machine. Rahimi owns eight machines that together provide 60,000 hours of machine time per year. Each unit of Model 12 requires three hours of machine time, and each unit of Model 15 requires 45 minutes or 0.75 hour of machine time. The unit contribution for Model 12 is $60 and for Model 15 is $30. Rahimi wants to identify the product mix that will maximize total contribution margin.

Required:

1. Formulate Rahimi's problem as a linear programming model.
2. Solve the linear programming model in Requirement 1.
3. Identify which constraints are binding and which are loose. Also, identify the constraints as internal or external.

OBJECTIVE

Problem 20-20 Product Mix Decision, Single and Multiple Constraints

DATA ANALYTICS

Patz Company produces two industrial cleansers that use the same liquid chemical input: Regular Strength and Heavy Duty. Regular Strength uses two quarts of the chemical for every unit produced, and Heavy Duty uses five quarts. Currently, Patz has 6,000 quarts of the material in inventory. All of the material is imported. For the coming year, Patz plans to import 6,000 quarts to produce 2,818 units of Regular Strength and 1,272 units of Heavy Duty. The detail of each product's unit contribution margin is as follows:

	Regular Strength	Heavy Duty
Selling price	$ 81	$139
Less variable expenses:		
Direct materials	(20)	(50)
Direct labor	(21)	(14)
Variable overhead	(10)	(15)
Contribution margin	$ 30	$ 60

Patz Company has received word that the source of the material has been shut down by embargo. Consequently, the company will not be able to import the 6,000 quarts it planned to use in the coming year's production. There is no other source of the material.

Required:

1. Compute the total contribution margin that the company would earn if it could import the 6,000 quarts of the material.
2. Determine the optimal usage of the company's inventory of 6,000 quarts of the material. Compute the total contribution margin for the product mix that you recommend.
3. Assume that Regular Strength uses three direct labor hours for every unit produced and that Heavy Duty uses two hours. A total of 6,000 direct labor hours is available for the coming year.
   a. Formulate the linear programming problem faced by Patz Company. To do so, you must derive mathematical expressions for the objective function and for the materials and labor constraints.
   b. Solve the linear programming problem using the graphical approach.
   c. Compute the total contribution margin produced by the optimal mix.

4. For Requirements 1 to 3, identify the data analytic model used and select and justify the data analytic type(s) used. See Exhibits 2.5 and 2.6, pp. 37, 40, for a review of data analytic types (descriptive, diagnostic, predictive, and prescriptive).

Problem 20-21 Product Mix Decision, Single and Multiple Constraints, Basics of Linear Programming

OBJECTIVE ◀ 3

EXCEL

Desayuno Products, Inc., produces cornflakes and branflakes. The manufacturing process is highly mechanized; both products are produced by the same machinery by using different settings. For the coming period, 200,000 machine hours are available. Management is trying to decide on the quantities of each product to produce. The following data are available:

	Cornflakes	Branflakes
Machine hours per unit	1.00	0.50
Unit selling price	$2.50	$3.00
Unit variable cost	$1.50	$2.25

Required:

1. Determine the units of each product that should be produced in order to maximize profits.
2. Because of market conditions, the company can sell no more than 150,000 boxes of cornflakes and 300,000 boxes of branflakes. Do the following:
   a. Formulate the problem as a linear programming problem.
   b. Determine the optimal mix using a graph.
   c. Compute the maximum contribution margin given the optimal mix.

Problem 20-22 Product Mix Decisions

OBJECTIVE ◀ 3

CMA

Calen Company manufactures and sells three products in a factory of three departments. Both labor and machine time are applied to the products as they pass through each department. The nature of the machine processing and of the labor skills required in each department is such that neither machines nor labor can be switched from one department to another.

Calen's management is attempting to plan its production schedule for the next several months. The planning is complicated by the fact that labor shortages exist in the community and some machines will be down several months for repairs.

Following is information regarding available machine and labor time by department and the machine hours and direct labor hours required per unit of product. These data should be valid for at least the next six months.

Monthly Capacity	Department		
	1	2	3
Labor hours available	3,700	4,500	2,750
Machine hours available	3,000	3,100	2,700

Product	Input per Unit Produced	1	2	3
401	Labor hours	2	3	3
	Machine hours	1	1	2
402	Labor hours	1	2	—
	Machine hours	1	1	—
403	Labor hours	2	2	2
	Machine hours	2	2	1

Calen believes that the monthly demand for the next six months will be as follows:

Product	Units Sold
401	500
402	400
403	1,000

Inventory levels will not be increased or decreased during the next six months. The unit cost and price data for each product are as follows:

	Product		
	401	**402**	**403**
Unit costs:			
Direct material	$ 7	$ 13	$ 17
Direct labor	66	38	51
Variable overhead	27	20	25
Fixed overhead	15	10	32
Variable selling	3	2	4
Total unit cost	$118	$ 83	$129
Unit selling price	$196	$123	$167

Required:

1. Calculate the monthly requirement for machine hours and direct labor hours for producing Products 401, 402, and 403 to determine whether or not the factory can meet the monthly sales demand.

2. Determine the quantities of 401, 402, and 403 that should be produced monthly to maximize profits. Prepare a schedule that shows the contribution to profits of your product mix.

3. Assume that the machine hours available in Department 3 are 1,500 instead of 2,700. Calculate the optimal monthly product mix using the graphing approach to linear programming. Prepare a schedule that shows the contribution to profits from this optimal mix. (*CMA adapted*)

OBJECTIVE ▶ **4**

**DATA
ANALYTICS**

Problem 20-23 Identifying and Exploiting Constraints, Constraint Elevation

Middleton Company produces two different metal components used in medical equipment (Component X and Component Y). The company has three processes: molding, grinding, and finishing. In molding, molds are created, and molten metal is poured into the shell. Grinding removes the gates that allowed the molten metal to flow into the mold's cavities. In finishing, rough edges caused by the grinders are removed by small, handheld pneumatic tools. In molding, the setup time is one hour. The other two processes have no setup time required. The demand for Component X is 900 units per day, and the demand for Component Y is 1,500 units per day. The minutes required per unit for each product are as follows:

	Minutes Required per Unit of Product		
Product	Molding	Grinding	Finishing
Component X	5	10	15
Component Y	10	15	20

The company operates one eight-hour shift. The molding process employs 36 workers (who each work eight hours). Two hours of their time, however, are used for setups (assuming both products are produced). The grinding process has sufficient equipment and workers to provide 600 grinding hours per shift.

The Finishing Department is labor intensive and employs 100 workers, who each work eight hours per day. The only significant unit-level variable costs are materials and power. For Component X, the variable cost per unit is $40, and for Component Y, it is $50. Selling prices for X and Y are $90 and $110, respectively. Middleton's policy is to use two setups per day: an initial setup to produce all that is scheduled for Component X and a second setup (changeover) to produce all that is scheduled for Component Y. The amount scheduled does not necessarily correspond to each product's daily demand.

Required:

1. Calculate the time (in minutes) needed each day to meet the daily market demand for Component X and Component Y. What is the major internal constraint facing Middleton Company?
2. Describe how Middleton should exploit its major binding constraint. Specifically, identify the product mix that will maximize daily throughput.
3. Assume that manufacturing engineering has found a way that will reduce the molding setup time from one hour to 10 minutes. Explain how this will affect the product mix and daily throughput.
4. For Requirements 1 to 3, identify the data analytic model used and select and justify the data analytic type(s) used. See Exhibits 2.5 and 2.6, pp. 37, 40, for a review of data analytic types (descriptive, diagnostic, predictive, and prescriptive).

Problem 20-24 Theory of Constraints, Internal Constraints

OBJECTIVE ◀ 4

Pratt Company produces two replacement parts for a popular line of Blu-ray disc players: Part A and Part B. Part A is made up of two components, one manufactured internally and one purchased from external suppliers. Part B is made up of three components, one manufactured internally and two purchased from suppliers. The company has two processes: fabrication and assembly. In fabrication, the internally produced components are made. Each component takes 20 minutes to produce. In assembly, it takes 30 minutes to assemble the components for Part A and 40 minutes to assemble the components for Part B. Pratt Company operates one shift per day. Each process employs 100 workers who each work eight hours per day.

Part A earns a unit contribution margin of $20, and Part B earns a unit contribution margin of $24 (calculated as the difference between revenue and the cost of materials and energy). Pratt can sell all that it produces of either part. There are no other constraints. Pratt can add a second shift of either process. Although a second shift would work eight hours, there is no mandate that it employ the same number of workers. The labor cost per hour for fabrication is $15, and the labor cost per hour for assembly is $12.

Required:

1. Identify the constraints facing Pratt, and graph them. How many binding constraints are possible? What is Pratt's optimal product mix? What daily contribution margin is produced by this mix?
2. What is the drummer constraint? How much excess capacity does the other constraint have? Assume that a 1.5-day buffer inventory is needed to deal with any production interruptions. Describe the drum-buffer-rope concept using the Pratt data to illustrate the process.
3. Explain why the use of local labor efficiency measures will not work in Pratt's TOC environment.
4. Suppose Pratt decides to elevate the binding constraint by adding a second shift of 50 workers (labor rates are the same as those of the first shift). Would elevation of Pratt's binding constraint improve its system performance? Explain with supporting computations.

OBJECTIVE **4**

Problem 20-25 TOC, Internal and External Constraints

Bountiful Manufacturing produces two types of bike frames (Frame X and Frame Y). Frame X passes through four processes: cutting, welding, polishing, and painting. Frame Y uses three of the same processes: cutting, welding, and painting. Each of the four processes employs 10 workers who work eight hours each day. Frame X sells for $40 per unit, and Frame Y sells for $55 per unit. Materials is the only unit-level variable expense. The materials cost for Frame X is $20 per unit, and the materials cost for Frame Y is $25 per unit. Bountiful's accounting system has provided the following additional information about its operations and products:

Resource Name	Resource Available	Frame X Resource Usage per Unit	Frame Y Resource Usage per Unit
Cutting labor	4,800 minutes	15 minutes	10 minutes
Welding labor	4,800 minutes	15 minutes	30 minutes
Polishing labor	4,800 minutes	15 minutes	—
Painting labor	4,800 minutes	10 minutes	15 minutes
Market demand:			
Frame X	200 per day	One unit	—
Frame Y	100 per day	—	One unit

Bountiful's management has determined that any production interruptions can be corrected within two days.

Required:

1. Assuming that Bountiful can meet daily market demand, compute the potential daily profit. Now, compute the minutes needed for each process to meet the daily market demand. Can Bountiful meet daily market demand? If not, where is the bottleneck? Can you derive an optimal mix without using a graphical solution? If so, explain how.
2. Identify the objective function and the constraints. Then, graph the constraints facing Bountiful. Determine the optimal mix and the maximum daily contribution margin (throughput).
3. Explain how a drum-buffer-rope system would work for Bountiful.
4. Suppose that the Engineering Department has proposed a process design change that will increase the polishing time for Frame X from 15 to 23 minutes per unit and decrease the welding time from 15 minutes to 10 minutes per unit (for Frame X). The cost of process redesign would be $10,000. Evaluate this proposed change. What step in the TOC process does this proposal represent?

21 International Issues in Cost Management

After studying this chapter, you should be able to:

1 ▸ Explain the role of the accountant in the international environment.

2 ▸ Explain the varying levels of involvement that firms can take in international trade.

3 ▸ Calculate exchange gains and losses so that accountants can manage foreign currency risk.

4 ▸ Explain how environmental factors can affect performance evaluation in the multinational firm.

5 ▸ Describe the role of transfer pricing in the multinational firm.

6 ▸ Discuss ethical issues that affect firms operating in the international environment.

Pryimak Anastasiia/Shutterstock.com

CRYPTOCURRENCY

at Nvidia

With dreams of winning money and perhaps a scholarship in esports tournaments, you have spent months practicing car control in Rocket League. You have the two-dimensional aspects of the game well under control and have moved on to aerial ball maneuvers. Unfortunately, your skills are lacking. Perhaps you would be better off with a newer, faster graphics processing unit (GPU). This would smooth out your slow, occasionally pixelated video. You would see the background details more clearly and would be a stronger asset for your team. Without one, you might be stuck at the bottom of the rankings forever. You start looking at the Nvidia site for a GPU in your price range.

Nvidia was founded in 1993 to make a new type of computer chip ideal for powering three-dimensional video games even before games could take advantage of the additional power. Since then, video games such as Grand Theft Auto (GTA), Defense of the Ancients (DOTA), World of Warcraft, and Call of Duty have been designed to take advantage of each new generation of GPUs from Nvidia and **AMD**. The new chips make backgrounds crisper—not muddled and pixelated—so that players can more easily see partially hidden Easter eggs and react to sudden movements. Once a new Nvidia GPU is incorporated into a video game, then gamers need to upgrade their chips. For example, GeForce supports League of Legends, Call of Duty: Modern Warfare, and Minecraft. If you play these games, you'll want the GeForce.

Nvidia has always considered gamers its main market, but cybercurrency miners also realized the power of the cards for mining cybercurrency. In 2018, GPUs were out of stock at major retailers around the world as the miners had bought up all available stock: the kind of people that were so desperate to get as many cards as possible in as short amount of time as possible to the point where they were renting entire Boeing 747s to ship GPUs to their mining farms. Graphics card prices had increased by two to three times the regular retail price, pricing gamers out of the market. Nvidia has reportedly asked retailers to stop selling its graphics cards to miners. The company wanted its cards to go to gamers instead of miners. So why did Nvidia want its GPUs to go to gamers rather than miners? The reason is loyalty. Cryptocurrency values fluctuate wildly. When that market crashes, miners sell their hardware on the gray market and gamers can then buy the cheaper GPUs and not buy them from Nvidia and AMD. GPU manufacturers cannot sell their inventory and may have to write it off at a huge loss. This is something AMD had to do back in 2014 after the crypto market crashed and used Radeon GPUs flooded the second hand market. More importantly, from a business perspective, a gamer is a more valuable customer than a miner. If you win a gamer's loyalty, they're more likely to buy again from you come upgrade time or purchase other products from you in the long run. Gaming market share is also a huge bargaining chip when it comes to game optimizations and studio partnership negotiations. As a company, you can get away with more if you have a bigger user-base, that's just the nature of the beast.[1]

In fiscal 2020, gaming will be worth an estimated $6.1 billion in revenue for Nvidia. However, the company is branching out into artificial intelligence (AI). Soon, Nvidia hopes that AI will lead to revenues of $6.5 billion, making it even more important than gaming. AI is used in a variety of applications, from mining customer data for sales tips to spotting cancers that doctors might miss. **Tesla** has developed its own hardware and software for autonomous driving. Other car companies are turning to Nvidia for chips that can be used for training autonomous-driving algorithms.

Jensen Huang, Nvidia CEO, said, "People thought we were a videogame company. But we're an accelerated computing company where videogames were our first killer app." The second killer app, its Data Center, will use AI and parallel processing.[2]

OBJECTIVE

Explain the role of the accountant in the international environment.

COST ACCOUNTING IN THE INTERNATIONAL ENVIRONMENT

Doing business in a global setting used to be a choice, but this is no longer true. The rapid, far-reaching advances in technology, communications, information technology, and transportation have made this a truly global economy. Now, the actions of companies and countries throughout the world are so intricately intertwined that the fortunes of one affect the fortunes of all. Currency fluctuations, deflationary environments, and overcapacity in manufacturing all affect the ability of U.S. companies to compete around the world.

Doing business in a global environment requires cost managers to shift perspective. While many aspects of business dealings remain the same, other aspects are quite different. The company doing business in both its home country and other countries may find that practices working well in the home country are working imperfectly or not at all in another country. Much of the difference can be related to the business environment—that is, the cultural, legal, political, and economic environment of the various countries. Just as a fish supposedly is not aware of water, we in the United States take our business environment for granted. We have grown accustomed to a market economy and to the concept of private property. We are accustomed to a legal system that enforces contracts. Our sense of ethics grew in tandem with the underlying environment. When the environment changes, ethical problems may arise. Different divisions of the same company may face different ethical problems; therefore, evaluating the ethical content of divisional decisions is common.

Where does the accountant fit into the global business environment? Business looks to the accountant for financial and business expertise. The accountant's job is not cut and dried. Knowledge, creativity, and flexibility are needed to help managers make decisions. We might take a cue from the IMA Statement of Ethical Professional Practice (given in Chapter 1) and consider competence. Good training, education, and staying up to date with one's field are important to any accountant. However, the job of the accountant in the international firm is made more challenging by the ambiguous and ever-changing nature of global business. Since

1 Khalid Moammer, "NVIDIA Asks Retailers to Stop Selling to Miners & Sell to Gamers Instead," *WCCFTech.com*, January 19, 2018, https://wccftech.com/nvidia-instructs-retailers-stop-selling-miners-sell-gamers/#:~:text =NVIDIA%20Asks%20Retailers%20To%20Stop%20Selling%20To%20Miners%20%26%20Sell%20To%20 Gamers%20Instead,-By%20Khalid%20Moammer&text=NVIDIA%20is%20reportedly%20asking%20retailers, for%20the%20past%20several%20months, accessed September 12, 2020.

2 Jack Hough, "How Nvidia Went from Gaming to AI to Riding with Mercedes," (June 26, 2020, updated June 28, 2020), https://www.barrons.com/articles/how-nvidia-went-from-gaming-to-ai-to-riding-with-mercedes-51593212698, accessed September 7, 2020.

much of the accountant's job is to provide relevant information to management, staying up to date requires one to read web-based stories and articles and books in a variety of business areas, including information systems, marketing, management, politics, and economics. In addition, the accountant must be familiar with the financial accounting rules of the countries in which the firm operates.

The remainder of this chapter will touch on various issues facing the multinational firm. Our focus is on the internal accountant and the interaction of cost and revenue management with those issues.

LEVELS OF INVOLVEMENT IN INTERNATIONAL TRADE

OBJECTIVE 2

Explain the varying levels of involvement that firms can take in international trade.

A **multinational corporation (MNC)** is one that owns and controls the production or distribution of goods and services in countries in addition to its home country. From this definition, we can see that the involvement of the MNC in international trade may take many forms. On a fairly simple level, the MNC may import materials and/or export finished products. On a more complex level, the MNC may be a large firm consisting of a parent company and a number of divisions in various countries.

In the international environment, the choice of company structure goes beyond the issue of centralized versus decentralized firm structure described in Chapter 10. While multinational companies are very often decentralized, with subsidiaries that are wholly owned by the parent firm, the many business environments in which the firm may operate have led to various company structures. Some of the choices are importing and exporting, wholly owned subsidiaries, and joint ventures.

Importing and Exporting

A relatively simple form of multinational involvement is importing and exporting. A company may import parts for production. Similarly, a company may export finished products to foreign countries. Even such simple transactions as importing and exporting can present new risks and opportunities for companies.

Importing A company may import materials for use in production or for resale. While this transaction may look identical to the purchase of materials from domestic suppliers, U.S. tariffs add complexity and cost. A **tariff** is a tax on imports levied by the federal government. Recall that freight-in is a materials cost. If an imported part has tariff (or duty) in addition to freight-in, this tax becomes part of the cost of materials. Companies search for ways to reduce tariffs. They may restrict the amount of imported materials, alter the materials by adding U.S. resources (to increase the domestic content and gain more favorable tariff status), or utilize foreign trade zones.

Foreign Trade Zones The U.S. government has set up **foreign trade zones (FTZs)**, areas that are physically on U.S. soil but considered to be outside U.S. commerce. Rooted in the ancient free-port concept, the FTZ was set up by Congress in 1934. Goods imported into an FTZ are duty-free until they leave the zone for sale in the United States. The United States has set up over 250 FTZs and 500 subzones. Because FTZs must be located near a customs port of entry, they are often located near seaports or airports. San Antonio, Texas, Fairbanks, Alaska, and Miami, Florida, are examples of cities with FTZs.[3] This has important implications for firms that import materials. Since tariffs are not paid until the imported materials leave the zone as part of a finished product, the company can postpone payment of duty and any associated loss

---

3 For information on foreign trades zones, see https://www.cbp.gov/border-security/ports-entry/cargo-security /cargo-control/foreign-trade-zones/about, accessed August 20, 2020.

of working capital. Additionally, the company does not pay duty on defective materials or on inventory that has not yet been included in finished products. Companies in FTZs can engage in warehousing and/or manufacturing. If the items leave the FTZ bound for non-U.S. destinations, there is no tariff due. If they leave the zone for U.S. destinations, then the tariff is due. Some raw materials have higher tariffs than the finished product. Once the materials are included in the finished product, the lower duty amount is paid—not the original duty on unfinished raw materials. Finally, some imported materials are subject to breakage or evaporative loss. Since that loss occurs in the FTZ, duty is never paid on the amount of the loss since it is never sold. **Example 21.1** shows how and why a company may choose to locate in an FTZ.

EXAMPLE 21.1

The HOW and WHY of Locating in a Foreign Trade Zone

Information:
Roadrunner, Inc., and Wilycoyote, Inc., both operate petrochemical plants that import volatile materials (i.e., chemicals subject to substantial evaporation loss during processing) for use in production. Roadrunner is an FTZ; Wilycoyote, Inc., operates an identical plant just outside the FTZ. Each plant purchases $400,000 of crude oil imported from Venezuela for use in chemical production. Each purchases the oil about three months before use in production, and the finished chemicals remain in inventory about five months before sale and shipment to the customer. About 30 percent of the oil is lost through evaporation during production. Duty is assessed at 6 percent of cost. Each company faces a 12 percent carrying cost.

> **Why:**
> The location of the plant in the FTZ means that duty is not assessed until the product leaves the zone. Duty on the evaporative loss is never paid by the plant inside the zone.

Required:

1. What is the amount of duty paid by Wilycoyote? By Roadrunner?

2. What is the amount of carrying cost associated with the duty paid by Wilycoyote? By Roadrunner?

3. What is the total duty-related cost for Wilycoyote? For Roadrunner?

4. What is the total savings on duty and carrying cost attributable to locating in an FTZ?

5. ***What if*** duty increased to 9 percent? Would it be more or less advantageous to be located in an FTZ?

Solution:

1. Duty paid by Wilycoyote = $400,000 × 0.06 = $24,000

   Duty paid by Roadrunner = $400,000 × 0.7 × 0.06 = $16,800

   (Only 70% of the oil is subject to duty since 30% is lost to evaporation and is not sold outside the zone.)

2. Carrying cost on duty paid by Wilycoyote = 0.12 × [(3 + 5)/12] × $24,000 = $1,920

   Carrying cost on duty paid by Roadrunner = 0

   (Duty is paid at the point of sale so there is no carrying cost on the duty.)

3. Total duty-related cost for Wilycoyote = $24,000 + $1,920 = $25,920

   Total duty-related cost for Roadrunner = $16,800

4. Total savings to Roadrunner for locating in FTZ = $25,920 − $16,800 = $9,120

5. If duty amount increases, then it is even more advantageous to locate in the FTZ, and Roadrunner would save more money compared with Wilycoyote.

Foreign trade zones provide additional advantages. For example, goods that do not meet U.S. health, safety, and pollution control regulations are subject to fine. Noncomplying foreign goods can be imported into FTZs and modified to comply with the law without being subject to the fine. Another example of the efficient use of FTZs is the assembly of high-tariff component parts into a lower-tariff finished product. In this case, the addition of domestic labor raises the domestic content of the finished product and makes the embedded foreign parts eligible for more favorable tariff treatment. Finally, logistics may be streamlined by using FTZ procedures, leading to quicker and more efficient clearance of customs, and moving the United States closer to the concept of a borderless economy.

In 2018, incoming zone shipments totalled over $793 billion annually.[4] While the paperwork involved in establishing an FTZ is extensive—and very expensive—reallocating the space of an existing FTZ is relatively easy. The owners of FTZs (typically, city or county authorities) can then work with companies to maximize the advantages of the zone.

For example, suppose that Worldwide Enterprises, an export-import company, is considering expansion and wants to build a distribution center in the southwest part of the United States. The distribution center must be convenient to the interstate highway system and to rail transportation. Additionally, because Worldwide imports a significant amount of inventory, it wants to establish the center in an FTZ. Suppose that a city in which the center might be located has an already established FTZ on 200 acres near its airport. The city has offered Worldwide the chance to purchase land in the zone on which to build the center. However, the land does not meet the company's criteria for rail and highway access. Worldwide has located a 10-acre parcel of land in the city that meets its transportation criteria but is not in the FTZ. Now what? The city is anxious to win Worldwide's center, as it will mean nearly 500 new jobs and a healthy increase in the city economy. Fortunately, the flexibility of FTZs makes it possible for the city to name Worldwide's preferred parcel of land a foreign trade subzone (and to reduce the airport FTZ area by 10 acres).

A final factor should be mentioned in connection with FTZs—possible political ramifications. By their nature, plants located in FTZs are engaged in international trade. For example, the government may levy high duties on certain items—such as foreign-made automotive parts—to encourage the use of domestic parts. An automobile company may choose to locate in an FTZ and import the foreign parts into the zone for installation in an automobile, which has a lower duty rate when shipped out of the zone. Components that have a high duty can be imported into the FTZ, used in manufacturing cars, and then the cars leave the zone at the much lower completed automobile rate. This helps U.S. companies to compete on an equal footing with their foreign competitors. Foreign car companies such as **Nissan Motor Company**, producer of the titan and frontier pickup trucks, finds that manufacturing in Canton, Mississippi, allows them to import Asian components at half the usual duty for final assembly in the United States as well as situating closer to their ultimate market. **BMW** has a manufacturing plant in Spartanburg, South Carolina. This has the political advantage of making their cars in the American market and contributing to the U.S. economy. Cost accountants must be aware of much more than narrow business interests in evaluating the advantages and disadvantages of international trade.

Exporting Exporting is the sale of a company's products in foreign countries. It is not necessary to have a production facility in the foreign country: finished products can simply be transported to the buyer. However, exporting is usually more complex than the sale of finished goods within the home country. Foreign countries have a variety of import and tariff regulations. The job of complying with the foreign rules and regulations often falls to the controller's office, just as compliance with U.S. tax regulations is an accounting function. Alternatively, a U.S. company may choose to work with an experienced distributor, familiar with the legal complexities of the other countries. In some cases, the distributor is wholly owned; in other cases, the distributor is a separate company.

---

4 See National Association of Foreign Trade Zones, "FTZ Basics and Benefits," https://www.naftz.org/ftz-resources /ftz-basics-benefits/, accessed October 13, 2020.

Wholly Owned Subsidiaries

A company may choose to purchase an existing foreign company, making the purchased company a wholly owned subsidiary of the parent. This strategy has the virtue of simplicity. The foreign company has established an outlet for the product, and the production and distribution facilities are already in place. For example, by 2015, **Whirlpool** expanded into the European market by acquiring some of the most popular brands of France, the United Kingdom, and Germany. In 2014 Whirlpool purchased **Indesit**, an Italian appliance brand that was the third-largest in Europe. It is now the largest appliance manufacturer in Europe—larger even than **Bosch** and **Siemens**. Whirlpool's challenge now is to ensure that customers can differentiate among the brands. The European companies have established a strong brand presence—in large part what Whirlpool purchased. Thus, buying wholly owned subsidiaries provided more advantages than simply establishing a Whirlpool manufacturing plant overseas.[5]

Outsourcing of technical and professional jobs is becoming an important issue for resource-conscious U.S. firms. **Outsourcing** is the payment by a company for a business function that was formerly done in-house. For example, some domestic companies outsource their legal needs to outside law firms rather than hiring corporate attorneys. In the context of the MNC, outsourcing refers to the move of a business function to another country. For example, **Texas Instruments (TI)** set up a Research & Development (R&D) center in Bangalore, India. The availability of underemployed college graduates in India created a combination of low wage rates and high productivity. However, the underdeveloped Indian infrastructure required considerable capital investment. TI installed its own electrical generators and satellite dishes, some hauled in by oxcart, to operate efficiently. TI's location in India also adds to its ability to access large new markets for its products.

Money is not the only resource saved when MNCs locate operations in foreign countries. Time is a valuable resource, and many companies have found that a global presence leads to time and quality enhancement. TI's global network of R&D facilities works simultaneously and around the clock on some projects. In one instance, a customer asked TI for a quote on a handheld bidding device for stock exchange traders. TI's Dallas, Texas, design group began working on the problem, and then, at the end of the day, transferred their work electronically to designers in Tokyo. The Tokyo group continued developing the design, and at quitting time, transferred the design to the Nice, France, design group. By the next day, the Dallas group had completed the design, quote, and a preliminary picture of the device.

PepsiCo, Inc., has also found that wholly owned subsidiaries can increase quality. Pepsi Foods International is the overseas Snack Foods division. It found that potato chips are the most popular snack, with a worldwide market of $4 billion, and worked to capitalize on that market to increase demand even more. It grew internationally by buying foreign competitors or entering into joint ventures. However, the chips were of uneven quality. To enforce uniform quality standards, new equipment was brought in to handle potatoes more gently and slice them more evenly. Chips and snack foods are "redesigned" to meet the local market's tastes. For example, Japanese Cheetos may be strawberry flavored. The Chinese do not like cheese on their Cheetos, so Chinese Cheetos are cheeseless. The company is developing a seafood-flavored Cheeto for this market.

The accountant must be aware of numerous costs and benefits of wholly owned subsidiaries. The varying tax structures and incentives of local authorities, as well as the overall educational level of the country and the infrastructure, all play a role in the accountant's assessment of costs and benefits.

Joint Ventures

On occasion, companies with the specific expertise needed by MNCs do not exist or are not for sale. A joint venture is an option that may work. A **joint venture** is a type of partnership in which investors co-own the enterprise. **General Electric Company (GE)** owns 51 percent of a medical systems venture with **Wipro, Ltd.** of India, now named Wipro GE Healthcare.

---

5 Keith Barry, "Whirlpool Reveals Plans for World Domination," *Reviewed.com*, September 4, 2015, https://www .reviewed.com/dishwashers/news/whirlpool-reveals-plans-for-world-domination, accessed August 21, 2020.

Initially, Wipro GE produced CT scanners, applications software, and ultrasound devices, including a 20-pound ultrasound unit that fits into the back of a car to enable Indian doctors to take the technology to remote villages. Wipro GE Healthcare expects significant growth of 12 to 13 percent per year in products in cardiology, infection treatment, and maternal and infant care.[6] More joint ventures include **Hewlett-Packard** and **Hitachi**, **Boeing** and **Embraer**, and **Apple Computer** and **Sharp Electronics**.

Sometimes, a joint venture is required because of restrictive laws. In China, for example, MNCs are not allowed to purchase companies or set up their own subsidiaries. Joint ventures with Chinese firms are required. Similarly, India and Thailand demand local ownership. **Loctite Corporation**, maker of Super Glue, runs joint ventures in both India and Thailand for that reason.

A special case of joint venture cooperation is the maquiladora. **Maquiladoras** are manufacturing plants located in Mexico that process imported materials and reexport them, tariff-free, to the United States. Originally designed to encourage U.S. firms to invest in Mexico, the program has now expanded to include other foreign firms, such as Nissan and **Sony**. Basically, the maquiladora enjoys special status in both Mexico, which grants operators an exemption from Mexican laws governing foreign ownership, and the United States, which grants exemptions from or reductions in custom duties levied on reexported goods. Most maquiladoras are located in cities bordering the United States to take advantage of ready access to U.S. transportation and communication facilities. The Mexican advantage is low-cost, high-quality labor. The structure of the maquiladora is flexible. Mexico permits different levels of involvement. The minimal level combines low risk with low cost savings. In this case, the U.S. firm transfers materials to an existing Mexican firm and imports them back in finished form. All hiring and operating of the Mexican plant is accomplished by the Mexican owners. The highest level of involvement offers both high risk and high cost savings. At this level, the U.S. firm owns the Mexican subsidiary and oversees all the operations.

Maquiladoras are an example of a government program to increase production that has worked well. Foreign investment has moved well beyond the border cities to a broad band of northern Mexico. Improvements in Mexican infrastructure, such as roads and communications, have enticed companies further into the interior, lowering nonlabor costs. While U.S. companies were originally drawn to the maquiladoras for the cheap labor (wage rates of approximately $1.50 per hour versus $17.50 per hour for U.S. assemblers), other reasons keep them. For example, Ford's plant in Chihuahua was built to satisfy export requirements for doing business in Mexico. Now, it supports Ford's sales to Mexico, establishing a marketing reason for the plant's presence.

No matter which structure the MNC takes, it faces issues of foreign trade. An important issue is foreign currency exchange. This is addressed in the next section.

FOREIGN CURRENCY EXCHANGE

OBJECTIVE 3
Calculate exchange gains and losses so that accountants can manage foreign currency risk.

When a company operates only in its home country, only one currency is used, and exchange issues never arise. However, when a company begins to operate in the international arena, it must use foreign currencies. These foreign currencies can be exchanged for the domestic currency using **exchange rates**, or the rate at which one currency will be exchanged for another. If the exchange rates never changed, problems would not occur. Exchange rates do change, however, often on a daily basis. Thus, a dollar that could be traded for 110 yen one day may be worth only 104 yen on another day. Currency rate fluctuations add considerably to the uncertainty of operating in the international arena.

The accountant plays an important role in managing the company's exposure to currency risk. **Currency risk management** refers to the company's management of its transaction, economic, and translation exposure due to exchange rate fluctuations. **Transaction risk** refers

6 "GE Merges Healthcare Unit with Wipro," *The Hindu*, October 3, 2009, https://www.thehindu.com/business/companies/GE-merges-healthcare-unit-with-Wipro/article16884454.ece, accessed September 3, 2020.

to the possibility that future cash transactions will be affected by changing exchange rates. **Economic risk** refers to the possibility that a firm's present value of future cash flows will be affected by exchange fluctuations. **Translation (or accounting) risk** is the degree to which a firm's financial statements are exposed to exchange rate fluctuation. Let's look more closely at these three components of currency risk and some ways in which the accountant can manage the company's exposure to them.

Managing Transaction Risk

Today's MNC deals in many different currencies. These currencies may be traded for one another depending on the exchange rate in effect at the time of the trade. The **spot rate** is the exchange rate of one currency for another for immediate delivery (i.e., today). Exhibit 21.1 lists some widely used currencies and their spot rates as of September 11, 2020. While the spot rates are surely different now, as you read this book, you can gain an idea of relative values. Changes in the spot rates can affect the value of a company's future cash transactions, posing transaction risk. Let's first get a feel for currency appreciation and depreciation before we progress to exchange gains and losses and hedging.

Currency Appreciation and Depreciation When one country's currency strengthens relative to another country's currency, currency appreciation occurs, and one unit of the first country's currency can buy more units of the second country's currency. **Example 21.2** shows how and why a firm may want to exchange one currency for another.

Exhibit 21.1

Spot Rates for Major Currencies
September 11, 2020*

	In U.S. $	Per U.S. $
Australia $	0.7283	1.37306
Canada $	1.3179	0.75878
Chinese Yuan	6.8344	0.14632
Euro	1.1848	0.84402
Great Britain Pound	1.2796	0.78149
Mexico Peso	21.2754	0.047
New Zealand $	0.6669	1.49948
Swedish Krona	8.7749	0.11396
Swiss Franc	0.909	1.10011
Japanese Yen	106.16	0.00942

*Markets Digest: Currencies, *The Wall Street Journal*, September 12–13, 2020, page B7.

EXAMPLE 21.2

The HOW and WHY of Exchanging One Currency for Another

Information:
Angell, Inc., has always purchased supplies from and sold finished goods to firms that deal in dollars. Recently, however, Angell has decided to purchase components from a Japanese company that requires payment in yen (¥), and it will sell finished product to a Brazilian company that will remit payment to Angell in Brazilian reals (R$). On June 1, Angell ordered components from the Japanese company costing ¥4,240,000 and sold finished goods to the Brazilian company with a selling price of $50,000 to be paid in Brazilian reals. The June 1 spot rates of U.S. dollars for yen and for Brazilian reals was:

$$\$1 = ¥106.0$$
$$\$1 = R\$ 5.60$$

EXAMPLE 21.2

(*Continued*)

Why:
Because different countries use different currencies, firms dealing with companies in other countries need to determine the value of an item in the other currency.

Required:

1. What is the cost of the ¥4,240,000 in dollars?

2. How many Brazilian reals will Angell receive from the Brazilian company in payment for the finished product?

3. *What if* the exchange rate of dollars for yen was $1 = ¥105? What is the cost of the ¥4,240,000 in dollars (rounded to the nearest dollar)?

Solution:

1. Angell will need $40,000 to purchase ¥4,240,000.

$$¥4,240,000/¥106 = $40,000$$

2. In payment by the Brazilian company, Angell will receive

$$$50,000 \times 5.60 = R\$280,000$$

3. Angell will need $40,381 to purchase ¥4,240,000.

$$¥4,240,000/¥105 = $40,381 \text{ (rounded)}$$

Suppose that last month $1 could buy 0.90 euro (€ is the symbol for euro), and now, a month later, $1 can buy 0.92 euro. The dollar has appreciated against the euro since it can buy more of them.

Alternatively, suppose that last month $1 could buy 0.90 euro, and now $1 can buy 0.85 euro. The dollar has depreciated against the euro since it can buy fewer of them. So, **currency appreciation** means that one country's currency has become relatively stronger and buys more units of another country's currency, and **currency depreciation** means that one country's currency has become relatively weaker and buys fewer units of another country's currency.

What about the euro? Has it appreciated or depreciated? If the dollar has appreciated, the euro must have depreciated. Let's look at the exchange rate in terms of euros. Last month, $1 could buy 0.90 euro, which means that:

$$€1 = $1/0.90 = $1.11 \text{ (rounded)}$$

Today, $1 could buy 0.92 euro, which means that:

$$€1 = $1/0.92 = $1.09 \text{ (rounded)}$$

And the euro buys fewer dollars than before.

Alternatively, when the dollar depreciates, the euro appreciates. If $1 = €0.85, then:

$$€1.0 = $1/0.85 = $1.18$$

And the euro then buys more dollars than the original $1.11.

Notice that if one currency appreciates, then the other has depreciated. Is this good or bad? That depends on whether you are buying goods in another country or selling them.

For example, in the late 1990s, various Asian currencies weakened vis-à-vis the dollar. This had an impact on trade between Asian countries and the United States. Disneyland and Universal Studios theme parks suffered from the decrease in Asian tourists. Even though the parks' admission prices had not changed, the dollar was relatively more expensive for Malaysian and Singaporean tourists, and they avoided Southern California tourist attractions, hotels, restaurants, and so on.

Exchange Gains and Losses An **exchange gain** is the gain on the exchange of one currency for another due to appreciation of the home currency. An **exchange loss** is a loss on the exchange of one currency for another due to depreciation of the home currency. Let's look at **Example 21.3** to see how exchange gains and losses are calculated.

EXAMPLE 21.3

The HOW and WHY of Calculating Exchange Gains and Losses

Information:
SuperTubs, Inc., based in Oklahoma, sells its line of whirlpool tubs at home and to foreign distributors. On February 15, Bonbain, a French distributor of luxury plumbing fixtures, orders 100 tubs at a price of $1,000 per tub to be delivered immediately and to be paid in euros on April 15. The selling price in euros is computed using the exchange rate in effect on February 15.

> Spot rates of euros for $1
> February 15 $1 = €0.892
> April 15 $1 = €0.898

> **Why:**
> Because different countries use different currencies, firms trading need to determine the cost of an item in the other currency. Frequently changing currency exchange rates mean that there may be gains or losses on the exchange.

Required:

1. On February 15, how much does SuperTubs expect to receive from Bonbain in euros in payment for the tubs?

2. On April 15, how much does SuperTubs actually receive from Bonbain in euros? What is that amount converted to dollars?

3. Did SuperTubs experience an exchange gain or loss on the transaction? Of how much in dollars?

4. *What if* the exchange rate of euros for $1 on April 15 was $1 = €0.89? How much would SuperTubs receive from Bonbain in euros? What is that amount converted into dollars? Would SuperTubs experience an exchange gain or loss on the transaction?

Solution:

1. SuperTubs expects to be paid (0.892 × $100,000) = €89,200

2. SuperTubs will be paid €89,200. Converted into dollars, it is

    (€89,200/0.898) = $99,332 (rounded)

3. SuperTub's exchange loss = $100,000 − $99,332 = $668

4. The February 15 exchange rate remains $1 = €0.892 so SuperTubs still expects to receive €89,200 ($100,000 × 0.892) but, converted into dollars, it is

    (€89,200/0.89) = $100,225 (rounded) and there would be an exchange gain of $225 ($100,225 − $100,000)

Transaction risk also affects the purchase of commodities from foreign companies. Suppose that on February 20, Video Services, Inc., (based in Los Angeles) purchases computers from Canon for $50,000, payable in yen (¥) on May 20. Assume the spot rate for yen is 107.5 per dollar on February 20. It is easy to see that Video Services' true payable is for 5,375,000 yen ($50,000 × 107.5). If the spot rate for yen is 108.7 on May 20, it will cost Video Services only $49,448 (¥5,375,000/108.7) to get enough yen to pay Canon.

Liability in dollars, February 20	$50,000
Liability in dollars, May 20	49,448
Exchange gain	$ 552

As we can see, the more favorable May 20 spot rate has resulted in an exchange gain. Clearly, transaction risk caused by the movement of foreign currency against the dollar must be taken into account by managers as it affects the prices paid and received for goods. Suppose management does not want to be involved in gambling on exchange rates. The following section on hedging explains how the accountant can manage a company's exposure to exchange gains and losses.

Hedging One way of ensuring against gains and losses on foreign currency exchanges is hedging. **Hedging** requires one to lock in a currency exchange rate in advance. Typically, a forward exchange contract is used as a hedge. The **forward contract** requires the buyer to exchange a specified amount of a currency at a specified rate (the forward rate) on a specified future date.

Let's return to Example 21.3 with SuperTubs' sale of $100,000 to the French company. The spot rate on February 15 was 0.892 euro per dollar. SuperTubs' problem is that it does not know what the exchange rate will be on April 15. If it is more than 0.892 euro per dollar, SuperTubs will receive less than the $100,000 anticipated in accounts receivable. Of course, if the rate is less, SuperTubs will receive more. But the difficulty is in predicting short-term exchange rate movements. SuperTubs may well decide it is in the business of manufacturing and selling tubs, not in the business of betting on exchange rate fluctuations. Therefore, it may forego the opportunity for exchange rate gains by hedging against exchange rate losses. **Example 21.4** explains how the hedging works.

EXAMPLE 21.4

The HOW and WHY of Hedging Currency Exchange Rates

Information:

SuperTubs, Inc., sold 100 tubs at a price of $1,000 per tub to be delivered immediately and to be paid in euros on April 15. SuperTubs is worried that the exchange rate of dollars for euros could change significantly within two months. In hopes of avoiding a potential loss on exchange, the company has decided to purchase a forward contract.

Spot rates of euros for $1	
February 15 spot rate of euros for $1	$1 = €0.892
April 15 forward rate of euros for $1	$1 = €0.894

Why:
A company may hedge against currency exchange fluctuations to avoid potential large losses on the exchange.

Required:

1. On February 15, how much does SuperTubs expect to receive from Bonbain in euros in payment for the tubs?

2. If SuperTubs purchases the forward contract, how many euros will it receive on April 15? What is that amount converted to dollars?

EXAMPLE 21.4

(Continued)

3. What is the premium SuperTubs paid for the forward contract?

4. ***What if*** the exchange rate of euros for $1 on April 15 was $1 = €0.898? How much would SuperTubs have received from Bonbain in euros? What is that amount converted into dollars? Would SuperTubs have experienced an exchange gain or loss on the transaction?

Solution:

1. SuperTubs expects to be paid (0.892 × $100,000) = €89,200

2. SuperTubs will be paid €89,200. Converted into dollars at the forward rate, it is

$$(€89,200/0.894) = \$99,776 \text{ (rounded)}$$

3. SuperTubs' premium = $100,000 − $99,776 = $224

4. SuperTubs would have received €89,200 that converted into dollars would be

$$(€89,200/0.898) = \$99,332 \text{ (rounded) and there would have been an exchange}$$
$$\text{loss of } \$668 (\$100,000 − \$99,332)$$

Of course, the hedging can also be done by agreeing to exchange dollars for a foreign currency at a future date. Recall the previous example of Video Services' purchase of 5,375,000 yen worth of computer equipment. At a spot rate of 107.5, Video Services expects to pay $50,000 to satisfy its liability. Video Services may fear that the rate will decline, say to 105 yen per dollar. If it did, Video Services would have to pay $51,190 (¥5,375,000/105) for the same 5,375,000 yen. A hedging transaction would resolve Video Services' uncertainty. Perhaps the forward rate is 128.7 yen per dollar. Then, Video Services would purchase a forward contract to purchase 6,500,000 yen on May 20 for $50,505 (¥6,500,000/128.7).

Liability in dollars, February 20	$50,000
Payment in dollars, May 20	(50,505)
Premium expense	$ 505

Hedging transactions can become much more complex than the foregoing example. Companies with significant transaction exposure may choose to hedge all or part of their exposure. Hedging may also be used as a tool to manage economic risk, which will be addressed in the following section.

Cryptocurrencies

We have long used physical items, such as beads, metal coins, dollars, or bank notes, as a means of exchange. The advent of electronic accounting for monetary assets has accustomed us to digital money and accepted digital means to accept deposits and pay bills and transfer money. It was a short step from this to true digital currency or cryptocurrency. **Cryptocurrency** is a means of exchange that is only available in electronic form. A cryptocurrency is originally centralized when it is created. But after issue, it usually works through a blockchain or distributed ledger technology. It is decentralized rather than centralized under the control of a country's banking system, and it is a public transaction base. Bitcoin and Ethereum are well-known and widely traded cryptocurrencies, but new cryptocurrencies continue to be created. Some cryptocurrencies can be used only within the confines of a game or particular activity, such as CryptoKitties, a blockchain game built on Ethereum. However, many cryptocurrencies can be used as a medium of exchange and can be traded on the open market. For example, on September 21, 2020, one ether (Ethereum cryptocurrency) was valued at $343.92 and one

Bitcoin was valued at $10,479.20. In a sense, cryptocurrencies are treated like physical assets like gold. They have a value and can be traded on the open market.[7]

Mining Cryptocurrencies use various timestamping schemes to "prove" the validity of transactions added to the blockchain ledger without the need for a trusted third party. The first timestamping scheme invented was the proof-of-work scheme. When cryptocurrency is produced, it is said to be mined. Within a cryptocurrency system, safety, integrity, and balance of the distributed ledgers that keep track of the transactions is ensured by individuals called *miners*. Basically, miners validate transactions using their own equipment and resources. In return, they receive new cryptocurrency as a reward. Mining is a resource-intensive process requiring sophisticated computers, chips, electricity, and cooling equipment. The Opening Scenario describing the Nvidia graphics chips illustrates the importance of using the most up-to-date equipment. The cost of these resources may or may not justify the mining effort. Most cryptocurrencies are designed to gradually decrease production of that currency, placing a cap on the total amount of that currency that will ever be in circulation.

Legality As of February 2020, Bitcoin was legal in the United States, Japan, the United Kingdom, Canada, and most other developed countries. The legal status of Bitcoin varies dramatically in other countries and must be looked at by specific country. While China does not outlaw holding Bitcoins, it is heavily restricted. Indian banks may not deal in Bitcoins, but the remaining legal status is murky.

Even where Bitcoin is legal, most of the laws that apply to other assets also apply to Bitcoin. Tax laws are the area where most people are likely to run into trouble. For tax purposes, Bitcoins are usually treated as property rather than currency. Bitcoin is generally not considered legal tender.[8] It is legal to mine Bitcoin in the United States, but since it's designated as a commodity, capital gains have to be reported for tax purposes.

On March 25, 2014, the U.S. Internal Revenue Service (IRS) ruled that Bitcoins will be treated as property for tax purposes, subjecting their sale to capital gains tax. In July 2019, the IRS started sending letters to cryptocurrency owners warning them to amend their returns and pay taxes.

The legal status of cryptocurrencies varies substantially from country to country and is still undefined or changing in many of them. Various government agencies, departments, and courts have classified Bitcoin differently. In China, banks are banned from handling cryptocurrency. In Russia, cryptocurrency is legal, but it cannot be used to pay for goods and services. Other countries accept, ban, or partially restrict the use of cryptocurrencies. Like many cryptocurrencies, Bitcoin is pseudonymous rather than anonymous. That is, the name of the owner is not specified, but it is possible to trace the transactions back through the blockchain to collect personal information on the user. In that sense, it is more difficult for countries to identify the owner since unlike a bank, user information is not collected and reported to a central agency. Cryptocurrencies can be more difficult for law enforcement to seize and subject to taxation.

Managing Economic Risk

Dealing in different currencies can introduce an economic dimension into currency exchange transactions. Recall that economic risk was defined as the impact of exchange rate fluctuations on the present value of a firm's future cash flows. The risk can affect the relative competitiveness of the firm, even if it never participates directly in international trade. Take a simple example based on the market for heavy equipment between 1981 and 1985.

---

7   According to Coindesk, https://www.coindesk.com/price/ethereum and https://www.coindesk.com/price
    /bitcoin, September 21, 2020, accessed September 21, 2020.
8   Mara Lesemann, "Is Bitcoin Legal?" *Investopedia*, February 3, 2020, https://www.investopedia.com/ask
    /answers/121515/bitcoin-legal-us.asp, accessed September 21, 2020.

Suppose that U.S. consumers can choose to purchase heavy equipment from either **Caterpillar** (based in the United States) or from **Komatsu** (based in Japan). Assume the price of one type of equipment is $200,000 from both makers. However, while Caterpillar truly means $200,000, Komatsu really is interested in 21,400,000 yen, its own currency. At an exchange rate of $1 equals 107 yen, the price of $200,000 is set. Now, suppose that the value of the dollar strengthens against the yen and the exchange rate becomes $1 equals 108 yen. To get the same 21,400,000 yen, Komatsu requires a price of only $198,148 (rounded). The cost structures of the two firms have not changed, neither has customer demand, but because of currency fluctuations, the Japanese firm has become more "competitive." Of course, as the dollar weakens, the position is reversed, and U.S. exports become relatively cheaper to foreign customers.

How does the accountant manage the company's exposure to economic risk? Most important is awareness of the risk by understanding the position of the firm in the global economy. As we can see in the Caterpillar-Komatsu example, the two firms were competitors and were linked through their customers' participation in the global marketplace. The accountant provides financial structure and communication for the firm. In preparing the master budget, for example, budgeted sales must take into account potential strengthening or weakening of the currencies of competitors' countries. Often, the controller's office is responsible for forecasting foreign exchange movements.

Hedging can provide another means of managing economic risk. For example, the Toronto Blue Jays (Major League Baseball), Toronto Maple Leafs (National Hockey League), and the Raptors (National Basketball Association) receive their revenues in Canadian dollars but pay their payroll expenses in U.S. dollars (due to the team traveling within the United States). The fall in the value of the Canadian dollar (the loonie) by nearly 20 percent in 2014 greatly increased the expenses payable in U.S. dollars. So for the Toronto Blue Jays, with a 2014 payroll of about $137 million, the fall in the value of the loonie was over $25 million. The Raptors and Maple Leafs were looking at an additional $14 million each. The teams anticipated a serious loss of profit in due to unfavorable exchange rate fluctuations. To prevent this, the Canadian teams typically hedge. **Maple Leaf Sports and Entertainment (MLSE)**, which runs the Maple Leafs and the Raptors among others, hedged about $100 million each year. The certainty of knowing the rate of exchange was worth the cost of about $350,000 to hedge the $100 million.[9]

DATA ANALYTICS

Typically a forward exchange contract is used as a hedge. The forward contract requires the buyer to exchange a specified amount of currency at a specified rate (the forward rate) on a specified future date. Companies collect data on currency fluctuations over a number of months and years for analysis. They use these data to forecast future fluctuations to determine whether the premium expense of hedging is worthwhile.

Let's return to Example 21.3 to look at SuperTubs' sale of $100,000 worth of tubs to the French company. The spot rate on January 15 was 0.82 euro per dollar. SuperTubs' problem is that it does not know what the exchange rate will be on March 15. If it is more than 0.82 euro, SuperTubs will receive less than the $100,000 anticipated in accounts receivable. Of course, if the rate is less, SuperTubs will receive more. But the difficulty is in predicting short-term exchange rate movements. SuperTubs may well decide it is in the business of manufacturing and selling tubs, not in the business of betting on exchange rate fluctuations. Therefore, it will forgo the opportunity for exchange rate gains by hedging against exchange rate losses. Here is how it might work using forward contracts.

Managing Translation Risk

Often, the parent company restates all subsidiaries' income into the home currency. This restatement can result in gain and loss opportunities on the revaluation of foreign currencies. It can also impact a subsidiary's financial statements and the related return on investment (ROI) and residual income computations. For example, **Walt Disney Company** noted in its first

---

9   Josh Rubin, "MLSE, Blue Jays Deal with Dollar Dive," *The Star*, January 25, 2015, https://www.thestar.com/sports /leafs/2015/01/25/mlse-blue-jays-deal-with-dollar-dive.html, accessed August 27, 2020.

quarter 2016 report that earnings for its studio networks, cable entertainment, and consumer products and interactive media were down due to unfavorable currency effects as the dollar strengthened against major currencies.[10]

Suppose you are a division manager based in Mexico. Your division earned 2,200,000 pesos this year, up from 2,000,000 pesos the year before, a 10 percent increase. Now, suppose that your income is translated into dollars. If the exchange rate last year was 20 pesos per dollar and the exchange rate this year is 25 pesos per dollar, your income figures translate into $100,000 ($2,000,000/20) income last year and $88,000 ($2,200,000/25) income this year. Suddenly, there is a 12 percent decrease in income. Similar unpleasant surprises await ROI and net worth computations. The potential for gain or loss on currency revaluation is particularly relevant for countries whose currencies are volatile—and depreciating relative to the home company's currency.

Foreign currency fluctuations also cause difficulties in evaluating the local manager's adherence to company policy. **Monsanto** faced this problem in the early 1980s. The company noticed declining sales in some of its foreign markets. The local managers were instructed to increase promotional expenditures. However, dollar-denominated reports showed no increases. Top management continued to press local managers to carry out instructions. Local managers were frustrated by their inability to convince higher management that they had increased expenditures, since the reports showed fewer dollars being spent. Eventually, local currency statements were placed alongside dollar-denominated reports. These comparative statements clearly showed that increased expenditures had taken place.

A simple numerical example may illustrate the problem. Assume that Multinational, Inc., has made a strategic decision to emphasize the production of technologically advanced, high-quality products. As a result, Multinational's top management has instructed its foreign division, FD, to increase expenditures on R&D. FD managers do increase R&D expenditures over the following four quarters as follows.

Quarter	Expenditures in Local Currency
1	LC 100,000
2	LC 110,000
3	LC 121,000
4	LC 133,100

As we can see, R&D expenditures have grown by 10 percent in each quarter. However, Multinational managers do not see this table. Instead, they see dollar-denominated reports. In order to translate local currency figures into dollars, we need the exchange rates for each quarter. Suppose the dollar has strengthened against the local currency and the quarterly exchange rates of $1 for units of local currency are 1.00, 1.20, 1.35, and 1.50. Then, FD's R&D expenditures in dollars would be as follows.

Quarter	Expenditures in Dollars
1	$100,000
2	91,667
3	89,630
4	88,733

What a difference! Not only does it appear that local managers have not increased expenditures, it looks as if they have actually decreased expenditures. Only by comparing the dollar-denominated figures with those denominated in local currency can Multinational see the two effects of an increase in R&D expenditures and the strengthening of the dollar. In this case, FD's increase was hidden in currency translation.

---

10 "The Walt Disney Company Reports Record Quarterly Earnings for the First Quarter of Fiscal 2016," *The Business Wire*, February 9, 2016, https://www.businesswire.com/news/home/20160209006737/en/Walt-Disney-Company -Reports-Record-Quarterly-Earnings, accessed August 27, 2020.

The objective of dollar-denominated internal reports is to measure all figures on the same basis. While this strategy may work at any one point in time, it may mislead managers when comparisons are made over time. The accountant must be aware of this source of translation risk.

OBJECTIVE 4

Explain how environmental factors can affect performance evaluation in the multinational firm.

DECENTRALIZATION AND PERFORMANCE EVALUATION IN THE MULTINATIONAL FIRM

Frequently, firms that are decentralized in the home country may exercise tighter control over foreign divisions, at least until they gain more experience with their overseas operations. Just as decentralization offers advantages for home country divisions, it also offers advantages for foreign divisions. Let's review some of those advantages and their impact on performance evaluation.

The MNC has great flexibility in creating types of divisions. Divisions are often created along geographic lines. IBM, for example, has divisional boundaries that organize production and sales for Asia Pacific, North America, Latin and South America, and Europe/Middle East/Africa. Product lines may afford a rationale for the creation of divisions. Many MNCs are diversified, manufacturing and selling a number of different products. The MNC may decide that the major difference is the type of product sold, not the country in which it is sold. Procter & Gamble (P&G), for example, operates through six industry-based sector business units: fabric and home care, baby and feminine care, family care and P&G ventures, beauty, grooming, and health care.[11]

Advantages of Decentralization in the MNC

The quality of information is better at the local level, and that can improve the quality of decisions. This is particularly true in MNCs, where far-flung divisions may be operating in a number of different countries, subject to various legal systems and customs. As a result, local managers are often in a position to make better decisions. Decentralization allows an organization to take advantage of this specialized knowledge. For example, Loctite Corporation has local managers run their own divisions. In particular, marketing and pricing are under local administration. Language is not a problem as local managers are in control. Similarly, local managers are conversant with their own laws and customs.

Local managers in the MNC are capable of a more timely response in decision making. They are able to respond quickly to customer discount demands, local government demands, and changes in the political climate.

In Chapter 10, we discussed the need for centralized managers to transmit instructions and the chance that the manager responsible for implementing the decision might misinterpret the instructions. The different languages native to managers of divisions in the MNC make this an even greater problem. MNCs address this problem in two ways. First, a decentralized structure pushes decision making down to the local manager level, eliminating the need to interpret instructions from above. Second, MNCs are learning to incorporate technology that overrides the language barrier and eases cross-border data transfer. Technology is of great help in smoothing communication difficulties between parent and subsidiary and between one subsidiary and another. For example, bar code technology "reads" package labels, eliminating the need for foreign language translation.

Just as decentralization gives the lower-level managers in the home country a chance to develop managerial skills, foreign subsidiary managers also gain valuable experience. Just as important, home country managers gain broader experience by interacting with managers of foreign divisions. The chance for learning from each other is much greater in a decentralized MNC. Off and on throughout the latter half of the twentieth century, a tour of duty at a foreign subsidiary has been a part of the manager's climb to the top. Now, foreign subsidiary managers may expect to spend some time at headquarters in the home office, as well.

---

11 Procter & Gamble Structure and Governance, https://us.pg.com/structure-and-governance/corporate-structure/, accessed August 28, 2020.

Measuring Performance in the Multinational Firm

It is important for the MNC to separate the evaluation of the manager of a division from the evaluation of the division. The managers' evaluations should not include factors over which they exercise no control, such as currency fluctuations, income taxes, and so on. Instead, managers should be evaluated on the basis of revenues and costs incurred. It is particularly difficult to compare the performance of a manager of a division (or subsidiary) in one country with the performance of a manager of a division in another country. Even divisions that appear to be similar in terms of production may face very different economic, social, or political forces. The manager should be evaluated on the basis of the performance he or she can control. Once a manager is evaluated, then the subsidiary financial statements can be restated to the home currency and uncontrollable costs can be allocated.

International environmental conditions may be very different from, and more complex than, domestic conditions. Environmental variables facing local managers of divisions include economic, legal, political, social, and educational factors.

Economic Factors

Some important economic variables are inflation, foreign currency exchange rates, income taxes, and transfer prices. For example, MNCs have invested heavily in developing countries. The result is that those countries have built considerable manufacturing capacity and are now competing aggressively around the world. This has led to lower prices and deflation on a global basis. As a result, MNCs, used to dealing with the inflationary environment of the 1990s and early 2000s, will have to shift gears to deal with possible deflation. In this case, cost control is essential.

Legal and Political Factors

Legal and political factors also have differing impacts. For example, a country may not allow cash outflows or may forbid the import of certain items. In the early 2000s, U.S. agricultural laws did not allow rooted plants to enter the country. This posed a problem for U.S. florists who sell poinsettias during the Christmas season. They need many poinsettias, but they do not have the greenhouse capacity to grow them throughout the rest of the year. Mexico provides an ideal growing environment for the plants. However, potted plants could not enter the United States. Plant science advances solved the importation problem. The plants were imported as cuttings that were quick cooled, bagged, and shipped in dry ice, clearing customs in this form, arriving at their destination within the 72-hour window. Further advances in plant science allowed growing of plants in sterilized soil or vermiculite; these can pass through customs. The result is a thriving poinsettia-growing industry in Mexico and many more of the colorful plants available for U.S. consumers.[12]

Educational, Infrastructure, and Cultural Factors

Educational, infrastructure, and cultural variables affect how the multinational firm is treated by the subsidiary's country. For example, Walmart now operates in 27 countries around the world from Argentina to Zambia but Brazil is not one of them. Walmart entered Brazil in 1996, opening its own stores and acquiring other stores. From the beginning the company had difficulty in its expansion to Brazil. Walmart's system of just-in-time restocking of shelves runs like a well-oiled machine in the United States. In Brazil, however, the company did not own its own distribution system, meaning that stores in Brazil had to process up to 300 deliveries daily versus 7 in the United States. On the cultural front, Walmart had to change its credit policies by accepting postdated checks—the most common form of credit in Brazil. Walmart also did not adapt to local consumer preferences. Brazilians prefer frequent promotions, they did not perceive value in Walmart's "every day low pricing."

---

12 Rodrigo Cervantes, "Poinsettias Are Mexico's Heritage to the Holidays—Thanks to a U.S. Diplomat," *kjzz.org*, December 24, 2016, https://kjzz.org/content/10532/poinsettias-are-mexicos-heritage-holidays—thanks-us-diplomat, accessed August 28, 2020.

In addition, they like to shop at multiple stores to find the best bargains. *Atacarejos* are popular in Brazil; these are variations of "cash and carry" stores. They are basically warehouse stores but without annual fees. In the end, Walmart's model simply did not work in Brazil and by 2018, the company had sold the majority of its Brazilian operations to a private equity company.[13] As the Walmart example shows, the data collected on Brazilian sales were analyzed to determine that the stores should be closed.

The need to provide education and infrastructure also affect the MNC. Many clothing distributors in the United States depend on factories in developing countries to do the manufacturing. However, first, those companies had to develop the area, putting in roads and communication equipment and providing training for workers.

Comparison of Divisional ROI

The existence of differing environmental factors makes interdivisional comparison of ROI potentially misleading. Suppose a U.S.-based MNC has three divisions, located in Brazil, Canada, and Spain, with the following information given in millions of dollars:

	Assets	Revenues	Income	Margin	Turnover	ROI*
Brazil	$10	$ 6	$ 3	0.50	0.60	0.30
Canada	18	13	10	0.77	0.72	0.56
Spain	15	10	6	0.60	0.67	0.40

*Rounded to two decimal places

On the basis of ROI, it appears that the manager of the Canadian subsidiary did the best job, while the manager of the Brazilian subsidiary did the worst job. But is this a fair comparison? Spain and Canada face very different legal, political, educational, and economic conditions. Inflation has been very high in South America compared to North America. Many South American firms have responded by adjusting reported financial amounts for inflation. Suppose in our example that the Canadian firm reports its assets at historical cost and that the Brazilian firm adjusts its assets for inflation. If inflation during the period the assets have been held has averaged 100 percent (not an unreasonable assumption in a country that has faced monthly double-digit inflation rates for years), then the historical cost of the Brazilian assets would be $5 million. The calculation is as follows:

$$X + 100\%X = \$10$$
$$X + 1.00X = \$10$$
$$2X = \$10$$
$$X = \$5$$

If we restate the Brazilian subsidiary's assets to historical cost, then the ROI would be 60 percent ($3/$5 = 0.6). If this computation is used, the Brazilian subsidiary appears to be the most successful, not the least. It should be noted that accounting for inflationary effects on income and assets is very complicated and that the simple restatement just shown is not a comprehensive approach. Additionally, top management is typically aware of the existence of differential inflation rates. Still, the lack of consistency in internal reporting may obscure interdivisional comparison, and the accountant must be aware of this problem.

Other environmental factors can differ between countries. A minimum wage law in one country will restrict the manager's ability to affect labor costs. Another country may prevent the export of cash. Still others may have a well-educated workforce but poor infrastructure (transportation and communication facilities). Therefore, the corporation must be aware of and control these differing environmental factors when assessing managerial performance. Exhibit 11.2 lists some environmental factors that may make interdivisional comparisons misleading.

---

13 CNBC, "Walmart Flopped in This Country in South America—Here's Why," December 10, 2018, https://www.cnbc.com/video/2018/12/10/walmart-brazil-advent-retail-wholesale.html, accessed October 13, 2020.

Other Factors Affecting Performance Evaluation The accountant in the MNC must be aware of more than business and finance. Political and legal systems have important implications for the company. Sometimes, the political system changes quickly, throwing the company into crisis mode. Other times, the situation evolves more slowly.

General Electric has been affected by drug trafficking in Colombia as the Colombian drug lords turned to appliance exporting as a means of laundering their U.S. profits. Honest U.S. and Colombian retail appliance dealers have been hurt by the smugglers' low prices. GE was forced to institute tough audit procedures to ferret out the illegal activity. The result was a drop in GE's market share in the Miami area and an increase in accounting expense.[14]

On occasion, the political structure may mean that standard U.S.-based methods of control may not "work" in foreign countries. For example, under the communist regime in the USSR, manufacturers received a budget, actual results were compared with the budget, and variances were computed. However, variance analysis did not have the same meaning that it has in the United States. If a company faced a variance, the solution was to send the plant's senior political operative to Central Planning Headquarters with a case of champagne or cognac. The hoped-for result was a change in the budget so that it matched actual results, and the variance disappeared. The business objective was not efficiency or effectiveness but a compliance with the central plan. While the Central Planning Headquarters no longer exists, this culture of altering the plan to match the actual results does continue to exist.

Multiple Measures of Performance Rigid evaluation of the performance of foreign divisions of the MNC ignores the overarching strategic importance of developing a global presence. The interconnectedness of the global company weakens the independence or stand-alone nature of any one segment. As a result, residual income and ROI are less-important measures of managerial performance for divisions of the MNC. MNCs must use additional measures of performance that relate more closely to the long-run health of the company. In addition to ROI and residual income, top management looks at such factors as market potential and market share. For example, when **Gillette** began to sell Oral-B toothbrushes in China, it knew that even a small market share would lead to huge sales volume. **Procter & Gamble**, **Bausch & Lomb**, and **Citicorp** are expanding into Indian and Asian markets for the same reason.

Additionally, the use of ROI and RI in the evaluation of managerial performance in divisions of an MNC is subject to problems beyond those faced by a decentralized company that operates in only one country. It is particularly important, then, to take a responsibility accounting approach and evaluate managers on the basis of factors under their control. For example, by 2019 the rise in Russia-U.S. tensions led to pro-Kremlin politicians to push for the end of **McDonald's** in Russia. To maintain its presence, McDonald's management worked to "Go Russian." McDonald's sources 98 percent of its supplies locally and advertises that fact heavily. As a result, in 2018 McDonald's has grown in Russia by 6 percent compared to its worldwide average growth of 1.5 percent. [15]

TRANSFER PRICING AND THE MULTINATIONAL FIRM

OBJECTIVE 5

Describe the role of transfer pricing in the multinational firm.

For the multinational firm, transfer pricing must accomplish two objectives, performance evaluation and optimal determination of income taxes. The basics of transfer pricing are covered in Chapter 10; international implications of transfer pricing are discussed here.

---

14 Michael Allen, "GE Tries to Get Tough with Dealers after Pressure by Colombian Gadfly," *The Wall Street Journal*, December 21, 1998, https://www.wsj.com/articles/SB914195024241976500, accessed September 5, 2020.

15 Thomas Grove, "In Russia, McDonald's Serves Local Fries and a Side of Realpolitik," *The Wall Street Journal*, November 8, 2018, https://www.wsj.com/articles/in-russia-mcdonalds-serves-local-fries-and-a-side-of -realpolitik-1541678402?mod=searchresults&page=1&pos=3, accessed September 14, 2020.

Performance Evaluation

Divisions are frequently evaluated on the basis of income and ROI. As is the case for any transfer price, the selling division wants a high transfer price that will raise its income, and the buying division wants a low transfer price that will raise its income. A problem arises in that transfer prices in MNCs are frequently set by the parent company. Therefore, the use of mandated transfer prices makes the use of ROI and income suspect. That is, they are not under the control of division managers and no longer serve as indicators of management performance.

Income Taxes and Transfer Pricing

If all countries had the same tax structure, then transfer prices would be set independently of income taxes. However, there are high-tax countries (like the United States) and low-tax countries (such as the Cayman Islands). As a result, MNCs may use transfer pricing to shift costs to high-tax countries and shift revenues to low-tax countries.

U.S.-based multinationals are subject to Internal Revenue Code Section 482 on the pricing of intercompany transactions. This section gives the IRS the authority to reallocate income and deductions among divisions if it believes that such reallocation will reduce potential tax evasion. Basically, Section 482 requires that sales be made at "arm's length." That is, the transfer price set should match the price that would be set if the transfer were being made by unrelated parties, adjusted for differences that have a measurable effect on the price. Differences include landing costs and marketing costs. Landing costs (e.g., freight, insurance, customs duties, and special taxes) can increase the allowable transfer price. Marketing costs are usually avoided for internal transfers and reduce the transfer price. The IRS allows three pricing methods that approximate arm's-length pricing. In order of preference, these are the **comparable uncontrolled price method**, the **resale price method**, and the **cost-plus method**. The comparable uncontrolled price method is essentially market price. The resale price method is equal to the sales price received by the reseller less an appropriate markup. That is, the subsidiary purchasing a good for resale sets a transfer price equal to the resale price less a gross profit percentage. The cost-plus method is simply the cost-based transfer price. Let's look at **Example 21.5** to calculate transfer prices using the comparable uncontrolled price method and the resale price method.

EXAMPLE 21.5

The HOW and WHY of Using the Comparable Uncontrolled Price Method, the Resale Price Method, and the Cost-Plus Method in Calculating Transfer Prices

Information:
ABC, Inc., has a number of divisions around the world. Division B (in the United States) purchases a component from Division C (in Canada). The component can be purchased externally for $38 each. The freight and insurance on the item amount to $5; however, commissions of $3.80 need not be paid.

Why:
These transfer prices are acceptable to the IRS for tax purposes.

Required:

1. Calculate the transfer price using the comparable uncontrolled price method.

2. Suppose that there is no outside market for the component that Division C transfers to Division B. Further assume that Division B sells the component for $42 and normally received a 40 percent markup on cost of goods sold. Calculate the transfer price using the resale price method.

EXAMPLE 21.5

(*Continued*)

3. Now assume that there is no external market for the component transferred from Division C to Division B and that the component is used in the manufacture of another product (i.e., it is not resold). Calculate the transfer price using the cost-plus method. Further assume that Division C's manufacturing cost for the component is $20.

4. ***What if*** freight and insurance were $4 per unit? How would that affect the comparable uncontrolled price? The cost-plus price?

Solution:

1. The comparable uncontrolled price is calculated as follows:

Market price	$38.00
Plus: Freight and insurance	5.00
Less: Commissions	(3.80)
Transfer price	$39.20

2. With no outside market for Division C, and a resale price for Division B, the transfer price is calculated as follows:

   $$\text{Resale price} = \text{Transfer price} + (\text{Markup percentage} \times \text{Transfer price})$$
   $$\$42 = 1.40 \times \text{Transfer price}$$
   $$\text{Transfer price} = \$42/1.40$$
   $$= \$30$$

3. Cost-plus transfer price = Manufacturing cost + Freight and insurance
   $$= \$20 + \$5$$
   $$= \$25$$

4. If freight and insurance decrease by $1, the comparable uncontrolled price and the cost-plus price would be $1 lower.

The determination of an arm's-length price is a difficult one. Many times, the transfer pricing situation facing a company does not "fit" any of the three preferred methods just outlined. Then, the IRS will permit a fourth method—a transfer price negotiated between the company and the IRS. The IRS, taxpayers, and the Tax Court have struggled with negotiated transfer prices for years. However, this type of negotiation occurs after the fact—after income tax returns have been submitted, and the company is being audited. The IRS has authorized the issuance of **advance pricing agreements (APAs)** to assist tax-paying firms to determine whether a proposed transfer price is acceptable to the IRS in advance of income tax filing. An APA is an agreement between the IRS and a taxpayer on the pricing method to be applied in an international transaction. It can cover transfers of intangibles (such as royalties on licenses), sales of property, provision of services, and other items. It is binding on both the IRS and the taxpayer for the years specified in the APA and is not made public.[16]

The super royalty provision of Section 482 was added in 1986 to require companies to value their intangibles more fairly. The IRS suspected that U.S. companies were transferring their intangibles (patents, copyrights, customer lists, etc.) to foreign subsidiaries at less than fair market value. For example, a U.S. pharmaceutical firm would develop a new drug and license its Puerto Rican subsidiary to produce it. The drug would then be purchased by the parent company for sale in the United States, and a royalty would be charged to the Puerto Rican subsidiary. The royalty rate, taxable income to the parent, was low but was similar to other third-party transactions. Thus, the IRS could not challenge it. The super royalty provision changed this situation by linking the transfer price of the intangible to the income attributable to the intangible.

---

16 https://www.irs.gov/businesses/corporations/apma; https://www.jct.gov/publications.html?func=startdown&id=3692

The IRS also regulates the transfer pricing of foreign companies with U.S. subsidiaries. A U.S. company that is at least 25 percent foreign owned must keep extensive documentation of arm's-length transfer pricing.

Of course, MNCs are also subject to taxation by other countries as well as the United States. Since income taxes are virtually universal, consideration of income tax effects pervades management decision making. Canada, Japan, the European Community, and South Korea have all issued transfer pricing regulations. This increased emphasis on transfer price justification may account for the increased use of market prices as the transfer price by MNCs. The most important environmental variable considered by MNCs in setting a transfer pricing policy is overall profit to the company—with overall profit including the income tax impact of intracompany transfers.

Managers may legally avoid income taxes; they may not evade them. The distinction is important. Unfortunately, the difference between avoidance and evasion is less a line than a blurry gray area. While some situations are clearly abusive, other tax-motivated actions are not. For example, an MNC may decide to establish a needed research and development center within an existing subsidiary in a high-tax country, since the costs are deductible. MNCs may have income tax-planning information systems that attempt to accomplish global income tax minimization. This is not an easy task.

OBJECTIVE

Discuss ethical issues that affect firms operating in the international environment.

ETHICS IN THE INTERNATIONAL ENVIRONMENT

As challenging as ethical decision making can be in the home country, there are even more problems when dealing internationally. Ethical codes differ widely among different countries. This makes it difficult for managers to maintain the same code of ethics in each country. For example, a bribe in one country is totally unacceptable and yet an expected way of doing business in another country. Child labor laws vary from country to country. As a result, managers in international business must know how to address differences in ethical standards around the world.[17]

A strong underlying system is important for enforcing contracts, and it provides the basis for confidence in ethical dealings. For some countries (e.g., the United States and western European countries), that system is legal with deviations punishable by law. For others (e.g., Japan and countries in the Middle East), it is cultural, and deviations are punished at least as severely by loss of honor. The importance of a strong underlying social code of conduct is clearly evident by its absence in illegal business dealings. For obvious reasons, you would be loathe to contact the police or district attorney about your purchase of low-quality methamphetamine. Similarly, in Iran or Venezuela, where foreign currency exchange is controlled by the government, a black market for U.S. currency exchange exists.

Other ethical problems with bribes and differing business laws exist. For example, bribery is illegal in the United States but is common in other countries. Afghanistan, Cambodia, Yemen, and the Ukraine are countries in which bribery is commonplace.

Another serious ethical problem arises with enforcement of local labor laws. Central American children can begin work at age 11. Youngsters in Thailand may begin work even earlier. Our own history includes immigrant children of 10 and 12 at work in the steel mills of Bethlehem, Pennsylvania. Many clothing and sporting goods companies are grappling with the issue of child labor in the manufacture of the products they sell. **Levi Strauss** hires its own inspectors to ensure that factories abroad are in compliance with local law. The Levi Strauss Code of Conduct states "Use of child labor is not permissible. Workers can be no less than 14 years of age and not younger than the compulsory age to be in school. We will not utilize partners who

---

17 David Ingram, "How to Address Differences in Ethical Standards and International Businesses," *The Houston Chronical,* September 15, 2020, https://smallbusiness.chron.com/address-differences-ethical-standards-international -businesses-5254.html, accessed October 15, 2020.

use child labor in any of their facilities. We support the development of legitimate workplace apprenticeship programs for the educational benefit of younger people." In addition, Levi Strauss has hired teachers to come to the factories to teach the young workers.[18] Still, it is clear that many underage (less than 14 years old in Guatemala) workers produce clothing for U.S. markets. Should companies enforce local labor laws more stringently? One corporate official pointed out that the company codes may be having some effect, since there are 12- and 13-year olds at work but no 8- or 9-year olds, as is the case in other countries. Also, the strict enforcement of rules can have a negative effect on local income. When companies have determined that suppliers used underage workers, they canceled their orders. As a result, factories fired a number of workers who were the sole support of their families. An ethical solution is not clear-cut.

A number of companies now focus on ethical behavior. Ethical sourcing with its insistence on continuous testing and evaluation is emphasized by **Patagonia**, **Starbucks**, **H&M**, and **Dr. Pepper Snapple Group**.[19] For example, Patagonia works to reduce pesticide use and to ensure that workers across the supply chain are treated fairly and provided safe working conditions. Starbucks attempts to ensure that each step of coffee growing, from planting through harvesting and purchasing, is done ethically. Third parties are used to verify that sourcing is ethical. H&M has committed to supply chain transparency by listing all suppliers on its website so that they can be checked. The bottom line is that ethical activity improves sustainability, working conditions, and the companies financial health.

---

18 "Levi Strauss & Co., Code of Conduct," University of Minnesota Human Rights Library, http://hrlibrary.umn.edu /links/levicode.html, accessed September 20, 2020.

19 Bennett O'Brien, "4 Companies Who Succeed by Focusing on Ethical Sourcing and Manufacturing," *TradeReady*, August 2, 2018, http://www.tradeready.ca/2018/topics/supply-chain-management/4-companies-succeed-focusing -ethical-sourcing-manufacturing/, accessed September 20, 2020.

SUMMARY OF LEARNING OBJECTIVES

LO1. Explain the role of the accountant in the international environment.
- Accountants must be aware of differing cultural, legal, political, and economic factors.
- The IMA Statement of Ethical Professional Practice requirement of competence means that accountants must stay up to date on accounting and all areas affecting international trade.

LO2. Explain the varying levels of involvement that firms can take in international trade.
- An MNC is one that owns and controls the production or distribution of goods and services in countries in addition to its home country.
- Imported goods may be subject to tariffs.
- FTZs may allow importing firms to avoid payment of duty.
- Firms may outsource functions, own foreign subsidiaries, and engage in joint ventures.

LO3. Calculate exchange gains and losses so that accountants can manage foreign currency risk.
- Changing currency exchange rates can affect income.
- If a country's currency can buy more of another country's currency, the first currency has become stronger. If a country's currency can buy less of another country's currency, the first currency has become weaker.
- Spot rates are currency exchange rates for immediate exchange. Future rates are currency exchange rates that are locked in until some time in the future.
- Cryptocurrencies are completely digital means of exchange and do have value on the open market.

LO4. Explain how environmental factors can affect performance evaluation in the multinational firm.
- Performance in the MNC is affected by economic, legal, political, and cultural environments in the different countries in which the MNC operates.
- Currency fluctuations may affect ROI and other performance measures.

LO5. Describe the role of transfer pricing in the multinational firm.
- MNCs can work to shift costs to subsidiaries in high-tax countries and profit to subsidiaries in low-tax countries.
- In the United States, there are four transfer pricing methods that are acceptable to the IRS: comparable uncontrolled price (market pricing), resale price, cost-plus price, and Advanced Pricing Agreements.

LO6. Discuss ethical issues that affect firms operating in the international environment.
- Ethical codes vary widely among countries.
- Strong underlying systems make it possible to enforce contracts.
- MNCs must reconcile differences in ethical codes to "do the right thing" according to their own code of ethics.

EXAMPLE 21.1	The HOW and WHY of Locating in a Foreign Trade Zone, page 1062
EXAMPLE 21.2	The HOW and WHY of Exchanging One Currency for Another, page 1066
EXAMPLE 21.3	The HOW and WHY of Calculating Exchange Gains and Losses, page 1068
EXAMPLE 21.4	The HOW and WHY of Hedging Currency Exchange Rates, page 1069
EXAMPLE 21.5	The HOW and WHY of Using the Comparable Uncontrolled Price Method, the Resale Price Method, and the Cost-Plus Method in Calculating Transfer Prices, page 1078

KEY TERMS

Advance pricing agreements (APAs), 1079

Comparable uncontrolled price method, 1078

Cost-plus method, 1078

Cryptocurrency, 1070

Currency appreciation, 1067

Currency depreciation, 1067

Currency risk management, 1065

Economic risk, 1066

Exchange gain, 1068

Exchange loss, 1068

Exchange rates, 1065

Foreign trade zones (FTZs), 1061

Forward contract, 1069

Hedging, 1069

Joint venture, 1064

Maquiladoras, 1065

Multinational corporation (MNC), 1061

Outsourcing, 1064

Resale price method, 1078

Spot rate, 1066

Tariff, 1061

Transaction risk, 1065

Translation (or accounting) risk, 1066

BRIEF EXERCISES

Brief Exercise 21-1 Duty-Related Costs of Locating in an FTZ

OBJECTIVE ◄ 2
Example 21.1

Aranda Company is an import-export company that relocated earlier this year in a foreign trade zone (FTZ) in a southwestern city. The company imports $760,000 of fabric from overseas for resale to clothing companies located in the United States. Aranda purchases and receives the fabric about four months before it is sold and shipped to customers; customers are billed and pay in two months. Duty is assessed at 15 percent of cost, and Aranda faces a 6 percent carrying cost.

Required:

1. What is the amount of duty paid by Aranda last year (before locating in the FTZ) and for this year after relocating to the FTZ?
2. What is the amount of carrying cost associated with the duty paid by Aranda last year and for this year after relocating to the FTZ?
3. What is the total duty-related cost for Aranda last year and for this year after relocating to the FTZ?
4. What is the total savings on duty and carrying cost attributable to locating in an FTZ?
5. *What if* some of the fabric turned out to be defective and had to be disposed of before sale and shipment to customers? Would it be more or less advantageous to be located in an FTZ in this case? Why or why not?

Brief Exercise 21-2 Currency Exchange

OBJECTIVE ◄ 3
Example 21.2

Chinook, Inc., purchases components from a Japanese company that requires payment in yen (¥); it sells finished product to a German company that pays in euros. On June 1, Chinook ordered components from the Japanese company costing ¥6,890,000 and sold finished goods to the German company with a selling price of $150,000 to be paid in euros. The June 1 spot rates of U.S. dollars for yen and for euros was:

$$\$1 = ¥106.0$$
$$\$1 = €0.84$$

Required:

1. What is the cost of the ¥6,890,000 in dollars?
2. How many euros will Chinook receive from the German company in payment for the finished product?
3. *What if* the exchange rate of dollars for yen was $1 = ¥108? What is the cost of the ¥6,890,000 in dollars (rounded to the nearest dollar)?

Brief Exercise 21-3 Gain or Loss on Currency Exchange

OBJECTIVE ◄ 3
Example 21.3

Goler Company, based in Illinois, sells its product at home and abroad. On March 1, Bondi Company, an Australian company, orders $30,000 worth of product to be delivered immediately and to be paid in Australian dollars (AUD$) on May 1. The selling price in Australian dollars is computed using the exchange rate in effect on March 1.

Spot rates of Australian dollars for $1	
March 1	$1 = AUD $1.40
May 1	$1 = AUD $1.37

Required:

1. On March 1, how much does Goler expect to receive from Bondi in Australian dollars in payment for the order?
2. On May 1, how much does Goler actually receive from Bondi in Australian dollars? What is that amount converted to dollars?
3. Did Goler experience an exchange gain or loss on the transaction? Of how much in dollars?
4. *What if* the exchange rate of Australian dollars for $1 on May 1 was $1 = AUD $1.39? How much would Goler receive from Bondi in Australian dollars? What is that amount converted into dollars? Would Goler experience an exchange gain or loss on the transaction?

OBJECTIVE **3**

Example 21.4

Brief Exercise 21-4 Hedging

On June 1, Marano, Inc., sold product for $50,000 to be delivered immediately to a Japanese customer and to be paid in yen on August 1. Marano is worried that the exchange rate of dollars for yen could change significantly within two months. In hopes of avoiding a potential loss on exchange, the company has decided to purchase a forward contract.

Spot rates of yen for $1
June 1 spot rate of yen for $1 $1 = ¥107.0
August 1 forward rate of yen for $1 $1 = ¥107.2

Required:

1. On June 1, how much does Marano expect to receive from the Japanese customer in yen in payment for the sale?
2. If Marano purchases the forward contract, how many yen will it receive on August 1? What is that amount converted to dollars?
3. What is the premium Marano paid for the forward contract?
4. *What if* the exchange rate of yen for $1 on August 1 was $1 = ¥108.0? How much would Marano have received from the Japanese customer in yen? What is that amount converted into dollars? Would Marano have experienced an exchange gain or loss on the transaction?

OBJECTIVE **5**

Example 21.5

Brief Exercise 21-5 Calculating the Comparable Uncontrolled Price, Resale Price, and Cost-Plus Price

Washington, Inc., has a number of divisions around the world. Division US (in the United States) purchases a component from Division N (in the Netherlands). The component can be purchased externally for $24.50 each. The freight and insurance on the item amount to $2.45; however, commissions of $2.00 need not be paid.

Required:

1. Calculate the transfer price using the comparable uncontrolled price method.
2. Suppose that there is no outside market for the component that Division N transfers to Division US. Further assume that Division US sells the component for $26.00 and normally receives a 30 percent markup on cost of goods sold. Calculate the transfer price using the resale price method.
3. Now assume that there is no external market for the component transferred from Division N to Division US and that the component is used in the manufacture of another product (i.e., it is not resold). Calculate the transfer price using the cost-plus method. Further assume that Division N's manufacturing cost for the component is $18.20.
4. *What if* commissions avoided were $2.25 per unit? How would that affect the comparable uncontrolled price? The resale price? The cost-plus price?

EXERCISES

Exercise 21-6 Characteristics of Cost Accounting in International Environment

OBJECTIVE ◀ 1

A close friend of yours is majoring in accounting and would like to work for an MNC upon graduation. Your friend is unsure just what courses would help prepare for that goal and wants your advice.

Required:

Advise your friend on the kind of courses that might prepare him/her for this goal.

Exercise 21-7 Foreign Trade Zones

OBJECTIVE ◀ 2

EXCEL

Cajas, Inc., is considering opening a new warehouse to serve the Southwest region. Aaron Garcia, controller for Cajas, has been reading about the advantages of FTZs. He wonders if locating in one would be of benefit to his company, which imports about 90 percent of its merchandise. Garcia estimates that the new warehouse will store imported merchandise costing about $3,450,000 per year. Inventory shrinkage at the warehouse (due to breakage and mishandling) is about 4 percent of the total. The average tariff rate on these imports is 20 percent.

Required:

1. If Cajas locates the warehouse in an FTZ, how much will be saved in tariffs? Why?
2. Suppose that on average, the merchandise stays in a Cajas warehouse for seven months before shipment to retailers. Carrying cost for Cajas is 12 percent per year. If Cajas locates the warehouse in an FTZ, how much will be saved in carrying costs? What will the total tariff-related savings be?

Exercise 21-8 Relevant Costs, Foreign Trade Zones

OBJECTIVE ◀ 2

EXCEL   SHOW ME HOW

Pacific Rim, Inc., is considering opening a new warehouse to serve the northwest region. Darnell Florian, controller for Pacific Rim, has been reading about the advantages of FTZs. He wonders if locating in one would be of benefit to his company, which imports its merchandise from Asia. Darnell estimates that the new warehouse will store imported merchandise costing about $16.78 million per year. Inventory shrinkage at the warehouse (due to breakage and mishandling) is about 8 percent of the total. The average tariff rate on these imports is 5.5 percent.

Required:

1. If Pacific Rim locates the warehouse in an FTZ, how much will be saved in tariffs? Why? (Round your answer to the nearest dollar.)
2. Suppose that, on average, the merchandise stays in a Pacific Rim warehouse for nine months before shipment to retailers. Carrying cost for Pacific Rim is 6 percent per year. If Pacific Rim locates the warehouse in an FTZ, how much will be saved in carrying costs? What will the total tariff-related savings be? (Round your answers to the nearest dollar.)
3. Suppose that the shifting economic situation leads to a new tariff rate of 13 percent and a new carrying cost of 6.5 percent per year. To combat these increases, Pacific Rim has instituted a total quality program emphasizing reducing shrinkage. The new shrinkage rate is 7 percent. Given this new information, if Pacific Rim locates the warehouse in an FTZ, how much will be saved in carrying costs? What will the total tariff-related savings be? (Round your answers to the nearest dollar.)

OBJECTIVE

SHOW ME
HOW

Exercise 21-9 **Currency Translation**

Sterling, Inc., is an export-import firm. On June 1, Sterling purchased goods from a British company costing £20,000. Payment is due in pounds on September 1. The spot rate on June 1 was $1.29 per pound, and on September 1, it was $1.34 per pound.

Required:

1. How much would Sterling have to pay for the purchase (in dollars) if it paid on June 1? How much would it have to pay for the purchase (in dollars) if it paid on September 1?
2. Calculate the spot rate of $1 against the pound on June 1 and September 1. (Round your answers to two significant digits.) Did the dollar strengthen or weaken against the pound during the three-month period?

OBJECTIVE

SHOW ME
HOW

Exercise 21-10 **Currency Gain or Loss**

Refer to Exercise 21-8. If Sterling paid for the purchase using the September 1 spot rate, what was the exchange gain or loss?

OBJECTIVE

SHOW ME
HOW

Exercise 21-11 **Hedging**

Permian Company engages in many foreign currency transactions. Company policy is to hedge exposure to exchange gains and losses using forward contracts. On July 1, Permian bought merchandise from a Canadian company for 120,000 Canadian dollars, payable on September 30. Exchange rates of $1 for Canadian dollars were as follows:

Spot rate, July 1	1.30
Forward rate, September 30	1.30
Spot rate, September 30	1.35

Required:

1. Did Permian Company buy or sell Canadian dollars for future delivery?
2. According to company policy, how many U.S. dollars did Permian pay for this purchase?

OBJECTIVE

SHOW ME
HOW

DATA
ANALYTICS

Exercise 21-12 **Comparing ROI**

Ariana Stratford, vice president for Newtronics, Inc., was reviewing the latest results for two divisions. The first, located in Baja California, Mexico, had posted income of $150,000 on assets of $1,500,000. The second, in Punt-on-Thames, England, showed income of $230,000 on assets of $2,000,000.

Required:

1. Calculate the ROI for each division.
2. Can a meaningful comparison be made of the British Division's ROI to the Mexican Division's ROI? Which of the four data analytic types—descriptive, diagnostic, predictive, or prescriptive—will Ariana use to assess the performance of each division? More than one type may be used. (See Exhibits 2.5 and 2.6, pp. 37, 40, for a review of data analytic types.) Explain.

OBJECTIVE

SHOW ME
HOW

Exercise 21-13 **Transfer Pricing**

Mitford Furniture Manufacturing, Inc., has a division in the United States that produces and sells furniture for discount furniture stores. One type of dining room set is made in the International Division in China. The dining room sets are sold externally in the United States for $450 each. It costs $17.50 per dining room set for shipping and $21 per dining room set for import duties. When the dining room sets are sold externally, Mitford Furniture Manufacturing spends $34 each for commissions and an average of $1.65 per dining room set for advertising.

Required:

1. Which Section 482 method should be used to calculate the allowable transfer price?
2. Using the appropriate Section 482 method, calculate the transfer price.

Exercise 21-14 Transfer Pricing and Section 482

OBJECTIVE ◀ 5

EXCEL SHOW ME
HOW

Colorworld, Inc., has a division in Indonesia that makes dyestuff in a variety of colors used to dye denim for jeans and another division in the United States that manufactures denim clothing. The Dyestuff Division incurs manufacturing costs of $2.68 for one pound of powdered dye. The Clothing Division currently buys its dye powder from an outside supplier for $3.80 per pound. If the Clothing Division purchases the powder from the Dyestuff Division, the shipping costs will be $0.34 per pound, but sales commissions of $0.05 per pound will be avoided with an internal transfer.

Required:

1. Which Section 482 method should be used to calculate the allowable transfer price? Calculate the appropriate transfer price per pound.
2. Assume that the Clothing Division cannot buy this type of powder externally since it has an unusual formula that results in a color particular to Colorworld's jeans. Which Section 482 method should be used to calculate the allowable transfer price? Calculate the appropriate transfer price per pound.

Exercise 21-15 Transfer Pricing and Section 482

OBJECTIVE ◀ 5

SHOW ME
HOW

Yukon, Inc., has a division in Canada, the Exterior Stain Division, which makes long-lasting exterior wood stain. Yukon has another U.S. division, the Retail Division, which operates a chain of home improvement stores. The Retail Division would like to buy the unique, long-lasting wood stain from the Exterior Stain Division since this type of stain is not currently available. The Exterior Stain Division incurs manufacturing costs of $13.45 for one gallon of stain. If the Retail Division purchases the stain from the Exterior Stain Division, the shipping costs will be $1.40 per gallon, but sales commissions of $0.75 per gallon will be avoided with an internal transfer. The Retail Division plans to sell the stain for $32.80 per gallon. Normally, the Retail Division earns a gross margin of 35 percent above cost of goods sold.

Required:

1. Which Section 482 method should be used to calculate the allowable transfer price?
2. Calculate the appropriate transfer price per gallon. (Round to the nearest cent.)

PROBLEMS

Problem 21-16 Exporting, Foreign Trade Zones

OBJECTIVE ◀ 2

DATA
ANALYTICS

Paladin Company manufactures plain-paper fax machines in a small factory in Minnesota. Sales have increased by 50 percent in each of the past three years, as Paladin has expanded its market from the United States to Canada and Mexico. As a result, the Minnesota factory is at capacity. Beryl Adams, president of Paladin, has examined the situation, analyzed relevant data, and developed the following alternatives.

1. Add a permanent second shift at the plant. However, the semiskilled workers who assemble the fax machines are in short supply, and the wage rate of $15 per hour would probably have to be increased across the board to $18 per hour in order to attract sufficient workers from out of town. The total wage increase (including fringe benefits) would amount to $125,000. The heavier use of plant facilities would lead to increased plant maintenance and small tool cost.

2. Open a new plant, and locate it in Mexico. Wages (including fringe benefits) would average $3.50 per hour. Investment in plant and equipment would amount to $300,000.
3. Open a new plant, and locate it in an FTZ, possibly in Dallas. Wages would be somewhat lower than in Minnesota but higher than in Mexico. The advantages of postponing tariff payments on parts imported from Asia could amount to $50,000 per year.

Required:

Advise Beryl of the advantages and disadvantages of each of her alternatives.

OBJECTIVE **Problem 21-17 Currency Translation, Hedging**

Langford Woodworks, Inc., manufactures custom window shutters on a job-order basis. Langford has invested heavily in precision woodworking equipment. As a result, the company has a reputation for producing excellent quality interior shutters. Sales are made in all 50 states. On July 1, Langford received orders from interior designers in Sweden and Japan. Al Langford, president and co-owner of Langford Woodworks, was delighted. The Swedish order for shutters is priced at $150,000. The order is due in Stockholm on September 1, with payment due in full on October 1. The Japanese order for shutters is $65,000. It is due in Tokyo on August 1, with payment due in full on October 1. Both orders are to be paid in the customer's currency. The Swedish customer has a reputation in the industry for late payment, and it could take as long as six months. Al has never received payment in foreign currency before and was concerned about fluctuations in exchange rates. He had his accountant gather data and prepare the following table of exchange rates.

	Exchange Rate for $1	
	Swedish Krona	Yen
Spot rate, July 1	8.60	107.60
30-day forward	8.64	107.61
90-day forward	8.65	107.60
180-day forward	8.69	107.55

Required:

1. If the price of the shutters is set using the spot rate as of July 1, how many krona does Al expect to be paid on October 1? How many yen does he expect on October 1?
2. Using the number of krona and yen calculated in Requirement 1, how many dollars does Al expect to receive on October 1? Will he receive that much? Which of the four data analytic types—descriptive, diagnostic, predictive, or prescriptive—is Al using to determine the probable amount? (See Exhibits 2.5 and 2.6, pp. 37, 40, for a review of data analytic types.) What is the value of hedging in this situation?

**DATA
ANALYTICS**

OBJECTIVE **Problem 21-18 Exchange Gains and Losses**

EXCEL

The following are the exchange rates of various currencies for $1 on July 1 and on October 1.

	July 1	October 1
Euro	0.84	0.86
Canadian dollar (CAD)	1.33	1.30
Yen	106.00	104.00

Required:

1. Indicate whether the dollar has strengthened or weakened against the euro, the Canadian dollar, and the yen.
2. A U.S. company purchases merchandise on July 1 from a French company for €8,700, payable on October 1. How much is the U.S. company's payable for the purchase on July 1? On October 1? Since the company paid on October 1, what is the amount of exchange gain or loss?

3. A U.S. company sells merchandise on July 1 to a French company for €8,700, payable on October 1. How much is the U.S. company's receivable for the transaction on July 1? On October 1? Since the French company paid on October 1, what is the amount of exchange gain or loss?

4. A U.S. company purchases merchandise on July 1 from a Canadian company for 40,000 Canadian dollars, payable on October 1. How much is the U.S. company's payable for the purchase on July 1? On October 1? Since the company paid on October 1, what is the amount of exchange gain or loss?

5. A U.S. company sells merchandise on July 1 to a Canadian company for 40,000 Canadian dollars, payable on October 1. How much is the U.S. company's receivable for the transaction on July 1? On October 1? Since the Canadian company paid on October 1, what is the amount of exchange gain or loss?

6. A U.S. company purchases merchandise on July 1 from a Japanese company for ¥2,000,000, payable on October 1. How much is the U.S. company's payable for the purchase on July 1? On October 1? Since the company paid on October 1, what is the amount of exchange gain or loss?

7. A U.S. company sells merchandise on July 1 to a Japanese company for ¥2,000,000, payable on October 1. How much is the U.S. company's receivable for the transaction on July 1? On October 1? Since the Japanese company paid on October 1, what is the amount of exchange gain or loss?

Problem 21-19 Transfer Pricing and Section 482

OBJECTIVE ◄ 5

The U.S. division of MegaBig, Inc., has excess capacity. MegaBig's European division, located in Lisbon, has offered to buy a component that would increase the U.S. division's utilization of capacity from 70 to 80 percent. The component has an outside market in the United States with a unit selling price of $12. The variable costs of production for the component are $6. Landing costs total $2 per unit, and an internal transfer avoids $1.25 per unit of variable marketing costs. The European and U.S. divisions agree on a transfer price of $9. The European division can purchase the component locally for $12.

Required:

Suppose you have scheduled a meeting with an IRS representative. What arguments would you make for an advance pricing agreement that would permit the use of the $9 price?

**DATA
ANALYTICS**

Elena Chavez is founder and CEO of Willowbank, Inc., which owns and operates several assisted-living facilities. The facilities are apartment-style buildings with 25 to 30 one- or two-bedroom apartments. While each apartment has its own complete kitchen, every building offers communal dining options and an on-site nurse who is available 24 hours a day. Residents can choose monthly meal options that include one or two meals per day in the dining room. Residents who require nursing services (e.g., blood pressure monitoring and injections) can receive those services from the nurse. However, Willowbank facilities are not nursing homes, all residents are ambulatory, and custodial care is not an option. In the five years it has been in operation, the company has expanded from one facility to five, located in southwestern cities. The income statement for last year follows.

Willowbank, Inc.
Income Statement for Last Year

Revenue	$11,520,000
Cost of services	8,064,000
Gross profit	$ 3,456,000
Marketing and administrative expenses	1,550,000
Operating income	$ 1,906,000

Elena originally got into the business because she had trouble finding adequate facilities for her mother. The concept worked well, and income over the past five years had grown nicely at 20 percent per year. However, Elena sensed clouds on the horizon. She knew that the population was aging and that her current clients would be moving to more traditional forms of nursing care. As a result, Elena wanted to consider adding one or more nursing homes to Willowbank. These nursing homes would be staffed around the clock with RNs and LPNs. The residents would likely have more severe medical problems and would be confined to beds or wheelchairs. Elena knew that quality care of this type was needed. So, she contacted Peter Merrion, her marketing manager, and Bernadette Velarde, her accountant, for a brainstorming session.

Peter: "Elena, I really like the concept. As you know, several of our facilities have faced seeing their long-term residents move out to local nursing homes. Not only are these homes of lower quality than what we could provide, but losing a resident is heartrending for the staff, as well as for the remaining residents. I like the idea of providing a transition from less care to more."

Bernadette: "I agree with you, Peter. But let's not forget the differences between assisted-living and full-time, nursing-home-type care. Our expenses will really increase."

Elena: "That's why I wanted to talk with both of you. As you know, Willowbank's mission statement emphasizes the need to make a profit. We can't continue to serve our residents and provide high-quality care if we don't make enough money to pay our staff a living wage and earn enough of a profit to smooth over the rough patches and continue to improve our business. Could the two of you look into this idea, and get back to me in a week or so?"

Throughout the following week, the three communicated by e-mail. By the end of the week, a number of possibilities had surfaced, and these were summarized in a message from Bernadette to the others.

TO: elena.chavez@willowbank.com, peter.merrion@willowbank.com
FROM: bernadette.velarde@willowbank.com
MESSAGE:

I've compiled the ideas from all of our e-mails into the following list. This may be a good starting point for our meeting tomorrow.

1. Buy an existing nursing home in one of our current locations.
2. Buy an existing nursing home in another city.
3. Build a new nursing home facility in one of our current locations.
4. Build a new nursing home facility in another city.
5. Build a wing on to one of our existing facilities. The Mesa Ridge facility has sufficient open land for an addition.

The next day, Elena, Peter, and Bernadette met again in Elena's office.

Elena: "I didn't realize there were so many possibilities. Are we going to have to work up numbers on each of them?"

Bernadette: "No, I think we can eliminate a few of them pretty quickly. For example, building a new facility would cost more than the other options, and it would involve the most risk."

Peter: "I agree, and I also think we might eliminate the purchase of an existing nursing home for the same reasons. Also, existing homes would not give us the option of building a facility that is state of the art and meets our needs, and it would lock us into a preexisting patient mix."

Elena: "I like that thinking. Let's restrict our attention to Option 5."

Bernadette: "I thought you might like that option, so Peter and I sketched out two alternatives for an extension of the Mesa Ridge building. We call the alternatives Basic Care and Lifestyle Care."

Peter: "There are different markets for each type of care. If we want to concentrate on Medicare and Medicaid patients, the reimbursement is lower, and we would want to offer the Basic Care option. Private insurance and private-pay patients could afford more services; if we are marketing to these patients, we could offer the Lifestyle Care option. Both alternatives provide high-quality nursing care. Basic Care concentrates on the quality nursing and maintenance activities. For example, the addition would have 25 double rooms, two nursing stations, two recreation rooms, a treatment room, and an office. The Lifestyle Care option adds physical and recreational therapy with a specially equipped gym and pool. That addition would have 30 single rooms, two nursing stations, a recreation room, a swimming pool, a hydrotherapy spa and gym, a treatment room, and an office. In each case, there would be cable TV and telephone hookups in each room and a buffer area between the nursing home and the apartments."

Elena: "Why the buffer area? Won't that add unnecessary cost?"

Peter: "It adds cost, but it will be well worth it. Remember that the nursing home patients are different from the apartment residents. Some of the patients will have advanced dementia. We'll lose apartment residents in a hurry if they have to be reminded every day of what might be in store for them later on."

Elena: "I see your point. Bernadette, what will these two plans cost? I'll tell you right now that I like the Lifestyle Care option better. It fits with our history of doing whatever we can to make life better for our residents."

Bernadette: "I've checked into the costs of putting on a new wing and operating both alternatives. Here's a listing."

Basic Care		Lifestyle Care	
Construction	$2,800,000	Construction	$4,000,000
Annual operating expenses:		Annual operating expenses:	
Staff:		Staff:	
RNs (3 × $50,000)	$ 150,000	RNs (3 × $50,000)	$ 150,000
LPNs (6 × $30,000)	$ 180,000	LPNs (6 × $30,000)	$ 180,000
Aides (6 × $24,000)	$ 144,000	Aides (6 × $30,000)	$ 144,000

Basic Care		Lifestyle Care	
Cooks (2 × $20,000)	$ 40,000	Cooks (1.5 × $20,000)	$ 30,000
Janitors (2 × $22,000)	$ 44,000	Janitors (2 × $22,000)	$ 44,000
		Physical and recreational therapists	
		(2 × $35,000)	$ 70,000
Other* (60% variable)	$400,000	Other* (60% variable)	$480,000
Debt service	$280,000	Debt service	$400,000
Depreciation (over 20 years)	$140,000	Depreciation (over 20 years)	$200,000

*Other includes supplies, utilities, food, and so on.

"In both cases, total administrative costs for Willowbank would increase by $60,000 per year. This seems high, but the increased legal and insurance requirements will add significantly more paperwork and accounting."

Elena: "All this sounds reasonable, but why is reimbursement such an important factor?"

Peter: "Well, if you admit Medicaid patients, the state will reimburse at most $60,000 per year. Private insurance policies will pay roughly $82,000 per year. We can charge up to about $120,000 for private patients, but this type of care is so expensive that many of these patients exhaust their funds and go on Medicaid. The nice aspect of Medicaid is that we can be virtually assured that we will operate at capacity."

Elena: "Can we cross that bridge when we come to it?"

Peter: "No, not really. Once the patient is a resident of our facility, it is hard to evict them. Also, while it is legal to force patients out before they go on Medicaid and to refuse to accept Medicaid patients, once we do accept Medicaid patients, we are prevented by law from evicting them—no matter how high our costs go."

Elena: "OK, it looks as if we have some hard work ahead of us to decide whether or not to get into this line of business."

Required

1. How did Elena, Bernadette, and Peter use the tactical decision-making model of Chapter 17?

2. Categorize each of the expenses for the Basic Care and Lifestyle Care options as flexible or committed. Further categorize the committed expenses as committed fixed or committed step costs.

DATA ANALYTICS

3. Calculate the break-even number of patients (in total and for each type of reimbursement) for each of the following scenarios (for fractional break-even amount, round up to the nearest higher whole number):

   a. Basic Care option, 20 percent private insurance, and 80 percent Medicaid
   b. Basic Care option, no Medicaid
   c. Lifestyle Care option, no Medicaid, 75 percent private insurance, and 25 percent private pay
   d. Lifestyle Care option, all insurance reimbursement

4. What is the markup percent of cost of services charged on the assisted-living expenses? What would the price per month for a Basic Care patient be if the same markup were used? For a Lifestyle Care patient? (Assume in both cases that occupancy is at 80 percent of capacity.)

5. What is the payback period for the new addition?

6. Suppose that Elena discovered a potential new market for the Lifestyle Care services, well-off immigrants from Europe and East Asia who moved to the United States to be closer to their children. Some of these immigrants would need the care offered by Lifestyle Care but would need to pay in their home currency. How would currency fluctuations affect Willowbank's revenue estimation? How might Elena handle potential currency fluctuations to reduce risk?

7. Research Assignment: In 1999, Congress passed a law restricting the ability of nursing homes to evict Medicaid patients. What led to the passing of these laws? Why would nursing homes accept Medicaid patients and later evict them? Is eviction of Medicaid patients still a problem? Discuss the legal and ethical issues in a nursing home's decision on whether to accept Medicaid patients.

Glossary

A

Abnormal spoilage spoilage that exceeds the amount expected under normal efficient operating conditions.

Absorption costing a costing method that assigns all manufacturing costs, including direct materials, direct labor, variable overhead, and a share of fixed overhead, to each unit of product.

Absorption-costing income income computed by following a functional classification.

Acceptable quality level (AQL) a predetermined level of defective products that a company permits to be sold.

Account analysis method a method used to estimate costs by classifying accounts in the general ledger as fixed, variable, or mixed.

Accounting information system a system consisting of interrelated manual and computer parts that uses processes such as collecting, recording, summarizing, analyzing (using decision models), and managing data to provide output information to users.

Accounting rate of return (ARR) the rate of return obtained by dividing the average accounting net income by the original investment (or by average investment).

Activity a basic unit of work performed within an organization. It also can be defined as an aggregation of actions within an organization useful to managers for purposes of planning, controlling, and decision making.

Activity analysis the process of identifying, describing, and evaluating the activities an organization performs.

Activity attributes financial and nonfinancial information items that provide descriptive labels for individual activities.

Activity-based cost (ABC) system a cost accounting system that uses both unit- and non-unit-based cost drivers to assign costs to cost objects by first tracing costs to activities and then tracing costs from activities to products.

Activity-based management (ABM) an advanced control system that focuses management's attention on activities with the objective of improving the value received by the customer and the profit received by providing this value. It includes driver analysis, activity analysis, and performance evaluation and draws on activity-based costing as a major source of information.

Activity-based responsibility accounting assigns responsibility to processes and uses both financial and nonfinancial measures of performance.

Activity capacity the ability to perform activities or the number of times an activity can be performed.

Activity dictionary lists the activities in an organization along with desired attributes.

Activity drivers measure the demands that cost objects place on activities.

Activity elimination the process of eliminating non-value-added activities.

Activity flexible budgeting the prediction of what activity costs will be as activity output changes.

Activity inventory a listing of the activities performed within an organization.

Activity output measure assesses the number of times the activity is performed. It is the quantifiable measure of the output.

Activity rate the average unit cost, obtained by dividing the resource expenditure by the activity's practical capacity.

Activity reduction decreasing the time and resources required by an activity.

Activity resource usage model a model that classifies resources according to their nature, which allows the assessment of changes in resource supply (and thus resource spending) as activity demand for the resource changes.

Activity selection the process of choosing among sets of activities caused by competing strategies.

Activity sharing increasing the efficiency of necessary activities by using economies of scale.

Activity volume variance the cost difference of the actual activity capacity acquired and the capacity that should be used.

Actual cost system a cost measurement system in which actual manufacturing costs are assigned to products.

Adjusted cost of goods sold normal cost of goods sold adjusted to include overhead variance.

Administrative costs all costs associated with the general administration of the organization that cannot be reasonably assigned to either marketing or production.

Administrative expense budget a budget consisting of estimated expenditures for the overall organization and operation of the company.

Advance pricing agreements (APAs) an agreement between the Internal Revenue Service and a taxpayer on the acceptability of a transfer price. The agreement is private and is binding on both parties for a specified period of time.

Allocation assignment of indirect costs to cost objects.

Allocative efficiency the point at which given the mixes that satisfy the condition of technical efficiency, the least costly mix is chosen.

Annuity a series of future cash flows.

Applied overhead the overhead assigned to production using a predetermined overhead rate.

Appraisal costs costs incurred to determine whether or not products and services are conforming to requirements.

Assets unexpired costs.

B

Backflush costing a simplified approach for cost flow accounting that uses trigger points to determine when manufacturing costs are assigned to key inventory and temporary accounts.

Balanced Scorecard a strategic-based performance management system that typically identifies objectives and measures for four different perspectives: the financial perspective, the customer perspective, the process perspective, and the learning and growth perspective.

Base period a prior period used to set the benchmark for measuring productivity changes.

Batch-level activities   activities performed each time a batch is produced.

Batch production processes   a process that produces batches of different products that are identical in many ways but differ in others.

Benchmarking   uses best practices as the standard for evaluating activity performance.

Bill of activities   specifies the product, product quantity, activity, and amount of each activity expected to be consumed by each product.

Binding constraint   constraints whose limited resources are fully used by a product mix.

Break-even point   the point where total sales revenue equals total costs (i.e., the point of zero profits).

Budgetary slack   the process of padding the budget by overestimating costs and underestimating revenues.

Budget committee   a committee responsible for setting budgetary policies and goals, reviewing and approving the budget, and resolving any differences that may arise in the budgetary process.

Budget director   the individual responsible for coordinating and directing the overall budgeting process.

Budget   a plan of action expressed in financial terms.

Business ethics   learning what is right or wrong in the work environment and choosing what is right.

Business sustainability   a company's ability to create value over the long term by measuring performance, managing risks, and communicating effectively to key stakeholders in a manner that consistently reflects the achievement of its strategy.

By-products   secondary products recovered in the course of manufacturing a primary product during a joint process.

C

Cannibalization   occurs when a special-order sale takes away from (or eats into) the sale of a regular product or service.

Capital budgeting   the process of making capital investment decisions.

Capital expenditures budget   a financial plan outlining the acquisition of long-term assets.

Capital investment decisions   decisions concerned with the process of planning, setting goals and priorities, arranging financing, and using certain criteria to select long-term assets.

Carrying costs   the costs of holding inventory.

Cash budget   a detailed plan that outlines all sources and uses of cash.

Causal factors   activities or variables that invoke service costs. Generally, it is desirable to use causal factors as the basis for allocating service costs.

Centralized decision making   a system in which decisions are made at the top level of an organization and local managers are given the charge to implement them.

Certified Internal Auditor (CIA)   an accountant certified to possess the professional qualifications of an internal auditor.

Certified Management Accountant (CMA)   an accountant who has satisfied the requirements to hold a certificate in management accounting.

Certified Public Accountants (CPAs)   an accountant certified to possess the professional qualifications of an external auditor.

Coefficient of correlation (r)   the square root of the coefficient of determination, which is used to express not only the degree of correlation between two variables but also the direction of the relationship.

Coefficient of determination (R^2)   the percentage of total variability in a dependent variable (e.g., cost) that is explained by the independent variable(s) (e.g., activity level). It assumes a value of between 0 and 1.

Committed resources   resources that are supplied in advance of usage. Because the amount of committed resource supplied may exceed the firm's demand for it, unused capacity is possible.

Common costs   the cost of a resource used in the output of two or more services or products.

Common fixed expenses   fixed costs that are not traceable to the segments and that would remain even if one of the segments were eliminated.

Comparable uncontrolled price method   the transfer price most preferred by the Internal Revenue Service under Section 482. The comparable uncontrolled price is essentially equal to the market price.

Competitive advantage   creating better customer value for the same or lower cost than can competitors or equivalent value for lower cost than can competitors.

Compounding of interest   paying interest on interest.

Constant gross margin percentage method   a joint cost allocation method that maintains the same gross margin percentage for each product.

Constrained optimization   choosing the optimal mix given the constraints faced by the firm.

Constraints   a mathematical expression that expresses a resource limitation.

Constraint set   the collection of all constraints that pertain to a particular optimization problem.

Consumable life   the length of time that a product serves the needs of a customer.

Consumption ratio   the proportion of an overhead activity consumed by a product.

Continuous budget   a moving 12-month budget with a future month added as the current month expires.

Continuous improvement   the relentless pursuit of improvement in the delivery of value to customers; searching for ways to increase overall efficiency by reducing waste, improving quality, and reducing costs.

Continuous replenishment   when a manufacturer assumes the inventory management function for the retailer.

Contribution margin   the difference between revenue and all variable expenses.

Contribution margin ratio   contribution margin divided by sales revenue. It is the proportion of each sales dollar available to cover fixed costs and provide for profit.

Contribution margin variance   the difference between actual and budgeted contribution margin.

Contribution margin volume variance   the difference between the actual quantity sold and the budgeted quantity sold multiplied by the budgeted average unit contribution margin.

Control   the process of setting standards, receiving feedback on actual performance, and taking corrective action whenever actual performance deviates significantly from planned performance.

Control activities   activities performed by an organization to prevent or detect poor quality (because poor quality may exist).

Control costs   costs incurred from performing control activities.

Controllable costs   costs that managers have the power to influence.

Controller   the chief accountant of an organization.

Control limits   the maximum allowable deviation from a standard.

Controlling   the monitoring of a plan through the use of feedback to ensure that the plan is being implemented as expected.

Conversion cost   the sum of direct labor cost and overhead cost.

Core objectives and measures   those objectives and measures common to most organizations.

Cost   the cash or cash equivalent value sacrificed for goods and services that are expected to bring a current or future benefit to the organization.

Cost accounting information system   a cost management subsystem designed to assign costs to individual products and services and other objects as specified by management.

Cost accumulation   the recognition and recording of costs.

Cost assignment   the process of associating manufacturing costs with the units produced.

Cost-based pricing   the process by which particular costs are marked up by a chosen percentage to arrive at the price for a product or service.

Cost behavior   the way in which a cost changes in relation to changes in activity usage.

Cost center   a responsibility center in which a manager is responsible for cost.

Cost leadership strategy   providing the same or better value to customers at a lower cost than offered by competitors.

Cost management   identifies, collects, measures, classifies, and reports information that is useful to managers in costing (determining what something costs), planning, controlling, and decision making.

Cost management information system   an accounting information subsystem that is primarily concerned with producing outputs for internal users using inputs and processes needed to satisfy management objectives.

Cost measurement   the process of assigning dollar values to cost items.

Cost objects   any item such as products, departments, projects, activities, and so on, for which costs are measured and assigned.

Cost of capital   the cost of investment funds, usually viewed as a weighted average of the costs of funds from all sources, where the weight is defined by the relative amount from each source.

Cost of goods manufactured   the total cost of goods completed during the current period.

Cost of goods sold   the cost of direct materials, direct labor, and overhead attached to the units sold.

Cost-plus method   a transfer price acceptable to the Internal Revenue Service under Section 482. The cost-plus method is simply a cost-based transfer price.

Cost reconciliation   determining whether the costs assigned to units transferred out and to units in ending work in process are equal to the costs in beginning work in process plus the manufacturing costs incurred in the current period.

Costs of quality   costs incurred because poor quality may exist or because poor quality does exist.

Cost-volume-profit graph   a graph that depicts the relationships among costs, volume, and profits. It consists of a total revenue line and a total cost line.

Cryptocurrency   a means of exchange that is only available in electronic form.

Cumulative average-time learning curve model   the model stating that the cumulative average time per unit decreases by a constant percentage, or learning rate, each time the cumulative quantity of units produced doubles.

Currency appreciation   one country's currency has become relatively stronger and buys more units of another country's currency.

Currency depreciation   one country's currency has become relatively weaker and buys fewer units of another country's currency.

Currency risk management   refers to the company's management of its transaction, economic, and translation exposure due to exchange rate fluctuations.

Currently attainable standards   a standard that reflects an efficient operating state; it is rigorous but achievable.

Customer perspective   a Balanced Scorecard viewpoint that defines the customer and market segments in which the business will compete.

Customer value   the difference between what a customer receives (customer realization) and what the customer gives up (customer sacrifice).

Cycle time   the length of time between the beginning and completion of a process.

Cycle time (manufacturing)   The length of time to produce a unit of product from the time materials are received (starting point) until the good is delivered to finished goods inventory (finishing point).

D

Data analytics   the process through which an organization utilizes various amounts and types of data to help connect strategy and other key goals to improved decision making throughout the organization.

Decentralization   the granting of decision-making freedom to lower operating levels.

Decentralized decision making   a system in which decisions are made and implemented by lower-level managers.

Decision making   the process of choosing among competing alternatives.

Decision model   a set of procedures that, if followed, will lead to a decision.

Decline stage   the stage in a product's life cycle when the product loses market acceptance and sales begin to decrease.

Defective product   a product or service that does not conform to specifications.

Degree of operating leverage   a measure of the sensitivity of profit changes to changes in sales volume. It measures the percentage change in profits resulting from a percentage change in sales.

Dependent variable   a variable whose value depends on the value of another variable. For example, Y in the cost formula $Y = F + VX$ depends on the value of X.

Deviation   the difference between the cost predicted by a cost formula and the actual cost. It measures the distance of a data point from the cost line.

Differentiation strategy   an approach that strives to increase customer value by increasing what the customer receives.

Direct costs   costs that can be easily and accurately traced to a cost object.

Direct fixed expenses   fixed costs that can be traced to each segment and would be avoided if the segment did not exist.

Direct labor   labor that is traceable to the goods or services being produced.

Direct labor budget   a budget showing the total direct labor hours needed and the associated cost for the number of units in the production budget.

Direct labor efficiency variance (*LEV*)   the difference between the actual direct labor hours used and the standard direct labor hours allowed multiplied by the standard hourly wage rate.

Direct labor rate variance (*LRV*)   the difference between the actual hourly rate paid and the standard hourly rate multiplied by the actual hours worked.

Direct materials   those materials that are traceable to the good or service being produced.

Direct materials price variance (*MPV*)   the difference between the actual price paid per unit of materials and the standard price allowed per unit multiplied by the actual quantity of materials purchased.

Direct materials purchases budget   a budget that outlines the expected usage of materials production and purchases of the direct materials required.

Direct materials usage variance (*MUV*)   the difference between the direct materials actually used and the direct materials allowed for the actual output multiplied by the standard price.

Direct method   a method that allocates service department costs directly to producing departments. This method ignores any interactions that may exist among service departments.

Direct tracing   the process of identifying costs that are specifically or physically associated with a cost object.

Discounted cash flows   future cash flows expressed in present value terms.

Discount factor   the factor used to convert a future cash flow to its present value.

Discounting   the act of finding the present value of future cash flows.

Discounting models   any capital investment model that explicitly considers the time value of money in identifying criteria for accepting or rejecting proposed projects.

Discount rate   the rate of return used to compute the present value of future cash flows.

Discretionary fixed expenses   costs incurred for the acquisition of short-term capacity or services, usually as the result of yearly planning.

Double-loop feedback   information about both the effectiveness of strategy implementation and the validity of assumptions underlying the strategy.

Downstream costs   costs incurred after production.

Driver analysis   the effort expended to identify those factors that are the root causes of activity costs.

Drivers   factors that cause changes in resource usage, activity usage, costs, and revenues.

Driver tracing   the use of drivers to assign costs to cost objects.

Drum-buffer-rope (DBR) system   the TOC inventory management system that relies on the drum beat of the major constrained resource, time buffers, and ropes to determine inventory levels.

Drummer   the major binding constraint.

Dumping   predatory pricing on the international market.

Duration-Based Costing (DBC)   A before-the-fact simplification of ABC that uses a single rate to assign overhead costs to cost objects and is as accurate as ABC assignments that use duration drivers.

Duration drivers   measure the demands in terms of the time it takes to perform an activity, such as hours of hygienic care and monitoring hours.

Dysfunctional behavior   individual behavior that conflicts with the goals of the organization.

E

Ecoefficiency   The ability to improve environmental performance while simultaneously improving economic performance.

Economic order quantity (EOQ)   the amount that should be ordered (or produced) to minimize the total ordering (or setup) and carrying costs.

Economic risk   refers to the possibility that a firm's present value of future cash flows will be affected by exchange fluctuations.

Economic value added (EVA)   the after-tax operating profit minus the total annual cost of capital.

Effectiveness   the manager's performance of the right activities. Measures might focus on value-added versus non-value-added activities.

Efficiency   the performance of activities. May be measured by the number of units produced per hour or by the cost of those units.

Electronic data interchange (EDI)   an inventory management method that allows suppliers access to a buyer's online database.

Ending finished goods inventory budget   a budget that describes planned ending inventory of finished goods in units and dollars.

Enterprise resource planning (ERP) software   software that has the objective of providing an integrated system capability—a system that can run all the operations of a company and provide access to real-time data from the various functional areas of a company.

Enterprise risk management (ERM)   the formal process of aligning an organization's overall desired level of risk taking with its strategy and then managing its top risks in a manner that maintains this alignment.

Environmental costs   costs that are incurred because poor environmental quality exists or may exist.

Environmental detection costs   costs incurred to detect poor environmental performance.

Environmental external failure costs   costs incurred after contaminants are introduced into the environment.

Environmental internal failure costs   costs incurred after contaminants are produced but before they are introduced into the environment.

Environmental prevention costs   costs incurred to prevent damage to the environment.

Equivalent units of output   the complete units that could have been produced given the total amount of productive effort expended for the period under consideration.

Error cause identification   a program in which employees describe problems that prevent them from doing their jobs right the first time.

Error costs   the costs associated with making poor decisions based on inaccurate product costs (or bad cost information).

Exchange gain   is the gain on the exchange of one currency for another due to appreciation of the home currency.

Exchange loss   is a loss on the exchange of one currency for another due to depreciation of the home currency.

Exchange rates   the rate at which one currency will be exchanged for another.

Executional activities   activities that define the processes of an organization.

Expected activity level   the level of production activity expected for the coming period.

Expected global consumption ratio   the proportion of the total activity costs consumed by a given product or cost object.

Expenses   expired costs.

Experience curve   relates cost to increased efficiency, such that the more often a task is performed, the lower will be the cost of doing it.

External constraints   limiting factors imposed on the firm from external sources.

External failure costs   costs incurred because products fail to conform to requirements after being sold to outside parties.

External linkages   the relationship of a firm's activities within its segment of the value chain with those activities of its suppliers and customers.

External measures   measures that relate to customer and shareholder objectives.

F

Facility-level activities   activities that sustain a factory's general manufacturing processes.

Failure activities   activities performed by an organization or its customers in response to poor quality.

Failure costs the costs incurred by an organization because failure activities are performed.

Favorable (F) variance a variance produced whenever the actual amounts are less than the budgeted or standard allowances.

Feasible set of solutions the collection of all feasible solutions.

Feasible solution a product mix that satisfies all constraints.

Feature costing assigns costs to activities and products or services based on the product's or service's features.

Feedback information that can be used to evaluate or correct steps being taken to implement a plan.

FIFO costing method a unit-costing method that excludes prior-period work and costs in computing current-period unit work and costs.

Financial accounting the branch of the accounting system that is concerned with the preparation of financial reports for users external to the organization.

Financial accounting information system an accounting information subsystem that is primarily concerned with producing outputs for external users and uses well-specified economic events as inputs and processes that meet certain rules and conventions.

Financial-based responsibility accounting system a system that assigns responsibility to organizational units and typically measures performance using only financial metrics.

Financial budgets that portion of the master budget that includes the cash budget, the budgeted balance sheet, the budgeted statement of cash flows, and the capital budget.

Financial measures measures expressed in dollar terms.

Financial perspective a Balanced Scorecard viewpoint that describes the financial consequences of actions taken in the other three perspectives.

Financial productivity measure a productivity measure in which inputs and outputs are expressed in dollars.

Five-year assets assets with an expected life for depreciation purposes of five years; light trucks, automobiles, and computer equipment fall into this category.

Fixed costs costs that in total are constant within the relevant range as the level of the cost driver varies.

Fixed overhead spending variance the difference between actual fixed overhead and applied fixed overhead.

Fixed overhead volume variance the difference between budgeted fixed overhead and applied fixed overhead; it is a measure of capacity utilization.

Flexible budget a budget that can specify costs for a range of activity.

Flexible budget variances the difference between actual costs and expected costs given by a flexible budget.

Flexible resources acquired as used and needed, these are a strictly variable cost. The quantity supplied equals quantity demanded, so there is no excess capacity.

Focusing strategy selecting or emphasizing a market or customer segment in which to compete.

Foreign trade zones (FTZs) areas physically on U.S. soil but considered to be outside U.S. commerce. Goods imported into a foreign trade zone are duty-free until they leave the zone.

Forensic accounting the action of identifying, recording, settling, extracting, reporting, and verifying past financial data or other accounting activities for settling current or prospective legal disputes or using such past financial data for projecting future financial data to settle legal disputes.

Forward contract requires the buyer to exchange a specified amount of a currency at a specified rate (the forward rate) on a specified future date.

Full-costing income see **absorption-costing income**.

Full environmental costing the assignment of all environmental costs, both private and societal, to products.

Full private costing the assignment of only private costs to individual products.

Future value the value that will accumulate by the end of an investment's life if the investment earns a specified compounded return.

G

Gainsharing An incentive mechanism that offers a bonus as a percentage of savings resulting from any employee-suggested improvements in quality or productivity.

Goal congruence the alignment of a manager's personal goals with those of the organization.

Goodness of fit the degree of association between Y and X (cost and activity). It is measured by how much of the total variability in Y is explained by X.

Growth stage the stage in a product's life cycle when sales increase at an increasing rate.

H

Half-year convention a convention that assumes a newly acquired asset is in service for one-half of its first taxable year of service, regardless of the date that use of it actually began.

Hedging requires one to lock in a currency exchange rate in advance. Typically, a forward exchange contract is used as a hedge.

Heterogeneity refers to the greater chances for variation in the performance of services than in the production of products.

Hidden quality costs opportunity costs resulting from poor quality.

High-low method a method for fitting a line to a set of data points using the high and low points in the data set. For a cost formula, the high and low points represent the high and low activity levels. It is used to break out the fixed and variable components of a mixed cost.

Hypothesis test of cost parameters a statistical assessment of a cost formula's reliability that indicates whether the parameters are different from zero.

Hypothetical sales value an approximation of the sales value of a joint product at split-off. It is found by subtracting all separable (or further) processing costs from the eventual market value.

I

Ideal standards standards that reflect perfect operating conditions.

Incentives the positive or negative measures taken by an organization to induce a manager to exert effort toward achieving the organization's goals.

Incremental approach the practice of taking the prior year's budget and adjusting it upward or downward to determine next year's budget.

Incremental unit-time learning curve model decreases by a constant percentage each time the cumulative quantity of units produced doubles.

Independent projects projects that, if accepted or rejected, will not affect the cash flows of another project.

Independent variable a variable whose value does not depend on the value of another variable. For example, in the cost formula $Y = F + VX$, the variable X is an independent variable.

Indirect costs costs that cannot be traced to a cost object.

Indirect materials direct materials that form an insignificant part of the final product.

Industrial engineering method a forward-looking method of determining through physical observation and analysis, just what activities, in what amounts, are needed to complete a process.

Industrial value chain the linked set of value-creating activities from basic raw materials to end-use customers.

Inherent risk the risk that exists absent of any risk management action to reduce or avoid the risk.

Innovation process a process that anticipates the emerging and potential needs of customers and creates new products and services to satisfy those needs.

Inseparability an attribute of services that means that production and consumption are inseparable.

Intangibility refers to the nonphysical nature of services as opposed to products.

Intercept parameter the fixed cost, representing the point where the cost formula intercepts the vertical axis. In the cost formula $Y = F + VX$, F is the intercept parameter.

Interim quality performance report a comparison of current actual quality costs with short-term budgeted quality targets.

Interim quality standards a standard based on short-run quality goals.

Internal business process perspective a Balanced Scorecard viewpoint that describes the internal processes needed to provide value for customers and owners.

Internal constraints limiting factors found within the firm.

Internal failure costs costs incurred because products and services fail to conform to requirements where lack of conformity is discovered prior to external sale.

Internal linkages relationships among activities within a firm's value chain.

Internal measures measures that relate to the processes and capabilities that create value for customers and shareholders.

Internal rate of return (IRR) the rate of return that equates the present value of a project's cash inflows with the present value of its cash outflows (i.e., it sets the NPV equal to zero). Also, the rate of return being earned on funds that remain internally invested in a project.

Introduction stage a product life-cycle stage characterized by preproduction and startup activities, where the focus is on obtaining a foothold in the market.

Inventory the money an organization spends in turning raw materials into throughput.

Investment center a responsibility center in which a manager is responsible for revenues, costs, and investments.

J

JIT manufacturing a demand-pull system that strives to produce a product only when it is needed and only in the quantities demanded by customers.

JIT purchasing a system that requires suppliers to deliver parts and materials just in time to be used in production.

Job-order costing system a cost accumulation method that accumulates manufacturing costs by job.

Job-order cost sheet a document or record used to accumulate manufacturing costs for a job.

Joint products two or more products, each having relatively substantial value, that are produced simultaneously by the same process up to a "split-off" point.

Joint venture a type of partnership in which investors co-own the enterprise.

Just-in-case inventory management a traditional inventory model based on anticipated demand.

Just-in-time inventory management the continual pursuit of productivity through the elimination of waste.

K

Kaizen costing efforts to reduce the costs of existing products and processes.

Kaizen standard an interim standard that reflects the planned improvement for a coming period.

Kanban system an information system that controls production on a demand-pull basis through the use of cards or markers.

Keep-or-drop decision a relevant costing analysis that focuses on keeping or dropping a segment of a business.

L

Lag measures outcome measures or measures of results from past efforts.

Lead measures (performance drivers) factors that drive future performance.

Lead time for purchasing, the time to receive an order after it is placed. For manufacturing, the time to produce a product from start to finish.

Lean manufacturing an approach designed to eliminate waste and maximize customer value; characterized by delivering the right product, in the right quantity, with the right quality (zero-defect), at the exact time the customer needs it and at the lowest possible cost.

Learning and growth (infrastructure) perspective a Balanced Scorecard viewpoint that defines the capabilities that an organization needs to create long-term growth and improvement.

Learning curve an important type of nonlinear cost curve that shows how the labor hours worked per unit decrease as the volume produced increases.

Learning rate expressed as a percent, it gives the percentage of time needed to make the next unit, based on the time it took to make the previous unit.

Life-cycle cost management actions taken that cause a product to be designed, developed, produced, marketed, distributed, operated, maintained, serviced, and disposed of so that life-cycle profits are maximized.

Life-cycle costs all costs associated with the product for its entire life cycle.

Linear programming a method that searches among possible solutions until it finds the optimal solution.

Linear programming model expresses a constrained optimization problem as a linear objective function subject to a set of linear constraints.

Line position a position in an organization filled by an individual who is directly responsible for carrying out the organization's basic objectives.

Long-range quality performance report a performance report that compares current actual quality costs with long-range targeted quality costs (usually in the 2–3% range).

Long run period of time for which all costs are variable (i.e., there are no fixed costs).

Loose constraints   constraints whose limited resources are not fully used by a product mix.

Loss   a cost that expires without producing any revenue benefit; a negative profit.

loss leader pricing   occurs when the price is set below cost (i.e., the product is sold or service is provided at a loss) to attract additional customers into the store who then also buy items with significantly positive profit margins.

M

Make-or-buy decision   a relevant costing analysis that focuses on whether a component (service) should be made (provided) internally or purchased externally.

Mandatory measures   measures that are required by regulators (e.g., concise and logical disclosure of significant risk factors) and thus companies must collect (and sometimes publicly disclose) such measures to comply with rules and regulations.

Manufacturing cells   a plant layout containing machines grouped in families, usually in a semicircle.

Maquiladoras   are manufacturing plants located in Mexico that process imported materials and reexport them, tariff-free, to the United States. Originally designed to encourage U.S. firms to invest in Mexico, the program has now expanded to include other foreign firms.

Margin   the ratio of net operating income to sales.

Margin of safety   the units sold or expected to be sold or sales revenue earned or expected to be earned above the break-even volume.

Marketing expense budget   a budget that outlines planned expenditures for selling and distribution activities.

Marketing (selling) costs   those costs necessary to market and distribute a product or service.

Market share   the proportion of industry sales accounted for by a company.

Market share variance   the difference between the actual market share percentage and the budgeted market share percentage multiplied by actual industry sales in units times budgeted average unit contribution margin.

Market size   the total revenue for the industry.

Market size variance   the difference between actual and budgeted industry sales in units multiplied by the budgeted market share percentage times the budgeted average unit contribution margin.

Markup   a percentage applied to base cost for the purpose of calculating price; the markup includes desired profit and any costs not included in the base.

Master budget   the collection of all area and activity budgets representing a firm's comprehensive plan of action.

Materials requisition form   a document used to identify the cost of raw materials assigned to each job.

Maturity stage   the stage in a product's life cycle when sales increase at a decreasing rate.

Maximum transfer price   the transfer price that will make the buying division no worse off if an input is acquired internally.

Measurement costs   the costs associated with the measurements required by a cost management system.

Method of least squares   a statistical method to find a line that best fits a set of data. It is used to break out the fixed and variable components of a mixed cost.

Minimum transfer price   the transfer price that will make the selling division no worse off if the intermediate product is sold internally.

Mixed costs   costs that have both a fixed and a variable component.

Mix variance   the difference in the standard cost of the mix of actual material inputs and the standard cost of the material input mix that should have been used.

Modified accelerated cost recovery system (MACRS)   a method of computing annual depreciation; defined as double-declining-balance method.

Monopolistic competition   a market that is close to the competitive market. There are many sellers and buyers, and low barriers to entry, but the products are differentiated on some basis.

Monopoly   a market in which barriers to entry are so high that there is only one firm selling a unique product.

Multinational corporation (MNC)   a corporation for which a significant amount of business is done in more than one country.

Multiple-period quality trend report   a graph that plots quality costs (as a percentage of sales) against time.

Multiple regression   the use of least-squares analysis to determine the parameters in a linear equation involving two or more explanatory variables.

Mutually exclusive projects   projects that, if accepted, preclude the acceptance of competing projects.

Myopic behavior   managerial actions that improve budgetary performance in the short run at the expense of the long-run welfare of the organization.

N

Net income   operating income less taxes, interest expense, and research and development expense.

Net present value (NPV)   the difference between the present value of a project's cash inflows and the present value of its cash outflows.

Net realizable value method   a method of allocating joint production costs to the joint products based on their proportionate share of eventual revenue less further processing costs.

Nondiscounting models   capital investment models that identify criteria for accepting or rejecting projects without considering the time value of money.

Nondiscretionary (or committed) fixed expenses   the annual expense associated with the multi-period category which is independent of actual usage of the resource. They essentially correspond to committed resources—costs incurred that provide long-term activity capacity.

Nonfinancial measures   measures expressed in nonmonetary units.

Nonproduction costs   those costs associated with the functions of selling and administration.

Non-unit-based drivers   factors, other than the number of units produced, that measure the demands that cost objects place on activities.

Non-unit-level drivers   explain the changes in cost as factors other than units change.

Non-value-added activities   activities either unnecessary or necessary but inefficient and improvable.

Non-value-added costs   costs that are caused either by non-value-added activities or the inefficient performance of value-added activities.

Normal activity level   the average activity level that a firm experiences over more than one fiscal period.

Normal costing system   a cost measurement system in which the actual costs of direct materials and direct labor are assigned to production and a predetermined rate is used to assign overhead costs to production.

Normal cost of goods sold   cost of goods sold *before* adjustment for an overhead variance.

Normal cost system   a cost system that uses predetermined overhead rates and actual costs for direct materials and direct labor.

Normal spoilage   spoilage that is expected with an efficient production process and that may require extra work to make the units saleable, or may result in the units being discarded.

O

Objective function   the function to be optimized, usually a profit function; thus, optimization usually means maximizing profits.

Objective measures   measures that can be readily quantified and verified.

Observable quality costs   those quality costs that are available from an organization's accounting records.

Offshoring   the situation when a function is outsourced to a company that is located outside of the country.

Oligopoly   a market structure characterized by a few sellers and high barriers to entry.

Operating assets   those assets used to generate operating income, consisting usually of cash, inventories, receivables, property, plant, and equipment.

Operating budgets   budgets associated with the income-producing activities of an organization.

Operating expenses   the money an organization spends in turning inventories into throughput.

Operating income   revenues minus expenses from the firm's normal operations. Income taxes are excluded.

Operating leverage   the use of fixed costs to extract higher percentage changes in profits as sales activity changes. Leverage is achieved by increasing fixed costs while lowering variable costs.

Operational activities   day-to-day activities performed as a result of the structure and processes selected by an organization.

Operational control information system   a cost management subsystem designed to provide accurate and timely feedback concerning the performance of managers and others relative to their planning and control of activities.

Operational cost drivers   those factors that drive the cost of operational activities.

Operational productivity measure   measures that are expressed in physical terms.

Operation costing   a hybrid of job order and process costing.

Operations process   a process that produces and delivers existing products and services to customers.

Opportunity cost   the net benefit sacrificed or forgone when one alternative is chosen over another.

Opportunity cost approach   a transfer pricing system that identifies the minimum price that a selling division would be willing to accept and the maximum price that a buying division would be willing to pay.

Optional measures   measures that are voluntary rather than required.

Ordering costs   the costs of placing and receiving an order.

Organizational cost drivers   structural and procedural factors that determine the long-term cost structure of an organization.

Outsourcing   relocating a business function to another company by paying them to perform this function rather than conduct it in-house.

Overapplied overhead   the overhead variance resulting when applied overhead is greater than the actual overhead cost incurred.

Overhead   all production costs other than direct materials and direct labor.

Overhead budget   a budget that reveals the planned expenditures for all indirect manufacturing items.

Overhead variance   the difference between the actual overhead and the applied overhead.

P

Partial productivity measurement   a ratio that measures productive efficiency for one input.

Participative budgeting   an approach to budgeting that allows managers who will be held accountable for budgetary performance to participate in the budget's development.

Payback period   the time required for a project to return its investment.

Penetration pricing   the pricing of a new product or service at a low initial price, perhaps even lower than cost, to build market share quickly.

Perfectly competitive market   a market (or industry) characterized by many buyers and sellers—no one of which is large enough to influence the market; a homogeneous product; and easy entry into and exit from the industry.

Performance reports   accounting reports that provide feedback to managers by comparing planned outcomes with actual outcomes.

Period costs   costs such as marketing and administrative costs that are expensed in the period in which they are incurred.

Perishability   an attribute of services that means that they cannot be inventoried but must be consumed when performed.

Perquisites   a type of fringe benefit over and above salary which is received by managers.

Physical flow schedule   a schedule that accounts for all units flowing through a department during a period.

Physical units method   a method of allocating joint production costs based on each product's share of total units.

Planning   setting objectives and identifying methods to achieve those objectives.

Postaudit   a follow-up analysis of an investment decision.

Post-purchase costs   the costs of using, maintaining, and disposing of a product incurred by the customer after purchasing a product.

Post-sales service process   a process that provides critical and responsive service to customers after the product or service has been delivered.

Practical activity level   the output a firm can achieve if it is operating efficiently.

Practical capacity   the efficient level of activity performance.

Predatory pricing   the practice of setting prices below cost for the purpose of injuring competitors and eliminating competition.

Predetermined overhead rate   estimated overhead divided by the estimated level of production activity. It is used to assign overhead to production.

Present value   the current value of a future cash flow. It represents the amount that must be invested now if the future cash flow is to be received assuming compounding at a given rate of interest.

Prevention costs   costs incurred to prevent defects in products or services being produced.

Price discrimination   charging different prices to different customers for essentially the same commodity.

Price elasticity of demand   measured as the percentage change in quantity divided by the percentage change in price.

Price gouging   when firms with market power (i.e., little or no competition) price products "too high."

Price (rate) variance   the difference between standard price and actual price multiplied by the actual quantity of inputs used.

Price-recovery component   the difference between the total profit change and the profit-linked productivity change.

Price skimming   a pricing strategy in which a higher price is charged at the beginning of a product's life cycle, then lowered at later phases of the life cycle.

Price standards   the price that should be paid per unit of input.

Primary activity   an activity that is consumed by a product or customer (i.e., a final cost object).

Prime cost   the sum of direct materials cost and direct labor cost.

Private costs   environmental costs that an organization has to pay.

Process   a series of activities (operations) that are linked to perform a specific objective.

Process-costing principle   the period's unit cost is computed by dividing the costs of the period by the output of the period.

Process creation   installing an entirely new process to meet customer and financial objectives.

Process improvement   incremental and constant increases in the efficiency of an existing process.

Process innovation (business reengineering)   the performance of a process in a radically new way with the objective of achieving dramatic improvements in response time, cost, quality, and other important competitive factors.

Process value analysis (PVA)   an analysis that defines activity-based responsibility accounting, focuses on accountability for activities rather than costs, and emphasizes the maximization of system-wide performance instead of individual performance.

Process value chain   the innovation, operations, and post-sales service processes.

Producing departments   a unit within an organization responsible for producing the products or services that are sold to customers.

Product diversity   the situation present when products consume overhead in different proportions.

Production budget   a budget that shows how many units must be produced to meet sales needs and satisfy ending inventory requirements.

Production Kanban   a card or marker that specifies the quantity the preceding process should produce.

Production (or product) costs   those costs associated with the manufacture of goods or the provision of services.

Production report   a report that summarizes the manufacturing activity for a department during a period and discloses physical flow, equivalent units, total costs to account for, unit cost computation, and costs assigned to goods transferred out and to units in ending work in process.

Productivity   producing output efficiently, using the least quantity of inputs possible.

Productivity measurement   assessment of productivity changes.

Product-level activities   activities performed that enable the various products of a company to be produced.

Product life cycle   the time a product exists—from conception to abandonment; the profit history of the product according to four stages: introduction, growth, maturity, and decline.

Profile measurement   a series or vector of separate and distinct partial operational measures.

Profit center   a responsibility center in which a manager is responsible for both revenues and costs.

Profit-Linkage Rule   for the current period, calculate the cost of the inputs that would have been used in the absence of any productivity change and compare this cost with the cost of the inputs actually used. The difference in costs is the amount by which profits changed because of productivity changes.

Profit-linked productivity measurement   an assessment of the amount of profit change—from the base period to the current period—attributable to productivity changes.

Profit-volume graph   a graphical portrayal of the relationship between profits and sales activity.

Pseudoparticipation   a budgetary system in which top management solicits inputs from lower-level managers and then ignores those inputs. Thus, in reality, budgets are dictated from above.

Q

"Quality of conformance"   conforming to the design requirements of the product.

Quality product or service   a product which meets or exceeds customer expectations.

Quantity standards   the quantity of input allowed per unit of output.

R

Realized external failure costs   the environmental costs caused by environmental degradation and paid for by the responsible organization.

Reciprocal method   a method that simultaneously allocates service department costs to all user departments. It gives full consideration to interactions among service departments.

Relevant costs (revenues)   future costs (revenues) that differ across alternatives.

Relevant range   the range over which an assumed cost relationship is valid for the normal operations of a firm.

Reorder point   the point in time at which a new order (or setup) should be initiated.

Required rate of return   the minimum rate of return that a project must earn in order to be acceptable. Usually corresponds to the cost of capital.

Resale price method   a transfer price acceptable to the Internal Revenue Service under Section 482. The resale price method computes a transfer price equal to the sales price received by the reseller less an appropriate markup.

Research and development expense budget   a budget that outlines planned expenditures for research and development.

Reshoring   refers to the return of previously offshored business functions to the original country of origin.

Residual income   the difference between operating income and the minimum required dollar return on a company's operating assets.

Residual risk   the risk that remains after any risk management action has been taken.

Resource drivers   factors that measure the demands placed on resources by activities and are used to assign the cost of resources to activities.

Responsibility accounting   a system that measures the results of each responsibility center and compares those results with some measure of expected or budgeted outcome.

Responsibility center   a segment of the business whose manager is accountable for specified sets of activities.

Return on investment (ROI)   the ratio of operating income to average operating assets.

Revenue center   a responsibility center in which a manager is responsible only for sales.

Revenue-producing life   the time a product generates revenue for a company.

Risk appetite   an organization's overall desired level of risk taking.

Risk response benefit   the difference between the inherent risk and the residual risk produced by the particular risk response.

Risk response cost   the incremental cost incurred by the company to implement a given risk response.

Risk response net benefit   the benefit of risk response minus the cost of risk response.

Robustness   exact conformance to the target value (no tolerance allowed).

Rolling budget   see **Continuous budget**.

Ropes   actions taken to tie the rate at which raw material is released into the plant (at the first operation) to the production rate of the constrained resource.

S

Safety stock   extra inventory carried to serve as insurance against fluctuations in demand.

Sales budget   a budget that describes expected sales in units and dollars for the coming period.

Sales mix   the relative combination of products (or services) being sold by an organization.

Sales mix variance   the sum of the change in units for each product multiplied by the difference between the budgeted contribution margin and the budgeted average unit contribution margin.

Sales price variance   the difference between actual price and expected price multiplied by the actual quantity or volume sold.

Sales-revenue approach   an approach to CVP analysis that uses sales revenue to measure sales activity. Variable costs and contribution margin are expressed as percentages of sales revenue.

Sales-value-at-split-off method   a method of allocating joint production costs based on each product's share of revenue realized at the split-off point.

Sales volume variance   The difference between actual volume sold and expected volume sold multiplied by the expected price.

Scattergraph   a plot of (X, Y) data points. For cost analysis, X is activity usage and Y is the associated cost at that activity level.

Scatterplot method   a method to fit a line to a set of data using two points that are selected by judgment. It is used to break out the fixed and variable components of a mixed cost.

Secondary activity   an activity that is consumed by intermediate cost objects such as materials and primary activities.

Sell or process further   a relevant costing analysis that focuses on whether or not a product should be processed beyond the split-off point.

Semi-variable cost   a cost that is variable in nature, but its rate of change is not constant.

Sensitivity analysis   a "what-if" technique that examines altering certain key variables to assess the effect on the original outcome.

Separable costs   are easily traced to individual products and offer no particular problem.

Sequential (or step) method   a method that allocates service department costs to user departments in a sequential manner. It gives partial consideration to interactions among service departments.

Services   a task or activity performed for a customer or an activity performed by a customer using an organization's products or facilities.

Setup costs   the costs of preparing equipment and facilities so that they can be used for production.

Seven-year assets   assets with an expected life for depreciation purposes of seven years; equipment, machinery, and office furniture fall into this category.

Shadow prices   the amount by which throughput will increase for one additional unit of scarce resource.

Short run   period of time in which at least one cost is fixed.

Simplex method   an algorithm that identifies the optimal solution for a linear programming problem.

Single-loop feedback   information about the effectiveness of strategy implementation.

Slope parameter   the variable cost per unit of activity usage, represented by V in the cost formula $Y = F + VX$.

Source document   a document that describes a transaction and is used to keep track of costs as they occur.

Special-order decision   a relevant costing analysis that focus on whether a specially priced order should be accepted or rejected.

Split-off point   the point at which the joint products become separate and identifiable.

Spot rate   is the exchange rate of one currency for another for immediate delivery (i.e., today).

Staff positions   a position in an organization filled by an individual who provides support for the line function; thus, a staff person is only indirectly involved with the basic objectives of an organization.

Standard bill of materials   a listing of the type and quantity of materials allowed for a given level of output.

Standard cost per unit   the per-unit cost that should be achieved given materials, labor, and overhead standards.

Standard cost sheet   a listing of the standard costs and standard quantities of direct materials, direct labor, and overhead that should apply to a single product.

Standard hours allowed   the direct labor hours that should have been used to produce the actual output (Unit labor standard $\times$ Actual output).

Standard quantity of materials allowed   the quantity of materials that should have been used to produce the actual output (Unit materials standard $\times$ Actual output).

Static budget   a budget for a particular level of activity.

Step-cost function   a cost function in which cost is defined for ranges of activity usage rather than point values. The function has the property of displaying constant cost over a range of activity usage and then changing to a different cost level as a new range of activity usage is encountered.

Step-fixed costs   a step-cost function in which cost remains constant over wide ranges of activity usage.

Step-variable costs   a step-cost function in which cost remains constant over relatively narrow ranges of activity.

Stock option   the right to purchase a certain amount of stock at a fixed price.

Stock-out costs   the costs of insufficient inventory.

Strategic-based control system (SBCS)   a high-level approach for translating a company's strategy into operational objectives whose performance is measured and linked to employee compensation.

Strategic cost management   the use of cost data to identify and develop superior strategies that will produce a sustainable competitive advantage.

Strategic decision making   choosing among alternative strategies with the goal of selecting a strategy or strategies that provide a company with reasonable assurance of long-term growth and survival.

Strategic positioning   the process of selecting the optimal mix of cost leadership, differentiation, and focusing strategies.

Strategy   choosing the market and customer segments, identifying critical internal business processes at which the firm must excel to increase customer value, and selecting the individual and organizational capabilities required to achieve the firm's internal, customer, and financial objectives.

Strategy map   a detailed graphical representation of an organization's strategic objectives and the cause-and-effect relationships that exist among them.

Stretch targets   targets that are set at levels that, if achieved, will transform the organization within a period of three to five years.

Structural activities   activities that determine the underlying economic structure of the organization.

Subjective measures   measures that are nonquantifiable whose values are judgmental in nature.

Sunk cost   a past cost that already has been incurred and cannot be affected by future actions.

Supplies   materials necessary for production but that do not become part of the finished product or are not used in providing a service.

Support departments   a unit within an organization that provides essential support services for producing departments.

Sustainable development   development that meets the needs of the present without compromising the ability of future generations to meet their own needs.

System   a set of interrelated parts that performs one or more processes to accomplish specific objectives.

T

Tactical cost analysis   the use of relevant cost and revenue data to identify the alternative that provides the greatest benefit to the organization.

Tactical decision making   choosing among alternatives with only an immediate or limited end in view.

Taguchi loss function   a function that assumes any variation from the target value of a quality characteristic causes hidden quality costs.

Tangible products   goods produced by converting raw materials through the use of labor and capital inputs such as plant, land, and machinery.

Target cost   the difference between the sales price needed to achieve a projected market share and the desired per-unit profit.

Target costing   a method of determining the cost of a product or service based on the price that customers are willing to pay. Also referred to as price-driven costing.

Tariff   the tax on imports levied by the federal government.

Technical efficiency   point at which for any mix of inputs that will produce a given output, no more of any one input is used than is absolutely necessary.

Testable strategy   set of linked objectives aimed at an overall goal that can be restated into a sequence of cause-and-effect hypotheses.

Theoretical activity level   the maximum output possible for a firm under perfect operating conditions.

Theory of constraints   method used to continuously improve manufacturing activities and nonmanufacturing activities.

Three-year assets   assets with an expected life for depreciation purposes of three years; most small tools fall into this category.

Throughput   the rate at which an organization generates money through sales.

Time/batches   it is time required to produce one batch for a batch process.

Time buffer   the inventory needed to keep the constrained resource busy for a specified time interval.

Time/units   it is time required to produce one unit of product for a continuous process.

Time-Driven Activity-Based Costing (TDABC)   a before-the-fact simplification method that simplifies Stage 1 by eliminating the need for detailed interviewing and surveying to determine resource drivers.

Time ticket   a document used to identify the cost of direct labor for a job.

Total budget variance   the difference between the actual cost of an input and its planned cost.

Total (overall) sales variance   the sum of the sales price and sales volume variances.

Total preventive maintenance   a program of preventive maintenance that has zero machine failures as its standard.

Total product   the complete range of tangible and intangible benefits a customer receives from a product.

Total productive efficiency   the point at which technical and price efficiency are achieved.

Total productivity measurement   an assessment of productive efficiency for all inputs combined.

Total quality control   an approach to managing quality that demands the production of defect-free products.

Total quality management   a philosophy that requires managers to strive to create an environment that will enable workers to manufacture perfect (zero-defects) products.

Traceability   the ability to assign a cost directly to a cost object in an economically feasible way using a causal relationship.

Traditional cost system   a cost accounting system that uses only unit-based activity drivers to assign costs to cost objects.

Traditional operation control system   a system that assigns costs to organizational units and then holds the organizational unit manager responsible for controlling the assigned costs.

Transaction drivers   measure the number of times an activity is performed, such as the number of treatments and the number of requests.

Transaction risk   refers to the possibility that future cash transactions will be affected by changing exchange rates.

Transfer prices   the price charged for goods transferred from one division to another.

Transfer pricing problem   the problem of finding a transfer pricing system that simultaneously satisfies the three objectives of accurate performance evaluation, goal congruence, and autonomy.

Transferred-in cost   the cost of goods transferred in from a prior process.

Translation (or accounting) risk   the degree to which a firm's financial statements are exposed to exchange rate fluctuation.

Treasurer   the financial officer responsible for the management of cash and investment capital.

Turnover   a measure that is found by dividing sales by average operating assets to show how productively assets are being used to generate sales.

U

Underapplied overhead   the overhead variance resulting when the actual overhead cost incurred is greater than the applied overhead.

Unfavorable (U) variance   a variance produced whenever the actual input amounts are greater than the budgeted or standard allowances.

Unit-level activities   activities that are performed each time a unit is produced.

Unit-level drivers   factors that measure the demands placed on unit-level activities by products and, therefore, may explain changes in cost as units produced change.

Unit standard cost   the product of these two standards: Standard price × Standard quantity ($SP \times SQ$).

Unrealized external failure (societal) costs   environmental costs caused by an organization but paid for by society.

Unused capacity   the difference between the acquired activity capacity and the actual activity usage.

Unused capacity variance   the difference between acquired capacity (practical capacity) and actual capacity.

Upstream costs   costs incurred prior to production.

Usage (efficiency) variance   the difference between standard quantities and actual quantities multiplied by standard price.

V

Value-added activities   activities that are necessary to achieve corporate objectives and remain in business.

Value-added costs   costs caused by value-added activities.

Value-added standard   the optimal output level for an activity.

Value chain   the set of activities required to design, develop, produce, market, distribute, and service a product (the product can be a service).

Value-chain analysis   identifying and exploiting internal and external linkages with the objective of strengthening a firm's strategic position.

Value stream   made up of value-added and non-value-added activities required to bring a product group or service from its starting point to a finished product in the hands of the customer.

Variable budget   see **flexible budget**.

Variable costing   a costing method that assigns only variable manufacturing costs to the product; these costs include direct materials, direct labor, and variable overhead. Fixed overhead is treated as a period cost and is expensed in the period incurred.

Variable cost ratio   variable costs divided by sales revenue. It is the proportion of each sales dollar needed to cover variable costs.

Variable costs   costs that in total vary in direct proportion to changes in a cost driver.

Variable overhead efficiency variance   the difference between the actual direct labor hours used and the standard hours allowed multiplied by the standard variable overhead rate.

Variable overhead spending variance   the difference between the actual variable overhead and the budgeted variable overhead based on actual hours used to produce the actual output.

Velocity   the number of units that can be produced in a given period of time (e.g., output per hour).

Vendor Kanban   a card or marker that signals to a supplier the quantity of materials that need to be delivered and the time of delivery.

W

Waste   anything customers do not value.

Weighted average costing method   a unit-costing method that merges prior-period work and costs with current-period work and costs.

Weighted average cost of capital   the proportionate share of each method of financing is multiplied by its percentage cost and summed.

Weight factor   a value used to assign weights to various joint products in accordance with their relative size, difficulty to produce, etc.

What-if analysis   see **sensitivity analysis**.

Withdrawal Kanban   a marker or card that specifies the quantity that a subsequent process should withdraw from a preceding process.

Work in process   consists of all partially completed units found in production at a given point in time.

Work-in-process inventory file   the collection of all job cost sheets.

Work orders   used to collect production costs for product batches and to initiate production.

Y

Yield variance   the difference in the standard material cost of the standard yield and the standard material cost of the actual yield.

Z

Zero-base budgeting   a method of budgeting in which the prior year's budgeted level is not taken for granted. Existing operations are analyzed, and continuance of the activity or operation must be justified on the basis of its need or usefulness to the organization.

Zero defects   a quality performance standard that requires all products and services to be produced and delivered according to specifications.

Check Figures

Check figures are given for selected exercises and problems.

Chapter 2

2-14
2. Cost of goods manufactured = $571,800
3. Conversion cost = $19.09

2-15
1. Ending inventory = $7,300
3. Cost of goods manufactured = $347,700
5. Overhead = $348,000

2-16
1. Cost of goods manufactured = $860,600
2. Cost of goods sold = $865,400

2-17
1. Finished goods ending inventory = $93,600
2. Cost of goods sold = $1,209,000
3. Operating income = $84,700

2-18
1. Cost of goods manufactured = $1,222,890
2. Cost of goods sold = $1,219,390

2-19
5. Operating income = $35,345

2-22
2. Cost of goods manufactured = $977,000
3. Conversion cost = $7.07

2-23
2. Operating income = $129,300

2-24
3. Total overhead = $300,000
4. Cost of goods manufactured = $706,000
5. Cost of goods sold = $708,000
6. Operating income = $122,200, 10.18%

2-28
1. Cost of goods manufactured = $5,018,000
3. Operating income = $1,048,250, 15.25%

2-29
1. Cost of goods manufactured = $154,000
2. Cost of goods sold = $169,400

2-30
1. Cost of services sold = $1,577,500
3. Operating income = $650,500

2-31
1. Cost of goods manufactured = $1,077,500
2. Operating income = $172,000

Chapter 3

3-10
3. Total fixed overhead cost = $2,500,000
6. Unit fixed cost = $50 per unit

3-14
2. Fixed activity rate = $2.46 per test

3-16
3. April cost = $4,214

3-19
2. Y = $174,769

3-20
3. Y = $94,140

3-21
1. $Y = \$17,350 + \$12X$

3-22
2. Y = $5,791

3-23
2. Y = $287,895

3-25
2. Total labor cost for 16 sets = $202,520

3-29
4. Charge/day = $124.80

3-31
1. Total unit variable cost = $210
3. Total unit variable cost = $222

3-33
3. Y = $91,815
4. Y = $87,195

3-34
2. Y = $63,696
3. Y = $69,031

3-35
1. Y = $9,025
2. Y = $9,227
4. Y = $9,375.80

3-36
2. Y = $34,896

Chapter 4

4-11
3. Underapplied overhead = $6,960
4. Unit cost = $8.8536

4-12
2. Findley: Underapplied overhead = $7,180
   Lemon: Overapplied overhead = $5,625

4-13
2. Overapplied overhead = $84,000

4-22
1. Total OH assigned: Model X = $171,000, Model Y = $129,000
2. Total OH assigned: Model X = $185,740, Model Y = $114,305

4-23
2. Total OH assigned: Model X = $129,001, Model Y = $171,002

4-28
2. Unit cost (ABC): Standard = $189.50, Deluxe = $571.00

4-31
1. Gross margin: Part 127 = $10.50, Part 234 = $11.97
2. Gross margin (loss): Part 127 = $16.60, Part 234 = $(18.54)

4-32
3. Unused capacity cost = $92,000

4-34
2. Overhead per unit: Cylinder A = $146.67, Cylinder B = $60.00
4. Overhead per unit: Cylinder A = $146.67, Cylinder B = $60.00
5. Overhead per unit: Cylinder A = $146.67, Cylinder B = $60.00

4-36
1. Percentage of total activity costs = 85%
2. Overhead per unit: Cylinder A = $100.44, Cylinder B = $83.20

4-37
3. Overhead per unit: Scientific = $5.95, Business = $1.61

Chapter 5

5-7
2. Total cost = $3,870

5-8
2. Total unit cost: June = $682, July = $654, August = $621

5-11
1. Job 86: Total job cost = $9,808
2. Job 88: Ending work in process = $13,760

5-12
3. Ending work in process = $42,972
4. Cost of goods sold = Job 115 = $22,496
5. Price of Job 115 = $28,120

5-14 3. Work in process, August 31 = $9,691
4. Cost of goods sold = $11,890
5. August sales revenue = $14,268

5-15 Operating income = $1,178

5-16 2. (d) Finished goods inventory = $1,010

5-17 2. Ending work in process = $2,500

5-18 2. Ending work in process = $12,890

5-20 3. Ending balance in work in process = $70,126
4. Cost of goods sold = $270,597

5-21 3. Cost of goods manufactured = $160,000

5-22 1. Bid price: Job 1 = $8,890, Job 2 = $16,926
2. Bid price: Job 1 = $9,821, Job 2 = $17,136

5-24 1. Unit bid price: Job 97-28 = $18.75, Job 97-35 = $60.00
2. Unit bid price: Job 97-28 = $14.67, Job 97-35 = $101.01

5-25 1. Total cost = $47.50
4. Price = $641.25

5-26 1. Total cost = $48.15
2. Total cost = $54.15

5-27 4. Profit = $18,951

5-28 1. Gross profit = $37

5-29 2. Gross profit = $644.46
4. Total price = $2,980.25

Chapter 6

6-12 2. Cost per haircut = $10

6-13 2. Unit cost = $11 per unit

6-14 4. (c) Cost of EWIP = $94,080
5. (d) Unit conversion cost = $10.54

6-15 Total costs accounted for = $5,364,000

6-16 1. Total units accounted for = 300,000
4. (b) Unit materials cost (FIFO) = $4.00

6-17 1. Total cost of goods transferred out = $388,000
2. Total units accounted for = 22,000

6-20 2. Cost of goods transferred out = $343,750

6-21 1. Total units accounted for = 70,000
2. Unit cost = $10.40 per equivalent unit

6-26 1. Total units accounted for = 135,000
3. Conversion cost = $5,871,150

6-27 3. Total unit cost = $77.420

6-28 Total costs accounted for = $738,720

6-29 Total costs accounted for = $738,720

6-35 2. Unit cost: Regular strength = $2.17, Extra strength = $2.17

6-37 2. Total unit cost = $8.50
3. Cost of units transferred out = $4,165,000

6-38 3. Total unit cost = $0.38
4. Loss due to spoilage = $684

Chapter 7

7-15 2. Total cost = $1.18

7-16 2. Total = $403.33

7-19 1. Total cost: Department A = $55,000, Department B = $55,000

7-20 2. Shampoo = $56.10 per MHr, Conditioner = $22.55 per MHr

7-21 2. Shampoo = $52.64 per MHr, Conditioner = $23.70 per MHr

7-22 2. Assembly = $14.00 per DLhr, Finishing = $8.18 per DLhr

7-23 2. Assembly = $13.70 per DLhr, Finishing = $8.36 per DLhr

7-24 2. Assembly = $14.09 per DLhr, Finishing = $8.12 per DLhr

7-27 2. Incremental value of further processing = $94,500

7-34 2. Additional contribution from further processing = $50,000

7-35 2. In-house members: Total = $233,584, Out-of-house members: Total = $41,293

Chapter 8

8-18 Total = $12,605,000

8-22 1. Ending cash balance = $1,493

8-23 1. Total = $202,080

8-24 Total cash receipts: August = $46,623, September = $58,105

8-25 1. Total: August = $22,350, September = $27,814
2. Total: July = $23,683, August = $25,644

8-26 1. Units produced = 2,580
2. DM to be purchased = 8,960

8-27 1. Total overhead costs = $200,760

8-30 1. Total = $3,026,000

8-31 7. Total unit cost = $78.41
8. Budgeted cost of goods sold = $2,626,687
9. Income before income taxes = $85,713

8-35 1. Total predicted overhead = $423,145
2. Total predicted overhead = $423,201

8-36 1. Total predicted overhead = $423,184
2. Total predicted overhead = $423,109

Chapter 9

9-12 2. Total standard cost = $30.20

9-13 1. SQ = 888,000 pounds
2. SH = 432,000 hours

9-14 1. MPV = $3,840 F, MUV = $36 U
2. LRV = $0, LEV = $900 U

9-17 1. Yield ratio = 0.90
2. SPy = $450.01
4. Direct material mix variance = $39,973.65 U

9-19 1. Yield ratio = 5
2. Standard cost = $3.60 per unit of yield

9-20 1. MPV = $4,809 F, MUV = $90 U
2. LRV = $16,000 U, LEV = $144,000 U

9-23 1. Direct materials = \$158,720, Direct labor = \$186,000
3. *MPV* = \$4,950 F, *MUV* = \$320 F
4. *LRV* = \$2,500 F, *LEV* = \$1,500 U

9-24 1. Standard variable overhead rate = \$2.22 per DLhr
2. Total variable overhead variance = \$4,920 U

9-25 1. *MPV* = \$8,160 U, *MUV* = \$1,560 F
2. *LRV* = \$525 F, *LEV* = \$5,400 U

9-27 1. *MPV* = \$5,416 F, *MUV* = \$6,480 U
2. *LRV* = \$730 F, *LEV* = \$8,100 U

9-28 2. *MPV* = \$2,800 F, *MUV* (Regular) = \$1,200 F
3. *LRV* = \$3,700 F, *LEV* (Regular) = \$5,600 U

9-29 1. Yield variance = \$42,750 F

9-30 1. Yield variance = \$20,685 F

9-32 4. *LEV* = \$7,600 F

9-35 2. Cost of goods transferred out = \$1,995,000

Chapter 10

10-9 1. Fruit Pouch residual income = \$200

10-10 1. *EVA* = \$(19,140)

10-12 1. Increased profit = \$152,00

10-13 1. North American = \$200,000
2. North American = 1.33%
3. North American = 8.33%

10-14 2. D's residual income = \$336

10-15 1. Residual income = \$51,000
2. ROI = 18.40%

10-16 1. Value of option = \$230,000

10-18 1. Maximum transfer price = \$3.45

10-19 1. Contribution margin = \$7,420,000

10-21 1. Contribution margin (Company) = \$118,500

10-23 3. Total addition to profits = \$768,000

10-26 1. Combined return on investment = 0.2321
2. Combined residual income = \$920,000

Chapter 11

11-12 1. Unit cost: Harvey = \$68.24, Curtis = \$81.84

11-13 1. Customer profitability = \$15,414,000

11-22 1. Cost per unit of average product = \$62.50
2. Cost per unit of average product = \$63

11-23 1. Unit cost: Villa = \$444.81, Verity = \$343.21

11-25 1. Total savings = \$2,675,000

11-26 4. Income before taxes (current) = \$191,250

11-27 1. Target cost = \$115 per unit
3. Design A: Profit per unit = \$15.43
4. Increase in benefits = \$800,000

11-29 1. After JIT unit cost = \$32.54

Chapter 12

12-20 1. Total: Fixed = \$1,394,000, Variable = \$2.16
4. Total: Fixed = \$504,000, Variable = \$2.16

12-21 2. Total = \$1,278,000
3. Cost reduction to maintain = \$9, Cost reduction to expand = \$12
4. Unit savings = \$12.53

12-22 2. Molding: *SQ* = 2,538,000 lbs., Engineering: *SQ* = 126,720 eng. hrs.

12-23 1. *C* = \$1,352
2. Unit non-value-added cost = \$455

12-25 1. Total actual costs = \$1,854,500
2. Total/Units = \$15.29
3. Total: 20,000 moves = \$165,000, 40,000 moves = \$290,000

Chapter 13

13-8 1. Theoretical conversion cost per unit = \$585
2. Applied conversion cost per unit = \$900

13-9 1. Cycle time (actual) = 40 minutes per laptop
2. Assignment per unit (actual) = \$80

13-16 1. (d) 208,000/1,300,000 = 16%
(g) 13,000/208,000 = 6.25%
(k) 5,200

13-19 1. Cycle time (theoretical) = 20 minutes per unit
2. Assignment per unit (theoretically) = \$20.00
4. Cost = \$20.00

13-20 1. MCE = 0.30

13-21 1. Theoretical cycle time = 80 minutes per model
2. Actual cycle time = 96 minutes per model

Chapter 14

14-9 2. Hidden cost = \$1,000,000

14-12 1. Total quality costs = \$540,000

14-13 2. Profit potential = \$5,520,000

14-15 2. (c) Bonus pool = \$110,400

14-21 1. Total environmental costs = \$24,637,500

14-23 1. Unit cost per pound: Org AB = \$1.08, Org XY = \$0.20

14-24 1. Treatment rate = \$0.10 per pound

14-25 1. Total quality costs = \$12,000,000

14-29 1. Total quality costs = \$1,396,500

14-30 1. Total quality costs: January = \$86,000, February = \$100,500

14-31 1. External failure costs: 20x4 = 33.2%, 20x5 = 36.1%

14-38 1. Total benefits = \$1,131,000, Total costs = \$1,179,000

14-39 1. Unit cost: Model XA2 = \$2.11, Model KZ3 = \$4.54

Chapter 15

15-6 1. Total time = 980 minutes
3. Time saved = 38.93 minutes per unit (41.33 for continuous)

15-9   1. Unit cost: Model A = $817.50, Model B = $625.63

15-10 2. Week 3: Average cost = $22.22

15-13 1. Value of productivity = $756,000

15-15 2. Price recovery = $514,400

15-16 2. Change in income = $300,000
4. Price-recovery component = $(420,000)

15-17 2. Average lunch cost = $8.50
3. Group A: Average lunch cost = $6.80

15-18 1. Group A: Average lunch cost = $6.17

15-22 1. Current system labor = 0.50

15-23 2. Increase in profits due to productivity = $40,000

15-24 3. Change I = $0, Change II = $495,000

Chapter 16

16-8   1. Contribution margin = $9.80
3. Operating income = $22,540

16-9   1. Break-even in units = 43,560 gas grills
2. Operating income = $1,205,625

16-10 1. Contribution margin ratio = 62%
3. Sales revenue for target profit = $13,298,387

16-11 1. Break-even in units = 14,600 units
2. Operating income = $95,900

16-12 1. Break-even in units = 90 jobs per month
4. Break-even in units = 67 jobs per month

16-13 Monthly revenue = $600,000

16-14 1. Break-even sales revenue = $4,060,000
2. Margin of safety = $8,285,000

16-15 1. Break-even units = 600 units

16-16 1. Net income after taxes = $570,150

16-17 1. Break-even units = 30

16-18 1. Break-even revenue = $937,500
2. Break-even point = $1,163,321

16-20 1. Contribution margin ratio = 0.4661
3. Operating income = $55,055
4. Margin of safety = $118,118

16-22 2. Revenue = $9,988,386

16-23 2. Revenue = $3,600,000

16-24 1. Break-even units = 400,000
3. Break-even units = 292,858

16-25 1. Operating income = $139,000
3. Break-even sales = $513,889

16-26 1. Total fixed expenses = $1,491,980

16-27 1. (a) Operating income = $1,025,000

16-29 3. Margin of safety = $90,000
4. Net income = $35,000

16-30 3. New break-even units = 41,860
5. New break-even units = 37,333

16-31 3. Margin of safety = $500,000

16-32 2. Operating income = $1,292,800
5. Margin of safety = $6,481,818

16-33 2. Revenue = $584,735
4. Revenue = $1,311,386

16-34 3. Percentage change in net income = 160%

16-35 3. Net income = $516,960

16-36 2. Total unit variable cost = $21

Chapter 17

17-8   1. Incremental loss per pair = $(0.20)

17-9   2. Maximum price = $58.43

17-11 1. Loss from accepting order = $(10,955)
3. Loss from accepting order = $(3,680)

17-12 1. Operating income = $962,500
2. Operating income = $962,500

17-13 1. Gross profit = $48,300

17-14 1. Total annual cost = $3,050

17-16 1. Operating income = $18,280
2. Operating income = $49,889

17-17 1. Net income = $3,150,000

17-19 2. Operating income = $1,749,000

17-20 1. Operating income = $58,250
2. Operating income = $45,400

17-22 2. Activity rate per procedure = $176

17-27 1. Total relevant costs: Lease and make = $51,000, Buy = $50,000
2. Total relevant cost: Make = $58,600, Buy = $50,000

Chapter 18

18-13 1. Markup percentage = 12%
2. Bid = $364,000

18-16 1. Minimum bid price = $25.03
2. Bid price = $31.19

18-18 2. Operating income = $13,950
3. Operating income = $1,800

18-19 2. Operating income = $31,890

18-20 1. Sales price variance = $500 U
2. Sales volume variance = $15,750 F

18-21 1. Product T: Sales volume variance = $680,000 F

18-22 1. Unit variable product cost = $5.00

18-24 1. Total cost = $1,476,000
2. Total cost = $1,008,000

18-25 3. (a) Operating income = $363,250

18-26 1. Cost of goods sold: Year 1 = $832,000, Year 2 = $956,000
2. Cost of goods sold: Year 1 = $672,000, Year 2 = $756,000

18-27 1. Operating income = $146,720

18-28 1. Contribution margin variance = $4,670 F
3. Sales mix variance = $406.64 F

18-29 2. Market size variance = $36,613 F

18-30 1. Contribution margin variance = $3,490 F

18-31 1. Net change in income = $(600)

18-33 2. Operating income = $785,000

18-34 1. Operating income = $2,455,000

18-35 1. Operating income = $(75,000)

18-36 1. Profit on first year = $675

18-37 1. Operating income = $272,400

18-38 1. Net income = $72,250

Chapter 19

19-7 1. Payback period = 3.00 years

19-8 3. CF = $108,155

19-9 1. NPV = $268,000

19-10 1. Payback period = 3.33 years

19-11 1. MRI equipment: NPV = $32,050

19-12 1. MRI equipment: Payback period = 2.83 years

19-13 3. NPV = $136,290

19-15 1. Payback period = 6.00 years

19-17 Project I: CF = $112,500

19-18 1. Present value = $3,411

19-19 3. NPV = $789,523

19-21 1. Scrubbers and treatment facility, NPV = $(85,208)

19-25 3. NPV = $16,297

19-27 2. Manual system, NPV = $452,000

Chapter 20

20-6 1. Annual ordering cost = $4,800
3. Cost of current inventory policy = $34,800

20-7 1. *EOQ* = 1,600
2. Total cost = $24,000

20-8 1. *EOQ* = 2,500
2. Ordering cost = $562.50

20-9 1. Reorder point = 1,260 units

20-10 1. *EOQ* = 120,000
2. Total cost = $720,000

20-11 1. *EOQ* = 40,000
2. Total cost = $720,000

20-12 1. *ROP* (small casings) = 48,000

20-13 Safety stock = 150

20-16 2. Total contribution margin = $16,685,000

20-18 1. *EOQ* = 12,000

Chapter 21

21-7 2. $241,500

21-8 3. New carrying cost = $7,444

21-9 1. June 1 = $25,800

21-11 2. Canadian $92,308

21-14 1. Transfer price = $4.09

21-17 1. Japanese order = 6,994,000 yen

21-18 5. Exchange gain = $694
7. Exchange gain = $363

Subject Index

Exhibits are indicated by *exh.* preceding the page number.

A

ABB. *See* Activity-based budgets (ABB)
ABC. *See* Activity-based costing (ABC)
ABM. *See* Activity-based management (ABM)
Abnormal spoilage, 243–244, 297
Absorption costing
  disadvantages of, 931
  income statement, 929–930, *exh.* 935
  inventory costs under, 929–930, *exh.* 934
  and profit measurement, 928–931
Absorption-costing income, 50
Acceptable quality level (AQL), 589
Accountability, 501
Account analysis method, 94–96
Accounting
  for activity-based costs, 55–56
  for actual overhead costs, 234
  for by-products, 351–353
  certification in, 18
  cost. *See* Cost accounting
  for cost of goods sold, 237–240, *exh.* 238
  for direct labor cost, 233, *exh.* 233
  for direct labor variances, 447–460
  for direct materials, *exh.* 232, 232–233
  for direct materials variances, 447–460
  ethical conduct and, 15–16, *exh.* 17
  financial. *See* Financial accounting
  for finished goods inventory, 235–236, *exh.* 236
  forensic, 11, 84–85, 889–891, 926–927
  for joint product costs, 343–351
  for joint production processes, 341–353
  lean. *See* Lean accounting
  for nonmanufacturing costs, 240
  for overhead, 233–234, *exh.* 235
  for overhead application, 234
  for overhead variances, 470–471
  responsibility. *See* Responsibility accounting
  role of management accountant in, 13–15
  for spoiled units in traditional job-order costing, 243–244
  for traditional costs, 55
  variance analysis and, 447–460
Accounting information system, 30–34
  cost management, 4–6, 32–35
  defined, 4, 30
  features of, 31
  financial, 4, 32
  importance of, 29–30
  operational model of, *exh.* 32
  subsystems, 4–6, 30, 31–35, *exh.* 36
Accounting rate of return (ARR), 977–978
Accounting records, 93
Accounting (translation) risk, 1070, 1076–1078

Accounts receivable aging schedule, 395–396
Acquisition costs, 1022–1027
Activity
  assigning costs to, 163–167, *exh.* 168
  batch-level, 168
  bill of, *exh.* 167, 167–168
  calculating availability, 92–93
  classification, 161–162, 168–169, 650
  control, 710
  cost behavior and, 88–93
  and cost information, *exh.* 879
  defined, 41, 88, 161, 650
  discretionary, 632
  environmental, 162, 707–708, *exh.* 733
  examples of, 41
  executional, 558
  facility-level, 168
  failure, 710
  flexible budget for actual level of activity, 406–407
  flexible budget for varying levels of, 404–405
  gathering necessary data, 162
  identification of, 162–163, 650
  illustrative example, 162–163
  inspecting, 634
  mixed cost behavior and, 93
  moving, 634
  non-value-added, 162, 633–634, 1027
  operational, 559, *exh.* 559, *exh.* 560
  organizational, and cost drivers, *exh.* 558, 558–559, *exh.* 560
  performance measurement of, 635
  primary, 161–162
  product-level, 168
  quality-related, 162
  scheduling, 633
  secondary, 161–162
  state-correction, 633
  state-detection, 633
  storing, 634
  structural, 558
  unit-level, 147–148, 168
  value-added, 162, 632
  value-chain, 556–558
  waiting, 634
Activity analysis, 631–635
Activity attributes, 161
Activity-based accounting systems, 6
Activity-based and traditional cost management systems comparison of, 54–59, *exh.* 57
Activity-based budgets (ABB), 408–412
  example, *exh.* 411
  flexible vs., *exh.* 410
  traditional vs., *exh.* 409
Activity-based cost accounting, 55–56
Activity-based cost control, 56–57
Activity-based costing (ABC), 8, 144–183
  activities, 160–169
  and activity-based management, 630–631

big data and, 166
CVP analysis vs., 842–844
and environmental costing, 737–738
health-care setting implementation, 145–146
job-order costing with, 241–243
and kaizen standards, 443
limitations of plantwide and departmental rates, 153–160
managing procurement costs using, 572–574
overview of, 146
process costing with no WIP inventories, 270
product life-cycle costs by category, *exh.* 946
product life cycle implications for, 946
rationale for, 157–159
simplification of, 169–181
standards and, 443
system implementing. *See* Activity-based costing (ABC) system
time-driven, 8, 169–173, 175–176
unit-level product costing, 147–153
users of, 159–160
Activity-based costing (ABC) system, 56, 160–181
  activity classification, 161–162, 168–169
  activity definition, 161
  activity inventory, 160–161, *exh.* 162
  approximately relevant, 169, 177–179
  assigning costs to activities, 163–167, *exh.* 168
  cost objects and bills of activities, *exh.* 167, 167–168
  data collection, 162
  design steps for, *exh.* 161
  equally accurate reduced, 169, 179–181
  flexible budgeting with data from, 408
  illustrative example, 162–163
  model of, *exh.* 161
  reducing size and complexity of, 169–181
Activity-based cost management system, 55–57, *exh.* 56, 717, 878–880
Activity-based customer costing, 576–577
Activity-based life-cycle cost reduction, 581–583
Activity-based management (ABM), 9, 56–57, 628–657, 775
  activity-based costing and, 630–631
  defined, 56, 630
  failure of implementation of, 650–651
  financial-based vs. activity-based responsibility accounting, 651–655, *exh.* 653–655
  financial measures of efficiency, 635–648
  implementation of, 648–651, *exh.* 649

model of, *exh.* 56, *exh.* 630
process value analysis and, 631–635
traditional vs., 57, *exh.* 57
two-dimensional model of, *exh.* 630
use of, 629
Activity-based performance report, *exh.* 645
Activity-based responsibility accounting
  assigning responsibility in, 652–653, *exh.* 653
  assigning rewards, 654–655, *exh.* 655
  defined, 651
  financial-based responsibility accounting vs., 651–655, *exh.* 653–655
  performance evaluation, 654, *exh.* 654
  performance measures, 653, *exh.* 654
  process value analysis and, 631–635
Activity capacity, 88–89, 646–648
  management, 646–648
Activity classification, 161–162, 168–169, 650
Activity dictionary, 161, 163, 650
  cardiology unit, *exh.* 164
Activity drivers, 81, 147–148, 631
  defined, 167
  non-unit-based, 56
  potential, 163
  for support departments, *exh.* 320
Activity efficiency, financial measures of, 635–648
Activity elimination, 634
Activity flexible budgeting, 643–646, *exh.* 644
Activity inventory, 160–161, *exh.* 162
Activity level
  choosing, 226
  expected, 226
  measures of, *exh.* 226
  normal, 226
  practical, 226
  theoretical, 226
Activity output measure, 81, 107, 631
Activity rates, 91–92, 157–159, 167–168
Activity reduction, 634
Activity resource usage model, 874–876
Activity selection, 634–635
Activity sharing, 634
Activity volume variance, 646–647
Actual cost system, 223
Actual fixed overhead (AFOH), 466–467
Actual overhead costs, 234
Actual variable overhead rate (AVOR), 462, 463–464, 465
Actual vs. budgeted usage, 327–328
Additional operating budgets, 390–391
Additional revenues, 735
Additive manufacturing (AM), sustainability through, 225
Adjusted cost of goods sold, 237

Administrative costs, 49
Administrative expense budget, 390, 391
Advanced technology, capital
    investments, 991–996
Advance pricing agreements (APAs), 1083
AFOH (actual fixed overhead), 466–467
After-tax cash flows
    computing, 986–991
    conversion of gross cash flows to,
        986–989
    final disposal, 991
    MACRS depreciation, 989–991,
        exh. 990, *exh.* 991
    operating cash flows, life of project,
        988–989
    Year 0, 986–987
After-tax profit targets, 824–826
After-the-fact simplification, 176–181,
    exh. 177
Allocation. *See also* Cost allocation
    cost assignment, 42
    cost separability and need for, 342–343
    defined, 42
    direct method of, 330–332, *exh.*
        331, 338–339, *exh.* 339
    objectives of, 320–322
    reciprocal method of, 336–339,
        exh. 339
    on relative market value, 346
    resource, 694
    sequential method of, 332–335, *exh.*
        333, 338–339, *exh.* 339
Allocation bases, 320
Allocation ratio, 180
Allocative efficiency, 783, *exh.* 785
AM (Additive manufacturing),
    sustainability through, 225
Annuity, 1000
APAs (advance pricing agreements), 1083
Applied overhead, 148–150. *See also*
    Overhead application
Appraisal costs, 710
Appreciation, currency, 1070–1071
Approximately Relevant ABC Systems,
    169, 177–179
AQL (acceptable quality level), 589
ARR. *See* Accounting rate of return (ARR)
Assets
    defined, 40
    five-year, 989
    operating, 506–507
    seven-year, 989
    three-year, 989
Asset utilization, 682
Assumed consumption ratios, 156
Assumed linkage, 42, 55
Auditors, certificate in internal auditing
    for, 18
Automated vs. manual systems, *exh.* 841
Average time per unit, cumulative
    average, *exh.* 117
AVOR. *See* Actual variable overhead
    rate (AVOR)

B

Backflush costing, 591–594
Balanced Scorecard, 672–695
    basic concepts of, 680–688
    company strategy, 676
    core objectives and measures, 682
    customer perspective, 682–683, *exh.* 683

customer value, 683
    defined, 676
    financial perspective, 681–682, *exh.*
        682
    incentive programs, 678–680
    learning and growth (infrastructure)
        perspective, 687–688, *exh.* 689
    linking measures to strategy,
        688–691
    performance measures, 678, 688–691
    process perspective, 684–687, *exh.* 687
    strategic alignment, 692–694
    strategy translation, 680, *exh.* 681
    sustainability, 694
Balance sheets, budgeted, 399, *exh.*
    399–400
Malcolm Baldrige National Quality
    Award, 708, 709
Base period, 785
Batch-level activities, 168
Batch production processes, 290
Before-the-fact simplification method,
    169–176
    DBC, 169, 173–176
    TDABC, 169–173, 175–176
Beginning inventory output, 283
Beginning WIP inventories, 277
Behavioral dimension
    of budgeting, 412–416
    of EVA, 515–516
Behavioral effects, drivers and, 639–640
Benchmarking, 642–643
Benefits
    comparing relevant costs and, 870
    direct, intangible, and indirect, *exh.* 994
    environmental, 735
    of ethical behavior/conduct, 16
    predicting, 869–870
    risk response net, 565–568
    of solar homes, 926
Best-fitting line
    method of least squares, 102, 103
    regression cost formula, 106
    scatterplot method, 102
BFOH (budgeted fixed overhead),
    466–467
Big data, 10, 36, 57
    ABC and, 166
    analysis of. *See* Data analytics
    and bookstores transformation, 875
    for budgeting in large retail firms, 393
    and capital investments in advanced
        technology, 993
    in construction, 241
    customer linkages and, 575
    customer loyalty and, 921
    customer service use of, 341
    inventory management and, 1027
    kaizen costing and, 642
    and performance measures, 677, 783
    process costing and, 277
    in professional golf, 516–517
    and quality management, 729
    in restaurant industry, 458
    sustainability and, 109
    in telecommunications, 841
Bill of activities, *exh.* 167, 167–168
Bill of materials, standard, *exh.* 451,
    451–452
Binding constraints, 1034–1038,
    1040–1041

Break-even point
    break-even analysis, 813–814
    contribution margin approach, 820–824
    defined, 815
    equation method for, 818–820,
        823–824
    target profit in units and sales
        revenue and, 815–824
    in units for multiproduct setting,
        826–830
Budgetary slack, 414
Budget committee, 375
Budget director, 375
Budgeted balance sheets, 399, *exh.*
    399–400
Budgeted costs, 327–328, 405
Budgeted fixed overhead (BFOH),
    466–467
Budgeted income statement, 392–393
Budgeted overhead, 147
Budgeted statement of cash flows, 394
Budgeted vs. actual usage, 327–328
Budgeting, 372–418
    activity-based budgets, 408–412
    activity flexible, 643–646, *exh.* 644
    behavioral dimension of, 412–416
    capital, 974
    data analytics for, 10, 393
    ethical issues, 412
    financial budgets, preparing, 375,
        394–402
    flexible budgets, 402–408, 414,
        643–646
    gathering information for, 377–378
    incremental approach to, 401
    operating budgets, preparing, 375,
        379–394
    participative, 413–414
    in planning and control, 373–378,
        exh. 374, 402–408
    process, 375–377
    purposes of, 374–375
    sustainability, 415
    zero-base, 401
Budgets
    activity-based, 408–412
    activity flexible, 643–646, *exh.* 644
    additional operating, 390–391
    administrative expense, 390, 391
    capital expenditures, 394
    cash, 394–399, *exh.* 395
    continuous, 375–376
    continuously updated, 377
    cost of goods sold, 388–389
    defined, 374
    direct labor, 384–386, *exh.* 644
    direct materials purchases, 382–384
    ending finished goods inventory,
        386–388
    financial, 375, 394–402
    flexible, 402–408, 414, 643–646
    marketing expense, 389–390
    master. *See* Master budget
    operating, 375, 379–394
    overhead, 386–387
    production, 379, 381–382
    realistic standards for, 414–415
    research and development expense,
        390–391
    sales, 379, 380
    static, 401, 403–404

types, 375–377
    variable, 405
Business ethics, 16. *See also* Ethical
    behavior/conduct; Ethics
    benefits of, 16
    standards for management accountants,
        16, *exh.* 17
Business reengineering, 653
Business sustainability, 12. *See also*
    Sustainability
By-products
    accounting for, 351–353
    characteristics, 351
    defined, 351
    as other revenue, 352–353
    as reduction in main products cost, 353

C

Cannibalization, 885
Capacity
    activity, 88–89, 646–648
    excess, 524
    multi-period service, 89
    planned utilization of, 469
    practical, 89, 470
    unused, 89, 92–93, 172
    used, 92–93
Capacity variances, 646–648
Capital, cost of, 513–515, 979
Capital budgeting, 974
Capital expenditures budget, 394
Capital investment, 972–1002
    advanced technology and
        environmental considerations,
        991–996
    computing after-tax cash flows,
        986–991
    decisions, 973–975
    internal rate of return, 979, 981–985
    nondiscounting methods, 975–978
    NPV method, 979–980, 982–985
    present value, 998–1002
Carbon dioxide (CO_2) emissions, smart
    meters for, 109
Carrying costs, 1021
    minimizing ordering costs and, 1022
    model for balancing acquisition and,
        1022–1027
    setup costs and, 1028–1029
Carrying inventory, *exh.* 1021
Cash budget, 394–399
    components of, 394–397, *exh.* 395
    constructing, 395–396, 397–399
Cash compensation, 518
Cash disbursements section, cash
    budget, 396
Cash equivalent value, 40
Cash excess or deficiency section, cash
    budget, 396
Cash flows
    budgeted statement of, 394
    computing after-tax, 986–991
    conversion of gross to after-tax, 986–989
    discounted, 978
    modified, with additional
        opportunity, *exh.* 984
    operating. *See* Operating cash flows
    present value of uneven series of, *exh.*
        999, 1000
    present value of uniform series of
        cash flows, *exh.* 999, 1000

Cash receipts budget, constructing with accounts receivable aging schedule, 395–396

Causal factors, 320

Causal relationships, 41, 42

Cellular manufacturing, 587, *exh.* 772, 772–773

Centralized decision making, 501

Central management, decentralization and, 503

Certificate in Internal Auditing, 18

Certificate in Management Accounting, 18

Certificate in Public Accounting, 18

Certifications, to management accountants, 18

Certified Internal Auditor (CIA), 18

Certified Management Accountant (CMA), 18

Certified Public Accountants (CPA), 18

Changeover times, 772

Charging rates, 322–327

CIA (Certified Internal Auditor), 18

Citizenship report, 12

CMA (Certified Management Accountant), 18

Codes of ethics, 16, *exh.* 17

Coefficient of correlation (r), 107–108

Coefficient of determination (R^2), 107, 112

Cognitive limitations, decentralization and, 502

Committed fixed expenses, 89

Committed resources, 89–90, 874–875, *exh.* 876

Common costs, 317

Common fixed expenses, 826

Comparable uncontrolled price method, 1082–1083

Comparative income statements, *exh.* 523

Compensation
cash, 518
income-based, 519
noncash, 519
stock-based, 518–519

Competition
enhanced, 503
error costs and, 59
global, 7
monopolistic, 917
perfectly competitive market, 916
in service industry, 7

Competitive advantage, 9, 555–556

Competitive pricing, 321

Compounding of interest, 998

Confidence intervals, 106, 109

Constant gross margin percentage method, 350–351

Constant sales mix, 834

Constrained optimization, 1034–1038

Constraint data, *exh.* 1036

Constraints
binding, 1034–1038, 1040–1041
defined, 8, 1034
theory of, 8, 1019–1020, 1038–1044

Constraint set, 1036
new, *exh.* 1044

Construction, big data and data analytics in, 241

Consumable life, 577–578

Consumable life-cycle viewpoint, 579, *exh.* 580

Consumption ratio, 154, 156–157
expected global, 179

Continuous budget, 375–376

Continuous improvement, 15, 630, 674, 694

Continuously updated budget, 377

Continuous replenishment, 1028–1029

Contribution margin, 820–824, *exh.* 821

Contribution-margin-based income statement, 816–818

Contribution margin ratio, 821

Contribution margin variance, 939–942

Contribution margin volume variance, 940–941

Control
budgets for, 373–378, *exh.* 374, 402–408
defined, 374
of environmental costs, 729–736
implications of cost behavior for, 90
of quality costs, 720–729
standard costing system in, 443
strategic-based systems. *See* Strategic-based control systems
total quality. *See* Total quality control (TQC)
traditional cost, 55

Control activities, 710

Control costs, 710

Controllable costs, 415

Controller, 13

Control limits, 456–457

Controlling, 14–15

Conversion cost, 47
calculating, 48
operation costing, 291

Core objectives and measures, 682

Corporate sustainability report (CSR), 12

Correlation
coefficient of, 107–108
illustrated, *exh.* 108
risk, 562

Cost accounting
activity-based, 55–56
in international environment, 1064–1065
system, setting up, *exh.* 222, 222–226
traditional, 55

Cost accounting information system, 5–6, 35

Cost accumulation, 222
cost measurement and cost assignment, relationship with, *exh.* 222
defined, 222
methods, comparison, *exh.* 265

Cost allocation, 317–355
accounting for joint production processes, 341–353
allocation bases, 320
budgeted vs. actual usage, 327–328
choosing support department method, 329–339
cost separability and need for, 342–343
departmental overhead rates and product costing, 339–341
departments, types, 318–319, *exh.* 319, *exh.* 320
ethical implications of, 353
fixed vs. variable bases, 329

multiple charging rates for, 324–327
objectives of, 320–322
from one department to another, 322–329
overview, 317–322
single charging rate for, 322–324

Cost analysis, tactical, 870, 878–880

Cost assignment, 40–43, 224–225
accuracy of, 41–43
to activity, 163–167, *exh.* 168
activity-based environmental, 737–738
approaches, *exh.* 444
cost accumulation and cost measurement, relationship with, *exh.* 222
of cost objects, 40–41, *exh.* 168
defined, 222
FIFO, 279–280
to inventories, 273
overhead, plantwide, 148–149
product, *exh.* 590
summarized, 42–43
traceability of, 41–42
tracing methods, 42
unit cost and, 224–225, 273, 279–280, 284–285
weighted average costing method, 284–285

Cost avoidance, 735

Cost-based pricing, 917–919

Cost-based transfer prices, 527–529
calculating, 528–529
full cost plus markup, 527–528
full-cost transfer pricing, 527
propriety of use, 528
variable cost plus fixed fee, 528

Cost behavior, 78–121
activities and, 88–93
basics of, 80–88
control and decision making implications, 90
defined, 80
forensic accounting role of, 84–85
learning curve and nonlinear, 112–118
managerial judgment, 118–119
methods of determining, 94–96
mixed, 87–88, 93
multiple regression, 109–112
nonlinear, 86, 112–118
profitability improvement and, 79–80
quantitative methods for cost separation, 96–106
reliability of cost formulas, 106–109
resources, 88–93
step-cost behavior, 90–93, *exh.* 91, *exh.* 92, *exh.* 571
sustainability and, 85

Cost center, 500

Cost control
activity-based, 56–57
traditional, 55

Cost drivers
non-unit, 842–845
operational, 559
organizational activities and, *exh.* 558, 558–559, *exh.* 560

Cost equation, constructing using results from multiple regression, 110–112

Cost flows
direct labor, 233, *exh.* 233

direct materials, *exh.* 232, 232–233
finished goods, 235–236, *exh.* 236
job-order costing, 231–241
manufacturing, *exh.* 239
operation costing, 292, *exh.* 292
overhead, 233–234, *exh.* 235
process costing, 264–267, *exh.* 267

Cost formulas
regression, 106
reliability of, 106–109

Cost information, 5, 34
activity and, *exh.* 879

Costing
ABC. *See* Activity-based costing (ABC)
absorption. *See* Absorption costing
backflush, 591–594
duration-based. *See* Duration-Based Costing (DBC)
environmental, 736–738
feature, 412
features and characteristics, 778
first-in, first-out. *See* FIFO (first-in, first-out) costing method
job-order. *See* Job-order costing
kaizen, 634, 640–642
operation, 221, 290–293
problems with accuracy, 155–156
process. *See* Process costing
product. *See* Product costing
standard. *See* Standard costing
target, 9, 583–585, 919–920
TDABC, 8, 169–173, 175–176
unit-level product, 147–153
value-stream, 777–780
variable. *See* Variable costing
weighted average, 282–287, 345–346

Cost leadership strategy, 555

Cost management
data analytics importance in, 36–40, *exh.* 37. *See also* Data analytics
factors affecting, 6–12
financial accounting vs., 4–6
impact of product life cycle on, *exh.* 945
importance of, 3–4
international issues in, 1062–1086
life-cycle, 577–585
standard costing system in, 443
strategic. *See* Strategic cost management

Cost management information system, 4–6, 32–35
cost accounting information system, 5–6, 35
integrated, 34
operational control information system, 6, 35, 90
organization-wide perspective, 34
other operational systems and functions and, 34

Cost management system
activity-based. *See* Activity-based cost management system
choice of, 57–59
ethics of choice of, 59
features of service firms and their interface with, *exh.* 219
JIT effect on, 589–594
traditional vs. activity-based, 54–59, *exh.* 57

Cost measurement, 222, *exh.* 222, 223
Cost objects, 40–41, 81
  assigning costs, 40–41, *exh.* 168
  bills of activities and, 167–168
  potential, 163
Cost of capital, 513–515, 979
Cost of goods manufactured, 50–51
  preparing statement of, 50–51
  statement of, 50–51, 236, *exh.* 237
  work in process, 51
Cost of goods sold, 51–54
  accounting for, 237–240, *exh.* 238
  adjusted, 237
  budget, 388–389
  defined, 50
  job-order cost sheet to determine
    balance of, 238–239
  normal, 237
  preparing statement of, 52
  statement of, 52, *exh.* 238
Cost-oriented viewpoint, 579
Cost-plus method, 1082–1083
Cost reconciliation, 273
Cost reduction, 581–583, 634–635, 681
  activity-based life-cycle, 581–583
  environmental, 735
  kaizen process, *exh.* 641
Cost(s)
  acquisition, 1022–1027
  administrative, 49
  appraisal, 710
  budgeted, 327–328, 405
  calculating by customer class, 924–925
  calculating markup on, 918–919
  carrying, 1021, 1022–1027, 1028–1029
  common, 317
  control, 710
  controllable, 415
  conversion, 47–48, 291
  customer, 575–577
  defined, 40
  direct, 41–42
  direct labor, 233, *exh.* 233
  distribution, avoidable, 522–523
  downstream, 45
  environmental. *See* Environmental costs
  error, *exh.* 58, 58–59, *exh.* 59
  external failure, 711, 732
  failure, 710–711, 732
  fixed. *See* Fixed costs
  forensic accounting pricing cases,
    role in, 926–927
  future, 873
  indirect, 41–42
  internal failure, 710, 732
  inventory, 929–930, 932–933, 1023
  irrelevant, 870, 873
  known, 835
  life-cycle, 578
  manufacturing, 46
  marketing, 49
  materials handling, 96–112
  measurement, *exh.* 58, 58–59, *exh.* 59
  mixed. *See* Mixed costs
  noncontrollable, 415
  nonmanufacturing, 46, 240
  nonproduction, 46, 49
  non-value-added. *See* Non-value-
    added costs
  operational system and, 264–268,
    exh. 267, *exh.* 268

opportunity, 873
ordering, 1020–1021, 1022
overhead. *See* Overhead
past, 873
period, 49
post-purchase, 555, 683, 736
predicting, 869–870
prevention, 710, 732
pricing policies and, 917–922
prime, 47–48
private, 732
product. *See* Product costs
production. *See* Production costs
quality. *See* Quality costs
relevant. *See* Relevant costs (revenues)
resource, assigning to activities,
  163–167
and revenue relationships, *exh.* 834
risk response, 565
semi-variable, 112–114, *exh.* 113,
  exh. 114
separable, 93–106, 342–343
service, 43–49
setup, 1021, 1028–1029
of solar homes, 926
step-fixed, 91–93, *exh.* 92
step-variable, 91
stock-out, 1021
sunk, 873
target, 9, 583–585, 919–920
total. *See* Total costs
traditional, 54–55
transferred-in, 265
unbundling of general ledger, *exh.* 167
unit. *See* Unit costs
unit standard, 442
upstream, 45
value-added. *See* Value-added costs
value-stream, *exh.* 776, *exh.* 779
variable. *See* Variable costs
Cost separability and need for
  allocation, 342–343
Cost separation, 93–106
Cost sheets, standard, *exh.* 445, 445–447
Costs of quality. *See* Quality costs
Cost view, 57
Cost-volume-profit analysis (CVP
  analysis), 812–847
  activity-based costing vs., 842–844
  after-tax profit targets, 824–826
  assumptions of, 833–835
  basic concepts, 816–818
  break-even point, 813–814,
    815–824, 826–830
  changes in variables, 835–841, *exh.*
    836, *exh.* 837
  ethical issues, 841
  graphical representation of, 831–835
  and JIT, 844
  multiple drivers, nonprofit entities,
    and, 845
  multiple-product, 826–831
  and non-unit cost drivers, 842–845
  overview of, 814–815
  risk and uncertainty, 836–840
  sales mix and, 828–830
  sensitivity analysis and, 840–841
  and strategic design decisions,
    719–720
Cost-volume-profit graphs, 832–833,
  exh. 833

CPA (Certified Public Accountants), 18
Cryptocurrency, 1063–1064,
  1074–1075
  legality of, 1075
  mining, 1075
CSR (Corporate sustainability report), 12
Cultural factors, 1079–1080
Culture, in strategic-based control
  systems, 675
Cumulative average-time learning
  curve model, 114–118, *exh.* 117
Currency appreciation, 1070–1071
Currency depreciation, 1070–1071
Currency risk management, 1069
Currently attainable standards,
  442–443
Current-period output, 277, 283
  categories of, 281
Current-period unit cost, 277
Current savings, 735
Customer costs, managing, 575–577
Customer linkages, 557, 574–577
Customer loyalty, 921
Customer orientation, 9
Customer perspective, 682–683,
  exh. 683
Customer service, big data use, 341
Customer value, 6, 33, 555, 683
Customer value-oriented viewpoint, 580
CVP analysis. *See* Cost-volume-profit
  analysis (CVP analysis)
CVP variables, changes in, 835–841,
  exh. 836, *exh.* 837
Cycle time, 173, 778
Cycle time (manufacturing)
  calculating, 685
  and velocity, 684–685

D

Damage, environmental, 732
Data
  actual, for performance evaluation
    purposes, *exh.* 328
  after-the-fact simplification, *exh.* 177
  big. *See* Big data
  budgeted, for product costing, *exh.*
    328
  constraint, *exh.* 1036
  electronic data interchange, 1029
  gathering, for ABC system, 162
  qualitative vs. quantitative, 38
  summary of sales and production,
    exh. 523
  for support and producing
    departments, *exh.* 330
Data analytics, 10–11, 36–40
  of big data. *See* Big data
  for budgeting, 10, 393
  in construction, 241
  customer loyalty and, 921
  defined, 10, 36
  descriptive, *exh.* 40
  diagnostic, *exh.* 40
  framework for, 36–39, *exh.* 37
  in job-order costing, 240–241
  make-or-buy decision, 880
  management accountant role in, 57
  predictive, *exh.* 40
  prescriptive, *exh.* 40
  price elasticity estimates using, 916
  role in cost management, 36–40, *exh.* 37

sustainability and, 44, 109
  types of, for cost management
    analyses, 39–40, *exh.* 40
Database management system, 30–31
Databases, 30–31
Data visualization tools, 11, 39
DBC. *See* Duration-Based Costing (DBC)
DBR (drum-buffer-rope) system, 1041,
  exh. 1041, *exh.* 1043
Decentralization, 498–531
  investment center, measuring
    performance of, 499–500, 505–517
  managers, measuring performance
    and rewards of, 517–519
  in multinational corporations,
    advantages of, 1078
  overview, 501–505
  reasons for, 502–503
  responsibility accounting, 500–501
  transfer prices, 520–529
  units of, 504
Decentralized decision making, 501
Decision making, 15
  capital investment, 973–975
  centralized vs. decentralized, 501
  control and, implications of cost
    behavior for, 90
  defined, 15
  keep-or-drop, 881–884
  lean accounting, 781
  make-or-buy, 876–890
  product costing and, 443–444
  quality cost information and,
    717–720
  relevant cost analysis in, 891–892
  sell or process further, 887–889
  special-order, 867–868, 885–887
  standard costing systems, 443–444
  strategic, 554–555, 719–720
  tactical. *See* Tactical decision making
Decision model, 870
Decline stage, product life-cycle, 578
Defective product, 710
Degree of operating leverage, 838–840
Delivery performance, 33, 683, 1040
Demand
  price elasticity of, 915–916
  resources, 874–875, *exh.* 876
  and supply, 914–915
Demand-pull system, 774
Departmental layout, *exh.* 772
Departmental orientation, 400–401
Departmental overhead rates
  application of, 150–153
  product costing and, 339–341
  unit cost computation, 155–160
Departmental rates
  limitations of, 153–160
  product costing data, *exh.* 154
  unit product cost, *exh.* 155
Departments
  cost allocation from one to another,
    322–329
  support. *See* Support departments
  types of, 318–319, *exh.* 319, *exh.* 320
Dependent variable, 96
Depreciation, 873
  currency, 1070–1071
  MACRS, 989–991, *exh.* 990, *exh.* 991
  straight-line, *exh.* 991
Descriptive data analytics, *exh.* 40

Deviation, *exh.* 102, 102–103
Diagnostic data analytics, *exh.* 40
Differential analysis, 889–891
Differentiation strategy, 555
Digital information technology, advances in, 7–8
Direct benefits, *exh.* 994
Direct costing. *See* Variable costing
Direct costs, 41–42
Direct fixed expenses, 826
Direct labor, 46
Direct labor budget, 384–386
    flexible budget, *exh.* 644
Direct labor cost, 233, *exh.* 233
Direct labor efficiency variance (LEV)
    accounting for, 455
    computing, 453–454
    defined, 455
    formula approach to, 454–455
Direct labor mix variance, 476
Direct labor rate variance (LRV)
    accounting for, 455
    computing, 453–454
    defined, 454
    formula approach to, 454–455
Direct labor variances
    calculating, 452–454
    disposition of, 458–460
    investigating, 455–458
    mix variance, 476
    responsibility for, 458
    yield variance, 476–477
Direct labor yield variance, 476–477
Direct materials, 46
    cost flows, accounting for, *exh.* 232, 232–233
Direct materials mix variance, 473–474
Direct materials price variance (MPV)
    accounting for, 452–455
    calculating, 447–452
    defined, 448
    timing of computation, 450–451
Direct materials purchases budget, 382–384
Direct materials usage variance (MUV)
    accounting for, 452–455
    computing, 447–452
    defined, 448
    timing of computation, 451–452
Direct materials yield variance, 474–475
Direct material variances
    disposition of, 458–460
    investigating, 455–458
    mix variance, 473–474
    price and usage variances, 447–455
    responsibility for, 457–458
    yield variance, 474–475
Direct method
    of allocation, 330–332, *exh.* 331
    comparison of sequential, reciprocal and, 338–339, *exh.* 339
Direct tracing, 42
Discounted cash flows, 978
Discount factor, 999
Discounting, 999
Discounting models, 975, 978
Discount rates, 979, 995–996, 999
Discounts and price increases, 1033
Discretionary activities, 632
Discretionary fixed expenses, 90
Discrimination, price, 923–925

Disposal
    final, of after-tax cash flows, 991
    of overhead variances, 150–151
Distribution costs, avoidable, 522–523
Divisional profit, 936
Divisional return on investment, 1080
Divisions, segments and
    measuring profit of, 934–937
    units of decentralization, 504
Double-loop feedback, 689
Downstream costs, 45
Driver analysis, 631–632
Drivers, 42
    activity. *See* Activity drivers
    and behavioral effects, 639–640
    cost. *See* Cost drivers
    duration, 167
    multiple, and CVP analysis, 826–831
    non-unit-based, 56, 81, 153
    performance, 677
    resource, 162–163, 164
    transaction, 167
    unit-based, 55, 81, 147–148
Driver tracing, 42
Drum-buffer-rope (DBR) system, 1041, *exh.* 1041, *exh.* 1043
Drummer, 1040
Dual charging rates, 326–327
Dual-rate vs. single-rate method, *exh.* 328
Due-date performance, 1029
Dumping, 923
Duration-Based Costing (DBC), 169, 173–176, 778, *exh.* 779
Duration drivers, 167
Dysfunctional behavior, 412

E

Ecoefficiency paradigm, 729–731, *exh.* 730
Economic factors, 1079
Economic order quantity (EOQ), 1022–1027
Economic risk, 1070, 1075–1076
Economic value added (EVA), 513–516
    behavioral aspects of, 515–516
    calculating, 513–515
    defined, 513
EDI (electronic data interchange), 1029
Educational factors, 1079–1080
Effectiveness, 407, 504
Efficiency, 407, 504, 635
    allocative, 783, *exh.* 785
    financial measures of, 635–648
    manufacturing cycle, 686–687
    productive, 783–786
    technical, 783, *exh.* 784
Efficiency variance. *See* Direct labor efficiency variance (LEV); Usage variance; Variable overhead efficiency variance
Electrical usage, smart meters for, 109
Electronic data interchange (EDI), 1029
Employee alignment, 688
Employee capabilities, 688
Employee empowerment, 588–589, 688, 775
Employee motivation, 688
Employees, grouping of, 587–588
Ending cash balance section, cash budget, 397

Ending finished goods inventory budget, 386–388
Ending work-in-process inventories, 270–277
Enterprise resource planning (ERP) software, 7, 34
Enterprise risk management (ERM), 560–568
    defined, 560
    inherent risk assessment, 562, *exh.* 563
    inherent risk response, 564–568
    key elements of portfolio risk management perspective, *exh.* 563
    key steps in, *exh.* 561
    monitoring process, 568
    net benefit of risk response, 565–568
    overview of, 560–561
    residual risks, *exh.* 563, 564–568
    risk acceptance response, 564, 566
    risk appetite, determining, 561, *exh.* 563
    risk assessment matrix, *exh.* 564
    risk avoidance response, 564, 566
    risk identification, 561–562
    risk reduction response, 564, 565
    risk response, 564–568
    strategic-based control systems and, 676
    strategy implementation using, 552–553
Environmental activities, 162, 707–708, *exh.* 733
Environmental benefits, 735
Environmental considerations, advanced technology and, 991–996
Environmental costs, 729–738
    activity-based assignments, 737–738
    classification by activity type, *exh.* 733
    defined, 732
    defining, measuring, and controlling, 729–736
    ecoefficiency paradigm, 729–731, *exh.* 730
    financial report/statement, 735–736, *exh.* 735–736
    information, using, 707–708
    overview of, 708
    post-purchase, 736
    product costs, 736–737
    reduction, 735
    relative distribution, *exh.* 734
    report, 732–734
    sources of, 736
Environmental detection costs, 732
Environmental external failure costs, 732
Environmental information, using, 707–708
Environmental internal failure costs, 732
Environmental prevention costs, 732
Environmental Protection Agency, 12
EOQ. *See* Economic order quantity (EOQ)
Equally Accurate ABC System, 169
Equally Accurate Reduced ABC Systems, 179–181
Equation method, break-even point, 818–820, 823–824
Equivalent units
    calculation of, 289
    with nonuniform inputs, 275–277
    of output, 271–272
Equivalent units and physical flow analysis, 271–272

FIFO method, 278–279
    transferred-in goods, 288–289, *exh.* 289
    weighted average method, 283–284, *exh.* 289
ERM. *See* Enterprise risk management (ERM)
ERP (enterprise resource planning) software, 7, 34
Error cause identification, 726
Error costs, *exh.* 58, 58–59, *exh.* 59
Errors, standard, 108–109
Ethical behavior/conduct
    accounting and, 15–16, *exh.* 17
    benefits of, 16
    standards for management accountants, 16, *exh.* 17
Ethics
    behavioral dimension of budgeting, 412
    choice of cost management systems, 59
    committed resources, 89–90
    cost allocation, 353
    and CVP analysis, 841
    international issues, 1084–1085
    manufacturing vs. service firms, 220
    negotiated transfer prices, 525
    pricing, 925, 947–948
    profit measurement, 947–948
    relevant costing and, 891
    tactical decision making, 891
EVA. *See* Economic value added (EVA)
Evaluation, performance. *See* Performance evaluation
Excess capacity, 524
Exchange gains, 1072–1073
Exchange losses, 1072–1073
Exchange rates, 1069
Executional activities, 558
Executional cost drivers, 558
Expected activity level, 226
Expected global consumption ratio, 179
Expenses, 40. *See also* Fixed expenses; Operating expenses
Experience curve, 114
Exporting, 1067
External benchmarking, 643
External constraints, 1034
External failure costs, 711
    environmental, 732
External financial reporting, product costs and, 46–49
External financial statements, 49–54. *See also specific types of statements*
External linkages, 557–558
External measures, 677
External users, 4, 32
Extraction, data analytics for, 11

F

Facility-level activities, 168
Factory burden. *See* Overhead
Factory within a factory, 587
Failure activities, 710
Failure costs, 710–711
    environmental, 732
Fairness (equity), government contract, 322
FASB (Financial Accounting Standards Board), 4, 5, 32, 35

Favorable variance, 447
Feasible alternatives, identifying, 869
Feasible set of solutions, 1036
Feasible solution, 1036
Feature costing, 412
Features and characteristics costing, 778
Federal False Claims Act (FFCA), 85, 926–927
Feedback
    from accounting information system, 31
    control function, 14
    defined, 14
    double-loop, 689
    on performance, 413
    single-loop, 689–690
    strategic, 689–690
FFCA (Federal False Claims Act), 85, 926–927
FIFO (first-in, first-out) costing method, 277–282
    compared with weighted average, 286–287
    physical flow analysis and equivalent units, 278–279
    production report and journal entries, 281, exh. 282
    unit cost and cost assignment, 279–280
Final disposal, after-tax cash flows, 991
Financial accounting
    cost management vs., 4–6
    information system, 4, 32
Financial Accounting Standards Board (FASB), 4, 5, 32, 35
Financial-based responsibility accounting
    activity-based responsibility accounting vs., 651–655, exh. 653–655
    assigning responsibility in, 652–653, exh. 653
    assigning rewards, 654–655, exh. 655
    defined, 651
    performance evaluation, 654, exh. 654
    performance measures, 653, exh. 654
Financial budgets, 375, 394–402. See also Budgets
    budgeted balance sheet, 399, exh. 399–400
    cash budget, 394–399, exh. 395
    defined, 375
    shortcomings of master budget process, 400–402
Financial measures, 677
    activity capacity management, 646–648
    of activity efficiency, 635–648
    activity flexible budgeting, 643–646
    benchmarking, 642–643
    drivers and behavioral effects, 639–640
    kaizen standards, role of, 640–642, exh. 641
    reporting value- and non-value-added costs, 635–638
    trend reporting non-value-added costs, 638–639
Financial perspective, 681–682, exh. 682
Financial productivity measure, 784
Financial report, environmental, 735–736, exh. 735–736

Financial statements, external, 49–54. See also specific types of statements
Financing section, cash budget, 397
Finished goods
    cost flows for, 235–236, exh. 236
    ending inventory budget, 386–388
    inventories, accounting for, 235–236, exh. 236
    job-order cost sheet to determine balance of, 238–239
First-in, first-out costing method. See FIFO (first-in, first-out) costing method
Five-year assets, 989
Fixed base vs. variable base, 329
Fixed cost behavior, 82–83, exh. 83
Fixed costs, 82–83
    account analysis to determine, 94–96
    allocation procedure, 324–325
    cost behavior, 80, 82–83, exh. 83
    defined, 80
    high-low method to determine, 97–99
    regression programs to determine, 103–106
    scatterplot method to determine, 99–102
    separating mixed cost behavior into variable cost and, 96–106
    step-fixed costs, 91–93
Fixed expenses
    common, 826
    direct, 826
    discretionary, 90
    nondiscretionary or committed, 89
Fixed overhead spending variance
    calculating, 466–468
    defined, 466–467
    interpreting, 469, exh. 469
Fixed overhead variances, 466–470
    calculating, 466–468
    four-variance analysis of, 466
    interpreting, 469–470
Fixed overhead volume variance
    calculating, 466–468
    defined, 467
    interpreting, 469–470
Fixed rate, 324–325
Flexible budget, 404–408, 414
    activity-based budgets vs., exh. 410
    activity flexible budgeting, 643–646, exh. 644
    for actual level of activity, 406–407
    direct labor hours, exh. 644
    example of, exh. 644
    performance reports, exh. 403, exh. 407, exh. 645
    static budgets vs., 403–408
    types of, 404
    for varying levels of activity, 404–405
Flexible budget variances, 405
Flexible resources, 89, 874, exh. 876
Focusing strategy, 556
Forecasting
    data analytics for, 10
    other variables, 378
    sales, 377–378, exh. 378
Foreign currency exchange, 1069–1078
    cryptocurrency, 1063–1064, 1074–1075

currency appreciation and depreciation, 1070–1071
    economic risk management, 1070, 1075–1076
    exchange rates, 1069
    gains and losses, 1072–1073
    hedging, 1073–1074
    process of, 1070–1071
    transaction risk, 1069–1074
    translation risk management, 1070, 1076–1078
Foreign trade zones (FTZs), 1065–1067
Forensic accounting
    cost behavior role in, 84–85
    cost management and, 11
    defined, 11
    differential analysis role in, 889–891
    pricing cases, role of costs in, 926–927
Forward contracts, 1073–1074
Four-variance analysis, 466
Four-variance method, 461–462
FTZs (foreign trade zones), 1065–1067
Full-costing income, 50
Full cost plus markup, 527–528
Full-cost transfer pricing, 527
Full environmental costing, 736
Full private costing, 736
Future costs, 873
Future value, 998

G
GAAP (Generally Accepted Accounting Principles), 32, 321
Gainsharing, 728
General ledger costs, unbundling, exh. 167
Generally Accepted Accounting Principles (GAAP), 32, 321
Gig economy, 7
Global competition, 7
Global issues. See International issues
Goal congruence, 412, 505, 517
Goodness of fit measures, 106, 107–108
Governance, data analytics for, 11
Graphical representation of CVP relationships, 831–835
Graphs
    cost-volume-profit, 832–833, exh. 833
    cumulative total hours and cumulative average time, exh. 117
    multiple internal binding constraints, exh. 1038
    multiple-period trend, exh. 725, exh. 726
    profit-volume, 831, exh. 832
    relative contribution, exh. 715
    relative distribution, environmental costs, exh. 734
    zero-defects quality, exh. 716
Gross cash flows, conversion to after-tax cash flows, 986–989
Grouping of employees, 587–588
Growth stage, product life-cycle, 578

H
Half-year convention, 989
Hedging, 1073–1074
Heterogeneity, 218–219
Hidden quality costs, 711
High-low method, 97–99

High point, 98–99
Human resource (HR) information system, 30
Hurdle rate. See Discount rates
Hybrid costing approach, 291
Hybrid setting, manufacturing firm, 290
Hypothesis test of cost parameters, 106–107
Hypothetical sales value, 348–349

I
IASB (International Accounting Standards Board), 32, 35
Ideal standards, 442
IMA. See Institute of Management Accountants (IMA)
Importing, 1065
Improvement
    continuous, 15, 630, 674, 694
    process, 652
    quality, incentives for, 726–728
Incentive pay for managers, 517. See also Managerial rewards
Incentive programs, 678–680
Incentives
    defined, 413
    monetary, 413, 728
    nonmonetary, 413, 726–727
    quality improvement, 726–728
    targets and, 692–693, exh. 693
Income
    absorption-costing, 50
    full-costing, 50
    impact of transfer pricing on, 520, exh. 520
    net, 816
    operating, 506
    residual, 510–512
    targeted, 815–824
Income-based compensation, 519
Income statements. See also Profit and loss statement
    absorption costing, 929–930, exh. 935
    budgeted, 392–393
    comparative, exh. 523
    contribution-margin-based, 816–818
    cost flows to, 240, exh. 241
    manufacturing firm, 50–54
    preparing, 53
    service organization, 54
    variable costing, 932–933, exh. 936
Income taxes, and transfer pricing, 1082–1084
Incremental approach to budgeting, 401
Incremental benefit, exh. 994
Incremental unit-time learning curve model, 118
Independent projects, 974
Independent variable, 96
Indirect benefits, exh. 994
Indirect costs, 41–42
Indirect materials, 46
Industrial engineering method, 94, 96
Industrial value chain, 556, 571
Information, role of, 501
Information systems capabilities, 688

Information technology, advances in, 7–8
Infrastructure factors, 1079–1080
Infrastructure (learning and growth) perspective, 687–688, *exh.* 689
Inherent risks, 562, *exh.* 563
    responding to, 564–568
Innovation process, 684
Inputs, productive, 275–277
Inseparability, 43, 218–219
Inspecting activity, 634
Institute of Management Accountants (IMA)
    certifications, 18
    Competency Framework, 10
    cost allocation objectives, 320–321
    on enterprise risk management, 561
    statement of ethical professional practice, 16, *exh.* 17, 1064
Intangibility, 43, 218
Intangible benefits, *exh.* 994
Intangible products, 43
Interactive viewpoint, 579–583
Intercept parameter, 96–97
Interest, compounding of, 998
Interim quality performance report, 722–723
Interim quality standards, 721–722
Interim standard report, 722–723
Internal benchmarking, 642–643
Internal business process perspective, 684
Internal constraints, 1034–1038
Internal customers, 9, 34
Internal failure costs, 710
    environmental, 732
Internal linkages, 557–558, *exh.* 569, 569–571
Internal measures, 677
Internal rate of return (IRR), 979, 981–982
    NPV vs., 982–985, *exh.* 983–984
Internal users, 4, 32
Internal value chain, *exh.* 569, 569–571
International Accounting Standards Board (IASB), 32, 35
International issues, 1062–1086
    cost accounting, 1064–1065
    cryptocurrency, 1063–1064, 1074–1075
    decentralization, advantages of in MNC, 1078
    ethical, 1084–1085
    foreign currency exchange, 1063–1064, 1069–1078
    international trade, 1065–1069
    multinational corporations/firms, 501, 1065, 1078–1084
    performance measures in MNC, 1079–1081
    transfer pricing, 1081–1084
International Standards Organization (ISO) 9000, 720
International trade, 1065–1069
    exporting, 1067
    foreign trade zones, 1065–1067
    importing, 1065
    joint ventures, 1068–1069
    wholly owned subsidiaries, 1068

Introduction stage, product life-cycle, 578
Inventory
    absorption costing for, 929–930, *exh.* 934
    activity, 160–161, *exh.* 162
    assigning costs to, 273
    beginning inventory output, 283
    beginning WIP, 277
    calculating cost of, 929–930, 932–933
    carrying, *exh.* 1021
    changes in under absorption and variable costing, *exh.* 934
    defined, 1039
    finished goods, accounting for, 235–236, *exh.* 236
    finished goods, ending inventory budget, 386–388
    JIT manufacturing effects on, 586–587
    justifying, 1021–1022
    lean manufacturing, 775, 1028–1032
    process costing with ending WIP, 270–277
    process costing with no WIP, 268–270
    valuation of, 273, 289–290
    variable costing for, 932–933, *exh.* 934
    work-in-process. *See* Work-in-process inventories
Inventory cost
    calculating, 929–930, 932–933
    defined, 1023
Inventory management, 1018–1046
    big data and, 1027
    constrained optimization, 1034–1038
    EOQ and, 1026
    improving performance, 1040–1043
    JIT, 1027–1034
    just-in-case, 1020–1027
    theory of constraints, 1019–1020, 1038–1044
Inventory valuation, 273, 289–290
Investment
    in advanced technology, 993–994
    in automated manufacturing processes, 992
    capital. *See* Capital investment
    return on, 499–500, 505–510
Investment center
    defined, 500
    EVA, 513–516
    measuring performance of, 505–517
    multiple measures of performance, 516
    residual income, 510–512
    ROI, 499–500, 505–510
IRR. *See* Internal rate of return (IRR)
Irrelevant cost, 870, 873
ISO 9000, 720

J
JIT (just-in-time)
    CVP analysis and, 844

and effect on cost management system, 589–594
effect on job-order and process-costing systems, 591
JIT inventory management, 1027–1034
JIT/Lean approach, 1028–1033
JIT manufacturing, 8, 585–594
    backflush costing, 591–594
    comparison of traditional manufacturing vs., *exh.* 589
    effect on cost management system, 589–594
    effect on job-order and process-costing systems, 591
    employee empowerment, 588–589
    grouping of employees, 587–588
    inventory effects of, 586–587
    lean manufacturing, 769
    objective of, 585–586
    plant layout pattern, 587, *exh.* 588
    process costing with no WIP inventories, 270
    and purchasing, 585–589, 769
    total quality control, 589
JIT purchasing, 586, 774
Job-order costing, 216–246
    activity-based costing in, 241–243
    data analytics in, 240–241
    description of, 227–231
    process costing comparison, *exh.* 265
    production process, 217–221
    setting up cost accounting system, *exh.* 222, 222–226
    specific cost flow description, 231–241
    use of, 217
Job-order costing system, 227–231
    accounting for spoiled units in traditional, 243–244
    defined, 227
    description of, 227–231
    JIT effect on, 591
    normal, 223
Job-order cost sheet, 227–228, *exh.* 228
    completed, *exh.* 236
    in determining balances of WIP, finished goods, and cost of goods sold, 238–239
    simplified, 230–231
Job-order procedures, 291
Job time tickets, *exh.* 229, 229–230
Joint product costs
    accounting for, 343–351
    constant gross margin percentage method to allocate, 350–351
    net realizable value method to allocate, 348–349
    physical units method to allocate, 343–345
    relative market value to allocate, 346
    sales-value-at-split-off method to allocate, 347–351
    weighted average method to allocate, 345–346
Joint production processes, accounting for, 341–353
    by-products, 351–353

cost separability and need for allocation, 342–343
joint product costs, 343–351
model of, *exh.* 342
Joint products, 341
Joint ventures, 1068–1069
Journal entries, production reports and, 281
Just-in-case inventory management, 1020–1027
Just-in-time inventory management, 1027–1034
Just-in-time manufacturing. *See* JIT manufacturing

K
Kaizen costing, 634, 640–642
Kaizen standards
    ABC and, 443
    cost reduction process, *exh.* 641
    role of, 640–642, *exh.* 641
Kanban process, *exh.* 1032
Kanban system, 1030–1033
Keep-or-drop decision, 881–884
Key performance indicator, 689
Known costs and prices, 835

L
Labor
    direct. *See specific entries*
    materials and, 472–477
Labor cost, direct, 233, *exh.* 233
Lag measures, 676–677
Lead measures, 677
Lead time, 1024
Lean accounting, 766–791
    decision making, 781
    defined, 768
    lean manufacturing, 768–775
    overview of, 767–768
    performance measurement, 781–783, *exh.* 782
    productive efficiency, 783–786
    total productivity measurement, 786–790
    value streams, 776–781
Lean manufacturing, 8, 768–775
    defined, 768, 769
    JIT inventory management and, 1028–1033
    perfection, pursuing, 774–775
    principles of lean thinking, 769–775
    pull value, 774
    value by product, 770
    value flow, 771–773
    value stream, 770–771
Learning and growth (infrastructure) perspective, 687–688, *exh.* 689
Learning curve, 112–118
    cumulative average-time, 114–118, *exh.* 117
    as experience curve, 114
    incremental unit-time, 118
    nonlinear cost behavior and, 112–118
    semi-variable cost behavior and, 112–114, *exh.* 113, *exh.* 114
Learning rate, 114

Least squares method, *exh.* 102, 102–103
Legal system
  cryptocurrency legality, 1075
  forensic accounting and, 11, 84–85, 889–891, 926–927
  legal factors in international performance measures, 1079
  pricing and, 922–927
LEV. *See* Direct labor efficiency variance (LEV)
Life cycle, product. *See* Product life cycle
Life-cycle cost management, 577–585
  defined, 579
  interactive viewpoint, 579–583
  product life cycle viewpoints, 577–579
  target costing, 583–585
Life-cycle costs, 578
Linearity assumption, 85–87
Linear programming, 1036–1038
Linear programming model, 1036
Line positions, 13
Linkages, 556–558
  assumed, 42, 55
  customer, 557, 574–577
  external, 557–558
  internal, 557–558, *exh.* 569, 569–571
  supplier, 557, 571–574
Local information, access to, decentralization and, 502
Long-range quality performance report, 725, 727–728
Long run, 88
Long-term contracts, 1028–1029
Loose constraints, 1034
Loss, 40
Loss leader pricing, 921–922
Lower control limit, 456
Low point, 98–99
LRV. *See* Direct labor rate variance (LRV)

M
MACRS. *See* Modified accelerated cost recovery system (MACRS)
Make-or-buy decision, 876–880
Management, activity-based. *See* Activity-based management (ABM)
Management accountants
  certifications, 18
  data analytics role of, 57
  ethical conduct standards for, 16, *exh.* 17
  international role of, 1064–1065
  responsibility accounting system and, 501
  role of, 13–15
Management by exception, 413
Managerial judgment, 118–119
Managerial rewards, 55, 518–519
  cash compensation, 518
  income-based compensation, 519
  noncash compensation, 519
  stock-based compensation, 518–519
Managers
  incentive pay for, 517
  measuring and rewarding performance of, 517–519
Mandatory measures, 677

Manual systems, automated system vs., *exh.* 841
Manufacturing, additive, 225
Manufacturing, lean. *See* Lean manufacturing
Manufacturing cells, 587, *exh.* 772, 772–773
Manufacturing cost flows, *exh.* 239
Manufacturing costs, 46
Manufacturing cycle efficiency (MCE), 686–687
Manufacturing environment, advances in, 7–8
Manufacturing excellence, 9
Manufacturing firm
  cost of goods manufactured, 50–51, 236, *exh.* 237
  cost of goods sold, 50, 51–54, 237–240, *exh.* 238, 388–389
  defined, 43
  departmentalization for, *exh.* 319
  hybrid setting, 290
  importance of unit costs to, 224
  income statement, 50–54
  JIT. *See* JIT manufacturing
  organizational chart, *exh.* 14
  vs. service firms, *exh.* 218, 218–220
  summary of cost flows for, *exh.* 239
Manufacturing management approaches, 8
  just-in-time (JIT) manufacturing, 8. *See also* JIT manufacturing
  lean manufacturing, 8. *See also* Lean manufacturing
  theory of constraints, 8. *See also* Theory of constraints
Manufacturing overhead. *See* Overhead
Maquiladoras, 1069
Margin, 506–508
  calculating, 506–507
  contribution. *See* Contribution margin
  defined, 508
  product (or segment), 881
  of safety, 837–838
Market-based transfer prices, 521–522, 526–527
Marketing costs, 49
Marketing expense budget, 389–390
Marketing viewpoint, product life-cycle, 578, *exh.* 578, *exh.* 580
Market price, 521–522
  calculating, 526–527
Market research method, 712
Market share, 942
Market share variance, 942–944
Market size, 942
Market size variance, 942–944
Market structure, 916–917, *exh.* 917
Markup
  calculating on costs, 918–919
  full cost plus, 527–528
Master budget
  components of, *exh.* 376
  criticisms/shortcomings of, 400–402
  defined, 375
  interrelationships, *exh.* 374
Materials
  direct. *See* Direct materials
  indirect, 46

labor and, 472–477
  standard bill of, *exh.* 451, 451–452
Materials handling cost, 96–112
  multiple regression results for, *exh.* 111
  regression results for, *exh.* 105
  scattergraph for, *exh.* 100
  spreadsheet data for, *exh.* 104
Materials requirements planning (MRP) system, 30
Materials requisition forms, 228–229, *exh.* 230, 291
Materials requisitions, 228–229
Maturity stage, product life-cycle, 578
Maximum transfer price, 521
MCE (manufacturing cycle efficiency), 686–687
Measurement
  cost, 222, *exh.* 222, 223
  environmental cost, 729–736
  financial. *See* Financial measures
  performance. *See* Performance measures
  profit. *See* Profit measurement
  qualitative vs. quantitative, 38
  quality cost, 711–713
Measurement costs, *exh.* 58, 58–59, *exh.* 59. *See also* Error costs
Measures and objectives
  customer perspective, *exh.* 683
  customer value, 683
  financial perspective, *exh.* 682
  innovation process, 684
  learning and growth perspective, *exh.* 689
  operations process, 684
  post-sales service process, 687
  process perspective, 684–687, *exh.* 687
Measures of output, 81. *See also* Output
Merchandising firms
  operating budgets for, 393–394
  product costs for, 45
Method of least squares, *exh.* 102, 102–103
Microsoft Power BI, 39
Milking the firm, 416
Minimum transfer price, 521
Mining cryptocurrency, 1075
Mixed cost behavior, 93
Mixed costs, 87–88
  activities and, 93
  cost behavior, 87–88, *exh.* 88, 93
  defined, 87
  quantitative methods for separating into fixed and variable components, 96–106
Mix variance, 472–477
  computing, 473–474
  defined, 472
  direct labor, 476
  direct materials, 473–474
  sales, 941–942
MNC (multinational corporation), 501, 1065, 1078–1084
Modified accelerated cost recovery system (MACRS), 989
  depreciation rates, 989–991, *exh.* 990
  methods of, *exh.* 991

Modified cash flows, *exh.* 984
Monetary incentives, 413, 728
Monopolistic competition, 917
Monopoly, 916–917
Moving activity, 634
MPV. *See* Direct materials price variance (MPV)
MRP (materials requirements planning) system, 30
Multinational corporation (MNC), 501, 1065, 1078–1084
Multi-period service capacities, 89
Multiple charging rates, 324–327
  calculating and using, 325–326
  fixed rate, 324–325
  total allocation, 326–327
  variable rate, 324
Multiple drivers, and CVP analysis, 845
Multiple performance measures, 416, 516, 1081
Multiple-period quality trend report, 724–725, *exh.* 725, *exh.* 726
Multiple-product CVP analysis, 826–831
  break-even point in units for, 826–830
  sales-revenue approach, 830–831
Multiple-product production, using same material, *exh.* 342
Multiple-product value stream, 777–778
Multiple regression, 109–112, *exh.* 111
Multiplier method, 711–712
Multiproduct firms, 828–830
Mutually exclusive projects, 975, 982–985
MUV. *See* Direct materials usage variance (MUV)
Myopic behavior, 416, 510

N
Negotiated transfer prices, 522–527
  advantages of, 526
  calculating, 526–527
  disadvantages of, 524–526
  ethical issues, 525
Net benefit of risk response, 565–568
Net income, 816
Net present value (NPV), 979–980
  IRR vs., 982–985, *exh.* 983–984
Net realizable value method, 348–349
New constraint set, *exh.* 1044
New product value stream, 770
Noncash compensation, 519
Noncontrollable costs, 415
Nondiscounting methods, 975–978
Nondiscounting models, 975, 978
Nondiscretionary fixed expenses, 89
Nonfinancial measures, 677
Nonlinear cost behavior, 86, *exh.* 86, 112–118
  cumulative average-time learning curve, 114–118, *exh.* 117
  semi-variable, 112–114, *exh.* 113, *exh.* 114
Nonlinearity of variable costs, 86, *exh.* 86
Nonmanufacturing costs, 46, 240
Nonmanufacturing firms, importance of unit costs to, 224

Nonmonetary incentives, 413, 726–727
Nonnegativity constraints, 1036
Nonproduction costs, 46, 49
Nonprofit entities, and CVP analysis, 845
Nonuniform application, of productive inputs, 275–277
Non-unit-based activity drivers, 56
Non-unit-based drivers, 56, 81, 153
Non-unit cost drivers, CVP analysis and, 842–845
Non-unit-level drivers, 56, 81, 153
Non-unit-related overhead costs, 153
Non-value-added activities, 162, 633–634, 1027
Non-value-added costs
    defined, 633
    formulas for, *exh.* 637
    reporting, 636–638
    trend reporting of, 638–639
Normal activity level, 226
Normal cost/costing system, 147, 223
Normal cost of goods sold, 237
Normal job-order costing system, 223
Normal spoilage, 243–244, 296, 297
NPV. *See* Net present value (NPV)

O

Objective function, 1035
Objective measures, 677
Objectives and measures
    core, 682
    customer perspective, *exh.* 683
    customer value, 683
    financial perspective, *exh.* 682
    innovation process, 684
    learning and growth perspective, *exh.* 689
    operations process, 684
    post-sales service process, 687
    process perspective, 684–687, *exh.* 687
Observable quality costs, 711
Observation, physical, 42
Offshoring, 876
Oligopoly, 917
Online analytic software, 8
On-time delivery, 683
Operating assets, 506
    calculating, 506–507
Operating budgets, 375, 379–394
    additional, 390–391
    administrative expense budget, 390, 391
    budgeted income statement, 392–393
    components of, 379
    cost of goods sold budget, 388–389
    direct labor budget, 384–386
    direct materials purchases budget, 382–384
    ending finished goods inventory budget, 386–388
    marketing expense budget, 389–390
    for merchandising firms, 393–394
    overhead budget, 386–387
    production budget, 379, 381–382
    research and development expense budget, 390–391
    sales budget, 379, 380
    for service firms, 393–394

Operating cash flows
    after-tax, 988–989
    estimates of, 992–993
Operating expenses, 1039
Operating income, 506
Operating leverage, 838–840
Operational activities, 559, *exh.* 559
    organizational activity relationship with, *exh.* 560
Operational and cost concepts, 264–268, *exh.* 265, *exh.* 267, *exh.* 268
Operational control information system, 6, 35
    resource usage and spending, 90
Operational cost drivers, 559
Operational measures, 1038–1040
Operational process system, *exh.* 265
Operational productivity measure, 784
Operation costing, 221, 290–293
    basic features of, 291–292, *exh.* 292
    defined, 291
    example, 293
Operations process, 684
Opportunity cost, 873
Opportunity cost approach, 521
Optimization. *See* Constrained optimization
Optional measures, 677
Order-filling costs, 49
Order fulfillment value stream, 770, *exh.* 770
Order-getting costs, 49
Ordering costs, 1020–1021, 1022
Organizational activities and cost drivers, *exh.* 558, 558–559
    operational activity relationship with, *exh.* 560
Organizational chart, manufacturing company, *exh.* 14
Organizational cost drivers, 558
Organizational positions, 13, *exh.* 14
Output
    activity measure, 81, 107, 631
    beginning inventory, 283
    current-period, 277, 281, 283
    equivalent units of, 271–272
    measures of, 81
Outsourcing, 876, 1068
Overall profit, 936
Overall sales variance, calculating, 938
Overapplied overhead, 149
Overhead, 46, 233–234
Overhead application
    accounting for, 234
    applied overhead, 148–150
    departmental rates, 150–153
    job-order costing system, 230
Overhead assignment, plantwide rates, 148–149
Overhead budget, 386–387
Overhead cost flows, 233–234, *exh.* 235
Overhead costs
    actual, 234
    actual fixed, 466–467
    budgeted, 147
    budgeted fixed, 466–467
    non-unit-related, 153
    overview, 460–461
    traceability of, 589–590, 776–777

unit cost computation of, 155–160
variance analysis, 460–472
Overhead rates
    actual variable, 462, 463–464, 465
    departmental, 150–153, 155–160, 339–341
    failure of unit-based, *exh.* 154, 154–155
    predetermined, 147, 226
    product costing and, 339–340
Overhead variances
    accounting for, 470–471
    calculation and disposition of, 149–150, 461–464
    defined, 149
    disposal, 150–151
    fixed, 466–470
    four-variance method for calculating, 461–462
    variable, 461–466

P

Padding the budget, 414
Partial measures
    advantages of, 785–786
    and changes in productive efficiency, 785
    disadvantages of, 786
    productivity, 783–785
Partial productivity measurement, 783–785
Participative budgeting, 413–414
Past costs, 873
Payback period, 976–977
Payroll information system, 30
Penetration pricing, 921–922
Perfection, pursuing, 774–775
Perfectly competitive market, 916
Performance
    of activity, assessing, 635
    delivery, 33, 683, 1040
    due-date, 1029
    feedback on, 413
    improving, 1040–1043
    of investment center, 499–500, 505–517
    of managers, 517–519
    multiple measures of, 416, 516, 1081
Performance drivers, 677
Performance evaluation, 327, *exh.* 328, 654, *exh.* 654, 1082
Performance measures
    big data and, 677, 783
    comparison, *exh.* 654, *exh.* 678, 1080
    establishing, 653, *exh.* 654
    lean accounting, 781–783, *exh.* 782
    linking to strategy, 688–691
    in multinational firms, 1079–1081
    multiple, 416, 516, 1081
    in strategic-based control systems, 676–678, *exh.* 678, 688–691
Performance reports, 14–15, *exh.* 15, *exh.* 403, *exh.* 407, *exh.* 645, 722–728
Period costs, 49
Perishability, 43, 218, 220
Perquisites, 517
Personal property, 989
Physical flow and equivalent units, 271–272

FIFO method, 278–279
    operation costing, 292, *exh.* 292
    transferred-in goods, 288–289, *exh.* 289
    weighted average method, 283–284, *exh.* 289
Physical flow schedule, 271, 288
Physical observation, 42
Physical standards, 721
Physical units method, 343–345
Planned ending cash balance section, cash budget, 397
Planned utilization of capacity, 469
Planning, 14
    budgets for, 373–378, *exh.* 374, 402–408
    standard costing system in, 443
    systems, 650
Plant layout pattern, 587, *exh.* 588
Plantwide overhead costs, 148–149, 155–160
Plantwide rates
    limitations of, 153–160
    product costing data, *exh.* 154
    unit product cost, *exh.* 155
Political factors, 1079
Postaudit, 993
Post-purchase costs, 555, 683, 736
Post-sales service process, 684, 687
Practical activity level, 226
Practical capacity, 89, 470
Predatory pricing, 84–85, 922–923
Predetermined conversion rate, 291
Predetermined overhead rates, 147, 226
Predictive data analytics, *exh.* 40
Prescriptive data analytics, *exh.* 40
Present value, 998–1002
    defined, 998
    net. *See* Net present value (NPV)
    tables of, *exh.* 1001–1002
    of uneven series of cash flows, *exh.* 999, 1000
    of uniform series of cash flows, *exh.* 999, 1000
Prevention costs, 710
    environmental, 732
Preventive maintenance, total, 1030
Price discrimination, 923–925
Price elasticity of demand, 915–916
Price gouging, 922
Price-recovery component, 788
Prices
    complexity of setting, 913–914
    increases in, discounts and, 1033
    known, 835
    lower, 1039
    market, 521–522, 526–527
    shadow, 1037
    transfer, 520–529
Price skimming, 922
Price standards, 442
Price variance
    defined, 447
    direct materials, accounting, 452–455
    direct materials, calculating, 447–452
    overall variance decomposed into, 443
    sales, 937–938
    timing of computation, 450–451

Pricing, 912–951
  basic concepts of, 914–917
  competitive, 321
  complexity of setting prices, 913–914
  cost and policies for, 917–922
  cost-based, 917–919
  demand and supply, 914–915
  ethical issues, 925, 947–948
  legal system and, 922–927
  loss leader, 921–922
  market, 521–522, 526–527
  market structure and, 916–917, *exh.* 917
  penetration, 921–922
  predatory, 84–85, 922–923
  price elasticity of demand, 915–916
  product life cycle, 944–946
  profit measurement and, 927–937, 947–948
  profit-related variance analysis and, 937–944
  strategic, 718–719
  target costing and, 919–920
  transfer. *See* Transfer pricing
Pricing policies, cost and, 917–922
Primary activity, 161–162
Prime cost, 47–48
Private costs, 732. *See also* Full private costing
Process, defined, 264
Process acceptance, 710
Process costing, 262–297
  activity-based costing and, 270
  big data and, 277
  cost flows and, 264–268, *exh.* 267
  with ending WIP inventories, 270–277
  FIFO method, 277–282, 286–287
  JIT manufacturing firms, 270, 591
  job-order costing comparison, *exh.* 265
  with no WIP inventories, 268–270
  operational and cost concepts, 264–268, *exh.* 265, *exh.* 267, *exh.* 268
  operation costing, 290–293
  production report, 267–268, 274–275, 281, *exh.* 282, *exh.* 286–287, 290, *exh.* 290–291
  service organizations, 269
  spoiled units, 295–297
  transferred-in goods, 287–290
  unit costs, 268, 273
  use of, 263
  weighted average method, 282–287
Process creation, 653
Process further decisions, 887–889
Process improvement, 652
Process innovation (business reengineering), 653
Process perspective, 684–687, *exh.* 687
Process procedures, 291
Process reliability, 1030–1032
Process value analysis (PVA), 631–635
  activity analysis, 632–635
  activity performance assessment, 635
  defined, 631
  driver analysis, 631–632
Process value chain, 684
Process view, 57

Producing departments, 318–319
  data for support departments and, *exh.* 330
  defined, 318
  direct method of cost allocation to, 330–332, *exh.* 331
  reciprocal method of cost allocation to, 336–338
  sequential (step) method of cost allocation to, 332–335, *exh.* 333
  steps in allocating support department costs to, *exh.* 319
Product acceptance, 710
Product costing
  activity rates and, 167–168
  comparison of methods, 159, *exh.* 159
  cost allocation, 327, *exh.* 328, 339–340
  decision making and, 443–444
  departmental overhead rates and, 339–341
  JIT effects on, *exh.* 590, 590–591
  job-order. *See* Job-order costing
  multiple-product value stream, 777–778
  plantwide and departmental data, *exh.* 154
  single-product (focused) value stream, 777
  standard costing systems, 443–444
  unit-based models, *exh.* 147, 147–153
Product costs, 43–49. *See also* Production costs
  assignment of in traditional vs. JIT manufacturing, *exh.* 590
  by-products as reduction in, 353
  different costs for different purposes, 44–45, *exh.* 45
  environmental, 736–737
  external financial reporting and, 46–49
  joint. *See* Joint product costs
  service costs and, 43–49
  by unit, *exh.* 155
Product diversity, 154
Product functionality, 583
Production budget, 379, 381–382
Production costs
  calculating, 48
  conversion costs, 47–48
  defined, 46
  direct labor, 46
  direct materials, 46
  overhead. *See* Overhead
  prime costs, 47–48
Production data, summary of, *exh.* 523
Production equal to sales, 834
Production Kanban, *exh.* 1031, 1031–1032
Production process, 217–221
  batch, 290
  ethics, 220
  manufacturing vs. service firms, 218–220
  unique vs. standardized products and services, 221
Production report, 267–268, 286, 290
  example, 274–275, *exh.* 282, *exh.* 286–287, *exh.* 290–291

five steps of, 274–275
  journal entries and, 281
Production viewpoint, product life-cycle, 578, *exh.* 579, *exh.* 580
Productive efficiency, 783–786
Productive inputs, nonuniform application of, 275–277
Productivity, 783
Productivity measurement
  defined, 768, 783
  partial, 783–785
  total, 786–790
Product-level activities, 168
Product life cycle, 944–946
  activity-based costing implications, 946, *exh.* 946
  consumable life-cycle viewpoint, 579, *exh.* 580
  cost in ABC categories, *exh.* 946
  defined, 577
  impact on cost management, *exh.* 945
  marketing viewpoint, 578, *exh.* 578, *exh.* 580
  production viewpoint, 578, *exh.* 579, *exh.* 580
  and profitability, *exh.* 945
  viewpoints, 577–579, *exh.* 578, *exh.* 579, *exh.* 580
Product line, profit by, 934–935
Product (or segment) margin, 881
Products
  continuum of services and manufactured, *exh.* 218
  defective, 710
  diversity of, 154
  functionality of, 583
  higher-quality, 1039
  intangible, 43
  joint, 341
  quality, 709
  and services, unique vs. standardized, 221
  tangible, 43
  value by, 770
Profile productivity measurement, 786–788
Profit
  calculating by customer class, 924–925
  calculating percent change in, 839
  divisional, 936
  measuring. *See* Profit measurement
  overall, 936
  by product line, 934–935
  target, after-tax, 824–826
  target, in units and sales revenue, 815–824
  variance analysis, 937–944
Profitability
  cost behavior knowledge to improve, 79–80
  product life cycle and, *exh.* 945
  of segments and divisions, 934–937
Profit and loss statement, *exh.* 781. *See also* Income statements
Profit center, 500
Profit-linkage rule, 788
Profit-linked productivity measurement, 788–790
Profit measurement, 927–937

absorption-costing approach, 928–931
  ethical issues, 947–948
  limitations of, 947–948
  reasons for, 927–928
  segments and divisions, 934–937
  variable-costing approach, 931–934, 935
Profit-related variances, analysis of, 937–944
Profit-volume graphs, 831, *exh.* 832
Propriety of use, cost-based transfer prices, 528
Pseudoparticipation, budgeting, 414
Pull system, 1028
Pull value, 774
Purchasing
  JIT, 586, 774
  JIT manufacturing and, 585–589, 769
  step-cost behavior, *exh.* 571
  sustainability, 574
PVA. *See* Process value analysis (PVA)

Q

Qualitative factors, tactical decision making, 870
Qualitative measurement, 38
Quality, defined, 709–710
Quality, of activity performance, 635
Quality control, total. *See* Total quality control (TQC)
Quality costs, 706–740
  activity-based cost management system, 717
  big data and, 729
  controlling, 720–729
  defined, 710–711
  environmental. *See* Environmental costs
  example by category, *exh.* 711
  hidden, 711
  information, and decision making, 717–720
  information, using, 707–708
  measurement, 711–713
  observable, 711
  optimal distribution of, 715–717, *exh.* 716
  overview of, 708, 709–713
  quality performance reports and, 722–728
  quality standards and, 721–722
  relative contribution graphs, *exh.* 715
  reporting, 713–717
Quality improvement incentives, 726–728
Quality information
  decision making and, 717–720
  using, 707–708
"Quality of conformance," 709
Quality performance reports, types of, 722–728
Quality product/service, 709
Quality-related activities, 162
Quality standards, 721–722
Quantitative measurement, 38
Quantitative methods for cost separation, 96–106

Quantity standards, 442
Qui Tam suits, 927

R

r (coefficient of correlation), 107–108
R^2 (coefficient of determination), 107, 112
R&D (research and development), allocation of costs, 322
Ratio
    allocation, 180
    assumed consumption, 156
    consumption, 154, 156–157, 179
    contribution margin, 821
    expected global consumption, 179
    variable cost, 821
Realized external failure costs, 732
Reciprocal method of allocation, 336–338
    comparison of direct, sequential and, 338–339, exh. 339
Reconciliation, 273
Regression programs, 103–106, exh. 105. See also Multiple regression
Relative market value, allocation based on, 346
Relative quality costs, multiple-period trend graph, exh. 726
Relative value unit (RVU), 445
Relevant costs (revenues)
    comparing, 870
    defined, 872
    and ethical behavior, 891
    tactical decision making and, 870, 872–873, 891–892
Relevant range, 82, 86, exh. 86, 834, exh. 834
Remote sensing, 109
Reorder point, 1024–1025, exh. 1025, exh. 1026
Required rate of return, 979
Resale price method, 1082–1083
Research and development (R&D), allocation of costs, 322
Research and development expense budget, 390–391
Reshoring, 876
Residual income, 510–512
    advantages of, 511–512
    calculating, 510–511
    defined, 510
    disadvantages of, 512
Residual risks, exh. 563, 564
    risk response and, 564–568
Resource allocation, 694
Resource costs, assigning to activities, 163–167
Resource drivers, 162–163, 164
Resources
    committed, 89–90, 874–875, exh. 876
    cost behavior and, 88–93
    defined, 88
    demand and supply, 874–875, exh. 876
    flexible, 89, 874, exh. 876
    identification of, 163
    supplied, 91–92
    used, 91–92
Responsibility accounting, 500–501
    activity-based vs. financial-based, 651–655, exh. 653–655
    defined, 500, 651

information and accountability, 501
    model, exh. 652
    responsibility centers, types of, 500
Responsibility centers, 55, 500
Responsibility report, 12
Restaurant industry
    big data development in, 458
    sustainability in, 444
Results orientation, budget, 402
Return on investment (ROI), 499–500, 505–510
    advantages of, 508–509
    calculating, 506–507
    defined, 506
    disadvantages of, 509–510
    divisional, comparison of for performance measures, 1080
    margin, 506–508
    turnover, 506–508
Revenue center, 500
Revenue enhancement, 581
Revenue growth, 681
Revenue-oriented viewpoint, 579
Revenue-producing life, 577
Revenues
    additional, 735
    by-products as other, 352–353
    calculating for break-even point and target profit, 815–824
    and cost relationships, exh. 834
    division of, exh. 821
    relevant. See Relevant costs (revenues)
Rewards, managerial, 55, 518–519
    cash compensation, 518
    income-based compensation, 519
    noncash compensation, 519
    stock-based compensation, 518–519
Reward system
    assigning rewards, 654–655, exh. 655
    comparison, exh. 655
Risk
    economic, 1070, 1075–1076
    transaction, 1069–1074
    translation (or accounting), 1070, 1076–1078
    and uncertainty, 836–840
Risk appetite, 561, exh. 563
Risk correlation, 562
Risk identification, 561–562
Risk management, 682. See also Currency risk management; Enterprise risk management
Risk monitoring, 568
Risk response benefit, 565–568
Risk response cost, 565
Risk response net benefit, 565–568
Robinson-Patman Act, 923
Robustness, 710
Robust quality view, 715–717, exh. 716
Robust zero-defects standard, 721
ROI. See Return on investment (ROI)
Rolling budget, 375–376
Root causes, driver analysis, 631–632
Ropes, 1041
RVU (relative value unit), 445

S

Safety stock, 1024
Sales
    forecasting, 377–378, exh. 378

production equal to, 834
    tax effects of, exh. 987
Sales budget, 379, 380
Sales data, summary of, exh. 523
Sales mix, 827–830
    constant, 834
    and CVP Analysis, 828–830
Sales mix variance, 941–942
Sales price variance, 937–938
Sales revenue, break-even point and target profit in units and, 815–824
Sales-revenue approach, 822, 830–831
Sales-value-at-split-off method, 347–351
Sales volume variance, 937–938
Salvage value, 995
Sarbanes-Oxley Act, 16
Scattergraphs, 99–102, exh. 100, exh. 101
Scatterplot method, 99–102, exh. 100, exh. 101
Scheduling activity, 633
Secondary activity, 161–162
Securities and Exchange Commission (SEC), 4, 5, 13, 32, 35
Segment managers, decentralization and, 503
Segments, profitability of divisions and, 934–937
Selling costs, 49
Sell or process further decisions, 887–889
Semi-variable cost behavior, 112–114, exh. 113, exh. 114
Sensitivity analysis, 840–841, 995
Separable costs, 93–106, 342–343
Sequential (step) method of allocation, 332–335, exh. 333
    comparison of direct, reciprocal and, 338–339, exh. 339
Service costs, 43–49
Service firms/organizations
    defined, 43
    departmentalization for, exh. 319
    features of and interface with cost management system, exh. 219
    importance of unit costs to, 224
    income statement for, 54
    job-order system. See Job-order costing
    manufacturing firm vs., exh. 218, 218–220
    operating budgets for, 393–394
    process costing with no WIP inventories, 269
    service costs, 43–49
Service industry, 7
Services
    continuum of manufactured products and, exh. 218
    defined, 43
    quality, 709
    unique vs. standardized, 221
Setup costs, 1021
    carrying costs and, 1028–1029
Setups, 1025–1026
Setup times, reducing, 772, 1029
Seven-year assets, 989
SH (standard hours allowed), 446–447
Shadow prices, 1037

Shared services centers (SSC), 317
Short life cycles, 585
Short run, 88, 869
Shutdown, avoidance of, 1030–1033
Simplex method, 1036
Single-and dual-rate methods, exh. 328
Single charging rate, 322–324
Single-loop feedback, 689–690
Single-product (focused) value stream, 777
Slope parameter, 97
Small-scale actions, 869
Smart meters, 109
Solar homes, costs and benefits of, 926
Source document, 222
Special-order decisions, 867–868, 885–887
Split-off point, 341
    sales-value-at-split-off method, 347–351
    sell at, 888–889
Spoiled units, 243–244, 295–297
Spot rate, 1070, exh. 1070
Spreadsheet data for materials handling cost, exh. 104
Spreadsheet for cumulative average-time learning model, exh. 117
SQ (standard quantity of materials allowed), 446–447
SQ and SH (standard quantities allowed), 446–447
SSC (shared services centers), 317
Staff positions, 13
Standard bill of materials, exh. 451, 451–452
Standard costing, 440–479
    direct materials and direct labor variance analysis and accounting, 447–460
    materials and labor mix and yield variances, 472–477
    overhead costs variance analysis, 460–472
    standard cost sheets, exh. 445, 445–447
    unit input standards, 442–444
    variances and, 441
Standard costing systems, 443–444
Standard cost per unit, 445
Standard cost sheets, exh. 445, 445–447
Standard errors, 108–109
Standard hours allowed (SH), 446–447
Standardized vs. unique products and services, 221
Standard quantities allowed (SQ and SH), 446–447
Standard quantity of materials allowed (SQ), 446–447
Standards
    activity-based costing and, 443
    currently attainable, 442–443
    establishing, 442–443
    ethical conduct, 16, exh. 17
    ideal, 442
    interim quality, 721–722
    kaizen, 443, 640–642
    physical, 721
    price, 442
    quality, 721–722
    quantity, 442
    realistic, for budgets, 414–415
    robust zero-defects, 721

Standards (*Continued*)
total quality management, 721
unit input, 442–444
value-added, 636
Standard variable overhead rate
(SVOR), 462, 463–464
State-correction activity, 633
State-detection activity, 633
Statement of cash flows, budgeted, 394
Statement of cost of goods manufactured,
50–51, 236, *exh.* 237
Statement of cost of goods sold, 52,
exh. 238
Static budgets, 401
actual performance comparison,
exh. 403
vs. flexible budget, 403–408
Step-cost behavior, 90–93
purchasing activity, *exh.* 571
step-cost function, 91, *exh.* 91
step-fixed costs, 91–93, *exh.* 92
step-variable costs, 91
Step-cost function, 91, *exh.* 91
Step-fixed costs, 91–93, *exh.* 92
Step (sequential) method of allocation,
332–335, *exh.* 333
comparison of direct, reciprocal and,
338–339, *exh.* 339
Step-variable costs, 91
Stock-based compensation, 518–519
Stock option, 518–519
Stock-out costs, 1021
Storing activity, 634
Straight-line method, depreciation,
exh. 991
Strategic alignment, 692–694
Strategic-based control systems, 672–695
Balanced Scorecard. *See* Balanced
Scorecard
challenges of, 673–674
company strategy, 676
defined, 675
elements of, *exh.* 675, 675–680
incentive programs, 678–680
linking measures to strategy, 688–691
overview of, 674–680
performance measures, 676–678,
exh. 678, 688–691
strategic alignment, 692–694
Strategic cost management, 552–596
basic concepts, 553–560
competitive advantage, 555–556
enterprise risk management, 552–553,
560–568
JIT manufacturing and purchasing,
585–594
life-cycle cost management, 577–585
objective of, 556
operational activities and drivers,
559, *exh.* 559, *exh.* 560
organizational activities and cost
drivers, *exh.* 558, 558–559, *exh.*
560
value-chain analysis, 568–577
value-chain framework/linkages/
activities, 556–558, *exh.* 557
Strategic decision making, 554–555,
719–720
Strategic feedback, testable strategy
with, 689–690

Strategic information availability, 688
Strategic positioning, 556
Strategic pricing, 718–719
Strategy. *See also specific strategies*
communication of, 692
defined, 556, 680
Strategy map, 690–691, *exh.* 691
Strategy translation, 680, *exh.* 681
Stretch targets, 678
Structural activities, 558
Structural cost drivers, 558
Subjective measures, 677
Subsystems, 4–6, 30, 31–35, *exh.* 36
Sunk cost, 873
Supplier and firm interaction, 584–585
Supplier linkages, 557, 571–574
Supplies, defined, 46
Supply
demand and, 914–915
resources, 874–875, *exh.* 876
Support department cost
allocation, 317, 329–339
benefits of allocating, 340–341
comparison of cost allocation
methods, 338–339, *exh.* 339
data for producing departments
and, *exh.* 330
departmental overhead rates
calculated with, 339–340
direct method of allocation, 330–332,
exh. 331, 338–339, *exh.* 339
reciprocal method of allocation,
336–339, *exh.* 339
sequential method of allocation,
332–335, *exh.* 333, 338–339,
exh. 339
steps in allocating to producing
departments, *exh.* 319
total cost, 336, 338
Support departments, 318–319
activity drivers for, *exh.* 320
cost allocation method, choosing,
329–339
defined, 318
total cost of, 336, 338
Sustainability
activity selection, 635
through additive manufacturing,
225
Balanced Scorecard, 694
big data and, 109
budgeting, 415
business, 12
by-products and, 352
concept of, 44
cost behavior and, 85
data analytics and, 44, 109
purchasing decisions, 574
reports, 12, 504–505
in restaurant industry, 444
solar homes, costs and benefits of,
926
tactical decision making and,
871–872
Sustainable development, 44, 729
SVOR (standard variable overhead
rate), 462, 463–464
System, defined, 30
Systems framework, 4–6, 30–36
Systems planning, 650

T
Tableau, 39
Tactical cost analysis, 870, 878–880
Tactical decision making, 866–893
activity resource usage model,
874–876
defined, 868
differential analysis role in forensic
accounting, 889–891
ethical issues, 891
illustrative examples of, 876–892
keep-or-drop decisions, 881–884
make-or-buy decision, 876–880
overview of, 868–869
process of, 869–870, *exh.* 871
qualitative factors, 870
relevant costs and revenues, 870,
872–873, 891–892
sell or process further decisions,
887–889
special order decisions, 867–868,
885–887
sustainability and, 871–872
Taguchi quality loss function, *exh.* 712,
712–713, *exh.* 713
Tangible products, 43
Target costing, 9, 583–585
model, *exh.* 584
and pricing, 919–920
short life cycles, 585
supplier and firm interaction,
584–585
Targeted income
contribution margin approach,
820–824
equation method for, 818–820,
823–824
as percent of sales revenue, 815–824
Targets, 678, 692–693, *exh.* 693
Tariffs, 1065
Tax effects of sale, *exh.* 987
TDABC. *See* Time-driven activity-
based costing (TDABC)
Technical efficiency, 783, *exh.* 784
Technology. *See also* Big data; Data
analytics
advanced, capital investments,
991–996
bookstore transformation and, 875
digital information, advances in, 7–8
Testable strategy, 689–690
Theoretical activity level, 226
Theory of constraints (TOC), 8,
1019–1020, 1038–1044
Three-variance analysis, 472, *exh.* 472
Three-year assets, 989
Throughput, 1038–1039
Time, for activity performance, 635
Time buffer, 1040–1041
Time-driven activity-based costing
(TDABC), 8, 169–173, 175–176
Time equations, 170, 172–173
Time horizon, 88
Timely response, decentralization and,
502
Time tickets, *exh.* 229, 229–230
Time to order to produce inventory,
1024
Timing of direct materials usage
variance, 451–452

Timing of price variance computation,
450–451
TOC. *See* Theory of constraints
(TOC)
Total allocation, 326–327
Total budget variance, 447
Total cash available section, cash
budget, 394
Total costs, 82–84
allocation and, 318. *See also* Cost
allocation
manufacturing, 51
product, calculating, 48
quality, multiple-period trend graph,
exh. 725
of support departments, 336, 338
Total hours, cumulative average, *exh.*
117
Total manufacturing costs, 51
Total preventive maintenance, 1030
Total product, 555
Total product costs, calculating, 48
Total productive efficiency, 783
Total productivity measurement,
786–790
Total quality control (TQC), 571, 589,
775, 1030
Total quality costs, multiple-period
trend graph, *exh.* 725
Total quality management, 9–10
Total quality management standard,
721
Total (overall) sales variance, 938
Total variable overhead variance,
461–462
Toyota Production System, 769
TQC. *See* Total quality control (TQC)
Traceability, 41–42, 589–590,
776–777
Tracing, methods of, 42
direct, 42
driver, 42
Traditional budgets, *exh.* 409. *See also*
Static budgets
Traditional cost accounting, 55
Traditional cost control, 55
Traditional cost management systems,
54–55
activity-based cost management
systems vs., 54–59, *exh.* 57
overview of, 55
Traditional cost system, 55
Traditional operation control system,
55
Transaction drivers, 167
Transaction risk, 1069–1074
Transfer prices, 520–529
comparable uncontrolled price
method for, 1082–1083
cost-based, 527–529
cost-plus method for, 1082–1083
defined, 520
market price, 521–522, 526–527
maximum, 521
minimum, 521
negotiated, 522–527
resale price method for, 1082–1083
setting, 520–529
Transfer pricing
impact on income, 520, *exh.* 520

income taxes and, 1082–1084
multinational firm and, 1081–1084
performance evaluation and, 1082
setting transfer prices, 520–529
Transfer pricing problem, 521
Transferred-in cost, 265
Transferred-in goods, 287–290
Translation (or accounting) risk, 1070,
1076–1078
Treasurer, 13
Trend reporting
multiple-period quality, 724–725,
exh. 725, *exh.* 726
non-value-added costs, 638–639
t statistics, 106–107, 109
Turnover, 506–508
calculating, 506–507
defined, 508
Two-variance analysis, 471, *exh.* 471

U

Unbundling general ledger costs, *exh.*
167
Uncertainty, risk and, 836–840
Underapplied overhead, 149
Unfavorable variance, 447
Unique vs. standardized products and
services, 221
Unit-based drivers, 55, 81, 147–148
Unit-based overhead rates, failure of,
exh. 154, 154–155
Unit-based product-costing models,
exh. 147, 147–153
Unit cost and cost assignment
FIFO, 279–280
importance to manufacturing firms,
224
importance to nonmanufacturing
firms, 224
process costing, 273
production of unit cost information,
225
weighted average costing method,
284–285
Unit cost calculation, 230–231, 273,
289
Unit cost computation of overhead
costs, 155–160
Unit cost information, production of,
225
Unit costs
comparison of, *exh.* 159
computation of, 230–231, 273, 289
current-period, 277
EWIP only, 273
importance to manufacturing firms,
224
importance to nonmanufacturing
firms, 224
with nonuniform inputs, 275–277
process costing, 268, 273
production of information on, 225
Unit input standards, 442–444
Unit-level activities, 147–148, 168
Unit-level drivers, 55, 81, 147–148
Unit-level product costing, *exh.* 147,
147–153
Unit overhead, 148–149

Units
break-even point and target profit in
sales revenue and, 815–824
break-even point for multiple-
product setting, 826–830
cumulative average time per, *exh.* 117
of decentralization, 504
equivalent. *See* Equivalent units
physical units method of cost
allocation, 343–345
product costs, *exh.* 155
relative value, 445
spoiled, 243–244, 295–297
standard cost per unit, 445
in traditional cost accounting, 55
Unit standard cost, 442
Unrealized external failure (societal)
costs, 732
Unused capacity, 89, 92–93, 172
Unused capacity variance, 647
Upper control limit, 456
Upstream costs, 45
Usage variance
actual vs. budgeted, 327–328
defined, 447
direct materials, 447–455
overall variance decomposed into, 443
timing of computation, 451–452

V

Value-added activities, 162, 632
Value-added costs, 632
formulas for, *exh.* 637
reporting, 636–638
Value-added standard, 636
Value by product, 770
Value-chain
defined, 9, 33
framework, 556–558, *exh.* 557
industrial, 556, 571
internal, *exh.* 569, 569–571
model of, *exh.* 33
process, 684
Value-chain analysis, 568–577
customer linkages, exploiting,
574–577
defined, 568
internal linkages, exploiting, *exh.*
569, 569–571
overview of, 568
supplier linkages, exploiting,
571–574
Value flow, 771–773, *exh.* 772
Value stream, 770–771, 776–781
costing, 777–780
costs and production hours, *exh.* 779
matrix approach to identifying, *exh.*
771
multiple-product, 777–778
new product, 770
order fulfillment, 770, *exh.* 770
reporting, 780, *exh.* 781
single-product (focused), 777
and traceability of overhead costs,
776–777
Value-stream box scorecard, *exh.* 782
Value-stream costs, *exh.* 776, *exh.* 779
Variable bases vs. fixed bases, 329

Variable budget, 405. *See also* Flexible
budget
Variable costing
income statement, 932–933, *exh.* 936
inventory costs under, 932–933,
exh. 934
and profit measurement, 931–934,
935
Variable cost plus fixed fee, 528
Variable cost ratio, 821
Variable costs, 83–84
account analysis to determine, 94–96
cost behavior, 80, 83–84, *exh.* 84
defined, 80, 83
division of revenue into, *exh.* 821
high-low method to determine, 97–99
nonlinearity of, 86, *exh.* 86
product, calculating, 48
regression programs to determine,
103–106
relevant range for, 86, *exh.* 86
scatterplot method to determine,
99–102
semi-variable costs, 112–114, *exh.*
113, *exh.* 114
separating mixed cost behavior into
fixed cost and, 96–106
step-variable costs, 91
Variable overhead efficiency variance,
462–464
computing, 463–464
interpreting, 465–466, *exh.* 466
Variable overhead spending variance,
462–464
computing, 463–464
interpreting, 464–465, *exh.* 465
Variable overhead variance, 461–466
calculating total, 461–462
interpreting, 464–466
Variable rate, 324
high-low method to determine, 97–99
Variable vs. fixed bases, 329
Variance accounts, closing balances in,
459–460
Variance analysis
accounting and, 447–460
direct materials and direct labor,
447–460
overhead costs, 460–472
of profit, 937–944
three-variance analysis, 472, *exh.* 472
two-variance analysis, 471, *exh.* 471
Variances
activity volume, 646–647
calculation and disposition of, 149–150
capacity, 646–648
contribution margin, 939–942
contribution margin volume, 940–941
direct labor, 452–460, 476–477
direct materials, 455–460, 473–475
favorable, 447
fixed overhead, 466–470
flexible budget, 405
market share, 942–944
market size, 942–944
mix, 472–477, 941–942
overall sales, 938
overhead. *See* Overhead variances

price, 443, 447–455, 937–938
sales mix, 941–942
sales price, 937–938
sales volume, 937–938
standard costing and, 441
total budget, 447
total (overall) sales, 938
unfavorable, 447
unused capacity, 647
usage, 327–328, 443, 447–455
variable overhead, 461–466
volume, 407, 466–470, 646–647,
937–938, 940–941
yield, 472–477
Velocity
calculating, 685
cycle time and, 684–685
Vendor Kanban, *exh.* 1031, 1031–1032
Visualization, data analytics for, 11, 39
Volume, in traditional cost accounting, 55
Volume variances, 407, 466–470,
646–647, 937–938, 940–941

W

Waiting activity, 634
Waste, 8, 775
Weighted average costing method,
282–287
FIFO compared with, 286–287
for joint product costs allocation,
345–346
physical flow and equivalent units,
283–284, *exh.* 289
production report, 286, *exh.* 286–287
unit cost and cost assignment, 284–285
Weighted average cost of capital,
513–515
Weight factor, 345
What-if analysis, 995
Wholly owned subsidiaries, 1068
Withdrawal Kanban, *exh.* 1031,
1031–1032
Work distribution matrix, 164
Work-in-process, 51
inventory file, 228
job-order cost sheet to determine
balance of, 238–239
Work-in-process inventories
beginning, 277
inventory file, 228
process costing with ending, 270–277
process costing with no, 268–270
Work orders, 291
World-class manufacturing, 769

Y

Yield variance, 472–477
computing, 475
defined, 472
direct labor, 476–477
direct materials, 474–475

Z

Zero-base budgeting, 401
Zero-damage point, 735
Zero defects, 710, 721
Zero-defects model, 715–717, *exh.* 716

Company Index

Exhibits are indicated by *exh.* preceding the page number.

A

Abbott Nutrition Supply Chain, One Chain Enterprise, 769
Abbott Nutrition Supply Chain, Sturgis, 769
Adventist Health White Memorial, 708
Advocate Aurora Health, 440–441
Advocate Good Samaritan Hospital, 9
Aetna, 651
Airbnb, 7, 78–80, 89
Amazon/Amazon.com, 12, 28–29, 81, 875, 881, 882
AMD, 1059
American Airlines, 867
American Eagle, 45
American Electric Power (AEP) Ohio, 12
American Express, 427–428
Apple/Apple Computer, 7, *exh.* 37, 107, 564, 928, 1065
Aquafina Water, 504
Arm & Hammer, 581
AT&T, 585, 641
Autodesk ADSK, 241

B

Ball Corp., 513
Baptist Health, 146
Barclays, 89, 876
Bausch & Lomb, 1077
Baxter International, 706–708
Bayer, 562
Berkshire Hathaway, Inc., 45
Best Buy, Inc., 816
BioNTech, 885
Black & Decker, 585
BMW, 1063
Boeing, 217, 867, 1065
BorgWarner, 585
Bosch, 768, 1064
Boston Scientific, Coyol, 769
Bristol Myers Squibb, 913
Brooklyn Nets, 44
Burger King, 1028

C

Canon, 638, 1069
Cardinal Health, 552–554, 560
Caterpillar, 1072
Cathay Pacific Airways Ltd., 373
Chemical Bank, 651
Chevron, 641
Chrysler, 585
Citicorp, 1077
Citrix Systems, Inc., 373
Clarus Technologies, 574
Cleveland Cavaliers, 44
Cleveland Clinic, 16

The Coca-Cola Company, 7, 377, 378, 513, 648, 674
Conlan Company, 217
ConocoPhillips, 375, 556
Costco, 921
CVS/CVS Health, 516, 884

D

Darden Restaurants, 444
Dell, 46, 876
Delta, 413, 866–868
DENSO, 768
DHL Express, 166
Dialpad Inc., 921
Disneyland. *See* Walt Disney Company
Domino Sugar Company, 49
Dow Chemical Company, 317, 633
Dow Terneuzen, 633
Dr. Pepper Snapple Group, 1081
Dr. Reddy's Laboratories Limited, 1018–1020

E

EGR, Inc., 769
Elgin Sweeper Company, 119
Eli Lily, 674
Embraer, 1065
Evides, 633
ExxonMobil, 556. *See also* Mobil

F

Federal Express/FedEx, 9, 12, 33, 85, 413, 974
Federal-Mogul, 651
15th Club, 517
Ford Motor Company, 341, 585, 648, 767, 769, 871–872, 881, 885–886, 1019, 1065
Frito-Lay, 504

G

Gamesa and Latin America Foods, 504
Gatorade, 504
GE Aviation, 113, 225
GE Healthcare, 885
General Electric (GE), 413, 503, 513, 585, 651, 674, 876, 1019, 1064, 1077
General Mills, 917
General Motors (GM), 674, 881, 936
Germantown, Tennessee, City of, 708
Gillette, 1077
Girl Scouts of America, 928
GlaxoSmithKline, 913
GLYNT.AI, 880
Gold Coin Group, 693
Google, 7, 90
Grede Foundries, Inc., 717

H

Haimen Pharmaceutical Factory, 457
H&M, 1081
Harley-Davidson, 585, 1029
Henkel Corporation, 502, 503
Henkel's Loctite, 503
Hershey, 674
Hewlett-Packard, 34, 317, 519, 585, 922, 1065
High Flight, 937
Hitachi, 1065
Honeywell, 572
Hyatt, 921

I

IBM, 317, 338–339, 375, 674, 1074
IBM Credit, 651
IBM Institute for Business Value, 575
Illinois Municipal Retirement Fund, 708
Indesit, 1064
Industrial Light & Magic, 217
Instacart, 7
Instagram, 812–814
Intel, 513, 585, 783
Ipsen, 626–628
Ipsen Pharma Biotech (Ipsen Signes), 626–628, 769

J

Jacksonville Naval Supply Center, 815
J.D. Powers, 220
JEA, 416
JetBlue Airways, 815
J.F. Dunn Construction, 241
John Deere, 585
Johnson & Johnson, 913, 947

K

Kellogg, 674, 917
KFC, 504
Kimberly-Clark Corp., 377
Komatsu, 1072
KPMG, 12
Kraft, 575
The Kroger Company, 2–4, 9, 677, 678, 884
KU Leuven Arenberg Library, 173

L

LafargeHolcim, 263–264
Lands' End, 54
Levi Strauss, 1080–1081
Lexus, 220
Lipton, 504
LNS Research, 729
Lockheed Martin, 377, 638
Loctite Corporation, 1065, 1074
Los Angeles Lakers, 44
Lufthansa AG, 373
LURA Group, 731

M

Mackay Memorial Hospital, 688
Macy's, 393
Maple Leaf Sports and Entertainment (MLSE), 1072
Marriott, 413, 921
Mars, Inc., 7
Martin Marietta Materials, 651
Marvel Studios, 216–217
Mary Greeley Medical Center, 708
Mastercard, 427–428, 564
Mattel, 946
Maxion, 768
Mayo Clinic, 814, 826
McDonald's Corporation, 43, 220, 1077
MEDRAD, 709
Memorial Sloan-Kettering Cancer Center, 219
Mercedes-Benz U.S. International, 586
Merck & Co., 5, 513, 913
Mercury Marine, 585
Merit Medical Systems, Inc., 650, 769
Metropolitan Life Insurance Company, 59
Michael Kors, 813
Mobil, 38. *See also* ExxonMobil
Mobility, 731
Monsanto, 1073
Motorola, 585
Mott's, 341
Mustang and Fusion, 342
Mylan, 925

N

Nabisco, 555
National Geographic, 813
National Restaurant Association, 458
Nationwide, 89
Nestlé/Nestlé Global, 378, 638, 766–768
NeXT, 928
Nike, 498–500, 513
Nissan Motor Company, 1063, 1065
Nordstrom/Nordstrom Department Stores, 393, 920
North Face, 393
Norwegian Cruise Lines, 921
Novartis, 913
Novopharm Ltd., 457
Nvidia, 1058–1060, 1071

O

Ocean Spray, 504
Oracle, 10, 876
Oregon Cutting Systems (OCS), 585, 587, 591
Owensboro Health, 146

P

Patagonia, 891, 1081
PepsiCo, 504, 1064
PepsiCo Americas Beverages, 504
PepsiCo Americas Foods, 504
PepsiCo Foods International, 1064
PepsiCo International, 504
Pfizer, 885, 912–913, 916
PGA, 516–517
Pixar, 928
Pizza Hut, 504
Pottery Barn, 919
PPG Industries, 372–373
PricewaterhouseCoopers, 501
Procter & Gamble (P&G), 7, 49, 504–505, 815, 1019, 1029, 1074, 1077
Procter-Silex, 219
Public Service Enterprise Group, 641

Q

Quaker Foods & Snacks, 504, 516, 917

R

Rite Aid, 884
The Ritz-Carlton, 641
Roche, 913
Royal Caribbean, 921
Royal Dutch Shell, 679, 694

S

Sabritas, 504
Saïd Business School at the University of Oxford, 575
Sam's Club, 504, 516
SAP, 10
Seaboard Foods, 352
Sears, 920
SeaWorld, 815
Sentieo, 677
7 For All Mankind, 47
Sew Sister Fabrics, 221
Sharp Electronics, 1065
Shell. *See* Royal Dutch Shell
Siemens, 1064
Singapore Airlines Ltd., 373
Smiths Medical, 1030
Snapchat, 812–814
Sony, 1065
Southwest Airlines, 46
Space Exploration Technologies Corporation/SpaceX, 566, 972–974
Standard Oil, 928
Starbucks/Starbucks Coffee, 88, 321, 813, 1081
Stillwater Designs, Inc., 7, 33
Susan's Fine Catering, 217

T

Taco Bell, 218, 504
Tennant Company, 716, 721–722, 725, 728

Tesco, 1027
Tesla, 1060
Texas Instruments (TI), 401, 1019, 1064
The Wall Street Journal, 891
Thomson Corporation, 641
3M Corporation, 415, 885–886
Toronto Blue Jays, 1072
Toronto Maple Leafs, 1072
Toronto Raptors, 1072
Toyota, 577, 638, 767, 769
Toys "R" Us, 585
Tropicana, 504
True Religion, 47
Twitter, 812–814
Tyco, 519

U

Uber, 7
Unilever, 915
United Way, 394
Universal Studios, 1067
University of Minnesota Medical Center, Fairview, 631
University of Oxford Saïd Business School, 575
University of Pittsburg Medical Center (UPMC), 144–146
UPS, 8, 12, 677
USAA, 516
U.S. Postal Service (USPS), 9, 33, 845, 916

V

Verizon, 641
Victoria's Secret, 38
VISA, 427–428
Volkswagen (VW), 318
Vought Aircraft Industries, Inc., 992

W

Walgreens Boots Alliance, 884
Wal-Mart Neighborhood Markets, 504
Wal-Mart/Walmart, 504, 585, 675, 884, 923, 928, 1029, 1075–1076
Walt Disney Company, 39, 219, 564, 838, 1067, 1072–1073
Wells Fargo, 15, 672–674, 676, 680
Westinghouse/Westinghouse Electric, 585, 711, 716
Whirlpool, 1064
Whole Foods, 513, 813
Wipro, Ltd./Wipro GE Healthcare, 1064–1065

X

Xerox, 585, 651, 678

Y

YouTube, 812–814
Yum! Brands, 7, 504

Examples

Examples for Chapter 2

2.1 The HOW and WHY of Calculating Prime Cost, Conversion Cost, Variable Product Cost, and Total Product Cost, page 48

2.2 The HOW and WHY of Preparing the Statement of Cost of Goods Manufactured, page 50

2.3 The HOW and WHY of Preparing the Statement of Cost of Goods Sold, page 52

2.4 The HOW and WHY of Preparing the Income Statement for a Manufacturing Firm, page 53

Examples for Chapter 3

3.1 The HOW and WHY of Forming an Equation to Describe Mixed Cost, page 87

3.2 The HOW and WHY of Calculating Activity Availability, Capacity Used, and Unused Capacity, page 92

3.3 The HOW and WHY of Using Account Analysis to Determine Fixed and Variable Costs, page 94

3.4 The HOW and WHY of Using the High-Low Method to Determine Fixed Cost and Variable Rate, page 97

3.5 The HOW and WHY of Using the Regression Results for Fixed Cost and Variable Rate to Construct and Use a Cost Formula, page 105

3.6 The HOW and WHY of Constructing a Cost Equation Using the Results from Multiple Regression, page 111

3.7 The HOW and WHY of Calculating the Cumulative Average-Time Learning Curve, page 115

Examples for Chapter 4

4.1 The HOW and WHY of Applied Overhead and Unit Overhead Cost: Plantwide Rates, page 148

4.2 The HOW and WHY of Overhead Variances and Their Disposal, page 150

4.3 The HOW and WHY of Departmental Overhead Rates: Their Assignment and Rationale, page 152

4.4 The HOW and WHY of Consumption Ratios, page 156

4.5 The HOW and WHY of Activity-Based Costing, page 157

4.6 The HOW and WHY of Assigning Resource Costs to Activities, page 165

4.7 The HOW and WHY of TDABC, page 170

4.8 The HOW and WHY of DBC, page 174

4.9 The HOW and WHY of Approximately Relevant ABC Systems, page 178

4.10 The HOW and WHY of Equally Accurate Reduced ABC Systems, page 180

Examples for Chapter 5

5.1 The HOW and WHY of Setting Up a Simplified Job-Order Cost Sheet, page 230

5.2 The HOW and WHY of Using a Job-Order Cost Sheet to Determine the Balances of Work in Process, Finished Goods, and Cost of Goods Sold, page 238

5.3 The HOW and WHY of Using Activity-Based Costing in Job-Order Costing, page 242

5.4 The HOW and WHY of Accounting for Normal and Abnormal Spoilage in a Job-Order Environment, page 243

Examples for Chapter 6

6.1 The HOW and WHY of Cost Flows: Process Costing, page 266

6.2 The HOW and WHY of Process Costing: Services with No WIP Inventories, page 269

6.3 The HOW and WHY of Physical Flow Analysis and Equivalent Units: EWIP Only, page 271

6.4 The HOW and WHY of Unit Cost, Inventory Valuation, and Cost Reconciliation: EWIP Only, page 273

6.5 The HOW and WHY of a Production Report, page 274

6.6 The HOW and WHY of Equivalent Units and Unit Costs with Nonuniform Inputs, page 275

6.7 The HOW and WHY of Physical Flow Analysis and Equivalent Units: FIFO Method, page 278

6.8 The HOW and WHY of Unit Cost and Cost Assignment: FIFO, page 279

6.9 The HOW and WHY of Physical Flow Analysis and Equivalent Units: Weighted Average Method, page 283

6.10 The HOW and WHY of Unit Cost and Cost Assignment: Weighted Average Method, page 284

Examples for Chapter 7

7.1 The HOW and WHY of Calculating and Using a Single Charging Rate, page 323

7.2 The HOW and WHY of Calculating and Using Multiple Charging Rates, page 325

7.3 The HOW and WHY of Allocating Support Department Costs to Producing Departments Using the Direct Method, page 331

7.4 The HOW and WHY of Allocating Support Department Costs to Producing Departments Using the Sequential (Step) Method, page 334

7.5 The HOW and WHY of Allocating Support Department Costs to Producing Departments Using the Reciprocal Method, page 336

7.6 The HOW and WHY of Using Allocated Support Department Costs to Calculate Departmental Overhead Rates, page 339

7.7 The HOW and WHY of Using the Physical Units Method to Allocate Joint Product Costs, page 344

7.8 The HOW and WHY of Using the Weighted Average Method to Allocate Joint Product Costs, page 345

7.9 The HOW and WHY of Using the Sales-Value-at-Split-Off Method to Allocate Joint Product Costs, page 347

7.10 The HOW and WHY of Using the Net Realizable Value Method to Allocate Joint Product Costs, page 349

7.11 The HOW and WHY of Using the Constant Gross Margin Percentage Method to Allocate Joint Product Costs, page 350

Examples for Chapter 8

8.1 The HOW and WHY of Constructing a Sales Budget, page 380

8.2 The HOW and WHY of Constructing a Production Budget, page 381

8.3 The HOW and WHY of Constructing a Direct Materials Purchases Budget, page 383

8.4 The HOW and WHY of Constructing a Direct Labor Budget, page 385

8.5 The HOW and WHY of Constructing an Overhead Budget, page 386

8.6 The HOW and WHY of Preparing the Ending Finished Goods Inventory Budget, page 387

8.7 The HOW and WHY of Preparing the Cost of Goods Sold Budget, page 388

8.8 The HOW and WHY of Constructing a Marketing Expense Budget, page 389

8.9 The HOW and WHY of Constructing an Administrative Expense Budget, page 391

8.10 The HOW and WHY of Constructing a Budgeted Income Statement, page 392

8.11 The HOW and WHY of Constructing a Cash Receipts Budget with an Accounts Receivable Aging Schedule, page 395

8.12 The HOW and WHY of Constructing a Cash Budget, page 397

8.13 The HOW and WHY of Constructing a Flexible Budget for Varying Levels of Activity, page 404

8.14 The HOW and WHY of Constructing a Flexible Budget for the Actual Level of Activity, page 406

Examples for Chapter 9

9.1 The HOW and WHY of Computing Standard Quantities Allowed (*SQ* and *SH*), page 446

9.2 The HOW and WHY of Computing the Direct Materials Price Variance (*MPV*) and Direct Materials Usage Variance (*MUV*), page 448

9.3 The HOW and WHY of Computing the Direct Labor Rate Variance (*LRV*) and Direct Labor Efficiency Variance (*LEV*), page 453

9.4 The HOW and WHY of Using Control Limits to Determine When to Investigate a Variance, page 456

9.5 The HOW and WHY of Closing the Balances in the Variance Accounts at the End of the Year, page 459

9.6 The HOW and WHY of Calculating the Total Variable Overhead Variance, page 461

9.7 The HOW and WHY of Computing the Variable Overhead Spending Variance and the Variable Overhead Efficiency Variance, page 463

9.8 The HOW and WHY of Computing the Fixed Overhead Spending Variance and the Fixed Overhead Volume Variance, page 467

9.9 The HOW and WHY of Computing the Mix Variance, page 473

9.10 The HOW and WHY of Computing the Yield Variance, page 475

Examples for Chapter 10

10.1 The HOW and WHY of Calculating Average Operating Assets, Margin, Turnover, and Return on Investment (ROI), page 506

10.2 The HOW and WHY of Calculating Residual Income, page 510

10.3 The HOW and WHY of Calculating the Weighted Average Cost of Capital and EVA, page 514

10.4 The HOW and WHY of Calculating Market-Based and Negotiated Transfer Prices, page 526

10.5 The HOW and WHY of Calculating Cost-Based Transfer Prices, page 528

Examples for Chapter 11

11.1 The HOW and WHY of Using Net Benefit to Evaluate Risk Response Alternatives, page 566

11.2 The HOW and WHY of Exploiting Internal Linkages to Reduce Costs and Increase Value, page 569

11.3 The HOW and WHY of Activity-Based Supplier Costing, page 573

11.4 The HOW and WHY of Activity-Based Customer Costing, page 576

11.5 The HOW and WHY of Activity-Based Life-Cycle Cost Reduction, page 581

11.6 The HOW and WHY of Backflush Costing, page 593

Examples for Chapter 12

12.1 The HOW and WHY of Value- and Non-Value-Added Cost Reporting, page 635

12.2 The HOW and WHY of Non-Value-Added Cost Trend Reporting, page 636

12.3 The HOW and WHY of Kaizen Costing, page 639

12.4 The HOW and WHY of Activity-Based Flexible Budgeting, page 643

12.5 The HOW and WHY of Activity Capacity Management, page 645

Examples for Chapter 13

13.1 The HOW and WHY of Calculating Cycle Time and Velocity, page 685

13.2 The HOW and WHY of Calculating Manufacturing Cycle Efficiency (MCE), page 686

13.3 The HOW and WHY of Strategy Mapping, page 690

Examples for Chapter 14

14.1 The HOW and WHY of Preparing a Quality Cost Report, page 714

14.2 The HOW and WHY of Preparing Interim Quality Performance Reports, page 722

14.3 The HOW and WHY of Multiple-Period Quality Trend Reporting, page 724

14.4 The HOW and WHY of Long-Range Quality Performance Reporting, page 727

14.5 The HOW and WHY of an Environmental Cost Report, page 733

14.6 The HOW and WHY of Activity-Based Environmental Cost Assignments, page 737

Examples for Chapter 15

15.1 The HOW and WHY of Cellular Manufacturing, page 773

15.2 The HOW and WHY of Value-Stream Product Costing, page 779

15.3 The HOW and WHY of Profile Productivity Measurement, page 787

15.4 The HOW and WHY of Profit-Linked Productivity Measurement, page 789

Examples for Chapter 16

16.1 The HOW and WHY of Basic Cost Calculations and the Contribution-Margin-Based Income Statement, page 816

16.2 The HOW and WHY of Calculating the Units Needed to Break Even and to Achieve a Target Profit, page 819

16.3 The HOW and WHY of Calculating Revenue for Break-Even and for a Target Profit, page 822

16.4 The HOW and WHY of Calculating the Number of Units to Generate an After-Tax Target Profit, page 824

16.5 The HOW and WHY of Calculating the Break-Even Number of Units in a Multiproduct Firm, page 828

16.6 The HOW and WHY of Calculating Margin of Safety, page 837

16.7 The HOW and WHY of Calculating Degree of Operating Leverage and Percent Change in Profit, page 839

Examples for Chapter 17

17.1 The HOW and WHY of Structuring a Make-or-Buy Decision, page 877

17.2 The HOW and WHY of Structuring a Keep-or-Drop Product Line Decision, page 882

17.3 The HOW and WHY of Structuring a Special-Order Decision, page 886

17.4 The HOW and WHY of Structuring a Sell at Split-Off or Process Further Decision, page 888

1128

Examples for Chapter 18

18.1 The HOW and WHY of Calculating a Markup on Cost, page 918

18.2 The HOW and WHY of Calculating Cost and Profit by Customer Class, page 924

18.3 The HOW and WHY of Calculating Inventory Cost and Preparing the Income Statement Using Absorption Costing, page 929

18.4 The HOW and WHY of Calculating Inventory Cost and Preparing the Income Statement Using Variable Costing, page 932

18.5 The HOW and WHY of Calculating the Sales Price Variance, the Sales Volume Variance, and the Overall Sales Variance, page 938

18.6 The HOW and WHY of Calculating the Contribution Margin Variance, page 939

18.7 The HOW and WHY of Calculating the Contribution Margin Volume Variance, page 940

18.8 The HOW and WHY of Calculating the Sales Mix Variance, page 942

18.9 The HOW and WHY of Calculating the Market Share Variance and the Market Size Variance, page 943

Examples for Chapter 19

19.1 The HOW and WHY of Calculating the Payback Period, page 976

19.2 The HOW and WHY of Calculating the Accounting Rate of Return, page 978

19.3 The HOW and WHY of Analyzing NPV, page 979

19.4 The HOW and WHY of Calculating the Internal Rate of Return, page 981

19.5 The HOW and WHY of Determining NPV and IRR for Mutually Exclusive Projects, page 984

19.6 The HOW and WHY of Calculating After-Tax Cash Flows, page 988

Examples for Chapter 20

20.1 The HOW and WHY of Calculating the EOQ, page 1023

20.2 The HOW and WHY of Reordering, page 1024

20.3 The HOW and WHY of Solving Constrained Optimization Problems with One Internal Constraint, page 1035

20.4 The HOW and WHY of Solving Linear Programming Problems with Two Variables, page 1036

20.5 The HOW and WHY of a Drum-Buffer-Rope System, page 1042

Examples for Chapter 21

21.1 The HOW and WHY of Locating in a Foreign Trade Zone, page 1062

21.2 The HOW and WHY of Exchanging One Currency for Another, page 1066

21.3 The HOW and WHY of Calculating Exchange Gains and Losses, page 1068

21.4 The HOW and WHY of Hedging Currency Exchange Rates, page 1069

21.5 The HOW and WHY of Using the Comparable Uncontrolled Price Method, the Resale Price Method, and the Cost-Plus Method in Calculating Transfer Prices, page 1078